PRINCIPLES OF BUSINESS & MANAGEMENT

PRINCIPLES OF
BUSINESS &
MANAGEMENT

PRACTICING ETHICS, RESPONSIBILITY, SUSTAINABILITY

OLIVER LAASCH

3RD EDITION

1 Oliver's Yard
55 City Road
London EC1Y 1SP

2455 Teller Road
Thousand Oaks
California 91320

Unit No 323-333, Third Floor, F-Block
International Trade Tower
Nehru Place, New Delhi – 110 019

8 Marina View Suite 43-053
Asia Square Tower 1
Singapore 018960

Editor: Matthew Waters
Development editor: Jessica Moran
Editorial assistant: Charlotte Hanson
Production editor: Sarah Cooke
Copyeditor: William Baginsky
Proofreader: Brian McDowell
Indexer:
Marketing manager: Lucia Sweet
Cover design: Francis Kenney
Typeset by: C&M Digitals (P) Ltd, Chennai, India
Printed in the UK by Bell and Bain Ltd, Glasgow
BB0345731

Library of Congress Control Number: 2023940584

British Library Cataloguing in Publication data

A catalogue record for this book is available from the British Library.

PRME
an initiative of the
United Nations Global Compact

CRME··
**Center for Responsible
Management Education**

ISBN 9781529610826
ISBN 9781529610819 (pbk)

CONTENTS

ONLINE RESOURCES FOR INSTRUCTORS   IX

CONTRIBUTORS   XI

PREFACE   XV

FOREWORD BY METTE MORSING   XIX

ABOUT THE AUTHOR   XXI

PRAISE FOR THE BOOK   XXIII

CHAPTER FEATURES GUIDE   XXV

PART A: BASICS   1

CHAPTER 1: MANAGEMENT IN CONTEXT   3
OLIVER LAASCH

CHAPTER 2: MANAGEMENT IN PRACTICE   41
OLIVER LAASCH

PART B: DIMENSIONS   71

CHAPTER 3: ETHICAL MANAGEMENT   73
OLIVER LAASCH

CHAPTER 4: RESPONSIBLE MANAGEMENT   115
OLIVER LAASCH

CHAPTER 5: SUSTAINABLE MANAGEMENT   151
OLIVER LAASCH

PART C: MODES OF MANAGEMENT   187

CHAPTER 6: ORGANIZING   189
OLIVER LAASCH AND ROGER N. CONAWAY

CHAPTER 7: BEHAVING 233
OLIVER LAASCH AND ALEXANDRA BARRUETA

CHAPTER 8: FOLLEADING 267
OLIVER LAASCH AND ALEXANDRA BARRUETA

CHAPTER 9: DECIDING 307
OLIVER LAASCH

CHAPTER 10: COMMUNICATING 349
OLIVER LAASCH, ROGER N. CONAWAY AND ALEXANDRA BARRUETA

CHAPTER 11: DIGITALIZING 385
ANNMARIE HANLON AND OLIVER LAASCH

CHAPTER 12: GLOCALIZING 429
OLIVER LAASCH AND ROGER N. CONAWAY

CHAPTER 13: STRATEGIZING 467
OLIVER LAASCH

CHAPTER 14: INNOVATING 505
OLIVER LAASCH AND BARBARA RIBEIRO

CHAPTER 15: ENTREPRENEURING 553
OLIVER LAASCH, XUAN YE AND HAIBO ZHOU

PART D: MANAGEMENT OCCUPATIONS 611

CHAPTER 16: SUPPLY MANAGEMENT 613
ZHAOHUI WU, OLIVER LAASCH AND RICK EDGEMAN

CHAPTER 17: OPERATIONS MANAGEMENT 649
RICK EDGEMAN, OLIVER LAASCH AND ZHAOHUI WU

CHAPTER 18: MARKETING MANAGEMENT 693
OLIVER LAASCH, DIRK C. MOOSMAYER, NATASHA CLENNELL AND ROGER N. CONAWAY

CHAPTER 19: PEOPLE MANAGEMENT 729
ROGER N. CONAWAY, ELAINE COHEN AND OLIVER LAASCH

CHAPTER 20: ACCOUNTING AND CONTROLLING   765
ULPIANA KOCOLLARI, ANDREA GIRARDI AND OLIVER LAASCH

CHAPTER 21: FINANCIAL MANAGEMENT   809
OLIVER LAASCH AND NICK TOLHURST

CASE STUDY ZONE   851

CASE STUDY I: NEW-WORLD MANAGEMENT AT PATAGONIA   853
OLIVER LAASCH

CASE STUDY II: YASH PAKKA: NATURALLY INSPIRED TO CHANGE THE WORLD   863
DANIEL A. DIAZ

CASE STUDY III: FAIRPHONING MANAGEMENT   875
OLIVER LAASCH

CASE STUDY IV: MANAGING ACCORDING TO THE SAGES AT GOOD-ARK   889
PINGPING FU AND QING QU

CASE STUDY V: MANAGING BY THE GRAM AT ALGRAMO   901
DANIEL A. DIAZ

CASE STUDY VI: GREYSTON'S BAKERS ON A MISSION TO SCALE OPEN HIRING®   913
OLIVER LAASCH, REUT LIVNE-TARANDACH AND MICHAEL PIRSON

APPENDIX   923
INDEX   927

ONLINE RESOURCES FOR INSTRUCTORS

The third edition of **_Principles of Business & Management_** is supported by an array of useful online resources for instructors to use as part of their teaching and student assessment. Log in or set up an account via **https://study.sagepub.com/laasch3e** to access:

- **Teaching guide** providing further support for those using the book in their teaching, including course design information, additional resource suggestions and Case Study Zone teaching notes.

- **PowerPoints** consisting of both a core set as well as a separate supplementary set per chapter, which can be downloaded, adapted and combined as needed.

- **Testbank** of multiple-choice questions to assess students as part of the course, particularly useful for large cohorts.

- **Chapter supplements** featuring more in-depth content for those wanting to dig a bit deeper into key topics and concepts.

- **Resource pack** to easily upload all of the above resources onto your university's online learning platform (e.g. Blackboard, Canvas or Moodle) and customize the content as required.

A dedicated YouTube channel has been created to house a brief lecture recording for each chapter of the book. To access the channel, use your smartphone to scan the QR code.

In addition to the instructor resources mentioned above, the author hosts a free online course open to all titled, 'Managing Responsibly: Practicing Sustainability, Responsibility and Ethics', available here: **https://www.coursera.org/learn/responsible-management**

CONTRIBUTORS

PIONEER INTERVIEWS

Chapter 1	Rakesh Khurana
Chapter 2	Henry Mintzberg
Chapter 3	Linda Treviño
Chapter 4	Archie B. Carroll
Chapter 5	John Elkington
Chapter 6	Simon Zadek
Chapter 7	Denise Rousseau
Chapter 8	Nancy J. Adler
Chapter 9	Roy Suddaby
Chapter 10	François Cooren
Chapter 11	Andreas Kaplan
Chapter 12	Geert Hofstede
Chapter 13	Mark Kramer
Chapter 14	R. Edward Freeman
Chapter 15	Muhammad Yunus
Chapter 16	Michael Braungart
Chapter 17	Sandra Waddock
Chapter 18	Philip Kotler
Chapter 19	Liz Maw
Chapter 20	Stefan Schaltegger
Chapter 21	Robert Costanza

PROFESSIONAL PROFILES

Chapter 1	Anonymous
Chapter 2	Kene Umeasiegbu
Chapter 3	Pia Poppenreiter
Chapter 4	Sudhir Kumar Sinha
Chapter 5	Judith Ruppert
Chapter 6	Thomas Hügli
Chapter 7	Clover Hogan
Chapter 8	Mariné Azuara
Chapter 9	Tommy Weir

Chapter 10	Thomas Hügli
Chapter 11	Yue Hu
Chapter 12	Laura Clise
Chapter 13	Cansu Gedik
Chapter 14	Ved Krishna
Chapter 15	Doru Mitrana
Chapter 16	Dinah Madiadipura
Chapter 17	Cecilia del Castillo
Chapter 18	Adela Metlicka Lustykova
Chapter 19	Erika Guzmán
Chapter 20	Daniel Ette
Chapter 21	Darminder Tiwana

TRUE STORIES

Edited by:

Chapter 1	Oliver Laasch
Chapter 2	Alexandra Leonor Barrueta-Sacksteder
Chapter 3	Alexandra Leonor Barrueta-Sacksteder
Chapter 4	Alexandra Leonor Barrueta Sacksteder and Daniele Eckert
Chapter 5	Oliver Laasch
Chapter 6	Oliver Laasch
Chapter 7	Oliver Laasch
Chapter 8	Alexandra Leonor Barrueta Sacksteder
Chapter 9	Alexandra Leonor Barrueta Sacksteder
Chapter 10	Oliver Laasch
Chapter 11	Oliver Laasch
Chapter 12	Alexandra Leonor Barrueta Sacksteder
Chapter 13	Alexandra Leonor Barrueta Sacksteder
Chapter 14	Alexandra Leonor Barrueta Sacksteder and Lucia Kirchner
Chapter 15	Alexandra Leonor Barrueta-Sacksteder and Ekaterina Ivanova
Chapter 16	Alexandra Leonor Barrueta Sacksteder
Chapter 17	Oliver Laasch
Chapter 18	Alexandra Leonor Barrueta Sacksteder and Judy Nagy
Chapter 19	Alexandra Leonor Barrueta Sacksteder
Chapter 20	Oliver Laasch
Chapter 21	Alexandra Leonor Barrueta Sacksteder

CASE STUDIES

Chapter 7	Oliver Laasch, Claus Dierksmeier
Chapter 9	Oliver Laasch, Daiteng Ren
Chapter 19	Rory Ridley-Duff, Michael Bull, Oliver Laasch
Case I	Oliver Laasch
Case II	Daniel A. Diaz
Case III	Oliver Laasch
Case IV	Pingping Fu and Qing Qu
Case V	Daniel A. Diaz
Case VI	Oliver Laasch, Reut Livne-Tarandach, and Michael Pirson

PREFACE

A TEXTBOOK FOR BUSINESS MANAGEMENT'S EMERGING NEW NORMAL

Most existing management textbooks have been and are 'propaganda' for keeping up the 'old normal' [1]. Instead, this textbook is meant to be fundamentally subversive 'propaganda' for a 'new normal of management'. Such 'professional' management assumes a positive role in society and for the planet. Professional managers manage ethically, responsibly, and sustainably. It is management whose underlying purpose is to reconstruct the economic machine from the inside, to 'regear' it from causing social, environmental, and ethical problems towards solving them, a form of positive subversion. This book is meant to be doubly subversive: subversive hopefully towards colleagues, so that they can subvert students.

Professional **management is ethical, responsible, and sustainable.** Professional management is getting things done ethically, responsibly, and sustainably and in the service of society and the planet [2–4].

It's about practices and practitioners. *Knowing about* ethics, responsibility and sustainability is not enough. Instead, we as managers have a responsibility to *become competent* in managing ethically, responsibly, and sustainably, through holistic, whole person training for professional management competence. The social practices perspective [5, 6] on management applied throughout the book shifts the attention to all the things we customarily do as managers, as well as to unique innovative practices like open hiring or employee self-management.

'Business' management. The title of the third edition includes the word 'business'. We have realized this change to call attention to the fact that the book includes both the customary chapters covered in an introduction to management book (e.g. deciding, communicating, organizing) and those more related to introduction to business courses (e.g. marketing, operations management, people management). Typically, business and management degree programmes teach either one of these courses, but not both. Accordingly, through this title change we hope to enable the use of this book across all business and management programmes.

NEW AND MORE ACCESSIBLE CHAPTERS

Among the 21 chapters in this third edition, there are two new chapters on the management modes of behaving (Chapter 7) and digitalizing (Chapter 11). The remaining chapters have been tightened and the contents updated. We have added another full-blown teaching case featuring the Indian company Yash Pakka's innovative biomimetic management practices. We have also updated, replaced, and added over 50 cases, pioneer interviews, true stories and practitioner profiles.

The new Behaving chapter expands on contents that in the previous edition formed part of the Folleading chapter. The decision to add a dedicated organizational behaviour chapter was based on both the prominent role of organizational behaviour in many introductory management course syllabi, and in order to tighten the overloaded Folleading chapter, which students had reportedly found somewhat overwhelming in coverage.

The new Digitalizing chapter responds to the significant transformation into a digital realm of management practices. One of the reviewers of the second edition made a very convincing argument that, like entrepreneuring and glocalizing, digitalizing had become a pervasive mode of management that most managers engage in.

While recognizing this, however, we also have followed student and educator feedback voicing concerns about the length and depth of some of the chapters. As a consequence, this new edition features somewhat shorter chapters throughout. In most chapters, some sections that seemed important but not essential have been moved into a supplementary online resources package which is available through Sage's companion website: **https://study.sagepub. com/laasch3e**

ACKNOWLEDGEMENTS

Books are never only the author's work. Considering the over 70 contributors to this manuscript, this phrase is even more true for *Principles of Business & Management*. My heartfelt thanks go out to the 16 chapter and case co-authors, each of them being distinguished experts in their respective fields, who have brought in a depth and topic expertise that I could never have reached on my own. I am grateful to the 20 pioneers, the 21 practitioners appearing as themselves, and the 21 anonymous protagonists featured in each chapter's 'True Story case'.

I am genuinely grateful for the exceptional support provided by everyone at Sage, in particular Matt Waters and Jess Moran, as well as the amazing team of sales representatives and course instructors around the world who ensure that this book's message about better forms of business and management reaches our future managers.

PLEASE BE IN TOUCH!

Introductory management courses fulfil a crucial role in shaping incoming management students' perspectives on what management is and can be [7]. Imagine if all the tens of thousands of introduction to management and business courses around the world taught ethical, responsible, and sustainable management as the new normal of business management! A vision like this can become a reality, but it requires all of us to work together. Transforming management education and transforming management to become management 'for the world', needs all of us to be connected in a network of like-minded change makers [8].

If you are a student, please join our LinkedIn student community by searching for the group named 'Managing Responsibly Network'. If you are a course instructor using this book, or interested in using this book, please join the LinkedIn group titled 'Principles of (Responsible) Management Instructors Network'.

Oliver Laasch

Berlin, May 15 2023

REFERENCES

1.   Cameron KS, Ireland RD, Lussier RN, New JR, Robbins SP. Management textbooks as propaganda. *Journal of Management Education.* 2003, 27(6): 711–729.
2.   Khurana R. *From higher aims to hired hands: The social transformation of American business schools and the unfulfilled promise of management as a profession.* Princeton: Princeton University Press, 2010.
3.   Donham P. Is management a profession? *Harvard Business Review.* 1962, 40(5): 60–68.
4.   Donham WB. The emerging profession of business. *Harvard Business Review.* 1927, 5(4): 401–405.
5.   Gherardi S. *How to conduct a practice-based study: Problems and methods* (2nd edn). Cheltenham: Edward Elgar, 2019.
6.   Price OM, Gherardi S, Manidis M. Enacting responsible management: A practice-based perspective. In: Laasch O, Suddaby R, Freeman RE, Jamali D, eds. *The research handbook of responsible management.* Cheltenham: Edward Elgar, 2020.
7.   Christopher E, Laasch O, Roberts J. Pedagogical innovation and paradigm shift in the introduction to management curriculum. *Journal of Management Education.* 2017, 41(6): 787–793.
8.   Muff K, Dyllick T, Drewell M, North J, Shrivastava P, Haertle J. *Management education for the world: A vision for business schools serving people and the planet.* Cheltenham: Edward Elgar, 2013.

FOREWORD BY METTE MORSING

Mette Morsing, Outgoing Head of PRME (Principles for Responsible Management Education), United Nations Global Compact

Principles of Business & Management provides a truly excellent overview of a burgeoning field of management with a focus on how new responsibilities and the UN's Sustainable Development Goals (SDGs) are taken on by management professionals to make business serve societal development. This book insists admirably and systematically on a 180 degrees turnaround to view management as a profession in service of society rather than taking on the conventional view on management as a discipline in service of individual businesses. While this may sound like a small rhetorical twist, that is not the case. Such a twist has been referred to as Capitalism 2.0. and this book's perspective on management makes the implications clear. Making societal development the core purpose of management practice is a far-reaching approach that challenges management practice – and management theory. It implies a shift from a business-centric focus to a society-centric focus in every small and large area of managerial decision-making. While it may seem obvious and perhaps even trivial to some, it is important to remember that this is not the way many managers are trained today around the world. And this is not the main message from many management textbooks taught in classrooms all over the world.

In 21 chapters, *Principles of Business & Management* challenges conventional management ideologies, or what is in the book referred to as 'old world management' by providing a 'new world management', importantly offering a journey on how to get there: 'transition world management'. With an ambition of introducing students to classical and recent management theorizing while at the same time ongoingly relating to current real-life business challenges in cases and business leader comments, this book does not try to simplify or downplay the complexity of the task for management in the context of dire global challenges. Readers are taken on a complex journey and invited to reflect and think for themselves. The book provides great overviews, definitions and insightful questions to inspire reflections and dialogue for current and next generation managerial decision-making to carefully consider how to support scientifically informed, socially inclusive and long-term planetary well-being.

While this book introduces its readers to responsible management at the individual firm level, it importantly discusses how responsible and sustainable development are related to management practices in society today. It encourages the reader to think about how systemic injustice, corruption, human rights abuse and climate change are issues of management, and not just externalities to be blamed on someone else or on 'the system'. I applaud the book for doing that. If our students – the world's future decision-makers – across disciplines, programmes and paradigms at business schools and universities today are to understand what responsible management is about, they must understand management as a practice that plays a key role for the interconnectedness of human beings and eco-systems across time and geographies for the world.

Oliver Laasch and his contributors have courageously decided to take out 'responsible' from the 'responsible management' title. I respect their trust in the self-fulfilling prophecies (a phrase they use themselves) and while I think we still need to remind managers about their new responsibilities, and that we have a long way ahead of us as management educators to do exactly that, I believe that the content and spirit of this book may in fact exactly contribute to stimulating future practitioners to integrate societal responsibility as a taken-for-granted ambition in any management practice.

Finally, the book's baseline respect for integrity, professionalism and inclusiveness is well aligned with the UN principles and values. The very fact that around 70 individuals have contributed to the production of the book is itself a testimony of the appreciation of the need to embrace many and not always aligned perspectives if we are to achieve societal and planetary betterment. And this is the real task facing modern managers. I congratulate the author and his team for the hard and careful work that has gone into producing this text, and I wish the book to be a cornerstone for new debates on responsible management.

Dr Mette Morsing
Outgoing Head of PRME (Principles for Responsible Management Education)
United Nations Global Compact

New York

an initiative of the United Nations Global Compact

ABOUT THE AUTHOR

Oliver Laasch is a Chaired Professor of Responsible Management at ESCP Business School, and an Adjunct Professor of Social Entrepreneurship at the University of Manchester. He previously filled academic full-time roles at the University of Manchester (UK), University of Nottingham Ningo (China), Steinbeis University Berlin (Germany), the Tecnologico de Monterrey (Mexico), and Seoul National University (South Korea), and visiting positions at the University of Tübingen's Global Ethic Institute and at Copenhagen Business School. His research interest lies in alternative business models and in responsible management.

Oliver is an Associate Editor of the journal, *Academy of Management Learning and Education* and has edited related special issues for the *Journal of Business Ethics*, *Journal of Management Education*, and *Organization & Environment*. He is a long-standing contributor to the United Nations Principles for Responsible Management Education (PRME) initiative. He edits the responsible management education book collection, has coordinated UN working groups, and founded the Center for Responsible Management Education (CRME). Oliver has co-edited *The Sage handbook of responsible management learning and education* as well as the *Research handbook of responsible management*.

Oliver has worked extensively as coach and consultant with dozens of companies and universities in staff and faculty development. He has also designed and taught a variety of full courses on bachelor, master's, PhD and executive education levels, including blended and massive open online courses such as the Coursera MOOC 'Managing Responsibly'.

ABOUT THE AUTHOR

PRAISE FOR THE BOOK

'The practice of management needs to move with the times, and today's business environment requires managers to take a much broader view of their responsibilities than was necessary in the past. This book provides the first comprehensive guide to this new management agenda – how those in management and leadership positions can contribute to sustainable development and social responsibility.'

Julian Birkinshaw FBA, Professor of Strategy & Entrepreneurship, London Business School, UK

'This book is an important and very timely contribution to the broader field of management. It convincingly shows that we have to rethink the very core of management, if we want to ensure its relevance in a society where sustainable business becomes the new normal. *Principles of Business & Management* will therefore be an indispensable reference work for anyone interested in the future of management education.'

Andreas Rasche, Professor of Business in Society, Copenhagen Business School, Denmark

'Another significant piece of work by Oliver Laasch, a warrior for responsible management in practice and education. The book, focusing on all moral and practical aspects of business leadership and management, has nothing less than the potential to create business as a force for good. Rich, engaging and colourful, with numerous examples, interviews, facts and stories, it is a joy to read. This should be on the bookshelf of existing and future business leaders and business management educators.'

Debbie Haski-Leventhal, Professor of Management, Macquarie Business School, Macquarie University, Australia

'I am happy to see this management book make a strong case for ethics and social responsibility. Companies are deeply affected by social problems that endanger livelihoods, social cohesion, and human values. Companies need to show that their company cares deeply about people and the planet.'

Philip Kotler, S.C. Johnson & Son Distinguished Professor of International Marketing (emeritus), Kellogg School of Management, Northwestern University, USA

'Sustainable management strategies are central to the success of our planet, our civilization, and the organizations that will thrive in the 21st century. Oliver Laasch guides the reader, managers and students alike, through the challenges, ethical dilemmas, and strategies that will lead to profound levels of success. We all have much to learn from Oliver Laasch and his perspective.'

Nancy J. Adler, S. Bronfman Professor Emerita in Management, McGill University, Montreal, Canada

'An excellent book that adeptly prepares students to become leaders in a new era of business that is shaped by societal grand challenges such as climate change, inequalities and resource scarcity. It enables students to understand the role and responsibilities of managers, and critically informs them how they can manage organizations to make a positive impact in the world. The book offers the latest in scholarly thinking and management approaches that come alive to students through vivid examples, cases and insightful interviews with top scholars and practitioners.'

Steve Kennedy, Associate Professor of Business Sustainability, Rotterdam School of Management, Erasmus University, Netherlands

'*Principles of Business & Management: Practicing Ethics, Responsibility, Sustainability* is a refreshing and welcome text in the field. By positioning Responsible Management as 'business as usual', it centres the profession of management in service of society and the planet. Thus the required knowledge, skills and competences to manage ethically, responsibly and sustainable are fully integrated with those associated with managing people and resources in an organisation.'

Carole Parkes, Professor of Responsible Management & Leadership, University of Winchester, UK

CHAPTER FEATURES GUIDE

The third edition of **Principles of Business & Management** includes a wide range of features to support and enhance your learning throughout. Look out for these invaluable features in each of the chapters as you read!

- Learning goals outline what you will gain from reading each chapter.

- **Facts** at the start of each chapter provide a fun, scary or impressive piece of information about a key topic.

- 'Spotlight' cases at the start of each chapter feature real companies from around the globe to aid your understanding of business and management practices.

- Key terms in chapter margins provide clear, concise definitions to save you having to interrupt your reading and search online.

- Sustainable Development Goals (SDG) icons connect the global goals for a better and more sustainable world, created by the United Nations (UN), with the relevant areas of management in the text so you can more easily recognise and link the two.

- Pioneer interviews in each chapter include the views and opinions of iconic thinkers in the fields of business and management as well as closing questions for your consideration.

- Professional profiles in each chapter include expert insight from practitioners across a range of different industries as well as closing questions for your consideration.

- 'True Story' cases in each chapter provide first-hand managerial insights with questions for your consideration to help deepen your understanding of how business people practice management in the most complex of situations.

- 'Digging Deeper' resources and worksheets provide advanced, hands-on coverage and activities to prepare you for management in the real world.

PART A

BASICS

CHAPTER 1

MANAGEMENT IN CONTEXT

OLIVER LAASCH

LEARNING GOALS

1. Understand how old-world management practices have formed our present world
2. Appreciate the complexities and tensions of transition-world management practices
3. Envision professional management practices in service of a new world

SCARY FACT

Among the Fortune Global 500 companies, most have climate-related targets (83%). Across other dimensions of nature, freshwater consumption (25%), chemical and plastic pollution (20%), forest and seabed loss (9%), biodiversity loss (5%) and nutrient pollution (<1%), targets are far lower [1].

SPOTLIGHT

NEW WORLD MANAGEMENT

Management practice in the outdoor company Patagonia has long been making headlines. Its practices have been called innovative, radical, and even fanatical. What is unique about these management practices and why does Patagonia use them?

A typical practice is, for instance, demarketing. Potential consumers are asked to think twice about whether they really need Patagonia's product and are encouraged to buy less

[2]. Management may also increase a product price on purpose, so that people buy less and pay the full cost of the product, including its environmental cost [3–5]. Patagonia aims to curb its growth by practicing 'controlled growth' [5]. Instead of using up its production resources, it works to replenish resources through restorative sourcing and production management practices [6].

(Continued)

Courtesy of patagonia

While most companies try to pay as little tax as possible, Patagonia has long assumed responsibility to pay a 'self-imposed tax', donating 1 per cent of its sales to environmental NGOs. In September 2022 founder Yvon Chouinard and his family ramped up this commitment by transferring their ownership shares to the Patagonia Purpose Trust and the Holdfast Collective, a group of climate- and biodiversity- supporting non-profit organizations [7].

'Patagonia's famous range' by Nicolas.Boullosa is licensed under CC BY 2.0

What these practices have in common is an attempt to innovate management in a way that makes it fit for purpose in a context characterized by pressing ethical, social, and environmental issues and crises like corruption, inequality, and climate change. As the founder Yvon Chouinard explains, these practices are 'based on wanting to be here 100 years from now' [8]: they are new world management practices.

SHAPE-SHIFTING CONTEXTS OF (UN) PROFESSIONAL MANAGEMENT

> People are suffering. People are dying. Entire ecosystems are collapsing. We are in the beginning of a mass extinction and all you can talk about is money and fairytales of eternal economic growth … How dare you! … How dare you pretend that this can be solved with just business as usual?
>
> Greta Thunberg at the 2019 UN Climate Action Summit [9]

What do Greta Thunberg's words have to do with management practices? What does the introductory case of Patagonia's management practices have to do with her statement? Can business management practices that may appear harmless, such as profit maximization, consumer marketing, and global supply chain management, really be blamed for much of what's wrong with the world? Conversely, could management possibly address, maybe even repair, many of these problems?

This chapter provides a reflective space for you to look for answers to these questions. We will discuss management's shape-shifting past, present, and future contexts. At the heart of this is how management practices have created and continuously recreate our day-to-day realities, and how they may shape future realities. We will consider the fact that management practices are influenced by their present context, but also influence and reshape their future context.

A **profession** is an occupation that serves society and the world. For instance, the medical profession serves a healthy world, the legal profession serves a just and fair world. Professional business management, in turn, should serve the goods and services the world needs and therefore all the people in it [10–12]. Due to the important role of professions, any unprofessional **practices** and practicing unprofessionally have the potential to do much harm. For this reason, most professions have a code of practice outlining 'professional conduct'. Such codes put forward practices that professionals should and should not engage in, and how they should practice. Examples are a medical doctor's Hippocratic Oath and the oaths that lawyers take before being allowed to practice. Such a professional code of practice has recently also been introduced for management [13, 14].

Translating this understanding of professionalism to management, we understand **professional management** as a particular type of management practice. To be called 'professional', this management practice requires both to be carried out in service of society and the planet, and to be carried out

Profession
a type of specialized occupation in service of society and the world

Professional practice
practicing and practices that serve society and the world in professional conduct

Professional management
management practice carried out with professional conduct and in pursuit of goals serving society and the world

with professional conduct. As we will discuss further in the next chapter, a manager up to the task will require both 'normal' management competence to get things done with people and resources, and an ability to manage ethically, responsibly, and sustainably. This book is designed to enable (aspiring) managers to develop both types of competences in an integrated way.

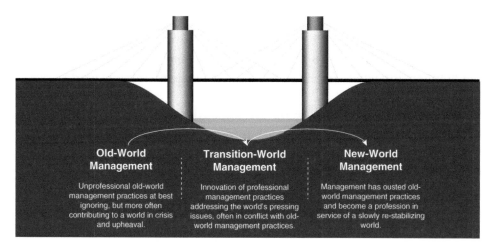

Old-World Management	Transition-World Management	New-World Management
Unprofessional old-world management practices at best ignoring, but more often contributing to a world in crisis and upheaval.	Innovation of professional management practices addressing the world's pressing issues, often in conflict with old-world management practices.	Management has ousted old-world management practices and become a profession in service of a slowly re-stabilizing world.

FIGURE 1.1 The changing contexts of (un)professional management

Credit: Slidemodel.com

In this chapter, you will first learn how management has developed unprofessional practices that do not live up to management's potential to serve and better the world. We call these practices 'old-world management' (see Figure 1.1). You will also learn how many of these practices have created, and are continuously recreating, some of the gravest problems we face in our world today. These include inequality, climate change, and the collapsing ecosystems which Greta Thunberg and many others have drawn attention to.

Secondly, we will discuss how many managers nowadays engage in innovative management practices and management innovation of new practices that are aimed at addressing the world's pressing issues. Great examples of such transition-world practices are the practices of demarketing and planned growth, which we have already been introduced to in the case of Patagonia. That these practices have been called not only 'innovative' but also 'radical' and 'fanatical' exemplifies the stark contrast and at times open conflict with still dominant old-world management practices that 'won't go down without a fight'.

Third, together we will envision a type of new-world management that ticks the boxes of a management profession in service of the world.

Management practices
activities that management
practitioners customarily
engage in

We will do so by actively identifying old-world **management practices** and introducing their new-world alternatives. This is urgent. No time to lose. Let's get to it!

OLD-WORLD MANAGEMENT

Martin Parker, the author of the book *Shut down the business school* [15] claims that 'Management has made the world that we live in. The world that we live in could now be destroyed by management … Now, more than ever, we need to rethink management' [16]. How can management have made the world we are living in and what kind of world is this management-made world?

HOW (UN)PROFESSIONAL MANAGEMENT MATTERS

For a moment, let us take a step back in time to think about one of the most amazing management innovations in history: factory production. It probably sounds like a very normal and unexciting practice from the perspective of a person, like you and me, living in the twenty-first century. However, the practice of factory production was revolutionary when it was invented in the 1850s, and with novelties like Ford's moving assembly line and robotic factories, it has kept reinventing itself until today [17].

Management innovation
invention and implementation
of a management practice that
breaks with 'normal' practices

Richard Arkwright, a tailor's son and self-made entrepreneur, is often credited as the **management innovator** who invented and implemented factory production (see the 'Factory production in a cotton mill' image) in the English village of Cromford [18]. Arkwright's textile factory ran on practices that were machine-aided flow production, where the item flowed through the production process while being transformed into the end product. This practice broke with past production practices based on individual workshop-based production by skilled craftspeople. Factory production, in contrast, centres on division of tasks that requires only lowly or semi-skilled workers [19–21]. This 'management innovation', an innovation of management practices [22–24] was in a way the invention of modern management itself, as factory production required supervision of semi-skilled labour by a manager [19].

Factory production in a cotton mill.

Look and Learn.

Arkwright's invention first changed lives in the village of Cromford, which experienced an influx of low-skilled migrant workers – mostly former farmers who became workers in the factory. The management practice of factory production was at the very heart of the industrial revolution and went

on to change the world. We still see urbanization and 'modern cities' fuelled by the influx of low-skilled workers. Factory-produced goods boosted global trade as global trade was required to ship the massive amounts of goods produced in factories to wherever they were in demand around the world. Factory production drove down the costs of products, and consumerism beyond the basic needs of people became possible. Due to a stable income from factories, compared to the income derived from the previously dominant agriculture, a sizeable middle class emerged, which in turn engaged in consumerism and which could be influenced by consumerist marketing.

The practice of factory production also 'produced' a world with a tension between capitalist and communist systems, and related practices. Capitalist practices are centred on the belief in human opportunities for people to 'work their way up' by accumulating private property and in efficient market-exchange of produced goods, by entrepreneurs just like Arkwright. Communist practices instead aim to 'free' and empower the workers 'enslaved' in factory production by commonly owned factories, abandoning property, and a (state) controlled exchange of goods.

11 November, the Chinese Singles' day, one of the world's biggest consumption festivals boosted with the help of Jack Ma's Alibaba.

Management innovation of factory production shows how practices in general, and management practices in particular, can change people's lives and the world for better or worse. This story of Arkwright also highlights the potential of (un)professional management both to positively contribute to the world and do considerable harm. On the one hand, without factory production, many of the people now living comfortable middle-class lives might still be caught in poor living conditions. On the other hand, without factory production we would not have today's overconsumption that has brought human existence on planet Earth to the brink of collapse.

This tension was obvious in the thoughts of management leaders in the early nineteenth century. In 1927 for instance, Mary Parker Follett, who has been called 'the prophet of management' [25–27], stressed that 'all professional business [wo]men assume grave responsibilities' [10]. Wallace Brett Donham, the second dean of Harvard Business School idealistically envisioned 'this new profession of business … with the sound evolutionary progress of civilization as its objective' [11]. However, he also warned that 'unless more of our business leaders learn to exercise their powers and responsibilities with a definitely

Mary Parker Follett: *"Finally, management, not bankers nor stockholders, is now seen to be the fundamental element in industry. It is good management that draws credit, that draws workers, that draws customers. Moreover, whatever changes come, whether industry is owned by individual capitalists or by the state or by the workers, it will always have to be managed. Management is a permanent function of business... Business as a public service, which carries with it a sense of responsibility for its efficient conduct. The profession of business management... must prepare themselves as seriously for this profession as for any other. They must realize that they, as all professional [wo]men, are assuming grave responsibilities, that they are to take a creative part in one of the large functions of society, a part which, I believe, only trained and disciplined [wo]men can in the future hope to take with success."*

Wallace Brett Donham: *"The development, strengthening, and multiplication of socially minded business [wo]men is the central problem of business. Moreover, it is one of the great problems of civilization, for such [wo]men can do more than any other type to rehabilitate the ethical and social forces of the community and to create the background which is essential to a more idealistic working philosophy... the development... of socially minded business [wo]men is the central problem of business... It is one of the great problems of civilization... unless more of our business leaders learn to exercise their powers and responsibilities with a definitely increased sense of responsibility toward other groups in the community (...) our civilization may well head for one of its periods of decline. (...) leaders who are competent to solve these problems are strangely missing."*

FIGURE 1.2   Visionary thought on the role of professional management

SOURCE: HUP Donham, Wallace B. (1). Harvard University Archives.

increased sense of responsibility towards other groups in the community (...) our civilization may well head for one of its periods of decline' [28]. Figure 1.2 shows more of their views.

THE REALITIES OF UNPROFESSIONAL MANAGEMENT PRACTICES

How do you think we humans have done as (un)professional managers in the last hundred years? What kind of management have we practiced and what kind of reality have we created? Here is a brief list of examples of how managerial practices invented in the last hundred years are linked to some of the most serious problems we now face:

- Practices of **continuous company growth** have led to an economic system that continuously produces more than the Earth is able to support while continuing to function as a suitable habitat for humanity.

- **Consumerist marketing** practices creating unnecessary wants have led people to overconsume. Population increases and an increase in the number of people having money to overconsume now exceed what our planet can support.

- Maintaining growth-consumption requires practices of **low-cost production**, which create a need for the cheapest possible, which leads to exploitative (ab)use of workers in low-labour-cost countries.

- Practices related to a **take–make–waste** production management have led to mountains of waste and quite literally islands of plastic waste floating in the oceans.

- Management evaluation practices based on **quarterly reporting** emphasize short terms and make long-term sustainable management practices unfeasible.

- The practice of **'exploiting' resources** has led to collapsing ecosystems, including forests and the ocean, a species extinction crisis, and an instrumentalization of human 'resources'.

- **Shareholder-value-based management** practices give priority to company owners, leading managers to treat all other stakeholders – e.g. communities, ecosystems, employees – as being of lower-importance.

- Executive payment practices, particularly related to **high-level pay** (CEO and other C-suite managers), produce and reproduce economic inequality.

- Practices of **paying women less than men** for the same job done maintain gender inequality.

- **Strategic human resources management** looking for only the 'best and brightest' leads to exclusion from the labour market, unemployment, and poverty.

- **Globalized supply chain management** has been linked to the collapse of local industries and their communities and contributes to climate change.

- Finance and accounting practices centred on **financial costs and value** create a management system that at best is ignorant about social and environmental cost and value, and at worst harms society and the environment.

All these practices are examples of what we call 'old-world management'. These practices have not only contributed to the critical situation we are now in, but are also misaligned with the needs of the troubled world we live in. We now realize that old-world management practices form a management occupation whose practices are not in the best interests of society and the Earth as a whole.

Engaging in these and similar practices makes a manager an **unprofessional manager**. For instance:

- You can be highly competent in marketing management, but if this marketing fuels unsustainable consumption, which harms society and adversely affects the Earth, you are not engaging in a professional management practice.

- You can be a 'pro' at cost accounting, but if you are not including social and environmental costs, you are not managing professionally.

- You might be the world's greatest strategist, but if you practice strategy in service of outcomes that do harm to society or the planet, you are not practicing professional management.

Unprofessional management practice
managerial practice not conducted in the service of society and the planet or without professional conduct

Professional management practice requires competence to carry out management tasks 'professionally',[1] whilst ensuring that the tasks themselves are in service of society and the Earth.

After reading this section you might feel that becoming a professional manager is a daunting task. Can we really avoid unprofessional practice if it seems to be so deeply embedded in the current management? At the same time, you may also be thinking about the potential that business management has to do good, such as creating fulfilling jobs, solving society's problems through business solutions, and producing amazing products and services. The next section and the next chapter discuss these kinds of questions, including the challenges and opportunities of practicing professional management in our current managerial world as it transitions towards professional, 'new-world' management.

TRANSITION WORLD MANAGEMENT

King Charles III of the United Kingdom summarized the current situation dramatically at the Davos Economic Forum when he challenged managers to engage in a 'paradigm shift, one that inspires action at revolutionary levels and pace ... we need a new economic model or the planet will burn ... and just think for a moment – what good is all the extra wealth in the world, gained from "business as usual", if you can do nothing with it except watch it burn in catastrophic conditions?' The World Economic Forum calls this 'The Great Reset' of our economic system [29]. Such a revolutionary new system will need professional management practices, and for this system to come into being we need to go through a transition from old-world to new-world management. For this transition, in turn, we need 'subversive' management that does away with inadequate management theories and practices, and instead promotes new theories and practices conducive to creating the world we want [30].

Transitions are understood as 'co-evolving processes in economy, society, ecology, and technology that progressively build up toward a revolutionary systemic change' [31]. Management currently operates in a world in the process of a revolutionary transition. It is a transition from an old world where management contributes to global issues and crises, to a new world where management must become a force for restoring and restabilizing the world. It is a systemic transition from management that parasitically uses the Earth, to a management that serves the world, which is a management for all the people in the world rather than just a few, and which restores the Earth to its previous healthy state [32].

Transitions
revolutionary systemic changes emerging from the co-evolution of economic, technological, social, cultural, and ecological changes

---

[1]We will discuss professional management competence in depth in Chapter 2.

The following sections reflect on the questions relating to this transition: What is the global transition in revolutionary systemic changes that we are involved in? It is a transition from the world being issue- and crisis-ridden to being more stable. This transition may happen either through a catastrophic forced transition – for instance, an acceleration of extinction due to the effects of climate change – or a global food crisis due to collapsing ecosystems, for example due to water issues, or extinction of insects such as bees. Or, hopefully, this transition will happen in the form of a human revolution in changes to ways of life. What can the role of managers and management be in that transition? What drivers and inhibitors will we encounter when trying to manage professionally in a transition world?

THE MESS WE ARE IN

In the initial words of this chapter, Greta Thunberg reminded us of some of the most salient global issues and crises humanity has created. We are living in an era of convergent grand crises [33]. The second millennium has seen an increasing interrelatedness and convergence of those crises towards a global mega-crisis triggered by multiple causes. Such challenges are increasingly systemic, interrelated and complex, and resist resolution which makes solving them a 'super wicked problem' [34, 35].

Humanity's global footprint is a way of measuring how much of our planet's resources are used for human production and consumption. A footprint of one would mean that on an annual basis we are using exactly the amount of resources the Earth can produce and replace. A footprint below one would imply we are using less than the Earth produces, and that it is restoring its resources. However, we are currently using up 1.75 Earths a year, so that each year we are getting closer to running out of natural resources. This means that humanity's resource consumption exceeds the reproductive capacity of our planet. This overconsumption is enabled by our economic system, which in turn is enabled by our (un)professional management practices [36].

Research published in two leading scientific journals, *Nature* and *Science*, has identified nine ecological boundaries (see Figure 1.3). Overstepping just one of these boundaries makes global catastrophes highly likely. We

Tough questions for the world's management in Davos.

are currently overstepping four of them, creating a very real risk of such catastrophes, among them climate change and species genetic diversity (species extinction). In summary, we are currently in an unsafe operating space for humanity on Earth. If the Earth's ecosystem should destabilize, it will no longer support human society as we know it [37, 38]. Further research has outlined how management practices need to change so less damage is inflicted and we step back from **planetary boundaries**, or even start to restore ecosystems [39, 40]. Patagonia's ecosystem restoration management practices are excellent examples, which need to be repeated on a large scale.

Planetary boundaries
ecological thresholds, which if overstepped threaten humanity's subsistence on the Earth

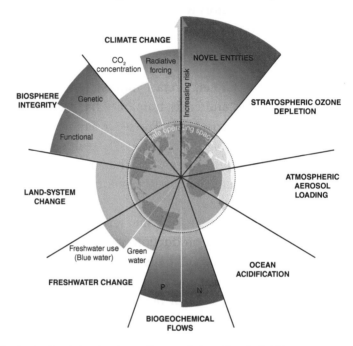

FIGURE 1.3   The planetary boundaries of a safe operating space for humanity on Earth [37]

Interestingly, CEOs in a large-scale global survey appear to lack an appreciation of these long-term risks. The only planetary boundaries related risk they fear is climate change and it comes fourth after the risks of cyber security, health, and macroeconomic volatility, thought before geopolitical conflict, and social inequality [41]. Even more importantly than appreciating the risks, there is a need for us as economic actors to understand and assume our role as global crisis makers. It has been suggested that we rename our Earth epoch from 'anthropocene' (the geological epoch in which humanity negatively impacts the planet as a whole) to 'capitalocene', as most of the human impacts have emerged from economic activity [42, 43].

Sustainable Development Goals (SDGs)
17 goals addressing humanity's social, environmental, and economic issues

The **Sustainable Development Goals (SDGs)** introduced by the United Nations (see Figure 1.4) have become a global movement that is influencing both management practice and management education. Addressing one or several of the SDGs, or at least not exacerbating the related issues, is an important step towards professional management practice. For instance, a recruiting manager could combat poverty (SDG 1) by creating recruitment practices that enable poor unemployed people to enter the workplace. A product research and development manager in a food company could manage her team to develop products with lower sugar and salt in order to contribute to good health and well-being (SDG 3). Any type of manager currently travelling for work could take climate action (SDG 13) by, wherever possible, using phone or internet meetings instead of flying to them, and by carbon-offsetting all flights still taken.

FIGURE 1.4 The Sustainable Development Goals

SOURCE: www.un.org/sustainabledevelopment The content of this publication has not been approved by the United Nations and does not reflect the views of the United Nations or its officials or Member States

MANAGERS' TRANSITIONAL ROLE

Forty-two per cent of CEOs mention their personal motivation as the main driver for their companies' sustainability initiatives [41]. The very powerful high-level managers say they are leading an integral part of their company's activities based on a personal preference to do good. Individual management practitioners, and not only those high up the ranks, matter and are critical in professional management and for the progress towards professional new world management.

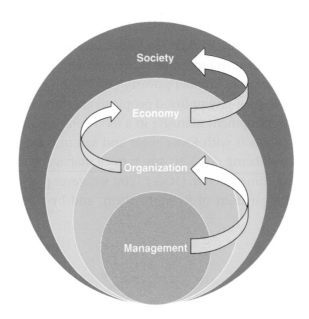

FIGURE 1.5   The layered nature of managerial influence

Figure 1.5 illustrates the central role of managers and management for a broad systemic shift towards ethics, responsibility, and sustainability. The figure illustrates how there are three broad change mechanisms that may well be triggered by a change in individual managers or groups of managers towards truly professional management. First, managers have the power to change business in their respective spheres of influence, regardless of their hierarchical position. A frontline manager may create a bubble of equity, diversity, and inclusion in managing their own team. A top-level manager can do the same for the company as a whole. Secondly, once the business has demonstrated success in transforming to more professional ways, its industry peers are likely to follow for competitive reasons. Companies from other industries and ultimately the economy as a whole could also follow the lead of innovative companies. Third, while the economy is changing, the impact on society of the overall economic system of industries and single companies becomes visible. For instance, consumers are educated through companies and now have some choice of sustainable and responsible products. Employees who have learned responsible practices in companies might transfer those to their individual lives. In developing countries, a waste recycling culture often starts first in companies and is then transferred to broader society. Companies leading in professional management activities often lobby politicians to foster public policies for ethics, responsibility, and sustainability.

The description of this chain of events is a highly idealized one. Change in reality is a process that starts at many other points. You could also identify social movements, consumers, or politicians as the individuals who trigger a particular change towards a better system, but the particular chains of beneficial events described here all start with management.

You might ask how one should engage in professional, new-world management practices if the whole system around us seems to be almost all unprofessional practices. How can management at Patagonia innovate practices so far away from the unprofessional norm? Management icon Peter Drucker once stressed how much 'normal' ways of doing management have become an institution: 'The emergence of management as an essential, a distinct and a leading institution is a pivotal event in social history. Rarely, if ever, has a new basic institution, a new leading group, emerged as fast as has management since the turn of this century' [44].

Professional managers at Patagonia realize that **institutional work** changes the institution of management. One type of institutional work refers to work to change what is institutionalized as 'normal' For instance, when Patagonia's management engages in restorative agriculture, it aims to establish this kind of agriculture as a new normal, where there is no exploitative unsustainable agriculture. A second type of institutional work is to try to maintain the 'old normal', for instance, when petroleum companies lobby against anti-carbon-emissions legislation. The third type of institutional work refers to creating new institutions, for instance, a profession of management, an entirely 'new normal'.

Institutional work
is work realized to maintain the 'old normal', to change it, or to create an entirely 'new normal'

User experience designer Emily advocating for the institutionalization of more advanced CO_2 management practices by her employer Amazon.

Jade Prevost Manuel / Shutterstock.com

DRIVERS AND INHIBITORS OF PROFESSIONAL MANAGEMENT

Transition-world management is characterized by the continuous struggle between forces that drive us to engage with professional new-world management, and the opposing forces, inhibitors dragging us back to old-world management (see Figure 1.6).

DRIVERS

We will now discuss four main drivers of professional management: First, main stakeholders like customers, employees, and civil society are increasingly expecting managers to contribute to society and the world through their

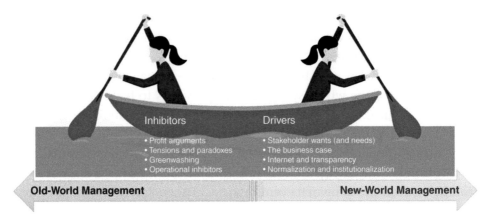

FIGURE 1.6   Inhibitors and drivers of professional management

CREDIT: Slidemodel.com

Business case
business opportunities arising
from ethical, responsible, and
sustainable management

companies. For instance, employees increasingly look for work with companies that have management practices that contribute to society. Many customers demand ethical, responsible, and sustainable products and services. They will boycott or rather 'buycott' companies that have been highlighted for their unprofessional management practices. Governments are increasing legislative pressure. Examples range from small advances, such as bans on disposable plastic bags in countries around the world, to the large-scale closing down of polluting factories in China. Last, but not least, civil society demands a change in management practices to address the world's pressing issues. For instance, air traffic in Sweden for the first time fell in response to the practice of 'flight shaming' and as Swedish people increasingly took 'no-flight pledges' [45]. Global movements like Black Lives Matter and Extinction Rebellion are attacking irresponsible practices in companies and society as a whole.

Secondly, there are many business opportunities in professional management in the service of society and the planet. As mentioned, professional management is attractive to many employees and customers, and there is a multi-billion dollar market for sustainable products around the world related to so-called LOHAS (lifestyles of health and sustainability). Using less of resources such as water and energy results in considerable cost savings. Management sensitive to social and environmental issues reduces the risk of a company being affected by the repercussions of related crises. In many cases, professional management is 'just good business'.

Third, with the worldwide use of mobile devices and social media it has become almost impossible to hide unprofessional behaviour. A clip of a manager's unprofessional behaviour can go viral within minutes. Such increased transparency incentivizes professional behaviour. Eighty-seven per cent of executives state that one of the main drivers for their responsible management activities is the mitigation of such risks to their brand. Another 64 per cent say they aim to increase their company's visibility in external responsible business rankings, which have become another widespread transparency mechanism [41]. Fourth, professional management practices in service of society and the planet are increasingly institutionalized. Norms like ISO 26000 for social responsibility and ISO 14000 for environmental management are present in most managerial workplaces. So are the United Nations Global Compact Principles relating to labour responsibility, human rights, corruption, and the environment. In addition, the Global Reporting Initiative's social and environmental reporting guidelines are widespread norms among managers. Many stock markets have launched sustainability indexes, such as the UK's FTSE4Good Index and the US's Dow Jones Sustainability Index and the Chinese Hang Seng Sustainability Index.

INHIBITORS

On the other hand, there are also widespread inhibitors of professional management. First, there are critical arguments related to profit. There is the old, but still very alive '**Friedman argument**', which implies that the only responsibility of managers is to make money. According to the late Nobel Prize Laureate in Economics, Milton Friedman, managers should not manage in the service of society and the planet as this takes away from their main profit-making responsibility. Others may question the motivation of managers who might be perceived to 'only be in it for the money', or to improve their reputation. A related argument suggests that one can only contribute to society and the integrity of the Earth in times of high profits and that such professional management cannot be maintained in times of economic hardship, for instance, during an economic crisis.

Friedman argument
the only managerial
responsibility is
to make profit

Second, there are often tensions and paradoxes between old-world and new-world management [46]. A management in service of society and the planet often requires prioritization. For instance, as a store manager in a supermarket, should you place unhealthy or high-revenue items at the cash register where people are more likely to buy them on impulse? Or should you rather place them further back in the store to make it less likely for these items to be purchased? We have a typical paradoxical situation here for professional management who want to both increase profit and ensure fewer people buy unhealthy products. The paradox is rooted in a contradiction between commercial business logic and the professional logic of serving society [47].

Third, stakeholders might accuse a manager of **greenwashing** when creating a misleading impression of the social, environmental, or ethical performance of a product or company. Many well-intentioned (and also less well-intentioned) companies have fallen through the 'greenwashing trapdoor' [48].

Greenwashing
creating a misleading impression
of social, environmental
and ethical performance

'Or could you take the train?' is a question asked by the airline KLM's fly responsibly campaign. Old-world greenwashing or new-world demarketing?

© 2020 KLM

"Dutch KLM flight attendants in Amsterdam airport before check-in" by Kristoffer Trolle is licensed under CC BY 2.0.

Once stakeholder confidence of a company's 'green credentials' is lost it is difficult to regain trust. To avoid greenwashing accusations, a professional manager aims to avoid exaggeration and misleading communication so that the professional management 'talk will match the walk'.

Fourth, there are also varieties of operational inhibitors. A survey among CEOs revealed how it is often (30%) hard to identify the business case. Forty-nine per cent of executives find it difficult to accommodate competing strategic priorities with professional management and strategy and forty-eight per cent encounter high complexity in integrating professional management practices throughout all business functions. Additional implementation issues are the lack of managers' professional management skills (24%) and difficulties engaging with external groups (30%). Executives also felt that the financial markets did not sufficiently recognize professional management efforts (34%) [41].

NEW-WORLD MANAGEMENT

'Management, like the combustion engine, is a mature technology that must now be reinvented for a new age' [49] concludes management thinker Gary Hamel. He had brought together a group of 35 eminent management specialists, C-suites that included managers at Google, UBS, and McKinsey, with academic management gurus like Henry Mintzberg and Peter Senge. This team of 'renegades', as they called themselves, jointly developed recommendations for a new world management, stating that management has to take the next evolutionary step. Interestingly, their first three recommendations all relate to management's role in society [49]:

1. Ensure that the work of management serves a **higher purpose**. Management, both in theory and in practice must orient itself to the achievement of **noble, socially significant goals**.

2. Fully embed the ideas of **community and citizenship** in management systems. There's a need for processes and practices that reflect the interdependence of all **stakeholder** groups.

3. Reconstruct management's **philosophical foundations**. To build organizations that are more than merely efficient, we will need to draw lessons from such fields as biology, political science, and theology.

Reinventing management as a whole will happen by reinventing one management practice at a time. Earlier in this chapter, we briefly discussed the invention and implementation of management practices that break with 'normal' practices, practices that go against the current paradigm and are 'management innovations'. In the case of Patagonia, we have seen new-world management innovations, such as demarketing, controlled growth, and restorative sourcing. The 'digging deeper' resource provided at the end of this chapter offers a non-exclusive list of old-world assumptions, and alternative new-world management practices and innovations that break with old-world practices. Throughout this book we will go deeper into many of these practices and examples.

Many of the management innovations in the table are related to ethics, social responsibility, and environmental sustainability. In the next sections we will first introduce these topics of professionalism and then explore what would be needed for management as a whole to become professional.

Reinventing management, however, cannot happen in a vacuum. It is a co-evolution with the economic system that makes management, and a co-evolution of the economic system made by management. What all of them have in common is a rupture with the 'mainstream' neoclassical and neoliberal economic thought that the previously dominant form of capitalism was built on. Underlying assumptions attacked are, for instance:

1. Humans are rational decision-makers → Irrational emotions and intuition explain human behaviours better than rational intellect.

2. Humans are utility maximizers → Common human behaviour, for instance, related to fairness, altruism, social capital, and vengeful behaviour, does not maximize utility.

3. Humans are egoistic and therefore competitive → We are more commonly social, collaborative, and caring.

4. Individual pursuit of wealth leads to social well-being → It has led to global and local economic and social inequality.

5. Private capital and unlimited wealth accumulation are necessary for capitalism to work and lead to well-being → Rather they lead to power imbalances that maintain the unhealthy interests of money elites.

6. There are no limits to economic growth and progress → We are nowadays meeting the social and environmental limits to growth, and social progress from growth is stalling.

7. Market exchange driven by the market equilibrium is the most efficient and effective, and therefore socially the most desirable form of exchange → Many of today's social and environmental issues have been caused by the glorification of market exchange.

8. Laissez faire! Economic behaviour must be freed and de-regulated, 'let the market do its thing' → There are negative consequences of 'capitalism unchained' and unregulated, for instance, related to free trade.

9. Neoclassical economics is a 'value neutral' 'positive' 'science' that describes and explains reality → Most neoclassical economics is unproven or is built on refuted assumptions on which the system of thought builds in spite of these flaws. Neoclassical economics rather than 'describing' reality is 'performative' as it becomes a self-fulfilling prophecy that changes reality.

10. Neoclassical economics is an all-embracing theory that adequately describes economic phenomena → It has blind spots such as economic phenomena related to feminist perspectives, like family economy.

Table 1.1 provides an overview of more recent alternative proposals for economic systems and observed digressions as to how actual economic behaviour increasingly contradicts neoclassical economic theory.

TABLE 1.1   Salient exemplary alternatives to the neoclassical economics that made our current capitalist system

Academic economics theories	
Heterodox economics [50–52]	An umbrella term for the long-established varieties of alternative economic theories disagreeing with neoclassical economics. So far, however, only a few Nobel Prize winners in economics have been heterodox economists.
Ecological economics [53, 54]	Studies human economies as subsystems of Earth's larger natural ecosystems.
Feminist economics [55]	Critically addresses phenomena that mainstream economics neglect (e.g. family economics, domestic work) and breaks with core assumptions (e.g. 'free' is not 'good' as it reshapes inequalities).
Observed and proposed shifts in economic behaviour	
Economy of the common good (Gemeinwohl Ökonomie) [56, 57]	A movement advocating for an alternative economic model that works towards the common good and cooperation before profit orientation and competition that have led to greed and uncontrolled growth.
Conscious capitalism [58, 59]	Proposes transformed but still capitalist practices for the conscious capitalist who pursues the ideal of capitalism as the most powerful system for social cooperation and human progress.
Purpose economy [60, 61]	A proposition for a new framing of the economic system based on the observation that economic systems are increasingly centred on the realization of individual, social, and societal purposes.
Bioeconomy [62, 63]	An economic system built dominantly on renewable natural resources and mimicking naturally sustainable biological processes.

ETHICS, RESPONSIBILITY, SUSTAINABILITY

The matrix in Figure 1.7 brings together the two criteria for professionalism, service, and professional conduct to illustrate four different types of management and managers.

Professional conduct and service closely relate to ethics, responsibility, and sustainability, the three **dimensions of professionalism** shown in Figure 1.8. These three dimensions are a recurrent theme of this book, with practical applications in each chapter. Sustainability, responsibility, and ethics overlap

Dimensions of professional
management
ethics, responsibility,
sustainability

significantly and strongly influence one another. However, they are centred on sufficiently distinct core concepts to make complementary valuable contributions to professional management.

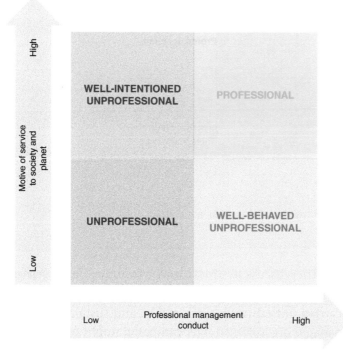

FIGURE 1.7 Types of (un)professional management and managers

CREDIT: Slidemodel.com

To further transition from old-world management to new-world management, old-world management practice should integrate ethics, responsibility, and sustainability into both their management conduct ('doing it right'), and the goals they serve ('getting the right things done'). Professional management therefore builds on ethical, responsible, and sustainable management.

- **Ethics** focuses on making the right decision in moral-dilemma situations [64] and builds on moral philosophy and behavioural ethics. Ethical management relies on conduct that embraces ethical behaviour and serves moral excellence.

- **Responsibility** deals with the relationship stakeholders, the various groups that affect or are affected by management including, for instance, employees, governments, and ecosystems [65]. Responsible management relies on conduct that fulfils its stakeholder responsibilities, and serves stakeholder value optimization.

- **Sustainability** focuses on social, environmental, and economic value for future generations [66]. Sustainable management favours conduct that balances social, environmental, and economic value, and serves to restore value through triple bottom line optimization [67].

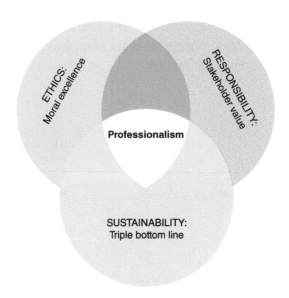

FIGURE 1.8   Dimensions of professionalism and 'good' management

CREDIT: Slidemodel.com

Professional management conduct
managing ethically, responsibly, and sustainably

Professional management service
managerial practice serving ethical, responsible, and sustainable goals and purposes

We will now further discuss **professional management conduct** and professional service. First, professional management conduct asks whether management is carried out ethically, responsibly, and sustainably. For instance, a marketing manager organizing a flyer campaign might engage in professional conduct by using biodegradable promotional materials (sustainability), ensuring that the contents are not discriminatory to any minority groups (ethics), and that it is not distributed to children (responsibility).

Second, **professional management service** is centred on whether and how management practice serves society and the Earth. For instance, the same marketing manager, while engaging in professional conduct, may not pursue professional service. Imagine if the marketing campaign they are organizing pursued the goal of promoting cigarettes (irresponsible due to health effects) or weekend flight trips (unsustainable due to increasing carbon emissions).

However, if their practice was aimed at, for instance, promoting a 'Veganuary'[2] vegan 'tastes like chicken' burger for KFC, we could claim they were pursuing professional goals related to ethics (less animal cruelty in chicken production), sustainability (less CO_2 emissions from plant

Food business management participating in 'Veganuary'

***

[2]A campaign joined by many food-related businesses in the United Kingdom, to promote vegan eating throughout January.

rather than animal production), and responsibility (towards customers by promoting healthier food options). Table 1.2 exemplifies some popular causes that could be addressed through managers' professional conduct and goals.[3]

TABLE 1.2   Professional management causes by dimension

Ethics (moral dilemma)	Responsibility (stakeholders)	Sustainability (triple bottom line)
- Human and natural rights	- Employee equity, diversity, and inclusion	- World water and ocean crisis
- Income inequality	- Labour standards	- Global warming
- Corporate governance	- Consumer rights and protection	- Deforestation and soil loss
- Fair competition	- Community well-being	- Overpopulation
- Corruption	- Supply chain practices	- Poverty and hunger
- Marketing ethics	- Good citizenship	- Ecosystem degradation
- Accounting ethics	- Respect for the law	- Biodiversity loss
- Use of artificial intelligence (AI)		

TOWARDS A NEW-WORLD MANAGEMENT PROFESSION?

As we have seen in the previous section, you and I can manage professionally if we make sure that we manage in the service of society and if we do so with professional conduct. Accordingly, professional management practice is something that managers can engage in. But does this make management as a whole a profession? No, 'not unless our economic system undergoes some revolutionary changes' [12]. We can see that the revolutionary change is underway, and that many think that it is time for management to step up. However, the concept that those who lead and 'manage our society's major private economic institutions might provide, or be responsible for providing, a public good is quite foreign to our customary way of thinking about management' [68].

1.   There is reason to believe that management is increasingly moving towards providing responsible **service to society**. For instance, over 700 business schools worldwide have committed to the United Nations Principles for Responsible Management Education initiative [69]. Pledging a professional MBA Oath originally launched at Harvard Business School and applied at over 5000 other MBA programmes, managers nowadays frequently commit to creating value for society ethically and responsibly [14, 70].

---

[3]Of course such a classification cannot be absolutely precise. A good example is corporate governance, which on the one hand fulfils the ethics criterion of the moral dilemma, but at the same time governs the stakeholder relationship between managers and company owners. The topic of poverty also has a sustainability characteristic in threatening the well-being of current and future generations, while having a responsibility dimension relating to managers' relationships to society and their role in furthering social welfare.

FIGURE 1.9   What makes a profession?

SOURCE: Adapted from [12]

For management to become a profession it would need the development of all four characteristics suggested in Figure 1.9 [12].

1.   A management profession needs a **process of qualification**. One could argue that with fairly standardized MBA programmes – accredited, for instance, through AACSB, EQUIS, or AMBA – we have that.

2.   One could argue that we also have a rather systematic **body of knowledge**. There are certain conceptual frameworks that are commonly covered in management degrees, such as Porter's five forces, balanced scorecards, the four Ps of marketing, the business model canvas, and cash flow analysis, which could be considered the parts of such a systematic body of knowledge.

3.   Management in general does not have a **professional enforcement organization**, like the Bar Association for lawyers, that would be able to license or ban managers from practicing. However, some management occupations, such as accounting (e.g. the American Institute of Public Accountants) and marketing (e.g. the Chartered Institute of Marketing) do have organizations that perform such a role. It is possible that the accreditation organizations mentioned above at

some point in the future might assume a similar role. In summary, we are not yet there, but professional management without a formally established management profession is still possible.

PRINCIPLES OF PROFESSIONAL MANAGEMENT IN CONTEXT

I. **Old-world management practices** have been instrumental in shaping the present world, both much of its progress, but also many of its issues.

II. We are living in a **'transition world'** characterized by varieties of **ethical, social, and environmental issues**, and by a **tension** between old and new world management.

III. Professional management addresses these issues by assuming a **responsibility to serve society and the world** as well as doing so in **professional conduct**.

IV. Professional management draws from the **dimensions of ethics, responsibility, and sustainability**.

V. Although any manager can work towards practicing management professionally, **making management a profession** requires considerable further institutional work.

MANAGEMENT GYM: TRAINING YOUR PROFESSIONAL SIX-PACK

Knowing

1. What are the main differences between old-world management and new-world management?

2. Define the three dimensions of professional management and elaborate on their unique characteristics, differences, and similarities.

3. Find up-to-date, in-depth information about one global issue and how it relates to managerial practice.

Thinking

4. Think about one management practice of your choice systemically by exploring its ripple effects on the world, close and far, over time.

5. Map the relationships between three social, environmental, or ethical issues.

6. Brainstorm ideas for management innovations that could make a real difference in terms of one of the global issues.

Acting

7. Engage in a new-world practice (can be a work or lifestyle practice) for one day.

8. For a week, stop engaging in one of your personal practices that impacts negatively on a planetary boundary.

9. Train yourself in one management practice that will improve your professional conduct.

Interacting

10. Write or respond to a social media post related to professional management to provoke reactions and engage in discussion.

11. Form a small group to jointly draw a mind map or rich picture that integrates your different views on one of the SDGs.

12. Put yourself into the shoes of someone who is as different as possible from you and try to see one global issue through their eyes.

Being

13. Reflect on who you want to be as a manager.

14. What are your personal values and how might they be drivers or inhibitors of your managing?

15. What are dos and don'ts for you as a manager? What are your aspirations? What are your hard limits?

Becoming

16. What seems most difficult to you about becoming a professional manager?

17. Reflect on one professional management issue in the form of a social media post in which you describe what it means to you personally.

18. Who do you want to become as a manager? Envision a future work day for yourself. What does your workplace look like? What will you wear? With whom will you meet and why? How do you feel?

SOURCE: Adapted from [71].

PIONEER INTERVIEW
RAKESH KHURANA

INTERVIEWER: OLIVER LAASCH

Rakesh Khurana is a Professor of Leadership Development at Harvard Business School, Professor of Sociology at Harvard University, and the Dean of Harvard College. He has contributed pioneering work, among others, on the professionalization of management, corporate leadership, and the role of business schools.

Courtesy of Rakesh Khurana

How it's going with the professionalization of management. Like many things in society it seems too slow and sometimes going in the wrong direction. But I am cautiously optimistic, or maybe ruggedly optimistic... A number of things have brought forward the necessity of a mindset shift, if not necessarily a professionalization project per se, in the way we institutionally define professions and managers.

A diverse community of management professionals. Just like in any healthy social group, you want to be sure there's a lot of diversity of perspectives, viewpoints, backgrounds, and experiences, and that it can be voiced. At the same time, it should also have a collective orientation toward shared responsibility and a community view that we are all part of a profession, and we have obligations to each other and as stewards meeting societal expectations.

Professionalization rituals. Business schools may want to think more explicitly about the role of rituals, myths, and ceremony which raise and elevate the notion that you are entering the profession no different than, for example, the white coat ceremony that might happen in medical schools, or when students are brought into the bar after law school. Business schools could be more intentional about thinking about the institutional infrastructure of what constitutes a profession, or at least heightens people's responsibilities and sense that they belong to something bigger than themselves.

Professionalizing management disciplines. How can business schools adapt their curriculums and infuse a normative meaning structure?... This means going beyond the traditional organizational behaviour courses and evolving them toward Selznick's model of institutional leadership. It also means that fields like strategy would anchor around sustainable strategy, and operations management around environment and climate. Finance and accounting would take into account the total costs of both the negative externalities and the positive

(Continued)

externalities and the total value created. So you could imagine in each of these areas a conceptual relationship that would lead to a meta-view that the purpose of a professional business education is to educate business and business leaders who have a positive impact on the broader society.

Challenging core tenets of neoliberal management. The ideas that... took the re-professionalization project off track are the neo-liberal anchored theories that the purpose of the firm is simply to maximize shareholder value. The idea that organizations have responsibilities or obligations to any stakeholder other than shareholders in the short term has been critically interrogated not only now by scholars, but more broadly normative pressures have come into that. I also think that the idea that the firm is simply a nexus of individual contracts, given the actual empirical and lived experiences and realities of most managers and executives, to paraphrase Max Weber, is now seen as belonging in the kindergarten of social thought. In that way, I think what we have seen is at least a sense that the paradigm and ideology of the neo-liberal or the financial conceptualization of the firm has been challenged.

Re-imagining capitalism and (de)growth. Poverty of imagination. Our students have an easier time imagining the end of the world than they can imagine modifications to capitalism. I think that's our fault, because we are not encouraging imagination among our students. I think growth is a complicated thing, because I want to separate growth from capitalism. A lot of social systems are oriented toward growth, family unit, churches, higher education institutions alike, there's an orientation toward growth. It can mean a lot of different things. In the material world it means something that has a specific set of consequences. But I want to disentangle this desire for growth and expansion which has been fairly universal for a long time. Then the question is if it is healthy or unhealthy. How are the benefits of growth distributed? If the benefits of growth distributed in the right place can, for example, lead to a more sustainable economy and sustainable environment. If you get the right growth to certain parts of developing economies... there are ways about thinking about the redistributive component.

QUESTIONS

1. Do you think there is such a thing as a management profession, and if so, do you feel part of it?

2. What do you think business schools could and should do for management professionalization? What is your school doing? What should it do?

3. Do you agree with the suggestions about which aspects of management should be re-thought and how? What specifically do you agree or disagree with? What would you add to the list and why?

PROFESSIONAL PROFILE
ANONYMOUS

This Professional Profile has been anonymized to protect the identity of the interviewee.

I am a corporate social responsibility (CSR) specialist at an Armenian telecommunications company.

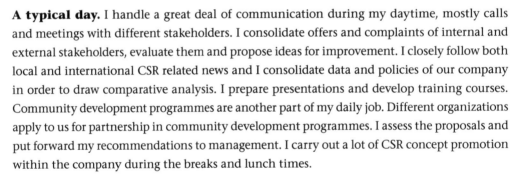

My position. I lead the CSR committee by coordinating the CSR strategy, its implementation and reporting according to sustainability reporting guidelines. My personal mission is to integrate responsibility into the company's day-to-day operations. We address organizational performance and improvement in socially responsible behaviour by applying the principles of the UN Global Compact, and the ISO 26000 standard.

A typical day. I handle a great deal of communication during my daytime, mostly calls and meetings with different stakeholders. I consolidate offers and complaints of internal and external stakeholders, evaluate them and propose ideas for improvement. I closely follow both local and international CSR related news and I consolidate data and policies of our company in order to draw comparative analysis. I prepare presentations and develop training courses. Community development programmes are another part of my daily job. Different organizations apply to us for partnership in community development programmes. I assess the proposals and put forward my recommendations to management. I carry out a lot of CSR concept promotion within the company during the breaks and lunch times.

Our Code of Ethics. Our Code of Ethics sets forth the principles and ethical standards for the professional conduct and responsibilities of employees. These principles and standards are used as guidelines during our daily professional activities. They constitute normative statements for all of us and provide guidance on issues that we may encounter in our professional day-to-day work.

Recommendations. To understand CSR we need to have an integrated understanding of economics, management, leadership, politics, procurement, social sciences, communication, diplomacy, environmental management, and finance. I also recommend speaking with friends, families, and colleagues to increase the number of people speaking the 'CSR language' around you.

(Continued)

Challenges. At first it was difficult to promote CSR and to make others speak about it. It took a few years to prove its importance. Other challenges were to differentiate CSR from philanthropy. CSR is mutually beneficial management, which begins with a sense of collective vision for the future and continues with difficult decisions about the balance between industrial production–consumption and environmental quality.

QUESTIONS

1. What drivers and inhibitors of professional management can you spot in this profile?

2. What connections to ethics, responsibility, and sustainability can you identify?

3. What other professional management practices could or should a company like this engage in?

TRUE STORY

SHOULD I STAY OR SHOULD I GO?

(Continued)

Who I am. My name is Armani and I have been in energy companies ever since I graduated from my undergraduate studies in civil and environmental engineering in Abu Dhabi. I have constructed many oil refineries and industrial gas stations in many places in the Middle East. I became interested in the project management side of things. After doing my MBA, I am now a managing director of a construction company that is a subsidiary of one of the world's top ten petroleum, or should I say 'energy', companies?

But who am I? Very recently my daughter Layla was born, a life event which made me rethink many things. While working in the petroleum business, I have seen many of the environmental problems that come with it. I have often witnessed colleagues' successful efforts at maintaining its unsustainable but profitable status quo at all costs, including greenhouse gas emissions, corruption, oil spills, sabotaging competing renewable and cleaner energy sources, you name it. Do I really want to be that person that makes loads of money, which leads to making the world a worse place? I cannot stand the idea that I am actively contributing with my work to that kind of world for Layla to live in.

Energized about who I could become. Just the other day I sat on a plane right next to a young professional who works for Tesla's Solar City business. I was struck about how similar her energy sector expertise was in comparison to mine, but how entirely different she felt about her job. She is convinced she is saving the world. Apart from the fact that we were travelling business class on a short-haul flight emitting carbon when we could have taken a high-speed train, our two respective impacts on the world couldn't be more different.

It made me think, 'I could do her job and save the world too!' It was then that I had an epiphany: What if I 'deserted' my own (oil) camp, and joined the renewable energies sector? What if I could help reduce the impact of big oil companies like my own employer and help to redeem myself?

Putting out my feelers. Energized by that epiphany, I got right to it. Being a LinkedIn aficionado I scanned my five thousand contacts to identify people in alternative energy businesses. I found 30 people on all hierarchical levels, from local supply chain coordinators to managing directors in alternative energy businesses ranging from hydropower to 'jellyfish batteries'. By the time I left the airport I already had three responses!

Is it worth it? As the responses came in, it reality hit me. I had not realized how specialized the competence profiles of people in alternative energy businesses had become. To enter at a similar level in the hierarchy and earn similar money, I would have to make considerable investment into a master's degree that would bring me up to speed for the job. This would mean less time for Layla, and in the short run less money for my family. I had idealistically assumed I could quit my current job and start somewhere else in a month or two.

(Continued)

Also, it would require me starting as a rookie in this new field, and I quite like my current reputation as 'the go to guy' with 'tons of experience'. More so, my family and I might have to move to another city, maybe even another country. I am still excited about this potential change and what it could mean for me and the world, but what should I actually do, and how?

QUESTIONS

1. Do you think Armani has engaged in (un)professional management practice?

2. Do you think Armani is an unusual case, or do you believe it is common for experienced managers to want to change their careers?

3. Imagine yourself in Armani's situation? What would you do? Why and how?

4. Under what circumstances (now or later in your career) can you imagine drastically changing your job?

DIGGING DEEPER: SOME OLD-WORLD VERSUS NEW-WORLD MANAGEMENT PARADIGMS AND PRACTICE

Old-world management	Old-world examples	New-world management	New-world examples
The bigger the better! Everything has to grow: Economies, companies, and revenues …	Growth is demanded by the stock market to increase share prices, which leads to practices of swallowing smaller, [companies] destroying the competition, and cannibalizing [your] own assets [72].	Small is beautiful [73]. There is an optimum economic size for economies and companies. Reaching this size might require degrowth or some limited growth [74].	Bio-beverage producer Neumarkter Lammsbräu has decided to limit its maximum optimal size as corresponding to the maximum amount of ingredients that can be sourced locally in the small German region of Neumarkter Oberpfalz in Bavaria [75, 76].
Globalize! Global is the future, local is backwards thinking.	Globally dispersed and hard-to-control supply chains like those of fast-moving consumer goods company P&G with 75,000 suppliers or oil company Total's 150,000 suppliers globally [77].	Glocalize! Find a balance between global and local, finding local solutions to global issues and vice versa.	Natura cosmetics company is locally sourcing while protecting the Brazilian Amazon region [78]. Weetabix breakfast cereal sources all of its wheat in a 50 miles radius [79, 80].

(Continued)

Old-world management	Old-world examples	New-world management	New-world examples
Abundance: The more consumption the better! Create new wants through marketing.	Invention of consumption festivals, such as Christmas shopping, Valentine's day (flower industry), China's 11/11 singles day [81], and black Friday.	Sufficiency: Not too little, not too much: Just enough! [82, 83] Serve needs, and de-market unnecessary wants to enable a frugal lifestyle [84].	Job sharing practices to enable self-sufficiency lifestyles: fewer employed working hours, less consumption, more free time, more doing it yourself [85].
Make it quick and easy! Everything has to be available on demand, without waiting times and for instant gratification.	Shanghai-based food delivery platform Ele.me (translates as 'Are you hungry NOW?') delivers food. Even the smallest snacks can be delivered via courier into homes, offices and libraries, etc.	Slow down, but do it well, and enjoy the process!	Slow food agriculture and preparation practices have taken hold around the world [86]. Slow entrepreneurship favours slow but stable and people-friendly entrepreneuring over quick success [87].
New is always better; old is less valuable.	Fast fashion practices like Zara's two-week clothing collection turnover [88].	Old is better, more valuable and beautiful.	MUD Jeans rents jeans to customers for a year, after which they come back and are resold to others with a story and the name of the previous owner(s) sewn into them [89].
Customer is king, always right and gets whatever they want. 'Give the lady what she wants' is a classic slogan. The customer knows best and we always satisfy their demand.	Some of the biggest global industries are built on the practice of selling things to customers that they want, but don't really need. Sometimes these are clearly unhealthy for them, society and the Earth. Prime examples are tobacco, alcohol, processed food, petroleum, and single-use plastic packaging.	The customer needs to be nudged to change behaviours. Stop enabling unsustainable behaviours, implying that sometimes customers should not be offered what they want if it is bad for them.	The global retailer Tesco phased out lunch-pack-size, high-sugar-content drinks typically consumed by small children against the opposition of mums [90]. Coronation Street's social marketing of sustainable lifestyles through their show.
The basis of strategy is competition, working against each other or 'killing off the competition' in order to be better and reach goals alone.	Hypercompetition practices, swift tactic micro-moves aimed at actively undermining other companies' competitiveness [91].	The basis of strategy is collaboration and co-opetition, working together to achieve goals together.	Competing Australian wine companies Accolade and TWE decided to cooperate by mutually bottling their wines in foreign markets [92].
Production and use are linear and run 'from cradle to grave': Make, use, waste.	Oceans have become the biggest grave of single-use plastic packaged products with Coca Cola, Pepsico, and Nestlé sticking out as the largest plastic polluters of oceans worldwide [93].	Production and consumption are circular 'from cradle to cradle': Recycle, use, reuse, recycle, use, reuse …	On the spot, a circular juice bar peels oranges, squeezes them, and 3D prints drink cups from the orange peels, so it is repacking the orange juice in its original natural packaging [94].
Designing things to break beyond repair, speeding up consumption cycles.	Planned redundancy practices like Apple's, which admitted to the practice of slowing down older models on purpose [95] or sealing off products so that they cannot be repaired.	Designing things to last and encouraging and enabling repairs.	The Dutch smartphone company Fairphone's modular design practices are aimed at making phones last longer and makes them as repairable as possible [96], therefore protecting customers' 'right to repair' [97].
Short-termism, immediate value creation.	Quarterly reporting practices are meant to continuously control management's performance and create transparency for investors [98].	Long-term orientation, long-run value creation.	The day Paul Polman became Unilever's CEO he abandoned quarterly reporting practices to redirect the attention to the company's long-term value creation. Many others have followed [99].

(Continued)

Old-world management	Old-world examples	New-world management	New-world examples
Exclusivity, creating scarcity by curbing access.	Luxury clothing cutting out labels of unsold items in order to make them unusable, create scarcity, and to maintain exclusivity [100]. Another common marketing management practice in varieties of businesses from supermarkets to financial services is 'redlining'. The practice consists of drawing an (imaginary) red line around typically poorer neighbourhoods. As a result, poor people, in spite of having less disposable income often have harder times accessing even essential products and paying considerably more than affluent customers [101].	Inclusivity, by giving access to otherwise marginalized groups.	Manifold bottom of the pyramid business practices, such as microfinance, to create access to goods and services for otherwise marginalized groups. For instance, the global construction materials corporate Cementos Mexicanos (CEMEX) uses the practice of 'bloqueras solidarias', where people who could not otherwise afford to pay for cement are given the opportunity to use CEMEX cement to make cement blocks as home building materials themselves. They can keep one of every two blocks they make, and the other is sold off by the company to fund the practice [102].
Private ownership.	Buying and owning products is still the standard mode of accessing use of most products from bikes and cars to clothing and power tools.	Shared ownership and 'use-only' practices.	Sharing platforms, such as Airbnb and Chinese bike sharing practices like those of Ofo or Mobike rely on 'use-only' practices.

POINTERS

The list of practices above exemplifies how opposing old-world and new-world principles relates to practices. You could use the list to dig deeper into one of the examples, or to think of more of your own examples that follow the same structure as the ones presented in the table.

WORKSHEET

YOUR PROFESSIONAL MANAGEMENT OATH

Original text	
I. I RECOGNIZE that any enterprise is at the nexus of many different constituencies, whose interests can sometimes diverge. While balancing and reconciling these interests, I will seek a course that enhances the value my enterprise can create for society over the long term. This may not always mean growing or preserving the enterprise and may include such painful actions as its restructuring, discontinuation, or sale, if these actions preserve or increase value.	
II. I PLEDGE that considerations of personal benefit will never supersede the interests of the enterprise I am entrusted to manage. The pursuit of self-interest is the vital engine of a capitalist economy, but unbridled greed can be just as harmful. Therefore, I will guard against decisions and behaviour that advance my own narrow ambitions but harm the enterprise I manage and the societies it serves.	
III. I PROMISE to understand and uphold, both in letter and in spirit, the laws and contracts governing my own conduct, that of my enterprise, and that of the societies in which it operates. My personal behaviour will be an example of integrity, consistent with the values I publicly espouse. I will be equally vigilant in ensuring the integrity of others around me and bring to attention the actions of others that represent violations of this shared professional code.	
IV. I VOW to represent my enterprise's performance accurately and transparently to all relevant parties, ensuring that investors, consumers, and the public at large can make well-informed decisions. I will aim to help people understand how decisions that affect them are made, so that choices do not appear arbitrary or biased.	
V. I WILL NOT PERMIT considerations of race, gender, sexual orientation, religion, nationality, party politics, or social status to influence my choices. I will endeavour to protect the interests of those who may not have power, but whose well-being is contingent on my decisions.	
VI. I WILL MANAGE my enterprise by diligently, mindfully, and conscientiously applying judgement based on the best knowledge available. I will consult colleagues and others who can help inform my judgement and will continually invest in staying abreast of the evolving knowledge in the field, always remaining open to innovation. I will do my utmost to develop myself and the next generation of managers so that the profession continues to grow and contribute to the well-being of society.	
VII. I RECOGNIZE that my stature and privileges as a professional stem from the honour and trust that the profession as a whole enjoys, and I accept my responsibility for embodying, protecting, and developing the standards of the management profession, so as to enhance that respect and honour.	

SOURCE: [14]

POINTERS

This worksheet is to help you reflect on what kind of management professional you want to become and to make an explicit commitment. The left column is the original text of the originally proposed 'Hippocratic Oath for managers' [14]. In the right-hand column you can write your own customized version of the oath inspired by the original text. If your business school has graduates swear some version of an oath, then you could use that. You could print the completed table and hang it near your desk as a visible commitment and a reminder to yourself. Alternatively, you could use the right-hand column to identify instances where managers have behaved according to that code or violated the code. For instance, how does the behaviour of managers that led to the ENRON scandal map onto the code?

REFERENCES

1. Where the world's largest companies stand on nature. www.mckinsey.com/capabilities/sustainability/our-insights/where-the-worlds-largest-companies-stand-on-nature. Published 2022. Accessed October 31 2022.
2. Schiller B. Patagonia asks its customers to buy less. www.fastcompany.com/1678676/patagonia-asks-its-customers-to-buy-less. Published 2011. Accessed January 7 2020.
3. Armstrong Soule CA, Reich BJ. Less is more: Is a green demarketing strategy sustainable? *Journal of Marketing Management*. 2015, 31(13–14): 1403–1427.
4. Kotler P, Levy SJ. Demarketing, yes, demarketing. *Harvard Business Review*. 1971, 49: 74–80.
5. Iddings S. Yvon Chouinard of Patagonia on controlled growth. https://community.intelligentfanatics.com/t/yvon-chouinard-of-patagonia-on-controlled-growth/266 Published 2017. Accessed January 7 2020.
6. Beer J. Patagonia founder Yvon Chouinard talks about the sustainability myth, the problem with Amazon – and why it's not too late to save the planet. www.fastcompany.com/90411397/exclusive-patagonia-founder-yvon-chouinard-talks-about-the-sustainability-myth-the-problem-with-amazon-and-why-its-not-too-late-to-save-the-planet Published 2019. Accessed January 1 2020.
7. Kolodny L. Patagonia founder just donated the entire company, worth $3 billion, to fight climate change. www.cnbc.com/2022/09/14/patagonia-founder-donates-entire-company-to-fight-climate-change.html Published 2022. Accessed November 11 2022.
8. Stifler-Wolfe E. Patagonia founder Yvon Chouinard is in business to save the earth – not Wall Street. www.esquire.com/style/mens-fashion/a27153682/patagonia-yvon-chouinard-sustainability-wall-street Published 2019. Accessed January 1 2020.
9. Thunberg G. Read Greta Thunberg's full speech at the United Nations Climate Action Summit www.nbcnews.com/news/world/read-greta-thunberg-s-full-speech-united-nations-climate-action-n1057861 Published 2019. Accessed January 14 2020.
10. Follett MP. Management as a profession. In: Metcalf HC, ed. *Business management as a profession*. Chicago: A. W. Shaw Company, 1927, pp. 73–87.
11. Donham WB. The emerging profession of business. *Harvard Business Review*. 1927, 5(4): 401–405.
12. Donham P. Is management a profession? *Harvard Business Review*. 1962, 40(5): 60–68.
13. Blok V. The power of speech acts: Reflections on a performative concept of ethical oaths in economics and business. *Review of Social Economy*. 2013, 71(2): 187–208.
14. Khurana R, Nohria N. It's time to make management a true profession. *Harvard Business Review*. 2008, 86(10): 70–77.
15. Parker M. *Shut down the business school*. Chicago: University of Chicago Press, 2018.
16. Laasch O, Jamali D, Freeman E, Suddaby R, eds. *The research handbook of responsible management*. Cheltenham: Edward Elgar, 2020.
17. II Thomas. The history and evolution of the factory. www.thomasnet.com/insights/the-history-and-evolution-of-the-factory Published 2020. Accessed February 4 2020.
18. BBC. Sir Richard Arkwright (1732–1792). www.bbc.co.uk/history/historic_figures/arkwright_richard.shtml Published 2014. Accessed January 15 2020.
19. Chapman SD. The textile factory before Arkwright: A typology of factory development. *Business History Review*. 1974, 48(4): 451–478.
20. Fitton RS, Wadsworth AP. *The Strutts and the Arkwrights, 1758–1830: A study of the early factory system*. Manchester: Manchester University Press, 1958.
21. Pollard S. Factory discipline in the industrial revolution. *Economic History Review*. 1963, 16(2): 254–271.
22. Birkinshaw J, Hamel G, Mol MJ. Management innovation. *Academy of Management Review*. 2008, 33(4): 825–845.
23. Hamel G. The why, what, and how of management innovation. *Harvard Business Review*. 2006, 84(2): 72.
24. Birkinshaw JM, Mol MJ. How management innovation happens. *MIT Sloan Management Review*. 2006, 47(4): 81–88.
25. Graham P. *Mary Parker Follett: Prophet of management*. Cambridge: Harvard Business Press, 1995.
26. Calas MB, Smircich L. Not ahead of her time: Reflections on Mary Parker Follett as prophet of management. *Organization*. 1996, 3(1): 147–152.

27. Simms M. Insights from a management prophet: Mary Parker Follett on social entrepreneurship. *Business and Society Review*. 2009, 114(3): 349–363.

28. Donham WB. The social significance of business. *Harvard Business Review*. 1927, 5(4): 406–19.

29. World Economic Forum. The Great Reset. www.weforum.org/great-reset Published 2020. Accessed June 21 2020.

30. Petriglieri G. Are our management theories outdated? https://hbr.org/2020/06/are-our-management-theories-outdated Published 2020. Accessed July 27 2020.

31. Loorbach D, Frantzeskaki N, Lijnis Huffenreuter R. Transition management: Taking stock from governance experimentation. *Journal of Corporate Citizenship*. 2015, 58: 48–66.

32. Muff K, Dyllick T, Drewell M, North J, Shrivastava P, Haertle J. *Management education for the world: A vision for business schools serving people and the planet*. Cheltenham: Edward Elgar, 2013.

33. Laasch, O, Ryazanova, O, & Wright, AL. 2022. Lingering Covid19 and looming grand crises: Envisioning business schools' business model transformations. *Academy of Management Learning & Education*, 21(1): 1–6.

34. Laszlo C, Zhexembayeva N. *Embedded sustainability: The next big competitive advantage*. Stanford: Stanford University Press, 2011.

35. Levin K, Cashore B, Bernstein S, Auld G. Overcoming the tragedy of super wicked problems: Constraining our future selves to ameliorate global climate change. *Policy Sciences*. 2012, 45(2): 123–152.

36. Global Footprint Network. Ecological footprint. www.footprintnetwork.org/our-work/ecological-footprint Published 2020. Accessed January 18 2020.

37. Steffen W, Richardson K, Rockström J, et al. Planetary boundaries: Guiding human development on a changing planet. *Science*. 2015, 347(6223): 1259855.

38. Rockström J, Steffen W, Noone K, et al. A safe operating space for humanity. *Nature*. 2009, 461(7263): 472.

39. Schaltegger S. Linking environmental management accounting: A reflection on (missing) links to sustainability and planetary boundaries. *Social and Environmental Accountability Journal*. 2018, 38(1): 19–29.

40. Whiteman G, Walker B, Perego P. Planetary boundaries: Ecological foundations for corporate sustainability. *Journal of Management Studies. 2013, 50(2): 307–336.*

41. PwC's 25th Annual Global CEO Survey: Reimagining the outcomes that matter. www.pwc.com/gx/en/ceo-agenda/ceosurvey/2022.html Published 2022. Accessed October 31 2022.

42. Moore, JW ed.. *Anthropocene or capitalocene? Nature, history, and the crisis of capitalism*. Oakland: Pm Press, 2016.

43. Haraway, D. (2015). Anthropocene, capitalocene, plantationocene, chthulucene: Making kin. *Environmental Humanities*, 6(1), 159–165.

44. Drucker PF. *The practice of management*. New York: Harper, 1954.

45. BBC. Sweden sees rare fall in air passengers, as flight-shaming takes off. www.bbc.co.uk/news/world-europe-51067440 Published 2020. Accessed January 19, 2020.

46. Van der Byl C, Slawinski N, Hahn T. Responsible management of sustainability tensions: A paradoxical approach to grand challenges. In: Laasch O, Suddaby R, Freeman RE, Jamali D, eds. *The research handbook of responsible management*. Cheltenham: Edward Elgar, 2020.

47. Radoynovska N, Ocasio W, Laasch O. The emerging logic of responsible management: Institutional pluralism, leadership, and strategizing. In: Laasch O, Suddaby R, Freeman RE, Jamali D, eds. *The research handbook of responsible management*. Cheltenham: Edward Elgar, 2020.

48. Taubken N, Leibold I. Ten rules for succesful CSR communication. In: *Responsible business: How to manage a CSR strategy successfully*. Chichester, West Sussex, UK: John Wiley & Sons, 2010.

49. Hamel G. Moon shots for management. *Harvard Business Review*. 2009, 87(2): 91–98.

50. Lawson T. The nature of heterodox economics. *Cambridge Journal of Economics*. 2006, 30(4): 483–505.

51. Dequech D. Neoclassical, mainstream, orthodox, and heterodox economics. *Journal of Post Keynesian Economics*. 2007, 30(2): 279–302.

52. Lee F. *A history of heterodox economics: Challenging the mainstream in the twentieth century*. London: Routledge, 2009.

53. Daly HE, Farley J. *Ecological economics: Principles and applications*. Washington: Island Press, 2011.
54. Costanza R. *Ecological economics: The science and management of sustainability*. New York: Columbia University Press, 1992.
55. Woolley FR. The feminist challenge to neoclassical economics. *Cambridge Journal of Economics*. 1993, 17(4): 485–500.
56. Felber C. *Die Gemeinwohl-Ökonomie*. Munich: Piper, 2018.
57. Meynhardt T, Fröhlich A. Die Gemeinwohl-Bilanz-Wichtige Anstösse, aber im Legitimationsdefizit. *Zeitschrift für öffentliche und gemeinwirtschaftliche Unternehmen*. 2017 (2–3): 152–176.
58. Mackey J, Sisodia R. *Conscious capitalism, with a new preface by the authors: Liberating the heroic spirit of business*. Boston: Harvard Business Review Press, 2013.
59. O'Toole J, Vogel D. Two and a half cheers for conscious capitalism. *California Management Review*. 2011, 53(3): 60–76.
60. Hurst A. *The purpose economy, expanded and updated: How your desire for impact, personal growth and community is changing the world*. Boise: Elevate Publishing, 2016.
61. Hurst A. Welcome to the purpose economy. www.fastcompany.com/3028410/welcome-to-the-purpose-economy Published 2014. Accessed February 6 2020.
62. European Commission. *A sustainable bioeconomy for Europe – strengthening the connection between economy, society, and environment: Updated bioeconomy strategy*. 2018.
63. D'Amato et al. Green circular, bio economy: A comparative analysis of sustainability avenues. *Journal of Cleaner Production*. 2017, 168, 716–734.
64. Crane A, Matten D. *Business ethics* (3rd edn). New York: Oxford University Press, 2010.
65. Freeman RE. *Strategic management: A stakeholder approach*. Cambridge: Cambridge University Press, 1984/2010.
66. Brundtland GH. *Presentation of the report of the World Commission on Environment and Development to UNEP's 14th Governing Council*. Nairobi, 1987.
67. Elkington J. *Cannibals with forks: The triple bottom line of 21st century business*. Gabriola Island: New Society Publishers, 1998.
68. Khurana R, Nohria N, Penrice D. Management as a profession. In: Lorsch JW, Zelleke A, Berlowitz L, eds. *Restoring Trust in American Business*. Cambridge: American Academy of Arts and Sciences, 2005.
69. PRME. Overview. www.unprme.org/about-prme Published 2007. Accessed November 23 2016.
70. Kornbluh E. Ten years on, HBS students revive the push for an MBA oath. www.hbs.edu/socialenterprise/blog/post/hbs-students-revive-the-push-for-an-mba-oath Published 2018. Accessed January 19 2020.
71. Laasch, O., Moosmayer, D., & Antonacopoulou, E. P. (2022). The interdisciplinary responsible management competence framework: An integrative review of ethics, responsibility, and sustainability competences. *Journal of Business Ethics, 187*, 733–757.
72. Neumarkter Lammsbräu. 100% Bio, 0% Kompromiss. www.lammsbraeu.de Published 2020. Accessed February 1 2020.
73. Liesen A, Dietsche C, Gebauer J. *Successful non-growing companies*. Degrowth Conference, Leipzig, 2014.
74. Webb J. How many suppliers do businesses have? How many should they have? www.forbes.com/sites/jwebb/2018/02/28/how-many-suppliers-do-businesses-have-how-many-should-they-have/#2bd287f69bb7 Published 2018. Accessed February 1 2020.
75. Balch O. Natura commits to sourcing sustainably from Amazon. www.theguardian.com/sustainable-business/natura-sourcing-sustainably-from-amazon Published 2013. Accessed January 31 2020.
76. Farming UK. Weetabix meets goal in sourcing wheat within 50 miles of its mill. www.farminguk.com/news/weetabix-meets-goal-in-sourcing-wheat-within-50-miles-of-its-mill_50123.html Published 2018. Accessed January 31 2020.
77. Weetabix. Weetabix re-commits to source wheat from local farmers www.weetabixfoodcompany.co.uk/press/news-archive/weetabix-re-commits-to-source-wheat-from-local-farmers Published 2016. Accessed January 31 2020.
78. Soo Z. Chinese consumers spend US$22 billion in first nine hours of Alibaba's Singles' Day shopping event. www.businessinsider.sg/chinese-consumers-spend-us22-billion-in-first-nine-hours-of-alibabas-singles-day-shopping-event Published 2019. Accessed November 30 2020.

79. Boulanger P-M. Three strategies for sustainable consumption. *SAPI EN S Surveys and Perspectives Integrating Environment and Society.* 2010, 3(2).
80. Alcott B. The sufficiency strategy: Would rich-world frugality lower environmental impact? *Ecological Economics.* 2008, 64(4): 770–786.
81. Bocken NM, Short SW. Towards a sufficiency-driven business model: Experiences and opportunities. *Environmental Innovation and Societal Transitions.* 2016, 18: 41–61.
82. Lynn T. 6 steps for living a self-sufficient lifestyle. https://oursimplehomestead.com/living-a-self-sufficient-lifestyle Published 2020. Accessed January 31 2020.
83. Pietrykowski B. You are what you eat: The social economy of the slow food movement. *Review of Social Economy.* 2004, 62(3): 307–321.
84. Stillman J. Slow business: The case against fast growth. www.inc.com/jessica-stillman/slow-business-fast-growth-is-not-good-for-the-company.html Published 2012. Accessed February 1 2020.
85. Nick. How Zara sells out 450+ million items a year without wasting money on marketing. https://beeketing.com/blog/zara-growth-story Published 2018. Accessed February 1 2020.
86. MUD Jeans. Start your circular journey here. https://mudjeans.eu/about-mud-method Published 2020. Accessed February 1 2020.
87. Collinson P. Tesco to stop selling lunchbox-size sugary Ribena and Capri-Sun. www.theguardian.com/business/2015/jul/28/tesco-stop-selling-childrens-high-sugar-drinks-ribena-capri-sun Published 2015. Accessed February 1 2020.
88. D'aveni RA. *Hypercompetition.* New York: Simon & Schuster, 2010.
89. Christ KL, Burritt RL, Varsei M. Coopetition as a potential strategy for corporate sustainability. *Business Strategy and the Environment.* 2017, 26(7): 1029–1040.
90. Greenpeace International. Coca-Cola, PepsiCo, and Nestlé found to be worst plastic polluters worldwide in global cleanups and brand audits. www.greenpeace.org/international/press-release/18872/coca-cola-pepsico-and-nestle-found-to-be-worst-plastic-polluters-worldwide-in-global-cleanups-and-brand-audits Published 2018. Accessed February 1 2020.
91. Barrett A. Juice bar turns orange peels instantly into bioplastic cups. https://bioplasticsnews.com/2019/09/10/juice-bar-orange-peels-bioplastic-cups Published 2019. Accessed February 1 2020.
92. McMahon J. Apple had way better options than slowing down your iPhone. www.wired.com/story/apple-iphone-battery-slow-down Published 2017. Accessed February 1 2020.
93. Fairphone. Spare parts: The most sustainable phone is the one you already own. https://shop.fairphone.com/en/spare-parts Published 2020. Accessed February 1 2020.
94. Design reality. What does the new 'Right to Repair' legislation mean for manufacturers and product designers? https://designreality.co.uk/journal/2019/right-to-repair Published 2020. Accessed February 1 2020.
95. Dallas G, Andrus J. Quarterly reporting: Too much of a good thing? www.icgn.org/quarterly-reporting-too-much-good-thing Accessed February 2 2020.
96. Walker O. The long and short of the quarterly reports controversy. www.ft.com/content/e61046bc-7a2e-11e8-8e67-1e1a0846c475 Published 2018. Accessed February 1 2020.
97. Brown C. How widespread is waste in luxury fashion? https://goodonyou.eco/waste-luxury-fashion Published 2019. Accessed February 1 2020.
98. Shannon J. From food deserts to supermarket redlining. www.bunkhistory.org/resources/3029 Published 2018. Accessed February 1 2020.
99. CEMEX. Bloqueras solidarias. www.cemexcolombia.com/sostenibilidad/asuntos-sociales/generamos-valor-compartido/vivienda-social-e-infraestructura/bloqueras-solidarias Published 2020. Accessed February 1 2020.

CHAPTER 2

MANAGEMENT IN PRACTICE

OLIVER LAASCH

LEARNING GOALS

1. Understand the process of practicing professional management
2. Gain insight into the elements that make a management practice
3. Build competence to engage in professional management practice

FUN FACT

Sustainability and responsibility practitioners globally earn an average of £76,182 (US$88,000), according to a global survey among 1,542 executives [1].

SPOTLIGHT

THE DAILY SOAP OF CARBON LITERACY

© Copyright ITV plc 2020

Coronation Street is the world's longest-running soap opera, watched by tens of millions of people across the United Kingdom and around the world. Many of its viewers may not realize that it is 'TV's greenest show' [2]. Neither might they **know** that they are being influenced to live a more sustainable life while watching *Coronation Street*. The programme is produced by the television network ITV, which has committed to 'being green' both in their daily management practices, and also by spreading sustainable practices through their programmes [3].

'Corrie', as fans affectionately call the show, has centred on practices of carbon literacy. Carbon literacy is the umbrella term for a set of everyday practices that aim to reduce climate change by creating the competence 'to reduce emissions, on an individual, community and organizational basis' [4]. On *Coronation Street*, the practice began with production manager Dan, who is passionate about environmental protection and has made promoting carbon literacy part of his job. Since then carbon literacy practices have become a team effort, and a collaborative practice involving virtually everyone, from actors, to make-up, set-building management, prop-store supervision, and on to executive production [5].

(Continued)

While efforts are centred on carbon reduction, they also address other ethics, sustainability, and responsibility topics. Instead of using large amounts of printed paper manuscripts, actors and the production crew now use tablets. Colleagues at the costumes department engage in ethical fashion practices, and set building managers have become re-use and recycling experts. When filming outside the main set, the CO_2 emissions involved with travel are a major part of managing to identify a location to film.

The production team at Corrie, however, is aiming at an even bigger impact. Through the programme's storyline, set, and characters, they promote sustainable living practices. For instance, there are electric-car charging stations, main characters discuss organic produce and food miles, and a 1980s themed wedding with upcycled clothing takes place.

PROFESSIONAL MANAGEMENT PRACTICE

Management is a practice that has to blend a good deal of craft (experience) with a certain amount of art (insight) and some science (analysis).

Henry Mintzberg [6]

In the previous chapter we introduced professional management as a particular type of practice. That **management** is a practice has long been stressed by iconic management thinkers like Peter Drucker and Henry Mintzberg [6–8]. But what does it mean to say management is a practice? As we have seen in the previous chapter, professional management is of utmost importance, but what is professional management practice, and how can we carry it out?

To answer these questions we first have to take a step back and ask, 'What is management?' When we say 'management' in the context of this book, we mean the practice of getting things done with people and resources. We will mostly focus on business management; however, the practice of management also takes place in a range of other organizations, like religious organizations, NGOs, and public administration. Management is also omnipresent in non-organizational settings. For instance, if you need to complete an assignment with people (e.g. the ones you study with) and resources (e.g. time, a study space, a book), then that assignment needs to be managed. Management also often happens ad hoc. For instance, you might be managing a project, an event, a citizen protest, or moving house.

It is time to link your everyday understanding of management with our criteria for professional management introduced in the first chapter: professional

> **Management**
> the practice of getting things done with people and resources

Management practice
management practices and the
practicing of management

management is **management practice** carried out with professional conduct and in pursuit of goals serving society and the world. This then implies that professional management means getting the right things (goals serving society and the world), done right (with professional conduct).

As illustrated in Figure 2.1, management practice includes both the actual 'doing' or 'carrying out' of management (practicing), and the common ways of doing management (practices). For instance, at ITV, when the production manager Dan does his job, he practices his job. That involves many different tasks on a daily basis, such as scheduling production crews, organizing locations, and participating in meetings. Some of his practicing relates to common practices and ones that are collaborative or shared – for example, meeting practices are common among many people in *Coronation Street*, across organizations, and across countries. So are carbon literacy training practices that involve people across *Coronation Street*, in different organizations and countries.

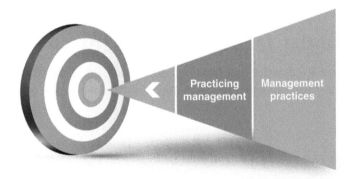

FIGURE 2.1   Professional management practice

CREDIT: Slidemodel.com

In this chapter we will first explore the process of practicing management, then explore the collaborative nature of management practices, and finally explore the competent management practitioners carrying out professional management practice.

PRACTICING MANAGEMENT

Henry Mintzberg has famously claimed that MBA programmes 'get it all wrong' by teaching management 'in theory' to people who have never practiced management. He said that 'to help develop people already practicing management is a fine idea, but pretending to create managers out of people who have never managed is a sham' [6]. Practicing management in real life is the only way to learn management, but what does practicing management mean?

We have established what professional management means.

The basic elements of **practicing management** can be grouped into three areas: management inputs, management process, and management output (see Figure 2.2). The main management inputs are the goals as aspired to as outcomes of practicing management, the people with whom to achieve them, and the resources used in achieving the goals. On the process stage, the two main criteria of evaluation are effectiveness (does management activity contribute to the goals set?) and efficiency (has the contribution been reached with the minimum resources necessary?). Outcomes are the management performance. Performance is usually evaluated in the light of the pre-set goals described in the input stage.

Practicing management
working with people and resources to achieve performance effectively, efficiently, and in line with pre-established goals

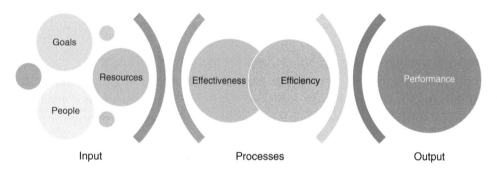

FIGURE 2.2   Practicing management

To take the next step towards professional management, these elements of the management process need to integrate sustainability, responsibility, and ethics. We will now look at how each element needs to change to integrate sustainability, responsibility, and ethics, and then develop and deepen this understanding in the chapters that follow.

INPUTS

Goals: Traditionally management goals have been centred on the ultimate achievement of increased competitiveness, which leads to above-average profits, which then benefits shareholders. Goals for a sales manager, for instance, might be to increase the number of deals made by their team. This rather narrow goal perspective must be broadened in professional management.

Goals
describe the aspired outcome of the management process

The **professional management** perspective requires **goals** that optimize the value created from management activity for all stakeholders, not just shareholders. A sales manager, for example, would need to consider whether the product they are selling is good, or at least not bad, for the customer, the environment, society at large and all stakeholders affected by or affecting the product. From a sustainability perspective, a fundamental

Professional management goals
create value for all stakeholders, in all three dimensions of the triple bottom line, and are of high moral quality

consideration of corporate goals must be that they are socially, environmentally, and economically sustainable and that they are not immoral from an ethics perspective.

Resources: Mainstream management considers any asset that helps to achieve goals as a resource. Necessary resources are often classified as either technical, social, or financial resources. Professional management abstains from seeing resources as a mere means for achieving goals. Instead resources are viewed through the three perspectives of sustainability, responsibility, and ethics. From a sustainability standpoint, resources are understood as one of three types of capital: social, environmental, or economic capital, and these need to be sustained through the management process. The capital thinking provides managers with a broader significance. Capital needs to be sustained.

Professional managers would, for example, withdraw from the excessive use of non-renewable environmental resources, such as petroleum and other extractive industry products, because using them would mean reducing, not sustaining, this environmental capital. A similar argument applies to the environment, which from an ethics of rights perspective is often considered to have rights far exceeding the management understanding of environment as mere resource. Finally, professional managers would not engage in financial transactions that put the economic capital of their company at risk, and instead would aim to sustain it.

People: The professional perspective requires that resources are distributed throughout the management process in a way that optimizes the value created with all stakeholders of the company. A professional manager of a product development team, for example, would use the creativity of their team to develop the product which yields the highest financial return to owners of the company. They would also consider the value the design creates for customers, how safe and satisfying the production processes are for employees, and consider whether the new product has the potential to include and develop otherwise marginalized suppliers. From an ethics standpoint, it is important that human beings are not instrumentalized as mere means to achieve goals, but rather as ends in themselves, who are nourished, protected, and treated with dignity, and whose well-being is a core concern. Professional managers invest in the education and welfare of the people they are working with.

PROCESSES

Effectiveness: Effectiveness is measured by the achievement of goals set. The question is whether the management process contributes to the achievement of pre-set goals. If the goals set in the input stage reflect the ethics, responsibility, and sustainability perspectives, then management must aim at the highest

Resources
assets used to achieve goals when practicing management

Professional management
resources are understood as social, environmental, and economic capital (triple bottom line), which are managed for the achievement of maximum stakeholder value, and of moral excellence

People
include varieties of human stakeholders such as subordinates and superiors, colleagues, customers, and communities. In professional management people not are simply means to an end, but whose protection and well-being should be a primary concern

Effectiveness
describes the degree to which the management process has contributed to the pre-established managerial goals

possible degree of accomplishment of those goals. Often however, goals are not aligned with all ethics, responsibility, and sustainability considerations. This means that in many cases, being effective and achieving goals may be unprofessional.

Imagine, for instance, a cigarette company that achieved a successful market entry into a country where few people smoked, and increased the number of people smoking through marketing. No doubt this could be seen as effective when assessed from the tobacco company management's goal-setting perspective. However, when the sustainability perspective is included, the effectiveness of the marketing management process is less favourable. Encouraging non-smokers to take up smoking affects the social capital, moving away from the healthier lifestyle of non-smoking. Viewed from a responsibility perspective, achievement of goals would include assessing the overall welfare created by the market access. Responsibility means asking how much welfare is created for company shareholders and the local economy, and asking how much stakeholder value is in turn destroyed through pulmonary diseases and other detrimental health effects among consumers. From an ethics of justice perspective, the market entry would be seen as unfair and immoral, asking how a company can enrich itself at the cost of killing thousands of people through pulmonary diseases.

Efficiency: While effectiveness focuses on the effect of management on the achievement of goals, efficiency scrutinizes the relationship between the resources used and the achieved output. In mainstream management, a management process is more efficient if it achieves the same output with fewer resources or a better output with fewer resources.

In **professional management** efficiency the same basic definition holds true. From a sustainability perspective the aim is to sustain or even renew social, environmental, and economic capital. The fewer resources that are used up, the better the process. The concept of eco-efficiency describes the amount of natural resources, such as water, energy, and raw materials that are used to produce a certain product or service. Along the same lines, professional

Imagine what it can do to your management process if key people go astray. A great example is when Adidas severed ties with rapper Ye (a.k.a. Kanye West) and his Yeezy brand over antisemitic comments expressed by him, violating the company's equality, diversity, and inclusion policy. The move resulted in an anticipated loss in company revenue of 5–8 per cent, disrupted store operations, cut supply relationships, and created public relations chaos [9]. After the outrage over Ye had calmed down Adidas management decided to sell remaining stock of 4 million shoes anyway, for approximately half a billion USD.

'Adidas Yeezy 350 Boost "Pirate Black"' by dj_boYo is licensed under CC BY-NC-SA 2.0.

Efficiency
describes the proportion of resource input per management output and vice versa.

Professional management effectiveness
is measured in the amount of triple bottom line value and stakeholder value created and the degree of moral excellence achieved

Professional management efficiency
consists of the relationships between the triple bottom line capital used and created, the stakeholder input and value created, and the moral issues encountered and moral excellence achieved throughout the management process

managers can think of social efficiency as an evaluation of their own manage-ment processes – for example, how much social welfare is created? Does my team enjoy work? Are employees growing as people in their work or are they exploited, leading to a loss of social capital? From a responsibility perspective, efficiency can be defined as stakeholder value created (or destroyed) per unit of production. Efficiency from an ethics perspective might aim at the lowest amount possible of amoral behaviour per unit of product or service. Such alternative interpretations of efficiency feed into professional management and are options for mainstream management thinking.

OUTPUTS

Performance
is the output of the management process, valued by its proximity to the predetermined goals

Performance: The output or performance of a management process may be interpreted by short-term profit. For a professional manager, short-term finan-cial performance must be considered together with other criteria to judge the success of the management process.

Sustainability thinking requires planning in long-term financial per-formance, including decisions such as selling sub-prime loans that make short-term money sense, but in the long run may threaten the sustainabil-ity of the company or the whole economic system that was demonstrated in the world economic crisis that began in 2007. For a **professional man-ager**, **performance** is not constrained by economic performance only, but rather is defined as a combination of social, environmental, and eco-nomic performance, known as the triple bottom line. From a responsibility perspective, a professional manager thinks in terms of the performance for all stakeholders, the value created for all groups related to the manage-ment activities. From an ethics perspective the professional manager would thoroughly scrutinize all facets of the management outcome for potentially immoral components.

Professional management performance
is a product of professional management effectiveness and efficiency achieved. Professional management must re-assess the criteria applied for evaluating performance as good or bad

MANAGEMENT PRACTICES

Iconic management scholar Sumantra Ghoshal has claimed that 'many of the worst management practices have their roots in a set of ideas that have emerged from academics … a dehumanization of management practice' [10]. For instance, he refers to excessive management control practices, cultivated by academic ideas, such as agency theory [11], that promote the idea that it is 'natural' for human beings to be spiteful in our own self-interest. Another example is an unhealthy overemphasis of competitive practices, fostered through Porter's five forces model [12, 13]. What 'makes' practices like these? How can we change them? How can we make whole 'bundles' of professional practices?

In Chapter 1, we looked at the definition of **management practices** as activities that management practitioners customarily engage in. Two elements in this definition are particularly important. First, 'customarily' stresses the normalized, taken-for-granted nature of these activities. They are common, normal, institutionalized. Practices like conducting meetings or employee 'pep talks' are perceived as just what you do and how you do things as a manager. Secondly, we use the plural form 'practitioners'. Practices are collective achievements. Many practitioners engage in practices like meetings or pep talks [14, 15]. Third, practices do not exist in isolation. They connect with other practices to form complex, entangled bundles of practices. Meetings may include pep talks, and pep talks in turn may relate to practices of employee performance review.

What bundle of practices might you need to manage a 'margin-free' supermarket in order to allow low-income consumers access to essential products at as low a cost as possible, in this case in the Indian state of Kerala?

Management practices activities that management practitioners customarily engage in

In this section we discuss the customary, collaborative, and interconnected nature of practices. First, we will explore the elements that 'make' a practice and how these elements connect practices, namely meanings, materials, and competences. Second, we will explore some bundles of distinct types of practices, such as strategizing, organizing, and communicating that managers typically engage in. Third, we will discuss how a particular practice involves many practitioners, so they are practiced collaboratively and across organizational boundaries.

WHAT PRACTICES ARE MADE OF

As illustrated in Figure 2.3, it has been suggested that practices are constructed of three elements [16]: (the logic and 'why' of practices); materials (the 'stuff' needed for the practice); and competences (practitioners' qualities necessary to practice). These elements are often shared between practices and therefore connect them. In the example of *Coronation Street*'s environmental protection practices of paperless work (use of tablets), the make-up department connects to paperless work in production management through shared materials (tablets and the absence of paper). All of them require the competence of carbon literacy. Paperless work practices also connect to other environmental practices, like recycling TV sets and using low-energy LED lighting as they share the aspirational meaning of becoming 'TV's greenest show'. We now introduce each of these elements and their importance for professional management practices.

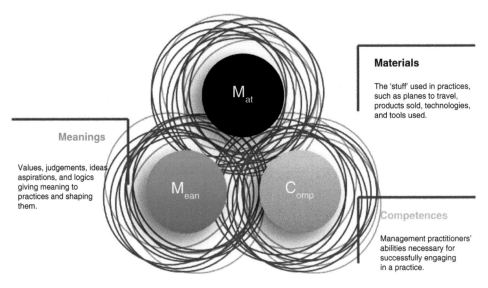

Materials

The 'stuff' used in practices, such as planes to travel, products sold, technologies, and tools used.

Meanings

Values, judgements, ideas, aspirations, and logics giving meaning to practices and shaping them.

Competences

Management practitioners' abilities necessary for successfully engaging in a practice.

FIGURE 2.3   Three elements of managerial practice(s)

CREDIT: Slidemodel.com

MEANINGS

Meanings
what is intended or conveyed
through a practice

In our current transition of management there is a **meanings** war going on. An excellent example is from the 2020 Davos World Economic Forum, where the then Prince Charles shared his meaning of management as needing a 'new economic model ... a *revolutionary* paradigm shift' [17]. Meanwhile, Donald Trump calls him and other advocates of change pessimists, alarmist, radical socialists, and 'perennial prophets of doom ... heirs of yesterday's foolish fortune-tellers'. Trump instead advocates old-world 'faith and confidence in the market system ... the American model as an example to the world of a working system of free enterprise that will produce the most benefits for the most people in the 21st century and beyond'.

In professional management practices, meanings clash in a very similar fashion. For instance, for one manager, aggressive sales practices in the housing market might simply mean a great financial year. For another manager, they might mean a great worry for the people who might not be able to pay back their loans in the future. Professional management practices swim in a complex melting pot of meanings related to 'business as usual', ethics, responsibility, and sustainability. Due to this hybrid logic of professional management, tensions and paradoxes between different meanings are inevitable and there is need for an awareness of these differences and they need to be handled carefully [18, 19].

Imagine a marketing manager in charge of optimizing sales by designing product positioning in supermarkets. On the one hand it makes sense to put high revenue items like sweets and soft-drinks right next to the checkout area, where people make 'impulse decisions' to buy in the last moment of their shopping. This means profit. On the other hand, you might be concerned about how unhealthy these items are, as an individual manager or if your company has a health agenda. Placing sweets at the checkouts encourages eating that can lead to health issues; it means harming people.

MATERIALS

Materials involved in management practices can be of a physical, tangible nature, like the tablets that replaced most of the paper in *Coronation Street* or the planes you use to fly to a sales conference. Materials can also be management tools and techniques like key performance indicators, or balanced scorecards. Materials can also be management techniques like cash-flow analysis or the reporting guideline you use for annual reports.

Materials
the 'stuff' used in practices

Materials may come with flaws in professionalism that aren't immediately obvious. For instance, imagine you are an office manager who promotes the practice of the 'paperless office', stopping print, and using mobile tablets instead. You might think this is a simple example of 'mundane materials' [20], but they and most other considerations are complex – a minefield! Considerations include: Tablets may use so much energy that your carbon footprint increases instead of decreases. If I use tablets produced by Apple, does that mean we are complicit in worker suicides, as reported by the company's main hardware provider Foxcon? [21] Can you be sure that your tablet is 'good' when the mobile devices industry appears to be involved in fuelling corruption, armed conflict, and exploitative labour conditions in some African regions through 'conflict' minerals used? [22] Will our older employees be able to use the tablets after they have used paper their whole lives? What materials we involve in practices matter in achieving professional management goals.

A professional practice could even be centred entirely on the material dimension. For instance, the precious metals company UMICORE has changed their sourcing management practices from mining such metals to recycling them, including electronic waste and spent batteries used in tablets [23, 24].

Plastic-free biodegradable packaging practices often rely on unusual materials like the banana leaves used by Rimping supermarket, Chiang Mai, Thailand.

Courtesy of perfect homes

COMPETENCES

Professional practice always relies on the **competence** of practitioners to carry out these professional practices (practices aimed at serving society and the planet), and to do so professionally (professional conduct as managing ethically,

Competence
the ability to carry out a practice

responsibly, sustainably). Competence is needed to get the right things done right. Such competence also requires basic 'mainstream' management competences, of being able to get the job done effectively and efficiently.

As crucially important as it is, such competence is in short supply. Wallace B. Donham, the second dean of Harvard Business School, said a hundred years ago that 'The development … of socially minded business men is the central problem of business… our civilization may well head for one of its periods of decline … leaders who are competent to solve these problems are strangely missing' [25]. Competence must change when management practices are transformed as 'the dramatic changes in management roles and the individual competencies required to implement them' impact on 'employees in the post-transformational organization' [26].[1]

Competent practitioner
someone who has mastered the practices of a role

We are in urgent need of an increase in professional management competence, but what is this and how do we get it? What makes a **competent professional management practitioner**? There is no list that covers all the competences necessary to become a competent management professional. Competence will comprise different factors, depending on the practitioner's characteristics and on the actual bundle of practices the practitioner engages in [26]. A female CEO with 40 years of work experience in charge of a medium-sized Kenyan family business selling food will require different professional management competences than a male middle-level manager in a fast-moving consumer goods multinational like P&G or Unilever. The competence for carbon literacy in *Coronation Street* requires different practices, and therefore different competences, as practitioners' roles vary across different departments, occupations, and hierarchies.

Professional management competence
to be and become, act and interact, know and think professionally

Despite these differences, we know that the basic building blocks (the 'sub-competences' of unique **professional management competence**) can be organized into six competence domains. They are: to know, think, act, interact, be, and become professional (Table 2.1) [27]. Achieving professional management competence, like any other competence, relies on a further set of sub-competences within each of these six sub-competence domains. Just as your abdominal muscles are crucial for keeping your body strong and upright, the professional management six-pack 'keeps you strong as a professional manager'. We have discussed above how the competences needed to be a management professional vary between people, practices, and contexts. Accordingly, everybody will need a different set of sub-competences in each domain

---

[1] The authors quoted here meant a transformation in typical corporate structures, a rather minor transformation in comparison to the transition from old-world to new-world management practices. The more drastic the transformation, the more drastic is the necessary change in competences.

of the six-pack. For instance, the managing director of *Coronation Street* might have a more strongly pronounced 'interact' competence to collaborate with diverse groups of stakeholders due to his position. The designers building sustainable features into the show's set are likely to rely more strongly on the 'interact' competence to communicate and create new realities so that viewers may pick up sustainable lifestyle practices. To be a competent professional management practitioner some competence in all domains of competences (to be and become, act and interact, know and think professionally) is needed.

TABLE 2.1   The professional management competence 'six-pack'

	Independent	Interdependent
Intellectual	**KNOW:** Knowing about ethical, social, and environmental issues related to management; to be able to identify and access trustworthy knowledge and filter out misinformation; ability to find knowledge for action …	**THINK:** To systemically evaluate the impact of management practices across stakeholders and contexts; to engage in critical moral reasoning to decide about the 'goodness' of practices; to think creatively 'outside normal management' to envision new practices …
Actional	**ACT:** Acting ethically, responsibly, sustainably; managing effectively and efficiently; overcoming resistance and barriers to action; making change happen; keeping up momentum …	**INTERACT:** Collaborating in diverse groups of actors and stakeholders; navigating tensions arising from distinct world views and agendas; cultivating ethical, responsible, and sustainable relationships; communicating to create new realities …
Personal	**BE:** Ethical, responsible, sustainable mindsets; professional identity; sense of duty and willingness to serve; strong moral character and aspirations; capacity for empathy with stakeholders …	**BECOME:** Capacity to put own interests aside; critical self-reflection; strength of will; self-direction; belief in the impact of own actions; react to conflict constructively; ability to navigate unprofessional temptations …

PRACTICES ACROSS MANAGERIAL MODES AND OCCUPATIONS

In the past, baseline managerial practices have centred on the sequence of tasks and practices of planning, organizing, leading, and controlling that were built on the framework first suggested by Henri Fayol in 1916.[2] While these practices may seem intuitively right to many, Henry Mintzberg in 1976 observed managers during their work and noticed that they did not actually engage in this set of practices, let alone in this sequence. Rather, managers dynamically switched between interpersonal roles (figurehead, leader, liaison), informational roles (monitor, disseminator, spokesperson), and decisional roles (entrepreneur, disturbance handler, resource allocator, negotiator) [30, 31]. Bartlett and Ghoshal observed in 1997 that managerial roles and related practices are not a persistent characteristic of management, but rather

---

[2]The tasks originally suggested by Fayol [28] were planning, organizing, commanding, coordinating, and controlling, but over the years were reframed as planning, organizing, leading, and controlling.

Modes of management
distinct bundles of
practices shaped by
distinct managerial tasks

are continuously reshaped as context, organizational forms, and managerial jobs change [26]. In this book, we call these distinct but overlapping bundles of practices that managers may engage in **modes of management**.

We will introduce modes that managers operate: organizing, folleading, deciding, communicating, digitalizing, glocalizing, strategizing, innovating, and entrepreneuring.

In this book we use the verb 'glocalizing' to express practices related to the ongoing post-globalization trend of navigating between local and global practices and their impact. Phenomena related to the recently invigorated importance of the local dimension include local, and indigenous production and consumption, local circular economy initiatives, as well as a resurgence of national and protectionist trade policies.

We use the term 'folleading' to refer to practices that involve working in groups, and to question the emphasis that has been placed on leading while downplaying the crucial role of following [31, 32]. Following practices have been shown to have a central place in contemporary trends of flatter managerial hierarchies (fewer people in formal leadership roles), democratic distributed management practices, and employee empowerment. A pioneer of folleading practices is the Brazilian company SEMCO and their 'management without managers' [33].

FIGURE 2.4   Modes of professional management practice

CREDIT: Slidemodel.com

Figure 2.4 shows how each of these modes of management is centred on a distinct object. For instance, entrepreneuring practices are typically centred on managing opportunity creation and exploitation, while strategizing is centred on making and implementing plans for goal achievement. Different managers engage in different mixes of these modes at different times and in different contexts. For instance, *Coronation Street*'s production manager Dan, at the beginning of his promotion of carbon literacy practices, might have engaged more heavily in practices related to innovating, entrepreneuring, and communicating his idea in order to make it a reality. Later on, these practices are likely to have reduced in intensity and given way to more strategizing, organizing, and folleading.

In Part C of this book, there are chapters dedicated to each one of these modes. The chapters in Part D each present a distinct occupation of management, including operations management, supply chain management, marketing management, people management, accounting, and financial management. While engaging in each of the modes of management, these managerial occupations rely on a unique specialized bundle of practices. The people management occupation, as an example, relies on practices related to the employee life-cycle (e.g. hiring, onboarding, capacitating) that 'normal' managers are only marginally involved in. Operations managers often use specialized practices related to quality and efficiency, such as Six Sigma process improvement, Kanban scheduling, or just-in-time production. Of course, the boundaries between the practices in modes and occupations are fluid. As an example, the innovating mode of management shares practices with the specialized research and development occupation. Further, 'normal' managers engage in some practices of the accounting occupation – for example, gathering information to feed into key performance indicators (KPIs).

Occupational practices specialized bundles of practices related to tasks carried out by a specialized managerial occupation

COLLABORATIVE PRACTICES

Each practice per definition relies on collaboration, or 'doing together' [14, 15]. In our initial example of *Coronation Street*, the practice of carbon literacy is collaboratively carried out among practitioners across the entire organization, from the set-building workshop, to the make-up room, to the film editing studio. We now highlight some typical collaborative practices of professional management.

First, practices related to ethics, responsibility, and sustainability (ERS) are often carried out in collaboration between specialized ERS managers and 'mainstream' managers who integrate ERS into their non-ERS roles (see Figure 2.5). **Specialized ERS managers**, on the one hand, have an explicit mandate to focus on ethics, responsibility, and sustainability as their main activity. For instance, Kene Umeasiegbu, the professional featured at the end of this chapter, is a specialized environmental sustainability manager at Tesco. There are now varieties of such roles, such as chief ethics officers, vice-president

Specialized ERS managers these are managers whose main role is specialized in practices related to ethics, responsibility, and sustainability

responsibility, ethics and compliance managers, and community managers. It has been suggested that these are emerging as new managerial professions as more focus is given to their important role for society and the world [34, 35]. Mainstream managers, on the other hand, are primarily concerned with commercial business operations in standard managerial roles and occupations. For mainstream managers to become professional managers, they need to integrate sustainability, responsibility, and ethics into their mainstream role, to 'mainstream' ERS [36, 37] – for instance, social marketing practices carried out by a 'mainstream' marketing manager, or a socially responsible investment conducted by a financial manager. There are also hybrid roles like a sustainable sourcing manager, or an environmental accountant.

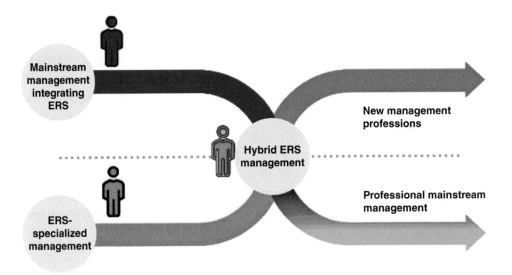

FIGURE 2.5 Types of ERS management and their professionalization potential

CREDIT: Slidemodel.com

Secondly, professional management practices also involve practitioners beyond organizational boundaries. Practices might require collaborative enactment between managers and their supply chain partners, together with customers, or with society more widely. Kene Umeasiegbu, in his professional profile at the end of this chapter, explains how carbon accounting only works if everybody along the supply chain is counting, and how there are no sustainable production practices without sustainable consumption. *Coronation Street*'s on-screen examples of responsible lifestyle practices directly link to their intention to move their viewers to engage in such practices. Corrupt practices are another example, as management corruption typically involves 'corruption practitioners' from different sectors of society. For example, if a manager 'bribes a government official to obtain a licence to operate, they jointly engage in the practices of corruption'.

Part B of this book more comprehensively introduces ethics, responsibility, and sustainability.

PRINCIPLES OF PROFESSIONAL MANAGEMENT PRACTICE

I.   Management is the practice of **getting things done with people and resources**.

II. Management practice includes both **practicing management**, the doing of management activities in general, and **management practices**, the customary ways of doing management.

III. Practicing management relies on putting together the **elements of the managerial process** including goals, people, and resources; effectiveness and efficiency; and performance.

IV. Practices of management are collaborative, and connect through the elements of **meanings, materials, and competences.**

V.   Practices of management relate to different **modes of management** (e.g. strategizing, organizing, innovating) and **management occupations** (e.g. people management, accounting).

John Sidanta from the straw supplier PRIMASTRAW showed a collaborative professional attitude in service of the planet when he said, 'It's the right decision ... we straw manufacturers have to cope' after Starbucks announced its 'strawless revolution' of stopping the use of plastic straws. It is important to note that Starbucks's move to ban straws meant they used plastic lids instead, which might produce even more plastic waste in comparison to the straws.

[38] Image source, Oliver Laasch

MANAGEMENT GYM: TRAINING YOUR PROFESSIONAL SIX-PACK

Knowing

1. What is the difference between practices of management and practicing management?

2. What are the main management modes and occupations and how are they different?

3. Approach a manager and ask them what it means for them to manage professionally.

Thinking

4. Look up a business person's (auto)biography (either online or in a book) to evaluate whether you would consider them to be a professional manager.

5. Imagine you are a manager of an airport front desk for a major airline. You are speaking to a customer who clearly has bought a ticket for her business trip through a collaborating airline. However, you cannot see or print her ticket from your system due to a technical error. The flight leaves in 45 minutes; the next one is tomorrow. What's your responsibility and what would you do?

6. Think about one management practice you are familiar with and identify which other practices it relates to and how.

(Continued)

Acting

7. Experiment with changing one thing you regularly do to make it more effective and more efficient.

8. Design and use indicators to evaluate the performance of one activity you often engage in.

9. Install and use a sustainability app on your phone to change one of your lifestyle practices to become more sustainable.

Interacting

10. Talk to a manager of your choice and ask if and how the topics of ethics, responsibility, and sustainability are relevant in the person's practice?

11. Have a look at the professional social network profiles of a couple of managers (e.g. on LinkedIn). What competences can you identify (e.g. through endorsed skills and others' references)?

12. Look at a company's corporate sustainability or responsibility report and think about one thing about their management practices that they could improve. Write to the company (often there is contact information at the end of the report) to suggest the idea.

Being

13. Do you think it would be a more natural role for you to be a 'mainstream' manager integrating ERS or a specialized ERS manager? Why?

14. What professional management practices do you think align well with your personal values and preferences? Which ones don't?

15. What do you think is or will be your unique style of practicing management? What meanings, materials, and competences do you think will be core to your management practice?

Becoming

16. Think about one situation where you had to manage (this could be either in a private or a professional role). How do you think you did? How would others describe what you did well and/or where you didn't do so well? What could have been done better? Do you think your management activity would be described as professional management? Why, or why not?

17. What personal practices do you use to keep yourself on track when 'the going gets tough'? What other practices, tricks, or tactics could you use?

18. Which of the modes of management do you think you could master most successfully? How would you make sure to practice management in this mode professionally?

SOURCE: Adapted from [27]

PIONEER INTERVIEW
HENRY MINTZBERG

INTERVIEWER: OLIVER LAASCH

Henry Mintzberg is arguably the world's most influential modern management thinker, including his tremendous contributions to understanding what managers do in practice.

On the impossibility of ignoring the social consequences of our managing. I don't see how you can manage any institution in society, whatever it is, and ignore the social consequences. That doesn't mean you go to the other and

Christinne Muschi/Getty Images

(Continued)

pretend you're a government. I don't want to be governed by corporations. I don't want them to decide, you know, what's moral or not.

On responsible management puzzles. They're loaded with puzzles, but their puzzles are both markets, and customers, and where things are going, and so on. I guess corporate social responsibility is a puzzle when you get stuck in both ends: there's a big fight in Canada now over a pipeline. Here the American company is building that pipeline. As the arguments are going, you can argue that we're creating employment, we're bringing energy to the world, those kinds of things. And some of the Aboriginal peoples on the route are saying you're not gonna do this in our backyard. That's irresponsible. They're saying, 'Creating employment is responsible.' Some of the Aboriginal tribes are saying, 'Yeah. We want it because we want the employment.' *So, you can get caught up in the two sides of this argument. Are you being decent?* You find justifications for self-interest, some of which are valid, maybe creating employment, but you're creating employment with some of the dirtiest energy in the world. And you're risking an oil spill in a very, very delicate part of the country. So, managers face puzzles all the time.

On the responsible action plane. In a recent book I talk about managing on an information plane, a people plane, and an action plane [40]. If you're not on the action plane, then it's harder to be responsible, because you're not plugged into the consequences of what's going on if you are always on an information plane. Robert McNamara[3] supposedly was a very sort of caring man, but he was a monster. His behaviours were monstrous. I don't care how much he claims to have been concerned. He was a numbers nut, so body counts became body counts. They weren't women and children, they were Vietnamese bodies, Việt Cộng bodies. So *management on an information plane, without getting to the action plane does not breed responsible behaviour.* That's one connection. You can carry out all the rules, more or less responsibly or irresponsibly. On the people level you can exercise the kind of leadership that is phony or you can access the kind of leadership that's authentic.

On face-to-face responsibility. Well, *you're always tentatively more responsible when your constituency is face to face and you have to face them.* I like to show two views of markets. One is a food market in Brazil and the other is the New York Stock Exchange. It's a lot easier to be responsible. I spent my share of time in markets in France especially in villages where I lived. That's the centre of community. Talk about responsibility: a person who is selling you turkey will take ten minutes to explain how to cook your turkey not because they're getting paid for it, but because there's a kind of communal relationship. It's not mercenary. It doesn't feel mercenary. The booths that are mercenary, just people – you can see them lined up behind one cheese thing and not behind another. Anybody who cheats their customers or doesn't even treat them nicely is not going to get revisited. Whereas in tourist trap places like in the Left Bank ['la Rive Gauche'] in Paris where nobody goes back to those restaurants. They're awful. I remember

---

[3]Robert McNamara was a US-American business executive, briefly serving as Ford's president, and then as Secretary of Defense. He played a major role in escalating the United States' involvement in the Vietnam war.

(Continued)

one posting a menu and they didn't even offer that menu inside. They were selling water for about ten times the price that they paid for it. They were completely irresponsible. Nobody would ever come back. So, that communal relationship certainly breeds more responsibility. Part of the problem now is that globalization is inconsistent with community. It undermines community. It undermines national sovereignty and it undermines community.

On responsibility to the ones closest to us. Well, *the most irresponsible thing you can do directly is mistreat your own people so they go home crying miserably.* God, the number of people who can't stand their bosses is so high and getting higher all the time. I can't believe it. Just mean management there is. We had a dean years ago. He was just such a mean person. People like that have no business running any organizations. They're irresponsible first of all to their own employees. There's so much of that going on.

On judging managers by their (ir)responsibilities. Flaws can be anything from bad breath to being killers. I mean, flaws can be anything. Obviously, irresponsibility is a flaw. For some companies, they don't mind. You read about Wells Fargo and they just seem to go from one crisis to another, or Uber under the previous guy. There's a blog on Uber you could look at that; I did with a colleague where she's in favour and I'm opposed. It's called Uber Uber über Alles [41]. *Too much responsibility can also be a flaw sometimes.* That's what happened with the chief executive of General Electric. He was so concerned with national issues and being on the business roundtable and all of these things that people are asking who is running the company. That was a flaw. He was too responsible. He was a statesman. The chief executive was out doing all kinds of wonderful deeds and not looking up to the story.

Note: This text is an abridged version of the interview conducted with Henry Mintzberg by Oliver Laasch, published in full as part of the *Research handbook of responsible management* [41].

QUESTIONS

1. If it is so impossible to ignore the social consequences of your managing, how come there appear to be frequent examples of managers doing exactly this?

2. How would you describe the relationship between managing on the action plane and face-to-face responsibility?

3. What modes of management practice can you spot in the interview text?

4. When you work as a manager, what kind of puzzles do you think you will encounter? What tactics could you use to solve them?

5. Do you agree that too much responsibility can be a flaw for a manager? If so, under what conditions? If not, why not?

6. What does management practice that assumes responsibility for the ones closest to us look like?

PROFESSIONAL PROFILE
KENE UMEASIEGBU

My name is *Kene Umeasiegbu* and I *head up the climate change and sustainable agriculture team at Tesco*. Prior to that I worked as a consultant for about five years in a number of consultancies including the Carbon Trust … but also around social and ethical issues like human rights and child labour. Prior to that I spent quite a big chunk of my career at Cadbury … a time in my career where I could reflect on my practice.

Courtesy of Kene Umeasiegbu

Acknowledging the complexity of practices. When you think about Tesco, we have thousands and thousands of product lines, and each of them would come with complex production systems. So as a business we look at it and say, 'Well gosh, where do we start?'

Mapping practices' impacts. We took another look at the way we've laid out an environmental sustainability agenda … We want to make a positive contribution where we can … we asked ourselves, 'What are the environments we have an impact upon?' and we laid out about five environments that we think account for 80 maybe 90 per cent of all the impacts we have. The first is … impact on the climate both through our own operations … but also through our supply chains … The sourcing of seafood has an impact on the marine environment. We have an impact on rainforests, which are a source of timber, soy, palm oil, and Amazonian beef. We also have an impact on farmlands, for instance, on agriculture in the Mediterranean region, in the UK here and in northern Africa. And then we also have our impact on freshwater bodies. … If we get it right, we'll be addressing at least 80 per cent of our environmental impacts.

What practices? When you come to addressing sustainability there are two ways you can go. One is how can we make production as efficient as possible and reduce as much as possible the environmental impacts of production? The customers look to us to take the lead because it's a complicated system and they don't understand it as well as we do. Then there is the consumption side of things. No matter how efficient and how well produced, if we waste 30 per cent of those resources when we over-consume, there's just no way to make production sustainable.

(Continued)

What we need to know as practitioners. Understanding the issues is just the foundation of an effective sustainability practitioner within business. Understanding the theory of the issue, the science of how to resolve it, is the start and the most important thing. Then, understanding how to make business address [the issues] in the light of commercial realities, of reputational realities, of the interests of investors, of the mandates of business to grow shareholder value, and of course of a practice ... trying to find the balance between quarterly results and the long-term focus.

Business sustainability careers. The job of a practitioner like me in-house is to find out how we find the right way to take these ideas as practitioners, as students, or whatever else, and how we embed it into the way we do business. You could choose a career to make this contribution as a consultant where you'll be the one doing the technical number crunching, always updating information and providing the footprint and the scientific evidence to make the case. That's an important role in the sustainability career sphere, but one could also play the role of being the person that takes this idea to market, the person who goes to the business and makes the business case.

I think there's a whole ecosystem of careers in sustainability. Each person would be best served by thinking about which area of this field plays well to their instincts as people to their values, and to the action logic. How do they organize their thoughts? If someone is of the view that the nature of business needs to be overhauled completely, and there's an argument for that, that the nature of consumption, the nature of capitalism, and value needs to be overhauled, perhaps that is someone more suited to policy conversations, to the transformation of the integral mental institution that is business.

Note: This text is an abridged version of the interview conducted with Kene Umeasiegbu by Frank Boons for the Massive Open Online Course 'Managing Responsibly' [42].

QUESTIONS

1. What role does professional practice play in Kene's management activity, and more widely at TESCO and in the food retail industry? What elements of the process of practicing professionally can you spot?

2. What (un)professional management practices does Kene allude to? What collaborative aspects of practices can you find?

3. Which of Kene's statements do you agree with? Which ones don't you agree with?

4. What different roles does Kene describe for practitioners who want to engage in changing management practices? Could you see yourself in these roles and do you think, for you, it would be more interesting to change a business from within or from the outside?

TRUE STORY
BETTING THE FARM

EDITED BY ALEXANDRA LEONOR BARRUETA-SACKSTEDER

Who I am. My name is Roberto and I have been the general manager at a hotel for 13 years. I began working as a bellboy out of high school and climbed the ranks from there until eventually I was promoted to manager. I come from a nearby village and worked hard to get where I am. I continue to put in the time and the work to help others from my village to get ahead in life. We were a normal, luxury hotel resort for tourists wishing to visit local ruins and monuments. Under my leadership we've expanded and now offer cultural tours and local food tastings as I think it's crucial to inform people about the local culture, which is dying out.

Why is everyone leaving? Six years ago we had a problem, people kept quitting their jobs at the hotel. We were losing money and time on all the training we were doing, and so I had to figure out a way to get them to stay. We started offering courses in hospitality, cooking and other fields related to the hotel, and for a while it seemed to be working, until I realized that people were taking the courses, getting the education and then leaving to find better jobs. There wasn't any loyalty to the company and I didn't know what to do. We even organized trash clean-up days with the local schools and sent our trucks and employees to help the students clean up the villages. This helped for a while but then the problems kept coming back.

(Continued)

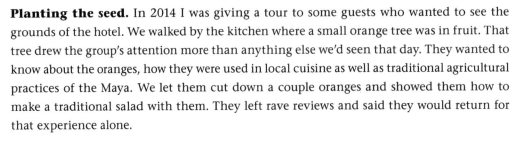

Planting the seed. In 2014 I was giving a tour to some guests who wanted to see the grounds of the hotel. We walked by the kitchen where a small orange tree was in fruit. That tree drew the group's attention more than anything else we'd seen that day. They wanted to know about the oranges, how they were used in local cuisine as well as traditional agricultural practices of the Maya. We let them cut down a couple oranges and showed them how to make a traditional salad with them. They left rave reviews and said they would return for that experience alone.

Fuelled with the good feedback, I asked the owner for a small plot of land to grow fruit trees on. He was sceptical but allowed me to grow the fruit as long as it didn't interfere too much with employees' scheduled work. Soon that small tree growing outside the kitchen became ten, then 50, then over 100 and we had to hire more people dedicated to the grove.

Something began to happen: Employees would come to work and bring their kids on weekends to walk through the grove. Using local agriculture had instilled a pride in them and their work. Our turnover numbers were down.

Thinking outside the pot. I continued to run the farm as a side project and it benefited the hotel in many ways. Guests loved our local flora and fauna tours and especially liked to know where their food was coming from. We now have over 500 fruit trees, including oranges, mandarins, lemons, limes, coconuts, and even pineapples! Turnover is at almost 0 per cent and we have a waiting list for potential employees. By creating the farm we have given jobs to people in the local village and as we learned about growing local produce they learned about their heritage too and were proud of it.

But now I have a dilemma. The farm was so successful that two things happened. Firstly, it has grown so big I can no longer manage the project as well as my general manager duties. Secondly, the owner of the hotel wants to set up other farms at different hotel locations to renew the local economy and bring the benefits of the farm to those villages as well. With my background and education, I felt good setting up the farm and running it initially but I feel that we need to hire someone to direct it and focus all their time on that, ideally someone young who can use social media, as my experience in this area is limited. However, my boss wants me to be in charge of the farming operation side of the business. I am also concerned about growing the farm to different locations. I know my village, I know the people, and even with that it took a lot of trial and error to find the right initiative to make them feel proud of their work. I feel like I would be out of my depth trying to expand it. What I would really like to do is hand over the project to someone I trust to do the right thing, with the right education and experience, and work in parallel with them while continuing my job as general manager, but I don't want to disappoint my boss by saying no, or the farm by abandoning it.

(Continued)

QUESTIONS

1. What type of ERS manager is Roberto?

2. How does Roberto's practice as general manager link to farming practice?

3. (How) Does Roberto engage in professional management practice?

4. Do you think Roberto should take the job and run all the new farms or not? Why and how?

5. How do different types of competences play a role in this story?

6. Think of an organization you've worked at or would like to work at. What practice could they engage in that benefits employees and the organization?

DIGGING DEEPER: PROFESSIONAL MANAGEMENT COMPETENCES

Interdependent competences

Thinking (Analysis)

Evaluating & deciding	Evaluative judgement, choosing & deciding
Using methodologies	Design & development, using analytical methods
Systemic-complex	Systemic appreciation, complexity thinking
Strategic-temporal	Temporal thinking, strategic planning
Divergent thought	Creative thinking, thinking in alternatives
Ethico-critical judgement	Critical thinking, ethical & values judgement

Interacting (Relation)

Relating to others	Cultivating relationships, stakeholder engagement, stewardship
Acting together	Cooperation, networked participation, team work, inter-work
Giving direction	Principled leadership, supervising others, advocacy & promotion
Mobilising others	Accessing others' competence, enabling, motivating, training
Communicating	Expressionality, receptive listening, 'good' communication
Handling difference	Embracing diversity, conforming-dissenting, generative conflict

Becoming, (Maturity)

Situated development	Situated learning, personal development
Intro-version	Reflexive introspection, handling emotions
Conversion	Personal commitment, self-responsibilisation
Self-management	Self-direction, professional work ethic, resilient persistence
Incorruptibility	Temperance & nonmaleficence, personal integrity, self-advocacy

Independent competences

Knowing (Knowledge)

Knowing disciplines	ERS domains knowledge, management specialisations knowledge
Situated knowing	Knowing context, knowing players, knowing rules
Knowledge qualities	Cross-cutting, actionable, conceptual, current
Sourcing knowledge	Knowledge generation, knowledge acquisition, experiential knowing
Handling knowledge	Information ethics, organising knowledge, dissemination
Interpreting knowledge	Recognising, contextualising, de/reconstructing

Acting (Action)

Managing activity	Resourcing activity, organising activity, implementation, completion
Mainstream managing	General administration skills, specialised management practices
Principled conduct	Moral action, responsible-sustainable behaviour, professional compliance
Managing ERS	Managing ERS issues &initiatives, using ERS tools
Impacting	Tackling ERS problems & opportunities, optimising impact
Transforming	Changing, integrating, innovating

Being (Character)

ERS mindset	Positive ERS affect, ERS attitudes, ERS aspirations
Morality	Moral consciousness, ethical and social values
Sociability	Empathy, approachability, respecting others, fairness, altruism
Agency	Self-efficacy, action orientation

Sources: [27]

POINTERS

This table is the outcome of a systematic review of which ethics, responsibility, and sustainability (ERS) management competences have been suggested by the literature [see paper cited in reference list item 27]. You could use the competences mentioned to reflect on which of these you believe you have, and which ones you are lacking. You could dig deeper into this, for instance, by looking up the original paper this table was published in [27]. From there you can read deeper into how a competence that you are interested in has been described and what can be done to increase that competence.

WORKSHEET

YOUR PROFESSIONAL MANAGEMENT SIX-PACK

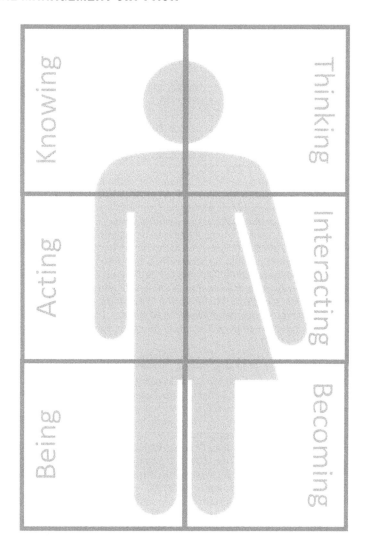

SOURCE: [27]

POINTERS

This worksheet can be used in many different ways. For instance, you could use it as a tool for self-reflection: to think about the professional or unprofessional sub-competences you have in each of the six fields. Alternatively, you could think about what kinds of competences would be necessary for you to master a particular practice of your choosing. You could also think about identifying a personal competence gap, comparing the competences you have with what you need for mastery. Finally, you could also explore how the different competences interrelate between the six fields. For instance, do your *knowing* competences match your *being* competences? Are there tensions or perhaps synergies?

REFERENCES

1. Acre. *The CR and sustainability salary survey.* London, 2020.
2. Slater C. Coronation Street named TV's greenest show. www.manchestereveningnews.co.uk/whats-on/film-and-tv/coronation-street-named-tvs-greenest-9577170 Published 2015. Accessed January 22 2020.
3. ITV. Environment. www.itvplc.com/socialpurpose/reducing-environmental-impact Published 2020. Accessed January 22 2020.
4. The Carbon Literacy Trust. The carbon literacy project. https://carbonliteracy.com Published 2020. Accessed January 22 2020.
5. Laasch O. Introduction: Responsible management in practice at Coronation St: MOOC managing responsibly. www.youtube.com/watch?v=ebAksdWkFNU&t=564s Published 2016. Accessed January 29 2020.
6. Mintzberg H. *Managers, not MBAs: A hard look at the soft practice of managing and management development.* Oakland: Berrett-Koehler Publishers, 2004.
7. Drucker PF. *The practice of management.* New York: Harper, 1954.
8. Drucker P. *Management: Tasks, responsibilities, practices.* New York: Truman Talley, 1974.
9. Felsted, A. Adidas-Kanye divorce is going to be expensive. Bloomberg. www.bloomberg.com/opinion/articles/2022-10-25/adidas-finally-ditches-kanye-west-and-yeezy-in-an-expensive-split?in_source=embedded-checkout-banner Published 2022. Last accessed July 18 2023.
10. Ghoshal S. Bad management theories are destroying good management practices. *Academy of Management Learning & Education.* 2005, 4(1): 75–91.
11. Jensen MC, Meckling WH. Theory of the firm: Managerial behavior, agency costs and ownership structure. *Journal of Financial Economics.* 1976, 3(4): 305–360.
12. Porter M. *Competitive strategy: Techniques for analyzing industries and competitors.* New York: The Free Press, 1980.
13. Porter ME. What is strategy? *Harvard Business Review.* 1996, 74(6): 25–40.
14. Gherardi S. Practice as a collective and knowledgeable doing. *Working Paper Series Collaborative Research Center Media of Cooperation.* 2019, 8.
15. Gherardi S. *How to conduct a practice-based study: Problems and methods* (2nd edn). Cheltenham: Edward Elgar, 2019.
16. Shove E, Pantzar M, Watson M. *The dynamics of social practice: Everyday life and how it changes.* Thousand Oaks: Sage, 2012.
17. Thompson M, Foster M. Prince Charles: We need a new economic model or the planet will burn. https://edition.cnn.com/2020/01/22/business/prince-charles-climate-davos/index.html?fbclid=IwAR0aCYGWuUAnjcPsshhOlIint2qSIqG4VisaOfzMk0OhwRkUXvVu5iN5rNU Published 2020. Accessed January 26 2020.
18. Van der Byl C, Slawinski N, Hahn T. Responsible management of sustainability tensions: A paradoxical approach to grand challenges. In: Laasch O, Suddaby R, Freeman RE, Jamali D, eds. *The research handbook of responsible management.* Cheltenham: Edward Elgar, 2020, pp. 2–39.

19. Radoynovska N, Ocasio W, Laasch O. The emerging logic of responsible management: Institutional pluralism, leadership, and strategizing. In: Laasch O, Suddaby R, Freeman RE, Jamali D, eds. *The research handbook of responsible management.* Cheltenham: Edward Elgar, 2020, pp. 420-437.

20. Yli-Kauhaluoma S, MikaPantzar, Toyoki S. Mundane materials at work: Paper in practice. In: Shove E, Spurling N, eds. *Sustainable practices: Social theory and climate change.* London: Routledge, 2013, 85–102.

21. Merchant B. Life and death in Apple's forbidden city www.theguardian.com/technology/2017/jun/18/foxconn-life-death-forbidden-city-longhua-suicide-apple-iphone-brian-merchant-one-device-extract Published 2017. Accessed January 26 2020.

22. Rayner T. You wouldn't buy a blood diamond, but do you own a conflict phone? www.androidauthority.com/conflict-minerals-883973 Published 2018. Accessed January 29 2020.

23. Umicore. Process. https://pmr.umicore.com/en/about-us/process Published 2020. Accessed January 26 2020.

24. Umicore. Recycling. www.umicore.com/en/industries/recycling Published 2020. Accessed January 26 2020.

25. Donham WB. The social significance of business. *Harvard Business Review.* 1927, 5(4): 406–419.

26. Bartlett CA, Ghoshal S. The myth of the generic manager: New personal competencies for new management roles. *California Management Review.* 1997, 40(1): 92–116.

27. Laasch, O., Moosmayer, D., & Antonacopoulou, E. P. The interdisciplinary responsible management competence framework: An integrative review of ethics, responsibility, and sustainability competences. *Journal of Business Ethics.* 2022. https://doi.org/10.1007/s10551-022-05261-4

28. Fayol H. *Administration industrielle et générale: Prévoyance, organisation, commandement, coordination, contrôle.* Paris: Dunod, 1916.

29. Mintzberg H. *The nature of managerial work.* New York: HarperCollins, 1973.

30. Mintzberg H. Rounding out the manager's job. *Sloan Management Review.* 1994, 36(1): 11–26.

31. Riggio RE, Chaleff I, Lipman-Blumen J. *The art of followership: How great followers create great leaders and organizations.* Chichester: John Wiley & Sons, 2008.

32. Uhl-Bien M, Pillai R. The romance of leadership and the social construction of followership. In: Shamir B, Pillai R, Bligh MC, Uhl-Bien M, eds. *Follower centered perspectives on leadership: A tribute to the memory of James R Meindl.* Greenwich: Information Age Publishing, 2007, 187–209.

33. Semler R. Managing without managers. *Harvard Business Review.* 1989, 67(5): 76–84.

34. Morelli J. Environmental sustainability: A definition for environmental professionals. *Journal of Environmental Sustainability.* 2011, 1(1): 1–9.

35. Brès L, Mosonyi S, Gond J-P, et al. Rethinking professionalization: A generative dialogue on CSR practitioners. *Journal of Professions and Organization.* 2019, 6(2): 246–264.

36. Maon F, Swaen V, Lindgreen A. Mainstreaming corporate social responsibility: A triadic challenge from a general management perspective. In: Idowu SO, Filho WL, eds. *Professionals' perspectives of corporate social responsibility.* Heidelberg: Springer, 2010, 71–96.

37. Idowu SO, Leal Filho W. *Professionals' perspectives of corporate social responsibility.* Berlin: Springer, 2009.

38. La Roche, J. Straw supplier says Starbucks is making the 'right decision'. https://finance.yahoo.com/news/straw-supplier-says-starbucks-making-right-decision-200507502.html?guccounter=1 Published 2018. Last accessed August 3 2023.

39. Mintzberg H. *Simply managing: What managers do – and can do better.* Oakland: Berrett-Koehler, 2013.

40. Mintzberg H, Breitner L. Uber Uber über alles. www.mintzberg.org/blog/uber-uber-uber-alles Published 2017. Accessed September 22 2020.

41. Laasch O, Jamali D, Freeman E, Suddaby R, eds. *The research handbook of responsible management.* Cheltenham: Edward Elgar, 2020.

42. Laasch O, Boons F, Randles S. Managing responsibly: Practicing sustainability, responsibility and ethics. www.coursera.org/learn/responsible-management Published 2016. Accessed January 28 2020.

PART B

DIMENSIONS

CHAPTER 3
ETHICAL MANAGEMENT

OLIVER LAASCH

LEARNING GOALS

1. Navigate ethical dilemma situations by applying moral reasoning
2. Analyse why people do right or wrong things
3. Use ethics management instruments to foster 'right' decisions and actions

IMPACTFUL FACT

Organizations with a strong ethical culture are 467 per cent more likely to positively influence employees' ethical behaviour (e.g. handling ethical risks, adhering to organizational values) than organizations with weak-leaning culture. Strongest ethical cultures companies outperform by approximately 40 per cent across business performance measures. [1].

SPOTLIGHT

UNMAKING THE UNFAIRPHONE

'Fairphone pop up' by Paul Miller is licensed under CC BY 2.0

The Amsterdam-based company Fairphone claims that 'from the earth to your pocket, a smartphone's journey is filled with unfair practices. We believe a fairer electronics industry is possible' [2]. Fairphone claims that the labour practices in both mineral mining and phone factories are mostly unfair. Their view is that the main minerals used in phones fuel conflicts, due to corrupt and violent supply chain practices. They also think that customers have a 'right to repair', while most phones are designed to make repair practices the least viable option in comparison to buying a new one [2, 3]. Fairphone instead guarantees fair labour practices in all their factories around the world. They have Fairtrade certified their mineral supply chain practices. Phone shells are produced from recycled plastic and so the carbon footprint of Fairphone's production is considerably reduced. Fairphone practices modular design, where customers can repair or upgrade their phones themselves by swapping components [3–5].

How has it worked out so far for the managers at Fairphone? Fairphone has consistently record-breaking scores for repairability [6]. An industry specialist has concluded that with Fairphone 'the only way is ethics' and that their practices are 'lightyears ahead of its competitors' [3]. Another commentary suggests that it is the most ethical and sustainable phone on the

(Continued)

market [5]. The same reviews also highlight that the phone is too pricey for its tech specs, but it's a sales hit anyway [3, 5]. Customers have even waited for months after they have prepaid new models through crowdfunding [7, 8].

Usually, strategizing means making sure that others are unable to copy any competitive advantage, in this case Fairphone's unique ethical practices. However, Fairphone's CEO Eva Gowens wants competitors to emulate and even improve these practices: 'We envision an economy where consideration for people and the planet is a natural part of doing business. This is why we are creating scalable and replicable models in our impact areas for the industry ... we need to transform the industry. The strongest signal that we can send is that there is a market' [5].

'Phone making with FairPhone' by PICNIC Network is licensed under CC BY-SA 2.0

Fairphone claims to make a 'phone that cares' and that 'caring is a radical act in a world that doesn't care' [9]. Is there anything radical or revolutionary in the way Fairphone practices management in the consumer electronics industry? Well, you could claim Fairphone is not just making fair phones, but attempting to unmake the industry's normal, uncaring practices of making 'unfair phones'.

ETHICAL MANAGEMENT

Managers engage in discretionary decision-making behavior affecting the lives and well-being of others.

Linda K. Treviño [10]

Does management have issues? The answer is yes. Managers working in organizations face a wide variety of ethical problems, dilemmas, and issues for which there is no one clear answer. Should I fire an older employee if they are performing less consistently, or should I keep that person as a reward for all the years served to the company? Should I invest in a climate change or a diversity initiative? Should I recommend that marketing campaign of unhealthy food products to children due to its profit potential?

Business **ethics** is about doing the right thing in such ethical problem situations and dilemmas. Managers must first understand that there is an ethical issue, then decide what is the right alternative to choose, and finally act accordingly. The more managers and employees do the 'right thing' and separate the acceptable from the unacceptable, the higher the ethical value creation will be. The management tool for achieving such value creation is ethics management, the management of **moral** dilemmas and issues. The practice of **ethical management** in turn is practicing ethically and engaging in ethical practices.

Figure 3.1 illustrates the ethical management process and how it maps onto sections of this chapter. In the first section of this chapter we will introduce basic concepts of business ethics, such as moral dilemmas, normative, and descriptive ethics, and ethics management. The second section sketches the ethics management process in its three phases: dilemma assessment, ethical behaviour analysis, and the application of ethics management tools.

Ethics
is the systematic consideration of right or wrong, using particular principles

Morality
describes norms, values, and beliefs of wrong or right held by a particular individual, group, or culture

Ethical management
means practicing management ethically and engaging in ethical practices

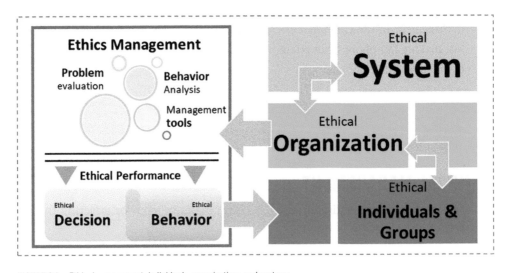

FIGURE 3.1   Ethical management, individuals, organizations and systems

Moral dilemma
a situation where right or wrong is questioned through a set of alternative actions that are likely to have significant effects on oneself and others and where the answer is not evident

MORAL ISSUES, DILEMMAS AND ETHICAL PROBLEMS

Ethics often deals with **moral dilemmas** and questions of right or wrong in a business context, but how do we identify issues? One may apply a simple scheme to identify a moral dilemma [11].

1. Is the decision to be taken likely to have significant **effects on others**?

2. Does the decision to be taken provide choices and **alternative actions**?

3. Is the decision perceived as **ethically relevant** (about moral right or wrong)?

As illustrated in Figure 3.2, **ethical problems** are not always dilemmas. Eth-ical problems can be divided into four broad types, based on the clarity of the moral judgement and the motivation of decision-makers to do the right thing.

Ethical problem
an issue centred on right or wrong decisions and behaviours

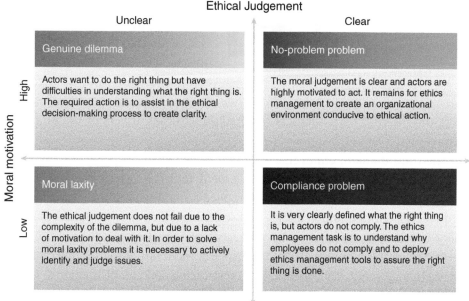

FIGURE 3.2   Types of ethical problems and approaches to addressing them

SOURCE: Aviva [12] Credit: Slidemodel.com

Determining whether a moral dilemma, issue, or conflict exists is import-ant in delineating the boundary between ethics, law, compliance, and gov-ernance topics, all of which play an important role in ethical management practice.

DOMAINS OF BUSINESS ETHICS

Business ethics, in its interdisciplinary nature, consists of three main domains illustrated in Figure 3.3. The first domain, normative ethics, relates to the field of moral philosophy. Normative ethics provides universally applicable rules for evaluating what should be considered right or wrong. Is it morally right to outsource jobs, to accept arms dealers as clients, or to take office material home?

Big pharma's ethical issues span individual, organizational, and system levels.

"Are your kids getting enough drugs?" by Loozrboy is licensed under CC BY-SA 2.0

Secondly, descriptive ethics explains why people do or don't act in a morally correct way. It explains how we make ethical decisions and how we act upon them. Descriptive ethics is mostly based on behavioural and organizational psychology as background disciplines: 'Why did Mr Li steal those office supplies from his company? Is it retaliation against his boss, or does he feel that it is fair to do so to compensate for what he perceives to be a lousy payment? What were the internal psychological factors and external drivers of his unethical behaviour?'

The third domain, ethics management, is rooted in management studies. It fulfils the function of applying management tools to foster morally excellent behaviour. Some of the tools typically applied are codes of ethics, ethics councils and officers, ethics training, audits, and screenings of employees. Ethics management in the application of ethics management tools largely relies on the clues derived from domains one and two. All three domains are absolutely necessary for ethical management. They are mutually reinforcing and complementary.

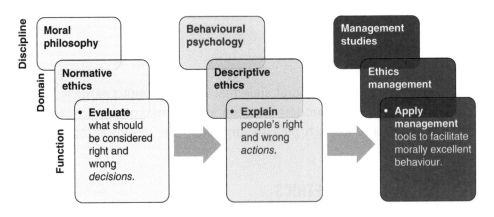

FIGURE 3.3 Functions, domains, and disciplines for ethical management

NORMATIVE ETHICS: EVALUATE WHAT'S RIGHT OR WRONG

Normative ethics
centred on ethical theories
of right and wrong to
solve ethical dilemmas

Normative ethical theories are based on moral philosophy, which is concerned with providing generally applicable rules for deciding what is right or wrong. In the following sections we will present three main streams of such ethical thought, as shown in Figure 3.4.

- **Consequentialism** judges by the consequences of one's actions [13, 14].

- **Deontology** (derived from the Greek word for duty) is based on the importance of duties and rules, and higher moral principles.

- **Virtue ethics** highlights that the 'good person' who lives a virtuous life, with a virtuous character, and virtuous practices will make right decisions.

We will propose a 'tripartite' approach to ethical theories, which acknowledges both advantages and disadvantages of all three theories, while stressing their complementary character [15].[1]

Let's think about how different normative ethics streams can provide insight into current dilemmas of the agricultural sector. With a dramatic decline in pollinating insects, artificial pollination using methods as varied as workers pollinating by hand to delivering pollen in soap bubbles has become a necessary agricultural management practice. Hot contenders being used already are robotic and AI solutions, including robotic drones shooting pollen at flowers. An episode of the dystopian sci-fi TV series *Black Mirror* thinks this scenario forward. After a (not unrealistic) wipe-out of pollinators, a tech company has successfully launched self-reproducing (nano-tech-enabled hives) robotic drones that behave like bees and self-regulate through swarm intelligence while communicating through a shared wireless connection. However, one R&D team member decides to programme the bees, as swarms, to every day hunt down (facial recognition) and 'take out' the person (e.g. a young woman who had shared an image of herself urinating on a war memorial) who has been tagged most often with a #DeathTo hashtag on social media [16].

Consequentialism might lead to the question of whether one person dying a day might not be worth it, if it creates a 'greater good' for masses of others. Deontology would, first of all, invoke the rule that you shall not kill. Looking at this through a virtue ethics lens, we would be concerned with the question of whether one bad action, however bad it is, should be used for an ethical judgement of a whole person's life. Finally, there is the intriguing underlying question of how to judge the ethical actions of an artificial intelligence and of the 'hybrid' intelligence (the R&D manager *with* the bee drones).

---

[1]While the three main ethical theories mentioned constitute the basis of moral philosophy and ethical reasoning, more recently, major alternatives have been developed that complement the traditional theories. Good examples are discourse ethics, which aims at ethical decisions through good communication, and feminist ethics that bases good decisions on good relations and empathy [11]. To keep complexity low and to stay in the scope and scale of this introductory ethics chapter, we will not elaborate on those theories in detail.

CONSEQUENTIALISM: JUDGE BY THE OUTCOME!

Consequentialism
the moral theory judging right or wrong based on outcomes

The moral philosophy called **consequentialism** is often presented as the counterpart to deontology. It is also called a teleological approach to ethics, derived from the ancient Greek word 'telos' for end. Both theories start from opposing assumptions. While deontology aims at applying ethical principles on actions, consequentialists are solely interested in the outcomes (ends) of those actions [17]. Consequentialism bases its assessment of right or wrong on the idea of hedonism that the only good is human happiness, which can be measured in terms of pleasure and pain. Thus, no matter the moral quality of the action, the good decision is always one that maximizes pleasure and minimizes pain.

The most prominently applied consequentialist theory is **utilitarianism**. Utilitarianism aims at creating maximum utility or welfare for all groups and individuals affected by a decision, behaviour, or in our case by an (un)professional practice. The fathers of utilitarian thinking were Jeremy Bentham and John Stuart Mill. Bentham described utilitarianism and the greatest overall happiness caused by a behaviour as the main end of ethical decision-making. Mill based his arguments on the central idea of welfare and the greatest happiness principle [37]. In contrast to egoism, which has also been subsumed under consequentialist thinking, the right decision is not the one making the decision maker most happy, but the one creating the greatest happiness for all involved: 'the greatest happiness for the greatest number' [18].

Making ethical decisions in the artificial pollination industry.

Utilitarianism
bases judgements of right and wrong on the principle of creating the greatest happiness possible for all affected by a decision

Mainstream economic thinking has often been related to utilitarian theory. Microeconomics, for instance, commonly analyses the utility of economic actors in order to find out what the rational economic decision should be. Welfare economics aims at maximizing the overall utility, and in this context, the welfare of all involved. Profit maximization, which has often been criticized as one of the main reasons for unethical decisions and business, is the maximization of utility for individuals, the owners of the business. Much of stakeholder management as described in the preceding chapter is based on

Overall Assessment Grade

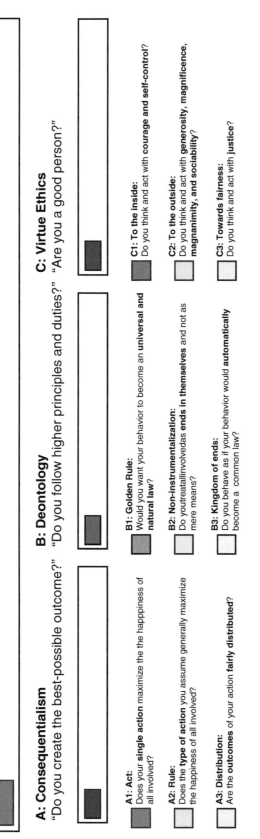

A: Consequentialism
"Do you create the best-possible outcome?"

A1: Act:
Does your **single action** maximize the the happiness of all involved?

A2: Rule:
Does the **type of action** you assume generally maximize the happiness of all involved?

A3: Distribution:
Are the **outcomes** of your action **fairly distributed**?

B: Deontology
"Do you follow higher principles and duties?"

B1: Golden Rule:
Would you want your behavior to become an **universal and natural law?**

B2: Non-instrumentalization:
Do youtreatallinvolvedas **ends in themselves** and not as mere means?

B3: Kingdom of ends:
Do you behave as if your behavior would **automatically** become a common law?

C: Virtue Ethics
"Are you a good person?"

C1: To the inside:
Do you think and act with **courage and self-control?**

C2: To the outside:
Do you think and act with **generosity, magnificence, magnanimity, and sociability?**

C3: Towards fairness:
Do you think and act with **justice?**

FIGURE 3.4 Major streams of moral philosophy

SOURCES: Adapted from [13, 14]

utilitarian thinking as it facilitates a consideration of all effects that a certain business activity has on the various groups that 'can affect or are affected' by the business activity [19].

Let us assume the example of outsourcing labour from the developed country France to a developing country such as India. For a well-rounded consequentialist analysis of a decision we propose approaching moral dilemmas such as the outsourcing decision through three consequentialist decision criteria:

1. **Act utilitarianism:** 'Does the single act I am conducting create more pleasure or pain?' To find out if the outsourcing should take place, a consequentialist would try to compare the outcomes for the main groups and individuals involved, such as the employees of the company. A simple consideration might be how much employment will be created in India compared to the employment lost in France. Another group might be customers. Is the value provided to customers greater or smaller with or without outsourcing? The same arguments can and must be created for all other involved parties.

2. **Rule utilitarianism:** 'Does the type of behaviour in general create more pleasure or pain?' The question here shifts from the single action to the type of action. Does outsourcing in general create more pleasure or pain? Is the socio-economic development in host countries greater than the loss in home countries? Do companies win or lose through outsourcing?

3. **Distribution fairness:** Are the costs and benefits created distributed fairly? While fairness is not a classic consequentialist argument, it has increasingly been integrated into utilitarian thinking in order to counter the common argument against utilitarianism, purely maximizing value, but not letting everyone benefit from the value created. Ask, for instance, do workers in developing countries benefit sufficiently in the way the company and customers do?

Many philosophers have completely rejected utilitarian thinking. The normative dialogue about deontology or teleology as the better theory for making ethical decision seems to have come to a stalemate [20]. Typical criticism of consequentialist thinking includes the feasibility and complexity of assessing the pleasure and pain involved for all parties; the danger of neglecting the interests of individuals and minorities; and the fair distribution of benefits [14].

DEONTOLOGY: 'FOLLOW HIGHER RULES AND DUTIES!'

Deontology
judges right or wrong by referring to higher duties that must be derived from universal rules

Deontology is an umbrella term for ethical theories that refer to higher duties derived from universal rules [17]. Deontological ethics and the related moral principles have largely been applied to ethical management, often with reference to the philosopher Immanuel Kant [21–23]. He proposed the 'categorical imperative' as the ultimate decision-making instrument for defining moral behaviour based on one's duties [24]. The categorical imperative is only the first of three of Kant's maxims to derive higher duties. According to Kant, every action to be considered right and good has to comply with the following three rules [24]:

1. **Universal law and the golden rule:** Would you wish everybody else to act the same way? Act as if by your action what you do would automatically become a natural law. Those questions have been summarized as 'the golden rule'. For instance, a manager who considers lying to one of their reports, who is also his personal friend, about the reasons for his layoff, would intrinsically propose the rule of 'lie if convenient'. Applying the golden rule, to check the ethics of his self-made rule, he would realize that if everybody always lied when convenient (when the rule had become a universal law), ultimately his organization and probably society as a whole would face severe problems.

2. **Non-instrumentalization. End in itself:** Do you treat (human) beings as means or as an end? It is undesirable to use human beings merely as 'instruments' for a certain purpose; instead your actions should be aligned to the good of humanity. Some authors have gone so far as to assume that if this maxim was taken seriously, management would not be able to operate. For instance, most businesses 'use' employees to fulfil a purpose that is different from the employees' ends. They are not ends in themselves [23]. Throughout this book we refrain from talking about human 'resources' (instruments) and instead refer to people management. We also discuss humanistic management that pursues the end of human well-being.

3. **The kingdom of ends:** Make sure that the maxims your actions are based on are acceptable to every other rational being. Would other rational beings who are part of the society or 'kingdom of ends' and who applied rules one and two judge as you did? To test if you are acting in the interests of every citizen in this kingdom of ends, a disclosure, also called the *New York Times* test, has been proposed. If you published your rule for behaviour on the front page of the *New York Times*, would rational beings agree? [25] In the business realm the respective question would be, 'Do I want our rules of behaviour to be published on the front page of all our company's communication channels, from annual report to website?'

There are other prominent examples of such higher rules. One important deontological philosopher is John Locke, who initiated the notion of natural, given rights of human beings, which ultimately resulted in today's powerful human rights movement [26, 27]. Another important example is John Rawls, who proposed justice as another universal, natural principle to derive duties from [28].

One typical criticism of deontology is that moral principles might often be conflicting. Imagine a situation where the moral principle of fairness opposes the principle of natural human rights. Which one should be considered more important and override the other? Imagine you are a manager at a medium-sized factory. There have been repeated thefts of employees' personal items. You know those items must be hidden in one of the employees' lockers. The fair thing to the ones who had been stolen from would be to search everybody's lockers. The human rights principle of protecting privacy would contradict this search. What should you do?

Another criticism is that moral principles if applied rigorously often lack practicability, and that deontological ethics only focuses on the actions, but neglects the outcomes of those actions [14]. In spite of extensive criticisms, deontological arguments are influential also for the other ethical theories. In virtue ethics, as an example, the virtue of justice can at the same time be used to derive deontological rules. Deontology and moral principles also play roles in consequentialist ethics. Interestingly, Kant's golden rule can also be interpreted for classical consequentialist, often economic thinking, which will be illustrated further in the following section [29].

VIRTUE ETHICS: 'BE A GOOD PERSON!'

Virtue ethics
judges decisions as right that are taken based on a virtuous mindset and congruent with a good, 'virtuous' life

Virtue ethics considers an ethical decision and behaviour to be right when it is conducted by a person with a virtuous character (a 'good' person) out of a virtuous motivation. A virtue is a combination of good traits of character, such as honesty, prudence, and wisdom.

There is a strong connection between virtues and values. One could say that a virtue is a series of lived values, which would lead to a good or virtuous life [13]. Interestingly, such a virtuous life is not only interpreted as good morally, but is also thought to lead to personal happiness, or *Eudemonia* in ancient Greek. Happiness in the sense of virtue ethics means activities that involve virtues and make appropriate use of our capacities. Happiness is generated through a way of life in which one functions optimally according to their purpose as a human being [30].

This idea of a good, virtuous life is also prevalent in many other philosophers' writings. Examples are Thomas Aquinas' new lifestyle or 'modus vivendi', and Confucian virtuous life, which is based on benevolence, propriety, and piety [31, 32]. Virtuousness is the fundamental criterion for deciding if a decision or action is good. Thus, an action conducted by a non-virtuous actor and/or out of a non-virtuous motivation is always bad, however good the outcome might actually be.

Virtue ethics has much to contribute to ethical management. Through its motivational aspect, and lasting perspective, it can provide distinct insights complementary to consequentialist and deontological ethics [15, 33, 34]. Modern virtue ethics has been applied in many ways to business ethics, from an entire corporation with a virtuous character to the virtuousness of a single manager [35, 36]. In practice, one can assess if an action is morally good or bad from a virtue ethics standpoint by assessing the virtues displayed in it. Each virtue is to be seen as an intermediate point, a 'golden mean', between two non-virtuous (vicious) behaviours. For instance, courage is located between cowardice and rashness, self-control between self-indulgence and prudishness.

Bragues [30] distils seven main virtues from Aristotle's original catalogue of 13 virtues that are especially relevant to management practice. The virtues identified are courage, self-control, generosity, magnificence, magnanimity, sociability, and justice. The following list groups the seven virtues into three main groups. It may help to assess ethical situations in the sense of 'What would a virtuous person do?'

1. **To the inside (courage and self-control):** A *courageous* person is able to overcome fear and risk when necessary for a higher goal. In a management context courage might lead to ethically favourable outcomes when the person needs to fight for the right outcomes against animosity, or to overcome the fear of risk in a social enterprise venture for a higher purpose. *Self-control* regulates our attraction to pleasure. The virtue of self-control can be understood as being a role model to others. Managers would, as an example, abstain from seducing others into bad practices and losing their self-restraint. Furthermore, managers would abstain from excessive marketing and from selling products that promise over-abundant pleasures, such as the newest fashion fad, high-fat meals, or pornography.

2. **To the outside (generosity, magnificence, magnanimity, and sociability):** Generosity is the virtue that regulates our desire for wealth. A manager who does not pursue wealth at all costs is more likely to abstain from engaging in ethically questionable practices. *Magnificence* strongly relates to generosity but refers to the ability to spend large sums for a worthy purpose. A large-scale example is Bill Gates, who through his foundation has donated 4.2 billion USD to improving health in developing countries. *Magnanimity* refers to a humble but articulated attitude towards honours and success. A manager with the virtue of magnanimity would neither brag with success nor shyly refrain from mentioning it, neither rush for success, nor endanger it by too risky adverse behaviour. *Sociability* is the virtue that results in a good-natured attitude towards others. Good nature may lead to morally favourable outcomes through the consideration of others in decision and behaviour.

3. **Towards fairness (justice):** The virtue of *justice* can be seen in obedience to law, or more broadly in thinking fairly. Acting justly and fairly includes both fairness in decisions and activities, and fairness in the outcomes of such activities. An example of lacking the virtue of justice would be a CEO passing up for promotion to vice-president of marketing a hardworking and competent brand manager in favour of the CEO's less qualified cousin. Another example would be a procurement manager trading inhumane labour conditions for thousands of workers in order to achieve a slightly cheaper product.

There is much criticism of virtue ethics being able to solve ethical dilemmas and being a guiding light for businesses management. The most extreme criticism is the one of incompatibility between virtue ethics and businesses as we know them. A manager who would thoroughly apply a virtue ethics philosophy would quickly put herself out of business [30]. A less drastic but equally powerful criticism of virtue ethics is its limited applicability to concrete dilemmas and situational ambiguity. We would need to know the entire personal history, thoughts, and motivation of the actor in order to authoritatively assess his or her virtuousness. Another difficulty in applying virtue ethics is the need to constantly re-assess the adequateness of virtues in a quickly changing world [14].

INTEGRATING AND OPERATIONALIZING TRADITIONAL THEORIES

All of the preceding ethical theories have been criticized. However, each also has specific strengths. In practice, mitigating the weaknesses of one theory by the strength of another can make ethical theory accessible and transform it into a powerful management tool [37].

Management decisions often draw from all three, outcome orientation (consequentialist), moral rules (deontology), and values in action (virtue) [38, 39]. An example is office theft. An employee might not do significant damage (no big negative outcome) by 'borrowing' an envelope for a letter to a friend. From a virtue ethics perspective, this act is highly unethical. It displays a lack of self-control, greed (the opposite of generosity), and unfairness towards the company and other employees who do not share the same benefit. One example of a deontological argument would be that the stealing employee acts against the golden rule. He would probably not want his action to become a general and natural law, as if everybody stole from the company it would probably go bankrupt and everybody, including the employee, would lose their jobs.

Helping managers understand how those moral theories can be integrated and used to make better decisions is crucial for ethical management. In this chapter we integrate the three main ethical theories, consequentialism, deontology, and virtue ethics through the perspective of ethical pluralism. In ethical pluralism the use of moral theories as a 'prism' helps to see an ethical dilemma in 'different colours', depending on which ethical theory is applied as lens [11]. This chapter's worksheet helps you to conduct a 360-degree ethics assessment using practical questions to guide an integrated ethical decision-making process.

DESCRIPTIVE ETHICS: EXPLAIN RIGHT AND WRONG ACTIONS

If we look at managerial scandals related to ethical issues, it often seems very clear from the outside what actions the managers should have performed if they had acted in an ethically correct way. Of course, they should not have falsified the books. Of course, pressuring employees into suicide is tragic and wrong. Unfortunately, for managers facing those decisions in practice, it is usually not as easy to make the right decision, even if knowing what should be done [40]. A variety of personal and external factors influence whether managers do the right thing. The domain of business ethics that analyses why people do or don't do the right thing is called **descriptive ethics**. Descriptive ethics is largely based on behavioural psychology, which is why it is often called behavioural ethics or moral psychology [41, 42, 43]. Descriptive ethics helps to describe, understand, influence, and predict the ethical behaviour of individuals and groups.

Descriptive ethics serves to describe, understand, influence, and predict moral behaviour of individuals and groups

THE ETHICAL DECISION-MAKING AND BEHAVIOUR MODEL

Research has shown that for a person to behave ethically, he or she needs to engage in four elements of ethical behaviour (see Figure 3.5). If an individual coincidentally acts (behaviour) in an ethically correct way, but without knowing why he or she does so (judgement), and without recognizing (awareness) that there actually is an ethical dilemma, it is neither an ethical decision nor ethical behaviour. Another person might be aware of an ethical dilemma and be motivated to do the right thing but might not be able to make the ethical judgement necessary to know what the right behaviour is. Such a person might either abstain from behaving in an ethically correct way out of insecurity or, even worse, engage in ethically incorrect behaviour out of ignorance.

Ethical decision-making and behaviour, and how people engage in the three elements are embedded in a process of person–situation interaction. First, the person influences the ethical decision and action through individual factors such as cognitive processes (how you think), affective factors (how you feel), and identity-based characteristics (who you think you are). Secondly, the influence that the situation exerts can be divided into issue-related factors (regarding the ethical dilemma) and situational factors (regarding the surrounding circumstances) [10, 42].

INDIVIDUAL AND SITUATIONAL FACTORS

Individual factors are all 'that are uniquely associated with the individual decision maker' [46]. Such individual factors can be approached from many different angles. Research suggests that your ethical decision-making and action depends on biological sex, what region you come from, what religion you adhere to, what your educational background is and what job you do. Another group of individual factors includes personal integrity, cognitive moral development, or how much 'moral imagination' you have [11, 42, 46].

Individual factors factors uniquely associated with the individual decision-maker that can be divided

Situational Factors

Issue e.g., moral integrity, framing, complexity

Context e.g., others, rewards & sanctions, organizational, tools, culture, industry, competitiveness

Behavior   Awareness

Motivation   Judgment

Individual Factors

Demographic e.g., age, gender, nationality, religion, education, employment

Psychological e.g., judgment, intelligence, locus of control, values, awareness

1. **Awareness:** The individual or group recognizes a potential moral dilemma.
2. **Judgment:** The individual has made a moral judgment upon what right means in this situation.
3. **Motivation:** The individual or group wants (has established a moral intent) behave right.
4. **Behavior:** The individual or group engages in the morally right behavior.

FIGURE 3.5   Situational and individual influences on elements of ethical decision and action

SOURCE: Adapted from [44, 45]

The first group includes demographic factors, and socio-economic factors, which are typically considered in a census or population statistics. The second group, psychological factors, is based on an individual's cognitive functions. Understanding individual factors in ethical decision-making may lead to valuable insights for ethical management.

The individual factors of ethical wrongdoing can be said to resemble a doctor's assessment of the causes of a patient's disease. Some authors have interestingly taken the perspective that bad ethics is a 'cognitive pathology', a disease that can be cured [39]. As an example we can consider two common individual drivers of unethical behaviour. Understanding that a specific misbehaviour stems from an individual perceiving work and private life as two different worlds, one with high and another one with low ethical standards [47], will require a different remedy from the situation where a manager acts unethically for hedonistic or egoistic reasons [48, 49].

A study by the Ethics Resource Center summarized the pressures to behave unethically perceived by employees of Fortune 500 companies, typical **situational factors**. The number one source of pressure was to keep their own job, followed by meeting personal financial obligations, and the pressure to

Situational factors
external factors that influence a decision and can be divided into issue-related and context-related components

meet quarterly earnings targets. Other items on the top ten list of pressures to behave unethically were to ensure the financial success of the company, to expand globally, to advance the individual's career, and, ironically, the pressure to uphold the company's brands and reputation [1].

Descriptive ethics proposes an extensive list of such situational factors influencing ethical behaviour. Issue-related situational factors that influence your ethical behaviour might be, for instance, how relevant, drastic, and severe you perceive an ethical issue to be. Another group of external, context-related factors includes the company's rewards systems, topics related to authorities and hierarchies, work roles and national and cultural contexts [11, 42, 46]. This chapter's 'Digging deeper' section summarizes the main individual and situational factors influencing ethical decisions and behaviours.

'Is it unethical to not tell my employer I have automated my job?' is a trending post on a job Q&A website by the user 'Etherable' [50]. We can imagine varieties of individual (e.g. is the person inclined to (ab)use their new free time; are they motivated to 'show off' with the achievement?) and situational factors (e.g. will they make themselves, colleagues, and work friends redundant if the employer knew?) to play a role in what they actually did.

Imagine you had written a program that takes care of your job, allowing you to get it done within two hours a week.

ETHICS MANAGEMENT

We will now introduce a set of **ethics management** tools. These tools aim at influencing situational and individual factors to increase the number of right decisions and behaviours.

Ethics management
the process of managing
ethical problems through
management tools

THE GOAL: MORAL EXCELLENCE THROUGH ETHICAL VALUE CREATION

Moral excellence
above-average ethical value creation

The goal of the ethics management process is **moral excellence**, which can be defined as above-average ethical value creation. A critical consideration is whether we should define 'above average' in relation to other actors, or in relation to a normative 'on average actors should do this or that'. In this chapter we endorse the application of the latter. The opposite of moral excellence can be called 'moral bankruptcy', a situation where management is so deeply involved in unethical practices that it has lost its moral licence to operate; it has lost its 'ethical profitability' [51, 52].

Ethical value creation
the sum of right and wrong decisions and behaviours in a specific entity and for a determined time period

To understand ethical management, we must rely on a solid understanding of what **ethical value creation** means. Management can keep track of infringements of ethical standards, by, as an example, conducting an anonymous survey among their employees to find out how many infringements of the code of ethics they have observed. This value, let's say an average of two infringements per employee per year, could then be used as a benchmark for the company's ethics management system. The goal might, for instance, be to reduce the observed ethical misconduct to one per employee per year within a timeframe of six months.

But is this enough? The company might realize that this one measurement does not provide accurate data. Employees might simply become better at hiding unethical behaviour. They might comply with the standards without any awareness as to why, or without making a judgement of their own. One measurement tool cannot provide the complete picture. To provide a concise, accurate picture of ethical value creation, it is important to apply a mix of measurement methods. We introduce three main approaches for assessing ethical value creation, as Figure 3.6 shows.

FIGURE 3.6　Ethical value assessment approaches

Moral development
an approach to measuring ethical value creation, based on the level of ethical reasoning of decision-makers in dilemma scenarios

MORAL DEVELOPMENT

The first approach to assessing ethical value creation aims at assessing the **moral development** of ethical decision-makers. The assumption is that the more competent moral actors are, the more ethical are the decisions made by them. As illustrated in Figure 3.7 Laurence Kohlberg divided moral development into six stages on three levels.

> The intermediate level of reasoning is called conventional. Most adults, among them managers, reason on this level, based on either Level 3 of conformity with society and mutual expectations, ('I do what is expected by my social group') or Level 4 focusing on what is good for society and the overall system ('I do what is right to maintain order') [53]. Managers with a lower moral development, the pre-conventional level either base their decision on Level 1, obedience and punishment ('I do anything that is not punished') or on Level 2 of interpersonal exchange ('if you do this, I do that'). The highest stage of moral development relies on 'principled' reasoning. On Level 5, managers orient their decisions towards a greater social contract that is based on individual rights, values, and in which some cases might stand above the law and general customs ('I do what is right to hold up the social contract'). On the last stage six, managers orient their decisions on self-chosen ethical principles as ultimate decision criterion ('I do what *I* know is right').

Based on Kohlberg's stages, schemes – mostly questionnaire-based – have been developed to assess an individual's moral development and ethical value creation [54]. Most of those questionnaires work by exposing decision-makers to hypothetical dilemma situations and asking them to recommend a course of action. The answers are then evaluated to find out on which level of ethical reasoning the individual argues [10, 55].

A recurrent criticism of moral development as proxy for ethical value creation is that it measures the potential cognitive ability to act ethically, which does not necessarily have to lead to *actual* ethical behaviour: Not everybody who knows what is right will also do the right thing. Nevertheless, many studies have shown that individuals with advanced moral development are significantly more likely to actually do the right thing [10].

While the moral development approach can only assess the capacity to make good decisions, the next approach focuses on ethics management practice, an 'implemented ethics' approach.

IMPLEMENTED ETHICS

The implementation of ethics management practices and tools can be used as another proxy for ethical value creation. The assumption is that groups and organizations that have ethics management tools such as codes of ethics, ethics training, or ethics policies are more likely to create ethical value.

Implemented ethics
an approach to measuring ethical value creation, based on the quantitative and qualitative level of ethics management practices implemented

An inventory of ethics practices and tools is the main methodology used to assess **implemented ethics**. Often this inventory is established using a checklist approach, where standard items of ethics practice are checked to establish the implemented ethics inventory.

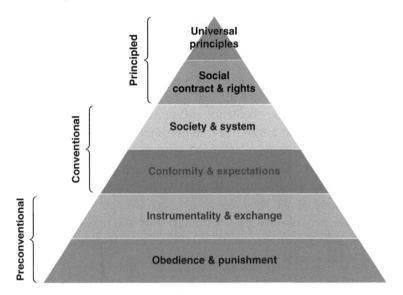

FIGURE 3.7   Ethical value creation models based on moral development

SOURCES: Adapted from Kohlberg [53]

The decision based on an item in the inventory or of a checklist is to be evidenced. For example, the inventory item 'human rights practices' would rely on evidence like a company's human rights policy, or a section on human rights in the code of ethics. Management may establish such a portfolio internally or use it to report their implemented ethics to external rankings, labels, and certifications such as the Ethisphere ranking or the Ethos label [56, 57].

OBSERVED BEHAVIOUR

The ethical value creation assessment approach of **observed behaviour** is usually based on quantitative surveys. Observed behaviour approaches usually focus on ethical misconduct as it is easier to identify than ethically correct actions. If the morally right decisions are taken, one might not even realize that a moral issue was looming. Managers might use internal survey mechanisms – for example, through information obtained from a whistleblowing hotline, to obtain quantitative data, or choose to conduct anonymous surveys.

An impressive overview of observed (un)ethical behaviour is established through macro-surveys that ask questions such as, 'How often do you observe

Observed behaviour
an approach to measuring ethical value creation based on the quantitative surveys of observed ethical (mis)behaviour

ethical misconduct in your team?', 'What are the biggest pressures on you to behave unethically?', or 'In how many incidents annually do you feel you do not comply with ethical standards?' [1, 58] A strength of the observed behaviour approach is that it captures actual (observed) ethical incidents. The first two assessment methods mentioned are mere 'surrogate indicators', which indicate that there might be an ethical issue [59]. The disadvantage of the observed behaviour approach lies in the lack of information on why individuals show a certain behaviour.

ETHICS MANAGEMENT TOOLS

Ethics management deploys a varied set of tools, stemming from both origins, mainstream business, and from specialized business ethics. Mainstream management tools are, for example, a new payment scheme that rewards ethically correct behaviour (people management), ethical key performance indicators (accounting), or including ethics in the company's mission statement (strategy). All of those are powerful tools influencing employees' ethical decision-making, but they must be complemented by specialized **ethics management tools**, such as codes of ethics, ethics councils, and ethics training. In the following sections we will provide greater insight into both types of tools.

Ethics management tools managerial means to improve ethical value creation

Figure 3.8 illustrates ethical value creation overall and how an organization depends on both types of ethics management instruments. They complement each other and create what we might call an ethical value creation margin. Such a margin describes the difference between ethical misbehaviour (unethical value creation) and ethically correct behaviour (ethical value creation). Just as a mainstream business value chain and its margin describe the difference between the financial costs of doing business and the total value added by its activity, an ethics value chain describes the difference between ethical misbehaviours and good deeds.

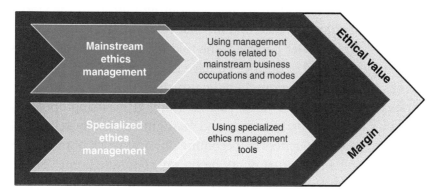

FIGURE 3.8   Ethics management tools and the ethical value creation margin

Ethical management behaviour describes a manager's ethical behaviour in his or her immediate sphere of managerial influence

The basis of ethical value creation is the **ethical behaviour of managers**. Such good ethical behaviour not only adds up to an organization's overall ethical value creation, it also serves as a role-model function of ethical leadership. A survey by the Ethics Resource Center [1] illustrates further: when supervisors were observed to behave unethically, 42 per cent of employees felt the pressure to do so too. Eighty-nine per cent observed ethical misconduct, but 40 per cent did not report it. Those negative behaviours were more than halved when supervisors were perceived as behaving ethically themselves. The pressure to compromise standards was reduced by 25 per cent, the observed misconduct by 45 per cent, and the number of unreported incidents of ethical misconduct was reduced from 37 per cent to only 3 per cent. When employees report misconduct, the large majority do so to their supervisors (86 per cent). The perceived behaviour of companies' top management has a similarly significant impact.

MAINSTREAM ETHICS MANAGEMENT TOOLS

Mainstream ethics management tools standard management instruments used throughout managerial modes and occupations to improve ethical value creation

Mainstream ethics management tools harness the standard instruments of management occupations and modes to manage ethical value creation. Later chapters will provide deeper insight into main managerial modes, like leading and organizing, and managerial occupations like financial management and marketing management, in order to explore how ethics, responsibility, and sustainability are a part of them. Mainstream management is crucial in ethics management in two ways.

However, often mainstream management practices are not what prevents unethical behaviour, but what causes it. It is then up to the individual to 'speak their values' and 'draw a line in the sand' [60], which is an immensely challenging task as illustrated by Emily McCrary-Ruiz-Esparz, who shared her experience in 'This is what happened when I stood up for ethics at work' [61]. She sums up the story by explaining: 'The company I worked for told me to inflate numbers and mislead customers and outright lie about the work we'd done. I confronted my boss who told me that I was mistaken, that's not what was going on. When I later persisted, she told me that if I wanted to have a good job, this is the kind of practice I'd have to get used to. I was gone within six months. And she was wrong.' Emily also shared all the workplace retaliation practices applied afterwards, such as being given inappropriate tasks, downgrading her work performance and 'gaslighting'. Emily tells us about the very personal consequences of 'becoming physically sick from the anxiety and … developing a new ritual of crying on my commute home'. She closes her account by explaining her underlying motivation of 'coming out' about this experience: 'I tell this story not to convince you that if you stand up for your ethics, everything will be okay. There's a chance it won't. I tell this story because standing up for your ethics is worth it. It was for me.'

Emily explains how 'normal' but unethical management practices at work make one's life miserable and how it's worth the consequences of doing something about it.

Ethical misconduct in particular modes and occupations. First, some occupations and modes of management seem to be more susceptible than others to ethical misconduct. A survey among 175 company leaders revealed that 53 per cent found sales to be the area of greatest concern; 51 per cent identified operations management, especially in emerging markets; and 20 per cent found accounting and finance a reason to worry [58]. A first and powerful step to foster good ethics across particular occupations and modes of management is to create formal ethics policies, such as an ethical sourcing policy for procurement, ethical marketing for customer relationship management, and an accounting ethics policy for accounting and controlling.

Support of ethical value creation by management. The second type of significance of mainstream ethics management tools lies in mainstream management's support of ethical value creation across other occupations and modes of management. For instance, members of the accounting and controlling occupation might implement ethical issue-related indicators in their work, such as the average number of ethical misconduct reports to an ethics hotline in a given period. In communication mode, managers can send messages about the desired ethical behaviour or conduct a monthly internal dilemma solution competition in the style of 'What would you do?' Further, people management has many ways of increasing ethical value creation, such as rewarding ethical behaviours in payment schemes; conducting ethics training; and considering ethical behaviour in performance evaluations. A survey among company leaders found that almost half of the participants (49 per cent) considered good ethical behaviour at least as important as mainstream business outcomes in employees' performance evaluation [58]. Eighty-one per cent of Fortune 500 companies have an assessment of employees' ethical conduct as one part of performance evaluation. Ninety-one per cent train their employees on ethics [1].

SPECIALIZED ETHICS MANAGEMENT TOOLS

Specialized ethics management tools
tools to manage ethics throughout the whole organization

Specialized ethics management tools have been developed specifically to manage ethical value creation. This set of tools is typically administered by the ethics and compliance department that specializes in the management of the organization's overall ethical value creation, but can also be applied by individual managers in their sphere of influence:

Moral leadership. Codes of conduct are probably the most commonly applied ethics management tools. Ninety per cent of those codes are meant as guidance for ethical decision-making and behaviour. They present a combination of ethical rules and values. Fifty-nine per cent of employees surveyed applied the code on their job most of the time and another 35 per cent applied the code sometimes [58]. Companies that have a better code of conduct are usually ranked higher for their ethics, responsibility, and sustainability performance [62]. The code of conduct is often the basis and a first step for subsequent ethics instruments deployed by organizations. It is important to get the code right (see Table 3.1).

TABLE 3.1 Quality criteria for codes of conduct

Analysis component	Component description
Public availability	A code should be made readily available to all stakeholders. What is the availability and ease of access to the code?
Tone from the top	Level at which the leadership of the organization is visibly committed to the values and topics covered in the code.
Readability and tone	What is the style and tone of the language used in the document? Is it easy to read and reflective of its target audience?
Non-retaliation and reporting	Is there a stated and explicit non-retaliation commitment and dedicated resources available for making reports of code violation? If so, is it presented clearly?
Commitment and values	Does the code embed corporate values or mission language? Does it identify the ethical commitments held to its stakeholders (e.g. customers, vendors, communities)?
Risk topics	Does the code address all of the appropriate and key risk areas for the company's given industry?
Comprehension aids	Does the code provide any comprehension aids (Q&As, FAQs, checklists, examples, case studies) to help employees and other stakeholders understand key concepts?
Presentation and style	How compelling (or difficult) is the code to read? This depends on layout, fonts, pictures, taxonomy, and structure.

SOURCE: Adapted from [62]

Organizational structure. Ethics departments and officers are usually the roles assigned to handle ethics management tools. Ethics departments and officers often fulfil a double role as they also cover the function of compliance with laws and regulations. The resulting ethics and compliance function can often be a considerable size and is best measured by the number of full-time employees in such departments. Fifty-five per cent of companies with an ethics and compliance officer have been found to employ 2–9 full-time employees dedicated full-time to the management of ethics and compliance, 18 per cent 0–1, 11 per cent 20–49, and 12 per cent more than 50 [58]. The job of the ethics officer has been described as crucial for ethical value creation, but as highly complex in practice. Ethics officers are often seen as 'troublemakers' who have little power and unclear job descriptions. To ensure ethics officers positively impact on ethical value creation, it has been recommended that they are positioned directly under the board of external directors (for greater independence from the managers they are to observe). Another recommendation is to clearly define and communicate ethics officers' job descriptions, and to pay extra attention to the moral profile of candidates [63, 64].

Feedback mechanisms. Whistleblowing, councils, ombudsmen, and audits are ethics management tools that fulfil a double function. On the one hand they serve to obtain information about ethical (mis)conduct. On the other hand, they provide feedback and advice. Whistleblowing (blowing the whistle is a symbol for making public others' misconduct) can be achieved through many different anonymous or personalized mechanisms. Ethics hotlines, where employees can report misconduct to an independent person, are widely applied. Ethics councils and ombudsmen are people that employees can contact for advice and support. Ethics audits are a third mechanism to detect misconduct where ethical value creation is checked systematically.

How can feedback mechanisms be managed most effectively? Of the people who did not report an ethical misbehaviour in a survey among Fortune 500 companies, 61 per cent stated that they did not believe that corrective action would be taken anyway. In most cases this is not true. Seventy-one per cent of people who have reported misconduct in a survey state that their reports were investigated and actions taken. The second biggest inhibitor for employee reporting (42 per cent) is that reporting channels were not confidential, which leads directly to fear of retaliation. Twenty-nine per cent of survey respondents did not report as they feared retaliation from co-workers, 28 per cent from top management, and 25 per cent from their direct supervisor. Unfortunately, this fear is rooted in a real risk. Fifteen per cent of respondents did not report as they had experienced retaliation when they reported previously. Retaliation ranged from other employees giving them the cold shoulder, to abuse, and exclusion from decisions [1].

ETHICS PROGRAMMES AND CULTURE

An ethics programme
a set of ethics management instruments combined to create ethical value

Ethics management tools are typically bundled to jointly form an **ethics programme**, which aims to maximize ethical value. Sixty per cent of Fortune 500 companies have an ethics programme consisting of at least six distinct ethics management instruments. Programmes may be a powerful start towards ethical value, but good ethics only become truly institutionalized and lasting when 'socialization of ethics' takes place, when doing the right thing has become part of the organizational identity and is its natural character [59, 65, 66].

An ethical culture
describes an organization's environment characterized by ethical values and behaviour

The consistent application of those programmes should lead to an ethical organizational culture, which in turn helps to stabilize ethical value creation. An **ethical culture** creates an environment where it is easy and natural to do the right thing in every decision and action.

Achieving ethical culture is a worthwhile endeavour both from an ethical value perspective and from a mainstream management perspective. Employees working in organizations with strong ethical cultures feel less pressure to compromise ethical standards. The observed ethical misconduct is more than halved and an average of 97 per cent of employees reported misconduct when they saw it [1]. Ethical culture also brings advantages for mainstream management, most notably an increase in the long-term value of the business, compliance with rules and regulations, and a heightened employee commitment to organizational mission and values [1, 58].

Imagine you could take a peek inside to see (un) ethical company cultures before you start a new job.

So, what is the secret to creating an ethical culture? Creating an ethical culture is a primary task of the ethics and compliance (E&C) department, but it is in need of allies. The main allies for the E&C department are the active support of the C-suite, the topmost managers in the company, the people management department, operations management, and the internal corporate communication department. Interestingly, the role of C-suite management is almost as important as that of the E&C department. The three largest hurdles to achieving ethical culture are:

1. Organizational complexity

2. Lack of support by middle managers

3. Lack of appreciation of ethical culture as a business driver [58]

In the past you would have needed to enter a workplace as a new employee to see first-hand if there was an ethical culture. Interestingly, nowadays there are websites like Glassdoor where former employees of companies leave their appreciation of the company, often providing quite a lively picture of (un)ethical business cultures [67].

THE PROCESS OF ETHICS MANAGEMENT

The **ethics management process** applies to all levels of management and the people managed. For example, the top manager who manages a corruption issue for the whole company will apply the same ethics management process as a sales manager who needs to decide whether to sell to a tobacco company or not. Figure 3.9 illustrates the process of ethics management in three main stages. At every stage, one of the three domains of business ethics is predominantly important. At stage one, the ethical problem evaluation, the focus is on understanding the issue and finding the right behaviour. The normative ethics stage delivers the answers to those questions by applying theories of moral philosophy to the situation at hand. In the next stage the main task is to understand why people do or don't act according to what has been defined as ethically correct. Descriptive ethics provides the answers by evaluating individual and situational factors that may be inhibitors and drivers of making the right decisions. At Stage 3, ethics management is the domain that delivers the right tools to manage ethical value creation.

The ethics management process
the management of ethical problems with the goal of achieving maximum ethical value creation

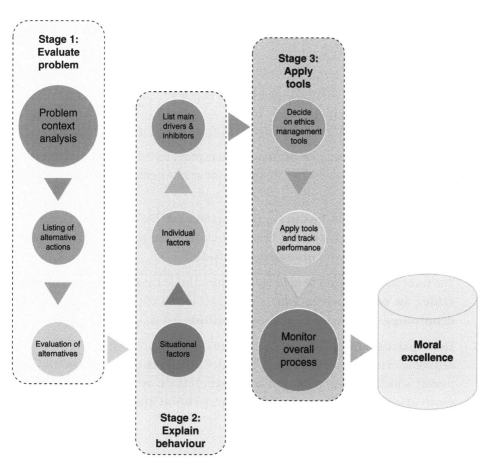

FIGURE 3.9 The ethics management process

At Stage 1 of the ethics management process, the evaluation of the ethical problem means deeply understanding the issue at hand. The first question to ask before the dilemma evaluation is whether the management challenge at hand is actually an ethical issue. Many problems that are commonly subsumed under the heading of ethics are not strictly ethical issues, but rather mainstream business challenges or legal compliance issues. Those issues have to be managed, but ethics management is not an adequate tool. Examples of typical ethical management issues are discrimination, sexual harassment, bribery, equal treatment of employees, advertising, occupational health and safety, unjust dismissal, financial issues, and pollution [68].

In the ethics management process we encounter a powerful concept that attempts to unify the long history of business ethics and the three main domains of the field in one easy-to-capture road map. The simplicity of description in this road map should not create the illusion of ethical management being simple. Achieving moral excellence is a highly complex process that can be described easily, but which needs a profound knowledge basis in normative and descriptive ethics, and knowledge of the tools of ethics management.

PRINCIPLES OF ETHICAL MANAGEMENT

I.   **Business ethics** is the interdisciplinary study of moral issues in business.

II. Business ethics is related to **morality**, as ethics provides the rules for deciding what is right or wrong, while morality explicitly describes right or wrong for a specific group and situation.

III. The three **domains of business ethics** are **normative ethics**, based on moral philosophy, **descriptive ethics**, based on **behavioural psychology**, and **ethics management**, based on **management studies**.

IV. The three major theories of moral philosophy, inside the domain of **normative ethics**, are **consequentialism**, based on achieving the best-possible outcome; **deontology**, based on rules; and **virtue ethics**, based on a virtuous life.

V.   **Descriptive ethics** aims to describe, understand, influence, and predict the ethical behaviour of individuals and groups. It is based on the **ethical decision-making** process, which revolves around the four stages of ethical **awareness, judgement, motivation, and behaviour,** and takes **individual and situational factors** into account.

VI. **Ethics management** is the process of managing ethical problems through management tools with the goal of improving ethical value creation.

VII. **Ethical value creation** can be assessed through the three approaches of moral development, implemented ethics, and observed behaviour.

VIII. **Ethics management tools** to achieve ethical value creation fall into the categories of mainstream, and specialized ethics management. Tools, if applied well, serve to create a self-reinforcing **ethical culture**.

MANAGEMENT GYM: TRAINING YOUR PROFESSIONAL SIX-PACK

Knowing

1. Define the following terms, and interrelate them: normative theories, descriptive ethics, and ethics management.

2. Define the following terms, and interrelate them: ethical management, morality, and behavioural ethics.

3. Look up the code of ethics of an industry of your choice. Find out about the typical ethical issues in that industry, past ethical issues (potential scandals?), and potential future issues.

Thinking

4. Choose a 'non-Western' moral philosophy like Confucianism or Ubuntu. What similarities and differences can you see with the Western theories introduced in this chapter? Do you think a shared 'world ethos' can be agreed upon across cultures? What ethical ideas or principles would be the main contenders for such a world ethos?

5. Imagine you work in a company's people management department (HR). You have just found out that when employees are let go, their severance pay is not paid. When former employees find this out it is classified as an accounting mistake and the payment is made. You hear from your colleagues that this is 'normal' across the company and that the senior management team approves. Consider the options for what you could do. Which one should you choose?

6. Use your 'moral imagination' to think about all the moral issues, implications, and consequences related to the (non)payment practice in the previous question. Think about it in relation to individuals, groups, organizations, economy, the country, and the world.

Acting

7. Write a code of ethics for a management occupation of your choice (e.g. marketing, accounting, operations management). Apply the quality criteria provided in this chapter.

8. Look up a company's website, examine their reports, and prepare an 'implemented ethics assessment' in which you list the ethical issues explicitly addressed by the company and the ethics management tools deployed.

9. Imagine you are the newly assigned ethics officer of a company of your choice. Write an ethics management plan for the company, describing a set of ethics management tools to be applied. Explain how this ethics management system will create ethical excellence and avoid ethically wrong decisions and actions.

Interacting

10. Talk to a manager about one specific moral issue they observe among colleagues. Try to understand together what the personal and situational factors are of why people do right or wrong in relation to that issue.

11. Engage a representative of a specific profession, company, or industry in a discussion on a typical ethical issue encountered in their professional sphere. Try to jointly analyse the person's behaviour and develop strategies to increase their ethical value creation. The exchange will probably be easier if you have a personal connection to this person.

12. Speak with one of your course mates about how they usually make ethical decisions and share how you do so with them. What role might your unique personal characteristics play in this (e.g. home culture, gender identity, upbringing)? How are your respective decision-making methods similar and/ or different?

(Continued)

Being

13. Reflect on how you make your ethical decisions. Think about occasions when you had to make a morally difficult decision. What were the main factors in your decision-making? Can you recognize any of the above normative theories or decision-making principles in the way you made your decision?

14. Moral issues are everywhere. Look around you and make a list of ten moral issues related to what you see.

15. What are the Top three core values and beliefs you cannot compromise on?

Becoming

16. Based on your cultural, religious, or family background, can you think of anything that you disagree with among the moral theories and values presented in this chapter? Can you imagine settings where there might be tensions or even conflict due to these disagreements with the theory? How could you handle such a situation?

17. Have you ever been in a situation, or can you imagine a situation, where you felt you knew what 'the right' thing to do was, but circumstances made it very difficult to actually do? What tactics can you use to do the right thing despite the difficulties? What will you do next time you are in a similar situation?

18. What personal qualities and habits do you think will help you to be an ethical manager? How can you obtain these?

SOURCE: Adapted from [69]

PIONEER INTERVIEW
LINDA K. TREVIÑO

INTERVIEWER: OLIVER LAASCH

Linda K. Treviño is a pioneer of the behavioural ethics movement who has shaped the way we understand (un) ethical management thought and action.

Understanding the psychology of (un)ethical behaviour. I think that both are extremely important. We need the normative ethics tools to help us decide what's right in a particular situation. But we all know that people don't always follow those prescriptions. So, we also need to understand the psychology of human decision-making and behaviour. Psychology can help us to figure out why people think and behave as they do, and that knowledge can inform how we structure organizations and lead people in an ethical direction.

Courtesy of Linda K. Treviño

Is it just lovely at the top? The study 'It's lovely at the top' demonstrated what many of us know intuitively – that top executives are often out of touch with what's happening at lower

(Continued)

levels in their organizations because information gets filtered and bad news often stops at lower levels. That doesn't just apply to ethics, but when it does, it has huge implications. If everything looks rosy and fine at the top, executives won't commit resources that are necessary to develop ethical cultures and ethical leadership in their organizations. I encourage organizations to do serious ethical culture assessments at least every few years to find out what employees are saying and doing. They then need to take the results of such assessments seriously and make necessary changes.

The top three recommendations for students to get business ethics right. First, I believe that it's so important to know yourself. Figuring out who you are, what your values are, and what you stand for before you enter the workplace can go a long way towards ensuring ethical behaviour because there will be challenges along the way. If you know what your values are, and work towards standing up for them, you are more likely to resist pressure to behave in ways that are inconsistent with those values.

Second, I encourage students to do their best to figure out what an organization's values are before joining it. This is because good values fit makes for happier employees generally. But it also helps to avoid the serious ethical challenges that employees sometimes face. If they've made a good match, they are more likely to agree with how their employer does business.

Third, it's important for students to understand their own responsibility for ethical leadership. They are in business school in part because they expect to be leaders. And, as leaders, they have a responsibility to design workplaces in ways that support ethical conduct and discourage unethical conduct. That applies to all sorts of things managers do, from setting goals to designing reward and punishment systems to conducting performance evaluations.

QUESTIONS

1. How do you think insights from psychology can be used to generate ethical management practices?

2. How would you design an ethical workplace? What would it look like and feel like to work in?

3. What do you think top managers and managers in general can do to avoid the 'it's lovely at the top' perspective?

PROFESSIONAL PROFILE
PIA POPPENREITER

I am Pia the CEO and co-founder of Ohlala, a paid dating app. We connect users to go on paid dates instantaneously in the safest way possible. After we founded Ohlala we raised money to finance the product development and when we launched, it went so well that we quickly took it to more cities in Germany and we started to take it abroad to New York City.

From investment banking to responsible management to founding Ohlala. I have a finance background and worked in investment banking. But I did some soul-searching and studied responsible management in Berlin. After graduation I founded my start-up. I'm a very data-driven structured person, but I also am incredibly happy that I studied

Courtesy of Pia Victoria Poppenreiter

responsible management. Finance gives the structure to data-driven work but having this ethics background helped me put a framework around products and the company so that we all have a good feeling working here.

Ethics is so abstract. Or is it? When I was studying ethics it was quite abstract. A couple of times I thought: What am I doing here? How could I possibly ever use this for my further career?... I only found out later that this is so valuable. It helped me... You're going through the cases and you're like: Why are we discussing this? Now I really think a lot back when we evaluate situations and how we derive decisions: How can I put a structure around the product and the company and the people working here? They need to feel comfortable acting with their own set of values, but still within the scope of the values that we created for the company. With Ohlala we're tackling a super tricky topic that is really stigmatized in public and there's a lot of explaining and judgement.

Hiring for ethics? We are hiring right now. I really look forward to starting the interview process when I get to talk to the people that are applying... We're really talking a lot about the issues and the ethical implications. The core of our whole being is that we have some prefixed rules that we constantly apply. First, we honour the integrity of our users. We ask, 'If we were a user would we want that to be done?' and that is actually really fundamental to how we make decisions.

Getting started with ethics. Start-ups are quite crazy, but actually we did have a code of ethics in place the first month. You have co-founders and you need to sit down and discuss

(Continued)

how you see the world, how you see the product, and where it should go. Then you really need to be aligned and you want to go in the same direction. So ethics was a huge component right at the beginning and we are constantly communicating this. We recently closed our financing round and we are now in the phase of professionalizing ethics within the company.

Inviting people to reconsider their worldviews. I know who I am and I know who we are at Ohlala and I know our product. That's the foundation of all my arguments if I'm being criticized. I think a lot of times it is due to a lack of understanding or miscommunication. You always try to find out what the problem actually is and to discuss it. Just maybe you invite the other person or the audience to question how they view the world. I am not saying that I'm right. It's just one perspective and I want to invite people to reconsider how to view the world. That's my approach without telling them what they have to think.

How to live with the critics, moral and otherwise? I know who I am and that my intentions are good. This is what you have to deal with when you are starting a socially tricky topic. It takes a while for people to understand what you really want to accomplish. People get a little information, not the full picture. At the end of the day I just hope that maybe a couple of years down the road people do know what I was up to and what my intentions were. Until then I knew what I was getting myself into and that not everyone's going to be totally fine with it. I believe over time connecting the dots, what we are doing will make sense. I'd like to be a role model for people to go and dare something, and as a woman that you know anything's possible.

Note: This text is an abridged version of the interview conducted with Pia Poppenreiter for the Massive Open Online Course 'Managing Responsibly' [70].

QUESTIONS

1. What (un)ethical practices and practicing can you identify in this case? What types of ethical issues are they related to (compliance, no problem, moral laxity, genuine dilemma)?

2. What ethical decision-making rules or principles can you spot in Pia's explanation?

3. What are the connections between legal, moral, and ethical considerations in what Pia describes? How do these change with Ohlala's international connections, for instance, in relation to New York?

4. How would you describe the role of ethics in the way Pia manages her start-up? How do you imagine she creates her 'moral structure' that works for all. What might a code of ethics for Ohlala look like?

TRUE STORY
THE PRICE IS RIGHT

EDITED BY ALEXANDRA LEONOR BARRUETA SACKSTEDER

Who I am. My name is Juan Torres and I am the founder and CEO of a small construction company in Latin America. I pride myself on the fact that I am the best at what I do and work with honesty and integrity.

Credit: Atstock Productions/Shutterstock.com

Although we are a small company with only 26 employees we regularly get big contracts. Because we use only the best materials we are also the most expensive firm and this often results in us losing bids. However, a common theme is being called in to redo work, which is done poorly by our competitors and ultimately the clients end up spending more money. Therefore we have a reputation of being the best option and have been getting more and more contracts. I have three children who are extremely successful at what they do and my friends often ask me why I don't train them to take over my company, particularly my eldest who specializes in finance and management. My answer is simple: They aren't engineers and wouldn't be as good as me. I would love to find someone to replace me but unfortunately, it looks like my company will die with me.

Way back when... In 2006 a highly placed government official approached me about a potential project. After several meetings, site visits and proposals I concluded that the entire project would cost $600,000 to complete. I sent in my proposal and the following week was called up by the official and asked to meet for coffee.

(Continued)

When I arrived at the coffee house I thought it was a bit strange, it was a very out of the way place, almost an hour out of the city and there was security making sure no one sat on the side the official was. When I sat down he began immediately by telling me that my company was the most expensive one. I explained why our costs were higher and he agreed that it was better to pay more for quality work. He also mentioned he knew several people who had worked with me and were very satisfied with the results.

Then came the proposal. I would do the job for $700,000, making $100,000 more than I had budgeted but would provide receipts for $1,450,000. He laid it out as a win–win situation, we'd both make money. I thanked him, got up, and left. The following day I sent him an email politely declining his offer explaining that I didn't have the time or resources to take it on at the moment.

Audit attack. Soon after I rejected the project, I was informed my organization would be audited, which was nothing new as it's normal for this to happen every few years. But then came the second and third audits. We had been audited three times in one year and it felt like they were trying to find something. They didn't but that didn't stop the inconvenience and disruption it caused our business. This has continued pretty consistently. Every couple of months my company is audited. I felt persecuted and attacked and it didn't take long for me to figure out that it was probably coming from the same official I had said no to.

An offer you can't refuse? Soon after the whole auditing ordeal began, the same official came to my office. He explained that they still had the project and didn't want to work with anyone else. He told me the offer was still on the table and once again, I refused. The next day we were informed of another audit. The day before yesterday, he came back and once again proposed the same offer making it clear that 'all my troubles' would go away if I agreed to help the government. I was given until the end of the week to respond and at this point I didn't know what to do. On the one hand I don't want to sacrifice my principles; on the other the audits are costing me money and slowing down my business as well as making my employees uncomfortable. Should I take the contract? Or should I keep suffering for doing the right thing? I don't know how long I can keep fighting.

QUESTIONS

1. How would you describe the situation Juan currently finds himself in using the terminology learned in this chapter?

2. What would you do? Would you take the contract or continue to decline the offer? Why? Is there a third alternative?

3. Look at one of the following documentaries or one with a similar theme: *War on Whistleblowers* by Robert Greenwald, *Citizenfour* by Laura Poitras, or *Risk* by Laura Poitras. Discuss similarities between this True Story and the documentaries. Put yourself in the shoes of the people in the documentary you watch – how would you have reacted in the same situation?

DIGGING DEEPER: THE ROLE OF INDIVIDUAL AND SITUATIONAL FACTORS

Demographic factors	Age	Age influences ethical decision-making, but in a highly situation-dependent way. In some situations, older employees were found to adhere to higher ethical standards; the same is true for older students. On the other hand, studies in different environments showed that younger managers had more ethical viewpoints than their older counterparts.
	Gender	Women seem to be more critical about ethical issues, behave with higher ethical standards, and be less likely to conceal their unethical behaviour. Interestingly, women tend to display stronger unethical behaviour patterns in unethical environments.
	National and cultural characteristics	The studies conducted in this factor often have a USA-centric approach, which needs to be questioned in a global context. Non-US citizens were found to behave more unethically from a US point of view. Other surveys – for instance, comparing Australia and South Africa – found that managers behaved equally ethically.
	Religion	Strong religiousness matters in the perception of the importance of ethical misconduct. There is no relationship in the strength of ethical behaviour between different denominations.
	Education	The general education level has been found to have only little influence on ethical decision-making and action. Nevertheless, the type of education has been found to play a role. Business majors have repeatedly been found to display weaker ethics than other majors. Specific ethics education, both in business schools and on the job showed an increase in the ethical reasoning of attendees.
	Employment	It has been found that on the one hand, the greater the work experience, the more ethically people respond. On the other hand, unethical behaviour has been found to increase with job ascension. For instance, CEO seniority was found to increase unethical behaviour. In most studies, however, executives are found to display higher ethics than students.
Psychological factors	Moral philosophy and ethical judgement	Individuals with more highly developed ethical judgement skills have been found to display higher ethical intentions and actions. Deontologically oriented individuals are ranked with higher ethical scores than consequentialists. Individuals display differing levels of moral development in private and professional life and use different reasoning mechanisms in different situations.
	Intelligence and need for cognition	Individuals of high intelligence have been found to be less ethically oriented than individuals of low intelligence. High need for cognition (the inclination to enjoy effortful cognitive activities) showed stronger contextual biases, but also inquired more into ethical issues.
	Locus of control	Individuals with an internal locus of control (who believe they can influence their environment) were more likely to act ethically than individuals with an external locus of control (who believe they cannot influence their environment).
	Values and attitudes	Idealistic individuals (who pursue strong values) act more ethically than relativistic individuals (who change values depending on situations). Individuals with Machiavellian attitudes (characterized by manipulative cunningness and deceit, often found among managers) and individuals with a high personal gain and money orientation are more likely to apply ethically questionable practices.
	Awareness and moral imagination	Individuals with a higher sensitivity for ethical issues (awareness) and who are able to creatively perceive many facets of issues and potential consequences (moral imagination) are more likely to make highly ethical decisions and act upon them.

SOURCE: Based on [11, 42, 46, 70]

Issue-related factors	Moral intensity	The relative importance of an ethical issue (moral intensity) strongly influences individuals' ethical decision-making process, especially, how much the potential harm (magnitude of consequences) will be, and how likely others will consider it to be acting unethically (moral social consensus). The greater the moral intensity, the more sophisticated the ethical judgement becomes, and this increases individuals' intentions to act in an ethically correct way.
	Moral framing	In different contexts, individuals might perceive the same issue as having different levels of importance. The moral intensity mentioned above differs from one situation to another. 'Depending on their environment (e.g. private or professional), ethical decisions and actions have been found to differ for individuals.' Certain personal situations, such as those involving peer pressure, might move individuals to treat the same moral issue with a different degree of moral intensity.
	Moral complexity	Issues and the capacity to correctly interpret and act upon them vary in complexity – e.g. because of their interrelatedness with other issues, the complexity of assessing the possible consequences, a lack of quality information, and conflicting moral principles applying to the same issue.
Context-related factors	Significant others	Individuals and groups with the potential to influence a person's ethics have been called 'significant others'. Both peer groups and top management have been found to be especially influential in individuals' ethical decisions and actions. Especially powerful are peers' reporting behaviour in terms of ethical misconduct, direct superiors' influence, and the tone provided by high-level executives.
	Rewards and sanctions	The higher the potential gain and the lower the potential sanction for an unethical behaviour, the more likely individuals are to engage in such behaviour. Incentive schemes to discourage unethical behaviour and encourage ethical behaviour have an important role to play.
	Organization size, structure and bureaucracy	Increasing the size of an organization has been found to favour ethical misconduct. Bureaucratic structures are assumed to have a negative effect on the ethics of individuals working within those structures.
	Ethics management tools	Ethics management tools have been found to potentially increase ethical behaviour when applied diligently. The best-researched tool is a code of ethics. Codes of ethics and subsequent actions for enforcement were found to further ethical awareness and behaviour and reduce employees' perceived pressure to behave unethically.
	Culture and climate	Ethical cultures in organizations have consistently been found to further ethical behaviour. Counter-intuitively, some studies have found that an ethical culture might also have negative influences on the effectiveness of whistleblowing mechanisms.
	National and cultural context	While there is little empirical research on how much ethical behaviour is embedded in a national culture, it is likely that the norms, customs, and regulations associated with a national culture will have an impact on an individual's ethical decisions and actions.
	Industry type	The supposition that ethical behaviour varies from industry to industry is supported by strong research evidence. Although research has been unable to rank industries' ethical performance, significant differences in ethical reasoning have been seen based in comparisons of two or a few industries.
	Competitiveness	Practices that increase competitive behaviour have been found to increase the perception of moral issues, and are likely to create ethical misconduct through higher pressure to perform.

SOURCE: Adapted from [13]

POINTERS

The table above show how individual and situational factors play into ethical decision-making and influence behaviour in many different ways. In this light, you could look at an ethical decision you have had to make yourself and reflect on which factors would best explain the decision you have taken.

360 DEGREE ETHICS ASSESSMENT

Overall Assessment Grade

[ ]

A: Consequentialism
'Do you create the best possible outcome?'

[ ]

A1: Act:
Does your **single action** maximize the happiness of all involved?

A2: Rule:
Does the **type of action** you assume generally maximize the happiness of all involved?

A3: Distribution:
Are the **outcomes** of your action **fairly distributed**?

B: Deontology
'Do you follow higher principles and duties?'

[ ]

B1: Golden Rule:
Would you want your behaviour to become a **universal and natural law?**

B2: Non-instrumentalization:
Do you treat all involved as **ends in themselves** and not as mere means?

B3: Kingdom of ends:
Do you behave as if your behaviour would **automatically** become a natural law?

C: Consequentialism
'Do you create the best-possible outcome?'

[ ]

C1: To the inside:
Do you think and act with **courage and self-control?**

C2: To the outside:
Do you think and act with **generosity, magnificence, magnanimity, and sociability?**

C3: Towards fairness:
Do you think and act with **justice?**

POINTERS

This worksheet is called a 360-degree ethics assessment because it views ethical dilemmas from different angles. Imagine you are the person facing the dilemma and thinking through alternative decisions and actions. Conduct a 360-degree ethics assessment for each course of action by following the following three steps:

Step 1. *Evaluate* the degree of fulfilment of each of the nine questions from A1 to C3 on a continuum from –5 = completely amoral to +5 = morally excellent and write your evaluation grades in the boxes to the left of the respective questions. Use the background information in the preceding chapters to assure the quality and depth of your assessment.

Step 2. *Calculate* the average evaluation grade per ethical theory (A, B, and C) by adding up the grades of all three questions and dividing them by three. Write the result down in the grey field under each respective theory. Also calculate the average grade for all three theories by summing the three theory grades and dividing them by three. Note down your result in the dark grey field under the text 'overall assessment grade'.

Step 3. *Compare* the assessment for your different alternatives of decision and action. In the comparison process you can and should also decide upon how to weight the different moral theories and questions. For instance, the utilitarian focus of the greatest happiness might be almost neglected in situations where the outcomes are not significant, while in the same situation the virtue-implications are drastic.

REFERENCES

1. LRN. *Benchmark of ethical culture.* https://lrn.com/en-gb/benchmark-ethical-culture-report-uk 2021. Accessed July 19 2023.
2. Fairphone. Our mission. www.fairphone.com/en/story Published 2020. Accessed February 4 2020.
3. Martin A. Fairphone 3 review: The only way is ethics? www.expertreviews.co.uk/mobile-phones/1411365/fairphone-3-review Published 2020. Accessed February 4 2020.
4. Glomb N. Fairphone 3 – faires, modulares Mittelklasse-Smartphone. https://blog.deinhandy.de/fairphone-3-faires-modulares-mittelklasse-smartphone Published 2019. Accessed February 4 2020.
5. Heathman A. Is the Fairphone 3 the most sustainable smartphone on the market? www.standard.co.uk/tech/fairphone-3-phone-specs-features-uk-price-and-release-date-a4221756.html Published 2019. Accessed February 4 2020.
6. Waag. Highest repairability score ever for Fairphone 2. https://waag.org/en/article/highest-repairability-score-ever-fairphone-2 Published 2015. Accessed February 2 2020.
7. Degeler A. Ethical smartphone company Fairphone raises €20 million in debt, crowdfunding, and VC financing. https://tech.eu/brief/ethical-smartphone-company-fairphone-raises-e20-million-in-debt-crowdfunding-and-vc-financing Published 2018. Accessed February 4 2020.
8. Best J. The gadget with a conscience: How Fairphone crowdfunded its way to an industry-changing smartphone. www.techrepublic.com/article/the-gadget-with-a-conscience-how-

fairphone-crowdfunded-its-way-to-an-industry-changing-smartphone Published 2014. Accessed February 4, 2020.

9. Fairphone. The phone that cares for people and planet. www.fairphone.com/en Published 2020. Accessed February 4 2020.

10. Treviño LK. Ethical decision making in organizations: A person-situation interactionist model. *The Academy of Management Review*. 1986, 11(3): 601–617.

11. Crane A, Matten D. *Business ethics*. New York: Oxford University Press, 2004.

12. Geva A. A typology of moral problems in business: A framework for ethical management. *Journal of Business Ethics*. 2006, 69(2): 133–147.

13. Hursthouse R. Virtue Ethics. *The Stanford Encyclopedia of Philosophy*. 2012. http://plato. stanford.edu/entries/ethics-virtue Accessed September 5 2012.

14. Bleisch B, Huppenbauer M. *Ethische Entscheidungsfindung* [Ethical decision making]. Zurich: Versus, 2011.

15. Whetstone JT. How virtue fits within business ethics. *Journal of Business Ethics*. 2001, 33(2): 101.

16. Kimbrough L. Bubbles, lasers and robo-bees: The blossoming industry of artificial pollination. https://news.mongabay.com/2020/07/bubbles-lasers-and-robo-bees-is-artificial-pollination-here-to-stay Published 2020. Accessed July 28 2020.

17. Alexander L, Moore M. Deontological ethics. In: *The Stanford Encyclopedia of Philosophy* (Fall 2008 Edition). 2008.

18. Mill JS. *Utilitarianism*. Forgotten Books, 1863/2008.

19. Freeman RE. *Strategic management: A stakeholder approach*. Boston: Pitman/Ballinger, 1983.

20. Scheffler S. *The rejection of consequentialism: A philosophical investigation of the considerations underlying rival moral conceptions*. New York: Oxford University Press, 1994.

21. Smith J, Dubbink W. Understanding the role of moral principles in business ethics: A Kantian perspective. *Business Ethics Quarterly*. 2011, 21(2): 205–231.

22. Micewski ER, Troy C. Business Ethics – deontologically revisited. *Journal of Business Ethics*. 2007, 72(1): 17–25.

23. Bowie NE. A Kantian theory of capitalism. *Business Ethics Quarterly*. 1998, 1: 37–60.

24. Kant I, Patton HJ. *Moral law: Groundwork of the metaphysic of morals*. New York: Routledge, 1785/2005.

25. Treviño LK, Nelson KA. *Managing business ethics* (5th edn). Hoboken, NJ: John Wiley & Sons, 2011.

26. Chappel V. *The Cambridge companion to Locke*. Cambridge: Cambridge University Press, 1994.

27. Sheridan P. Locke's moral philosophy. In: *The Stanford encyclopedia of philosophy* (Winter 2011 edition). Retrieved from https://plato.stanford.edu/entries/locke-moral Published 2011. Accessed July 2 2012.

28. Rawls J. *A theory of justice*. Revised edition. Cambridge: Harvard University Press, 1999.

29. Roemer JE. Kantian equilibrium. *The Scandinavian Journal of Economics*. 2010, 112(1): 1–24.

30. Bragues G. Seek the good life, not money: The Aristotelian approach to business ethics. *Journal of Business Ethics*. 2006, 67(4): 341–357.

31. Weston A. *A 21st century ethical toolbox*. New York: Oxford University Press, 2008.

32. McInerny R, O'Callaghan J. Saint Thomas Aquinas. *The Stanford Encyclopedia of Philosophy*. 2010. https://plato.stanford.edu/entries/aquinas

33. Koehn D. A role for virtue ethics in the analysis of business practice. *Business Ethics Quarterly*. 1995, 5(3): 533–539.

34. Audi R. Virtue ethics as a resource in business. *Business Ethics Quarterly*. 2012, 22(2): 273–291.

35. Moore G. Re-imagining the morality of management: A modern virtue ethics approach. *Business Ethics Quarterly*. 2008, 18(4): 483–511.

36. Moore G. Corporate character: Modern virtue ethics and the virtuous corporation. *Business Ethics Quarterly*. 2005, 15(4): 659–685.

37. Robbin Derry RMG. Ethical theory in business ethics: A critical assessment. *Journal of Business Ethics*. 1989, 8(7): 521.

38. Bazerman MH, Messick DM. On the power of a clear definition of rationality. *Business Ethics Quarterly*. 1998, 8(3): 477–480.

39. Curlo E, Strudler A. Cognitive pathology and moral judgment in managers. *Business Ethics Quarterly*. 1997, 7(4): 27–30.

40. Gentile MC, ed. *Educating for values-driven leadership: Giving voice to values across the curriculum.* New York: Business Expert Press, 2013.

41. Greene J. From neural 'is' to moral 'ought': What are the moral implications of neuroscientific moral psychology? *Nature Reviews Neuroscience.* 2003, 4(10): 846–850.

42. Treviño LK, Weaver GR, Reynolds SJ. Behavioral ethics in organizations: A review. *Journal of Management.* 2006, 32(6): 951–990.

43. Haidt J. The new synthesis in moral psychology. *Science.* 2007, 316(5827): 998–1002.

44. Jones TM. Ethical decision making by individuals in organizations: An issue-contingent model. *The Academy Management Review.* 1991, 16(2): 366–395.

45. Rest JR. *Moral development: Advances in research and theory.* New York: Praeger, 1986.

46. Ford RC, Richardson WD. Ethical decision making: A review of the empirical literature. *Journal of Business Ethics.* 1994, 13(3): 206.

47. Carr AZ. Is bluffing ethical? *Harvard Business Review.* 1968: 143–153.

48. Ralson DA, Egri CP, Reynaud E, et al. A twenty-first century assessment of values across the global workforce. *Journal of Business Ethics.* 2011, 104(1): 1–31.

49. Moran G. Is it unethical to not tell my employer I've automated my job? www.fastcompany.com/90357964/is-it-unethical-to-not-tell-my-employer-ive-automated-my-job?partner=rss&utm_source=rss&utm_medium=feed&utm_campaign=rss+fastcompany&utm_content=rss?cid=search Published 2019. Accessed July 28 2020.

50. Swamy KM. Focus on moral bankruptcy through money laundering case studies of Nigeria and Russia – proposal for a new approach to financial statements analysis. *Journal of Financial Management & Analysis.* 2000, 13(1): 59–68.

51. Swamy KMR. Financial management call for a new approach to ethical-based financial statements analysis. *Journal of Financial Management & Analysis.* 2009, 22(2): 70.

52. Kohlberg L. Stages of moral development. *Moral Education.* 1971, 1: 23–92.

53. Gibbs JC, Basinger KS, Fuller D. *Moral maturity: Measuring the development of sociomoral reflection.* Hillsdale, NJ: Lawrence Erlbaum Associates Inc., 1992.

54. Rest J, Turiel E, Kohlberg L. Level of moral development as a determinant of preference and comprehension of moral judgments made by others. *Journal of Personality.* 1969, 37(2): 225–252.

55. Empresa Socialmente Responsable. In Centro Mexicano para la Filantropia [Mexican Center for Philanthropy], 2012.

56. Ethisphere Institute. In Centro Mexicano para la Filantropia [Mexican Center for Philanthropy], 2012.

57. Gatewood RD, Carroll AB. Assessment of ethical performance of organization members: A conceptual framework. *The Academy of Management Review.* 1991, 16(4): 667–690.

58. *Ethics and compliance leadership survey report.* New York, 2012.

59. Gentile MC. *Giving voice to values: How to speak your mind when you know what's right.* Yale: Yale University Press, 2010.

60. McCrary-Ruiz-Esparza E. This is what happened when I stood up for ethics at work. www.fastcompany.com/90462318/this-is-what-happened-when-i-stood-up-for-ethics-at-work Published 2020. Accessed July 28 2020.

61. Erwin PM. Corporate codes of conduct: The effects of code content and quality on ethical performance. *Journal of Business Ethics.* 2011, 99(4): 535–548.

62. Adobor H. Exploring the role performance of corporate ethics officers. *Journal of Business Ethics.* 2006, 69(1): 57–75.

63. Hoffmann WM. Repositioning the corporate ethics officer. *Business Ethics Quarterly.* 2010, 20(4): 744–745.

64. Balmer JMT, Fukukawa K, Gray ER. The nature and management of ethical corporate identity: A commentary on corporate identity, corporate social responsibility and ethics. *Journal of Business Ethics.* 2007, 76(1): 7–15.

65. Duh M, Belak J, Milfelner B. Core values, culture and ethical climate as constitutional elements of ethical behaviour: Exploring differences between family and non-family enterprises. *Journal of Business Ethics.* 2010, 97(3): 473–489.

66. Glassdoor. Glassdoor. www.glassdoor.co.uk/index.htm Published 2020. Accessed July 28 2020.

67. Laasch, O., Moosmayer, D., & Antonacopoulou, E. P. (2022). The interdisciplinary responsible management competence framework: An integrative review of ethics, responsibility, and sustainability competences. *Journal of Business Ethics*, 187, 733–757.

68. Liedekerke Lv, Dubbink W. Twenty years of European business ethics – past developments and future concerns. *Journal of Business Ethics*. 2008, 82(2): 273–280.

69. Laasch O, Boons F, Randles S. Managing responsibly: Practicing sustainability, responsibility and ethics. www.coursera.org/learn/responsible-management Published 2016. Accessed January 28 2020.

70. O'Fallon MJ, Butterfield KD. A review of the empirical ethical decision-making literature: 1996–2003. *Journal of Business Ethics*. 2005, 59(4): 375–413.

CHAPTER 4

RESPONSIBLE MANAGEMENT

OLIVER LAASCH

LEARNING GOALS

1. Be able to use core responsible management tools
2. Understand how to manage the creation and balancing of stakeholder value
3. Conduct stakeholder assessment and excel in stakeholder management

INTRIGUING FACT

Among CEOs 53% say consumers are among the stakeholders that influence their strategies most. Also influential are employees (44%), governments (41%), regulators (30%), communities (27%), suppliers (25%), boards (23%), the investment community (20%), non-government organizations (NGOs) and media (12% each) [1].

SPOTLIGHT

STAKEHOLDERS, LET'S PLAY!

LewisTsePuiLung

The Danish LEGO company, best known for its colourful interlocking plastic bricks, calls itself a 'stakeholder-driven brand' that manages 'the responsible way'. The LEGO company's 'zero impact director' Andrew McMullen stresses the importance of the 'ability to rethink the way you fundamentally create value for your customers and shareholders ... the purpose of LEGO is ... not to sell bricks [but] ... to get kids to play and be creative' [2].

LEGO has four value propositions. The 'play promise' for customers is directly related to the company's product. The 'planet promise' commits to creating a positive social and environmental impact. The 'partner promise' involves teaming up with suppliers in order to mutually create value, and the 'people promise' specifically refers to the purpose of being jointly successful with employees. Each promise fulfils a distinct value proposition LEGO has created, an explicit strategy to create stakeholder value [3].

How does LEGO work with those stakeholders? Management at LEGO conducted a 'materiality assessment' through which they identified important issues to be addressed. Out of 58 potential issues, LEGO identified 36 relevant (material topics), 15 top topics, and eight topics categorized as most important. LEGO assesses the needs of stakeholders through 'respectful stakeholder dialogue' as the basis for collaborative stakeholder engagement [3].

(Continued)

Courtesy of Andy Priestner

Customers: LEGO aims to satisfy and educate their customers at the same time. LEGO engages with kids (the 'LEGO builders') and parents mainly through the issues of product safety, education ('learning manifesto'), and an extensive collaboration with parents. **Employees**: LEGO engages with employees about the main issues of gender diversity, motivation and satisfaction, work–life balance, and health and safety. **Partners and suppliers:** Topics addressed with partners are the sustainability of materials (polymers), anti-corruption policies, auditing, supplier responsibilities towards their own stakeholders. **Environment:** Issues related to the environment at LEGO are energy efficiency, waste reduction, recycling, and the end-of-life of the product [3]. They have made a commitment to have their bricks made from 100 per cent non-fossil-fuel plastic by 2032, involving a financial commitment of several billions of US dollars. 'We are testing lots of different materials right now, and we have to test many that do not work before we find something that works', says the LEGO company's chief executive Niels B. Christiansen [2, 4]. In late 2023 Lego announced they had to abandon three years worth of work to produce PET bricks from recycled plastic bottles as it would actually have increased their carbon footprint. However, they remain committed to the 2032 goal [112].

Apart from interaction with its four primary stakeholders, the company also interacts with secondary stakeholders, such as broader society through the LEGO foundation, with the government through lobbying, and with local communities through community development programmes. In its annual 'progress report', LEGO provides performance data for all stakeholders. Joining in 2003, LEGO has been one of the early companies participating in the world's biggest responsible business and management initiative, the United Nations Global Compact.

RESPONSIBLE MANAGEMENT

What does it mean to say that 'business' has responsibilities? Only people can have responsibilities.

Milton Friedman [5]

The words of Milton Friedman, Nobel Prize in Economics laureate, embody the essence of this chapter. We are presenting responsibility in the management context as a personal responsibility: Responsible *management*. Stressing management and the manager as responsible is a deliberate move away from the abstract organizational responsibility we evoke if we call it *corporate* social responsibility or responsible *business*. People learn to be responsible, not organizations, businesses, and corporations.

Friedman, however, was arguably the most prominent opponent of management's responsibility. The quote is followed by a critical litany of what it would lead to if managers assumed professional responsibility:

> He is to refrain from increasing the price of the product in order to contribute to the social objective of preventing inflation, even though a price increase would be in the best interests of the corporation. Or that he is to make expenditures on reducing pollution beyond the amount that is in the best interests of the corporation or that is required by law in order to contribute to the social objective of improving the environment. Or that, at the expense of corporate profits, he is to hire 'hardcore' unemployed instead of better qualified available workmen to contribute to the social objective of reducing poverty [5].

Originally, these examples by Friedman were meant to be outrageous, to cause reactions along the lines of 'obviously, a manager should never do this!' However, if we engage in professional management, these are exactly the things that we are meant to do. The professional manager's service to society and professional conduct overrides their commitment to the organization, including profit generation.

For a professional manager, professional conduct implies that wherever the organization's benefit is achieved at the cost of the many stakeholders that make up society, professional responsibility supersedes the responsibility to make profit. Professional managers are not just the 'hired hands' of a business who have to blindly follow orders, but rather they seek to achieve 'higher aims' through professional management practice [6]. Professional management is **responsible management** as it assumes responsibility for its impacts on the myriad of groups that affect and are affected by management, so-called stakeholders [7]. The LEGO company's stakeholder promises are an excellent illustrative example.

Responsible management voluntarily assumes professional accountability for harmonizing stakeholder value in response to social, environmental, and economic issues

There are many questions to consider for a thorough understanding of responsible management:

- What are the responsibilities of a manager?

- What is responsible management?

- Who should management create value for?

- Should companies (such as LEGO) care so much about their suppliers and the environment, or should they rather focus on responsibilities to their customers and/or their employees?

In this chapter we will sketch a picture of responsible management that is practiced for the good of a broad set of stakeholders with the higher aim of harmonizing stakeholder value [8]. In the first section we provide an overview of the development of the field of responsible management. We will discuss central concepts, such as Archie B. Carroll's responsibility pyramid. We will explore the current state of understanding and implementation and provide an outlook on the likely future development of the field.

The second section focuses on the in-depth explanation of frameworks, such as social performance, that are at the centre of responsible management practice. We will distinguish between corporate social responsibility, accountability, responsiveness and performance, and provide an initial insight into the field of stakeholder theory. The third section illustrates stakeholder management, which has the assessment and subsequent management of stakeholder relations at its core (see Figure 4.1).

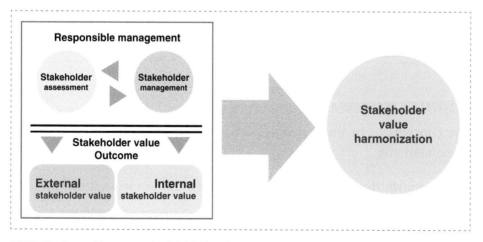

FIGURE 4.1   Responsible management and stakeholder value

Companies that give paid leave for election days (where these fall on weekdays as in the US) have elements of individual and corporate citizenship.

CONCEPTUALIZING RESPONSIBLE MANAGEMENT

Defining responsible management is not an easy task. A study summarizing common definitions of responsibility in a management context found 37 distinct definitions. However, there are five common elements in a majority of those definitions. The percentages in parentheses describe how many of the surveyed definitions the term was contained [44].

- Stakeholder thinking (88%)

- Social dimension (88%)

- Economic dimension (86%)

- Voluntary character of assuming responsibility (80%)

- Environmental dimension (59%)

ASSESSING SOCIAL PERFORMANCE

Management's social performance
an umbrella term for assessment methods for the degree of responsibility assumed through a management practice

A range of different concepts have been used to analyse the degree of responsibility assumed. Those methods have been summarized under the umbrella concept of social performance. More particularly, we focus on **management's social performance** (MSP). The following paragraph summarizes central frameworks for the assessment of MSP. The frameworks can be applied on many levels, from a single responsible management practice, to evaluating a whole business's bundle of management practices. Assessing MSP can be done either qualitatively or quantitatively [52, 53].

QUALITATIVE ASSESSMENT

The concepts to be illustrated as part of a qualitative social performance assessment are:

1. **Responsibility categories**, following Archie B. Carroll's responsibility pyramid

2. **Social responsiveness framework**, which assesses how management reacts to stakeholder claims

3. **Issues maturity**, which explains how advanced management is in the issues it covers

4. **Implementation stages**, which show the degree to which stakeholder responsibilities are embedded into management processes.

As illustrated in Table 4.1, these four categories jointly allow for a multi-faceted appreciation of MSP[1].

TABLE 4.1   Dimensions of social performance

Application level	Responsibility category	Stakeholder responsiveness	Issues maturity	Implementation stages
1	Economic	Reactive	Institutionalized	Isolated
2	Legal	Defensive	Consolidating	Managerial
3	Ethical	Accommodative	Emerging	Strategic
4	Discretionary	Proactive	Latent	Civil

Responsibility category. The first social performance dimension answers the question, 'Which category of responsibilities do you fulfil?' Carroll (see 'Pioneer interview' at the end of this chapter) describes a sequence of four categories of economic, legal, ethical, and discretionary responsibilities (see Figure 4.2) [34, 54, 55].

Responsibility category describes the type of responsibility assumed by management and is based on Carroll's four categories of economic, legal, ethical and discretionary responsibilities

1. The logic of the pyramid is that management first assures survival by fulfilling economic responsibilities, such as making profit and paying employees.

2. What follows are legal responsibilities, by complying with laws, such as labour or environmental regulations.

3. At the next stage, management takes on ethical responsibilities, required by moral standards, but not formalized through laws – for instance a decision to increase workplace safety beyond the legally required level.

4. The final stage comprises discretionary responsibilities, which are not required by any of the preceding levels. Those are 'nice' things to do, but not necessarily morally enforceable. Management is philanthropic or discretionary – for instance, when giving donations for disaster relief.

---

[1]The four qualitative assessment methodologies mentioned here are just some of the many that have been applied to assess MSP.

What would be the responsibility category of a supermarket that sells only products from Black-owned companies?

A great example for assuming a discretionary responsibility is the Soul Food Supermarket project, a Black-owned supermarket that has made its cause to sell only products from other Black-owned companies. Social equality movements like Black Lives Matter have made active racial empowerment a cause that is very visible in society. However, making the economic empowerment and solidarity between Black people something core to management of this retailer goes beyond a responsibility that would be usually required by moral or legal norms. That's what makes it the assumption of a discretionary responsibility. It also serves as an inspiration for potential other 'cause-related retailers'. As an example, imagine there was a supermarket where buying something does not only give you a product, but where every product bought also contributes to another worthy cause. While shopping, you would continuously decide not only what you want, but also what kind of world you want to create with the money you spend [56].

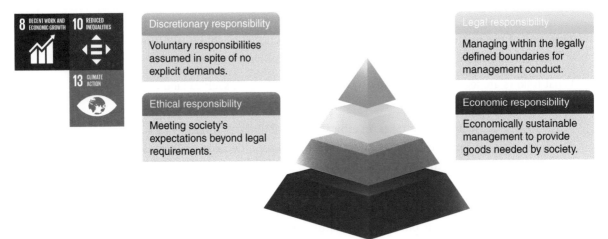

FIGURE 4.2   Carroll's social responsibility pyramid

SOURCE: adapted from [34, 54, 56], Credit: Slidemodel.com

Stakeholder responsiveness describes the manner in which management answers to stakeholder claims and is typically divided into reactive, defensive, accommodative, and proactive

Stakeholder responsiveness. The second dimension of MSP poses the question, 'How do you respond to stakeholder claims?' There are different levels of responsiveness.

1. The lowest level of responsiveness is **reactive** behaviour, where management tries to deny the validity of stakeholders' claims and their resulting responsibility.

2. On the **defensive** level, management accepts its responsibilities, but tries to avoid them.

3. At the **accommodative** stage, management accepts stakeholder claims and acts upon the resulting responsibilities.

4. Management on the final level is **proactive**. It anticipates stakeholder claims and acts upon them even before claims are made explicitly.

These stages of responsiveness are also called the RDAP scale, an abbreviation consisting of the four letters of the stages of responsiveness [57]. Responsiveness changes over time, as certain issues become more or less 'normal' for companies to react to. For instance, when LEGO first committed to stop using petrol-based plastics, this was a proactive move, as society had not demanded such a radical shift. However, in the early 2020s, as net positive, or zero-impact goals for companies became increasingly normal, such a move seemed more like an ethical responsibility that was expected by society.

Issues maturity. This dimension answers the question, 'How well established are the issues I am responding to?' The goal is to find out whether management practice addresses the baseline of issues or rather approaches an innovative frontier [58]. We can break this into three levels.

Issues maturity describes the degree of acceptance of an issue divided into institutionalized, consolidated, emerging, and latent issues

1. The lowest level of issues maturity is **engagement** with issues that are completely institutionalized. An example is management focusing on addressing human rights issues in the workforce (e.g. health, non-discrimination, minimum wage), a topic that is well institutionalized through many international norms.

2. On the next level we find management that tackles **consolidated** issues, which have not yet reached a high level of institutionalization, but which are well accepted as common management practice. For instance, the disclosure and aggressive mitigation of carbon emission is not yet completely institutionalized. Nevertheless, measuring, reporting, and addressing carbon emissions have already become consolidated practices and management has frequently made commitments to zero carbon emissions.

3. Managers might also become pioneers by addressing **emerging** issues, for which there is only a very basic awareness.

4. They might even open up new ground through addressing **latent issues** that are yet to reach public awareness [59].

Implementation stages describe the degree of integration of responsible management into practices, processes, and structures. Levels of implementation are isolated, managerial, strategic, and civic implementation

Implementation stages. The fourth and final dimension of MSP management addresses stakeholder responsibilities. The underlying question is, 'How deeply embedded are management's stakeholder responsibilities in management practices, processes, and structures?'

1. On a **rudimentary** level, management commonly applies isolated policies, which are a weakly integrated ad-on.[2] For instance, manufacturing plants often comply with local legislation and additionally with norms (such as the ISO 14000 for environmental management) required by clients or the mother company.

2. The second stage of **managerial** implementation considers stakeholder responsibilities in core processes and practices.

3. The **strategic** implementation stage additionally considers stakeholder responsibilities an integral element of strategic planning. Management would, for instance, aim at a strategic positioning of its products through the assumption of stakeholder responsibilities. As an example, a soft drink producer might change its products from industrial sugar basis to organically produced fruit juices. Management would at the same time assume its customer responsibility of providing a healthy product and strategically position its product.

4. On the **civic** implementation stage, management has not only succeeded in its stakeholder responsibilities internally, but additionally acts as a change agent for responsible management practices externally, inspiring business partners, suppliers, and even clients to do the same.

It can be argued, for instance, that management of the UK's National Health Service (NHS) and of other major customers of the Malaysian rubber gloves producers Top Glove and WRP has not yet reached a civic stage of responsible management implementation. Strong evidence was found by the *Guardian* newspaper that both companies engaged in forced labour practices, including withholding Nepalese and Bangladeshi workers' passports, lost limbs due to unsafe conditions, wages less than half of the Malaysian minimum wage, workers driven into debt through 'recruitment feeds', and who had illegally been withheld their pay, all of this while wearing Top Glove's branded uniforms with the motto 'Be honest and no cheating'. The companies together supplied 40 per cent of the gloves used by the NHS. If the accusations were true, almost every second NHS patient for whom gloves were used would have been made complicit in supporting forced labour, otherwise known as modern-day slavery [60].

---

[2]In Zadeck's article, this level was originally called 'compliant' and he proposed an additional defensive level as a first stage. In order to integrate his model into the overall CSP framework, these two features have been altered.

STAKEHOLDER MANAGEMENT

At the very core of responsible management is management in a network of stakeholder relationships. Management's social performance depends on how this 'myriad of groups and relationships' [66] is navigated. The ultimate goal of **stakeholder management** is the creation of value for all those different groups that 'affect or are affected' the creation of value for stakeholders [7]. Stakeholder management practice as illustrated earlier in Figure 4.1 consists of practices of stakeholder assessment and stakeholder interaction.

Stakeholder management the process of managing relationships with the various groups, individuals, and entities that affect or are affected by an activity

THE GOAL: STAKEHOLDER VALUE HARMONIZATION

What does **stakeholder value** actually mean? This abstract term can be translated into concrete indicators for each individual stakeholder group, such as satisfaction for customers, employee welfare, or return on investment for shareholders. For other stakeholders, such as NGOs, governments or the media, indicators developed to measure the value created for them might be somewhat more complex. The crucial question to answer is,

Forced labour is a common phenomenon of irresponsible management in otherwise legal businesses, particularly, in manufacturing and agriculture.

'us-embassy-and-usaid-delegations-visit-to-hm-factory_36936071754_o' by USEmbassyPhnomPenh is licensed under CC BY-ND 2.0

'What is their stake in the company?' Once the mutual relationship between a particular stakeholder and the company has been understood, how management could create value for the stakeholder and vice versa becomes easier to define. One thing becomes clear: stakeholder value means something different from one stakeholder to another, which makes stakeholder management a highly complex, multi-dimensional task. The resulting contemporary understanding of stakeholder management is that 'the question of *who* and what really counts should be replaced by the question of *how* value is created in stakeholder relationships' [67].

Stakeholder value the degree of satisfaction of either single stakeholders or of all stakeholders of a specific activity

Is stakeholder value intended to benefit external stakeholders only, and not management and their organizations? There is sound evidence that excellence in stakeholder management also increases financial business performance [68–70]. Good stakeholder management often benefits internal and external stakeholders and creates shared value [71, 72]. The idea of managing in a way that benefits both management and society and internal and external stakeholders sounds nice, but what are the fundamental aspects or guidelines to be followed by such a shared-value-creating management?

- First, the primary goal of any management activity must be the **harmonization of stakeholder value** in the short, medium, and long run [8, 73, 74]. R. Edward Freeman proposes the notion of 'harmonizing the interests of stakeholders … because harmony in music is the idea that even though the notes are different, they sound good together' [8].

- Second, such value harmonization must **consider the entire complex mesh of stakeholder relations** throughout management's sphere of influence [39, 75].

- Third, managers must understand **that connectedness and synergies** among stakeholders require a holistic understanding and management of those relationships: 'No stakeholder stands alone' [69]. For instance, when LEGO's management commits to stop using petrol-based plastics, they do this for the environment as a stakeholder. However, this decision will have a dramatic impact on their supplier stakeholders as well, as they will have to rebuild their processes around different materials. It might also affect the 'play promise' to customers as new materials might result in different ways to play with LEGO.

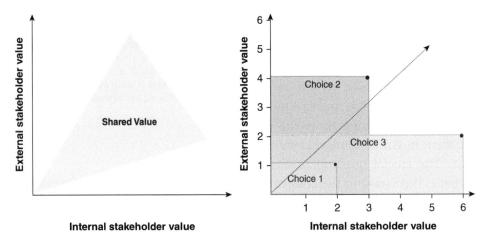

FIGURE 4.3   Shared value and stakeholder value harmonization

SOURCE: Left: adapted from [71]. The version on the right is the author's elaboration.

SHARED VALUE AND STAKEHOLDER VALUE HARMONIZATION

The broader rules for stakeholder value creation mentioned in the preceding section require an additional, more concise decision-making framework for stakeholder value creation. Figure 4.3 provides such a framework. The graphs illustrate the relationships between internal (e.g. owners, employees) and external (e.g. government, community) stakeholder value creation. The image on the left describes a corridor of shared value, where both stakeholder groups have a close-to-equal share of the value creation. The image on the right compares the value created by three alternative management choices with different amounts and distributions of stakeholder value creation on a numeric scale. The numbers represent the cumulative amount of stakeholder value created internally and externally.

Let's imagine the Head of Corporate Responsibility of an information technology company like Google, SAP, or Microsoft has received proposals to spend their department's budget on one of the following:

Choice 1. A philanthropic community volunteering campaign

Choice 2. Developing a mobile app that helps private customers lead a more environmentally friendly life

Choice 3. An energy-efficiency programme for the company's server infrastructure

How should the manager decide which option to choose? We propose two basic criteria for stakeholder value harmonization, a maximization maxim, and a fairness maxim:

1. The **maximization of stakeholder value maxim** suggests that Choice 1 is not attractive as the overall value of 2 (the box area) is topped by Choices 2 and 3, which would both create a value of 12. How should they decide between those two remaining options?

2. The **fairness in distribution** maxim suggests that the manager in the case of two equal options should choose the option that provides a fairer distribution of value created. Proponents of equality as the fairness criterion would opt for Choice 2, which is closer to the 45-degree line of equal distribution between internal and external stakeholders.[3]

Anti-piracy operations, likely to have been made necessary by the shared value created between the Haradheere's community investors and the piracy in stock exchange management.

'091112-N-9500T-170.JPG' by Photograph Curator is marked with CC PDM 1.0

The decision pattern mentioned above is just one of many proposed patterns for the creation of stakeholder value. Other prominent proposals include, for instance, the idea of stakeholder democracy [76, 77], where stakeholders should have a say in

---

[3]The traditional argumentation of neo-classical economics would be that Choice 3 is the right one as the company's internal stakeholders are the creators and subsequently owners of value, which should then also benefit them most.

decisions regarding company value creation. Further, there is stakeholder governance, which focuses corporate governance mechanisms on the creation of stakeholder value (instead of shareholder value) as the main governance criterion [78, 79].

Take the example of the cooperative pirate stock exchange in the Somali city of Haradheere. Mohamed, one of the founders and a former pirate, explains the 'success story', which includes both commercial value for 'the company' and community value: 'Four months ago, during the monsoon rains, we decided to set up this stock exchange. We started with 15 "maritime companies" and now we are hosting 72. Ten of them have so far been successful at hijacking. The shares are open to all and everybody can take part, whether personally at sea or on land by providing cash, weapons or useful materials … we've made piracy a community activity.' In addition, community members turned investors, like Sahra, a young divorcee, seem to receive value: 'I am waiting for my share after I contributed a rocket-propelled grenade [received in alimony from her ex-husband] for the operation … I am really happy and lucky. I have made $75,000 in only 38 days since I joined the "company"' [80]. Clearly, there is shared value between the company and this community member. Does this make it a good company? Creating shared value will only lead to responsible results if the value is created for 'the right' stakeholders, and if all relevant stakeholders have been considered. We will now discuss **stakeholder assessment** as the tool that helps us in this task.

Stakeholder assessment
the process of understanding stakeholders and their relationship to a specific activity. It can be subdivided into the processes of stakeholder identification and prioritization

STAKEHOLDER ASSESSMENT

The main prerequisite for creating stakeholder value is to understand the stakeholders. Easier said than done. Stakeholders may differ considerably in their characteristics and in their relationship to management. One can easily imagine that a loyal customer requires a very different stakeholder management strategy than an aggressive customer group, a governmental representative, or an NGO like Greenpeace. Understanding stakeholders and their relationships with the company can be subdivided into the two steps of stakeholder identification and prioritization.

Stakeholder identification typically involves the mapping of stakeholders and relationships. Figure 4.4 presents an exemplary stakeholder map, the main tool for stakeholder identification. The AA 1,000 stakeholder engagement standard recommends asking the following questions to guide stakeholder identification [50]:

1. **Dependency.** Groups or individuals who are directly or indirectly dependent on management's activities, products or services and associated performance, or on whom management is dependent in order to operate

2. **Responsibility**. Groups or individuals to whom management has, or in the future may have, legal, commercial, operational or ethical/moral responsibilities

3. **Tension**. Groups or individuals who need immediate attention from management regarding financial, wider economic, social or environmental issues

4. **Influence**. Groups and individuals who can have impact on management's or a stakeholder's strategic or operational decision-making

Stakeholder mapping helps to identify main groups of stakeholders. Internal stakeholders form part of the company's internal organizational structure, such as employees and owners. External stakeholders are mainly outside the organizational boundaries [7, 39, 81]. Primary stakeholders have a direct connection with the company. Connections may be of many different natures, such as legal connections (e.g. governments), involvement in exchanges (e.g. direct suppliers), or physical proximity (e.g. local community). Secondary stakeholders do not have such a connection but might be connected indirectly through primary stakeholders. Secondary stakeholders might be of equal or even higher importance than the primary ones. For instance, a third-tier supplier who triggers a scandal due to inhumane working conditions might be more critical than a 'well-controlled' direct supplier [57].

Social stakeholders are individuals or groups of human beings currently alive, as opposed to non-social stakeholders, such as animals, the natural environment, or future generations. Social stakeholders, in contrast to non-social stakeholders, can voice their concerns, which has profound implications for the management of their relationships [81, 82], especially if the stakeholder status of the natural environment has been discussed extensively. The main question is whether nature should be seen as a stakeholder in its own right, and should therefore qualify for protection, or nature is only an instrument for the satisfaction of human needs [82–84]. The last and broadest differentiation exists between stakeholders and non-stakeholders who do not have any relationship with the company [85]. To create a stakeholder map the following three-step approach is recommended:

1. **Identify the focal entity**, which provides the perspective from which the stakeholder analysis is conducted. Such entities can be anything from a single management decision, to a practice, a manager, or even company management as a whole.

2. **List all relevant stakeholders**, for now independently from the type or strength of relationship to the focal entity.

3. **Group** the stakeholders into the categories mentioned before and organize your map based on those categories.

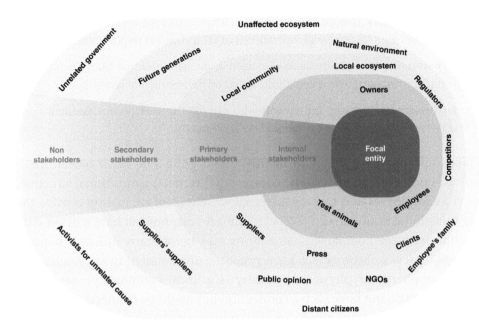

FIGURE 4.4   Categorized stakeholder map

Credit: Slidemodel.com

After stakeholder identification, stakeholders need to be understood and ranked in priority. Many frameworks have been developed to analyse and prioritize stakeholder groups, preparing the decision on whom/what (not all stakeholders are humans – e.g. ecosystems, animals, or plant species) to involve. Surveys as to which stakeholders companies most commonly consider reveal intriguing insights [1, 86–91].

- First are prominent stakeholder groups that are repeatedly ranked as high priority. Customers, employees, investors and governments are such groups.

- Second, the importance of stakeholder groups differs over time and across different situations (e.g. stable versus turbulent economic macro-climate) and who you ask (e.g. middle management or CEO).

- Third, non-social stakeholder groups and aggressive NGOs, which in the past have been shown to exert critical influence on management's success or failure, are not represented among prioritized stakeholders.

These three observations provide important arguments for not going by generalized importance, but rather using stakeholder prioritization tools on a case-by-case basis and frequently updating the results.

Figure 4.5 summarizes three of the most commonly applied approaches for assessing stakeholders.

1. Mitchel, Agle and Wood [85] used a Venn diagram to explain the salience (importance) of a stakeholder in the three dimensions abbreviated as 'PUL': **P**ower (How strong is the stakeholder's potential influence over management?); **U**rgency

(How quickly is a reaction to the claim required?); and **L**egitimacy (How 'rightful' is the stakeholder's claim?). The most important stakeholder is the one that combines all three categories, a so-called definite stakeholder.

2. Savage et al. use a collaboration–harm grid which combines the negative power of the stakeholder to pose a threat to management (yes/no) with the power to cooperate (yes/no). This gives rise to four types of stakeholders: stakeholder type 4, a 'mixed blessing' stakeholder, should be involved in collaboration. This stakeholder on the one hand has a high potential to collaborate, but also has the power to harm. Collaboration in this case will also serve to 'keep an eye' on the stakeholder, and make sure that they do not exert their power to harm management [92].

3. The simplest but very powerful form of stakeholder prioritization is the core-strategic-environmental framework. Core stakeholders are the most important ones, as they are crucial to the existence of the company. The second most important category is strategic stakeholders, which if unattended to do not threaten the survival of the company, but

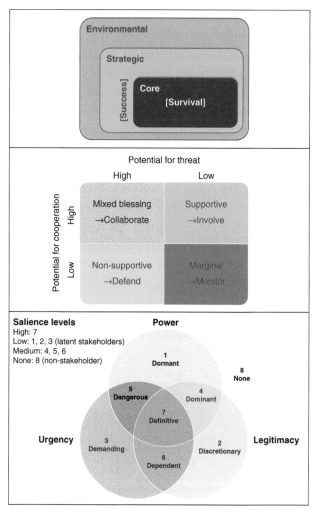

FIGURE 4.5   Stakeholder prioritization approaches

SOURCES: Left [85]; middle [92]; right [81].

its success. The third group – environmental stakeholders – should not be confused with the natural environment as a stakeholder. Environmental stakeholders are all the stakeholders that exist in the company's surroundings, but they are not important for its survival nor for its success.

All these prioritization methods fulfil different functions and provide the best results when applied in combination. It is important to consider that stakeholder prioritization is an ongoing process. The importance of stakeholders changes over time [67]. Once stakeholders have been mapped and prioritized, it is time to start engaging with those that are relevant.

STAKEHOLDER ENGAGEMENT

Stakeholder engagement consists of practices of interaction with stakeholders and can be subdivided into stakeholder communication and the co-creation of joint activities

Stakeholder engagement is subdivided into two phases, which often unfold iteratively and in parallel. Stakeholder communication aims to create a deeper understanding of the prioritized stakeholders and the co-creation of joint activities.

Stakeholder communication should happen in a dialectic pattern. Managers should both talk and listen to the prioritized set of stakeholders [15, 93–95]. A key communication task is to identify the importance of certain issues for stakeholders. This process is called **materiality** assessment and is a central point of understanding how to create value for different stakeholders. The underlying logic is that the more important or material a certain topic or issue is for a stakeholder, the more value will be created if the topic is addressed by the company. A typical analysis tool for materiality assessment is a materiality chart, such as the one in Figure 4.6. Responsible management issues are analysed by deriving an overall priority, from the importance of an issue to both management (horizontal axis) and stakeholders (vertical axis). Such an assessment is the basis for an informed decision about which issues should be given priority by management.

Materiality describes the shared importance of a specific issue to both company and stakeholders

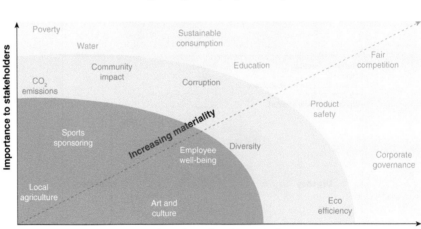

FIGURE 4.6   Exemplary materiality assessment

CREDIT: Slidemodel.com

The ultimate step of stakeholder management is the co-creation of activities to address issues jointly between company and stakeholders. Establishing a portfolio of issues and related stakeholders that helps to keep track of the value created for stakeholders and the mitigation of issues is recommended. As mentioned in the LEGO example, the identification of the company's four main 'promises' to stakeholders resulted from a materiality assessment. Table 4.2 provides practical guidance on how to conduct stakeholder engagement in five main 'modes' [96].

TABLE 4.2 Modes of stakeholder engagement

Level/mode	Information	Consultation	Deciding together	Acting together	Supporting
Typical process	Presentation and promotion	Communication and feedback	Consensus building	Partnership building	Community development
Typical methods	Leaflets, media, video	Surveys, meetings	Workshops Planning for real strategic choice	Partnership bodies	Advice, support, funding
Initiator stance	'Here's what we are going to do.'	'Here are our options – what do you think?'	'We want to develop options and decide actions together.'	'We want to carry out joint decisions together.'	'We can help you achieve what you want within these guidelines.'
Initiator benefits	Apparently least effort	Improves chances of getting it right	New ideas and commitment from others	Brings in additional resources	Develops capacity in the community and may reduce calls for service
Issues for initiator	Will people be willing to consult?	Are the options realistic? Are there others?	Do we have similar ways of deciding? Do we know and trust each other?	Where will the balance of control lie? Can we work together?	Will our aims be met as well as those of other interests?
Needed to start …	Clear vision, identified audience, common language	Realistic options, ability to deal with responses	Readiness to accept new ideas and follow them through	Willingness to learn new ways of working	Commitment to continue support

SOURCE: [96]

PRINCIPLES OF RESPONSIBLE MANAGEMENT

I. **Responsible management** voluntarily assumes accountability for social, economic, and environmental issues related to its stakeholders and aims to harmonize stakeholder value.

II. **Stakeholder management** consists of administration practices centred on stakeholders and aiming at the harmonization of stakeholder value.

III. **Stakeholder value** is created in many different ways and differs from stakeholder to stakeholder. An aspiration of responsible management is to create **shared value** between external and internal stakeholders.

IV. **Management social performance (MSP)** is a framework that aims to define the degree of responsibility achieved by management. It provides an estimate of the amount of stakeholder value created.

V. The process of **stakeholder management** consists of two tasks – stakeholder assessment (understanding stakeholders) and stakeholder engagement (interacting with stakeholders).

VI. **Stakeholder assessment** involves practices of **stakeholder identification**, through which stakeholders are mapped, and **stakeholder prioritization**, through which stakeholders' characteristics are understood and prioritized for engagement.

VII. **Stakeholder engagement** consists of practices of **stakeholder communication**, through which direct contact with stakeholders is established, and the **co-creation** of activities, through which stakeholders and management start to collaborate.

MANAGEMENT GYM: TRAINING YOUR PROFESSIONAL SIX-PACK

Knowing

1. Define the following terms and explain how they are interrelated: (a) responsible management (b) stakeholder, and (c) shared value.

2. List the four levels of stakeholder responsiveness, and give a real responsible management example for each.

3. Look up a CR report of a company of your choice and identify how the company prioritizes stakeholders.

Thinking

4. Pick one specific responsible management practice and analyse its social performance.

5. Imagine you are a logistics company's fleet manager. You have been asked to decide whether or not to adopt alternative fuels for your vehicles. What distinct stakeholder value implications does either option have? Which technology do you think will lead to more responsible fleet management?

6. Which one of the three stakeholder prioritization approaches in this chapter do you think is the most appropriate one for a professional manager and why?

Acting

7. Imagine you are the owner of a small grocery store in the suburb of one of the world's capitals. Conduct a complete stakeholder assessment, including a stakeholder map, a stakeholder prioritization, and a materiality assessment. Based on this analysis, create three concrete lines of action that such a business could implement in order to create more stakeholder value.

8. Exchange one of your personal hygiene products (e.g. shampoo, lotion, deodorant, toothbrush) with a different one that better harmonizes stakeholder value.

9. Expand your sphere of responsibility by doing one thing to which you would usually say, 'That's not my responsibility.'

Interacting

10. Approach a real business's responsibility department (most CSR reports have an email address) and propose a concrete idea for the creation of additional stakeholder value. Be clear and concise, and follow up on the topic until you receive feedback from the business. Document the exchange.

11. Form a small group and conduct a stakeholder role-play centred on the question, 'Should sales restrictions be put on the German arms producer Heckler & Koch's (H&K) grenade launcher XM25 and, if so, what restrictions should be applied?' Have different members of the group assume different roles and develop their respective back stories (e.g. an H&K sales manager; the head of R&D; a war victim who had been injured by a similar launcher; a prospective client who would not disclose his identity; a representative of the German government; a member of the local chamber of commerce; a member of an NGO for peace). Conduct the role-play and draft a sales policy that harmonizes stakeholder value while doing this.

12. Post an article, picture, or video about a stakeholder issue of your choice on social media and briefly comment on what your position on the issue is.

Being

13. Train your empathy by envisioning what the world looks like from a stakeholder's perspective. From the following stakeholders, pick the one that you initially feel least empathy for: a worker in a sweatshop garment factory; a male chick in the chick culling practice; an employee working under abusive supervision.

     Most likely you will have to inform yourself about the chosen stakeholder to develop empathy.

14. Remember an occasion when you felt you acted responsibly. Why do you think you felt the need to do so?

15. Watch a movie that is related to an (ir)responsible practice and think about how it relates to your values and who you are as a person. Examples include *Blood Diamond; Enron: The Smartest Guys in the Room; Horrible Bosses;* and *Don't Look Up.*

Becoming

16. Think about a situation you had to manage (this could be either in a private or a professional role). Do you think others would describe you as a responsible manager and why?

17. Identify someone in your personal sphere of influence (your stakeholder) and do something that is valuable for them. How did it make you feel before, during, and after?

18. What do you think are, or will be, the main obstacles that keep you from harmonizing stakeholder value in your current or future job? Envision personal characteristics or habits that could help you to overcome these obstacles. What could you do right now to start developing or strengthening these characteristics and habits?

SOURCE: Adapted from [97].

PIONEER INTERVIEW
ARCHIE B. CARROLL

INTERVIEWER: OLIVER LAASCH

Archie B. Carroll has been a leading figure in the responsible management and CSR movements for decades, including his signature creation, the CSR pyramid.

From corporate to management responsibility?
It is true that, historically, the sphere or domain of responsible management has concentrated primarily on the organization level rather than the (lower) managerial levels. This may be because the Business and Society and Social Issues in Management academic disciplines have been more closely aligned with the broader field of Strategic Management, for example, in the Academy of Management (AOM), than with the fields of Organizational Behaviour (OB) or Human Resource Management

Courtesy of Archie Carroll

(Continued)

(HRM). In the past couple of decades, however, that has begun to change and we are now observing researchers addressing managerial and behavioural levels, which more closely align with middle management and supervisory management. Academics from OB and HRM are now more frequently addressing RM issues and they naturally pivot towards the management processes.

Responsible management means implementing CSR. One major reason the attention is shifting towards the managerial level of responsibility is because most firms today have pretty much accepted the paradigms of CSR, sustainability and responsible management, and now increasing attention is being given to the implementation stage and that occurs at the managerial level and the employee level. So, it's natural that the entire hierarchy of the organization is now being researched and taught. Coming from a 'management' academic background, I sought to pursue this topic early on with my book of readings titled *Managing Corporate Social Responsibility* [98] and I guess that has influenced my attention on the managerial levels in my own work. Related to this, much of my writing and teaching has focused on the managerial level in the topic of business ethics where it has a natural fit. In fact, I think the topic of business ethics is more a managerial one than a philosophical one. In other words, I think it is easier to know what the right thing to do (philosophy) is than to actually do it (management). Of course, some of my philosophy colleagues may not agree with this. In any event, both are important.

The business case for responsibility. If you talk to most folks today, especially business people who are our primary target audience along with those training to be business people, the 'business case for CSR or RM' is pretty much accepted and appears to be the primary driver in business decision-making. There are a few 'true believers' who still argue via ethical reasoning, but in business schools, at least, the business case seems to dominate. Having said that, we cannot abandon the business case thinking as a done deal. We need to provide a business rationale for what organizations are doing. Businesses began as the primary economic institutions in society though they are now multipurpose, social institutions. This is one reason I have placed the economic responsibility at the base of my Pyramid of CSR [99]. Research has demonstrated that business people agree with this and most see this as the starting point in discussing responsible management or corporate responsibility. In capitalist societies, the shareholders or owners are still a primary stakeholder who must be considered. In addition, the focus on tensions and paradoxes is inevitable and also vitally important.

Core concepts of responsibility. We extrapolated three core concepts that we thought were present in each. We concluded that each included these core concepts: *value*, *balance*, and *accountability*. We then named this a VBA model or framework.

(Continued)

We thought of the fundamental element underlying the entire business-and-society field, and the first of these concepts, appears to be the generation of value. *Value* is created when business meets society's needs by producing goods and services in an efficient manner while avoiding unnecessary negative externalities. Each of the constructs is concerned about business generating value or benefit to society.

We also thought each concept rested on the notion of *balance*. A degree of balance is necessary in addressing and responding appropriately to potentially conflicting stakeholder interests and/or ethical standards. The concept of *balance* is not new. Drucker argued that the notion of balancing stakeholder interests dates back to the 1920s and Berle & Means [100] indicated that while serving the interests of society as a whole, corporations must balance a variety of claims by various groups in the community. We argued that balance was a process component of the VBA framework whereby businesses would be required to take active steps to achieve appropriate balance among competing stakeholders' interests and claims. We think the concept of balance is present in all these competing and complementary frameworks. Acting in an accountable manner is the third notion common to all the frameworks.

Accountability implies that business and its agents, while attempting to fulfil their economic, legal, ethical, and philanthropic responsibilities [101] must acknowledge and take responsibility for their actions and decisions and take steps to rectify failures and ensure that they don't happen again. Accountability also implies the importance of trustworthiness and transparency.

Note: This text is an abridged version of the interview conducted with Archie B. Carroll by Oliver Laasch, published in full as part of the Research handbook of responsible management [102].

QUESTIONS

1. How does Archie Carroll connect the topics of managerial responsibility and ethics?

2. Do you agree with his view that responsible management equals 'just' implementing CSR? Is there more to it that is not covered by CSR? Should CSR actually *be* a part of responsible management?

3. What other drivers of responsible management activity can you imagine that are *not* related to the business case for responsibility?

4. How do you think a professional manager could use the VBA framework? Give an example.

PROFESSIONAL PROFILE
SUDHIR KUMAR SINHA

My name is Sudhir Kumar Sinha and I am Head of Corporate Social Responsibility (CSR) for Cipla Ltd, which is one of the world's largest generic pharmaceutical companies with a presence in over 170 countries. It was established in 1935 and is headquartered in Mumbai.

Responsible management tasks. Main tasks are managing and heading the corporate responsibility (CR) respectively CSR operations; devising CR policies and procedures; advising the management on issues associated with CR/sustainability standards; streamlining the CR/CSR process and ensuring adherence to the CR/ CSR standards. I also conceptualize and implement community development initiatives. Managing the entire gamut of operations

Courtesy of Sudhir Kumar Sinha

including financial, statutory compliances, and administrative functions. Building and managing positive perception; maintaining close coordination with the top management and employees. Finally, I am carrying out assessment studies and am responsible for disclosure and CR as well as sustainability reporting.

My daily practice. I evaluate and assess the company's business decisions and activities according to sustainability parameters, and accordingly communicate with the top management and board. I intensely engage with the team, management and employees and identify the sustainability strengths and gaps. Often I plan and evolve policies, strategies, action plan and measurement processes in consultation. I also engage with external stakeholders on material issues and plan strategies to address them. I monitor and manage the management information system (MIS) routinely and draw inferences from the analyses, and send in recommendations to the management. Also, I am responsible for all communications and accountable to all stakeholders in addressing their expectations and concerns. I design and implement financial systems, policies and procedures in line with Cipla's objectives to facilitate internal financial control. Some days I also screen new projects and evaluate project reports to assess viability of projects, predictable cash flow and growth opportunities. I constantly engage in relationship building with external stakeholders. I am pushing to integrate employee volunteering into the Cipla's culture. I frequently interface with the CR teams horizontally, for instance, with the teams working in plants of the company in order to supplement and reinforce Cipla's overall

(Continued)

CR and social commitments. Finally, I frequently represent Cipla as well as the sector at various international and national CR forums, academic discussions and through ensuring space in various national and international committees.

Recommendations to other responsibility practitioners. I have the following seven recommendations:

1. *Positioning of CSR.* Work hard for CR/CSR function to be strategically positioned in the organization under the board or CEO.

2. *CSR v/s CR.* Don't endorse a charity-led-philanthropy model of CSR. Even philanthropy has to be replaced with strategic philanthropy. Broaden the horizon of CSR; go for strategizing a multi-stakeholders model of corporate responsibility.

3. *Raising the bar.* Keep updating the knowledge on evolving universal consensus on understanding and great practices of corporate responsibility, and accordingly set new targets by raising the bar of CR standards each time for your company.

4. *Stand up firm.* Rather function as 'whistleblowers' than merely as CSR managers, and stand firm and show perseverance until issues and concerns are understood in the organization.

5. *Join networking.* Join local as well as international professional networks and actively participate in discussion. Contribute and simultaneously learn from the network.

6. *Involve the C-suite.* Encourage your CEO and senior management to attend and join CR and sustainability forums as well as public discourse. Facilitate their understanding of corporate responsibility from the viewpoint of overarching responsibilities of the business.

QUESTIONS

1. How do you think Sudhir's responsible management practice is different from a 'mainstream' manager's responsible management practice?

2. Which one of Sudhir's recommendations do you think will be most applicable to your present or future job? How does it apply?

3. What do you think are the likely top-ten stakeholders of managers in a pharmaceutical company like Cipla?

4. Which do you imagine to be the most 'material' issues in a company like Cipla?

TRUE STORY

LICENCE TO ... LICENSE?

EDITED BY ALEXANDRA LEONOR BARRUETA SACKSTEDER AND DANIELE ECKERT

Who we are. What happens when your values as a company change? When do we change how we do business as well? Hello! My name is Josh and I've been working as a member of the board, general director, and sometimes consultant to my firm for a while now. The organization I work for is very large and relatively well known in Latin America. For the last few years I've been taking it through a total transformative process. My organization operates in the sectors of Education and Health. It is committed to building relationships that value life and wellness. Some of our products include crutches, sporting goods, thermal bags, and school supplies.

Licensing drama. One of the biggest advantages our organization possesses is our licensing agreements for popular characters for some of our products, particularly in the school supply division. Targeted mainly at young consumers, these products generate significant revenue.

(Re)Discovery. In 2007 we went through a massive restructuring. We repositioned the entire brand to better fit our targets when it came to human, social, and environmental issues. We began to focus on how our actions were impacting our customers and their communities and used surveys, interviews, and other methods of data collection to see how we were doing.

(Continued)

Through our research, we realized that we had drifted away from our company culture. Our founders had focused on specific issues they wanted to work on and help solve, something we were no longer doing. We had become a profit-driven organization, focusing more on solving financial issues than those closer to our founders' vision.

The right fit. As we went through this transformation, we realized that although we knew a lot about the market for school supplies, we'd never entered a classroom or talked to parents, teachers, counsellors or students. We knew about school supplies; we didn't know about education. To remedy this, in 2009 we hired a pedagogical consulting service that brought together educators to help us understand how we could potentially be damaging society through our work in the educational sector. Moreover, how were we helping society?

Our team came back with a problem: licensed products harm children's education. They were creating problems amongst families because they catalysed bullying situations at school and led to family conflict when these same families couldn't afford the more popular products. From this new insight emerged a crucial question: Given our brand positioning, did the commercialization of these products fit the current strategy?

The decision. At the time, we were implementing a new model of management where decisions were no longer being made top to bottom; rather, the problems were shared and discussed by employees. We wanted everyone, not just senior management, to identify and deal with different business-related issues. Following this model, we opened the debate regarding licensed products to all our employees.

Finances were particularly discussed during this period – the licensed products were profitable; they drove the sales of other products. Some employees worried that if we stopped using them, sales would drop across the board. Not only was this a concern to our employees but echoing opinions were received from our customers, distributors, retailer networks, and representatives.

We continued to question our strategy. Our research team had said that there are children coming into education nowadays with mobility difficulties, needing support materials that did not exist in the market. We agreed that this was important and launched our Diversity on the Street project, which worked to develop, along with consumers (and their caregivers), products that could solve some of the difficulties they were facing.

Diversity on the Street was an easy consensus to reach; we thought it was important and it matched our brand positioning. However, the debate over licensed products kept going.

We now had decisions to make. Should we discontinue the products? Should we focus on creating things that didn't create conflict and invest in the 'educational' aspect of our products? What about the partners we had created the products with, and the companies we'd purchased the licensing agreements from?

(Continued)

Throughout the process, we'd attempted to adopt an attitude of recognizing that one can't just look at financial advantage. Sometimes looking out for society and our communities is worth more but was this the case here?

QUESTIONS

1. What different stakeholders and stakeholder issues can you identify in this case?

2. Would you consider Josh a responsible manager? Why or why not?

3. What would be the 'professional' thing to do and how does it relate to responsible management? What do you think they should do? Why?

DIGGING DEEPER: QUANTITATIVE CORPORATE SOCIAL PERFORMANCE ASSESSMENT

As will be shown in the following example, the qualitative social performance framework introduced in the last section can be translated into a quantitative assessment for planning or evaluating management's responsibility initiatives.

How can we compare the world's largest hotel chain with the world's largest coffeehouse brand? The MSP model provides a framework for comparing management across the most different industries. Management in both companies has responsible sourcing practices, which will be the subject of analysis.

Management at **Starbucks** has pioneered its responsibility towards community stakeholders in the supply chain through its Coffee and Farmer Equity (CAFE) practices, which support small local farmers in their community development and integrates them into Starbucks' fair trade network to provide communities with a decent income. Starbucks procured 367 million pounds of coffee (86% of their global purchase) through the CAFE Practices programme in 2011 [62]. The signature practice of **Intercontinental Hotel Group (IHG)** for involvement with community stakeholders in the supply chain is the IHG Academy, a training programme preparing individuals from local communities to work in the hotel sector. The IHG Academy annually trains 5,000 students, mostly in China, but also in other countries like the UK and the USA. Students are offered permanent jobs in IHG after graduating from the programme [63, 64].

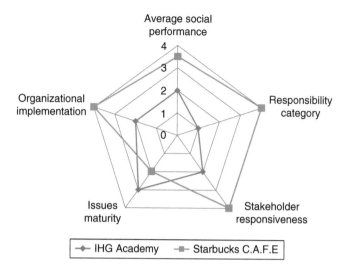

Average social
performance

Organizational
implementation

Responsibility
category

Issues
maturity

Stakeholder
responsiveness

→ IHG Academy   ■ Starbucks C.A.F.E

FIGURE 4.7 Comparing responsible sourcing practices

In the MSP analysis (see Figure 4.7), we find widely varying results for both companies' responsible management practices. For the responsibility category, Starbucks can be placed on level 4, discretionary responsibilities, as the programme is far exceeding the scope of what would be morally required from the company. IHG's management's activity would be categorized as economic responsibility (Level 1), as the company mentions as the reason for creating the academy that they 'have found it difficult to attract and retain talented employees in the region' [referring to China] as the reason for implementing their programme [63]. Starbucks' management's stakeholder responsiveness can be assessed as proactive (Level 4). When Starbucks' management began with CAFE there was barely any fair-trade activity in the agricultural sector and no for-profit company showing a comparable degree of involvement. SB's management proactively anticipated small communities (the stakeholder) necessity. The IHG Academy follows good practice examples of other companies with similar programmes (e.g. Cisco's Networking Academy [65]) and the often-made claim for hotels to be more closely involved with their communities. Those features suggest accommodative stakeholder responsiveness (Level 3). The issues maturity for SB's responsible management practices can be categorized as consolidating (Level 2). The issue community development through fair trade in the coffee industry is a mature topic, which has been well consolidated among stakeholders. IHG's topic of economic community development in the hotel industry is a fairly new, emerging issue (Level 3). The organizational implementation of Starbucks' practices has exceeded the strategic level (strategic positioning of Starbucks through its deeply implemented responsibility practices) and can be placed on a civil stage (Level 4), where Starbucks has long been a role model inspiring other actors inside and outside its industry to improve their practices. IHG's implementation is managerial (Level 2), as the programme is embedded into central management practices and processes (e.g. people management and hotel operations), but has not yet found application on a strategy level.

Those findings result in an average CSP score of two out of four for Intercontinental's responsible management practice and 3.5 out of 4 for Starbucks'.

The preceding concepts imply a qualitative sequence and quantitative indicators to rank social performance. All of those measures can only be lagging indicators for the true goal of responsible management, the creation of stakeholder value. The third part of this chapter illustrates the tool of stakeholder management for the creation of stakeholder value and the central instrument in responsible management.

POINTERS

You could use this example as inspiration for your own quantitative assessment of different companies. Further, you could assess whether you would have quantified the qualitative information differently. Another interesting exercise would be to look up these two companies' up-to-date responsibility practices and see how your assessment today would differ.

THE STAKEHOLDER MANAGEMENT DASHBOARD

Stakeholder and materiality assessment for _____

3. Stakeholder prioritization
Which ones are the most important stakeholders to consider?

Power (P): Stakeholder has power to influence management

Urgency (U): Swift reaction to stakeholder claim required

Legitimacy (L): Stakeholder is making a legitimate 'rightful' claim

P

L

U

3. Materiality assessment
How important are these issues to stakeholders and management?

Importance to management

Importance to stakeholders

1. Stakeholder screening
Who and what are the relevant stakeholders?

1.
2.
3.
4.
5.
6.
7.
8.
9.
10.

2. Issues screening
Which ones are the relevant social, environmental, and ethical issues?

A.
B.
C.
D.
E.
F.
G.
H.
I.
J.

POINTERS

You may use this worksheet to assess stakeholders and issues related to a variety of focal entities. You could, for instance, assess the stakeholders related to one management activity, practice, particular manager, department or product of a business branch or business unit. In order to manage the information on the figures you might want to use the numbers and letters on the left-hand side to populate the images on the right. If you are using this sheet as a group, we recommend you use a poster-sized copy.

REFERENCES

1. Gupta A, Raghunath A, Gula L, Rheinbay L, Hart M. *The decade to deliver: A call for business action.* New York: Accenture, 2019.
2. George S. Lego to ditch virgin fossil plastics by 2030. www-edie-net.cdn.ampproject. org/c/s/www.edie.net/amp-news/5/Lego-to-ditch-virgin-fossil-plastics-by-2030 Published 2020. Accessed February 11 2020.
3. LEGO. *Progress Report.* 2011.
4. The Local. Lego to turn all its bricks 'green' by 2030. www.thelocal.dk/20200203/lego-to-turn-all-its-bricks-green-by-2030-denmark Published 2020. Accessed February 11 2020.
5. Friedman M. A Friedman doctrine: The social responsibility of business is to increase its profits, *New York Times*, 13 September 1970.
6. Khurana R. From higher aims to hired hands: The social transformation of American business schools and the unfulfilled promise of management as a profession. Princeton: Princeton University Press, 2010.
7. Freeman RE. *Strategic management: A stakeholder approach.* Cambridge: Cambridge University Press, 1984/2010.
8. Carroll AB, Adler NJ, Mintzberg H, et al. What 'are' responsible management? A conceptual potluck. In: Laasch O, Suddaby R, Freeman RE, Jamali D, eds. *The research handbook of responsible management.* Cheltenham: Edward Elgar, 2020, pp. 56-72.
9. Carroll AB, Laasch O. From managerial responsibility to CSR and back to responsible management. In: Laasch O, Suddaby R, Freeman RE, Jamali D, eds. *The research handbook of responsible management.* Cheltenham: Edward Elgar, 2020, pp. 84-90.
10. Mawer S. Corporate to management social responsibility: Extending CSR to MSR guided by Mary Parker Follett. Salford: University of Salford, 2016.
11. Sprunger M. An introduction to Confucianism. *VI Confucianism: The religion of social propriety.* 2011. https://urantiabook.org/world-religions#confucianism Accessed 29 August 2011.
12. Melzer U. 50 biblische Erfolgsgrundlagen im Geschäftsleben – 23. Kapitel – Gib den Zehnten! In *Word* Press, 2011.
13. Beekun RI, Badawi JA. Balancing ethical responsibility among multiple organizational stakeholders: The Islamic perspective. *Journal of Business Ethics.* 2005, 60(2): 131–145.
14. Siwar C, Hossain MT. An analysis of Islamic CSR concept and the opinions of Malaysian managers. *Management of Environmental Quality: An International Journal.* 2009, 20(3): 290–298.
15. O'Brien T, Paeth S. *Religious perspectives on business ethics: An anthology.* Lanham: Rowman & Littlefield, 2007.
16. Hemingway CA, Maclagan PW. Managers' personal values as drivers of corporate social responsibility. *Journal of Business Ethics.* 2004, 50(1): 33–44.
17. Ramasamy B, Yeung MCH, Au AKM. Consumer support for corporate social responsibility (CSR): The role of religion and values. *Journal of Business Ethics.* 2010, 91(1): 61–72.
18. Brammer S, Williams G, Zinkin J. Religion and attitudes to corporate social responsibility in a large cross-country sample. *Journal of Business Ethics.* 2007, 71: 229–243.
19. Melé D. Ethics in management: Exploring the contribution of Mary Parker Follett. *International Journal of Public Administration.* 2007, 30(4): 405–424.
20. Schilling MA. Decades ahead of her time: Advancing stakeholder theory through the ideas of Mary Parker Follett. *Journal of Management History.* 2000, 6(5): 224–242.

21. Simms M. Insights from a management prophet: Mary Parker Follett on social entrepreneurship. *Business and Society Review*. 2009, 114(3): 349–363.
22. Donham WB. The social significance of business. *Harvard Business Review*. 1927, 5(4): 406–419.
23. Bowen HR. Social Responsibilities of the Businessman. New York: Harper, 1953.
24. Carroll AB. Corporate social responsibility: Evolution of a definitional construct. *Business & Society*. 1999, 38(3): 268–295.
25. Laasch O. Just old wine in new bottles? Conceptual shifts in the emerging field of responsible management. *CRME Working Papers*. 2018, 4(1).
26. Adler NJ, Laasch O. Responsible leadership and management: Key distinctions and shared concerns. In: Laasch O, Suddaby R, Freeman RE, Jamali D, eds. *The research handbook of responsible management*. Cheltenham: Edward Elgar, 2020, pp. 100-112.
27. Miska C, Mendenhal ME. Responsible leadership: A mapping of extant research and future directions. *Journal of Business Ethics*. 2018, 148(1): 117–134.
28. Dillon PJ. Identity, justice, and social responsibility: Micro-foundations of CSR. *Academy of Management Proceedings*. 2014(1): 10425.
29. Willness CR, Jones DA, Strah N, Rupp DE. Corporate social responsibility at the individual level of analysis: Research findings that inform responsible management 'in the wild'. In: Laasch O, Suddaby R, Freeman RE, Jamali D, eds. *The research handbook of responsible management*. Cheltenham: Edward Elgar, 2020, pp. 375-391.
30. Friedman M. A Friedman doctrine: The social responsibility of business is to increase its profits, New York Times, 13 September 1970.
31. A heavyweight champ, at five foot two: The legacy of Milton Friedman, a giant among economists. *The Economist*, 2006.
32. Levitt T. The dangers of social responsibility. *Harvard Business Review*. 1958, 36(5): 41–50.
33. Husted BW, Salazar JDJ. Taking Friedman seriously: Maximizing profits and social performance. *Journal of Management Studies*. 2006, 43(1): 75–91.
34. Carroll AB. The pyramid of corporate social responsibility: Toward the moral management of organizational stakeholders. *Business Horizons*. 1991: 225–235.
35. Implementing the partnership for growth and jobs: Making Europe a pole of excellence on corporate social responsibility. Brussels: European Union, 2006.
36. Habisch A, Jonker J, Wegner M, Schmidpeter RE. *Corporate social responsibility across Europe*. New York: Springer, 2005.
37. The United Nations global compact. www.unglobalcompact.org Published 2011.
38. Principles of responsible management education. www.unprme.org Published 2011.
39. International Standard ISO 26000: Guidance on Social Responsibility. Geneva: International Organization for Standardization, 2010.
40. Waddock SA, Bodwell C, Graves SB. Responsibility: The new business imperative. *Academy of Management Executive*. 2002, 47(1): 132–147.
41. Visser W. The age of responsibility: CSR 2.0 and the new DNA of business. Chichester: Wiley, 2010.
42. Laasch O, Flores U. Implementing profitable CSR: The CSR 2.0 business compass. In: *Responsible Business: How to Manage a CSR Strategy Successfully*. Chichester: John Wiley & Sons, 2010: 289–309.
43. Visser W. CSR 2.0: The new era of corporate sustainability and responsibility. *CSR Inspiration Series*. 2008, 1.
44. Dahlsrud A. How corporate social responsibility is defined: An analysis of 37 definitions. *Corporate Social Responsibility and Environmental Management*. 2006, 15(1): 1–13.
45. Garriga E, Melé D. Corporate social responsibility theories: Mapping the territory. *Journal of Business Ethics*. 2004, 53: 51–71.
46. Matten D, Moon J. 'Implicit' and 'explicit' CSR: A conceptual framework for a comparative understanding of corporate social responsibility. *The Academy of Management Review*. 2008, 33(2): 404–424.
47. Misani N. The convergence of corporate social responsibility practices. *Management Research Review*. 2010, 33(7): 734–748.
48. *Briefing: Corporate Accountability*. London: Friends of the Earth, 2005.

49. Valor C. Corporate social responsibility and corporate citizenship: Towards corporate accountability. *Business and Society Review*. 2005, 110(2): 191–212.

50. AccountAbility. *AA1000 Accountability principles standard 2008*. London: AccountAbility, 2008.

51. Vanberg VJ. Corporate social responsibility and the 'game of catallaxy': The perspective of constitutional economics. *Constitutional Political Economy*. 2007, 18(3): 199–222.

52. Wood DJ. Corporate social performance revisited. *The Academy of Management Review*. 1991, 16(4): 691–718.

53. Wartick SL, Cochran PL. The evolution of the corporate social performance model. *The Academy of Management Review*. 1985, 10(4): 758–69.

54. Carroll AB. A three-dimensional conceptual model of corporate performance. *Academy of Management Review*. 1979, 4(4): 497–505.

55. Schwartz MS, Carroll A. Corporate social responsibility: A three-domain approach. *Business Ethics Quarterly*. 2003, 13(4): 503–30.

56. Black Business. Introducing the first black-owned supermarket carrying all black-owned products. www.blackbusiness.com/2019/03/soul-food-market-first-black-owned-supermarket-carry-all-black-owned-products.html Published 2019. Accessed July 28 2020.

57. Clarkson MBE. A stakeholder framework for analyzing and evaluating corporate social performance. *Academy of Management Review*. 1995, 20(1): 82–117.

58. Martin R. The virtue matrix: Calculating the return on corporate. *Harvard Business Review*. 2002, 80(3): 68–75.

59. Zadeck S. The path to corporate social responsibility. *Harvard Business Review*. 2004, 82: 125–132.

60. Ellis-Petersen H. NHS rubber gloves made in Malaysian factories linked with forced labour. www.theguardian.com/global-development/2018/dec/09/nhs-rubber-gloves-made-in-malaysian-factories-accused-of-forced-labour Published 2018. Accessed July 28 2020.

61. Orlitzky M, Schmidt FL, Rynes SL. Corporate social and financial performance: A meta-analysis. *Organization Studies*. 2003, 24(3): 403–441.

62. Baer E. Lessons from Starbucks: Building a sustainable supply chain. *GreenBiz*, 2012.

63. Corporate responsibility report. *Intercontinental Hotels* Group, 2012.

64. Ashley C, Brine PD, Lehr A, Wilde H. The role of the tourism sector in expanding economic opportunity. *Corporate Social Responsibility Initiative Report*. 2007, 23.

65. Cisco Networking Academy. CISCO, 2012.

66. Freeman RE, McVea J. A stakeholder approach to strategic management. *Darden Business School Working Paper*. 2001, 1(2).

67. Myllykangas P, Kujala J, Lehtimäki H. Analyzing the essence of stakeholder relationships: What do we need in addition to power, legitimacy, and urgency. *Journal of Business Ethics*. 2010, 96(1): 65–72.

68. Hillman AJ, Keim GD. Shareholder value, stakeholder management, and social issues: what's the bottom line? *Strategic Management Journal*. 2001, 22(2): 125–139.

69. Berman SL, Wicks AC, Kotha S, Jones TM. Does stakeholder orientation matter? The relationship between stakeholder management models and firm financial performance. *The Academy of Management Journal*. 1999, 42(5): 488–506.

70. Preston LE, Donaldson T. Stakeholder management and organizational wealth. *The Academy of Management Review*. 1999, 24(4): 619–620.

71. Porter M, Kramer M. The competitive advantage of corporate philanthropy. *Harvard Business Review*. 2002, 80(12): 56–68.

72. A renewed EU strategy 2011–14 for corporate social responsibility. Brussels: European Union, 2011.

73. Jensen MC. Value maximization, stakeholder theory, and the corporate objective function. *Business Ethics Quarterly*. 2002, 12(2): 235–256.

74. Freeman RE. Managing for stakeholders: Trade-offs or value creation. *Journal of Business Ethics*. 2010, 96(1): 7–9.

75. Sachs S, Post JE, Preston LE. Managing the extended enterprise: The new stakeholder view. *California Management Review*. 2002, 45(1): 6–28.

76. Crane A, Matten D, Moon J. Stakeholders as citizens? Rethinking rights, participation, and democracy. *Journal of Business Ethics*. 2004, 53(1–2): 107–122.

77. Matten D, Crane A. What is stakeholder democracy? Perspectives and issues. *Business Ethics: A European Review.* 2005, 14(1): 6–13.
78. Freeman RE, Reed DL. Stockholders and stakeholders: A new perspective on corporate governance. *California Management Review.* 1983, 25(3): 88–106.
79. Edward Freeman R, Evan WM. Corporate governance: A stakeholder interpretation. *Journal of Behavioral Economics.* 1990, 19(4): 337–359.
80. Ahmed M. Somali sea gangs lure investors at pirate lair. www.reuters.com/article/us-somalia-piracy-investors-idUSTRE5B01Z920091201 Published 2009. Accessed July 28 2020.
81. Buchholtz AK, Carroll AB. *Business and Society.* Scarborough, Canada: Cengage 2008.
82. Fitch HG. Achieving corporate social responsibility. 1976, 1(1): 38–46.
83. Starik M. Should trees have managerial standing? Toward stakeholder status for non-human nature. *Journal of Business Ethics.* 1995, 14(3): 207–217.
84. Driscoll C, Starik M. The primordial stakeholder: Advancing the conceptual consideration of stakeholder status for the natural environment. *Journal of Business Ethics.* 2004, 49(1): 55–73.
85. Mitchel RK, Agle BR, Wood DJ. Toward a theory of stakeholder salience: Defining the principles of who and what really counts. *Academy of Management Review.* 1997, 22(4): 853–886.
86. Doing good: Business and the sustainability challenge. London: Economist Intelligence Unit, 2008.
87. Pohle G, Hittner J. *Attaining sustainable growth through corporate social responsibility.* Somers: IBM Institute for Business Value, 2008.
88. Lacey P, Cooper T, Hayward R, Neuberger L. *A new era of sustainability: UN global compact-accenture CEO study 2010.* New York: Accenture Institute for High Performance, 2010.
89. Lacey P, Hayward R. The UN global compact-accenture CEO study on sustainability 2013: Architects of a better world. New York: Accenture, 2013.
90. The state of corporate responsibility: Setting the baseline. *Corporate Responsibility Magazine.* 2010. www.thecro.com Accessed September 4 2011.
91. E&Y. Six growing trends in corporate sustainability. Ernst & Young, 2012.
92. Savage GT, Nix TW, Whitehead CJ, Blair JD. Strategies for assessing and managing organizational stakeholders. *Academy of Management Executive.* 1991, 2: 61–75.
93. Conaway RN, Laasch O. Communicating business responsibility: Strategies, concepts and cases for integrated marketing communication. New York: Business Expert Press, 2012.
94. Morsing M, Schultz M. Corporate social responsibility communication: Stakeholder information, response and involvement strategies. *Business Ethics: A European Review.* 2006, 15(4): 323–338.
95. Hemmati M. Multi-stakeholder processes for governance and sustainability: Beyond deadlock and conflict. London: Earthscan, 2010.
96. Wilcox D. *The guide to effective participation.* London: Partnership.org, 1994.
97. Laasch O, Moosmayer D. Competences for responsible management: A structured literature review. *CRME Working Papers.* 2015, 1(2).
98. Carroll AB, ed. *Managing corporate social responsibility.* Boston: Little Brown, 1977.
99. Carroll AB. The pyramid of corporate social responsibility: Toward the moral management of organizational stakeholders. *Business Horizons.* 1991, 34(4): 39–48.
100. Berle AA, Means GC. *The Modern Corporation and Private Property.* New York: Routledge, 1932/2017.
101. Carroll AB. A three-dimensional conceptual model of corporate performance. *Academy of Management Review.* 1979, 4(4): 497–505.
102. Laasch O, Jamali D, Freeman E, Suddaby R, eds. *The research handbook of responsible management.* Cheltenham: Edward Elgar, 2020.
103. *Our common future.* New York: United Nations, 1987.
104. Fioravante PL. Corporate philanthropy: A strategic marketing consideration. *Journal of Applied Business and Economics.* 2010, 11(3): 91–96.
105. Bruch H, Walter F. The keys to rethinking corporate philanthropy. *MIT Sloan Management Review.* 2005, 47(1): 49–55.

106. Godfrey PC. The relationship between corporate philanthropy and shareholder wealth: A risk management perspective. *The Academy of Management Review.* 2005, 30(4): 777–798.

107. Moir L, Taffler R. Does corporate philanthropy exist?: Business giving to the arts in the U.K. *Journal of Business Ethics.* 2004, 54(2): 149–161.

108. Matten D, Crane A. Corporate citizenship: Toward an extended theoretical conceptualization. *The Academy of Management Review.* 2005, 30(1): 166–179.

109. Altman BW, Vidaver-Cohen D. A framework for understanding corporate citizenship: Introduction to the special edition of business and society review 'corporate citizenship for the new millennium'. *Business and Society Review.* 2002, 105(1): 1–7.

110. Matten D, Crane A, Chapple W. Behind the mask: Revealing the true face of corporate citizenship. *Journal of Business Ethics.* 2003, 45(1–2): 109–20.

111. Austin J, Reficco E. Corporate Social Entrepreneurship. *HBS Working Paper Series.* 2009, 101(9).

112. Cooban, A. Lego drops plans to make bricks from recycled plastic bottles 25 September 2023. https://edition.cnn.com/2023/09/25/business/lego-abandons-recycled-plastic-bottle-bricks/index.html.

CHAPTER 5

SUSTAINABLE MANAGEMENT

OLIVER LAASCH

LEARNING GOALS

1. Explore the rise of sustainable development as an issue
2. Get to know essential tools of sustainable management
3. Learn to manage the triple bottom line

STAGGERING FACT

Ninety-nine per cent of the CEOs of the world's largest companies say sustainability issues are important to their future success [1].

SPOTLIGHT

SPOTLIGHT

FROM MISSION ZERO TO CLIMATE TAKE-BACK

Interface

Management at Interface present themselves as *'Radical Industrialists'* [2]. Interface manufactures and sells carpet tiles. Managing a carpet business is not the easiest starting point on the journey to sustainable development. Plastics used in carpet production are usually petroleum based and the glue is often toxic. The production process is energy intensive, and creates large amounts of CO_2. Nevertheless, in 1994 Interface's management declared its 'Mission Zero', to become truly sustainable, without any negative social, environmental and economic impacts by 2020 [3]. The final goal, however, is to become not only a business that does no harm, but one that has a net positive impact, a restorative business [4]. Interface's late founder Ray Anderson called this journey 'climbing Mount Sustainability', difficult, but not impossible [5, 6].

Interface started to produce carpet in 1973. The product itself comes with an initial environmental benefit due to 'Modular Flooring' practice [7]. Producing carpet tiles as opposed to large full-floor carpet sheets means that only the most-used tiles of the carpet in a room have to be replaced and disposed of, and there are fewer offcuts and less waste. Management declared they would follow

Interface

a 'less is more' philosophy in 1994. Their efforts quickly showed tangible results, reducing the average consumption of fibre by 10 per cent in just 12 months. Since then it has been a journey

(Continued)

of continuous management innovations. For instance, there is the ReEntry® programme to recover used carpet tiles from customers and recycle them into new products [8]. The 'Cool Carpet' practice allows customers to participate in a carbon-offsetting scheme [9]. Production management uses smart conveyor belts, the 'Intelliveyor', which stops when there is no product to be moved and saves considerable amounts of energy [4]. All products include an Environmental Product Declaration (EPD) of its complete environmental impact, including global warming, abiotic depletion, and the water footprint [10–12].

Mission Zero was accomplished ahead of time. It had required efforts of management across departments, hierarchies, and locations. For instance, Adrian, a site manager for Interface in Northern Ireland, explains how 'after 25 years driving innovation and business change, Interface recently announced success on our "Mission Zero" commitment to reduce our environmental footprint and have no negative impact by 2020. Looking forward with optimism, we are committed to becoming a Carbon Negative Company, taking more carbon out of the air than emitting, by 2040. And as of January 2019, every flooring product that Interface sells is carbon neutral across its full life-cycle through innovation and the purchase of a small number of offsets. We are … now focused on setting our sights higher through our Climate Take Back commitment, which aims to create a movement to reverse global warming' [13].

To become 'net positive' and to have a positive environmental, social, and economic impact, management at Interface is now engaging in a wider variety of innovative practices. For instance, Net-Works is a sourcing practice with both positive social and environmental impacts. It involves paying fishermen, often from marginalized communities, to collect and sell discarded fishing nets floating in the oceans to Interface as a production input [14]. Sustainable management at Interface translates into sustainable living practices as customers use their products at home [15]. For instance, 'Biophylic Design' practices help people to reconnect to nature by bringing it back into our living space through the use of nature-like designs [16].

Most importantly, Interface's practices related to net-zero and net-positive goals have prepared the ground for the surge in net-zero practices in the 2020s, including corporate giants like Amazon, entire industries like the UK aviation industry, cities like Tokyo, and entire countries like Germany [17–21].

SUSTAINABLE MANAGEMENT

> The TBL's [Triple Bottom Line] stated goal from the outset was system change – pushing toward the transformation of capitalism ... a genetic code, a triple helix of change for tomorrow's capitalism, with a focus on breakthrough change, disruption, asymmetric growth (with unsustainable sectors actively sidelined), and the scaling of next-generation market solutions.
>
> John Elkington [22]

Should management care about humanity's survival on Earth? Should it concern itself with the protection of the planet, including all of its species? However lofty this might sound, it is the exact aspiration of sustainable management. Management's environmental, social, and economic value creation, its triple bottom line, is the central element of sustainable management. Such management, if successful, may sustain or even restore our planet's social, environmental, and economic systems. **Sustainable management**, such as the practices at Interface, is management's contribution to trying to achieve sustainable development of the world, including the survival of the human race.

This chapter will first provide a systematic overview of factors that have led to today's global unsustainable society, describe the status quo, and provide an outlook on future scenarios of development. We also discuss the historic events that have led to the development of central theoretical concepts and global institutions involved in setting the stage for sustainable management.

The second section introduces the most important theoretical concepts for analysing sustainability. It also introduces the Brundtland definition of sustainable development and illustrates different approaches to interpreting sustainability. Central topics include the systemic, holistic approach of sustainability, the degree of change that is needed to reach sustainability, and whether sustainability can be reached through economic growth. We will address whether de-growth should be the new paradigm. Finally, we describe three kinds of capital: environmental, social, and economic, and illustrate how sustainable development can only be reached if governmental, business, and civil sectors become sustainable together (see Figure 5.1).

The final part of this chapter places the **triple bottom line** concept of social, environmental, and economic performance at the centre of sustainable management practices. This approach helps us to achieve the goal of a neutral or even positive overall value creation in the three dimensions. We apply the

Sustainable management sustains and balances social, environmental, and economic capital in the short, medium, and long run

Sustainable development a development that meets the needs of the present without compromising the needs of future generations

Triple bottom line refers to combined social, environmental, and economic impacts

tool of footprinting, which provides a sum of a specific impact, such as water usage or jobs creation, and the tool of product life-cycle assessment (LCA). LCA sums up those impacts throughout all stages of a product's production, use, and end of useful life.

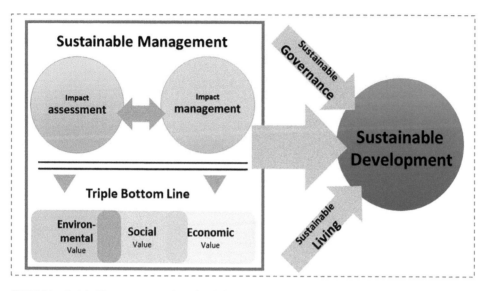

FIGURE 5.1   Sustainable management and sustainable development

STATUS QUO AND THE FUTURE

The last time that we could have claimed that humanity was living a sustainable existence on planet Earth was in 1970, when we had an overall environmental footprint of 1. We were using up exactly the amount of natural resources that the planet could replenish [29]. In 2011, the world population reached seven billion and common estimates suggest that there will be almost ten billion people on the planet in 2050 [30]. The human footprint has almost reached two times the Earth's long-term carrying capacity. This means that around summertime every year the Earth's population has used up one entire planet's worth of natural resources for the respective year. This day is called the 'world overshoot day' (see Figure 5.2). This means we are moving towards an inability to sustain all human lives, disaster, as we deplete Earth's resources each year. As environmental resources, such as water, food, and ecosystems become scarcer, world population keeps growing, and the impacts of climate change increase, we head further towards a grim future.

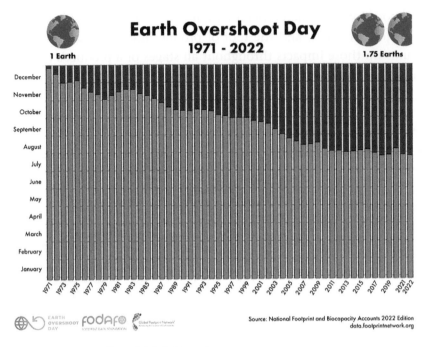

FIGURE 5.2   The development of humanity's footprint over time

SOURCE: www.footprintnetwork.org/our-work/earth-overshoot-day

What is the outlook for the future? Many scenarios exist. For instance, the famous independent scientist James Lovelock was of the opinion that efforts to reach sustainable development, especially to stop climate change, are in vain. He believed society should prepare to survive the inevitable catastrophe rather than try to stop it [31]. The WBCSD's Vision 2050 represents the other extreme, in which ten billion people will be able to live sustainably within the planet's resource limits from 2050 onwards [30]. WBCSD suggests that the time from 2010 to 2020 could be called the 'turbulent teens', a time in which the path to sustainable development has become clear through much energy, dynamism, and activity in many levels of society. From 2020 to 2050, according to WBCSD, we are in a transition phase in which a constant change in all parts of society will happen and sustainable development will be reached. As illustrated in Figure 5.3, four future scenarios appear likely [32]:

An idealistic guide for action and an ultimate vision of what sustainability could look like is the 'Doughnut' model for sustainable development (see Figure 5.4) [33]. It suggests that there are two fundamental aspects we need to get right in order to achieve sustainable development. Sustainability, first, builds up on a social foundation of minimum human and humane needs (e.g. health, housing, equality, safety, and justice) that need to be fulfilled, while staying inside an ecological ceiling (e.g. stopping biodiversity loss, curbing freshwater withdrawals, and reversing ocean acidification). The model suggests that we have to avoid, or rather stop, two basic problems at all costs:

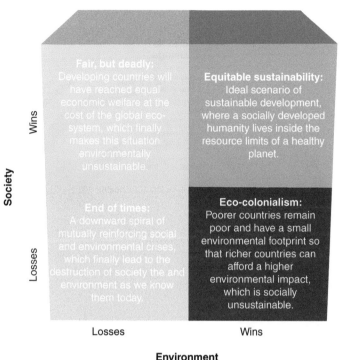

FIGURE 5.3   Scenarios of (un)sustainable global development

CREDIT: Slidemodel.com

1. **Social shortfalls:** Repair the current shortfall in fulfilling the human/social needs and redistribute needs fulfilment more evenly across the planet, genders, and socio-economic groups.

2. **Environmental overshoot:** Stop our overshoot in terms of using up too much of our planet's resources to survive as humanity.

This can and has been translated to the individual level, or regional level. The city of Amsterdam was the first city to adopt the Doughnut Economy approach. They use the Amsterdam City Doughnut as a policy development instrument. This includes economic policy affecting businesses and their management fundamentally [34] to align their responsible and sustainable management practices by addressing both humanistic shortfalls and environmental overshoots [35].

CONCEPTS OF SUSTAINABLE MANAGEMENT

The term sustainability has been a buzzword since the early 2000s. Unfortunately, the proliferation of a term does not necessarily increase our understanding. The report, *Our Common Future*, published by the United Nations

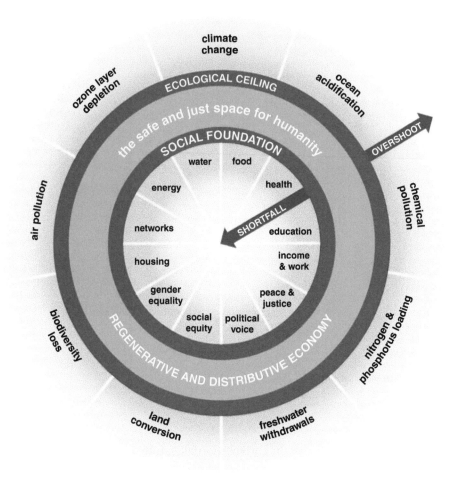

FIGURE 5.4   The Doughnut model of sustainable development

SOURCE: [33]

World Commission on Environment and Development (WCED) [24] defines sustainable development as development that 'meets the needs of the present, without compromising the needs of future generations'. This simple phrase implies much more than first meets the eye. The central term is intergenerational justice: what we do today must meet our needs and should not interfere with the needs of coming generations. We do not actually know what the needs of future generations are, so the only thing we can do is to abstain from destroying basic prerequisites for needs fulfilment, which serve as a basis for our offspring. Needs should also not be confused with superficial wants. We can assume that many of the amenities of 'modern' society rather serve to fulfil superficial wants, instead of profound needs, such as food, shelter, and belonging.

THE THREE DIMENSIONS OF SUSTAINABILITY

Sustainability at its core is about handling the three dimensions of environmental, social, and economic value. We will now discuss three main frameworks aimed at analysing these three dimensions.

As illustrated in Figure 5.5, in the left side's Venn diagram, truly sustainable development can only be reached if it is based on social, environmental, and economic co-development. If a country such as China focused mainly on economic and social development, such developments would be equitable (fairness between the civil and private business sectors), but neither bearable nor viable. For example, the missing environmental development and quality has led to an unbearable amount of air pollution in China's major cities, and non-renewable resources would be used up. Economic growth will no longer be viable if those resources need to be bought at horrendous prices through external trade when internal, non-renewable resources have been used up completely.

The circle model has been translated into a less complex model of mutually interdependent pillars, all necessary to carry 'the roof' of sustainable development, as illustrated in the middle visual of Figure 5.5 [26]. The third visual in Figure 5.5 expresses how economic activity is limited to society's potential to consume and how society's growth in turn is limited to the planet's environmental resource base.

> **Sustainability** describes the degree to which a situation will maintain (sustain) environmental, social, and economic capital

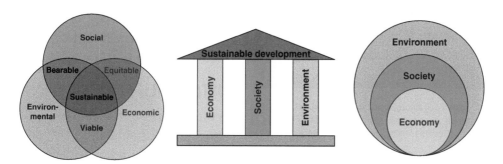

FGURE 5.5 Models of the three dimensions of sustainable development [25, 26]

A deeper analysis can be reached by understanding the three dimensions as different types of capital. In simple terms, economic development is an increase in the quality and quantity of financial capital. Social development implies an increase in the quality and quantity of social capital, and environmental development an increase in the quality and quantity of environmental capital. Accordingly, sustainable development must be development that increases all three types of capital simultaneously, or at least does not decrease any of them [36].

- **Social capital** is value directly embodied in human beings. Social capital on the one hand comprises individual, so-called human capital, including knowledge, skills, values, physical health, and personal well-being. On the other hand, social capital also comprises capital that is collectively created by interaction inside groups of human beings, such as joint values, culture, and collective welfare.

- **Environmental capital** (often called 'natural capital') comprises the amount of both renewable and non-renewable natural resources. Resources here should not be narrowly misunderstood as material production inputs, but also as non-material services provided by the natural environment such as recreational value, realized while enjoying nature or flower pollination by bees. A qualitative measure of environmental capital avoids the narrow, instrumental output focus by also considering the internally valuable characteristics of the biosphere, such as the resilience of ecosystems, or the richness of interconnections represented by high biodiversity.

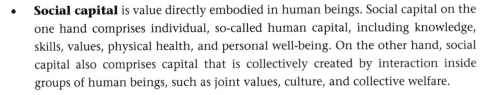

- **Economic capital** can be expressed in monetary terms. It comprises tangible assets (often called 'man-made capital') such as machines or production facilities, intangible assets such as customer loyalty or brand value, and financial resources, such as cash flows or a certain revenue margin. Economic capital can be attributed to an individual company or to the economic system as a whole.

As the failure of 'weak' politics and management 'as usual' to achieve effective change has become apparent, more radical 'strong' sustainability thinking as demanded by Extinction Rebellion is becoming a mainstream attitude.

'Rebellion Day: Brisbane' by larissawaters is marked with CC0 1.0

These three types of capital form the foundation of the triple bottom line business application of sustainability [27, 37], which we look at in more detail later in this chapter.

SUSTAINABILITY FOOTPRINTS

Sectoral contributions to reaching global sustainability are perhaps intuitively understandable. As shown in Figure 5.7, we will reach global sustainability only if people live sustainable lifestyles, businesses are managed sustainably, and nations are governed sustainably. If just one level does not make a commitment to sustainable development, global sustainability is impossible [36].

A footprint sums up one or several types of environmental, social or economic impacts for one pre-defined entity

But what commitment is needed to become sustainable? The **footprinting** methodology provides a clear answer: all 'entities', including people, organizations, and entire states, should not use up more environmental resources than the planet can reproduce. Footprinting can also establish single footprints for specific environmental impacts of management, such as a water footprint (e.g. water usage per product), or a CO_2 footprint (e.g. CO_2 emissions per employee). The footprinting methodology has not only been applied to the environmental dimension, but also to the social and economic dimensions. Management can for instance measure the social community impact (e.g. volunteering hours per employee) or the economic return (e.g. revenue per dollar spent) through footprints.

A specific type of footprint measures the relationship between the entity's resource usage and planetary resource reproduction. If a footprint corresponds to the planet's resource replenishing capacity, also called 'biocapacity', it is expressed with the number 1, meaning that exactly 'one planet is used' [38, 39]. The situation is neutrally **sustainable**. If the footprint is smaller than 1, fewer resources are used up than are replenished; the situation is restoratively sustainable or just **restorative.** An example is Cargill's watershed restoration mentioned below, aiming to add more water to the reserves than water taken out. If more natural capital is used up than the biosphere can replenish, the footprint is greater than 1, and the situation is **unsustainable**. Accordingly, each entity must achieve a footprint of one or lower to reach a sustainable situation in any of those three sectors.

Sustainable
resource usage and reproduction rate are equal

Restorative
fewer resources are used up than reproduced

Unsustainable
resource usage exceeds the resource reproduction rate

As illustrated in Figure 5.6, most developed countries far exceed the biocapacity of their national territories with a tendency to worsen the situation by reducing their biocapacity through environmental depletion and increasing their impact through growing consumption [40].

In spite of large-scale footprint initiatives, like the Carbon Disclosure Project [41], the footprint of the business sector is less well documented. However, the general consensus is that truly sustainable business management is still utopian. The crucial question to change this unsatisfactory situation is: what tools does each sector need to become sustainable?

Management at Cargill recently announced 'science-based targets' to restore water reserves in quantity and quality in 'priority watersheds' affected by their operations.

For the governmental sector, shaping public policies for sustainability is crucial to reach sustainable governance. The private sector's efforts must be centred on the development of sustainable lifestyle practices (sustainable living) and the business sector must manage the life-cycle of their products so that the overall social, environmental, and economic impact becomes either neutral or restorative (sustainable management).

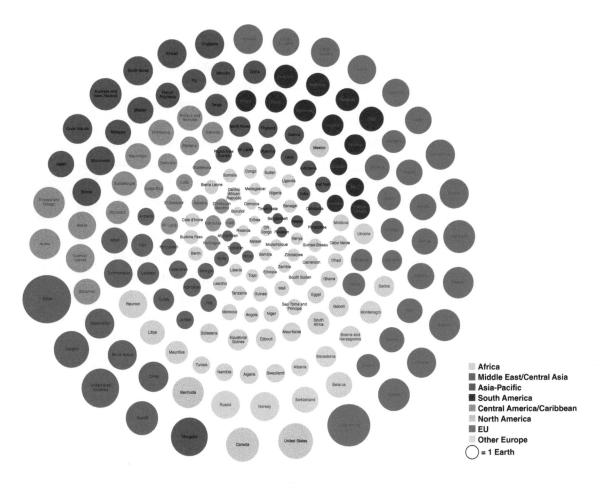

FIGURE 5.6   How many Earths do we need if the world's population lived like…

SOURCE: Global Footprint Network www.footprintnetwork.org

A great example of how different sectors interact in sustainability is that of Rebecca and Neil who thought of social and environmental sustainability when they got married during the coronavirus crisis. The couple had taken seriously the UK government's social distancing advice (social sustainability) and ensuring that they did not add more plastic waste to the environment (environmental sustainability). This was made possible by the REELshield Flip Visors produced by the social enterprise Plastic Free Planet. The visors are made from Forest Stewardship Council certified paper board and cellulose from wood pulp for the clear, mist-free screen, making them both recyclable and home compostable. Rebecca explained that 'especially after lockdown, our wedding was an opportunity to create a positive new normal and to be more environmentally conscious in our decision making' [42].

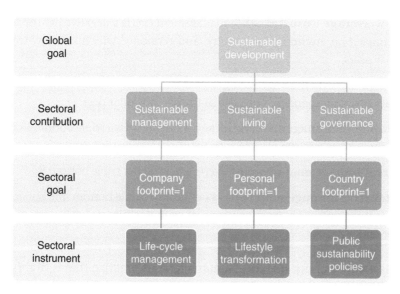

FIGURE 5.7 Sectoral contributions to sustainability

TRIPLE BOTTOM LINE MANAGEMENT

Management at Innocent Drinks claims that their mission is to 'strive to do business in a more enlightened way, where we take responsibility for the impact of our business on society and the environment, aiming to move these impacts from negative to neutral or (better still) positive. It's part of our quest to become a truly sustainable business where we have a net positive effect on the wonderful world around us' [43]. The statement embodies what **triple bottom line management** in a business means. They provide the perfect definition, including a 'net positive impact' and defining the key measurement tool, the triple bottom line, as 'business, society and environment'. In order to measure the triple bottom line, sustainability management has to consider all three impacts made, or as they put it, to 'take responsibility for the impact of our business'. Management must measure and manage all impacts in order to create a neutral to positive triple bottom line of social, environmental, and economic impacts.

> **Triple bottom line management** comprises practices influencing environmental, social, and economic bottom lines in order to reach a neutral or positive triple bottom line

THE GOAL: A NEUTRAL TO POSITIVE TRIPLE BOTTOM LINE

The **triple bottom line** (also TBL or 3BL) of environmental, social, and economic value is often paraphrased as the three Ps of sustainability, Planet, People, Profit [27, 37, 44]. When management assesses the triple bottom line, how will they know if their practice is sustainable? The following three types of management link different triple bottom line results to the classifications of unsustainable, sustainable, and restorative management [36].

> **Triple bottom line** refers to combined social, environmental and economic value

1. **Below-average unsustainable** management exerts a negative net-triple bottom line impact on environment, society, and economy, which is below the one of similar peers.

2. **Average-unsustainable management** exerts a net negative triple bottom line impact that corresponds to the normal impact of similar peers.

3. **Sustainable management** exerts a small net negative triple bottom line impact that does not exceed the planetary systems' restorative capacity.

4. **Neutral impact management** exerts a neutral net triple bottom line.

5. **Restorative management** exerts a net positive triple bottom line impact, which means it replenishes at least one type of capital, while not depleting any of the other ones.

Does this mean that, for instance, a management practice that is highly profitable, socially neutral, and only 'a little bad' for the environment is sustainable or maybe even restorative? To be truly sustainable or restorative, management must be sustainable in each of the three dimensions. As an example, imagine a management practice that is good to all its stakeholders and has reached a situation where its environmental impact is neutral. The business is socially restorative and environmentally sustainable. Unfortunately, the management practice was too costly and therefore not economically sustainable, which makes it overall an unsustainable management practice. This argument holds true in many scenarios and leads us to the two main meta-tasks of sustainability management, balancing and sustaining all three types of capital [36].

Figure 5.8 stresses the importance of balancing and sustaining when managing the three capitals. When management does not sustain one type of capital, it threatens the overall sustainability of management activities. Not sustaining social capital may cause a situation in which social groups start actively opposing management – for example, labour union protests triggered by exploitative (not socially sustaining) management practice. Further, the lack of balance among the three capitals causes problems due to mutual interdependence. Balancing here refers to creating a mutually reinforcing co-development of social, environmental, and economic capital or to protecting from favouring one capital at the expense of others, and to making trade-offs when necessary. The final goal is to create what John Elkington [46] calls a triple win or win–win–win situation for business, society, and environment.

In this section, we examine closely how to manage in order to create a positive or even restorative triple bottom line, which requires managing **impacts** across the three dimensions of the triple bottom line management. Sustainable management in practice is about accounting and managing positive or

Impact
a negative or positive
environmental, social, or
economic value created

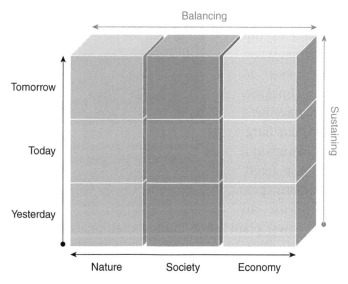

FIGURE 5.8 Sustainable management as balancing and sustaining the three capitals

SOURCE: Adapted from [45]

negative environmental, social, and economic impacts. Impacts should then add up to a neutral or positive triple bottom line. The next sections then introduce tools for assessing impacts and provide guidance on impact management for the good of environment, society, and economy.

IMPACT ASSESSMENT

The triple bottom line has been criticized as a mere 'article of faith', 'vague, confused and often contradictory' [47]. Accounting for just the economic bottom line can be difficult and has led to a number of business scandals. Accounting for the three interconnected bottom lines is a highly complex task.

In this section, we examine appropriate tools to assess the triple bottom line. These help to make social and environmental issues more manageable. We also provide an overview of social and environmental indicators and describe a toolbox of methods for 'making sustainable development operational' [48]. Chapter 18 will look at these indicators in greater detail.

LIFE-CYCLE ASSESSMENT AND IMPACT INVENTORY

Before impacts can be managed, it is necessary to map them. The product life-cycle model illustrated in Figure 5.9 can be used to provide a complete overview of impacts at all stages, from the extraction of the first raw material and sourcing of first inputs to the end of the product's or service's useful life.

Life-cycle assessment enables us to sum up different impacts across stages of the life-cycle even in complex cases. Imagine, for instance, management at ISCC (the Indian Singareni Collieries Company), which, on the one hand, powers its operations (production stage) with an

The Indian Singareni Collieries Company (ISCC) have set up solar power plants to fuel their coal mining operations: 'Oh sweet irony!'

'File: The Singareni Collieries Company Limited.png' by Pashamohammad444 is licensed under CC BY-SA 4.0

impressive solar power plant while mining coal, one of the most polluting forms of energy generation (use stage of the coal life-cycle) [49].

Life-cycle assessment the practice of mapping environmental, social, and economic impacts along the stages of production, use, and the end-of-useful life of a product

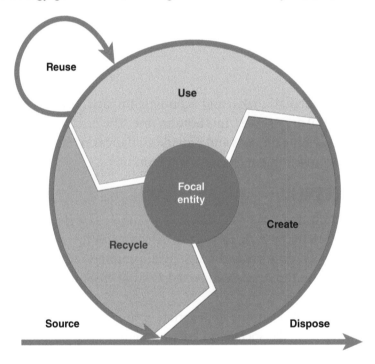

FIGURE 5.9   The life-cycle model

CREDIT: Slidemodel.com

Life-cycle impact inventory an extensive list of a company's impacts resulting from a cumulative life-cycle assessment, summing up all impacts of a business along with all products and services in its portfolio

Management needs to map and measure environmental, social, and economic impacts through all stages of the life-cycle. The final goal of this mapping process is to establish a complete **life-cycle impact inventory**, summing up all impacts for all products and services a company offers. Table 5.1 provides an inventory of exemplary impacts throughout the three stages and the three impact types, exemplified by Samsung Electronics [50].

TABLE 5.1 Exemplary company life-cycle-impact[1] portfolio for Samsung Electronics [50]

	Social	Environmental	Economic
Production	Employee education of 29,300 people, with an average of 87 hours per person and education cost of 977 USD per person.	'Reduction in GHG emission (relative to sales) by 31 per cent from the level in 2008, resulting in 5.11 tons of CO_2 per 88,800 USD [100,000 KRW] revenue.	Direct economic value creation of 130 billion USD out of which 99 billion USD have been redistributed to suppliers, 12 billion USD to employees, and the remainder reinvested or distributed to other stakeholders.
Use	Total customer enquiries and complaints accounted for 57 million.	Ratio of eco-products is 91 per cent of Samsung's products that were classified as eco-products with above average performance in material reduction, energy usage, and toxicity.	Economic (cost) savings for clients through energy savings were between 17 and 88%. A price cap on repairs of products stimulates longer product usage through incentives for repairs and savings.
End-of-useful life	100% PVC/BFR-free laptop models. Those chemical substances would otherwise result in toxic waste, harmful to human health [51].	Through an end-of-life, take back scheme, 1.06 million mobile phones have been recovered in Korea. Samsung has over 2,000 collection points in 61 countries.	In-kind donations of used electronic products for low-income communities increased the community's economic capital.

A company's overall life-cycle assessment is an accumulative measure of the company's products and services life-cycles.[2] Life-cycle assessment (LCA) was traditionally applied to understand environmental impacts. However, it has been broadened to take into account environmental, social, and economic impact in the sustainability management context [23, 52, 53].

- Typical impacts summarized through an **environmental life-cycle assessment** (ELCA) are impacts on water, air quality, and biodiversity.

- The assessment of economic factors is often called **life-cycle costing** (LCC). It might include the amount of wages paid, economic value added or profit made per life-cycle stage.

- Assessing social life-cycle impacts through a **social life-cycle assessment** (SLCA) may require a more complex approach to developing measurable indicators than the first two categories. Valuable support for identifying these indicators can be

---

[1]Many of the impacts mentioned in this table are relative impacts expressed in percentages. For the purpose of establishing a company's triple bottom line, total impacts expressed through sums are preferable.

[2]Life-cycle assessment can be conducted for both products and services. For the sake of simplicity, we will use the word 'product' to jointly refer to products and services.

found in the Global Reporting Initiative and the Dow Jones Sustainability Index [54]. Social life-cycle assessment is an emerging tool crucially important to the social dimension in sustainable management [55–57].

The process of life-cycle assessment can be subdivided into the following stages (see Figure 5.10) [58–60].

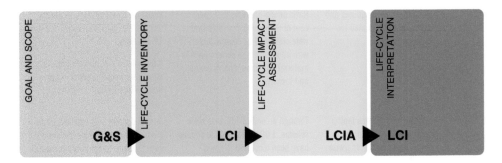

FIGURE 5.10   Stages of the life-cycle assessment process

1. Defining the **goal and scope (G&S)** of LCA first serves to develop a deep understanding of why the assessment is conducted. In the context of sustainable management, the primary goal should be a complete description of all environmental, social, and economic impacts as a basis for subsequent management activities. A secondary goal might be to create comparability with other products or alternative practices. For example, a company might consider substituting petroleum-based diesel with biodiesel in its processes, and it needs to compare the triple bottom line of both products before making a decision to improve its sustainability performance. Another secondary goal might be external communication purposes and the creation of transparency about the company's impacts. Defining the scope of the assessment involves defining the product system to be analysed and setting the boundaries of the LCA – the parts of the system that will be included in the assessment. Figure 5.11 illustrates the application of different scopes for a greenhouse gas emissions life-cycle assessment according to the Greenhouse Gas Emissions Protocol (Greenhouse Gas Emissions Protocol: https://ghgprotocol.org/guidance-built-ghg-protocol). [61] This type of assessment is often behind organizations' claims of being 'net zero' or 'climate positive', which can mean a very different impact depending on which scope of assessment such statements are based on and what types of greenhouse gases are included. The scope of a life-cycle assessment defines which of those stages will be included and in what detail. The ideal scope for a maximum quality sustainable management would be a complete inclusion of all functions in the greatest depth possible.

2. A **life-cycle inventory (LCI)** serves to quantify all inputs and outputs of the product's life-cycle. This inventory consists of the three stages of data collection,

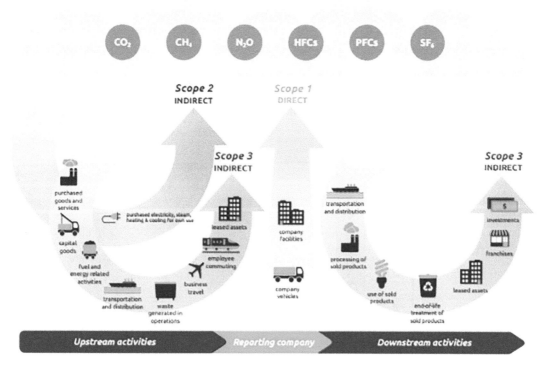

FIGURE 5.11 Greenhouse gas emissions scopes as an example of defining scope

SOURCE: https://ghgprotocol.org/blog/you-too-can-master-value-chain-emissions

data calculation, and the allocation of flows and releases. Central to the stage of data collection is the development and measurement of quantifiable indicators for inputs and outputs in all three dimensions. Inputs are, for instance, the amount of water used (environmental), the number of employees (social), and the capital invested (economic). Related examples for output are the water quality after the production process (environmental), employee well-being (social), and the profit made (economic). At the stage of data calculation the measurements made are related to specific process and functional units. Few processes result in only one product output. Therefore, the allocation of flows and releases to respective products in processes helps to reach a clear picture of the impact of a single product or service.

3. The stage of conducting a **life-cycle impact assessment (LCIA)** serves to evaluate the significance of impacts listed in the inventory and organizes them for analysis and management purposes. Impacts at this stage refer to real-life outcomes caused by the life-cycle. Figure 5.12 illustrates different types of data organization. For instance, sustainable management might need to specify the product's 'water footprint'. A company could plan to use the economic savings generated from a new energy efficient product as a sales argument, and therefore it needs to know the single impact of 'economic savings per customer'. The company could plan to fundamentally redesign the product's end-of-life and require

understanding of the 'end-of-use impact' in all three dimensions. LCIA pursues the final goal of categorizing life-cycle inventory data by their importance. Importance can depend on the size of the impact, the negative or positive external consequences of the impact and its instrumental value for the business.

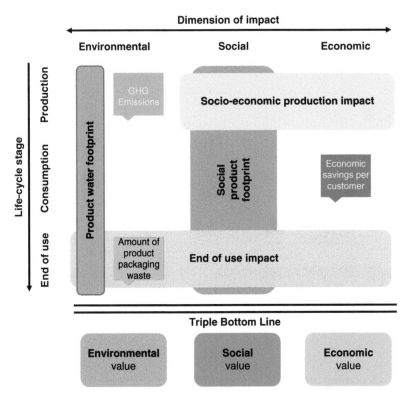

FIGURE 5.12 Exemplary application of impact assessment, life-cycle management, and footprints

4. **Life-cycle interpretation (LCI)** is the connecting element between life-cycle assessment and impact management. At the interpretation stage, the task is to plan actions based on the outcomes of the life-cycle process.

IMPACT MANAGEMENT

The management of environmental, social, and economic impacts is based on a sound life-cycle assessment. It is the core task of sustainable management. The basic goal of impact management must be centred on the aspiration of achieving sustainable or restorative outcomes of management activity. Similar to financial performance, the cumulative triple bottom line of all activities adds up to its sustainability performance. Thus, any person in the company should base their actions on the following simple set of principles:

• **Optimize triple bottom line impacts** to move towards sustainability. Optimizing impacts does not always mean reducing negative and increasing positive impacts. A company that is highly profitable (positive economic impact) might be so at the cost of its social and environmental bottom lines. In this case the company should actually re-invest the positive economic bottom line into boosting the social and environmental bottom lines.

- **Eliminate waste** in whatever form. Wasting resources will result in an unnecessary loss of environmental, social, and economic capital and automatically reduces triple bottom line performance.

- **Scale** your sustainable management practices to have a larger impact. Grow your own activities and inspire others to share your good practices inside and outside your business.

Whenever sustainable management practices are based on a sound life-cycle analysis and a systemic understanding of environmental, social, and economic dimensions of sustainable development, they enable the manager to make a lasting impact for the best of planet, people, and profit.

PRINCIPLES OF SUSTAINABLE MANAGEMENT

I. **Sustainable development** is a development that meets the needs of present generations without compromising the needs of future generations.

II. **Three types of capital** have to be sustained and balanced in order to reach sustainable development: environmental, social, and economic capital. Those three capitals comprise elements measured by the triple bottom line.

III. The **triple bottom line** sums up all environmental, social, and economic impacts of an activity.

IV. **Unsustainable management** has a negative triple bottom line; **sustainable management** is neutral; and **restorative management** has a positive triple bottom line.

V. **Sustainable management** is the process of managing in a way that reaches a neutral or positive triple bottom line.

VI. The **process of sustainable management** is based on the tool of product life-cycle impact management and can be subdivided into two main activities of impact assessment and impact management.

VII. Product **life-cycle impact management** administers all environmental, social, and economic impacts of a product or service through the stages of production, use, and end of useful product life.

VIII. The **stages of life-cycle impact management** are 1) goal and scope definition, 2) life-cycle inventory, 3) life-cycle impact assessment, and 4) life-cycle interpretation.

MANAGEMENT GYM: TRAINING YOUR PROFESSIONAL SIX-PACK

Knowing

1. Look up some ancient and/or indigenous stories about sustainable and unsustainable practices and identify something we can learn from them about sustainable management.

2. Prepare a mind map that interrelates the following terms: triple bottom line, sectoral sustainability, sustainable management, restorative management, and life-cycle assessment.

3. Look up detailed information on the nine planetary boundaries. You might want to explore how management practice impacts on these boundaries (e.g. *Journal of Management Studies* article by Gail Whiteman and colleagues [28]). You might also want to explore how the planetary boundaries relate to the United Nations Sustainable Development Goals (SDGs) featured in the first chapter of this book.

Thinking

4. Engage with two other people by together drawing a 'rich picture' (see how to do this online) that describes a major sustainability issue, all of its interrelations and impacts now and later, here and elsewhere.

5. We have presented Interface as a company pioneering sustainable management practices. However, in early 2020 they let go their CEO, who in his role had engaged in sustainable management, due to ethical misconduct, which had been revealed through a whistleblowing employee (the entire story is online). Use this example as a reflection about how ethics, responsibility, and sustainability need to come together for a truly professional manager.

6. Compare two products of two different brands by assessing their main triple bottom line impacts. Decide which of the two products is the more sustainable one by ranking both products on a scale of 0 (highly unsustainable) to 10 (highly restorative).

Acting

7. Prepare a life-cycle assessment for one product that you use frequently and identify one environmental, social, and economic impact per life-cycle stage. Research online if necessary.

8. Innovative paper-like materials like 'stone paper' (also called mineral paper) and Npulp (also called straw paper) have been presented as more sustainable alternatives to 'normal' paper. Imagine you are a representative of a major recycled paper maker and have to analyse what competitive threat this new material poses to you. Your line manager tasks you with writing a one-page briefing answering the question: In which part of the life-cycle are these innovations better than normal recycled paper, and in which parts worse?

9. Prepare the sustainability product portfolio of one company of your choice. Prepare a one-page proposal for how to make one product of the portfolio an environmentally restorative product.

Interacting

10. With a partner, watch and critically discuss a clip entitled 'The story of stuff', available online. It illustrates a high-speed life-cycle assessment of our main production and consumption practices.

11. Look up three terms in which you are interested in the online 'Sustainability dictionary' (https://sustainabilitydictionary.com), Wikipedia, or a similar online resource. Suggest an improvement to at least one definition using the site's comment back function.

12. Get in touch with a company of your choice to explain an idea for a more sustainable management practice. You can do so through hotlines, online contact forms, or the contact provided in the company's sustainability report. Document their reaction.

Being

13. Evaluate yourself. Are you a proponent of more moderate or more radical sustainability? Define your personal stance.

14. Imagine a typical Tuesday in your life in the year 2050, from waking up until going back to bed. Where and how do you live? How do you work? How do you move around? With whom do your spend your time? What does the environment look like? What are typical challenges and how do you tackle them? How have your work and/or private practices changed?

15. How does it make you feel to think about the consequences of climate change? How do you think it makes others feel – e.g. a Somalian fisherman, a middle-level manager in a petroleum business, or an Australian seven-year-old?

Becoming

16. Imagine a restorative management practice that you could engage in. Watch yourself doing this practice. What would it entail? What would it feel like to engage in? How would others react? What kind of support or resistance do you think you would encounter?

17. Use an online footprinting tool to assess a personal footprint, such as your modern slavery footprint, CO_2 footprint, or water footprint. How would your personal practices need to change in order to halve this footprint?

18. How do you feel about your available job choices in relation to their impact on sustainable development? Do you feel that you can pick a job in which you can be a sustainable manager, or that you have no choice other than being an 'unsustainable' manager in your next job? What practices or tactics could you use to engage in sustainable management?

SOURCE: Adapted from [65]

PIONEER INTERVIEW
JOHN ELKINGTON

INTERVIEWER: OLIVER LAASCH

John Elkington is arguably the most influential pioneer of the sustainable management movement and the creator of powerful ideas, including the triple bottom line.

The breakthrough wave? In some parts of the world, that last wave will never come; elsewhere it may be achieved for short periods of time, then be lost. Sustainability is a dynamic state, a resolution of forces in tension, so depends on the quality of leadership (and followership/implementation) over time. Fundamentally, it is a cultural (and civilizational) challenge. Changing mindsets does not guarantee the necessary changes in behaviour, and the cultures that lock in unsustainable behaviours may require a paradigm shift to change sufficiently. We think a fifth – breakthrough – wave will begin to build.

Zeronauts. Zeroing is possible for any company, any industry, in the sense that 'the impossible takes a little longer', as the US Army Corps of Engineers used to say. But it depends on a timely alignment of drivers and on leadership. At a time when most leaders are defensive or incremental in this space, and elsewhere, the chances are that breakthrough change will come in fits and starts. Zero-based targets help jolt leaders and C-suites out of complacency, and need well-designed financial incentives and recognition-based rewards (and penalties) to sustain the necessary levels of change.

Unreasonable people. The point is, as the playwright George Bernard Shaw put it, reasonable people adapt themselves to the world as they find it, whereas unreasonable people can imagine a different world, different realities. So in the early stages, anyone who aims to change the system in which people currently operate is going to be seen as unreasonable. Our future depends on the success of the more positive among them.

(Continued)

Mind the gatekeepers. I am answering this set of questions on a Eurostar train to Paris, for a session organised by the supply chain management firm EcoVadis for a growing group of major corporate customers. Such organizations are helping to drive triple bottom line considerations through supply chains, as are market gatekeepers.

Unreasonable leaders for systems change. We need all sorts of innovation for sustainable business. Clayton Christensen talks in terms of enabling, sustaining and efficiency forms of innovation, all of which have a role to play here. But we are at a point in all of this where incremental innovation must increasingly give way (or lead) to innovation that drives the necessary system change. Which is where unreasonable leaders come in again. This is an agenda we tackle in our report, 'Breakthrough: Business leaders, market revolutions', and in a book with former PUMA CEO Jochen Zeitz, called *Tomorrow's bottom line*.

QUESTIONS

1.   What do you think John means with breakthrough waves, paradigm shifts, and systems change? How do those terms belong together in the sustainability context? How might these relate to the four scenarios mentioned early on in this chapter?

2.   John talks about profiles of 'Zeronauts', gatekeepers, and unreasonable people. What kind of profiles and personal characteristics do you think a sustainability leader needs to have nowadays? What would you call them?

3.   At the time this interview was conducted John forecast that the breakthrough wave of sustainability would arrive in the early 2020s. Do you think this has happened yet? Will it happen?

---

[3]This interview was conducted in 2013.

PROFESSIONAL PROFILE
JUDITH RUPPERT

My name is Judith Ruppert and I am an environmental consultant at a Western Australian environmental management consultancy.

Courtesy of Judith Ruppert

A typical day at work. For an Environmental Impact Assessment (EIA), for example, I do background research about the site I am assessing, which includes finding out about the, for example, biological, hydrological, geological, and social/cultural situation onsite. I then do a risk assessment, analysing the probability and potential consequences of the project. After that, I would give recommendations on how to mitigate potential adverse effects. For more business-related topics, I would do research on different ways of improving energy efficiency and reducing carbon or water footprints. I'd then put together a management plan and a presentation and liaise with the client on how to best convey the message to employees. There are of course also more mundane tasks to do such as data entry, reviewing energy or carbon data and making sure everything is on track and compliant. When I'm out in the field, I would walk through environmentally sensitive areas, counting animal scat or finding tracks and nests to be able to assess the likely occurrence of a species.

Juggling bottom lines. Every day we have to juggle the economic interests of our clients with the environmental and social impacts of a big infrastructure, mining or oil and gas project, especially in Australia, where the resource sector is a major part of the economy, environmental and social impacts are often significant and given the fact that many projects in Western Australia affect indigenous communities, which represents a whole different level of social impacts than the usual neighbouring properties issue. As environmental practitioners, we have the responsibility to protect the environment as good as we can while not stifling the national resource industry, which in some situations is a big challenge. Barrow Island for example is a class A nature reserve off the coast of northern Western Australia, which now has LNG and oil being extracted from it – probably one of the most controversial projects in Australia, which requires a balance act between economic and environmental interests.

(Continued)

Navigating trade-offs. The main challenge being an environmental consultant is the balance act between the triple bottom line factors: ideally, you want to achieve the best environmental and social outcomes possible, but this is often being stifled by economic and especially financial interests. As the market is very competitive in Western Australia, the project budgets are usually very tight, which often leads to decisions based on 'best information available' and 'the best solution for the resource industry' rather than the best outcomes for the environment and indigenous communities.

QUESTIONS

1. What concepts and tools mentioned in this chapter's main text can you spot in Judith's words? Which core concepts and tools are absent? Why?

2. What examples of the social, environmental, and economic dimensions of sustainability can you find in Judith's story? What relationships between these three dimensions can you spot?

3. Could you imagine being an environmental consultant like Judith or would you prefer to work as an internal sustainability director like Kene (see practitioner profile in Chapter 2)?

TRUE STORY
(FLIGHT) SHAME ON ME

Who I was, am, and should be. My name is Olivier and I am a frequent traveller. Or rather, should I say, I used to be one?

Careful what you wish for. I still remember the first time I flew, a trip to London with my grandparents, still a young teenager. It got me hooked. I loved to watch out of the window fascinated by the sea and the picturesque English landscape moving by under us. The trip made

(Continued)

such a big impression on me that for a long time while growing up I wondered how I could work in a job where I could travel all the time and get to know the world.

A dream come true? Last year I did over 40 roundtrips to some 30 different destinations. Mostly, these were business trips with a handful of holidays in between. While doing so I have ticked many of the boxes for my personal 'see before you die' places across the globe, the Peruvian Amazon and Mongolia's steppes, Tokyo's Sumos and Mexico's Lucha Libre, Icelandic geysers, and Dubai's skyscrapers, Cape Town's Table Mountain and Rio's Sugarloaf Mountain, you name it, I have probably been there. It's a dream, isn't it? But something doesn't feel quite right.

What's wrong in this picture? So here's what doesn't make sense in this picture. I am a very environmentally conscious person. I haven't owned a car in over a decade to save emissions, and at some point considered not to have kids as I firmly believe we are too many people on this planet already. How on earth can I then be travelling the planet with these 'carbon bombs' that are planes? Also, seeing the amount of single-use plastic waste I cause on overseas trips makes me feel sick and guilty: a new cup for every sip, a plastic box for every meal, a plastic bag for three nuts and a raisin … I don't want to be a part of this anymore.

Trying to calm my conscience. Most of the time when I travel I do so to train others in sustainable, responsible, and ethical management. I want to believe that maybe, just maybe, I can influence enough people on every trip to reduce their carbon emissions so that I have a 'net positive' impact. I doubt it though. So I have begun to take other baby steps. I now always bring my own water bottle and fill it up from the tap before I board a plane. When given the chance, I order vegan on-board meals to avoid the emissions from dairy and meat. I refuse silly plastic packaged mini-items.

Who's friend, who's foe? I am not quite sure what to think about typical airline practices. On the one hand, there have been so many good pieces of news in the airline industry recently: zero carbon emission goals, edible food boxes, and biofuels. On the other hand, most flight attendants still decline to fill up my water bottle and force me to use plastic cups as 'it's our airline's policy'. Every time I see another advertisement that promotes 19-euros weekend plane trips or to 'just fly' when there is a perfectly fine

(Continued)

train to go on, I want to lose faith in humanity. But whose fault is it really? Are we as travellers 'making' those super-unsustainable practices, or is it the airline management and pricing schemes? Probably both.

Minor acts of rebellion. Recently I happened to have what I feel was a major win. I paid for carbon offsetting of three major trips out of my own pocket (some 150 euros per transcontinental trip) assuming, in the worst case to have to pay it myself to ease my conscience. However, I then submitted them for reimbursement as part of my normal travel expenses. My employer paid it without further questions! I still think it was rather an oversight than a purposeful action for sustainability. What an opportunity for sneakily normalizing carbon offsetting as a taken-for-granted reimbursement practice! So I sent a message to a dozen or so environmentally conscious colleagues to let them know what had happened so that they could do the same. Did they? Will they? I am not sure yet.

Envisioning bigger steps. After all, every flight with or without carbon offsetting is one too many considering the climate change mess we are in. So what to do? I am trying to figure out alternative ways of travel, but expect that much of it would imply a major struggle with my employer. Things I have been looking into are, for instance, organizing trips actively with multiple events along the way or in the same location, so that there is 'less carbon per event'. How much influence I can have on individual events' scheduling, and that I might have to say no to events that don't fit the logistics, are likely to cause major difficulties. I have also looked into radically different means of transportation, including travelling to the Americas via boat and taking long-distance train lines like the Orient Express between Europe and China. I could work while travelling on my laptop, but the travel time and possibly higher costs might be a real issue. Also, I am a young father and really want to be with my family more. So maybe, what I have to do is to change jobs, or to drastically change how I do my job. Decisions, decisions.

QUESTIONS

1. Do you think how you travel has anything to do with your being a professional manager or not?

2. Conduct a basic brainstorming life-cycle assessment for a typical flight you have taken in the past. What kind of impacts can you think of beyond the ones that Olivier mentions?

3. Changing jobs to avoid flights? Isn't he going a bit too far?

DIGGING DEEPER: SUSTAINABLE DEVELOPMENT INDICATORS

See: https://sdgs.un.org/goals and https://unstats.un.org/sdgs/indicators/indicators-list/

An important factor that prevents reaching global sustainability is the constant growth of world population and the footprint-growing effect of economic development on the environmental footprint of under-developed countries (see Figure 5.6) [63, 64].

One approach to solve the population issue appears to be to live in smaller families, 'small planet, small families' [65]. Most economically developed countries have a fertility rate close to or below the rate of 2.0 (two children per woman) (e.g., Germany 1.41, USA: 2.06 Singapore: 0.78), which means that the population of those countries is decreasing. Most of the least developed countries have a fertility rate far beyond the replacement rate of 2 (e.g. Cambodia: 2.78, Afghanistan: 5.64, Niger: 7.52, Honduras: 3.01) [66–68]. If we take the fertility-reducing effects of socio-economic development as given, one can assume that to reduce stress on the global resource, we would only need to bring social and economic development to all developing countries. Their fertility rates would drop, humanity's environmental impact would drop, and the world population would shrink itself to a sustainable level. There are several problems with this assumption, which will be illustrated in the following section.

The Kuznets curve is named after the economist Simon Kuznets, who revolutionized the understanding of relationship between economic development and wealth inequalities. The Kuznets curve helps us to understand the effect of an aspired future economic development of poor countries and sustainability. The curve evaluates the impact economic development has on the two crucial components of sustainable development, environmental degradation [69] and the degree to which wealth is equally distributed between the rich and the poor [70]. Figure 5.13 suggests that economic development affects

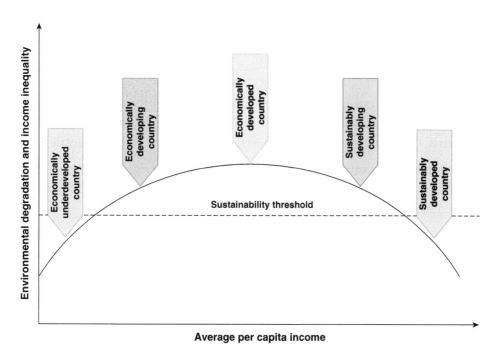

FIGURE 5.13 The sustainability Kuznets curve and country development stages

wealth inequality and environmental degradation in an inverted u-shaped pattern. Economic development in economically underdeveloped countries creates an increase in income inequality, increased differences between rich and poor people, and additional environmental degradation through the pollution created by increased economic activity. The sustainability threshold marks the level of inequality and pollution that is unsustainable in the long run. Thus, the parts of the Kuznets curve (K_1) that are located above this sustainability threshold are unsustainable: pollution exceeds Earth's carrying capacity and inequality increases above the socially bearable level.

Assume that a country's usual economic development follows the path of economic development before focusing on social and environmental development. Thus, at the peak of economic development efforts, we would assume such countries would begin focusing on reducing environmental impact and increasing social equality. Countries based on this scheme can be divided into five categories.

Economically underdeveloped countries have little inequality, as most people are homogenously poor. Because of low levels of consumption and economic activity, the country's environmental impact is within the planetary resource limits. Countries such as Afghanistan and Niger represent this stage.

Economically developing countries increase inequality, as lucrative entrepreneurial opportunities of economic development initially increase in only a minority of society. The environmental impact of the country begins to exceed the planetary resource limits because of the higher exploitation of the country's natural capital and lower eco-efficient production methods. Prominent examples are Thailand, Mexico, and Brazil.

Economically developed countries decrease income inequality but start to create a major middle class society. This group shares the benefits of economic development through equitable wages and employment schemes. Negative environmental impact, however, decreases because of more eco-efficient production schemes. Good examples for this stage are South Korea and, on a more advanced level, the USA.

Sustainably developing countries have reached high equality through developing a solid middle class and reducing the country's footprint through mainstreaming sustainable production and consumption patterns. Good examples are Japan, Germany, and many Nordic countries.

Sustainably developed countries are characterized by an almost equal distribution of wealth and a global environmental footprint that is within the planetary resource threshold, while providing an advanced standard of living. Such countries do not currently exist.

There are two main hurdles to reaching sustainable development. First, the vast majority of the world population lives in countries that are either underdeveloped or developing. If we believe in the Kuznets curve, those countries will become much more unsustainable, before they start to reduce their negative social and environmental impact. The crucial question is whether the planetary system can resist this increase in environmental and social stress. If not, are we moving towards a global showdown of crises as described in the first chapter of this book? Second, none of the developed countries has reached the level of a sustainably developed country, which would be necessary for globally sustainable development. Will developed countries be able to make the transition towards a truly sustainable situation? Fortunately, a large group of specialists agree that the social and environmental Kuznets curves can be altered by public policies [71–73]. The following two types of strategies are recommendable for the first four categories of countries.

Strategy 1. Economically underdeveloped and developing countries (Types 1 and 2) should harness the learning of already economically developed and sustainably developing countries. They should become fast-learners in sustainable development by deploying methodologies and technologies tried and tested in the countries of Categories 3 and 4. The policy goal must be to achieve economic growth and welfare, while keeping inequality and pollution inside the sustainability threshold.

Strategy 2. Economically developed and sustainably developing countries (Types 3 and 4) must follow the primary goal of increasing equality and decreasing their industries' and citizens' environmental impact into the planetary resource limits.

POINTERS

This section invites you to dig deeper into the (un)sustainable development implications of local footprints and population growth. You could play with distinct scenarios. For instance, if developing countries like Nigeria would bring down their exceptionally high fertility rate, how would that change their possibility of allowing a higher per-capita footprint? Also, you could critically explore the frameworks used here. For instance, empirical evidence suggests that the Kuznets curve's main proposition (higher income, lower pollution/inequality) can be true, but is not always so. Why, how, and when?

WORKSHEET

LIFE-CYCLE ASSESSMENT

Source	Use	Dispose
Create	Recycle and Reuse	

POINTERS

This worksheet can be used in many ways. After you have picked a focal entity (typically, products or service, but also event or activity) you could list main impacts, issues, or stakeholders per life-cycle stage. Five items per stage would be extensive enough, but still a manageable number. Alternatively, you could focus on one main item per stage and research it in depth. You could do this either for assessment, or to list distinct impact management practices for each stage. If you are using this worksheet as a group, we recommend using a poster-sized copy.

REFERENCES

1. Gupta A, Raghunath A, Gula L, Rheinbay L, Hart M. *The decade to deliver: A call for business action.* New York: Accenture, 2019.
2. Radical industrialists interface. *Greenbiz.* www.greenbiz.com/business/engage/enterprise-blogs/radical-industrialists Published 2012. Accessed April 1 2012.
3. Environmental. *InterfaceFLOR*, 2012.
4. Case study. *InterfaceFLOR.* Bradford Metropolitan District Council, 2012.
5. BIC. InterfaceFLOR. www.bitcni.org.uk/success-story/interface-flor Published 2020. Accessed 2020.
6. Mount Sustainability. LaGrange: *InterfaceFLOR*, 2012.
7. Interface. TacTiles: The easy way to install modular flooring without glue. www.interface.com/EU/en-GB/about/modular-system/TacTiles-en_GB Published 2020. Accessed February 18 2020.
8. History. *InterfaceFLOR*, 2012.
9. Squarely focused on cool programs for a warm planet. LaGrange: *InterfaceFLOR*, 2007.
10. Carpet tile: GlasBac, type 6 nylon. LaGrange: *InterfaceFLOR*, 2011.
11. InterfaceFLOR's new era in sustainability reporting: Full product transparency. *Ethical Performance*, 2010.
12. Giving you the complete picture – InterfaceFLOR's EPDs. *InterfaceFLOR*, 2012.
13. Lurgan Mail. Interface achieves Platinum status. www.lurganmail.co.uk/business/interface-achieves-platinum-status-1–9208023 Published 2020. Accessed February 18 2020.
14. Interface. The Net-Works Programme. www.interface.com/EU/en-GB/about/mission/Net-Works-en_GB Published 2020. Accessed February 18 2020.
15. Interface. BREEAM Contribution. www.interface.com/EU/en-GB/about/modular-system/BREEAM-en_GB Published 2020. Accessed February 18 2020.
16. Interface. An introduction to biophilic design. www.interface.com/EU/en-GB/campaign/biophilic-design/Biophilic-Design-en_GB Published 2020. Accessed February 18 2020.
17. Press Association. World sees growing move towards net zero emissions goals – analysis. www.eveningexpress.co.uk/news/uk/world-sees-growing-move-towards-net-zero-emissions-goals-analysis Published 2020. Accessed February 18 2020.
18. Takahashi R. Ambitious zero emission Tokyo plan wins praise, but begs for action. www.japantimes.co.jp/news/2020/01/26/national/zero-emission-tokyo-plan/#.XkvceaIWY7w Published 2020. Accessed February 18 2020.
19. Topham G. UK air industry sets zero carbon target despite 70% more flights. www.theguardian.com/business/2020/feb/04/uk-air-industry-sets-zero-carbon-target-despite-70-more-flights Published 2020. Accessed February 18 2020.

20. Mace M. 49% of world's GDP now covered by net-zero targets, study says. www.euractiv.com/section/climate-environment/news/49-of-worlds-gdp-now-covered-by-net-zero-targets-study-says Published 2020. Accessed February 18 2020.

21. George S. Amazon commits to net-zero by 2040 following staff protests. www.edie.net/news/6/Amazon-commits-to-net-zero-by-2040-following-staff-protests Published 2019. Accessed February 18 2020.

22. Elkington J. 25 years ago I coined the phrase 'Triple Bottom Line': Here's why it's time to rethink it. https://hbr.org/2018/06/25-years-ago-i-coined-the-phrase-triple-bottom-line-heres-why-im-giving-up-on-it Published 2018. Accessed February 18 2020.

23. Kloepffer W. Life cycle sustainability assessment of products. *The International Journal of Life Cycle Assessment.* 2008, 13(2): 89–95.

24. *Our common future.* New York: United Nations, 1987.

25. Barbier E. The concept of sustainable economic development. *Environmental Conservation.* 1987, 14(2): 101–110.

26. *2005 World summit outcome.* New York: United Nations, 2005.

27. Elkington J. *Cannibals with forks: The triple bottom line of 21st century business.* Gabriola Island: New Society Publishers, 1998.

28. Whiteman G, Walker B, Perego P. Planetary boundaries: Ecological foundations for corporate sustainability. *Journal of Management Studies.* 2013, 50(2): 307–336.

29. *Living planet report 2010: Biodiversity, biocapacity and development.* Gland: WWF International, 2010.

30. *Vision 2050: The new agenda for business in brief.* Geneva: World Business Council for Sustainable Development, 2010.

31. Lovelock J. *The vanishing face of Gaia.* New York: Basic Books, 2010.

32. Elkington J. *Raising our game: Can we sustain globalization?* London: SustainAbility, 2007.

33. Raworth K. *Doughnut economics: Seven ways to think like a 21st-century economist.* Vermont: Chelsea Green Publishing, 2017.

34. Wray S. Amsterdam adopts first 'city doughnut' model for circular economy. www.smartcitiesworld.net/news/news/amsterdam-adopts-first-city-doughnut-model-for-circular-economy-5198 Published 2020. Accessed July 29 2020.

35. Pirson M. A humanistic narrative for responsible management learning: An ontological perspective. *Journal of Business Ethics.* 2020, 162: 775–793.

36. Laasch O, Conaway R. *Responsible business: Managing for sustainability, ethics, and citizenship.* Monterrey: Editorial Digital ITESM, 2013.

37. Elkington J. What is the triple bottom line? *Big Picture TV,* 2011.

38. Global Footprint Network. *Footprint* Basics, 2011. https://www.theguardian.com/business/2018/jul/23/starbucks-straws-ban-2020-environment https://www.gov.uk/guidance/straws-cotton-buds-and-drink-stirrers-ban-rules-for-businesses-in-england

39. Wackernagel M, Rees W. *Our ecological footprint.* British Columbia, Canada: New Society, 1996.

40. Moore EBD, Goldfinger S, Oursler A, Reed A, Wackernagel M. *The ecological footprint atlas 2010.* Oakland: Global Footprint Network, 2010.

41. CDP. Disclosure, insight, action. www.cdp.net/en Published 2020. Accessed February 20 2020.

42. Campbell M. World's first couple get married wearing plastic-free face shields. www.euronews.com/living/2020/07/28/world-s-first-couple-get-married-wearing-plastic-free-face-shields Published 2020. Accessed July 29 2020.

43. Being sustainable. *Innocent.* www.innocentdrinks.co.uk/us/being-sustainable Published 2012. Accessed March 3 2012.

44. Savitz AW, Weber K. *The triple bottom line: How today's best-run companies are achieving economic, social and environmental success and how you can too.* San Francisco: Jossey-Bass, 2006.

45. Laasch O, Conaway R. *Responsible business: The textbook for management learning, competence, innovation.* Sheffield: Greenleaf, 2016.

46. Elkington J. Towards the sustainable corporation: Win–win–win business strategies for sustainable development. *California Management Review.* 1994, 36(2): 90–101.

47. Norman W, MacDonald C. Getting to the bottom of 'Triple Bottom Line'. *Business Ethics Quarterly*. 2003, 14(2): 243–262.

48. Hunkeler D, Rebitzer G. The future of life cycle assessment. *The International Journal of Life Cycle Assessment*. 2005, 10(5): 305–308.

49. Saurabh. Indian coal miner plans 550 megawatt solar projects to power operations. https://cleantechnica.com/2018/02/27/indian-coal-miner-plans-550-megawatt-solar-projects-power-operations Published 2018. Accessed July 27 2020.

50. Samsung. *Global harmony with people, society and environment: 2011 sustainability report*. Suwon: Samsung Electronics, 2012.

51. Why BFRs and PVC should be phased out of electronic devices. In *Greenpeace International*, 2010.

52. Starting life cycling. *Life Cycle Initiative*, 2010.

53. Zamagni A. Life cycle sustainability assessment. *The International Journal of Life Cycle Assessment*, 2012: 1–4.

54. *Dow Jones Sustainability World Indexes Guide Book*. Zurich: SAM Indexes, 2011.

55. Dreyer LC, Hauschild MZ, Schierbeck J. A framework for social life cycle impact assessment. *The International Journal of Life Cycle Assessment*. 2006, 11(2): 88–97.

56. Jørgensen A, Finkbeiner M, Jørgensen MS, Hauschild MZ. Defining the baseline in social life cycle assessment. *International Journal of Life-Cycle Assessment*. 2010, 15(4): 376–384.

57. Swarr TE. Societal life-cycle assessment – could you repeat the question? *International Journal of Life-Cycle Assessment*. 2009, 14(4): 285–289.

58. Rebitzer G, Ekvall T, Frischknecht R, et al. Life-cycle assessment part 1: Framework, goal and scope definition, inventory analysis, and applications. *Environment International*. 2004, 30(5): 701–720.

59. *ISO/FDIS 14040 environmental management: Life cycle assessment, principles and framework*. Geneva: International Standardization Organization 2006.

60. *Life cycle assessment: Principles and practice*. Reston: Scientific Applications International Corporation, 2006.

61. Greenhouse Gas Protocol https://ghgprotocol.org/guidance-built-ghg-protocol Last accessed August 6 2023.

62. Interface Inc. Interface issues statement in response to lawsuit by terminated CEO. www.prnewswire.com/news-releases/interface-issues-statement-in-response-to-lawsuit-by-terminated-ceo-301006159.html Published 2020. Accessed February 21 2020.

63. United Nations Department of Economic and Social Affairs. Sustainable development: The 17 goals. https://sdgs.un.org/goals Last accessed August 6 2023.

64. United Nations Department of Economic and Social Affairs. SDG indicators. https://unstats.un.org/sdgs/indicators/indicators-list Last accessed August 6 2023.

65. Laasch O, Moosmayer D. Competences for responsible management: A structured literature review. *CRME Working Papers*. 2015, 1(2).

66. Population matters. Smaller families means better life for all. https://populationmatters.org/smaller-families Published 2020. Accessed February 19 2020.

67. Central Intelligence Agency. *The world factbook*, 2012.

68. Janowitz BS. An empirical study of the effects of socioeconomic development on fertility rates. *Demography*. 1971, 8(3): 319–330.

69. Adserà A. Changing fertility rates in developed countries. The impact of labor market institutions. *Journal of Population Economics*. 2004, 17(1): 17–43.

70. Grossman GM, Krueger AB. Economic growth and the environment. *Quarterly Journal of Economics*. 1995, 110(2): 353–378.

71. Kuznets S. Economic growth and income inequality. *The American Economic Review*. 1955, 45(1): 1–28.

72. Yandle B, Bhattarai M, Vijayaraghavan M. Environmental Kuznets curves: A review of findings, methods, and policy implications. *Property and Environment Research Center (PERC)*. 2004, 2(1).

73. Panayotou T. Demystifying the environmental Kuznets curve: Turning a black box into a policy tool. *The Review of Economics and Statistics*. 2002, 84(3): 541–551.

PART C

MODES OF MANAGEMENT

CHAPTER 6

ORGANIZING

OLIVER LAASCH AND ROGER N. CONAWAY

LEARNING GOALS

1. Organize yourself
2. (Re)Structure your organization for ethics, responsibility, and sustainability
3. Shape organizational dynamics for professionalism

ENCOURAGING FACT

Among CEOs, 44 per cent believe or strongly believe that their organizations will have been transformed to achieve net zero carbon emissions by 2030, while 37 per cent don't rule out the possibility. Another 10 per cent don't believe such a transformation will have been achieved [1].

SPOTLIGHT

MAVERICK ORGANIZING AT SEMCO

'Who's in charge here? No one!' While one might think this kind of unusual setting in an organization is a lack of organizing, it actually is the main organizing principle at the Brazilian company SEMCO [2]. Organizing practices include, for instance, employees picking their own bosses and evaluating them twice a year. They also decide their working hours and wage [3]. Meetings are voluntary and at board meetings two seats are reserved for any member of the organization who turns up first, regular board member or not. There is no mission statement, no people management department, or headquarters [3]. Self-managed work teams who are in charge of all aspects of production and set their own budgets and production goals, invent and reinvent products. These autonomous work teams can even hire and fire co-workers and bosses with a democratic vote. A quarter of profits are shared with workers [4]. There is a 'survival

GRUPO SEMCO

'Democratic management at Semco' by dgray_xplane is licensed under CC BY-ND 2.0

manual' that outlines some of the most basic 'soft' practices, like the dress code, namely that there is no dress code [5, 6]

Before Ricardo Semler, at the time just 21 years old, took over the company from his father in times of economic depression, SEMCO used to be organized very differently [3, 7, 8]. Change started with a bang, when Ricardo fired 60 per cent of Semco's top management who didn't want to go along with the changes [3]. Changes were made one at a time, starting with what now seems the small step of allowing

flexible working hours to beat Sao Paolo's traffic, and then with the bigger step of letting workers set their own wages [3]. The radical changes he made to SEMCO's organizing structures and processes earned Semler titles like 'the anti-CEO' [9] who manages from his hammock, 'subversive' [2], a 'corporate rebel' [10], and a 'radical boss' [3]. Ricardo likes to call himself a 'maverick' [11]. There was even a party to celebrate the successful revolution against business as usual, in the form of the ten-year anniversary of Ricardo last having to make a decision [3]. Semler likes to joke about the paradox that 'my former employees still work for me' at the same time saying that they cannot be described as normal 'employees' any more [8].

(Continued)

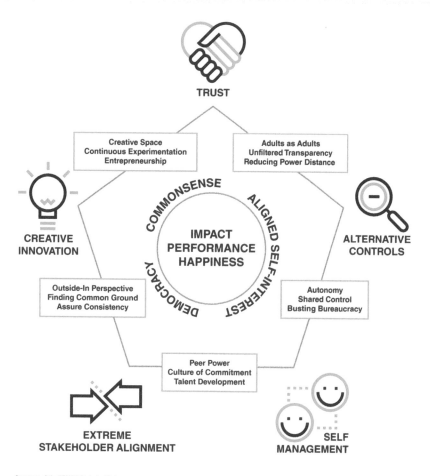

Courtesy of the SEMCO Style Institute

To some this sounds like chaos. Can you successfully manage a company that is organized like this? However, sales grew 286 per cent between 1990 and 1996 [4]. SEMCO's value increased from 4 million USD to 160 million USD in 2003, and the number of employees increased from 900 to 3,000 [2]. Employee turnover was minimal and SEMCO has become one of Brazil's favourite employers [3]. Ricardo Semler claims to have shifted the purpose of work from making money to making 'the workers, whether working shifts or top executives, feel good about life' [12]. Employees have more free time than in most other businesses, and a genuinely happy work culture [13].

No wonder that the 'SEMCO Style practices' of organizing have drawn much attention [14]. Management at SEMCO has helped others, including managers from over 150 Fortune 500 companies, to learn these organizing practices [4]. It has even launched an institute that trains others in the over 100 SEMCO Style practices [14] and provides resources 'to dig deeper' into individual practices [15].

PROFESSIONAL ORGANIZING

Once you have a clear picture of your priorities – that is your values, goals and high leverage activities – organize around them.

Stephen Covey [16]

The **organizing** mode of management manifests in many forms. Managers have the liberty to organize their own area of influence in this manner, which best serves performance goals. However, they are also part of others' organizing practices and of a surrounding organizational design. Such a design prominently includes the topics of hierarchies, authority, job positions, and functions. Organizing also includes the task of identifying communication channels, assigning tasks and responsibilities, and establishing accountability. In the SEMCO example we have seen how organizing can involve a type of 'de-organizing', an active move away from 'hard' organizational structures. Organizing has also been described as 'the design and evolution of the social structures comprising modern complex **organizations**, as well as the adaptation of those structures' [17]. This definition presents organizing as forming and changing organizations. Organizing often but not necessarily results in an organization. Organizing also happens outside organizations. For instance, you could organize your next family vacation (a united action from the coordinated parts of accommodation, travel, on-site activities, etc.). Such ad-hoc organizing does not necessarily result in an organization. However, you might also be the manager of a travel agency where organizing someone's family vacation becomes one of the organizing practices of the organization (travel agency), together with other organizing practices, like organizing colleagues' work schedules, or who reports to whom.

Core to an organization is a shared purpose that members pursue through the organization, and a shared commitment to organizational values. A professional organization then is one where the organizational purpose is related to serving society and the planet and where the values are in line with ethical, responsible, and sustainable conduct of organizational members. **Professional organizing** in turn means to engage in professional conduct by organizing ethically, responsibly, and sustainably. It also means to engage in professional service by creating organizations that serve society ethically, responsibly, and sustainably, or to change existing organizations accordingly.

This chapter's focus is on professional organizing and **professional organizations**. As illustrated in Figure 6.1, we are exploring the role of professional organizing that both shapes organizational structures and dynamics and is influenced by them. In the first section of this chapter we will discuss

Organizing
to arrange the parts so that they form a whole for united action

Organization
a social structure built to pursue the creation of value in line with its purpose and values

Professional organizing
both organizing ethically, responsibly, and sustainably as well as shaping organizations that serve society and the planet

Professional organization
serves society and the planet through the professional conduct of organizational members, characterized by ethics, responsibility, and sustainability

how to organize structures for ethics, responsibility, and sustainability, such as sustainable routines, chief ethics officers, or stakeholder engagement platforms. In the second section, we will discuss how to organize the dynamics to construct more ethical, responsible, and sustainable organizations.

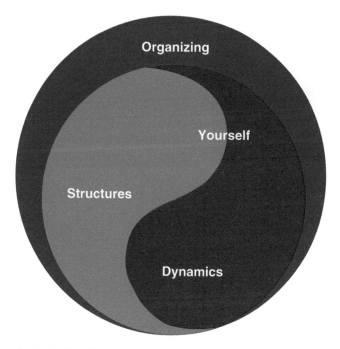

FIGURE 6.1   Areas of professional organizing

CREDIT: Slidemodel.com

ORGANIZING YOURSELF

In Chapter 2, we defined management as the practice of getting things done with people and resources. The emphasis in organizing is on *getting things done*, or as we defined earlier in this chapter, organizing as forming a united whole for action, 'getting organized'. Before organizing external structures and dynamics, a key prerequisite is to organize ourselves.

One of the most common types of unprofessional management manifestations lies in managers who cannot get things done, however many people and resources they have, as they cannot organize themselves – for instance, managers who do not stick to deadlines, who make others work overtime to patch up their own lack of organizing, or who might even end up burnt out, or neglecting family and friends. Many personal organizing practices can also have major ethics, responsibility, and sustainability (ERS) implications. For instance, to attend a meeting, do you

The airline industry has taken a hit as travel organizing changed in response to 'flygskam', flight shaming.

take the first flight in the morning or do you take a train the day before and stay in a hotel? The difference in carbon emissions is considerable. Do you plan your work travel by 'Googling' everything, causing large amounts of CO_2 emissions [18], or do you use a 'restorative' search engine like Ecosia that plants trees for every search? Such personal organizing habits and sustainable work practices matter [19]. Figure 6.2 illustrates three areas of good practice for organizing yourself, each of which we will have a closer look at in the following sections.

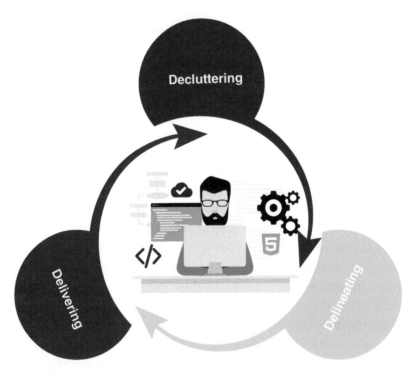

FIGURE 6.2   The 3Ds of organizing oneself

CREDIT: Slidemodel.com

DECLUTTERING

Decluttering refers to all practices that relate to getting rid of what is unnecessary, and organizing what we actually need and want to do well. While it sounds mundane, decluttering practitioners, like the global 'tidying up' guru Marie Kondo, claim it's 'magical' [20]. That 'stuff' to get rid of may be material, virtual, mental, or even relational [21]. For instance, you might decide to stop collaborating with a friend because the work they do distracts you from what you really want to do. Or you might decide to throw away old project files you were keeping 'just in case' to make sure that what you are currently working on is not hidden behind 'the old stuff'. Decluttering means organizing for efficiency in terms of getting things done and creating space to concentrate. It relates to the notion of beginning 'with the end in mind' [16]. You only retain what is essential for action.

A very helpful tool for organizing what is needed for action is the '5S' methodology of workplace organization as illustrated in Figure 6.3 [22, 23]. It starts with sorting, only keeping the items in a location that are really needed, no more, no less. The remaining items are then set in order, so they are accessible for use. If a file containing supplier contacts is used frequently, it should be readily available on a desktop, not buried in a hard-to-reach folder. Shining, making what you keep better and more beautiful, is required to keep what you really need functional and pleasant to work with. How about 'beautifying' your work relations by inviting your closest co-workers to the occasional cup of tea, or by polishing up your desk to get rid of those coffee stains? Marie Kondo would say that whatever you keep should 'spark joy' [20, 24], so make it 'pretty' and enjoyable to use. Systemizing what you have then ensures that your new order is clearly visible and understandable, and therefore easy to maintain. Finally, to sustain your order it is important to recurrently run through this cycle and to stay ready for agile action. In work environments where ERS might still be seen as an 'add-on' to 'normal' responsibilities, creating additional spaces to be ethical, responsible, and sustainable may be essential for a professional manager.

> Decluttering involves practices of both reducing our 'stuff' and making what we keep most useful for action

DELINEATING

Delineating involves two main practices, delineating what you do and what you don't as well as delineating how you use time. To delineate what to do (or not), the 'Eisenhower matrix' (Figure 6.4) is a simple but powerful tool. It is built on the distinction between urgent (needs immediate attention) and important (the outcome matters) tasks. For professional management, urgency and importance could be assessed – for instance, in terms of the social consequences. A task might be urgent, as an immediate reaction might be required to avoid harming stakeholders. A task could be important, for instance, as the future of our planet depends on it (e.g. think about restorative practices).

> Delineating practices involve both delineating what you do and don't do, as well as delineating how you use your time and others'

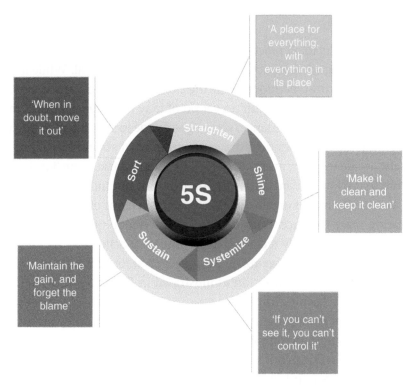

FIGURE 6.3   The 5S of workplace organization

CREDIT: Slidemodel.com Source: Adapted from [22]

The matrix suggests that you should only do important tasks yourself, the urgent-important ones immediately, and schedule a time for the non-urgent but important ones. Non-important and non-urgent tasks should not be done by anyone, as they are mere time-wasters. The recommendation for urgent but non-important tasks is to delegate them, or if delegation is not feasible, not to do them either. The underlying rationale is only to do what needs doing, and this way to save some time and headspace to do it well. This might also be achieved by identifying the problems and tasks that might not need your attention as they solve themselves, or others might solve them automatically if you don't intervene. Most importantly, it requires the ability to say no to others, be it managers or reports, who might order or nudge you into doing their tasks [25].

Secondly, delineating time is centred on the question of what to do when and how, in order to save time (i.e. time management). It has long been clear that the managerial role involves a wide variety of often complex tasks [26, 27], therefore good time management is important for busy managers [25]. There is a long list of effective time management practices – for instance, setting aside sacrosanct, shielded, quiet hours during which the important things get done without interruption, or reserving buffer time for unexpected but urgent and important work that needs to be done right away. Practices of delineating time might also serve to protect others' time – for instance, by starting and ending appointments and meetings on time [28].

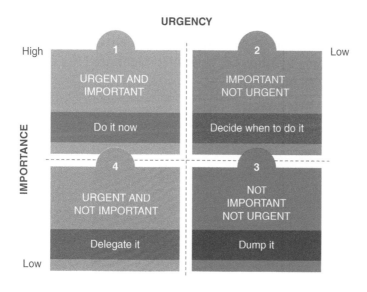

FIGURE 6.4   Eisenhower matrix

CREDIT: Slidemodel.com

DELIVERING

Once you have delineated what the right things to do are, it comes to **delivering** them at the right quality level, and at the right time. But what does this mean? It is a balance between the two extremes of the Chinese 'Cha bu duo' (差不多), translating as *'just* good enough' and Sigmund Freud's being anal retentive [29], which means trying to get every smallest detail right. For some tasks getting it right might mean doing it *just* well enough for it to be acceptable. For instance, you might use 'cha bu duo' delivery to send an implicit message to the recipient of the output that *you* should not be doing it in the future. Also, the quality delivery of some tasks might not make a difference to its usefulness or to the task's stakeholders. Doing the right tasks 'cha bu duo' might free time to really get the other tasks right that require delivery with the highest level of attention to detail, the more common meaning of 'getting it right'.

Many professionals use tools to plan the delivery of tasks such as Gantt charts like the one in Figure 6.5. The chart presents a weekly delivery

Delivering
getting the right things done right, and right on time

planning of (imaginary) Mansi, who manages store operations at a medium-sized fashion retailer. You see how she distributes deliverables in different categories (e.g. meetings and reporting) throughout her work week, ranging into the weekend, in order to be ready for her Sunday Mandarin Chinese course. When she allocates time, she makes sure to always add an additional 30 per cent on top of how long she thinks it will take to make sure she really gets it done on time, and she starts early with tasks, often distributing them over several days before the delivery deadline to deliver right on time. Also, she appears to leave ample time for other activities that might need her attention.

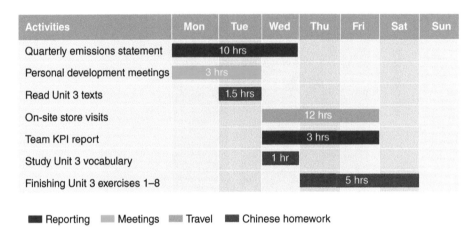

FIGURE 6.5   Exemplary Gantt chart of a head of store operations

CREDIT: Slidemodel.com

ORGANIZING 'HARD' STRUCTURES

Organizational structure is the formal framework organizations adopt to control how managers and employees conduct their activities and move towards organizational goals. The framework often includes the following aspects:

1. **Lines of command** (Who reports to whom?)

2. **Spans of management** (How many report to one?)

3. **Chains of command** (Who tells whom what to do?)

4. **Roles and responsibilities** (Who is responsible for what?)

5. **Channels of communication** (Who speaks to whom, how, and reporting what?)

7. **Organizing authority** (Who makes which decisions?)

Often, these structures appear in written form as operational guidelines, published in a handbook, posted on a website, or included in company

Organizational structure
the formal framework organizations adopt to control how organizational members conduct their activities to move toward organizational goals

presentations. The organizational structure is intended to coordinate organizational members' actions to ensure the organization moves towards the fulfilment of its purpose, while staying true to its values.

Should I prefer a highly bureaucratic so-called **mechanistic form of organizing** with static roles and responsibilities, with the main goal of efficiency? Or should I organize organically with flexible roles, flat hierarchies, and a high degree of decentralization? From a professional management perspective, many arguments speak for **organic organizing**. Employees' personal freedom and natural relationships and responsibilities are at the heart of the organic organization form. Organic structures may enable the social interaction necessary for professional management and also provide an excellent precondition for connection to stakeholders. Employees in an organic structure may feel a higher degree of personal accountability for making sustainable, responsible, and ethical choices. Proponents of a mechanistic structure, however, might claim that employees need strict control in order not to behave unethically, irresponsibly, and unsustainably. Another consideration relates to organic organizing's emphasis on flexibility and dynamics. Mechanistic organizational structures have too little flexibility to allow for the often radical change necessary to create professional organizations [30].[1]

Some organizations swiftly adopt dramatically different structures on their path to moral excellence, triple-bottom line and stakeholder management. In contrast, other organizations incrementally develop new structures. By whatever method an organization chooses to restructure itself towards professional management, the following clusters of questions will have to be addressed:

- **Creation.** Should there be a specific department or area exclusively coordinating ethics, responsibility, and sustainability topics? Should we create new related job roles? What new policies, programmes, and processes are required?

- **Integration.** How is professional management integrated – for instance, into existing job descriptions, departmental structures, or mission and vision statements?

- **Alignment.** How do we achieve harmony between existing structures and new professional ones? How do we align new structural elements with the organization's purpose (vision and mission statements), and with organizational culture?

> Mechanistic organizing emphasizes rigid top-down, centralized and standardized structures
>
> Organic organizing emphasizes flexible bottom-up, decentralized, adaptable dynamics

---

[1]The distinction between mechanistic and organic organizing was originally presented as part of the 'contingency approach', which suggested that mechanistic organizing works better in stable environments, while organic organizing is better suited to complex dynamic environments. While the case of SEMCO fits this description, both the case of Premium Cola in Chapter 13 and of Allsafe in the following chapter contradict these assumptions, as does the highly organic organizing in stable environments and industries.

- **Naming.** What do we call what we do? Is it ethics, responsibility, sustainability, responsibility, maybe all three of them or something else entirely? Maybe the organization should use a specific cause, like diversity, CO_2 reduction, or community well-being to name programmes, departments, and job positions.

- **Displacement.** How do we deal with situations where existing processes, jobs, or even whole departments need to be replaced by newly created structures? Should we even dismantle structures entirely because they are unethical, irresponsible, or unsustainable?

- **Communication.** What mechanisms can we create to make sure that both internal and external stakeholders are informed transparently, and empowered to co-construct the organization?

- **Empowerment.** What do the different structural elements need to fulfil their function? What hierarchical level are responsibility officers to be placed on? What budget is given to a sustainability department? What authorities and responsibilities are attributed to job positions? What mechanisms for training, improvement, and guidance are implemented?

In the following section, we review typical organizational designs in order to understand what broad structures to organize ethics, responsibility, and sustainability are available.

TYPES OF ORGANIZATIONAL DESIGN PATTERNS

The bureaucratic hierarchical organization that used to be considered 'ideal' [31] is nowadays just one of many valid organizational designs. Today we find a confusing flurry of different types of organizational architectures. Is the hierarchy deep or flat? Is it structured around groups, processes or classic departments? Organizational design is crucial for professional organizing.

For instance, vertical hierarchical organizational structures reduce communication effectiveness and cause messages to be filtered, refined, and shortened. Such a communication issue might cause severe problems when a CEO wants to communicate the company's new responsibility vision. If the message is not understood on all hierarchical levels, the programme is doomed to fail from the beginning. Deeper hierarchies may also distance the realities on the operational management plain [32]. For example, senior managers' perceptions of ethics in the organization tend to be significantly more positive than more junior employees' perceptions [33].

What is the right design for a professional organization? The answer is, of course, it depends. Figure 6.6 sums up the five most common organizational designs and how they may influence professional management. Each organizational design provides different advantages and disadvantages for transformation into a professional organization. In the introductory case, SEMCO had achieved a transformation from a self-contained organization (first type in the figure) to a horizontal organization (second type in the figure). It resulted in increased employee welfare, a great example of how management can create stakeholder value through professional organizing. We will now briefly introduce the less commonly known types of hollow, modular, and virtual organizations.

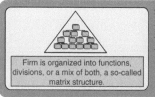

Self-contained: Conduct of processes without external support
→ Great control over companies' activities and responsibilities.
→ External stakeholder collaboration is impeded through contained nature.
→ Strong hierarchies might impede changes in organizational structure.

Firm is organized into functions, divisions, or a mix of both, a so-called matrix structure.

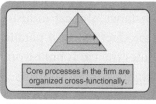

Horizontal: Core-process and team focus
→ Responsible business structures must organize around making core processes more responsible.
→ Opportunity to achieve responsible business programmes through team initiatives, such as green teams.
→ Quick change is possible due to flexible structure.

Core processes in the firm are organized cross-functionally.

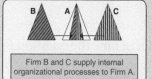

Hollow: Outsourcing of internal processes
→ Make sure outsourcing does not create sub-optimal labour standards or additional environmental or ethical issues.
→ Parts of the responsible business infrastructure, such as a CSR hotline can be created in an outsourcing fashion.
→ Experience in the outsourcing process may help to manage responsible business activities in collaboration with external (stakeholder) providers.

Firm B and C supply internal organizational processes to Firm A.

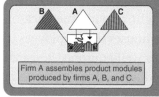

Modular: Modular production
→ Great potential for improving one's own product module for better social and environmental performance.
→ Create an eco-system for sustainable innovation together with other module producers.
→ Possibility to flexibly innovate or substitute modules that are not responsible enough without having to abandon the whole product or service.

Firm A assembles product modules produced by firms A, B, and C.

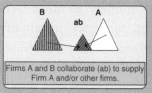

Virtual: Joint ventures
→ Great potential to pool know-how and resources with other organizations in order to quickly react to social, environmental, or economic opportunities and challenges.
→ Possibility to beta-test new responsible business structures without greater risk.
→ If virtual organization succeeds, it should be transformed to a non-virtual, independent structure.

Firms A and B collaborate (ab) to supply Firm A and/or other firms.

FIGURE 6.6   Organizational design patterns

SOURCE: Based on [34]

HOLLOW ORGANIZATION

Hollow organizations only fulfil core value, adding functions themselves and outsourcing others. Most of today's organizations are to some degree hollow.

If an organization does not see ethics, responsibility, or sustainability as core functions, it might get outsourced to external service providers. This is dangerous, as professional management requires substantial attention to detail, knowledge about the internal workings of the company, and an insider's perspective to be implemented credibly and successfully. Outsourcing other processes, especially production to developing countries, requires equally close professional attention. Scandals have been related to ethical, social, and environmental issues in outsourcing facilities.

MODULAR ORGANIZATION

In modular organization, a company assembles sub-modules to a product or service. Professional organizing in a modular organization is often based on improving single critical modules of a product. For instance, the car industry has made great strides towards a less unsustainable product by, in a parallel fashion, improving the different components or modules the car is built from: alternative engines, like hybrid, hydrogen, or electric engines; improvements in weight and aerodynamic design; and re-charging technologies in brake systems.

VIRTUAL ORGANIZATION

The same industry also provides us with great examples of how the question for more sustainable products creates so-called virtual organizations. Virtual organizations, often joint ventures of two or more companies, do not create great new structures, but rather borrow from the mother companies. For instance, one company's people management department might provide the back-office work, while another partner of the joint venture houses the employees in their offices or provides well-equipped research facilities. Major car producers, often direct competitors, have formed joined ventures to quickly produce new battery technology, a critical technology, urgently needed for more sustainable vehicles. Virtual organizations can be created and dismantled quickly with the changing tides of social, environmental, and economic opportunities and challenges.

Virtual organizations for electric mobility.

ORGANIZATIONAL ARCHITECTURE AND ITS PROFESSIONAL ELEMENTS

What is the role in professional organizing of sustainability departments, ethics hotlines, chief responsibility officers, multi-stakeholder forums, and responsibility programmes? They are but a few of the structural elements typically created by managers to support their efforts to become a professional organization. These structuring elements, their location, their connections, hierarchies, and responsibilities together form an organizational architecture for ethics, responsibility, and sustainability, the structures in which professional managers work. **Organizational architecture** refers to the totality of organizational structure and implies an ordered connectivity between its various elements. Whether a small, medium, or large enterprise, it will have architecture (structure) or a form by which it operates. We will now provide an overview of **structural elements** related to ethics, responsibility, and sustainability. Table 6.1 introduces the most common groups of such structural elements and their respective functions.

> Organizational architecture
> refers to the totality
> of organizational
> structure constructed of
> interconnected and aligned
> organizational elements

> Structural elements
> the building blocks of an
> organizational architecture

TABLE 6.1 Structural elements

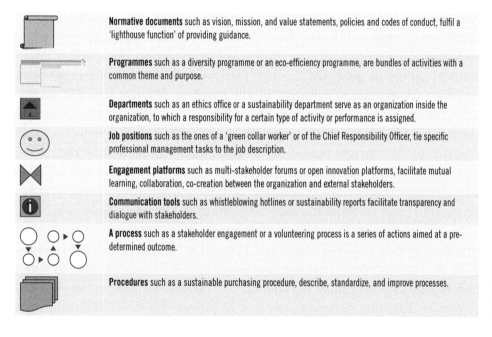

	Normative documents such as vision, mission, and value statements, policies and codes of conduct, fulfil a 'lighthouse function' of providing guidance.
	Programmes such as a diversity programme or an eco-efficiency programme, are bundles of activities with a common theme and purpose.
	Departments such as an ethics office or a sustainability department serve as an organization inside the organization, to which a responsibility for a certain type of activity or performance is assigned.
	Job positions such as the ones of a 'green collar worker' or of the Chief Responsibility Officer, tie specific professional management tasks to the job description.
	Engagement platforms such as multi-stakeholder forums or open innovation platforms, facilitate mutual learning, collaboration, co-creation between the organization and external stakeholders.
	Communication tools such as whistleblowing hotlines or sustainability reports facilitate transparency and dialogue with stakeholders.
	A process such as a stakeholder engagement or a volunteering process is a series of actions aimed at a pre-determined outcome.
	Procedures such as a sustainable purchasing procedure, describe, standardize, and improve processes.

These structural elements can be integrated into a typical organizational chart as in Figure 6.7. Such an organizational architecture for ethics, responsibility, and sustainability provides the infrastructure for professional management. An organizational chart which is the scaffold of the architecture can be divided into four main areas.

- **Top management.** The highest tier of managers is led by the CEO.

- **Board of directors.**[2] The board serves as a control mechanism and includes internal and external directors, and committees focusing on core topics.

- **Staff function.** These support functions provide central services important to the work of line functions.

- **Line functions.** These main functions are directly involved in the main value-creating activities of the company. Which functions to include in staff and line functions depend on the focus of the particular organization.

Elements of professional organizational structure are located inside, around, and in between those areas. In the following section, we will discuss some parts of the structure to exemplify salient elements.

NORMATIVE DOCUMENTS

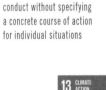

Normative documents provide broad guidance on service to society and the planet as well as professional conduct without specifying a concrete course of action for individual situations

Normative documents are important when individuals in companies find discretional, often weakly structured situations without a particular procedure to follow a 'normative infrastructure'. Not every action in an organization can and should be governed through particular rules. It is natural that organizations set strategic preferences, ideally based on different issues of materiality (see Chapter 4). For instance, the organizational architecture mentioned above does not have any structural elements related to CO_2 reduction that would provide concrete procedures to employees. This might be due to the fact that this company produces a service, not a product that would require a CO_2-intensive production process. The company might have made a strategic decision to focus on more material (relevant to stakeholders) lines of action.

Nevertheless, an office manager might, for instance, be faced with a decision to either buy a new, more energy-saving printer or to keep an old, less environmentally friendly one. A fleet manager might have to decide whether to invest in company cars with more horsepower or in hybrid technology. In such discretionary decisions, normative documents provide guidance. The company's mission statement might state, 'We aim to become the most environmentally friendly company in our sector.' The values statement might translate this into 'respect for the environment'. The code of ethics might specify that the environmental impact has to be taken into consideration in all decisions, and there might even be an environmental policy that specifies CO_2 reduction as a goal. The following list illustrates different normative documents and how they can be used to create an infrastructure for professional management.

---

[2]The board is a structure resulting from the concept of corporate governance. Corporate governance will be illustrated in greater detail in Chapter 21 as corporate governance was originally developed as a tool to manage the relationship with shareholders and other owners.

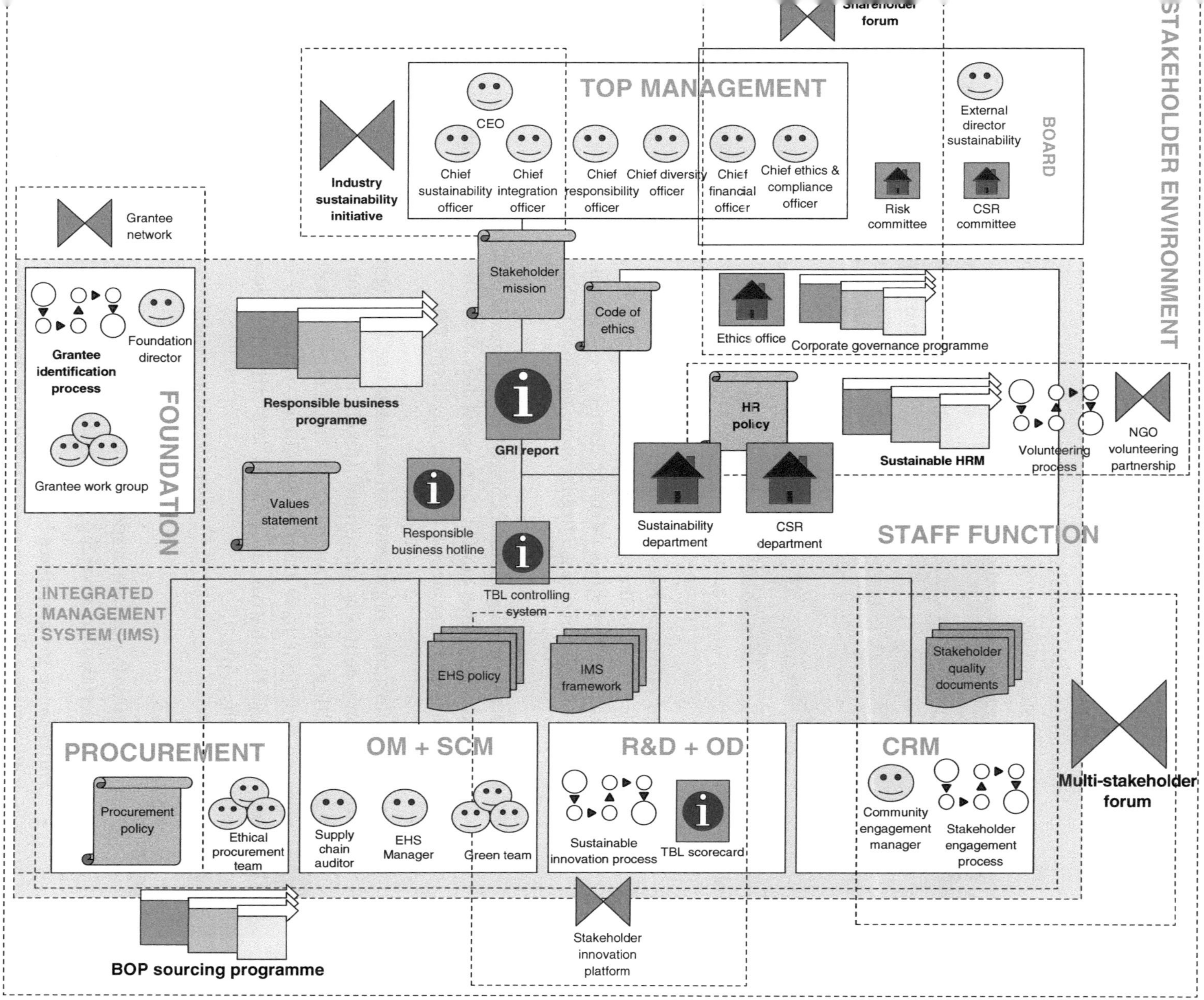

FIGURE 6.7 Exemplary professional organizing architecture

- The **vision** describes what the organization should ultimately become. The vision statement should describe how the professional organization should look at the end of its transformation process.

- The **mission** defines what the business should be and do in the present to fulfil its purpose. Organizational mission statements may include triple bottom line, stakeholder, and ethical considerations. Some organizations also draft particular mission statements for focus topics in professional management (e.g. missions for sustainability, stakeholders, diversity, or CO_2 topics). For instance, the hostelling organization HI USA states its mission is 'To help all, especially the young, gain a greater understanding of the world and its people through hostelling' [35].

Hostelling International's Mission
© 2020 Hostelling International USA

- **Values statements** highlight the values that should be the underlying fabric of organizational culture and which should guide all actions taken.

- A **code of ethics** provides rules for ethical decision-making or highlights specific ethical issue areas of the organization with the goal of fostering morally correct behaviour. Codes of ethics might be drafted for the whole organization or for single areas and topics (e.g. integrity/anti-corruption code or an ethical sourcing code).

- **Policies** state the organization's official stance regarding ERS topics. Policies are often broad summaries of what the business does or does not do in a certain area of action (e.g. environmental, people management, PR).

In the professional organizational architecture in Figure 6.7 we see the organization's centrally important stakeholder mission, the ethics code, and a resulting values statement. In the example, both the HR and the sourcing functions have their own policies, which are integrated into ERS programmes. Normative documents are also the foundation of other structural elements.

PROGRAMMES

Programmes do not form a specific new organizational structure, but a joint activity undertaken by several company departments.

Programmes
bundles of activities and
structural elements with a
common theme and purpose

- **Multi-cause programmes** bundle a wide variety of different causes and typically embrace all parts of the organizational architecture. An iconic example is Marks and Spencer's Plan A, bundling the retailer's most important areas of

social and environmental initiatives in one strategic plan. Al Programmes like this include activities for many different causes to further professional conduct and ERS in many parts of the organization. In our exemplary architecture (Figure 6.7) the 'responsible business programme' is the organization's flagship programme.

- **Cause-centred programmes** have a narrower scope as they focus on a few or single causes. Figure 6.8 provides an exemplary programme structure for the company AT&T including, for instance, a waste management programme – e-waste, the built environment of the company, and hazardous waste. What can be seen here is how cause-related programmes interrelate and are often managed simultaneously by a core team and by different mainstream business functions. For example, product stewardship is partly managed by the marketing department and the diversity programme by the people management department.

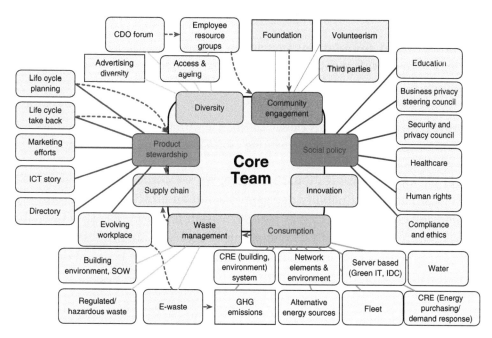

FIGURE 6.8   Exemplary programme structure at AT&T

SOURCE: [36] Source: AT&T (2011). Sustainability. Retrieved December 18 2012 from About AT&T: www.att.com/gen/landing-pages?pid=7735. Courtesy of AT&T Intellectual Property. Used with permission.

DEPARTMENTS

The more meaningful ERS programmes become, the more likely it is also that a **department** for the topic is created

- **Stand-alone ERS departments** may be called sustainability departments or corporate responsibility departments. Often the term office (e.g. ethics office or disability office) is used for smaller departments. While only managing few ERS

Department
an organizational entity to which responsibility for a certain type of activity and performance is assigned

activities themselves, they enable and coordinate the professional management efforts of many others.

- If **integrated into mainstream departments**, professional management is implemented from the inside of 'normal' departments. A marketing department might have a responsible marketing programme, or people management an employee well-being programme. Often an independent job position is created external to the department, supervising and supporting implementation across functions.

A peculiar element of organizational ERS architecture is foundations. Traditionally, foundations were largely separated from main business activities. Therefore they work differently from a stand-alone ERS department. Nevertheless, foundations have increasingly become involved in professional conduct across companies' value chains:

- **Independent foundations** are typically financed through a budget representing a fixed percentage of the company's profits, or even through company owners' private funds. They usually serve as grant givers to what are often social or philanthropic projects external to the company.

- **Integrated foundations** closely collaborate with both staff and main business functions as a partner in implementing professional management activities.

In our exemplary organizational structure, we see corporate social responsibility (CSR) and sustainability departments and an ethics office, all centrally located and closely connected as part of the staff function. The structure also shows how a multitude of ERS management activities are dispersed through different functions and organizational entities, such as the board of directors, its foundation, and top management.

JOB POSITIONS

An ERS job position includes core tasks related to ERS

With the importance of professional management practices, a variety of **jobs** have emerged **that revolve around ERS**. Related job descriptions can be divided by hierarchical levels and the organizational entities the job is located in.

- **Top management positions** for ERS carry many names, mostly beginning with the c for chief; chief responsibility officers (CRO), chief sustainability officer (CSO), and the chief ethics and compliance officer (CECO) are common job titles. Most of the c-level positions have high influence on the company's strategic decision-making as they are one or two steps away from the CEO of the company [37]. Managers in c-level roles often lead company-wide ERS departments and are in close contact with other leaders to jointly take measures throughout the company. At board level, directors are often assigned to assure professional conduct.

- In **middle and line management,** managers, directors, and vice-presidents (VPs) are typical titles of executives in charge of ERS. Middle and line managers often have a strong mainstream business function expertise coupled with specialized knowledge in the ERS area that is most relevant to their work. Middle managers often carry a term related to a certain cause or issue in their job title. Examples are the global sustainability director, the VP of diversity, or the CO_2 manager.

- **Green collar workers** are employees with operational jobs that actively work on social and environmental value creation. Examples for this might be the janitor or caretaker who, as part of their daily routines, makes sure that lights are switched off, and heating and air conditioning do not use too much energy. Such people can make a great difference to a company's ERS performance [38]. A related term is **green teams**, groups of employees whose task it is to improve environmental performance on an operational level.

The organization in our example (Figure 6.7) has created three c-level ERS positions and has one external board director in charge of responsibility topics, the director of the corporate foundation, an environment health and safety (EHS) manager, and one community engagement manager. On the operational level, the company has various teams working on ERS, such as the ethical procurement team. Internal employees working in ERS management must often interact and engage with the many groups of external stakeholders through engagement platforms that enable collaboration.

ENGAGEMENT PLATFORMS AND COMMUNICATION TOOLS

Engagement platforms are forums specifically created to facilitate collaboration with stakeholders. Such platforms can come in many forms, such as meetings (e.g. a quarterly shareholder meeting), collaboration events (e.g. volunteering campaigns), web-based platforms (e.g. an open-innovation platform). We can identify two typical engagement platforms:

Engagement platform facilitates mutual learning, collaboration, and co-creation between organizational members and stakeholders

- **Partnership-based engagement** is based on a close long-term relationship built with one or a few stakeholders. Engagement platforms are typically customized to the necessities of the partners. Information about and outcomes of the engagement are often disseminated internally. Processes of partnership-based engagement are often highly standardized.

- **Community-based engagement** instead has the goal of engaging with many stakeholders simultaneously. In this form of engagement, it is often not the company–stakeholder relationship that is dominant, but rather the relationship and co-creation process between stakeholders.

The organization described in our example is involved in an industry sustainability initiative in which top management engages with other leaders of companies to further industry transformation towards sustainability, the grantee network of the foundation, a periodic volunteering campaign for community engagement, an open innovation platform through which employees, clients and NGOs are involved in co-creating new sustainable products, and an annual stakeholder forum event.

Communication tools fulfil an important function in the professional organization infrastructure. They serve to maintain the connection to a broad group of stakeholders, as a mutual feedback line, and to use communication to create new realities. The main communication tools in our example are a sustainability report, a stakeholder hotline, and a sustainability controlling system for the company's line functions. Communication tools are described extensively in Chapter 10.

PROCESSES AND PROCEDURES

One of the main challenges in implementing ERS management activities in organizations is operationalization throughout all departments, functions, and hierarchies. The main solution for this challenge is processes. Wherever people work for a certain output, there is a **process**, more or less structured, to achieve this outcome. If we succeed in implementing processes for ERS management throughout the organization, we succeed in operationalizing it. Chapter 15 ('Operations Management') describes the design and continual improvement of professional performance through processes, procedures, and management systems. Here we will provide a short glimpse of two different ways processes can be used as structures for ERS:

- **Specialized processes** for professional management are procedures with ERS topics at their core and as their primary purpose. In our example, the stakeholder engagement process and the volunteering process illustrate such specialized processes.

- **Integrated processes** define actions important for ERS as part of mainstream business processes. Examples are the sustainable innovation process, which centrally considers the triple bottom line as one action of the normal innovation process. The responsible sourcing process from our example also illustrates this.

Procedures are formalized, usually written descriptions of processes. Often different procedures are integrated and jointly form a management system, administering many or even all processes of a company. The difference between procedures and the normative documents described at the beginning of this section is that

Communication tool
in professional organizing, it serves to exchange information, and to co-create new professional realities

Process
a series of actions leading to an outcome

Procedure
a process description that serves to standardize and improve processes

normative documents answer the 'what' question: 'What should be achieved?' Procedures instead answer the 'how' question: How can we achieve it? Normative documents are the starting point of organizational structuring elements; procedures are the completion. In order to construct a professional organization infrastructure, we have to run through an **organizational development** process that happens through the more fluid dynamics discussed next.

Organizational development the process of leading an organization towards its goals by changing its structures and culture

ORGANIZING 'FLUID' DYNAMICS

The first section of this chapter has introduced rather 'static', 'solid' building blocks, elements that can be integrated into an organizational architecture. In this second section, we will discuss the dynamics of how to create, maintain, and change those structures. Companies have frequently tried to remake themselves unsuccessfully [39]. Developing organizational structures, or restructuring towards ethical, responsible, and sustainable practices is an equally challenging, possibly even more challenging, task due to the paradigmatic differences with 'management as usual'. We will now explore how practices envisioning the professional organization, professional culture, organizational learning, and organizational change are at the centre of successfully creating a professional organization.

ENVISIONING THE PROFESSIONAL ORGANIZATION

What is the goal of re-inventing or re-structuring an organization for professional management? Figure 6.9 is an overview of the process of sustainability management, responsibility management, and ethical practices. Stages of professional growth models are valuable tools for qualitatively analysing how professional an organization's structures, activities, and performance are [40]:

- **Ethics performance** represents how morally desirable decision-making in the organization is. An organization weakly developed in the ethical dimension is on the amoral first stage, while a perfectly developed business is on the ethical stage, where moral dilemmas resolve in the most ethical decisions possible. The benchmark stage three in the ethics dimension is an ethically responsive organization that actively manages the main ethical dilemmas occurring in the organization's sphere of influence [41].

- **Responsibility performance** illustrates a continuum of different organizational behaviour patterns with regard to stakeholders. The continuum pictures a company's defensive behaviour, denying responsibilities at one end to a civil position where the organization even promotes stakeholder responsibility in other actors at the other end. The benchmark situation in the responsibility dimension is managerial implementation where social responsibility is embedded into all core processes of the company [42].

- **Sustainability performance** ranges from a largely undeveloped organization that is below average in sustainability even in comparison to a typical company in its industry, to the perfect situation of a restoratively sustainable organization that is able to simultaneously create social, environmental, and economic capital. The benchmark situation in the sustainability dimension is a situation where the organization produces a sustainable triple bottom line, one that is inside the planetary resource limits [43]. Many organizations have recently committed to 'net positive' goals where they aim to restore social, environmental, and/or economic capital [44]. For instance, IKEA has committed to becoming 'climate positive' by 2030, including intriguing plans to store carbon through both forest management and their products [45].

IKEA's organizing towards 'climate positive'

The dashed line through the middle in Figure 6.9 illustrates the implementation benchmark, a minimum requirement for professional organizations. An organization cannot be called 'professional' – nor can a management activity or a process – if the commitment implemented and the development path chosen do not lead to the fulfilment of the minimum ethics, responsibility, and sustainability requirements represented by the benchmark.

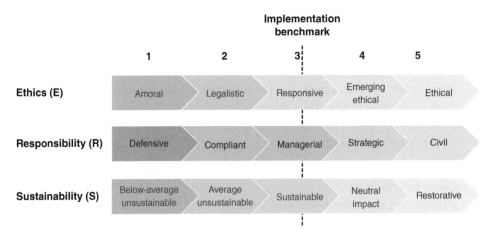

FIGURE 6.9   Development paths towards a professional organization

SOURCES: Based on [41–43, 46]

Let us imagine you are in charge of ERS at a company that after a self-assessment has realized it is on Stage 1, which gives you one point for each of the three dimensions, a sum of 3 in total. Reaching a performance sum of 15, where all three dimensions are fulfilled at level 5, or even just reaching the benchmark of 3 in all dimensions (performance sum of 9) may feel daunting. To make it achievable, we recommend simultaneously pursuing two types of tactics:

- **Small steps and single dimensions**. It will be much easier to subsequently develop the organization if the goal is not to achieve excellence simultaneously in all three dimensions and if the goal is not to jump to the highest stage possible in one go.

- **Balance between the dimensions**. It will always be easier to make the next step towards a higher level in one dimension than in others. This step can then prepare the ground for improvement in the other dimensions. For instance, it might be a small step to move from the compliant responsibility (R2) stage to the managerial stage (R3) by integrating stakeholder concerns into your existing quality management system. This step might also help you to move the company from a below-average unsustainable situation (S1) to an average sustainable situation. It might be that the integration of stakeholders into the quality management system also improves social and environmental indicators. Those indicators can now be used to benchmark and recognize areas of necessary opportunity in comparison to other companies that are on the stage of average unsustainability (S2).

PROFESSIONAL ORGANIZING PATTERNS

Professional organizing often applies the set of micro-practices that are illustrated in Figure 6.10. These patterns are built on the observation that originally ethics, responsibility, and sustainability practices were practiced at the periphery of an organization, as opposed to being part of the core practices of an organization. For instance, tobacco and petroleum companies have been big spenders on philanthropic and corporate social responsibility initiatives, largely without changing their core business practices that have immensely detrimental impacts on society and the environment.

Professional organizing depends on both 'trimming' practices that are bad and adding practices that are good. Trimming practices may be particularly challenging if bad practices are at the very core of the organization. For instance, Marks and Spencer uses the cooperating practice when working with the vertical farming company Infarm. Together, they have installed smart vertical farming units in the food retailer's stores, growing herbs and vegetables right in-store [47]. This practice is also likely to imply practices of trimming as the space taken up by the vertical farming units has to replace other food

Vertical farm in a Marks and Spencer store, achieved through cooperative organizing with Infarm.

Samuel Cane @ Marks & Spencer

Organizational culture describes the shared values, attitudes, and beliefs underlying the decisions made and actions in an organization

production-storage-sales practices such as refrigeration or inbound logistics chains for fresh produce.

The professional organizing patterns management applies depend on the initial situation. Some organizations, especially social enterprises, may be 'born responsibility oriented' and will only need to grow what they are doing well anyway. Other organizations might have to patch responsible business activities to mainstream core activities and to trim irresponsible practices. Some organizations might even have to 'close shop', to dissolve and re-invest the capital into a venture without irresponsible and unprofessional core practices.

CULTURE

Organizational culture has been called the DNA of an organization [49]. Culture, like the DNA, determines what an organization, including all its members, naturally is and does, as exemplified in Figure 6.11 for a fictional organization. Making ERS part of the organizational culture should ideally make it second nature to every organizational member to act ethically, responsibly, and sustainably from small, apparently mundane, decisions and behaviours, to the biggest ones.

How can managers foster an ethical, responsible, and sustainable culture? Transforming an organization's culture typically requires the following activities [50, 51]:

1. **Attention.** On what do stakeholders, especially employees, focus their attention? Professional managers can create this focus by praising employees' professional performance, criticizing aspects of their unethical behaviour, and communicating professional organizational values to stakeholders. By re-directing stakeholder attention to organizational values, leaders will encourage professional management throughout the organization and direct attention to sustainable objectives and values.

2. **Reactions to crises.** Crises small and large tend to reveal a manager's true nature because emotions in tense situations tend to reveal the way people really feel about an issue. Typically, professional managers will respond either ethically or unethically,

responsibly or irresponsibly in times of crisis, which shows who they really are to followers.

3. **Role modelling.** A manager's actions say more about company values than many words and messages. Individuals as role models have a crucial influence on the behaviour of followers. Managers may lead a green office programme, participate in sustainable activities, or show other professional actions.

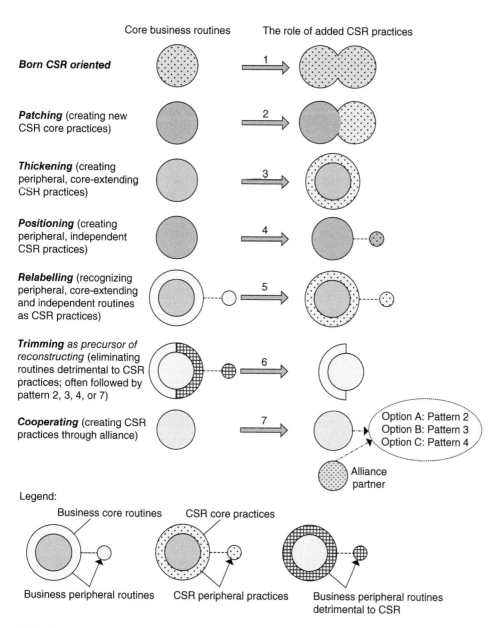

FIGURE 6.10 Professional organizing patterns

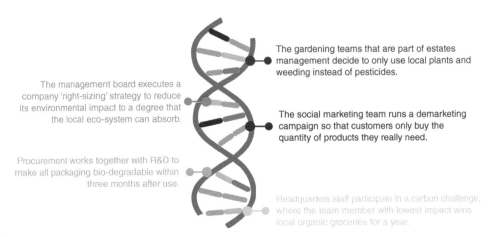

The gardening teams that are part of estates management decide to only use local plants and weeding instead of pesticides.

The management board executes a company 'right-sizing' strategy to reduce its environmental impact to a degree that the local eco-system can absorb.

The social marketing team runs a demarketing campaign so that customers only buy the quantity of products they really need.

Procurement works together with R&D to make all packaging bio-degradable within three months after use.

Headquarters staff participate in a carbon challenge, where the team member with lowest impact wins local organic groceries for a year.

FIGURE 6.11   Manifestation of a 'green' organizational DNA

CREDIT: Slidemodel.com

1. **Allocation of rewards.** Managers often control decisions about pay increases, promotions, or advancement within the organization. These particular decisions will communicate a strong message about the importance of sustainability performance. A professional manager who rewards such performance and financially backs ethical practices will promote organizational change towards professionalization.

2. **Criteria for selection and dismissal.** Recruiting, selecting, and hiring individuals with sustainability experience communicate these values both inside and outside the organization. Likewise, employees who are dismissed because of a lack of ethical integrity show other employees the importance of ethical criteria. We will discuss more about these processes in Chapter 17.

What is fascinating about the interplay of professional business structures and culture is their complementary nature. It has been claimed that creating an organizational infrastructure for professional business renders a professional culture unnecessary and vice versa. One fact is certain: structure and culture both have the potential to be enablers of organizational infrastructure for professional business.

ORGANIZATIONAL LEARNING

Continuous learning for ERS is crucial [52]. Organizational learning is based on both the learning of organizational members and that of the organization as a whole. The learning organization framework illustrates the practice of learning organizations through five main elements (Figure 6.12) [53].

An organization engaged in professional learning will need to foster ethical, responsible, and sustainable mental models among its organizational members. Such mental models may often clash with taken-for-granted business

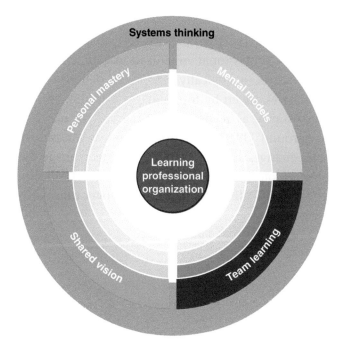

FIGURE 6.12   The learning organization framework

CREDIT: Slidemodel.com

assumptions. For instance, people might have to get used to 'We can't have our cake and eat it' as ERS mental models might clash with classic commercial business case mental models [54]. These members will need to achieve mastery of ERS in their personal sphere of influence, to develop professional competence, as we discussed in Chapter 2.

In order to generate learning beyond the individual, organizational learning requires organizational members to develop a shared vision of what the professional organization is meant to look like. It also requires the interweaving of individuals' learning processes through learning in teams. Finally, all these elements of organizational learning are to be connected through systems thinking as all of them together make the learning organization. Systems thinking is also required in order to place professional organizational learning in a larger moral, stakeholder, and planetary system, which it is meant to serve.

MANAGING CHANGE

Organizational change is often required to move towards a structure and culture undergirding improved ERS performance. Change usually occurs as continuous change in which organizations develop in a natural, often unintentional pattern of **incremental changes** over longer periods of time [55].

Organizational change
the process of changing structures and culture

Incremental change
is pervasive, distributed and often happens unintentionally, incrementally, and over an extended period of time

Incremental change is often 'pervasive' and distributed, spanning the entire organization. It therefore has the potential to generate a deeply rooted shift towards becoming a professional organization [56]. The opposite type of change, **episodic change**, typically consists of deliberate, centralized strategic change initiatives driven by top management [55]. Episodic change has been framed, for instance, as 'reengineering, right sizing, restructuring, cultural change, and turnaround' [39]. This section addresses professional management of organizational change, and we examine how to manage the change process of becoming a professional organization. Figure 6.13 illustrates both how human change typically influences performance over time, and typical stages of the change process.

Episodic change focuses, centralizes, and typically happens deliberately, driven by top management as part of strategic change initiatives

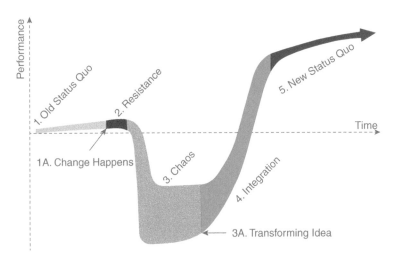

FIGURE 6.13   Performance throughout stages of the change process

SOURCE: Adapted from [57]; Slidemodel.com

Change management the process of transforming an organization towards a pre-set goal, by overcoming barriers and facilitating drivers for change

Change management is aimed at avoiding barriers, particularly employee resistance (corresponding to stage 2 in Figure 6.13) to episodic, radical change. When it comes to change for professional business, the process becomes even more complex as it then involves the various drivers and inhibitors to be found among the different stakeholder groups. When management decides to re-structure and move towards ERS, the process may create its fair share of internal and external resistance. Resistance is a normal phenomenon of any change. Why do some organizational transformations fail? There are eight typical errors occurring in change management [58]:

1. **Not establishing a great enough sense of urgency.** 'Well over 50% of the companies I have watched fail in this first phase,' change scholar Kotter [39] noted. He emphasized how difficult it is for leaders to move employees out of their comfort

zones. At least 75 per cent of a company's management must be convinced that business as usual is unacceptable for transformation to work. Top leadership must ensure managers are on board for successful professional management transformation. A sense of urgency for professional transformation can, for instance, be created by referring to the competitive threat of companies implementing ERS, or by upcoming regulation.

2. **Not creating a powerful enough guiding coalition**. A professional management 'coalition' typically will be those employees and managers who support the transformation. This coalition will grow as the process continues or the change may not be successful.

3. **Lacking a vision**. This refers to a clear vision that states that the future professional organization will push it on the path of organizational change.

4. **Under-communicating the vision by a factor of ten.** Frequently, change management stumbles over how it communicates the change. An error can be made in tending towards minimal communication with few attempts at letting employees know about the new vision. Similarly, the message might not be clear and understandable to most employees. Equally, the message may be clear, but may not be trusted as professional leaders act inconsistently with the message.

5. **Not removing obstacles to the new vision**. Obstacles inevitably arise once change is underway. For instance, the old structure may not allow for innovation and creativity in job positions. If a new structure is created, unconventional activities must be considered by leaders and given legitimacy. Overly hierarchical structures also may be an impediment and must be dealt with. For instance, Ricardo Semler decided to fire almost his entire senior management team as they did not support the change.

6. **Not systematically planning for and creating short-term wins.** Every organization undergoing a significant organizational change needs short-term successes to keep morale up. Part of the change process requires an achievable goal to be set within the first year.

7. **Declaring victory too soon.** Vision or momentum may be lost even when an organization achieves success in 'picking the lowest hanging fruits' over several years. Professional managers may feel like 'we've made it' and lose motivation to change further, never achieving the harder, more deep-rooted change.

8. **Not anchoring changes in the corporation's culture.** This final error occurs when progress towards professional management does not become an integrated part of organizations' structures and culture. Changing culture (and mindsets) towards the triple bottom line, stakeholder thinking, and moral excellence is a central aspect of change management.

These eight errors may occur when organizations are transforming their structures. Change management is a complex dynamic process and organizations must plan well and avoid pitfalls when they begin the move towards becoming a professional organization. Table 6.2 [59] presents a similar change model, centred on change for responsibility that closely relates to Kotter's dont's.

TABLE 6.2   Stages of CSR implementation

Stages of CSR Implementation	Explanation
1. Conduct a 'zero assessment'.	Identify current CSR practice (Cramer et al., 2004; Maignan et al., 2005).
2. Develop CSR goals within the organization's mission, vision, and strategy.	Identify what the organization wants to achieve and how to achieve it (Doppelt, 2003; Lyon, 2004; Were, 2003).
3. Gain top management support.	Senior managers determine strategy and without their support become critical barriers to CSR implementation (Doppelt, 2003; Were, 2003).
4. Gain employee support to ensure they own CSR as part of their work–life activities.	This requires involvement of a cross-section of employees in zero assessment and effective communication of CSR mission and vision, reinforced though training (Cramer et al., 2004, 2006; Maignan et al., 2005; Were, 2013).
5. Gain support from external stakeholders.	External stakeholders include groups affected by the organization or that affect the organization (e.g. suppliers, distributors, wider community). Selecting organizations with similar CSR beliefs helps to consolidate the reorientation of the business (Castka et al., 2004; Cramer et al., 2004; Maignan et al., 2005).
6. Prioritize change effort and focus on achieving it.	This is an acknowledgement of how the change implementation requires the application of finite management and other resources (Doppelt, 2003).
7. Measure progress and fine-tune the process.	CSR implementation is an iterative approach (Cramer et al., 2004; Porter and Kramer, 2006).
8. Anchor change.	Ensuring the organization's activities result in mutual benefits for it and the society in which it operates (Porter and Kramer, 2006; Were, 2003).
9. Reorder the implementation system.	Reordering reflects the continuous nature of the process, where states may occur simultaneously, shaped by the situations faced by the organization (Doppelt, 2003).

For full references to the citations in this table, see Lindgreen et al. [59].

PRINCIPLES OF PROFESSIONAL ORGANIZING

I.   Professional organizing involves **organizing yourself, structures,** and **dynamics**.

II. The '3D' of organizing oneself are **decluttering, delineating,** and **delivering**.

III. Professional **organizational architecture** integrates **structural elements** of responsible organizations (normative documents, programmes, departments, job positions, engagement platforms, communication tools, processes, procedures) into **organizational design patterns** (self-contained, horizontal, hollow, modular, virtual).

IV. A main goal of **organizational development** in a responsible organization must be to simultaneously reach or exceed benchmarks in triple bottom line performance, stakeholder value creation, and moral excellence.

V.   Professional organizing **dynamics** consist of organizing **patterns**, organizational **learning**, **culture**, and **change management**.

MANAGEMENT GYM: TRAINING YOUR PROFESSIONAL SIX-PACK

Knowing

1. Explain and relate the following terms: Sustainability report, whistleblowing hotline, values statement.

2. Explain and interrelate the following terms: Organizational learning, mental models, and systems thinking.

3. Look up the social responsibility or sustainability website of a company you find interesting and identify three of its professional organizing patterns.

Thinking

4. Look up the website of SEMCO or another company of your choice and assess where the company is located on the responsible business performance scale in the three dimensions of sustainability, responsibility, and ethics.

5. Imagine you were part of the management board committee of a major retailer in your country at the beginning of the Covid-19 outbreak. What re-organizing measures would you propose to the board to fulfil your professional, positive role in society?

6. Management of a building construction company claims that 'respecting LGBTQ+ is in our DNA'. In what kind of practices do you think this DNA might manifest?

Acting

7. Look at a company's responsibility or sustainability report and draw a figure of the responsible organizational architecture.

8. Apply the three Ds of being organized to one task in your private or professional life.

9. Use the 5S of workplace organizing to reorganize your computer.

Interacting

10. Talk to a manager (e.g. among your friends, family, and acquaintances, or on a professional social media network like LinkedIn) and ask them what it means for them to organize professionally, ethically, responsibly, and sustainably.

11. Interview someone (e.g. your course mate) about how they organize and compare this with your organizing style.

12. Use the Eisenhower matrix to identify a task that could be delegated and do so.

Being

13. Where would you place your natural delivery style on a continuum between 'cha bu duo' and being 'anally retentive'?

14. Do you prefer organic or mechanistic organizing?

15. Would you prefer working in a more hierarchical organization or one that is 'flat'?

Becoming

16. Have others told you that you sometimes over-organize or under-organize? What could you do to find a balance?

17. Would people describe you as an 'organized person'? Why (not)?

18. How do you think you should organize your work and private life to find harmony and happiness in both?

SOURCE: Adapted from [60].

PIONEER INTERVIEW
SIMON ZADEK

INTERVIEWER: OLIVER LAASCH

Simon Zadek is a co-creator of main stakeholder management standards like the AA1000 series. His *Harvard Business Review* article 'The path to corporate responsibility' outlines

(Continued)

the stages of organizational learning for responsibility, which have been discussed in this chapter.

What stage of professional organizing do you think organizations are typically on nowadays? Many major corporations, notably those stewarding premium brands, have reached the managerial level on many issues, beyond denial and compliance. A small number have strategic aspirations for selected aspects of their sustainability footprint that can be inverted to create business value. First-generation companies are starting without legacy

Courtesy of Simon Zadek

constraints and are racing ahead, albeit at smaller scale. Just a small number of companies, or more correctly their leaders, see that the real deal is one that has to include broad-ranging changes in our economic governance, and profound changes in our financial system.

How to reach scale? The simple answer is product, process, people, and public policy, the four Ps. New products, redesigned business processes, citizens who behave differently as consumers and voters, and public policies that shape markets to incentivize the right business behaviour.

Accountable organizations? Businesses are in general very accountable, but the right balance of what they are accountable for has been lost. Intended beneficiaries of private financial capital deserve a decent return, but not at any cost, just as fund managers should be incentivized but not to take excessive risk or to trade at the cost of the real economy. We need different accountability, not more or less, if sustained prosperity and reasonable equity is to be ensured. And no, we do not have that right balance of accountabilities today. We have made some gains, but the sway of history remains in the wrong direction.

QUESTIONS

1. How can you use the organizational development paths presented in this chapter to interpret Simon's first statement about the stage of professional organizing?

2. What parallels do you see between the four Ps of Simon's organizing and the professional organizing described in this chapter?

3. What are the implications of Simon's statement about 'accountability' for professional organizing?

PROFESSIONAL PROFILE
THOMAS HÜGLI

My name is Thomas and I am the Chief Communication and Corporate Responsibility Officer (CCRO) of AXA Winterthur, a leading all-line insurer in Switzerland.

Courtesy of Thomas Hügli

My responsibilities. The CCRO is a direct report to the CEO and has a dotted-line reporting relationship to the AXA Group CCRO in Paris, France. The CCRO role is not designed to be a full-time occupation, but rather a governance position. As one of AXA's primary voices on corporate responsibility (CR) and advisor to senior management, the CCRO drives and articulates our three-legged CR strategy (employee engagement, stakeholder management, flagship programme) at regional and local levels to position AXA as a responsible corporation, in order to achieve our ambition to become the preferred financial services company. Through effective leadership and in line with the Group CR strategy, he is responsible for building a strong CR strategic plan and targeted key performance indicators (KPIs) in order to embed CR into core business processes. This aims to provide proof of AXA's commitment and to leverage this proof in order to build trust among all of AXA's key stakeholders.

Organizing strategies. The company's mission, vision, values, and business strategy form the basis of our work, and they are therefore also reflected in the CR Charter and the CR Strategy. We conduct a self-assessment each year to see what progress we've made. This is based on economic, social, and environmental aspects, with reference to the Dow Jones Sustainability Index (DJSI), on which AXA Group has been listed since 2007. Important instruments in connection with conservation include our environmental strategy with its focus on climate protection and resource use, and our energy guideline, which defines the benchmarks for efficient, low-impact, and climate friendly use of energy at AXA Switzerland in order to meet the internal targets of AXA Group and comply with statutory provisions (Energy Act, CO_2 law, as well as applicable cantonal energy laws).

Organizational structures. As regards organizational structure, the Corporate Responsibility Committee defines, approves, and periodically reviews the CR strategy; ensures its integration into the overall company strategy; and approves the guidelines and directives, standards, and processes concerning CR management. The Committee meets twice a year and includes members of the Executive Board, the Chief Communication and Corporate Responsibility Officer (chair),

(Continued)

and the Head of Public Affairs and CR, who is in charge of implementing the CR strategy at the operational level. She and her team are part of the Communication and CR department. They work with CR ambassadors, who are responsible for implementing specific departmental activities, together with the department head. AXA Group issues an Activity and Corporate Responsibility Report, which also includes projects and key figures of AXA Winterthur.

QUESTIONS

1. What main organizing structures and dynamics can you see at play in Thomas's description?

2. What relationships can you see between organizing and strategizing in Thomas's work?

3. Would you say Thomas is a professional manager? If so, what makes him one? If not, why not?

TRUE STORY
WHAT AN UNPROFESSIONAL MESS!

Hi there. My name is Monica and I am an international supply chain manager at KitchCo, a medium-sized European company that produces kitchenware. My role revolves around the making and delivery of sales agreements. I mainly manage the relationship with our clients, mostly national and international retailers and ensure their order is delivered according to specifications.

Managing the/in chaos … Being junior in our sales and marketing team, I do not have the authority to sign the contract. Frankly, I am happy I don't have to. I am not sure I want

(Continued)

to have the responsibility for possibly making mistakes worth thousands, at times millions of euros. My line manager Callum, the head of sales, is the one who signs. Dealing with Callum is a rather stressful part of my job because, frankly, he's a mess. His office looks as if a bomb has exploded in there. As a consequence, he frequently loses documents in the chaos, or worse, he forgets that he actually had them.

What an opportunity! Two months ago something very exciting happened. I was able to secure an order from SellMart, a major international retailer to whom we had wanted to sell for years. They were known to be picky, but if we could do a good job on the first order, they promised to place a regular major follow-up order. Callum was excited. However, being busy with the daily nitty gritty, he did not read the contract and agreements thoroughly as he wanted to get it signed quickly. He seemed distracted and overloaded with filling in the performance reviews of everyone on his quite big team. Also, it appeared to me signing contracts was the least favourite part of his job. He often seemed to procrastinate reviewing and signing until the last moment before due date, meaning he had very little time left to check it thoroughly.

Bleeding money. This time it was bad, bad, bad! Callum checked the contract so sloppily that he did not notice several main clauses of contract fulfilment. To begin with, he missed that the quotation was meant to be calculated in USD, but he calculated it in euros. This meant that we were losing money on the contract from day one, as we were contractually obliged to sell at a price below our own costs. Also, he did not realize the quote should include all logistics costs for delivery to Barcelona. He simply assumed products would be (as with other contracts) delivered to Rotterdam, the much cheaper option.

When the shit hits the fan. We decided to 'beg for mercy' and called Annika, the buyer at SellMart, to ask for permission to adjust the quote to cover at least our costs. 'With all due respect, this is your problem', was her answer. Callum's reaction was to 'give her the finger'. Fortunately, we were not on a video call. But the problems didn't stop there, as Callum had missed that the contract had a clause demanding a particular shade of blue, to which our products were close, but not exact. So on top, KitchCo even had to pay an additional fine for non-compliance. Needless to say that there were no follow-up orders. This was embarrassing for KitchCo, for our team, for me, and one of the most stressful times I have lived through at work.

(Continued)

QUESTIONS

1. What organizational structure elements can you spot throughout the story?

2. What issues do you see with Callum's and maybe Monica's personal organizing practices? What would you do differently?

3. Make a list of the actors and of the way(s) in which their organizing and behaviour in this story is (un)professional.

4. In what ways do organizational structures and dynamics interact with personal organizing in this story?

5. How come Callum has not been fired yet? Have a guess at what kind of organizational dynamics might be at play here, keeping Callum in position in spite of his shortcomings.

DIGGING DEEPER: ORGANIZING EXTREMES

Earlier on we explored approaches to organizing at the extremes of mechanistic and organic organizing. In this section, we will briefly outline further extremes of organizing. The understanding of an organization varies greatly and opposing viewpoints often exist in parallel in organizations. For instance, one department in the same company might be led in a highly individualistic way, while another one relies on collectivist, culture-based interaction.

Differentiation, similar to Frederick Taylor's Division of Labour, means everybody takes the part of the work that allows them to specialize in work that best corresponds with their capabilities.	**Integration** is focused on organizing to re-assemble the specialized contribution to a coherent whole, usually a product, service, or a process.
Hierarchy relies on tight centralized structuring, including strict definitions of authority, lines of control, and communication.	**Holacracy, heterarchy, and anarchy** share an emphasis on dynamics, freedom, 'destructuring', flattening, decentralization, and local self-organizing.
Formal organizing refers to the explicitly established, defined and communicated organizational elements.	**Informal organizing**, sometimes called shadow organizing, refers to the implicit unspoken organizing that happens naturally.

Structural primacy refers to the recurrent patterns of organizational life that shape human behaviour.	Agency is human beings' capacity to act independently from structures.
Individualistic organizing stresses individual employees' performance and responsibility.	Collectivistic organizing stresses collective organizational level performance and responsibility as individuals can only act in groups.
Realism stresses non-negotiable universally applicable rules, laws, or standards as the main orientation for organizing that apply to everyone, with no room for reinterpretation.	Constructivism emphasizes that organizing is based on beliefs that are socially constructed between organizational members and other stakeholders.
Instrumentalism emphasizes organizing by a small group of dominant members who use others and the organization to accomplish goals.	Institutionalism emphasizes the intrinsic value of the organization as a whole as they become 'institutions' whose goals organizational members serve.

POINTERS

Which of these opposing viewpoints do you believe are compatible and how? You could also dig deeper into one of these viewpoints. For instance, you could explore anarchical organizing or how to organize a holocracy.

WORKSHEET

KOTTER'S TRANSFORMATIONAL CHANGE TOOL

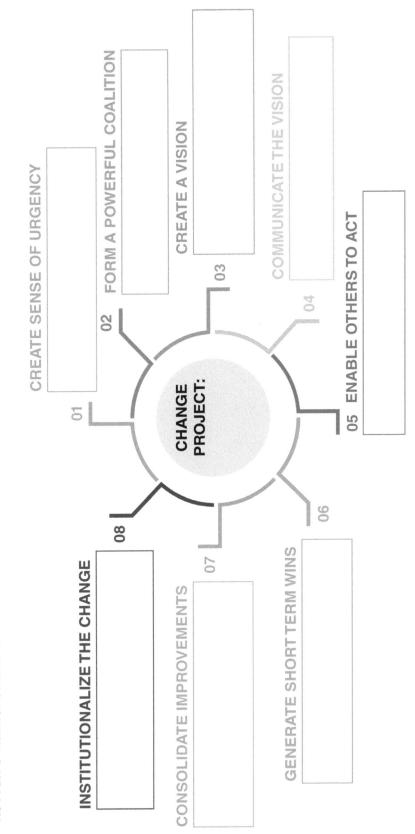

CREATE SENSE OF URGENCY

FORM A POWERFUL COALITION

CREATE A VISION

COMMUNICATE THE VISION

ENABLE OTHERS TO ACT

CHANGE PROJECT:

01

02

03

04

05

06

07

08

INSTITUTIONALIZE THE CHANGE

CONSOLIDATE IMPROVEMENTS

GENERATE SHORT TERM WINS

POINTERS

You can use this worksheet to plan a future change project, or to analyse why a past change project was successful or not.

REFERENCES

1. Gupta A, Raghunath A, Gula L, Rheinbay L, Hart M. *The decade to deliver: A call for business action*. New York: Accenture, 2019.
2. Caulkin S. Who's in charge here? No one. www.theguardian.com/business/2003/apr/27/theobserver.observerbusiness7 Published 2003. Accessed March 19 2020.
3. Baker M. Ricardo Semler: The radical boss who proved that workplace democracy works. http://mallenbaker.net/article/inspiring-people/ricardo-semler-the-radical-boss-who-proved-that-workplace-democracy-works Published 2016. Accessed March 19 2020.
4. Killian K, Perez F, Siehl C. *Ricardo Semler and Semco SA Thunderbird Case#*. A15-98–0024, 1998.
5. Semco. *Manual de sobrevivência*. São Paulo: Semco, 2020/2000.
6. Semco Style Institute. The simple manual on survival. https://semco.style/toolkit/alternative-controls/the-simple-manual-on-survival-sample Published 2020. Accessed March 20 2020.
7. Semco. Company history. www.semco.com.br/en/about-us Published 2020. Accessed March 20 2020.
8. Semler R. Why my former employees still work for me. *Harvard Business Review*. 1994, 72(1): 64–74.
9. Vogl A. The anti-CEO. *Across the board*. 2004, 41(3): 30–36.
10. Borges I. Why Semco doesn't want your company to be like Semco. https://corporate-rebels.com/guest-post-semco Published 2019. Accessed March 20, 2020.
11. Semler R. *Maverick! The success story behind the world's most unusual workplace*. New York: Random House, 1993.
12. Killian K, Perez F, Siehl C. *Ricardo Selmer and Semco SA* Phoenix: Thunderbird School of Management, 1998.
13. Koisser H. Harald Koisser macht Mut Folge 23: Führungslos erfolgreich. www.die-wirtschaft.at/die-wirtschaft/harald-koisser-macht-mut-folge-23-fuehrungslos-erfolgreich-98808 Published 2013. Accessed March 20 2020.
14. Semco Style Institute. Welcome to Semco Style toolkit. https://semco.style Published 2020. Accessed March 20 2020.
15. Semco Style Institute. Building careers on the fly. https://semco.style/toolkit/self-management/building-careers-fly-sample Published 2020. Accessed March 20, 2020.
16. Covey S. *The 7 habits of highly effective people*. New York: Free Press, 1989.
17. Heugens PP, Scherer GA. When organization theory met business ethics: Toward further symbioses. *Business Ethics Quarterly*. 2010, 20(4): 643–672.
18. BBC. 'Carbon cost' of Google revealed. http://news.bbc.co.uk/1/hi/7823387.stm Published 2009. Accessed July 29 2020.
19. Johri A. Open organizing: Designing sustainable work practices for the engineering workforce. *International Journal of Engineering Education*. 2010, 26(2): 278.
20. Kondō M. *The life-changing magic of tidying up: The Japanese art of decluttering and organizing*. Berkeley: Ten Speed Press, 2014.
21. Knowledge@Wharton. Marie Kondo at work: Can your office 'spark joy'? https://knowledge.wharton.upenn.edu/article/marie-kondo-work Published 2019. Accessed March 25 2020.
22. Fabrizio T, Tapping D. *5S for the office: Organizing the workplace to eliminate waste*. New York: Productivity Press, 2006.
23. Moulding E. *5S: A visual control system for the workplace*. Milton Keynes: Author House, 2010.

24. Lin A. Lean in real life: Tidying up with Marie Kondo. https://tulip.co/blog/lean-manufacturing/lean-in-real-life-tidying-up-with-marie-kondo Published 2019. Accessed March 25, 2020.

25. Blair GM. Personal time management for busy managers. *Engineering Management Journal.* 1992, 2(1): 33–38.

26. Oshagbemi T. Management development and managers' use of their time. *Journal of Management Development.* 1995, 14(8): 19–34.

27. Mintzberg H. *The nature of managerial work.* New York: HarperCollins, 1973.

28. Lussier R. *Management fundamentals: Concepts, applications, skill development* (4th edn). Mason: Cengage, 2008.

29. Straker D. Freud's psychosexual stage theory. http://changingminds.org/explanations/learning/freud_stage.htm Published 2020. Accessed March 26, 2020.

30. Lawrence PR, Lorsch JW. *Organization and environment: Managing differentiation and integration.* Irwin: Homewood, 1969.

31. Weber M. *Economy and society.* Berkeley: University of California Press, 1978.

32. Mintzberg H, Laasch O. Mintzberg on (ir)responsible management. In: Laasch O, Suddaby R, Freeman E, Jamali D, eds. *The research handbook of responsible management.* Cheltenham: Edward Elgar, 2020.

33. Trevino LK, Weaver GR, Brown ME. It's lovely at the top: Hierarchical levels, identities, and perceptions of organizational ethics. *Business Ethics Quarterly.* 2008, 18(2): 233–252.

34. Anand N, Daft RL. What is the right organization design? *Organizational Dynamics.* 2007, 36(4): 329–344.

35. HI USA. Blog. www.hiusa.org/about-us/hiusa-news/how-to-choose-hostel Published 2020. Accessed July 29 2020.

36. Sustainability. *About AT&T,* 2011.

37. Group W. CSO back story: How chief sustainability officers reached the C-suite. http://weinrebgroup.com/wp-content/uploads/2011/09/CSO-Back-Story-by-Weinreb-Group.pdf Published 2011.

38. Heaney SA. How to embed sustainability into the business enterprise? *Executive Forum – Boston College Center for Corporate Citizenship.* Blog, 2012.

39. Kotter JP. Leading change: Why transformation efforts fail. *Harvard Business Review.* 1995, 73(2): 55–67.

40. Ditlev-Simonsen CD, Gottschalk P. Stages of growth model for corporate social responsibility. *International Journal of Corporate Governance.* 2011, 2(3): 268–287.

41. Reidenbach RE, Robin DP. A conceptual model of corporate moral development. *Journal of Business Ethics.* 1991, 10(4): 273–284.

42. Zadeck S. The path to corporate social responsibility. *Harvard Business Review.* 2004, 82: 125–132.

43. Laasch O, Conaway RN. *Responsible business: Managing for sustainability, ethics and global citizenship.* Monterrey: Editorial Digital, 2013.

44. Hollender J. Net positive: The future of sustainable business. *Stanford Social Innovation Review.* 2015.

45. Ikea. What does being climate positive mean for IKEA? https://about.ikea.com/en/sustainability/becoming-climate-positive/what-is-climate-positive Published 2020. Accessed September 24, 2020.

46. Zadeck S. The path to corporate responsibility. *Harvard Business Review.* 2004, 82(12): 125–132.

47. Marks and Spencer. Marks & Spencer partners with infarm to bring urban farming to its London stores. https://corporate.marksandspencer.com/media/press-releases/5c2f8d61 7880b21084450f5e/marks-and-spencer-partners-infarm-to-bring-urban-farming-to-its-london-stores Published 2020. Accessed March 23 2020.

48. Yuan W, Bao Y, Verbeke A. Integrating CSR initiatives in business: An organizing framework. *Journal of Business Ethics.* 2011, 101(1): 75–92.

49. Hickman GR. *Leading organizations: Perspectives for a new era* (2nd edn). Thousand Oaks: Sage, 2010.

50. Schein E. *Organizational culture and leadership.* San Francisco: Jossey-Bass, 1985.

51. Sims RR. Changing an organization's culture under new leadership. *Journal of Business Ethics*. 2000, 25: 65–78.
52. Laasch O, Moosmayer D, Antonacopoulou E, Schaltegger S. Constellations of transdisciplinary practices: A map and research agenda for the responsible management learning field. *Journal of Business Ethics*. 2019, https://doi.org/10.1007/s10551-020-04440-5.
53. Senge P. *The fifth discipline: The art and practice of the learning organization*. New York: Random House, 1990/2010.
54. Hahn T, Figge F, Pinkse J, Preuss L. Trade-offs in corporate sustainability: You can't have your cake and eat it. *Business Strategy and the Environment*. 2010, 19(4): 217–229.
55. Weick KE, Quinn RE. Organisational change and development. *Annual Review of Psychology*. 1999, 50(50): 361–386.
56. Laasch O. An actor-network perspective on business models: How 'being responsible' led to incremental, but pervasive change. *Long Range Planning*. 2018, 52(3): 406–426.
57. Satir V, Banmen J. *The satir model: Family therapy and beyond*. Palo Alto: Science & Behavior Books, 1991.
58. Kotter JP. Leading change: Why transformation efforts fail. *Harvard Business Review*. 1995, 73(2): 59–67.
59. Lindgreen A, Swaen V, Harness D, Hoffman M. The role of 'high potentials' in integrating and implementing corporate social responsibility. *Journal of Business Ethics*. 2011, 99(1): 73–91.
60. Laasch, O., Moosmayer, D., & Antonacopoulou, E. P. (2023). The interdisciplinary responsible management competence framework: An integrative review of ethics, responsibility, and sustainability competences. *Journal of Business Ethics, 187*, 733–757.

CHAPTER 7

BEHAVING

OLIVER LAASCH AND ALEXANDRA BARRUETA

LEARNING GOALS

1. Analyse and understand ethical, responsible, and sustainable behaviours in organizations
2. Learn about human motivation, power, and team dynamics in organizations
3. Get to know extreme work behaviours and how to navigate them

WORRYING BEHAVIOURAL FACT

In a survey of over 2,000 people across the globe, 78 per cent witness incivility at work at least once a month, and 70 per cent witness it at least two to three times a month. Examples are insults, false rumours, dirty looks, social isolation, or being disruptive. The main drivers of such behaviours are stress at work, work overload, anger, weakened workplace relations, a disconnect through increased technology use, and a lack of self-awareness [1].

SPOTLIGHT

TROUBLE IN THE GOOGLE PARADISE
OLIVER LAASCH

'Google Campus' by AndyRobertsPhotos is licensed under CC BY 2.0

Google (aka Alphabet Inc.) is well known for going above and beyond when it comes to offering all the perks that keep organizational members motivated. Access to good food, health services from massages to on-site doctors, flexible work arrangements, free time for pet projects, allowing for family time, enabling a healthy balance between work life and private life, as well as the stylish and creativity-oozing Google Campuses can be seen to satisfy the physiological and safety needs of employees, in turn leading to a sense of belonging, high self-esteem, and personal fulfilment in the workplace [2]. Google also caters to higher motivational needs, such as self-realization in the workplace, by supporting employees in their career progression in and across the various technology businesses of the conglomerate, in a mind-boggling variety of career paths, and across global locations [3, 4].

However, over the last couple of years there has been the occasional but recurrent protest cloud hanging over the Google paradise. The trouble started with global employee walkouts in the thousands in 2018. They protested against the company's practices dealing with sexual misconduct, abuse of power, and general unhappiness with equity, diversity, and inclusion practices [5]. Since then similar protests have become a regular practice of Google employees, most recently protesting against the corporation's artificial intelligence work with the Israeli government [6] and the involvement in drone strike related technologies for the US government [7].

Google has long encouraged employees to speak up by using the 'don't be evil' motto and its code of conduct. However, ex-employees who had been fired after speaking up against Google's sales of cloud technologies to migration authorities claim that by doing so Google violates

(Continued)

its very own code of conduct and, with it, employee contracts [8]. Some employees claim there is a regular retaliation practice against workers who speak out against their employer's actions [9], including alleged firing for unionization movements and doing so illegally [10]. They claim that Google damages its own culture by cracking down on worker activism [11].

"moveon.org protest" by Photographing Travis is licensed under CC BY 2.0.

WORK LIFE AND ORGANIZATIONAL BEHAVIOUR

Professional management is embedded in our working lives and in how we and other people behave in organizations. On the one hand it is central to the lived experience of managers, the life at work while practicing management, including, for instance experiences of power, identity, inequality, and insecurity [12]. Therefore, the intention behind this chapter is to reconnect to how managers' vocational lives unfold through their engagement at work [13].

The following sections have elements of two main streams of organizational behaviour. On the one hand there is much of the 'traditional' **organizational behaviour** centred on how to deal with dysfunctional aspects of people's behaviour such as misbehaviours, stress, or lack of motivation. On the other hand, we will also cover 'positive' organizational behaviour, emphasizing aspects related to human flourishing, emotions like love and forgiveness, and altruism in the workplace [14–16].

Behaviour in organizations, of course, entails a wide variety of broader topics such as organizing structures, folleading, communication, and decision-making, each of which is covered in a dedicated chapter of this book. In this particular chapter, however, we will have a closer look at fundamental psychological and sociological aspects of management-related organizational behaviour, including motivation, power, deviance, and group behaviours (see Figure 7.1).

Managerial work
life describes the lived experience of people practicing management

Organizational behaviour
describes how people behave in organizations.

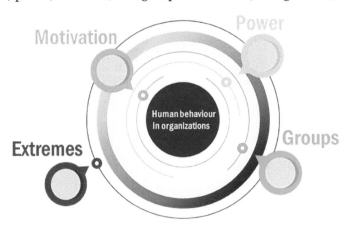

FIGURE 7.1   Organizational behaviour topics covered in this chapter

MOTIVATION

Why do we do *what* we do? Is it a self-drive that guides us or is it external factors out of our control? Maybe, it is both or something else entirely? Such questions related to work **motivation** have recently seen a resurgence with the growing popularity of working from home and all the challenges and opportunities this entails, including the opportunity to considerably reduce our work CO_2 footprint

Motivation
the willingness to do something often related to a person's desires or aversions

from commuting. A common heuristic for describing the role of motivation that performance depends on the interplay between someone's motivation and their competence (ability to carry out an activity effectively) is the following equation:

Performance = Function of (Competence × Motivation)

We will first introduce three traditional **theories of motivation** to then move on to two more contemporary theories.

Content theories of motivation explain 'what' motivates people

MASLOW'S HIERARCHY OF NEEDS

The arguably most popular content theory of motivation is Maslow's hierarchy of needs [17]. As illustrated in Figure 7.2, the hierarchy consists of five levels (or hierarchies) of human needs that range from the basic, low level (the need to eat or sleep) all the way up to the complex, high level (self-fulfilment). The underlying idea is that the lowest level of unsatisfied need is the most important to someone at any given time. For example, someone who is hungry is likely to be more driven by the need to eat than by the need to belong or be loved. An employee who is being paid below the living wage and is struggling to feed their family will be motivated more by a pay rise than by a commendation by their boss.

FIGURE 7.2 Maslow's hierarchy of needs with exemplary quotes

Adapted with permission.

SOURCE: Adapted from [17]

HERZBERG'S MOTIVATION–HYGIENE THEORY

Another need-based theory is Herzberg's motivation–hygiene theory. Rather than dividing needs into hierarchies, Herzberg distinguishes between hygiene needs (baseline needs like working conditions or security) and motivation needs (like recognition or growth). When people are unhappy with their job, they often state the *lack of* hygiene needs as a reason, but when they were satisfied, they tend to acknowledge the *presence of* motivation needs, so we can think of hygiene factors as *dissatisfiers* and motivation factors as *satisfiers*. Interestingly, this implies that at work you can be at the same time very satisfied and unsatisfied, motivated and unmotivated. You might be motivated because you have an interesting job that fulfils you, but at the same time dissatisfied because you feel the job is stressful, insecure, or you are not being paid enough. One interesting argument for working from home is that it puts many hygiene factors in the hands of the employees themselves and therefore reduces the dissatisfaction (at least that can be blamed on the organization) from not satisfying these needs.

FROM TAYLORISM TO THEORIES X, Y, AND Z

As early as 1911, Frederick Taylor theorized that employees would do as little work as possible unless they are motivated by financial gain [18]. As illustrated in Table 7.1, McGregor [19] called Taylor's and similar views 'Theory X'. He

TABLE 7.1   Theories X, Y, and Z

	Theory X	Theory Y	Theory Z
Motivation	People don't want to work and have to be motivated through money or threats.	People are self-motivated and want to work.	Self-driven to work but also driven by a desire to see organization succeed.
Leadership	Authoritarian, leaders exert absolute control.	Participative leadership while still retaining control.	More guide or coach than manager.
Power and authority	Leaders have most (if not all) power through coercion, control and threats.	Individuals are self-managed and self-controlled.	Implicit power through loyalty to collective, higher purpose.
Innovation	Security is more important than ambition.	Individuals can innovate.	The whole is better than the sum of its parts.
Responsibility	Avoidance. People need firm instructions and direction.	Acceptance. People seek out responsibility.	Collective. Responsibility is shared.

SOURCE: Adapted from [19, 22, 23]

argued that Taylor's view of employees in general being inherently lazy, disliking work, and being motivated by money alone was pessimistic at best, factually wrong at worst. Theory Y, on the other hand, described people putting in effort as natural – having self-direction and control and commitment to goals, wanting more responsibility and being capable of creativity and innovation – and that Theory X ignored all the good that could come from motivation. McGregor was also careful to point out that Theory X and Theory Y worked together, they were opposite ends of the same spectrum, which implied that, depending on the person and situation, both or either one can explain why we behave in a certain way [20]. The Japanese scholar Ouchi later added Theory Z, which focuses on the collective dimension of motivation. Theory X emerged from observations about Japanese management, which typically emphasizes trust among and with workers, loyalty and an interest in teamwork. Another important distinction is that McGregor's theories focused on the organization and management (leading) while Ouchi focused on the attitudes and responsibilities of the workers themselves (following) [21, 22].

PROCESS THEORIES OF MOTIVATION

Process theories of motivation help to understand how motivation 'happens' – for instance, through processes of self-determination or goal-setting. We will now briefly introduce four of the most popular process theories:

> Process theories of motivation explain the process of how people get motivated

- **Self-determination theory** [24] is centred on the idea that individual behaviour is self-determined through intrinsic motivational drivers. Intrinsic motivation (due to internal rewards like enjoyment or satisfaction from an activity) is in principle more powerful than extrinsic motivation (external rewards like a bonus or a good evaluation) [25]. Extrinsic rewards may even decrease motivation as they replace the more powerful intrinsic motivation [26]. Intrinsic core elements motivating people are autonomy (being self-directed), competence (mastering the action), and relations (attachment to others and higher purpose) [25, 27].

- **Expectancy theory** [28, 29] explains how people's motivation changes in relationship to expected outcomes. It implies that people have the highest motivation for the behaviour that promises the most favourable consequences, while also considering the effort necessary to reach those benefits.

- **Goal-setting theory** [30] is centred on how we are more motivated when working towards a clear goal (or set of goals). Goal-setting theory is well supported and indicates that a manager who sets clear goals, provides feedback, and increases the difficulty of goals when required will help increase motivation [30, 31]. Goal-setting theory closely relates to the 'management by objectives' style [32]. While goals in goal-setting theory are often understood as 'given' to subordinates by superiors, in practice, goals are often co-developed.

- An **equity theory of motivation** [33] explains a person's workplace motivation by their perception of the input (e.g. effort, work hours, education) output (e.g. wage, praise) ratio, which they compare to their peers'. If their own ratio is less favourable than that of peers, they perceive an unpleasant tension and engage in varieties of behaviours to reduce that tension. For instance, they might reduce their input, cognitively distort inputs/outputs (e.g. 'maybe, I am really not working *that* hard'), or in the most extreme case resign from the job.

A HUMANISTIC VIEW ON MOTIVATION

A humanistic view on motivation centred on the use of motivation to ensure work is good for people, and that people can be motivated as a whole human being at work

Now that we have a sound overview of both the content and processes of motivation it is important to critically reconsider how motivation has been framed and used. First, motivation has the potential to be understood as a management 'tool' to make people work harder, or to 'make them do what you want'. Such a 'use' of motivation instrumentalizes human beings as mere means to the end of performance, output, and ultimately profit. It robs people of their dignity, their inherent worth, which should be independent from their work productivity [34]. A more **humanistic** understanding of motivation, however, is centred on how creating the conditions for motivating work can increase a person's well-being, and to achieving personal fulfilment through it [35]. This implies a managerial shift in mindset from using motivation to ensure that 'people are good for work' to using motivation to ensure that 'work is good for people'.

Secondly, motivation, particularly of managers and business leaders, has often been presented as if it should be centred on a very narrow set of contents of motivation that represent only a part of human nature. Evolutionary theory suggests that human beings have four main motivational drives that explain their behaviour: the drive to acquire (e.g. to grow a company), to defend (e.g. to protect your market share from competitors), to bond (e.g. to form friendships at work), and to comprehend our place in the environment (e.g. to gain personal insights through work) [36]. It is worrying that conventional management theory and business school teaching's mantras like 'profit first' (acquire) or 'beat the competition!' (defend) are stressed as legitimate motivations, while the drives to bond ('it's nothing personal, it's just business'), and comprehend ('don't overthink this') are often delegitimized as 'unprofessional' for people in business. Teaching this behaviour in business schools may well have turned in a self-fulfilling prophecy, creating a type of two-drive managers with almost psychopathic traits [37].

POWER

Power is ubiquitous [38], it is everywhere around us and in us, a pervasive aspect of our social structures, including organizations and society as a whole [39]. Practices like those of management produce and reproduce power [39, 40]. For instance, the practice of enormous executive payments, (re)produces inequality between rich and poor, and therefore the skewed power relations between the 'top and bottom'

Power is everywhere and may take the form of influence over others or of influencing with others

During the football World Cup in Qatar, the football association FIFA decided to wield their power over players by advising their referees to give a yellow card to any player wearing a One Love bracelet in support of LGBTQ+ inclusion. Such a gesture would have meant further unwanted attention to the suppressive power structures upheld against same sex relationships by the Qatari government, with FIFA already being under pressure for deciding to hold the World Cup in a country notorious for human rights abuses, and with one of the worst environmental impacts in the history of the World Cup [45]. Resistance against being silenced came in many forms, from whole teams symbolically covering their mouths, and major sponsorships being withdrawn in protest, to journalists provocatively wearing the bracelet during interviews [45].

of societies [41]. Power can be negative – for instance, it keeps a 'bad regime' like the fossil fuel industry in place, but it may also be a positive, generative force – for instance, when it serves as the 'glue' that holds together a business in times of crisis [39]. Power structures and power relations come in the form of organizational rules or how resources (e.g. financial or time) are commonly allocated to people. Depending on how these power structures affect different groups of people, they may be either one, a source of empowerment or a source of disempowerment and suppression. Individuals and groups can actively generate and use power in three different, but interrelated ways [42–44]:

- **'Power over'** is centred on obtaining and maintaining influence over others, to 'make others do things' that serve the actor's interest.

- **'Power with'** revolves around the idea that power is generated through interaction between actors that co-define shared interests and co-generate power to pursue them together.

- **'Power to'** do or achieve something is centred on the notion of power as a means to something else, a generative force that can make things (happen).

The employee walkouts at Google are an excellent example for how these three patterns of power interact in practice. Employees attempted to generate the 'power to' effect 'real change' in relationship to perceived sexism, sexual harassment, racism, and inequality-exacerbating practices. They attempted to do so using 'power with' the thousands of co-workers joining the protests. The attempt at gaining 'power over' Google's practices, however, partly backfired, as opposing parts of Google's management made their own 'power over' move by demoting two of the main protest organizers. One of them, 'Claire Stapleton, a marketing manager at YouTube, said she was demoted and told to take medical leave, even though she wasn't ill' [47]. As illustrated in Table 7.2, we can distinguish two divergent views on power in greater detail on how power is practiced, the processes of influence, and the role of conflicts like the one in this case.

TABLE 7.2 Divergent views on power

	Influence over others	Influencing with others
Root metaphor	Power over (coercive control)	Power with (coactive collaboration)
Nature of power	An object, something one has, a capacity or resource	An effect, something one does, a process or practice
Core practice	Overpowering and controlling others	Emancipating and empowering each other
Process of influence	One-sided influence increasing one's power: dividing power	Mutual influence increasing joint power: generating power
Role of conflict	Conflict as threat to existing power structures	Conflict as opportunity for fairer power relations

SOURCE: Based on [38, 42, 46]

For professional management, it is crucial to exert influence in a network of stakeholders and actors [32], some of whom you can team up to 'influence with' and others who you might have to gain influence over. To do so you might want to consider which sources of power to tap into. Here are the five main sources illustrated by short examples [49]:

1. **Legitimate power** (legal or contractual relationship). An Italian retailer insists that a manufacturer takes back goods that are not compliant with European minimum environmental standards and receives a contractually agreed fine for late delivery.

2. **Coercive power** (controlling punishment). A weapons producer abstains from doing business with a potential customer under suspicion of human rights abuses.

3. **Reward power** (controlling rewards). A company lobbying for extended LGBTQ+ rights might financially support a political party's election campaign with related legislation on their agenda.

4. **Referent power** (appealing personal characteristics). Charismatic pioneers like Ann Roderick from The Body Shop or Dean Anderson from InterfaceFlor have influenced industry peers to adopt sustainable management practices.

5. **Expert power** (expertise and knowledge). A net positive management expert influences entire organizations to reorganize their management practices to restore the natural environment.

Please note that these 'sources' of power are strongly related to the 'power over others' perspective.

EXTREME WORKPLACE BEHAVIOURS

Workplace behaviours that are unusual, abnormal or in other ways extreme are a core concern for professional management to address and they often hit close to home. We will focus on deviant behaviours that are not the norm, and toxic behaviours that frequently lead to dysfunctional workplaces [50–52].

DEVIANT BEHAVIOUR

Deviance means to err from what is considered 'normal' [53]. When someone within an organization (in leading or following roles) purposely breaks customs, policies, or rules we say that they are engaged in **deviant behaviour** [54]. Figure 7.3 provides examples of typical deviant behaviours. Refusing to work, stealing, sabotaging a product launch, spreading malicious rumours, calling in sick (when not actually sick) or even watching pornography at work are all considered negatively deviant behaviours [55, 56].

Deviant behaviour purposely breaking customs, policies, or rules, out of either positive or negative intentions

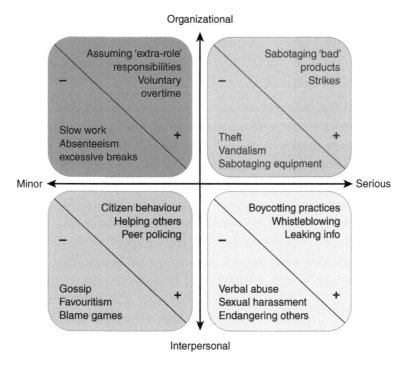

FIGURE 7.3 Types and examples of negative and positive deviance

SOURCE: Based on [54, 56, 57]

For instance, a study in the USA found, that three out of every four employees reported having stolen at least once from their employer [58]. It is of vital importance that we not only understand these behaviours and their underlying causes, but also how to avoid them. Not enough pay, social pressures from colleagues, bad attitudes, job uncertainty or ambiguity, unclear or unfair rules, lack of perceived justice or simply the violation of employee trust are all considered to significantly increase negative deviant workplace behaviour [59]. Workplaces that have higher employee satisfaction, better perceptions of their managers and an environment that is considered 'fair' have fewer incidents of deviant behaviour [55, 60].

Conversely, there is much potential in encouraging **positive deviance** [61, 62]. Practitioners engaging in positive deviance behave in a norm-violating way, but they do so for some form of greater good, honourably and constructively, so to say [56, 63]. Examples of positive deviant behaviours include whistleblowing, speaking out against immoral superiors, or engaging in 'extra-role' behaviours like helping others [64, 65], and voluntary **organizational citizenship behaviours** [51]. It might also include major or also minor rebellious behaviours like 'spitting into the shrimp salad' when everyone is watching at a company party to protest against this environmentally unsustainable food choice [66]. Going beyond social and environmental industry norms is also positive deviance [67]. The power of positive deviance is that it may be a force for positive transformation, possibly raising the bar to achieve more ethical, responsible, and sustainable standards of what *is* normal.

TOXIC WORKPLACE BEHAVIOURS

Toxic workplace behaviours describe individuals' (in leading or following roles) destructive behavioural habits that may render themselves and their environment dysfunctional [68–70]. Such behaviours may include, for instance, unjustified micromanagement, humiliating others, and passive-aggressiveness [68].

The consequences of toxic followership and leadership [71] are manifold. They may discourage organizational citizenship behaviour [51], increase negative workplace deviance [72], and negatively impact workplace satisfaction and commitment [73]. Such behaviours may spread and result in a downward spiral of increasingly toxic, dysfunctional workplaces and organizations [74, 75]. People working in such toxic environments have been found to suffer from a variety of negative consequences like 'impaired judgment, irritability, anxiety, anger, an inability to concentrate and memory loss' [50]. Toxic behaviour and toxic leadership in particular may be rooted in mental health conditions, and people engaging in toxic behaviour may need professional help just like the people suffering from their behaviours, but in a different way. Particularly, narcissist, manic depressive, passive aggressive and emotionally disconnected leader behaviours can have their origin in underlying mental health conditions as illustrated in Table 7.3 [76]. People displaying these behaviours may often not be aware of them.

Positive deviance
a behaviour or practice erring from the norm for an honourable reason and/or positive outcomes

Organizational citizenship behaviours
positive contributions to the organization, usually outside their job-description

Toxic workplace behaviours
exhibit dysfunctional and destructive characteristics

TABLE 7.3 Potentially pathological toxic behaviours

Type	Behaviour	Coping recommendations
Narcissist	Selfish, inconsiderate, demand excessive attention, feel entitled, pursue power and prestige at all cost.	Convey respect. Acknowledge their need to be recognized and accepted. Show empathy.
Manic depressive	Contagious energy and ebullience, talent to draw people to them, prone to volatile outbursts, behavioural extremes (very good or very bad).	Get them to go to psychotherapy and take medication?
Passive aggressive	Express negative feelings indirectly, shy away from confrontation, are outwardly accommodating but obstructive in an underhand way.	Confront passive-aggressive behaviours consistently, point out inconsistencies. Never argue or correct denials, just back away, leaving them to reflect.
Emotionally disconnected	Literal-minded, display little imagination, are unable to describe or recognize their feelings. They have difficulty interpreting emotional signals from others.	Openly communicate feelings and the reasoning behind them. Work with them to establish coping routines and mechanisms.

SOURCE: Adapted from [76]

It is management's professional responsibility to counteract toxicity, but what can be done about toxic colleagues? A first step is spotting toxic behaviours and practice in others (or yourself). Detecting toxicity is a precondition for immunity against the 'allure of toxic leaders' [46]. Once this has been achieved you can take action to 'detox' – for instance, by actively 'managing' your dysfunctional leader [153], or, if you are in a position to do so, to even coach them [76]. Table 7.4 provides an overview of common toxic behaviours, corresponding to different types of toxic personalities and coping tactics.

GROUP AND TEAM BEHAVIOURS

Working in **groups** is an ever-present aspect of managerial work lives and crucial to management effectiveness. On the one hand, most people strive for acceptance and avoid group exclusion [80]. Feelings of belonging are strongly related to motivation and work satisfaction [81]. Well-designed, closely knit, well-incentivized, functioning groups are found to be immensely effective [82]. On the other hand, when people don't identify with a group they are part of, it can lead to conflict, lower motivation, and reduced organizational citizenship behaviours [83]. Sometimes, when we have very strongly identifiable groups within an organization, we see the members of our group as being better than everyone else. This is called **ingroup favouritism**, a clique-like behaviour. Everyone who isn't part of our group or belongs to another group is part of the outgroup. This strong sense of group identity becomes problematic when it causes conflict, animosity, and fierce conflict between different groups within the same organization.

Group
a set of people who 'belong together' – for instance, due to a shared sense of identity, similar characteristics, or close relations

Ingroup favouritism
describes behaviours based on the idea that members are better and outsiders are all the same

TABLE 7.4   Toxic behaviours and how to cope with them

Type	Behaviours	Coping recommendations
The self-promoter	• Changes behaviour according to who is present. • Won't accept responsibility for mistakes. • Will help (if there is something in it for them). • Accepts praise and credit (even if they don't deserve it). • Acts only in own best interest.	• Try to stay objective; is the behaviour harmful or just annoying? • Offer consistent, balanced, feedback. • Talk about what self-promotion activities are acceptable.
The abusive supervisor	• Ridicules followers. • Makes followers do extra (not in work description). • Inconsiderate of followers' work–life balance. • Gossips and speaks poorly about followers. • Publicly shames followers. • Reminds people of past mistakes and failures. • Tells followers they aren't good enough.	• Build awareness by engaging in open dialogue. • Suggest management training. • Hold an intervention with other employees. • In extreme cases, leave.
The unpredictable one	• Prone to outbursts. • Lets their mood define workplace climate. • Lets mood define how they speak to people. • Expresses anger without expressing underlying reason. • Causes others to attempt to 'read' moods, to gauge how to react. • Affects emotions of others. • Difficult to gauge approachability as it often changes.	• Use the sandwich method if you need to deliver bad news or criticism: good news, bad news, good news again. • Communicate how their behaviour affects you. • Remain as calm as possible when outbursts occur. • Walk away if necessary to give them time to calm down.
The narcissist	• Exhibits personal entitlement. • Takes for granted they deserve to be at the top. • Believes they are more capable than everyone else. • Believes they are special. • Thrives on compliments and overt admiration.	• Use flattery if you think it will help. • Phrase demands by telling them how it will help them. • Be positive before offering negative or critical feedback. • Maintain your expectations, they are unlikely to change even if it bothers you or others.
The authoritarian	• Controls how tasks are completed. • Invades privacy (for the sake of control). • Does not allow for new methods or ideas. • Ignores ideas they disagree with. • Inflexible with workplace policies, even in special circumstances. • Wants to be the one to decide whether something is important or not.	• Praise their attention to detail. • Offer ideas in a non-critical way. • Provide extra details to ease their fear of ambiguity. • Give in if the situation or task doesn't really affect you (choose your battles). • Do not take it personally.

SOURCES: Based on [76, 78, 79]

'McDonald's' by MatHelium is licensed under CC BY-NC-ND 2.0.

'Why sustainability is a team sport' reads the headline of an article on the Greenbiz outlet. The text argues that CEOs and C-suite executives often have little power to implement changes unless they get the thousands of different teams motivated and involved that make an organization. McDonald's vice president for corporate responsibility illustrates this further by drawing attention to the fact that the vast marjority of McDonald's outlets are 'owned and operated by independent business people … They have a lot of power in our system. That means we can't dictate from on high' [84].

https://search-production.openverse.engineering/image/3f6d18dc-81cb-47c2-930b-1b84d7fdf3a7

We call groups centred on the achievement of a particular goal a **team**. The process of team development typically runs through five stages (see Figure 7.4) [85–87]. Forming is the honeymoon stage when members are excited to start and get to know other members. Relationships begin to develop but the team isn't very productive yet. Once the initial excitement wears off, we enter the storming stage. Conflict may develop, personalities may clash, members may question leadership or authority. These 'growing pains' are normal and necessary. Once conflicts can be resolved in a healthy way, individual strengths start to shine through, delegation becomes more common, and everyone begins to settle into teamwork in the norming phase. In stage four, performing, ideally teams are working well and are performing according to their group goals. However, this is also where things might get tricky again. If you've skipped a previous stage (particularly storming in order to avoid conflict) the performing stage might not materialize. If so, make sure to go back to previous stages and redo what was missing. Finally, once the project is over, adjourning occurs. The team disbands, new teams are formed, and the process is repeated.

Core to teamwork are the complementarities and synergies that can arise from people working together. There are nine roles crucial to a team's effectiveness and goal achievement (see Figure 7.5) [88]. Members performing one of these roles will have a unique set of both strengths and weaknesses. These weaknesses are

Team
a group of interdependent people who work together to achieve a goal

'allowable' as they are traits or behaviours that in some contexts are seen as weaknesses but in the right role are just a trade-off that comes with the role's strength. As an example, if you are in the team worker role, to avoid confrontation is an allowable weakness, as it aligns with the strength of being cooperative. If you were in the 'shaper' role, however, avoiding conflicts would not be an allowable weakness, as it does not go well with the role's main strength of being challenging. One person can perform any given role, or multiple roles within a team and, as a person develops, their roles can even change. The ideal team is well balanced and includes and makes space for all the unique roles.

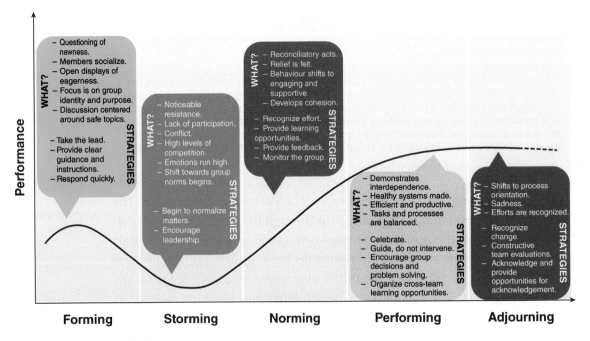

FIGURE 7.4   Phases of team development

SOURCE: Adapted from [85, 87]

Diverse teams have often been praised for their complementarities. At the same time, there is the need for equality and inclusion of women in the workplace. Both forces come together in all-female enterprises like the interior design agency Roar led by Pallavi Dean who describes the strength of her very homogenous female team: 'I've come across designers who are driven by ego and style, but women, I've found, have a much different approach, coming from a more empathetic place. Of course, there are men who are detail-orientated and women who are macro-thinkers, but women, in general, biologically we're nurturers and carers' [89]. On the other hand, there might also be conflict emerging from similarly homogeneous team compositions

Action

Has drive to overcome obstacles.
- **Strengths:** Challenging, dynamic, thrives on pressure.
- **Weakness:** Prone to provocation. Offends people's feelings.

Shaper

Turns ideas into actions and organizes tasks.
- **Strengths:** Practical, reliable, efficient.
- **Weakness:** Somewhat inflexible. Slow to respond to new possibilities.

Implementer

Finds errors, polishes and perfects.
- **Strengths:** Painstaking, conscientious, anxious.
- **Weakness:** Inclined to worry unduly. Reluctant to delegate.

Completer Finisher

Thought

Generates ideas and solves hard problems.
- **Strengths:** Creative, imaginative, free-thinking.
- **Weakness:** Ignores incidentals. Too preoccupied to communicate effectively.

Planter

Sees all options and judges accurately.
- **Strengths:** Sober, strategic and discerning
- **Weakness:** Lacks drive and ability to inspire others. Can be overly critical.

Monitor Evaluator

Provides rare knowledge and skills.
- Strengths: Single-minded, self-starting, dedicated.
- **Weakness:** Contributes only on a narrow front. Dwells on technicalities.

Specialist

People

Clarifies goals, delegates effectively.
- **Strengths:** Mature, confident, identifies talent.
- **Weakness:** Can be seen as manipulative, offloads own share of work.

Coordinator

Listens and averts friction.
- **Strengths:** Cooperative, perceptive and diplomatic
- **Weakness:** Indecisive in crunch situations. Avoids confrontation.

Teamworker

Explores opportunities, develops contacts.
- **Strengths:** Outgoing, enthusiastic, communicative.
- **Weakness:** Over-optimistic, loses interest once initial enthusiasm expires.

Resource Investigator

FIGURE 7.5   Team member roles

SOURCE: Adapted from [88]

as exemplified by the experience of Samantha Brick. She founded a women-only TV company in order to break through the glass ceiling in male-dominated TV production, but ironically crashed due to the destructive workplace dynamics unfolding in her team: 'Though I will not absolve myself of all guilt, I believe the business was ruined by the destructive jealousy and in-fighting of an all-female staff. Their selfishness and insecurities led to my company's demise. When I needed the so-called "Sisterhood", believe me, it just wasn't there' [90].

Psychological safety in groups is not only crucial for group performance [91], but also a crucial element of managing for diversity and inclusion. Psychological safety allows the unique individuals that make a diverse team to express their unique characteristics, heritage, and identity, including elements like race and ethnicity, gender and sexual orientation, as well as background and family status. Figure 7.6 illustrates different group dynamics depending on the status of psychological safety and group performance standards [92]. It can be used, for instance, to assess a working group of yours, in your job or for a university assignment, by writing down observations of your group dynamics in the respective quadrant. The most favourable outcomes are achieved in the upper right quadrant, where both psychological safety and performance standards are high. If your group is not in this quadrant, what can you do to get everyone there? Do you think there might be differences in the psychological safety felt by different group members. If so, why? You can use arrows to indicate measures that would take you from the zone you are currently in to the learning zone.

> **Psychological safety** describes the situation in a group where members feel safe to speak up freely without fear of negative consequences

PRINCIPLES OF BEHAVING IN ORGANIZATIONS

I. **Organizational behaviour** describes how people behave in organizations and is a core aspect of managerial work life, both in the form of one's own behaviour and that of others.

II. **Motivation** is willingness to do something. Popular content theories of motivation include Maslow's hierarchy of needs, Herzberg's motivation-hygiene framework, Theories X, Y, and Z. There are also theories of the motivation process, such as goal-setting and expectancy theory.

III. **Deviant behaviours** and **toxic workplace behaviours** cause friction within the organization and may lead to positive or negative change.

IV. When **working in teams** it is important to understand the phases of **team development**, **roles of individual team members**, and **psychological safety** in order to create inclusive, effective, and responsible teams.

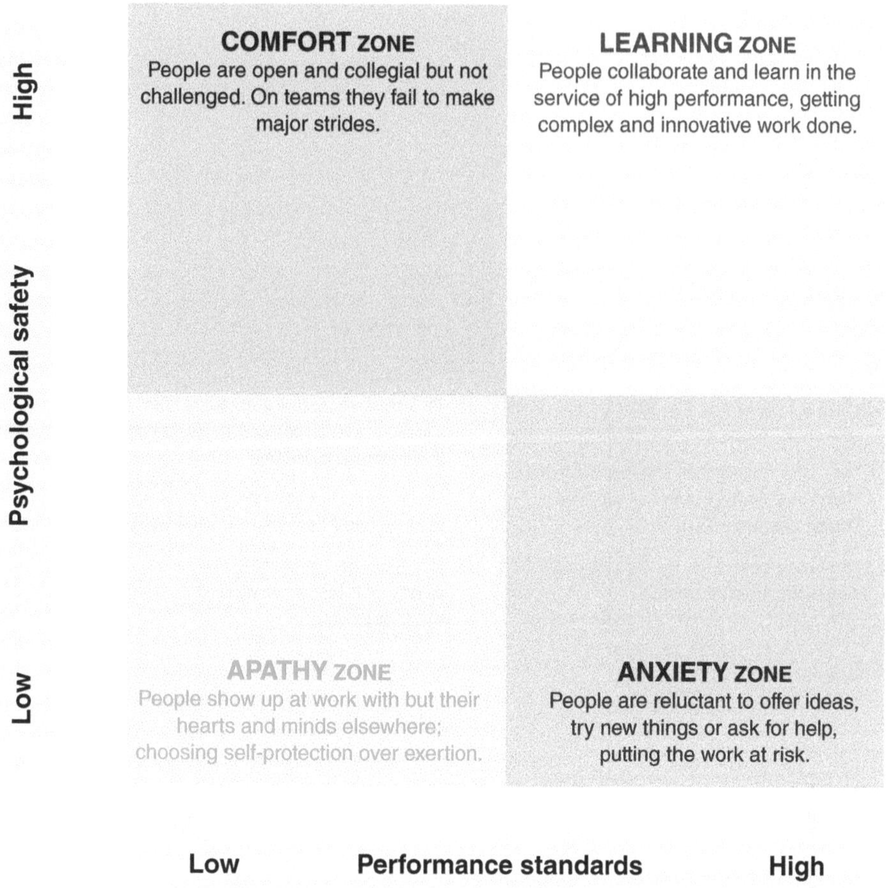

FIGURE 7.6   Psychological Safety and Team Dynamics

IMAGE SOURCE: Adapted from https://amycedmondson.com/psychological-safety-%E2%89%A0-anything-goes and Edmondson, A. (1999). Psychological safety and learning behavior in work teams. *Administrative Science Quarterly*, 44(2), 350–383.

MANAGEMENT GYM: TRAINING YOUR PROFESSIONAL SIX-PACK

Knowing

1. What common elements can you identify among Maslow's hierarchy of needs, Theories X and Y, and self-determination theory?

2. Skim read the chapter again to find out the different roles conflict plays in folleading and organizational behaviour.

3. Access Chaleff's follower typology and compare it to Kelley's. What main differences and similarities can you identify?

Thinking

4. Brainstorm to identify ten potential moral issues for each leading and following role.

5. Allsafe production team leaders have recently been trained to always behave as team coaches? What are the implications of this move from a situational leadership perspective?

6. Imagine your working group has run into a situation where one member has stopped to contribute and accuses another member of being a dictator. How could you analyse this dynamic using concepts covered in this chapter?

(Continued)

Acting

7. Look at five different online petitions and decide which one to follow and sign.

8. Write a ten-item code of ethics for responsible followership.

9. Motivate yourself using goal-setting theory: establish a personal goal and divide it into smaller, more attainable mini-goals. Write a concise, clear and timely plan. (Bonus points if your goal helps with a good cause!)

Interacting

10. Talk to someone you know who is often in a leading position and find out what they say, and which type of leading, among the ones introduced in this chapter, they practice.

11. Form a small group and discuss your motivators. What drives each person? What motivational theory (or theories) best explains each individual? How do you explain the differences (or lack thereof)? Discuss.

12. Assume a follower role in a situation where you would normally have led. Listen to others, follow instructions, and observe what happens to others and to you.

Being

13. Think of a time when your behaviour has been deviant. How did it make you feel? What was the outcome?

14. Who is your favourite 'rebel' character (can be real, from a book, movie, etc.)? How and why did you identify with the character?

15. What kind of power do you possess in which situations (e.g. expert, reward, power, etc.)?

Becoming

16. Think about one situation when you had to lead (this could be either in a private or a professional role). Do you think others would describe you as a responsible leader? Why?

17. Identify one negative power structure which either suppresses you or which you benefit from. How could you develop power to counteract?

18. Identify your ideal leader and follower profiles. What kind of folleader do you want to be? How can you develop competence to be more in line with those profiles?

SOURCE: Adapted from [93].

PIONEER INTERVIEW
DENISE ROUSSEAU

INTERVIEWER: OLIVER LAASCH

Denise Rousseau is one of the most influential organizational behaviour scholars. In particular, her work on trust in organizations, the psychological contract, and evidence-based management is not only academically groundbreaking, but also of enormous practical relevance.

The psychological contract (PC) is an individual's system of beliefs (or mental model if you prefer) regarding an exchange relationship between that person and another. The other may be a manager, team, employer, or some other entity with which the person interacts. Ethical concerns are the heart of the PC in that

Courtesy of Denise Rousseau

www.heinz.cmu.edu/faculty-research/profiles/rousseau-denisem

(Continued)

people form beliefs regarding what is appropriate reciprocity, the obligations they and the other party are committed to fulfil to each other.

PC beliefs over time reflect the quality of the exchange, including whether higher-order goals and values are met in employment, marriage, friendship, or community ties. In low-quality exchanges only limited goals and values may be served, perhaps in working for Uber or the Amazon warehouse. In high-quality exchanges, deeper human needs for growth and values related to service and community may be served, perhaps for those performing public service roles. EDI concerns reflect a higher-order set of values like safety or interpersonal respect and thus add depth and value to the PC exchange.

Numerous forms of PC exist, more arm's length and economic in some settings and more relational in others. Labour law contributes to employee beliefs in obligations and of course those vary widely by country and, in the US, by state.

How to *not* violate the psychological contract. PCs reflect a vulnerability in that we act today in anticipation of a commensurate response by the other party to the exchange. If either fails to fulfil its 'perceived obligations' the other can be harmed. Avoiding harms to our exchange partners is a fundamental feature of reciprocity in human society. Reciprocity builds trust and creates resources we don't have on our own.

Violation means wilful failure to keep or honour one's obligations. Most often we think about it in terms of employers who fail to keep commitments employees understand them to have made regarding everything from job security to respectful treatment. There are many reasons why an exchange partner might not be able to meet its obligations (health issues, business constraints, etc.) but 'wilful' violation occurs when one party has the capacity to honour its commitments and out of self-interest chooses not to. Downsizing or closing a plant while the business is strong is exploitive, even if done for 'future strategic reasons'. There are alternatives the employer is choosing to ignore. The resulting violation in the eyes of employees generates anger and losses for employees that are unjustifiable in their eyes. Acknowledging the existence of PCs offers a basis for making changes that honour the spirit of the deal even when all its terms cannot be met. In recent years, employers have often chosen to ignore those obligations. A good employer enhances its reputation by making adjustments in a way that shows care for the well-being of its workforce.

Practicing evidence-based management. The key features of managers who make decisions based on evidence are these: using multiple sources of evidence *and* paying attention to the trustworthiness or quality of the evidence. Four types of evidence are pertinent to management decisions: organizational evidence (using reliable organizational data, quantitative and qualitative, that are checked to reduce errors and increase their accuracy and relevance to decisions); scientific evidence (bodies of research supporting use of specific management practices, like compensation systems or selection processes); stakeholder evidence (concerns expressed by people affected

(Continued)

by decisions, from workers to clients and the community); and practitioner evidence (insight experience practitioners have regarding effective solutions or ways to make a decision).

A great example of an evidence-based management practice is the consulting firm that developed an intervention to promote psychological safety (PS) in organizations, first by commissioning a rapid evidence assessment of the scientific literature on predictors of PS, identifying organizational conditions that promote or impede PS, asking experienced practitioners how they have reinforced PS in their work units, and finally building stakeholder focus groups to capture the lived experience of high and low PS. The firm then combined information into guidance for interventions that it then developed and implemented. Last, the efficacy of these interventions was assessed using an established PS measure developed by Amy Edmondson, allowing the firm to learn what worked well and what didn't.

Stakeholder concerns are perhaps the most neglected aspect of evidence gathering in management decisions. Managers often choose to ignore stakeholders they fear will attempt to influence their decisions or impose constraints. This avoidance is at the heart of decisions we come to view as unethical. Attention to stakeholders upfront (not after the fact) is critical in broadening our thinking about the implications of the decisions we make.

The crucial role of trust. Trust is the willingness to be vulnerable to the actions of another, and it is *the* social lubricant. An exchange of goods and services, or labour and compensation has no future without trust. Low trust requires vigilance and tight controls while high trust is more open and cooperative. The psychological contract is inherent to trust in that if we have exchanges in which the parties work to avoid harming each other and meeting important needs we have the basis of sustained trust. Stakeholders know how a company treats its workers and its contractors. It is important evidence of the trustworthiness of the company and a reason why a reputation for trustworthiness is so valuable.

QUESTIONS

1. Take stock of your own psychological contracts (PS). Who are your contracts' exchange partners, and what unwritten expectations do you have towards them? How have your PSs been violated in the past and how might you have violated others' PSs?

2. Imagine a particular decision related to ethical, responsible, or sustainable management. What types of evidence do you think you should consider and how?

3. What practices could you engage in to build or protect the trust of others in you, and what practices could you use to build your own trust towards others involved in your work life?

PROFESSIONAL PROFILE
CLOVER HOGAN

My name is Clover Hogan. I'm a 23-year-old climate activist and the founder and executive director of a youth nonprofit called Force of Nature.

Courtesy of Clover Hogan

Declaring myself an activist. I grew up in tropical North Queensland, Australia, where I developed a very early love for the natural world. At the age of 11, I discovered documentaries that showed the harm we were causing to our planet, which filled me with grief, despair, frustration, as well as determination and inspiration from the people who were putting their lives on the line in order to platform these issues and draw attention to them. So, I declared myself an activist over the dinner table at the age of 11.

The powerful's feeling of powerlessness. What was interesting was I left school and started working in sustainability, from working at Impossible Foods, the company in Silicon Valley that makes meat from plants, through to working with John Elkington … What I realized working in those different spaces was that people in existing seats of power, who, from the outside have a lot of influence, often feel the most powerless of all. As I started to see that powerlessness, I also recognized that in my peers and young people, there were mounting feelings of powerlessness, of despair, which often manifested by way of eco-anxiety, feelings of grief and frustration in response to the climate ecological crisis.

What we do at Force of Nature. We are now four years old and a 12-person team. We really exist to mobilize mindsets for climate action. We run programmes with young people around the world to help them turn eco-anxiety into agency, and bring them into conversation with those in powerful positions to challenge the business-as-usual mindset.

We have led a lot of research at the intersection of climate and mental health and found through the largest ever survey conducted on mental health and climate that 56 per cent of young people believe that humanity is doomed, and over 70 per cent of young people experience eco-anxiety. And we found that a lot of us feeling powerless stems, not exclusively from the enormity of the climate crisis, but more specifically in response to inaction in the face of it.

(Continued)

A typical day at work. Is there such a thing? It really does change every single day. I'm very lucky in that I get to meet a lot of interesting people in my work, I do a lot of speaking engagements. In one day, I might in the morning deliver a workshop to a hundred business leaders, then at midday, do a keynote for a festival, speaking to civil society. Amidst that, I might be taking client calls, setting up partnerships, as well as having the team calls with Force of Nature. In the evening, I might be working with a school or on volunteering on a personal level. So, I get to do a lot of things, which is really cool. The most energizing part of my job is connecting with people and establishing new partnerships.

My job responsibilities. As the Executive Director, my two primary responsibilities are making sure that money is coming in, so that we can pay people and support the young people in our community, and establishing partnerships that facilitate the growth of Force of Nature.

A lot of my focus at the moment is around fundraising. We have ambitious fundraising targets to enable exciting projects this year, including training up young people to become change-makers in business and policy, hosting activists retreats, launching season three of the Force of Nature podcast, and starting a micro grant scheme to fund activists at the grassroots.

Climate change and work–life disruption. I don't think the problem is a lack of caring, I think the problem is that a lot of us don't feel empowered to care and to take action. That definitely extends to the workplace … A lot of young people don't really want to work for companies that aren't aligned with their values. Business leaders are quite scared because young people are consciously quitting, because they want to see real action, not just empty promises and greenwashing.

An ability to imagine and disrupt. Young people, I think we're at a unique advantage to create change. Unlike our predecessors, unlike people who are older, we haven't necessarily been around long enough to conform to systems that fundamentally change in order to solve the climate crisis. And so we have a natural kind of disruptive tendency, we have an ability to see new ways for things to be done. We have an innate imagination, a sense of moral absolutism and justice.

How to move from climate anxiety to climate action? We need to shift from anxiety to action. It is less of a linear transition. Eco anxiety is not something that we should try and run away from. Eco anxiety is a very rational, healthy response to the climate crisis, and serves as an internal alarm, telling us that something is wrong … We've gotten so good at a culture of switching off and sleepwalking. There's something in our culture that is fundamentally broken, and we need to do something about it … Anxiety can be that incredible catalyst and the thing that sparks us but it's necessary to sustain that action.

Use your emotions! Develop emotional literacy and identify what you're feeling, whether it be anxious, frustrated, sad, or apathetic. Once you have that grip on how you're feeling, talking to other people is very powerful … Once you've addressed your emotions, spoken to other people, connected into community, you can begin to think how you want to channel those

(Continued)

emotions into action. Find the specific problem within the climate crisis that ignites a fire in you, whether it's food waste, education, or prison reform … It is really important to marry up the problem you're passionate about with the skills that you innately have, or that you want to develop in order to solve it.

Emotions in the workplace. We've gotten so good as a culture of sleepwalking toward this cliff of climate collapse. And that's why emotions are so important when the issue is overwhelming … Even if we have differences in opinion around how to solve the climate crisis, I think the unifying factor is these emotions. That is where our humanity lies – in the shared grief and anxiety and frustration and even apathy that people might feel. Emotions are often swept under the rug or disallowed in professional 'spaces'. We are taught to leave our emotions at the door … I think that's changing … generationally that is shifting.

QUESTIONS

1. What role does power play in Clover's account?

2. Do you agree with Clover's attitude towards emotions?

3 Have you ever felt eco-anxiety yourself or heard of others who do? What role might there be for climate anxiety in business management?

4. Do you think young people really can play a powerful role in business, just as Clover suggests?

TRUE STORY
DON'T GET YOUR HOPES UP

Hello everyone. Hi folks, my name is Christian and I am a CSR trainer working out of Germany. This story is about when I thought I had arrived at my dream job at StoneBite, training company employees in CSR, training the trainers, and developing innovative materials.

(Continued)

The build-up. I had worked as an external trainer for StoneBite for several years and had gotten to know my boss-to-be as an extremely hospitable and kind person, always complimenting my skills and telling me how much all the participants loved me, and how important I was to them. I was walking on sunshine. However, when I started to work for StoneBite full time, my world was turned upside down. My boss and now immediate line manager appeared to feel threatened by me and tried to keep me small wherever she could. Within the first two weeks of arrival she demoted me from being managing director of the project to project coordinator, assuming the managing director position herself. My motivation and workplace commitment started to drop dramatically at this very point.

'Upside Down, office setting of the other planet, saying goodbye to his colleague (Timothy Spall as Bob Boruchowitz) and dog, 2012 Canadian-French romantic science fiction film, written and directed by Juan Diego Solanas, starring Jim Sturgess' by Wonderlane is licensed under CC BY 2.0.

Verschlimmbessern: In German we have a word to describe the dynamic when things get worse through efforts of trying to improve: Verschlimmbessern. I tried to speak openly to my boss, but she began to gaslight me, telling me I was being paranoid and a whiner. From that point on she continuously belittled me, was micro-managing and checking every single one of my work emails saying my orthography was not good enough (notwithstanding that my high school major was German language). There was no rational reasoning with my boss, although I tried incessantly. I vividly remember a session where I insisted to get to the bottom of some of her criticism, in which for three hours straight she responded to every single question of mine with an unrelated new accusation instead of an answer.

Power-group dynamics. At this time, there were very few companies where one could work as CSR trainer, so colleagues had few other places to go. Several colleagues had given up their previous jobs to work in the project, and several depended on it for their visa, or for future career progression. At some point I walked in on my married boss and the second in command in an apparently compromising situation which added to the feeling that nobody could stay neutral, and there seemed conflicts of interest wherever I looked. While initially feeling supported and understood by co-workers, as the rupture between my boss and me became increasingly apparent to the outside, people started to openly take her side, while in confidence with me kept telling me that they were sorry for doing so. In one conversation my boss explicitly told me, 'Nobody likes you here.'

Work anxiety, coping, and revenge. As a consequence, I felt on edge all the time. I did rarely dare to speak up to anybody about my concerns and hid my true feelings behind a wall of faked indifference and meaningless small talk. I felt afraid of the many little acts of vengeance. One episode particularly stuck in my head: in spite of setting up much of the CSR training project,

(Continued)

and having trained many of the participating companies, as well as all the trainers working with companies, I was ex-post deleted from the project documentation. It was tempting to plot my own revenge. At some point in time, I felt I wanted to formally blow the whistle on my boss as I felt she was embezzling public funds into StoneBite's operations outside the funded project. But I felt afraid to do so, even when I had long left the company.

Get out! After about half a year, I took the decision to give up trying to fix my work life at StoneBite. It took me about two months to find a new job. When I told my boss that I had scored a very prestigious job at a competing organization, she explicitly told me, 'You shouldn't get your hopes up: You don't have what it takes.' The new job turned out to be 'a walk in the park' in comparison to what I had gone through.

QUESTIONS

1. What do you think is the role of psychological patterns in this case, for instance, the psychological contract, psychological safety, emotional resignation?

2. What toxic and deviant workplace behaviours can you detect in this case?

3. What observations have you made about the group processes, motivational processes, and power dynamics in this case? How could they have been managed better?

4. What would you have done? Would you have remained quiet as well? Would you have 'blown the whistle'?

DIGGING DEEPER: BEHAVING LIKE A CLIMATE REBEL[94]

As tensions rise over insufficient commitment and actions to both avoid climate change and prepare for its consequences, varieties of movements against climate change have taken to more extreme practices. Use the following descriptions of these movement's practices to think about how we could productively translate what they do and how they do things into a business context.

1. **Reflect on your boundaries and potential consequences.** Being a climate rebel means disrupting a possibly convenient (albeit unsustainable) status quo and therefore is likely to cause tensions, potentially aggression, or tangible negative consequences. What consequences might your rebellion have, and where are your personal boundaries when it comes to the type of rebellious practices you would engage in?

2. **Problematize taken-for-granted but unquestioned behaviours:** Activists from the group Tyre Extinguishers deflate SuV tyres to make owners feel that their practice of using climate-damaging SuVs in urban settings is 'not ok' even though it is widely accepted [95]. What unsustainable but unquestioned behaviours could you problematize in your work context, and how would you best do that?

3. **Block unsustainable behaviours through civil disobedience:** Members of the German activist group Die Letzte Generation have frequently blocked airport infrastructure in order to disrupt the climate-damaging practice of short-haul flying [96]. What unsustainable work practices could you block and how?

4. **Find grey zones or illegal but non-enforced spaces for change:** The Phantom Planters use 'guerilla tactics' to plant trees around the world in treeless, unused green spaces without gaining permission of these spaces' owners [97]. What kind of legal grey areas, non-enforced spaces, or possibly even legal but frequently unused spaces could you use to rebel against unsustainable practices?

5. **Embrace the minor rebellions:** One would think that wearing a wrist band would not be such a big deal, yet at the Quatar football World Cup FIFA threatened players with yellow cards if they should wear the One Love wristband in support of LGBTQ+ rights. As a consequence many journalists, commentators, and fans wore the wristband in protest [98]. What 'small' but meaningful protest practices could you engage in in the workplace?

6. **Don't let the discussion about the means mute out the message.** Frequently, public opinion agrees with activists' causes but still is bothered by actions taken. There is a danger that important discussions about the social and environmental concerns behind protests are muted by criticism of the means. If this should happen in your rebellious practices, how could you steer the discourse back towards the main purpose of your actions?

POINTERS

This section allows you to dig deeper into rebellious, more extreme types of leading and following. You could, for instance, reflect on how some of their practices could be translated to a managerial workplace, or what role they could play in your personal work life.

WORKSHEET

DETECTING PROBLEMATIC BEHAVIOURS

I observe this behaviour …	Never	Very infrequently	Occasionally	Frequently	Very frequently
Significant decisions made without information	1	2	3	4	5
Micro-managing and over-control	1	2	3	4	5
Ineffective negotiation	1	2	3	4	5
Lying or engaging in other unethical behaviours	1	2	3	4	5
Ineffective coordination and managing	1	2	3	4	5
Acting in a brutal or bullying manner	1	2	3	4	5
Inability to deal with new technology and change	1	2	3	4	5
Favouritism	1	2	3	4	5
Failing to seek appropriate information	1	2	3	4	5
Lack of clarity about expectations	1	2	3	4	5
Acting in an insular manner	1	2	3	4	5
Inability to develop and motivate others	1	2	3	4	5
Ineffective communication	1	2	3	4	5
Telling people only what they want to hear	1	2	3	4	5
Lack of skills to do the job	1	2	3	4	5
Acting inappropriately in interpersonal situations	1	2	3	4	5
Inability to prioritize and delegate	1	2	3	4	5
Exhibiting inconsistent, erratic behaviour	1	2	3	4	5
Inability to understand a long-term view	1	2	3	4	5
Engaging in behaviours that reduce credibility	1	2	3	4	5
Inability to make appropriate decisions	1	2	3	4	5
Unwillingness to change mind	1	2	3	4	5

SOURCE: Adapted from [217]

POINTERS

For each line, circle the number that reflects your observation. This worksheet may help you to identify problematic behaviours you or others around you may be engaging in. Please read the small text upon completion.

All items in bold letters are incompetences, whereas cursive text indicates toxic behaviours. Tally up final scores for each type and identify if there is a bigger issue with incompetence or toxicity. Can you address both in the same way? How would you correct the incompetence? How would you correct the toxic behaviour? Discuss which one is worse.

REFERENCES

1. Christine Porath. Frontline work when everyone is angry. https://hbr. org/2022/11/frontline-work-when-everyone-is-angry?utm_source=social&utm_ medium=linkedingroup&utm_campaign=recommendations&utm_id=hbr *Harvard Business Review.* November 9 2022.
2. Benson, T. How does Google motivate their staff? www.teamtactics.co.uk/blog/google-motivate-staff Published 2023. Accessed August 8 2023. www.teamtactics.co.uk/blog/2016/01/28/google-motivate-staff
3. Google. Here's your guide to find your career path. https://grow.google/intl/ALL_au/guide-career-path Last accessed August 8 2023.
4. Google Careers. https://careers.google.com Last accessed August 8 2023.
5. The Guardian. www.theguardian.com/technology/2018/nov/01/google-walkout-global-protests-employees-sexual-harassment-scandals Published November 1 2018. Last accessed August 8 2023.
6. Bloomberg. Google workers protest $1.2 billion Israeli contract. www.bloomberg.com/news/articles/2022-08-31/google-workers-step-up-protests-of-1-2-billion-israeli-contract?leadSource=uverify%20wall Published August 31 2022. Last accessed August 8 2023.
7. Business and Human Rights Resource Centre. www.business-humanrights.org/en/latest-news/the-business-of-war-google-employees-protest-work-for-the-pentagon Published April 4 2018 in the *New York Times.* Last accessed August 8 2023.
8. The Guardian. Google breached its own 'don't be evil' motto, ex-employees' lawsuit claims. www.theguardian.com/technology/2021/nov/30/google-dont-be-evil-ex-employees-lawsuit Published November 30 2021. Last accessed August 8 2023.
9. The Guardian. Google worker activists accuse company of retaliation at 'town hall'. www.theguardian.com/technology/2019/apr/26/google-worker-activists-accuse-company-of-retaliation-at-town-hall Published April 27 2019. Last accessed August 8 2023.
10. Paresh Dave. Google violated U.S. labor laws in clampdown on worker organizing, regulator says. www.reuters.com/article/us-alphabet-google-labor-idUSKBN28C35V *Reuters.* Published December 2 2020. Accessed December 3 2020.
11. Vox. Google employees protest the company's 'attempt to silence workers'. www.vox.com/recode/2019/11/22/20978537/google-workers-suspension-employee-activists-protest Published November 22 2019. Last accessed August 8 2023.
12. Knights D, Willmott H. *Management lives: Power and identity in work organizations.* London: Sage, 1999.
13. Gherardi S. *How to conduct a practice-based study: Problems and methods* (2nd edn). Cheltenham: Edward Elgar, 2019.
14. Luthans F. Positive organizational behavior: Developing and managing psychological strengths. *Academy of Management Perspectives.* 2002, 16(1): 57–72.
15. Luthans F. The need for and meaning of positive organizational behavior. *Journal of Organizational Behavior.* 2002, 23(6): 695–706.
16. Bakker AB, Schaufeli WB. Positive organizational behavior: Engaged employees in flourishing organizations. *Journal of Organizational Behavior.* 2008, 29(2): 147–154.
17. Maslow AH. A theory of human motivation. *Psychological Review.* 1943, 50(4): 370–396.
18. Taylor FW. *The principles of scientific management.* Vol. 202. New York, 1911.
19. McGregor D. Theory X and Theory Y. In. Vol 358: *Organization Theory,* 1960: 374.
20. Kopelman RE, Prottas DJ, Davis AL. Douglas McGregor's Theory X and Y: Towards a construct-valid measure. *Journal of Managerial Issues.* 2008, 20(2): 255–71.
21. Ouchi WG. A conceptual framework for the design of organizational control mechanisms. *Management Science.* 1979, 25(9): 833–848.
22. Ouchi WG. Theory Z: *How American business can meet the Japanese challenge* (Vol. 13). Reading: Addison-Wesley, 1981.
23. Mallette LA. Theory Pi-engineering leadership not your Theory X, Y or Z leaders. Paper presented at: 2005 IEEE Aerospace Conference, 2005.
24. Gagné M, Deci EL. Self-determination theory and work motivation. *Journal of Organizational Behavior.* 2005, 26(4): 331–362.
25. Pink DH. *Drive: The surprising truth about what motivates us.* London: Penguin, 2011.

26. Deci EL. Effects of externally mediated rewards on intrinsic motivation. *Journal of Personality and Social Psychology.* 1971, 18(1): 105–115.
27. Deci EL, Ryan RM. A motivational approach to self: Integration in personality. Paper presented at Nebraska Symposium on Motivation, 1991.
28. Vroom VH. *Work and motivation.* New York: Wiley, 1964.
29. Porter LW, Lawler EE. *Managerial attitudes and performance.* Homewood: Irwin-Dorsey, 1968.
30. Locke EA, Latham GP. New directions in goal-setting theory. *Current Directions in Psychological Science*, 2006, 15: 265–268.
31. Locke EA, Latham GP. Goal setting theory. In O'Neil HF, Drillings M, eds. *Motivation: Theory and research.* 1994: 13–29.
32. Maak T, Pless NM. Responsible leadership in a stakeholder society: A relational perspective. *Journal of Business Ethics.* 2006, 66: 99–115.
33. Adams JS. Towards an understanding of inequity. *The Journal of Abnormal and Social Psychology.* 1963, 67(5): 422–436.
34. Pirson M, Dierksmeier C, Goodpaster K. Human dignity and business. *Business Ethics Quarterly.* 2014, 24(3): 501–503.
35. Melé D. 'Human quality treatment': Five organizational levels. *Journal of Business Ethics.* 2014, 120(4): 457–471.
36. Lawrence PR, Nohria N. *Driven: How human nature shapes our choices.* San Francisco: Jossey-Bass, 2001.
37. Lawrence PR, Pirson M. Economistic and humanistic narratives of leadership in the age of globality: Toward a renewed Darwinian theory of leadership. *Journal of Business Ethics.* 2015, 128(2): 383–394.
38. Watson M. Placing power in practice theory. In: Hui S, Shove E, Schatzki T, eds. *The nexus of practices: Connections, constellations, practitioners.* London: Routledge, 2017: 169–182.
39. Foucault M. *Discipline and punish: The birth of the prison.* New York: Pantheon, 1977.
40. Bourdieu P. *Outline of a theory of practice.* Cambridge: Cambridge University Press, 1977.
41. Beal BD, Astakhova M. Management and income inequality: A review and conceptual framework. *Journal of Business Ethics.* 2015, https://doi.org/10.1007/s10551-015-2762-6.
42. Carlsen A, Clegg SR, Pitsis TS, Mortensen TF. From ideas of power to the powering of ideas in organizations: Reflections from Follett and Foucault. *European Management Journal.* 2020, https://doi.org/10.1016/j.emj.2020.03.006.
43. Arendt H. *On violence.* Orlando: Harcourt, 1970.
44. Follett MP. *Creative experience.* New York: Longman, Green, 1924/1951.
45. Time. The 'One Love' LGBTQ rights armband is causing a stir at the Qatar World Cup. https://time.com/6235503/one-love-armband-qatar-world-cup Published November 21 2022. Last accessed August 8 2022.
46. Lipman-Blumen J. The allure of toxic leaders: Why we follow destructive bosses and corrupt politicians – and how we can survive them. Oxford: Oxford University Press, 2006.
47. Fernández-Campbell A. Google employees say the company is punishing them for their activism. www.vox.com/2019/4/23/18512542/google-employee-walkout-organizers-claim-retaliation. Published 2019. Accessed April 7, 2020.
48. Goss D, Jones R, Betta M, Latham J. Power as practice: A micro-sociological analysis of the dynamics of emancipatory entrepreneurship. *Organization Studies.* 2011, 32(2): 211–229.
49. French JRP, Raven BH. The bases of social power. In: Cartwright D, ed. *Studies in social power.* Ann Arbor: University of Michigan Press, 1959: 150–167.
50. Appelbaum SH, Roy-Girard D. Toxins in the workplace: Affect on organizations and employees. *Corporate Governance.* 2007, 7(1): 17–28.
51. Zellars KL, Tepper BJ, Duffy MK. Abusive supervision and subordinates' organizational citizenship behavior. *Journal of Applied Psychology.* 2002, 87(6): 1068–1076.
52. Tepper BJ, Henle CA, Lambert LS, Giacalone RA, Duffy MK. Abusive supervision and subordinates' organization deviance. *Journal of Applied Psychology.* 2008, 93(4): 721–732.
53. Clinard MB, Meier RF. *Sociology of deviant behavior* (14th edn). Belmont, CA: Wadsworth, Cengage Learning, 2011.
54. Robinson SL, Bennett RJ. A typology of deviant workplace behaviors: A multidimensional scaling study. *Academy of Management Journal.* 1995, 38(2): 555–572.
55. Everton WJ, Jolton JA, Mastrangelo PM. Be nice and fair or else: Understanding reasons for employees' deviant behaviors. *Journal of Management Development.* 2007, 26(2): 117–131.

56. Appelbaum SH, Iaconi GD, Matousek A. Positive and negative deviant workplace behaviors: Causes, impacts, and solutions. *Corporate Governance.* 2007, 7(5): 586–598.

57. Spreitzer GM, Sonenshein S. Toward the construct definition of positive deviance. *American Behavioral Scientist.* 2004, 47(6): 828–847.

58. Appelbaum SH, Iaconi GD, Matousek A. Positive and negative deviant workplace behaviors: Causes, impacts, and solutions. *Corporate Governance: The International Journal of Business in Society.* 2007, 7(5): 586–598.

59. Litzky BE, Eddleston KA, Kidder DL. The good, the bad, and the misguided: How managers inadvertently encourage deviant behaviors. *The Academy of Management Perspectives.* 2006, 20(1): 91–103.

60. Peterson DK. Deviant workplace behavior and the organization's ethical climate. *Journal of Business and Psychology.* 2002, 17(1): 47–61.

61. Mertens W, Recker J, Kohlborn T, Kummer T-F. A framework for the study of positive deviance in organizations. *Deviant Behavior.* 2016, 37(11): 1288–1307.

62. Marsh DR, Schroeder DG, Dearden KA, Sternin J, Sternin M. The power of positive deviance. *BMJ.* 2004, 329(7475): 1177–1179.

63. Warren DE. Constructive and destructive deviance in organizations. *Academy of Management Review.* 2003, 28(4): 622–632.

64. Demerouti E, Bakker AB, Gevers JM. Job crafting and extra-role behavior: The role of work engagement and flourishing. *Journal of Vocational Behavior.* 2015, 91: 87–96.

65. Van Dyne L, LePine JA. Helping and voice extra-role behaviors: Evidence of construct and predictive validity. *Academy of Management Journal.* 1998, 41(1): 108–119.

66. Välikangas L, Carlsen A. Spitting in the salad: Minor rebellion as institutional agency. *Organization Studies.* 2019, https://doi.org/10.1177/0170840619831054.

67. Walls JL, Hoffman AJ. Exceptional boards: Environmental experience and positive deviance from institutional norms. *Journal of Organizational Behavior.* 2013, 34(2): 253–271.

68. Kusy M, Holloway E. *Toxic workplace! Managing toxic personalities and their systems of power.* New York: Wiley, 2009.

69. Offerman LR. When followers become toxic. *Harvard Business Review.* 2004, 82(1): 54–60.

70. Thomas TA, Gentzler K, Salvatorelli R. What is toxic followership? *Journal of Leadership Studies.* 2016, 10(3): 62–65.

71. Tepper BJ. Consequences of abusive supervision. *Academy of Management Journal.* 2000, 43(2): 178–190.

72. Mitchell MS, Ambrose ML. Abusive supervision and workplace deviance and the moderating effects of negative reciprocity beliefs. *Journal of Applied Psychology.* 2007, 92(4): 1159–1168.

73. Mehta S, Maheshwari GC. Consequence of toxic leadership on employee job satisfaction and organizational commitment. *Journal of Contemporary Management Research.* 2013, 8(2): 1–23.

74. Goldman A, Van Fleet DD, Griffin RW. Dysfunctional organization culture. *Journal of Managerial Psychology.* 2006, 21(8): 698–708.

75. Goldman A. Company on the couch: Unveiling toxic behavior in dysfunctional organizations. *Journal of Management Inquiry.* 2008, 17(3): 226–238.

76. Kets De Vries M. Coaching the toxic leader. *Harvard Business Review.* 2014, 92(4): 100–109.

77. Tavanti M. Managing toxic leaders: Dysfunctional patterns in organizational leadership and how to deal with them. *Human Resource Management.* 2011, 2011: 127–136.

78. Schmidt AA. *Development and validation of the toxic leadership scale.* College Park: University of Maryland, 2008.

79. Universal Class. Ten difficult workplace personalities and how to deal with them. www.universalclass.com/articles/business/difficult-workplace-personalities-and-how-to-deal-with-them.htm Published 2020. Accessed July 3 2020.

80. Leary MR, Allen AB. Belonging motivation: Establishing, maintaining, and repairing relational value. In: Dunning D, ed. *Frontiers of social psychology. Social motivation.* New York: Psychology Press, 2011: 37–55.

81. Tabassi AA, Abu Bakar AH. Training, motivation, and performance: The case of human resource management in construction projects in Mashhad, Iran. *International Journal of Project Management.* 2009, 27(5): 471–480.

82. Wageman R. Interdependence and group effectiveness. *Administrative Science Quarterly.* 1995, 40(1): 145–180.

83. Kidwell Jr RE, Mossholder KW, Bennett N. Cohesiveness and organizational citizenship behavior: A multilevel analysis using work groups and individuals. *Journal of Management.* 1997, 23(6): 775–793.

84. GreenBiz. Why sustainability is a team sport. www.greenbiz.com/article/why-sustainability-team-sport Published February 21 2013. Last accessed August 8 2023.

85. Tuckman BW, Jensen MAC. Stages of small-group development revisited. *Group & Organization Studies.* 1977, 2(4): 419–427.

86. Bonebright DA. 40 years of storming: A historical review of Tuckman's model of small group development. *Human Resource Development International.* 2010, 13(1): 111–120.

87. Tuckman BW. Developmental sequence in small groups. *Psychological Bulletin.* 1965, 63(6): 384–399.

88. Belbin MR. *Management teams: Why they succeed or fail.* (3rd ed). Oxford, UK: Elsevier, 2010.

89. White G. A woman's place: Inside the UAE's all-female workplaces. www.thenational.ae/lifestyle/a-woman-s-place-inside-the-u-a-e-s-all-female-workplaces-1.981646 Published 2020. Accessed July 9 2020.

90. Brick S. Catfights over handbags and tears in the toilets: When this producer launched a women-only TV company she thought she'd kissed goodbye to conflict... www.dailymail.co.uk/femail/article-1168182/Catfights-handbags-tears-toilets-When-producer-launched-women-TV-company-thought-shed-kissed-goodbye-conflict-.html Published 2009. Accessed July 9 2020.

91. Singh B, Winkel DE, & Selvarajan TT. Managing diversity at work: Does psychological safety hold the key to racial differences in employee performance? *Journal of Occupational and Organizational Psychology.* 2013, 86(2): 242–263.

92. Edmondson A. Psychological safety and learning behavior in work teams. *Administrative Science Quarterly.* 1999, 44(2), 350–383.

93. Laasch O, Moosmayer DC, & Antonacopoulou EP. The Interdisciplinary Responsible Management Competence Framework: An integrative review of ethics, responsibility, and sustainability competences. *Journal of Business Ethics.* 2022, 1–25, https://doi.org/10.1007/s10551-022-05261-4.

94. Primetime. How to raise a rebel manager. https://primetime.unprme.org/2022/05/12/how-to-raise-a-rebel-manager Published May 12 2022. Last accessed August 8 2023.

95. Tyre Extinguishers. We are the tyre extinguishers. www.tyreextinguishers.com Published November 11 2022. Last accessed August 8 2023.

96. Tagesspiegel. 2022, Ankündigung im Bayrischen Rundfunk: 'Letzte Generation' möchte Flughafenbetrieb am BER mit Ballons lahmlegen. www.tagesspiegel.de/berlin/letzte-generation-mochte-flughafenbetrieb-am-ber-mit-ballons-lahmlegen-4312822.html Last accessed August 8 2023.

97. The phantom planter. Blog. www.thephantomplanter.org Last accessed August 8 2023.

98. ESPN. Why did FIFA ban the LGBTQ OneLove armband at the World Cup? www.espn.co.uk/football/fifa-world-cup/story/4808986/why-fifa-banned-lgbtq-onelove-armband-at-world-cup-in-qatar Published November 21 2022. Last accessed August 8 2023.

99. Erickson A, Shaw B, Murray J, Branch S. Destructive leadership: Causes, consequences and countermeasures. *Organizational Dynamics.* 2015, 44(4): 266–272.

CHAPTER 8

FOLLEADING

OLIVER LAASCH AND ALEXANDRA BARRUETA

LEARNING GOALS

1. Appreciate the entangled nature of leading and following

2. Explore how to follow and lead ethically, responsibly, and sustainably

3. Understand the main frameworks to analyse and understand professional organizational behaviour

DISCONCERTING FACT

Among 4394 executives surveyed from more than 120 countries, only 12 per cent strongly agreed that their leaders have the right mindsets to lead them forward [1].

EYE-LEVELLING AT ALLSAFE

OLIVER LAASCH AND CLAUS DIERKSMEIER

Imagine a type of followership where leaders only work a half day because they are not needed during the other half. ... *And by lunchtime I go home* is the main title of a bestselling leadership book by Detlef Lohmann, owner–manager of Allsafe, a medium-sized automobile and aerospace supplier company in Germany [2].

Allsafe has become famous for its unique practice called 'eye-level' leadership ('Augenhöhe' in German) [3]. The practice is based on the core principle of freedom for responsibility: if given freedom, employees will use it responsibly for the best of themselves and the company. Eye-level leadership is practiced by tearing down hierarchies; dissolving departments; abandoning controls; letting employees decide freely to spend company money; having no fixed work hours; and having access to all financial and even competitively sensitive information [4, 5].

(Continued)

© Allsafe GmbH & Co. KG

IMAGE SOURCE: [6]

Germany's leading manager magazine *Handelsblatt* featured Allsafe as one of the 'world's craziest companies … breaking away from the normal management logic [and achieving] success based on new rules of management' [7]. Employees feel eye-level leadership increases their well-being, self-worth perception, and happiness [8, 9]. Frank, who works in production, shares that 'feeling that I have as an employee: I am important as a human being' [10].

Purchasing manager Simon reflects on more hierarchical leadership styles by suggesting that 'you can also make money with a strongly hierarchical structure … To what extent this is fun is another question.'

A key feature of eye-level leadership is that it is distributed. Everyone engages in both leading and following practices at one time or another, as there are very few fixed formal leadership positions. Ute, a senior financial manager, uses the example of how roles change in different projects: 'I'm always actively involved, either as a leader or a participant in such a project.' 'I'm here … I'm the boss you're talking to right now', says accounting clerk Jonas reporting on a conversation with a customer who wanted to speak to his 'boss'. As a consequence, employees across Allsafe feel that they are leaders and decision-makers. As Theo, an engineer, explains, they engage in a form of 'co-entrepreneurship … lived in many areas through this independence [and] personal responsibility'. People practicing eye-level management have the freedom to follow and lead, whichever is in the interest of their common purpose.

"Jack Sealey Warehouse" by toolstop is licensed under CC BY 2.0.

FOLLOWING AND LEADING: TWO SIDES OF THE SAME COIN

Bosses are not necessarily good leaders; subordinates are not necessarily effective followers. Many bosses couldn't lead a horse to water. Many subordinates couldn't follow a parade.

Robert E. Kelley [11]

The case of Allsafe shows how leading and following, in practice, cannot be separated. Practices of following and leading are inseparably entangled when groups of people pursue a common purpose [12]. Achieving that shared purpose depends on successfully practicing '**folleading**', the entangled dynamics of following and leading.

Talking about leaders and followers as if leadership and followership were stable attributes of particular people, fixed roles so to speak, is problematic and misleading. Most people, at some point in their career, will predominantly engage in practices of leading and at another time predominantly in following; we all follow and we all lead. Working in a group and across different groups, the same person in some situations will lead, in others follow, in some situations both. Following and leading are not two different currencies, they are two sides of the same coin.

Therefore, it has been suggested that strictly distinguishing between fixed 'leaders' and 'followers' is an outdated world view [13–16], a remnant of a past that is inadequate for our present and future [17]. Folleading requires a shift in the way we think: 'Followership is not part of leadership, leadership is part of followership.' [18] Instead they are one entangled bundle of practices, 'mutually interwoven leadership/followership' [19], a 'yin–yang of followership–leadership' [20] that exists in 'essential interdependence' [21]. Folleading, for instance, in the case of eye-level leadership at Allsafe, might mean not to be leading followers, but rather leading leaders [22]. Management practitioners in the folleading mode may find themselves dynamically engaging in different practices of leading and following.

In parallel, it has been noted that we are slipping into a 'followership crisis' [13]. Following might appear dull and 'not sexy' or 'trendy' [23–27] due to the cult that has been built around business leaders from Muhammad Yunus and Elon Musk to Steve Jobs and Jack Ma. 'Everyone wants to be a leader', which makes assuming a follower role less desirable, merely a temporary stepping-stone towards a leading position. In consequence, when assuming a follower role, people are increasingly critical and less persistently loyal.

The chapter overview in Figure 8.1 expresses the inseparable, intimate entanglement of following and leading, revolving around the pursuit of a

The folleading
mode of management is centred on the inseparable practices of leading and following in pursuit of a group's common purpose

common purpose. It also expresses how folleading is grounded in and inter-woven with the complex tapestry of work life and organizational behaviour. Finally, it shows how folleading practices should be guided and protected by professionalism. Each of these areas will be explored further in a dedicated section of this chapter.

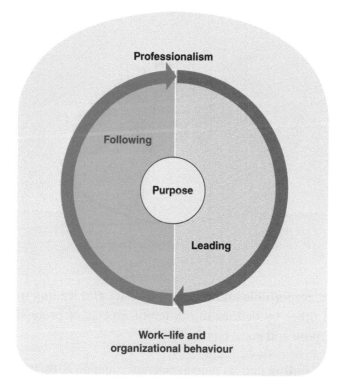

FIGURE 8.1   Folleading in context

PROFESSIONAL FOLLEADING

Effective folleading requires tuning into the continuously evolving dynam-ics and changing roles in follower–leader dynamics. It needs a focus on the quality of the ever-changing relational dynamics and how follower and leader characteristics influence that relationship [28, 29]. However, to follead profes-sionally, one has to be more than 'effective'. Imagine, for instance, you were a very effective follower boosting a cigarette company's sales promotion to new customer groups as your main purpose. Imagine, you might be an effec-tive follower 'doing whatever it takes' for the common purpose, maybe even playing 'little dirty tricks'. Effective for what and in what way is the question. **Professional folleading** requires the pursuit of a common goal that is in service of society and the world, and to do so in an ethical, responsible, and sustainable way (see Figure 8.2).

Professional folleading to effectively follow and lead toward a purpose that serves society and the planet, while engaging in ethical, responsible, and sustainable conduct

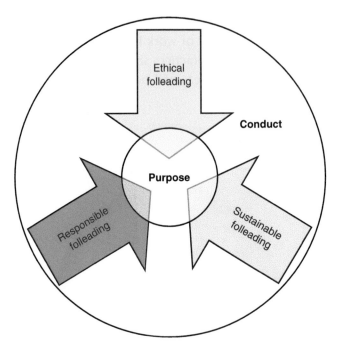

FIGURE 8.2   Integrating ethical, responsible, and sustainable purpose and conduct

Sustainable, responsible and ethical following and leading mutually complement each other by delineating different aspects of professional folleading's good purpose and good conduct:

- **Ethical folleading** pursues morally relevant common goals, while engaging in ethical conduct. Ethical folleading is at times also called moral leadership or followership [30].

- **Sustainable folleading** describes the dynamics between followers and leader pursuing common social, environmental, and economic sustainability goals. Sustainable folleading groups might be a work team, a whole organization, or even a complete region, or a whole industry together pursuing a positive triple bottom line impact.

Responsible folleading
refers to the practice of building responsible leader–follower relationships throughout a stakeholder network for a common purpose

- **Responsible folleading** is directed towards common purposes related to the creation of stakeholder value and does so by nurturing responsible follower–leader relationships. In addition, responsible folleaders are enmeshed in an extended leader–follower network of varieties of stakeholders. Folleading relationships span far beyond hierarchical or intra-organizational relationships. Responsible folleaders are stakeholder followers and leaders [31, 32].

As illustrated in Figure 8.3 the **responsible folleading** perspective provides a much broader view of the leader–follower relationship. As mentioned before, practitioners often dynamically switch between and engage in following and leading at different times and in different situations. But who are these followers and leaders? Traditionally, we used to think of them as the members of an organization, such as the employees of Allsafe, or *Vogue* (covered later in the chapter). In mainstream business thinking, followers are usually understood to be subordinate employees of leaders further up the hierarchy. However, leaders and followers can be distributed across a wider network of stakeholders, far beyond organizational boundaries. From a stakeholder perspective, however, responsible leaders and followers might be varieties of individuals with different backgrounds. Responsible folleading is a multi-stakeholder process that requires additional social skills and mental flexibility from managers as they assume different roles of responsible folleaders. Those roles include, for instance, being a visionary, a storyteller, or a servant folleader to stakeholders [31–33].

When WhatsApp faced a backlash to its end-to-end encryption from governments all around the world fearing its use for criminal or subversive activities, a spokesperson took the lead by responding that 'rolling back [end-to-end encryption] will make us all less safe, not more'. In parallel, Mark Zuckerberg reaffirmed his commitment to 'private, encrypted services where people can be confident what they say to each other stays secure' [34]. While they were fighting the battle for user freedom of speech and anonymity, on the ground there also were masses of users who were pivotal to the change, for instance in Afghanistan where after only two days citizens had protested a WhatsApp ban so vehemently that it was lifted completely [35].

Examples of the consequences of responsible management might include consumers being led to more responsible consumption patterns, or product development managers in businesses following trending Pinterest users focusing on sustainable consumption. Politicians might be lobbied to create public policies for sustainability, responsibility, and morality, while conversely politicians might also find business managers follow their social and environmental initiatives, such as in the case of the European Union's Green New Deal. Suppliers might follow their buyers' lead in sustainability or vice versa.

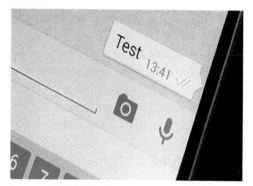

A responsible folleading stakeholder that spans the world and across sectors, striving for privacy protection.

'Blaue Haken WhatsApp' by jfrigger is licensed under CC BY-SA 2.0

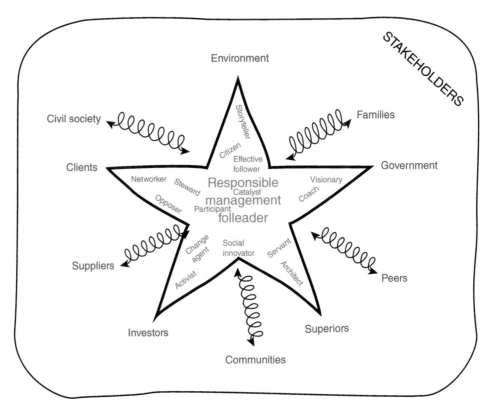

FIGURE 8.3   The roles involved in responsible folleading

SOURCE: Adapted from [31–33]

FOLLOWING

Following
means to go after a common purpose, often under the direction of leaders

What does good **following** look like? Does it simply mean to obediently carry out whatever a leader, or 'the boss', requests? An interesting take comes from Anna Wintour, editor in chief of the fashion magazine *Vogue*:

> You need someone who can push you, that isn't pulling you back … It is important to empower those who work with you because you are nothing, nothing without a good team. It is really, really important to surround yourself with a team whose opinions you trust, who are not in any way frightened of disagreeing with you and you have to listen [36].

Surprisingly, Wintour, who is infamous for her extremely assertive, at times intimidating, attitude towards others, does not stress obedience as characteristics of good followers, but wants a type of following characterized by 'pushing' and 'disagreeing'. She also stresses how much formal leaders 'have to follow direction when "listening" as they follow their "good team" that they are "nothing without"'. Paradoxically, good leaders have to be good followers too. For instance, imagine if Wintour decided to publish an issue on a topic she knew nothing about. Would it be better to flounder about like a ship lost at storm, or to find someone who *did* know about the subject and temporarily reverse roles for the good of the organization?

TYPES OF FOLLOWING

In this section we will explore different profiles of **followers**. It is important to keep in mind that practitioners might be predisposed to follow in a certain way, but may also actively change the way they follow to develop a profile more suited to the situation. Kelley's followership types presented in Figure 8.4 explore what the characteristics of effective followership are.

Follower
a practitioner engaging in the practice of following

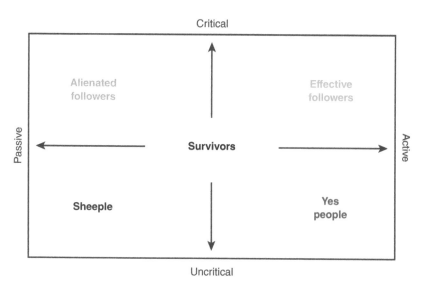

FIGURE 8.4 Kelley's follower types

SOURCE: [37]

The typology is built on two main dimensions: the degree of critical thinking and the active engagement of followers. An independent, critically thinking follower won't be afraid of providing constructive feedback and contributing ideas to the conversation. Dependent, uncritical thinkers, on the other hand, will remain quiet and blindly do what their leader asks of them, never questioning anything. Speaking of engagement, followers who are actively engaged tend to participate actively and have a strong sense of ownership, while passive followers are at the other end of the spectrum and barely participate [37]. Along the spectrum, we can identify five distinct types of followers:

1. **Sheeple** ('Sheep people') are passive, dependent followers with no critical thinking. They don't have a particularly strong sense of responsibility and don't show initiative. They have a 'not my job' mentality where they perform exactly what is asked of them and nothing else. Highly controlling, autocratic leaders might prefer sheeple.

2. **Yes people** are active and seem to be doing something on the surface, but are nevertheless dependent on their leader and unwilling to use critical thinking. Often characterized as being brainwashed, they only agree with a leader when questioned and can be 'aggressively accommodating'. Leaders with low self-confidence or insecurities regarding their judgement or decisions tend to surround themselves with yes people who boost their ego.

3. **Alienated followers** 'are over it'. They have the ability to be independent and think critically but are extremely passive in their roles. They have gradually become cynical and most commonly just do what is asked of them. They are frequently unhappy and unfulfilled in their roles.

4. **Survivors** exist somewhere 'stuck in the middle' between other types. They adapt to the situation and have a 'better safe than sorry' mentality. They typically survive change as they can flexibly mould into whatever form of following suits changing situations.

5. **Effective followers** are both active and independent critical thinkers. They are the ones we might want to hire and the ones we might want to be. They self-manage and are brave. They can commit to something outside or beyond themselves, and they continuously build up their competence to pursue the common purpose.

Effective following
means to be courageous, honest, and credible using self-management skills to hone competencies and to fully commit to the common purpose

Given that **effective following** has been presented as an ideal type, let's have a closer look at the skills required.

First, effective following requires **self-management**. Good followers can not only accept and take on responsibilities that are delegated to them, but they also see themselves as equals (at 'eye level' as they would say at Allsafe) to their leaders, actively managing their own affairs and requiring very little direction from superiors. Interestingly, effective following means practice that is similar to good leading: acting autonomously, working independently, not being afraid of speaking your mind, and thinking outside the box, while putting yourself in other people's shoes.

Secondly, effective following means **committing to a higher purpose 'beyond'** their own or the leader's benefit. Effective following means being not only engaged and excited at work but also standing up to others when they believe things are taking a turn contrary to that purpose. Effective followers see leaders as (possibly temporary) elements in the pursuit of that higher purpose.

Third, effective following means **increasing one's competence to pursue the purpose**. Effective followers are self-starters who identify the competences that are lacking or continually push themselves to improve. Effective following means not being afraid to perform unfamiliar tasks as these are seen as opportunities to improve rather than risks to fail.

Fourth, effective following means **being brave** enough to speak inconvenient truths or poke holes in flawed strategies, to call out mistakes and suggest better, different, new ideas.

FOLLOWER ACTIVISM

Follower activism has proven to be a powerful lever for addressing some of our biggest ethical, social, and environmental causes and for opposing unethical, irresponsible, or unsustainable leaders. Follower activism describes a type of followership with little direction from leaders or without leaders, and at times against leaders.

As illustrated in Figure 8.5, a crucial question is the extent to which followers are engaged (similar to Kelley's passive–active follower dimension), whether they are for or against, and with whom or what they engage. Interestingly, engagement here can mean engagement for or against, with or without a leader. The continuum features those who do not engage whatsoever at one end, and 'diehards' that engage to the extreme at the other end. While following has been called an 'art' that may create great leaders [38], engaged followers might also break a leader.

> Follower activism
> consists of follower-led practices that engage against 'bad' leadership or for good causes`

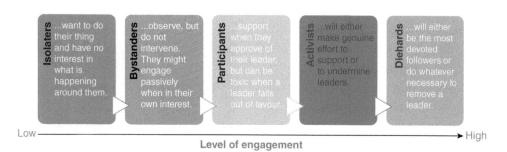

Low ——————————————————————→ High
Level of engagement

FIGURE 8.5 Follower engagement typology

SOURCE: [39]

SOCIAL MOVEMENTS

One type of follower activism is seen in **social movements** [40] for ethics, responsibility, and sustainability, which often co-emerge with an iconic leader figure such as Greta Thunberg in the Fridays for the Future movement. At

> Social movement
> a loosely directed effort by a large group of followers in the pursuit of a common goal

times large, leaderless, distributed follower networks *are* the movement – for instance, in the social-media-enabled Hong Kong independence movement. At times leaders 'kick off' a movement, and a large followership takes over with sporadic distributed leaders emerging temporarily and merging back into the follower crowd, as with the '#MeToo' movement.

There are many similar follower-led movements in the world of management, such as the socially responsible investment movement [41] or the responsible management education movement [42]. What often happens is that movements go from 'tweets to streets' [43]. A similar pattern is seen where large follower movements go 'from the streets to the suites' [44], such as in the case of the German biotech movement, with managers furthering the aims of the movement from within corporations.

FOLLOWER OPPOSITION

Follower opposition
a follower identity developed by
practitioners who act against leaders

Follower activism can also take the form of follower opposition, where practitioners develop a follower identity that goes *against* leaders [45]. Unethical, irresponsible, or unsustainable leadership practices might require toppling 'or reducing the power of a 'toxic leader' as a necessary first step in developing responsible organizational practices [46]. Therefore, being a 'good' follower means to stop following or to actively sabotage, attack, oppose, or ignore leaders.

Follower opposition can assume many forms. Ethical followers might, for instance, call out leaders' immoral behaviour by using whistleblowing practices [47, 48]. Practitioners might also decide to 'unfollow' leaders or to fix the unprofessional aspects. Former followers might plan a 'coup' to become a more responsible, sustainable, or ethical leader instead of the one currently in charge.

Again, Anna Wintour provides us with an excellent example. In spite of Wintour's pro-fur stance [49], some editors at British *Vogue* decided not to follow her lead as head of content, while others did [50]. Former *Vogue* cover models have aggressively campaigned against Wintour's use of *Vogue* to promote

Controversial pro-fur ad published in the British *Vogue*.

fur. Modelling agencies have asked their clients to 'unfollow' by walking out of fashion shows featuring fur. One of the most striking acts of opposition was when a young woman whirled a dead raccoon from a fur farm onto Wintour's plate at a restaurant in Manhattan. When asked how she was able to pull off that stunt, she replied that 'There are many people at … *Vogue* who wanted to help me … I soon got a call telling me she was going to be at the Four Seasons.' [49]

LEADING

Now that we have explored practices of following, it is time to have a close look at practices of **leading** followers towards a goal or purpose in an ethical, responsible, and sustainable way. Goals may be understood as goals of the leader, their organization or of the followers, or ideally, all three of them aligned in one goal [51]. We will first discuss the leadership process before going on to look at different leadership behaviours, and finally exploring varieties of leadership style from autocratic and Machiavellian to transformative and servant leadership.

Leading
comprises the practice of directing, influencing, and enabling followers to pursue and attain a goal or purpose

LEADERSHIP PROCESS

As discussed early on in this chapter responsible (fol)leading relies on a process through which responsible leaders and followers achieve a common purpose. When it comes to leading an organization towards ethics, responsibility, and sustainability, experienced leaders recommended three main areas of practice for this process [53]:

1. **Creating direction.** Leaders must convincingly convey the vision and goals associated with the change to be implemented. Good practices are:

   a. **Framing and delivery of the message.** Avoid 'gloom and doom', and frame sustainability as a positive message of opportunities. Use vivid examples and involve emotions and creativity. Use the language of business, of financial factors and feasibility. Appeal to employees' inherent motivation to do the right thing by reframing the activities in the light of social value.

   b. **Initiating, implementing, and advising.** Make sure you have a powerful initiator who can launch the change, someone to do the detailed work and implementation, and an expert in an advisory role.

   c. **Focusing the effort.** Do not lose energy by trying to convince sceptics but focus on the early adopters who can use their energy to carry on.

2. **Building alignment.** Leaders must ensure the initial implementation of internal responsible management practices.

a. **Implementing internal business practices.** If internal processes and structures are in place for sustainability, employees do not necessarily have to *believe* in sustainability to make it happen. Structures that were mentioned as especially important are job functions and controlling systems based on sustainability indicators, communication and feedback systems, and a company-wide sustainability training system.

b. **Engaging with stakeholders.** Sustainability goals cannot be reached alone. Leaders must collaborate in a broader stakeholder system to build long-term partnerships and try also to convince other companies to do the same thing.

c. **Integrating sustainability in products, and services.** Integrating sustainability here creates a constant reminder to all involved in the production process and in consuming products and services. Implementation also has the potential to create new revenue streams and show the business case for sustainability.

3. **Maintaining commitment.** Reaching sustainability, and stakeholder responsibility is a long run goal. Accordingly, it is of crucial importance for successful sustainability leaders to ensure that followers' commitment is maintained over long periods of time.

a. **Treating employees as important competent human beings.** When employees are treated as carriers of the organization's sustainability knowledge, skills, and culture this may reduce employee rotation, increase motivation and keep the sustainability movement alive.

b. **Building reputation.** Once a company has created a reputation for being an ethical, sustainable, and responsible business this becomes a self-fulfilling prophecy. Stakeholders expect the company to stay the course. The organization will be held accountable for non-compliance with the reputational image created.

c. **Engaging in networks.** Sustainability and responsibility networks, such as industry initiatives, are an external anchor that helps maintain efforts.

LEADERSHIP STYLES

Situational leadership suggests that the most effective leadership style varies from one situation to another.

What different leadership styles should one apply? Is there a perfect or ideal leadership style? The underlying idea of **situational leadership** is that different styles are differently well suited to distinct situations.

Fred Fiedler's pioneering contingency model suggests that leader characteristics and their corresponding styles are fixed [54]. To find out which type of leader one is 'naturally', they developed the Least Preferred Coworker (LPC) scale. LPC is a questionnaire to identify if you naturally lean towards a people-centred or task-centred leadership style. Different leaders therefore suit different situations and the main task for effective leadership is to match leaders and situations [55]. The three most relevant factors that folleading situations can be distinguished by are:

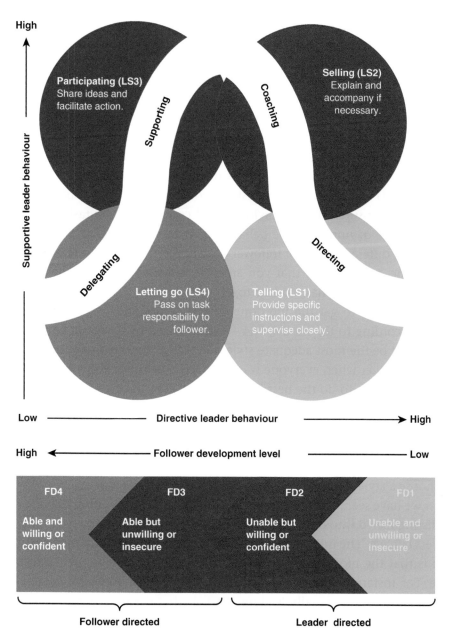

FIGURE 8.6 Follower characteristics and situational leadership styles

SOURCE: Adapted from [56]

1. **Leader–follower relations quality.** How much trust and other positive relational factors characterize the relationship between leader and followers?

2. **Task structure.** Are tasks clear and structured or vague and unstructured?

3. **Leader position power.** How much power does the leader have by virtue of their position to influence group members – for instance, through reward or punishment?

Unlike Fiedler, Hersey and Blanchard did not think leaders have just one fixed style. Rather, they could to some degree adjust their leadership style to different situations. As illustrated in their life-cycle model of leadership (Figure 8.6) [56], they observed that over time followers in groups typically get more mature and therefore leadership styles have to adjust to this fundamental change in the situation. Their model distinguishes the different leadership styles (LS1–4) using the two dimensions, concern for people resulting in supportive or non-supportive behaviours, and concern for the task, translating into directive or non-directive behaviours. It then matches these leadership styles with different levels of follower development (FD1–4).

Imagine, for instance, that you are a team leader of one of the assembly teams at Allsafe that has worked together for the last five years. Everybody is perfectly able to get the job done, and is secure and motivated to do so (FD4). According to the model, LS4 – characterized by delegating and letting go – would be the most adequate style of leading. Now imagine the situation five years earlier when everyone was new to the task, but very motivated and excited, wanting to do the best job possible (FD2). In this past setting, LS2 – coaching and selling – would be the best match. Usually group composition changes over time, implying that not every follower will be on the same development level, and that leaders might have to apply different leadership styles in the same situation at the same time, as they lead different group members, or choose a style that matches the majority of group members.

As we have seen, it is the case with following and also leading that they can be distinguished into different styles, depending on how actively or passively leaders behave. The full-range leadership model's [57, 58] underlying assumption is that the more active a leader is the more effective is their leadership style. For instance, someone practicing a laissez-faire leadership style could be described as not actually leading at all, as that person is actively avoiding the responsibility of leading whenever possible. The inspirational motivation type, transformation leadership style, instead is likely to be more effective, as it actively inspires followers to reach challenging goals.

The full range of leadership styles can be divided into two larger types, transactional and transformational, plus the 'laissez-faire style', each of which can in turn be split up into the further substyles and the laissez-faire style. For leaders to be truly effective, they must display both transactional and transformational leading.

- First, **laissez-faire leading** is characterized by having a distinct lack of leadership initiative. It is both passive and ineffective and a typical answer regarding what a laissez-faire leader actually does would accurately be: not much.

- Secondly, **transactional leading** means to clearly communicate requirements, roles, policies, and responsibilities and make sure these are followed with positive and negative rewards.

- Third, **transformational leading** arouses and transforms followers' attitudes, motivations, and beliefs, acting as agents of change. Leaders provide direction, inspiration, vision, and emotional connection, and operate on a plane above self-interest.

In this section, we have introduced main frameworks that illustrate how different leadership styles can be used to different effectiveness levels. However, the styles presented in these sections only represent a small selection of the full breadth of different leadership styles and phenomena. Given the introductory nature of this chapter, we cannot discuss each in depth, but Table 8.1 provides a helpful overview. As you move from top to bottom among these styles, you will notice that the leadership styles develop from the 'bad, ugly, and old-fashioned' towards the 'nice, good, and progressive' styles of leadership. However, as mentioned earlier on, this does not mean that the styles further down the table are necessarily the less effective ones, or the ones that are always preferable. After all, the 'best' or most effective style of leading will be a question of fit between a practitioner's 'naturally effective' style and the situational factors.

TABLE 8.1   Varieties of leadership styles

Style	Description of practice	This type of leading might manifest, for instance, as ...
Machiavellian leadership [59]	Controlling others through deception, guile, and/or manipulation.	... lying or cheating to obtain what the leader wants.
Autocratic leadership [60]	Controlling decisions and allowing little, if any, input from group members.	... holding a meeting, spending the whole time talking, and not allowing anyone to contribute new ideas.
Bureaucratic leadership [61]	Emphasizing specific rules, systems and lines of authority for followers.	... not listening to others if they haven't approached the leader through the appropriate channels.
Institutional leadership [62–64]	Leaders who prioritize the institutional values and characters or the organization.	... develop strategies to increase respect and legitimacy for a leader's organizations.
Shared/distributed leadership [65]	Sharing power and influence, while being transparent, encouraging autonomy and being open to new ideas.	... allowing others to self-organize to find solutions to problems collaboratively.
Charismatic leadership [66–68]	Relying on charm, eloquence of communication, persuasion and force of personality to motivate followers to get things done or create change.	... delivering a highly motivational speech encouraging employees' productivity.

(Continued)

TABLE 8.1 (Continued)

Style	Description of practice	This type of leading might manifest, for instance, as …
Authentic leadership [69]	Building honest and open relationships with followers by valuing their input and following an ethical foundation.	… taking followers' advice and making changes to the organization, management or even the leader herself.
Servant leadership [70, 71]	Pursuing the main objective to serve the group of followers.	… asking everyone to perform a task, and then being the first one to do it.
Spiritual leadership [72]	Leading out of a spiritual motivation and upon a shared vision, of hope/faith, altruistic love, emphasis of workplace spirituality, and spiritual thriving.	… talk about having faith in the organization and caring about followers' spiritual needs.
Ethical leadership [73]	Guiding behaviour by moral principles (*the right thing*) and in line with personal or organizational values.	… putting their position at risk by standing up for *the right thing*.
Responsible leadership [74, 75]	Fostering responsible relations and outcomes in and through a stakeholder-follower network.	… make sure a new project is not going to damage the environment or the community before beginning, no matter how profitable.
Sustainability Leadership [76] [77]	Assuming a responsibility for understanding and acting on sustainability challenges.	… actively exploring a sustainability issue's complexity and co-implementing solutions with others.
Sustainable leadership [78]	Sustainable leadership assumes a responsibility for particular leadership goals and purposes beyond one's own tenure, by protecting resources, aligning the leadership context and preparing one's successors.	… identifying and developing others to be able to assume one's own role in the future in a way that allows them to continue in alignment with past leadership.

Julian Adyeri Omalla affectionately known as 'Mama Cheers' is an authentic and charismatic Ugandan service leader.

Business Star Africa

Often different styles of leading blend, as in the case of Julian Adyeri Omalla, with her unique life-story giving her an air of charisma while being authentically down to earth. She started off as a poor schoolteacher's daughter selling fruit from a wheelbarrow and being defrauded by her first business partner and is now the CEO of her diversified agribusiness empire, including a women's cooperative, poultry farm, and her original juice business known by the leading brand name 'Cheers' [79]. Julian still has an iron work ethic: 'When I'm launching a new product, I sleep at 10.00 pm and get up at 2.00 am to work and sleep again at 5.00 am.' Another characteristic is that she genuinely cares for the people she employs:

'The biggest problem in Uganda is unemployment ... I know what to do – we can create more employment ... I am delighted when I employ people and see them work and educate their children. I encourage my employees to develop themselves, to save money, buy land, and build houses for themselves' [80].

Leaders apply principles of **glocal leadership**, adjusting practices for both global and local stages. Glocality 'is defined as experiencing the global locally or through local lenses' [81], which refocuses the perspective of global leadership onto the local differences [82]. Leading glocally often connects to local cultural characteristics, institutions, power relations, environment, as well as social and environmental needs and issues. Glocal leadership means recognizing that there are global needs (e.g. upholding human rights or reducing CO_2 emissions) that require upholding in spite of local differences. At the same time, leading glocally tunes into the different ways of leading across locations and they all might be equally valid. This could mean, for instance, applying Igbo and Yoruba-style (local cultural-philosophical systems) leadership for the common good in Nigeria [83], while paying particular attention to the societal duties embedded in the role model of the 'responsible merchant' in Germany [84].

Glocal leadership
practice responds to both
global and local contexts

In the past, leadership theory implicitly assumed what can be described as a 'colonial' attitude by suggesting that Western or Anglo-Saxon leadership styles and theory are 'the' right way to lead. Responsible leadership, however, requires respect for and a sensitivity to indigenous ways of leading and following. **Indigenous leadership** emerges from and evolves with indigenous communities and, as such, is highly subjective and varied. Common themes include a strong sense of self and a humanistic, long-term, egalitarian, and adaptive viewpoint [85–87]. Often aspects of indigenous leadership can become resources for re-thinking leadership globally. For instance, the indigenous Mexican Mayan principle 'following we lead' ('tusbej u'uy t'aan') [88], can serve as inspiration for global folleading. Figure 8.7 summarizes how typical leadership styles differ across regions, due to both glocal and indigenous influences, while being made increasingly more uniform due to global pressures for conformity.

Indigenous leadership
practice emerges from and
with indigenous people's
culture and context

PRINCIPLES OF FOLLEADING

I. **Professional folleading** means effectively following and leading towards a purpose that serves society and the planet, while engaging in ethical, responsible, and sustainable conduct.

II. **Responsible folleading** is the practice of building responsible leader–follower relationships throughout a stakeholder network for a common purpose.

III. **Effective followers** are courageous, honest and credible. They self-manage and hone skills to fully commit to a common purpose. Other types of followers include: **sheeple, yes people, alienated followers,** and **survivors.**

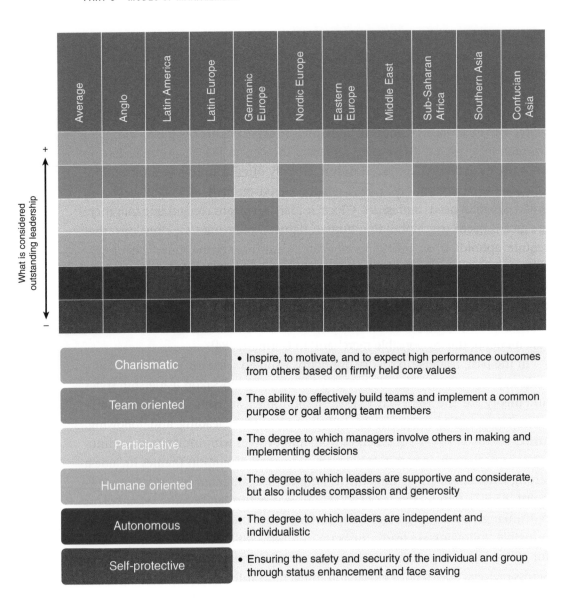

FIGURE 8.7 Typical leadership behaviours across regions

SOURCE: Built with data from [89]

IV.   Followers are also classified by their level of engagement, from low to high: **isolates, bystanders, participants, activists, and diehards.**

V.   Followers who unite for 'the common good' and lead change may do so through **follower activism, a social movement** or **follower opposition.**

VI.   The three main areas of practices for leading an organization towards ethics, responsibility and sustainability are: **creating direction, building alignment,** and **maintaining commitment.**

VII. **Situational leadership** suggests that the best leadership style varies and adapts to different situations. The full range leadership model suggests that effective leaders display both **transactional** and **transformational** leading.

MANAGEMENT GYM: TRAINING YOUR PROFESSIONAL SIX-PACK

Knowing

1. What elements are shared between ethical, responsible, sustainable, and sustainability leadership? What are the unique differences?

2. Skim read the chapter again to discover the different roles conflict plays in folleading.

3. Research Chaleff's follower typology and compare it to Kelley's. What main differences and similarities can you identify?

Thinking

4. Identify ten potential moral issues for each leading and following role.

5. Allsafe production team leaders have been trained to always behave as team coaches. Applying a situational leadership lens, consider the implications of this move.

6. Imagine your working group has encountered a situation where one member has stopped contributing and accuses another member of being a dictator. What should group leaders and followers do, and how?

Acting

7. Look at five different online petitions and consider which one you would follow and sign.

8. Write a ten principles code of ethics for responsible followership.

9. Actively lead in a situation where usually you would have followed and follow in a situation where usually you would have led.

Interacting

10. Talk to someone you know who is often in a leading position and find out which type of leading, among the ones introduced in this chapter, they practice.

11. Form a small group and discuss your usual follower or leader behaviour. If you were to work in this group on a project, how would you assign roles based on this discussion?

12. Assume a follower role in a situation where you would normally have led. Listen to others, follow instructions and observe what happens when the dynamics are switched up.

Being

13. What type of follower do you think you naturally are? What type of leadership comes most naturally to you?

14. If you were leading, what kind of followers would you prefer to have? If you were following, what type of leading would you feel most comfortable with?

15. Rank the leadership and followership styles you consider most/least desirable. Consider the factors influencing your decision.

Becoming

16. Think about a situation in which you have had to lead (this could be either in a private or a professional role). Do you think others would describe you as a responsible leader? Why/why not?

17. Think about a situation in which you had to lead. How could you use the situational leadership framework to learn from this situation for future occasions?

18. Identify your ideal leader and follower profiles. What kind of folleader do you want to be? How can you develop competence to be more in line with those profiles?

SOURCE: Adapted from [90].

PIONEER INTERVIEW
NANCY J. ADLER

INTERVIEWER: OLIVER LAASCH

Nancy J. Adler has conducted iconic research on cross-cultural leadership, management, and organizational behaviour [91], including questions of gender and female leadership [92–95]. Over the years she has studied many subjects closely related to responsible management, such as management and business as agents of world benefit [96, 97], the dehydrated language of management [98, 99], leading beautifully [100–103], as well as leadership and management scholarship that 'dares to care' [104, 105].

Courtesy of Nancy J. Adler

Responsible management and/versus responsible leadership. I believe leadership and management are distinct. Both are necessary, but leadership predominantly asks the question 'To what end?' Management primarily asks the question, 'How do we get there?' I still think that Warren Bennis's insightful observation – 'We are over-managed and under-led' – is true for the world as a whole, for individual countries, and for companies as well as organizations [106]. From a management perspective, we ask questions about efficiency and effectiveness, or about the bottom line and stock performance. We unfortunately often ask those management questions without previously asking the companion leadership question: 'Are we producing something that's of value to society?'

The responsibility to walk away. Years ago, Harvard Business School offered insight into the ethical and responsible nature of its career planning philosophy, when it advised: Unless you have at least a year's salary in the bank, don't pretend that you are an ethical manager. Their clear challenge to managers was that, unless you can walk away from a job without it doing severe damage to your family's well-being, to their home, the literal roof that is over their head, and unless you can continue to provide clothing, food, etc., then don't tell me you have the choice to act ethically. One of the first steps in being an ethical manager, therefore, is to save enough money, so that if you discover that the organization you are working for is not a good fit with your goals, values and ethics, you can leave.

Debunking some female leadership myths. I initially accepted the published descriptions differentiating how men managed and led as compared with the approaches of most women. However, the more I conducted my own research, the more

(Continued)

I questioned the generally accepted characterizations. The research described women as more inclusive, more caring, and less hierarchical than men. Those conclusions, however, had been reached primarily by comparing men at higher levels in the organization with women at lower levels. This was surprising because already in 1977, Rosabeth Moss Kanter [107] reported in her seminal book, *Men and Women of the Corporation,* based on her excellent study of employees and managers working across 16 levels of the US Civil Service, that if you hold hierarchical level constant, the behaviours of men and women are fairly similar. Both women and men at the most senior levels focus more on strategy and policy, less on relationships, and more on achieving critical tasks. Male and female employees at lower levels in the organization also share a similar focus and priorities. At lower levels, both women and men focus less on strategy and show more interest in relationships.

Tapping into leadership diversity. If a company selects its leaders from the population as a whole, rather than from just half the population (men), on average, they will have better leaders. If your company only promotes men into senior leadership and my company promotes both men and women, the chances (statistically speaking) are high that my company will outperform your company. Why? Because, on average, my company will have a more talented leadership team because they have been drawn from a larger pool of candidates [108]. That same statistical argument applies to global companies and organizations that select people from around the world for their senior leaders. Of course, the company has to know how to manage the cross-cultural diversity such broad-based hiring creates. When cultural diversity is present, there is the potential for cultural synergy … Synergy is even more important today when we need creative ideas to address the world's biggest challenges, from climate change to world peace [109]. Similarly for women, the goal is not simply to bring more women into the organization and promote them into the most senior positions. Rather it is to synergistically leverage the diverse strengths of men and women once they are in the organization and working together. The goal is to benefit from the advantages of diversity – the synergies – and not simply to have more women present or to simply attempt to mitigate the assumed problems that bringing in more women might hypothetically cause.

Leading beautifully. Singer/songwriter Phil Ochs stated, 'In such ugly times, the only true protest is beauty'. When we think about responsible management, and such issues as the environment, we have many examples of atrocious behaviour, examples of things being done wrong. We don't need to look far to see them. What we need to ask is: Where is the beauty in this ugliness? And how could we create more beauty?

As human beings, we crave beauty, in all its forms. In terms of strategy, William McDonough and Michael Braungart [110] helped us to understand that 'less bad is not good'. Likewise, less ugly is not beautiful. Yet we continue to believe that less war is peace. It isn't. That less pollution is a vibrant, healthy environment. It isn't. Beauty is what a thriving society looks like, not simply a society with less war, or fewer guns, or less pollution. Ending war is necessary, but not sufficient

(Continued)

for peace. Reducing pollution is necessary, but not sufficient for a healthy, thriving environment. Beauty isn't about going from negative to neutral; it's about moving from negative to positive. *So, not only sustainable management, but management that restores, that makes things better, more beautiful.* Yes, where the environment, society as a whole, organizations, and people flourish. You don't want to aim for sustainable ugliness. The goal is beauty. The goal is not 'good enough', even if 'good enough' is sustainable.

Note: This text is an abridged version of the interview conducted with Nancy J. Adler by Oliver Laasch, published in full as part of the *Research handbook of responsible management* [111].

QUESTIONS

1. Do you think you will be able to assume your responsibility to walk away if necessary?

2. Do you think men and women follow and lead differently? What are the implications for people with non-binary gender identities?

3. What, for you, would it mean to lead or follow beautifully?

PROFESSIONAL PROFILE
MARINÉ AZUARA

My name is Mariné and I am an Administration and Public Relations Leader for a power plant in Mexico that is part of the global power company AES. I am an accountant by original training, and I have an MBA.

My responsibilities. I am responsible for improving the relationship between the company and the community, including local authorities. In addition, I manage the administration, general services, and accounts payable. I also lead internal and external programmes and social responsibility activities. Furthermore, I am responsible for the running of the PR department.

Courtesy of Mariné Azuara

What I do during a day at work. I typically establish and manage activity programmes with the community and monitor its needs. I also manage donations from the company to communities and coordinate community visits, including schools although mainly universities, to the plant. I frequently manage local authority permissions, and the document control area (monitoring archives management, managing information from the data system, planes control, etc.).

Another key aspect is managing the general services area and monitoring the implementation of the activity plans for buildings, offices, rooms, among many others. This includes the management of the chauffeur's service, coordinating events (celebrations), the AES recreational club, vehicles fleet, cell phones, buildings, lawyers and travel. I even handle petty cash and contract cleaning, gardening, plumbing and consulting for the entire plant. I also lead in the management of expatriate documentation and analyse the plant's costs and capital projects. I communicate necessary information to staff.

Ethics, responsibility, and sustainability in my job. These three topics not only play an important role in my work, but my position is governed by these concepts in all the activities that I do. In AES we have five values: safety first, act with integrity, fulfilling commitments, strive for excellence and enjoy the work. Fulfilling these values is a matter of responsibility and ethics, and all the values are present in my duties. It is more than customer service, it is being a good neighbour and a good companion, with a joint social responsibility, talking internally and externally. Acting ethically is a way of life in AES, which in turn makes us responsible for our actions with the values and code of conduct.

(Continued)

Fulfilling both concepts of 'responsibility and ethics,' I can ensure that I can be sustainable. That is what AES requires from me. To meet the standards, we are certified with ISO9001, ISO14001 and OHSAS 18001, with best practices in the ISO26000 and SA8000, and fulfilling the requirements of the World Bank. My role is not operational; it is a support area. However, it is very important for energy availability – the overall objective of the company.

Stakeholder effectiveness is extremely important for my position to achieve results that satisfy stakeholders' goals. In my role, I manage the relationship with the community, employees, some of the suppliers, and shareholders.

QUESTIONS

1. Mariné's job title indicates that she is a 'leader'. When you first read her title, would you have imagined that her job is how she described it? In your view, to what degree does the job title reflect the scope of the role?

2. Whom does Mariné lead, whom does she follow? What are her typical practices of leading and following?

3. What might standards like the ones of the World Bank and of ISO14001 have to do with folleading?

4. What societal contributions and/or professional conduct aspects can you identify in Mariné's profile?

TRUE STORY
STAGING A COUP

EDITED BY ALEXANDRA LEONOR BARRUETA SACKSTEDER

Hello everyone. My name is Andrea and I was completing my undergraduate degree in Finance and Economics. While studying in China, I had been working at a small international

(Continued)

company for a couple years part-time in training when it became apparent that I had a knack for managing. Most of the employees began to turn to me with their issues and I served as a sort of unofficial liaison between the foreign employees and the Chinese owner as communication and misunderstanding issues were quite common.

That summer, our manager quit. He was an Australian man and for the most part had done a good job at making sure everything was running smoothly. The owner took over as manager and promoted me to official head of foreign affairs: my job was to make sure everything went smoothly with the foreign (non-Chinese) employees, and that they were happy and productive.

This is where it gets difficult. It soon became apparent that the owner had no experience and no business managing a team of people. It started out with small things at first. Our salaries would arrive a couple of days late because of 'system' or 'bank' problems; a student would be placed in the wrong level or with the wrong teacher, but things started to get worse.

Our owner/manager would regularly have shouting matches in the middle of the office and would often insult and speak condescendingly to clients. She began to verbally abuse staff, repeatedly telling one individual that he was too short to be respected. Our office environment went from feeling like we were a family to torture, and people were either quitting or being fired for no apparent reason.

I loved my job and the organization I worked for but was no longer happy working in that environment. I dreaded coming into work every day and knowing she was going to find something to complain about or blame me for. I received several (better paying) job offers during this time but always scheduled a meeting with her to inform her and she always said that she needed my help and was happy with my progress, so I stayed.

Six months after she had taken over as a manager, in a staff meeting during which she was not present, a matter was brought up and it became apparent to everyone that she had been lying to certain people. Everyone left the meeting shocked and disappointed and several of the people I was managing approached me saying that they no longer trusted the organization and would be submitting their resignation.

(Continued)

The 'coup'. I requested a meeting with the other person who had been managing the organization, an old friend of the owner who had worked there for ten years. She had taken on the role of junior manager and was second in command. After four hours we realised that a lot of things were going to have to change, but the first thing that needed to happen to save the business was for the owner to step down as manager and just act as a silent, non-present owner.

We asked her for a meeting and both explained to her that more than half our staff had threatened to quit and that we were unhappy as well. We gave her several examples of where she had discouraged staff and explained why we thought it would be better for everyone if she was no longer present and let us run the business as her agents.

She wasn't happy to hear this and called a staff meeting with everyone during which she attempted to get employees to state that they were actually unhappy with me and the junior manager, but they held their ground and in the end she agreed to step down and only come to the office once a week for update meetings with us.

Success ... kind of. It worked! After two months people were happier, numbers were up and turnover was down, and the office was slowly returning to a productive, healthy and safe work environment. But then the owner began stopping by twice a week to 'use the wi-fi because the one in her home broke', then three times a week because she had 'forgotten something'.

One month later she was at the office every day, micro-managing everything we did and turning the office into a toxic, unhappy workspace once again. The junior manager left, telling me our boss would never change. I was torn. On the one hand I loved my job and my colleagues were amazing, hardworking people. On the other ... the stress of dealing with this woman every day was making me sick. Should I stay and sacrifice my own happiness for my employees, or should I move on to greener pastures?

QUESTIONS

1. Who leads, who follows in this case? Do they do so effectively and professionally? Why (not)?

2. What cultural differences and dynamics might be at play here between leaders and followers?

3. If you had been in Andrea's shoes, what would you have done differently? Why and how? What should she do next?

DIGGING DEEPER: HISTORIC MILESTONES AND STREAMS IN MANAGEMENT AND LEADERSHIP THOUGHT

Table 8.2 illustrates how mainstream management theory can provide many insights for ethical, responsible and sustainable management practice. While many of the established management theories include elements of professional management, the first and second decades of the twenty-first century have seen an exponential increase. There is broad consensus among management scholars that ethical, responsible, and sustainable management 'is here to stay'.

TABLE 8.2   Milestones in modern leadership, followership, and management thought

Stream of thought	School	Proponents	Thought	Interpretation and significance for responsible management
Science and administration	Administrative learning	Henri Fayol	The management process consists of the tasks of planning, organization, commanding, coordination and control. Management should be guided by a diverse set of principles, from principle 1, the division of work to principle 14, the team spirit [112].	Responsible management must explore the integration of sustainability, responsibility and ethics in each of the management tasks. The 14 principles of management must be extended to consider responsible management considerations.
	Scientific management	Frederick Winslow Taylor	Management must analyse the efficiency of workers' tasks through scientific methods and then give workers the right (often monetary) incentives to perform more efficiently and increase productivity [113].	Thinking of employees merely in terms of efficiency and functioning through extrinsic functioning may result in abusive management patterns that contrast with a stakeholder value perspective on employees, which advocates human development through work.
	Fordism	Henry Ford	Management should concentrate on increasing the efficiency of production through standardization of processes and products.	Standardized and mechanistic production processes on the one hand have the potential to lead to eco-efficiency in the usage of natural resources, but on the other hand the value of such mechanistic work for workers has to be questioned.
	Bureaucracy	Max Weber	The ideal form of organization is authority-based bureaucracy, which is characterized by the subdivision of work into elementary tasks, performed by specialists, whose positions are organized hierarchically and governed through a system of abstract rules. Promotion is based on seniority and achievement for the organization [114].	The rigid structures envisaged by bureaucratic management conflict with the stakeholder view of the firm, where flexibility, multiple perspectives, and a spider's-web of relations, responsibilities and communication channels are imperative.
Contingencies and structure	Organizational contingencies	Peter Lawrence and Jay W. Lorsch	Organizations must adapt their structure and management practice to changing environmental conditions, so-called contingencies [115].	The global issues and crises affecting both general society and organizations are strong contingencies, which according to situational management require new, responsible forms of organization.
	Contingency model of leadership	Fred E. Fiedler	Different situations require different leadership styles (measured by so-called leadership perception scores, LPCs) for the effectiveness of outcomes. Leaders must be matched with the adequate situation or vice versa [54].	The organizational transformation in responsible management requires effective leadership, adapted to a varied set of contingencies.
	Strategy and structure	Alfred Chandler	Organizational structure must follow the organizational strategy [116].	Responsible management must do both, integrate the triple bottom line, stakeholders, and morality into strategy and subsequently develop adequate business structures, to put those strategies into practice.

(Continued)

TABLE 8.2   (Continued)

Stream of thought	School	Proponents	Thought	Interpretation and significance for responsible management
Human relations and behaviour	Humanistic–relational leadership	Mary Parker Follett	Individuals, business and society can't be separated. People are the most important element of any organization. Institutional hierarchies should be replaced by a network of groups. It is important to allow for different opinions and shared control, to not exert power 'over' others, but use power 'with' others [117, 118].	Responsible managers can't think of their employees as separate from society, or of their business as an isolated unit. They will also acknowledge that employees are extremely important, more so than mechanical or industrial components. Absolute control is not something to be desired, and to be responsible we must share power on an individual, group and institutional level.
	Human relations	Elton Mayo	Social and psychological processes are more important for employee productivity than monetary incentives. Human relations inside groups have to be managed and an authoritarian leadership style should be substituted by democratic leadership [119].	The human relations approach in work groups can be transferred to broader stakeholder groups related to companies. Stakeholder democracy is the responsible management counterpart to democratic leadership.
	Theory X and theory Y	Douglas McGregor	The attitude managers have towards their employees determines managers' behaviour. Managers perceiving employees as inherently lazy (theory X) will use authoritarian and control-based leadership style. Managers perceiving employees as self-motivated (theory Y), will create a trust-based environment where employees can fully develop themselves and their tasks [120].	Theory Y reflects the stakeholder value approach of responsible management by focusing on co-creation of employee and organizational value.
	Leadership theory	Chester Barnard	Organizations are social systems and managers inside this system have to balance employee orientation with performance orientation [121].	In responsible management, employee orientation must be substituted by the broader stakeholder orientation versus performance orientation thinking. The antagonistic relationship between both is weaker in responsible management as, in the perfect case, performance is redefined as general stakeholder performance instead of pure shareholder performance.
	Motivation theory	Frederick Herzberg	Herzberg explains employee motivation through both satisfiers (e.g. professional success and appreciation), and dissatisfiers (e.g. work conditions, company reputation) [122].	Responsible management practices interpreted through the lens of Herzberg's theory must be considered highly motivating for employees. Those practices reduce the dissatisfiers (e.g. bad reputation or work conditions) and strengthen many of the satisfiers (e.g. meaningfulness of work, self-fulfilment through work).
Mathematics	Management science	Patrick Blackett	Management science, also called 'operations research' bases managerial decisions on the scientific, mostly statistical analysis and mathematical modelling [123].	Management science can be a valuable tool for modelling, measuring, and managing the complex social and environmental effects caused by managerial decision-making.
	Decision theory	Herbert A. Simon	Right decisions in management are made based on mathematical models.	Decision theory requires integration of the triple bottom line, stakeholder value, and moral considerations into decision modelling.
Systems, dynamics, and complexity	Evolutionary management and chaos theory	Karl Weick, Peter Senge	Management and organization should be decentralized for more flexibility, less hierarchy, and less planned, evolutionary development, which underlies a constant learning and sense-making process [124–127].	A flexible and evolving management system is likely to adapt more quickly to the changes necessary to implement responsible management practices.

Stream of thought	School	Proponents	Thought	Interpretation and significance for responsible management
	Systems theory	Norbert Wiener; Hans Ulrich	Organizations are to be managed as self-regulating and organizing, complex and interconnected systems that interact with other external systems, such as markets, governments, and society [128].	Systems-based management is a valuable pre-condition for the implementation of responsible management activities, which aim at a holistic management that interacts with and benefits the various stakeholder systems, and the surrounding environment.
	Work environments	Kurt Zadek Lewin	Environments of work and managerial action can be divided as authoritarian, democratic and laissez-faire environments [129].	A democratic work environment is likely to deliver best responsible management results, as it facilitates stakeholder engagement at eye level.
Efficiency	Lean management	Taiichi-Ohno	Lean management aims at the elimination of any resource usage that does not increase value for customers. The main process is to reduce 'waste', and increase quality, which jointly constitute operational efficiency.	Lean management can be applied on responsible management by substituting the customer value through stakeholders focusing on the saving of natural resources in the production process.
Practice	Empirical success research	Peter Drucker	Good management principles should be derived from empirical practice experience. What works in practice should be considered good management.	Responsible management requires the development of good practices, following the principles of sustainability, responsibility, and ethics.
	Organization-management ethnography	Henry Mintzberg	We have to understand management by observing 'what managers really do', their actual managerial work practice(s) and the manager's job, in their organizational environments.	Responsibility has to be anchored in what managers actually do across the elements of their job from information and action to the people plane, including practices of leading, communicating, linking, controlling, and doing themselves.
	Practice-based studies	e.g. Joseph Raelin, Richard Whittington, William B. Gartner	Focus on the practices that make managerial reality (e.g. strategizing, entrepreneuring, leading practices) [130–132] often centred on the 'socio-material' nature of management, including the practitioner and her/his materials (e.g. tools and technologies), and is interested in competence and the meanings of these practices [133, 134].	Ethics, responsibility and sustainability have to be practiced and understood as continuously emerging anew through the practicing of management. So there can be few one-fits-all solutions or prescriptions for being a responsible manager, but managers can foster their competence to practice ethically, responsibly, and sustainably.
Followership [135]	Leader-centric	Frederick Winslow Taylor Paul Herseyand Ken Blanchard	Followers are the recipients or moderators of leader influence, exhibiting little resistance or initiative.	Focusing only on the development of managers can cause followers to 'fall through the cracks', leading to an environment inconducive to followers' growth, progress and innovation.
	Follower-centric [37]	Hogg, Kelley, Shamir	Leadership is constructed by followers. Followers 'make' leaders emerge and disappear.	Managers' following practices can make and break both responsible and irresponsible leaders.
	Relational view [136]	e.g. Lord, Herrold, Follett	Followers and leaders mutually shape and influence each other.	Following and leading should foster a healthy relationship between people in follower and leader roles.

POINTERS

This section allows you to dig deeper into where today's leadership theory has come from. For instance, you could use this timeline to explore how the role of followers and following practices have been characterized through the leadership lenses presented here. Going back to have a close look at the sources included in the table offers a fascinating walk through the evolving perspectives on folleading.

WORKSHEET

MAPPING LEADERSHIP JOURNEYS

1) Challenge the status quo

A challenge could be to critically attack existing irresponsible products, structures, and behaviors.

2) Inspire a shared vision and goals

The challenge has to be translated into concrete proposals for improvement, summarized into a concrete vision and goals.

3) Empower others to follow

Stakeholders must be given the means, (e.g. knowledge, financial resources or platforms) to follow the goals.

4) Model the way

Establish milestones, propose activities, and processes to achieve the goals of the stakeholder community.

5) Encourage others to act

Ensure on an operational level that following stakeholders do the right things to make the shared vision a reality.

POINTERS

You can use this worksheet, for instance, to envision a leadership process for a goal you would like to achieve, or to analyse why a past leadership process might have succeeded or failed.

REFERENCES

1. Ready DA, Cohen C, Kiron D, Pring B. The new leadership playbook for the digital age. *MIT Sloan Management Review.* 2020.
2. Lohmann D. *... And by lunchtime I go home: An altogether different way to lead a company to success.* BoD – Books on Demand, 2014.
3. *Augenhöhe* (Documentary) 2015. A Brandes, Franke, Hansen Luinstra, Trebien Film.
4. Lohmann D. *...und mittags geh ich Heim.* Vienna: Linde, 2012.
5. Lohmann D, Lohmann U. *...und heute leg ich los.* Vienna: Linde, 2016.
6. Allsafe. *Nachhaltigkeitsbericht 2019: Ihr Erfolg mit sichtbarer Haltung.* Engen, 2020.
7. Handelsblatt. Die verrücktesten Firmen der Welt. 29 July 2016.
8. Boons F, Laasch O, Dierksmeier C. Assembling organizational practices: The evolving humanistic business model of Allsafe. 6th Asian SME Conference, 2018, Tokyo.
9. Laasch O, Dierksmeier C, Livne-Tarandach R, Pirson M, Fu P, Qu Q. Humanistic management performativity 'in the wild': The role of performative bundles of practices. Academy of Management Annual Conference, 2019, Boston.
10. Practices at Allsafe. Interview with Allsafe representative. 2018.
11. Kelley RE. In praise of followers. *Harvard Business Review.* November 1998.
12. Chaleff I. *The courageous follower: Standing up to & for our leaders.* New York: Berrett-Koehler, 2009.
13. Fisher PD. *New giants rising: How leaders can help people and companies grow during the followership crisis.* New York: Taylor & Francis, 2018.
14. Blom M, Alvesson M. Less followership, less leadership? An inquiry into the basic but seemingly forgotten downsides of leadership. *Management.* 2015, 18: 266–282.
15. Stech EL. A new leadership–followership paradigm. In: Riggio REC, Chaleff I, Lipman-Blumen J, eds. *The art of followership: How great followers create great leaders and organizations.* Vol. 146. Hoboken: John Wiley & Sons, 2008: 41–52.
16. Rost J. Followership: An outmoded concept. In: Riggio RE, Chaleff I, Lipman-Blumen J, eds. *The art of followership: How great followers create great leaders and organizations.* Vol. 146. Hoboken: John Wiley & Sons, 2008: 53–64.
17. Van Vugt M, Hogan R, Kaiser RB. Leadership, followership, and evolution: Some lessons from the past. *American Psychologist.* 2008, 63(3): 182.
18. Adair R. Developing great leaders, one follower at a time. In: Riggio RE, Chaleff I, Lipman-Blumen J, eds. The art of followership: How great followers create great leaders and organizations. Hoboken: John Wiley & Sons, 2008.
19. Küpers W. Perspectives on integrating leadership and followership. *International Journal of Leadership Studies.* 2007, 2(3): 194–221.
20. Srinivasan J, Holsinger JW. The yin–yang of followership–leadership in public health. *Journal of Public Health.* 2012, 20(1): 95–98.
21. Hollander EP. The essential interdependence of leadership and followership. *Current Directions in Psychological Science.* 1992, 1(2): 71–75.
22. Rubenstein H. The evolution of leadership in the workplace. *Vision.* 2015, 9(2): 41–49.
23. Baker SD. Followership: The theoretical foundation of a contemporary construct. *Journal of Leadership & Organizational Studies.* 2007, 14: 50.
24. Bennis W. Introduction. In: Riggio RE, Chaleff I, Lipman-Blumen J, eds. *The art of followership: How great followers create great leaders and organizations.* Vol. 146. Hoboken: John Wiley & Sons, 2008, pp. xxiii–xxvii.
25. Epitropaki O, Sy T, Martin R, Tram-Quon S, Topakas A. Implicit leadership and followership theories 'in the wild': Taking stock of information-processing approaches to leadership and followership in organizational settings. *The Leadership Quarterly.* 2013, 24(6): 858–881.

26. Kelley RE. Rethinking followership. In: Riggio RE, Chaleff I, Lipman-Blumen J, eds. *The art of followership: How great followers create great leaders and organizations.* Vol. 146. Hoboken: John Wiley & Sons, 2008: 5–16.

27. Uhl-Bien M, Riggio RE, Lowe KB, Carsten MK. Followership theory: A review and research agenda. *The Leadership Quarterly.* 2013, 25(1): 83–104.

28. Phillips AS, Bedeian AG. Leader–follower exchange quality: The role of personal and interpersonal attributes. *Academy of Management Journal.* 1994, 37(4): 990–1001.

29. Dienesch RM, Liden RC. Leader–member exchange model of leadership: A critique and further development. *Academy of Management Review.* 1986, 11(3): 618–634.

30. Gini A. Moral leadership and business ethics. *Journal of Leadership & Organizational Studies.* 1997, 4(4): 64–681.

31. Pless NM. Understanding responsible leadership: Role identity and motivational drivers. *Journal of Business Ethics.* 2007, 74: 437–456.

32. Maak T, Pless NM. Responsible leadership in a stakeholder society: A relational perspective. *Journal of Business Ethics.* 2006, 66: 99–115.

33. Jaén MH, Reficco E, Berger G. Does integrity matter in BOP ventures? The role of responsible leadership in inclusive supply chains. *Journal of Business Ethics.* 2020, https://doi.org/10.1007/s10551-020-04518-0:1–22.

34. Doffman Z. Serious new encryption warning for all WhatsApp and iMessage users. *Forbes.* www.forbes.com/sites/zakdoffman/2020/06/24/new-warning-issued-for-all-whatsapp-and-imessage-users-serious-threat-to-security/#31f714ec48e6 Published 2020. Accessed July 8 2020.

35. Mehrdad E. How citizen uproar halted Afghanistan's ban on WhatsApp and Telegram. *Fast Company.* www.fastcompany.com/40498985/after-citizen-uproar-afghanistan-ends-a-ban-on-whatsapp-and-telegram?cid=search Published 2017. Accessed July 8 2020.

36. MasterClass. Anna Wintour teaches creativity and leadership (Official trailer) MasterClass. www.youtube.com/watch?v=j7BkeFy_L94. Published 2019. Accessed June 8 2020.

37. Kelley RE. The power of followership: How to create leaders people want to follow, and followers who lead themselves. Bantam Dell. New York, 1992.

38. Riggio RE, Chaleff I, Lipman-Blumen J. *The art of followership: How great followers create great leaders and organizations.* Vol. 146: Hoboken: John Wiley & Sons, 2008.

39. Kellerman B. *Followership: How followers are creating change and changing leaders.* Boston: Harvard Business School Press, 2008.

40. Tilly C, Wood LJ. *Social movements, 1768–2008.* London: Routledge, 2020.

41. Arjaliès D-L. A social movement perspective on finance: How socially responsible investment mattered. *Journal of Business Ethics.* 2010, 92(1): 57–78.

42. Haertle J, Parkes C, Murray A, Hayes R. PRME: Building a global movement on responsible management education. *The International Journal of Management Education.* 2017, 15(2): 66–72.

43. Gerbaudo P. *Tweets and the streets: Social media and contemporary activism.* London: Pluto Press, 2012.

44. Weber K, Rao H, Thomas LG. From streets to suites: How the anti-biotech movement affected German pharmaceutical firms. *American Sociological Review.* 2009, 74(1): 106–127.

45. Collinson D. Rethinking followership: A post-structuralist analysis of follower identities. *The Leadership Quarterly.* 2006, 17(2): 179–189.

46. Lipman-Blumen J. *The allure of toxic leaders: Why we follow destructive bosses and corrupt politicians – and how we can survive them.* Oxford: Oxford University Press, 2006.

47. Carollo L, Pulcher S, Guerci M. Whistleblowing as a crucial practice for responsible management. In: Laasch O, Suddaby R, Freeman RE, Jamali D, eds. *The research handbook of responsible management.* Cheltenham: Edward Elgar, 2020.

48. Alford CF. Whistleblowing as responsible followership. In: Riggio RE, Chaleff I, Lipman-Blumen J, eds. *The art of followership: How great followers create great leaders and organizations.* Hoboken: Jossey-Bass, 2008: 237–251.

49. Tuck A. Stars come out against Vogue 'fur hag' Wintour. www.independent.co.uk/news/stars-come-out-against-vogue-fur-hag-wintour-1282720.html Published 1997. Accessed June 8 2020.

50. Petter O. British Vogue advert for fur trade causes confusion over magazine's stance under new editor. www.independent.co.uk/life-style/british-vogue-fur-trade-advert-fashion-magazine-stance-peta-clothing-editor-a8151831.html Published 2018. Accessed June 8 2020.

51. Bateman TS, Snell SA. *Management.* New York: McGraw-Hill, 2011.

52. Kouzes JM, Posner BZ. *The leadership challenge.* Chichester: Wiley, 2002.
53. Quinn L, Dalton M. Leading for sustainability: Implementing the tasks of leadership. *Corporate Governance.* 2009, 9(1): 21–38.
54. Fiedler FE. A contingency model of leadership effectiveness. *Advances in Experimental Social Psychology.* 1964, 1: 149–190.
55. Fiedler FE, Chemers MM, Mahar L. *Improving leadership effectiveness: The leader match concept.* New York: Wiley, 1976.
56. Hersey P, Blanchard KH. Life cycle theory of leadership. *Training and Development Journal.* 1969, 23(5): 26–34.
57. Avolio BJ, Bass BM. *Developing potential across a full range of leadership: Cases on transactional and transformational leadership.* Hove, East Sussex: Psychology Press, 2001.
58. Bass BM, Avolio BJ, Jung DI, Berson Y. Predicting unit performance by assessing transformational and transactional leadership. *Journal of Applied Psychology.* 2003, 88(2): 207.
59. Christie R, Geis FL. *Studies in Machiavellianism.* New York: Academic Press, 2013.
60. De Hoogh AH, Greer LL, Den Hartog DN. Diabolical dictators or capable commanders? An investigation of the differential effects of autocratic leadership on team performance. *The Leadership Quarterly.* 2015, 26(5): 687–701.
61. Weber M. *The theory of economic and social organization.* New York: Oxford University Press, 1947.
62. Selznick P. *Leadership in administration: A sociological interpretation.* Evanston: Row, Peterson, 1957.
63. Radoynovska N, Ocasio W, Laasch O. The emerging logic of responsible management: Institutional pluralism, leadership, and strategizing. In: Laasch O, Suddaby R, Freeman RE, Jamali D, eds. *The research handbook of responsible management.* Cheltenham: Edward Elgar, 2020.
64. Greenwood R, Oliver C, Suddaby R, Sahlin-Andersson K. *The Sage handbook of organizational institutionalism.* Thousand Oaks, CA: Sage, 2008.
65. Pearce CL, Conger JL. *Shared leadership: Reframing the hows and whys of leadership.* London: Sage Publications, 2002.
66. Conger JA, Kanungo RN. Toward a behavioral theory of charismatic leadership in organizational settings. *Academy of Management Review.* 1987, 12(4): 637–47.
67. Vlachos PA, Panagopoulos NG, Rapp AA. Feeling good by doing good: Employee CSR-induced attributions, job satisfaction, and the role of charismatic leadership. *Journal of Business Ethics.* 2013, 118(3): 577–588.
68. Van Knippenberg D, Sitkin SB. A critical assessment of charismatic–transformational leadership research: Back to the drawing board? *The Academy of Management Annals.* 2013, 7(1): 1–60.
69. Luthans F, Avolio B, J. Authentic leadership development. In: Cameron K, Dutton JE, Quinn RE, eds. *Positive Organizational Scholarship: Foundations of a New Discipline.* San Francisco: Berrett-Koehler, 2003: 241–271.
70. Greenleaf RK. *Servant leadership: A journey into the nature of legitimate power and greatness.* New York: Paulist Press, 1977.
71. Patterson KA. *Servant leadership: A theoretical model.* Regent University, 2003.
72. Fry LW. Toward a theory of spiritual leadership. *The Leadership Quarterly.* 2003, 14(6): 693–727.
73. Brown ME, Treviño LK, Harrison ME. Ethical leadership: A social learning perspective for construct development and testing. *Organizational Behavior and Human Decision Processes.* 2005, 97(2): 117–134.
74. Maak T, Pless NM. Responsible leadership in a stakeholder society: A relational perspective. *Journal of Business Ethics.* 2006, 66(1): 99–115.
75. Miska C, Mendenhal ME. Responsible leadership: A mapping of extant research and future directions. *Journal of Business Ethics.* 2018, 148(1): 117–134.
76. Metcalf L, Benn S. (2013). Leadership for sustainability: An evolution of leadership ability. *Journal of Business Ethics.* 112(3), 369–384.
77. Ferdig MA. Sustainability leadership: Co-creating a sustainable future. *Journal of Change Management.* 2007, 7(1), 25–35.

78. Hargreaves, A., Fink, D. (2004). The seven principles of sustainable leadership. *Educational Leadership.* 61(7), 8–13.

79. DUL. *'Mama Cheers': Everyone's favourite juice maker.* Published 2016. Accessed July 9 2020.

80. Lionesses of Africa. Julian Adyeri Omalla: 'Mama Cheers', everyone's favourite juice maker. www.lionessesofafrica.com/lionesses/#/lioness-julian-omalla Published 2020. Accessed July 9 2020.

81. Roudometof V. Theorizing glocalization: Three interpretations. *European Journal of Social Theory.* 2015, 19(3): 391–408.

82. Mendenhall ME. Leadership and the birth of global leadership. In Osland J, Bird A, Oddou GR, Maznevski ML, Stevens M, Stahl GK, eds. *Global leadership: Research, practice and development* (2nd ed.). London: Routledge, 2013: 13–32.

83. Ogunyemi K, Obiorah O. Responsible managers for the common good: African Igbo and Yoruba perspectives on responsible management. In: Laasch O, Suddaby R, Freeman RE, Jamali D, eds. *The research handbook of responsible management.* Cheltenham: Edward Elgar, 2020.

84. Looser S, Schwalbach J. 'Honorable Merchant' and 'Handshake Quality': Interpretations of individually responsible leadership. In: Laasch O, Suddaby R, Freeman RE, Jamali D, eds. *The research handbook of responsible management.* Cheltenham: Edward Elgar, 2020.

85. Stewart D, Verbos AK, Birmingham C, Black SL, Gladstone JS. Being Native American in business: Culture, identity, and authentic leadership in modern American Indian enterprises. *Leadership.* 2017, 13(5): 549–570.

86. Verbos AK, Kennedy DM, Gladstone JS. 'Coyote was walking...': Management education in Indian time. *Journal of Management Education.* 2011, 35(1): 51–65.

87. Mika JP, Colbourne R, Almeida S. Responsible management: An indigenous perspective. In: *Research handbook of responsible management.* Edward Elgar Publishing, 2020.

88. Marcos S. Deconstructing captivities: Indigenous women reshaping education and justice. In: Champagne D, Abu-Saad I, eds. *Indigenous and minority education: International perspectives on empowerment.* Israel: Negev Center for Regional Development, 2005.

89. GLOBE. Culture groups. https://globeproject.com/results/clusters/southern-asia?menu=cluster#cluster Published 2020. Accessed April 18 2020.

90. Laasch, O., Moosmayer, D., & Antonacopoulou, E. P. (2023). The interdisciplinary responsible management competence framework: An integrative review of ethics, responsibility, and sustainability competences. *Journal of Business Ethics, 187,* 733–757.

91. Adler NJ, Gundersen A. *International dimensions of organizational behavior.* Mason: Cengage, 2007.

92. Adler NJ, Izraeli DN. *Competitive frontiers: Women managers in a global economy.* Cambridge: Blackwell, 1994.

93. Adler NJ. Global leadership: Women leaders. *Management International Review.* 1997, 37(1): 171–196.

94. Adler NJ. Global managers: No longer men alone. *International Journal of Human Resource Management.* 2002, 13(5): 743–760.

95. Adler NJ, Osland JS. Women leading globally: What we know, thought we knew, and need to know about leadership in the 21st century. *Advances in Global Leadership.* 2016, 9: 15–54.

96. Adler NJ. Global business as an agent of world benefit: New international business perspectives leading positive change. In: Scherer A, Palazzo G, eds. *Handbook of research on global corporate citizenship.* Cheltenham: Edward Elgar, 2008: 374–401.

97. Adler NJ. Corporate global citizenship: Successful partnering with the world. In: Manz CC, Cameron KS, Manz KP, Marx RD, eds. *The virtuous organization: Insights from some of the world's leading management thinkers.* Singapore: World Scientific, 2008: 181–208.

98. Adler NJ. The artistry of global leadership: Going beyond the dehydrated strategies of management, economics, and politics. *Journal of Leadership Studies.* 2015, 9(1): 48–51.

99. Seifter H, Buswick T, Adler NJ. Going beyond the dehydrated language of management: Leadership insight. *Journal of Business Strategy.* 2010, 31(4): 90–99.

100. Adler NJ, Delbecq A. Twenty-first century leadership: A return to beauty. *Journal of Management Inquiry.* 2018, 27(2): 119–137.

101. Ippolito L, Adler NJ. Shifting metaphors, shifting mindsets: Using music to change the key of conflict. *Journal of Business Research.* 2018, 85: 358–364.

102. Adler NJ, Ippolito LM. Musical leadership and societal transformation: Inspiration and courage in action. *LEARNing Landscapes.* 2016, 9(2): 23–47.

103. Adler NJ. Finding beauty in a fractured world: Art inspires leaders – leaders change the world. *Academy of Management Review.* 2015, 40(3): 480–494.

104. Adler NJ, Hansen H. Daring to care: Scholarship that supports the courage of our convictions. *Journal of Management Inquiry.* 2012, 21(2): 128–139.

105. Adler NJ. Leadership artistry: Daring to care. *Organizational Aesthetics.* 2012, 1(1): 5–10.

106. Bennis WG, Nanus B. *Leaders: The strategies for taking charge.* New York: Harper & Row, 1985.

107. Kanter RM. *Men and women of the corporation.* New York: Basic Books, 1977/2008.

108. Jelinek M, Adler NJ. Women: World-class managers for global competition. *Academy of Management Perspectives.* 1988, 2(1): 11–19.

109. Szkudlarek B, Nardon L, Osland J, Adler NJ, Lee ES. When context matters: What happens to international theory when researchers study refugees. *Academy of Management Perspectives.* 2021, 35(3), https://doi.org/10.5465/amp.2018.0150.

110. McDonough W, Braungart M. *Cradle to cradle: Remaking the way we make things.* New York: North Point Press, 2002.

111. Laasch O, Jamali D, Freeman E, Suddaby R, eds. *The research handbook of responsible management.* Cheltenham: Edward Elgar, 2020.

112. Fayol H. *Administration industrielle et générale: Prévoyance, organisation, commandement, coordination, contrôle.* Paris: Dunod, 1916.

113. Taylor FW. *Principles of scientific management.* New York: Harper, 1911.

114. Weber M. *Economy and society.* Berkeley: University of California Press, 1978.

115. Lawrence PR, Lorsch JW. *Organization and environment: Managing differentiation and integration.* Irwin: Homewood, 1969.

116. Chandler AD. *The visible hand: The managerial revolution in American businesses.* Cambridge: Belknap Press, 1977.

117. Schilling MA. Decades ahead of her time: Advancing stakeholder theory through the ideas of Mary Parker Follett. *Journal of Management History.* 2000, 6(5): 224–242.

118. Parket LD. Control in organizational life: The contribution of Mary Parker Follett. *Academy of Management Review.* 1984, 9(4): 736–745.

119. Mayo E. *The human problems of an industrial civilization.* New York: The Macmillan Company, 1933.

120. McGregor D. *The human side of enterprise.* New York: McGraw Hill, 1960.

121. Barnard CI. *The functions of the executive.* Cambridge: Harvard University Press, 1939/1968.

122. Herzberg F. One more time: How do you motivate employees? *Harvard Business Review.* 1987, 65(5): 109–120.

123. Hillier FS, Lieberman GJ. *Introduction to Operations Research* (4th edn). San Francisco: Holden-Day, 1986.

124. Malik F, Probst GJB. Evolutionary management. *Cybernetics and Systems: An International Journal.* 1982, 13(2): 153–174.

125. March JG. Bounded rationality, ambiguity, and the engineering of choice. *The Bell Journal of Economics.* 1978, 9(2): 587–608.

126. Senge P. *The fifth discipline: The art and practice of the learning organization.* New York: Random House, 1990/2010.

127. Weick KE. *Sensemaking in organizations.* Thousand Oaks, CA: Sage, 1995.

128. Stürm JR. *The new St. Gallen management model: Basic categories of an approach to integrated management.* New York: Palgrave Macmillan, 2005.

129. Lewin K, Lippitt R, White RK. Patterns of aggressive behavior in experimentally created social climates. *Journal of Social Psychology.* 1939, 10(2): 271–301.

130. Gartner WB, Stam E, Thompson N, Verduyn K. Entrepreneurship as practice: Grounding contemporary practice theory into entrepreneurship studies. *Entrepreneurship & Regional Development.* 2016, 28(9–10): 813–816.

131. Raelin J. From leadership-as-practice to leaderful practice. *Leadership.* 2011, 7(2): 195–211.

132. Whittington R. Strategy practice and strategy process: Family differences and the sociological eye. *Organization Studies.* 2007, 28(10): 1575–1586.

133. Gherardi S. *How to conduct a practice-based study: Problems and methods* (1st edn). Cheltenham: Edward Elgar, 2012.

134. Shove E, Pantzar M, Watson M. *The dynamics of social practice: Everyday life and how it changes*. Thousand Oaks, CA: Sage, 2012.
135. Uhl-Bien M, Riggio RE, Lowe KB, Carsten MK. Followership theory: A review and research agenda. *The Leadership Quarterly*. 2013.
136. Uhl-Bien M. Relational leadership theory: Exploring the social processes of leadership and organizing. In: Werhane P, Painter-Morland M, eds. *Leadership, gender, and organization*. Heidelberg: Springer, 2011: 75–108.

CHAPTER 9

DECIDING

OLIVER LAASCH

LEARNING GOALS

1. Decide ethically, responsibly, and sustainably
2. Get to know different characteristics of choice situations
3. Practice whole-person decision-making: intuitive, rational, creative and relational

WHAT A FACT!

Only 20 per cent of executives in a global survey say they have excellent decision-making practices, while a majority say much of the time they devote to decision-making is used ineffectively [1].

SPOTLIGHT

DECISIONS, DECISIONS, DECISIONS AT YASH PAKKA

In 1992 KK Jhunjhunwala, the CEO of Yash Paper made the decision to tour around the world on a motorcycle and to hand over the reigns to his son Ved Krishna [2]. Ved transformed the company to become Yash Pakka (translates as 'packaging with a soul' [3]) a world-leading biodegradable food packaging company based in Faizabad, India. He recently decided to 'fire himself as a CEO in order to now work from a place of deeper purpose' as head of strategy [4].

Making important decisions at Yash Pakka is not an exclusive practice of high-level managers like Ved. The interaction between people at Yash Pakka has been described by a visitor as 'distributed decision-making, self-organizing pods responsible to one another as peers from a commitment perspective, and completely free to make their own decisions about the way they work' [5]. For everyone to make business decisions across hierarchical levels seems highly unusual, particularly in the Indian culture characterized by high risk aversion and high power distance [6, 7]. Just as unusual seems the story of how distributed decision-making practices came about: During times of communal violence between Hindu and Muslim unrest in 1999 managers were unable to travel to the factory for a month, only to find out that when they could, the workers living close to the plant had

(Continued)

made all decisions themselves and kept things running successfully on their own. The decision was made to keep and nurture these non-hierarchical decision-making practices for the future [5, 6].

Decision-making practices at Yash Pakka are fundamentally collective and group based. Decision-making typically happens in teams

Courtesy of Susan Basterfield

called 'Sanghs'. There is also the regular practice of meeting every morning before work to focus, share information and meet everyone [5, 8]. Key information is on display for everyone to inform decision-making [5]. Decision-making is further supported by information technologies, and the board even has a separate IT committee [9].

In 2012, burnt out personally and with the company on a downward spiral, Ved took a bold creative decision. Instead of incrementally looking for profitability or cost-effectiveness in order to fix the problems, Ved decided to creatively steer into a new market, building on his and the company's strengths by starting to focus on biodegradable packaging. He later explained that his simplified decision algorithm was built on three beliefs: 1) Everything happens for a reason (e.g. the crisis giving rise to opportunity). 2) Build on what you have (e.g. their sustainable operations). 3) Go big (e.g. accelerating growth by buying machines with a production capacity multiple times the current demand) [2].

A final key area of decision-making relates to the creative biodegradable product design of Yash Pakka's disposable food packing 'Chuk'. Ved steered his team towards design decisions guided by the question, 'What would nature do?' For instance, in nature packaging (think banana peels) decomposes and is integrated in the natural cycle once it has fulfilled its natural packaging purpose. Chuk therefore degrades within some six weeks under any conditions, even if (as nature would do it) simply left where it was used, for instance on the street or in people's back yards. Similarly, they decided to go against the custom of using white packaging, a common symbol for cleanliness, as opposed to the natural brown colour of the fibres used. Producing the white colour would have meant using harmful bleaching processes, during which a large proportion of the primary material would be lost. They decided to keep the natural brown colour, which is 'what nature would have done'. By doing so they decided to accept the trade-off between environmental performance, and user preferences.

DECIDING PROFESSIONALLY

Decision-making is the heart of administration ... the logic and psychology of human choice.

Herbert Simon [10]

The deciding mode of management centred on identifying alternatives and choosing between them

As the above quote suggests, **deciding** is central to management. As we have seen in the introductory case of Yash Pakka, decisions come in varieties of shapes and sizes. Traditionally, decision-making in management centred on 'rational' choice. This type should prioritize a commercial, economic rationality with the goal of maximizing profit, growth, and similar financial measures. The 'economic man' or 'homo oeconomicus' makes decisions that are rational and maximize economic value.

Whole-person decision-making involves rational, intuitive, creative, and relational practices

However, at Yash Pakka, decisions go beyond rationality. Deciding requires improvisation [11], is multi-dimensional [12], and engages the **whole person**, the whole human being. It includes, for instance, personal experience, relationships, emotions, preconceptions, values, competences, and human error. Again, in the words of Herbert Simon in the introductory quote, it is a 'human choice'. Managers are not just the 'rational fools' that classic economic theory describes them as [13]. In this chapter we follow the call to 'open up decision-making', consider aspects of commitment and action, history, experience, affect, inspiration as well as the dynamic linkages in networks of decisions as there are never 'isolated' or 'single' decisions. They are a network [14]. Beyond rational decision-making we are able to use powerful intuition, creativity, and relations with others when deciding [15]. As illustrated in Figure 9.1, this chapter embraces whole-person decision-making, which includes rational, intuitive, creative, and relational practices facilitating more holistic, 'better' decisions. We will first explore the challenging nature of decision-making by exploring different characteristics of choice situations and how they may make it more likely for certain mistakes to occur. We then look at different types of decision-making processes. The chapter's last section juxtaposes the four different modes of decision-making: deciding rationally, intuitively, creatively, and relationally.

Professional decision-making deciding ethically, responsibly, and sustainably

Better decisions also mean deciding ethically, responsibly, and sustainably. This type of decision-making is at the centre of **professional** management conduct, in order to assume a role in service of society and the planet. Making 'good' decisions as a manager centrally means not only making effective decisions but ethical, responsible, and sustainable decisions. The World Economic Forum recently stressed that the global and local ethical, social, and environmental problems we are facing are 'fundamentally changing the traditional context for decision-making. The inconsistencies, inadequacies and contradictions of multiple systems – from health and financial to energy and education – are more exposed than ever amidst a global context of concern for lives, livelihoods and the planet. Leaders find themselves at a historic crossroads, managing short-term pressures against medium- and long-term uncertainties' [16].

FIGURE 9.1   A whole-person model of professional decision-making

THE CHALLENGING NATURE OF DECISION-MAKING

Making good management decisions according to McKinsey [1] depends on three main good practices:

1.   'Make decisions at the right level, often by delegating.'

2.   'Make decisions that align with corporate strategy and allocate resources to high-value projects.'

3.   'Commit to decisions once they are made.'

Doesn't this sound easy? Unfortunately, such 'one size fits all' advice may only provide very rough guidance as decision situations [17] vary considerably. Therefore, in the following sections we will explore how to assess choice situations, and then move on to describe typical types of decision-making mistakes.

ASSESSING CHOICE SITUATIONS

Choice situations [17] vary considerably, which has important implications for how decisions are made and what it means to make a good decision. We will first discuss four central parameters of choice situations, each of which significantly influences how we approach a decision.

Imagine you are the customer service counter manager of China Eastern at the local Chinese airport of Ningbo. A customer has a valid ticket which he booked through one of your partner airlines. However:

1. Due to a software integration issue between the airlines, you cannot see the booking in your system, a problem you have never encountered before (unprogrammed decision).

2. It would be fair to reissue his ticket so that he can board the plane and he demands that you to do so in an upset manner (logic of appropriateness).

3. However, you cannot print the boarding pass, which in turn means that the customer will miss his flight (logic of consequence) which leaves in just 45 minutes (high urgency).

4. This in turn means he will lose his connection flight in Shanghai, and a major business meeting in Copenhagen (certainty).

5. You are not quite sure how your superiors will react if you simply issue a new ticket without receiving payment for it (uncertainty).

The parameters of this case are represented in choice situation 3 in Figure 9.2. These case parameters strongly influence how you approach the decision and what choice you make. Even if one parameter changes, the situation changes. For instance, imagine you called your line manager and they tell you (with certainty) it is fine to issue a new ticket and that there will be no negative repercussions for you. Or imagine this was a programmed, frequently occurring situation and your company has given you a standard operating procedure that explicitly states that the customer has the right to receive a new ticket and boarding pass even if the ticket could not be found.

(UN)PROGRAMMED DECISIONS

The vast majority of decisions are 'programmed', meaning that they occur frequently, and are a normal, recurrent part of work life [18]. Think about the distributed day-to-day decisions necessary at Yash Pakka: What actions do we have to make if a colleague does not come to work? What happens after a customer places an order? Chapter 17 provides varieties of decision-making tools to deal with these 'standards'. For instance, standard operating procedures provide guidance for these choices by prescribing decision rules of what kind

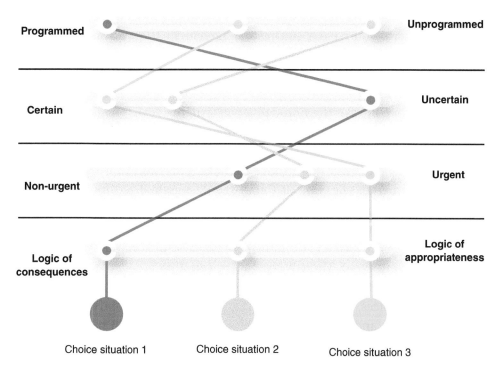

FIGURE 9.2 Different combinations of characteristics leading to varied choice situations

CREDIT: Slidemodel.com

of action should be taken in which event. This is also called 'recognitional' decision-making as the core action is to recognize a standard decision situation and to take the predetermined action. There is no choice involved [19]. Typically, programmed decisions are highly structured, as they are well understood due to their frequent occurrence.

The opposite type, unprogrammed decision-making [18] does, however, involve choice as the crucial part of decision-making, as these decisions are typically 'one off' or unusual decisions that vary considerably in their characteristics. Ved Krishna's decision at Yash Pakka about how to stop the 'downward spiral' of the company is such an unprogrammed decision. In this chapter, we will focus mostly on unprogrammed decisions as they require complex choices such as Ved's decision to reorient the whole company towards biodegradable packaging. Typically, unprogrammed decisions are unstructured as there is little opportunity to understand the problem and choice alternatives from past occasions.

(UN)CERTAINTY OF OUTCOMES?

A certain situation would be where a decision-maker knows the outcomes of all alternatives. Imagine you are a manager about to take a decision not to follow up on your commitment to deliver to your customer by their deadline. Further, imagine you have a contractual agreement to pay a fine of 10,000 USD for non-delivery. You know from several other suppliers who have been in that situation that this particular customer will not only make you pay the fine, but also that they will never order from you again. There is certainty about these outcomes of the non-delivery alternative.

At the other end of the spectrum, we have **uncertainty**, where none of the alternative outcomes can either be known or estimated by using probabilities. For instance, you might have to make a decision to venture into an entirely new market (e.g. one of Cape Town's marginalized township communities mostly inhabited by people who are ultra-poor) with a unique new product (e.g. a solar charging kiosk). You have no way of estimating what the probability of success is (e.g. of improving the lives of community members, and still breaking even). There is absolute uncertainty.

Between these two extreme points on the spectrum, we have risk. In the case of risky choices, the decision-maker can assign a probability to the alternative outcomes and in this way calculate how likely it will be that one or another outcome materializes. Decision-makers can sometimes take action to make an uncertain decision a risky decision, or a very risky decision a less risky decision by gathering additional information. For instance, you could interview people in the township to learn about their views on the product, hear how likely they think your equipment will get damaged or stolen, or you could conduct an experiment and pilot test what happens if you provide the product in just one township.

(NON)URGENCY OF TIMING?

Different choices come with different timings. **Urgent decisions** are time sensitive. To be effective, they have to be taken in a small time window. **Non-urgent decisions**, on the other hand, remain effective even if taken at a future point in time. Urgency of decisions changes over time, such as once distant deadlines move closer over time. For example, in sustainability management, decisions are all 'about time' [20], whether as the consequence of unsustainable decisions which, although certain, are far in the future, or where there is an urgent crisis, like the climate crisis, which requires immediate action. In principle any manager's decisions could be either urgent or non-urgent in nature. However, there are certain fast-paced industries where speed is of the essence, such as fast fashion where clothing has to be sold before it is 'out of fashion'; food production where supply chain decisions are time sensitive due to food's perishable nature; or high-tech and pharmaceutical industries where patents might

run out. The management consultancy McKinsey recently reported that managers are making decisions in the 'age of urgency' [1]. Crises like the Covid-19 pandemic are likely to occur more and more frequently and at an accelerated pace, as we have overstretched the environmental, social, and economic limits of our planet.

A brewery deciding to add alcohol-based hand sanitizer to their product portfolio.

Courtesy of BrewDog

Imagine the urgency of decision-making when the pandemic hit and millions of businesses depending on bricks-and-mortar customer footfall were robbed of any income. Big decisions had to be made quickly as costs (e.g. rent and salaries) accumulated, while revenues froze. For instance, the owner of the Spanish fast-fashion corporation Inditex (e.g. Zara, Pull & Bear stores) quickly decided to shift business to online retail by closing a large number of bricks-and-mortar stores for good after a Covid-related sales slump of 44 per cent [21]. Management at the Scottish craft-beer brewery and restaurant chain BrewDog took an urgent decision to produce hand sanitizers (product name 'Punk Sanitiser'), responding to a societal need following a dangerous shortage of the product [22, 23].

LOGIC OF CONSEQUENCE OR APPROPRIATENESS?

A traditional view on decision-making is that decisions are or should be based on a **'logic of consequences'** [24]: 'What will be the different outcomes (consequences) if I choose this or that alternative?' However, we are increasingly aware that there is at least an equally prevalent **logic of appropriateness** involved in decision-making: 'What would be the appropriate decision for a person like me in a situation like this?' Choice situations can be placed on a continuum with a pure logic of consequences at one end and a pure logic of appropriateness at the other. Imagine you are a female team manager in a medium-sized Egyptian garment factory who has observed that the CEO's favourite new machine is underperforming in comparison to the previous models used. The consequence is that everyone's production numbers go down and production becomes more inefficient overall in a situation where the numbers don't look good anyway. Now your boss, the head of production, is about to order another one of the CEO's favourite, but ineffective, machines. In your culture, it is highly unusual to contradict a superior's

Logics of consequence typical for choice situations that are largely devoid of expectations of customary behaviours

Logic of appropriateness typical for choice situations that are largely imbued with expectations of customary behaviours

judgement or to criticize (high power distance). On one similar occasion in the past your boss had told another colleague to shut up and do his job. In this situation, you are likely to assume a logic of 'appropriateness' following the cultural norms and social pressures not to speak up. If this choice situation was dominated by a logic of consequence, you most likely would have decided to speak up.

Logics of appropriateness may come in multiple forms, such as 'institutional logics' [25] – for instance, the 'logic of commerce', which suggests it is appropriate for a business manager to maximize profits, reduce costs, grow business, and defeat competitors. Managers in other organizations – for instance, in a religious organization – might operate under a logic of appropriateness that emphasizes caring for people's spiritual well-being, obeying moral principles, and being a role model. Often different logics of appropriateness mix in managerial decision-making. For example, if you consider yourself a responsible manager, there are the multiple logics of appropriateness of your many and varied stakeholders to consider [26]. There can be many types of tensions, trade-offs and paradoxes to consider [27, 28]. What your supplier considers appropriate might contradict what your community or family consider an appropriate decision. Making decisions based on appropriateness is socially complex. It also includes your environment's tolerance for outcomes, which could be high if your out-of-the box solutions are acceptable, or low if decisions are meant to be made 'according to script'. There might also be peer pressures, or political pressures, which make it hard to take what you know is the right decision, despite social pressures to take a different decision [29].

MODES OF DECISION-MAKING

Traditionally, there has been a preference for the rational mode of decision-making. However, as illustrated in Table 9.1, deciding rationally is only one of four main modes of decision-making together with deciding intuitively, creatively, and relationally. Each mode is differently suited to different choice situations and decision-making processes. For instance, you might prefer to evaluate choices rationally or leave it to a group, so you can justify it later. Rationally, you could say, 'the facts show it is the right choice'; relationally, you could say, 'the group decided', as justifications. If you got stuck with a decision, because there seemed to be no good choices, you might want to 'go creative' and identify new out-of-the box alternatives. If you feel there is too much urgency to engage in a lengthy rational analysis or group process, a quick gut decision based on your intuition might be an attractive mode of decision-making to choose.

TABLE 9.1   Characteristics of the four modes of decision-making

	Rational	Intuitive	Creative	Relational
In short	'Analyse facts objectively!'	'Listen to your gut!'	'Think outside the box!'	'Let's decide together!'
Ideal	Taking the one 'right' decision based on deliberation and perfect information	The quickest and 'best' decisions come from listening to your gut	Generating new unusual choice alternatives and using your imagination	Tapping into collective intelligence and being inclusive
Dominant stage of decision-making	Evaluating alternatives: collecting information and analysing it systematically	Intuitive identification and choice of alternatives, as well as foresight of consequences	Generating alternatives: broadening the pool of choice alternatives	Developing group objectives; choosing alternatives collectively
Downsides	Bounded rationality	The justification problem of intuition	Mental creativity locks	Groupthink
Typical methods	Decision trees, probability matrices	Tacit intelligence, 'the gut'	Brainstorming, associative exercises	Thinking hats, devil's advocate, Delphi method

Different modes are often interconnected in the same decision-making process. Imagine you are a product manager of a food business. Due to environmental and health issues, you have to make a decision on which alternative products to processed meat you could provide. You might, for instance, define the problem and develop objectives relationally, involving a group of stakeholders like customers, farmers, researchers, health specialists, carbon accountants, and marketing people specializing in sustainable consumption. You might then engage in creative brainstorming to identify a wide variety of choice options (e.g. lab-grown meat, tofu-based alternatives, insect protein, robotic farming). Then you might go on to rationally evaluate the alternatives with a decision tree, while intuitively trusting your gut to assign different probabilities to the outcomes for which you don't have any objective numbers yet. You might finally carry your analysis back into the stakeholder group for a vote to pick an alternative. We will now briefly introduce each of these four modes.

DECIDING RATIONALLY

Making decisions rationally and deliberatively follows the ideal of the rational choice [31, 32] that is made based on complete knowledge of all facts. These facts are meant to be analysed systematically, and choices to be made objectively, applying cold reason without allowing any subjective emotions, beliefs or values to play a role. This underlying *modus operandi* can be applied to varieties of parts of the decision-making process. For instance, you might aim to rationally forecast outcomes of decisions using decision trees and probabilities; forecast your competitors' or customers' behaviour using 'prisoner's dilemmas' and utility curves; or rank different alternatives based on quantitative evaluation criteria. We will now discuss several core features shared across:

Rational decision-making to decide objectively based on a systematic analysis of facts

- **Data.** Search for (ideally) big quantitative data, possibly aided by management information systems, mobile apps, or additional data collection tools like customer surveys, or industry data reports and statistical analysis.

- **Outcome probabilities.** Where possible, you should prefer objective probabilities (derived mathematically from reliable data) instead of subjective probabilities ('guesstimation' derived from subjective judgement).

- **Decision criteria.** A key distinction is between *must* criteria ('knock out' criteria, which lead to exclusion of an alternative if not fulfilled) and *want* criteria (leading to a higher appreciation of an alternative).

- **Weighting of value.** Depending on what underlying logic is applied (e.g. financial bottom line versus triple bottom line, or commercial versus social welfare logic), different types of value might be included or excluded from the analysis, or weighted differently when a choice is made.

BOUNDED RATIONALITY

Bounded rationality describes human beings' inability to ever be entirely rational

Notions like 'people are people' or 'human error' express the limits of human rationality. These limits can, for instance, be due to our limited information processing capability, or to our inherently subjective nature through which personal values or emotions influence decision-making. Herbert A. Simon coined the term '**bounded rationality**' [10, 33]. He suggests that instead of trying to make the 'perfect decision' ('optimizing'), realistically, we should rather try to make a decision that is 'good enough' ('satisficing') [10, 34]. Satisficing makes use of 'fast and frugal heuristics' [35], rules of thumb and minimum criteria, like 'focus on the 20 per cent of your customers that make 80 per cent of your revenue', that help us understand if a decision is good enough. It helps to avoid 'paralysis by analysis', where no decision is made as you never get to the end of the optimum 'rational' analysis.

Environmental sustainability management and making sustainable decisions with all its complexities (from global impacts to complex socio-environmental systems) is an excellent field for rules of thumb and other complexity reducing measures to deal with the boundedness of human rationality. For instance, the Swedish fast-food chain MAX Burgers was globally the first (starting in 2008) to use carbon labelling, providing information on a burger's carbon footprint similar to the more common calories and ingredients labels: 'This initiative gives power to our customers as it allows them the opportunity to choose meals not only from taste or health but also from climate impact' [36]. More recently, MAX Burgers made headlines by launching the world's first climate-positive burger [37]. It is a great example of a satisficing decision, as this might not be the most climate friendly burger possible, but it satisfices the minimum condition of being at least climate positive.

USING DECISION TREES

As an example of how to use the core instrument of rational decision-making, the decision tree [19], let's revisit the example of fridge doors in a supermarket we introduced earlier on (see Figure 9.3). Imagine you are the head of the energy management team of a market leading supermarket chain. You are scheduled to present your decision recommendation in a meeting with the VP of operations tomorrow. Since your company has signed up to the Carbon Disclosure Project, your

From carbon labelling to the first climate-positive burger at MAX in Sweden.

© 2020 MAX Burgers AB

performance is measured by how well you can both keep energy costs down and reduce overall carbon emissions. The new CEO tries to position your company as the 'green industry leader'.

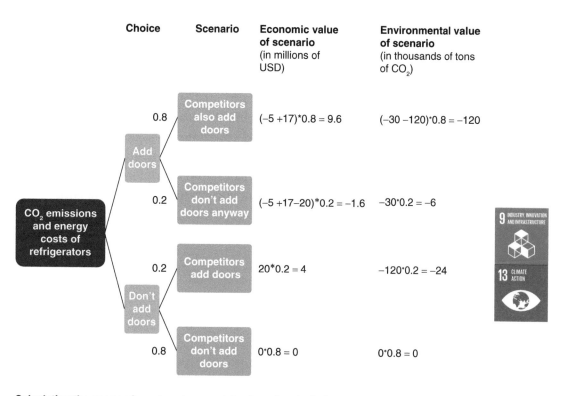

Calculating the economic and environmental value of each choice:
Add doors: Economic: 9.6-1.6 = 8 million USD; Environmental: −120−6 = −126 thousand tons of CO_2 emissions
Don't add doors: Economic: 4 million USD; Environmental: −24 thousand tons of CO_2 emissions

FIGURE 9.3   Using a decision tree to evaluate alternative scenarios

You are thinking about adding doors, which would cost you $5 million USD, but would also save $17 million in energy costs in the first year. If you add doors, you would save 30 thousand tons of CO_2 emissions. Because your company is a market and opinion leader in the retail industry, you believe that if you add doors others are likely to follow (80% likelihood), reducing the industry's overall carbon emissions by another 120,000 tons of CO_2. If competitors were not to follow, however, you know from pilot studies and focus groups that your supermarket would lose roughly $20 million USD in revenues, the reason being that customers would grow frustrated by the fact that your stores were the only ones in which they had to open the fridge door every time they reached for a product. If you decided not to add doors, the rest of the industry is considerably less likely to do so without your leadership (20%), in which case you would gain $20 million USD in additional revenues from customers who change to your supermarket for the convenience of not having to open doors when they reach for products. All things considered, you would recommend fixing doors to the refrigerators, as it would beat the alternative both in the likely money saved and in the likely amount of carbon reductions.

DECIDING INTUITIVELY

Deciding intuitively relies on 'direct knowing' without conscious reasoning

Intuitive decision-making means knowing without thinking, at least without deliberating consciously [38]. Intuition is associated with 'thinking fast'. It is a system of thought that is automatic, frequent, emotional, stereotypic, and unconscious, as opposed to 'thinking slow', a system that is slow, effortful, infrequent, logical, calculating, and conscious [30]. Intuition can help to transcend 'the bounds of cerebral rationality' [14] by trusting your 'gut' [39], knowing from within [40] through unconscious [38] practices of 'intuiting' [41]. Intuition can fulfil three main functions in decision-making [42]:

1. Intuitive expertise → decision-making

2. Intuitive creation → problem solving

3. Intuitive foresight → appreciation of consequences

THE IMPORTANCE OF INTUITION

Even Herbert Simon, the godfather of the rational decision-making field, early on highlighted the role of intuition and emotions in management decision-making [15], and it is a common mode of managerial decision-making [43]. Intuition is particularly important when making decisions related to ethical, responsible, and sustainable management. For instance, in a management context characterized by dynamic, quick, at times overwhelming environments, the types of deliberative decision-making rules and principles presented in Chapter 3 may not be the best fit. Intuitive ethics [44] or moral intuition [45–47], intuitively knowing what is the right thing to do, seem much better suited. Further, in sustainable management, intuition can provide a way to make decisions, where rationality would not allow us to 'take it all in'. For instance, think about a complex sustainability-oriented decision with all its social, environmental, and economic ramifications near and far.

How are we able 'out of nowhere' to make often excellent decisions without even thinking about them? Moreover, such decisions are often more effective than the deliberative decisions we would have made instead [48–51]. If it is not rational thought, what are the resources that intuitive judgement taps into? Figure 9.4 summarizes the different types of intuition and what source each of them taps into.

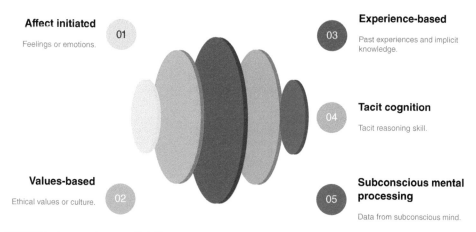

Affect initiated
01
Feelings or emotions.

Values-based
02
Ethical values or culture.

Experience-based
03
Past experiences and implicit knowledge.

Tacit cognition
04
Tacit reasoning skill.

Subconscious mental processing
05
Data from subconscious mind.

FIGURE 9.4   Layers and sources of intuition

SOURCE: Adapted from [7]; Credit: Slidemodel.com

INTUITION'S JUSTIFICATION PROBLEM

Making 'good' effective intuitive decisions strongly depends on the characteristics of a choice situation and the experience and expertise of the decision-maker [52]. But how can you evidence, prove, or justify that you have made the right decision and that you have not fallen prey to unproductive subconscious biases? This is known as **justification problem of intuition** [53]. It is a problem of accountability, of proving that you took a 'good' decision, particularly if there might be undesired or even disastrous, or life-threatening consequences for people or the environment [54]. For instance, in people management and finance, not only are intuitive decisions very common due to the complex nature of

The justification problem of intuition
refers to difficulties in proving that an intuitive decision is 'good' based on the process, as there is no explicit, visible, reasoning process as evidence

typical choice situations in these settings, but also intuition is seen as critical due to the potential of huge human and financial consequences [55, 56]. Here are three main ways to mitigate the justification problem:

1. Train your intuition. You could proactively learn to make better intuitive decisions so that others learn to 'trust in your gut' [57].

2. Choose intuition intentionally. You can argue that you have deliberately, not arbitrarily chosen to be intuitive as the situation required you to do so. Some managers have a general preference for intuitive over rational–deliberative decision-making [58], entrepreneurial managers on average have a stronger intuitive tendency than 'normal' managers [59], and people have a general tendency to use intuitive reasoning when in a happy mood, less likely if sad [60]. It can be advantageous to distance yourself from such automatic behaviour and to deliberately apply intuition instead of rationality when the situation demands it, for instance, when identifying entrepreneurial opportunities [61].

3. Practice 'intuitive rigour'. You could demonstrate your 'intuitive rigour' by describing the practices you use to boost your intuition effectiveness – for instance, showing that you are using the practices presented in Figure 9.5.

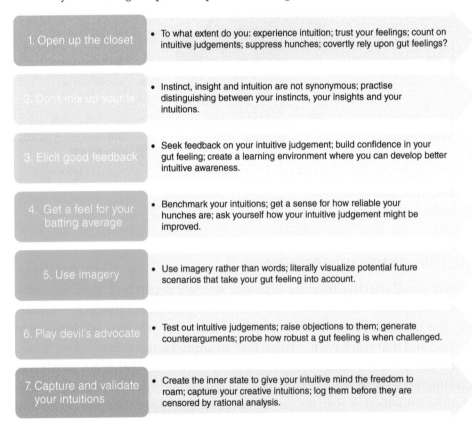

FIGURE 9.5 Practices for improving intuitive choice

SOURCE: Adapted from [39]

DECIDING CREATIVELY

Arguably, there is no quote that better expresses the need for creative problem solving in ethical, responsible, and sustainable management than 'We cannot solve our problems with the same kind of thinking that we used to create them'.[1] As we have argued in the opening chapter of this book, the 'normal' underlying logic of management has done much to steer the world into the multiple social, environmental, and economic crises we are facing today. Therefore, we cannot stress enough how important it is to 'decide out of the box' of normal management thought, and to critically question every decision that is based on 'conventional management wisdom' [62]. The main aspects of creativity are captured in the list below [63]:

Deciding creatively means to generate new and original valuable answers

1. **Person.** While certain personal characteristics play a role, in principle anyone can engage in creative management decision-making [64]. However, developing one's creative potential may require personal development, learning, and continuous practice.

2. **Place.** Place[2] refers to the forces at play in the environment that may promote or impede creativity. Different places may provide a differently suitable breeding ground for creativity. This includes the social context of the workplace [65] like colleagues' openness to novel ideas and time that is ring-fenced for creative work [64, 66]. The place (and time) also provides the issues and problems to be addressed in creative problem solving.

3. **Process.** The creative process relies on divergent and convergent thinking and distinct sub-processes like ideation and germination, which we will have a closer look at in the next section.

4. **Product.** Products or outcomes of a creative process can be of a cognitive or material nature, of 'hand or mind' [63]. Creative ideas manifest as 'artefacts' – for instance, in the form of an image, a technology, an invention, or a composition.

Creative process and practices. The creative process is centred on an interplay between divergent and convergent thinking. While divergent thinking starts from a problem and generates multiple alternative answers [67], convergent thinking narrows down alternatives, ultimately leading to a single solution [68]. Divergence helps to create new ideas, while convergence serves to evaluate the value of new ideas [68]. As illustrated in Figure 9.6, the creative decision-making process therefore relies on both divergent thinking and convergent thinking, often in multiple iterative cycles [69].

---

[1]The quote has often been misattributed to Albert Einstein while its actual origin has not been confirmed conclusively.
[2]Place was originally called 'press', making reference to how these forces mould people and their creativity.

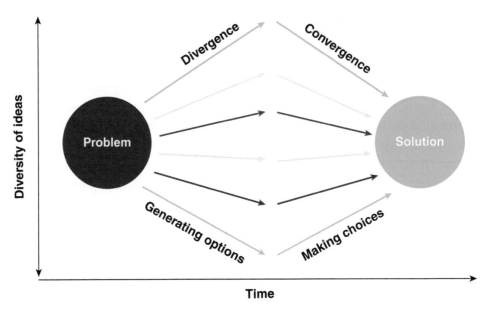

FIGURE 9.6   Divergent and convergent thinking in the creative decision-making process

SOURCE: Adapted from [70]

The creative process can be described as a bundle of creative practices that interact with each other. The following creative practices interacting in the creative process have been identified [71, 72]:

1. **Preparation.** Getting fixated on a problem and exploring its characteristics

2. **Incubation.** A deep subconscious internalization of the problem

3. **Intimation.** The creative practitioner feels a solution emerging

4. **Illumination.** Creative ideas burst from the subconscious into the conscious: an 'aha!' moment

5. **Verification**. Ideas are consciously tested and applied

Originally, these practices were understood as a linear process running from preparation all the way through to verification. However, more recent research has found that these and further creative practices are used in an iterative way and a more random sequence [69].

Unlocking creativity. There is a long list of potential inhibitors of managerial creativity, ranging from stress and fear, to societal norms and fear of criticism, to constraints of time and money [73]. Creative decision-making is also commonly inhibited by ten typical 'mental locks' that can be avoided [74, 75]. The following description can be used as a screening tool, to make sure you or people you work with don't lock up their creative potential in these mindsets. The divergent part of the creative process is particularly vulnerable to these mental locks:

1. 'The right answer': Search for multiple answers!

2. 'That's not logical': Illogical answers may be valuable too!

3. 'Follow the rules': Not following the rules leads to novel answers!

4. 'Be practical': A theoretical focus may stifle the flow of ideas!

5. 'Play is frivolous': Play is creative!

6. 'That's not my area': New answers can only be found in new areas!

7. 'Avoid ambiguity': Being ambiguous allows for multiple interpretations and new ideas!

8. 'Don't be foolish': Goofing around might stir up new ideas!

9. 'To err is wrong': Erring along new paths leads to new places!

10. 'I'm not creative': Believe in your innate creativity!

Furthermore, techniques like brainstorming, association exercises, provocations and unreasonable questions, disordering, or reversing the original questions as well as back casting are creativity techniques to unleash your creative thought [76, 77].

DECIDING RELATIONALLY

Early on in this chapter, we discussed decisions based on a 'logic of appropriateness' that is centred on social norms and expectations. One may even argue that we always engage in **relational decision-making** as we and our decisions are always enmeshed in a web of stakeholder relationships [78] each of which comes with a different logic of decision-making [26]. While this type of relational complexity is an inescapable reality of managerial decision-making, managers can also decide to deliberately seek out relational decision-making. It has been argued that there are many ways in which relational or group decision-making can be harnessed to generate both better decision-making processes and better decision outcomes:

Deciding relationally emphasizes the social dynamics of decision-making

- **Effectiveness.** In smaller groups, making decisions together may lead to a pooling of group members' thought faculties and the amount of information available [79, 80]. You might also get access to the 'collective intelligence' of large groups – for instance, by using collaborative social media tools [97, 98], or even including artificial intelligence in your group decision-making [83]. Therefore, it has been argued that more effective decisions can be made by pooling resources and achieving synergies in groups. However, later on we will discuss the problem of groupthink, which may lead to group decisions that are inferior to individual decisions.

- **Transfer of responsibility.** There may be many reasons for wanting to transfer the responsibility for a decision to a larger group of people. You might not want to take the whole blame if risky decisions lead to undesirable outcomes, or you might want not to be the only person who will be challenged if decisions are not socially desirable. Conversely, you might want to empower others by giving them authority to make decisions or use a democratic vote to make sure that what is decided reflects the majority's preference.

- **Inclusiveness.** Including stakeholders in decision-making is an essential piece of responsible management. Making responsible decisions and making decisions responsibly starts with making stakeholder voices heard [84]. Through inclusion and participation, passive stakeholders of a decision may even become co-responsible actors shaping decisions and outcomes themselves. From an instrumental perspective, including stakeholders in the decision-making process is likely to lead to stronger buy-in to the decision outcome. It may decrease potential opposition and increase support in implementing the decision.

Participative decision-making. In the relationship between 'boss and subordinates' [85] participative decision-making is a core aspect of 'high involvement management', which has been found to be positively related to performance [86] and job satisfaction [87]. Thinking about management in the service of society, to be considered responsible, decision-making must facilitate the participation of stakeholders that affect or are affected by the decision [88, 89]. Figure 9.7 presents a continuum of participative decision-making [85]. It runs from entirely 'autocratic' decision-making, where the original decision-maker does not involve stakeholders at all (telling and selling), to 'consultative' modes where stakeholders are asked to provide input into the decision ultimately to be taken by the original decision-maker (consulting), to 'collaborative' modes, where decisions require consensus from the stakeholder group (sharing, delegating, democratizing) [85, 90, 91].

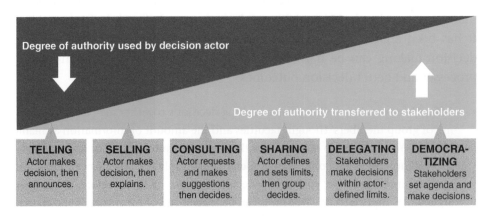

FIGURE 9.7   Continuum of stakeholder participation types in decision-making

SOURCE: Integrated from [85, 88, 92]

If you are the person with the original authority to make the decision, how do you choose which style of relational decision-making to pursue? Ethical decision-making based on stakeholder democracy principles is a fundamental aspect of responsible management [92]. Achieving as much participation as possible from the stakeholders of a decision in the making is therefore a normative, imperative and a moral obligation for a responsible manager [93]. Such a combination of participative and stakeholder management [94–96] requires a thorough assessment of the varieties of forces and contingencies that determine the degree and type of participation that can be achieved in a given choice situation [85–91]. For instance, a decision might be urgent, leaving little time for any time-intensive stakeholder participation. When responding to an emergent crisis, group decision-making might just take too long. How committed is the group to making 'good' decisions? How well is the group involved functioning? Can the group handle the level of complexity of the decision at hand? Are you legally or contractually allowed to let others participate or even make the decision? Do you have enough information to make the decision on your own, and conversely, are you able to share decision-critical, potentially confidential information with the group?

Mitigating groupthink. Who needs to fight over good ideas if we can all agree on a bad one? Groupthink has been blamed for everything from the explosion of space shuttles to low grades for students' group assignments [97]. Paradoxically, while in theory pooling decision-making resources in a group should lead to better decisions, making decisions in a group frequently leads to 'defective decision-making' [98], and decisions that are less effective than an individual's. 'How could we have been so stupid?' is the perplexed question victims of groupthink often ask themselves. The reason is that particularly homogeneous, close, cohesive groups often tend to over-emphasize conformity and uniformity.

The Australian Rachael Robertson had to keep peace while still making effective decisions in one of the world's most extreme environments, the Antarctic.

Courtesy of Renato Granieri

'Arctic Spitsbergen Magdalena Fjord Mountain Glacier Zodiac-Renato Granieri 2012-IMG2058183 Lg RGB[2][14].jpg' by Traveloscopy is licensed under CC BY-ND 2.0

Ideas for improvement or criticism might not be brought forward in order not to upset the peace. Take it from Rachael Robertson, who managed 'a mixed bag of projects' in an isolated Antarctic camp with a team of 17 people she had not even picked herself: 'I have grave concerns for any team that, explicitly or implicitly, strives just for harmony at the expense of productivity and respect. It's dangerous, dysfunctional behaviour still continues; it just goes underground so the illusion of harmony remains … it stifles innovation. People are often too afraid to put up their hand and offer a different view or opinion … it's unsafe both physically and mentally' [99]. This type of close-knit group may tend towards group polarization (pun intended) in the form of overly strong agreement on potentially inferior decision options [100]. These issues are often rooted in the following attitudes and behaviours [101, 102]:

- Illusion of invulnerability
- Belief in inherent group morality
- Collective rationalization
- Stereotypes of outsiders
- Self-censorship
- Illusion of unanimity
- Pressure on dissenters
- Self-appointed mindguards

Ensuring a diverse group composition and that critical points are raised are the principal remedies for groupthink. Groupthink can be mitigated by using techniques aimed at increasing the quality and effectiveness of group decisions:

- The **nominal group technique** is centred on eliminating early convergence of group ideas by 'keeping ideas apart'. Group members meet up but develop their thought independently and silently. Then a facilitator records all ideas publicly. Next, participants may seek verbal explanation about details or ambiguities of each idea. Ideas may be combined or added, but not eliminated. Once all ideas are clear and complete, participants rank ideas and vote on which one to pursue [103].

- The **Delphi technique** builds on anonymity to allow people to express their unique, honest, and critical thought. While it was originally meant to catch experts' opinions on a topic [104, 105], the method is particularly helpful when capturing stakeholders' distinct perspectives, their unique expertise [106]. Group members do not meet, but submit their unique ideas to a facilitator who in turn re-shares them with all group members. In the next round, group members adjust their own ideas based on new aspects introduced in others'

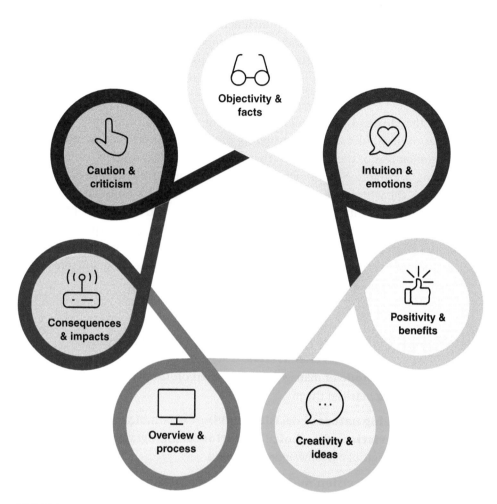

FIGURE 9.8   Group roles for lateral thinking

SOURCE: Adapted from [111]; Credit: Slidemodel.com

ideas. Over several rounds, the experts' ideas tend to converge to include all experts'/stakeholders' ideas, thus building an integrative idea reflecting all perspectives.

- **Appreciative inquiry** moves away from the group's focus on problem solving to a focus on shaping a desired 'good' future [107, 108]. Stakeholders engage in a positive appreciation of the status quo and create a positive vision exercise of the future they want. Processes and practices that work well and that are likely to build that future are then designed and implemented [109].

- The **devil's advocate** technique is used to question a group's potentially premature adoption of a preferred decision by assigning the role of the devil's advocate to one or several group members. Their role is to actively find flaws and to critically challenge other group members defending the decision. It has been found that this method tends to lead to even more effective decisions when the devil's advocate is genuinely opposing the solution, not just hypothetically [110].

- Using the **thinking hats** method offers the opportunity to tap into all four modes of decision-making by assigning different decision-making roles to different members of the group (see Figure 9.8), symbolized by each team member wearing a metaphorical or actual hat whose colour symbolizes their role. For instance, the white data and information hat closely relates to rationality; the red hat involves intuition, the green hat creativity; and finally, the blue hat is about steering the relational decision-making process. The purple hat stands for the consequences of the decision in the long run and on stakeholders. A variation of the thinking hats could be to wear hats representing different stakeholders' views on a decision.

PRINCIPLES OF PROFESSIONAL DECISION-MAKING

I.   The **deciding mode** of management is centred on **identifying alternatives and choosing** between them.

II. The **challenging nature of decision-making** can be mitigated by an assessment of **characteristics of a choice situation** ((un)programmed, (un)certain, (non)urgent, logic of outcome/appropriateness).

III. **Whole-person decision-making** involves rational ('Analyse facts objectively!'), intuitive ('Listen to your gut!'), creative ('Decide outside the box!'), and relational practices ('Let's decide together!').

IV. Deciding **rationally** emphasizes complete **information and an optimum choice**, with practices often centred on **decision trees**. It needs to deal with **bounded rationality**.

V.   Deciding **intuitively** emphasizes **implicit spontaneous knowledge**, with practices centred on tapping into different **layers of intuition**. It requires attention to the **justification problem** of intuition.

VI. Deciding **creatively** emphasizes the generation of large quantities and varieties of **new and unique ideas**, using cycles of **divergent and convergent** thought. It requires attention to **creativity locks**.

VII. Deciding **relationally** emphasizes pooling individuals' decision resources and inclusiveness, while often using **participative decision-making** practices. It requires attention to the **groupthink** problem.

MANAGEMENT GYM: TRAINING YOUR PROFESSIONAL SIX-PACK

Knowing

1. What connections and overlaps can you identify between rational, intuitive, creative, and relational decision-making?

2. Try to visually integrate rational, intuitive, creative, and relational decision-making.

3. Look up ten different creativity techniques online. Write a one-paragraph description for each of them. Make sure the sentence includes basic characteristics and assumptions, content related to the process or procedure, and how it could be used in an ethics, responsibility, or sustainability management context.

Thinking

4. Imagine, you are the owner–manager of a medium-sized local family business. The production manager Heimana, in return for favours, has been giving jobs to unqualified people considered unemployable, often members of the local community. Heimana is your brother-in-law. What different logics of appropriateness play a role and how might each suggest a distinct decision?

5. Use the 'thinking hats' technique (individually, not in a group setting) to solve a problem of your choice. Note down each hat's contribution to the process.

6. Assess a choice situation based on the choice characteristics introduced. What does this mean for your decision-making in this situation?

Acting

7. Identify and download a mobile app that supports decision-making. Use it for a week, write a one-page review of your experience including what you found helpful, and make suggestions about how the app could be improved.

8. Make a decision intuitively, note it down. Then prepare a rational decision tree for the same decision as if you had not decided yet.

9. Write a one-page implementation plan for a decision you have taken recently.

Interacting

10. In a small group of 4–6 people use one of the group decision techniques presented in this chapter on a decision of your choice.

11. Draw a visual – e.g. an image, map, or diagram that expresses an Intuitive insight you have had recently. Ask someone else for their feedback on your visual.

12. Ask three people to take part in the decision-making process of a real decision you have to take. What type of stakeholder participation have you chosen and why?

Being

13. Think about two recent decisions. Which do you think is your natural decision-making mode – rational, intuitive, creative, or relational? Or is it a combination?

14. Use the practices for improving intuitive choice presented in this chapter for a week and document what you did in a short reflective diary entry every day.

15. Observe yourself while engaging in a creative decision-making process (e.g. together with a partner). Which of the mental locks to creativity can you spot in what you say and do?

Becoming

16. What kind of decisions are most important in your private and/or professional life?

17. Think about three 'bad' decisions you have taken. Why were they bad, and how could you improve your decision-making in the future?

18. Do you sometimes make decisions that are unnecessary, which you could leave to someone else without major consequences, and this way reduce your 'mental load' a bit? Conversely, what decisions should you definitely not leave to someone else?

SOURCE: Adapted from [112]

PIONEER INTERVIEW
ROY SUDDABY

INTERVIEWER: OLIVER LAASCH

Roy Suddaby is a pioneering thought leader in the field of organizational institutionalism. He has been recognized, among others, for his research understanding 'institutional work'

(Continued)

[113–115], how people can change what is 'normal' and 'taken for granted' around them, including what is considered rational or logical. As alternatives to pure rationality, he has explored re-enchantment [116] and 'magical thinking' [117].

Myths of economic rationality. Let me back up a little bit here and talk about this idea of myths of rationality, which really comes from Max Weber [118] and his discussion of this process of ongoing rationalization of the world. We understand quite well what that means in present day terms, and that is that we are subject to these inexorable processes of industrialization of the world. Sometimes it's referred to as McDonaldization [119], but it's based on this economic rationality that we need bigger factories to get these ever-increasing economies of scale so that we can feed the world. Meyer and Rowan [120] in their paper talk about this as being rational myths because we don't know where these myths of rationality come from. While there is some kind of *prima facie* demonstration of effectiveness of industrialization and rationality, what we tend to forget is that Weber talked about this process as producing this massive disenchantment with the world, this feeling of ennui. It sometimes is referred to as this iron cage that we get trapped in, these webs of meaning of our own making.

Imagining alternative management worlds. I think that the role of the manager is to understand that these myths of rationality are not above and beyond human agency, that we have the capacity and ability to change our world view. So, responsible managers' jobs are really to re-enchant our institutions, re-enchant our government, re-enchantment of our institutions of commerce. In part, that means stepping away from this idea that bigger and cheaper is the way to human salvation. There are alternative realities out there that allow us to create a viable means of human existence and a viable means of feeding the world, but it doesn't have to occur on an industrial scale that involves this degree of disenchantment. I think that there are opportunities for re-enchantment in modes of production that don't rely on this sort of mix of rationality that everything has to be done on a massive industrial scale. That is, we need to change the dialogue or discourse by which we have this conversation about what it means to be a manager. I think that managers need to acquire this idea of moving away from a notion that we're trapped by the world the way it is and to imagine alternative worlds.

Thinking institutional reflexivity. We need to develop a degree of institutional reflexivity rather than the focus on this ongoing process towards legitimacy that we're doing things just because other organizations or other actors are doing them. We need to think a little bit about authenticity and ideas to do things because they're the right thing to do, not necessarily because everyone else is doing them. I have written about this in a paper about craft, magic,

(Continued)

and re-enchantment of the world [116], but it really is designed to look at the other half of Weber's argument. That is that it isn't always about inexorable rationalization. There is a humanistic element to industrialization that tends to get overlooked.

QUESTIONS

1. Do you think Roy suggests that managers should generally not be rational?

2. On what kind of criteria do you think decisions are taken in the 'normal' world, and how?

3. is this different from the decisions to be taken in the 'alternative worlds' Roy suggests managers should imagine?

4. Can you spot instances of intuitive, creative, rational, and relational decision-making in what Roy describes?

PROFESSIONAL PROFILE
TOMMY WEIR

My name is Dr Tommy Weir, and I'm the founder and CEO of Enaible, a company that helps business leaders improve the productivity of their workforce. I'm passionate about helping leaders become the best they can.

The real depth of my calling started 20 years ago while I attended a doctoral seminar and thought, 'Every employee deserves to be led by a great leader.' Since then, I've been committed to making this happen: coaching CEOs, discovering the power and role of

Courtesy of Tommy Weir

(Continued)

data science in leadership, and writing a handful of books for which I have earned numerous accolades, including #1 best-seller status on Amazon.

Leading and deciding with artificial intelligence. In October 2016, I studied and learned about applied AI and how companies like Media Lab, Sony Labs, and Google are doing such innovative and progressive things with AI. This is when I had my 'aha moment', leading me to discover the link between AI and leadership. Two years later, in 2018, I hired a rock-star team of data scientists and opened the world's first Leadership AI Lab. Combining 20 years' experience in leadership research and coaching CEOs with AI, we've solved the productivity paradox and created Enable: AI-powered leadership. And this resolved a private frustration that I've lived with, how can I impact leaders at scale? AI makes this possible and even more. Now, even if a manager is average or poor, Enable gives them a surrogate in the form of our Leadership Recommender™.

A typical day at work? I'm still on the hunt for a typical day. And the day I have planned rarely plays out according to what's on my calendar. I guess this is one of the benefits of running a fast-growing company. I'm energized by the twists and turns. My time is generally split between supporting sales, product vision, helping out customers get maximum value from Enable, and shaping the world's thinking about machines learning and humans leading. My favourite part of the day is engaging with customers, they are why we jump out of bed every morning … helping them become the best they can, then better.

Making decisions. For me, decision-making needs to be informed and quick. In a typical day, I make dozens of decisions that need to be made instantaneously, otherwise I'd hold up our team's progress. Oftentimes, I find myself drawing on my decades of experience coaching CEOs and reflecting on the advice I would have given them. I'm highly conscious of the reality that when I make a decision, my perspective is limited and I'm not aware of all of the needed information. This problem isn't limited to me, thus the value of our AI Leadership Recommender™. Noting that leaders have limited visibility, suffer from subjective bias and skewed by the present moment, we need help – this is why Enable's Leadership Recommender™ continuously mines data that companies have, identifies what will help employees to be as productive as possible and then acts like a coach and makes personalized, prioritized recommendations.

The importance of knowing when you're right. My biggest challenge is recognizing when I am right and when it's just an opinion. Right now, I'm very conscious of this as I had a stretch of thinking others may be right, yet in hindsight we had to go back and rework what we had done. In hindsight, this cost us valuable time. Balancing my ideas and others is always a thin and contentious line. This is in addition to the typical cash management challenges of every fast-growing business.

Some advice. Have an ambitious appetite, create an environment where others succeed, act decisively, keep the focus, micro-monitor without micromanaging and never accept good enough as good enough. That's my general leadership advice.

(Continued)

At a more macro level, my advice is to embrace the reality that humans and machines are better together. AI is a resource that should be used to make the human worker the best they can be. I've realized that AI is better at parts of leadership than we will ever be, just as there are parts that it can't do yet. If you fail to leverage AI, you'll fail to reach your peak.

QUESTIONS

1. What type of decisions do you think Tommy typically engages in – for instance, are they planned or unplanned? Are they characterized by risk, certainty or uncertainty? Rational, creative, intuitive, or group decisions?

2. Tommy strongly advocates the integration of human decision-making and AI. What kind of ethics, responsibility, or sustainability issues might arise from human and AI deciding together? What opportunities might there be?

3. What tactics does Tommy mention he uses to deal with his own bounded rationality?

TRUE STORY

STICKING TO MY GUNS

EDITED BY ALEXANDRA LEONOR BARRUETA SACKSTEDER

That's me: My name is Fade and my passion for responsible management and sustainability is profound. In addition to my Managing Responsibly Coursera MOOC, I have successfully

(Continued)

completed several courses in sustainability, which I am able to embed into my work. I believe in practicing what I preach. So, as well as supporting gender equality through my not-for-profit organization, I raise funds for women entrepreneurs in poorer countries, for example, Burkina Faso, Pakistan, Bangladesh, and Philippines. I also use social media to highlight and write articles about climate change and responsible management, in order to promote a sustainable world, for future generations. Recently, I managed to begin a recycling initiative in my building, which surprisingly took real effort. I believe small contributions like this from all of us, can help make a large difference collectively.

To begin at the beginning ... A couple of years ago, I was offered an opportunity abroad to work with several businesses in Bangladesh by SpeakCorp (based in the United Kingdom), with whom I was contracted as a consultant. At a briefing with the CEO, he requested I ensure that I sought opportunities for contracts from the company INK and to report back such opportunities. This was advanced rather forcibly and I was to be surreptitious. It was against this backdrop that my work was to be scoped. In effect I was being asked to carry out the very minimum of work and limit the deployment of the expertise, for which I was being engaged, to generate extra revenue for SpeakCorp, at INK's expense.

It was immediately clear what I was being asked to do: not work entirely in the client's interest. I felt awkward and a little contemptuous of the CEO for asking me to do this. I also felt it wasn't fair on INK who were rightfully expecting a fully supportive service.

Dilemmas, dilemmas. On arrival in Bangladesh, I was met with several scenarios, on which I had not been briefed. INK was further down the line with the project than previously thought. I realized that contrary to scaling back (so as to generate further revenue for SpeakCorp), I would not be meaningfully engaged, without extending the scope of work. I could not betray the trust of those on whose behalf I was working (Dilemma 1) but did not want to be party to an agenda that was not in the best interest of the client (Dilemma 2).

(Continued)

Taking matters into my own hands. By this time, I was aware that there were legitimate grounds for consulting work, not stipulated by an unethical agenda. Consequently, I emailed SpeakCorp, outlining the situation and requesting permission to provide this important groundwork. Several emails and phone calls later, with no response, I took the decision to move ahead. I prepared a report of critical success factors and an action plan. Unbeknown to me (probably understanding I wasn't pursuing ulterior motives, which was not the purpose of my role), SpeakCorp was undermining me. As a consequence, my relationship with both SpeakCorp and INK broke down. This happened before I could email the contents of a diagnostic report, so the contract terminated, without this important piece of information.

Can you believe these people? Approximately two weeks after my arrival back in the United Kingdom, I received a call from INK, requesting this information, which I had largely prepared on my own initiative, to underpin the success of the project. SpeakCorp would also have found it invaluable, both were desperate for it, as a means to forward plan and raise finance. At this point I felt that SpeakCorp was trying to take advantage of me and took the commitment and dedication with which I had undertaken my role, to mean I could be manipulated or used. I was rather irritated at what I considered the gall of asking, given the circumstances.

QUESTIONS

1. What main factors would you consider if making this decision? How are these factors interlinked?

2. If you were Fade, what would be your (different) decisions if you decided intuitively, rationally, collectively, or creatively?

3. What would you do if you were in Fade's shoes?

DIGGING DEEPER: EVALUATING ALTERNATIVES ETHICALLY, RESPONSIBLY, SUSTAINABLY

The matrix in Table 9.2 is a support tool for the evaluation of alternative decisions by considering the mainstream condition (solution effectiveness, SE), conditions for ethics, responsibility, and sustainability (moral value, stakeholder value, triple bottom line impact). In an ideal world, a manager rationally pursuing a good decision would assess the fulfilment of each of those categories. He might use a scale between 0 and 5, with 0 meaning not fulfilled and 5 completely fulfilled. For example, an alternative that will solve the problem at hand without any risk of failure would be evaluated as 5; an alternative that has no potential to solve the problem would be 0. A solution that is completely immoral would be evaluated as 0 and one that has no potential to deliver negative moral consequences would be 5.

The manager would then decide how strongly each of these factors should be reflected in the decision to be made. The manager defines an influence factor or weighting (wv) between 0 per cent and 100 per cent for each of the categories. The influence factors of all categories should jointly add up to 100 per cent. If all of them were equally important, each would have an influence factor of 25 per cent. The most extreme 'mainstream' old world manager would assign 100 per cent to the solution effectiveness and zero per cent in other categories. The only thing that counts is the organizational problem to be solved, no matter what the consequences. Consider a managing director of an NGO, for instance, who has the goal of alleviating AIDS and would focus their decision-making purely on the stakeholder value created for AIDS patients. This person would probably assign a 100 per cent of the weighting to the indicator for stakeholder value. There are many weighting situations in between those two extremes.

TABLE 9.2   Responsible decision-making matrix

	Effectiveness	ERS Value			
	Solution-effectiveness (SE) * wc_{SE}	Moral value (MV) * wc_{MV}	Stakeholder value (SV) * wc_{SV}	Triple bottom line impact (TL) * wc_{TL}	Sum
A1					
A2					
(...)					
A3					
Decision:					

To select a final alternative, a manager might choose between different choice practices:

1. Managers who *maximize* the overall value from the decision would choose the alternative that generates the biggest overall sum.

2. Managers who *satisfice* will use the first alternative that fulfils a pre-defined requirement. If the original problem was a manufacturing production method that polluted a nearby river, the manager might pick the first alternative that does not pollute.

3. Managers typically have to make decisions in a nexus of competing claims and responsibilities. Therefore, the most viable option for an ethical, responsible, and sustainable manager probably is to *optimize*, which is to choose the one alternative that best responds to competing claims while usually making compromises and incurring trade-offs between alternatives.

A manager might realize that all alternatives contradict responsible management, in which case it becomes necessary not only to make a single decision but to re-examine the organizational and personal framework in which the decision is to be made. In the most extreme case, a manager might decide to leave the organization, or if they have change-agent power, to actively effect profound change.

Here is an example. Imagine you were an assistant to the CEO of a multinational consulting company and you are in charge of organizing the annual budgeting meeting with the local managing directors of the company's four main business regions, USA/Canada, Europe, Latin America, and Australasia. Until this year, those meetings had always been conducted in the corporate headquarters in Paris. With the company's substantially increased revenue from sustainable business consulting the CEO has decided also to integrate the values of sustainability, responsibility, and ethics into the company's core activities, to make sure the consultancy is 'walking the talk'. The budget meeting is meant to be a first landmark event for doing so. Your task now is not only to plan a successful meeting, but to do so with 'good' conduct, optimizing the triple bottom line, stakeholder value, and moral value of the meeting decision. The three alternative meeting formats to be considered are:

- **A2 Classic on-site:** All managing directors travel to the headquarters: carbon impact of plane travel, advantages of face-to-face meeting experience, not walking the talk of sustainable business (immoral).

- **A2 On-site + carbon offsetting:** All managing directors travel, but the company pays for carbon offsetting to make the travel carbon neutral: cost of carbon offsetting, time required by managers.

- **A3 Web meeting:** The company invests in a sophisticated online meeting solution and nobody has to travel: time saved, loss of face-to-face experience, inconvenience for and inexperience of 'old-school managers' when using web meetings, distractions through office environment.

TABLE 9.3 Applying the integrative decision-making matrix

	Solution-effectiveness (SE) x wc_{SE}	Triple bottom line impact (TI) x wc_{TL}	Stakeholder value (SV) x wc_{SV}	Moral value (MV) x wc_{MV}	Sum
A1	5 x 0.25	1 x 0.25	2 x 0.25	1 x 0.25	2.25
A2	5 x 0.25	2 x 0.25	2 x 0.25	3 x 0.25	3.00
A3	2 x 0.25	3 x 0.25	1 x 0.25	5 x 0.25	2.75

Following your CEO's instructions to consider all responsible management aspects equally, you have given the same weighting factor of 0.25 to each of the four condition types. After considering all the above-mentioned aspects you have come up with a way of describing the situation. Alternative 2, the on-site meeting with carbon offsetting, is your preferred choice, as it combines perfect solution effectiveness (satisfying the need for an effective meeting) with an improved triple bottom line (much lower CO_2 emissions, slightly higher cost through offsetting), equal stakeholder value, and an increase in moral value through 'walking the talk' of sustainable business. You are worried, though, about increasing criticism of carbon offsetting as a 'not good enough' solution and flight shaming might still cause the company problems.

POINTERS

You could use this section to make your own decision, or to redesign the matrix. You could also use it as a basis for building a decision tree, or to explore changes in the decision-making algorithm. How might the external environment, like the emergent practice of flight shaming, change the value of decisions? Finally, you could critically evaluate whether this type of decision-making is doomed to fail due to our bounded rationality and time constraints. Is it 'too academic'?

WORKSHEET

CUTTING THE PROBLEM TO THE (FISH)BONE

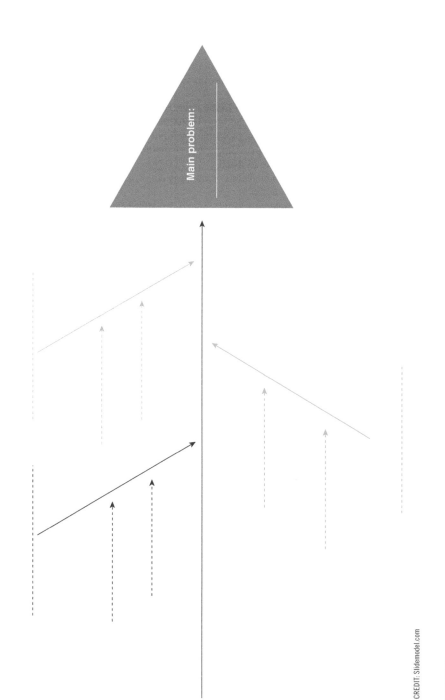

Main problem:

CREDIT: Slidemodel.com

POINTERS

Start by writing down the problem in the fish's head, then the primary causes of the problem at the top of the green, red, and blue arrows. Finally, fill in the sub-causes for the fishbone of each colour. Feel free to add your problem – for example, by leaving some dotted lines empty, or by adding additional lines. Once you have understood the problem, the detail provides a powerful information base for identifying effective solution alternatives that address these causes.

REFERENCES

1. McKinsey. *Organization practice: Decision making in the age of urgency.* Published 2019.

2. Krishna V. Nature based packaging, Ved Krishna, TEDxPSITKanpur. *TEDx Talks.* Published 2018. www.youtube.com/watch?v=cxQc6Mz_c3U&t=1s Accessed June 15 2020.

3. The Pulp and Paper Times. Yash Pakka steps up with three kinds of paper domains to serve food segment. www.youtube.com/watch?v=QiVSD0CHTkQ&t=309s Published 2020. Accessed June 15 2020.

4. Leadermorphosis. Ep. 42: Ved Krishna on self-management in an Indian paper factory. https://leadermorphosis.co/pages/episodes/ved-krishna-on-self-management-in-an-indian-paper-factory?utm_campaign=meetedgar&utm_medium=social&utm_source=meetedgar. com Published 2020. Accessed June 15 2020.

5. Basterfield S. Mango season: Self-management in India. www.linkedin.com/pulse/mango-season-susan-basterfield Published 2016. Accessed June 16 2020.

6. Gill L. This Indian company has been exploring self-management for two decades. https://corporate-rebels.com/this-indian-paper-company-runs-with-self-management-for-two-decades Published 2020. Accessed June 15 2020.

7. Robbins SP, DeCenzo DA, Coulter M. *Fundamentals of management: Essential concepts and applications* (9th edn). Harlow: Pearson, 2015.

8. Chuk. Yash Papers Limited. www.youtube.com/watch?v=-UL75GxJOe8 Published 2019. Accessed June 15 2020.

9. Singal A. A happy coincidence that led this entrepreneur to take a step towards compostable packaging. www.entrepreneur.com/article/334801 Published 2019. Accessed June 15 2020.

10. Simon HA. *Administrative behavior.* New York: Simon & Schuster, 1997/1947.

11. Eisenhardt KM. Strategic decisions and all that jazz. *Business Strategy Review.* 1997, 8(3): 1–3.

12. Eisenhardt KM, Zbaracki MJ. Strategic decision making. *Strategic Management Journal.* 1992, 13(2): 17–37.

13. Sen AK. Rational fools: A critique of the behavioral foundations of economic theory. *Philosophy & Public Affairs.* 1977, 6(4): 317–344.

14. Langley A, Mintzberg H, Pitcher P, Posada E, Saint-Macary J. Opening up decision making: The view from the black stool. *Organization Science.* 1995, 6(3): 260–279.

15. Simon HA. Making management decisions: The role of intuition and emotion. *Academy of Management Perspectives.* 1987, 1(1): 57–64.

16. World Economic Forum. The great reset. www.weforum.org/great-reset Published 2020. Accessed June 21 2020.

17. Cohen MD, March JG, Olsen JP. A garbage can model of organizational choice. *Administrative Science Quarterly.* 1972, 17(1): 1–25.

18. Soelberg P. Unprogrammed decision making. Paper presented at Academy of Management Proceedings, 1966.

19. Klein GA, Calderwood R. Decision models: Some lessons from the field. *IEEE Transactions on Systems, Man, and Cybernetics.* 1991, 21(5): 1018–1026.

20. Bansal P, DesJardine MR. Business sustainability: It is about time. *Strategic Organization.* 2014, 12(1): 70–78.

21. Jolly J. Zara owner to close up to 1,200 fashion stores around the world. www.theguardian.com/business/2020/jun/10/zara-owner-to-close-up-to-1200-fashion-stores-around-the-world Published 2020. Accessed June 25 2020.

22. Butler S. BrewDog begins making hand sanitiser amid shortages in UK. www.theguardian.com/business/2020/mar/18/brewdog-begins-making-hand-sanitiser-shortages-uk Published 2020. Accessed June 25 2020.

23. Butler S. First batch of BrewDog hand sanitiser turned down by local hospital. www.theguardian.com/business/2020/apr/02/brewdog-hand-sanitiser-turned-down-local-hospitals-scotland Published 2020. Accessed June 25 2020.

24. March JG, Olsen JP. The logic of appropriateness. In: Goodin RE, ed. *The Oxford handbook of political science.* Oxford: Oxford University Press, 2004.

25. Ocasio W, Thornton PH, Lounsbury M. Advances to the institutional logics perspective. In: Greenwood R, Oliver C, Lawrence TB, Meyer RE, eds. *The Sage handbook of organizational institutionalism* (2nd edn). Thousand Oaks, CA: Sage, 2017: 509–531.

26. Radoynovska N, Ocasio W, Laasch O. The emerging logic of responsible management: Institutional pluralism, leadership, and strategizing. In: Laasch O, Suddaby R, Freeman RE, Jamali D, eds. *The research handbook of responsible management.* Cheltenham: Edward Elgar, 2020.

27. Hahn T, Preuss L, Pinkse J, Figge F. Cognitive frames in corporate sustainability: Managerial sensemaking with paradoxical and business case frames. *Academy of Management Review.* 2014, 39(4): 463–487.

28. Van der Byl C, Slawinski N, Hahn T. Responsible management of sustainability tensions: A paradoxical approach to grand challenges. In: Laasch O, Suddaby R, Freeman RE, Jamali D, eds. *The research handbook of responsible management.* Cheltenham: Edward Elgar, 2020.

29. Gentile MC. *Giving voice to values: How to speak your mind when you know what's right?* Yale: Yale University Press, 2010.

30. Kahneman D. *Thinking, fast and slow.* New York: Macmillan, 2011.

31. Simon HA. A behavioral model of rational choice. *The Quarterly Journal of Economics.* 1955, 69(1): 99–118.

32. Boudon R. Beyond rational choice theory. *Annual Review of Sociology.* 2003, 29: 1–21.

33. Reinhard S. What is bounded rationality. In: Gigerenzer G, Selten R, eds. *Bounded rationality: The adaptive toolbox.* Cambridge: MIT Press, 2001: 13–36.

34. Brown R. Consideration of the origin of Herbert Simon's theory of 'satisficing' (1933–1947). *Management Decision.* 2004, 42(10): 1240–1256.

35. Todd PM. Fast and frugal heuristics for environmentally bounded minds. In: Gigerenzer G, Selten R, eds. *Bounded rationality: The adaptive toolbox.* Cambridge, MA: MIT Press, 2001: 5–70.

36. Max Burgers. Sustainability. www.maxburgers.com/climate-positive/sustainability Published 2020. Accessed June 29 2020.

37. Max Burgers. The world's first climate-positive burgers to be launched. www.maxburgers.com/about-max/news/news-and-press-releases/worlds-first-climate-positive-burgers Published 2018. Accessed June 29 2020.

38. Sinclair M, Ashkanasy NM. Intuition: Myth or a decision-making tool? *Management Learning.* 2005, 36(3): 353–370.

39. Sadler-Smith E, Shefy E. The intuitive executive: Understanding and applying 'gut feel' in decision-making. *Academy of Management Perspectives.* 2004, 18(4): 76–91.

40. Hodgkinson GP, Langan-Fox J, Sadler-Smith E. Intuition: A fundamental bridging construct in the behavioural sciences. *British Journal of Psychology.* 2008, 99(1): 1–27.

41. Crossan MM, Lane HW, White RE. An organizational learning framework: From intuition to institution. *Academy of Management Review.* 1999, 24(3): 522–537.

42. Sinclair M. Misconceptions about intuition. *Psychological Inquiry.* 2010, 21(4): 378–386.

43. Dane E, Pratt MG. Exploring intuition and its role in managerial decision making. *Academy of Management Review*. 2007, 32(1): 33–54.

44. Haidt J, Joseph C. Intuitive ethics: How innately prepared intuitions generate culturally variable virtues. *Daedalus*. 2004, 133(4): 55–66.

45. Gigerenzer G. Moral intuition = fast and frugal heuristics? *Moral Psychology*. 2008, 2: 1–26.

46. Woodward J, Allman J. Moral intuition: Its neural substrates and normative significance. *Journal of Physiology*. 2007, 101(4–6): 179–202.

47. Zollo L, Yoon S, Rialti R, Ciappei C. Ethical consumption and consumers' decision making: The role of moral intuition. *Management Decision*. 2018, 56(3): 692–710.

48. Mousavi S, Gigerenzer G. Risk, uncertainty, and heuristics. *Journal of Business Research*. 2014, 67(8):1671–1678.

49. Klein GA. *The power of intuition: How to use your gut feelings to make better decisions at work.* New York: Random House, 2007 (2004).

50. Cosier RA, Aplin JC. Intuition and decision making: Some empirical evidence. *Psychological Reports*. 1982, 51(1): 275–281.

51. Dane E, Rockmann KW, Pratt MG. When should I trust my gut? Linking domain expertise to intuitive decision-making effectiveness. *Organizational Behavior and Human Decision Processes*. 2012, 119(2): 187–194.

52. Salas E, Rosen MA, DiazGranados D. Expertise-based intuition and decision making in organizations. *Journal of Management*. 2010, 36(4): 941–973.

53. Hales SD. The problem of intuition. *American Philosophical Quarterly*. 2000, 37(2): 135–147.

54. Walsh M. Accountability and intuition: Justifying nursing practice. *Nursing Standard*. 1997, 11(23): 39–41.

55. Miles A, Sadler-Smith E. 'With recruitment I always feel I need to listen to my gut': The role of intuition in employee selection. *Personnel Review*. 2014, 43(4): 606–627.

56. Hensman A, Sadler-Smith E. Intuitive decision making in banking and finance. *European Management Journal*. 2011, 29(1): 51–66.

57. Sadler-Smith E, Burke LA. Fostering intuition in management education: Activities and resources. *Journal of Management Education*. 2009, 33(2): 239–262.

58. Andersen JA. Intuition in managers: Are intuitive managers more effective? *Journal of Managerial Psychology*. 2000, 15(1).

59. Allinson CW, Chell E, Hayes J. Intuition and entrepreneurial behaviour. *European Journal of Work and Organizational Psychology*. 2000, 9(1): 31–43.

60. De Vries M, Holland RW, Witteman CL. Fitting decisions: Mood and intuitive versus deliberative decision strategies. *Cognition and Emotion*. 2008, 22(5): 931–943.

61. Kickul J, Gundry LK, Barbosa SD, Whitcanack L. Intuition versus analysis? Testing differential models of cognitive style on entrepreneurial self-efficacy and the new venture creation process. *Entrepreneurship Theory and Practice*. 2009, 33(2): 439–453.

62. Lozano R. Creativity and organizational learning as means to foster sustainability. *Sustainable Development*. 2014, 22(3): 205–216.

63. Rhodes M. An analysis of creativity. *The Phi Delta Kappan*. 1961, 42(7): 305–310.

64. Xu F, Rickards T. Creative management: A predicted development from research into creativity and management. *Creativity and Innovation Management*. 2007, 16(3): 216–228.

65. Amabile TM. *Creativity in context: Update to 'The social psychology of creativity'*. Boulder: Westview, 1983/2018.

66. Henry J. *Creative management*. London: Sage, 2001.

67. Guilford JP. *The nature of human intelligence*. New York: McGraw-Hill, 1967.

68. Cropley A. In praise of convergent thinking. *Creativity Research Journal*. 2006, 18(3): 391–404.

69. Lubart TI. Models of the creative process: Past, present and future. *Creativity Research Journal*. 2001, 13(3–4): 295–308.

70. Kaner S. *Facilitator's guide to participatory decision-making*. New York: Wiley, 2014.

71. Wallas G. *The art of thought*. London: Jonathan Cape, 1926.

72. Sadler-Smith E. Wallas' four-stage model of the creative process: More than meets the eye? *Creativity Research Journal*. 2015, 27(4): 342–352.

73. Groth J, Peters J. What blocks creativity? A managerial perspective. *Creativity and Innovation Management*. 1999, 8(3): 179–187.

74. Von Oech R. *A whack on the side of the head: How to unlock your mind for innovation*. New York: Warner Books, 1983.

75. Kreitner R. *Principles of management* (11th edn). Mason: Cengage, 2009.

76. Summers I, White DE. Creativity techniques: Toward improvement of the decision process. *Academy of Management Review*. 1976, 1(2): 9–108.

77. Geschka H. Creativity techniques in product planning and development: A view from West Germany. *R&D Management*. 1983, 13(3): 169–183.

78. Carroll AB, Adler NJ, Mintzberg H, et al. What 'are' responsible management? A conceptual potluck. In: Laasch O, Suddaby R, Freeman RE, Jamali D, eds. *The research handbook of responsible management*. Cheltenham: Edward Elgar, 2020.

79. Winquist JR, Larson JR. Information pooling: When it impacts group decision making. *Journal of Personality and Social Psychology*. 1998, 74(2): 371–377.

80. Stasser G, Titus W. Pooling of unshared information in group decision making: Biased information sampling during discussion. *Journal of Personality and Social Psychology*. 1985, 48(6): 1467–1468.

81. Malone TW, Laubacher R, Dellarocas C. The collective intelligence genome. *MIT Sloan Management Review*. 2010, 51(3): 21–31.

82. Bonabeau E. Decisions 2.0: The power of collective intelligence. *MIT Sloan Management Review*. 2009, 50(2): 45–52.

83. Metcalf L, Askay DA, Rosenberg LB. Keeping humans in the loop: Pooling knowledge through artificial swarm intelligence to improve business decision making. *California Management Review*. 2019, 61(4): 84–109.

84. Hunton JE, Hall TW, Price KH. The value of voice in participative decision making. *Journal of Applied Psychology*. 1998, 83(5): 788–797.

85. Tannenbaum R, Schmidt WH. How to choose a leadership pattern. *Harvard Business Review*. 1958, 36(2): 95–101.

86. Lawler EE. *High-involvement management: Participative strategies for improving organizational performance*. San Francisco: Jossey-Bass, 1986.

87. Kim S. Participative management and job satisfaction: Lessons for management leadership. *Public Administration Review*. 2002, 62(2): 231–241.

88. Matten D, Crane A. What is stakeholder democracy? Perspectives and issues. *Business Ethics: A European Review*. 2005, 14(1): 6–13.

89. Moriarty J. The connection between stakeholder theory and stakeholder democracy: An excavation and defense. *Business and Society*. 2014, 53(6): 820–852.

90. Vroom VH, Yetton PW. *Leadership and decision-making*. Vol. 110: Pittsburgh: University of Pittsburgh Press, 1973.

91. Vroom VH, Jago AG. *The new leadership: Managing participation in organizations.* Upper Saddle River, NJ: Prentice-Hall, 1988.

92. Verkerk MJ, Leede J, Nijhof AH. From responsible management to responsible organizations: The democratic principle for managing organizational ethics. *Business and Society Review.* 2001, 4(106): 353–379.

93. Sashkin M. Participative management is an ethical imperative. *Organizational Dynamics.* 1984, 12(4): 5–22.

94. Fassin Y, Deprez J, Van den Abeele A, Heene A. Complementarities between stakeholder management and participative management: Evidence from the youth care sector. *Nonprofit and Voluntary Sector Quarterly.* 2017, 46(3): 586–606.

95. Branch KM. Participative management and employee and stakeholder involvement. In: Baker KA, ed. *Management benchmarking study.* Washington: Washington Research Evaluation Network, 2002, pp. 1-27.

96. Maclagan P. Corporate social responsibility as a participative process. *Business ethics: A European review.* 1999, 8(1): 43–49.

97. Janis IL. Groupthink. *Psychology Today.* 1971, 5(6): 43–46.

98. Janis I. Groupthink. In: Griffin E, ed. *A first look at communication theory.* New York: McGraw-Hill, 1991: 235–246.

99. Robertson R. I spent a year leading a team in complete isolation in Antarctica: Here are 4 strategies you need right now. www.fastcompany.com/90525132/i-spent-a-year-leading-a-team-in-complete-isolation-in-antarctica-here-are-4-strategies-you-need-right-now Published 2020. Accessed July 8 2020.

100. Whyte G. Groupthink reconsidered. *Academy of Management Review.* 1989, 14(1): 40–56.

101. Janis IL, Mann L. *Decision making: A psychological analysis of conflict, choice, and commitment.* New York: Free Press, 1977.

102. Aldag RJ, Fuller SR. Beyond fiasco: A reappraisal of the groupthink phenomenon and a new model of group decision processes. *Psychological Bulletin.* 1993, 113(3): 533.

103. Delbecq AL, Van de Ven AH. A group process model for problem identification and program planning. *The Journal of Applied Behavioral Science.* 1971, 7(4): 466–492.

104. Helmer O, Rescher N. On the epistemology of the inexact sciences. *Management Science.* 1959, 6(1): 25–52.

105. Landeta J. Current validity of the Delphi method in social sciences. *Technological Forecasting and Social Change.* 2006, 73(5): 467–482.

106. Geist MR. Using the Delphi method to engage stakeholders: A comparison of two studies. *Evaluation and Program Planning.* 2010, 33(2): 147–154.

107. Cooperrider DL, Srivastva S. Appreciative Inquiry in organizational life. In: Pasmore W, Woodman R, eds. *Research in organization change and development.* Greenwich: JAI Press, 1987: 129–169.

108. Cooperrider D, Srivastva S. The gift of new eyes: Personal reflections after 30 years of appreciative inquiry in organizational life. In: *Research in Organizational Change and Development.* 2017, 25: 81–142.

109. Beveridge AJ, Godwin L, Pavez I. Inquiring into change and innovation for greater responsibility through an appreciative inquiry lens. In: Laasch O, Suddaby R, Freeman RE, Jamali D, eds. *The research handbook of responsible management.* Cheltenham: Edward Elgar, 2020.

110. Nemeth C, Brown K, Rogers J. Devil's advocate versus authentic dissent: Stimulating quantity and quality. *European Journal of Social Psychology.* 2001, 31(6): 707–720.

111. De Bono E, Zimbalist E. *Lateral thinking.* London: Penguin, 1970.

112. Laasch, O., Moosmayer, D., & Antonacopoulou, E. P. (2023). The interdisciplinary responsible management competence framework: An integrative review of ethics, responsibility, and sustainability competences. *Journal of Business Ethics, 187,* 733–757.

113. Lawrence TB, Suddaby R, Leca B, eds. *Institutional work: Actors and agency in institutional studies of organizations.* Cambridge: Cambridge University Press, 2009.

114. Lawrence TB, Suddaby R. Institutions and institutional work. In: *The SAGE handbook of organization studies.* Thousand Oaks, CA: Sage, 2006: 215–254.

115. Lawrence T, Suddaby R, Leca B. Institutional work: Refocusing institutional studies of organization. *Journal of Management Inquiry.* 2011, 20(1): 52–58.

116. Suddaby R, Ganzin M, Minkus A. Craft, magic and the re-enchantment of the world. *European Management Journal.* 2017, 35(3): 285–296.

117. Ganzin M, Islam G, Suddaby R. Spirituality and entrepreneurship: The role of magical thinking in future-oriented sensemaking. *Organization Studies.* 2019. https://doi.org/10.1177/0170840618819035.

118. Weber M. *The Protestant ethic and the spirit of capitalism.* New York: Routledge, 1905/2013.

119. Ritzer G. *The McDonaldization of society.* Newbury Park: Pine Forge Press, 1992.

120. Meyer JW, Rowan B. Institutionalized organizations: Formal structure as myth and ceremony. *American Journal of Sociology.* 1977, 83(2): 340–363.

CHAPTER 10

COMMUNICATING

OLIVER LAASCH, ROGER N. CONAWAY
AND ALEXANDRA BARRUETA

LEARNING GOALS

1. Communicate your responsible management activities effectively
2. Create new 'better' realities *through* communicative action: 'Twalking'
3. Plan and execute stakeholder communication

PARADOXICAL FACT

In a 2022 survey of 704 US-based directors, over 90 per cent of company board members report having discussed topics related to data security and talent management, around 50 per cent report having discussed carbon emissions or climate change, and fewer than 30 per cent human rights issues [1].

TALKING THE WALK AT HAIER

OLIVER LAASCH AND DAITENG REN

The Chinese consumer goods corporation Haier has stunned the management world. Haier's CEO Zhang Ruimin has been hailed as an inspiring management innovator. The Rendanheyi (人单合一; translates as people–goal integration) management style he invented at Haier creates a super-agile innovation culture based on fluid structures [2, 3]. Observers have also been flabbergasted at the speed-of-light transformation of Haier that Zhang was able to realize [4]. One of the secrets behind it might just be communication.

Zhang Ruimin is a vivid and versatile communicator. You may have seen him on stage 'making a show' as headliner at the Global Peter Drucker Management Forum in Vienna or seen him thoughtfully listening in the audience [5]. He has been nicknamed 'the

(Continued)

Haier Hammer', due to an episode where he literally thrashed low-quality product batches with a hammer to communicate a future with no tolerance for mediocre quality [4]. The mastery of communication and its use to create new futures does not stop with Haier's CEO but is built in throughout the company.

A major trend on the Chinese Weibo social network (similar to X, formerly Twitter) were posts related to air-pollution-related baby health concerns like 'Is your baby always coughing?' [6]. Users frequently tagged Haier as a producer of air-filters [6, 7], to which they responded by inviting users into the 'Good Air' user group [8] on COSMOplat, Haier's open innovation social media network which enabled stakeholders to communicate directly with Haier's staff [9].

'Everyone is welcome to reply, let us work together to create the future air conditioner' [10]. Many stakeholders followed this invitation, including Hu Ding, a worried father who took the lead together with one of Haier's innovation managers to co-shape the new air conditioner-filter 'Baby Joy', fine-tuned to protect the health of babies and young children [11, 12].

COMMUNICATING PROFESSIONALLY AND EFFECTIVELY

Watch a manager and you will see someone whose work consists almost exclusively of talking and listening.

Henry Mintzberg [13]

The **communicating mode** of management is complex and multidimensional as it consists of speaking and listening, acting and observing. It involves a variety of stakeholders as communication partners, like colleagues (superiors, and managed), customers, shareholders, communities, and media. It requires communicating formally – for instance, in an annual report – and informally 'at the water cooler'. Managers have to be proficient communicators, not only using their physical but also their virtual presence. It involves explicit verbal communication as much as implicit communication through action like 'Haier's hammer' featured in the introductory case. You may communicate directly, or indirectly through others, and others through you. Communicating can be both a way to transmit information about an existing reality or to construct messages that form new realities.

While the risk of bad communication practices is significant, the opportunities of good communication are equally important. A great example of

The communicating mode of management is centred on the exchange of information through messages

how both of these dimensions come together culminates in Mark Zuckerberg's statement, 'I started this place, I run it … I'm responsible for what happened here', assuming full personal responsibility for letting third parties use Facebook's user data without permission. In the same statement he announced a three-year programme to improve responsible user data management for the future [14]. Communicating professionally can make or break a manager and their organization. Greenwashing accusations, which reveal the imbalance between a company's talk and walk can cause immense and lasting damage. A single imprudent remark can cost millions of dollars in stock value. Especially during times of crisis, communication can even save or destroy lives.

In this chapter, we focus on effective professional communication (see Figure 10.1). **Effective communication** may mean different things, depending on how you view communication. First, if you see communication as the transmission of a message, effective communication means that your message 'goes through' to the receiver. In the public relations context, we might add that we want 'the right' message to get through, in order to have people like us, to create 'stakeholder goodwill'. Secondly, if you see communication as something that can make change happen, effective communication takes a much more literal meaning: Does the communication have an effect? Does it impact on reality? Might it create a new reality, change an existing one, or possibly maintain an existing reality in spite of opposing forces? Communication that is at best ineffective and empty, or at worst unfounded, untruthful, or misleading has been called 'business bullshit' and related practices 'business bullshitting' [15, 16, 17)]. Given how much of management is related to communicating, there is a danger that one engages in 'bullshit management', which is primarily concerned with inconsequential empty talk [18].

What does **professional communication** mean then? First of all, it means that the communicator is a competent, proficient communicator. For instance, being able to send a clear, focused message that is appealing and easy to understand is part of communicating professionally. However, it also means communicating to fulfil a positive role in society. For instance, to send a misleading message to make the public believe your company is not bankrupt while it actually is would not qualify as professional communication, no matter how proficiently executed. Finally, professional communication requires professional conduct that is ethical, responsible, and sustainable. For instance, a flyer campaign using non-recycled material and toxic high-gloss ink cannot be considered professional communication as it is not environmentally sustainable.

In this chapter, we will explore how to practice such effective professional communication. We will first discuss the communication process centred on

Effective communication may either mean to get the message through, or to affect reality

Professional communication means to communicate proficiently, in order to fulfil a positive societal role, and in an ethical, responsible, and sustainable manner

the transmission of messages. Secondly, we will explore practices of 'twalking', centred on the relationship between talk and walk, between what you communicate and what you do. Third, we will explore how to communicate with varieties of different stakeholders. Fourth, we will introduce tactics of communicating in a tailored manner, adjusting communication by employing specialized stakeholder communication tools.

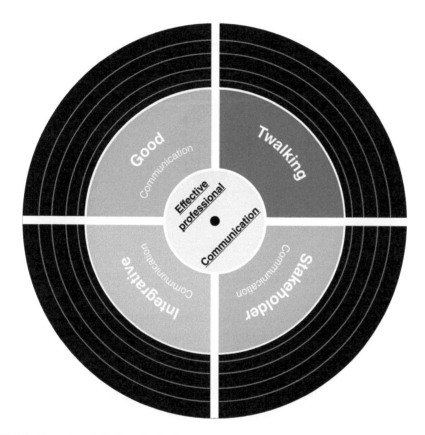

FIGURE 10.1   The practice of effective professional communication

CREDIT: Slidemodel.com

GOOD COMMUNICATION

This section explores different views and guidelines for 'good' communication. A typical way of communicating is focused on the transmission of messages. From this perspective, effective communication means that the message has been heard and understood. We will now discuss the underlying communication process, and practical advice on how to shape a good message that will be heard and understood.

EFFECTIVE TRANSMISSION OF MESSAGES

Sender
the person with whom
the message originates

Receiver
the person who receives
the original message

When the management communication process (see Figure 10.2) begins, a manager serves as the **sender**. This person communicates a message to **receivers**, who might be, for instance, the general public, investors, employees, and others. We could analyse the transmission process from the opposite perspective as well – for instance, starting with activists belonging to Greenpeace as original senders of a message, and company managers addressed as receivers.

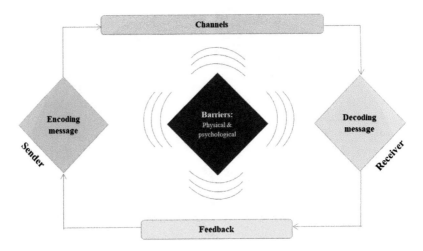

Figure 10.2   The communication 'transmission' process

Message
the unique combination
of words and symbols,
including tone and style

Channels
the medium
through which the
message moves

The message should be accurate, transparent, and adapted to its audience in an understandable way. The **message** is the unique combination of words and symbols the sender chooses to communicate. It involves the speaker's tone and *attitude* towards the content. It also involves the *style,* which is the *way* the speaker communicates – for example direct or indirect with information, formal or informal in presentation, or public oriented or company oriented. In many cases, a speaker's communication style becomes obvious to listeners but may not be obvious to the speaker. Communication style in responsible management should be adjusted to the distinct stakeholder groups, for example the general public, government officials, or employees.

The speaker's message may travel via various channels. Figure 10.3 provides an overview of typical communication **channels** used in a responsible management context. External communication may involve, for instance, media relations, television coverage, interviews, websites, and social media. Internal communication channels may include inter-company emails, phone calls, and social media messaging. 'Rich' communication channels include face-to-face communication or videoconferencing. These channels have many sensory cues or information about the message. 'Lean' channels include email and web-based channels such as interactive blogs, posts on Facebook, or text messages. These channels have fewer information cues, which result in a greater chance of the message being misinterpreted. Channel choice has an important role in effective communication and is determined by the importance of the message, its complexity, timeliness, and other factors.

FIGURE 10.3   Responsibility communication channels

SOURCE: Adapted from [19]

Effective communication may be hindered by *selective perception and misinterpretation* in both the sender and receiver. These interferences work against accurate understanding and are commonly called **barriers**, which may be either physical or psychological. The source of a physical barrier is external to the speaker and includes situational or cultural factors. Environmental noise, interruptions, or distractions are sources of external interference. Psychological

Barriers
any internal or external factors that interfere with accurate understanding

Encoding
the interpretative process of analysing the audience and crafting the message

barriers may be the mental preoccupation of the speaker with another person, mental distractions with a work issue, or simply daydreaming, all of which interfere with accurate understanding. These psychological barriers may inhibit both encoding and decoding of the message. The **encoding** process occurs when the sender turns an idea into a message and involves forming words and selecting non-verbal symbols to shape the message. In face-to-face communication, videoconferencing, or television broadcasting, the sender accentuates the message with eye contact, facial expressions, gestures, and other nonverbal symbols.

Decoding
the process by which the receiver interprets the words and symbols in the message

Once the message is sent, the receiver of the message begins **decoding**, which is the process of interpreting the meaning of words and symbols. Terms related to responsible management may lack a common understanding between sender and receiver. Customers may understand the very basic term 'sustainability' as referring merely to environmental topics, while many companies understand 'sustainability' as an integrated set of activities involving social, environmental, and economic factors. In this particular case, effective communication has to ensure that the term sustainability when used by a business is decoded with the same meaning as customers.

The encoding and decoding process are imperfect at best because of the sender's and receiver's tendency to perceive selectively. Barriers include any interference in the environment, culture, language, non-verbal communication, or other factors that negatively influence the perception and interpretation of the message. Noticeably, we tend to use words at various levels of abstraction in our messages. With so many abstract meanings of the words that we use – for example, 'sustainability' – one can understand how easy it is to communicate poorly. It is truly amazing that we can understand each other at all!

Feedback
verbal and non-verbal responses exchanged between sender and receiver

Communicating is usually a *two-way* process that includes **feedback** and verbal and non-verbal responses exchanged between sender and receiver, much like a tennis match. One communicator 'serves' a message to another communicator who sends a response back as feedback. The communication process can best be described as a relationship between people, a process whereby senders and receivers interact dynamically with each other. The decision outcome is often 'constructed' and modified when feedback is taken into account in multiple recurrent rounds of communication. This constructive process illustrates the dynamic view of communication.

SHAPING AN EFFECTIVE MESSAGE

When we consider the communication process as dynamic and relational, we move towards effective communication. We now identify several time-tested principles of management communication, which serve as a foundation or basis for shaping effective messages [20, 21].

1. **Adapt to your audience.** Effective communication means understanding the audience of stakeholders and knowing with whom you are communicating. Audience adaptation does not mean telling stakeholders what they want to hear. It means that they understand the meaning of the message. Too often we try to present our company or ourselves in the best way, focusing on who we are and how we do things. Consider several key questions: What are the primary interests of my stakeholders? What are their attitudes and beliefs about my sustainable activity? What is the size and what are the demographics of my audience? What is their level of understanding?

2. **Clarify your purpose.** If you are communicating for your company about a specific social activity, what do you want to say about it? What's the main idea?

3. **State your message clearly.** Use words so that the message intended will be the message the audience receives. Clearly construct the message and choose words they will understand. Be transparent in what is said without trying to hide meaning. In some cases, communicators may want to be 'strategically ambiguous'. They may be deliberately vague until a company decision is reached or a crisis has passed. Ideally, state your message transparently and understandably.

4. **Stay on topic.** When forming your message, steer 'clear of unrelated or loosely related subjects that just happen to be on your mind. It means not slathering on a pile of data and details that obscure the bottom-line message' [22]. Addressing just one topic gives the message greater impact than including many topics that may get lost in importance. It focuses the reader or listener on what you are communicating.

5. **Be complete and accurate.** Ensure the message is free from errors. Ineffective communication, for example, creates the danger of social and environmental topics being (mis)judged as superficial or having hidden agendas. A deadline may determine how quickly you communicate, but despite these time limitations, ensure that the facts of your message are as accurate as possible. An ever-present controversial topic in management communication is transparency. Responsible management advocates and stakeholders require transparency, but how much internal information can a manager possibly reveal to stakeholders without endangering its trade secrets?

6. **Communicate your goodwill.** Personalize your message and build goodwill with consumers, customers, and other stakeholders. Use their names in the message or address them personally. The goodwill message involves a 'selfless' tone, one that focuses on the receiver instead of the sender. A goodwill message will communicate understanding. It seeks to build or maintain a positive relationship. This principle of communication is essential to involvement and interaction with stakeholders.

7. **Communicate with credibility.** The audience's perception of our integrity and credibility influences how every single message we communicate is received. If the audience views the company or sender as trustworthy, they tend to believe the message. It also implies consistency between what a company says and what it does. If all other principles of communication are incorporated into a message except credibility, the communication will not be effective.

RESPONSIBLE COMMUNICATION

Effectiveness in the form of having one's message heard is important. However, it neither ensures that it is actually a 'good' message, nor that the communication process is good, ethical, responsible, and sustainable. We will now briefly introduce two frameworks that can be used to ensure a communication process that includes all important stakeholders, leading to morally desirable outcomes and shaping good, 'non-violent' (see below) messages.

CREATING IDEAL SPEECH SITUATIONS

The ideal speech situation is less focused on the structure of a somewhat 'static' communication process than on aspects of a 'good' process. Communication outcomes are morally good if they reflect a truth arrived at through free and inclusive participation in a discourse, an ideal speech situation [23, 24]. Outcomes might be a decision or an agreement on a course of action such as a new business strategy or entering a new market. Ideal speech situations are created by adhering to these principles:

1. **Open access.** From a stakeholder responsibility perspective everyone affected by the topic of discussion should be enabled to participate. For instance, discussing a decision to move a manufacturing plant close to a rural community requires giving access to a variety of groups, such as community members, environmental groups, company managers, government bodies, etc. Access barriers might take many different physical and psychological forms, including different languages, insecurities or status, or the monetary cost of attending.

2. **Free speech.** Participants can call into question any proposal, introduce any proposal into the discourse, and express attitudes, wishes, and needs. Reasonable, rational arguments brought forward have to be heard, no matter who brings them forward. This principle is concerned with making sure that everyone can speak freely without fear of consequences, like losing their job, or being bullied after having made an unpopular point, or one that is not what the more powerful members of a discourse want to hear. For instance, it would not be free speech if some community members felt that they could not argue against the plant for environmental reasons as they knew the mayor who wants the additional tax income might make life difficult for them later on.

3. **Protecting the communication process.** No speaker ought to be hindered from inside the discourse or outside the discourse from making use of their rights under points 1 and 2 [23].

In summary, the ideal speech principles are about shaping a situation in which discourse arrives at 'good' outcomes, through a good communication process, an ethical discourse [24].

SHAPING 'NON-VIOLENT' MESSAGES

Non-violent communication (NVC) has also been called non-exploitative, compassionate, and collaborative communication [25, 26]. NVC starts from the observation that the way we usually communicate frequently fosters conflicts, for instance, by blaming, shaming, or coercing others with our statements: Why didn't you listen? This is rubbish! Shouldn't you have read the manual? In some situations, generating conflict through such antagonistic communication might be intended and necessary. Where it is not, however, NVC, enables us to communicate in a way that builds harmonious and healthy relationships by considering both our underlying needs and those of our communication partners [27]. In the 'transmission' perspective of communication, people are presented as imperfect senders and receivers. NVC, however, makes human beings and their relationships the core concern. The following four steps are geared towards achieving this:

1. **Observations (facts).** First state the neutral facts based on an observation you made. For instance, if the subject of our communication is reducing carbon emissions in your office, you might start out by making this observation: 'When I came in early this morning, I observed that almost half of the team had left their computer screens on standby overnight. In some cases the whole computer was still on. I just had a quick check, and considering the size of our office, this has caused roughly the same amount of carbon emissions as a return flight to Australia.'

2. **Feelings (emotions).** You would then proceed by stating the feelings this provoked in you: 'This upset me and made me feel very worried about the future.' At this stage, it might be easy to fall back into the habit of violent communication, where you blame others for your feelings by saying things like, 'I was disappointed by you'.

3. **Needs (values).** Then explain to your communication partners what you believe are the underlying reasons for your feelings: 'You probably noticed that I am a very environmentally conscious person, and that I hope to be able to inspire my colleagues and friends to care about the environment too.' The recommendation here is to make it subjective and personal, as opposed to referring to wider objective facts like 'Everybody knows, we are screwing up our planet', as this implicitly puts blame and fault on others 'who should have known better'.

4. Requests (actions). Finally, you would request, or rather suggest actions, but without insisting that your requests are fulfilled (which would be coercion): 'Would you please consider switching off your screens when you leave the office, and maybe when you go for lunch or you are in meetings?'

When communication partners reply, again, non-violent communication should be conducted based on the same principles. For instance, you would acknowledge and address your communication partners' underlying needs and values. For instance, if a colleague says, 'How can I think about pressing this silly little button if I have to run to catch my bus every afternoon because I can hardly get my work done', you could reply along the lines of, 'I empathize with the need to get home on time and get a good rest and respect the value of giving private life its protected space and time.'

TWALKING: COMMUNICATION—ACTION

Why is it important to think about the relationship between communication and action, talk and walk, speaking and doing? As in the introductory case, we can, for instance, communicate by doing something – smashing sub-standard products with a hammer. When we tell the truth or lie, what we say represents, or doesn't represent, our actions. Communicating might also represent future realities – for instance talking about plans or a mission statement to promote them. So, communication and actions can be interconnected as 'truth', we report what we have done (we have walked the talk). They may also be connected as consequence: 'we do what we say' (we *will* walk the talk). Or it could even be the self-fulfilling-type of prediction: We tell you we will be like this in the future (talk the walk). We are never only talking, never only acting, talking and walking are always related, one entangled practice of **twalking** [28].

Twalking
refers to the inseparable dynamics between talk and walk, between saying and doing

Decoupling
happens when a communicator separates what they are doing from what they are saying

A lie is **decoupling** what is said from what is true, the talk from the walk: 'Yes, Mum, I brushed my teeth.' Or: 'No your honour, we did not bribe the government official.' Another type of decoupling, which we will discuss in depth is greenwashing – for instance, when BP changed their slogan to 'Beyond Petroleum' (the talk), while their operations were predominantly petroleum related (the walk). There are many different forms of decoupling – many bad, others potentially good. In aspirational talk, managers may communicate the aspiration of becoming a net-positive company that restores the environment (the talk), while currently (the walk) having a strong negative impact on the environment. Whether this claim is bad greenwashing or good aspirational talk depends on one question: Will management be able to live up to their aspirations and create a company that will be net positive in the future?

Consider, for instance, the case of Sasol, a South African integrated energy and chemical company. Their management was collaborating with North West University to find ways of producing what they call 'green coal' or 'clean coal' [29]. This clean coal would be charcoal produced by extracting coal stored in slime ponds combined with grass and animal waste. Protesters challenged Sasol's management to desist from misleading the country and the world with this 'false solution … [which emits] carbon in the extraction process of the coal, when transporting the coal, making the product and even when it is burned' [30]. The talk–walk dynamics of this case are intriguing. We can observe a bad decoupling, and intentions of making 'greener coal', and activists calling it a bluff,

and questioning the desirability of both their talk and of their aspirational goal of green coal.

GREENWASHING: TALK THAT MISREPRESENTS WALK

A communication effort that evokes a misleading impression of ethics, responsibility, or sustainability is called **greenwashing**. In such a situation the communicator is not walking the talk, which has the potential to inflict immense reputational damage. An

Sasol executives receive a memorandum from activists criticizing their talk and walk related 'clean coal'.

Chante' Ho Hip

iconic greenwashing example is that of BP mentioned above [31]. An excellent checklist for spotting greenwashing in your own and others' communication are the 'seven sins of greenwashing' [32].

Figure 10.4 describes four different positions that communicators can assume. Each position is distinguished by low or high intensity of communication and low or high stakeholder value creation [15]. A justified *greenwash* accusation occurs when the intensity of communication of responsible activities exaggerates the actual stakeholder value created. Responsible management usually displays high stakeholder value creation and a justified high activity in communicating this performance, a *high-balance* situation. In a *low balance* situation, management mirrors low stakeholder performance with little communication about social and environmental topics. A *shy* communicator displays high stakeholder performance but decides to limit the intensity of communication. In order to avoid justified greenwash accusations, management should avoid communication activities covering stakeholder performance before it has been realized.

The **greenwash trapdoor** refers to a situation whereby a company tries to gain reputational advantage from falsely claiming high stakeholder value creation, but is 'caught in the act', resulting in a loss of trust and damage to the company's reputation. What is worse, such a company is likely to be trapped by being forced to improve their activities for stakeholders to counter bad publicity without at the same time getting a reputational advantage from it, as their 'good deeds' remind stakeholders of their past wrongdoings. To avoid the 'greenwash trapdoor' [33] communicators should make sure always to balance walk and talk, moving in a straight line from a low balance to a high balance between stakeholder value and communication. Alternatively, they could go the safe route and improve the walk, to go from low balance to shy by increasing stakeholder value, and then moving from shy to high balance by starting to communicate about what the company is doing.

Greenwashing
refers to a communication practice that creates a misleading impression of a company's ethics, responsibility, or sustainability performance

Greenwash trapdoor
a failed attempt at increasing reputation by greenwashing, resulting in continuously low reputation even if stakeholder value is increased afterwards

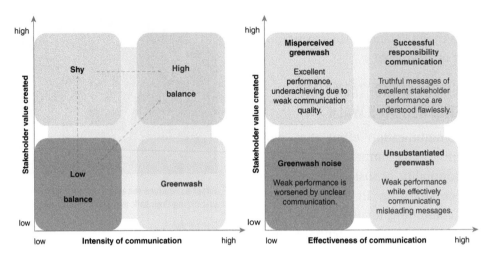

FIGURE 10.4   What management is saying–doing (left) and how stakeholders perceive it (right)

SOURCE: Left adapted from [19]; right adapted from [34]

The grid on the right in Figure 10.4 illustrates the type of perceptions stakeholders might arrive at. The vertical dimension in the grid on the right represents stakeholder value created and the horizontal dimension represents the effectiveness of communication.

The lower left quadrant, **greenwash noise**, illustrates how management lacks minimal efforts to add value to the environment and communication effectiveness. Management may say publicly, 'we're green', but their communication does not have compelling information to back up its claims and their efforts have little or no impact on the environment or stakeholders. Such communication is often confusing to stakeholders because of its unclear messages and statements.

The upper left quadrant, **misperceived greenwash,** illustrates how management adds good stakeholder value through its activities, but lacks effective ways to communicate the results. Managers might not have been able to adapt their communication to their audience and were not able to achieve stakeholder support for their message and socio-environmental activities.

The lower right quadrant, **unsubstantiated greenwash**, illustrates how communication is strong, but is based on inferior value to stakeholders. Management communicates effectively, but the messages are not based on the necessary performance. The picture of stakeholder performance is misleading.

Finally, the top right quadrant, **successful responsibility communication,** highlights how managers maximize value added to stakeholders and effectively communicate this good performance to stakeholders. Achieving this balance is sometimes difficult but is a recommended goal for professional managers.

COMMUNICATION THAT 'MAKES' REALITIES: TALK THAT MAKES WALK

Earlier in this chapter, we explored how to communicate well, if you consider communication to be 'transmission' of a message about reality. However, if we take 'twalking' seriously, communication never only transmits or represents an existing reality. It can also make new realities. After saying 'Let's dance', your walk will most likely look very different from the walk after yelling 'Run!'. 'To say something is to do something;…by saying something we are doing something' [35].

Communication is rarely only a transmission of a stable reality [36]. Through communication we can also alter reality and how it is being perceived [37}. Through communication we can (re)shape the past (e.g. by the way you talk about past events), the present (e.g. by presenting current events in different ways), and future realities (e.g. by communicating plans). Such communication is '**performative**', meaning that it 'does' things with reality [35, 38, 39].

The **communicative constitution** of organization perspective goes one step further by suggesting that organization *is* communication [36, 40]. Organization is a network of communication episodes [41], as communication is 'one of the various practices that collectively constitute the organization' [36]. This means that managers, when communicating in their respective organizational contexts, are continuously making and remaking the organization, as communication is organization.

Performative communication is 'talk that makes walk', as it maintains, deconstructs, and reconstructs existing realities, or constructs new realities

Communicative constitution of organization (CCO) is a perspective from which we understand how communication makes organization, as it is organization

The managers of Otto's Coffee House and Kitchen in the English town of Sevenoaks decided to fill up their store's floor with 15,000 discarded coffee cups. They then went on to force customers who did not bring their reusable cup, but wanted a coffee from this shop anyway, to wade through this sea of waste to the counter. Customers who did bring their own cup were served at the door. What kind of coffee shop do you think they constituted with this implicit communication campaign? What message did the cups convey for them? [42].

www.famouscampaigns.com/2021/08/the-walk-of-shame-redefined-ottos-coffee-house-kent

Using performative and constitutive communication as a manager has very practical implications for how you communicate. For instance, while communication as transmission focuses on 'cleanly' transmitting 'the right', unaltered message, performative communication might aim to get stakeholders involved in reshaping, or 'co-constructing' the message. Transmission-style communication is looking for consensus, while performative communication uses disagreement as a force that shapes communication and realities [43]. We will now discuss core phenomena of performative communication and their relevance for managerial communication.

Aspirational talk, 'talking the future into existence'. Managers may use aspirational talk to present a vision of ethical, responsible, and sustainable management in the future that clearly contradicts the current reality [39]. For instance, you may try to talk responsibility into being even though the current reality is a fundamentally irresponsible one. Ideally, such aspirational talk would become a self-fulfilling prophecy, where future responsible walk will match today's responsible talk. Aspirational talk creates a tension between lived reality and aspiration. Managing this tension is crucial to successful aspirational responsibility communication. For instance, others may actively disengage with the aspirational vision of the future reality because they feel it is unrealistic given the current circumstance. If this happens, the aspirational talk may lead to a vicious cycle where the current situation becomes even worse. However, it may also create a virtuous cycle, where the aspirational talk leads to solving tensions between talk and walk, and a motivation and commitment, pulling others towards making the aspired reality come into existence [44].

Textual agency, 'the things texts can do and things that communicate'. Messages and texts can do many things. Texts can be actors in performative communication too [45]. For instance, a manager may organize all their activity following the key performance indicators outlined in the text of their organization's balanced score card. Managers' lived realities may be shaped by the things texts do or may shape texts to influence others' lived realities. Texts, for instance, a one-page overview outlining a new responsibility agenda, may even be at the centre of a whole company's responsible transformation [46]. We can distinguish between three types of documents containing these statements and how they make realities [45, 47]:

1. **Assertives** state and confirm realities. For instance, a plaque in a company lobby might assert that you are in an equal opportunity workplace.

2. **Commissives** commit signatories of a text to a certain action. An example is a memorandum of understanding that outlines business partners' responsibilities and commits them to act according to these responsibilities.

3. **Directives** authorize or ban actions. For instance, a purchasing process standard operating procedure directs the task to be carried out in a specific way.

Highlighting the role of texts as communicators also reminds us that it is not only human beings who communicate, but also things that communicate for us and which may often develop a life of their own. An excellent example is, for instance, when automated algorithms or non-human chatbots send messages that might not be what had been intended originally. For managers, this means you can create multiple presence(s) (intended or not) through varieties of 'things' and 'cyborgs' of things and people, in different locations and at different points in time [48, 49].

   Polyphony and ventriloquism, 'the voices making reality'. The question of who is talking and whose voice and message we hear is a crucial aspect of communication. On the one hand, we may hear many diverging 'polyphonic' voices, multiple – at times contradictory – messages [50]. In the transmission perspective on communication, this is not desired. In performative communication and particularly responsibility communication, polyphony is often desired. For instance, responsible managers have to listen to the many different voices and values to learn about the manifold external and internal stakeholders' realities [51]. To the inside of an organization, hearing and engaging with the polyphonic voices of all majority and minority groups is crucial in establishing the talk and walk of diversity management [52].

   On the other hand, we may also make our own voice heard through others. Communication as 'ventriloquism' means managers speaking through others [49, 53]. One's message might be heard more widely and become more credible when others repeat it as their own. However, this might also imply that we might well not be the ventriloquist sending the message, but the 'dummy' being instrumentalized in repeating someone else's message, possibly even unknowingly.

STAKEHOLDER COMMUNICATION

It has been stressed that 'communicating and interacting responsibly with a broad range of diverse internal and external stakeholders in daily managerial practice … is key to responsible management' [43]. At the same time, **stakeholder communication** is not unique to *responsible* management. Whomever we communicate with is a stakeholder of what we do and say and might even belong to several stakeholder groups. So stakeholder communication is really just 'communication'. Communication is always stakeholder communication.

Stakeholder communication an ongoing dialogue with a group or individual who affects or is affected by something

STAKEHOLDER AUDIENCE ANALYSIS

Earlier in this chapter, you learnt to apply communication principles by first analysing your audience. This section discusses how to analyse your audience of stakeholders and to conduct an analysis of specific stakeholder characteristics.

Have you distinguished the types of stakeholders?

- Which one is primary?
- Which one is intermediate?
- Which one is secondary?

Do you understand the stakeholder?

- What does the stakeholder know?
- What does the stakeholder feel?
- What does the stakeholder want to know and feel?
- What can the stakeholder do?

Do you understand your relationship to the stakeholder? (Have you determined your goals?)

- What does your company want the stakeholder to know?
- What does your company want the stakeholder to feel?
- What does your company want the stakeholder to do?

Is your company perceived as credible by the stakeholder?

- Is your company considered reliable and believable?
- What does your company need to do to gain the stakeholder's trust?

FIGURE 10.5 Stakeholder profiling questionnaire

SOURCE: Adapted from [54]

As a communicator you must first make a comprehensive assessment of the stakeholder group(s) with whom you want to communicate and identify that group's purpose, mission, and interests. Is your goal to inform or persuade the stakeholder? What do you want them to know, do, or feel? Communication principle 2 will be applied when you clarify your communication purpose or goal. Use the questions in Figure 10.5 to help you analyse your stakeholders.

Management in companies often aims to communicate to diverse stakeholders with just a single message. Examples are CEO letters, press releases, and sustainability reports. These reports communicate to multiple groups at one time, such as investors, government entities, employees, and customers. If a crisis occurs, a CEO may speak to the public through the media, but the message reaches many stakeholders. Such messages need to consider what they 'do' when reaching main stakeholder groups and what stakeholder reactions mean to you and your company:

1. We define a **primary stakeholder** as the one you most want to develop a relationship with and primarily send the message to.

2. A **secondary stakeholder** might read your communication or learn about the information but is not the one to whom the original message was directed.

3. An **intermediate stakeholder** may be one who simply forwards the message to others. The media, for instance, may serve as intermediate stakeholders by announcing your company's activities to customers or investors.

Understanding what a stakeholder 'feels' means that your message anticipates the emotions of those who receive it. When you communicate, receivers often respond emotionally, positively or negatively, to a particular activity and those feelings of stakeholders must be taken into account. Communicators must also take into account what a stakeholder *wants* to know and feel. You may be answering one question while the stakeholder is thinking about a completely different question. Thus, stakeholder analysis intersects with the purpose of your message and will consider the questions in Figure 10.6. The assessment will identify the primary stakeholder, seek to understand what that stakeholder knows and feels, understand the relationship with the stakeholder, and accurately assess your own credibility with the stakeholder.

STAKEHOLDER COMMUNICATION STRATEGIES

What is our purpose when communicating with different stakeholders? Do we simply want to inform them, gather feedback on what we have done, or perhaps get new ideas? To achieve each of these, and other goals of stakeholder communication, we need to use different communication strategies [55]. We will now illustrate four main stakeholder communication strategies (see Figure 10.6) [56].

First, the **stakeholder information strategy** is essentially a one-way communication process. Communication is viewed by a company as 'telling, not listening' and may be persuasive in nature. Management releases information about activities to the public [55]. For instance, management at the Spanish energy company Iberdrola chose to run a social media information campaign through their Facebook page, where they regularly updated group members about their Smartgrid initiative aimed at higher energy efficiency. To keep the message clear, communicators at Iberdrola dealt with the few user comments received by redirecting them to their customer service hotline [56].

Second, the **stakeholder response strategy** [55] relies on a two-way communication process identified by communication flowing to and from stakeholders. The company listens to comments or feedback about its responsible activities and even changes or modifies its activities as a result. Management might listen to user feedback on their past initiatives to shape future activities.

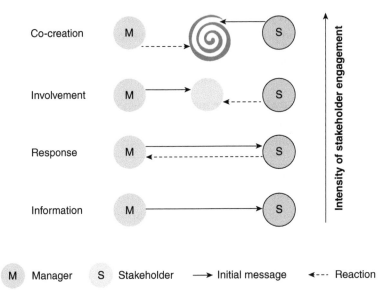

Co-creation   M

Involvement   M

Response   M

Information   M

S

Intensity of stakeholder engagement

M Manager   S Stakeholder   → Initial message   ◄--- Reaction

FIGURE 10.6   Stakeholder communication strategies

SOURCE: Adapted from [55, 56]

Management may also seek explicit endorsements from some stakeholders. For instance, communicators at the Chinese technology company IFLYTEK used a blended online–offline response strategy involving multiple stakeholders. They asked a doctor offline for feedback on how their AI may help doctors improve work efficiency and decrease work stress. This response was then posted to the Chinese Weibo network (the Chinese equivalent of Twitter), which triggered further online stakeholder feedback [56].

Third, a **stakeholder involvement strategy** [55, 56] builds a dialogue or relationship with stakeholders in which stakeholders actively co-shape existing activities [56]. Management communicators and stakeholders engage in 'sense making' of ideas, activities, and behaviours. For instance, the Shanghai-based airline China Eastern asked their followers on Weibo to contribute to their 'gesture of love' campaign, aimed at promoting traditional Chinese family values. Many users did post the expected pictures of loved ones, including young families and grandparents. However, there were also posts not in line with the existing purpose of the initiative – for instance, a young gay man who shared his heartbreak and kept doing so with the same 'gesture of love' hashtag years later. Finally, much of the communication was 'tweetjacked' by a flood of posts from angry customers trying to get a response from management related to poor customer service and lost luggage [56].

Fourth, using a **stakeholder co-creation strategy** [56], management signals openness to receive stakeholder ideas for new actions and works together with stakeholders to materialize their ideas. The initial example of Haier receiving stakeholder ideas through open social media network COSMOplat and co-creating the 'Baby Joy' air conditioner filter is an excellent example of a stakeholder co-creation communication strategy.

PRINCIPLES OF COMMUNICATING PROFESSIONALLY

I.   **Professional communication** means communicating proficiently to fulfil a positive societal role, and in an ethical, responsible, and sustainable manner.

II. **Effective management communication** may either mean getting the message through, or to affect reality.

III. **Shaping effective messages** can be summed up in the seven principles of audience adaptation: purpose clarification, message clarity, topical conciseness, completeness and accuracy, goodwill creation, and credibility.

IV. **Responsible communication** focuses on communication practices centered on virtuously involving stakeholders in communication, for instance, in the form of creating **ideal speech situations** and on engaging in **non-violent communication**.

V.   **Twalking** refers to the various ways in which communication and enacted reality relate to each other and to **greenwashing**, whereby communication presents a distorted image of reality, and to **performative communication** that shapes new realities.

VI. A thorough **stakeholder analysis** assures the appropriateness of communication for distinct stakeholder groups.

VII. **Stakeholder communication patterns** with an increasing intensity of stakeholder engagement involve information, response, involvement, and co-creation strategies.

MANAGEMENT GYM: TRAINING YOUR PROFESSIONAL SIX-PACK

Knowing

1. Define and interrelate decoupling, greenwashing, constitutive communication, and ideal speech situations.

2. Describe and compare the seven rules of effective communication with the principles of non-violent communication.

3. Find and familiarize yourself with one case for each of the four stakeholder communication strategies.

Thinking

4. Imagine a chain of negative, unethical, irresponsible, or unsustainable events that could be triggered in a managerial workplace by not applying non-violent communication principles.

5. Look up five news items issued by companies within the last month about social, environmental, and ethical issues (e.g. using news.google.com) and try to find signs of greenwashing or de-coupling for each of them.

6. Think about how the meaning of one statement of your choice could change for three different contexts with significantly different stakeholders.

(Continued)

(Continued)

Acting

7. Imagine you are a product manager at a video streaming platform in charge of making sure no inappropriate content is live-streamed. Write a ten-point checklist that the people monitoring live streams can use to either shut them down or keep them open.

8. Put yourself in the shoes of the public relations manager of an actual company that has recently had a scandal. Write a 100-word press release about it.

9. Think about one concrete topic you want to communicate about and sketch up an integrated communication plan by writing different texts for different channels corresponding to the respective receivers on each channel.

Interacting

10. Find a fake news item on social media shared by one of your contacts and do some research to prove it is fake. Reply to the news item to debunk it.

11. Think about one thing someone either in your private or professional life has done to upset you. Discuss it with the person using non-violent communication.

12. Invent a hashtag or an activity (e.g. like #MeToo or the ice bucket challenge) and try to make it go viral on social media. Design what you put out there to have a positive effect ethically, responsibly, or sustainably.

Being

13. Would you personally rather see communication as transmission of messages or as twalking?

14. Considering your cultural and family background, how would you describe your typical communication style?

15. What kind of 'barriers' to receiving others' messages in the way they are intended do you think you personally might have due to your cultural background, experiences, or personal preferences?

Becoming

16. Have a look at the social media posts you have shared in the past. What do you think is their overall impact on the world and how could you improve them?

17. Think about a situation where you were misunderstood or where something you said caused conflict. How could you use effective or non-violent communication to communicate 'better' in similar future situations?

18. When working, how do you balance private and operational communication? Do you think everyone around you is happy with this balance? What do you think you could do to improve this?

SOURCE: Adapted from [62]

PIONEER INTERVIEW
FRANÇOIS COOREN

INTERVIEWER: OLIVER LAASCH

François Cooren is arguably the most influential pioneer researching how communication shapes organizations and creates new realities.

Situational response-ability. I think a responsible manager is someone who does not hesitate to respond. You might have a situation where you could say, 'Well, that's not my concern. That's out of my hands', or 'There's nothing I can do'. In some contexts, it

Courtesy of François Cooren

(Continued)

could be acceptable as a response. A responsible manager is really someone who is able at least to reflect on his or her capacity to respond to a specific situation.

When we face a situation, this situation tells us something. This situation can contradict what we think matters. So we are also responding to the world that we are facing. We are reacting to it. That's part of the picture of what it means to be a responsible manager. In my own definition, responsible management is to respond to what the situation dictates. It means that you have agency, and you can make a difference.

The importance of listening. But you have to also listen to everything that might matter in a given situation. You have to be as open as possible to the complexity of a situation. You cannot just imagine what the situation might be. You also have to listen to people who are often representing aspects of a given situation, stakeholders. Stakeholders are people who are representing, in the stronger sense of the term, to represent, to make present, concerns of an aspect of a situation, for example, environmental organizations, representatives of local population, government, economic partners.

Finding out what we are. We used to think that what an organization is, is only what the official spokesperson is talking about. This is what we are. This is what we do. In CSR, communication has been this kind of transmission view of communication: We communicate about what we are and we hope that the environment is going to accept this view of what we are. Well, wait a minute, of course, we have a say on what we are as an organization and as a group of people about what we do, and so on. But other people also have a say regarding what we are. This is a dialogue that evokes different groups and different stakeholders in which we can really try to define who we are and what we do, and even what we want to do.

Talking into being. A manager can certainly talk into being a specific form of responsible management, but they also have to take into consideration that they are not the only one in the organization and outside the organization. Yes, certainly there are the managers who can talk sustainable, responsible and ethical organization into being. Yes, they can and they should actually. Because of their status and authority, they certainly have an important voice in the organization and maybe their responsibility is to initiate, certainly, to be responsive to this kind of initiative. The hope is that it's something that is going to be taken up, which people can appropriate, and apply.

Doing things with words. In traditional management we try to oppose speaking with acting, but speaking is also acting. To speak is to do things with words. It's to interest, to persuade, to convince, to seduce to some extent. This is an important aspect of these aspirations. There is this very nice article by Christensen and colleagues [39] about aspirational talk. It's an important point they are making, which is that aspirational talk can make a difference. There is no other way to change an organization.

(Continued)

We have to believe in the power of words. But also to do is to speak, to some extent, because our actions speak for themselves. We have to be aware of this communication of everything we do. People are not only looking at our words but also our deeds.

The dummy and the ventriloquist. We are the bearers of ideas, of ideologies, of preoccupation concerns and so on. What we call an organizational culture in many respects is this idea that we are the ventriloquist of specific values, of specific principles, which are supposed to direct or inform our actions.

People keep invoking values, principles, protocols, rules, policies, and so on, in order to say, you know, this is not what I say, this is what the facts show. This is what these policies require. It's interesting because there are effects of responsibilities in these activities. But at the same time, the ventriloquist could be accused of promoting a lack of responsibility, because you could say: 'It's not my fault. That's what the policies require.' Or 'It's not my fault. That's what the shareholders want.

As soon as we communicate, we have to be aware and vigilant about what we decide the ventriloquist requires. There is our automatism sometimes. We have almost mechanical reactions. We become a real dummy. The responsibility of the dummies is precisely to be vigilant about what is speaking through them. It's easy for us to just say that's what the CEO wants, that's what the shareholders want, that's what the clients want. It's a way to very quickly close the discussion and to say, 'There is no other way'. We are constantly doing that because it's lending weight to what we are saying. It's a source of authority because it says, 'You know it's not me.' When we are always on the voice of our masters, it's very monophonic. It's always repeating the same thing. We are always applying the same recipe, the same algorithm.

Documents doing things. Let's say we have an organization that tries to lay out its CSR principles. These are important documents. We could say that they are just for show, a cynical viewpoint. But this text might make a difference, to force people or an organization to do what it claims to do. Writing down CSR principles or mission statements or any kind of document that presents what the organization strives for; you can use these documents to make them do things, at the internal or external level. This idea of textual agency. We know the power of texts in organizations in general. That's where the stability of an organization or an institution comes from. It's not only from the text, but the texts are certainly a way to stabilize the organizer. It's also a source of authority. Precisely because it's a source of authority, a source of action. It dictates what the organization is supposed to be.

The texts are also dummies and ventriloquists because texts speak on behalf of the organization. That's what the organization is on paper. Of course, we might try to downplay its importance, but what the organization is on paper is still the organization. It's an aspect of the organization that could make a difference.

(Continued)

QUESTIONS

1. How do you think situational response-ability and listening go together?

2. What different forms of twalking can you spot across François' text and how do they interrelate?

3. What ventriloquists do you think speak through you? Whose dummy are you? Are you also a ventriloquist and who might be your dummies?

PROFESSIONAL PROFILE
THOMAS HÜGLI

My name is **Thomas Hügli,** and I am the Chief Communication and Corporate Responsibility Officer (CCRO) of AXA Winterthur, a major insurance company in Switzerland.

A typical day. My daily tasks mostly include observing the CR topics of the national political debate that also affect our work, such as the turnaround in energy policy, mobility in the future, or the new transparency and capital requirements. They also include thinking more deeply about CR. These ideas then become part of the statements or presentations we use in response to internal and external

(Continued)

enquiries. I also spend a lot of time talking with team members about operational decisions, meeting with customer segment boards, or holding stakeholder communication meetings in order to further establish the views and meaning of corporate responsibility within the organization.

ERS communication. AXA's mission says that 'we help customers live their lives with more peace of mind'. In this context, responsibility is an inherent part of our mission: As a company whose business it is to protect people over the long term, we have a responsibility to leverage our skills, resources, and risk expertise to build a stronger and safer society. Our CR charter communicates a shared set of commitments that will guide us as a professional team in integrating CR into AXA's core business and culture. Main points in the charter are 'monitor and control the honesty and accuracy of our messages' (e.g. avoid misrepresenting the CR aspects of our insurance products or services), 'strive to communicate how we run our business in a responsible way' (e.g. highlight how our business benefits society), and 'be exemplary regarding environment, and walk the talk' (e.g. look for ways to reduce our own impacts on the environment as regards travel, paper consumption, and energy use). Our Compliance Guide and Code of Ethics govern topics such as the whistleblower policy, money-laundering, data protection, and compliance reporting obligations.

QUESTIONS

1. Would you describe Thomas as a CSR professional or a communications professional? How do both roles come together here?

2. What types of 'good' communication can you spot in the way Thomas describes his work?

3. What instances of twalking can you identify?

TRUE STORY
FAIR(Y) TALES

Doing my work well and doing some good. My name is Alaida and I work as an international marketing manager in SFib, a Chinese company that produces fibres for all kinds of products. My role is to represent the company internationally, and to market our products to major retailers and cleaning product brands around the world. I am not really interested in making a career and climbing up the hierarchy, but I genuinely enjoy the interaction with my colleagues and customers, meeting new people and old friends when going to international trade fairs. Also, for me it is essential that I really want to do the job I do well. This includes, of course, doing it sustainably, responsibly, and ethically. This brings the occasional challenges and tension particularly in the communication that happens at trade fairs.

Proper communication etiquette? When going to international fairs, for some reason, my Chinese colleagues are fascinated by overweight people. They appear to process that in many different ways, the most obvious ones being finger pointing and laughing at them, the more hidden ones including taking pictures behind (and of) their back and sharing these on WeChat, a Chinese social media platform similar to Facebook and WhatsApp. For me that's an insult, incredibly unprofessional, and immature. When I first saw this, I didn't want to make a scene in front of the customer. However, I later told the girls, but they just laughed and didn't see any problem. I then talked to their boss, the director of sales, who didn't see any problem either. She had even commented positively on the WeChat posts sharing the pictures. What's worse, many of SFib's customers are also her followers on WeChat. When we were back in the office, I did a workshop of dos and don'ts on international fairs, including other observations like eating in the sales booth, and actively ignoring customers while doing so. However, I am doubtful that these efforts will make any difference. Me not being Chinese I feel it is immensely difficult to 'get through' culturally and after all they have been doing it this way for over ten years before I even started working at SFib.

Why make your own if you can use others'? One of the most embarrassing moments in my professional career was when at another trade fair all of a sudden a gentleman started yelling at us. As it turned out, he was an ex-customer of ours. He had shared his packaging design with us in the past, and apparently someone in SFib had decided to simply copy the very same design, word-by-word, same colour, same size for our own brand product. We were displaying

(Continued)

this product at the fair, which had triggered the customer's very understandable tantrum. My colleagues put the product away so that he would leave. After such an episode, and knowing what had happened, I was sure they had learnt their lesson. Boy, was I ignorant. They not only kept selling the product in the pirated design, but even brought it to the next trade show. I later learnt that this kind of thing was not a blunder, but a normal practice. For instance, when we launched another own-brand product, I started talking to the design team for the new logo. When our CEO heard this she said, 'We have logos already, why don't you just pick one instead of going through all that trouble?' To my surprise she had a whole book with logos of existing international brands: 'Why don't you just pick one of these?'

Spinning an eco-yarn. I have long been concerned about our plastic fibres' environmental impact. When being washed, the friction releases small micro-plastic particles, which then end up in the environment. The impacts on water ecosystem and our food chain are likely to be immense. We cannot keep doing this. I talked about this with the CEO and, as it turned out, she and her husband who worked on developing new products had been thinking about it and already had some ready-made product ideas they had not launched yet. As it turned out they were not sure how to position them. So I started nudging them. For instance, I forwarded mails from customers demanding sustainable products, and focused on conversations at international fairs, seeking out clients I thought would be interested. I then introduced the CEO to many of these customers. I have also won over some of my colleagues, 'parroting' my green message. For instance, I forwarded clips about the dangers of micro-plastics. I was so excited to learn that we would launch a recycled PET yarn and new bamboo fibre already on the next trade fair! I was even asked to design the flyer, the recycled yarn. I used an image of a PET bottle floating in the ocean.

QUESTIONS

1. Analyse each of the communication episodes, using concepts and tools that have been introduced in this chapter. What role do you think cultural differences may have played?

2. If you were Alaida, (how) would you have communicated differently in order to achieve the respective goals in these cases?

3. What role did other communicators play in Alaida's efforts at doing her job well and doing some good? How do you think these respective communication episodes reflect on the company?

4. How could you use day-to-day communication in your (future) job to achieve ethical, responsible and sustainable conduct and outcomes? What challenges do you think you might encounter?

DIGGING DEEPER: INTEGRATIVE STAKEHOLDER COMMUNICATION

Integrative stakeholder communication [33] aims at tight-knit, consistent communication – for instance, across stakeholders, different channels, communication tools, online and offline, internal and external, formal and informal, verbal and non-verbal, walk and talk. It is an approach that combines 'the most appropriate and effective methods for communicating and building relationships and customers and other stakeholders' [57]. We will briefly outline such integration for different communication tools and channels, for internal and external, as well as formal and informal communication.

Integrative stakeholder communication describes communication aimed at consistently integrating communication

COMMUNICATION TOOLS AND CHANNEL INTEGRATION

As illustrated in Table 10.1, distinct communication tools and their respective channels may be differently adequate for communicating with different stakeholders. For instance, via a social media platform like Facebook or WeChat you will probably communicate to end-consumers, while a professional social media network like LinkedIn is likely to be more highly frequented by employees, suppliers, and competitors.

TABLE 10.1 Stakeholder communication tools matrix

	Employees	Customers	Government	Community	Owners	Suppliers	Media
Cause-related marketing	5	1	5	5	3	5	3
Social marketing	1	1	5	3	5	3	5
Issues & crisis communication	1	3	3	3	1	3	1
Codes of conduct	1	3	5	5	5	1	5
Formal reports	3	5	3	3	1	5	3
Mission & vision	1	5	3	3	1	5	5
Social media	1	1	5	3	5	3	1

1=highly appropriate, 3=somewhat appropriate, 5=not very appropriate

A successful example of integrated communication is the movie-theatre chain, Cinépolis's *'Del amor nace la vista'* campaign, which translated reads 'Love gives birth to eyesight'. Management at Cinépolis used various communication channels – clips before movies; installations like their 'eye meter' counting the number of eyes cured; employees personally addressing customers; newspaper coverage, and many others – to fundraise for cataract eye surgery for people from low-income communities. They managed to communicate with a diverse set of stakeholders, including customers, employees, governmental institutions, and eye doctors' associations [58]. Another excellent example was when the management at Reckitt Benckiser aggressively counter-communicated across channels against Donald Trump's message that their disinfecting products could be injected to cure Covid-19 [59].

INTERNAL–EXTERNAL COMMUNICATION

Responsible management marketing and communication tools are directed to internal and external stakeholders. We first examine communication within the organization. **Internal operational communication** [60] describes how communication functions internally. Integrated as part of the organization's plan of operation, internal communication may flow along authority lines drawn in the formal organizational chart (downward, upward, and horizontal communication). Internal communication means employee discussions involve work-related tasks and further the organization's primary goals. It has been emphasized how ethics, responsibility, and sustainability communication must begin with top management as a boardroom priority [19]. Responsibility is managed in an interdisciplinary way across a company and requires direction, coordination, and support from top management.

While traditionally internal communications have been a one-way route – pushing out information that management requires employees to know so that they can do their jobs better – today's employees want to be engaged. Employee communications need to move from push to pull, from delivering messages to encouraging dialogue, from a communiqué to a conversation. In this way, employees will be better equipped to contribute to business objectives, raise issues that can benefit the business, feel more valued and motivated, and act as the voice of the business in the hundreds of daily interactions. Internal social networking tools are effective. Participative dialogues may prove effective with employees such as stakeholder conference calls, participative webinars, virtual conferences and meetings, and online company talk sessions. All these tools can help brand responsibility activities internally among employees.

External operational communication is equally important. It exists when organization members communicate with stakeholders outside the organization to achieve the organization's work goals. External communication fits closely to the marketing and public relations functions and the variety of messages an organization sends to the public. Such messages include press releases, advertisements through traditional media, and branding efforts. External communication involves online media such as blogs, Facebook, Twitter, communication on corporate websites, and dialogue with customers about sustainability (see the 'Digging deeper' section on online communication). Beyond these organization-level communication tools, the myriad of daily communication episodes with customers and suppliers, employee families and communities are powerful ways of reaching external stakeholders. Internally effective two-way, open, collaborative, and participative communications with employees may support them to become ambassadors externally also.

Internal operational communication consists of the structured communication within the organization that directly relates to achieving the organization's work goals

External operational communication occurs when employees communicate with people and groups outside the organization to achieve the organization's work goals [60]

INFORMAL–FORMAL COMMUNICATION

Communication flows throughout an organization in different directions among employees. **Informal communication** tends to increase when organizations move through periods of instability, acquisition, or personnel change, primarily when information is lacking about such events. Rumours may feed the informal communication channels. As a result, management may try to control or eliminate altogether the informal communication channels. Supervisors may complain that socializing keeps employees from their jobs and management may believe that employees are wasting company time.

However, there is also an increasing appreciation of how much work is actually being done and how much is managed through informal chats. Therefore, the grapevine cannot and should not be eliminated from an organization, but it can be accepted and managed as part of it. There needs to be a balance between creating overly restrictive boundaries for the informal channels and giving too much freedom to employees to communicate on the job about personal matters and through informal channels. An unhealthy organizational climate will exhibit signs of excessive personal communication, including rumours and inaccurate information. Managers who promote a healthy communication climate give ample information to employees whenever possible and are transparent. This helps to reduce an over-active, inaccurate organizational grapevine.

> Informal communication does not follow through the organization's formal channels and is often not of an 'operational' nature

POINTERS

What kind of communication do you consider more important for professional management, internal or external, formal or informal? Why? Think about some company scandal you have heard about. What kind of messages do you think the main actors should have communicated in which channels and to whom? What should have been the integrated message to be sent?

WORKSHEET

NON-VIOLENT COMMUNICATION PING PONG

	Sender	Receiver
Observation (facts)	I have observed that …	Observation leading to this conversation.
Feelings (emotions)	This makes me feel …	What does the other person feel?
Needs (values)	Because my need for … is not met.	What are the person's needs and values at play here?
Request (action)	Would you be willing to …?	What action could I take to address this?

SOURCE: Based on [26]

POINTERS

You could, for instance, use this worksheet to practice non-violent communication (NVC) talk and listening, being sender and receiver with a partner, and then switching roles, engaging in a non-violent conversation about different topics. You could also use the sheet to analyse an exchange you have had in the past and see to what degree it was non-violent, and how you could have done it better.

REFERENCES

1. Segal M. PwC survey: More than half of boards lack a strong understanding of ESG strategy or risks. www.esgtoday.com/pwc-survey-more-than-half-of-boards-lack-a-strong-understanding-of-esg-strategy-or-risks Published 2022. Last accessed August 11 2023.
2. Frynas JG, Mol MJ, Mellahi K. Management innovation made in China: Haier's Rendanheyi. *California Management Review*. 2018, 61(1): 71–93.
3. Ruimin Z, Michelman P. Leading to become obsolete. *MIT Sloan Management Review*. 2017, 59(1): 79–85.
4. Bryant L. Transformation at the speed of Haier. https://postshift.com/transformation-at-the-speed-of-haier Published 2015. Accessed April 26 2020.
5. China.org.cn. Zhang Ruimin lights the fire of management change. www.china.org.cn/business/2018-12/03/content_74233673.htm Published 2018. Accessed April 26 2020.
6. Anonymized user. Do you find that your baby is always coughing? http://weibo.com/haier Published 2013. Accessed April 26 2020.
7. User anonymized. Problems with air discovered. http://weibo.com/haier Published 2013. Accessed April 26 2020.
8. Anonymized user. Group member management. http://diy.haier.com/pc/community/group?groupId=60074 Published 2019. Accessed April 26 2020.
9. Haier. COSMOplat. http://diy.haier.com Published 2020. Accessed April 26 2020.
10. Anonymized user. Haier asks you to be an air conditioning designer. http://bbs.haicr.com/activity/98829.shtml Published 2013. Acccssed April 26 2020.
11. Anonymized user. Customize the Baby Joy air conditioner for pregnant women and babies. http://diy.haier.com/raphael/works/detail?id=309. Published 2016. Accessed April 26, 2020.
12. Anonymized user. Baby Joy air conditioner for pregnant women and babies. http://diy.haier.com/raphael/works/detail/?id=309 Published 2016. Accessed April 26 2020.
13. Mintzberg H. Rounding out the manager's job. *Sloan Management Review*. 1994, 36(1): 11–26.
14. Castillo M. Facebook's Mark Zuckerberg: 'I'm responsible for what happened' with data privacy issues. www.cnbc.com/2018/04/04/mark-zuckerberg-facebook-user-privacy-issues-my-mistake.html Published 2018. Accessed April 27 2020.
15. Spicer A. Shooting the shit: The role of bullshit in organisations. *M@N@GEMENT*. 2013, 16(5), 653–666.
16. Spicer A. Playing the bullshit game: How empty and misleading communication takes over organizations. *Organization Theory*. 2020, 1(2), 2631787720929704.
17. Ferreira C., Hannah, D., McCarthy, I., Pitt, L., & Lord Ferguson, S. (2022). This place is full of it: Towards an organizational bullshit perception scale. *Psychological Reports*, 125(1), 448–463.
18. Sułkowski Ł. On bullshit management – the critical management studies perspective. *Economics and Sociology* 2019, 12(1), 302–312.
19. Taubken N, Leibold I. Ten rules for successful CSR communication. In: *Responsible business: How to manage a CSR strategy successfully*. Chichester/West Sussex: John Wiley & Sons Ltd, 2010.
20. Locker KO. *Business and administrative communication* (10th edn). Boston: McGraw-Hill, 2003.
21. O'Hair D, Friedrich GW, Dixon LD. *Strategic communication in business and the professions*. Boston: Houghton Mifflin, 1995.
23. Habermas J. The theory of communicative action: Lifeworld and systems, a critique of functionalist reason. Chichester: Wiley, 1981/2015.
24. Habermas J. *Moral consciousness and communicative action*. Cambridge: MIT Press, 1990.
25. Rosenberg M. Living nonviolent communication: Practical tools to connect and communicate skillfully in every situation. Louisville, KY: Sounds True, 2012.
26. Rosenberg MB. *Nonviolent communication: A language of compassion*. Encinitas: Puddledancer Press, 2002.
27. CNVC. What is NVC? www.cnvc.org/learn-nvc/what-is-nvc Published 2020. Accessed May 3 2020.

28. Schoeneborn D, Morsing M, Crane A. Formative perspectives on the relation between CSR communication and CSR practices: Pathways for walking, talking, and t(w)alking. *Business & Society.* 2020, 59(1): 5–33.

29. Lepedi M. NWU students experiment green coal for energy. www.sabcnews.com/sabcnews/nwu-students-experiment-green-coal-for-energy Published 2019. Accessed April 30 2020.

30. Ho Hip C. Sasol held accountable in global climate strike. https://sandtonchronicle.co.za/236706/sasol-held-accountable-in-global-climate-strike Published 2019. Accessed April 30 2020.

31. Williams J. Beyond petroleum: Is BP finally moving from rhetoric to reality? www.cityam.com/beyond-petroleum-is-bp-finally-moving-from-rhetoric-to-reality Published 2020. Accessed July 30 2020.

32. Terrachoice. The sins of greenwashing: Home and family edition. Published 2010.

33. Conaway R, Laasch O. Communication in responsible business: Strategies, concepts, cases. New York: Business Expert Press, 2012.

34. Horiuchi R, Schuchard R, Shea L, Townsend S. *Understanding and preventing greenwash: A business guide.* San Francisco: BSR, 2009.

35. Austin JL. *How to do things with words.* Oxford: Oxford University Press, 1962.

36. Schoeneborn D, Trittin H. Transcending transmission: Towards a constitutive perspective on CSR communication. *Corporate Communications.* 2013, 18(2): 193–211.

37. Haack P, Schöneborn D, Wickert C. Talking the talk, moral entrapment, creeping commitment? Exploring narrative dynamics in corporate responsibility standardization. *Organization Studies.* 2012, 33(5–6): 815–845.

38. Gond J, Cabantous L, Harding N, Learmonth M. What do we mean by performativity in organizational and management theory? The uses and abuses of performativity. *International Journal of Management Reviews.* 2016, 18(4): 440–463.

39. Christensen LT, Morsing M, Thyssen O. CSR as aspirational talk. *Organization.* 2013, 20(3): 372–393.

40. Fairhurst GT, Putnam L. Organizations as discursive constructions. *Communication Theory.* 2004, 14(1): 5–26.

41. Blaschke S, Schoeneborn D, Seidl D. Organizations as networks of communication episodes: Turning the network perspective inside out. *Organization Studies.* 2012, 33(7): 879–906.

42. Abery L. The 'walk of shame' redefined: Otto's Coffee House, Kent. www.famouscampaigns.com/2021/08/the-walk-of-shame-redefined-ottos-coffee-house-kent Published 2021. Last accessed August 11 2023.

43. Schoeneborn D, Trittin H, Cooren F. Consensus vs dissensus: The communicative constitution of responsible management. In: Laasch O, Suddaby R, Freeman RE, Jamali D, eds. *The research handbook of responsible management.* Cheltenham: Edward Elgar, 2020.

44. Winkler P, Etter M, Castelló I. Vicious and virtuous circles of aspirational talk: From self-persuasive to agonistic CSR rhetoric. *Business & Society.* 2020, 59(1): 98–128.

45. Cooren F. Textual agency: How texts do things in organizational settings. *Organization.* 2004, 11(3): 373–393.

46. Laasch O. An actor–network perspective on business models: How 'being responsible' led to incremental, but pervasive change. *Long Range Planning.* 2018, 52(3): 406–426.

47. Searle John R. *Expression and meaning: Studies in the theory of speech acts.* Cambridge: Cambridge University Press, 1979.

48. Fairhurst GT, Cooren F. Leadership as the hybrid production of presence(s). *Leadership.* 2009, 5(4): 469–490.

49. Cooren F. Action and agency in dialogue: Passion, incarnation and ventriloquism. Amsterdam: John Benjamins Publishing, 2010.

50. Castelló I, Morsing M, Schultz F. The construction of corporate social responsibility in network societies: A communication view. *Journal of Business Ethics.* 2013, 115(4): 681–692.

51. Christensen LT, Morsing M, Thyssen O. The polyphony of values and the value of polyphony. *Journal for Communication Studies.* 2015, 8(1): 9–25.

52. Trittin H, Schoeneborn D. Diversity as polyphony: Reconceptualizing diversity management from a communication-centered perspective. *Journal of Business Ethics.* 2017, 144(2): 305–322.

53. Cooren F. Communication theory at the center: Ventriloquism and the communicative constitution of reality. *Journal of Communication.* 2012, 62(1): 1–20.

54. Andrews DC, Andrews WD. *Management communication: A guide.* Boston: Houghton Mifflin, 2004.

55. Morsing M, Schultz M. Corporate social responsibility communication: Stakeholder information, response and involvement strategies. *Business Ethics: A European Review.* 2006, 15(4): 323–338.

56. Laasch O, Barrueta-Sacksteder AL, Conaway RN, Gomez-Segovia A, Shi M. Co-creation in Europe and China: Revisiting CR communication strategies in social media. Paper presented at: Academy of Management Proceedings, 2018.

57. Belch GE, Belch MA. Advertising and promotion: An integrated marketing communications perspective. Boston: McGraw-Hill Irwin, 2009.

58. Laasch O, Conaway R. 'Making it do' at the movie theatres: Communicating sustainability in the workplace. *Business Communication Quarterly.* 2011, 74(1): 68–78.

59. Guardian. 'Don't inject Lysol': Maker of household cleaner hits back at Trump virus claim. www.theguardian.com/world/2020/apr/24/trump-lysol-injection-claim-maker-hits-back Published 2020 Accessed April 26 2020.

60. Lesikar RV, Petit JDJ. *Business communication: Theory and practice.* Homewood: Richard D. Irwin, 1989.

61. Doing good: Business and the sustainability challenge. London: The Economist, 2008.

62. Laasch, O., Moosmayer, D., & Antonacopoulou, E. P. (2023). The interdisciplinary responsible management competence framework: An integrative review of ethics, responsibility, and sustainability competences. *Journal of Business Ethics, 187,* 733–757.

CHAPTER 11

DIGITALIZING

BY ANNMARIE HANLON & OLIVER LAASCH

LEARNING GOALS

1. Appreciate the trend and developments of digitalization
2. Know what it means to work and manage digitally
3. Understand how to digitalize business across managerial practices

FACT FOR THOUGHT

The majority of both low and high digital maturity companies use digitalization to cut carbon emissions (53% of low maturity and 69% of high maturity companies) and to reduce their use of natural resources (58% and 67%) [49].

SPOTLIGHT

SHADES OF DIGITAL IN THE FIBRE BUSINESS

A fibre-producing company is probably not among the first candidates one would expect to be a leader in digitalization or environmental sustainability practices. Yet management at the Austria-headquartered global corporation Lenzing not only produces fibres for varieties of applications, from home textiles to clothing and technical textiles, they also offer impressive examples of how to successfully engage in the twin transformations of digitalization and sustainability.

'We know that moving towards a circular economy is vital to address the enormous textile waste challenges of the industry', recognizes Christian Skilich, Lenzing's Chief Pulp Officer [72]. Digitalization plays a major role in acting on this insight, as we can see

www.lenzing.com/lenzing-group/locations

in the sustainability report, which features a section dedicated to digitalization and sustainability [79]. Among others, they have developed 'fibrecoin', a blockchain-based system that allows them to trace their fibres' origin and destination as well as a related digital fibre certification [79]. Key to the Lenzing management's mission of informing and educating customers about sustainable clothing purchasing is an interactive eShop that

(Continued)

enables consumers to make informed purchases of sustainable clothing and home textile products and that fosters customer engagement. The eShop is also an integral element of the 'digital first' strategy adopted by management at Lenzing's TENCEL™ brand [94].

https://www.lenzing.com/newsroom/image-archive/browsepage/1?cat=24&chash=58&cHash=f1dc29d79dd0164a1e12bc467343e381

Printed with permission of Lenzing

Lenzing not only has a dedicated digital innovation department [79], but also ensures that digitalization runs across other areas of the business such as marketing, supply, and production management, as well as many aspects of work life. Remote working is enabled by the somewhat more 'mundane' but essential digital practices like ensuring cyber security and safely e-signing key documents [79]. Digital work life also extends to special events and celebrations using digital media production. This ranges from a professionally-produced 'virtual opening event' of their sustainable Lyocell fibre manufacturing plant in Thailand [80], to generating online hype when the crew of Avatar II wore Lenzing fibre at the movie's world premier [95].

All of these efforts to digitalize and 'sustainabilise' management are very laudable. However, it seems crucial to acknowledge that producing more fibres, even more environmentally sustainable and digitally enhanced ones, can never beat the sustainability improvements of simply using and re-using the already produced fibre for longer. From this perspective, Lenzing's recent moves to increase clothing sales through their digital presence can be seen as an example of where digitalization leads to less sustainable, not more sustainable, outcomes.

DIGITALIZING

'By adopting a "twin transition" approach, leaders can bring the digital and sustainability agendas together to future-proof their organizations." World Economic Forum [12].

Digitalization has been enabled through access to the internet which is over 63 per cent worldwide, although this varies from 98 per cent in northern Europe to 25 per cent in Middle Africa [99]. Further, over six billion people worldwide own a mobile device [100]. Accordingly, **digitalizing** has become a pervasive mode of our managerial practices. We use digital systems daily, from smartphones and apps to websites and software [18], to such an extent that it is difficult to carry out many managerial jobs without a device [18] where our managerial actions and activities are mediated by a connected device. Similarly, main management occupations and business functions centrally rely on digitalization, from block chain traceability in supply management, and the dominance of digital marketing in marketing management, to AI applications in screening applications in people management and digitally customized mass production in operations management.

Professional digitalizing requires us to not only be competent in a digital world of managerial work, but also to navigate this world ethically, responsibly, and sustainably. Ideally, in the digitalizing mode of management, a digitally professional manager would even use digitalization to pursue a broader contribution to society and our natural environment. Digitalization is a key factor shaping our global future and with it affecting many of the United Nations Sustainable Development Goals, such as quality (digitalized) education in relation to SDG4 and SDG11 by producing smart-sustainable cities and communities.

Ethics, responsibility, and sustainability are intimately entangled with digitalization, for better or worse. For instance, we can achieve a reduction of 20 per cent of global carbon emissions in key industries through digitalization [44]. But this is not an automatic effect, as digital infrastructure also comes with increased CO_2 emissions. In addition, it depends on our digital work practices – for instance, when it comes to digital clutter like unnecessary, undeleted emails, which keep servers using energy, resulting in humongous amounts of CO_2 emissions [39]. There are also ethical opportunities and issues. For instance, as more than half of the jobs previously carried out by human beings might become partially automated, a four-day (or less) working week with a better work–life balance and more meaningful work is in reach [121]. But automation also comes with the

Digitalizing
is the mode of practice centered on online, virtual and/or computational elements

Professional digitalizing
means to manage digital work life ethically, responsibly, and sustainably, as well as using digitalization to achieve ethics, responsibility, and sustainability goals for society and the planet

ethical dilemma of 'losing jobs to machines' [32]. Equally, digitalization has responsibility themes like that of digital inclusion. Of 2.7 billion people, 34 per cent of the global population do not use the internet, even though 5 per cent live in areas covered by 3G or 4G service [33]. Calling company management to offer digitally inclusive services is in order to bridge this digital divide.

FIGURE 11.1   Areas of digitalizing management

DIGITALIZATION BASICS

As illustrated in Figure 11. 2, digitization, digitalization, and digital transformation are closely associated and can be seen as different stages in a process of moving from analogue and physical to digital. **Digitization** is the material process of converting analogue streams of information (e.g. a video tape) into digital bits (1s and 0s). **Digitalization** instead is the way individual domains of social life are restructured around digital communication and media infrastructures [14]. For business management it means a centring of particular practices and processes around the use of digital technologies. **Digital transformation** goes one step further by moving beyond a change in one area to digitalizing an entire organization, its processes, products and services. It means reimagining business management for our digital age [111].

Digitization
the conversion of analogue streams of information into digital bits

Digitalization
a restructuring around digital technologies

Digital transformation
integration of digital practices and technologies across business functions of an organization

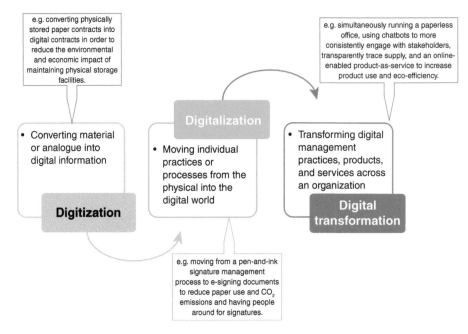

FIGURE 11.2   The process of digital transformation

Source: Adapted from [51].

DIGITAL TECHNOLOGIES

Digital technologies use and store data as discrete digits, as opposed to analogue machines relying on physical data

Digital technologies are varied, including for instance, networked (e.g. Internet of Things) and distributed systems (e.g. blockchain), the application of technology (e.g. 3D printing) on to training technology to perform human tasks (e.g. artificial intelligence, chatbots). Often particular digital technologies have multiple applications and frequently a particular digital practice relies on

The Mongolian Hard Rock Band's manager teamed up with the CEO of ARD management [56], usually in Fintec applications, to realize what they claimed was the world's first 'Meta-Rock Concert' [6]. The Mongolian version of the metaverse is where they planned to have the concert take place [83].

multiple digitalization technologies. For instance, Fintech practices in the financial services industry range from big data to blockchain technologies, which are in turn also used as part of Insurtech in the insurance industry [52, 65].

Table 11.1 offers an introduction to some key technologies and their ethics, responsibility, and sustainability implications.

TABLE 11.1   Salient digitalization technologies, examples and evaluation

Digitalization technology		Applications		Issues	
Definition	Advantages	General	ERS	General	ERS
The Internet of Things (IoT): A vast array of objects with sensing and actuating devices that collect, analyse and share data across other objects, programs, and platforms [73]	Devices collect and send data without the need for human intervention [112], save time, e.g. as smart speakers provide daily summary about weather, traffic and daily agenda	Smart devices including smartphones, smart watches, smart speakers and refrigerators	Smart home energy management systems [128], sustainable precision agriculture systems [1], wearable healthcare management devices [7]	Security can be an issue where devices are hacked, and there are privacy concerns over how and where user data is shared	Responsibility for harm of autonomously acting things [127], e-waste from appliances [105]
Blockchain: A distributed or shared record system known as a ledger	Data is not controlled by a single person, records are transparent, there is greater database integrity as records cannot be amended	Food safety – e.g. Carrefour supermarket uses blockchain to track food products from the farm to the store [51]	Food supply tracing (Pham et al., 2022), blockchain-based carbon credit management [85]	Supercomputers require large energy supplies; once made, errors in the ledger cannot be corrected	Over-hype (e.g. of blockchain-crypto currencies), blockchain power asymmetry [81], responsible blockchain governance [106] high energy demand and CO_2 impacts [155]
Additive manufacturing: A three-dimensional printing process using materials in layers [61]	Can be lower cost than other options, simple set-up	Prototype fabrication in sectors such as jewellery, manufacturing, healthcare	Humanitarian supply printing [21], sustainable production management [24]	Printing can be slow, material (additive) costs are high	Unauthorized duplication and counterfeiting of protected products, designs, and even counterfeited security seals [64, 93], unclear liability when printed products fail [58], environmental issues with energy use, recyclability and reuse of prints [5, 47]

(Continued)

TABLE 11.1   (Continued)

Digitalization technology		Applications		Issues	
Definition	Advantages	General	ERS	General	ERS
Artificial intelligence (AI): A technology that identifies, interprets and learns from data to achieve predetermined goals [35]	Speeds up processes, removes the need for repetitive tasks	Personal AI assistants supporting professionals, e.g. in accounting, also chatbots are based on AI	AI-based stakeholder relationship management [16], sustainable logistics, supply chain, and operations coordination by AI, and agriculture management [11]	Large data sets are needed, machine learning, a sub-category of AI needs mathematical models which may be biased	Security and privacy, bias and fairness [74], who is responsible for harm done by AI [127], toxic data risks [13], control of energy and resource consumption [25]?
Chatbots: Also known as talkbots, chatterbots, bots and intelligent virtual assistants (IVAs) [114], chatbots are autonomous agents which respond to questions based on pre-defined rules or machine learning	Provide a swift response, can personalize conversations, can be flexible and direct consumers to a real-life agent, considered cost effective	Facebook Messenger which provides consumers with responses to specific queries	Stakeholder relationship management, such as smart chatboxes in a library [17]; offering support where human respondents might be scarce – e.g. in healthcare management or disaster management [27, 120]	Might not always be able to respond, leaving the user dissatisfied, may contain bias depending on earlier questions	Confidentiality, privacy and information disclosure concerns (Norouzi et al., 2023), potential misdiagnosis or inappropriate treatment of users (Norouzi et al., 2023)

DIGITALIZATION'S TECHNOLOGY ADOPTION TRENDS

The larger digitalization trend is driven by a variety of digital technology trends that have radically transformed many of our work and private practices. We will now briefly illustrate some of the key digitalization trends and how each of them builds on the growth in use of a particular digital technology.

Mobile access acceleration. Everyone, access anything, anywhere, any time! By 2025 the number of worldwide mobile users is expected to exceed 7.4 billion and the number of mobile devices 18 billion [103] – that's nearly 2.4 devices per person! Applications on devices have improved to provide a near-desktop experience, with access to documents, online banking, mobile wallets, voice notes, instant messaging and video calling enabling citizens to access official documents, pay bills, travel locally and internationally, share information and still use the device as a telephone.

A key enabler of mobile access is **cloud computing**. It means that we no longer need devices with large storage capacity, nor do we need to wait to download materials we can store and access via the cloud. Whether you realize it or not, you're using cloud services. Many of these services are free to access until you reach your allocated space and payment is due. However, the growth of cloud computing has generated requirements for massive data centres. The centres use electricity 24/7 and account for 1 per cent to 1.5 per cent of global electricity use [66]. Yet it's claimed these are more efficient than each of us running our own personal storage facility.

Cloud computing is the ubiquitous, convenient, on-demand network access to a shared pool of configurable computing resources (e.g. networks, servers, storage, applications, and services) that can be rapidly provisioned and released with minimal management effort or service provider interaction (Mell & Grance, 2019)

The rise of 'hybrid' learning and competence. Increasingly, our daily practices rely not only on our own human capacity to engage in them – many of the things we are able to do require both human capacity and nonhuman digital technology, a form of **hybrid competence** [76], such as wearable tech. In particular, we are increasingly relying on artificial intelligence (AI) to complement our own competence. AI's 'ability to interpret external data correctly, to learn from such data, and to use those learnings to achieve specific goals and tasks through flexible adaptation' [68] may boost our capacity to carry out a variety of tasks. AI varies from super-intelligent to more basic machine learning. **Machine learning** performs simple tasks, such as:

Hybrid competence combines human and non-human capacities to carry out a particular practice

Machine learning refers to processes in which AI increases its capacity to analyse and carry out tasks without external instruction

- Speech recognition – controlling devices, voice search

- Image identification – tagging photographs, identifying cancerous cells in x-rays

- Statistical assessments – highlighting fraudulent or unusual behaviour in online banking

Machine learning is particularly strong in assessing large data sets and studies the patterns to recognize and predict future examples. This means it is dependent on significant amounts of data to provide a more accurate response.

Super-intelligent AI is still work in progress. This takes machine learning and applies a human approach, recognizing emotions. For example, Soul Machines [116] provides software for colleagues and universities that helps new students to more easily enrol and engage. They do this by using digital assistants – lifelike online support staff who greet the student, remember previous conversations and recognize if students don't fully understand aspects of the conversation. To do this, the data set comprises hundreds of thousands of photographs of people showing different emotions – happy, sad, confused. The digital assistants look lifelike and represent a range of student profiles, customizing the student journey.

It's important to remember that artificial intelligence is just that – *artificial* and not human, so some decisions may seem unfair or inappropriate as the machines running the processes do not consider the individual's situation. AI may encourage unethical behaviour, such as discriminating against specific groups where there may be less data, or providing advice which could be harmful. The European Union is working on a European AI Strategy from which legislation will follow [37]. This will provide guidelines for the development and application of AI within an ethical framework. For management practitioners relying on any type of hybrid competence, being aware of and feeling responsible for the machine parts of our managerial practice are crucially important aspects of professional digitalization.

Business analytics
practices rely on quantitative methods to find meaning in data to inform business decision-making

Availability of real-time and big data. Large amounts of data for **business analytics** [43] are now available in seconds. For instance, if you work in an advertising agency, you can log into your web-marketing dashboard and immediately see which adverts are performing best – and worst. You can assess whether this is based on a day of the week, or the use of specific words or images. You can assess how long people spend on a webpage and in an app and whether they are new or returning visitors. Similarly, based on ongoing recording and sensors in vehicles, real time data is used in the logistics sector where delivery companies provide real-time updates on a driver's location and expected delivery time.

Practices like data scraping or crawling have the potential to generate real-time data, which facilitates faster decision-making and enables organizations to respond more quickly. Benefits of real-time data for different business functions include:

- Marketing teams being able to change creative materials based on response rates, which improves marketing performance

- Operations managers being able to direct staff to busier checkouts in supermarkets, resulting in fewer abandoned baskets at checkouts where people are bored waiting in a queue

- Accounting teams having faster access to results, which means they can instantly gain the data needed when it's needed, saving time filling in requests for data

Big data
refers to large amounts of data from new digital data sources which may offer new solutions or solutions to business problems that could not be addressed without it

There are also challenges, as managing such volumes of data requires expertise. For example, Unilever receives millions of messages from customers every year and to make sense of the data, Unilever has invested heavily in **big data** [98] using over 35 datacentres worldwide. The raw data is added to 'data lakes' where vast amounts of unstructured data start their journey. From here, specialist data managers, architects, engineers, experts and analysts process the data, using machine learning [51]. The 'Vs' [98] is a helpful framework to assess and manage big data:

- **Volume.** The amount of data handled can go up to hundreds of petabytes – for instance, from Twitter data feeds, webpage or app clickstreams, or sensor-enabled equipment.

- **Velocity.** The speed at which data is retrieved and acted on. Some technologies operate in real time evaluation and action.

- **Variety.** Refers to the many types of data and their unstructured nature, which makes fitting it into a relational database challenging. For instance, text, audio, and video data will require additional pre-processing.

- **Value.** The value of a particular big data set for a particular purpose needs to be discovered and 'mined' before it can be realized.

- **Veracity.** Refers to the degree of truthfulness and reliability of the data used.

The blending of realities. The boundaries between digital and physical realities are increasingly blurred as digital worlds and physical spaces increasingly blend into each other. Isn't it exciting how additive printing allows us to move digital designs into the real world within the shortest of times? Or think about how virtual reality technologies allow us to enter and interact with digital worlds as if we were there physically.

However, there are also more controversial forms of blending, where stakeholders might become involuntary subjects to blended physical-non-physical spaces. Digitally capturing our physical moves (and sounds) in an almost ubiquitous technological surveillance network is an example of that. Further, digital technologies may alter our perception of the world (e.g. through our search engines' personalized 'filter bubble'), frequently without users even recognizing it.

Digitalization in retail outlets is a contentious issue. Proponents see varieties of business advantages, ranging from avoiding theft by recognizing the faces of known shoplifters [91] and automatically verifying alcoholic beverage shoppers' age using face scans [97], and on to eye-tracking devices to optimize shoppers' exposure to high-margin products [113]. **Criticism of such applications, however, raises concerns about shoppers' privacy, data collection, and disclosure of such surveillance [46]. The author of this book found the experience of suddenly and without explanation being shown on a big screen in a British Asda supermarket disorienting and eerie at best.**

An automated algorithm asserting eBay's 'fantastic prices on child labour'.

DIGITAL MANAGEMENT AND WORK LIFE

Work life
is the time engaged in work-related practices and how it relates to one's life more broadly

A key element in successful digitalizing is to get digital work dynamics right, to make digitalization a natural and value-adding element of managerial **work life**.

PEOPLE'S ROLE AND THEIR DIGITAL COMPETENCE

Companies' digital transformations and innovations often fail due to a lack of attention to the people dimension of digitalization. Digitalization processes commonly over-attend to the technological side, but neglect how people use technologies as part of their lives. It is crucial not to leave people in the dark about upcoming digitalization moves, and to clearly lay out the purpose and advantages of the moves, and to confront their fears about digitalization (e.g. relating to job losses, or not being able to cope with new technology) [123].

Digital competence
describes the qualities of individuals and organizations that enable them to enact digitalizing practices proficiently

Digital competence includes the awareness, attitude and ability of individuals to use digital tools and facilities to identify, access, manage, integrate, evaluate, analyse and synthesize digital resources, construct new knowledge, create media expressions, and communicate with others, in the context of specific life situations, in order to enable constructive social action and to reflect upon this process. Managers in the digitalizing mode have to be able to recognize, harness, and foster their teams' and their own digital competence.

DIGITAL WORKERS

Digital workers
are individuals doing their work with a strong reliance on digital technologies

Getting a digitalized work life right also matters for **digital workers**. There are opportunities for more flexible work arrangements, saving time on commuting, and a better work–life balance. However, there are also risks related to a blurring of work and private time when digital workers are expected to

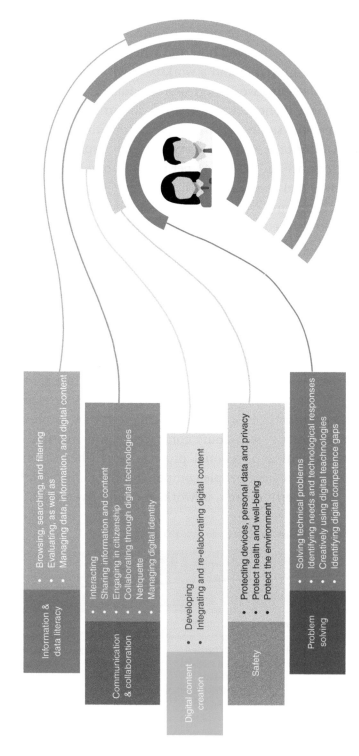

FIGURE 11.3 Digital Competence(s) Framework

IMAGE SOURCE: Adapted from [125]

The labels shown in the figure:

- **Information & data literacy**
  - Browsing, searching, and filtering
  - Evaluating, as well as
  - Managing data, information, and digital content

- **Communication & collaboration**
  - Interacting
  - Sharing information and content
  - Engaging in citizenship
  - Collaborating through digital technologies
  - Netiquette
  - Managing digital identity

- **Digital content creation**
  - Developing
  - Integrating and re-elaborating digital content

- **Safety**
  - Protecting devices, personal data and privacy
  - Protect health and well-being
  - Protect the environment

- **Problem solving**
  - Solving technical problems
  - Identifying needs and technological responses
  - Creatively using digital teachnologies
  - Identifying digital competence gaps

be 'always on', working to schedules determined by non-human (possibly inhumane) algorithms or automated tasks, and subject to the privacy implications of online worker surveillance and monitoring [121].

Digital technology has changed how and where we work, depending on access to transport, fast internet and a workspace within the home. On the one hand, this enables some workers greater freedom, as they don't need to commute and can save money on travel, which in turn reduces their carbon footprint. It also enables some workers to spend more time with their families and friends. On the other hand, not everyone has a space to work within their home. For instance, in the UK 41 per cent of homeowners during the Covid-19 lockdowns had to adapt their home to make space to work [126], with many using bedrooms. Many of these people felt resentful about this. Home working also reduced the notion of work–life balance, which is considered to be 'the relationship between work and non-work aspects of individuals' lives, where achieving a satisfactory work–life balance is normally understood as restricting one side (usually work), to have more time for the other' [70].

Not just where we work, but also how we work is changing as digitalization progresses. The notion of a regular income and single employer has been replaced with a more fluid approach that has given rise to a variety of new digital worker types, as illustrated in Table 11.2. While some people work with a single company for a fixed salary, others work as 'eLancers' on short projects (e.g. creative designers), on demand for an employer when there is work available on zero-hours contracts (e.g. delivering food), as 'gig workers' for specified occasional projects (e.g. Uber drivers) or as 'crowd workers' where several people compete for the same work via companies such as peopleperhour.com, upwork.com, and fiverr.com.

TABLE 11.2   Digital worker types, examples, and ERS considerations associated with their job

Types of digital roles			Examples of ethics, responsibility, and sustainability (ERS) implications	
Type	Description	Example jobs	Examples of ERS benefits	ERS concerns
Nine to fivers	Nine to fivers work from a single place of employment with limited mobility and flexibility	Virtual customer service representative, remote technical support specialist, remote sales representative, virtual assistant [59]	e.g. confidentiality, job security, stable work routines allowing for healthy work–life balance [122], lower carbon footprint of 'virtual commutes' than traditional commutes [45, 78]	e.g. health risks through tight scheduling or inadequate home workplace [124], possibly stressful to maintain productivity at home [118]

Types of digital roles			Examples of ethics, responsibility, and sustainability (ERS) implications	
Type	Description	Example jobs	Examples of ERS benefits	ERS concerns
ICT-based mobile workers	ICT-based mobile workers engage in a form of remote work which is not dependent on a fixed location	Multi-site managers, regional–global sales people [38]	Personal autonomy to shape working style and place [57], opportunity to reduce CO2 emissions if working from low-additional-power-consumption spaces [40]	Limited privacy and interruptions [57], ergonomic and psychosocial risks [57, 109, 119]
Digital nomads	Digital nomads are location-independent knowledge workers, who engage in nomadic practices characterized by intense mobility without fixed workplaces, times, or organizational anchors	Remote software developer, digital marketing consultant [102]	Opportunities for international mobility and freedom [53], flexibility to choose and change home location(s) [36, 84], opportunity to care for family on site when needed [89], opportunity to live a low-environmental-impact life day today, without impacts associated with e.g. owning a car or maintaining a flat [3]	Ethical concerns, such as limited job security and loneliness [20, 53], cybersecurity risks [28], reinforcing inequalities [53], difficult for employer to ensure their duty of care due to hard-to-manage local workplace risks [89], social and cultural impact [53], and environmental impacts from frequent flying [3]
Mobile knowledge workers	Mobile knowledge workers perform work beyond an organization's premises	Health workers, such as home health aides, survey researcher (by conducting surveys in various locations such as shopping centres, car parks)	Place-based inclusivity and diversity [54], flexibility [54], personal fulfilment [54]	Ethical concerns, such as income inequality, intellectual property and ownership [54], and well-being issues arising from lack of routine [15]
eLancers	Performing work over the internet as part of the 'gig economy'. They can be self-employed workers or employed by an organization on an hourly or project-based contract	Freelance or rather e-lance graphic designers, writers, web developers, or social media specialists employed on a project-to-project basis [92]	Freedom to choose clients [2], personal growth in an increasing network and with an opportunity to continuously learn and update skills [26]	Concerns about intellectual property, privacy, confidentiality, and discrimination, lack of workers' social protection and development [2], potential lack of respect for clients and little reliability and commitment to work [71]

(Continued)

TABLE 11.2   (Continued)

Types of digital roles			Examples of ethics, responsibility, and sustainability (ERS) implications	
Type	**Description**	**Example jobs**	**Examples of ERS benefits**	**ERS concerns**
On-demand workers	On-demand workers are in continuous employment relationship with an organization but without a pre-defined volume of work and remuneration. Workers and employer manage availability for work and demand through online platforms	On-demand delivery driver or cleaning professionals [92]	Personal flexibility and freedom to work when and where it suits worker [48, 110]	Limited job security, lack of access to benefits and social benefits, and potential to be exploited [48]
Prosumer workers	Prosumers are workers who produce and consume digital knowledge with limited or without any contractual agreements	Food, energy, and shelter prosumers [77]	Consumer empowerment [77], prosumers' contribution to sustainability challenges [77], resilience, e.g. through distributed co-prosumption of energy [31]	Potential lack of prosumer accountability for outcomes [77], rebound effects resulting from lack of control over prosumer behaviour leading to ecological imbalance and resource depletion [31, 77]
Gig workers	Gig workers are workers who attain ad hoc projects from online specialized platforms and agencies or sell products and services online	Personal shopper, virtual assistant [92]	Accessibility to gigs for workers with diverse backgrounds [75], flexibility, e.g. for family care [41]	Potential discrimination and unequal bargaining power, lack of social protection, lack of professional development opportunities [75, 108]
Crowd workers	Crowd workers are both amateur and professional freelancers who work on virtual micro-tasks in a project-based manner on which the price is set by auction	Jobs on platforms of AppJobber, Microworkers and Crowdtasks	High autonomy and flexibility [30], accessibility of work force for varieties of stakeholders, and opportunities for resource efficiency [22, 34]	Job insecurity [8], power asymmetries between crowd sourcer and crowd worker [29], and lack of fair compensation [30]
Wikinomics	Wikinomics are qualified workers who voluntarily collaborate without hierarchy, pressure or compensation to gather, maintain up-to-date and share knowledge through the Web	Volunteer content creator, contributor-community managers [87]	Transparency of contribution and originator [82]	Accuracy and reliability of the information that they contribute to online communities [50], privacy and security of the data that they gather and share [4], intellectual property issues [86]

SOURCE: Adapted from [104]

As illustrated in Table 11.2, each of these worker types comes with distinct ethical, responsibility, and sustainability opportunities and challenges. Professional management in the digitalizing mode implies managing so that such opportunities for each worker type are realized and challenges are addressed. For instance, if you are in charge of managing a team of prosumer workers, you would want to make sure that the opportunities of consumer empowerment are realized through the work dynamics, while also ensuring that there are no negative effects from the potential challenge of prosumers' lack of accountability for their work.

BLENDED WORK LIVES

The Covid-19 crisis accelerated the transition towards fully digital and blended work lives. This resulted in blurred boundaries between working from home and living at work. The typical 9 to 5 job is no longer the main way we work. **Blending** in a largely digital work environment takes many forms.

Blending
in digital work refers to a blurring or loss of boundaries between aspects of work life that used to be clearly delineated

1. We might have blended physical–digital work practices. While many meetings take place online, it is common to also have the occasional in-person catchup. Even if we are working online and our employer might not have dedicated offices any more, there will still be our own physical workspace – maybe at home, in a café, or in a coworking space.

2. Products and services are also often blended. As an example, in additive manufacturing with 3D printing, design may take place entirely online, but a product still needs to be printed.

3. There might be blending and loss of clear boundaries between work and private time and spaces. Spare space in some digital workers' bedrooms might, for instance, double as a workplace.

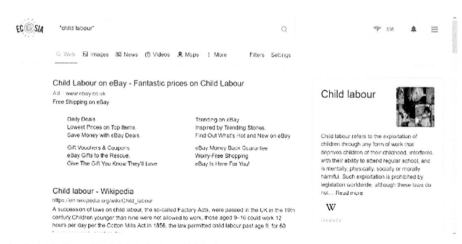

An automated algorithm asserting eBay's 'fantastic prices on child labour'.

4. And then there are blended human–nonhuman online interactions – for instance, if a person engages with a chatbot, or if you are working together with some form of artificial intelligence (such as a digital assistant) that takes care of routine tasks for you.

For managers in digitalizing mode it is a crucial element of their responsibility to ensure that this blending of work life is managed in the most ethical, responsible, and sustainable way for the people managed, oneself, and the organization.

DIGITAL WORK WELLBEING AND IMPACTS

Digital well-being [63] in the workplace encompasses a wide variety of elements, including emotional elements like feelings of trust online, isolation, mental well-being, stress, physical well-being related to sedentary lifestyles, eye strains from screen use, as well as social elements like feelings of isolation and trust online, or in extreme cases even becoming 'digital work otakus' – unable to engage in social work life outside the digital realm. Figure 11.4 offers an overview that connects these digital well-being concerns to digital management practices building on managers' digital competence, which in turn allows a manager to actively foster positive impacts of digital work life and to proactively mitigate potential negative impacts on digital workers and stakeholders.

Digital well-being is centred on digitalizing practices and interaction with technology's influence on human well-being

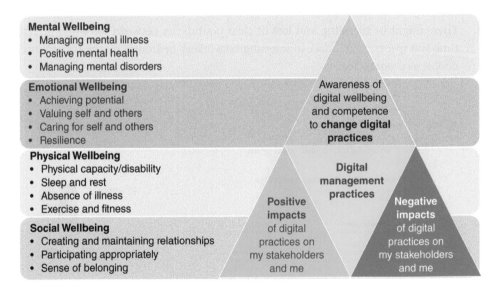

FIGURE 11.4   Digital well-being

IMAGE SOURCE: Adapted from Jisc [62]

In the digitalizing mode, managers have a responsibility for the digital well-being of employees and those they manage, as well as stakeholders including families, communities, customers, among many others.

The actions digitalizing managers might take to achieve this are varied. For instance, one could address physical well-being related to sedentary work lives by installing Peloton-bike workstations, or encouraging managed colleagues to join certain online meetings while exercising, and/or being outside. One could counteract a stressful, always-on culture by discouraging or even disabling work-related messaging during certain times of the day. On the customer side, it could involve proactively designing digital products so that they maximize their positive impacts on users and minimize the negative ones.

Not only should professional managers assume responsibility for the impact of their digitalizing practices on human beings in terms of digital wellbeing, but also for their environmental impact. For instance, professional digitalizing requires being aware of, mitigating, and offsetting the environmental impact of digital work life. This could involve practices such as actively tracking and managing the carbon impact of emails and digital infrastructure more widely. It should also involve active management of digital electronics equipment, from mobile devices to headsets and laptops, in particular when it comes to electronic waste management. It could also involve actively scheduling and placing occasional on-site meetings in a way that allows team members to choose the most environmentally friendly means of transport and, by default, offsetting and paying for all travel emissions.

DIGITALIZING BUSINESSES: BUSINESS MODELS AND BUSINESS FUNCTIONS

Digitalizing businesses requires both the digitalization of the higher-level business model and of all of the more fine-grained digitalization in individual business functions.

A distinction can be made between digital business models and digitalized business models. **Digital business models** are wholly centred on digital market offers and are often 'born digital' (see Table 11.3), while digitalized business models more selectively include digitalized practices across functions of an originally non-digital business model. Digital and digitalized business models both rely on digitalizing business functions, albeit to different degrees.

Digital business models generate digital value propositions and/or fully digitalized value creation, exchange, and capture of value

TABLE 11.3 Types of digital business models

Type of business model	Examples	
	Mainstream	ERS
E-commerce/marketplace	Zappos, Amazon, Alibaba	Rêve En Vert, 4ocean
On-demand	Uber, DiDi, Getir	Too Good to Go, OurBike
Subscription-based	Netflix, Salesforce	Elmo car, Ethical Consumer
Hidden revenue generation	Google, Facebook	Ecosia, Good Search
Freemium	Spotify, Mailchimp	EcoRise, Coursera, Bikemap
Peer-to-peer marketplace	Airbnb, eBay, Etsy	Trash Nothing, Olio, Vinted
Ad-supported	Twitter, Quora	Environment + Energy LEADER
Open source model	GitHub, RedHat	Creative Commons, Open-Seneca
Ecosystem	Microsoft, SAP	Greenly, EARTHLY, SDGs in Action

We will now further explore the unique ways in which digitalizing takes place in some of the main business functions.

SUPPLY MANAGEMENT

Supply management is a business function for which typically the technology is in place and there are widespread systems available. Major IT firms such as IBM have created dedicated groups of people to enable organizations to introduce these systems. This means that to succeed in this area, all competitors are adopting digital business processes. The sharing of data has enabled the growth and further development of digitalization across the supply chain.

As a network of organizations and resources the supply chain widely uses the Internet of Things (IoT), connecting devices along each stage of the product journey. For example, the automotive manufacturing supply chain has led the way in adopting the IoT and is experiencing real growth, such that the market size of the automotive IoT is forecast to reach USD219 billion in 2026, from USD115 billion in 2021 [117]. From the moment a car enters the supply chain IoT is in place. The raw materials are scanned as they move from the factory into the production line, so manufacturers can plan production and reduce downtime. As the car is built sensors are added to all major functions, such as motion detectors to remove potential collisions, radars that identify speed limits, GPS navigation and video cameras, as well as car diagnostics which are connected to the car's central computer and link back to the car showroom responsible for the sale and subsequent maintenance of the car. As vehicles are connected to sensors and software they regularly exchange data with both the driver and the car maintenance garage. So a car may be available with an app that monitors the car's location, its energy use as well as being able to lock or unlock the doors, start the air conditioning or heating.

Blockchain, or digital record keeping improves transparency in the supply chain. According to [42] 'blockchain can greatly improve supply chains by enabling faster and more cost-efficient delivery of products, enhancing products' traceability, improving coordination between partners, and aiding access to financing.' As food security has become an important factor for retailers, using blockchain enables supermarkets to understand where produce has come from. For example, if a supermarket discover insects in a bag of frozen vegetables they can trace the supply back to the farm – and the field – where the vegetables were grown and take action to ensure this is not repeated.

There are downsides to blockchains. If someone makes an error, it can never be corrected. New information can be added, but the error and the details of the person who made it remain visible. From a sustainability perspective, blockchains require huge computing processing power, which leads to significant energy consumption, but in some cases it is a vital tool to enable citizens to keep their identity online where passports or other documents have been destroyed in times of conflict.

OPERATIONS MANAGEMENT

Improving the management of business processes can be supported by the digitalization of operations management. For instance, data can be shared at different stages of operations management so that decisions as to whether to replace, reduce, reuse and recycle can be taken.

Using the IoT, technology and systems are in place with advanced analytics which can identify problems before the customer is aware of them. For example, remote asset monitoring in the case of security alarms, which are managed in a central location through a software dashboard, can identify a broken sensor or failing battery before a facilities manager has realized there is an issue. Software monitoring can collect data and, using artificial intelligence, (AI) recommend suitable solutions, such as updating software or changing a network to optimize its use. AI can also be used to automate inventory control at times when the network is least busy.

Amazon is well known as a large online retailer, but what is less well known is its development of a software system for operations management. It has developed its own operations management processes such as speedy order picking, which is traditionally labour intensive and has had negative PR as workers complain they aren't allowed to take breaks. The introduction of the Sparrow robot [55] is a faster way to identity and pick goods ready for distribution but it is not without its critics as there are concerns that robots will remove the need for human workers.

MARKETING AND COMMUNICATIONS

Digitalization offers real-time data from the numbers of people looking at a product on a website, to measuring the success or failure of a communications campaign – within hours. One area that has seen growth is chatbots, which were first introduced in the 1960s [114] and are familiar across many websites. At the start, chatbots were basic and the technology was not in place to realize their full potential. Superfast internet has facilitated the development of speedier responses that don't suffer from a time-lagged answer.

AI chatbots use more natural language and can sound like a member of staff. In some cases they might even be more trusted than humans [114]! The capabilities of chatbots are based on machine learning – capturing the questions and providing relevant answers, as when a response is unacceptable, the chatbot gathers this and better information can be supplied. Chatbots also provide a rich seam of data, gathering frequently asked questions from customers, which means marketing teams can ensure they provide relevant answers in their communications material.

The downsides are that chatbots are dependent on the information given, which can be wrong or incomplete, or engage in non-productive machine

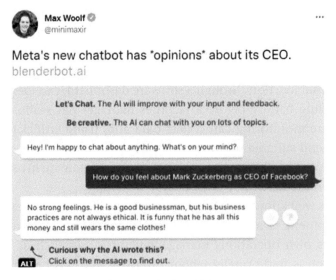

https://hothardware.com/news/metas-ai-chatbot-calls-zuckerberg-creepy-manipulative-unethical

learning, which in turn leads to incorrect, offensive, or unethical responses. For instance, Meta's BlenderBot 3 provided racist responses to some questions and Meta explained it was still a work in progress and acknowledged that it wasn't 'at human level' and did make mistakes [88].

PEOPLE MANAGEMENT

Considering the digital business framework (see Figure 11.2) it may be thought that this is an internal rather than external function. However, digitalization within people management impacts external factors too. Staff are the customers as well as the people involved with the systems. IoT, AI and data are used across five main areas of people management within centralized systems:

- **Recruitment and selection processes** include job applications via LinkedIn and AI-automated selection processes whereby individuals' details are scored and those with the highest scores are submitted to HR for review. In situations where companies receive large numbers of applications, this is a way to speed up the process. Google, for example, receives over 3 million job applications a year!

- **Development and training management** take time and in the past may have involved manual records. Using data within the systems, an organization can identify who has – or has not – completed mandatory and desirable training, automatically sending reminders and, where there is noncompliance, advise the employee's manager.

- **Performance management** through the use of apps or connected systems ensure that employees' records are held centrally and enables comparison between teams and across departments, which means that problems can be identified earlier.

- **Data and analytics** can be captured enabling informed decisions to be made – for example, decisions about hiring processes and how they might be improved, as well as building teams with specific skill sets.

Blockchain is also used in people management. For example, LG CNS (Jaeheun, 2022), a subsidiary of Korean manufacturer LG Corporation, has streamlined how their staff access their offices, pay for beverages in the coffee shop, access their salary details and manage their identity. Instead of a plastic swipe card used to access the building, an app contains their digital identity. Instead of cash or a credit card to pay for coffee, the same app can be used and when employees want to access their employment history, they use the same app. The data comes from different sources such as the payroll team, building security and their bank details. Combining the different elements into one app enables employees to control their identity and if, for example, they change their address, they only need to change it in the app which will automatically make the changes in the other areas.

The challenge is that organizations can monitor employees more closely than before and all employees would require access to a smartphone to be involved in the process, which could exclude some people.

ACCOUNTING AND FINANCE

Accounting and finance are based around systems. This is one business function which in most cases adopted digitalization quickly. As requirements in accounting and finance are often defined in legislation, the capabilities and resources are allocated as a priority. Digitalization has been in place for many years as most employees are paid electronically using cloud-based systems. Governments across Europe are adopting digitalization and encouraging organizations to adopt digital accounting systems, keeping one shared record online.

The use of blockchain technology (shared record) saw the development of decentralized currencies or cryptocurrency, a digital currency which is stored online. You might think of it as a digital wallet, but as there is an absence of regulation, it's a risky digital wallet and is illegal in several countries. There are over 8,000 cryptocurrencies [10] and one of the best-known is Bitcoin which is accepted as a payment method in many countries. Cryptocurrency is accepted as a payment by Wikipedia, Microsoft and Twitch – as well as by many smaller stores, coffee shops and pizza restaurants [9].

But there are downsides, and regulators in Germany are seeking to regulate its use to prevent money laundering and protect consumers [107]. Another issue is concern about the impact on the environment as the energy required to gather (mine) Bitcoin is equivalent to the total energy consumption of Norway [90], making it an unsustainable currency. This has seen some companies announcing that they can no longer accept cryptocurrency.

PRINCIPLES OF DIGITALIZING

I.   Digitalization and sustainability have been called the 'twin transformation' of our times, implying the need to search for synergies between these two world-reshaping trends.

II. The digitalizing mode of management involves all three, digitization (transforming analogue to digital data), digitalization (transforming individual practices to be centred on digital technologies), and digital transformation (building predominantly digital businesses).

III. The practice of digitalizing is heavily centred on technology involving, among others, artificial intelligence, big data, additive printing, blockchain, and the Internet of Things.

IV. Digital work lives take place in the midst of tension between potential advantages such as increased flexibility and self-determination, and challenges such as surveillance and achieving digital wellbeing. Professional management's role is to foster the realization of opportunities while addressing the challenges.

V. The digital maturity of an organization requires the successful adoption and alignment of digital technologies across all main business functions.

MANAGEMENT GYM: TRAINING YOUR PROFESSIONAL SIX-PACK

Knowing

1. What is digital competence and how does it relate to professional competence?

2. Describe the different levels of digital maturity using real-life examples.

3. List the ethics, responsibility, and sustainability implications of three different digital technologies of your choice.

Thinking

4. Choose a business you use regularly, such as a coffee shop or sports club. How far advanced is their digital maturity and what do you imagine the environmental footprint of their digitalizing to be?

5. What do you think are the main challenges for organizations in advancing their digital maturity and how do these challenges differ regionally and depending on the size of the organization?

6. Use an artificial intelligence tool to help you summarize knowledge about a particular cause, such as carbon neutrality or social inclusion. Critically evaluate the process and outcome.

Acting

7. Assess your digital competence using the digital competence framework presented in this chapter and/or online offers like the EU's digital competence tool https://digcomp.digital-competence.eu

8. Experiment as a crowd worker, sign up for a crowd platform (e.g. Fiverr, Upwork) and offer a service. Reflect on the experience. Did you obtain any work and if you did, was it worth it?

9. Imagine you are an employee of a company of your choice and you are in charge of producing a list of potential environmentally sustainable digitalization initiatives tailored to the company's characteristics. Prepare that list, considering the characteristics of the company chosen.

Interacting

10. Together with a family member, compare their digital competence to yours. What are the differences and why?

11. Form a small group and discuss the ethics of artificial intelligence, automation, and/or virtual reality.

12. Find and discuss with a chatbot a particular company's ethics, responsibility, or sustainability challenges.

Being

13. Reflect on the digitalization technologies you use most and why. What do they mean for your social and environmental impact?

Becoming

16. What challenges and opportunities do you think digital work life and management might present to you personally and how do you think you should best act on them?

(Continued)

Being	Becoming
14. What are the upsides and downsides of your use of digital technology?	17. Identify and use an AI-based teacher – e.g. a sustainability education chatbot – to learn something new about ethics, responsibility, or sustainability.
15. What are the most important ethics, responsibility, or sustainability implications of digitalization for you?	18. How would you personally practice digital work life in the most sustainable, ethical, and responsible way?

Laasch, O., Moosmayer, D., & Antonacopoulou, E. P. (2023). The interdisciplinary responsible management competence framework: An integrative review of ethics, responsibility, and sustainability competences. *Journal of Business Ethics, 187,* 733–757.

PIONEER INTERVIEW
ANDREAS KAPLAN

INTERVIEWER: OLIVER LAASCH

Andreas Kaplan is a pioneering professor and opinion maker in digitalization, ranging from business uses of alternative realities, artificial intelligence, and mobile devices to social media marketing use and digital mass customization.

Courtesy of Andreas Kaplan

Digital revolution – the good, bad, and the ugly!
On a very abstract level, one can look at this question either optimistically or pessimistically, and I largely prefer the positive alternative. Let's take an example. In the business world, supply chains and the logistics and transportation sector account for approximately 10 per cent of global GDP, and 10 per cent of global CO_2 emissions. If we increase supply chain efficiency through artificial intelligence, blockchain technologies, and the Internet of Things, we can substantially improve the world's sustainability.

On the other hand, however, due to those same technologies, many employees might lose their jobs and fall into long-term unemployment. We might recall what a Russian historian, Aleksandr Solzhenitsyn, once stated, saying that the battle line between good and evil runs

(Continued)

through the heart of every (wo)man. We could certainly say the same about the world's digital revolution. It will all depend on how companies and society in general deal with this digital transformation and what they use it for.

Digitalizing ethically, responsibly, sustainably. Many jobs will disappear and be carried out by machines. On the other hand, many new jobs will evolve, whose nature we do not even know yet. Most likely, not everybody who loses their job due to the digital transformation will be able to find new, higher-quality employment. It is essential that all different groups in society take part in this digital journey and that nobody is left behind. This is a question of ethical and responsible management. I would hope human beings are always at the centre of the digital transformation.

Then there is the link between digitalization and sustainability, which I will illustrate with the example of the future metaverse – i.e. virtual worlds: several studies warn of an increase in carbon emissions due to the extremely large amounts of energy required by virtual reality technology. Conversely, virtual worlds might also considerably reduce pollution by reducing the need for travel and commuting and replacing physical goods with virtual ones. It will be a matter of calculating which option will be more advantageous in terms of sustainability. One can only remain optimistic and ask both governments and corporations to be smart in developing the metaverse (and digitalization in general), to use it responsibly, and, more generally, to ensure that the metaverse is beneficial for both the planet and its inhabitants.

Digital managing and leading. The more digitalization transforms the workplace in an unprecedented way, the more managers will need to adopt a leadership style that builds trust. Employees might be scared of their futures or unsettled and overwhelmed by technological change. Leadership skills such as humane, ethical, open, and transparent management will be essential. In addition, managers will need to be specialists in assessing competencies and skills to detect the best position for each employee in such a hybrid system that includes people and AI, augmented reality, and the like. Managers will need to become both data-driven decision-makers and empathetic mentors.

Digital users versus rulers of the world? More than a decade ago, in 2010, we published an article on the challenges and opportunities of social media, titled 'Users of the world, unite' [69]. Social media helped people unite, raise their voices, and collectively fight for their cause. Information could be spread quickly on platforms such as Facebook or Twitter. Just think of the Arab Spring, a series of anti-government protests and uprisings against oppressive regimes that spread across the Middle East and North Africa, during which social media played a decisive role in facilitating interaction and communication among participants in these rebellions.

Since the article was published, we have seen AI evolve. Social media, newly powered by AI, are increasingly being used to spread fake news and manipulate entire groups of people. Social media went from being a facilitator of democracy to a serious threat to it. The political consulting

(Continued)

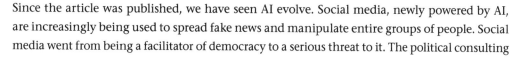

firm Cambridge Analytica, for instance, used the data of several million Facebook users to strongly manipulate public opinion in events such as the 2016 US presidential election and the 2016 Brexit referendum. This consequently created an outcry and called for governments and corporate leaders to develop legal frameworks and ethical standards for the use of AI-driven social media. For us, this was the trigger to write a second article, exactly ten years after the first one, titled 'Rulers of the world, unite' [69].

The digital business school? First, let's ask ourselves whether a fully digitalized business school would make sense. This could be the case if participants cannot afford air fares or living expenses, need to take care of children or sick or disabled family members, or are unable to travel to campus. These business schools would also work for students interested only in the content of the studies or the degree itself. However, they might lose out in several respects since studying is more than just learning new material and acquiring knowledge. There is also, among other things, the exchange between students in class and, even more so, outside the classrooms over a cup of coffee or a glass of wine.

In the future, the metaverse might provide an entirely new virtual environment to in which study and provide new possibilities, surpassing many of today's online institutions. Students will immerse themselves in the metaverse to participate in courses, work on group assignments, or join extracurricular activities to socialize virtually. Going even further, at some point in time, human teachers might be replaced by AI-driven machines, holograms, bots or humanoids. Although this won't happen for a while, we might be wrong in thinking (and hoping) that students will always prefer human instructors over artificially intelligent ones. In a similar vein, a study conducted by the IE University in Spain found that one-fourth of Europeans would prefer AI-driven systems to govern rather than human politicians who might be corrupt or ideologically motivated. Only the future will tell what will happen and what a fully digital school will look like.

QUESTIONS

1. Prepare a list of the positive and negative ethics, responsibility, and sustainability impacts of digitalization mentioned by Andreas. Looking at that list, do you think digitalization will makes a more ethical, responsible, or sustainable world, or conversely one that is more unethical, irresponsible, and unsustainable?

(Continued)

2. Do you think digitalization as it is practiced today empowers 'users' or 'rulers' of the work? Do we see an ongoing democratization of the digital world, or do we see it being subdued?

3. Would you personally want to live and study and work in applications like the metaverse and with virtual AI creatures? Why? Why not?

PROFESSIONAL PROFILE
YUE HU

Digital trading. I am the marketing manager out of Shanghai for a global ecommerce website called PlayerAuctions, a platform facilitating in-game assets trading amongst players. You can think of us as eBay for gaming goods – video game accounts, in-game gold, items, and power levelling services – all goods are virtual. Players deliver their digital assets online and we, as the middleman and an escrow party, secure and verify the transactions. So yes, there is no shipping or logistics. Everything happens over the internet with no physical traces.

Courtesy of Yue Hu

Digital working. Digitalization is not only reflected in our business model, but also in the way we work. We have offices in China, the Philippines, Hong Kong and the US. Our parent company is in Korea

(Continued)

and our market in North America and Europe. A Zoom meeting is held twice a week to go over important matters. During the Covid-19 pandemic, as many other companies in the gaming territory, our business grew significantly. However, we moved our Manila office to a smaller office space, not only to save costs, but also because there is just no need for everyone to work physically at the office every single day. For example, for the marketing department, all my team members have their weekly targets, which are easy to track and evaluate remotely. Theoretically there is no need for them to work in an office at all. Having said that, face-to-face interactions amongst team members are still a necessity for team cohesiveness and morale. After collecting our team members' opinions, we decided that everyone goes to the office once a week, on Fridays. While there is still a debate over the productivity and satisfaction of remote working, so far, it works well for us.

Digital marketing. I discovered my interest in marketing in college. Creativity, strategy, branding, these things fascinated me as a student as I buried myself in David Ogilvy's biography and binge-watched *Mad Men*. However, after I started my first job in a small agency under BBDO, I realized how difficult it is to measure performance in the traditional landscape of advertising. I decided to try something new and so I went to the UK for a master's degree. After that, I started an internship in a digital firm in London and since then I embarked on my career in digital marketing.

In the digital world, creativity meets math. Every idea you conceive, every line you write, and every design you make, you face an instant result in concrete numbers – click through rate, bounce rate, conversion rate, etc. It can be brutal, but also exciting. As a professional in digital marketing, you not only need to be sensitive about the nuances of language and culture, you also have to comprehend the basics of coding, tracking and analysing. And if you are interested in both sides of the world, digital marketing can be a fun ride for you too.

QUESTIONS

1. What elements of digital work life and digital business models can you spot in Yue's work profile?

2. What ethics, responsibility, and/or sustainability implications can you find in Yue's work?

3. How would you practice Yue's job if you wanted to do it the most professional possible way?

TRUE STORY

FEAR AND LOATHING IN DIGITAL WORK

sf_freelance/shutterstock.com

Hi, my name is Chris and I applied for a job at an international training firm to lead the 'making us digital' team. Digital transformation takes many forms and one way to accelerate the process is to engage new staff. The firm already had new technology in different parts of the business. The key was joining the dots and bringing the different aspects together and promoting the achievements to the outside world.

My digital dream job, or is it? This was my dream job. I'd graduated in business and marketing and this was a significant step from a previous assistant role I worked in, where I had been supporting digital project management. As cutting-edge new technology was involved the recruitment took place through a combined employer–university partnership, known as a knowledge-transfer partnership. This is a three-way partnership between the firm, the university and me. My official title was KTP (Knowledge Transfer Partnerships) associate and there were benefits for all. The university gained funding to manage the role, the firm gained government funding for part of the role and I gained a mentor from the university to coach me along the journey, as well as significant training and the ability to gain a professional qualification. It's a great way to bring technology into a firm and for an individual to accelerate their career. Plus many major firms across the UK have been involved with KTP projects and the programme has a successful track record.

(Continued)

I'd checked Glassdoor, the employer review, site and the reviews seemed amazing, so many 5 stars. An occasional 2 or 3 star, but that was the minority so I assumed these were just unhappy people. The firm was an award-winning business with great clients and great opportunities.

At the interview I met the university professor who was managing the university partnership and could provide access to more training. Although I was based in the firm's office, technically I was employed by the university so one day a week I would be back to examine tech solutions further and gain training. The firm had a great work–life balance policy with a right to ignore emails sent outside working hours.

Off to a great start. My first day arrived and the firm had moved from allocated desks to hot-desking. This was so exciting. I could pick where I wanted to sit whenever I went into the office, although some of the best spots in smaller booths seemed to be reserved in advance. HR organized a trolley for me to store my personal stuff and this was placed into a locker at the end of each day. IT sorted out a laptop, headset and mobile phone and HR took me though a whole week of induction. The MD was super enthusiastic and kept popping in to see me to ask what changes I'd made and I thought this was really funny as I'd literally been there for a few days.

The first three-way meeting took place and a program of work was agreed with key milestones. I set up meetings with the different IT stakeholders to understand and map the different technologies being used in the firm to see where integration or replacement could take place. The people I was working with were great and very supportive but seemed to be holding back from giving me all the information. I also started client focus groups to better understand their needs and where there were roadblocks that impacted the services being delivered. In a couple of months I'd gained a good overview and was working with the university to carry out an experiment to test the introduction of artificial intelligence in several places. This was ground-breaking and could save the company money in travel costs and had a great impact on sustainability. Instead of flying to New York to deliver training, there were alternative options to offer this in a virtual environment.

No digital boundaries, it seems. The MD was keen for me to attend a training conference that many staff were booked into and I was thrilled with the opportunity to travel overseas within a few months. The professor seemed a little reluctant to support this but added that if I was attending as an observer this would be great experience. Two months later I was on a flight to Las Vegas and the conference started. I've never been a big drinker and am happy to go out and stick to water or orange juice, but on the first evening the group were doing shots – all led by the MD. I said no a few times, but felt pressured and in the end I drank more than I've ever done before. The next day I felt pretty unwell. We'd got to our rooms by 3am and at 6am my phone was ringing. One of the team members said the MD wasn't able to deliver a presentation,

(Continued)

so had asked me to do it. I was terrified. Speaking to a crowd of at least 100 people, badly hungover and not knowing as much about the firm. The slides were sent to me and I felt that I had no choice. I got onto the stage and basically read the slides. It was the worst presentation I've ever done. In fact it was so bad there were no questions from the audience. As I looked to the back of the room, I saw the MD was there and didn't look happy.

We got back two days later and the emails were piling up. The MD was sending emails at 9pm, 10pm, 11pm and midnight and they all needed a response before 7am. At the next three-way meeting – they were every two weeks – we talked about the conference and I mentioned the volume of emails. The conference presentation was, according to the MD, 'a great opportunity to showcase your skills'. The emails were 'part of how we work'. So I didn't feel like I could say anything in the room as it sounded like I was moaning about everything when I'd been given such a great opportunity. The professor had a separate meeting with me afterwards and probed, asking more about the conference so I explained what had happened. I mentioned the emails coming through at all times of the day and night that all required an urgent response. I didn't want them to mention this, so they agreed we would review the situation in two weeks' time. At this time I'd worked there for three months.

Pretty bad but looking good online. Two weeks later I saw the prof first and then we had the three-way meeting. The prof raised the emails and this was dismissed with a 'Well, I don't really expect Alex to look at them at those times, but Alex doesn't usually respond very quickly to anything, in fact, several people have said Alex is very slow at work. I was devastated and exhausted. I'd been working night and day to stay ahead, as well as weekends, yet I was still learning about the job.

As I'd started to make friends in the firm, I discovered that I was the third person in the role. The first person left after eight weeks, the second person lasted three months. I could be the record as it was six months and I was still just about there. I wasn't entirely surprised but said the firm looked good on Glassdoor, then discovered that employees were encouraged, with the MD coming to their desk and saying, 'Have you left a great review on Glassdoor yet?' The glowing reviews meant the business looked good to the outside world. I started to think about the few negative reviews (poor management, lack of understanding, toxic environment) and realized every time there was a single negative review, a bunch of positive reviews turned up. Someone in IT told me they even created extra, fake employee email addresses to add more and more of these.

Letting the world know. At the next three-way review meeting the prof brought up the issue of emails and general pressure and the MD's response was, 'Alex doesn't seem able to cope

(Continued)

with this job so we won't be approving the probation.' At this stage the decision had been made for me. I worked my notice and updated my CV.

Three months after I left I added my own review to Glassdoor: 'The firm looks great on the outside, but the culture is toxic as others have said. Watch out for some great reviews appearing soon to improve the star rating but be aware, they're probably fake.'

QUESTIONS

1. Which of the troubles described in this true story do you think are unique to a digitalized workplace?

2. If you were in Chris's shoes, what would you have done differently, if anything? What would have been the most responsible and ethical course of action?

3. Do you think reviewing employees on Glassdoor or similar sites is a helpful practice, and, if so, in what way, and if not, why not?

DIGGING DEEPER: WEB COMMUNICATION 1.0, 2.0, AND 3.0

Adapted from [19]

The first (1.0) version of the web was a static one-way information system. Users were rather passive recipients of information prepared by institutions with enough technical know-how and financial resources to establish a webpage. The possibilities to 'communicate back' were restricted to mail applications. With Web 2.0 a change from static to dynamic took place. Users evolved to become co-creators of many different kinds of content and applications such as video, text, or even software (e.g. the open-source movement). The web also became mobile and omnipresent with an exponentially increasing number of mobile devices, which would often save information in the web 'cloud' instead of locally on the device. Web 2.0 was also characterized by its social component, where offline social life was transferred on a massive scale to online platforms. In Web 3.0, increasingly, online activity was so embedded in offline 'real life' that distinguishing the two spheres became increasingly difficult. A 'metaverse', neither online nor offline was created. In Web 4.0, finally the web is dominated by non-human artificial intelligence (e.g. chatbots and artificial virtual assistants) that makes automated decisions while also being able to learn. These decisions do not 'stay' online but unfold in an increasingly 'blended' reality (e.g. automatic driving and facial recognition systems).

As described in Table 11.4, each version of the web brings typical advantages and challenges to communicating online, which can still be observed when companies adapt a communication style in the continuum between Web 1.0 and 4.0. All three types of the web co-exist simultaneously and companies can make an active choice about which one is best suited to their communication aims regarding responsible management. Management that wants to co-create value with stakeholders will use a strong Web 2.0 strategy in order to maximize exchange and co-creation possibilities with stakeholders. A different company, at a time of crisis, might try to gain control of the content shared on the web to mitigate reputational damage and would choose to communicate through a traditional Web 1.0 homepage, which does not allow publicly visible reactions to content to be shared. A third company's management might aim to connect their real-life products to the virtual world through activities in the realm of Web 3.0 and the management of a fourth company, an insurance company, might use fintech (financial services based on new technologies) together with a wearable bracelet to monitor insurance customers' (ir)responsible health behaviour.

TABLE 11.4 Advantages and disadvantages of communication styles related to different types of the web

Type of web	Communication pattern	Advantage	Disadvantage
1.0, content diffusion	Few users putting information online for others to see.	Complete control over content and answers.	Restricted possibility for dialogue and co-creation with stakeholders.
2.0, user generation	Everyone generating and adapting contents in social interaction.	Democratization of communication and enhanced possibility to interact with stakeholders.	Unstructured, hard to grasp and control flow of information.
3.0, semantic web	Local and human-controlled machine-to-machine communication in both physical and virtual realities.	Possible to create real-life change and increase the eco-efficiency of lifestyles.	Potential to block change for sustainable behaviours by keeping them in their own personalized world.
4.0, intelligent ubiqituous web	Continuous, often hidden exchange of information between humans and artificial intelligence making joint decisions in a blended reality.	Ease of use, due to the integrated and automated nature in daily life.	Dangers from 'transparent' human beings and artificial intelligence making decisions over human lives.

POINTERS

As all four types of the web now exist in parallel, you might dig deeper into this topic by, for instance, thinking about how the different web types and their channels suit different types of messages to reach different stakeholders. Also, there are intriguing questions; for instance, on Web 3.0, how do automated non-human communicators and human communicators communicate with and challenge each other? What are the potential dangers and opportunities in each web? How could you shape a message that spans all four webs?

WORKSHEET

Describe the typical user-stakeholder #1

Describe the typical user-stakeholder #2

Describe the typical user-stakeholder #3

User motivation

Describe the perceived usefulness across user types

Describe the perceived ease of use across user types

Summarize the attitude toward using the technology

Your thoughts on the likely or actual use of the technology and impacts on the user stakeholders.

POINTERS

This stakeholder-adapted version of the versatile technology acceptance model (Davis, 1989) can be used in a variety of helpful ways – for instance, to better understand how to improve the actual use of a digitalization technology, or to assess its likely future use as well as its impact on key non-/user stakeholders.

REFERENCES

1. Abu, N., Bukhari, W., Ong, C., Kassim, A., Izzuddin, T., Sukhaimie, M., … Rasid, A. (2022). Internet of Things applications in precision agriculture: A review. *Journal of Robotics and Control (JRC), 3*(3): 338–347.
2. Aguinis, H., & Lawal, S. O. (2013). eLancing: A review and research agenda for bridging the science–practice gap. *Human Resource Management Review, 23*(1): 6–17.
3. Alexandra, K. (2020). Leave only footprints: Why digital nomads and sustainability are a match made in heaven. https://nofootprintnomads.com/nomadism/nomad-lifestyle/digital-nomads-sustainability Last accessed August 13 2023.
4. Ali, S., Islam, N., Rauf, A., Din, I. U., Guizani, M., & Rodrigues, J. J. (2018). Privacy and security issues in online social networks. *Future Internet, 10*(12): 114.
5. AMFG. (2020). How sustainable is industrial 3D printing? https://amfg.ai/2020/03/10/how-sustainable-is-industrial-3d-printing Last accessed August 13 2023.
6. ARD. (2022). The Hu plans to host a virtual concert in the metaverse in partnership with ARD. https://ardholdings.com/en/thehumetaverse Last accessed August 13 2023.
7. Atanasova, G. L., Atanasov, B. N., & Atanasov, N. T. (2022). Fully textile dual-band logo antenna for IoT wearable devices. *Sensors, 22*(12): 4516.
8. Bayudan-Dacuycuy, C., & Kryz Baje, L. (2021). Decent work in crowdwork: Gendered takeaways from an online survey in the Philippines. https://pidswebs.pids.gov.ph/CDN/PUBLICATIONS/pidsdps2111.pdf Last accessed August 2023.
9. Beigel, O. (2023). Who accepts bitcoin as payment? https://99bitcoins.com/bitcoin/who-accepts Last accessed August 13 2023.
10. Best, R. de. (2023). Number of cryptocurrencies worldwide from 2013 to February 2023. www.statista.com/statistics/863917/number-crypto-coins-tokens Last accessed August 13 2023.
11. Bhargava, A., Bhargava, D., Kumar, P. N., Sajja, G. S., & Ray, S. (2022). Industrial IoT and AI implementation in vehicular logistics and supply chain management for vehicle mediated transportation systems. *International Journal of System Assurance Engineering and Management, 13*(Suppl 1): 673–680.
12. Blüm, S. (2022). What is the 'twin transition' – and why is it key to sustainable growth? www.weforum.org/agenda/2022/10/twin-transition-playbook-3-phases-to-accelerate-sustainable-digitization Last accessed August 13 2023.
13. Bogani, R., Theodorou, A., Arnaboldi, L., & Wortham, R. H. (2022). Garbage in, toxic data out: A proposal for ethical artificial intelligence sustainability impact statements. *AI and Ethics*: 1–8.
14. Brennen, J. S., & Kreiss, D. (2016). Digitalization. In K. B. Jensen & R. T. Craig (Eds), *The international encyclopedia of communication theory and philosophy* (pp. 1–11). Chichester: Wiley.
15. Charalampous, M., Grant, C. A., Tramontano, C., & Michailidis, E. (2019). Systematically reviewing remote e-workers' well-being at work: A multidimensional approach. *European Journal of Work and Organizational Psychology, 28*(1): 51–73.
16. Chatterjee, S., & Chaudhuri, R. (2022). Adoption of artificial intelligence integrated customer relationship management in organizations for sustainability. *Business under crisis, Volume III: Avenues for innovation, entrepreneurship and sustainability*. London: Palgrave Macmillan: pp. 137–156.
17. Ciappelloni, R., Avellini, L., Marenzoni, L., & Serenelli, F. (2020). *Smart chatbots as virtual assistants in the Library*. Sanita'Pubblica Veterinaria.

18. Cochoy, F., Licoppe, C., McIntyre, M. P., & Sörum, N. (2020). Digitalizing consumer society: Equipment and devices of digital consumption. *Journal of Cultural Economy, 13*(1): 1–11. doi:10.1080/17530350.2019.1702576.

19. Conaway, R., & Laasch, O. (2012). *Communication in responsible business: Strategies, concepts, cases.* New York: Business Expert Press.

20. Constantinescu, V. (2022). Achieving peace of mind as a digital nomad: A privacy guide. www.bitdefender.co.uk/blog/hotforsecurity/achieving-peace-of-mind-as-a-digital-nomad-a-privacy-guide Last accessed August 13 2023.

21. Corsini, L., Aranda-Jan, C. B., & Moultrie, J. (2022). The impact of 3D printing on the humanitarian supply chain. *Production Planning & Control, 33*(6–7): 692–704.

22. Crowdworker. (2023). Who are the typical crowdworkers? www.crowdworker.com/who-are-the-typical-crowdworkers Last accessed August 13 2023.

23. Davis, F. D. (1989). Perceived usefulness, perceived ease of use and user acceptance of information technology. *MIS Quarterly, 13*(3): 319–339.

24. de Mattos Nascimento, D. L., Mury Nepomuceno, R., Caiado, R. G. G., Maqueira, J. M., Moyano-Fuentes, J., & Garza-Reyes, J. A. (2022). A sustainable circular 3D printing model for recycling metal scrap in the automotive industry. *Journal of Manufacturing Technology Management, 33*(5): 876–892.

25. Dell. (2022). The AI sustainability paradox: And how to solve it. Retrieved from www.cio.com/article/415787/the-ai-sustainability-paradox-and-how-to-solve-it.html

26. Digitaltrainee. (2023). Why people love digital trainee? Retrieved from https://digitaltrainee.com/knowledge/benefits-of-digital-marketing-freelancers

27. Dilmegani, C. (2023, 2 February). Chatbots in healthcare: Top 6 use cases & examples in 2023. https://research.aimultiple.com/chatbot-healthcare Last accessed August 13 2023.

28. Donovan-Stevens, A. (2021). The new age of the digital nomad and the threats that come along with it. https://tbtech.co/blockchain/security-and-data/the-new-age-of-the-digital-nomad-and-the-threats-that-come-along-with-it Last accessed August 13 2023.

29. Durward, D., Blohm, I., & Leimeister, J. M. (2016). Crowd work. *Business & Information Systems Engineering, 58*: 281–286.

30. Durward, D., Blohm, I., & Leimeister, J. M. (2020). The nature of crowd work and its effects on individuals' work perception. *Journal of Management Information Systems, 37*(1): 66–95. doi:10.1080/07421222.2019.1705506.

31. Dütschke, E., Galvin, R., & Brunzema, I. (2021). Rebound and spillovers: Prosumers in transition. *Frontiers in Psychology, 12*: 636109.

32. Economist. (2018). A study finds nearly half of jobs are vulnerable to automation: That could free people to pursue more interesting careers. www.economist.com/graphic-detail/2018/04/24/a-study-finds-nearly-half-of-jobs-are-vulnerable-to-automation Last accessed August 13 2023.

33. Edison Alliance. (2023). The first alliance to accelerate digital inclusion. www.weforum.org/impact/digital-inclusion Last accessed August 13 2023.

34. Elbanna, A., & Idowu, A. (2021). Crowdwork as an elevator of human capital. A sustainable human development perspective. *Scandinavian Journal of Information Systems, 33*(2): 103–136.

35. Enholm, I. M., Papagiannidis, E., Mikalef, P., & Krogstie, J. (2022). Artificial intelligence and business value: A literature review. *Information Systems Frontiers, 24*(5): 1709–1734.

36. Erkilic, G. (2021). Digital marketing consultant job description: A complete guide for 2022. https://digitalagencynetwork.com/digital-marketing-consultant-job-description-a-complete-guide Last accessed August 13 2023.

37. EU. (2023). A European approach to artificial intelligence. https://digital-strategy.ec.europa.eu/en/policies/european-approach-artificial-intelligence Last accessed August 13 2023.

38. Eurofound. (2019). ICT-based mobile work. www.eurofound.europa.eu/observatories/eurwork/industrial-relations-dictionary/ict-based-mobile-work Last accessed August 13 2023.

39. Euronews. (2020). Digital cleanup day: Delete an email – save the planet, urge environmentalists. www.euronews.com/2020/04/21/digital-cleanup-day-declutter-your-devices-to-help-the-planet-urge-environmentalists Last accessed August 13 2023.

40. Evreka. (2023). 5 Environmental benefits of remote working. https://evreka.co/blog/the-environmental-benefits-of-remote-working Last accessed August 13 2023.

41. Fuller, J., Raman, M., Bailey, A., & Vaduganathan, N. (2020). Rethinking the on-demand workforce. *Harvard Business Review, 98*(6): 96–103.

42. Gaur, V., & Gaiha, A. (2020). Building a transparent supply chain blockchain can enhance trust, efficiency, and speed. *Harvard Business Review, 98*(3): 94–103.

43. Gavin, M. (2019). Business analytics: What it is and why it's important. https://online.hbs.edu/blog/post/importance-of-business-analytics Last accessed August 13 2023.

44. George, M., O'Regan, K., & Holst, A. (2022). Digital solutions can reduce global emissions by up to 20%: Here's how. www.weforum.org/agenda/2022/05/how-digital-solutions-can-reduce-global-emissions Last accessed August 13 2023.

45. Govtech. (2020, September 29). What is a virtual commute? Answer: A time of reflection, apparently. www.govtech.com/question-of-the-day/what-is-a-virtual-commute.html#:~:text=The%20idea%20is%20to%20help,like%20a%20miniature%20meditation%20session Last accessed August 13 2023.

46. Graves, J. (2019, July 12th 2019). Asda denies using facial recognition cameras on its customers in Preston amid privacy concerns. www.lep.co.uk/business/asda-denies-using-facial-recognition-cameras-its-customers-preston-amid-privacy-concerns-665351 Last accessed August 13 2023.

47. Griffiths, L. (2021). Is 3D printing really sustainable? www.tctmagazine.com/additive-manufacturing-3d-printing-industry-insights/latest-additive-manufacturing-3d-printing-industry-insights/is-3d-printing-sustainable-green-technology Last accessed August 13 2023.

48. Guda, H., & Subramanian, U. (2019). Your uber is arriving: Managing on-demand workers through surge pricing, forecast communication, and worker incentives. *Management Science, 65*(5): 1995–2014.

49. Gurumurthy, R., Schatsky, D., & Camhi, J. (2020). Uncovering the connection between digital maturity and financial performance. www2.deloitte.com/us/en/insights/topics/digital-transformation/digital-transformation-survey.html Last accessed August 13 2023.

50. Hajli, M. N., Sims, J., Featherman, M., & Love, P. E. D. (2015). Credibility of information in online communities. *Journal of Strategic Marketing, 23*(3): 238–253. doi:10.1080/0965254x.2014.920904.

51. Hanlon, A. (2022). Digital marketing: Strategic planning & integration (2nd revised edition): Sage Publications.

52. Hargrave, M. (2022). Overview of insurtech and its impact on the insurance industry. www.investopedia.com/terms/i/insurtech.asp Last accessed August 13 2023.

53. Hensellek, S., & Puchala, N. (2021). The emergence of the digital nomad: A review and analysis of the opportunities and risks of digital nomadism. *The flexible workplace: Coworking and other modern workplace transformations*, Marko Orel, Ondřej Dvouletý and Vanessa Ratten (eds). SpringerLink: pp. 195–214.

54. Holford, W. D. (2019). The future of human creative knowledge work within the digital economy. *Futures, 105*: 143–154.

55. Holt, K. (2022). Amazon's latest robot picker for warehouses uses AI to identify objects. www.engadget.com/amazon-robot-arm-picker-warehouse-sparrow-ai-computer-vision-210545438.html?guccounter=1&guce_referrer=aHR0cHM6Ly93d3cuZ29vZ2xlLmNvbvbS8&guce_referrer_sig=AQAAAD9p7wtacDs8td2RyUJoxseitobzlIPViISI1kKnO9fQQU_ampS8cWBNbFsbMpOhmbswtJEESIbJ9sbBCgXwO37x1axqXY9hRTxk913egSyXCdgjxzPJknCZf6iTPxdZMcXZg8s0GPZlemsCk16TGqoTWlAe42FIvU0qCDhukUCV Last accessed August 13 2023.

56. Hu, T. (2023). The Hu in #metaverse – first Mongolian band in the meta universe. www.google.com/search?q=%22The+Hu%22+metaverse&source=lmns&tbm=vid&bih=1297&biw=2560&rlz=1C1GCEB_en&hl=en&sa=X&ved=2ahUKEwi7lIHxpoj9AhV5sicCHVd0A_sQ_AUoA3oECAEQAw#fpstate=ive&vld=cid:4ee0bbac,vid:lSa40TQLLow Last accessed August 13 2023.

57. Hyrkkänen, U., Vanharanta, O., Kuusisto, H., Polvinen, K., & Vartiainen, M. (2022). Predictors of job crafting in SMEs working in an ICT-based mobile and multilocational manner. *International Small Business Journal*: 02662426221129157.

58. Iliff, C. C. (2017). Printing in 3D: Who's liable for product failures? www.propertycasualty360.com/2017/10/19/printing-in-3d-whos-liable-for-product-failures/?&slreturn=20230208060431 Last accessed August 13 2023.

59. Indeed. (2022, updated February 16 2023). Remote workforce definition (with how to find a remote job). https://ca.indeed.com/career-advice/finding-a-job/remote-workforce-definition Last accessed August 13 2023.

60. Jae-heun, K. (2022). LG CNS launches blockchain-based mobile ID service. www.koreatimes.co.kr/www/tech/2022/12/129_341655.html Last accessed August 13 2023.

61. Jandyal, A., Chaturvedi, I., Wazir, I., Raina, A., & Haq, M. I. U. (2022). 3D printing – a review of processes, materials and applications in industry 4.0. *Sustainable Operations and Computers, 3*: 33-42.

62. Jisc. (2020). Digital wellbeing for you, your colleagues and students: Briefing paper for practitioners. https://bdcdei-prod-media.s3.eu-west-1.amazonaws.com/documents/JB0019A_DIGITAL_WELLBENG_PRACTITIONERS_BRIEFING_PAPER_NOV19_WEB_v2.pdf Last accessed August 13 2023.

63. Jisc. (2023). Digital wellbeing – the impact of technologies and digital services on people's mental, physical and emotional health. https://digitalcapability.jisc.ac.uk/what-is-digital-capability/digital-wellbeing Last accessed August 13 2023.

64. Joyce, J. (2017). Unauthorised 3D printing: What use are intellectual property rights? www.taylorwessing.com/en/interface/2017/intellectual-property-rights-and-emerging-technologies/unauthorised-3d-printing---what-use-are-intellectual-property-rights Last accessed August 13 2023.

65. Kagan, J. (2022). Financial technology (fintech): Its uses and impact on our lives. www.investopedia.com/terms/f/fintech.asp Last accessed August 13 2023.

66. Kamiya, G. (2022). Data centres and data transmission networks. Retrieved from IEA: https://www.iea.org/energy-system/buildings/data-centres-and-data-transmission-networks Last accessed August 13 2023.

67. Kaplan, A. M., & Haenlein, M. (2010). Users of the world, unite! The challenges and opportunities of social media. *Business Horizons, 53*(1): 59–68.

68. Kaplan, A., & Haenlein, M. (2019). Siri, Siri, in my hand: Who's the fairest in the land? On the interpretations, illustrations, and implications of artificial intelligence. *Business Horizons, 62*(1): 15–25.

69. Kaplan, A., & Haenlein, M. (2020). Rulers of the world, unite! The challenges and opportunities of artificial intelligence. *Business Horizons, 63*(1): 37–50.

70. Kelliher, C., Richardson, J., & Boiarintseva, G. (2019). All of work? All of life? Reconceptualising work-life balance for the 21st century. *Human Resource Management Journal, 29*(2): 97–112.

71. Kissane, D. (2015). Do freelance marketers need a code of ethics? www.doz.com/marketing-resources/do-freelance-marketers-need-a-code-of-ethics Last accessed August 13 2023.

72. Köfner, D. (2022). Lenzing and Renewcell sign large-scale supply agreement further closing the loop in fashion [Press release]. www.lenzing.com/newsroom/press-releases/press-release/lenzing-and-renewcell-sign-large-scale-supply-agreement-further-closing-the-loop-in-fashion Last accessed August 13 2023.

73. Koohang, A., Sargent, C. S., Nord, J. H., & Paliszkiewicz, J. (2022). Internet of Things (IoT): From awareness to continued use. *International Journal of Information Management*, 62: 102442.

74. Kooli, C., & Al Muftah, H. (2022). Artificial intelligence in healthcare: A comprehensive review of its ethical concerns. *Technological Sustainability*, 1(2): 121-131. https://doi.org/10.1108/TECHS-12-2021-0029.

75. Kuhn, K. M. (2016). The rise of the 'gig economy' and implications for understanding work and workers. *Industrial and Organizational Psychology, 9*(1): 157–162.

76. Laasch, O., Moosmayer, D., & Arp, F. (2020). Responsible practices in the wild: An actor–network perspective on mobile apps in learning as translation(s). *Journal of Business Ethics, 161*(2): 253–277.

77. Lang, B., Dolan, R., Kemper, J., & Northey, G. (2021). Prosumers in times of crisis: Definition, archetypes and implications. *Journal of Service Management, 32*(2): 176–189.

78. Laurie Clarke, G. B. (2021, September 20). The practical ways to reduce your carbon footprint (that actually work). www.wired.co.uk/article/reduce-carbon-footprint Last accessed August 13 2023.

79. Lenzing. (2022). Digitalization. https://reports.lenzing.com/sustainability-report/2021/material-aspects/digitalization-cyber-security/digitalization.html Last accessed August 13 2023.

80. Lenzing Group. (2022). Lenzing Thailand – digital opening event: Behind the scenes. www.youtube.com/watch?v=nBo2STuAJUk Last accessed August 13 2023.

81. Longstaff, S. (2019). Blockchain: Some ethical considerations. https://ethics.org.au/blockchain-some-considerations Last accessed August 13 2023.

82. Madden, T. (2007). Wikinomics: How mass collaboration changes everything. www.minneapolisfed.org/article/2007/wikinomics-how-mass-collaboration-changes-everything Last accessed August 13 2023.

83. Mäenpää, A. (2022). Rock music in metaverses: A step towards new era. https://chaoszine.net/rock-music-in-metaverses-a-step-towards-new-era Last accessed August 13 2023.

84. Mancinelli, F. (2020). Digital nomads: Freedom, responsibility and the neoliberal order. *Information Technology & Tourism, 22*(3): 417–437.

85. Marchant, G. E., Cooper, Z., & Gough-Stone, P. J. (2022). Bringing technological transparency to tenebrous markets: The case for using blockchain to validate carbon credit trading markets. *Natural Resources Journal., 62*(2): 159.

86. Marinova, D., & Raven, M. (2006). Indigenous knowledge and intellectual property: A sustainability agenda. *Journal of Economic Surveys, 20*(4): 587–605.

87. McGinley, C. (2019, updated March 10 2022). Community managers: What they do & how to be a great one. https://blog.hubspot.com/marketing/great-community-management-tips Last accessed August 13 2023.

88. Meta. (2022). BlenderBot 3: An AI chatbot that improves through conversation. https://about.fb.com/news/2022/08/blenderbot-ai-chatbot-improves-through-conversation Last accessed August 13 2023.

89. Meyer, C. (2022). Remote work risk hits the road with digital nomads. www.asisonline.org/security-management-magazine/articles/2022/07/remote-work-risk-hits-the-road-with-digital-nomads2 Last accessed August 13 2023.

90. Moneysupermarket. (2021). As interest in cryptocurrencies and NFTs continues to grow, so too does the discussion around its energy consumption. But just how big is Bitcoin's energy bill? www.moneysupermarket.com/gas-and-electricity/features/crypto-energy-consumption/#:~:text=Based%20on%20the%20number%20of,annual%20energy%20consumption%20of%20Norway Last accessed August 13 2023.

91. Moore, J. (2022). UK retailer Co-Op's use of facial recognition cameras faces legal challenge from privacy campaigners. www.ifsecglobal.com/video-surveillance/co-op-facial-recognition-cameras-face-legal-challenge-privacy-data-protection Last accessed August 13 2023.

92. Moran, A. (2020, June 26). 20 Gig economy jobs to make some extra income. www.careeraddict.com/gig-economy-jobs Last accessed August 13 2023.

93. NanoMatriX. (2023). 3D-printed counterfeits on the rise: How to protect your brand. www.nanomatrixsecure.com/3d-printed-counterfeits-on-the-rise-how-to-protect-your-brand Last accessed August 13 2023.

94. Ng, R. (2021). Lenzing launches TENCEL™ eShop, the industry's first e-commerce platform managed by a fibre manufacturer [Press release].

95. Ng, R. (2022). Lenzing and RCGD Global bring eco-couture to the spotlight at the world premiere of 'AVATAR: The Way of Water'. www.lenzing.com/newsroom/press-releases/press-release/page?tx_news_pi1%5Bnews%5D=1280&cHash=815822b6f3936fd7129200e74466271b Last accessed August 13 2023.

96. Norouzi, Z., Amirkhani, F., & Babaii, S. (2023). Counselor bots as mental healthcare assistants and some ethical challenges. In *Social robots in social institutions*. Amsterdam: IOS Press: pp. 100–109.

97. Norton, J. (2023, January 12 2023). Supermarkets call for new laws that let them use AI to verify a customer is over-18 when buying alcohol – as figures show shop assistants are regularly abused when asking for ID. www.dailymail.co.uk/sciencetech/article-11623569/Supermarkets-call-new-laws-let-use-AI-verify-customers-18-buying-alcohol.html Last accessed August 13 2023.

98. OCI. (2022). What is big data? www.oracle.com/uk/big-data/what-is-big-data Last accessed August 13 2023.

99. Petrosyan, A. (2022a). Global internet penetration rate as of July 2022, by region. https://www.statista.com/statistics/269329/penetration-rate-of-the-internet-by-region/

100. Petrosyan, A. (2022b). Mobile internet usage worldwide. https://www.statista.com/topics/1145/internet-usage-worldwide/#topicOverview

101. Pham, C., Nguyen, T.-T., Adamopoulos, A., & Tait, E. (2022). Blockchain-enabled traceability in sustainable food supply chains: A case study of the pork industry in Vietnam. In *Information Systems Research in Vietnam: A Shared Vision and New Frontiers.* Springer: pp. 65–81.

102. Profiletree. (2022, December 23). Top 5 benefits of hiring a digital marketing consultant. https://profiletree.com/top-5-benefits-of-hiring-a-digital-marketing-consultant Last accessed August 13 2023.

103. Radicati. (2021). Mobile Statistics Report, 2021–2025. The Radicati Group Inc. www.radicati.com/wp/wp-content/uploads/2021/Mobile_Statistics_Report,_2021-2025_Executive_Summary.pdf Last accessed August 13 2023.

104. Rainoldi, M., Ladkin, A., & Buhalis, D. (2022). Blending work and leisure: A future digital worker hybrid lifestyle perspective. *Annals of Leisure Research*: 1–21. https://doi.org/10.1080/11745398.2022.2070513.

105. Razip, M. M., Savita, K., Kalid, K. S., Ahmad, M. N., Zaffar, M., Rahim, E. E. A., ... Ahmadian, A. (2022). The development of sustainable IoT E-waste management guideline for households. *Chemosphere, 303*: 134767.

106. Reiff, N. (2021). Governance: Blockchain tech's greatest problem. www.investopedia.com/investing/governance-blockchain-techs-greatest-problem Last accessed August 13 2023.

107. Reuters. (2022). Germany calls for global regulation of crypto industry. www.reuters.com/markets/currencies/germany-calls-global-regulation-crypto-industry-2022-12-14 Last accessed August 13 2023.

108. Ro, C. (2022). Why gig work is so hard to regulate. www.bbc.com/worklife/article/20220308-why-gig-work-is-so-hard-to-regulate Last accessed August 13 2023.

109. Robelski, S., & Sommer, S. (2020). ICT-enabled mobile work: Challenges and opportunities for occupational health and safety systems. *International Journal of Environmental Research and Public Health, 17*(20): 7498.

110. Rockmann, K. W., & Ballinger, G. A. (2017). Intrinsic motivation and organizational identification among on-demand workers. *Journal of applied psychology, 102*(9): 1305.

111. Salesforce. (2023). What is digital transformation? www.salesforce.com/eu/products/platform/what-is-digital-transformation/#:~:text=Digital%20transformation%20is%20changing%20the,both%20online%20and%20in%20person Last accessed August 13 2023.

112. Sarker, I. H., Khan, A. I., Abushark, Y. B., & Alsolami, F. (2022). Internet of Things (IoT) security intelligence: A comprehensive overview, machine learning solutions and research directions. *Mobile Networks and Applications*: 1–17.

113. Schwab, P.-N. (2021, April 28). The interest of eye tracking in the retail sector [Guide 2021]. www.intotheminds.com/blog/en/eye-tracking-retail-sector Last accessed August 13 2023.

114. Shaalan, A., Tourky, M. E., & Ibrahim, K. (2022). The chatbot revolution: Companies and consumers in a new digital age. In A. Hanlon & T. L. Tuten (Eds), *The Sage handbook of digital marketing* (pp. 369): Sage Publications.

115. Sharif, M. M., & Ghodoosi, F. (2022). The ethics of blockchain in organizations. *Journal of Business Ethics, 178*(4): 1009–1025. doi:10.1007/s10551-022-05058-5.

116. SoulMachines. (2021). How humanized AI is transforming education at scale. www.soulmachines.com/2021/10/how-humanized-ai-is-transforming-education-at-scale Last accessed August 13 2023.

117. Statista. (2022). Internet of Things (IoT). Retrieved from www.statista.com/topics/2637/internet-of-things/#topicOverview

118. Thomas, M. (2019). Nine to five work hours: Are employees really productive? www.worksmartpeo.com/xpanel/nine-five-work-hours-employees-really-productive Last accessed August 13 2023.

119. Tremblay, D.-G., & Thomsin, L. (2012). Telework and mobile working: Analysis of its benefits and drawbacks. *International Journal of Work Innovation, 1*(1): 100–113.

120. Tsai, M.-H., Chen, J. Y., & Kang, S.-C. (2019). Ask Diana: A keyword-based chatbot system for water-related disaster management. *Water, 11*(2): 234.

121. Vargas Llave, O. (2021). Digitalisation and working time. www.eurofound.europa.eu/data/digitalisation/research-digests/digitalisation-and-working-time Last accessed August 13 2023.

122. Verasai, A. (2023). Why 9-to-5 is not that bad. www.thehrdigest.com/why-9-to-5-is-not-that-bad Last accessed August 13 2023.

123. Viana Vargas, R. (2022). How human capital makes or breaks digital innovation. https://blogs.lse.ac.uk/businessreview/2022/10/26/how-human-capital-makes-or-breaks-digital-innovation Last accessed August 13 2023.

124. Vuka. (2019). Why the 9–5 schedule could be harming your health. https://vuka.co/blog/why-the-9-5-schedule-could-be-harming-your-health Last accessed August 13 2023.

125. Vuorikari, R., Kluzer, S., & Punie, Y. (2022). The digital competence framework for citizens: With new examples of knowledge, skills and attitudes. Publications Office of the European Union. https://data.europa.eu/doi/10.2760/115376 Last accessed August 13 2023.

126. Willems, M. (2022). 9m bedrooms have vanished as nearly half of all homeowners change property to suit post-pandemic needs. www.cityam.com/9m-bedrooms-have-vanished-as-nearly-half-of-all-homeowners-change-property-to-suit-post-pandemic-needs Last accessed August 13 2023.

127. Woodin, S. L. (2021). *SUITCEYES Scoping report on law and policy on deafblindness, disability and new technologies.* https://osf.io/preprints/socarxiv/uv5fe Last accessed August 13 2023.

128. Zhou, B., Li, W., Chan, K. W., Cao, Y., Kuang, Y., Liu, X., & Wang, X. (2016). Smart home energy management systems: Concept, configurations, and scheduling strategies. *Renewable and Sustainable Energy Reviews, 61*: 30-40.

CHAPTER 12

GLOCALIZING

OLIVER LAASCH AND ROGER N. CONAWAY

LEARNING GOALS

1. Analyse global and local management contexts
2. Map your glocal activities and their implications
3. Understand how to manage ethically and responsibly in a glocal work environment

ENCOURAGING FACT

When asked if they take action on global sustainability goals with their companies, 81 per cent of top managers say yes [1]!

SPOTLIGHT

LOCALIZING A GLOBAL CORPORATION IN THE AMAZON: THE NATURA WAY

www.naturabrasil.com

In a multinationally managed corporation with its roots firmly in the Brazilian Amazon, management at the beauty company Natura seems to be all about glocal. With Natura & Co's global brands Body Shop, Avon, Aesop, and their original brand Natura, they are the fourth biggest global beauty corporation [2]. At the same time, they have made a firm commitment to caring for their local origins.

Natura's 'reason for being' to 'create and sell products and services that promote the harmonious relationship of the individual with oneself, with others and with nature' translates into the tagline 'Beauty care that cares' [3]. From there varieties of ethical, social, and environmental core commitments have been integrated into their management practices and products. Their commitments are often linked to varieties of global certification schemes like the US-originated BCorp movement or the Union for Ethical Biotrade (UEB) with roots in Switzerland.

OUR COMMITMENTS

100% Vegan   Amazon Forest Ingredients   No Animal Testing   Climate Commitment

OUR CERTIFICATIONS

Ecological Packaging   Natural Origin Formulas

www.naturabrasil.com

(Continued)

Their flagship commitments tightly link the global corporation to the local Amazon. They support the Amazon through their commitment to Amazon-sourced ingredients, claiming that their 'R & D scientists … work directly with over 30 local communities in the Amazon region – including more than 300 families – to help them develop sustainable business models that benefit the forest.' They aim to preserve the unique interlinked local cultural heritage, communities, and ecosystem [4].

Natura is committed to the protection of the rainforest, 12 million hectares in total [5], and channelling global revenues into the use of the Amazon rainforest, which in turn creates further incentives for its communities to protect it. Again, the glocal dimension of these management practices becomes obvious when reflecting on the Amazon's role in capturing carbon and fighting global warming, and being a global biodiversity hotspot. Local sustainability, caring for the Amazon and global sustainability caring for the planet merge in glocally sustainable management [6].

www.naturabrasil.com

Management at Natura exemplifies how the glocalizing mode requires shifting attention and activity back and forth from local to global.

GLOCALIZING

If we get lost in reversing globalization, we will lose the ability to apply technology to the world's unmet needs and overcoming the grand challenges at global scale.

Frans van Houten [1]

We wake up every day to global and local air pollution problems, exhausted water resources, and depleted forests. Those global challenges require local solutions and, equally, local challenges require global solutions. In a **glocalizing** mode, managers can span the global and local, contributing to both society and the planet. Glocalizing management also has important implications for professional management conduct. Corruption, offshoring, human rights abuses, differing environmental standards are all glocal issues typically encountered by glocal managers. Glocally responsible management can also provide localized solutions fuelled by global activities, as seen in the case of Natura.

Glocalizing
a mode of management that integrates global and local issues and solutions

Should foreign companies cease operations in Russia during the country's invasion of Ukraine in order to generate economic pressure against the war? The Japanese clothing retailer Uniqlo first announced that the company was not shutting down stores in Russia, the CEO Tadashi Yanai stating that 'clothing is a necessity of life', a statement that is questionable considering the global over-supply of clothing. Insiders assumed that the actual reasons related to fears of negatively affecting Uniqlo's buoyant Chinese market. However, stores were then shut down after all, a move that was justified on the grounds that it was increasingly difficult to operate in the Russian business environment [7].

'Mall' by cacaoboy is licensed under CC BY-SA 2.0.

Glocally responsible management
is at the same time globally and locally responsible, excelling in intercultural ethics by creating value for stakeholders around the world, and in every location, and is locally and globally sustainable

Glocally responsible management is as much about globalizing responsibly as it is about localizing responsibly. It is about both complying with international sustainability, responsibility, and ethics standards, and adjusting responsible management conduct to manifold locations [8]. It is about addressing very local sustainability challenges, understanding and creating value for glocal stakeholders, and making ethically right but culturally tolerant decisions in any local values system. Glocally responsible management aspires to be globally valid as well as locally relevant.

In this chapter we will illustrate four core areas of the glocalizing mode of management (see Figure 12.1). First, *understanding glocalization* requires an appreciation of how and why the world has simultaneously become more globalized and localized. Secondly, *managing glocalized business* requires us to understand the characteristics of distinct types of glocal businesses – for instance, an ethnocentric or transnational type. Third, we will explore common *glocalization management practices* like foreign direct investment and global transfer pricing, and explore their ethical, stakeholder, and triple bottom line implications. Finally, *glocalized management* is centred on tools, such as cross-cultural ethics, to manage responsibly in a glocal workplace.

UNDERSTANDING GLOCALIZATION

Glocalization describes the phenomenon of inseparably entangled globalization and localization [9, 10]. It describes both global activities and strong adaptation to local circumstances [10], and understanding how local circumstances may influence global activities.

Glocalization describes global activities with a strong adaptation to local circumstances and local activities connecting to global circumstances

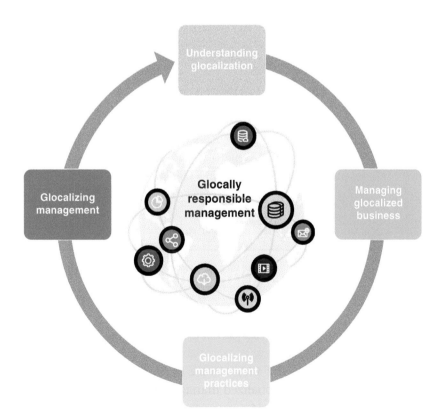

FIGURE 12.1   Glocalizing management areas of practice

Credit: Slidemodel.com

In the most extreme case, global and local can aggressively affect each other. This can work both ways. There was 'glocalization' – for instance, when Trump's US government unilaterally bailed out of the Paris climate agreement, imposing its local preferences on the global community of states suffering the consequences of climate change. 'Globalization' happens when, for instance, global standards, principles and practices are imposed on local settings at the expense of better suited local solutions [11]. Responsible management has to be mindful of both extremes in order not to repeat such patterns when glocalizing. Instead, it should focus on harmonizing both arenas, global, and local.

GLOBALIZATION

Glocalization
refers to the increased importance of global standards, relations, and flows

Globalization involves the integration of world economies as actors from different nations engage in trading goods, services, and ideas as well as competing on a global basis. This concept of globalization has often been characterized as a mix of internalization, Westernization, liberalization, and universalism. Also we are now managing in a globalized world of ethical, social, and environmental issues from the climate crisis to blatant inequality and deadly pandemics.

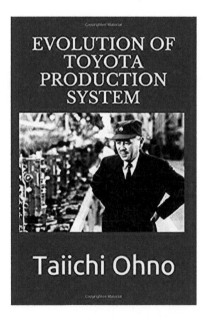

Japanese management practices like Kaizen and Poka-yoke have taken the operations management world by storm.

Globalization has changed the very nature of the economy, business, and management [12], including globalized management practices like the Toyota production system. The impact of economic globalization on the planet has made glocalizing responsible management an imperative. Globalizing today means management must undertake a parallel expansion in responsibility to global stakeholders. How can managers' glocalizing respond to the challenges of globalization? A first step is to appreciate the following main drivers, outcomes, and managerial implications of globalization:

1. **Global media.** Globalization involves the proliferation and predominance of media around the globe, connecting the world. Perhaps no better vehicle draws worldwide attention to global poverty, water shortages, the spread of disease as well as to management scandals.

2. **Global connectivity.** The growth of information and communication technology and access to the internet continues to accelerate. Yet paralleling the decline in smartphone costs, there is an increasing environmental impact from used smartphones. Might the extension of mobile internet access to poorer population shave a levelling effect on global society?

3. **Global transportation.** Faster and cheaper transportation enables globalized travel for both business or leisure. Yet the proliferation of aircraft and shipping has an immense environmental impact. Reducing the impact presents a major challenge.

4. **The rise of BRICS.** Glocally responsible managers will understand major shifts in economic powers and trade relationships. Brazil, Russia, India, China, and South Africa (BRICS) represent emerging economies with rapidly increasing GDPs. Practices in BRICS countries commonly have a significant environmental impact, raise ethical practice issues, and amplify inequality. Managers in these countries also face such challenges when maintaining sustainable supply chains and developing ethical employment practices.

5. **Global challenges and opportunities.** Moving out of a domestic into a global setting provides both immense challenges and immense opportunities. Global challenges are manifold, and include corruption, poverty, and global warming. A glocally responsible manager may find opportunities to do much good both on a global level and within host countries.

6. **Multinationals versus countries.** A decline in the global political power of countries is mirrored by multinational corporations' gain in power. Multinationals' revenue nowadays frequently exceeds the GDP of entire countries. Multinationals that outsource operations overseas, for example, may take advantage of less stringent laws regarding workplace conditions, employee treatment, or safety standards. Conversely, multinationals may also step up and assume roles in global society, which previously were the responsibilities of country governments, including health, labour rights, security, providing basic infrastructure and services.

7. **Global identity and affiliations.** Globalized business is creating less attachment to country citizenship and identity. People tend to identify less with a culture or community and more with personal affiliations or professional classifications.

8. **Global norms and organizations.** The new business geography involves working under the governance of global organizations that promote management norms for companies, such as the Organization for Economic Co-operation and Development (OECD), and the World Trade Organization (WTO). There are also global nonprofits, such as the Fair Labor Association and the Marine Stewardship Council whose de facto standards exert tremendous influence on glocal management practices.

LOCALIZATION

Strictly speaking, there is no such thing as 'global' management. Managing outside domestic borders means operating in a different location, not on a superior 'global' level. Global businesses operate locally in many different places. This fact is embedded in the megatrend of localization, including the following aspects:

I. **Anti-global trade movements**. These movements are critical of multinational corporate expansion and the resulting spread of consumerism, commercialization and capitalization [13], which are sometimes compared to a new form of colonization that either crowds out local differences or grabs local resources – for instance, through the practice of 'cultural appropriation'. Anti-glocalization movements such as Attac fight against global tax havens, and for a globalization tax and limits to free trade [14].

II. **New political nationalism.** The twentieth century has been the stage of a resurgence of nationalist governments. The effects of this new nationalism are manifold, including protectionist trade policies and trade wars like the one between China and the US. Another example is the abuse of national resources at the expense of global sustainability, as in the case of Brazil's former president, Bolsonaro, selling out and destroying the Amazon rainforest [15]. It has also resulted in political dissolution, as in the case of Brexit threatening a decline in human rights standards, and environmental and social legislation [16]. However, political nationalism has also led to the reinforcement of what are perceived as local cultural values and strengths, such as the restoration of Confucianism in China [17].

III. **Local production and consumption.** The local production and consumption movement includes, for instance, local circular economies or local currencies like the Bristol pound that can only be spent in this city [18]. Such schemes are often driven by a rationale of 'supporting our local economy' – for instance, for job creation. They may also relate to sustainability concerns – for instance producing and consuming locally (and seasonally) or reducing the CO_2 impact from transportation. Local and regional production/consumption may support local biodiversity, or local varieties and species. It may also serve to preserve local knowledge or crafts – for instance, the use of healing plants in the Amazon, and the culture of communities collecting them as in the Natura case.

Disney management between cultural appreciation and appropriation.

'Coco Review!' by AntMan3001 is licensed under CC BY-SA 2.0

IV. **Globalization as a local opportunity.** Localization may also be geared towards using global links to attract resources. For instance, the Republic of Ireland attracts corporations from around the globe with low taxes. Additionally, Disney has shown instances of both cultural appropriation and appreciation, cancelling a costume from the Polynesian-inspired movie Moana following accusations of cultural misappropriation, and praise for its positive cultural appreciation of the Mexican culture in the movie Coco.

MANAGING GLOCALIZED BUSINESS

Managerial glocalizing is substantially influenced by the type of glocal business one is working in. We will introduce frameworks to assess the different types of **international businesses** and their respective implications for management.

International business refers to commercial transactions taking place between two or more countries

GLOCAL RESPONSIBILITY ATTITUDE

The global responsibility pyramid provides a framework for assessing a company's attitude towards glocal responsibility [19]:

1. Make a profit consistent with expectations for international businesses.

2. Obey the law of host countries as well as international law.

3. Be ethical in your practices, taking host-country and global standards into consideration.

4. Be a good corporate citizen, especially as defined by the host country's expectations.

Managers will have to decide if and how their own responsible glocalizing will be in line with the company's attitude. Ideally, they would use the four levels as a checklist to earn a profit in the economic bottom line while simultaneously obeying the law, maintaining sound ethical practices, and being a good glocal citizen.

GLOCALIZATION STANCE

Different companies operating globally take their own distinct stance towards global–local relationships. A core question is what culture management practices should they follow – for example, home country, global, or local cultures [20–22]?

• **Ethnocentric**. Considers its own domestic 'home' culture as superior and therefore 'colonizes' other locations with practices and products like the ones at home

• **Polycentric**. Adjusts to multiple similar local cultures – for instance, multiple locations of consumers with similar tastes, or similar market characteristics

• **Regiocentric**. Applies one cultural practice per region, treating the entire region as the same and does not adapt to local conditions in different sub-regions

• **Geocentric**. Considers the whole world as a single market to be covered by a one size fits all integrated type of practice

While this 'EPRG' framework was developed in the context of international marketing practice, it can well be applied to the customization of any type of management practice. For instance, it may guide what style of management dominates a company in their local subsidiaries, or how management deals with religious diversity.

GLOCAL COMPANY TYPES

International firms form distinct patterns with regard to motivations in strategy, structure, and responsible managerial practices [23]. The original descriptions are adapted from Bartlett et al. [24] and include two additional international company types important in responsible management, the global-sourcing company and export businesses:

1. **Global-sourcing companies (GSC)** usually have operations and markets confined to one country but have far-reaching global supply chains which create an urgent need to assure responsible business practices among suppliers abroad. The main activity for GSCs is to implement extensive supply chain tracing, control mechanisms to know suppliers and their sustainability, responsibility, and ethics practices.

2. An **export business (EB)** is a company that produces local domestic products for a foreign market. EBs must be sure that local practices are in line with the expectations of global customers. It is crucial that the highest sustainability, responsibility, and ethics standards are met to satisfy increasingly critical customers' high standards.

3. Managers of businesses with an **international mentality** 'tend to think of the company's overseas operations as distant outposts whose main role is to support the domestic parent company in different ways, such as contributing incremental sales to the domestic manufacturing operations' [24]. Managers in essence see the company as domestic. The big challenge in glocally responsible management for businesses with an international mentality is to achieve a sufficient degree of localization in foreign operations in order to truly understand local stakeholders and issues.

4. **Multinational firms** begin to emphasize localization and responsiveness to national cultural differences. Managers in foreign operations are likely to be 'highly independent entrepreneurs, often nationals of the host country' [24]. This multinational mentality allows responsible managers to depend on localized knowledge and decision-making power. Such multinational firms, due to local flexibility and engagement, are well equipped to effectively develop solutions to local social and environmental issues.

5. **Global companies**' managers tend to 'think in terms of creating products for a world market and manufacturing them on a global scale in a few highly efficient plants, often at the corporate center' [24]. The globe is the market rather than local markets. In a global company, responsible managers may have the fascinating possibility of creating value for global stakeholders, and to address truly global sustainability challenges, but have to remain mindful of local challenges. For instance, the Swedish

fashion retailer H&M saw widespread protest and vandalism of their stores in response to a culturally insensitive ad in their online store [25].

6. A **transnational firm** mentality is 'more responsive to local needs while capturing the benefits of global efficiency' [24]. A balance is reached between centralization in the parent company, applying its capabilities and resources in foreign subsidiaries. Transnational firms typically have strong global sustainability, responsibility, and ethics standards, while being able to effectively customize those standards to local practices, issues, needs, and culture.

The South African Economic Freedom Fighters protest against an image promoting a hoodie with the print COOLEST MONKEY IN THE JUNGLE modelled by a young Black boy.

Twitter/EFF

Table 12.1 summarizes the characteristics of these different international business configurations and compares them with purely domestic businesses to provide recommendations for glocally responsible management.

TABLE 12.1 Global companies and management recommendations

Types of company	Characteristics					Responsible management recommendations
	Global sourcing	Foreign markets	Foreign operations	Global strategy	Foreign localization	
Purely domestic businesses	no	no	no	no	no	Focus on domestic responsible business strategy and actions.
Export businesses	no	yes	no	no	no	Focus on domestic responsible business strategy and make both product, and process adjustment to foreign requirements.
Globally sourcing companies	yes	no	no	no	no	Focus on domestic responsible business strategy and actions but scrutinize global suppliers.
International mentality	yes/no	yes/no	yes/no	no	no	Shape a domestic responsibility strategy but align foreign responsible business activities with local stakeholder needs and sustainability issues.
Multinational firms	yes	yes/no	yes	no	yes	Shape independent responsible business strategies and actions for each location that are consistent but not connected.
Global companies	yes	yes	yes	yes	yes/no	Shape a globally responsible business strategy giving primary concern to global issues and stakeholders.
Transnational firms	yes	yes	yes	yes	yes	Achieve a glocally responsible business strategy that considers both global and local issues and stakeholders equally.

SOURCE: Adapted from [24]

Glocalizing practices increase the integration of global and local

GLOCALIZATION MANAGEMENT PRACTICES

Consider the **glocalization management practices** at the company 4Ocean, which sells bracelets made from recycled ocean plastic globally to fund its local ocean clean-up operations [26]. Trade, foreign markets, global sourcing, foreign direct investment, and global partnerships are examples of management practices that drive glocalization. Each of those practices bears different challenges related to the triple bottom line, to stakeholder relations, and specific ethical dilemmas. Each practice also has specific areas of opportunity to do good (see Table 12.2).

Glocalization management for Sustainable Development Goal 14, Life under Water by 4Ocean

Here are some core considerations relevant across these practices:

- **Glocal stakeholders.** In the glocalizing mode, management is automatically influenced by and influences additional stakeholders glocally. Such stakeholders might be workers in a foreign subsidiary plant or a global environmental NGO like Greenpeace.

- **Glocal externalities.** Externalities are effects of one's actions that are incurred by others. Glocally responsible management must map glocal externalities and take action to internalize them.

- **Fairness of distribution.** Global management practice has been considered unfair. Two prominent examples are job loss in developed countries through outsourcing activities, and wages in developing countries that are often perceived as too low.

- **International development.** Glocal practices may contribute to economic and social development. Examples are know-how transfer, and raising local environmental and social standards.

TABLE 12.2   The responsible management of glocalizing practices

1. Global sourcing	2. Global trade	3. Foreign market presence	4. Foreign subsidiaries	5. Global alliances
Issues in outsourcing and offshoring	Environmental impact of logistics	Local sustainability awareness	Foreign direct investment (FDI)	Joint causes
Support for bad labour practices and corruption	Transfer pricing	Promotion of responsible consumption patterns	International mergers and acquisition (M&A)	Shared competences
Supply chain tracing	Fair trade	BOP markets	Global transfer pricing and taxation	Infrastructure sharing
BOP sourcing (see below)	Ethical trade	Local production and consumption	Local development	Cross-sector partnerships

1. GLOBAL SOURCING

Responsible **global sourcing** relies not only on external verification but also on ongoing self-assessment. A company's own standards applied internally are transferred through responsible sourcing and supply chain management to sourcing partners in the supply chain. Common practices are a responsible sourcing policy, codes of conduct for suppliers, and supplier development programmes with a focus on ethics, responsibility, and sustainability.

Global sourcing
the process of procuring inputs internationally

BOP SOURCING

The **bottom of the pyramid (BoP)** market refers to the globally underserved low-income consumers, who make up more than half of the world population. What is the role of small, medium, and large businesses in the **BoP** market? It has been argued that there is an urgent need for responsible international management to proactively integrate BoP countries [27]. There are two main practices for doing so:

Bottom of the pyramid (BoP)
refers to approximately four billion people worldwide living with very low income, at 'the bottom of the income pyramid'

- **Country identification.** First, managers should seek out viable suppliers from countries that fall into the BoP criteria. Buying from suppliers from such countries is meant to translate into economic development, more employment, and rising wages.

- **Supplier identification.** The second **BoP sourcing** model is to directly engage with suppliers and with people at the base of the pyramid who are known for their poverty reduction practices.

BoP sourcing
refers to sourcing activities involving small and medium enterprises at the base of the pyramid

BoP sourcing is attractive. For instance, The World Economic Forum suggests that strengthening the food value chain in developing countries meets two important goals. First, private sector businesses open up opportunities in a 'growing, profitable and largely untapped market' and second, 'poor communities, innovative approaches can improve livelihoods' [28]. Such sourcing can be highly decentralized, locally adapted and focused, which makes it an excellent tool for achieving a high degree of local adaptation and simultaneously creating value. When responsible managers encourage their companies to tap into the BoP market, they can in many settings achieve a strong economic competitive advantage in their domestic or global market and garner better community and stakeholder relationships.

OUTSOURCING

Outsourcing
involves a third-party company providing a service or process that used to be provided internally

Offshoring
activities that were done domestically are now carried out abroad

Another critical area for responsible business on a global scale is **outsourcing**. Often outsourcing comes with **offshoring**. A common motivation for companies in economically developed countries is to outsource for labour cost reduction. Another is to be able to concentrate on core processes and leave secondary processes to other companies that specialize in them. Both can be achieved abroad by lower labour costs, and often the same or even better skill levels in developing countries.

Both practices, outsourcing and offshoring, may lead to social, environmental, and ethical issues if not managed responsibly (see Chapter 14).

Responsible trade
a practice that mitigates negative impacts of trade and harnesses trade to do good

Sustainable trade
refers to trade as a tool for further sustainable development

2. GLOBAL TRADE

Global trade has been widely criticized for many of the ailments of the global economic system. On the other hand, trade also has the potential to reduce economic inequalities and to create a truly inclusive global economic system. Managing **responsible trade** means considering both facts.

SUSTAINABLE TRADE

While **trade**, especially the environmental impact of global logistics, poses a challenge to sustainable development, it may also serve as a tool for redistributing wealth globally, and for further economic and social development. The 'Winnipeg Principles' for trade and sustainable development' [29] were published in response to criticisms that the World Trade Organization did not effectively address sustainable development [30]:

1. **Efficiency and cost internalization.** Use as few resources as possible and make sure you pay the full external costs (e.g. pollution) of the traded good or service.

2. **Equity.** Use trade to actively promote equity between developing and developed countries.

3. **Environmental integrity:** Ensure that trade remains within the regenerative capacity of ecosystems.

4. **Subsidiarity.** Make sure that the corporate policies are in line with the highest local jurisdiction, international standards and, if necessary, for sustainability, exceed them.

5. **International cooperation.** Cooperate with international trade bodies to achieve sustainable development and resolve disputes in a fair dialogue.

6. **Science and precaution.** Base your decisions on scientific insights regarding the interaction of trade and the social and environmental systems. If in doubt about the effect of a trade activity, act with caution.

7. **Openness.** Communicate trade activity and the effects of it openly to stakeholders and participate in the dissemination and creation of knowledge on the intersection of trade and international development.

FAIR TRADE

In **fair trade** buyers provide, typically to small-scale producers, various guarantees with the goal of creating greater equity between trade partners in developing and developed countries. Guarantees given to producer partners in the trade relationship include a fair price, above the market level, long-term supplier relationships, and support in the social development of producer communities [31].

Fairtrade International (also known as the Fairtrade Labelling Organization, FLO) is an umbrella organization overseeing over 20 fair trade organizations and helping to administer fair trade globally. Such oversight groups provide fair trade labels and certification for farmers and producers worldwide [32].

Fair trade
a trading partnership, based on dialogue, transparency, and respect that seeks greater equity in international trade

ETHICAL TRADE

Ethical trade
aims to assure the avoidance of ethical issues in global supply chains

Fair trade mostly creates value for local community stakeholders, producers in fair trade partnerships, while **ethical trade** mostly focuses on the employee stakeholders of producing companies in developing countries. Most ethical issues in trade can be found in the working conditions of employees' factories, which is why ethical trade is often associated with assuring compliance with international labour standards [31].

For instance, the ethical trading initiative (ETI) provides detailed guidance on how to ensure the ousting of bad labour practices in global supply chains, and to promote good practices such as the payment of a living wage, adherence to human rights, and humane treatment [33].

3. FOREIGN MARKETS

When glocal management ventures into **foreign markets**, maybe introducing a new product, there is ample chance to do good or bad. It may transfer valuable technologies, provide access to (better) products, and shape 'good' consumption patterns. However, non-domestic products may also destroy important old-established industries or promote unsustainable consumption patterns.

Foreign market seeking
refers to practices of expanding beyond the domestic home market

In particular, international companies with high brand power in foreign markets find themselves in an ambassadorial role. The new middle classes, especially in India and China and other BRIC countries, are at a crossroads that might either lead to new, more sustainable consumption patterns, or to a misguided unsustainable consumerist pattern. It may be difficult for managers entering foreign markets not to take the easy path of promoting consumerism, which is more certain of short run sales and is crucially important for commercially successful market entry.

Market analysis will focus on what natural resources are available in the country and the availability of adequate labour, capital resources, or government support. Geopolitical factors, cultural diversity, and legal issues will be considered equally. A company also conducts analysis of its own core resources and capabilities. Analysing economies of scale will be involved in decisions about transportation or creating a subsidiary manufacturing plant abroad. The following are popular forms of market entry that provide a promising competitive and responsible position:

- **Sustainable market innovation.** Companies seeking to enter foreign markets may have a differentiation advantage over market incumbents if entering the market with an innovative product serving society and the environment. Such a 'sustainable market innovation strategy' could involve actively seeking out highly unsustainable foreign markets and aiming to actively change products and consumption patterns towards sustainability. It may involve cause-related marketing highlighting the product's social and environmental features, and social marketing to change consumers' behaviour patterns towards sustainable living.

- **Sustainable infrastructure.** A foreign location might lack recycling systems, renewable energy sources, know-how for responsible management, or even access to clean drinking water. Many businesses have the potential to create or be involved in creating such sustainable infrastructure through products and services. It can also involve addressing local sustainable development issues through the companies' operations, which on the one hand contribute to locally sustainable development and on the other create goodwill among the stakeholders involved.

- **Serving a BoP market**. Understanding a BoP market means we must first 'stop thinking of the poor as victims or as a burden and start recognizing them as resilient and creative entrepreneurs and value-conscious consumers' [34]. The extreme poor are defined by the UN as the proportion of the population whose income (purchasing power parity) is less than US $1 a day, or the poorest one-fifth in a nation's consumption. To access a BoP market, the crucial considerations are: How do low-income consumers consume? Where and what do they buy? What is the optimum price and packaging size? Most importantly: What are the most important needs of those consumers currently underserved?

4. INTERNATIONAL SUBSIDIARIES

Working with **international subsidiaries** involves varieties of glocalizing management practices. We will present three common practices, **foreign direct investment (FDI)**, international mergers and acquisitions (M&A), and transfer pricing.

FOREIGN DIRECT INVESTMENT (FDI)

FDI assets abroad can range from production facilities to personnel operating a facility or working in marketing. FDI may involve acquisitions, purchasing or leasing existing production facilities to launch a new production activity, or greenfield investment, which refers to construction of new operational facilities from scratch.

Responsible FDI should make sure to avoid ethical issues in the process (e.g. indirectly supporting corrupt governments), include local stakeholder interests (e.g. local government and employees), and support locally sustainable development (e.g. through economic development and poverty alleviation). FDI provides excellent potential for economic development. Financial investment in other countries may help to strengthen economies and, with them, socio-economic systems.

The long-term commitment implied by an FDI increases credibility and underlines the serious intentions of investing companies. This in turn can serve as a basis to develop long-lasting relationships for local development and, with it, international development. International development and responsible business can build mutually reinforcing systems through which shared value between host country and company can be created [35].

MERGERS AND ACQUISITIONS (M&A)

In **mergers**, two companies are integrated on an equal footing, while **acquisitions** imply a power imbalance in favour of the acquiring company. Management may pursue M&A for a variety of reasons and each choice involves considerations about sustainability, ethics, and responsibility for both companies.

The motivation for acquiring or merging with a foreign company may be manifold. It may be to seek to acquire resources that are not available or are too expensive domestically. The decision to acquire internationally may involve new technologies or research and development capabilities, such as in the case of low-cost software development in India. M&A might also be motivated by joining forces to increase (responsible) competitiveness. Management might look to access local cheap labour, unique local commodities, or lower taxes and government support.

International subsidiaries are business units located in foreign countries

Foreign direct investment (FDI) means to (partly) own and control a foreign company, and involves tangible or intangible assets transferred abroad

Mergers
refer to two companies voluntarily becoming one and financial investments on a mutual basis

Acquisitions
refer to the voluntary or forced takeover of another firm's assets

Due diligence
describes the process of
assessing the economic, social,
environmental, and ethical
implications of an M&A

For whichever reason managements engage in M&A, responsible managers must embed ethics, responsibility, and sustainability in the process. Assessments should consider potential issues, such as bad work conditions or human rights violations in countries where labour is inexpensive, and impact on the environment. The process of checking the economic, social, environmental, and ethical implications of a merger or acquisition is called **due diligence**.

In M&A, there are at least two core stakeholders. On the one hand, the glocalizing manager relates to trading partners in the market. The norms relating to market operations may focus on profit, for example. On the other hand, a glocalizing manager also determines how to relate to employees in the other company in an M&A. Managers may develop irresponsible attitudes towards employees 'to treat a person as an object [that they bought and own] or a means of achieving goals beyond that person him/herself' [36]. Respecting employees as individuals and ends in themselves, not merely as the means to achieving a successful consolidation or acquisition is key.

TRANSFER PRICING

Transfer pricing
the rates paid within a company
when products or services are
transferred from a subsidiary
in one country to another
country and subsidiary

Transfer pricing refers to the rates a parent company charges for its products or services to subsidiaries, or the rates its subsidiary or division charges to the company's foreign subsidiary or division. Transfer pricing may also occur between the rates two subsidiaries charge each other when they engage in trade.

Domestic governments often have difficulty taxing the income of multinational enterprises, and ethical issues arise over tax and transfer pricing. Tax rates, for instance, may differ between the home country's domestic operation and the tax rate of its foreign subsidiary. Ethical dilemmas and questions that might arise include:

- Should I pay higher domestic taxes to strengthen the home country or should I promote foreign investment to pay less tax abroad?

- Should I engage in manipulative transfer pricing tactics to avoid paying taxes [37]?

- How much is a fair profit for parties involved in transfer pricing?

Transfer pricing can have a 'dramatic impact on the allocation of an international business's taxable profits among the countries in which it operates' [38]. Accordingly, it can be a practice that either creates greater equity between countries or increases inequalities. Responsible managers, when confronted with taxing and transfer pricing issues, can develop codes of ethics or establish sets of values for a company which cares for the well-being of other stakeholders domestically and abroad. This way managers can foster social justice and optimize taxes.

5. INTERNATIONAL STRATEGIC ALLIANCES

International **strategic alliances** involve 'the cooperative relationship between two or more organizations that range from shared information and research to joint ventures where minority partners are subcontracted to provide local market access and distribution channels' [39]. All three types of such alliances go beyond normal market transactions but fall short of mergers [40]:

Strategic alliances are medium- to long-term relationships created for a common purpose of the partners involved

- **Scale alliances** pool similar assets so each firm can conduct business activities in which they already have experience.

- **Link alliances** combine complementary resources to expand into a new area.

- **Vertical and horizontal alliances** differ on whether levels are added to the value chain (vertical) or companies align on the same level (horizontal).

Strategic alliances can be based on many different types of relationships and typically involve minority ownership, especially **cross-sectorial alliance**, in which, for instance, businesses and NGOs, or businesses and governmental agencies, develop joint actions for a shared social, environmental, economic, or ethical goal which are of great interest in responsible management. The alternative to a cross-sectorial alliance is a sectorial alliance that involves players from the same sector such as the Chinese and UK bike sharing companies Youon and Cycle.Land [41].

Cross-sectorial alliances involve partners from different sectors (business, public, civil society) engaging in joint activity for a common purpose

To successfully tackle global, social, and environmental issues, neither one business alone, nor one sector alone can provide and scale solutions. There is a never-ending variety of different combinations of international strategic alliances. NGOs can form strategic alliances with other NGOs to exert stronger stakeholder influence on a large multinational corporation. International interest groups that specialize in particular environmental issues, harmful products or materials sold to children, or mistreatment of certain groups of people may form link alliances to jointly change policies and regulations.

Cycle.Land agrees to run Youon's UK operations as part of an international alliance.

Vertical alliances may be formed between a government agency and a small, new business using innovative packaging for a product. Companies may form horizontal alliances to combine R&D and technology to improve their sustainable performance with particular products or manufacturing processes. Or companies may provide budgets to collaborate with not-for-profit organizations to tackle social problems. A key glocalizing task is to develop a system of powerful glocal alliances in order to co-create solutions in the most effective way.

GLOCALIZING MANAGEMENT

This last section will explore core practices of (g)localizing management, of adapting it to local conditions while keeping in mind the global dimension.

GLOCALIZING TO LOCAL CONTEXTS

What distinguishes responsible management in Latin America from that in Europe, or in Africa? Understanding the regional context of and approaches to management are essential for the glocalizing mode of management. How do responsible management approaches differ across countries? Two main approaches have been identified, each applying to a distinct set of countries or regions [42]:

- **Explicit responsibility** (e.g. in the US) consists of policies that assume responsibility for some societal interests. Typical are voluntary activities by individual corporations that combine social and business values and address issues perceived as important to meet particular stakeholder expectations.

- **Implicit responsibility** (e.g. in the European Union) takes a broader systemic perspective by considering management's role within institutions across society and society's concerns. Typical are values, norms, and rules that result in requirements to address stakeholder issues and that define the obligations of corporate actors in collective rather than individual terms.

Understanding if you are managing responsibly in either an explicitly or implicitly inclined context is crucial.

This may include local priority issues, like indigenous rights in Canada or Australia; local certification like Empresa Socialmente Responsible (ESR) in Mexico; key certification organizations like BCorp in North America; iconic local cases like Aramex in Jordan; educational programmes like the Leuphana MBA in sustainability management in Germany [43]; regional (public) policies like Europe's Green New Deal [44]. The 'Diamond Model' (see Figure 12.2) helps to assess such local context attributes in a systematic and connected fashion by exploring a location's strategic context, local input and demand conditions, as well as related industries [45, 46]. It can be used to craft local actions to achieve both, to be a good locally responsible citizen, and at the same time to be locally competitive.

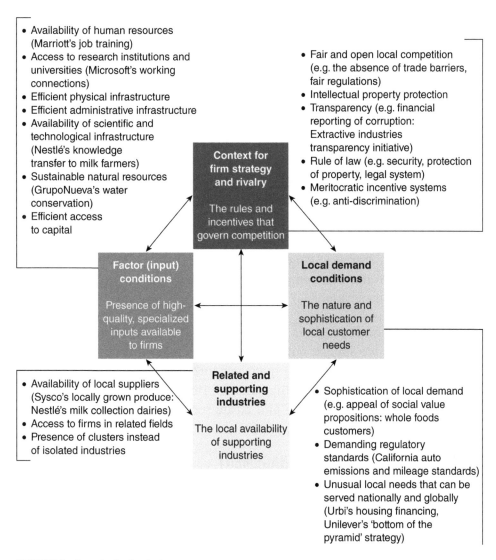

- Availability of human resources (Marriott's job training)
- Access to research institutions and universities (Microsoft's working connections)
- Efficient physical infrastructure
- Efficient administrative infrastructure
- Availability of scientific and technological infrastructure (Nestlé's knowledge transfer to milk farmers)
- Sustainable natural resources (GrupoNueva's water conservation)
- Efficient access to capital

- Fair and open local competition (e.g. the absence of trade barriers, fair regulations)
- Intellectual property protection
- Transparency (e.g. financial reporting of corruption: Extractive industries transparency initiative)
- Rule of law (e.g. security, protection of property, legal system)
- Meritocratic incentive systems (e.g. anti-discrimination)

Context for firm strategy and rivalry

The rules and incentives that govern competition

Factor (input) conditions

Presence of high-quality, specialized inputs available to firms

Local demand conditions

The nature and sophistication of local customer needs

Related and supporting industries

The local availability of supporting industries

- Availability of local suppliers (Sysco's locally grown produce: Nestlé's milk collection dairies)
- Access to firms in related fields
- Presence of clusters instead of isolated industries

- Sophistication of local demand (e.g. appeal of social value propositions: whole foods customers)
- Demanding regulatory standards (California auto emissions and mileage standards)
- Unusual local needs that can be served nationally and globally (Urbi's housing financing, Unilever's 'bottom of the pyramid' strategy)

FIGURE 12.2 Assessing local context

SOURCE: [47]

A comparison between home and host country can be conducted using a 'double-diamond' model that may serve to analyse differences in both domestic and foreign locations [47]. We have adapted the model to reflect the specific considerations important for an assessment focused on responsible management:

1. The **context for responsible competitiveness** describes the rules and incentives that govern responsible management. You might want to check the social and environmental laws and regulations to see if there are governmental incentive

programmes available, and also the degree to which ethics, responsibility, and sustainability are already part of the business culture in a specific location, and if there are local codes or certification.

2. The **related and supporting networks** are local groups of companies, NGOs, or governmental institutions that promote or oppose responsible management. Such groups might be local lobbyists, a local chamber of commerce, an industry-sustainability initiative, or a local UN Global Compact chapter.

3. **Sustainable factor conditions** refer to the availability of high-quality, specialized inputs for responsible management, including the workforce's responsible management competence, sustainably sourced materials, and financing opportunities.

4. **Local stakeholder demand conditions** describe the nature and sophistication of local stakeholders: Is there a local demand for sustainable innovation products by the customer stakeholder? How strongly do communities demand involvement by companies? How inclined are employees to work in a responsible organization?

The double diamond model can be used both ways, inside-out and outside-in. In our examples we applied outside-in thinking, asking: How does the local environment enable responsible management? Managers should also apply the opposite, inside-out thinking, asking: How can responsible business improve the local infrastructure and create social and environmental value across the four dimensions?

CULTURALLY RESPONSIVE MANAGEMENT

The proverb 'When in Rome, do as the Romans do' carries much wisdom for responsible management. However, glocalizing managers must balance global standards with respect for local cultural differences.

INTERCULTURAL COMPETENCE

Intercultural competence refers to the ability to cope with cultural differences

A glocalized working environment presents unique cultural challenges and contexts, making **intercultural management competence**, knowledge, skills, and attributes (KSA) indispensable for managerial effectiveness [48].

Knowledge. A manager must acquire knowledge about culture, appropriate rules of interaction and customs [49]. A responsible manager should receive country-specific training to gain knowledge of the culture's sustainability standards and ethical practices.

Skills. Skills include 'foreign language competence, adapting to the behavioural norms of a different cultural environment, effective stress-management, or intercultural conflict resolution' [48].

Personal attributes. These include personality traits, leadership qualities, learned 'ways of working', and tolerance of ambiguity. A responsible manager should develop qualities in cultural identity, avoiding biases, and avoiding ethnocentrism.

Professional managers must be able to manage sustainable performance, stakeholder relations and ethical practices across different cultural settings, and work effectively with stakeholders from different cultural backgrounds at home and abroad.

GLOCAL CULTURAL DIMENSIONS

What can responsible managers do to prepare themselves for effectively managing situations with intercultural issues? Geert Hofstede's set of dimensions of cultural identity provides valuable insights into organizational and national differences in culture [50]:

1. **Individualism** refers to cultures with loose ties between individuals, while **collectivism** describes cultures in which individuals are typically embedded into strong groups.

2. **Power distance** describes the acceptance and expectation of power to be distributed unequally.

3. **Uncertainty avoidance** describes to what degree individuals fear unknown or uncertain situations.

4. **Masculinity** refers to countries with very distinct gender roles, while **femininity** to countries where gender roles are similar.

5. **Long-term orientation** aims at the maximization of future reward, while **short-term orientation** is oriented to past, present, and immediate future.

6. **Indulgence** refers to fun-loving cultures, while **constraint** describes cultures that curb human drives through strict social norms.

These dimensions offer valuable insights for responsible management. For instance, if working with people from a strong masculinity culture, feminist equal employment programmes will probably encounter resistance. In countries with short-term orientation, the concept of sustainability might not be accepted as easily as in a country with a strong long-term orientation. It has been suggested that organizational cultures change much more quickly than national cultures [51], implying that an organization's unique responsibility culture is possible instead of a national host country culture that might 'not be there yet'.

Anglo
Confucian Asia
Eastern Europe
Sub-Saharan Africa
Latin America
Middle East
Nordic Europe
Southern Asia

FIGURE 12.3   Glocal leadership cultures

SOURCE: Adapted from [52]

In addition, management and leadership cultures differ considerably across regions and nations. The GLOBE study found the groups of distinct local leadership cultures illustrated in Figure 12.3. Being mindful of local management culture [53] and differing styles of responsible management [54] provides important cultural acumen for the glocalizing manager [55]. Table 12.3 provides an overview.

TABLE 12.3   How GLOBE dimensions manifest glocally

	Description	Highest regional/ country scores	Lowest regional/ country
Uncertainty avoidance	Extent to which members of an organization or society strive to avoid uncertainty by reliance on social norms, rituals, and bureaucratic practices to alleviate the unpredictability of future events.	Germanic Europe, Nordic Europe/ Austria, Denmark	Eastern Europe, Latin America, Middle East/ Russia, Hungary
Power distance	Degree to which members of an organization or society expect and agree that power should be unequally shared.	No clusters/Russia, Spain	Nordic Europe/ Denmark, Netherlands
Institutional collectivism	Degree to which organizational and societal institutional practices encourage and reward collective distribution of resources and collective action.	Anglo, Confucian Asia, Germanic Europe/Denmark, Singapore	Eastern Europe, Latin America/ Greece, Hungary
In-group collectivism	Degree to which individuals express pride, loyalty and cohesiveness in their organizations or families.	Confucian Asia, Eastern Europe, Latin America, Middle East, Southern Asia/Egypt, China	Anglo, Germanic Europe, Nordic Europe/Denmark, Netherlands

	Description	Highest regional/ country scores	Lowest regional/ country
Gender egalitarianism	Extent to which an organization or a society minimizes gender role differences.	Eastern Europe, Nordic Europe/ Sweden, Denmark	Middle East/South South Korea, Egypt
Assertiveness orientation	Degree to which individuals in organizations or societies are assertive, confrontational, and aggressive in social relationships.	Eastern Europe, Germanic Europe/ Spain, US	Nordic Europe/ Sweden, New Zealand
Future orientation	Degree to which individuals in organizations or societies engage in future-oriented behaviours such as planning, investing in the future, and delaying gratification.	Germanic Europe, Nordic Europe/ Denmark, Canada	Eastern Europe, Latin America, Middle East/ Russia, Argentina
Performance orientation	Extent to which an organization or society encourages and rewards group members for performance improvement and excellence	Confucian Asia, Germanic Europe/ US, Taiwan	Nordic Europe/Russia, Argentina
Humane orientation	Degree to which individuals in organizations or societies encourage and reward individuals for being fair, altruistic, friendly, generous, caring, and kind to others.	Southern Asia, Sub-Saharan Africa/ Indonesia, Egypt	Germanic Europe, Latin Europe/ Germany, Spain

SOURCES: Based on [53, 56]

CULTURALLY INCLUSIVE MANAGEMENT

The aspiration of culturally inclusive **diversity management** is to create a multicultural workplace that respects and nourishes cultural differences while providing equal opportunities [57]. Glocally responsible management has to construct an **inclusive workplace**. Are all groups and individuals: [58]

Cross-cultural diversity management
to manage a workforce composed of people from diverse cultures

1. Equally welcome to participate in decision-making?

2. Equally informed about important decisions made in the workplace?

3. Equally invited to formal and informal meetings and social events?

A glocally inclusive workplace
values and nurtures harmonic differences within the workforce

While diversity management is often a formal task of the people management occupation, it should be on every manager's agenda. Genuine integration does not happen through the company's policies alone, but through the personal initiative of managers at all levels. Responsible managers in a glocally diverse workplace should foster a mentality of inclusivity. Inclusivity in international management implies that workers from different backgrounds, such as cultures, religions, and races can work together harmoniously, develop respect for individual differences, and develop tolerance as an ethical workplace standard.

Diversity in responsible management cannot be limited to employees, who represent only one out of many stakeholder groups to be included in decisions. Responsible managers must transfer the principles of diversity management and inclusion to a broad set of stakeholders, from community members, to suppliers, and NGOs.

CROSS-CULTURAL ETHICS

Cross-cultural ethics
ethical decision-making
under influence of different
cultures' values

What types of **ethical issues** may glocally responsible managers face? A good example is corruption (including graft, kickbacks, and preferential treatment) [59]. While Western and global responsibility standards judge corruption as unethical, some local cultures see it as a legitimate cost of doing business. How do we make decisions where there are contradictions in cultural morality?

Glocally responsible managers often face situations and practices very different from their own culture. Managers may further realize that a country's culture is not a unitary, 'internally coherent system of values and beliefs' [60] but find fragmented cultural beliefs and competing sets of norms and practices. One way of addressing this complex moral diversity would be to find a set of universally acceptable ethical 'base norms' that can serve as a common ground for decisions that are acceptable for all cultures involved: focusing on our commonalities rather than our differences.

The idea of such a 'world ethos' aims at highlighting the core elements of a shared global ethic. No matter what cultural and religious context we come from, we can typically agree upon a set of shared ethical values and principles [61, 62]. A group of Muslim, Jewish, and Christian scholars proposed an interfaith declaration that comprised the following four shared principles [63]:

1. **Justice** (fairness)

2. **Mutual respect** (love and consideration)

3. **Stewardship** (trusteeship)

4. **Honesty** (truthfulness).

Basing ethical decisions and practices on shared principles and values is a promising approach to solving intercultural conflicts. However, critics claim that different cultures' ethical standards share no commonalities, which is why they have to be understood and managed independently [64].

What cultural ethical conflicts might occur? Considering the following types of conflicts [65] will be helpful for responsible managers in identifying appropriate solutions.

1. **The values of two cultures lead to opposite conclusions**. That is, one culture appears to be right and believes the other is wrong. For instance, a hiring decision based on gender or social status over technical ability may be acceptable in one culture, while the other culture will consider this practice unacceptable.

2. **A rule is morally important to one culture but not important to the other**. For example, a culture may view gift giving to bosses or key stakeholders as morally wrong while the other culture views it as an acceptable practice, not because the practice is morally good but because it does not have significant moral importance.

3. **Cultures agree on the same ethical value but circumstances create different interpretations of what is acceptable**. Different cultures may agree on the environmental damage caused by pollution, yet national conditions related to industrial development and construction may create less strict standards for air quality and environmental preservation in one culture than in another.

Responsible managers must engage in intensive communication with the other culture to determine the category of conflict they are facing and to work on viable compromises. Otherwise they engage in guessing or speculation that may lead to more intense conflict.

PRINCIPLES OF GLOCALIZING

I. **Glocally responsible management** integrates global and local responsibility. This means managing glocal moral issues and intercultural ethics successfully; creating value for stakeholders around the world, and in every location; and proactively addressing glocal sustainability issues.

II. **Glocalization** is a mixture of the words global and local and describes global activities with a strong adaptation to local circumstances and vice versa.

III. We can distinguish different characteristics of glocalized businesses. Their **glocalization attitude** may be ethnocentric, polycentric, regiocentric, or geocentric (**EPRG**). **Global businesses** include globally sourcing companies, export businesses, international mentality businesses, multinational firms, global companies, and transnational firms.

IV. Important **considerations** for glocally responsible business conduct are global stakeholders, global externalities, fairness of distribution, and international development.

V. There are varieties of managerial **glocalization practices**, including international sourcing, global trade, foreign markets, foreign subsidiaries, and strategic alliances.

VI. **Glocalizing management** entails glocalizing to local contexts, culturally responsive management, and cross-cultural ethics.

MANAGEMENT GYM: TRAINING YOUR PROFESSIONAL SIX-PACK

Knowing

1. What is glocally responsible management?

2. Define three types of responsible trade. Explain differences and communalities.

3. Find information on two main glocalization practices of Unilever (or another highly glocalized company).

Thinking

4. Japan's preference for whale meat is a global challenge caused by local preferences. What do you think is more important, the maritime ecosystem or cultural diversity?

5. How would you change practices of globalization so that it becomes globally and locally sustainable?

6. Imagine you are a manager in a global business from your home country that takes an extremely ethnocentric approach. Name five problems this approach might cause.

Acting

7. Imagine you are preparing your company's first move abroad. Prepare a ten-point list of the biggest cultural differences by comparing each country's cultural dimensions (Hofstede and/or GLOBE).

8. Write a code of responsible glocal management conduct.

9. Imagine you are an auditor who is tasked with assessing a company's (you choose which) compliance with the ten Global Compact Principles (available online). Investigate each principle from the company's news coverage or reports and summarize your findings in one sentence for each of the ten Principles.

Interacting

10. Ask someone if they are for globalization and/or localization and why. Discuss and compare with your point of view.

11. Analyse the sustainability report of an international company and develop one recommendation for improvement. Using the contact information provided in the report or on the company's website, email your recommendation to the company and follow up on any answers.

12. Come up with an extreme nationalistic or ethnocentric statement and argue for it with a partner, who should argue against it. Who wins by applying what tactics? Then swap roles.

Being

13. Have you personally benefited from globalization or localization, or suffered from it? If so, how and why?

14. Would you consider yourself more of an ethnocentric or cosmopolitan person? Why do you think so and how does this manifest in your life?

15. What characteristics of people from other cultures do you admire and which do you not? Why?

Becoming

16. What practices are you engaged in that fuel 'bad globalization'? How could you change that?

17. Think about a situation where you felt a cultural tension, or even a conflict. What tactics could you apply to cope with similar future situations?

18. What part of your cultural background and moral values might be difficult for other cultures? What could you do to mitigate potential tensions?

SOURCE: Adapted from [66]

PIONEER INTERVIEW
GEERT HOFSTEDE

INTERVIEWER: OLIVER LAASCH

Geert Hofstede was a pioneer studying the cultural dimensions of management. Many of the concepts bear important insights for responsible managers, which is why his work provides excellent guidance for all who aim to be interculturally responsible managers.

(Continued)

Localized growth–profit–sustainability preferences. My article [67] showed that perceived goals of business leaders differ considerably across countries. In countries where power is seen as more important, staying within the law is less important; where personal wealth is important, responsibility towards employees counts less; where innovation is stressed, patriotism is not stressed; a stress on this year's profit opposes profits ten years from now; and growth is not sought everywhere to the same extent, and too much striving for growth opposes responsibility towards society, which to me includes sustainability. My article is not about how to change these things, but about how the changing economic weight of the various countries will affect the global picture.

Colonialization through management myths? My article [68] showed how management books were based on American values and preached management practices that did not fit the culture of many other societies, including some that even in the USA itself were not really applied.

Going glocal and back. Responsible managers should learn about cultural differences when dealing with other societies and might learn from other societies when operating in their own. And the USA is no longer the world's example, on the contrary. Management schools should teach about culture, and management students should get international experience.

No universal standard of responsibility? What is responsible in one culture may not be responsible in another. Long-term orientation is certainly an asset. I am not sure differences along the dimension of indulgence versus restraint are relevant to sustainability; more research would be needed to prove that.

A new base for economics! Management is rooted in economic thinking, but economics itself needs a new base – it is not a matter of rational choices because there is no universal rationality; it is not an exact science but a social, even a moral science. Fortunately, the number of economists discovering this is increasing. Examples are books like one by the young Czech economist Tomás Sedlácek published in Czech in 2009 and in English as *Economics of good and evil: The quest for economic meaning from Gilgamesh to Wall Street* (Oxford: Oxford University Press, 2011). Two Dutch professors of economics have written books on economics and culture in which they use my categories: Eelke de Jong, *Culture and economics: On values, economics and international business* (London: Routledge, 2009) and Sjoerd Beugelsdijk with Robbert Maseland, *Culture in economics: History, methodological reflections, and contemporary applications* (Cambridge: Cambridge University Press, 2011). And there are more.

(Continued)

QUESTIONS

1. Have a look at Geert Hofstede's article on the perceived goals of business leaders. How are the dynamics he describes in this article important for glocalizing?

2. Can you think of examples of US or Western-style management theories and practices that are a poor fit in other locations and cultures?

3. What do you think would be features of a new economic thought that could provide the base for truly glocally responsible management?

PROFESSIONAL PROFILE
LAURA CLISE

Hi, my name is Laura Clise and I am the Sustainable Development Director at AREVA, a world leader in nuclear energy and a significant, growing player in renewable energies with 48,000 employees worldwide.

My responsibilities. I am responsible for the development and deployment of AREVA's North American sustainable development strategy, supporting the continued integration of sustainable development into regional business strategy.

A typical work day. I might start my day by reviewing a request for a proposal with one of our businesses that requires input or environmental management programmes along with information on our use of diverse business subcontractors. That might be followed by a conference call led by an environmental think tank on the topic of scenario planning regarding the US energy mix in 2030. Perhaps at some point during the day, I'll edit a blog post regarding a colleague's perspective regarding her first sustainability conference experience as an engineer

(Continued)

whose full-time job is not focused on sustainability. There are always plenty of emails, including requests to participate in roundtable discussions regarding energy and climate or to speak at conferences on the importance of including climate in business education.

A typical day is variety. But while the topic or issue may shift, there is a common thread of facilitation, collaboration, change management, and communication.

Integrating ERS. Sustainability, responsibility, and ethics play a central role in my job – both in terms of aligning internal stakeholder understanding and action and engaging external stakeholders in dialogue and partnership. We are a more effective company when sustainability, responsibility, and ethics are resonant in our activities and technologies. Through our product and service innovation, we have the opportunity to support environmental and social responsibility objectives and yet our global energy challenges are not limited to technology. There is need for engagement in public dialogue to increase the understanding of transitioning to a clean energy economy that sustains economic prosperity, our planet, and the global community.

QUESTIONS

1. What elements of the global and local dimensions of Laura's work can you find? How do glocal and local interact in her work?

2. Laura works in a nuclear energy company. What are the implications for Laura's responsible and sustainable 'glocalizing' practices?

3. If you were in Laura's shoes, what would you do just the same, what differently?

TRUE STORY

MAKING ME COMPLICIT

EDITED BY ALEXANDRA LEONOR BARRUETA SACKSTEDER

Hey there, my name is Beatriz and I am a 29-year-old international management professional. After my bachelor's in international commerce and master's in management, I have been

(Continued)

working in companies in Asia, Europe and North America. I consider myself a responsible person, take extra care to live sustainably in my private life, and try to always do the right thing. I love interacting with people and try to surround myself with good people around me. In the shops I buy from I am notorious for always bringing my own Tupperware and bags as I don't want to create any more waste than necessary. I sometimes even think I might not want to have kids because there are too many on this planet anyway … tough decision. In some situations, doing the right thing or even knowing what the right thing is, is just a bit harder than in others, as you will also see from one of the toughest challenges I have faced so far in my professional career. I will tell the story exactly as it went down when I was working in the leading European homeware company HOME Limited as a purchasing manager.

Chinese issues. As part of the usual process with international companies, a certification agency inspects the factories where the product is being made. A reputable international agency appointed by RetailY, was due to inspect our facilities in China. To my disappointment, our factories failed the inspection on three sub-categories. Ding, the manager of the Chinese facilities explained that the inspectors asked for a bribe. But since we abided by international standards (ISO 14000, BSCI, etc.), he couldn't do anything to stop the negative results. Jenny, the quality assurance manager in Europe, was confident we could fix those minor issues and pass another inspection within a week. Next week, we received the certificate with positive results.

European issues. As major international retailers, RetailY requested some samples for testing. To my surprise, our products did not pass the test, as they contained higher levels of a chemical regulated by European standards – this chemical, being harmful to animals and plants, but non-toxic for humans. We immediately contacted our supplier to report this issue. Since our products had been exported to Europe for years, the chemical levels should have been kept within European standards. This was a surprise to RetailY (as it was a surprise to us) because we trusted our Chinese supplier who we had been working with for over 15 years. RetailY decided to continue dealing with us as long as we fixed the problem and made new products for them.

What to do? Jenny, Steve and the managing director, Jay, had several meetings trying to solve this issue. The company decidedly had the responsibility of supplying new items for RetailY. But what should we do with all the products with higher levels of that chemical? The management team was aware that those products did not meet European standards. But we do not test our shipments often. Maybe the Chinese supplier had been using the chemical for a long time and we just hadn't noticed until now.

(Continued)

Are you kidding me? A couple of weeks later, RetailY received new products with chemical levels within the European standards. Just by accident, Jenny told me that Steve had decided to re-pack the toxic products into our standard boxes and sell them in the domestic market via different channels. I confronted Steve and explained how uncomfortable the decision made me feel. I was complicit in a situation I hadn't wanted to be involved with in the first place. I mentioned the possibility to report HOME Limited to the European Commission.

No worries, we've been bad before. Steve showed me how the chemical was slightly higher than the European standard and that it was harmless to humans. Steve claimed that our company was always doing its best to protect the environment, providing different examples of what we do at our factories in Europe. He even shared a similar experience he had in the past with another company he worked in. The company sold Christmas lights although they were known to be faulty and posed a fire hazard. He stressed that what our current company was doing did not endanger human lives – probably assuming that because other companies were doing worse things, I wouldn't make a big deal out of the situation.

Did I sell out on my ideals? In the end, I decided not to take any further action. Even today, three years later I am still not quite sure that I made the right decision, and, had I acted differently, what I could have done.

QUESTIONS

1. What local and global norms, practices, and standards do you see interacting in this case?

2. Why and how did things go wrong here? What do you think is the root cause? Whose fault is it?

3. What would you have done if you were in Beatriz's shoes?

DIGGING DEEPER: NORMS AND PRINCIPLES OF GLOCALLY RESPONSIBLE MANAGEMENT

There are many codes, initiatives, and even certification for international businesses (see Table 12.4). Apart from signalling to others that a business is doing everything right, such codes can also serve as a self-assessment tool. In the following we will focus on two main codes for international business and management: the OECD Guidelines for Multinational Enterprises and the United Nations Global

Compact (GC) Principles. Both norms are different in nature, but equally important in their coverage of responsible business topics and issues typically encountered in international business conduct. Additionally, we illustrate the Caux Roundtable Principles for Responsible Globalization [69], which are not as well known as the other two norms, but which add a proactive dimension to the discussion.

TABLE 12.4   Comparison of guidelines for responsible international management

United Nations Global Compact	OECD Guidelines for Multinational Enterprises	Caux Round Table Principles for Responsible Globalization
Human rights **Principle 1.** Businesses should support and respect the protection of internationally proclaimed human rights. **Principle 2.** Make sure that they are not complicit in human rights abuses.	**Disclosure** Enterprises should ensure that timely, regular, reliable and relevant information is disclosed regarding their activities, structure, financial situation and performance. **Employment and industrial relations** Enterprises should, within the framework of applicable law, regulations and prevailing labour relations and employment practices assure responsible labour practices.	**Principle 1.** The responsibilities of businesses: Beyond shareholders towards stakeholders As responsible citizens of the local, national, regional and global communities in which they operate, businesses share a part in shaping the future of those communities. **Principle 2.** The economic and social impact of business: towards innovation, justice and world community
Labour **Principle 3.** Businesses should uphold the freedom of association and the effective recognition of the right to collective bargaining. **Principle 4.** The elimination of all forms of forced and compulsory labour. **Principle 5.** The effective abolition of child labour. **Principle 6.** The elimination of discrimination in respect of employment and occupation. **Environment** **Principle 7.** Businesses should support a precautionary approach to environmental challenges. **Principle 8.** Undertake initiatives to promote greater environmental responsibility; and **Principle 9.** Encourage the development and diffusion of environmentally friendly technologies. Anti-corruption **Principle 10.** Businesses should work against corruption in all its forms, including extortion and bribery (UNGC, 2011).	**Environment** Enterprises should (…) take due account of the need to protect the environment, public health and safety, and generally conduct their activities in a manner contributing to the wider goal of sustainable development. **Combatting bribery** Enterprises should not, directly or indirectly, offer, promise, give, or demand a bribe or other undue advantage to obtain or retain business or other improper advantage. Nor should enterprises be solicited or expected to render a bribe or other undue advantage. **Consumer interest** When dealing with consumers, enterprises should act in accordance with fair business, marketing and advertising practices and should take all reasonable steps to ensure the safety and quality of the goods or services they provide. **Science and technology** Enterprises should promote the diffusion and transfer of technologies, and promote local collaboration for know-how creation. **Competition** Enterprises should follow the norms of fair competition, such as non-price fixing, collusion, and output restrictions. **Taxation** It is important that enterprises contribute to the public finances of host countries by making timely payment of their tax liabilities. In particular, enterprises should comply with the tax laws and regulations in all countries in which they operate and should exert every effort to act in accordance with both the letter and spirit of those laws and regulations.	Businesses established in foreign countries (…) should also contribute to the social advancement of those countries. (…) Businesses should contribute to economic and social development not only in the countries in which they operate, but also in the world community at large. **Principle 3.** Business behaviour: Beyond the letter of law towards a spirit of trust Businesses should recognize that sincerity, candour, truthfulness, the keeping of promises, and transparency (…) but also to the smoothness and efficiency of business transactions, particularly on the international level. **Principle 4.** Respect for rules To avoid trade frictions and to promote freer trade, equal conditions for competition, and fair and equitable treatment for all participants, businesses should respect international and domestic rules. **Principle 5.** Support for multilateral trade Businesses should support the multilateral trade systems of the GATT/World Trade Organization and similar international agreements. They should cooperate in efforts to promote the progressive and judicious liberalization of trade and to relax those domestic measures that unreasonably hinder global commerce, while giving due respect to national policy objectives. **Principle 6.** Respect for the environment A business should protect and, where possible, improve the environment, promote sustainable development, and prevent the wasteful use of natural resources. **Principle 7.** Avoidance of illicit operations A business cooperates with others to eliminate bribery, money laundering, or other corrupt practices. It should not trade in arms or other materials used for terrorist activities, drug traffic or other organized crime.

POINTERS

You could dig deeper into these codes, for instance, by comparing similarities and differences; by looking up businesses that claim to adhere to these codes; by researching news stories of businesses breaking these codes, or by critically evaluating if these codes are enough or if they should be amended.

WORKSHEET

ASSESSING GLOCALIZING LOGICS

	Ethnocentric	Polycentric	Regiocentric	Geocentric
	'Our home country's practices are best and we do it this way everywhere else.'	'There are similar locations suited to the same type of practices.'	'One practice works best for the whole region, there is no need for further local adaptation.'	'There is an integrated "middle ground" practice that on average works best everywhere.'

POINTERS

Use this table to analyse the underlying glocalization logics of, for instance, a practice, statement, strategy, manager, business or sector. Each line of the table can be used for a different object to be assessed. Start by writing down what it is you are assessing in each cell in the far-left column. Then assess aspects of which glocalizing logic it shows and write a couple of words or a note in the corresponding cell explaining why you think so.

REFERENCES

1. Gupta A, Raghunath A, Gula L, Rheinbay L, Hart M. *The decade to deliver: A call for business action.* New York: Accenture, 2019.
2. Wikipedia. Natura&Co. https://en.wikipedia.org/wiki/Natura_%26_Co Published 2020. Accessed April 15 2020.
3. Natura. Our reason for being. www.naturabrasil.com/pages/about-us# Published 2020. Accessed April 15 2020.
4. Natura. Care about relationships. www.naturabrasil.com/pages/beauty-that-empowers-a-network-of-care Published 2020. Accessed April 15 2020.
5. Natura. Natura helps conserve 1.8 million hectares of standing forest. www.naturabrasil.com/blogs/blog-do-brasil/natura-helps-conserve-1-8-million-hectares-of-standing-forest Published 2019. Accessed April 15 2020.
6. Natura. Care about the planet. www.naturabrasil.com/pages/care-about-the-planet-a-sustainable-timeline Published 2020. Accessed April 15 2020.
7. Insider. Uniqlo closes its stores in Russia, days after its CEO pledged to keep them open because 'clothing is a necessity of life'. www.businessinsider.com/uniqlo-closes-stores-in-russia-reversing-pledge-to-keep-them-open-2022-3?r=US&IR=T#:~:text=Uniqlo%20closes%20its%20stores%20in,is%20a%20necessity%20of%20life Published 2022. Last accessed August 14 2023.
8. Husted BW, Allen DB. Corporate social responsibility in the multinational enterprise: Strategic and institutional approaches. *Journal of International Business Studies.* 2006, 37: 838–849.
9. Robertson R. Glocalization. *The International Encyclopedia of Anthropology.* 2018: 1–8.
10. Robertson R. Glocalization: Time-space and homogenisation-heterogenization. In: *Global modernities.* Thousand Oaks, CA: Sage, 1995, pp. 25–44.
11. Andrews DL, Ritzer G. The grobal in the sporting glocal. *Global Networks.* 2007, 7(2): 135–153.
12. Doh J, Husted BW, Matten D, Santoro M. Ahoy there! Toward greater congruence and synergy between international business and business ethics theory and research. *Business Ethics Quarterly.* 2010, 20(3): 481–502.
13. Fontenelle IA. Global responsibility through consumption? Resistance and assimilation in the anti-brand movement. *Critical Perspectives on International Business.* 2010, 6(4): 256–272.
14. Attac. Attac: Overview. www.attac.org/en/overview Published 2020. Accessed April 16 2020.
15. Phillips D. Bolsonaro declares 'the Amazon is ours' and calls deforestation data 'lies'. www.theguardian.com/world/2019/jul/19/jair-bolsonaro-brazil-amazon-rainforest-deforestation Published 2019. Accessed April 16 2020.
16. Bloodworth A. Brexit Britain could be a human rights 'weak link', fears equality committee. https://eachother.org.uk/brexit-human-rights-weak-link Published 2019. Accessed April 16 2020.
17. Page J. Why China is turning back to Confucius. www.wsj.com/articles/why-china-is-turning-back-to-confucius-1442754000 Published 2015. Accessed April 16 2020.
18. Rogers J. Bristol pound is just one example of what local currencies can achieve. www.theguardian.com/local-government-network/2013/jun/17/bristol-pound-local-currencies Published 2013. Accessed April 16 2020.
19. Carroll AB. Managing ethically with global stakeholders: A present and future challenge. *Academy of Management Executive.* 2004, 18(2): 114–120.
20. Shoham A, Rose GM, Albaum G. Export motives, psychological distance, and the EPRG framework. *Journal of Global Marketing.* 1995, 8(3–4): 9–37.
21. Perlmutter HV. The tortuous evolution of the multinational corporation. *Columbia Journal of World Business.* 1969, 4(1): 9–18.
22. Wind Y, Douglas SP, Perlmutter HV. Guidelines for developing international marketing strategies. *Journal of Marketing.* 1973, 37(2): 14–23.
23. Tulder R van. The multinational perspective on responsible management: Managing risk-responsibility trade-offs across borders. In: Laasch O, Suddaby R, Freeman RE, Jamali D, eds. *The research handbook of responsible management.* Cheltenham: Edward Elgar, 2020, pp. 241–259.

24. Bartlett CA, Ghoshal S, Beamish PW. *Transnational management: Text, cases, and readings in cross-border management.* London: McGraw-Hill, 2008.

25. Fortin J. H&M Closes stores in South Africa amid protests over 'monkey' shirt. www.nytimes.com/2018/01/13/world/africa/hm-south-africa-protest.html Published 2018. Accessed April 19 2020.

26. 4Ocean. About 4Ocean. https://4ocean.com/about Published 2020. Accessed April 19 2020.

27. Choi CJ, Kim SW, Kim JB. Globalizing business ethics research and the ethical need to include the bottom-of-the-pyramid countries: Redefining the global triad as business systems and institutions. *Journal of Business Ethics.* 2010, 94: 299–306.

28. World Economic Forum. The next billions: Business strategies to enhance food value chains and empower the poor. www.weforum.org/reports/next-billions-business-strategies-enhance-food-value-chains-and-empower-poor Published 2009. Accessed September 26 2020.

29. International Institute for Sustainable Development. *Trade and Sustainable Development Principles.* Winnipeg: IISD, 1994.

30. Tisdell C. The Winnipeg Principles, WTO and sustainable development: Proposed policies for reconciling trade and the environment. *Sustainable Development.* 2001, 9(4): 204–212.

31. Smith S, Barrientos S. Fair trade and ethical trade: Are there moves toward convergence? *Sustainable Development.* 2005, 13: 190–198.

32. Huybrechts B, Reed D. Fair trade in different national contexts. *Journal of Business Ethics.* 2010: 147–150.

33. ETI. ETI Base Code. *Ethical Trading Initiative.* Published 2012.

34. Prahalad CK. *The fortune at the bottom of the pyramid: Eradicating poverty through profits.* Upper Saddle River, NJ: Pearson Education, 2006.

35. Laasch O, Yang J. Rebuilding dynamics between corporate social responsibility and international development on the search for shared value. *KSCE Journal of Civil Engineering.* 2011, 15(2): 231–238.

36. Sejersted F. Managers and consultants as manipulators: Reflections on the suspension of ethics. *Business Ethics Quarterly.* 1996, 6(1): 67–86.

37. Carbaugh RJ. *International economics.* Mason, OH: Thompson South-Western Publishers, 2010.

38. Pricing OT. About Transfer Pricing. *OECD Better Policies for Better Lives.* www.oecd.org/ctp/transferpricing/abouttransferpricing.htm. Published 2012. Accessed November 28, 2012.

39. Porter M. *Competitive strategy: Techniques for analyzing industries and competitors.* New York: The Free Press, 1980.

40. Daniels JD, Radebaugh LH, Sullivan DP. *International business: Environments and operations.* Upper Saddle River, NJ: Pearson Education, 2013.

41. Liao R. China's Youon expands into Europe as other bike startups backpedal worldwide. https://techcrunch.com/2018/10/31/youon-expands-into-europe Published 2018. Accessed April 19 2020.

42. Matten D, Moon J. 'Implicit' and 'explicit' CSR: A conceptual framework for a comparative understanding of corporate social responsibility. *Academy of Management Review.* 2008, 33(2): 404–424.

43. Visser WAM, Tolhurst N. *The world guide to CSR: A country-by-country analysis of corporate sustainability and responsibility.* Chichester: Wiley, 2010.

44. *The CSR navigator: Public policies in Africa, the Americas, Asia and Europe.* Eschborn: GTZ, 2007.

45. Porter M. The competitive advantage of nations. *Harvard Business Review.* 1990: 73–93.

46. Porter M, Kramer M. Strategy and society: The link between competitive advantage and corporate social responsibility. *Harvard Business Review.* 2006, 84(12): 78–92.

47. Moon HC, Rugman AM, Verbeke A. A generalized double diamond approach to the global competitiveness of Korea and Singapore. *International Business Review.* 1998, 7(2): 135–150.

48. Johnson JP, Lenartowicz T, Apud S. Cross-cultural competence in international business: Toward a definition and a model. *Journal of International Business Studies.* 2006, 37(4): 525–543.

49. Lustig MW, Koester J. *Intercultural competence: Interpersonal communication across cultures.* Boston: Allyn and Bacon, 2003.

50. Hofstede G. *Culture's consequences: International differences in work-related differences.* Thousand Oaks, CA: Sage, 1980.

51. Hofstede G, Fink G. Culture: Organisations, personalities and nations: Gerhard Fink interviews Geert Hofstede. *European Journal of International Management.* 2007, 1(1/2): 14–22.
52. GLOBE. Culture groups. https://globeproject.com/results/clusters/southern-asia?menu=cluster#cluster Published 2020. Accessed April 18 2020.
53. House RJ, Hanges PJ, Ruiz-Quintanilla SA, et al. Cultural influences on leadership and organizations: Project GLOBE. *Advances in Global Leadership.* 1999, 1(2): 171–233.
54. Waldman DA, De Luque MS, Washburn N, et al. Cultural and leadership predictors of corporate social responsibility values of top management: A GLOBE study of 15 countries. *Journal of International Business Studies.* 2006, 37(6): 823–837.
55. Javidan M, House RJ. Cultural acumen for the global manager: Lessons from project GLOBE. *Organizational Dynamics.* 2001, 29(4): 289–305.
56. GLOBE. An overview of the 2004 study: Understanding the relationship between national culture, societal effectiveness and desirable leadership attributes. Published 2020. Accessed April 15, 2020.
57. Cox T. *Creating the multicultural organization: A strategy for capturing the power of diversity.* San Francisco: Jossey-Bass, 2001.
58. Mor Barak ME. *Managing diversity: Toward a globally-inclusive workforce.* Thousand Oaks, CA: Sage, 2011.
59. Mahoney JF. Aspects of international business ethics. *Advances in Management.* 2012, 5(3): 11–16.
60. Bailey W, Spicer A. When does national identity matter? Convergence and divergence in international business ethics. *Academy of Management Journal.* 2007, 50(6): 1462–1480.
61. Küng H. A global ethic in an age of globalization. *Business Ethics Quarterly.* 1997, 7(3): 17–32.
62. Küng H. *Global responsibility: In search of a new world ethic.* London: Continuum Publishing Company, 1991.
63. Webley, S. The Interfaith Declaration: Constructing a code of ethics for international business. *Business Ethics: A European Review.* 1996, 5(1): 52–57.
64. Tsalikis J, Seaton B. The International Business Ethics Index: European Union. *Journal of Business Ethics.* 752007: 229–238.
65. Hendry J. Universalizability and reciprocity in international business ethics. *Business Ethics Quarterly.* 91999: 405–420.
66. Laasch, O., Moosmayer, D., & Antonacopoulou, E. P. (2023). The interdisciplinary responsible management competence framework: An integrative review of ethics, responsibility, and sustainability competences. *Journal of Business Ethics, 187,* 733–757.
67. Hofstede G. Business goals for a new world order: Beyond growth, greed and quarterly results. *Asia Pacific Business Review.* 2009, 15(4): 481–488.
68. Hofstede G. Cultural constraints in management theories. *Academy of Management Perspectives.* 1993, 7(1): 81–94.
69. Draft. *Principles for responsible globalization.* Saint Paul, MN: Caux Round Table, 2002.

CHAPTER 13

STRATEGIZING

OLIVER LAASCH

LEARNING GOALS

1. Integrate ethics, responsibility, and sustainability into your strategizing
2. Assess your social, environmental, and ethical strengths, weaknesses, threats and opportunities
3. Achieve responsible competitiveness

IMPRESSIVE FACT

Over one quarter of medium-sized and big businesses in the UK have a climate change strategy in place [1].

SPOTLIGHT

OPEN (BOTTLE) STRATEGIZING AT PREMIUM-COLA

The Hamburg-based company now called 'Premium' was founded 'by accident'. The iconic German brand Afri-Cola had been sold and the new owner had unilaterally changed the recipe and taste without consulting their loyal customers first [2]. One of the upset customers, Uwe Luebbemann, gathered a group of like-minded people to protest against this type of 'closed' strategic decision-making. The group then decided to make their own 'Premium-Cola', based on the original Afri-Cola recipe and started to build a 'Premium' company based on radically open decision-making [3].

Premium's strategizing practices are different 'from the bottom up', comments a journalist [4]. As Elena, part of Premium's management explains, they 'are trying to rethink capitalism' [4]. Their strategizing is based on democratic principles in order to find agreement among all involved [4]. Their strategizing 'board' consists of a chatroom and a mail list to which almost everyone (also 'externals') has access, explains Anna-Lilja, 'the first contact for people who want to know more about Premium-Cola' [4].

Identifying strategic issues, developing strategies, and implementation are all done openly and collectively by this group consisting of over 1,650 people [5]. However, in cases where consensus cannot be reached, Uwe in his role as 'central organizer' is allowed to make a decision [5]. Strategizing includes issues as varied as how to position Premium through advertising, reducing prices to benefit customers and distributors, and actively shrinking sales numbers to increase quality [5].

Premium's strategic operating model includes the principle of 'transfer' so that anyone can use it in their own company [6]. Premium even helps others to use their know-how in an 'open

franchise' model [7]. Strategizing at Premium is built on collaboration and friendly, trust-based relations, be it with customers, suppliers, or at times competitors like Coca-Cola [3]. Managers at Premium pride themselves on not having engaged in a single written contract in over ten years and not having been involved in a single law suit with their partners either [4, 8].

SOURCE: [4]

However, Premium's strategizing also requires protective practices so that their unique business model remains intact. Only people recommended by someone who is already on Premium's strategizing mail list can join, as 'curious competitors might otherwise use the information against us (which unfortunately has happened already)' [9]. Another strategizing practice is 'emergency exclusion' through which members of the strategizing collective can be ousted if they have done considerable damage [9].

PROFESSIONAL STRATEGIZING

What else could a strategic management process be, other than how to improve the business model, which is nothing more than how the company creates value for its customers, employees, suppliers, communities and financiers. Any strategic management process that is not oriented around such value creation, could probably be improved.

R. Edward Freeman [10]

Strategizing is a common starting point for many other management practices. Whatever management mode or occupation we scrutinize, it will, if managed well, be aligned with strategic goals or purposes. To understand how

Strategizing
is the mode of management
centred on achieving goals
through strategy practices

all of the commitments and actions related to, for instance, organizing, communicating, people management, or accounting are integrated and coordinated, we have to understand how strategizing underpins each of them.

A worldwide survey among CEOs has shown that the integration of ethical, responsible, and sustainable management with strategizing is being taken seriously. Fifty-nine per cent stated that they need to integrate environmental, social and governance issues much more with **strategy**. Thirty-four per cent said those topics have to be integrated more. Only seven per cent aimed at the same or less integration [11]. In the next iteration of the survey, management was already much further down the road. CEOs responded that they had largely completed the integration and that the new task was to deeply embed professional management throughout the main operational functions like accounting and supply chain management [1].

Professional strategizing has been discussed, criticized, and glorified. Strategic corporate social responsibility and philanthropy have seen a peak in interest ever since strategic management guru Michael Porter teamed up with the NGO specialist Mark Kramer, and jointly started to study and promote how strategy relates to society and vice versa [12–14]. The topic of strategic management and socio-environmental value goes back to the very roots of the field of strategizing. Igor Ansoff, often cited as creator of the term 'strategic management' and the field itself, highlighted the importance of strategic (social) issues management as a cornerstone of strategizing [15].

Professional strategizing is centred on how social and environmental value creation becomes integrated into the strategizing process.

The **strategizing process** consists of four types of practices. First, strategizing involves defining the strategic direction by shaping the strategic purpose (e.g. in the form of **vision and mission statements**) and objectives. Secondly, context analysis serves to identify strategically relevant internal and external factors. Third, **strategy formulation** practices relate to making alternative strategies explicit. Strategies can be developed for varieties of application areas, such as single initiatives, functions, a specific business unit, or an entire corporation. Fourth, **strategy execution** translates strategies into action, such as governance and organizing, change management activities, leading and entrepreneurial practices. As illustrated in Figure 13.1, the strategizing process is circular and iterative. This process does not necessarily have to begin with shaping objectives. Strategizing practices should constantly be aligned and realigned to achieve responsible competitiveness. Resulting strategies can be planned or unplanned (emergent) [16], and often happen in many strategizing episodes in which strategies are crafted and recrafted iteratively [17].

Strategy
is an integrated and coordinated set of commitments and actions aimed at achieving a goal or purpose

Professional strategizing
refers to the integration of socio-environmental factors into the core strategizing process in order to create social, environmental, and economic value

Strategizing process
consists of the shaping of purpose and objectives, analysing the context, formulating strategies, as well as executing them

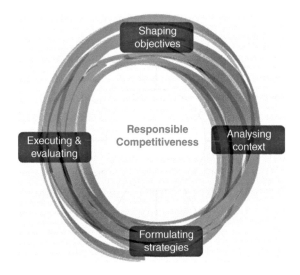

FIGURE 13.1 Strategizing process

RESPONSIBLE COMPETITIVENESS

What's a 'good' strategy? A simple answer is that it is a strategy that achieves its goals and larger purpose. An even better strategy achieves goals that relate to professional management, that are in service of society and the planet. The best strategy, however, is the one that additionally achieves those goals ethically, responsibly, and sustainably, through what we have previously called 'professional conduct'.

The field of strategic management suggests yet another answer, namely that a good strategy leads to an advantage over competitors. Such a strong position can take different forms. For businesses a competitive advantage is believed to be reflected in the performance and value of companies' stocks. Hence, a company achieving a **competitive strategic advantage** is supposed to ren-

> **Competitive strategic advantage**
> refers to an advantageous strategic position achieved in competition with peers

der above-average returns to shareholders and other owners [18]. However, in a professional management context, above-average returns do not necessarily have to be of a financial nature; nor do they have to be a return for the owners. An above-average stakeholder value creation can define competitiveness in the eyes of virtually any stakeholder group. For instance, the German automobile supplier Allsafe is not only a highly competitive market leader among peers, but also a leader in

Competitive advantages at Allsafe Germany

Collaborative strategic advantage
an advantageous strategic position achieved in collaboration with peers

Co-opetition
describes the complementary nature of collaboration and competition as bases of strategizing

Responsible competitiveness
is the achievement of a competitive advantage as above-average value creation for a wider range of stakeholders

Irresponsible competitiveness
is the achievement of a competitive advantage at the cost of stakeholders

the creation of value for their employees in the market for talent [19]. Both are competitive advantages.

While still a taken-for-granted assumption among many strategists, assuming competitive advantage as an indicator of a 'good' strategy is controversial. Competitive advantage is built on the underlying assumption that goals are competitive, that strategic purpose and goals have to be competitive, implying that if one achieves them, the other competitor doesn't. It has been suggested that 'realizing purpose' is better than strategic competitive advantage [10]. In professional strategizing, goals may often be of a **collaborative** nature – for instance, to join forces in order to achieve one of the sustainable development goals. Also, we have seen in the Premium case at the beginning of the chapter what a strategy based on collaboration and positive relationships can achieve.

The basis of strategizing can therefore be competition, collaboration, or even both. A well-known phenomenon is **co-opetition** where industry peers collaborate on some aspects to achieve their goals and compete on others [20]. For instance, car manufacturers Renault, Nissan, and Mitsubishi collaborate in a joint venture to develop more environmentally friendly technologies while also competing against each other for a market share of their end product [21].

What we are looking for in professional strategizing is **responsible competitiveness**, a situation where management achieves a competitive advantage by creating more value for a wider set of stakeholders than their competitors. A survey among executives revealed that over half (54 per cent) believed that responsible management activities give them an advantage over their most significant competitors [22]. But you cannot always 'have your cake and eat it' due to frequent strategic tensions between achieving goals and creating value for one or another stakeholder group [23]. The strategy field has often stressed the value of a 'sustained' competitive advantage, one that endures over time as it is hard to imitate. However, some organizations like Fairphone (Chapter 3) or Premium (in this chapter) might not actually want to sustain their responsible competitive advantage. Instead, they want competitors to imitate their more ethical, responsible, and sustainable management practices in order to improve their industry in the case of Fairphone, or even the economy at large in the case of Premium. Accordingly, responsible competitiveness may well be only temporary, but deliberate.

Irresponsible competitiveness, on the other hand, occurs when management achieves competitiveness at the cost of their stakeholders – for example, when a company abuses monopoly power to charge customers an exorbitant price for a subpar service or product, or when producing products that beat competitors' products using exploitative labour conditions. Promoting irresponsible competitiveness has no place in professional strategizing as it contradicts both principles of service to society, and of professional conduct.

SHAPING STRATEGIC PURPOSE AND OBJECTIVES

One of the best known statements of a strategic objective or vision started with the words, 'I have a dream …' by Martin Luther King [24]. Those words have been a guiding light for immense social progress and value creation, including the recent Black Lives Matter movement. We will now focus on strategizing tools related to vision, mission, and strategic objectives. The purpose is to achieve an alignment of strategizing practice with such goals serving as 'lighthouses' for truly professional strategizing [25]. For instance, management at Oxfam, one of the longest established fair-trade social businesses, has declared its purpose and mission to end poverty. The ice-cream business Ben and Jerry's has implemented a dual vision statement. While the social mission statement delineates the company's commitment to 'improve the quality of life locally, nationally and internationally', the economic mission aims at operating 'the company on a sustainable financial basis of profitable growth, increasing value for our stakeholders' [26]. Premium's founding purpose was to bring back the taste of the old Afri-Cola.

In his book *Strategic management: A stakeholder approach*, Edward Freeman makes the case for considering and involving stakeholders from the very beginning of strategizing. Not living up to stakeholders' expectations will inevitably force any business and its management into decline. So management has to readjust its strategic priorities based on a stakeholder assessment or active involvement and readjust its mission statements to reflect stakeholders' needs [27, 28]. The mission statement serves as a 'formal commitment' and 'key indicator' [29] for professional strategizing that is aimed at 'meeting the claims of various stakeholders' [30]. It specifies how strategizing pursues its ultimate responsibility to serve the needs of stakeholders [18].

Defining what an organization wants to achieve and be is usually done in the natural flow from a long-term vision to an actual mission statement, to short and medium-term objectives and finally concrete short-term goals. Vision, mission, and objectives are used, not only for giving direction to whole organizations, but also to single business units, business functions or even a specific business activity such as a project (see Chapter 10).

A **vision statement** expresses 'strategic intent', which often suggests using overarching stretch goals, which require innovative measures to be reached [29]. It is crucial to search for a mutually reinforcing relationship between a vision's social, environmental, and economic components. For instance, a costly vision of becoming the world's biggest charity donor company would not be in accordance with the vision of being the market's cost leader.

Vision statement delineates what management ultimately wants to achieve

Mission statement
defines what management and
its organization is and does at
a certain point in time, typically
including market, customers,
products, processes, and values

While the vision statement gives *future* direction, the **mission statement** defines what the organization is and does right now. Mission statements answer the question, 'What is your business?' [30], describing what the organization exists for and therefore what management should be doing [29]. The answer to this question covers typical markets, customers, main products and processes as well as values. In order to include stakeholders' perspectives on what the company is and how it should conduct its business a dialogue-based stakeholder assessment process is needed. Some strategic management classics recommend a management-exclusive mission development approach [30]. Exclusively focusing on the core stakeholder group managers is likely to assure full support from this group, but risks losing other stakeholders' support for subsequent strategic and tactical moves because the mission statement is so unbalanced. Premium-Cola is an excellent counter-example of a stakeholder-inclusive approach.

Purpose-driven business mission at Unilever.

Strategic objectives and goals are goals in line with the vision and mission, and more concrete medium- and long-term 'to-dos'. Often 'objectives' refers to specific quantitative targets, such as 'sustain a 40 per cent debt/equity ratio' or 'Source 100% of our agricultural raw materials sustainably' [31]. Goals on the other hand refer to qualitative intentions in the same time frame, such as 'design products to delight customers while maximizing the conservation of natural resources' [32].

Strategic objectives and goals
translate vision and mission
to medium- and long-
term operational goals

It is important to understand that while the strategic direction setting practices related to vision, mission, and objectives are often the starting point of strategizing, there has to be a constant readjustment of this initial position throughout subsequent strategizing activity. Strategy is a circular progression in which the starting and finish line should be redrawn continually by a consistent, comprehensive examination of the various environments surrounding the company' [33].

ANALYSING THE STRATEGIC CONTEXT

As illustrated in Figure 13.2, organizations exist in external and internal strategic environments, defining the basic conditions for all strategic decision-making. The internal environment is represented through the company's value chain, which provides a broad picture of the company [34]. The external environment can be subdivided into two layers. The first layer is the industry environment [34] and the second is the general macro environment surrounding particular industries. The internal and external stakeholder environments considered in a stakeholder assessment are a key element of this analysis (see Chapter 4).

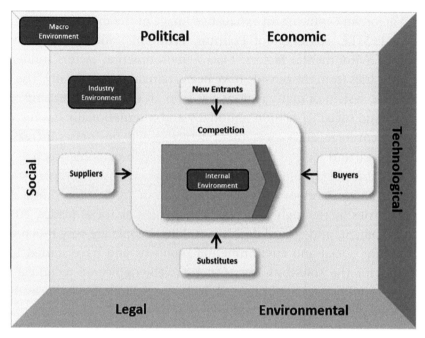

FIGURE 13.2   Strategic environments

Strategizing has two different ways of looking at the origin of competitive advantage. The environmental view focuses on a company's external environment as a source of competitive advantage. To put it simply: The company management that chooses the right industry and operates in the right macro environment will be competitive. The resource-based view attributes competitiveness to internal factors, the internal environment. In practice, both environments and their role in achieving competitive advantage can hardly be separated [35].

There is a strong mutually influencing relationship between professional strategizing and the environments, a mutual strategic relationship. Through **inside-out linkages** the internal environment positively or negatively influences social, environmental, and economic factors of its external environment. For instance, banks' irresponsible subprime lending strategies led to a global economic crisis in 2007 lasting for many years and affecting billions of people. Conversely, **outside-in linkages** describe how factors related to the external social and natural environment influence management's strategizing [13]. For instance, legislation phasing out petroleum-based combustion engines

Inside-out linkages describe how the internal environment influences the external environment

Outside-in linkages describe the influence of external factors on the internal company environment

around the world influences the car industry's strategizing. The essence of professional strategizing is to harness those linkages in order to create shared value strategies that are good for management and stakeholders.

EXTERNAL ENVIRONMENT ANALYSIS

A useful acronym capturing an exhaustive image of the macro environment's factors is PESTLE, standing for Political, Economic, Social, Technological, Legal and Environmental factors. Macro-environmental factors influencing whole industries from the outside have been changing dramatically. The overall economic system of many regions has seen an extensive 'greening'. Environmental and social legislation nationally and internationally has increased in number, coverage, and enforcement, which is why businesses increasingly encounter legal and societal pressure. Population demographics such as poor, or so-called base-of-pyramid, and ageing customers foster industry change adapting to those developments. The culture in many developed and developing countries increasingly embraces values such as social justice, sustainable development, and ethical decision-making. People are very much aware of threatening social and environmental problems and have started to feel responsible for the solutions. Increasingly, well-engineered technical solutions to predominantly environmental, but also social, problems are available, and increasingly they are being adopted.

On the industry level, the five forces of industry attractiveness, commonly known as Porter's five forces, describe the basic characteristics of an industry's environment: competition, supplier, customer bargaining power, threat of new entrants, and threat of substitute products [34]. Factors related to professional management have shaken up many industries. Many customers request more sustainable products and services. Substitute products with improved social or environmental characteristics have become increasingly attractive. The task of reinforcing the upstream value chain's social and environmental performance is forcing companies to radically transform their supplier relationships. Established industry incumbents are increasingly competing on sustainability.

While those developments constitute challenges, in some cases even threats to be taken seriously by management in businesses of all sizes and shapes, the opportunities are at least equally significant. Social entrepreneurs and green technology companies have successfully broken down long-established industry entry barriers. An excellent example is Nobel Peace Prize winner Muhammad Yunus who was able to enter the banking business with his group-lending and microcredit-based Grameen Bank. Figure 13.3 illustrates a wide variety of professional management factors changing the basic parameters of industry strategizing.

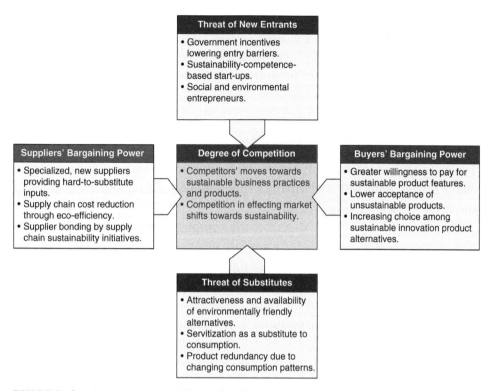

FIGURE 13.3 Exemplary socio-environmental forces influencing the industry environment

SOURCE: Adapted from [34]

External factors are likely to cause turbulent changes, which require extensive observation in order to be aware of external threats and opportunities. The following are common techniques used to achieve an ongoing environmental analysis [18]:

1. Environmental **scanning** helps to identify early signs of changes. For instance, car manufacturers might have scanned the first alternative engine technologies in the 1980s.

2. **Monitoring** provides ongoing observation of environmental trends. Any company producing end-consumer products is well advised to monitor the ever increasing LOHAS (Lifestyles of Health and Sustainability) consumer trend in order to identify the moment when a critical mass is reached for attacking this highly attractive new market segment.

3. **Forecasting** provides a future projection of anticipated outcomes as detected throughout the monitoring process [36]. As early as 1993, Toyota's forecast of environmental constraints due to future increased fuel prices and damage to the environment led to the birth of the company's groundbreaking Prius, the first mass-produced and competitively priced alternative to traditional combustion engines [37].

4. **Assessing** is the final step in an external environmental analysis in terms of the importance and timing of a strategic answer. An increasing number of companies have concluded that the overall sustainability trend requires a strategic answer. For this reason, the Coca Cola Company and SAP, among many others, have created high-level job positions such as Chief Sustainability Officer and Sustainable Strategy Director [38, 39].

INTERNAL ENVIRONMENT ANALYSIS

Typically applied internal environment analysis instruments include the value chain model, reflecting a company's functional areas [34] and an analysis of the resources a company is endowed with.

Value chain
is a description of a company's activities as they are bundled into functions

The **value chain** model describes the complete company and all its activities as they are bundled into business functions such as people management, procurement and marketing.[1] In the original value chain model the intended outcome was a maximum financial margin resulting from the difference between the cost caused and the value created by all the business functions as a whole. This allows the mapping of every single function's contribution to the financial margin, either by cost reduction or value creation for customers.

For professional strategizing, a three-dimensional (social, environmental, economic) value chain model as illustrated in Figure 13.4 seems more appropriate. It results in a triple bottom line margin [25] in turn consisting of social, environmental, and financial–economic margins. Every function not only produces a certain economic cost and value, but does the same in the social and environmental dimension:

1. A simplified **social margin** of a tobacco company, for instance, might be the difference between the social cost of health problems caused and the social value created by employing thousands of people.

2. The **environmental margin** of an eco-tourism business might be the difference between the environmental value of the ecosystems protected for tourist activity and the environmental cost of CO_2 emissions caused by the tourists while travelling to their destination.

Each function and every business exhibit a different social–environmental–economic cost and value structure, resulting in a unique triple margin. After analysing the triple margin of a single business function, the overarching goal should be to reach at least a positive overall triple margin, preferably for each function. Every function in the value chain can be matched with responsible management

---

[1]Typically, the specialized managerial occupations are practiced in these functions.

for triple value creation. Examples include sustainable innovation for the research and development function and sustainable packaging for outbound logistics. The marketing function has a specialized cause-related marketing tool, and triple bottom line accounting falls under the accounting function.

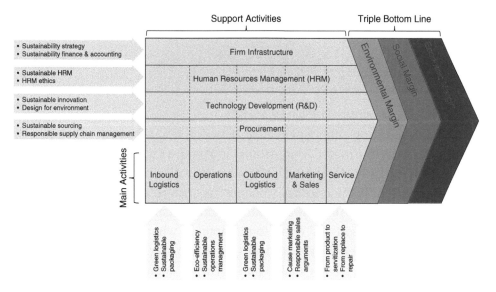

FIGURE 13.4   The responsible management value chain

SOURCE: Inspired by [13]

The **resource-based view of strategizing**, unlike the value chain model, does not scrutinize single business functions, but a company's resources and how they contribute to the achievement of competitive advantage, ideally a lasting, sustained competitive advantage. A resource can be physical (e.g. buildings, technology), human (e.g. knowledge and skills) or organizational (e.g. organizational rules and controls, management systems) [35, 40, 41]. Resources require strategic management that harnesses them optimally [29].

Resources can lead to different types of competences. A **competence** is something a company is good at, while a core competence is central to a company's strategy and competitiveness. The most valuable type of competence is a distinctive competence, being a competitively valuable activity that a company performs better than competitors and therefore leads to a competitive advantage [42]. A company's resource portfolio usually offers manifold competences and might offer one or several core competences. Distinctive competencies on the other hand are rare as not every company has one. Strategizing may be aimed at actively fostering resources and resulting competences in order to create distinctive competences.

Resource-based view of strategizing
aims to explain how resources and their management contribute to the achievement of competitive advantage

Competence
is something an organization and its management are good at

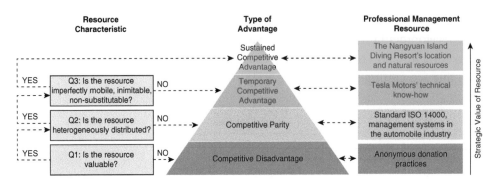

FIGURE 13.5   Professional management, resources and types of competitive (dis)advantages

SOURCE: Adapted from [43]

There is a strong interdependence between resources and the different kinds of strategic positions. As illustrated in Figure 13.5, three main questions may help to identify the strategic characteristics of a competence [35, 43]. If the first question 'Is the resource valuable?' is answered negatively it leads to a competitive disadvantage. If a resource is not valuable, in most cases it will still create a certain cost and effort to maintain it, which is a disadvantageous situation in comparison with competitors. For instance, the organizational culture resource of regularly making anonymous donations without any tax or reputational advantage directly from departments' budgets might be valuable and personally satisfying for the manager directing those funds to a good social cause, but certainly not for the company as a whole. The costs might lead to a competitive disadvantage in comparison with competitors that do not have an organizational donation culture.

If a resource is valuable but answers the second question, 'Is the resource heterogeneously distributed?' negatively, it will encounter competitive parity. For instance, most manufacturing companies nowadays reap cost efficiencies and environmental benefits from having certified environmental management systems. While this helps each of them, none can reap a competitive advantage in comparison to others. On the other hand, if the question is answered in the affirmative, the company is able to reach a temporary competitive advantage. For example, Tesla's unique electric vehicle (EV) patents have put them ahead of the competition. However, due to its founder Elon Musk's aspiration to promote electric mobility, these patents have been made openly available to competitors [44]. Tesla's competitive advantage from the EV know-how resource is temporary until

Strategic positioning at TESLA.

competitors have managed to catch up by translating these patents into their own EV know-how.

If the third question, 'Is the resource hard to imitate?' is answered in the affirmative it leads to a genuinely sustainable competitive advantage. For instance, the eco-tourism resort Nangyuan Island in the gulf of Thailand has such a unique resource. The island, with its romantic, unique setting and eco-system, cannot really be copied and this is therefore most likely to lead to a truly sustained competitive advantage. In spite of being hard to imitate, the resort has encountered a threat to its main core competence by increased diving traffic in the surrounding coral reefs, overfishing, and residual waste by its customers and island visitors [45].

STRENGTHS WEAKNESSES OPPORTUNITIES THREATS (SWOT) ANALYSIS

A simple and useful tool for analysing an organization's environment is **SWOT** (Strengths Weaknesses Opportunities Threats) **analysis**, which summarizes the external and internal analysis in the same management tool. Strengths and weaknesses are the outcome of the internal company environment analysis as described earlier, while threats and opportunities are the outcomes of the external company environment analysis (see Figure 13.6).

SWOT analysis
an environmental assessment tool that sums up helpful (Strengths) and harmful (Weaknesses) internal and external factors (Opportunities and Threats)

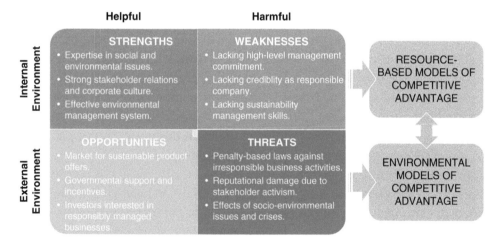

FIGURE 13.6   Exemplary professional management SWOT analysis

The overarching message for professional strategizing is that the business environment externally and internally is changing drastically, particularly across its social and environmental factors. This requires professional strategizing responding to those changes [46, 47].

FORMULATING STRATEGIES

On the basis of sound external and internal environment analysis, strategists formulate strategies. In a business management context, there is a 'strategy hierarchy in which corporate goals guide business unit strategies and business unit strategies guide functional tactics' [48]:

1. **Corporate level strategies** answer the question, 'In how many markets do I want to compete and how many stages of my value chain activities do I perform myself?'

2. **Business level strategies** give guidance on 'How to manage a strategic business unit competing on a certain product market'.

3. 'How do single business functions support the overarching strategic objectives?' is the question to be answered by the **functional level strategies**.

Together, these three strategy levels constitute the strategic backbone of a company to which various other strategies covering additional situations can be attached. Additional strategies might, for instance, be an internationalization strategy for global expansion, a cooperative strategy for alliance arrangements, and a competitive rivalry strategy for direct confrontation with competitors.

CORPORATE LEVEL STRATEGY

The **corporate level strategy** defines how to manage a company that is competing in more than one market, each being covered by a distinct business unit. Increasing the number of business units and markets is called **diversification**, while the process of decreasing the number of business units is called **divestment**. Running a number of parallel businesses competing in unconnected markets is called **horizontal integration**, while the process of managing businesses on a number of different levels of the value chain in the same industry is called **vertical integration**. Vertical integration can be forward, owning businesses engaged in the main businesses' distribution activities, or backward, owning businesses producing the main businesses' input [18].

An excellent example for corporate level strategy-making is strategizing at Clorox (Figure 13.7). While the flagship product Clorox bleach is perceived as harmful to the environment and potentially to users' health, diversification strategies strongly focus on businesses with a superior social and environmental impact. Clorox bought the company Burt's Bees, an organic personal care products business. This **unrelated diversification** activity is mirrored by a highly **related diversification** of launching the Green Works brand, which competes in Clorox's main market for cleaning products with a strong design for environment approach as Green Works' main distinctive feature.

By both strategic diversification moves, Clorox aims at greening the larger corporation. The strategic acquisition of Burt's Bees enables learning from their pioneering environmentally friendly management approach. The motivation of Clorox for the Green Works move can be manifold. Very similar features

Corporate level strategy defines in how many markets a company competes (horizontal integration) and to what degree the business performs activities throughout its upstream and downstream supply chain (vertical integration)

Increasing the number of business units and markets competing is called **diversification**, while the process of decreasing the number of business units is called **divestment**

Related diversification is a new business that has a close link to a company's previous business, while **unrelated diversification** lacks such a relationship

of Green Works and Clorox products make a 'strategic cannibalization' plan a likely rationale: sales in low-environmental performance Clorox products are to be replaced by the Green Works sustainable innovation products. Due to customers' increased willingness to pay for Green Works due to its environmental features, this might not only be a clever way of transitioning Clorox's business to a better overall environmental performance, but also an attractive tactic to increase profit margins.

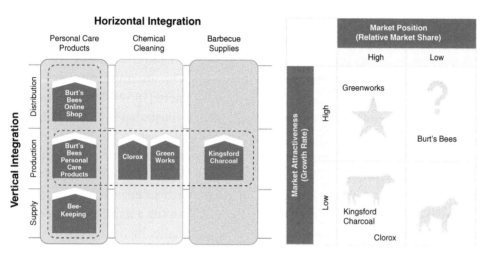

FIGURE 13.7 Corporate-level strategizing at The Clorox Company

The Boston Consulting Group (BCG) matrix is a frequently used tool for analysing and crafting diversification strategies based on each business unit's market share and growth prospects. The BCG matrix helps to analyse the portfolio of the diversified business units of a corporation in order to give recommendations for strategic diversification moves. The market growth criterion is a proxy for a business unit's market attractiveness, while the relative market share is a proxy for the evaluation of the overall competitive strength of a business unit [42, 49].

Figure 13.7 uses the BCG matrix on the Clorox case. A business unit classified as in the star category operates not only in an attractive market, but also holds a strong market position. For instance, General Electric's wind energy sector business unit falls into the star category. Its 1.5 MW series has been the most widely deployed wind turbine installed globally and was involved in a neck-to-neck race for market leadership with the Danish company Vestas [50, 51]. Wind power is an attractive market with the global wind power volume growing continuously [52]. The strategic value of business units marked as question marks cannot be their respective market position, which is weak. For instance Burt's Bees at the time of acquisition had a low market share but held strategic learning potential. Cash cows are well-positioned products

in markets with a limited growth rate and should be 'milked' while showing strong performance, which is the case with both the traditional Clorox brand and its substitute Green Works. Together, they are overall unlikely to gain higher market share but promise steady income taken together. Dogs are business units with a weak market position in an unattractive market. The strategic recommendation for a business unit in this situation is 'dogs must be killed'. They weaken the overall position of the company.

BUSINESS UNIT LEVEL STRATEGY

The **business unit level strategy** delivers answers to the question of how to manage a strategy in a specific product market from the perspective of the strategic business unit operating in this market: Who are my customers? What product do I offer? How do I reach those customers [18, 29]? There are four generic market strategies in a two-by-two matrix as illustrated in Figure 13.8 [34]. Strategic management may either compete on a low cost and resulting price or the differentiation of their product. Differentiation here means any product or service feature (excluding a low price) that makes consumers buy, so called 'non-price buyer's value' [53]. Companies can pursue such strategies based on different market scopes. A broad market scope means grasping a significant part of the overall market, while a narrow scope relates to a smaller niche market.

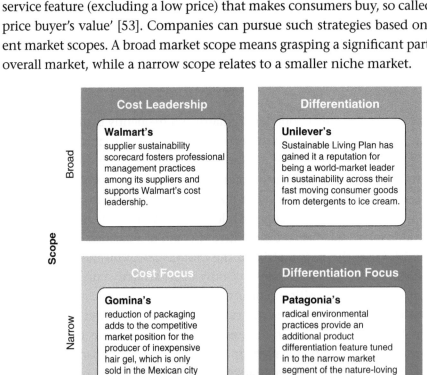

FIGURE 13.8   Professional strategizing and strategic positioning

SOURCE: Adapted from [53]

Strategists have to be cautious not to navigate into 'stuck in the middle' situations – they aim to simultaneously achieve low price and high product differentiation – as this strategy according to this matrix cannot lead to a competitive advantage [34, 54]. However, developments towards more effective production methods, highly effective information systems and flexible manufacturing have given rise to successful integrated cost leadership/differentiation strategies that avoid stuck in the middle [18, 29] situations.

Professional management can have a strong influence on the two crucial factors: price and differentiation, leading or supporting a beneficial strategic market position. It can lead to major cost savings from increased efficiency in natural resource usage [55] and at the same time achieve a 'sustainability premium' due to customers' higher willingness to pay for sustainable innovation products [56]. In the past such products have often been perceived as niche products and services (narrow scope) for the green idealists. However, nowadays ethical, responsible, and sustainable offers support all kinds of strategic positions (see Figure 13.8).

Business unit level strategizing requires a thorough internal value chain analysis. Based on the internal value chain analysis, management can understand how each and every functional unit contributes to the current strategic positioning. For instance, Walmart found that sustainability in the procurement and inbound logistics function might strongly support its price-leadership position. The introduction of its sustainable packaging scorecard was a logical consequence and brought not only significant reductions in energy usage and packaging waste (improving environmental margin), but also additional cost reduction in logistics and procurement [57–59]. Walmart's people management function, which in the past has been characterized as extremely low cost, or rather 'low-wage', was meant to contribute to its cost-leadership position too. Nevertheless, cheap human 'resources' ultimately turned out to be a rather costly strategy due to immense reputational damage when it drew broad public attention and resistance because of its exploitative characteristics [60, 61].

FUNCTIONAL LEVEL STRATEGIZING

Functional level strategizing seeks to develop strategies that support the business unit's strategic positioning from the inside of a specific function such as marketing or accounting. Single functions or departments can contribute to support the bases of competition, cost or differentiation. In order to reach cost leadership, a function has to facilitate low costs by highly efficient processes. To reach high differentiation the function's innovation capability and quality management are crucial [29].

Professional management, in the people management department for example, has immense potential to create both cost leadership and differentiation. For instance, Dell aims to support its mass customization-differentiation

Functional level strategizing aims at the development of strategies of single business functions that support a company's overall strategy

strategy with its strong people diversity strategy: '… we are committed to being a place where our team members can combine their varied experiences and creativity to achieve innovative solutions for a diverse customer marketplace' [62, 63]. Professional management, especially eco-efficiency activities in the inbound logistics and procurement functions often have immense potential to drive down supply chain costs and support a cost–leadership strategy. Sus-

Diversity and inclusion at Dell.

tainable product innovation in the research and development function can facilitate product innovation, delivering additional diversification from new socially and environmentally friendly product features. These are just a few of many mechanisms enabling professional management, as part of a functional strategy, to feed into other strategic positioning activities.

EXECUTING

The 'on-the-road' test of a strategy that looked magnificent on the drawing board can reveal significant practical complications. When CEOs were asked about what keeps them from implementing a fully integrated strategic approach to professional management, 43 per cent referred to competing strategic priorities and 39 per cent mentioned the difficulty of implementing strategy across business functions [11]. This difficulty is even more meaningful when considering the evidence that there are greater returns on a professional management strategy to be realized the more integrated it is into core business functions [22]. The task of aligning business at all levels and in all spheres to bring the strategy into every corner of the business is the main task of strategy execution.[2]

HARDWIRING AND SOFTWIRING

Enacting strategy involves both the 'soft' human elements and the 'hard' non-human elements of strategy execution [64]. First, **softwiring** refers to the social–human and knowledge component of implementation [65]. Secondly,

---

[2]Through strategic control, for example, by using key performance indicators and balanced scorecards (see Chapter 20). Strategic control is the process of evaluating the effects, success, or failure of the strategy, and readjusting parts of the strategy to achieve the company's purpose, goals, and responsible competitive advantage.

hardwiring of a strategy aligns the business infrastructure, corporate governance, and organizational structure with the chosen strategy. Companies often make the mistake of overemphasizing the hardwiring while neglecting softwiring. A five-year survey among more than 1,000 companies from 50 countries revealed that the drivers of effectively executed strategy were not the structural components. The number one reason for failure in strategy implementation was missing information (54%), followed by insufficiently defined decision rights (50%), and human motivators (26%). In only 25 per cent of the cases were structural considerations given as a reason for failure in strategy execution [66].

Strategy implementation typically requires strategic change: the more powerful the strategy, the more drastic the change; the bigger the change, the higher the social resistance to change. To address such resistance, there is change management, a form of **softwiring** dimension. Other softwiring tools are strategic leadership and strategic entrepreneurship practices [18]. Corporate culture management practices can deeply root a new strategy in the 'character of the company's internal work climate and personality' [42].

> **Softwiring**
> implements professional management strategies throughout the organization's social fabric

For instance, Procter and Gamble (P&G) introduced its 50 billion dollar strategy to achieve a major part of their projected revenues from sustainable innovation products. In order to execute this market-level strategy throughout the different business units, a major part of the company had to be changed considerably towards improved social and environmental performance [67, 68]. P&G's strategic innovation programme substituted traditional research and development (R&D) with the new C&D (connect and develop) approach involving a broad set of external and internal stakeholders. Aligning this stakeholder-based innovation model is a crucial part of the softwiring necessary for implementing the 50 billion dollar strategy [69, 70].

> **Hardwiring**
> of a professional management strategy refers to its implementation in the organizational infrastructure

Hardwiring is commonly achieved by using two main practices. First, organizational governance mechanisms assure consistency between the strategic goals and performance and owners' expectations. Recent definitions increasingly broaden this towards congruence not only with owners but also with general stakeholder expectations. The three main corporate governance mechanisms are executive pay, the concentration of ownership, and the board of directors [18].

Sustainable innovation products at P&G.

© Jonathan Weiss/Shutterstock.com

First, a board of directors consciously chosen from a broad and balanced set of stakeholders can greatly contribute to sound stakeholder performance of the overall business. Second, ensuring the alignment of organizational structure ensures that 'the firm's formal reporting relationships, procedures, controls, and authority and decision-making processes' are contributing to the successful implementation of the chosen strategy. Thus, 'the correct organizational structure is a design that best supports the execution of strategy' [71]. The trend towards the introduction of high-level-high-impact executive job positions for ethics, responsibility, and sustainability is a salient development towards an organizational structure, more suited to rolling out a sustainability strategy successfully [72]. Whether the organizational structure includes the information management mechanisms necessary for establishing a facts-and-figures-based strategy control system will be discussed in more detail in the following section.

PRACTICING STRATEGIES AS ALIGNED ACTIVITIES

Starbucks strategic activity system in Korea

If a strategy is 'alive' and therefore effective crucially depends on if it is actually lived and practiced, or conversely, if it only exists 'on paper'. In order to find out if your idealized 'paper strategy' corresponds to your 'de facto' practiced strategy, activity maps, also called synergy maps [54], which map main activities and practices and how they connect, are a great tool. These maps serve to align activities with the aspired strategic positioning goal, be it differentiation or price leadership. Activity maps also help to find synergies between activities, also called 'strategic fit'. For example, Figure 13.9 shows how Starbucks South Korea's local differentiation strategy was executed through an activity network, adding to the overall differentiation of Starbucks' value proposition [73].

After expanding into South Korea, Starbucks quickly experienced aggressive imitation by local competitors. Nevertheless, Starbucks' set of unique buyers' value-creating activities helped the company to transfer the competitive advantage achieved in other countries to this new location. For instance, Starbucks' often hailed CAFE (Coffee and Farmer Equity) programme is an

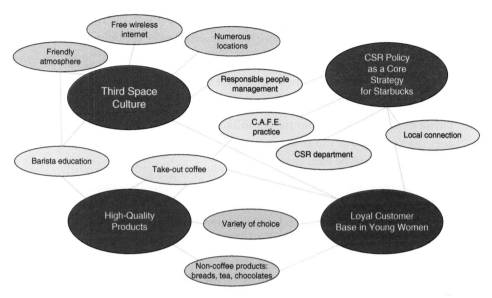

FIGURE 13.9   Strategic alignment at Starbucks Korea

important factor leading to its high-quality products, which are in turn one of the main reasons why the company can charge a price premium for its products [74]. Another salient point is Starbucks' 'third-place' culture. Starbucks' value proposition strongly relies on creating a comfortable third place, where customers spend their time after the first and second places: home and work. That third-place culture depends on a subset of professional management-related activities, one being the high people-management standards at Starbucks reflected in its constantly high Great Place to Work rankings. Starbucks' 'Barista' training then aims at translating employees' good work experience to a 'home away from home' feeling for customers. 'Baristas are the face of Starbucks. They create uplifting experience for the people who visit our stores and make perfect beverages – one drink and one person at a time' [75].

EXECUTING THROUGH BUSINESS MODELS

The **business model** (see Chapter 15) is often understood as the way strategies are implemented. It is no coincidence that the most prominent business model tool is called the Strategyzer business model canvas.[3] The business model consists of a unique 'value logic' [76, 77], built from the following value functions:

Business model
the unique formula of an organization's value proposition, creation, exchange, and capture

---

[3]www.strategyzer.com

1. **Value proposition.** What kind of value does the organization offer to whom? For instance, how and in what form do customers, employees, communities, and other stakeholders benefit from the business?

2. **Value creation.** How does the organization create value? For instance, what are its main production activities or operations necessary for creating value?

3. **Value exchange.** How does the organization exchange value? For instance, how does the value get to the stakeholders it is meant to be for: through marketing distribution, or maybe local outlets?

4. **Value capture.** How is the value created by an organization captured? For instance, how are costs and revenues produced, how do they result in a company margin, and how do internal and external stakeholders capture value from company operations?

In order to execute a strategy, company activities related to all four value functions must be aligned with the strategy. This way the business model forms a unique activity system through which the strategy is enacted and practiced [78]. For instance, Apple's high-end differentiation strategy relies on a customer value proposition of high-quality and high-end design, while depending on highest-standard production processes as their value creation, a value exchange through the iconic Apple stores and the Apple 'Geniuses', and on the ability to maintain high margins through which they capture value.

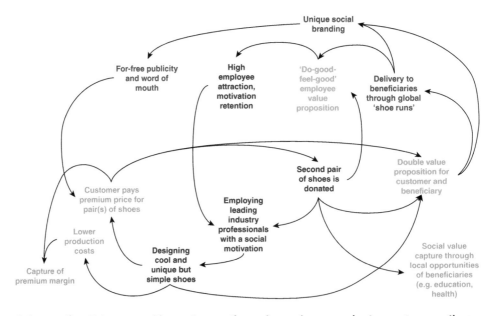

Colour coding: Value proposition, **value creation, value exchange, and** value capture **practices.**

FIGURE 13.10   Practices enacting the TOMS business model

SOURCE: adapted from [19, 79]

Another excellent example is TOMS which has achieved unique strategic differentiation through its one-for-one business model. TOMS customers never buy just one product (be it a pair of shoes or glasses), but also a second one for someone in need. Figure 13.10 illustrates how this business model and the underlying strategy simultaneously achieve social and commercial goals, what we have called 'responsible competitiveness'. You will see how their business model, and with it the strategy, is enacted in a tightly knit bundle of practices, each fulfilling part of the functions of value proposition, creation, exchange, and capture. Frequently, strategic activity systems are built around a central core practice like one for one. Another great example covered in this book is Greyston Bakery's business model built around the practice of 'open hiring' (see Chapter 19 and Case study VI).

PRINCIPLES OF STRATEGIZING

I. The goal of **professional strategizing** is the achievement of **responsible competitiveness**, the achievement of a competitive advantage in the form of above-average value creation for wider stakeholders.

II. The **strategizing process** consists of four types of practices: (1) shaping objectives, (2) analysing context, (3) shaping strategies, and (4) evaluating strategies.

III. **Mission and vision statements** are a 'lighthouse' for any strategizing activity and therefore should integrate social and environmental in addition to economic aspirations.

IV. The three **strategic environments** are the company's internal environment, the industry, and the macro-environment. In each, professional management factors play a crucial role.

V. The **strategy hierarchy** consists of corporate strategies for a company with several strategic business units: the business unit strategy, and the functional strategy.

VI. Professional strategizing can create valuable **diversification advantages** on the corporate level, support **strategic positioning for business units**, and support **functional strategizing contributions** to the overall organizational strategy.

VII. **Executing** professional management strategies is based on 'hardwiring' them into organizational structure, and 'softwiring' them into the human community.

VIII. **Activity maps** can be used to evaluate to what degree the practiced strategy corresponds to the idealized strategy 'on paper' and to find out how strategic activities align with each other.

IX. Strategies are practiced as **business models'** value proposition, creation, exchange, and capture.

MANAGEMENT GYM: TRAINING YOUR PROFESSIONAL SIX-PACK

Knowing

1. Describe the four phases of the strategizing process and give an example of a typical management task for each phase.

2. Mention the three levels of the strategy hierarchy and describe one strategic choice to be made for each level.

3. Describe the difference between the following:

   - collaborative advantage versus competitive advantage
   - inside-out linkages versus outside-in linkages
   - hardwiring versus softwiring.

Thinking

4. Research the strategic move of L'Oréal acquiring The Body Shop, and the later move of Natura buying The Body Shop from L'Oréal. Use the BCG matrix to categorize both brands and evaluate the strategic value of the move for each.

5. Look up the most recent sustainability or responsibility report of Reliance: use your analysis to decide whether the company's social and environmental activities are aligned with any of their strategic business units' strategizing.

6. Identify any questionable strategizing in this case:

   P&G, Unilever, and Henkel held talks to implement an industry-wide programme to improve the environmental performance of detergents. Management agreed to shrink the amount of packaging used but to keep prices unchanged, despite saving materials, and later to collectively raise prices [80].

Acting

7. Rewrite the mission statement of a company of your choice, integrating social and environmental considerations. Then rewrite the strategic objectives based on the new statement.

8. Draw an activity map of a responsible management practice of your choice.

9. Design a future strategic management approach. What would be the top three professional strategizing principles?

Interacting

10. Read or listen to an interview with a sustainability strategy practitioner, such as Melissa Vernon, Director of Sustainable Strategy at Interface.

11. Put yourself in the shoes of the stakeholders of a questionable strategizing practice such as competitor bashing, predatory pricing, or monopolizing. Who are the main stakeholders of the practice chosen, and what (dis) value do they get out of it?

12. Look up the business model section in the annual report of a FTSE100 company. Together with a partner compare how the company integrates ethics, responsibility, or sustainability into the business model. Discuss how they could improve.

Being

13. What kinds of strategic practices would you personally consider unfair, or as contradicting your values?

14. Do you think your personality lends itself to collaborative or competitive strategizing?

15. Imagine you have just started your dream job. How would you strategize in this job? What would be a typical strategic goal? What kind of strategies would you formulate and why?

Becoming

16. Develop and execute a set of coordinated actions (a strategy) for a personal goal of yours. Reflect on the issues you might encounter in this personal strategizing.

17. Do you think you've got what it takes to be a professional strategist? How could you develop your professional strategizing skills further?

18. Conduct a SWOT analysis of a personal career goal and formulate a strategy to achieve it.

SOURCE: Adapted from [81]

PIONEER INTERVIEW
MARK KRAMER

INTERVIEWER: OLIVER LAASCH

Courtesy of Mark Kramer

Mark Kramer has pioneered the topic of strategy and society together with the strategic management guru Michael Porter. They developed immensely influential ideas, among them 'shared value'.

Integrating strategy and society. Well, I certainly do not think we are there yet. I would say that Michael [Porter] and I have both been pleased and surprised by the resonance that the shared value idea has had all over the world, and by the number of companies that have managed to make this thinking part of their strategies. So there is certainly a movement.

Shared value becomes the strategy, but as we talked about before, it is not just strategy. We also need new tools around measurement and decision-making. Because of the social dimension that we are adding, the strategy is not well measured or evaluated by the existing corporate strategy tools.

The need to go beyond shared value. I certainly think that shared value does not replace sustainability or corporate responsibility. There are things that companies should and must do to be responsible citizens of the world. Those things are not necessarily going to contribute to their profit or to their competitive advantage. Those are the true areas of corporate responsibility. And they remain even if they do not create shared value.

Scaling up! So we think shared value represents a new and important opportunity for business and a new and tremendously important opportunity for society by bringing global corporations to the table to help address social problems, not just by writing cheques to non-profits or NGOs, but by actually using their capabilities in a profit-seeking way to solve social issues. We're able to generate a level of scale and impact that very, very few NGOs are able to generate. The scale of impact the companies can have when they decide that they want to solve a social issue, not just to be nice or to look good but because it is in the company's economic interest to do so, is tremendously powerful, and this is why Michael [Porter] and I are so hopeful about the positive impact that shared value can have in the world.

(Continued)

Embedding across management functions. One quick thought, as we have worked with companies, we have seen that moving towards a shared value strategy is a journey that takes quite a few years. It is really a different way of thinking at every level. It is not just the CEO thinking differently about strategy. It has to influence the behaviour of people in the operating level and people within the operations of each division.

And so what we have seen is that for this really to influence the thinking and really become embedded in the company takes not just one project or two projects or a shared value department that is off to the side like CSR often is. It is rather an executive education process that goes throughout the company – a lot of internal communication. We have to begin to look at the social dimension of people's performance and how we compensate and reward and promote them if we are serious about this. It really requires every operation within the company from procurement to HR, from marketing to research and development, to be undertaken with a different lens. However, maybe it takes years for a company really to embed this approach in all aspects of its operations.

QUESTIONS

1. Do you think professional strategizing always has to achieve shared value? Why (not)?

2. What limitations to shared value does Mark describe?

3. Mark stresses the need to assess people's social performance. How could that be done? What practices and actions do you consider promising?

4. Why does Mark describe companies as one of the most promising organization types for scaling up?

PROFESSIONAL PROFILE
CANSU GEDIK

My name is **Cansu Gedik,** and I am a project coordinator at Mikado Consulting, a Turkey-based consultancy that crafts innovative solutions for sustainable development.

(Continued)

Strategizing practice. My responsibilities include building and executing the corporate responsibility and sustainability strategy, planning and preparing the sustainability reports, and development and coordination of community investment projects of the companies we work with. I have been coordinating the 'Business and Human Rights Capacity Development Programme', a one-year project consisting of training and mentoring for participant companies funded by the Consulate General of the Netherlands in Turkey.

A day at work. Strategic planning for sustainability takes a significant amount of my time, especially when we have new clients, when we revise our yearly plans with our existing clients, and when we embark on new projects. I assist and coordinate the processes and activities that serve the corporate responsibility strategies of the companies we work with. Planning and content management for sustainability reports of our clients take a considerable amount of time and effort, especially in the first six months of the year. I prepare training content for our corporate training. I carry out research on various subjects related to responsible management and sustainability. I follow the global corporate responsibility and sustainability agenda and share relevant information with our stakeholders on our blog and social media accounts.

Theory for practice. While consulting companies in responsible management, we carry out a very similar process to the strategizing process introduced in this chapter. With the Sustainability Committees of our clients, we revise the vision and mission statements and prepare a sustainability policy statement. We realize SWOT analysis, taking both internal and external environments into account and decide on the strategy and a set of actions. We guide them in implementing the strategy. This involves both 'hardwiring' and 'softwiring'. Softwiring is especially important since it enables a change in corporate culture. In order to achieve this transformation, we provide training, introduce a sustainability approach to leadership mechanisms, encourage employee volunteering, etc. We constantly review, evaluate, and improve the strategy.

QUESTIONS

1. What elements of Cansu's job profile relate to which concepts in this chapter, and how?

2. Do you think Cansu has an interesting job? What would you change in her personal sphere of influence to become an even better strategist?

TRUE STORY

STRATEGIZING FOR THE GREATER GOOD

EDITED BY ALEXANDRA LEONOR BARRUETA-SACKSTEDER

My name is Saalih, and I am a 23-year-old aspiring social entrepreneur. I have always had the desire to learn and help people along the way, particularly the neglected ones. As some of my colleagues would say, the only thing that gets me excited usually entails me assisting people in need with something. Throughout the years I have been involved with several social projects and events to help people, I have managed several youth social organizations in different countries like Cyprus, Zambia and Tanzania. However, managing a newly initiated social enterprise was the epitome of my management career so far. Throughout this experience I learned about how management requires well calculated actions and strategies.

The 'short' of it. With the shortage of sustainable energy and electricity distribution in sub-Saharan Africa, my team and I came up with an innovative solution to generate a sustainable alternative for power generation by simply using the waste residues we collect in the communities. We founded Green Energy (GE) with the goal of assisting people in rural counties to get affordable and reliable access to power/electricity. The Enterprise was founded by four core team members and the team grew from then on. However, it is important to highlight that the founders of this enterprise had very minimal experience when it came to strategically leading a social enterprise of such calibre. The founding team were mostly driven by their desire for change in their communities. But little did they know that the experience of managing a social venture would be a rollercoaster ride compared to the conventional management positions they held before.

(Continued)

CEO who? In 2016, the founding team created a leadership policy defining each person's role. From the start, the team made a unanimous agreement to let Joe be the Chief Executive Officer (CEO). Joe was very passionate, but his enthusiasm for the organization proved to be lacking as GE wasn't making any progress in the technological aspect of the company: they weren't acquiring the necessary machinery and were unsure of where and how to set up new plants. It was discussed that Joe didn't have the necessary background in engineering related to gas and energy and in 2017 an annual meeting was held to check the progress of GE. It was during this meeting that Joe immediately agreed to step down for the good of the company and Jenny took over as the new CEO.

With a new CEO, the company experienced a lot of progress, particularly in the technical area. The first biogas plant was built in Kitwe and began a process of hiring key employees to share GE's vision with. Although things were improving, this new CEO didn't have an engineering background either and questions began arising regarding the complexity of the industry GBEC was dealing with and her lack of expertise in the field.

Making a decision. Upon the company's founding, goals had been strategically road mapped, goals that were not being met at the expected rate. This in part was due to the fact that the electricity and gas sector requires technical knowledge and experience to manage a growing firm in this field and so it was suggested that management outsource the CEO position and hire someone with more technical know-how and an engineering background, and could therefore help GE achieve its set goals.

Based on the progress reports submitted by Jenny for 2017 and 2018, at 2019's general meeting, the founders had to choose to go with Jenny's philosophy of learning during the process and entrust her with the position as she has proven that she gets things done, regardless of the pace, or the founders will be forced to choose an external but experienced manager to bring fast impact to the company and the target communities in general.

Growth strategies. From the founding, GE underwent two major managerial phases with two different managers using entirely different styles. Under Joe's lead, and considering they were a new market entrant, GE adopted entry strategies operating on 'shy' mode with the goal of observing market flow, keeping prices down and studying existing or potential competition, but finances weren't great and it was clear that they were missing a piece of the puzzle. Funds were difficult to acquire, forcing Joe to strategize ways to bring in investment, holding events and inviting public figures to contribute by being ambassadors of change, for instance. Under Jenny's management GBEC went through a paradigmatic shift in growth strategies as she leaned more into an aggressive approach where she was looking to set the price of the biogas produced and units of electricity sold to existing products in the market. When scepticism arose on this particular approach applied, she responded by saying, 'If we think what we are offering isn't on par with the already existing products, then we will be failing our own vision'.

(Continued)

Looking at both strategies implemented, I can identify a few shortcomings, but I am still sceptical as to which one was the right approach for GE out of the two.

QUESTIONS

1. Prepare a SWOT analysis for the decision at hand. How could the resource-based view help us to better understand what is going on here?

2. Do you think 'failing our own vision' is an option in this case? What would it imply? What's the problem?

3. Throughout the short history of this company, what was good strategizing, what not so good?

4. What role do different people play in the strategizing process described here?

DIGGING DEEPER: DELIBERATE, UNREALIZED, AND EMERGENT TYPES OF STRATEGIES

Strategizing is often idealised as a linear progression of crafting a strategy, implementing it, and reaping the benefits. However, in reality this ideal is rarely reached. For instance, crafted strategies may be unrealistic, or environmental forces may not allow them to be realized. Henry Mintzberg [16] offers a more realistic and diverse set of strategy paths, which are illustrated in Figure 13.11 and listed below:

1. Intended strategies that get realized; these may be called **deliberate strategies**

2. Intended strategies that do not get realized, perhaps because of unrealistic expectations, misjudgements about the environment, or changes during implementation; these may be called **unrealized strategies**

3. Realized strategies that were never intended, perhaps because they weren't intended from the outset or perhaps because, as in 2. they were displaced along the way; these may be called **emergent strategies**

In particular, in the volatile era of 'grand crises' in which we are living [82], having a more flexible, responsive, less top-down, and more ad hoc way of strategizing is crucial for success [83].

FIGURE 13.11   Types of strategies

SOURCE: Adapted from Mintzberg [16], Credit: Slidemodel.com

POINTERS

This excerpt from Henry Mintzberg's seminal work on different patterns in strategy formation [16] calls our attention to how important the unplanned types of strategizing can be in practice. It serves as a counter-narrative to this chapter's simplified presentation of apparently plannable and controllable strategizing practice.

WORKSHEET

SWOT ANALYSIS

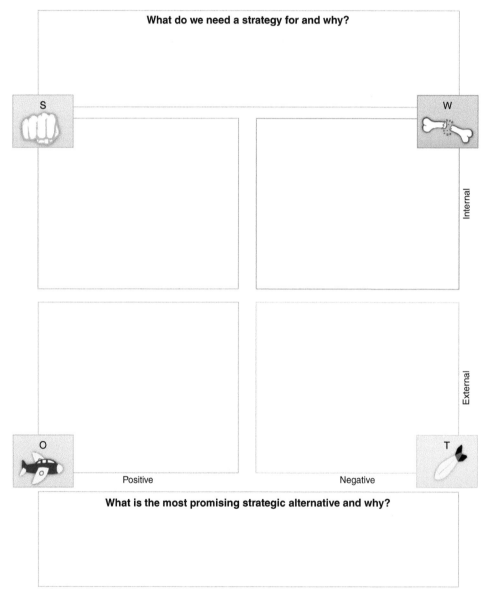

CREDIT: Slidemodel.com

POINTERS

One way of filling in this worksheet is from top to bottom, starting with the purpose of the strategy, then the situational analysis (the SWOT), leading to the identification of a promising strategy.

REFERENCES

1. Office for National Statistics. Data and analysis from Census 2021: Climate change insights, business and transport, UK: February 2023. www.ons.gov.uk/economy/environmentalaccounts/articles/climatechangeinsightsuk/february2023 Last accessed August 15 2023.

2. Premium. Oekologie. http://galerie.premium-cola.de/betriebssystem/oekologie Published 2020. Accessed March 11 2020.

3. Premium-Cola. Geschichte. http://galerie.premium-cola.de/betriebssystem/system-geschichte Published 2020. Accessed March 12 2020.

4. Beha S. Premium Cola: Von Grund auf anders. https://newmanagement.haufe.de/organisation/gleicher-lohn-keine-40-stunden-woche-konsensdemokratie-premium-cola Published 2019. Accessed March 11 2020.

5. Luedicke MK, Husemann KC, Furnari S, Ladstaetter F. Radically open strategizing: How the premium cola collective takes open strategy to the extreme. *Long Range Planning.* 2017, 50(3): 371–384.

6. Premium-Cola. KMU-Projekt. http://galerie.premium-cola.de/betriebssystem/kmu-projekt Published 2020. Accessed March 12 2020.

7. Premium-Cola. Soziales. http://galerie.premium-cola.de/betriebssystem/soziales Published 2020. Accessed March 12 2020.

8. Premium-Cola. 06. Modul 'Handschlag'. http://galerie.premium-cola.de/betriebssystem/soziales/193-modul-handschlag Published 2020. Accessed March 12 2020.

9. Premium-Cola. Schutz. http://galerie.premium-cola.de/betriebssystem/schutz Published 2020. Accessed March 12 2020.

10. Freeman ER, Laasch O. Pioneer interview with Edward Freeman. In: Laasch O, Conaway RN, eds. *Principles of responsible management: Glocal sustainability, responsibility, ethics.* Mason: Cengage, 2015, p. 106.

11. Oppenheim J, Bonini S, Bielak D, Kehm T, Lacey P. *Shaping the new rules of competition: UN Global Compact Participant Mirror.* New York: McKinsey & Company; 2007.

12. Porter M, Kramer M. Philanthropy's new agenda: Creating value. *Harvard Business Review.* 1999, 77(6): 121–130.

13. Porter M, Kramer M. Strategy and society: The link between competitive advantage and corporate social responsibility. *Harvard Business Review.* 2006, 84(12): 78–92.

14. Porter M, Kramer M. The competitive advantage of corporate philanthropy. *Harvard Business Review.* 2002, 80(12): 56–68.

15. Ansoff IH. Strategic issue management. *Strategic Management Journal.* 1980, 1(2): 131–148.

16. Mintzberg H. Patterns in strategy formation. *Management Science.* 1978, 24(9): 934–948.

17. Hendry J, Seidl D. The structure and significance of strategic episodes: Social systems theory and the routine practices of strategic change. *Journal of Management Studies.* 2003, 40(1): 175–196.

18. Hitt MA, Ireland RD, Hoskisson RE. *Strategic management: Competitiveness and globalization.* Mason: Thomson Southwestern, 2007.

19. Boons F, Laasch O, Dierksmeier C. Assembling organizational practices: The evolving humanistic business model of Allsafe. 6th Asian SME Conference, Tokyo, 2018.

20. Christ KL, Burritt RL, Varsei M. Coopetition as a potential strategy for corporate sustainability. *Business Strategy and the Environment.* 2017, 26(7): 1029–1040.

21. Alliance Ventures. Investing globally in next-generation mobility. www.alliance-2022.com/ventures Published 2020. Accessed March 14 2020.

22. Pohle G, Hittner J. *Attaining sustainable growth through corporate social responsibility.* Somers: IBM Institute for Business Value, 2008.

23. Hahn T, Figge F, Pinkse J, Preuss L. Trade-offs in corporate sustainability: You can't have your cake and eat it. *Business Strategy and the Environment.* 2010, 19(4): 217–229.

24. King ML. Jr. I have a dream. *American Rhetoric.* www.americanrhetoric.com/speeches/mlkihaveadream.htm Published 1963. Accessed June 8 2011.

25. Elkington J. *Cannibals with forks: The triple bottom line of 21st century business.* Gabriola Island: New Society Publishers, 1998.

26. Ben and Jerry's mission statement. *Ben & Jerry's.* www.benjerry.com/activism/mission-statement Published 2011. Accessed June 28 2011.

27. Freeman RE. *Strategic management: A stakeholder approach.* Cambridge: Cambridge University Press, 2010.
28. Freeman RE. Stakeholder theory. In: School DB, ed. *Business Roundtable: Institute for Corporate Ethics,* 2009. Retrieved August 23, 2013.
29. Hill CWL, Jones GR. *Strategic management: An integrated approach.* Boston, MA: Houghton Mifflin, 2001.
30. David FR. *Strategic management: Concepts.* Upper Saddle River, NJ: Pearson, 2007.
31. The plan: Small actions, big differences. *Unilever sustainable living plan.* www.sustainable-living.unilever.com/the-plan Published 2010. Accessed June 6 2011.
32. Collis DJ, Montgomery CA. *Corporate strategy: Resources and the scope of the firm.* New York: Irwin/McGraw-Hill, 1997.
33. Humphreys J. The vision thing. *Sloan Management Review.* 2004, 45(4): 96.
34. Porter M. *Competitive strategy: Techniques for analysing industries and competitors.* New York: The Free Press, 1980.
35. Barney J. Firm resources and sustained competitive advantage. *Journal of Management.* 1991, 17(1): 99–120.
36. Saffo P. Six rules for effective forecasting. *Harvard Business Review.* 2007, 85(7/8): 122.
37. Taylor A. Toyota: The birth of the Prius. *CNN Money.* http://money.cnn.com/2006/02/17/news/companies/mostadmired_fortune_toyota/index.htm Published 2006. Accessed June 12 2011.
38. Galbraith K. Companies add chief sustainability officers. *The New York Times.* 2009.
39. Vernon M. From supply chain to business development: Sustainability as business advantage at InterfaceFLOR. *Net Impact.* www.netimpact.org/displaycommon.cfm?an=1&subarticlenbr=3720 Published 2011. Accessed June 12 2011.
40. Wernerfelt B. A resource-based view of the firm: Ten years after. *Strategic Management Journal.* 1995, 16: 171–174.
41. Wernerfelt B. A resource based view of the firm. *Strategic Management Review.* 1984, 5: 171–180.
42. Thompson AA, Strickland AJ, Gamble JE. *Crafting and executing strategy: The quest for competitive advantage.* New York: McGraw-Hill, 2005.
43. Mata FJ, Fuerst WL, Barney JB. Information technology and sustained competitive advantage: A resource-based perspective. *MIS Quarterly.* 1995, 19(4): 494–505.
44. Musk E. All our patents belong to you. www.tesla.com/blog/all-our-patent-are-belong-you 2014.
45. Nangyuan Island. *Nangyuan Island Dive Resort.* 2010. https://www.nangyuan.com/
46. Lubin DA, Esty DC. The sustainability imperative. *Harvard Business Review.* 2010, 88(5): 42–50.
47. Waddock SA, Bodwell C, Graves SB. Responsibility: The new business imperative. *Academy of Management Executive.* 2002, 47(1): 132–147.
48. Hamel G, Prahalad CK. Strategic intent. *Harvard Business Review.* 1989, 67(3): 63–76.
49. Morrison A, Wensley R. Boxing up or boxed in? A short history of the Boston Consulting Group Share/Growth Matrix. *Journal of Marketing Management.* 1991, 7(2): 105–129.
50. Wind shear: GE wins, Vestas loses in wind-power market race. *Environmental capital.* http://blogs.wsj.com/environmentalcapital/2009/03/25/wind-shear-ge-wins-vestas-loses-in-wind-power-market-race Published 2008. Accessed May 29 2011.
51. Wind turbines. *GE Energy.* www.ge-energy.com/products_and_services/products/wind_turbines/index.jsp Published 2011. Accessed May 29 2011.
52. International wind power market update 2010. *BTM Consult.* www.btm.dk/public/Selected_PPT-WMU2010.pdf Published 2010.Accessed May 29 2011.
53. Porter M. *Competitive advantage: Creating and sustaining superior performance.* New York: The Free Press, 1985.
54. Porter M. What is strategy? *Harvard Business Review.* 1996, 74(6): 61–78.
55. *Eco-efficiency: Creating more value with less impact.* Geneva: World Business Council for Sustainable Development, 2000.
56. Barbier EB, Markandya A, Pearce DW. Environmental sustainability and cost-benefit analysis. *Environment and Planning.* 1990, 22(9): 1259–1266.
57. Wal-Mart unveils 'Packaging scorecard' to suppliers. Walmart Corporate. 2006.
58. Packaging progress. Walmart Corporate. 2010.

59. Arzoumanian M. Walmart updates scorecard status. Packaging-online.com, 2008.

60. Maclay K. UC Berkeley study estimates Wal-Mart employment policies cost California taxpayers $86 million a year. *UC Berkeley News.* 2004.

61. Dube A, Jacobs K. *The hidden cost of Wal-Mart jobs.* Berkeley: UK Berkeley Labor Center, 2004.

62. Diversity and inclusion. Dell: About us. 2011.

63. Forsythe J. Leading with diversity. *The New York Times.* www.nytimes.com/marketing/jobmarket/diversity/dell.html Published 2004. Accessed May 31 2011.

64. Laasch O. An actor-network perspective on business models: How 'being responsible' led to incremental, but pervasive change. *Long Range Planning.* 2018, 52(3): 406–426.

65. Wit MD, Wade M, Schouten E. Hardwiring and softwiring corporate responsibility: A vital combination. *Corporate Governance.* 2006, 5(4): 491–505.

66. Neilson GL, Martin KL, Powers E. The secrets to successful strategy execution. *Harvard Business Review.* 2008, 86(6): 61–70.

67. Laasch O, Flores U. Implementing profitable CSR: The CSR 2.0 business compass. In: *Responsible business: How to manage a CSR strategy successfully.* Chichester: John Wiley & Sons, 2010, pp. 289–309.

68. King H. The view from the C-suite: P&G's Len Sauers. *GreenBizcom.* www.greenbiz.com/blog/2010/06/28/view-c-suite-pgs-len-sauers. Published 2010. Accessed June 3 2011.

69. Huston L, Sakkab N. Connect and develop: Inside Procter & Gamble's new model for innovation. *Harvard Business Review.* 2006, 84(3): 58–66.

70. Ma M. How 'Open' should innovation be? *Psychology Today.* www.psychologytoday.com/blog/the-tao-innovation/200903/how-open-should-innovation-be Published 2009. Accessed June 3 2011.

71. Werther WB, Chandler D. *Strategic corporate social responsibility: Stakeholders in a global environment.* Thousand Oaks, CA: Sage, 2010.

72. Luijkenaar A, Spinley K. *The emergence of the chief sustainability officer: From compliance manager to business partner.* Amsterdam: Heidrick & Struggles, 2007.

73. Cha S, Ahn S, Suh J, Yoo B, Kim H. *Proposal: Rainwater harvesting at Starbucks.* Seoul: Seoul National University, Graduate School of Civil and Environmental Engineering, 2008.

74. C.A.F.E. Practices generic evaluation guidelines 2.0. *Starbucks Corporate.* www.scscertified.com/retail/docs/CAFE_GUI_EvaluationGuidelines_V2.0_093009.pdf Published 1997. Accessed May 31 2011.

75. Retail careers. *Starbucks Corporate.* www.starbucks.com/career-center/retail-positions Published 2011. Accessed May 31 2011.

76. Laasch O. Beyond the purely commercial business model: Organizational value logics and the heterogeneity of sustainability business models. *Long Range Planning.* 2018, 51(1): 158–183.

77. Osterwalder A, Pigneur Y. *Business model generation.* Chichester: Wiley, 2010.

78. Casadesus-Masanell R, Ricart JE. From strategy to business models and onto tactics. *Long Range Planning.* 2010, 43(2): 195–215.

79. Laasch O, Conaway R. *Responsible business: The textbook for management learning, competence, innovation.* Sheffield: Greenleaf, 2016.

80. Wearden G. Unilever and Procter & Gamble fined £280m for price fixing. *Guardian.* www.guardian.co.uk/business/2011/apr/13/unilever-procter-and-gamble-price-fixing-european-commission Published 2011. Accessed May 29 2011.

81. Laasch, O., Moosmayer, D., & Antonacopoulou, E. P. (2023). The interdisciplinary responsible management competence framework: An integrative review of ethics, responsibility, and sustainability competences. *Journal of Business Ethics, 187,* 733–757.

82. Laasch, O., Ryazanova, O., & Wright, A. L. Lingering COVID and looming grand crises: Envisioning business schools' business model transformations. *Academy of Management Learning & Education.* 2022, 21(1), 1–6.

83. Haslam, S., & Shenoy, B. *Strategic decision making: A discovery-led approach to critical choices in turbulent times.* London: Kogan Page Publishers, 2018.

CHAPTER 14

INNOVATING

OLIVER LAASCH AND BARBARA RIBEIRO

LEARNING GOALS

1. Explore innovative management and the management mode of innovation
2. Get to know different types of innovations, from innovating practices to systems, from commercial to social innovation
3. Understand what makes responsible innovation through the innovation process and outcomes

FACT FOR THOUGHT

While agreeing that innovation is a team effort, only 15 per cent of top managers consider their teams as innovation leaders, 28 per cent consider them as 'advancers', while over half considered them as innovation 'implementers' or 'beginners' [1].

SPOTLIGHT

SPOTLIGHT

OPEN PATENTING AND OTHER KINDS OF CRAZY AT TESLA
BY LAYLA MOHAMMED

'FANUC Robot Assembly Demo for Elon at Tesla' by jurvetson is licensed under CC BY 2.0

Imagine for a moment you are Tesla's CEO Elon Musk and have spent billions of US dollars on innovation, research, and development. Luckily, all this is protected by patents so that the competition can't just copy your work and catch up with you too easily. Then one fine day you take to the Tesla Blog and write 'All our patents belong to you.' You state that you will not pursue any lawsuits against those who want to use Tesla's innovative technology in 'good faith' [2]. Doesn't that seem a bit strange? However, what might sound crazy from a commercial point of view, might be the most sane thing to do if you think in terms of environmental sustainability.

Tesla's open patenting practice, a mixture of open innovation and open source, fully aligns with Tesla's mission 'to accelerate the world's transition to sustainable energy' and 'driving the world's transition to electric vehicles' [3]. Open patenting seems necessary to accelerate the development of innovative electric vehicle technologies. Allowing other manufacturers to use Tesla's patents helps foster knowledge within the industry. Additionally, developing a robust electric vehicle market provides Tesla with advantages like boosting the charging infrastructure and technology collaborations. Innovators at Tesla are aware that tackling the global carbon crisis requires cooperative efforts to scale the use of their environmental friendly technologies.

(Continued)

Not only are patenting practices innovative at Tesla, most prominently, their product innovation has manifested itself in a range of electric vehicles even including a truck. There is also the 'immense' manufacturing process innovation, that is Tesla's entirely solar-powered 'gigafactories' [4, 5]. Moving on to the personal transportation practices innovation in progress, namely the plan to sell

'The Tesla Patent Wall at HQ, now set free' by jurvetson is licensed under CC BY 2.0

self-driving vehicles that make their owners some money. Being part of the Tesla fleet, they can be rented out to others while not in use instead of being idly parked in your driveway. Elon Musk also has innovated his personal management control practices: 'I move my desk around to wherever the most important place is for the company and then I sort of maintain a desk there over time to come and check in on things' [6]'

However, not all new and innovative is necessarily 'good' and innovative practices often have a personal dimension. For instance, there is SpaceX, the business model innovation that is Musk's interplanetary 'travel company', pursuing the ultimate goal of setting up a human colony on Mars [7]. Many critics consider SpaceX a vanity project [8] and some, like the author of

this textbook, believe that Musk should rather invest the corresponding money into survival on Earth, rather than building escape routes for the rich and wealthy. Also, Musk's handling of the new acquisition of Twitter (now known as 'X') was widely criticized for the large-scale job losses, the banning of users critcising him, and the rise of hate speech. However, there are also innovative management practices, for instance, when Musk asked his followership on X to vote for him to leave his job as CEO. The answer was he should, and his reply was that he would do so once he had found 'someone foolish enough to take on the job'. (https://www.theguardian.com/commentisfree/2022/dec/20/elon-musk-twitter-ceo-poll)

INNOVATING

'**Innovation**' is the process of bringing something new into the world, through a combination of intellectual and practical ingenuity ... a future-creating activity: by bringing something new into the world, it changes the world itself [9].

As illustrated in Figure 14.1, we are in the middle of two waves of innovation driving and being driven by two parallel industrial revolutions. First, **novelties** like industrial ecology, biomimicry, and circular supply chains are part of the sustainability revolution. These novel solutions are a response to the new normal characterized by pressing societal and environmental issues. Moreover, business management needs to innovate in order to stop being part of the problem by continuously recreating the social and environmental mess humanity is in, a 'great reset' so to say [10]. Secondly, artificial intelligence, virtual reality, and blockchain are novelties that have surged as part of the wave of innovation that has come to be known as the fourth industrial revolution [11]. This means that nowadays being a competent management professional means to engage in **innovation professionally**. It means to be able to both handle high tech as part of the job, and to be able to innovate for ethics, responsibility, and sustainability. It is time to put management's intellectual and practical ingenuity to good work.

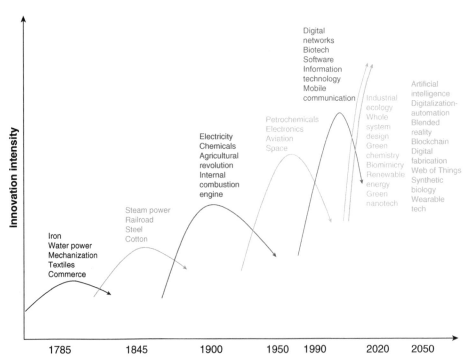

FIGURE 14.1   Waves of innovation and related transformation of management, business, and the economy

SOURCE: adapted from [11–14]

Figure 14.1 presents an overview of topics covered in this chapter. We will first discuss the nuts and bolts of the innovation process. This includes basic elements like novelty exploration and exploitation, as well as the innovation funnel. We will then look at varieties of innovation and different innovation frameworks, such as frugal innovation, traditional R&D management, and workplace innovation. Finally, we will discuss the principal approaches to 'good' innovation, namely social innovation, sustainability-oriented responsible innovation, and innovation ethics.

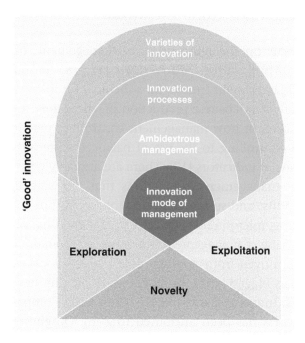

FIGURE 14.2   Mapping the innovating mode of management

THE INNOVATING MODE OF MANAGEMENT

What form does the **innovating mode** of management take? What is the relationship between management and innovation? What are typical practices at this intersection? The innovating mode of management comprises the following three forms:

The innovating mode of management comprises practices related to management innovation, innovative management, and to managing innovation

1. **Innovative management**. Management and managers need to be innovative. Innovativeness and creativity are consistently among the most requested competences in managerial job descriptions. Managing creatively and innovatively means to apply unusual or novel management practices and solutions.

2. **Managing innovation**. Managers often engage in innovation management, be it in the form of creating new products, business models, or developing new

production technologies. In spite of the importance of these three practices related to the innovating mode of management, barely any introduction to a management textbook has an innovation or technology chapter.

3. **Management innovation**. Management guru Gary Hamel suggests that 'Management, like the combustion engine, is a mature technology that must now be reinvented for a new age' [15]. Others like Dan Pink have offered an even more pessimistic outlook suggesting, that 'management is a technology from the 1850s … it's the wrong technology; even if you make it awesome it's the fundamentally wrong technology' [16]. To prove our relevance to today's world and our right to exist, management itself needs to be reinvented.

Management innovation
invention and implementation
of management practices
that depart from the norm

We will now focus on the reinvention of management, one practice at a time through **management innovation** [17, 18]. Prominent examples of mainstream management innovations include, for instance, how Toyota's production and related Japanese production practices took the world of manufacturing by storm, or how management controlling practices moved from purely financial controlling to the use of balanced scorecards with predominantly non-financial indicators [17]. There are arguably even more examples for 'responsible' management innovations that innovate management for ethics, responsibility, and sustainability. Think, for instance, of practices like carbon accounting, microfinance, cause-related marketing, or open hiring.

Consider the case of management innovation at Wahaha, a company that within a decade moved from producing juices for a local school district to becoming China's biggest drink producer [19]. Wahaha has even competed successfully with industry giants like the Coca Cola Company and Pepsico. Much of its success has been attributed to Zong Qinghou's (the company chairman) variety of management innovations. These were mostly incremental in nature, but added up. They used guerrilla marketing techniques, evading urban competitors by focusing on the fragmented rural economy, while common wisdom was to gear marketing practices to the urban centres. Their 'innovation by importation' incremental product innovation practices involved quickly copying competitors' products, but adding an incremental innovation twist to them to draw market demand. Against common custom and a normally hierarchical business culture they kept a flat organizational hierarchy, and did not have VPs, which enabled Zong to stay responsive in China's volatile emergent market. It was also unusual to build a personal relationship directly between CEO and small-scale distributors, in order to foster long-term trust. This supply chain management innovation was connected to a financial management innovation whereby the dealer would pay 10 per cent of their expected revenue upfront and also guaranteeing them additional profit later on [20].

How does one become a (serial) management innovator like Mr. Zong? Figure 14.3 lists and describes the four main necessary practices for management innovators.

AMBIDEXTROUS MANAGEMENT: EXPLORATION AND EXPLOITATION

Zong Qinghou built China's largest soft drinks empire using continuous management innovation.

In this section we will have a close look at the innovation process, including the **exploration** and **exploitation** of novelty and typical challenges. The management mode of innovating requires a varied set of competences related to the *creation* of innovation, what we call 'exploration', as well as the *use and dissemination* of innovation, its 'exploitation'.

Exploration
practices relate to searching novelties and developing innovations

Exploitation
practices relate to using a novelty and generating value through it

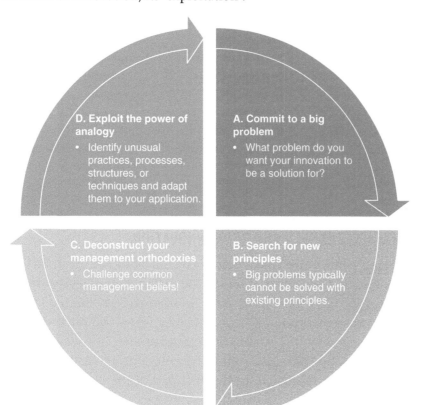

FIGURE 14.3 The process of management innovation
SOURCE: Adapted from [20, 21]

Being able to do both has been described as the '**ambidexterity**' [23–25] that innovation practitioners need, to be competent to explore novelties, and to exploit them, typically for commercial gain or some type of social or environmental value creation. Becoming ambidextrous in innovation requires developing a complex mix of entrepreneurial, leadership, and administrational competences [24, 26]. For instance an ambidextrous leader would need to be able to both engage in transformational leadership to explore novelty and in transactional leadership to exploit it [27]. Managers need to be able to work in and integrate structures and processes that allow for both novelty exploration and exploitation [28]. However, integrating them too closely may also lead to 'cross-contamination', where you get stuck in the middle with a dysfunctional mixture of exploration and exploitation that may lead to varieties of innovation failures [29]. Table 14.1 provides an overview of the distinct characteristics of exploration and exploitation through management [23].

TABLE 14.1   Ambidextrous management integrating innovation exploration and exploitation

	Innovation exploration management	Innovation exploitation management
Strategic intent	Innovation, growth	Cost, profit
Critical tasks	Adaptability, new products	Operations, efficiency
Novelty type	Breakthrough innovation	Incremental innovation
Competencies	Entrepreneurial	Operational
Structural design	Adaptive, loose	Formal, mechanistic
Controls and rewards approach	Milestones, growth	Margins, productivity
Culture promoted	Risk taking, speed, flexibility, experimentation	Efficiency, low risk, quality, customers
Leadership role	Visionary, involved	Authoritative, top down

SOURCE: Adapted from [23]

EXPLORATION: FUNNELS AND OPEN INNOVATION

The thinking behind the **innovation funnel** is to control that there are continuously ideas and innovations in the making, at all levels of maturity. As illustrated in Figure 14.4, ideas, a mix of internal and external knowledge, start with a problematization process, whereby issues and opportunities that could be addressed by innovations are identified and assessed. In the subsequent ideation phase, potential innovative solutions are searched, which are then developed and evaluated. In this first part of the process the emphasis is on exploration, shifting to exploitation in the second part. Next, feasible innovations are implemented and commercialized so that finally they can be used and generate actual value. One of the main goals is that at any given point in time, there are innovations at different stages in the funnel, so that it becomes a pipeline of innovations that continuously transform problems into ideas into value-generating innovations.

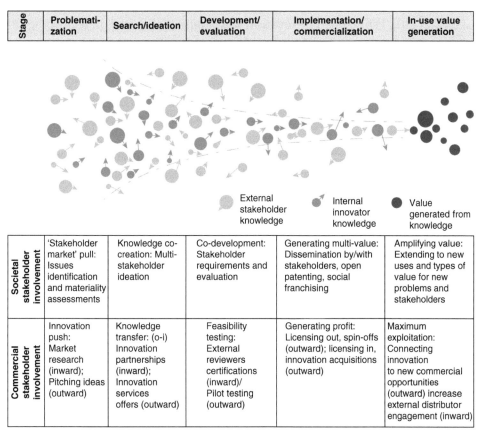

Stage	Problemati- zation	Search/ideation	Development/ evaluation	Implementation/ commercialization	In-use value generation
Societal stakeholder involvement	'Stakeholder market' pull: Issues identification and materiality assessments	Knowledge co-creation: Multi-stakeholder ideation	Co-development: Stakeholder requirements and evaluation	Generating multi-value: Dissemination by/with stakeholders, open patenting, social franchising	Amplifying value: Extending to new uses and types of value for new problems and stakeholders
Commercial stakeholder involvement	Innovation push: Market research (inward); Pitching ideas (outward)	Knowledge transfer: (o-i) Innovation partnerships (inward); Innovation services offers (outward)	Feasibility testing: External reviewers certifications (inward)/ Pilot testing (outward)	Generating profit: Licensing out, spin-offs (outward); licensing in, innovation acquisitions (outward)	Maximum exploitation: Connecting innovation to new commercial opportunities (outward) increase external distributor engagement (inward)

FIGURE 14.4   The innovation funnel of novelty exploration

SOURCE: adapted from [29–33]; CREDIT: Slidemodel.com

The funnel in Figure 14.4 has open boundaries. While business innovation in the past was very much a 'closed' process happening inside companies, mostly in the R&D department, innovation is now predominantly an **open innovation**, involving knowledge from inside and outside company boundaries [35]. It is a distributed type of innovation happening in interaction between varieties of innovation actors and stakeholders [36, 37] throughout an innovation ecosystem [38, 39]. If innovators choose to actively engage not only commercial actors (e.g. customers, suppliers, competitors), but also a wide variety of societal stakeholders (e.g. NGOs, community members, government agencies) [40], innovation funnels can become a powerful means of generating value, addressing both societal problems and those of the planet.

Open innovation
a distributed innovation process emphasizing knowledge flows across organizational boundaries, both inbound and outbound

Open innovation can be a tool for managers in companies of all sizes, inside and outside research and development roles [41]. For instance, social media are a powerful means of cost effectively tapping into external knowledge and passing on inside knowledge to external stakeholders for their innovation activities [30]. While open innovation was originally focused on technological products and processes innovation [33], it has also shown its value in different innovations, such as business models [42] and practices [43]. Figure 14.5 is an illustration of how innovators may choose from different modes of open innovation [34], and different innovation search paths [44]. Core questions to ask when configuring open innovation are:

1. Which **parts of the innovation funnel** do you want to open up (e.g. problematization and ideation might be open, while you might close development and evaluation, or vice versa)?

2. How big **a variety of and number of innovation partners** do you want to work with [34]?

3. **How far** will you search to access external knowledge (e.g. your own industry and home market, or beyond)?

4. Will you choose **experiential** (action-centred) **or cognitive** (thought-centred) novelty **search heuristics** [44]?

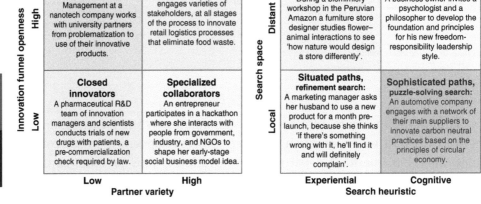

FIGURE 14.5   Configurations of open innovation

SOURCE LEFT: adapted from [34]; SOURCE RIGHT: adapted from [44]

EXPLOITATION: INNOVATION DIFFUSION, IMPLEMENTATION, AND USE

Absorptive capacity
the ability to recognize the value of new knowledge and to use it for the generation of value

Absorptive capacity was originally focused on the generation of commercial value [45] and on dynamically improving the strategic position [46] of managers' own organizations. This may mean, for instance, improving one's competitiveness through a novel production method or generating revenue by introducing an innovative product to the market. However, for absorptive capacity as a competence of responsible managers [47], we understand value additionally to include many types of value for internal and external stakeholders. Imagine, for instance, an ordinary commercial bank that, due to its managers' high absorptive capacity, is able to 'absorb' the novel practice of microfinance into their operations. Further, imagine this bank's operations management was able to integrate microfinance into their mobile banking app and this way give access to banking services to millions of poor people in rural areas. While the bank might not gain from this commercially, they generate social value through their absorptive capacity. Increased absorptive capacity requires four main sub-competences [46]:

1. **Knowledge acquisition**. The ability to identify and acquire valuable new knowledge

2. **Assimilation**. The ability to interpret, comprehend, and learn from new knowledge

3. **Transformation**. The ability to integrate new knowledge into existing processes and practices

4. **Exploitation**.[1] The ability to build new knowledge into a new device (e.g. a new product, service, process, practice) that generates value

High levels of absorptive capacity will help managers and their organizations to excel in innovation exploitation, centred on the application, dissemination, and use of an innovation.

Figure 14.6 integrates several main concepts that help us understand the exploitation process. The basis of the figure is the bell-curve that expresses the types of adopters (also users or customers) of innovations, their numbers and sequence [48].

For instance, we see that the very first adopter groups are innovators themselves and that this group accounts for roughly 2.5 per cent of the overall number of potential adopters of an innovation. Adopters in

While insects are an excellent innovative food from a sustainability and nutritional angle, mainstream adoption around the world is still thwarting the growth of the business of insect farming for human consumption.

'File:Everbruggen 20151115 5673 (22514085983).jpg' by Erwin Verbruggen from Amsterdam, The Netherlands is licensed under CC BY-SA 2.0

---

[1]Note that exploitation in the absorptive capacity context is understood somewhat more narrowly than the wider definition we suggested earlier on in this section.

this group have a profile characterized as that of a 'technologist', someone who knows and deeply understands the innovation's qualities, and can understand early-stage flaws and how they can be fixed. The figure also highlights two types of common challenges.

1.   There is a **chasm** between the visionary early adopters and the pragmatic early majority. Crossing the chasm requires a substantial shift in managing and marketing the innovation's adoption [49].

2.   There is also the **innovator's dilemma** [50], namely whether management should keep focusing on exploiting an 'old innovation' once it is approaching maturity in adoption, or if it should instead refocus on a new, potentially disruptive, innovation to its own market. The dilemma is that the former brings the advantage of maximizing the immediate exploitation of the value generation potential of the old innovation, while the latter holds the promise of participating in the exploitation of a future innovation. Conversely, the former comes with the risk of another company disrupting exploitation of the current innovation, while the latter bears the risk of missing out on exploitation of the old innovation while backing a future innovation that might well fail to disrupt the industry and market.

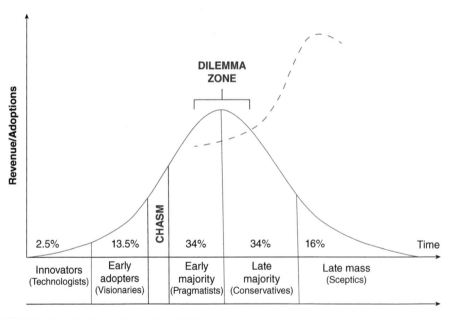

FIGURE 14.6   Dynamics of innovation adoption and diffusion
SOURCE: Adapted from [47–49]

Particularly, for disruptive or 'flashy' innovations the hype cycle illustrated in Figure 14.7 provides invaluable insights [51]. The hype cycle has been used to map where on the cycle innovations are, from block chain and cryptocurrencies to lab-grown meat, and carbon innovations like carbon insetting. In a nutshell, the hype cycle describes the relationship between an innovation's potential and its actual capacity as it develops. While actual capacity grows as the innovation is improved over time, it is first overtaken by inflated expectations of what it can or could do to change, or even save the world. That's the hype. As the limitations of the innovation become apparent, expectations fall rapidly, typically even below the innovation's actual capacity to generate value. Then begins the road to recovery when innovators' main task is simultaneously to improve the innovation's capacity and to rebuild adopters' expectations until these match each other on the plateau of productivity.

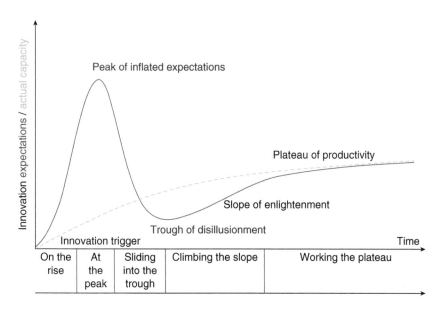

FIGURE 14.7 The hype cycle
SOURCE: Adapted from [50, 51]

The hype cycle can help us to understand the different dynamics in responsible and sustainable management. An interesting example is the innovative management accounting practice of carbon labelling, whereby the amount of carbon emission a product has generated throughout its supply chain is communicated on its packaging. Carbon labelling was at first hyped in the sustainability management community for its potential to revolutionize sustainable consumption, to influence customers' environmental purchasing behaviour such that there would be a massive decrease in carbon emissions. However, then consumers 'didn't quite get it', and only a few industry leaders adopted it. This led to disillusionment and major adopters, like the retail chain Tesco which had pledged to label all of their products, dropped the practice [53]. However, carbon labelling is now on the road to recovery, possibly soon entering the plateau stage where expectations to achieve important CO_2 reductions match its actual potential [54].

The hype cycle has been criticized for not mapping perfectly onto all innovation trajectories in practice [52]. However, it still provides a helpful guide in recognizing what phase the innovation is in, both for innovators and adopters. For instance, it might remind you not to believe the hype! As an innovator, you might dampen the hype early on to pre-empt a potentially deadly drop into the trough of disillusionment. If you have experienced the drop, it might remind you that there is a road to recovery. Imagine, for instance, past disillusionment with photovoltaic solar power which after the initial hype was declared to have failed as being too costly ever to be a viable alternative source of energy. Yet now, after having crept up the slope of enlightenment, solar power around the world has become even cheaper than coal, the previously cheapest mass source of energy [55].

VARIETIES OF INNOVATION

Innovations come in many forms, shapes, and patterns. In this section, we will have a look at these varieties of innovation to map their unique aspects, and how they can be of use to managers in the innovating mode.

FORMS OF NOVELTY

Novelty is at the very core of innovating. The context of novelty may range from something that was previously unknown to the world, an industry, a company, or even a department. Novelty can take many different forms:

- **Invention versus innovation**. Inventions are novelties that have no precedent; they are something new to the world. Innovation, however, typically creates by changing something in existence or putting it to new use. For instance, virtual reality (VR) devices were invented in the late 1970s, while virtual reality phone headsets emerging after 2015 are an innovation based on that past invention.

- **Creativity versus innovation**. Creativity is centred on creating novel ideas, while innovation additionally involves the use and application of that novelty, often as a solution to a particular problem or need. You might have many creative ideas for how to address our planet's looming biodiversity collapse. For instance, the film maker David Attenborough's creative idea that 'maybe we could enable *everyone* to experience and protect the beauty of coral reefs' becomes an innovation through Atlantic Productions' VR Dive where anyone can experience the Great Barrier Reef's biodiversity through a virtual reality dive [56].

- **Radical versus incremental innovations**. There are novelties which have a big impact and big changes, quasi synonymously known as radical, breakthrough, or disruptive innovations [57, 58]. Such innovations may disrupt the dominant existing structures, technologies or industries; they may be game changers for an entire field. For instance, dockless bikesharing business models (e.g. Ofo or Mobike), and carsharing (e.g. Uber or Didi) have disrupted personal transportation in big Chinese cities from privately owned vehicles to access to transportation. They have also disrupted taxi industries around the world. Then there are incremental innovations, minor novelties, changes, upgrades, or improvements. Incremental innovations are often also continuous innovations, a series of many smaller incremental innovations over time. A great example is the continuous incremental innovation of bike sharing business models from municipality-organized fixed stations, to commercial dockless bike-sharing of traditional pedal bikes, on to e-bikes, scooters, and e-scooters [59].

- **Innovation, technology, technical skills, and techniques**. A technology is scientific knowledge converted to a practical problem-solving application. So new technologies are typically also innovations. However, not all innovations are technologies as they do not always involve the application of scientific knowledge. Using and adopting new technologies in management processes, products, or services are important aspects of managerial practice. In addition, managers often have to adjust their practice to wider technological changes in the business environment. Think, for instance, about what blockchain currencies mean for bank management or what virtual online teamwork means for managing a team. A technique refers to specific procedures or methods applied to solve a problem. For instance, prioritization of tasks is a technique used to manage the problem of being short of time. Technical management skills then refer to competences that relate to using the technologies and techniques necessary for getting the management job done.

- **Technology push versus market pull**. If novelty in technology or other innovations drive new market demand, that is called technology push. If, however, an innovation is generated in response to existing market demand, this is called market pull. For instance, in the context of sustainability-oriented innovation, there is as much a technology push, for instance, with new-to-the world innovations like blockchain. However, there is also a market pull for sustainability innovation by the varieties of sustainable consumption movements like Lifestyles for Voluntary Simplicity (LOVOS), Lifestyles of Health and Sustainability (LOHAS), and strategic consumers who 'vote with their buck' for a more sustainable world.

INNOVATION TYPES AND FRAMEWORKS

What do managers innovate and how? The most commonly known framework distinguishing four different types of innovation is the so-called Oslo typology [60]:

1. **Product innovation** 'is the introduction of a good or service that is new or significantly improved with respect to its characteristics or intended uses. This includes significant improvements in technical specifications, components and materials, incorporated software, user friendliness or other functional characteristics.'

2. **Process innovation** 'is the implementation of a new or significantly improved production or delivery method. This includes significant changes in techniques, equipment and/or software.'

3. **Market(ing) innovation** 'is the implementation of a new marketing method involving significant changes in product design or packaging, product placement, product promotion or pricing'.

4. **Organizational innovation** 'is the implementation of a new organisational method in the firm's business practices, workplace organisation or external relations'.

However, as illustrated in Table 14.2, innovation frameworks have different strengths for practice. Some answer questions about 'who innovates where' (actors and place), 'how to innovate' (techniques), 'what to innovate' (objects), and 'what to innovate for' (purpose). The table serves as an overview of topics covered in this chapter. Some of the frameworks, like open innovation and management innovation, have already been covered. Others like innovating for sustainability will be covered later on. Yet others like retrovation or classic R&D management won't be covered in depth, but you are invited to explore them further by using the references in the table.

TABLE 14.2　Varieties of innovation frameworks

	Framework	Description	Example
Actor and place, 'Who innovates where?	**Distributed innovation** [36, 37]	Innovation involving collaboration between different types of actors with different capabilities across locations in an innovation system.	Tesla enabled distributed innovation by allowing anyone to use their patents.
	Open innovation [61]	Emphasizing knowledge flows across organizational boundaries, both inbound and outbound.	Haier's Cosmoplat social network engages Haier's staff and varieties of external stakeholders in collaborative innovation.
	Workplace innovation [62, 63]	Innovation of workplace practices in the workplace by employees and aimed at their own well-being.	At the manufacturer of load securing systems Allsafe, office staff have innovated the practice of supporting production line colleagues whenever production volumes peak (see Chapter 8).
	Job crafting [64, 65]	Employees redesigning their own job and generating a novel job profile.	A chief communications officer focuses on environmental responsibility topics, until his role is changed to chief communications and responsibility officer.
	Innovative work behaviour [66]	Generating, promoting and implementing novelties in the workplace.	Production manager Dan promoted a novel CO_2 literacy programme at *Coronation Street* (see Chapter 2).

	Framework	Description	Example
	Employee-driven innovation [67, 68]	Innovations by varieties of employees across an organization.	The browser gaming company Goldfire Studios blocks out time for employees to work on any side projects on Friday afternoons.
	Management innovation [18, 22]	Managers generating novel management practices.	Bernie Glassman, founder of Greyston Bakery, invented the people management practice of open hiring.
	User/customer innovation [69, 70]	Innovations in products or services generated by its ('lead') users/customers ('prosumers = producers + consumers').	Surfers invented the first skateboard for 'sidewalk surfing' by fixing roller skate wheels to a surfboard a decade before companies started producing them.
Techniques: How to innovate?	**R&D management**	Lab-based innovation, resembling academic research processes and lab-like experimentation.	A pharmaceutical company develops a new vaccination.
	Biomimicry/Bio-inspiration [71, 72]	Innovations following the question, 'How would nature do this?'	Yash Pakka's management (see Chapter 9) has innovated food packaging that biodegrades wherever it is left, just as nature would do it with leaves.
	Retrovation/ renovation [73, 74]	Innovation inspired by previously extinct realities that are brought back in an adapted form to fit today's world.	The lifestyle innovation of the Paleo Diet ('cave man diet') is a dietary innovation inspired by ancient eating habits.
	Backcasting	Envisioning a future state and tracing back ('backcasting') innovations that might get us to that future state.	The catastrophic vision of what the world in 2050 would look like if we were not to change humanity's ways has led to varieties of sustainability innovations aimed at avoiding this scenario.
	Eco-efficiency	Innovations driven by the quest for reducing the environmental resource input and/or increasing the output (see Chapter 17).	Waitrose supermarket innovated food delivery trucks that are fuelled with biomethane from food waste, reducing both emissions from other fuels, and turning waste into energy [75].
	Bricolage [76, 77]	Innovations that 'make do' with what is at hand by creatively recombining what is available.	Innovative management of a mission hospital uses what is at hand in rural India. Poor patients are entrusted with a piglet several months before their elective surgery is scheduled. Its increase in value covers the medical bill [78].
	Design innovation	The inventive combination of features for a particular user or purpose.	Management at Fairphone has recombined existing technologies, features, and practices for the purpose of environmental and social fairness.
	Frugal innovation [79, 80]	'Good-enough' inexpensive innovations aimed at serving the needs of poorer users by focusing on core functions and tailored performance levels.	The Indian entrepreneur Arunachalam Muruganantham invented a simple machine that could produce functional low-cost menstrual sanitary pads after he learnt that his wife could not afford pads due to their excessive price [80]. 

(Continued)

TABLE 14.2   (Continued)

	Framework	Description	Example
Objects: Innovating what?	**Products/services innovation**	Novel offers for customers.	Products to be offered as services like MUD Jeans which leases jeans to customers.
	Practices innovation [82, 83]	Changing meaning or tools, or the competences required to carry out a practice.	Commercial bike sharing companies have not only innovated the logistics practices of dockless bikes, but in parallel also users' personal transportation practices.
	Processes innovation [84]	Replacing or changing the elements or series of actions of a process.	Amazon has patented a bracelet for the warehousing process, which tracks workers' movements and vibrates to point them in the desired direction [85].
	Organizational innovation [60, 86, 87]	New organizational methods or structures changing internal or external relations and structures by generating and adopting innovations.	BCorps is a novel type of 'hybrid' organizational structure that balances purpose and for-profit elements.
	Business model innovation [88–90]	Innovating organizations' value proposition, creation, exchange, and capture.	The one-for-one business model, first innovated by TOMS is centred on a value proposition for both the actual product buyer and a second beneficiary who does not pay.
	Systems innovation [91, 92]	Novelty in the form of a change of larger socio-technical and complex adaptive systems.	Changing the transportation supply–demand systems from combustion engine to electric engines.
Purpose: Innovating for what?	**Commercial innovation**	Using innovation to reap commercial benefits (e.g. profit, growth, or competitive advantage).	The 3M corporation is known for its innovation-based commercial success, including groundbreaking inventions like the Post-it note.
	Responsible innovation [93, 94]	Ensuring an innovation's positive (or at least not negative) outcomes, and a stakeholder- inclusive process.	Tesla engaging in efforts to ensure that their auto-pilot does not cause (further) accidents.
	Social innovation [95]	Innovations aimed at addressing a social need, issue, or opportunity.	Muhammad Yunus's microfinance innovations address the social issues of poverty and gender inequality.
	Innovation for sustainability [96–98]	Creating more (often environmentally) sustainable alternatives.	Circular economy innovations aim to reduce or eliminate residual waste entirely.
	Institutional innovation [99, 100]	Changing taken-for-granted (institutionalized) aspects of society, often through social movements.	The degrowth movement tries to change the taken-for-granted economic growth paradigm by institutionalizing degrowth as a viable novel alternative.

'GOOD' INNOVATION

'Good' innovation generates good futures through good conduct in the innovation process

We started this chapter with a quote about how innovation means creating new futures, ideally 'good' futures. The purpose of a **'good' innovation** therefore, on the one hand, would be to generate good futures. On the other hand, not all good ends (good futures) justify bad means. Good and ethical conduct in the innovation process are another necessary condition for 'good' innovation.

This section discusses complementary frameworks for good innovation, with social innovation and innovation for sustainability pursuing the purpose of creating socially desirable and sustainable futures. Responsible innovation ensures an innovation process that is geared towards desirable outcomes for society and avoids negative consequences by collaborating with stakeholders. Innovation ethics, finally, is concerned with moral issues as they may occur at different stages of the innovation process.

Latosha Stone with Proper Gnar engaging in social business model innovation.

Credit: Proper Gnar

SOCIAL INNOVATION

Social innovation that addresses a social need better than existing practices [101] has been hyped for its potential to improve society. It may equally address grand societal challenges [102] or societal inefficiencies (e.g. social innovation in work and employment to better serve the need for meaningful and dignified work [103]).

Figure 14.8 illustrates the social innovation process. Imagine, for instance, the social innovation of 'Black-owned enterprises', which have recently experienced a new hype driven by the Black Lives Matter movement and prominent supporters like the singer Beyoncé who launched a directory of Black-owned businesses [104]. However, a similar social innovation has been around since the 1970s [105] and, if you count its resemblance with the *Green Book*, a travel guide featuring Black-friendly businesses during times of US segregation, since 1936 [106]. Consider, for instance, Latosha Stone, owner manager and innovator ('the agent' of this social innovation process) of Proper Gnar, the world's first Black female-owned skateboard company [107]. This social innovation addresses multiple social causes in parallel, racial economic empowerment, and transforming a male-dominated sport towards gender equality. New ideas like this are likely to be constrained by the taken-for-granted institution that is the male-dominated skateboarding sport and industry [108–110], but also enabled by institutionalized gender equality and diversity structures. Actions like innovating this unique ownership profile then change the social practices existent in the social system, for instance, in the 'intra-group' (e.g. female Black entrepreneurs), inter group (e.g. relationship between female and male, Black and non-Black skateboarders), and extra group (e.g. wider society's gender practices).

Social innovation addresses a social need, issue, or opportunity through a novel practice or institution

As early as 1987, management guru Peter Drucker claimed that 'social innovation has clearly become management's new dimension' [112]. He explained that management's strength for social innovation comes from its competence

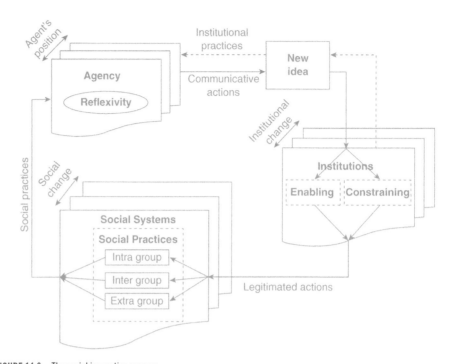

FIGURE 14.8   The social innovation process

Reprinted from *Social Innovation: Technological Forecasting and Social Change*, Volume 82, 2014, with permission from Elsevier.

SOURCE: [110]

to direct and organize as it 'is the specific practice that converts a mob into an effective, purposeful, and productive group'. This is particularly important as 'the mob' of social innovators is one distributed through all sectors of society [113]. While social innovation happens across sectors, and often in collaboration between sectors, it is often closely related to social entrepreneurship, particularly, in the business management context [111, 114]. Interestingly, many of the most iconic social innovations are responsible *management* innovations such as socially responsible investment, supported employment, microfinance, fair trade, and emissions trading [113]. There are three typical characteristics found in the most important social innovations, which can serve as valuable guidance for social innovators [115]:

1. They are usually new **combinations or hybrids** of existing elements, rather than being wholly new in themselves.

2. Putting them into practice involves **cutting across** organizational, sectoral or disciplinary boundaries.

3. They leave behind compelling **new social relationships** between previously separate individuals and groups, which matter greatly to the people involved, contribute to the diffusion and embedding of the innovation, and fuel a cumulative dynamic whereby each innovation opens up the possibility of further innovations.

Figure 14.9 further illustrates the stages that the most successful social innovations typically run through, from first 'prompts' of a social need and ideas for addressing it, to more concrete proposals and working prototypes. Next are advances in the innovation in which they are self-sustaining, onto their scaling, and then fulfilling the ultimate goal of systemic change, implying that the original need or issue has been addressed fully and widely.

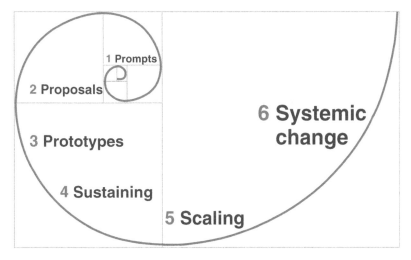

FIGURE 14.9 Stages of social innovation

SOURCE: [95]

SUSTAINABILITY-ORIENTED INNOVATION

However, as illustrated in Figure 14.10, **sustainability oriented innovation** embraces the balance between economic, social, and environmental impacts of the innovation process and practice. As we have covered social innovation in the last section, here we will predominantly focus on the environmental dimension. Sustainability-oriented innovation may be centred on an improved impact of varieties of objects of innovation, such as business models, a technology, or practice. Built on the life-cycle model previously introduced in the sustainable management chapter, such innovations can be focused on a better impact in a product or service's production (including sourcing), use, or end-of-life stage.

Sustainability-oriented innovation
is centred on innovating more (often environmentally) sustainable alternatives

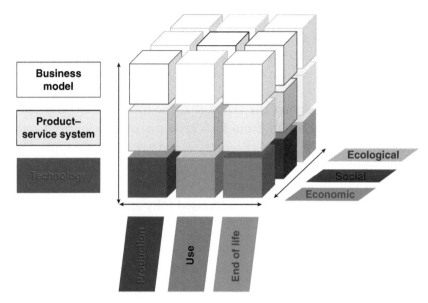

FIGURE 14.10   The sustainability innovation cube

Source adapted from: [96]. Reproduced with permission.

Sustainability-oriented innovation ultimately is meant to enable both business and private citizens' practices in order to decrease our footprint on planet Earth, and often change in both practices goes hand in hand as exemplified by the following quote by the property developer behind Dubai's Sustainable City neighbourhood:

> People came here primarily for the savings in community fees and service fees, but in no time they adopted the lifestyle of sustainability. Everything here is sustainable: we have sorting at source in the kitchen, and on the doorstep. We have made it easy to practice. Residents feel they are giving to the community and to nature, and to their children eventually, because we have a responsibility to safeguard the planet for them, so they feel happy and guilt-free. When you are in a community like this, you feel it, and you deliver the message to others [116].

The Natural Step's four science-based systems' conditions serve as high-level guidance on what characteristics of an entity can be considered unsustainable and are therefore worthy of being addressed by an innovation that improves the environmental impact: 'In a sustainable society, nature is not subject to systematically increasing:

1. concentrations of **substances from the Earth's crust** (such as fossil CO_2 and heavy metals)

2. concentrations of **substances produced by society** (such as antibiotics and endocrine disruptors)

3. **degradation** by physical means (such as deforestation and draining of groundwater tables)

4. and in that society ... there are **no structural obstacles to people**'s health, influence, competence, impartiality and meaning' [117]

A more complex and detailed framework for environment-oriented innovation is the Design for Environment approach (see Figure 14.11) [118], whose four main principles we will discuss briefly based on innovation in laundry detergents.

1. For instance, Tru Earth's highly concentrated laundry strips follow a *design for dematerialization*. They have reduced the product's weight by 94 per cent in comparison to traditional liquid or powder-based detergent, resulting in an immensely decreased transportation impact. They have also stopped using plastic packaging altogether [119].

2. *Design for detoxification* can be exemplified by the Belgian company Ecover's entirely plant-based laundry detergents that do not add phosphates (as usual detergents do) to our water [120].

3. *Design for revalorization* is at play when the Hulme Community Garden Centre in Manchester fills whichever used containers customers bring with their bio-detergent, this way giving back value to otherwise useless packaging from marmalade jars to cooking oil buckets.

4. Blueland is an example of *design for (economic) capital protection and renewal*. Their business model is centred on selling tablets from which customers can make their own detergents to be filled into Blueland's stylish containers [121].

RESPONSIBLE INNOVATION

The field of **responsible innovation** has grown out of concerns regarding the positive and negative impacts of innovation on society and the environment. Responsible innovation calls for managers to critically reflect upon the consequences of innovation and steer it towards societal and environmental goals. Its central mission is that of 'doing good' while also 'avoiding harm' [122]. Managers are encouraged to anticipate the potential impacts of innovation, assess their own values and assumptions, engage with a range of different actors to understand their needs and concerns, and develop a strategy that responds to the knowledge gained when taking these steps. Responsible innovation considers both responsible processes and outcomes.

Responsible innovation centred on fostering innovation practice that does good while avoiding harm through both innovation process and outcome

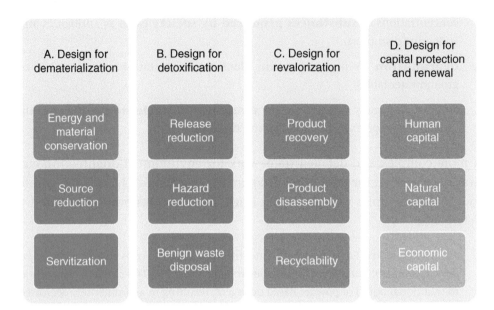

FIGURE 14.11   Design for environment principles
Source: adapted from [117]

- The **processes** of responsible innovation consist of the institutional and organizational practices that seek to lead to responsible outcomes.

- These **outcomes** can be new products, services, or organizational processes being designed and implemented inside and outside organizations.

IMPACTS OF INNOVATION

The practice of responsible innovation has, therefore, two main objectives: first, to steer innovation towards socially desirable outcomes, such as those outlined by the sustainable development goals (SDGs); second, to avoid potential negative impacts of innovation on society and the environment. It is useful here to think about the differences between *intended* and *unintended* impacts of innovation.

- **Intended impacts** are the outcomes from innovation processes that we expect to achieve as we innovate. Generally, intended impacts will focus on the positive outcomes brought about by innovation as we try to avoid any potential detrimental consequences of innovation. For a new product, service or organizational process, intended impacts are about what we expect different user groups affected by these innovations to gain – that is, the value that we seek to generate through innovation amongst these groups.

- **Unintended impacts** are those outcomes that we did not expect or explicitly plan to achieve. They can be both positive and negative. For example, a new product, service or organizational process may prove to be useful to certain user groups in ways we did not anticipate. On the other hand, users and other people, as well as the environment, may be adversely affected by the innovation in ways we were not able to foresee.

Following from the above, central to the idea of responsible innovation is the assumption that innovation processes and outcomes are not inherently bad or good and that responsible innovation is context dependent. Likewise, we should not take for granted the fact that services or products that reach the market are invariably desirable or socially acceptable. Taking into account that innovation can produce both intended and unintended impacts, part of our duty of care is trying to understand or unveil, as early as possible, the potential impacts of innovation. At the same time, we must acknowledge that there are limits as to how much we can foresee its consequences.

Given that different people and parts of the environment can be affected by the positive and negative impacts of innovation in different ways, it is crucial to think about the principle of **co-responsibility**, or in other words, *shared responsibilities* that underpin responsible innovation. Shared responsibility is promoted through transparent and inclusive processes, where society and innovators become *mutually responsive* to each other to achieve the ethical acceptability, sustainability, and societal desirability of innovation processes and their marketable products [123]. This means that, although we do it in different ways, we should all be committed to steering innovation towards desirable societal goals, such as solutions to an ageing society or a cleaner industry that uses low-carbon alternatives.

Innovation **co-responsibility** is practiced when innovation stakeholders and actors are mutually responsive to each other

GUIDING QUESTIONS AND PRINCIPLES

It has been stressed that responsible innovation needs to ensure that innovation needs to enjoy wide public acceptance, for which users and citizens in general must be involved in an open dialogue following these guiding questions:

1. Could the innovation I am pursuing be **controversial**?

2. What are the potential **ethical concerns** raised by the innovation?

3. Will my innovation be **publicly acceptable**? If not, why?

To ensure innovation processes and outcomes are 'responsible' we can put in place, or *operationalize*, a set of key dimensions of responsible innovation. These are anticipation, reflection, inclusion, and action [93, 94, 124]. These dimensions should not be treated as a 'checklist' but be used as guiding principles or, better, as a flexible and open set of goals designed to inform responsible innovation practices. We can call them the ARIA framework for responsible innovation (see Figure 14.12).

Anticipation What are the potential impacts of the innovation being proposed?	Reflection What are my assumptions and beliefs regarding the proposed innovation?	
Inclusion Who should I engage with?	**Action** How can I translate knowledge and insights into a plan?	How acceptable is my plan?

FIGURE 14.12   The ARIA canvas of responsible innovation practice

Artificial intelligence (AI) can provide great examples for the practice of responsible innovation. For management at technology companies that rely on big data, AI innovations have become a competitive priority. More broadly, managerial work will increasingly rely on AI. However, the use of AI does not come without its share of controversy. For instance, innovators at the software business Sage develop AI for managing accounting, finances, operations, and people. Their mission is to 'make admin invisible' as it would be taken over entirely by AI actors [125]. For instance, they offer 'smart assistant' natural language chatbots for accountants that can answer client questions, even those related to particular financial information [126].

Innovators at Sage developed their own approach to the responsible management of AI based on five core principles. These principles were designed to be applied within Sage but also apply to management AI technology more widely [125]:

1. AI should **reflect the diversity of the users** it serves; that means that teams building AI should involve people from diverse backgrounds.

Sage's mission is to let AI do the admin work so that people 'can spend more time doing what they love'.

andresr/Getty Images

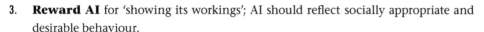

2. AI must be **held to account – and so must users**; AI should be transparent so we understand how it makes decisions.

3. **Reward AI** for 'showing its workings'; AI should reflect socially appropriate and desirable behaviour.

4. AI should **level the playing field**; AI should be used to democratize access to technology and not the other way around.

5. AI will **replace, but it must also create**; AI automation should be designed in ways that create opportunities for humans to enhance their professions.

With these principles, managers at Sage attempt to address a range of responsible innovation considerations. Intriguingly, we could understand these principles as the first code of ethics to be obeyed by non-human managers. The title of the principles ('The ethics of code') gives it away. These are ethical guidelines to be obeyed by the code that is AI, ethical guidelines for artificial managers.

INNOVATION ETHICS

Innovative management and innovative businesses come with a variety of ethical issues throughout the innovation process, as we discussed earlier in this chapter [127]. We will now highlight several salient and recurrent types of such issues in different stages of the innovation process.

> Innovation ethics
> concerned with ethical issues
> along the innovation process
> and in innovation outcomes

Planned obsolescence as motivation for innovation.[2] **Planned obsolescence** is often the starting point for generating novelty as creating novelty quickly makes the older version obsolete and creates a market for new commercial revenues. Particularly in the context of product development and innovation or where revenue is generated from quickly changing fashions (e.g. clothing, cars, and consumer electronics), planned obsolescence is a taken-for-granted but profoundly immoral core practice. It destroys value for users and creates enormous amounts of unnecessary waste, worsening the planet's environmental condition. There are four main types of planned obsolescence: contrived durability ('made to break'); incompatible software updates that make still intact older hardware redundant; perceived obsolescence (e.g. 'last year's fashion'); and prevention of repair (e.g. 'glued' electronics) [130].

> Planned obsolescence
> a value-destroying innovation
> and design practice deliberately
> making things useless or
> redundant, typically out
> of commercial interest

Issues in testing innovations. A morally loaded question in innovation is testing its effects on users. On the one hand, we would not want innovations to negatively affect humans. On the other hand, testing new products

---

[2]The 'irresponsible management innovation' of the practice of planned obsolescence has been attributed to Alfred P. Sloan, head of General Motors in the late 1930s, early 1940s,, who introduced annual updates of car design to convince consumers to buy a new car every year as the US car market had reached saturation [128]. It had a further boost as a managerial method to increase consumption as a way out of the Great Depression [129].

or innovations (e.g. cosmetics, medicine) more generally on animals has animal welfare implications. However, testing innovations on human subjects requires caution, for instance, of privacy and people's right to give informed consent to participate. Supermarkets have experimented with eye-tracking devices to redesign stores in a way that maximizes sales, and others live-tested facial recognition devices to deter thieves [131]. Another issue is what to do when tests do reveal potentially harmful impacts of an innovation. The more time that is spent on an innovation, the more money and personal effort is invested. Therefore, innovators might be tempted to 'make it work' in spite of potential ethical issues or likely consequences revealed during testing. The older an innovation project, the more valuable it is and the harder it is to 'throw it away' [127]. Early and ongoing consideration of detrimental effects and early testing may mitigate this issue.

Moral issues in intellectual property. Once an innovation has been realized, a critical question arises: Whose innovation is it? Who holds the legal (and moral) property rights and how can they be protected? Consider, for example, counterfeiting and end-user piracy in the clothing, entertainment, or publishing industries [132]. Moral issues in intellectual property are equally prevalent between companies and their management, however. For instance, Amazon's Alexa Fund has repeatedly been accused of copying innovative technologies and business models after gaining access to start-ups' confidential information when investing in them. In some cases, Amazon's management allegedly founded competing businesses pushing these start-ups out of the market [133]. However, there might be important social downsides to property protection as well. For instance, should innovations with positive social or environmental impact be 'owned' and controlled by a few, or rather should they be socialized in the public interest? At times these considerations might luckily converge, such as in the case of Tesla, which is strategically open to fostering innovation around its patents and while doing so promoting more eco-innovations related to electric mobility.

The ugly underbelly of implementing innovations. Often seemingly successful innovations come with (partially) hidden ethical issues, or might become corrupt over time. For instance, innovative sharing economy business models were originally hailed for their potential to use idle resources (e.g. your spare room in the case of Airbnb) more (eco)efficiently. However, while implementing the innovation, moral issues have emerged. A prominent example is the increased scarcity of local housing and subsequent rent inflation as living space is used commercially for Airbnb [134]. Another controversial case relates to Huawei's leadership in innovating 5G mobile internet around the world. Due to allegations and rising suspicions that their technology might be being used unethically, the company's management fell from grace, even resulting in some high-level legal procedures. Huawei, on the other hand, suggested these were false accusations made by foreign actors attempting to protect their own country's companies' inferior technologies from superior Huawei technology [135].

PRINCIPLES OF INNOVATING

I. **Innovation** means creating, using, and disseminating novelty, something new.

II. The **innovating mode** of management comprises practices related to management innovation, innovative management, and to managing innovation.

III. **Ambidextrous management** requires the ability to explore and generate novelty and to exploit and use it.

IV. Helpful innovation frameworks for exploitation are diffusion adoption curves and the hype cycle, and for exploration the innovation funnel and open innovation.

V. Typical **issues** encountered in the innovation process are **the chasm**, the **innovator's dilemma** and **hypes**.

VI. **Good innovation** generates **good futures** through **good conduct** in the innovation process, relying on social innovation, innovation for sustainability, responsible innovation, and innovation ethics.

MANAGEMENT GYM: TRAINING YOUR PROFESSIONAL SIX-PACK

Knowing

1. Create a mindmap that interrelates the concepts of open innovation, social innovation, and management innovation.

2. Find and compare three lists online that present recent top innovations for sustainability. Which one do you think is the innovation with the most potential?

3. Find a real example of an innovation that you would consider controversial and come up with one to three reasons why.

Thinking

4. Analyse five innovations of your choice and place them on the respective section of the innovation diffusion and hype curves. If applicable, place them in one of the six stages of social innovation. Based on this analysis, decide what the next step would be to push this innovation 'to the next level'.

5. Use the sustainability innovation cube to think of one innovation for each of the 27 cubes formed by its 3x3x3 dimensions.

6. Use the social innovation process model to analyse one well-documented historical social innovation of your choice.

(Continued)

Acting

7. Have a look at *The open book of social innovation* and use one of the social innovation techniques introduced there.

8. Download and test a trial version of some form of mobile app that supports management, entrepreneurship, organizing or leadership. How helpful did you find the app? How do you think it would be used ideally, and how could the technology be improved?

9. Identify a new technology that has not yet reached the market. Based on the ARIA goals of responsible innovation (anticipation, reflection, inclusion and action), write a one-page programme for operationalizing those four goals.

Interacting

10. Approach a friend or a family member and present the example you picked of a controversial innovation. Ask them if they agree with you or not and to explain why. Reflect on the differences or similarities of your opinions. What do they mean to you?

11. Ask three friends or family members what they think are one or two of the most pressing issues facing society and to speak about them for no more than one minute. Record or make notes of their statements and then analyse them. Can you think of any ways in which innovation can help address the challenges identified?

12. Together with a partner or in a small group, identify one innovation and try to attach as many of the innovation types learnt in this class to it as possible, e.g. 1. Innovation X is social innovation because … 2. Innovation X is frugal innovation because … Which member of the group can build the most valid sentences like these?

Being

13. What is your basic attitude towards a particular innovation or new technology of your choice? For instance, are you sceptical, scared, neutral, or enthusiastic about it? What might that mean for your managerial use of and involvement in innovation?

14. How do you experience the effects on your personal and professional lives of the currently building digitalization and sustainability waves of innovation?

15. Which of the following do you think comes most naturally to you: innovative management, managing innovation, or management innovation?

Becoming

16. Have you ever been part of hyping an innovation or on the trough of disillusionment? What could you learn or have you learnt from this experience for future behaviour?

17. How do you think you could become a more ambidextrous person, being able to both explore and exploit novelty?

18. What social need in your environment do you personally care about and how could you engage in social innovation to address it?

Laasch, O., Moosmayer, D., & Antonacopoulou, E. P. (2023). The interdisciplinary responsible management competence framework: An integrative review of ethics, responsibility, and sustainability competences. *Journal of Business Ethics, 187*, 733–757.

PIONEER INTERVIEW
R. EDWARD FREEMAN

INTERVIEWER: OLIVER LAASCH

R. Edward Freeman is one of the most influential responsible and ethical management thinkers. He is the father of stakeholder thinking.

Inventing management that 'rocks'. I would take 'management sucks' to be a subsidiary of the 'business sucks' story. The principles are probably not terribly different. The problem

(Continued)

is what management is. Dan Pink has a great way to say it: 'Management is like the television, not a tree. We invented it.' One way to get out of management sucks is to get out of the idea that management is about telling people what to do. Maybe it's about enabling people to manage themselves and to lead themselves. I think that's built-in in organizations around, extrinsic, if–then rewards. But building an organization around intrinsic rewards where people are trying to master a particular thing, and they have autonomy to do it. They have some sense of purpose. Again, it's just Dan Pink [136] in his book named *Drive*. We know that works. 'If–then rewards' work. They work in certain circumstances, but for most of

Courtesy of R. Edward Freeman

twenty-first-century jobs, they don't work. In fact, they made things worse. So, understanding how we go from management in this old view of telling people what to do, to enabling people to manage themselves and to lead themselves, to think about leadership in their organization, not leaders. Right? Again, we see this happening in places where the idea of the manager knowing more, telling people what to do is just not true. So, I'm very encouraged by some of the places where you see this sort of enabling self-leadership, self-management.

Innovating the role of money. In the old story of business where it's all about the money, we try and bolt on anything that will make it more morally acceptable. Some people bolt on ethics. 'Spend the money, but don't screw people.' Or some people try to bolt on sustainability: 'It's really about the money, but don't ruin it for our children.' Some people try to bolt on responsibility: 'It's really about the money, but don't do these bad things.' It seems to me the problem in all of that is, to make a difference here, it's not about bolting on one of those three things or all three of them. It's about changing the idea that this is about the money. Money is important: I have got to make red blood cells to live, but the purpose of my life is not to make red blood cells. Business has to make profits to live, but making profits isn't the purpose of business.

If the purpose of business is not to make profits, then why do entrepreneurs start a company? They start it because they want to make a difference. They see the world differently. So, changing the edges of this by bolting on ethics, or sustainability, or responsibility, or all three is a little like moving the deck chairs on the *Titanic*. What you really have to do is change the basic idea. To change the basic idea, I think you have to, among other things, change the unit of analysis. This is not about economic transactions. It's about creating value in relationships with stakeholders over time and seeing how those interests grow together and doing it with a sense of purpose and doing it with a sense of values and ethics all at the same time.

(Continued)

Note: This text is an abridged version of the interview conducted with R. Edward Freeman by Oliver Laasch, published in full as part of the *Research handbook of responsible management* [137].

QUESTIONS

1. How do you think we would need to reinvent management so that it rocks?

2. If we use the metaphor of management that is more like 'red blood cells' to come up with innovative ideas, what would the new management look like?

3. How could we use ethics, responsibility, and sustainability as a basis for innovating management in a way that is not 'just like moving the deck chairs on the *Titanic*'?

PROFESSIONAL PROFILE
VED KRISHNA

I am Ved Krishna, Strategy Head, Yash Pakka Limited. We work towards finding and providing compostable packing solutions for a cleaner planet.

A typical day. There is a very thin line for work and play for me as all I do leads me towards a more meaningful life. I love mornings, wake up at 4 am, practice yoga, meditate, read, write,

(Continued)

and plan. I am undergoing a master's programme so I then dedicate a couple of hours towards the same. 11 am to 4 pm goes in team interaction and direct business and then I try to spend a couple of hours reading before winding down and spending time with family. I am off to sleep by 10 pm.

Biomimicry-based innovation. We work on solving some real challenges and my role is primarily focused towards products and innovation. We keep searching for solutions and work on our own developments.

We are aware that all packing solutions lie in nature and hence the entire innovations team has to understand

Courtesy of Ved Krishna

biomimicry. Nature packages everything and does so in amazing ways. We search for ways we can become more observant, aware, and conscious so that we can learn and adapt. The challenges include both products and processes.

HOW TO EMPOWER COLLEAGUES' INNOVATIVENESS?

1. **Competence building**. It is really important to have clear role profiles for people and then be able to objectively assess and train for the gaps.

2. **Utilizing the digital space more and more**. We have the possibilities of statistics so much more today. We need to build on the same. We should be able to provide each person with the right dashboard and it should be pre-emotive not post-event analysis like profitability statements.

3. **Standardization**. It is so important to build and train for standardization. All innovations need to sit on top of a certain standard discipline, else all we get is a very subjective mismatch of heroism and jingoism.

4. **Values**. Clarity and alignment are a must. What would the organization want to work with? For example, for us humans respect is really important. We would like to ensure at all points that we maintain that value. We also work with the idea of growing the pie with social and environmental bottom lines. So at times the decision for profitability will be superseded by an environmental or societal aspect.

(Continued)

QUESTIONS

1. List all novelties and innovations that you can spot in Ved's explanation.

2. What other sustainable packaging solutions do you think we could possibly find in nature? Where and at what part of nature would you start looking?

3. How do you think Ved's management philosophy and principles may foster or inhibit the innovativeness of other people in his company?

4. How and why do you think Ved is or is not an innovative person?

TRUE STORY

LEVELLING THE FIELD

COEDITED BY ALEXANDRA LEONOR BARRUETA SACKSTEDER AND LUCIA KIRCHNER

Girl up! Hi, I am Missy. Responsible management is so important to me. Responsible management is definitely key in every area of business, but I think it's especially important in HR – where people are a first focus – where taking a responsible management approach can make a big difference. Certainly I have come across several challenges and issues during my career path, just like the one I am about to describe.

(Continued)

In the beginning ... At the time, I was working for a big internet company as Technical Talent Sourcer. My job was similar to the one of a classical recruiter. My main task was to attract and to recruit the best talents for the company. This meant that I was dealing with only passive candidates, who did not apply directly for a job but who were approached directly by me through different channels. Moreover 'best talent' referred to prospects who were exceptional, hence usually above the average.

To identify the best talents, CVs were evaluated on several criteria (e.g. previous employers, size of projects, kind of responsibilities and educational background). When the educational background was considered, the quality of the school (e.g. ranking) was examined as well and considered quite important.

An issue arises. I began to notice a trend that could potentially lead to a problem. Top schools, especially MBAs, are often located in Western countries and they are expensive. As an example, the *Financial Times* Global MBA Ranking for 2018 lists the 100 top MBAs; as is clearly visible from the list, the majority of them are actually based in the most wealthy countries in the world. Still focusing on MBA, the average tuition rates in 2016 ranged from less than $30,000 for Birmingham Business School to around $135,000 for the top four US programmes.

Ultimately, I realized that it was possible that these circumstances could lead to the exclusion of candidates with an underprivileged background – people who could not afford to study in such expensive schools. Moreover, usually top companies hire employees from other big names, employees that are likely to get their first job thanks to their studies in top schools. This could lead to a vicious circle, resulting in the exclusion of candidates with a less privileged background.

Action! Having identified this as potential bias, I tried to take action on it. Firstly, I made my stakeholders aware of this potential bias by providing more data about school ranking (e.g. *Financial Times* School Ranking, as well as the country's local ranking) to broaden the panorama of schools we could potentially hire from. As well, when speaking with a candidate, I started

(Continued)

to gather more information about their school (e.g. special programmes or ranking within the specific country) to better inform my stakeholders. I also asked my stakeholders not to be only focused on the school factor, but also take other criteria more into consideration (e.g. skills and results achieved during candidates' careers).

With this approach, I was able to diversify the pool of candidates I presented to my stakeholders, including candidates with an unprivileged background.

Success! By changing the selection criteria slightly and focusing on other elements of selection like skills or measurable results rather than focusing solely on the reputation of the school they had graduated from, I was able to not only improve the pool from which we were selecting candidates but also give new opportunities to qualified individuals regardless of their background.

QUESTIONS

1. Is what Missy describes an innovation and, if so, what kind of innovation is it?

2. Would you consider what Missy describes a responsible innovation? Based on which criteria would or wouldn't you do so?

3. What do you think might be the impact of the innovation she proposes – for instance, in relation to global economic inequality?

DIGGING DEEPER: SUSTAINABILITY BUSINESS MODEL PATTERNS AND ARCHETYPES

To innovate business models that are environmentally, socially, and economically sustainable is an essential practice for responsible managers [90]. Fortunately, we do not necessarily have to invent sustainability business models from scratch as there are well-known, understood, and practiced sustainability business model types. First, Figure 14.13 presents higher-level archetypes and examples in the categories of technological, social, and organizational innovations.

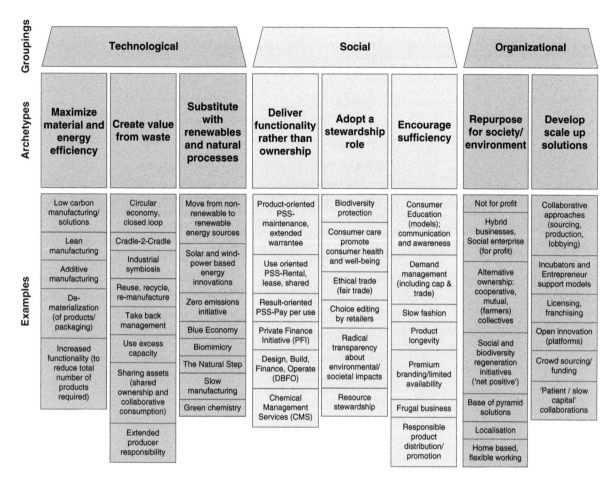

FIGURE 14.13   Sustainability business model archetypes

The patterns presented in Table 14.3 provide a somewhat more detailed distinction based on each business model type's primary value creation, including different combinations between environmental, social, and economic value focus.

TABLE 14.3   Sustainability business model patterns

Primary associated value creation (group)[a]	SBM pattern groups	Associated value creation (group and pattern)[a]
Mainly economic	G1 Pricing and Revenue Patterns	Primary: mainly economic/Secondary: social-economic
	P1.1 'Differential pricing'	Social-economic
	P1.2 'Freemium'	Social-economic
	P1.3 'Innovative product financing'	Mainly economic
	P1.4 'Subscription model'	Mainly economic
	G9 Service & Performance Patterns	Primary: mainly economic/Secondary: ecologic-economic
	P9.1 'Pay for success'	Mainly economic
	P9.2 'Product-oriented services'	Mainly economic
	P9.3 'Result-oriented services'	Ecologic-economic
	P9.4 'Use-oriented services'	Ecologic-economic
Social-economic	G7 Access Provision Patterns	Primary: social-economic/Secondary: multiple
	P7.1 'Building a marketplace'	Social-economic
	P7.2 'E-transaction platforms'	Social-economic
	P7.3 'Experience-based customer credit'	Social-economic
	P7.4 'Last-mile grid utilities'	Social-economic
	P7.5 'Value-for-money degrees'	Social
	P7.6 'Value-for-money housing'	Mainly Social
	G10 Cooperative Patterns	Primary: social-economic/Secondary: none
	P10.1 'Cooperative ownership'	Social-economic
	G2 Financing patterns	Primary: social-economic/Secondary: mainly economic
	P2.1 'Crowdfunding'	Mainly economic
	P2.2 'Microfinance'	Social-economic
	P2.3 'Social business model: no dividends'	Social-economic
Social	G6 Giving Patterns	Primary: social/Secondary: none
	P6.1 'Buy one, give one'	Social
	P6.2 'Commercially utilized social mission'	Social
	G8 Social Mission Patterns	Primary: social/Secondary: social-economic
	P8.1 'Expertise broker'	Social
	P8.2 'Market-oriented social mission'	Social
	P8.3 'One-sided social mission'	Social
	P8.4 'Social business model: empowerment'	Social-economic
	P8.5 'Two-sided social Mission'	Social

Primary associated value creation (group)[a]	SBM pattern groups	Associated value creation (group and pattern)[a]
Mainly ecological	G3 Ecodesign Patterns	Primary: mainly ecological/Secondary: ecologic-economic
	P3.1 'Hybrid model/Gap-exploiter model'	Ecologic-economic
	P3.2 'Maximise material productivity and energy effiency'	Mainly ecological
	P3.3 'Product design'	Mainly ecological
	P3.4 'Substitute with renewables and natural processes'	Mainly ecological
	G4 Closing-the-Loop Patterns	Primary: mainly ecological/Secondary: ecologic-economic
	P4.1 'Co-product generation'	Ecologic-economic
	P4.2 'Industrial symbiosis'	Ecologic-economic
	P4.3 'Online waste exchange platform'	Ecologic-economic
	P4.4 'Product recycling'	Ecologic-economic
	P4.5 'Remanufacturing/Next life sales'	Mainly ecological
	P4.6 'Repair'	Mainly ecological
	P4.7 'Reuse'	Mainly ecological
	P4.8 'Take back management'	Mainly ecological
	P4.9 'Upgrading'	Mainly ecological
Integrative	G11 Community Platform Patterns	Primary: integrative/Secondary: none
	P11.1 'Sharing symbiosis'	Integrative
	G5 Supply Chain Patterns	Primary: integrative/Secondary: multiple
	P5.1 'Green supply chain management'	Mainly ecological
	P5.2 'Inclusive sourcing'	Mainly social
	P5.3 'Micro distribution and retail'	Social-economic
	P5.4 'Physical to virtual'	Mainly economic
	P5.5 'Produce on demand'	Mainly economic
	P5.6 'Shorter supply chains'	Integrative

SOURCE: [139]. Reproduced with permission.

POINTERS

You could go deeper by comparing the two tables to see where and how the identified patterns and archetypes overlap. Or take an existing unsustainable business model and look through the patterns and archetypes to identify a viable sustainable business model pattern. For either one of these activities, it would be helpful to have a close read of the two original papers as well as looking up further details about particular patterns. For instance, what do inclusive source or freemium business models mean?

WORKSHEET

RESPONSIBLE MANAGEMENT INNOVATION CANVAS

Old-world management orthodoxy		Responsible management innovation	
Management-as-usual management practice	**Underlying beliefs and assumptions**	**Alternative beliefs and assumptions**	**More responsible, novel management practice**
Strategic hiring: Screen, test, and interview job applicants until you are sure they are the best fit for the job.	*We want the best of the best for the job.*	*We need the right jobs for people who cannot get a job elsewhere.*	*Open hiring: Anyone who puts their name on a list will be offered a job, no CVs seen, no questions asked.*

SOURCE: adapted from [22]

POINTERS

Following the example related to hiring practices provided in the first line, you can start to use this canvas in any column. First, you might start all the way to the right as you have already identified a responsible management innovation and work your way back to the left in order to understand how and why it replaces another management-as-usual practice. Secondly, you could start with an unusual responsible management belief like the belief in economic degrowth and identify responsible management innovations (realized or hypothetical) based on that belief, which in turn imply the 'old-world' assumptions and practices it breaks with. Third, you could also go from left to right by starting with an unethical, irresponsible, unsustainable, or otherwise outdated practice and work your way all the way to the right, identifying a responsible management innovation to replace that practice. Finally, you could identify an 'old world' management assumption, identify old-world practices upheld by it, and ideate alternative beliefs and practices.

REFERENCES

1. LeBleu L. The relationship that can make or break a business (infographic). www.forbes.com/sites/servicenow/2020/05/04/the-relationship-that-can-make-or-break-a-business-infographic/#410d54b51117 Published 2020. Accessed August 13 2020.

2. Musk E. All our patent are belong to you. www.tesla.com/blog/all-our-patent-are-belong-you Published 2014. Last accessed July 31 2023.

3. Tesla. About Tesla. www.tesla.com/about Published 2020. Accessed July 4 2020.

4. Tesla. Tesla gigafactory. www.tesla.com/en_GB/gigafactory Published 2020. Accessed July 4 2020.

5. Cooke P. Gigafactory logistics in space and time: Tesla fourth gigafactory and its rivals. *Sustainability.* 2020, 12(5): 2044.

6. Dyer J, Gregersen H. Tesla's innovations are transforming the auto industry. www.forbes.com/sites/innovatorsdna/2016/08/24/teslas-innovations-are-transforming-the-auto-industry/#2df55cbe19f7 Published 2016. Accessed April 7 2020.

7. Kennedy D. Trump praises Elon Musk's historic SpaceX mission as a 'great inspiration'. https://nypost.com/2020/05/30/elon-musks-historic-spacex-mission-makes-successful-launch Published 2020. Accessed July 4 2020.

8. Hiltzik, M. Column: The Bezos-Branson-Musk space race is a huge waste of money and scientifically useless. www.latimes.com/business/story/2021-07-06/jeff-bezos-richard-branson-elon-musk-space-race Published 2021. Last accessed July 31 2023.

9. Grinbaum A, Groves C. What is 'responsible' about responsible innovation? Understanding the ethical issues. In: Owen R, Bessant J, Heintz M, eds. *Responsible innovation.* Chichester: Wiley, 2013.

10. World Economic Forum. The Great Reset. www.weforum.org/great-reset Published 2020. Accessed June 21 2020.

11. Schwab K. *The fourth industrial revolution.* New York: Crown Business, 2017.

12. Lubin DA, Esty DC. The sustainability imperative. *Harvard Business Review.* 2010, 88(5): 42–50.

13. Hargroves K, Smith MH. *Natural advantage of nations.* London: Earthscan, 2005.

14. Elkington J. *Green swans: The coming boom in regenerative capitalism.* New York: Fast Company Press, 2020.

15. Hamel G. Moon shots for management. *Harvard Business Review.* 2009, 87(2): 91–98.

16. Pink D. Management is an outdated technology. www.youtube.com/watch?v=bgCdSnLrHJo Published 2012. Accessed February 21 2020.

17. Birkinshaw JM, Mol MJ. How management innovation happens. *MIT Sloan Management Review.* 2006, 47(4): 81–88.

18. Birkinshaw J, Hamel G, Mol MJ. Management innovation. *Academy of Management Review.* 2008, 33(4): 825–845.

19. Zong QH. Greetings. https://en.wahaha.com.cn/aboutus/aboutuswelcome.htm Published 2020. Accessed July 15 2020.

20. Xu F, Nash WR. Wahaha's management innovation. Paper presented at: 11th European Conference on Creativity and Innovation, Faro, 2011.

21. Laasch O, Conaway R. *Responsible business: The textbook for management learning, competence, innovation.* Sheffield: Greenleaf, 2016.

22. Hamel G. The why, what, and how of management innovation. *Harvard Business Review.* 2006, 84(2): 72.

23. O'Reilly CA, Tushman ML. The ambidextrous organization. *Harvard Business Review.* 2004, 82(4): 74–81.

24. March JG. Exploration and exploitation in organizational learning. *Organization Science.* 1991, 2(1): 71–87.

25. Duncan RB. The ambidextrous organization: Designing dual structures for innovation. *The Management of Organization.* 1976, 1(1): 167–188.

26. Dover PA, Dierk U. The ambidextrous organization: Integrating managers, entrepreneurs and leaders. *Journal of Business Strategy.* 2010, 31(5): 49–58.

27. Jansen JJP, Vera D, Crossan M. Strategic leadership for exploration and exploitation: The moderating role of environmental dynamism. *Leadership Quarterly.* 2009, 20(1): 5–18.

28. Jansen JJ, Tempelaar MP, Van den Bosch FA, Volberda HW. Structural differentiation and ambidexterity: The mediating role of integration mechanisms. *Organization Science.* 2009, 20(4): 797–811.

29. Hansen EG, Wicki S, Schaltegger S. Structural ambidexterity, transition processes, and integration trade-offs: A longitudinal study of failed exploration. *R&D Management*. 2019, 49(4): 484–508.

30. Mount M, Martinez MG. Social media: A tool for open innovation. *California Management Review*. 2014, 56(4): 124–143.

31. Chesbrough HW. *Open innovation: The new imperative for creating and profiting from technology*. Boston: Harvard Business Press, 2003.

32. Bonazzi FLZ, Zilber MA. Innovation and business model: A case study about integration of innovation funnel and business model canvas. *Revista Brasileira de Gestão de Negócios*. 2014, 16(53): 616–637.

33. Clark KB, Wheelwright S. *Managing new product and process development: Text and cases*. New York: Free Press, 1993.

34. Lazzarotti V, Manzini R. Different modes of open innovation: A theoretical framework and an empirical study. *International Journal of Innovation Management*. 2009, 13(4): 615–636.

35. Chesbrough H, Bogers M. Explicating open innovation: Clarifying an emerging paradigm for understanding innovation. In: Chesbrough H, Vanhaverbeke W, West J, eds. *New Frontiers in open innovation*. Oxford: Oxford University Press, 2014: 3–28.

36. Metcalfe JS, Coombs R. Organizing for innovation: Co-ordinating distributed innovation capabilities. In: Foss N, Mahnke V, eds. *Competence, governance, and entrepreneurship: Advances in economic strategy research*. Oxford: Oxford University Press, 2000: 209–231.

37. Howells J, James A, Malik K. The sourcing of technological knowledge: Distributed innovation processes and dynamic change. *R&D Management*. 2003, 33(4): 395–409.

38. Rohrbeck R, Hölzle K, Gemünden HG. Opening up for competitive advantage: How Deutsche Telekom creates an open innovation ecosystem. *R&D Management*. 2009, 39(4): 420–430.

39. Chesbrough H, Kim S, Agogino A. Chez Panisse: Building an open innovation ecosystem. *California Management Review*. 2014, 56(4): 144–171.

40. Wayne Gould R. Open innovation and stakeholder engagement. *Journal of Technology Management and Innovation*. 2012, 7(3): 1–11.

41. Vanhaverbeke W. Rethinking open innovation beyond the innovation funnel. *Technology Innovation Management Review*. 2013, 3(4): 6–10.

42. Chesbrough H. Why companies should have open business models. *MIT Sloan Management Review*. 2012, 48(2): 22–28.

43. Hautz J, Seidl D, Whittington R. Open strategy: Dimensions, dilemmas, dynamics. *Long Range Planning*. 2017, 50(3): 298–309.

44. Lopez-Vega H, Tell F, Vanhaverbeke W. Where and how to search? Search paths in open innovation. *Research Policy*. 2016, 45(1): 125–136.

45. Cohen WM, Levinthal DA. Absorptive capacity: A new perspective on learning and innovation. *Administrative Science Quarterly*. 1990, 35(1): 128–152.

46. Zahra SA, George G. Absorptive capacity: A review, reconceptualization, and extension. *Academy of Management Review*. 2002, 27(2): 185–203.

47. Dzhengiz T, Niesten E. Competences for environmental sustainability: A systematic review on the impact of absorptive capacity and capabilities. *Journal of Business Ethics*. 2020, 162(4): 881–906.

48. Rogers EM. *Diffusion of innovations*. New York: Simon & Schuster, 2010.

49. Moore GA, McKenna R. *Crossing the chasm: Marketing and selling high-tech products to mainstream customers*. New York: HarperCollins, 1991.

50. Christensen C. *The innovator's dilemma: When new technologies cause great firms to fail*. Cambridge: Harvard Business Review Press, 2013.

51. Fenn J, Blosch M. Understanding Gartner's hype cycles. www.gartner.com/en/documents/3887767 Published 2003/2018. Accessed July 19 2020.

52. Dedehayir O, Steinert M. The hype cycle model: A review and future directions. *Technological Forecasting and Social Change*. 2016, 108: 28–41.

53. Vaughan A. Tesco drops carbon-label pledge. www.theguardian.com/environment/2012/jan/30/tesco-drops-carbon-labelling Published 2012. Accessed July 19 2020.

54. Carbon Trust. Product carbon footprint certification and labelling. www.carbontrust.com/what-we-do/assurance-and-certification/product-carbon-footprint-certification-and-labelling Published 2020. Accessed July 19 2020.

55. Morton A. Wind and solar plants will soon be cheaper than coal in all big markets around world, analysis finds. www.theguardian.com/environment/2020/mar/12/wind-and-solar-plants-will-soon-be-cheaper-than-coal-in-all-big-markets-around-world-analysis-finds Published 2020. Accessed July 19 2020.

56. Attenborough D. VR Dive. www.attenboroughsreef.com/vr_dive.php Published 2018. Accessed July 16 2020.

57. Bower JL, Christensen CM. Disruptive technologies: Catching the wave. *Harvard Business Review.* 1995, 73(1): 43–53.

58. McDermott CM, O'Connor GC. Managing radical innovation: An overview of emergent strategy issues. *Journal of Product Innovation Management.* 2002, 19(6): 424–438.

59. Moon-Miklaucic C, Bray-Sharpin A, De La Lanza I, Khan A, Re LL, Maassen A. *The evolution of bike sharing: 10 questions on the emergence of new technologies, opportunities, and risks.* Washington: World Resources Institute, 2019.

60. *Oslo manual: Guidelines for collecting, and interpreting innovation data.* Paris: OECD Publishing, 2005.

61. Chesbrough HW. The era of open innovation. *MIT Sloan Management Review.* 2003, 44(3): 35–41.

62. Oeij P, Rus D, Pot FD. *Workplace innovation: Theory, research and practice.* Cham: Springer, 2017.

63. Badham R, Ehn P. Tinkering with technology: Human factors, work redesign, and professionals in workplace innovation. *Human Factors and Ergonomics in Manufacturing & Service Industries.* 2000, 10(1): 61–82.

64. Bizzi L. Responsible job crafting. In: Laasch O, Suddaby R, Freeman RE, Jamali D, eds. *The research handbook of responsible management.* Cheltenham: Edward Elgar, 2020.

65. Tims M, Bakker AB, Derks D. Development and validation of the job crafting scale. *Journal of Vocational Behavior.* 2012, 80(1): 173–186.

66. Yidong T, Xinxin L. How ethical leadership influence employees' innovative work behavior: A perspective of intrinsic motivation. *Journal of Business Ethics.* 2013, 116(2): 441–455.

67. Kesting P, Ulhøi JP. Employee-driven innovation: Extending the license to foster innovation. *Management Decision.* 2010, 48(1): 65–84.

68. Wallace JC, Butts MM, Johnson PD, Stevens FG, Smith MB. A multilevel model of employee innovation: Understanding the effects of regulatory focus, thriving, and employee involvement climate. *Journal of Management.* 2016, 42(4): 982–1004.

69. Von Hippel E. *Democratizing innovation.* Cambridge: MIT University Press, 2005.

70. Morrison PD, Roberts JH, Von Hippel E. Determinants of user innovation and innovation sharing in a local market. *Management Science.* 2000, 46(12): 1513–1527.

71. Mead T. *Bioinspiration in business and management.* New York: Business Expert Press, 2018.

72. Mead T, Jeanrenaud S, Bessant J. Factors influencing the application of nature as inspiration for sustainability-oriented innovation in multinational corporations. *Business Strategy and the Environment.* 2020. https://doi.org/10.1002/bse.2564.

73. Suddaby R, Laasch O. Responsible management as re-enchantment and retrovation. In: Laasch O, Suddaby R, Freeman E, Jamali D, eds. *The research handbook of responsible management.* Cheltenham: Edward Elgar, 2020.

74. Ertimur B, Chen S. Adaptation and diffusion of renovations: The case of the paleo diet. *Journal of Business Research.* 2019. https://doi.org/10.1016/j.jbusres.2019.06.015.

75. Spring Wise. UK supermarket debuts delivery trucks fuelled by food waste. www.springwise.com/uk-supermarket-debuts-delivery-trucks-fueled-food-waste Published 2017. Accessed July 25 2020.

76. Lévi-Strauss C. *The savage mind.* Chicago: University of Chicago Press, 1966.

77. Halme M, Lindeman S, Linna P. Innovation for inclusive business: Intrapreneurial bricolage in multinational corporations. *Journal of Management Studies.* 2012, 49(4): 743–784.

78. Jesudian G. Innovative financing for rural surgical patients: Experience in mission hospitals. *CHRISMED Journal of Health and Research.* 2016, 3(3): 207–213.

79. Zeschky M, Widenmayer B, Gassmann O. Frugal innovation in emerging markets. *Research-Technology Management.* 2011, 54(4): 38–45.

80. Weyrauch T, Herstatt C. What is frugal innovation? Three defining criteria. *Journal of Frugal Innovation.* 2017, 2(1): 1–17.

81. Venema V. The Indian sanitary pad revolutionary. www.bbc.co.uk/news/magazine-26260978 Published 2014. Accessed July 25 2020.

82. Nee RC. Creative destruction: An exploratory study of how digitally native news nonprofits are innovating online journalism practices. *International Journal on Media Management*. 2013, 15(1): 3–22.

83. Shove E, Trentmann F, Wilk R. *Time, consumption and everyday life: Practice, materiality and culture*. Oxford: Berg, 2009.

84. Davenport TH. *Process innovation: Reengineering work through information technology*. Cambridge: Harvard Business Press, 1993.

85. Solon O. Amazon patents wristband that tracks warehouse workers' movements. www.theguardian.com/technology/2018/jan/31/amazon-warehouse-wristband-tracking Published 2017. Accessed July 25 2020.

86. Daft RL. A dual-core model of organizational innovation. *Academy of Management Journal*. 1978, 21(2): 193–210.

87. Damanpour F. *Organizational innovation: Theory, research, and direction*. Cheltenham: Edward Elgar, 2020.

88. Schaltegger S, Lüdeke-Freund F, Hansen EG. Business cases for sustainability: The role of business model innovation for corporate sustainability. *International Journal of Innovation and Sustainable Development*. 2012, 6(2): 95–119.

89. Chesbrough H. Business model innovation: Opportunities and barriers. *Long Range Planning*. 2010, 43(2): 354–363.

90. Kennedy S, Bocken N. Innovating business models for sustainability: An essential practice for responsible managers. In: Laasch O, Suddaby R, Freeman RE, Jamali D, eds. *The research handbook of responsible management*. Cheltenham: Edward Elgar, 2020.

91. Berkhout F. Normative expectations in systems innovation. *Technology Analysis and Strategic Management*. 2006, 18(3–4): 299–311.

92. Girod SJG, Whittington R. Change escalation processes and complex adaptive systems: From incremental reconfigurations to discontinuous restructuring. *Organization Science*. 2015, 26(5): 1520–1535.

93. Stilgoe J, Owen R, Macnaghten P. Developing a framework for responsible innovation. *Research Policy*. 2013, 42(9): 1568–1580.

94. Long TB, Iñigo E, Blok V. Responsible management of innovation in business. In: Laasch O, Suddaby R, Freeman RE, Jamali D, eds. *The research handbook of responsible management*. Cheltenham: Edward Elgar, 2020: 606–623.

95. Murray R, Caulier-Grice J, Mulgan G. *The open book of social innovation*. London: The Young Foundation, 2010.

96. Hansen EG, Grosse-Dunker F, Reichwald R. Sustainability innovation cube–a framework to evaluate sustainability-oriented innovations. *International Journal of Innovation Management*. 2009, 13(4): 683–713.

97. Rennings K. Redefining innovation: Eco-innovation research and the contribution from ecological economics. *Ecological Economics*. 2000, 32(2): 319–332.

98. Schaltegger S, Wagner M. Sustainable entrepreneurship and sustainability innovation: Categories and interactions. *Business Strategy and the Environment*. 2011, 20(4): 222–237.

99. Ruttan VW, Hayami Y. Toward a theory of induced institutional innovation. *The Journal of Development Studies*. 1984, 20(4): 203–223.

100. Hargrave TJ, Van de Ven AH. A collective action model of institutional innovation. *Academy of Management Review*. 2006, 31(4): 864–888.

101. Howaldt J, Schwarz M. *Social innovation: Concepts, research fields and international trends*. Dortmund: Sozialforschungsstelle Dortmund, 2010.

102. Grimm R, Fox C, Baines S, Albertson K. Social innovation, an answer to contemporary societal challenges? Locating the concept in theory and practice. *Innovation: The European Journal of Social Science Research*. 2013, 26(4): 436–455.

103. Pot F, Dhondt S, Oeij P. Social innovation of work and employment. In: Franz H, Hochgerner J, Howaldt J, eds. *Challenge social innovation*. Berlin: Springer, 2012: 261–274.

104. Akers Z. Directory of black owned businesses. www.beyonce.com/black-parade-route Published 2020. Accessed July 26 2020.

105. Black Enterprise. About. www.blackenterprise.com Published 2020. Accessed July 26 2020.

106. Wallenfeldt J. The Green Book travel guide. www.britannica.com/topic/The-Green-Book-travel-guide Published 1936. Accessed July 26 2020.

107. Black Enterprise. Introducing the first black woman-owned skateboard company. www. blackenterprise.com/introducing-the-first-black-woman-owned-skateboard-company Published 2020. Accessed July 26 2020.

108. Atencio M, Beal B, Wilson C. The distinction of risk: Urban skateboarding, street habitus and the construction of hierarchical gender relations. *Qualitative Research in Sport and Exercise.* 2009, 1(1): 3–20.

109. Bäckström Å. Gender manoeuvring in Swedish skateboarding: Negotiations of femininities and the hierarchical gender structure. *Young.* 2013, 21(1): 29–53.

110. Red Bull Skateboarding. Skateboard like a girl. (https://www.redbull.com/int-en/pushing-forward-skateboard-like-a-girl) 2019.

111. Cajaiba-Santana G. Social innovation: Moving the field forward. A conceptual framework. *Technological Forecasting and Social Change.* 2014, 82: 42–51.

112. Drucker PF. Social innovation: Management's new dimension. *Long Range Planning.* 1987, 20(6): 29–34.

113. Phills JA, Deiglmeier K, Miller DT. Rediscovering social innovation. *Stanford Social Innovation Review.* 2008, 6(4): 34–43.

114. Phillips W, Lee H, Ghobadian A, O'Regan N, James P. Social innovation and social entrepreneurship: A systematic review. *Group and Organization Management.* 2015, 40(3): 428–461.

115. Mulgan G, Tucker S, Ali R, Sanders B. Social innovation: What it is, why it matters and how it can be accelerated. *Skoll Centre for Social Entrepreneurship Working Paper.* 2007.

116. Chudy J. Faris Saeed: The man who built utopia. www.arabianbusiness.com/construction/423093-faris-saeed-the-man-who-built-utopia Published 2019. Accessed July 9 2020.

117. The Natural Step. Our sustainability principles: The rules of the game to accelerate change. www.thenaturalstep.de/solution/sustainability-principles Published 2020. Accessed July 26 2020.

118. Fiksel J. *Design for environment.* McGraw-Hill, 2010.

119. Tru Earth. Finally, an eco-friendly laundry detergent, that's as sensitive on your skin as it is to the environment. www.tru.earth Published 2020. Accessed July 26 2020.

120. Ecover. Laundry. www.ecover.com/laundry Published 2020. Accessed July 26 2020.

121. Blueland. The future of laundry has arrived. www.blueland.com Published 2020. Accessed July 26 2020.

122. Voegtlin C, Scherer AG. Responsible innovation and the innovation of responsibility: Governing sustainable development in a globalized world. *Journal of Business Ethics.* 2017, 143(2): 227–243.

123. von Schomberg R, Hankins J. *International handbook on responsible innovation.* Cheltenham: Edward Elgar, 2019.

124. Ribeiro B, Smith R, Millar K. A mobilising concept? Unpacking academic representations of responsible research and innovation. *Science and Engineering Ethics.* 2017, 23(1): 81–103.

125. Sage. *The ethics of code: Developing AI for business with five core principles.* London: Sage, 2017.

126. Thomas-Bryant K. Five positive ways artificial intelligence will impact accountants. www. sage.com/en-gb/blog/artificial-intelligence-will-impact-accountants Published 2019. Accessed July 15 2020.

127. Fassin Y. Innovation and ethics ethical considerations in the innovation business. *Journal of Business Ethics.* 2000, 27(1–2): 193–203.

128. Zallio M, Berry D. Design and planned obsolescence: Theories and approaches for designing enabling technologies. *The Design Journal.* 2017, 20(1): 3749–3761.

139. London B. *Ending the depression through planned obsolescence.* 1932.

130. Packard V, McKibben B. *The waste makers.* Harmondsworth: Penguin, 1963.

131. Graves J. Asda denies using facial recognition cameras on its customers in Preston amid privacy concerns. www.lep.co.uk/business/asda-denies-using-facial-recognition-cameras-its-customers-preston-amid-privacy-concerns-665351 Published 2019. Accessed July 26 2020.

132. Easley RF. Ethical issues in the music industry response to innovation and piracy. *Journal of Business Ethics.* 2005, 62(2): 163–168.

133. Mattioli D, Lombardo C. Amazon met with startups about investing, then launched competing products. Published 2020. Retrieved from www.wsj.com/articles/amazon-tech-startup-echo-bezos-alexa-investment-fund-11595520249 Accessed July 26 2020.
134. Presenza A, Panniello U, Messeni Petruzzelli A. Tourism multi-sided platforms and the social innovation trajectory: The case of Airbnb. *Creativity and Innovation Management.* 2020: 1–16.
135. Vaswani K. Huawei: The story of a controversial company. www.bbc.co.uk/news/resources/idt-sh/Huawei Published 2019. Accessed July 26 2020.
136. Pink DH. *Drive: The surprising truth about what motivates us.* London: Penguin, 2011.
137. Laasch O, Jamali D, Freeman E, Suddaby R, eds. *The research handbook of responsible management.* Cheltenham: Edward Elgar, 2020.
138. Bocken NMP, Short SW, Rana P, Evans S. A literature and practice review to develop sustainable business model archetypes. *Journal of Cleaner Production.* 2014, 65: 42–56.
139. Lüdeke-Freund F, Carroux S, Joyce A, Massa L, Breuer H. The sustainable business model pattern taxonomy: 45 patterns to support sustainability-oriented business model innovation. *Sustainable Production and Consumption.* 2018, 15: 145–162.

CHAPTER 15

ENTREPRENEURING

OLIVER LAASCH, XUAN YE AND HAIBO ZHOU

LEARNING GOALS

1. Explore characteristics of different types of entrepreneurs and entrepreneuring
2. Get to know common practices throughout the entrepreneuring process
3. Get a grasp on entrepreneurial ethics and plan your 'good venture'

ENCOURAGING FACT

There are two million social economy enterprises in Europe alone, representing 10 per cent of all businesses. More than 11 million people – about 6 per cent of the EU's employees – work for social enterprises [1].

SPOTLIGHT

UTOPIAN (AD)VENTURE MANAGEMENT

'Fusion Festival 2012' by Libertinus is licensed under CC BY-SA 2.0

'The ideological goal of our conjoint action is … a self-determined life, aloof from capitalistic restraints and exploitation interests and to make utopias for us a real life experience by turning model experiments into actually viable options' [2]. What sounds a bit like an anti-capitalist manifesto describes the opportunity that the founders of one of the world's most successful music, art, and lifestyle festivals aimed to grasp. For over 20 years the Fusion

Festival has been gathering hundreds of thousands of guests on an abandoned military base between Berlin and Hamburg. Through this venture, guests and festival makers alike live the aspired utopia, breaking with many taken-for-granted assumptions of what is 'normal', a 'parallel society of a special kind, looking for a possibly better world' they call Kulturkosmos [3].

On the surface, you might think the utopia resides in the personal freedom and expression lived at Fusion, where guests can let go of the normal pressures of society. You might also think it was utopian to have an entirely vegetarian event for four days in a world hooked on meat. However, the utopia is rooted much more deeply in the entrepreneurial management of this venture, its business model breaking with many taken-for-granted capitalist practices.

For instance, Fusion eschews the usual commercial goals of increasing revenues through sales promotion, as they refrain from engaging in advertising of any kind. They even discourage visitors from sharing their images or videos on what they call 'SocialDirtWorks' (derogatory expression for social networks) [4]. Managing a 'normal' capitalist enterprise would seek growth at all costs, while Fusion has limited its paying guests to a maximum of 70,000. When demand

(Continued)

exceeds supply, 'normal' entrepreneurs would cash in on being able to charge more. The Fusion team, however, manages over-demand by raffling off tickets at an accessible price. Whoever isn't drawn doesn't attend [2]. Neither has the venture team had any financial gain from drink sales, usually a lucrative income stream at festivals. Instead they rely on independent NGOs to sell drinks as fundraising activities [3].

Neither are the organizers your 'normal' team of Silicon Valley-type young creatives, or your typical team of entrepreneurs: 'We form a free community of fellow campaigners from various backgrounds, whose life realities, professions and domiciles may differ profoundly, but who are all willing to contribute their free time to this shared venture' [2], '200 very different groups as well as many kick-ass lone fighters' [3]. Working at a 'normal' commercial enterprise, you would expect to be paid, yet Fusion predominantly relies on unpaid volunteer 'supporters'. Surprisingly, supporters don't only have to apply for the job with a letter of motivation, but also their application may be turned down if they don't seem to fit the motivation and mindset of Fusion [5, 6].

The success of Fusion has, however, been damp-ened recently, even threatening survival of the utopian venture. Amidst political tensions, and, as Fusion supporters hint, made-up safety concerns raised by a new police chief, Fusion was on the verge of being called off, which the team called an attack on the 'freedom of art and culture' [7], the beating utopian heart of Fusion. After involving the press and successful legal proceedings, however, the team was able to go ahead, just to be called off after all when the Coronavirus crisis struck [8].

PROFESSIONAL ENTREPRENEURING

Managers must convert society's needs into opportunities for profitable business.

Peter Drucker [9]

Entrepreneuring is centred on venturing practice, which creates value by bringing together resources with an opportunity

Entrepreneuring [10, 11] is the process [12–14] and practice(s) [15, 16] of creating new valuable realities. This might happen, for instance, in the form of solving a social–environmental problem [17, 18] or new organizations opening new markets [19]. It means creating value by bringing together resources to pursue an opportunity [20] in a 'venture', the 'package' in which resources are tied together [21] and in which they create value while travelling through time and space [22]. Making this package is entrepreneuring's main practice of 'venturing'. For instance, the Fusion Festival is a venture to create an alternative reality free from society's pressures. The package of this venture ties together varieties of resources, from money, to cultural capital in the form of music and arts, to personnel in the form of volunteering support, on to the military base where it takes place.

Why are we talking about entrepreneuring in a management textbook? It has been suggested that 'entrepreneurial management may be seen as a **'mode of management'** [23]. Apart from managing entrepreneurially, most managers are also involved in a particular business venture. You might be part of an entrepreneurial project, either your own or another company's, or possibly even founding your own venture, or working in an SME that often requires most of its work to be carried out in the entrepreneuring mode.

Entrepreneuring mode of management is centred on venturing in the pursuit of opportunities

As expressed in Peter Drucker's quote above, managers' natural characteristics include converting society's needs into business opportunities, a core feature also of entrepreneuring. Such needs-to-opportunity conversions may be 'big moves', turning grand challenges into opportunities [24] – for instance, when building a social enterprise that fights poverty and empowers women like Muhammad Yunus's Grameen Bank. Equally, it might consist of 'everyday seizing moments' of opportunity [11], the individual 'entrepreneurial act' [22] – for instance, when realizing that there is a customer group whose life your product could make easier or more sustainable. To engage in professional entrepreneuring not only requires assuming this important societal role, it also requires a certain entrepreneuring competence, to be effective in converting needs and the related opportunities into value. Finally, **professional entrepreneuring** requires professional conduct, to be conducted sustainably, responsibly, and ethically. If done so, this will result in what we call a 'good venture'.

Professional entrepreneuring to effectively turn society's needs into value while engaging in professional conduct

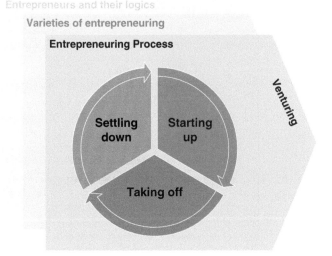

FIGURE 15.1   Mapping professional entrepreneuring

As illustrated in Figure 15.1, we will start this chapter by exploring varieties of forms of entrepreneuring, such as distinct entrepreneurial logics of action, hybrid entrepreneuring, and the characteristics of entrepreneurs. We will then focus on the process of business venturing with its phases of starting up, growing up, and settling down (maturity). We will close the chapter by unpacking typical ethical issues and responses throughout the entrepreneurial process.

ENTREPRENEURS AND THEIR LOGICS OF ACTION

Our answer to the somewhat controversial question 'Who is an **entrepreneur**?' [25] is that anyone and everyone who engages in entrepreneuring practice is an entrepreneuring practitioner. In this section we will discuss the entrepreneurial manager and their logics of action.

Entrepreneurs
are practitioners who engage in
the practice of entrepreneuring

ENTREPRENEURS' TRAITS

Practitioners who make competent and successful entrepreneurs often possess typical entrepreneurial traits as illustrated on the left side of Table 15.1 [26, 27]. However, even individuals without a very strong entrepreneurial personality can practice entrepreneurially, if behaving according to the dimensions of entrepreneurial orientation on the right side of the table [28].

TABLE 15.1   Characteristics of entrepreneurs and entrepreneuring

The 'big five' entrepreneurial personality traits	Dimensions of an entrepreneurial orientation of practice
High need for achievement: propensity to take responsibility for outcomes	**Autonomy:** independent action by an individual or team aimed at bringing forth a business concept or vision and carrying it through to completion
High risk-taking propensity: seeking opportunities in spite of the risks faced while doing so	**Innovativeness:** a willingness to introduce newness and novelty through experimentation and creative processes aimed at developing new products and services, as well as new processes
Internal locus of control: belief in oneself to be able to influence outcomes	**Proactiveness:** a forward-looking perspective characteristic of a marketplace leader who has the foresight to seize opportunities in anticipation of future demand
High self-efficacy: goal orientation and ability to build personal competence necessary to achieve goals	**Competitive aggressiveness:** an intense effort to outperform industry rivals. It is characterized by a combative posture or an aggressive response aimed at improving position or overcoming a threat in a competitive marketplace
High extraversion: positive energy levels invested in building and maintaining relationships	**Risk taking:** making decisions and taking action without certain knowledge of probable outcomes; some undertakings may also involve making substantial resource commitments in the process of venturing forward

SOURCES: adapted from [27, 28]

Productive motive
for entrepreneuring is initiated by desiring meaningful work such as delivering innovation to generate value for stakeholders

Unproductive motive
for entrepreneuring consists of value-extracting behaviour to appropriate existing value and externalize costs, potentially reducing others' overall welfare in the process or even destroying positive value(s)

Entrepreneurs are often constructed and presented in a very positive light, even as heroes [29]. Therefore, the traits-based literature on entrepreneurs has focused primarily on the 'good in people' – such as positive psychological characteristics (as indicated in Table 15.1). However, 'sometimes the same creative energy that drives an entrepreneur has its source in destructive internal needs that can ruin a career or a company' [30]. Related unproductive or even destructive entrepreneuring motives could both be driven by external factors, such as institutionalized 'rules of the game', or by the 'dark triad' of malevolent and egocentric qualities. Entrepreneurial personality traits are presented in Table 15.2 [31, 32].

TABLE 15.2   Dark triad, unproductive motive, and ethics issues

Dark triad characteristics	Unproductive motive/behaviour	Ethics issues
Narcissism: feeling superior, self-presumed greatness, belief that others should admire and serve them without expectation of reciprocation	Rent-seeking not bothered by moral dilemmas; value appropriation (taking without giving in return); view venture as a direct reflection of their own greatness	They are unlikely to want others to view their ventures as unscrupulous, but behind closed doors they would be unfazed by doing whatever it takes to be successful
Machiavellianism: Cynical, little concern for the well-being of others, self-interested	Maximizing personal gain and short-term profits with little thought given to broader and long-term repercussions; focusing on short-term wins; engaging in an appropriative rent-seeking orientation in which relationships involve taking as much as possible while minimizing reciprocation	Taking shortcuts on product quality, overcharging for services, taking advantage of employees, use of a litigatory competitive strategy

| Psychopathy: Callous, insensitive to others' needs, lack remorse, life perspective is every person for themselves, viewing others as prey or fellow predators | Rent-seeking; externalizing costs; dominance and coercion are the way to achieve cooperation and for an individual to maximize personal gains. | Gamble with others' money if the opportunity presents itself, pick out individuals who are vulnerable or easily dominated as stakeholders of whom they can take advantage while offering little in return |  |

SOURCES: synthesized from [31, 33–37]

The table also illustrates the kind of ethical issues that are likely to arise from these traits. This is an important consideration as 'If you build that foundation, both the moral and the ethical foundation, as well as the business foundation, and the experience foundation, then the building [the venture constructed] won't crumble' [38]. Therefore, the ethical issues arising from an entrepreneur's potentially 'dark' personality traits deserve reflexive attention for the sake of the venture's success. A curious related anecdote features John Mackey, the very much admired ecopreneur, founder of Whole Foods, and bestselling author of *Conscious capitalism: Liberating the heroic spirit of business* [39]. For seven years John used the alias Rahodeb (an anagram of his wife's name Deborah) and posted anonymous comments like 'I really like John Mackey's hair' or bashing their competitor OATS as 'floundering around hoping to find a viable strategy that may stop their erosion. Problem is that they lack the time and the capital now'. Ironically, this activity came to light when Mackey tried to take over OATS [40].

TYPES OF ENTREPRENEURS

While entrepreneurial traits and an entrepreneurial orientation of practice are found across entrepreneurs, they differ considerably in their profiles. Entrepreneurs are frequently classified in the following ways:

- **By venturing experience.** An *enterprising person* is a potential entrepreneur but is not engaged in a venture, while *nascent* entrepreneurs are in the process of starting their venture, and a *novice* is running their first venture. The more experienced entrepreneurs are *portfolio entrepreneurs* who run several ventures in parallel, and *serial entrepreneurs* have already run multiple ventures in the past [41, 42].

- **By traits–venture mix**. Entrepreneurs can also be characterized by a mixture of their personal traits and characteristics of their venture. For instance, a *diamond* is 'a visionary dreamer leading transformative ventures', while *stars*, 'are charismatic individuals building personality brands'. *Transformers* are 'change makers, reenergizing traditional industries' and a rocket ship is 'analytical thinkers making strategic improvements' [43].

- **By financial success of their business venture**. *Gazelles* are the entrepreneurs who start high-growth businesses with at least one million USD in revenue, and whose sales double every four years, while *unicorns* are start-ups with a value of over 1 billion USD before initial public offering [44]. Maybe we could call entrepreneurs successfully running small businesses 'ants' [45, 46].

- **By position in an organization**. *Founders* are entrepreneurs that are in the process of creating a new venture or who have created it in the past [47]. *Owner-managers* often manage small businesses in an entrepreneurial way [48]. They might be the founder too, or manage the business entrepreneurially, due to the volatile environment small businesses often operate in [49]. *Intrapreneurs* work in an entrepreneurial way in an established business, often using the business's resources to create or tackle opportunities [50, 51].

- **By attitude towards business ventures**. *Lifestyle entrepreneurs'* purpose in running a business venture is to increase their quality of life by, for instance, being more independent or increasing their income [52–54], while *career entrepreneurs* are interested in succeeding with their venture and making a career out of it [55, 56].

- **By entrepreneuring work patterns**. *Butterfly entrepreneurs* are opportunity spotters 'flitting from one pretty flower to the next', but not necessarily getting a lot of hands-on work done, while *bees* focus on one opportunity to get the work done [57]. Often members of entrepreneurial teams complement each other as both characteristics are necessary.

Entrepreneurial manager
a practitioner with both management and entrepreneuring competence, able to turn opportunities into value while administering resources

In the context of this book, we are most interested in when entrepreneuring and management come together – that is, entrepreneuring as a mode of management. We are looking for the **'entrepreneurial manager'** [23], who is competent in managing as part of the entrepreneuring practice or competent in entrepreneuring as part of their management practice. In practice, entrepreneurs often also act as managers when running their venture; they are entrepreneurs who manage: managing entrepreneurs. Equally, managers often entrepreneur – for instance, when pursuing an opportunity for an established business, they are managers who entrepreneur: entrepreneuring managers. Managers might also be part of a founder team of a new business venture or work in a startup business and engage in its entrepreneuring practices.

Aren't managers and entrepreneurs quite different? For instance, it has been suggested that the entrepreneuring 'pursuit of opportunity is distinguished from administrative tasks that involve managing resources. Some of the practices that contribute to the successful management of resources inhibit the pursuit of opportunity' [20]. So there seems to be an inherent tension between management's 'administrative' and 'entrepreneuring' modes. Managers are often described as 'doers' administering existing resources to keep fulfilling organizational goals, while entrepreneurs are often described as 'creators' or 'makers' who generate new realities. It has been found, for instance, that entrepreneurs typically have a higher tolerance for ambiguous situations than managers [58] and entrepreneurs on average have a higher motivation for achievement [59]. Entrepreneurs have a higher preference for making autocratic rather than consensus-based decisions, are more motivated by extrinsic (e.g. a high income) than intrinsic factors (e.g. personal achievement), and prefer more agile market-oriented structures to functional hierarchic structures [60]. Entrepreneurs love challenges much more than managers and see themselves as dreamers, and risk takers [61]. However, managers and entrepreneurs also share many similarities. For instance, they both show a high commitment to work, are energetic, need to have control, and most interestingly, both equally love to manage [61]!

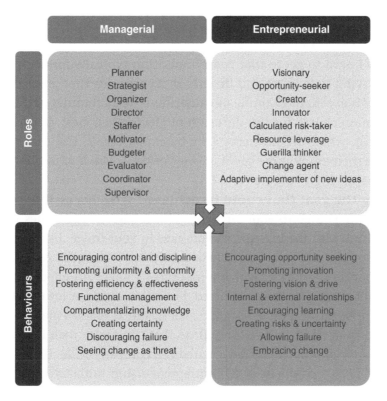

FIGURE 15.2   The complex entrepreneurial manager profile

SOURCE: adapted from [62, 63]

In Figure 15.2, we provide an overview of how both entrepreneurial and managerial practitioners' characteristics may come together in the practitioner profile of the entrepreneurial manager. It becomes clear how complex and at times paradoxical it can be to live the professional life of an entrepreneurial manager: for instance, to find the right balance or swap back and forth between the roles of an organizer and a guerilla thinker. Imagine on the same day engaging with behaviours promoting uniformity and behaviours promoting innovation.

ENTREPRENEURING LOGICS OF ACTION

In the entrepreneuring mode we behave differently. It has been found that entrepreneuring practitioners, whether they are classical 'full time' entrepreneurs or entrepreneurial managers, typically apply three different logics of action [64, 65]: causation, effectuation logic [66, 67], and bricolage logics [68, 69].

Causation
to select among given means
(resources) to achieve a
predetermined goal (end)

Acquiring and managing resources to achieve a predetermined goal [70]. Imagine you go to a restaurant and order a particular dish. The chef will apply causation logic when gathering the necessary ingredients for the dish [70]. The underlying question of entrepreneuring with a **causation** mode of action is 'What do I need to get this done?' or 'What do I need to get to that goal?' Causation typically follows predictive logic in trying to forecast and linearly move towards that predicted future [66, 70]. An excellent example of causation is Tesla founder and CEO Elon Musk's 'master plan' for the diffusion of electric vehicles: '1. Create a low volume car, which would necessarily be expensive. 2. Use that money to develop a medium volume car at a lower price. 3. Use *that* money to create an affordable, high volume car' [71].

Effectuation
to imagine possible new
goals (ends) using a given
set of means (resources)

Seeing the goal that could be achieved with accessible resources [70]. Imagine you go to your kitchen and think about the dishes you could possibly cook with the ingredients you have in your fridge. In **effectuation** the question shifts to 'What can I do with this?' or 'What goals could I achieve, what opportunities tackle, with the resources I have?' In effectuation logic, there is not one future to be predicted, but rather different futures that could be made from the accessible resources. For instance, management at the food retailer Tesco decided to use the resources that come with their immense scale to address social problems. They created the company-wide 'Using our Scale for Good' [72], a corporate social entrepreneurship initiative tackling social issues that they had the most effective resources to address. As an example, the 'tackling food waste' venture connected to the resources in their global food supply chain network and 'improving health' to their close relationship with customers' eating habits as a unique resource.

It has been suggested that the 'normal' manager is more likely to apply causation logic (see Figure 15.3), while typical entrepreneurs are more likely to use effectuation logic. Accordingly, in the entrepreneuring mode of management we will frequently switch back and forth between both logics.

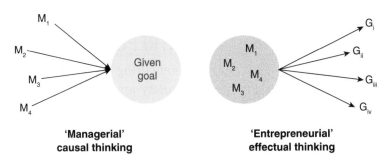

FIGURE 15.3 Causal versus effectual reasoning

SOURCE: adapted from [73]

Another unique logic of entrepreneuring action is **bricolage**, which is grounded in the idea that entrepreneuring commonly starts out with very few resources, but frequently builds something important. It performs the paradoxical magic trick of 'creating something from nothing' [74]. Most business ventures start out with very limited financial resources, usually less than 5,000 USD, and limited access to other sources of capital [74], making do with scarce resources, throwing them together, and 'making do' [75]. Entrepreneurship follows a logic of bricolage (French for 'tinkering') [76] and can be contrasted with 'engineering' logic whereby you would aim to use purpose-made ideal resources to design the ideal venture [69]. In bricolage, instead, ideal resources are not available, so entrepreneurs have to engage in an iterative process of 'tinkering' to iteratively make it work with the non-ideal available resources at hand [75]. The bricolage logic of entrepreneuring lends itself particularly to resource-poor environments where you have to 'make do' with what you have. It is a 'bottom-up' perspective on entrepreneuring and innovation that often relies on (localized) knowledge and social capital as the main resources [77].

For instance, the start-up venture Smart Air showed entrepreneurial bricolage in a variety of ways. Instead of spending resources on production lines, they relied on a do-it-yourself manufacturing model, where customers put their air filter together for themselves. Nor did they manufacture any of the parts, but instead relied on another bricolage type of entrepreneuring. Its product is based on the 'life-hack' of strapping an inexpensive filter frame in front of a normal household fan [78]. Instead of building up resource intensive distribution channels, Thomas Talhelm, the entrepreneur behind Smart Air, sold it via the Chinese Taobao e-commerce platform, and instead of spending a large amount on marketing, the innovative cost-effective design could be sold at a considerably lower price than any other air purifier on the market [79].

Entrepreneurial bricolage a logic of action in which one makes do with what is available, even if it is not ideal, put together in a new way to create value

Smart Air's DIY low-cost bricolage air filter consisting of a filter frame and Velcro to strap it in front of any common household fan.

'Smart Air Filters' by Kai Hendry is licensed under CC BY 2.0

VARIETIES OF ENTREPRENEURING

Entrepreneuring may assume a marvellous variety of shapes, sizes, and timings. However, all of them are built from '**entrepreneurial acts**' [22]. Entrepreneuring in one case may consist of an individual short-lived act such as seizing the opportunity to offer fruit from your garden to your neighbours. Equally, millions of entrepreneurial acts may form an enormous global enterprise like the electric car manufacturer Tesla. Entrepreneurial acts and related practices – customary, typical entrepreneurial acts – can be carried out in a variety of different ways and in a variety of contexts. We will now explore different mechanisms for and forms of entrepreneurial acts coming together in entrepreneuring.

Entrepreneurial act is the smallest building block of different forms of entrepreneuring

FORMS OF ENTREPRENEURING

Most people probably associate entrepreneuring with the creation of new businesses. However, as illustrated in Table 15.3, new business venturing is just one of the forms that entrepreneuring can take. We will now briefly introduce each of the three salient forms of entrepreneuring – new business venturing, corporate intrapreneuring, and institutional entrepreneurship.

TABLE 15.3   Prominent types of entrepreneuring

	Practice	Entrepreneur	Intention	Example
New business venturing	Creating a new business	Business (co) founder	Creating a new organization to realize an opportunity and to create value	Blake Mycoskie's TOMS Shoes business providing shoes to those who need them
Intrapreneuring	Acting entrepreneurially from the inside of an established organization	Organizational member, typically in some leading role	a) Tackling internal organizational change opportunities b) Using organizational resources to tackle a new external opportunity	Unilever's 'Sustainable Living Plan' (50 sustainability opportunities), created by former CEO Paul Polman
Institutional entrepreneurship	Venturing to create 'a new normal'	Any role	Changing taken-for granted (institutionalized) aspects – e.g. of society, economy, or an industry	Greta Thunberg's environmental movement

First, entrepreneuring is commonly understood as creating a **new business venture**, entrepreneuring as organization creation [19]. Such business ventures typically create value by seizing a commercial and/or social opportunity. The entrepreneurial practitioner in focus is the founder, or the founder team. For instance, TOMS Shoes is a business that was founded in order to both seize an opportunity to give shoes to people in need, and to make a profitable business out of it [80]. While we will mostly discuss entrepreneuring in a business venturing context, much of the rest of the chapter, particularly the phases of the entrepreneuring process, can easily be applied to corporate **intrapreneuring** and institutional entrepreneuring.

Intrapreneuring refers to members' of an organization who realize opportunities inside or from inside an established organization [50, 51]. Such opportunities may be to either transform the organization or to seize an external opportunity – for instance, to enter into a new promising market. Often, both internal transformation and seizing an external opportunity go hand in hand. Professional intrapreneuring in the ethics, responsibility, and sustainability context has gained considerable attention, due both to the immense power and resources of established corporations to tackle social goals, and to their often 'irresponsible' nature that is in need of internal transformation. Intrapreneurship is particularly prominent as a means of transforming companies to become more socially and environmentally responsible. Such social intrapreneurs typically engage in the following practices [81, 82]:

1. **Championing.** Continuously advocating for the integration of social and business value as a central tenet for the company

2. **Communicating.** Particularly articulating the rationale and importance of the transformation; actively listening to various stakeholders and speaking to them in ways that reveal how social action is relevant to their needs and interests

3. **Creating innovative solutions.** New resource configurations, actions, and relationships. They are not managers of the status quo but creators of a new, sometimes disruptive, one

4. **Catalysing for change.** Inspiring and creating synergies in the work of others

5. **Coordinating.** Effectively reaching across internal and external boundaries, mobilizing, and aligning interests and incentives

6. **Contributing.** Supporting the success of others rather than being perceived as building a new power centre, they are team players who enable other groups

7. **Calculating shrewdly.** Cognizant of the realities of the corporate environment, they are cost-conscious and mindful of the bottom line. Change is not framed in terms of ideals or intentions, but in terms of aligned incentives

8. **Assessing.** How fast and far they can move the transformational process within the realities of the organization

New business venturing is a form of entrepreneuring centred on the creation of new organizations

Intrapreneurship members of an established organization seize opportunities to change the organization from the inside or to use the organization to tackle new external opportunities

However, not all social intrapreneurs act in the same way. As illustrated in Figure 15.4, there are at least four substantially different species in the social intrapreneurial animal kingdom. Intrapreneurial roles consist of two tactical ones (Donkey and Wolf) and two strategic ones (Giraffe and Beaver), with the former requiring high-level strategizing, and the latter getting the work done. Each role in turn may emphasize more societal values (Giraffe and Wolf) or other organizational values (Beaver and Donkey), implying that social intrapreneurs have to be able to flexibly switch back and forth between social and commercial logics. Social intrapreneurs typically play each of those roles at some point in their professional lives. Accordingly, successful intrapreneuring requires the competence to move between these different roles as required by changing circumstances [83]. They are highly competent 'activists in suits' [84].

Societal values

Organizational value

The head in the clouds, but feet firmly planted on the ground

Ability to see threats and opportunities from a distance.
Reach opportunities that others cannot quite stretch to.
Distinguish trends from routine incidents in the landscape.

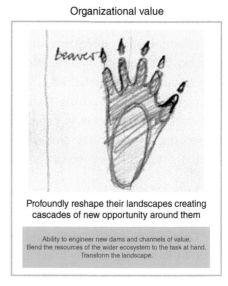

Profoundly reshape their landscapes creating cascades of new opportunity around them

Ability to engineer new dams and channels of value.
Bend the resources of the wider ecosystem to the task at hand.
Transform the landscape.

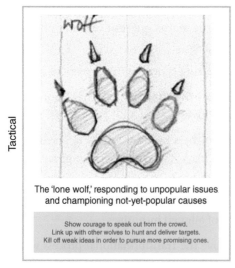

The 'lone wolf,' responding to unpopular issues and championing not-yet-popular causes

Show courage to speak out from the crowd.
Link up with other wolves to hunt and deliver targets.
Kill off weak ideas in order to pursue more promising ones.

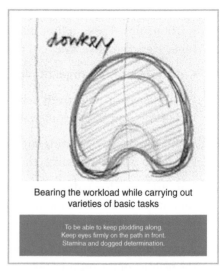

Bearing the workload while carrying out varieties of basic tasks

To be able to keep plodding along.
Keep eyes firmly on the path in front.
Stamina and dogged determination.

FIGURE 15.4 The social intrapreneurship taxonomy

SOURCE: [83]

Institutional entrepreneurs leverage resources to seize an opportunity in order to create new, institutionalized, taken-for-granted practices or to transform existing ones [85–87]. While institutional entrepreneuring sometimes happens in or through organizations, or leads to the creation of new organizations [88], it can happen entirely outside the organizational sphere – for instance, in the form of a social movement.

Paradoxically, institutional entrepreneurship is a form of 'embedded agency', which means that you are trying to change the rules of the game you are playing, while being bound by the same rules you are trying to change [89, 90]. The process of institutional entrepreneurship [91], therefore often includes some type of rule breaking, be it on a grand scale like Greta Thunberg's civil disobedience, in the form of Fridays for the Future or small symbolic acts like 'spitting in the salad' [92]. It also includes the caretaker/janitor who, acting as a 'workplace vigilante' and making it 'taken for granted' that everyone will always switch off their computer when going home, is a local institutional entrepreneur [93]. Another example is the beauty company Deciem whose management decided to engage in an institutional entrepreneurial act by boycotting the hyper-consumerist institution of Black Friday. They closed both their online and physical stores that day 'for a moment of nothing', to deinstitutionalize the practice of Black Friday as they said that it is bad for both consumers and the planet [94]. Institutional entrepreneurship often relies on the interplay of many distributed institutional entrepreneurs [95]. The institutional entrepreneurship process consists of three main sets of practices [87]:

1. **Positioning.** Institutional entrepreneurs need to be seen as legitimate among a diverse set of stakeholders.

2. **Theorizing.** They need to create alternatives, to theorize new practices that could become the new normal, through both discourse and political means.

3. **Institutionalizing.** The new practices are made the 'new normal' ('institutionalized') by connecting them to stakeholders' routines and values.

In the context of the necessary transformation from old-world to new-world management, a 'new normal of management', all three forms of entrepreneuring are crucial. For it to be a transformation, we need institutional entrepreneurs who change what is taken for granted about management, businesses and the economy, as in the case of Fusion which aimed to 'make utopias for us a real life experience by turning model experiments into actually viable options'. We need innovative sustainable Davids (new business ventures), and greening Goliaths that use their juggernauted size and resources to address sustainability issues large-scale, driven by intrapreneurs [96].

Institutional entrepreneurship entrepreneuring to create or change taken-for-granted practices

Further, entrepreneuring may shift among these three forms and exist in more than one of them at a time. For instance, the founding team at Fairphone (see Chapter 3) started out as an activist group of institutional entrepreneurs who wanted to change the taken-for-granted, unfair practices of the electronic devices industry. They became founders of the new business venture Fairphone, which is close to reaching maturity. It has grown to a size at which individuals across the company are soon likely to engage in corporate entrepreneuring, using Fairphone as a vehicle for corporate social entrepreneuring.

COMMERCIAL, SOCIAL, AND HYBRID ENTREPRENEURING

Traditionally, entrepreneuring efforts have often been understood as pursuing economic opportunities, and building profitable businesses very much in a commercial, market-oriented way driven by a capitalistic logic [97, 98]. However, there are varieties of entrepreneuring that are predominantly driven by a logic different from a capitalist-style commercial logic. Examples are many, including bottom-of-the pyramid entrepreneurship [99], spiritual entrepreneurship [100], cultural entrepreneurship [101], sports entrepreneurship [102], and family entrepreneurship [103]. The most prominent examples are social entrepreneurship [104], emphasizing a social welfare logic and mission [105], and ecopreneurship [104, 106], following an environmental logic and mission.

Hybrid entrepreneuring describes entrepreneuring practices that listen to multiple logics, not only the commercial one

To be economically viable, even entrepreneuring activities that are focused on non-commercial, social or environmental missions, also, to some degree, follow a 'money-making' logic. Therefore, they are **hybrid** ventures, partly commercial, partly non-commercial, that are managed according to multiple, hybrid, or even heterogeneous logics beyond the commercial one [98, 107]. It has also been argued that the majority of ventures and business organizations are hybrid rather than commercial, as they typically integrate parts of other logics such as corporate social responsibility, religious, as in Islamic banking, governmental, as in private–public or state-owned enterprises, and family, as in the enormous number of family businesses in the world [108].

Business ventures that appear to be entirely commercially driven may also have a surprising social logic. An excellent example is the Nigerian start-up Kobo360, which provides mobile cashless money services for professional lorry/truck drivers. On the surface their venture adds value by saving drivers and their companies the time necessary for paying out, receiving, and handling cash, an important factor in the logistics industry where time is quite literally money. However, the app also tackles the issue of cash-based corruption and frequent armed robberies that targeted the large amounts of cash drivers usually carried [109, 110].

The varieties of organizations created through those ventures can be placed on different sections of a 'hybrid spectrum' (see Figure 15.5). These ventures and corresponding organizations typically span varieties of sectors, not only the business sector, but also the public/governmental, and civil society 'third sector' [111].

The founders of Kobo360 (Obi Ozor and Ife Oyedele) ventured with a mobile payment that offers both commercial and social value to professional truck drivers across Nigeria, Ghana, Kenya, Uganda, Burkina Faso and Ivory Coast.

Printed with permission of Kobo360

Managing a venture according to hybrid logics, and the respective stakeholders that correspond to those logics can be challenging. Here are two main types of challenges in such ventures:

- **Tensions and trade-offs.** Hybrid venture management requires navigating tensions and making trade-offs between commercial and social logic when these contradict: 'You can't have your cake and eat it' [113]. However, they don't always have to contradict, as frequently there is a business case for ethics, responsibility, and sustainability [114]. This type of 'dual goal management' often requires innovative approaches, and can benefit from using unique combinations of logics as a valuable differentiator [115].

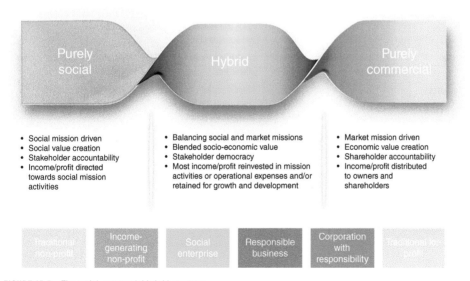

FIGURE 15.5 The social-commercial hybrid spectrum

SOURCE: adapted from [112], elaborated with elements from slidemodel.com

- **Mission drift.** As hybrid organizations work with dual missions, commercial and social, they often, over time, experience what is called a 'mission drift' [116, 117]. For instance, a venture that starts out with an entirely social mission might increasingly be steered by commercial stakeholders, such as financiers to fuel business growth, or traditional commercial managers that replace the original founder team as the venture grows. The social mission might 'drift' too much towards the commercial end of the spectrum. Conversely, commercial enterprises might drift towards a social mission [118], which in turn might be seen as critical by traditional commercial stakeholders.

As illustrated in Table 15.4 there are three main types of social entrepreneurs engaged in social and hybrid entrepreneuring. The social bricoleur typically addresses local social problems and opportunities by improvised, little resource-intensive solutions, using whatever is at hand. They can do so as they have superior problem knowledge, being so close to the social opportunity to be addressed. The social constructionist instead spots systemic 'voids', social needs that are not addressed by the 'normal' actors, be it government or business. The third type, social engineers, create better ways of addressing a social need than the current incumbents serving this need.

TABLE 15.4   Roles of social entrepreneurs

	Social bricoleur	Social constructionist	Social engineer
Theoretical inspiration	Hayek, local, contextualized nature of opportunities	Kirzner, 'systemic changes in expectations'	Schumpeter's 'creative destruction'
Opportunity	Perceives local opportunities to address local social needs	Builds structures to provide goods and services addressing social needs that governments, agencies, and businesses cannot	Creates more effective or efficient social systems designed to replace existing ones
Scale	Typically small scale, local in scope	Small to large scale, local to international	Potential to disrupt existing order globally
Resources	Uses existing local resources, tends not to rely on external resources	Needs important external resources (government, charities, NGOs, etc.) to support the structure	Finds their own resources; preserves its independence
Pro/Con	Flexibility to face social problems, self-reliant Addresses only local social needs	Scalable and exportable model in different regions Needs time and effort for fundraising, control by professionals and volunteers	Revolutionizes and replaces existing institutions, in-depth impact Uniqueness of the founder, tension and conflicts with industry incumbents being disrupted

SOURCE: Adapted from [119]

Often, the same entrepreneur and their enterprises move between these different roles. For instance, Muhammad Yunus with his Grameen Bank first acted as a bricoleur, using his own money to fund small loans and his intimate knowledge of the local Bangladeshi social structures to provide micro-loans to the rural poor [120, 121]. Building on this local bricolage, Yunus then assumed the role of a social constructionist, scaling and exporting microfinance practices globally, where they addressed similar problems of under-served communities with inadequate access to financial means, a problem then often neglected by governments. Finally, Yunus with Grameen developed into a social engineering role, disrupting varieties of existing industries. This included big banks that had long ignored poorer populations and the traditional informal money lenders industry, which often had abused its local monopoly position in order to charge cut-throat interest rates, or worse [120, 122].

ENTREPRENEURING PROCESS

In the previous section, we discussed how entrepreneuring comes in all sizes, shapes, logics, and motivations. We will keep this variety of entrepreneuring in mind, while now focusing on a new business venture creation type of entrepreneuring. The types of new business ventures vary considerably – social or commercial, local or global, virtual or bricks and mortar, among others.

However, as illustrated in Figure 15.6, new business ventures typically share a very similar underlying process centred on the three main elements – opportunity, resources, and the entrepreneurial team [21]. As ventures grow and develop, while responding to developments in the environment, the relative weight of each element may shift considerably. For instance, when starting up, there is usually an immense perceived opportunity while entrepreneurs have only few resources. In the settling-down phase of entrepreneuring where the enterprise has been developed to maturity, the situation is typically reversed. Ample resources might have been accumulated over time, and the opportunity is likely to have decreased over time as others compete.

Not only the weight, but also the nature of each element is likely to change over time. For instance, in the start-up phase, financial resources might initially come from 'family, friends, and fools', later from venture capitalists, and possibly even from the stock market if there should be an initial public offering (IPO). The **entrepreneuring process** is centred on aligning and balancing these three main elements. There are three main practices entrepreneurs engage in to manage opportunity, resources, and the team:

Entrepreneuring process can be understood as managing a venture by connecting opportunity, resources, and the team

1. Entrepreneurs connect opportunities to resources, mostly through **communication**. They might communicate their perception of an opportunity to potential investors and supporters to access financial resources – for instance, using a business plan. They communicate the opportunity to their venture team to keep them motivated and to create a shared vision to work towards. They might communicate with regulators in order to explore the regulatory conditions for the venture, and with stakeholders

to explore their potential engagement in seizing the opportunity, their concerns, or advantages resulting from the enterprise.

2. Entrepreneurs and their teams apply innovation and **creativity** to navigate the ambiguity and uncertainty of how value will be created while seizing the opportunity. Creative practices might relate to innovating a new type of business model, a new product like lab-grown meat, or a practice innovation such as open hiring (see Chapter 19).

3. Entrepreneurs offer **leadership** in navigating external forces and a constantly changing environment (e.g. regulatory changes, public opinion or regulatory pressures) [123]. They lead to managing the resources in the most effective manner and to shaping and structuring the venture. For instance, Pia Poppenreiter had to provide leadership in navigating public opinion, regulatory pressures, and her venture's internal ethical foundation in relation to her controversial dating app Ohlala.

In the following two sections we will have a closer look at the three elements of the entrepreneuring process, and at how they relate to the venture environment.

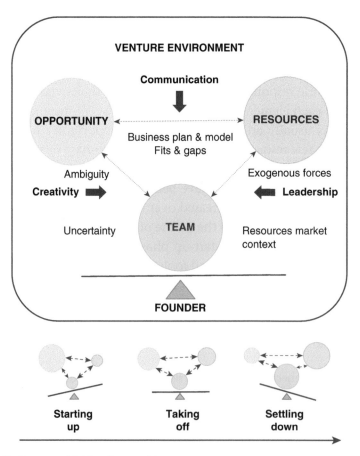

FIGURE 15.6   The Timmons model of the entrepreneurial process

SOURCE: adapted from [21]. Adapted with permission.

OPPORTUNITIES, RESOURCES, AND THE TEAM

The entrepreneurial process often begins by identifying an opportunity to create value. What counts as an **opportunity** very much lies in the eyes of different entrepreneurs. For instance, a commercial entrepreneur might not consider a barely profitable but effective technology for ocean clean-up to be an opportunity. An ecopreneur, however, might see an immense environmental restoration opportunity, which is also economically feasible. There are three main types of practice for identifying [124] market opportunities, each of which is differently useful under different conditions of demand and supply [124–126]:

Entrepreneuring opportunity consists of an unrealized potential to create value through a venture

1. **Recognizing opportunities.** If there is both demand and supply, accessing an opportunity relies on creating a venture that brings both together [126]. To do so entrepreneurs typically 'connect the dots' [127] – they recognize patterns of shifts, changes, and trends creating new matches between supply and demand, and opportunities to connect them [128]. In order to be able to do this, entrepreneurs need to acquire intimate knowledge of the market. They need to be competent entrepreneuring practitioners and require creativity to connect supply and demand [129]. In a social or ecopreneurship context, additional knowledge of social and environmental issues (demand) and solutions (supply) is key [130]. For instance, BRAC, an entrepreneuring NGO in Bangladesh recognized that there was both a demand for microfinance among ultra-poor women, and a supply of microfinance offers [131]. Their venture consisted of bridging the 'institutional void' and bringing supply and demand together [132].

2. **Discovering opportunities**. There are also situations where there is either a clear demand but no visible matching supply or vice versa. Unlike opportunity identification, where supply and demand only have to be 'found', opportunity discovery requires either supply or demand to actively be generated. An excellent example is Hector Castillo, founder of the Mexican 'Circo Volador' (translates as 'Flying Circus'). The social enterprise helps former street gang members to build professional employment skills. Hector had his supply of social services ready, his commitment to helping alleviate gang-related issues, although he knew little about the gangs' needs and demand. In order to discover the matching demand to his supply, he created a radio programme produced for and with street gang members. By doing so he was able to better understand gang members, including their needs, and the resulting demand for professional development opportunity. Hector had discovered the missing demand for the opportunity, which his social enterprise was to address [124].

3. **Creating opportunities.** Entrepreneurs might also actively create opportunities, including the creation of both supply and demand [126]. An excellent example of opportunity creation involving both commercial and institutional entrepreneurship is the Alaska-based entrepreneur Lowell Wakefield. Over the course of over 30 years

he not only created both supply and demand for the King Crab fishery industry, but also co-created the laws and regulations, such as quality and hygiene standards governing this industry [133].

While research on entrepreneuring has focused on the more attention-grabbing topic of opportunities, the vast majority of the world's enterprises, however, are not driven by opportunity, but by necessity. There are hundreds of millions of 'necessity entrepreneurs' in the world [134, 135]. These typically small-scale, individual proprietor enterprises range from street food stalls to gardening services. They are driven due to a lack of access to jobs to generate an income, driving them to become self-employed entrepreneurs. The entrepreneuring process of necessity entrepreneurship is significantly different, as opportunity entrepreneurs are drawn to, or rather pulled into entrepreneuring out of their own motivation, while necessity entrepreneurs are pushed to become entrepreneurs due to basic economic needs [136].

Entrepreneuring resources consist of varieties of different capital used to seize an opportunity

Seizing an opportunity to create value requires **resources**, the second main element of the entrepreneuring process. An entrepreneur might use financial, social, and human capital [137], cultural capital, legitimacy, goodwill, or even political capital to seize an opportunity. An important insight about resources is the difference between capital and resources. Capital only creates value once it has been turned into a resource for action. What kinds of resources and how much of them a venture needs and uses significantly influences entrepreneuring practices [18].

For instance, the resourcing practices (practices of accessing resources) [138] might consist predominantly of 'bootstrapping' creative ways of working with few financial resources, instead tapping into the entrepreneur's human capital of creatively making it work, or into their social capital of family, friends, and other supporters. Or an entrepreneur with strong political capital and legitimacy as resources might be able to seize an opportunity for a large-scale governmental contract without having major financial or human capital to tap into. The entrepreneur in this example would be able to seize the opportunity of this contract by turning their political capital into financial resources (payment for the contract), and financial resources into human resources by hiring specialists competent to fulfil the contract. The main mechanism of resourcing is to increase the resources available by transferring a less valuable resource into a more valuable one in order to seize the opportunity at hand. Expressions like 'making meatballs without meat' [139] or turning lead into gold [137] have been used to describe the power of resourcing practices. These metaphors express the potential and crucial importance of resourcing practices to create value where there was none by constructing the right mix of resources to seize an opportunity.

'Team entrepreneurship' reminds us that, although often dominant, individual entrepreneurs rarely get the job done themselves: the **entrepreneurial team** is crucial [140, 141].[1] This collective perspective of entrepreneuring goes beyond the 'lone hero' perspective of entrepreneurship, and in the most extreme case stresses the importance of 'entrepreneurialism', a culture of distributed entrepreneurship, where everyone acts entrepreneurially together with everyone else [95]. Therefore, entrepreneurial teams may range from typical 'founder couples' where two entrepreneurs create and steer a venture together, to entrepreneurial management approaches, where everyone in a venture is expected to act entrepreneurially. For instance, in our introductory case of Fusion, there was no principal entrepreneurial figure, but rather a changing team consisting of a variety of different people, an entrepreneurial 'collective'. Here we rather focus on the more common perspective of smaller founder teams. At the core of practices of venture team formation there is the balance to be struck between familiarity and complementarity. Founder teams are most effective if members are both similar enough to be able to work together closely, and different enough to mutually complement each other, creating a bigger team and competence pool [142]. Core factors influencing the functionality of such a team are the ownership of equity among team members, how autonomously they can make strategic decisions, and how coherently they can come together as a team [143].

Entrepreneurial teams are the people working together to seize an opportunity

NAVIGATING THE VENTURE ENVIRONMENT

Entrepreneuring connects to its economic, social, and natural environment in a variety of different ways, the venture-environment nexus [144]. For instance, opportunities and resources emerge in the environment, entrepreneurs relate to varieties of stakeholders in their environment, and impact their environment. Professional entrepreneuring needs to pay particular attention to their stakeholder environments, moral customs context, as well as local economic, social, and environmental capital [145]. According to the annual Global Entrepreneurship Monitor (GEM), entrepreneuring contexts and their relationship to entrepreneurs differ considerably around the world. This includes differences in local framework conditions like funding opportunities, entrepreneurial motivation, culture, and venture characteristics (see Figure 15.7) [146].

The metaphor of the **entrepreneurial ecosystem** has been used to describe how local context decisions may support and foster entrepreneuring

Entrepreneurial ecosystem comprises local conditions that affect entrepreneuring

---

[1]The focus in this chapter is uniquely on entrepreneurial teams. Other 'teaming' practices are discussed in Chapter 8.

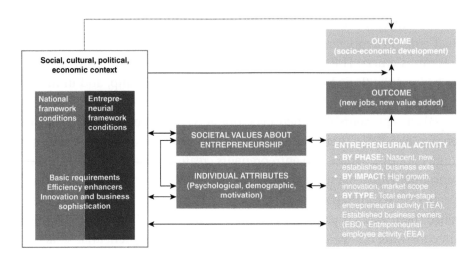

FIGURE 15.7   The GEM framework for assessing national entrepreneurial contexts

SOURCE: adapted from [146]

[147]. Local conditions can, for instance, relate to politics, finance, culture, support, human capital, and markets [148]. These conditions may be local in a nation, region or city [149] or also online [150]. Healthy entrepreneurial ecosystems have been found to significantly influence entrepreneurial success [151].

We will now highlight some core aspects of entrepreneurial ecosystems and how they relate to entrepreneuring practices:

1. **Industry clusters.** Clusters of similar businesses (see Chapter 12) offer entrepreneurs of a particular industry access to specialized knowledge and ideas, markets, and prospective employees [153, 154]. Examples of such clusters range from Silicon Valley, birthplace of the likes of Apple and Google, to Berlin's alternative eco-startup cluster that has produced businesses like the tree-planting search engine Ecosia and the travel carbon offsetting business Atmosfair.

2. **Business incubators and accelerators.** Business incubators are a combination of spaces and activities especially set up to provide an environment for new and young ventures. For instance, the University of Cape Town's Bertha Center for Social Entrepreneurship provides such a space to support social business generation. Related support for entrepreneuring practices range from simply providing an address and accessible workspace, to networking events and opportunities, to specialist support, facilities and equipment, educational programmes, and often facilitate access to finance. An iconic example is Y Combinator, an incubator that engages very early-stage entrepreneurs in a three-month programme to develop their idea. It culminates in an event in which the best graduates receive initial business funding. For instance, Airbnb and Dropbox came out of this programme [155].

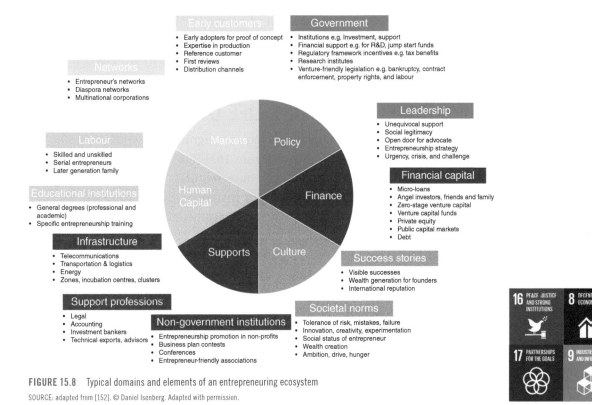

FIGURE 15.8 Typical domains and elements of an entrepreneuring ecosystem

SOURCE: adapted from [152]. © Daniel Isenberg. Adapted with permission.

3. **Regulation.** Navigating the regulations that govern setting up and running a venture can be a major hassle and can even threaten venture success. The World Bank's Doing Business Index ranks how easy it is to run a business in different countries with one main indicator being the ease of setting up a business in the first place. New

Zealand and Singapore have long been in the top five of that list. Main regulations considered include investor protection, enforcing contracts, and paying taxes [156]. An excellent example is the successful local 'embedding' of migrant entrepreneurs from Syria in the Swedish business context [157]. Sweden has been top-ranked on the Doing Business Index, which is likely to play a role in the success of migrant entrepreneurs.

A quite literal link to the environmental eco-system is another key aspect of the entre-preneurial environment – for instance, in the case of the Colombian venture Caguan Expeditions. The venture is a social enterprise

Entrepreneuring for peace is the motto of a venture employing former FARC guerrilla fighters as tour guides, who give guests an insight into how they used to live in the remote rainforest during times of war.

@caguanexpeditions and @remandoporlapaz

centred on the peaceful reintegration of previous FARC fighters into society. Of course, its entrepreneurial environment is strongly linked also to the societal and political conditions of a country that had been in violent conflict for over 50 years before the peace treaty in 2013 [158].

THE BUSINESS VENTURE LIFE CYCLE

A venture **life cycle** consists of the different phases ventures typically run through: starting up, setting up, and settling down

Managing an entrepreneurial venture requires significantly different practices at different phases of its **life cycle**. Figure 15.9 illustrates five typical phases which ventures run, and how each phase requires a different managerial focus, style and practices [159, 160]. For instance, in a venture's first phase (existence), the focus is on creativity as management needs to prove that the venture offers a novel concept of creating value. However, management in the second phase (survival) needs to show that it has sufficient control over resources to keep the venture alive. Direction is the managerial focus. This change in main venture management tasks typically leads to a leadership crisis between the first and second phase, where creativity is practiced at the expense of direction. One of the most challenging tasks in venture management is to switch gears, and from management practice phase to phase of venture growth.

In the following sections we introduce the main entrepreneuring practices during the venture life cycle. The simplified version of the life-cycle consists of three phases [161], starting up (creating a working venture), taking off (growth and development) [162], and settling down (maturity and reorientation).

STARTING UP: CREATING AND SUSTAINING THE VENTURE

Start-up phase
the emphasis is on developing a venture and scaling it up

Everything begins when you have identified an opportunity and have made a decision to seize it.[2] The **start-up** stage is all about showing you have a viable enterprise by creating a small, almost prototype version of it and about accessing the resources necessary to develop the venture further. During the start-up phase the emphasis therefore is on developing the business idea successively from a proof of principle to a working prototype, a first sellable product or service [162]. However, equally important is the development of a viable business model and business plan.

Business model
the unique formula of an organization's value proposition, creation, exchange, and capture

Business modelling and planning. The **business model** is a 'value logic' of how a company proposes (value proposition), creates (partners, activities, resources), exchanges (customer relationships, segments, channels), and captures (cost and revenue structure) value [98, 163]. It is a 'value model',

---

[2]Creativity and innovation techniques are immensely helpful during the start-up phase. Chapters 9 and 14 introduce relevant creative decision-making and innovation techniques, which is why we do not cover them in this chapter.

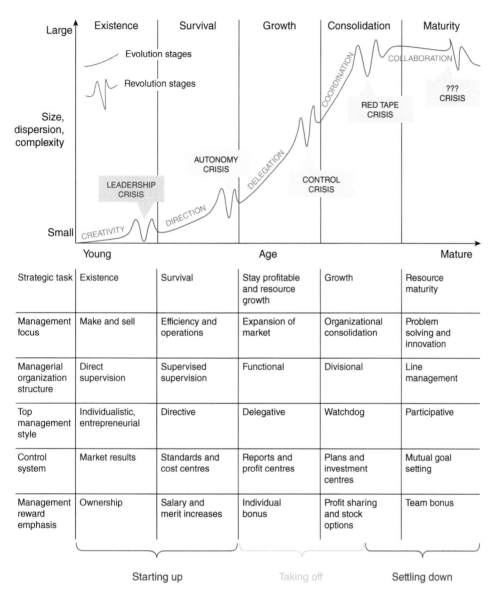

FIGURE 15.9 Entrepreneurial management across stages of the business venture cycle

SOURCES: adapted from [62, 159, 160]

which reconnects to our definition of the entrepreneuring process as a process of creating value by combining resources to pursue an opportunity. Business model canvases like the one shown in Figure 15.10 have arguably become the most frequently used tool in venture creation.

While business model descriptions provide a high-level overview, **business plans** fill in all the detail. Great business plans commonly focus on the following elements [164]: people, opportunity, context, as well as risk and reward. This information is often structured in the following way [161, 165]:

Business plan
the detailed overview of a business venture

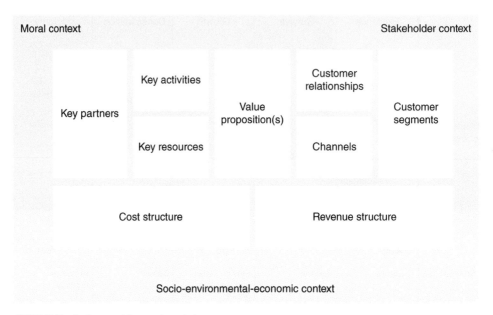

FIGURE 15.10   Business model canvas in context
SOURCE: adapted from [145, 163]

1.   **Executive summary.** Value logic, short and snappy, taglines, and hooking the interest of the audience.

2.   **Company**. Aims, objectives, vision, legal form, location(s) and facilities.

3.   **Situation**. Market (e.g. size, growth, competitors); contextual SWOT analysis, success factors.

4.   **Strategy**. Target market (segments), positioning, marketing.

5.   **Organization**. Organizational structure, controls, implementation, operations plan.

6.   **Finances.** Assumptions and financial scenarios, financial key indicators, break-even analysis, projected cash flows over time, projected profit and loss (P&L), performance ratios.

Extensive, detailed business plans can be converted into elevator pitches (short speeches introducing the venture), or pitch slide decks (short presentations of the venture) adjusting them to different audiences and situations. Business plans fulfil both internal and external functions. Internally, they serve as orientation to keeping the venture on track. Externally, business plans are used to present the venture to external stakeholders, most prominently to financiers in funding.

Funding. While funding the enterprise is a concern throughout the entire life cycle, it is often considered critical to get these first funds during the start-up phase and then again to finance future growth and development.

Four typical sources of external finance during start-up are private equity investors, banks loans, and overdrafts [161]. The most common initial source of funding, however, is the founder(s) private funds, family friends, fools (the '3Fs') [166], and bootstrapping [46]. Table 15.5 provides an overview of financing practices from early-stage bootstrapping to initial public offering, 'going public' as an often desired type of growth funding in the take-off phase (see also Chapter 21).

TABLE 15.5   Financing methods

Method	Practices, details and variations
Bootstrapping. Funding the venture with limited personal capital and stretching resources, which can be stressful as the entrepreneur carries the entire risk personally, but allows decision-making to be made independently of external funders	- Working from your home to save rent costs - Loans on personal property - Trade credits from suppliers, paying after 30–90 days - Factoring, selling your receivables to a collecting company - Letters of credit from customer - Buying equipment on instalments - Leasing instead of buying equipment
FFF funding. Investment, financial or in-kind from people close to the entrepreneur (friends and family) or others excited about the venture ('fools'), but inexperienced	- **Emotional risk** of disappointing or financially harming the ones closest to the entrepreneur - Potentially **volatile nature of 'fools'** as they might wish to quickly retrieve money if things don't go so well, or if investment does not pay off quickly enough
Goodwill (and in-kind) financing taps into stakeholders' positive attitude towards the venture and its related social or environmental cause to generate resources. If not financial donations, these resources are not of a monetary nature, but in-kind, such as volunteering support or donations, or saving money	- **Volunteering:** Employees and external stakeholders may donate their labour force - **Subsidies, grants and tax cuts** from governmental agencies often reward sustainability, responsibility and ethics-related ventures - **Donations** could be financial, but also in-kind such as equipment or products for sale (e.g. in charity shops)
Crowdfunding raises finance from a large audience (typically online), with each individual providing a very small amount	Crowdfunding works better the more **emotionally engaging** the venture is. Funds could be donations or tied to receiving a predetermined product or service in case the funding is successful
Loans and overdrafts. Traditional financing options available at banks and other financial institutions	While fixed-term loans offer comparatively low interest rates, bank overdrafts are more flexible
Angel investor. A venture-experienced individual investing their private capital and becoming a co-owner	Angel investors might rely more on their gut feeling and a personal link to the entrepreneur, at times becoming an active member of the venture team. *Dragons' Den, Shark Tank* and similar TV shows provide an excellent insight into the practice
Venture capitalists. Professional representing an investment company when providing capital in return for an equity stake in the venture	Venture capitalists often engage in extensive due diligence on the viability of the business plan, or may serve as mentors for entrepreneurs
Growth capital. Funding proven business model and products to accelerate growth, in exchange for equity, normally minority shares.	Normally, only attracted by proven and highly scalable business. Shareholders can retain control of the company

(Continued)

TABLE 15.5   (Continued)

Method	Practices, details and variations
Private equity (PE). Buy equity (or a mix with convertible loan), mostly gaining control, often alongside with management from previous owners	Invest only in mature business, make use of significant level of debt to maximize equity return. PE firms control or heavily influence the business strategy
Mezzanine. A debt instrument between equity and loans. It is structured as an unsecured loan with a warrant.	Used mainly when existing senior debts reached limit and banks will not allow for further loans. It is more expensive than normal loan due to higher risk for holder
Convertible bonds. A debt with conditions attached. Often, if conditions are not satisfied, it may be transformed into equity	Usually used by private equity to increase management shares ratio or by public company to decrease interest paid on bonds
Debenture/bonds. Unsecured and secured loan, which can be issued in public or private market	If issued on public market it requires a credit rating agency to provide credit quality note
Initial public offering. An IPO involves listing a more mature venture on a stock market, often in order to access large amounts of growth capital	Listing a venture requires immense efforts, including legal proceedings and road-shows. Being stock listed comes with increased oversight, rules, regulations, and often reduced entrepreneurial discretion
Shareholder recapitalization. Requires shareholders to inject more capital to strengthen the company balance sheet	It is required in case the company suffers important loss. It can also invite new shareholders to invest
Debt for equity swap. An agreement for the creditors to see the loans converted into company equity	It is an effective way to lower the debt level of the company
Turnaround. Investment in equity/debt coupled with professionals with experience in turning around a difficult situation	It is one of the last safeguards before company liquidation

Here are some typical questions to be considered when deciding which financing options to choose:

1. Should I finance using equity or debt?

2. How simple or tedious is it to access the financing?

3. What are the chances of success to access the option?

4. How flexibly can I dispose of the funds?

5. How do the financing arrangements influence my entrepreneurial discretion?

6. How much ownership of my venture do I have to give up in return for financial resources?

7. What non-financial benefits might I get from one or another financing option?

8. What are potential emotional or personal costs in comparison across options?

9. How well does the person or institution involved fit my venture?

10. How well does the type of capital fit the stage and context my venture is in?

As the venture characteristics change over time, typical forms of financing change too. Figure 15.11 illustrates how legitimacy, resources, and risk reduction that frequently come with firm size, age, and available information affect the access and preference for different financing forms [167].

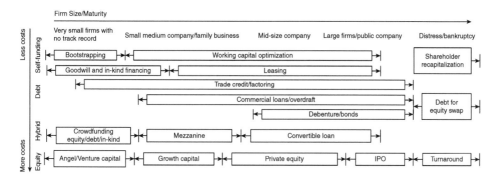

FIGURE 15.11   How typical financing forms change as ventures develop

SOURCE: adapted from [167]

Being involved in social entrepreneuring or ecopreneuring dramatically increases the funding avenues available. Also, these ventures often have access to financing below market rate, some forms without interest or pay back obligation [168]. Related financing methods range from the multi-trillion dollar movement of socially responsible investment to impact investing and microfinance. Figure 15.12 describes the whole spectrum of potential investors and their motivations and typical behaviours.

TAKING OFF: CONSOLIDATING AND SCALING THE VENTURE

After the start-up phase, the venture should be ready for **take-off**. There should be a promising viable business model that is ready to be consolidated and scaled, to improve and grow. The venture has been born, but it still has to 'grow up', implying that it has both to learn and get bigger.

Take-off phase
the emphasis is on consolidating
a venture and scaling it up

This phase has also been called the 'growth phase' [161]. However, in the context of professional management, we have to question if there should be a universal growth paradigm for ventures. How about rather thinking about optimum size than growth? Some ventures by their very nature are meant to be smaller – for instance, to serve an environmental niche market. Other ventures, in spite of being commercially viable, should perhaps not survive at all if their social or environmental impact is negative. In addition, rapid growth might lead to the irresponsible behaviour of growth at all cost – for instance, unnecessarily aggressive behaviour against competitors, or burnt-out employees due to the often stressful nature of rapid growth. It has been found that

Traditional Philanthropy

- Seeks to maximize social return

- Majority of applied funds not viewed as type of investment

- May engage in programme related investments

- 'Evaluation' used to assess relative social impact

- Often invests endowment in traditional capital institutions

Venture Philanthropy

- Seed capital for innovative social or economic programmes

- No market ROI

- Documented SROI

- Application of venture capital practice within philanthropic context

Community Debt Financing

- Positive financial return (fixed rate)

- Positive assumed social impact

- Modest financial returns on investment compared to market rates

- Includes CDFIs

Community Development Equity

- High risk

- No liquidity event

- Financial returns minimized

- Probably never going to get major money out, so how do you assess risk/reward?

Social Equity Investors   ←—————————————————————————————

Angel Investors and Social Venture Capital

- Seed funding of business start-ups

- Seeks market rate financial returns

- 'Qualitative' or anecdotal social impact assessment

- 'Do no harm' screen or perhaps facilitate some type of social good

Socially Responsible Investment Funds

- Seeks market rate financial returns

- Seeks to minimize negative social, environmental or other impacts

- Proactive social, environmental, or other screen for investing

- Engages in social audits and 'follow-along' monitoring

- Shareholder activism

Traditional Capital Institutions (Banks, Mutual Funds, etc.)

- No calculation of SROI

- Seeks to maximize financial return

- May engage in CRA lending, but not part of core mission

- Analysts simply 'observe' performance and make no direct effort to influence the operation of the investee corporation

- May engage in traditional philanthropy by making grants to non-profit organizations

- No thought of SROI

—————————————————————————→ **Private Equity Investors**

FIGURE 15.12   Spectrum of social enterprise financing

SOURCE: adapted from [168]

slow, steady growth most strongly correlates with firm survival [169]. Maybe, we should instead think about developing certain qualities of a venture, as opposed to predominantly growing or 'scaling' it, a shift from up-scaling to right-scaling ventures, meaning both reaching the right size and growing in the right way [170].

Growth strategies. Assume you have successfully established your main product in a market. Where should you grow? Figure 15.13 suggests four possible answers to this question. First, you could focus on market penetration, to grow further in the same market and with the same product by, for instance, increasing marketing or buying a competitor. Market growth might also fuel company growth, as observed in the extreme increase in demand for web conferencing platforms like Zoom or Microsoft Teams during and after the Coronavirus outbreak. You could also use a product development strategy and stay in the same market but launch a new product to the customers and in the context you are familiar with. For instance, TOMS Shoes became just TOMS when it widened its portfolio in the same fashion market segment to include sunglasses.

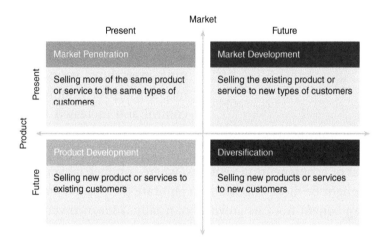

FIGURE 15.13   The Ansoff matrix of development and growth strategies

SOURCE: [171] Credit: slidemodel.com

If you are ready to venture into a new market, you could engage in a market development strategy, selling existing products to new customer groups. For instance, a company selling only online could venture into the bricks and mortar high-street shopping market; it could sell a product only sold in the domestic market in a new international market; or, if it had only been selling business-to-business, it could also enter the business-to-consumer market. Finally, you could apply a diversification growth strategy, where you engage in a new market with a new product. For instance, venture management might decide they want to enter a highly attractive market, but don't think their current product will find demand in this market (see also Chapter 13 on formulating strategies).

Collaborative growth strategies. A venture in its take-off phase is likely to have scarce resources and might lack the know-how to enter new markets or develop new products. Therefore, collaborative practices, where the venture management actively seeks partners for growth, are a typical strategy.

Cycle.land offers local knowledge about regulations, contacts with regulators, and user-learning initiative to Youon's market-extension to London.

Angel Sharp Media

For instance, the Chinese bike sharing company Youon set up a joint venture with Oxford-based Cycle.Land to enter the UK market, while Cycle. Land gains a powerful ally in their mission to sustainably disrupt urban transportation [172, 173]. Figure 15.14 introduces different forms of working with others to replicate or scale a venture. The main downsides to partnering, however, are that you will have to give up control over part of your operations and take on the risk of not running everything yourself. Common mechanisms for dealing with loss of control and increased risk are either contractual arrangements outlining partners' expected behaviours, or to have partners inject their own equity.

For social or ecopreneuring ventures, where commercial goals are not the priority, it might be more important to replicate the positive impacts of your venture than benefit from its growth financially. Your own venture does not need to necessarily grow (scale up) in order to replicate the value of addressing the social opportunity. Using the practice of **social franchising**, others can do that for you [174]! Social franchising implies that franchisees replicate the venture's 'blueprint including its commercial and social business model using their own resources' [175]. This way the franchising venture maintains control over the way the franchisees run their organization through adherence to the blueprint. Another main advantage is that the social franchising contract might involve a payment back to the core venture, bringing in additional cash-flows while not incurring costs. A pioneering social franchising case is Greenstar, which started out as a social enterprise as early as 1991 [176]. Greenstar has built a network of over 7,000 franchised clinics and 70,000 retail outlets, which now account for over half of Pakistan's contraceptives distributed through the private sector [177].

Social franchising
a contractual agreement through which franchisees replicate the venture's operations and impact

SETTLING DOWN: REORIENTING OR LETTING GO

Settling down phase
a venture has achieved maturity or failed, which places the emphasis on the 'what now?' question

Imagine, you have consolidated your venture, have reached the venture goals and maybe also your personal goals as an entrepreneur. Or alternatively, your venture might have run into a dead end, or even failed. So what's next? We will now discuss three main scenarios in the **settling down phase** – venture

Dissemination	Strategic alliance	Licensing	Franchising	Joint venture (JV)	Wholly owned
A variety of idea transfer between companies/ stakeholders with low level of commitment.	An arrangement between two or more companies in the same industry to accomplish a designated objective.	An arrangement involving a fee for the use of intellectual property, brand, design, and business programmes. Governed by principles of contract law.	An arrangement for use of full business model, marketing and brand names in new market.	Two or more business entities combine their resources to pursue a single project.	Parent firm creates the entire operation from scratch (or through acquisition).
Common approaches: Dissemination for Awareness (developing an identity and profile) and Dissemination for Action (expecting a change of practice).	Win–win situation (e.g. access to strong brand in exchange for access to emerging technology). Limited scope and function. Does not have the same legal protections as a JV or franchise.	Varying degree of support and training provided to licensee. Often based on patented technology and common in manufacturing industries. Profits limited to fees.	Governed by franchise legislation, franchisor and franchisee established as separate companies. The former provides support and training. Fees: upfront (franchise fee) plus % of the revenue (royalty fee).	Operated as a partnership, typically creating a new company to operate. All parties participate in the management of the JV and owe fiduciary duties of loyalty and care.	Subsidiary is an incorporated entity; parent firm maintains complete control over its operation and keeps all the profits (or losses). Detailed cost sharing agreement recommended for asset transfer/ taxation purposes.
Benefits: possibility for normative change as movement grows.	**Benefits**: include customization, flexibility in the agreement with partners.	**Benefits**: increased control and ownership, a revenue source for resource – limited founding organization.	**Benefits**: increased control and reduction of risk of non-compliance and brand dilution while benefiting from clear information flow.	**Benefits**: include leverage of partners' funding and other resources.	**Benefits**: include complete control over operations, strong economic benefit to founding organization if successful, potential for scalability.
Risks: loss of control over impact, target, brand. Trend to be a movement, not an organization.	Risks: include resource intensity, risk of partner organization failure, splintering of ideas across partners.	Risks: include exposure to quality dilution, loss of brand control and IP, loss of core expertise necessary to deliver effectively.	Risk: increased resource intensity of franchisor, need to codify processes and systems.	Risks: necessity to design a balanced governance structure, threat to alienation of core innovation strength due to centralization of activity in the JV.	Risks: include important initial investment, potential of capital loss, loss of context and cultural fit when organization expands.

FIGURE 15.14 A continuum of forms to achieve scale through collaboration
SOURCE: adapted from [174]

failure, exit of the entrepreneur, and corporate entrepreneurship. In all three scenarios the emphasis is on how the settling down phase can set up the venture and/or the entrepreneur for a new cycle of entrepreneuring.

Failure. Entrepreneurs dread failure and its bedfellow bankruptcy. Employees will lose their jobs; customers might not get the products they paid for; suppliers and financiers might not get paid. For social and ecopreneurial ventures it also means that their social and environmental missions have failed. A prime example is the formerly third-largest Chinese bike-sharing company Bluegogo. It went bankrupt after just 12 months of operations, abandoning offices in rapid retreat, not paying back customers' deposits, and having burnt 600 million RMB (119 million USD), with rumours that the previous CEO had fled the country [178, 179]. Similarly, the failure of the Israeli battery-swapping company Better Place meant the demise of a business model that was well on the way towards revolutionizing personal transport towards environmental sustainability [180].

What causes entrepreneurial failure? External triggers may include an economic downturn, a decline in market or industry structure, other arising opportunities into which venture equity is reinvested, and even bad luck. Prominent internal triggers are the lack, or mismanagement, of financial resources, inadequate management competence, or the entrepreneur's personal character [161]. There are typical venture–entrepreneur behaviour patterns that lead to failure. Using frogs as a metaphor for the entrepreneur–venture behaviour that has led to failure, Table 15.6 provides an overview of typical failure patterns.

TABLE 15.6   Entrepreneur–venture failure patterns

Failure pattern	Cause of death	Organization size at time of failure	
		Small	Big
Boiled frog	Cooked to death due to inaction in spite of a 'heating' up venture environment	The hardworking, introverted, family firm	The (s)lumbering giant
Drowned frog	Swallowing too much water while trying to do too much	The ambitious entrepreneur	The conglomerate king-maker
Bullfrog	Being dragged to the bottom of the pond by the financial burden of spending money not earned yet	The small firm flash	The money-messing megalomaniac
Tadpole	Starving to death when running out of resources	The failed start-up	The big project failure

SOURCE: adapted from [181]. Adapted with permission.

While never pretty, failure is a common reality of the entrepreneuring process that needs to be navigated and managed well, ideally by falling forward by maximizing gains from the venture while mitigating losses [182]. Failure management practices may range from attempting often lengthy turnarounds back to solvency and profitability to exiting early in order to minimize financial, emotional, and reputational costs of failure [183]. The entrepreneuring process can become cyclical even after failure, either as entrepreneurs might learn from the failed venture in a future successful venture, or as assets of bankrupt enterprises might be bought up to provide the basis for a continuance of the venture of a new form, a 'phoenix venture' [161].

Entrepreneurial exit. Entrepreneurs may decide to renounce leadership of their ventures. This might happen at many stages of the venture process – for instance, a young venture being bought up by a bigger industry player which aims to bring them to full potential. It might even happen decades after the venture has reached maturity – for instance, because the entrepreneur wants to retire. A common scenario of entrepreneurial exit is when the business has just reached maturity and the founder's job might be better suited to be filled by a skilled manager than an entrepreneur. Common exit questions include the following:

- Do I want to exit financially, **'harvest my investment'** by selling my equity share, and/or is it a leadership exit as I want to **retire from running the venture** and look for a successor?

- What does my exit mean for the venture, its **mission, employees, and values**?

- **Whom can I trust** to own and/or control the venture and carry it into the future?

- What is the right **timing of exit** – for instance, related to the changing value of the company, or to ensure a smooth transition?

Common forms of exit include the following:

1. **Acquisition** by another company – for instance, the sustainable cosmetics pioneer The Body Shop was bought up first by L'Oréal and then sold on to Brazilian natural cosmetics company Natura. While social enterprises particularly might suffer a loss of legitimacy if bought up by a 'big bad corporation', many of them have managed to use the acquisition conditions as a Trojan horse to make the buyer organization more ethical, responsible, or sustainable [184].

2. Through **management buy out and buy in**, either current managers become co-owners, or an external management team buy themselves in. An interesting case is where a community bank's management collectively retired as protest against its acquisition by a commercial bank, and re-founded the community bank [185].

3. Through **'hereditary' succession**, founders might pass on the helm to an 'heir', typically a family member taking over a family business [186, 187]. However, the founders of enterprises with a strong social mission have also been found to actively promote a worthy new leader who is not a family member to inherit the position [188].

The entrepreneuring process becomes a cycle if members, after exiting one venture, engage in a new venture and become 'serial entrepreneurs'.

Corporate entrepreneuring. Early on in this chapter we briefly discussed the profiles of intrapreneurs, entrepreneurs tackling opportunities from inside an established business. Intrapreneurs often engage in corporate entrepreneuring, creating new ventures from inside a now mature company. The underlying purpose of these ventures typically is to keep a mature organization innovative. Corporate entrepreneurship offers another set of practices [189] through which the entrepreneurial process can become an entrepreneuring cycle:

- Through **internal corporate venturing**, the venture stays innovative by creating an entrepreneurial architecture [62]. The intended outcome is the creation of new ventures from inside, often in the form of 'spin-offs' based on innovations created inside the mature company, but wrapped into a new business model, which are spun off to create stand-alone entities. These spin-offs could either compete for external equity 'to bring the market inside', or run on equity provided by the parent company. These spin-offs often assume the form of employee entrepreneurship, where a previous employee of the mature venture becomes a founding managing director in the new venture [190, 191].

- In **external corporate venturing**, a mature venture 'buys in' innovation from often younger, innovative ventures. For instance, Coca Cola bought a share in the natural smoothies company Innocent to buy in an innovative, more healthy product option [192]. Mature firms use corporate venture capital to acquire or partner with external firms [193]. A great example is Patagonia (see Chapter 1), which runs Tin Shed Ventures, their venture capital fund, investing in new ventures in disruptive socially and environmentally responsible companies [194].

- Corporate entrepreneuring may, at times, go beyond just the peripheral creation or support of new ventures. It may also refer to the **corporate strategic renewal** of the core business. The entire mature venture starts anew by changing its core business, tackling a new opportunity. For instance, IBM has gone through an entire makeover, a strategic renewal consisting of a change in core business from a computing hardware company and computer producer, to a computing services company, a consultancy [195]. Corporate entrepreneurship in the form of strategic renewal holds great promise for the urgent sustainability transition our economy has to go through. Imagine a petroleum company that transfers its core business exclusively to renewable energy, or a metal mining company that moves to 'urban mining', extracting precious metals only by recycling electronic waste.

PRINCIPLES OF PROFESSIONAL ENTREPRENEURING

I. The **entrepreneuring mode of management** is centred on venturing in the pursuit of opportunities. An **entrepreneurial manager** is a practitioner with both management and entrepreneuring competence, able to turn opportunities into value while administering resources.

II. Entrepreneuring logics of action include **causation** (looking for resources based on predetermined goals), **effectuation** (identifying goals that can be achieved with accessible resources), and **bricolage** (creatively making do with the resources available).

III. There are varieties of entrepreneuring, including new business venturing, intrapreneuring, and institutional entrepreneurship, each of which could follow a commercial, social, or hybrid logic.

IV. The entrepreneuring process is centred on managing its three main elements of **opportunity**, **resources**, and **team**.

V. The entrepreneuring process runs through the three main phases, each centred on distinct typical practices – **starting up** (business modelling/planning and funding), **taking off** (growth and collaboration) and **settling down** (entrepreneurial exit, failure and corporate entrepreneuring).

MANAGEMENT GYM: TRAINING YOUR PROFESSIONAL SIX-PACK

Knowing

1. Interrelate the terms intrapreneuring, employee entrepreneuring, corporate venturing, starting up and settling down. You will have to look up some terms in sources outside this chapter.

2. Match the following terms: manager, entrepreneur, effectuation, and causation.

3. Read and summarize the biography of an entrepreneur of your choice.

Thinking

4. Where on the hybrid spectrum would you place OXFAM, Reliance Industries, and CEMEX?

5. Look at the UN social development goals and think about one related opportunity you could tackle through a venture. What resources and team would you need to assemble to get started? What would your business model look like?

6. Imagine you live in an isolated and impoverished farming community and there is a drought that keeps everyone from farming. You are running out of food and have no income. The only thing you own is a bicycle. You have water from a groundwater well outside the village, but no pump to irrigate the fields. What venture could you build to serve the pressing needs with the resource accessible to you?

Acting

7. Write a one-page executive summary on the current entrepreneuring environment of your home country – for instance, using databases mentioned in this chapter.

8. Use a business model canvas to design a venture of your choice.

9. Write a summary business plan (around five pages) for a venture of your choice, making sure to cover all main contents expected from such a document.

Interacting

10. Join an entrepreneuring-themed group on a social media platform you are active on. 'Take a sniff' to get a feel for what people are talking about, what current opportunities there are, and how you could become an active part of that group. For instance, post, comment, or 'like' something.

11. Think about one venture idea of your choice and prepare a 60-second elevator pitch about it. Pitch the idea to three different people … ideally on an actual elevator ride.

12. Speak to two different people who are entrepreneurs, run a small business, or have been self-employed. Ask them about their experience, their main learning and what advice they have for you. How do their respective experiences compare?

Being

13. Which of the following modes do you think you lean towards most naturally – bricolage, effectuation or causation?

14. Which of your personal characteristics do you think (would) make you a good entrepreneur? Which ones don't? Take one of the many quizzes available online to self-assess your entrepreneurial potential.

15. Imagine a day in your life as an entrepreneurial manager. Where would you work? What would be typical activities? How would you go about them? What would be challenges, what would you enjoy? What values would be important in your work and why?

Becoming

16. Remember a time when you perceived an opportunity. How did you react and interact with the opportunity? What could you have done to build a venture around this opportunity?

17. Think about something you don't like, find problematic, unfair, irresponsible, or unsustainable. What kind of venture could you see yourself engaging in to change that aspect of your reality?

18. Often ventures challenge common wisdom by envisioning a future that is not real(istic) yet. How would you go about convincing financiers, your family, your team, customers, and other stakeholders to 'buy into your vision'? How do you build an entrepreneurial 'reality distortion field' around you and pull others into it?

Laasch, O., Moosmayer, D., & Antonacopoulou, E. P. (2023). The interdisciplinary responsible management competence framework: An integrative review of ethics, responsibility, and sustainability competences. *Journal of Business Ethics*, 187, 733–757.

PIONEER INTERVIEW
MUHAMMAD YUNUS

INTERVIEWED BY NISHA PANDEY, MICHAEL PIRSON, AND SATISH MODH; EDITED BY XUAN YE AND OLIVER LAASCH

Muhammad Yunus is a Professor of Economics, and one of the world's most successful social entrepreneurs. He was awarded the Nobel Peace Prize in recognition of his work to fight poverty and empower women with his Grameen Bank social enterprise.

Entrepreneuring to turn banking upside down.

We created the Grameen Bank in a challenge where we said the right question is not whether people are creditworthy or not. The great question is whether the banking system is people worthy or not. You have created the banking system, which is totally unworthy of people; it doesn't help the people and deprives people. So we have to create a new system. When we talk about that financial system we talked about microcredit coming back. The banking system was dependent on collateral only, exclusively. So we have to undo that. Grameen Bank means a social business banking bank, meaning that we talk about social business, a business to solve people's problems rather than to make money.

'Professor Muhammad Yunus: Building Social Business Summit' by University of Salford is licensed under CC BY 2.0

Social enterprises changing systems. We have no intention of making money by running businesses. So we created a microcredit bank as a social business. In social business there's no intention of owners making personal profits. The idea, or concept of social business has to mean to be in the financial system, also in the business system. It is the core of redesigning the entire system. We bring investment for creating social business to solve problems that we see around us, problems of water, problems of healthcare, problems of activities for the unemployed young people.

Two kinds of enterprises. There are two kinds of business, one to follow self-interest by creating a profit maximizing business, and another is a system of businesses for the common interests, which are not driven by profit maximization. It's driven by zero personal interest. We don't want to make any money because we are interested in solving people's problems. That's when the social business idea comes in. If we created social business on the first day, it would not be like this. Because they were selfish. We are so busy making money [that] we didn't care whether we're destroying the world by pollution, by global warming, by wealth concentration, by massive unemployment.

(Continued)

In praise of the emerging entrepreneurs. They find opportunities, tiny opportunities to make a living for themselves. That's what the informal sector is all about. I said this [informal sector] is the wrong terminology used by conventional economists to express the fact that they are not doing the right thing. I said they are doing the right thing! We should call it the emerging entrepreneur sector. These are all entrepreneurs on the edge. They are on their own. They are not bothering anybody. They are selling things on the street. They're making things at home and selling them to other people. They are on their own and nobody helps them. Why isn't there support? If I am calling it an emerging entrepreneurial sector, this is what is the seedbed of entrepreneurship. We should be applauding it. We should be feeling extremely happy to support them rather than kind of saying that they are doing the wrong thing.

Social venture capital for the emerging sector. We make sure that instead of job seekers they become entrepreneurs. They can become entrepreneurs provided we can provide the financing for them. That's where the social business venture capital is very important. We have done that in Bangladesh as a side programme financial institution. Anybody who has an idea to start a business, we come and invest and we become a partner. It's venture capital. (…) We get a partnership with you. So you work for the business and make it successful and over time you return the money that we gave you. Because we are a social business we are not interested in making profit out of you. You keep the profit, we just help you to overcome the problem. You return the money that we gave you and that's done and then all the business is yours.

Note: This text is part of a webinar entitled 'Muhammad Yunus on Social Business Post COVID-19', which was hosted by the Indian Humanistic Management Association. For more information. Please visit http://humanisticmanagement. international

QUESTIONS

1. Do some background research on Grameen Bank to get an idea about its history (including controversies), impacts, and future outlook.

2. How are entrepreneuring practices from the 'emerging entrepreneurs sector' different from 'normal' entrepreneuring practices?

3. How can an enterprise with 'no intention of making money' survive and what do you believe it takes to manage such an enterprise?

PROFESSIONAL PROFILE
DORU MITRANA

My name is Doru and I am an environmental and social activist, and managing director of MaiMultVerde (MuchMoreGreen), the NGO I co-founded to achieve environmental and social impact by developing educational, advocacy, entrepreneurship and volunteering projects, programmes and campaigns in Romania.

My responsibilities. I am in charge of coordinating the overall activity of the organization in line with the status, values, aim, and objectives. I work with the management team to set the yearly strategy and objectives, and work over the year to accomplish them. I also represent the organization in relation to public authorities, companies, board members or fellow organizations. Finally, I am in charge of the fundraising function of the organization.

A typical day. The daily routine includes tasks across varieties of different areas of the business:

- **Financial management**. Approving payments, checking financial and fiscal reports, forecasts, etc.

- **HR management**. Status meeting with all staff or specific departments or projects team, but also counselling and discussions, planning and evaluating, interviewing when necessary

- **Fundraising**. Setting up meetings, exchanging e-mails or telephone calls with representatives of active and potential funding organizations, private or public

- **Project management**. Keeping a close relationship with the project managers, for a close eye on the project status

- **Communication**. Articles, interviews, press conferences, online/social media reactions. Keeping permanent contact with all relevant stakeholders and continuously acting as liaison between the inner and outer part of the organization.

Challenges. Here is a list of the main challenges I encounter: (1) Resisting the 'temptations' of other sectors, like a nine-to-five, cosy, well-paid job with no extra worries in the public or private sector. (2) Having a lot of patience in waiting for the true social and environmental results to show up. (3) Having to convince everyone, everyday that the way you are promoting

(Continued)

is the right way, that you are not just an extravagant, exotic being but you actually understand the world around you and choose to be different because different is what we need to be.

Recommendations. Social entrepreneurship has a very strong, personal motivation. Starting a social-value-adding venture must be preceded by an introspective analysis of the entrepreneurs and their true motives, aspirations, and beliefs. Walking the talk, staying in the public eye with the head up high and allowing public scrutiny and input in the decisional process, are key elements for success in this sector.

QUESTIONS

1. Do you see Doru as an entrepreneur or a manager? How does your judgement relate to his apparent characteristics and tasks?

2. If you were Doru, under what conditions do you think you would stop resisting 'the temptations of other sectors'? What do you think these temptations might be?

3. At what stage of the entrepreneuring process life cycle do you think Doru and his venture are and why?

TRUE STORY

HEALTHY ENTREPRENEURING TIDBITS

EDITED BY ALEXANDRA LEONOR BARRUETA-SACKSTEDER AND EKATERINA IVANOVA

That's me. Hi, I am Lyuda and I never wanted to be an entrepreneur, because it is a colossal responsibility. As a woman, I always wanted to be on maternity leave, I wanted to have a happy family, a well-paid job. I went to university because it was expected. Then I completed a graduate programme at a university in the UK, worked at a major multinational petroleum company, and realized that it was enough of life abroad for me and I wanted to go home to Russia.

(Continued)

I really liked being and living in the corporate world. Being a tall girl I did modelling, but did not find it challenging enough, since little depends on the model herself. I guess if I look into my hobbies, it shows that I'm a health nut. I sometimes do Pilates, yoga or stretching. My body adapts very quickly, which is very cool. I guess I have to thank my mom and dad for forcing me to take ballet when I was younger even though I hated it with all my heart.

The power of inspiration. While I was taking an MBA programme in Moscow, I had a whole course at MIT. When our study group went to MIT, I took a required course called 'Entrepreneurship Developer'. They said that we had to learn it and know it, inside and out. We had two amazing lecturers there. They were constantly making us question what we knew by asking: 'Who are entrepreneurs?' Are they self-made people, who don't need any education? Or are they people who have studied entrepreneurship?

On one memorable occasion, we were around Boston's main square, where they have all of these start-ups and a main incubator. They took us there and showed us a Google Map. They zoomed in and showed us our location. Then they zoomed out and showed us all of Cambridge and Boston. Then they told us that within walking distance there are 50 companies valued at more than a billion dollars, and they all were created here. After these words our entire group, all 40 people, were restless. We thought about how these people had found strength in themselves, because we have a completely different mentality. We have very few entrepreneurs in Russia, we do not have this entrepreneurial culture. In our country it was always important to hold a prestigious position and become a headliner in the news.

Cambridge is a small paradise. It was amazing and absolutely magical to be there. We took part in a global conference, where the leaders of different start-ups gave talks, and answered questions. We were inspired.

Inspiration is the challenge, once you have that the rest is easy. I noticed that people in Boston were very health-conscious. They didn't eat junk food, worked out, etc. Even the Starbucks has healthy snacks readily available.

No coincidences or shortcuts. Too quickly, it was time to return to Russia and time to hand in our final projects. I couldn't stop thinking about the healthy snack culture in Boston and so developed my project around this and passed. I was done with my MBA. I got a job as a financial advisor but couldn't put healthy snacks out of my mind and after seven or eight months I still couldn't find any in Russia.

(Continued)

My mentor during the MBA knew about my idea and when my husband ran into him one day they got to talking about me. My mentor mentioned to my husband that there had been so much interest in my project. When discussing it later he encouraged me by saying, 'It's now or never. Follow your dream.' I used my own savings to launch my business with a goal of giving people the opportunity to eat delicious food while still being healthy.

Following my dream. I registered a company right before the New Year, opened an account, and hired my first employee, a technologist and we discussed ideas. The goal was to make a high-quality healthy product, but without preservatives. He said it was impossible. I told him that it was possible, I saw it in the US. He said that this is impossible, it is better to order everything from the US and repack it but I wanted my company to be in Russia. I wanted my production to be local. I wanted to give back to my country.

We spent the next eight months on R&D, we developed 'gentle processing' technology and understood how to make a product without preservatives. We now source 85 per cent of ingredients from abroad, since local suppliers cannot provide us with the level of quality we expect. We started our sales and just eight months later we were already profitable. My company became the first one to offer the healthy snack 'YumMe' on the Russian market. We also recently made the first healthy snack product for children in Russia that meets all strict national regulations for children's products.

My dream is that any person in the Russian Federation will have an opportunity to buy our YumMe. So that there would be access, so that he/she can afford it at least once a month or once a week. It is important to remember that we are role models for younger generations, they follow our behaviour. It is useless to say that chips are bad if you eat them yourself. Our country is big and I really want to reach out to almost every citizen. The challenge now is this, do I continue to source 85 per cent of ingredients from abroad, or follow my dream and help my country by accepting lower standards?

QUESTIONS

1. What kinds of taken-for-granted assumptions challenged this venture? How did Lyuda deal with them?

2. Do you think the venture lives up to its aspirations of helping Russia? How, how not? What would you have done differently to live up to these aspirations even more? Would you classify this as a social or commercial enterprise, maybe, an eco-enterprise?

3. Do you think this is an example of professional entrepreneuring? Does it realize a social opportunity for society? Do you think it has been conducted competently? Is it ethical, responsible, and sustainable?

4. If you were in Lyuda's shoes, what would be your next move?

DIGGING DEEPER: RESPONSIBLE SMALL AND MEDIUM SIZED ENTERPRISES (SMES)

SMEs significantly contribute to job creation in most countries. The contribution of SMEs to GDP ranges from little less than 10 per cent in Albania, to over 70 per cent in Germany [196]. In summary: 'SMEs matter' [197]. The management in SMEs differs from that in large companies. Most prominently, SME management is typically more entrepreneurial. Table 15.7 summarizes the main differences between SMEs and large companies, and their implications for responsible entrepreneurial management [198–200].

TABLE 15.7   Comparing large companies and SMEs, and the implications for responsible management

		Large enterprise	SME	Implications for responsible entrepreneurial management
Organization structure	**Top management**	CEO	Owner-Manager	Owner manager has bigger discretion in implementing or not implementing responsible business, as they are not accountable to external shareholders.
	Business development stage	Mature	Early development stage	Responsible business in SMEs needs to be managed more flexibly and intuitively than in large companies, due to the need for often quick reactions, and because of weakly developed management systems and little standardization of processes.
	Range of products and services	Diversified	Specialized	The specialized nature of SMEs makes it easier to develop innovative solutions to sustainability challenges in the company's area of expertise, but more difficult in outside areas.
	Structure	Departments	Positions (multi-functional)	Incumbents of SME jobs that include responsible management as part of the job description will encounter competing activities and priorities.
	Decisions and responsiveness	Deep hierarchies, extensive communication and decision processes	Flat hierarchies, uncomplicated communication and decision processes	Decisions in SMEs can be taken quickly, which gives them the potential to proactively react to stakeholder claims and to provide solutions to social and environmental issues that arise.
	Structural responsiveness	Rigidity	Flexibility	Potential for quick decision-making for responsible business implementation in SMEs.
Strategy	**Planning**	Long-term strategies	Short- to medium-term tactics	In SMEs, grassroots initiatives, providing punctual responsible business initiatives that grow to a company-wide responsible management infrastructure.
	Competitors	Enemy	Industry colleagues	High potential for industry collaboration – e.g. in strategic partnerships between 'industry colleagues'.
	Basis of competition	Price or differentiation	Relationships, cooperation, flexibility, service	Important functions of responsible business activities in SMEs are the networking aspect, the building of social capital, and the possibility of increasing competitiveness.
Marketing and communication	**Marketing partner**	Business-to-consumer (B2C)	Business-to-business (B2B)	Marketing and communication of responsible business in SMEs must be directed at industry clients and networks, instead of the end consumers, who are the primary target of responsible business communication in large companies.
	Marketing environment	Market	Network	Collaborative, responsible business activities can serve as marketing activities inside the SME network.
	Appearance	Visible on national and global scale	Invisible on supra-regional level, but high visibility in local community	External stakeholder pressures influence SMEs only on a local scale.

		Large enterprise	SME	Implications for responsible entrepreneurial management
	Codification	High, many explicit responsible business instruments	Low, implicit integration of responsible business into 'what we do'	In contrast to large companies, responsible business in SMEs are unlikely to have codes of conduct, values statements, or even mission statements. While SMEs usually 'do' responsible business, they often do not refer to it using this term. Often the terminology is neither well defined nor well understood.
	Basis of relationships	Brand	Trust	Responsible business must rather focus on building trust with key stakeholders, rather than marketing a brand to a broader set of stakeholders.
Environment and embeddedness	*Supply chain position*	End-consumer company, or higher-tier supplier	Lower-tier supplier or revalorizer	SMEs are often 'drawn to responsible business activities through market pressure by higher tier suppliers or end-consumer companies.
	Systemic embeddedness	Market mechanism	Relational mechanism	SMEs can create responsible business solutions in local networks, instead of focusing on larger markets.
	Glocalization	Global	Local	Local 'good citizen' activities in the community are more emphasized than distant global responsibilities, such as sustainable development.
	Community relationship	Intruder	Member	SMEs are in an excellent position to relate to local communities.
	Locus of responsibility	Anonymous corporation	Single individual	Owner-managers and other employees in SMEs can assume personal responsibility on the job that directly translates into organizational responsibility.
	Power and outreach	Power to create large-scale solutions	Local power	Little power and outreach of SMEs often leads to an attitude along the lines of 'We cannot do that anyway. Let the big ones do it.'
Finance and capital	*Decisive capital*	Economic	Social	Social capital, especially in personal business networks might be more crucial for the SME's success than the economic capital in the books. Responsible business can be used to increase social capital.
	Internal financing	Economies of scale	Limited resources	Little budget for responsible business, unless it pays back directly. The business case is critical.
	Ownership	External ownership	Individual or family ownership	Potential differences in distribution of profits, and importance of individual or family values in responsible business conduct.
	Rationale	Profit maximizing	Owner satisfaction	Owner-manager has high discretion regarding the use of SME funds, either to maximize profits for personal wealth or to internally invest into social or philanthropic topics, even if those should not have a strong business case.
	Funding	Outside	Inside	Due to restricted access to outside capital, SMEs might not be able to raise lump-sum funds for the transformation to responsible business practices.
People management	*Company–employee relationship*	Formalized, neutral, impersonal	Mutually dependent, personal	Potential ethical dilemmas through companies and employees mutually abusing the dependent and close personal relationship.
	Employee roles	Well defined and rigid	Vague and flexible	SMEs often have the potential to improve their employees. responsibility role definitions.
	Employee profile	Professionalized and specialized	Generalists	It might be difficult in SMEs to train employee specialists in responsible management.
	Responsibilities and tasks	Specialists	Multi-taskers	Other tasks might strongly compete with responsible business in the employees' job description.
	Attitude towards responsibility	Impersonalized responsibility, I am just one cog in the enormous machine.	Immediate responsibility – we are the business	Higher personal accountability of employees.

SOURCES: Synthesized [198–202]

POINTERS

You could use this table to reflect on how entrepreneurial management practices differ in bigger and smaller organizations. What does entrepreneurial management look like in a family business or an NGO?

WORKSHEET

TRIPLE-LAYERED BUSINESS MODEL CANVAS

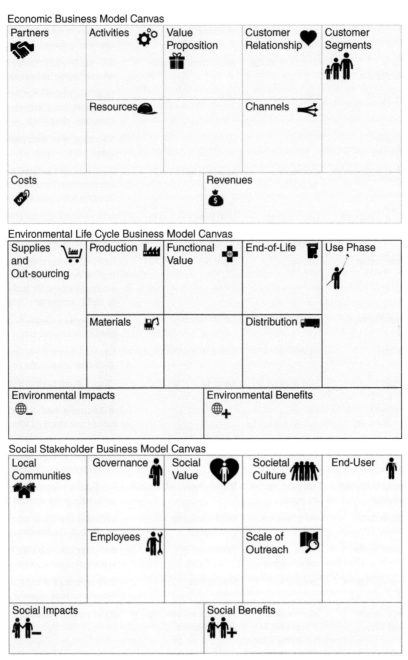

SOURCE: [203]

POINTERS

Use this canvas to creatively plan a new venture, or to analyse an existing one's economic, social, and environmental business model.

REFERENCES

1. European Commission. *Social economy in the EU.* 2018.
2. Kulturkosmos. Kulturkosmos: More than just a project. https://kulturkosmos.de/index_en.php Published 2019. Accessed May 10 2020.
3. Kulturkosmos. What is fusion? www.fusion-festival.de/en/x/festival Published 2020. Accessed May 10 2020.
4. Fusion. Hinweise. https://archiv.fusion-festival.de/2019/de/2019/hinweise/wissenswertes-zur-fusion-von-a-bis-z Published 2019. Accessed May 15 2020.
5. Fusion. Supporter. https://kulturkosmos.org/supporter#/whySupporter Published 2020. Accessed May 10 2020.
6. Anonymous Fusion Supporter. Application process at fusion. Interview with author, Frankfurt, 2019.
7. Stürzenhofecker M, Thurm F. Streit um das Fusion Festival. www.zeit.de/gesellschaft/zeitgeschehen/2019–05/laerz-fusion-festival-polizei-zugang-privatgelaende-sicherheitskonzept-musikfestival Published 2019. Accessed May 10 2020.
8. Fusion. Fusion Festival 2020 findet nicht statt. www.fusion-festival.de/de/x/festival/fusion-festival-2020-findet-nicht-statt Published 2020. Accessed 2020.
9. Drucker P. *The essential Drucker.* New York: HarperCollins, 2001.
10. Rindova V, Barry D, Ketchen DJ Jr. Entrepreneuring as emancipation. *Academy of Management Review.* 2009, 34(3): 477–491.
11. Antonacopoulou EP, Fuller T. Practising entrepreneuring as emplacement: The impact of sensation and anticipation in entrepreneurial action. *Entrepreneurship & Regional Development.* 2020, 32(3–4): 257–280.
12. Hjorth D, Holt R, Steyaert C. Entrepreneurship and process studies. *International Small Business Journal.* 2015, 33(6): 599–611.
13. Steyaert C. 'Entrepreneuring' as a conceptual attractor? A review of process theories in 20 years of entrepreneurship studies. *Entrepreneurship and Regional Development.* 2007, 19(6): 453–477.
14. Steyaert C. A qualitative methodology for process studies of entrepreneurship: Creating local knowledge through stories. *International Studies of Management & Organization.* 1997, 27(3): 13–33.
15. Gartner WB, Stam E, Thompson N, Verduyn K. Entrepreneurship as practice: Grounding contemporary practice theory into entrepreneurship studies. *Entrepreneurship & Regional Development.* 2016, 28(9–10): 813–816.
16. Johannisson B. Towards a practice theory of entrepreneuring. *Small Business Economics.* 2011, 36(2): 135–150.
17. Anderson AR. Cultivating the Garden of Eden: Environmental entrepreneuring. *Journal of Organizational Change Management.* 1998, 11(2): 135–144.
18. Mair J, Battilana J, Cardenas J. Organizing for society: A typology of social entrepreneuring models. *Journal of Business Ethics.* 2012, 111(3): 353–373.
19. Hjorth D. Entrepreneuring as organisation-creation. In: Hjorth D, Holt R, Steyaert C, eds. *Handbook of research on entrepreneurship and creativity.* Cheltenham: Edward Elgar, 2014: 97–121.
20. Stevenson HH, Jarrillo-Mossi JC. Preserving entrepreneurship as companies grow. *The Journal of Business Strategy.* 1986, 7(1): 10–24.
21. Timmons JA, Spinelli S, Tan Y. *New venture creation: Entrepreneurship for the 21st century.* Vol 6. New York: McGraw-Hill/Irwin, 2004.
22. Bruyat C, Julien P-A. Defining the field of research in entrepreneurship. *Journal of Business Venturing.* 2001, 16(2): 165–180.
23. Stevenson HH, Jarillo JC. A paradigm of entrepreneurship: Entrepreneurial management. *Strategic Management Journal.* 1990, 11: 17–27.
24. Markman GD, Waldron TL, Gianiodis PT, Espina MI. E Pluribus Unum: Impact entrepreneurship as a solution to grand challenges. *Academy of Management Perspectives.* 2019, 33(4): 371–382.
25. Gartner WB. 'Who is an entrepreneur?' is the wrong question. *American Journal of Small Business.* 1988, 12(4): 11–32.
26. Baum JR, Locke EA. The relationship of entrepreneurial traits, skill, and motivation to subsequent venture growth. *Journal of Applied Psychology.* 2004, 89(4): 587.

27. Zhou H, Huang L, Kuo T-K. Determinants of small firm growth: An exhaustive analysis using conceptual and statistical approaches. *International Review of Entrepreneurship*. 2018, 16(4): 525–564.

28. Dess GG, Lumpkin GT. The role of entrepreneurial orientation in stimulating effective corporate entrepreneurship. *Academy of Management Perspectives*. 2005, 19(1): 147–156.

29. Anderson AR, Warren L. The entrepreneur as hero and jester: Enacting the entrepreneurial discourse. *International Small Business Journal*. 2011, 29(6): 589–609.

30. Kets de Vries MF. The dark side of entrepreneurship. *Harvard Business Review*. 1985, 63(6): 160–167.

31. Hmieleski KM, Lerner DA. The dark triad and nascent entrepreneurship: An examination of unproductive versus productive entrepreneurial motives. *Journal of Small Business Management*. 2016, 54(1): 7–32.

32. Baumol WJ. Entrepreneurship: Productive, unproductive, and destructive. *Journal of Business Venturing*. 1996, 11(1): 3–22.

33. Dutton K. *The wisdom of psychopaths: Lessons in life from saints, spies and serial killers*. New York: Random House, 2012.

34. Brown TA, Sautter JA, Littvay L, Sautter AC, Bearnes B. Ethics and personality: Empathy and narcissism as moderators of ethical decision making in business students. *Journal of Education for Business*. 2010, 85(4): 203–208.

35. Chatterjee A, Hambrick DC. It's all about me: Narcissistic chief executive officers and their effects on company strategy and performance. *Administrative Science Quarterly*. 2007, 52(3): 351–386.

36. Jones DN. What's mine is mine and what's yours is mine: The Dark Triad and gambling with your neighbor's money. *Journal of Research in Personality*. 2013, 47(5): 563–571.

37. Jonason PK, Koenig BL, Tost J. Living a fast life: The Dark Triad and life history theory. *Human Nature*. 2010, 21(4): 428–442.

38. Kravis H. Avatar of American finance. www.achievement.org/autodoc/page/kra0int-2 Published 2010. Accessed March 30 2016.

39. Mackey J, Sisodia R. *Conscious capitalism, with a new preface by the authors: Liberating the heroic spirit of business*. Boston: Harvard Business Review Press, 2013.

40. Martin A. Whole Foods executive used alias. www.nytimes.com/2007/07/12/business/12foods.html Published 2007. Accessed May 29 2020.

41. Alsos GA, Kolvereid L. The business gestation process of novice, serial, and parallel business founders. *Entrepreneurship Theory and Practice*. 1998, 22(4): 101–114.

42. Erikson T. Towards a taxonomy of entrepreneurial learning experiences among potential entrepreneurs. *Journal of Small Business and Enterprise Development*. 2003, 10(1): 106–112.

43. Rottenberg L. *Crazy is a compliment: The power of zigging when everyone else zags*. London: Penguin, 2016.

44. Aldrich HE, Ruef M. Unicorns, gazelles, and other distractions on the way to understanding real entrepreneurship in the United States. *Academy of Management Perspectives*. 2018, 32(4): 458–472.

45. Van Praag CM. Business survival and success of young small business owners. *Small Business Economics*. 2003, 21(1): 1–17.

46. Winborg J, Landström H. Financial bootstrapping in small businesses: Examining small business managers' resource acquisition behaviors. *Journal of Business Venturing*. 2001, 16(3): 235–254.

47. Fauchart E, Gruber M. Darwinians, communitarians, and missionaries: The role of founder identity in entrepreneurship. *Academy of Management Journal*. 2011, 54(5): 935–957.

48. Carland JW, Hoy F, Boulton WR, Carland JAC. Differentiating entrepreneurs from small business owners: A conceptualization. *Academy of Management Review*. 1984, 9(2): 354–359.

49. Moran P. Personality characteristics and growth-orientation of the small business owner-manager. *International Small Business Journal*. 1998, 16(3): 17–38.

50. Pinchot G, Pellman R. *Intrapreneuring in action: A handbook for business innovation*. New York: Berrett-Koehler Publishers, 1999.

51. Pinchot G. *Intrapreneuring: Why you don't have to leave the corporation to become an entrepreneur*. New York: HarperCollins, 1985.

52. Business Dictionary. Lifestyle entrepreneur. www.businessdictionary.com/definition/lifestyle-entrepreneur.html Published 2020. Accessed May 16 2020.

53. Schine GL. *How to succeed as a lifestyle entrepreneur: Running a business without letting it run your life.* Dearborn Trade, 2003.

54. Moazzez N. How to become a lifestyle entrepreneur: 10 easy steps to follow. https://navidmoazzez.com/lifestyle-entrepreneur Published 2020. Accessed May 16 2020.

55. Henderson R, Robertson M. Who wants to be an entrepreneur? Young adult attitudes to entrepreneurship as a career. *Career Development International.* 2000, 5(6): 279–287.

56. Cassar G. Money, money, money? A longitudinal investigation of entrepreneur career reasons, growth preferences and achieved growth. *Entrepreneurship and Regional Development.* 2007, 19(1): 89–107.

57. Ayu A. Entrepreneur personalities: The butterfly vs. the bee. www.inc.com/ariana-ayu/entrepreneur-personalities-the-butterfly-vs-the-bee.html Published 2016. Accessed May 16 2020.

58. Schere JL. Tolerance of ambiguity as a discriminating variable between entrepreneurs and managers. Paper presented at Academy of Management Proceedings, 1982.

59. Stewart WH, Roth PL. A meta-analysis of achievement motivation differences between entrepreneurs and managers. *Journal of Small Business Management.* 2007, 45(4): 401–421.

60. Ohe T, Honjo S, Macmillan IC. Japanese entrepreneurs and corporate managers: A comparison. *Journal of Business Venturing.* 1990, 5(3): 163–176.

61. Malach-Pines A, Sadeh A, Dvir D, Yafe-Yanai O. Entrepreneurs and managers: Similar yet different. *The International Journal of Organizational Analysis.* 2002, 10(2): 172–190.

62. Burns P. *Entrepreneurship and small business: Start-up, growth and maturity.* New York: Palgrave Macmillan, 2011.

63. Morris MH, Kuratko DF, Covin JG. *Corporate entrepreneurship and innovation.* Mason, OH: Cengage Learning, 2010.

64. Bacharach SB, Bamberger P, Sonnenstuhl WJ. The organizational transformation process: The micropolitics of dissonance reduction and the alignment of logics of action. *Administrative Science Quarterly.* 1996, 41(3): 477–506.

65. Bacharach SB, Mundell BL. Organizational politics in schools: Micro, macro, and logics of action. *Educational Administration Quarterly.* 1993, 29(4): 423–452.

66. Dew N, Read S, Sarasvathy SD, Wiltbank R. Effectual versus predictive logics in entrepreneurial decision-making: Differences between experts and novices. *Journal of Business Venturing.* 2009, 24(4): 287–309.

67. Harms R, Schiele H. Antecedents and consequences of effectuation and causation in the international new venture creation process. *Journal of International Entrepreneurship.* 2012, 10(2): 95–116.

68. Fisher G. Effectuation, causation, and bricolage: A behavioral comparison of emerging theories in entrepreneurship research. *Entrepreneurship Theory and Practice.* 2012, 36(5): 1019–1051.

69. Duymedjian R, Rüling C-C. Towards a foundation of bricolage in organization and management theory. *Organization Studies.* 2010, 31(2): 133–151.

70. Sarasvathy SD. Causation and effectuation: Toward a theoretical shift from economic inevitability to entrepreneurial contingency. *Academy of Management Review.* 2001, 26(2): 243–263.

71. Musk E. Master plan, part deux. www.tesla.com/de_DE/blog/master-plan-part-deux Published 2016. Accessed May 15 2020.

72. Tesco. *What matters now: Using our scale for good: Tesco and society. Report 2013.* Cheshunt, 2014.

73. Read S, Sarasvathy S, Dew N, Wiltbank R. *Effectual entrepreneurship.* London: Routledge, 2010.

74. Baker T, Nelson RE. Creating something from nothing: Resource construction through entrepreneurial bricolage. *Administrative Science Quarterly.* 2005, 50(3): 329–366.

75. Garud R, Karnøe P. Bricolage versus breakthrough: Distributed and embedded agency in technology entrepreneurship. *Research Policy.* 2003, 32(2): 277–300.

76. Lévi-Strauss C. *The savage mind.* Chicago: University of Chicago Press, 1966.

77. Andersen OJ. A bottom-up perspective on innovations: Mobilizing knowledge and social capital through innovative processes of bricolage. *Administration & Society.* 2008, 40(1): 54–78.

78. Talhelm T. Do air purifiers remove PM2.5? www.quora.com/Do-air-purifiers-remove-PM2-5 Published 2019. Accessed May 16 2020.

79. Smart Air. Do HEPAs and the Smart Air DIY Purifier actually work? https://smartairfilters. com/cn/en/our-data-does-the-smart-air-diy-purifier-work Published 2020. Accessed May 16 2020.

80. Naeini A, Dutt A, Angus J, Mardirossian S, Bonfanti S. A shoe for a shoe, and a smile. *Business Today*. www.businesstoday.in/magazine/lbs-case-study/toms-shoes-shoes-for- free-cause-marketing-strategy-case-study/story/219444.html Published 2015. Updated. Accessed February 13 2019.

81. Austin JE, Leonard HB, Reficco E, Wei-Skillern J. Social entrepreneurship: It's for corporations too. In: Nicholls A, ed. *Social entrepreneurship: New models of sustainable social change*. Oxford: Oxford University Press, 2006: 169–180.

82. Austin J, Reficco E. Corporate social entrepreneurship. *International Journal of Not-for-Profit Law*. 2008, 11: 86–92.

83. SustainAbility. *The social intrapreneur: A field guide for corporate change makers*. London: SustainAbility, 2008.

84. Carollo L, Guerci M. 'Activists in a suit': Paradoxes and metaphors in sustainability managers' identity work. *Journal of Business Ethics*. 2017, 148(2): 249–268.

85. Hardy C, Maguire S. Institutional entrepreneurship. In: Greenwood R, Oliver C, Suddaby R, Sahlin-Andersson K, eds. *The Sage handbook of organizational institutionalism*. London: Sage, 2008: 198–217.

86. Dorado S. Institutional entrepreneurship, partaking, and convening. *Organization Studies*. 2005, 26(3): 385–414.

87. Maguire S, Hardy C, Lawrence TB. Institutional entrepreneurship in emerging fields: HIV/AIDS treatment advocacy in Canada. *Academy of Management Journal*. 2004, 47(5): 657–679.

88. Tracey P, Phillips N, Jarvis O. Bridging institutional entrepreneurship and the creation of new organizational forms: A multilevel model. *Organization Science*. 2011, 22(1): 60–80.

89. Battilana J, D'aunno T. Institutional work and the paradox of embedded agency. In: Lawrence T, Suddaby R, Leca B, eds. *Institutional work: Actors and agency in institutional studies of organizations*. Cambridge: Cambridge University Press, 2009: 31–58.

90. Garud R, Hardy C, Maguire S. Institutional entrepreneurship as embedded agency: An introduction to the special issue. *Organization Studies*. 2007, 28(7): 957.

91. Battilana J, Leca B, Boxenbaum E. How actors change institutions: Towards a theory of institutional entrepreneurship. *Academy of Management Annals*. 2009, 3(1): 65–107.

92. Välikangas L, Carlsen A. Spitting in the salad: Minor rebellion as institutional agency. *Organization Studies*. 2019, https://doi.org/10.1177/0170840619831054.

93. DeCelles KA, Aquino K. Dark knights: When and why an employee becomes a workplace vigilante? *Academy of Management Review*. 2015, https://doi.org/10.5465/amr.2017.0300.

94. Paddison L. Why some brands are leading a Black Friday boycott. www.huffingtonpost. co.uk/entry/black-friday-rei-deciem-boycottx Published 2019. Accessed May 17 2020.

95. Randles S, Laasch O. Theorising the normative business model (NBM). *Organization & Environment*. 2016, 29(1): 53–73.

96. Hockerts K, Wüstenhagen R. Greening Goliaths versus emerging Davids: Theorizing about the role of incumbents and new entrants in sustainable entrepreneurship. *Journal of Business Venturing*. 2010, 25(5): 481–492.

97. Austin J, Stevenson H, Wei-Skillern J. Social and commercial entrepreneurship: Same, different, or both? *Entrepreneurship Theory and Practice*. 2006, 30(1): 1–22.

98. Laasch O. Beyond the purely commercial business model: Organizational value logics and the heterogeneity of sustainability business models. *Long Range Planning*. 2018, 51(1): 158–183.

99. Dolan C. The new face of development: The 'bottom of the pyramid' entrepreneurs. *Anthropology Today*. 2012, 28(4): 3–7.

100. Fonneland T. Spiritual entrepreneurship in a northern landscape: Spirituality, tourism and politics. *Temenos-Nordic Journal of Comparative Religion*. 2012, 48(2).

101. Klamer A. Cultural entrepreneurship. *The Review of Austrian Economics*. 2011, 24(2): 141–156.

102. Ratten V. Sport-based entrepreneurship: Towards a new theory of entrepreneurship and sport management. *International Entrepreneurship and Management Journal*. 2011, 7(1): 57–69.

103. Heck RK, Hoy F, Poutziouris PZ, Steier LP. Emerging paths of family entrepreneurship research. *Journal of Small Business Management*. 2008, 46(3): 317–330.

104. Schaper M. The essence of ecopreneurship. *Greener Management International*. 2002, 22: 26–30.

105. Pache A-C, Santos F. Inside the hybrid organization: Selective coupling as response to competing institutional logics. *Academy of Management Journal*. 2013, 56(4): 972–1001.

106. Schaltegger S. A Framework for ecopreneurship. *Greener Management International*. 2002(38): 45–58.

107. Radoynovska N, Ocasio W, Laasch O. The emerging logic of responsible management: Institutional pluralism, leadership, and strategizing. In: Laasch O, Suddaby R, Freeman RE, Jamali D, eds. *The research handbook of responsible management*. Cheltenham: Edward Elgar, 2020.

108. Laasch O. The business model is dead: Long live the organizational value model! www.bos-cbscsr.dk/2018/09/04/organizational-value-model Published 2018. Accessed May 23 2020.

109. Ozor O. Kobo360: Keeping Africa moving. http://media.kobo360.com/kobo360-keeping-africa-moving Published 2020. Accessed May 27 2020.

110. Munshi N. Tech start-ups drive change for Nigerian truckers. www.ft.com/content/c6a3d1f2-c27d-11e9-a8e9-296ca66511c9 Published 2019. Accessed May 27 2020.

111. Ridley-Duff R, Bull M, Laasch O. Entrepreneurship: Value-added ventures. In: Laasch O, Conaway RN, eds. *Principles of responsible management: Glocal sustainability, responsibility, ethics*. Mason, OH: Cengage, 2015.

112. Alter K. *Social Enterprise Typology*. San Francisco: Virtue Ventures, 2007.

113. Hahn T, Figge F, Pinkse J, Preuss L. Trade-offs in corporate sustainability: You can't have your cake and eat it. *Business Strategy and the Environment*. 2010, 19(4): 217–229.

114. Hahn T, Preuss L, Pinkse J, Figge F. Cognitive frames in corporate sustainability: Managerial sensemaking with paradoxical and business case frames. *Academy of Management Review*. 2014, 39(4): 463–487.

115. Yin J, Chen H. Dual-goal management in social enterprises: Evidence from China. *Management Decision*. 2019, 57(6): 1362–1381.

116. Mersland R, Strøm Rø. Microfinance mission drift? *World Development*. 2010, 38(1): 28–36.

117. Ebrahim A, Battilana J, Mair J. The governance of social enterprises: Mission drift and accountability challenges in hybrid organizations. *Research in Organizational Behavior*. 2014, 34: 81–100.

118. Laasch O, Pinkse J. How the leopards got their spots: Embedding responsibility into business models as strategic response across spaces of institutional complexity. *Long Range Planning*. 2019, https://doi.org/10.1016/j.lrp.2019.101891.

119. Zahraa SA, Gedajlovic E, Neubaum DO, Shulman JM. A typology of social entrepreneurs: Motives, search processes and ethical challenges. *Journal of Business Venturing*. 2009, 24(5): 519–32.

120. Yunus M. The Grameen Bank. *Scientific American*. 1999, 281(5): 114–119.

121. Yunus M, Moingeon B, Lehmann-Ortega L. Building social business models: Lessons from the Grameen experience. *Long Range Planning*. 2010, 43(2): 308–325.

122. Bateman M. The rise and fall of Muhammad Yunus and the microcredit model. *International Development Studies Working Paper*. 2014, 1(1).

123. Kempster S, Cope J. Learning to lead in the entrepreneurial context. *International Journal of Entrepreneurial Behavior & Research*. 2010, 16(1): 5–34.

124. González MF, Husted BW, Aigner DJ. Opportunity discovery and creation in social entrepreneurship: An exploratory study in Mexico. *Journal of Business Research*. 2017, 81: 212–220.

125. Chetty S, Karami M, Martín OM. Opportunity discovery and creation as a duality: Evidence from small firms' foreign market entries. *Journal of International Marketing*. 2018, 26(3): 70–93.

126. Sarasvathy SD, Dew N, Velamuri SR, Venkataraman S. Three views of entrepreneurial opportunity. In: Acs ZJ, Audretsch DB, eds. *Handbook of Entrepreneurship Research*. Springer, 2003: 141–160.

127. Baron RA. Opportunity recognition as pattern recognition: How entrepreneurs 'connect the dots' to identify new business opportunities. *Academy of Management Perspectives*. 2006, 20(1): 104–119.

128. Baron RA, Ensley MD. Opportunity recognition as the detection of meaningful patterns: Evidence from comparisons of novice and experienced entrepreneurs. *Management Science*. 2006, 52(9): 1331–1344.

129. Ozgen E, Baron RA. Social sources of information in opportunity recognition: Effects of mentors, industry networks, and professional forums. *Journal of Business Venturing*. 2007, 22(2): 174–192.

130. Hanohov R, Baldacchino L. Opportunity recognition in sustainable entrepreneurship: An exploratory study. *International Journal of Entrepreneurial Behavior & Research*. 2018, 24(2): 333–358.

131. Mair J, Marti I. Entrepreneurship in and around institutional voids: A case study from Bangladesh. *Journal of Business Venturing*. 2009, 24(5): 419–435.

132. Mair J, Marti I, Ventresca MJ. Building inclusive markets in rural Bangladesh: How intermediaries work institutional voids. *Academy of Management Journal*. 2012, 55(4): 819–850.

133. Alvarez SA, Young SL, Woolley JL. Opportunities and institutions: A co-creation story of the king crab industry. *Journal of Business Venturing*. 2015, 30(1): 95–112.

134. Giacomin O, Janssen F, Guyot J-l, Lohest O. Opportunity and/or necessity entrepreneurship? The impact of the socio-economic characteristics of entrepreneurs. *MPRA Paper*. 2011, 29506.

135. Fuentelsaz L, González C, Maícas JP, Montero J. How different formal institutions affect opportunity and necessity entrepreneurship. *BRQ Business Research Quarterly*. 2015, 18(4): 246–258.

136. Dencker J, Bacq SC, Gruber M, Haas M. Reconceptualizing necessity entrepreneurship: A contextualized framework of entrepreneurial processes under the condition of basic needs. *Academy of Management Review*. 2019, https://doi.org/10.5465/amr.2017.0471.

137. Clough DR, Fang TP, Vissa B, Wu A. Turning lead into gold: How do entrepreneurs mobilize resources to exploit opportunities? *Academy of Management Annals*. 2019, 13(1): 240–271.

138. Keating A, Geiger S, McLoughlin D. Riding the practice waves: Social resourcing practices during new venture development. *Entrepreneurship Theory and Practice*. 2014, 38(5): 1–29.

139. Feldman MS, Worline M. Resources, resourcing, and ampliative cycles in organizations. In: Cameron K, Spreitzer G, eds. *Oxford handbook of positive organizational scholarship*. Oxford: Oxford University Press, 2011: 629–641.

140. Cooney TM. What is an entrepreneurial team? *International Small Business Journal*. 2005, 23(3): 226–235.

141. Reich RB. Entrepreneurship reconsidered: The team as hero. *Harvard Business Review*. 1987, 87(3): 77–83.

142. Lazar M, Miron-Spektor E, Agarwal R, Erez M, Goldfarb B, Chen G. Entrepreneurial team formation. *Academy of Management Annals*. 2020, 14(1): 29–59.

143. Knight AP, Greer LL, De Jong B. Start-up teams: A multidimensional conceptualization, integrative review of past research, and future research agenda. *Academy of Management Annals*. 2020, 14(1): 231–266.

144. York JG, Venkataraman S. The entrepreneur–environment nexus: Uncertainty, innovation, and allocation. *Journal of Business Venturing*. 2010, 25(5): 449–463.

145. Laasch O, Conaway R. *Responsible business: The textbook for management learning, competence, innovation*. Sheffield: Greenleaf, 2016.

146. Bosma N, Hill S, Ionescu-Somers A, Kelley D, Levie J, Tarnawa A. *Global entrepreneurship monitor: 2019/2020 Global report*. London: Global Entrepreneurship Research Association, 2020.

147. Acs ZJ, Stam E, Audretsch DB, O'Connor A. The lineages of the entrepreneurial ecosystem approach. *Small Business Economics*. 2017, 49(1): 1–10.

148. Isenberg DJ. How to start an entrepreneurial revolution. *Harvard Business Review*. 2010, 88(6): 40–50.

149. Feld B. *Startup communities: Building an entrepreneurial ecosystem in your city*. New York: John Wiley & Sons, 2012.

150. Sussan F, Acs ZJ. The digital entrepreneurial ecosystem. *Small Business Economics*. 2017, 49(1): 55–73.

151. Suresh J, Ramraj R. Entrepreneurial ecosystem: Case study on the influence of environmental factors on entrepreneurial success. *European Journal of Business and Management.* 2012, 4(16): 95–101.

152. Isenberg D. The entrepreneurship ecosystem strategy as a new paradigm for economy policy: Principles for cultivating entrepreneurship. Babson Park, MA: Babson Entrepreneurship Ecosystem Project, Babson College, 2011.

153. Pitelis C. Clusters, entrepreneurial ecosystem co-creation, and appropriability: A conceptual framework. *Industrial and Corporate Change.* 2012, 21(6): 1359–1388.

154. Porter ME. *The Competitive Advantage of Nations.* New York: Simon & Schuster, 1990.

155. Y Combinator. Y Combinator created a new model for funding early stage startups. www.ycombinator.com Published 2020. Accessed May 23 2020.

156. The Worldbank. Doing business: Measuring business regulations. www.doingbusiness. org/en/rankings# Published 2020. Accessed May 23 2020.

157. Evansluong Q. *Opportunity creation as a mixed embedding process: A study of immigrant entrepreneurs in Sweden.* Jönköping: Jönköping University, 2020.

158. Expeditions C. El audaz proyecto de ecoturismo de la Farc en Caquetá. www. caguanexpeditions.co/blog/el-audaz-proyecto-de-ecoturismo-de-la-farc-en-caqueta Published 2020. Accessed May 27 2020.

159. Lewis VL, Churchill NC. The five stages of small business growth. *Harvard Business Review.* 1983, 61(3): 30–50.

160. Greiner LE. Evolution and revolution as organizations grow. *Harvard Business Review.* 1972, 50(4): 37–46.

161. Burns P. *Entrepreneurship and small business.* New York: Palgrave Macmillan, 2016.

162. Bolton BK, Thompson J. *Entrepreneurs: Talent, temperament, technique.* London: Routledge, 2004.

163. Osterwalder A, Pigneur Y. *Business model generation.* Chichester: Wiley, 2010.

164. Sahlman WA. How to write a great business plan. *Harvard Business Review.* 1997, 75(4): 98–109.

165. Sørensen HE. *Business development: A market-oriented perspective.* Wiley Chichester, 2012.

166. Kotha R, George G. Friends, family, or fools: Entrepreneur experience and its implications for equity distribution and resource mobilization. *Journal of Business Venturing.* 2012, 27(5): 525–543.

167. Berger AN, Udell GF. The economics of small business finance: The roles of private equity and debt markets in the financial growth cycle. *Journal of Banking & Finance.* 1998, 22(6–8): 613–673.

168. Emerson J. The blended value proposition: Integrating social and financial returns. *California Management Review.* 2003, 45(4): 35–51.

169. Zhou H, van der Zwan P. Is there a risk of growing fast? The relationship between organic employment growth and firm exit. *Industrial and Corporate Change.* 2019, 28(5): 1297–1320.

170. Laasch O. An actor-network perspective on business models: How 'being responsible' led to incremental, but pervasive change. *Long Range Planning.* 2018, 52(3): 406–426.

171. Ansoff HI. Strategies for diversification. *Harvard Business Review.* 1957, 35(5): 113–124.

172. Liao R. China's Youon expands into Europe as other bike startups backpedal worldwide. https://techcrunch.com/2018/10/31/youon-expands-into-europe Published 2018. Accessed April 19 2020.

173. Milukaite A. Welcome to Cycle.land. www.cycle.land/about Published 2020. Accessed May 25 2020.

174. Hurley K. *From social enterprise to social franchise: An introductory guide to achieving scale through replication.* Toronto: Canadian Community Economic Development Network (CCEDNet), 2016.

175. Tracey P, Jarvis O. Toward a theory of social venture franchising. *Entrepreneurship Theory and Practice.* 2007, 31(5): 667–685.

176. McBride J, Ahmed R. *Social franchising as a strategy for expanding access to reproductive health services: A case study of the Green Star Service Delivery Network in Pakistan.* Karachi: Social Marketing Pakistan, 2001.

177. Greenstar. Greenstar Social Marketing (GSM). www.greenstar.org.pk/family_planning Published 2020. Accessed May 25 2020.

178. Haas B. Anger as Chinese bike sharing firm shuts up office with riders' deposits: Bluegogo, China's third largest bike sharing company, reported to be in financial

trouble. www.theguardian.com/world/2017/nov/17/anger-as-chinese-bike-sharing-firm-shuts-up-office-with-riders-deposits Published 2017. Accessed May 25 2020.

179. Wikipedia. Bluegogo. https://en.wikipedia.org/wiki/Bluegogo Published 2020. Accessed May 25 2020.

180. Christensen TB, Wells P, Cipcigan L. Can innovative business models overcome resistance to electric vehicles? Better Place and battery electric cars in Denmark. *Energy Policy*. 2012, 48: 498–505.

181. Richardson B, Nwankwo S, Richardson S. Understanding the causes of business failure crises. *Management Decision*. 1994, 32(4): 9–22.

182. McGrath RG. Falling forward: Real options reasoning and entrepreneurial failure. *Academy of Management Review*. 1999, 24(1): 13–30.

183. Shepherd DA, Wiklund J, Haynie JM. Moving forward: Balancing the financial and emotional costs of business failure. *Journal of Business Venturing*. 2009, 24(2): 134–148.

184. Sarason Y, Dean TJ. Lost battles, Trojan horses, open gates, and wars won: How entrepreneurial firms co-create structures to expand and infuse their sustainability missions in the acquisition process. *Academy of Management Perspectives*. 2019, 33(4): 469–490.

185. Marquis C, Lounsbury M. Vive la résistance: Competing logics and the consolidation of US community banking. *Academy of Management Journal*. 2007, 50(4): 799–820.

186. Ling C, Lifen Y. Hereditary succession: The inheritable management and creation in clannish enterprises. *Management World*. 2003, 6: 89–96.

187. Stavrou ET, Kleanthous T, Anastasiou T. Leadership personality and firm culture during hereditary transitions in family firms: Model development and empirical investigation. *Journal of Small Business Management*. 2005, 43(2): 187–206.

188. Ellis M. *What is responsible leadership in practice?* Sheffield: Sheffield Business School, Sheffield Hallam University, 2020.

189. Miles MP, Covin JG. Exploring the practice of corporate venturing: Some common forms and their organizational implications. *Entrepreneurship Theory and Practice*. 2002, 26(3): 21–40.

190. Burgelman RA. A process model of internal corporate venturing in the diversified major firm. *Administrative Science Quarterly*. 1983, 28(2): 223–244.

191. Chesbrough H, Rosenbloom RS. The role of the business model in capturing value from innovation: Evidence from Xerox Corporation's technology spin-off companies. *Industrial and Corporate Change*. 2002, 11(3): 529–555.

192. Slaughter of the Innocent? Or is Coke the real deal? *The Independent*, April 12 2009.

193. Keil T. Building external corporate venturing capability. *Journal of Management Studies*. 2004, 41(5): 799–825.

194. Tin Shed Ventures. About/history. www.tinshedventures.com/about Published 2020. Accessed January 10 2020.

195. Agarwal R, Helfat CE. Strategic renewal of organizations. *Organization Science*. 2009, 20(2): 281–293.

196. Ayyagari M, Beck T, Demirguc-Kunt A. Small and medium enterprises across the globe. *Small Business Economics*. 2007, 29(4): 415–434.

197. Morsing M, Perrini F. CSR in SMEs: Do SMEs matter for the CSR agenda? *Business Ethics: A European Review*. 2009, 18(1): 1–6.

198. Fuller T, Tian Y. Social and symbolic capital and responsible entrepreneurship: An empirical investigation of SME narratives. *Journal of Business Ethics*. 2006, 67(3): 287–304.

199. Spence LJ. CSR and small business in a European policy context: The five 'C's of CSR and small business research agenda 2007. *Business and Society Review*. 2007, 112(4): 533–552.

200. Perrini F, Russo A, Tencati A. CSR strategies of SMEs and large firms. Evidence from Italy. *Journal of Business Ethics*. 2007, 74(3): 285–300.

201. Murillo D, Lozano JM. SMEs and CSR: An approach to CSR in their own words. *Journal of Business Ethics*. 2006, 67(3): 227–240.

202. Mandl I. *CSR and Competitiveness – European SMEs Good Practice*. European Commission, 2005.

203. Joyce A, Paquin RL. The triple layered business model canvas: A tool to design more sustainable business models. *Journal of Cleaner Production*. 2016, 135: 1474–1486.

PART D

MANAGEMENT OCCUPATIONS

CHAPTER 16

SUPPLY MANAGEMENT

ZHAOHUI WU, OLIVER LAASCH
AND RICK EDGEMAN

LEARNING GOALS

1. Understand the complex systemic nature of supply and demand networks
2. Work with supply partners to build ethical, responsible, and sustainable supply and demand
3. Develop circular supply and demand systems

POSITIVE SIGNS?

The number of women in the Chief Supply Officer position increased from 9 per cent in 2016 to 17 per cent in 2020, while 39 per cent of the total supply workforce were women [1].

SPOTLIGHT

TOWARDS SUSTAINABLE SUPPLY SYSTEMS IN CHINA WITH TETRA PAK

The Swedish Tetra Pak (TP) is the world's leading food processing and packaging company. Since its entry into China in 1972, TP has been an influential player in the emerging Chinese dairy industry. The company has leveraged its packaging technology to shape the industry's supply and demand system. Sustainability is an integral part of TP's strategy including ambitious goals like becoming 'Planet Positive' [2], and constructing a circular economy [3]. They work with stakeholders, including government ministries, universities, NGOs, and garbage collectors, along both TP's upstream and downstream supply. We will have a closer look at some of TP's supply management practice from sourcing raw materials, to production, to use, to end-of useful lifetime.

Plant-based responsible raw materials are central to responsible sourcing practices at TP [4]. One key component of milk cartons is wood-based paper. Therefore, TP's management actively promotes sustainable forest management efforts. TP is working closely with the WWF, the China Green Foundation (CGF) and the forestry authority. To engage with the customers they supply, TP's key account management teams support new customers' plant, development,

www.tetrapak.com

improving processes, technology, quality development, and administration. In addition, they recruit professional consulting companies to provide specific services for the customer, covering 50 per cent of the consultancy fee. In return, TP

(Continued)

requires a guaranteed purchasing volume. TP also offers equipment financing. SME customers may pay only 20 per cent upfront, and once they have purchased a certain amount of packaging annually, TP excuses the remainder of the debt.

Post-consumer recycling of a product as durable as Tetra Pak's multi-layers of paper, plastic, and aluminium is challenging [5]. However, TP's management has set a 40 per cent recycling target which they claim 'raised the importance of recycling – both within and outside Tetra Pak. It helped us align partners along our value chain, and significantly improve recycling awareness and infrastructure along the way'.

TP adopted a proactive approach, and has remained one step ahead of Chinese law, referring to its used packaging as 'misplaced resources' [6]. TP works with recycling companies, schools, NGOs, waste collectors and local governments to help establish a sustainable collection and recycling system. TP has supported the China Packaging Association, which drafted the first circular economy law, and supports others to build a sustainable supply and demand system [4].

www.tetrapak.com

TP's supply management sought out paper mills and material companies which were willing to produce renewed materials and promote the development and application of those materials to increase recycling capacity. They discovered that by separating the raw materials in cartons, the value of recycled materials increased by nearly a third. Then they established a recycling network by offering a higher price for used packages (compared to waste paper). In addition, TP provides technical support to both individual and large-scale waste collectors. These efforts are crucial for co-constructing a future sustainable supply and demand system.

PROFESSIONAL SUPPLY MANAGEMENT

Production processes are often dispersed around the globe. Suppliers, focal companies and customers are linked by information, material and capital flows. In line with the value of the product comes the environmental and social burden incurred during different stages of production.

Stefan Seuring and Martin Müller [7]

This chapter discusses how to manage the system of companies, stakeholders, and management practices connected through supply and demand. This is critical because, as managers, we must approach sustainability challenges holistically to attain optimal system performance throughout the supply and demand system. Several factors lead firms to pursue sustainable **supply management**, including the demand to meet common standards such as ISO 14000, evolving supplier compliance policies. The implementation of environmental and social initiatives requires cooperation between buyer and seller for the adoption of responsible supply policies. Challenges may include reluctant suppliers, fragmented standards and data across global supply systems, and the risk of losing suppliers that cannot meet the challenges involved [8].

What should a 'good' supply system look like, one that is good for society and the planet and in which supply and demand actors engage in professional conduct? The main tasks in **professional supply management** are to:

1. Inspire, support, and lead supply partners to become more responsible businesses and create value for all supply-system **stakeholders**.

2. Develop a supply system including supplier, clients, and users that is efficient in its **triple bottom line** and effective in its **triple top line**.

3. Minimize the number of **ethical issues** and incidents of misconduct throughout the supply system.

In Chapter 5, we analysed stakeholder value, triple bottom line impacts, and ethical issues along the stages (production, use, end-of life) of a product or service. This way we were able to describe and understand all impacts of a product from beginning to end. Managing the whole supply system translates this theoretical insight into practical application. Supply management ranges from the extraction of raw materials, to the transformation to a product, through use by the customer, and final efforts to recycle the product or service. This whole system of activities follows the logic of the life-cycle which makes supply management the perfect tool to manage the sustainability, responsibility, and ethics of a product from beginning to end.

The process of sustainable supply management can be described in three phases (see Figure 16.1). First, 'Understanding the supply system' explores complex and adaptive supply systems, often with a high prevalence of small- and medium-sized enterprises. We will also provide tools to graphically map supply systems. Secondly, 'Managing from inside the supply system' involves principles and certifications for supply system incumbents. We will discuss tools to engage with supply partners upstream and downstream. Third, in 'Closing the loop' the focus is on methods of creating circular structures, as in an ecosystem, that help to re-integrate products at the end of their useful life into earlier stages of the life cycle.

Supply management centred on managing networks of supply and demand as well as managing from within these networks.

Professional supply management competently optimizes the triple bottom line, stakeholder value, and ethical performance from the first production activity, through use, until the end-of-useful life and beyond

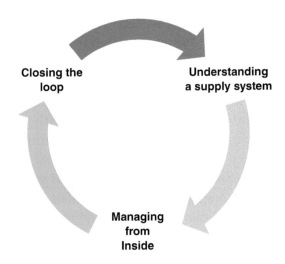

Closing the
loop

Understanding
a supply system

Managing
from
Inside

FIGURE 16.1   The sustainable supply management process

UNDERSTANDING THE SUPPLY SYSTEM

The **supply system** of a product or service is a series of interconnected value-creating (production/supply) and depleting (consumption/demand) activities from the first raw material to the final user. When we talk about managing supply we take the perspective of a particular company inside the supply system, a so-called **focal company**. A specific company's supply system is an extension of the focal firm, ordinarily the end buying firm or an original equipment manufacturer (OEM), which produces end-products that are then sold under a different brand name. Focal firms can also be dominant suppliers inside the system as we have seen in the case of Tetra Pak.

A high percentage of production operations typically take place in a company's supply system. As supply systems become more complex and companies continue to outsource, a significant portion of their carbon footprint lies in the supply system. Researchers and practitioners now call for an extended view of supply systems, arguing that institutional actors such as NGOs and governments often carry out operational tasks of supply systems [9, 10]. Recognition of these actors is important because they represent different stakeholder groups. Responsible supply management means to mobilize, coordinate, and engage in joint decision-making across a wide variety of stakeholder groups.

A good example of the effects of supply management activities is China's energy supply. As it builds its industrial capacity, China is demanding more energy. Over the past decade, renewable energy has become an important part of its energy portfolio. However, the total percentage of

Supply system
a series of interconnected value-creating and value-depleting activities

Focal company
the organization from which perspective the supply system is analysed and managed

renewable energy usage is actually decreasing as the total demand for energy is going up. Overall, developing countries are far less efficient in using energy in their economies. In addition, the Chinese government considers energy efficiency a social issue as well as a business and environmental concern – increasing pollution from coal power production has created a public health crisis and social unrest, with citizens protesting about the lack of transparency in government reporting of air quality and mine safety.

At the same time, environmental management of suppliers is ever more challenging because increasing numbers of suppliers are overseas, often in developing countries. OEMs need to develop and implement viable environmental frameworks, cultivate supplier awareness and create capabilities across cultural and national boundaries, monitoring suppliers' sustainability practices. Basically, supply managers must quantify and document the environmental footprint of the entire system.

SUPPLY NETWORKS

The Swedish sportswear manufacturer Houdini has managed to close the loop in a spectacularly creative way by offering the 'Houdini Menu' to their customers. Ingredients of the menu were grown with soil derived from composted Houdini shirts [11]). What changes do you think needed to be made to the supply–demand system for this project to succeed?

https://houdinisportswear.com/en-eu/campaigns/the-houdini-menu

Supply networks typically consist of multiple tiers of suppliers and buyers, many levels of interaction and a high degree of dynamism within the system, a 'network of firms engaged in manufacturing and assembly of parts to create a finished product' [12].

By looking at the links among buyers and suppliers it is possible to assess which are the critical companies in a network and what the risks are. The more connections a company has the more critical its role. If a company with multiple connections suffered disruption (e.g. as a result of

a fire or a strike) the effects would be felt throughout the network.. When the United States implemented tariffs on imports from China, many downstream buyers who relied on a critical supplier in China experienced shortages. The shortage of personal protection equipment as well as other items like toilet paper during the Covid-19 pandemic quickly revealed who the critical suppliers were, although they were unnoticed before the pandemic.

Each entity in the network has its own agenda, sometimes acting in concert with other members of the network, sometimes on its own. As such, a supply network constitutes a '**complex adaptive system**' [13]. A complex adaptive system emerges over time into a coherent form, then organizes and adapts itself with no single entity managing or controlling it.

Complex adaptive system
dynamic networks of suppliers and buyers engaging in complex dynamics of supply and demand

Each member of the network can manage its own actions, based on internal and external mechanisms, but the system evolves based on a complex interdependence of many variables. The members of a complex adaptive system interact with each other and with their environment. In addition, the members evolve together and with their mutual environment [13]. This idea – of the mutual interplay of all members of a supply network with their environment – will inform the following discussion. A first step to managing this complex network is mapping the supply system.

MAPPING SUPPLY ARCHITECTURES

What are the basic elements of **supply architecture**? Supply 'chains' in the narrow traditional view are a series of individual companies involved in the joint production of an end-product. From the perspective of any one company (the 'focal company'), there is an upstream (where products come from) and a downstream (where products go to) supply chain. However, as illustrated in Figure 16.2, supply systems are much more dynamic and complex.

Supply architecture
a description of the elements and interconnections of a supply and demand system

1. They should rather be called **supply-and-demand** systems, as they include both suppliers and consumers demanding the product and extracting value from it.

2. There are **no chains, but loops** where products and services at later stages are redirected to newly becoming inputs at earlier stages or in other supply loops.

3. We must think of **supply loops** (in the plural), in order to consider the second, third, and n-order supply loops that products are involved in after they have run through the first order supply loop. For instance, the outdoor clothing company Patagonia promotes the sales of their products on eBay, a **second-order supply loop**, attaching to the first order supply loop of a product bought 'first-hand', unused.

Second-order supply loops are based on products or services left over from a first-order supply loop, which after a revalorization process are given a 'second life', as a different type of product

Mapping supply systems may enable **traceability** as a crucial baseline condition for tracking ethics, responsibility, and sustainability concerns in supply systems. An intriguing related anecdote is when the investigative group Public Eye traced back the costs and wages paid to produce a hoodie of Zara's 'sustainable' clothing line. According to their calculations, Zara must have paid only one-third of a living wage. Zara's parent company Inditex's code of conduct, however, requires a payment of at least a living wage for workers and their families [15]. This contrasts with the not so modest income of Inditex's owner Amancio Ortega, who with a net worth of $85 billion was declared 'the richest

Traceability
the capacity to track impacts of products and services throughout the supply system

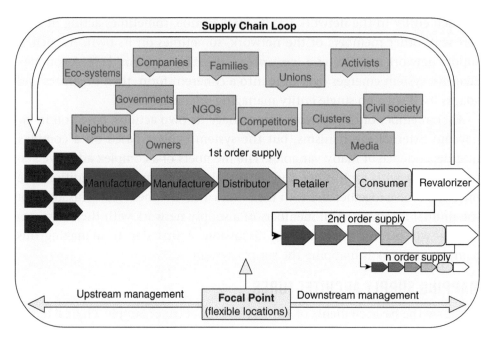

FIGURE 16.2   Mapping the supply–demand system

SOURCE: [14]

man in the world' by Forbes [16]. Traceability is elevated to a whole new level with novel blockchain-based supply chain transparency technologies.

In order to construct effective and 'good' supply systems, managers must take action to influence all three dimensions – ethics, responsibility, and sustainability.

- **Ethics.** Managers must design supply systems and take action to reduce the ethical dilemmas and misconduct inside the supply system. This might, for instance, imply stopping sourcing from a country known for human rights abuses, or not selling to customers with bad moral implications, such as tobacco companies.

- **Responsibility.** Managers must create stakeholder value across 'the extended network of responsibility' established by all of the stakeholders of the supply system.

- **Sustainability.** Managers can, as an example, design products that can easily be re-valorized at the end of their life and transferred to n-order supply loops, where value lasts longer than in the first-order supply system.

A more complex depiction of supply-and-demand relationships are maps of industrial ecosystems. Figure 16.3 illustrates how single actors (left), such as an oil refinery, a lake, and a cement plant can be connected in a so-called industrial ecosystem. Industrial ecosystems will be illustrated

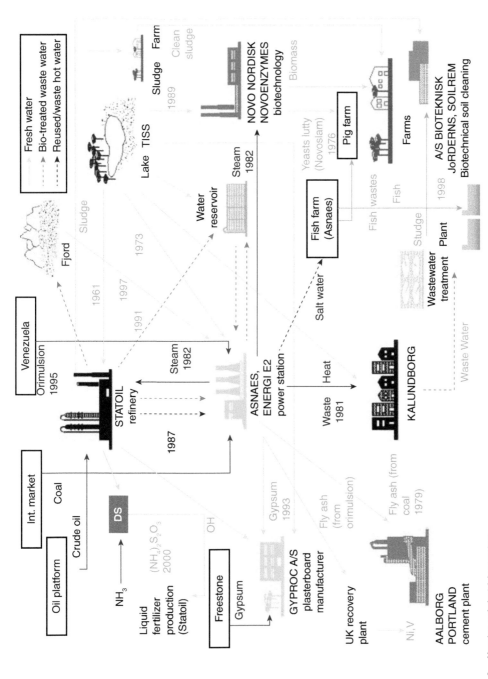

FIGURE 16.3 Mapping an industrial ecosystem

SOURCE: [17] Reproduced with permission.

in greater detail in a later section, but the map is a great tool to illustrate the importance of depicting complex systems. The industrial ecosystem depicted is not fiction, but a real structure developed in Kalundborg, Denmark.

Industrial ecosystems are not the only networks that supply systems are entangled with. They might also be embedded in other types of super-systems. Thus, mapping supply systems should, whenever possible, include the linkages to those two super-systems. Other prominent systems are responsible clusters, industries, and communities, which are explained with their specific characteristics in Table 16.1.

TABLE 16.1   Prominent types of sustainability-related economic sub-systems

Type of system	Aspiration	Entity
Industrial ecosystems	Achieve a locally self-sustaining, **zero-waste system**	Proximate industrial activities with the potential to connect in their resource usage
Sustainability clusters	Reach maximum **synergies**, resulting in highest social, environmental and economic **competitiveness** among related industries	Similarity and topical relatedness of locally concentrated industries
Sustainable value chains	Create a sustainable value chain of single **products**	Chain of production and consumption from first raw-material extraction to last value extraction from product through ultimate end-consumer
Sustainable industry	Create a sustainable industrial system of production and consumption, including **several related products**	Businesses and consumers connected through the same industry
Sustainable community	Self-sufficiency, **social welfare**, and sustainable **environmental impact** of a community	Businesses, citizens, and public actors shaping a joint community.

SOURCE: [18]

SOCIAL SUSTAINABILITY IN THE SUPPLY NETWORK

In the following sections, the primary focus will be on the direct environmental impact of supply. Nevertheless, one needs to keep in mind that supply networks, of course, have enormous economic and social impacts as well. For instance, among stakeholders of the supply network, issues such as inclusion and modern slavery in sourcing and processing resources must be considered consciously [19, 20]. As just one of many possible examples, tungsten – the material that causes a mobile phone to vibrate – is often extracted from mines in the Democratic Republic of the Congo via state sponsored slavery [21]. Such social supply management is an important element of supply system management. As most of those impacts occur in international client–supplier relationships we discuss social supply system topics, such as human rights, working conditions, and socio-economic development, in Chapter 12.

MANAGING FROM INSIDE THE SUPPLY SYSTEM

The first step in supply management is to be clear about the position of your company in the supply system. You have to find out where your company, the focal company, is located in the supply and demand system. Your position might be defined by the section of the network it is placed in. The company might, for instance, be a lower tier supplier, or an end-product producer. Your position might also be defined by the type of function the company fulfils in the supply system – manufacturer, distributor, retailer, or revalorizer.

It is no longer true that supply and demand systems are dominated by the client who challenges suppliers to comply with their standards. Those client companies are usually big multinationals with a myriad of mostly medium-sized or even small supplier companies. We have seen the case of Tetra Pak, where the company, a packaging supplier, actively engages with clients out of the dairy products industry. It seems like the question of 'Who buys from whom?' should be reframed to, 'Who leads whom in the effort for a more sustainable system, for quality and excellence?' Starting from this question we can define two types of roles in responsible supply systems:

1. **Responsible supply leaders** actively engage with others to support and nudge them towards becoming better companies and creating more sustainable supply and demand.

2. **Responsible supply followers** respond to supply and demand leaders' efforts.

Many companies in the middle positions of supply systems are leaders in some relationships and followers in others. We will take both perspectives, one of a big client company engaging with suppliers, and the other a typical SME company engaging with clients. The following sections aim to provide guidance for developing a partnership and the management efforts to be made on both sides: leaders and followers, clients and suppliers. The supply management practices that will be illustrated are supplier engagement, standardization and certification, and the application of quality management in supply systems.

ENGAGEMENT PRACTICES

Supply system engagement
collaborative practices among
supply-chain partners

How can supply leaders ensure that partners are acting sustainably, creating value for their stakeholders, and displaying moral excellence in dealing with ethical issues? The tools for creating such responsible supply systems are typically called **supply system engagement** tools. Such supply system engagement can be implemented upstream (supplier engagement) or downstream (client engagement). As clients are usually the supply leaders, supplier engagement, where buyers engage with their suppliers, is the more common practice. Supply leaders may harness a wide variety of potential tools to engage with suppliers.

Figure 16.4 provides an overview of the responsible management activities that aim at improving responsible supply performance. The percentages state the proportion of respondents in an international survey on sustainable supply management that relied on respective engagement practice to improve responsible supply performance. Interestingly, the same survey found out that many supply system engagement practices, such as incentivizing suppliers to share sustainability expertise and providing them with tools, policies, and processes, reduced operating costs for both suppliers and buyers [22].

The following five rules for successfully managing the responsible supply system can provide valuable guidance for responsible supply managers [23]:

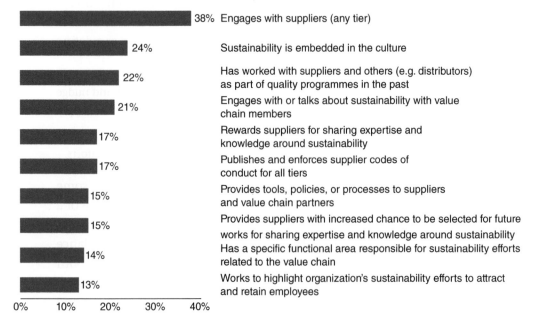

FIGURE 16.4   Engagement practices that can improve responsible supply performance

SOURCE: [22]

1. **Be a role model.** Establish and manage an internal responsible management programme before you engage with suppliers to improve their operations.

2. **Multiply through the system.** Extend your responsible management programmes into your supply system. Lead, multiply, and collaborate with your suppliers to duplicate good results in your own company.

3. **Extend your sphere of engagement.** Know your suppliers better and map your entire sphere of engagement with the goal of extending the influence you have in making the overall system more responsible, even in areas you had not known or accessed before.

4. **Establish a responsible sourcing programme**. Formalize your responsible sourcing practices in an explicit programme that covers the main principles of your responsible sourcing policy, goals, and lines of activities.

5. **Establish transparency and traceability.** For continual supply system improvement processes, information is the key. Make sure you implement mechanisms, such as audits, indicators, or verifiable supply system codes of conduct to ensure compliance and measure outcomes.

An especially powerful mechanism to create supply system transparency is the use of standardization and certification.

STANDARDIZATION AND CERTIFICATION IN THE SUPPLY SYSTEM

To manage a wide variety of relationships throughout the system, there is a need for standardization and certification. At the same time, this can be used actively by managers at supplying companies to signal compliance.

TABLE 16.2   Salient standards and certification for supply system companies

Certification	Description
ISO 9000	ISO 9000 is a globally applied norm for quality management. It often serves to establish the scaffold for an integrated management system that can then also include other management subjects, such as environmental or health and safety management.
ISO 14000	ISO 14000 certifies environmental management systems and is structured similarly to ISO 9000.
EMAS	The Eco-Management and Audit Scheme (EMAS) is an environmental management norm that extends the coverage of ISO 14000.
SA 8000	SA (social accountability) is a certifiable norm that focuses on labour rights in global supply systems.
ISO 26000	ISO 26000, also called ISO SR (social responsibility) cannot be certified, but can provide guidance for implementation and a common language for responsible business inside the supply systems.

One should bear in mind that standards and certification create entry barriers protecting a focal company and allow it to charge a price premium (e.g. grass-fed beef, organic produce). At the same time, attaining the standards and certification requires operational changes and can therefore increase the cost of doing business. Management often conducts cost–benefit analyses to determine what standards and certification make sense.

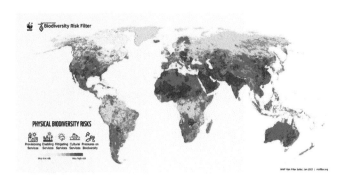

https://riskfilter.org/map-gallery

ISO 9000 and ISO 14000 are management standards. ISO 9000 deals with quality management, while ISO 14000 addresses environmental management. They provide guidance and tools for companies and organizations to help ensure that their services and products meet customer needs, that quality is consistently improved, and that their processes meet regulatory requirements.

Supply system standardization should be complemented by a supply risk assessment. For instance, the WWF has built an impressive database that maps the very substantive reputational, physical, and regulatory biodiversity risks across supply sourcing locations globally, accessible here: https://riskfilter.org/map-gallery[24].

LOGISTICS[1]

Logistics
the management of resource flows between a point of departure and a goal destination

Logistics plays a crucial role in the supply system. It provides the necessary transport of goods and even services inside the supply-and-demand network. From a focal company's perspective, logistics include both inbound and outbound logistics. Inbound logistics are concerned with delivering inputs to the production process, while outbound logistics deliver finished products and services to the customer. Logistics are also a crucial part of the management of worldwide supply networks as will be described in the last section of this chapter.

---

[1]The paragraph on logistics has been reproduced from Laasch and Conaway [14].

Depending on a company's offer and the related production processes, logistics can be very intensive in natural resources and harmful to the environment. Typical environmental issues are noise, air pollution, traffic congestion, 'land consumption' (the land occupied by roads, railways, airports), and packaging waste. Typical negative social impacts of logistic activity are road accidents and pulmonary diseases. The logistic network leading to most products is worldwide connected and involves complex transportation practices. In order to move logistics practices towards sustainability, it is helpful to understand the

During the Coronavirus pandemic, supermarkets, pharmacies, and even pet stores managed the increased demand for home delivery logistics by partnering with delivery services like Ele.me and Deliveroo, whose 'normal' food delivery traffic had plummeted.

typical conflicts of interest between efficient logistics and sustainable development. The following list presents some of the most salient paradoxes of 'green logistics' [25]:

1. **Minimizing costs.** A crucial competitive factor of logistics is the ability to provide transportation at the lowest cost possible. This is contrasted by the urgent need to internalize external environmental costs mentioned above. Internalization of those external costs would increase costs of the logistics activity immensely.

2. **Speed, flexibility, reliability.** Unfortunately, the means of transportation fulfilling those basic logistics requirements (such as planes and trucks) also do more harm to the environment than the less desired alternatives (such as ships and trains).

3. **Hub and spoke.** Using centralized hub and spoke logistical networks creates a highly concentrated negative impact at the centre of logistic networks.

4. **Warehousing and just-in-time logistics.** The just-in-time movement has drastically reduced the number of goods stored. A result is that much of the storage has been transferred 'to the streets', increasing the overall number of goods being moved and their negative environmental impact.

5. **E-commerce.** Small, individual shipments are required by the logistical structures of e-commerce. Such methods significantly decrease the efficiency of logistics by requiring more packaging and customized transportation. The related last-mile challenge (delivering large quantities of individual goods 'to the door') has gained strategic importance for on-line retailers (e.g. Amazon) brick-and-mortar retailers (Kroger), and even restaurants.

Actions to mitigate the negative impact of logistics rely on two basic approaches. On the one hand, one could reduce the impact of logistic activities while maintaining or growing the volume. On the other hand, the logistic volume could be reduced. In the following list, you will find some typical practices which may result in one of the approaches mentioned or in some cases a combination of both:

1. **Transport impact transparency.** The social and environmental impact of transportation is often hidden. While many products are labelled by the country of origin, this only provides a basic impression of the overall transport activities necessary. Some industries and single companies have started to increase the transparency of their impact. Food miles, which describe the distance travelled by food products, are a good example. Block chain technology, together with RFID and emerging 5G, is an integral part of data collection, monitoring and planning to ensure supply network transparency and product traceability.

2. **Eco-efficient logistics.** Eco-efficiency (see Chapter 17) aims at improving the ratio between economic output and the required input of natural resources. For the logistics sector this ratio is highly important. Eco efficient logistics aim to reduce the environmental impact of a given logistic activity. The cumulative negative impact might not be reduced at all.

3. **Reverse logistics.** Recycling only works if products at the end of their useful life-cycle are transported back to be re-integrated into the production process. This is the main task of reverse logistics, which makes it a crucial part of a circular and sustainable economy. Reverse logistics may also have ecological downsides, such as in the case of returns management. Many companies provide convenient financial and logistic take-back schemes for unsold goods. Such returns management systems create an incentive to order more than is actually needed.

4. **E-commerce (retailing) logistics.** E-commerce has often been described as more environmentally friendly, due to the reduction of resource-intensive brick-and-mortar store networks. It is not yet sure if this trend leads to more or less environmentally friendly logistics. Research suggests that the home-delivery services connected to e-commerce are less polluting than customers picking up the bought item in the shop themselves [26]. However, many customers would not have bought certain items in the first place if they weren't available from the convenience of their homes through e-commerce.

5. **Servitization logistics.** Complementing or substituting products by services often reduces the necessity to transport a physical product. Servitization models are for instance 'repair instead of replace' and 'rent instead of own'.

6. **Local production and consumption networks.** Increasingly local production and consumption networks substitute the need for extensive global logistics practices. Such a development is not necessarily always more sustainable.

Focusing only on the environmental impact, in some cases local production may be less sustainable than foreign production plus importation – for instance food products. The reason may lie in local differences in productivity and refrigeration efforts [27].

CLOSING THE LOOP

Methods for **closing the loop** that we will discuss in this section are industrial ecology, the circular economy, closed-loop supply networks, and end-of-life product design. Those methods are closely related, overlap and often work in a complementary pattern, which is why many of the concepts and contents covered under one heading also apply to others.

Closing the loop
methods to create circular structures that, like an eco-system, help to re-integrate products at the end of their useful life into earlier supply stages

INDUSTRIAL ECOLOGY

Since before the industrial revolution, economies have operated on the 'take-make-waste' paradigm – a world of unlimited resources and unlimited area to put our waste. The fact is, however, that we live in a limited world. In nature, materials are recycled, with one organism's waste becoming food for another. Take the example of a cow pasture: cows eat grass and drop excrement in their wake. Bacteria grow on the dung, breaking it down into simpler compounds. Fungi can then grow on the faeces, while some of the nutrients return to the soil to fertilize the following year's grass crop, when the next generation of cows shows up again to eat.

Just as ecology examines the flow of material and energy through the pasture (or other systems in nature,) **industrial ecology** emulates those

Industrial ecology
mimics ecological systems when designing industrial systems

TABLE 16.3   Comparison of natural and technological systems

Organizational Level	Biosphere	Technosphere
Systems	Environment	Market
	Ecosystem	Eco-industrial park
	Ecological niche	Market niche
	Food web	Supply system/product life cycle
Population and Products	Organism	Company
	Food (meat, fruit, seed, etc.)	Finished product or service
Processes	Succession	Economic growth and decline
	Natural selection	Competition
	Adaptation	Innovation
	Mutation	Design for environment
	Anabolism/catabolism	Manufacturing/waste management

flows through an industrial system. It is a multi-disciplinary field concerned with shifting industrial process from linear (open loop) systems, in which resource and capital investments move through the system to become waste, to a closed loop system where waste can become inputs for new processes. Along with material and energy flows, it focuses on product life-cycle planning, design and assessment; eco-design; extended producer responsibility ('product stewardship'); co-location of industrial facilities ('industrial symbiosis'); and eco-effectiveness. Table 16.3 shows other analogous features and characteristics of natural and technological systems.

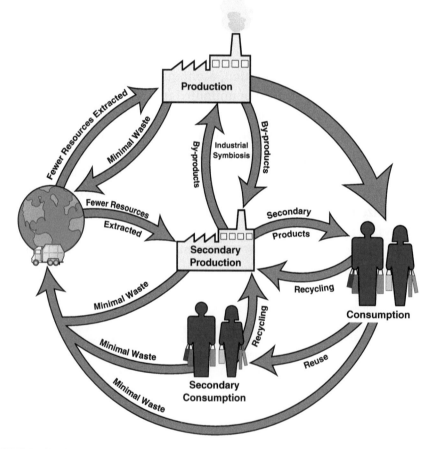

FIGURE 16.5   Closed loops and circular economies in an industrial ecology

Reprinted with permission of King County, WA, USA

Circular economy
a production–consumption system that creates circular flow of materials and energy where the by-product of one process is used as the raw material for the next

THE CIRCULAR ECONOMY

The concept of a **circular economy** (CE) was proposed as a development strategy to address the disparity between economic growth and the lack of raw materials and energy. It originated with industrial ecology, building on the notion of loop-closing, and has been pursued as a potential strategy to solve existing environmental and economic development problems.

At the centre of the closed economy is the circular flow of materials and energy through multiple processes – as in industrial symbiosis, the by-product of one process to be used as the raw material for the next. It includes both production processes and consumption activities. The most basic goal is efficiency. At the next level, the main objective is to develop a network that benefits both production systems and environmental protection. Core practices include:

- **Resource cascading.** Resources can be used several times, if usage is ordered by the resource quality required at different usage stages.

- **Shared infrastructure.** Companies can share facilities and other types of infrastructure in order to increase the resource efficiency of infrastructure usage.

- **Exchange of by-products.** By-products that are of no value to one company can be of value to another company or consumer.

- **Waste recycling.** Waste can be re-integrated into the production and consumption process.

Finally, the development of the eco-city, eco-municipality, or eco-province is one of the most prominent environmental movements in China. Whereas the eco-industrial park focuses only on sustainable production, the eco-city includes the notion of sustainable consumption. Western concepts of the circular economy include ideas such as:

- **Waste is food.** Just as biological nutrients can be composted, technical 'nutrients' – plastics, metals, and other man-made materials – are designed to be used again.

- **Diversity is strength.** Systems with multiple connections and scales are more shock-resistant than systems designed solely for efficiency.

- **Renewable energy.** Ultimately, energy should flow directly from the source to the process.

- **Systems thinking.** Understanding how systems fit together, including non-linear dynamics.

True circularity requires the collective consideration of many stakeholders, as can be seen in Figure 16.6. The circular economy necessitates consideration of a longer, networked chain of stakeholders that begins with those initially extracting resources that are transformed by manufacturers into items that are delivered to converters. Converters assemble or otherwise transform these into goods that are delivered to brands and brands have these distributed to retailers and sellers. Consumers acquire these goods, use them and – historically – dispose of them. Local concerns – municipalities, haulers and composters – then deal with this 'waste'. In the circular economy waste is composed of organic nutrients (e.g. resources), technological nutrients, and residual (true) waste, with the role of reprocessors being to separate and redeploy organic and technological nutrients for further use, with manufacturers making use of these nutrients. Ideally, there will be zero residual waste, so that a goal of circular economy companies is to drive down and drive out residual waste. Driving the concerns of various circular economy stakeholders are various social, environmental, economic, or political factors. These factors vary by stakeholder segment.

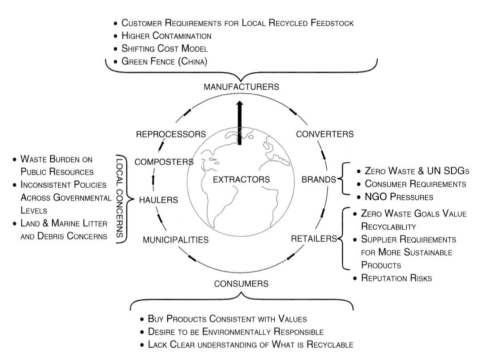

FIGURE 16.6   Typical circular economy stakeholders

SOURCE: adapted from [28]

Closed-loop supply networks recover materials post-consumer for reuse by the same company chain

CLOSED-LOOP SUPPLY NETWORKS

In contrast to the circular economy wherein one company's waste can be another company's raw material, a **closed-loop supply network** recovers materials for reuse by the same company – a 'cradle-to-cradle' approach to manufacturing. Traditional supply 'chains' flow forward: materials, components, and sub-assemblies move from upstream suppliers and contract manufacturers to downstream consumer brands and vendors (e.g. distributors, retailers) and eventually to consumers.

A closed-loop supply system requires a **reverse supply flow**. It begins with the used products being taken back through various channels. For example, field engineers from Honeywell's Industrial Automation and Control division make decisions regarding which printed wiring assemblies can be repaired on site, and which need to be shipped back to the company's manufacturing facility for more extensive processing. Along the same lines, Xerox leases copiers to customers and sends technicians into the field to service their machines as necessary. The technicians visit the customers and either repair the leased machines or take back old or damaged components.

The process of adding value to a product or service, usually at the end of its useful life, is called **revalorization** [29]. In order to close the supply or to channel products to a secondary supply network a preliminary step has to be to revalorize the products parts of it or materials. The following are prominent revalorization techniques: repair, refurbishment, remanufacturing, recycling, upcycling, and downcycling. When repair, refurbishment or remanufacturing are not possible, returns are recycled. If a product is disassembled before recycling, components are sent back to different tiers of the forward supply flow and reused, closing the loop. Standard components (e.g. computer memory chips) and salvaged raw materials (silver or copper) can be sold in secondary markets. When components are not disassembled before recycling, the process often becomes one of 'grind and sort'. This option is less desirable because it recovers less value. In the worst case scenario, certain materials (plastics or rubber, for instance) are incinerated as fuel or sent to a landfill.

Reverse supply flow
a structure that channels resources back from their end of life to be re-integrated into the supply network

Revalorization
the process of adding value to a product or service, usually at the end of its useful life, in order to re-integrate it into earlier stages of the supply flow

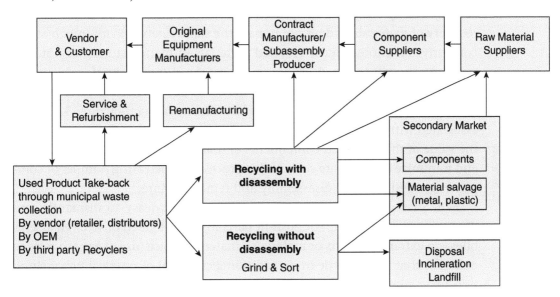

FIGURE 16.7   Closed-loop supply network

SOURCE: [30]. Reprinted with permission.

Figure 16.7 shows these choices and the options presented by each. The most efficient approach is the smallest loop (in the lower left corner) service and refurbishment. The least efficient starts with raw materials (upper right corner,) traces an open loop around the perimeter of the processes, and ends with incineration or landfill (lower right corner,) often the case with plastics and rubber. 'Downcycling' is a 'middle-of-the-road' option, with some materials going to recycling and some to the dump. Remanufacturing is not possible for many supply networkss. In several cases, the processing cost of remanufacturing is higher than the price of new products. In widely dispersed manufacturing supply networks, particularly those in which production is carried out in multiple locations, transportation costs for refurbishment prohibit the practice.

An unusual recycling practice happens in the life insurance secondary market where companies like the German policendirekt buy insurance policies from customers who would have cancelled them otherwise.

Courtesy of Policen Direkt

END-OF-LIFE (EOL) DESIGN

End-of-life (EOL) design focuses on creating products that minimize negative impacts at the end of the product's useful life span

The last part of closing the loop is **end-of-life (EOL)** design. EOL design and manufacture closes the supply loop by eliminating waste, improving reuse, refurbishment, and recycling efficiency and efficacy.

When recycling becomes mandatory and a company merely seeks to comply, it may outsource the process. This is cost effective, but it offers little recovery of materials. It does not impact the supply network, inasmuch as the company can choose to use recycled materials in manufacturing or not. If a company chooses to recycle in-house, it faces the choice of simple recycling of materials (where reusing the recycled materials becomes the natural choice), or recycling with disassembly and refurbishment/remanufacture. The costs associated with the additional handling are mitigated and often surpassed by the value of the recovered components or materials. To maximize the benefits and minimize the ultimate costs of this process, an increasing number of companies are designing for disassembly and remanufacture.

EOL Strategies include modular product designs (easy to dismantle and direct components), snap- or push-fit parts instead of glued or screwed assemblies (no extraneous parts or materials), material choice (use of easy-to-recycle materials that require little or no additional chemical or physical processing), non-toxic components (to minimize any impact the recycling process may have), and use of common materials (as opposed to separating, sorting, and processing different materials). Figure 16.7 shows how products and 'wastes' flow between different levels of providers and consumers in a closed-loop or circular system.

An example is the carpet manufacturer Interface previously featured in Chapter 5. When traditional carpet wears out, it is generally torn out and replaced, the old carpet being downcycled (some of the nylon pile can be recycled, but some pile and all the backing goes into the garbage). The materials are mostly lost, becoming useless (and possibly hazardous) landfill. At the same time, the carpet manufacturer must extract more raw materials to make new carpets. Interface adopted a new process, an updated product and a novel business model. Their carpet features easily separated, completely recyclable backing and pile. Rather than installing entire rolls of carpet, they manufacture smaller carpet squares with visual designs that piece together with non-obvious seams. And they lease the carpets to customers, making themselves responsible for the upkeep. When a section of carpet wears out, Interface replaces just the work-out section – not necessarily the entire installation. They maintain possession of the worn material, with the ability to recycle it into new, ready-to-install carpet. While the initial cost of creating and manufacturing the product were high, they can offer a green product while remaining competitive – because of their business model and reduced costs for raw materials.

PRINCIPLES OF PROFESSIONAL SUPPLY MANAGEMENT

I.   A **responsible supply network** is one that optimizes the triple bottom line, stakeholder value, and ethical performance from the first production activity, through use, until the end of useful life and beyond.

II.   A **progressive view of the supply network** assumes a complex system view of interdependent organizations supplying and demanding that includes loops where products and services at later stages are re-channelled to newly becoming inputs at earlier stages, and that includes n-order supply loops that products are involved in after they have run through the first order supply loop.

III. **Managing the supply network** includes engagement techniques, certification, and norms, quality management, eco-efficiency, and effectiveness.

IV.   **Closing the loop** refers to methods to create circular structures that, like an ecosystem, help to re-integrate products at the end of their useful life into earlier supply stages.

V.   Frameworks that help to close the loop are, among others, **circular economy, the closed-loop supply, industrial ecosystems, and end-of-life design.**

MANAGEMENT GYM: TRAINING YOUR PROFESSIONAL SIX-PACK

Knowing

1. Look up more information on the different supply standards described in this chapter, as well as three more that are not mentioned. Evaluate their similarities and differences in a table of your own design.

2. Look up the differences and similarities between closed-loop supply, circular economy, and industrial ecosystems.

3. Research at least one practice example of each of the revalorization techniques mentioned in this chapter.

Thinking

4. There is an argument that our supply systems are so ridden with ethical, social, and environmental issues, that no human being can ever truly be 'good', as any of our consumption moves fuel climate change, biodiversity loss, modern day slavery, and a myriad of other issues. Do you agree? If so, what would need to happen to change this?

5. This chapter mostly covers upstream supply management activities. How do you think managers can involve clients downstream?

6. Think of a local business in your area. How could this business start building an industrial ecosystem? To which other businesses could it sell its waste? Which other businesses could it use waste from?

Acting

7. Use a digital tool for supply system analysis like the tools that help you to map supply, or that help you to calculate the footprint of a product or service – e.g. for CO_2 or modern slavery.

8. Design a supply system (e.g. in a one-page drawing, on a flipchart or using some software) that tightly integrates the ecosphere and technosphere in a sustainable way.

9. Write a one-page report on how 'good' the supply system of one company of your choice is. Use a supply chain management standard (from this chapter or others) to analyse the company's reports or news coverage.

Interacting

10. Critically analyse the supply network related to a company's claims about what it does about zero deforestation, carbon neutrality, being net zero and climate positive, etc.. Based on your findings, post a critical analysis either assuring the validity of their claims, or pointing to inadequacies in them (e.g. in the 'Managing Responsibly Network' group on LinkedIn).

11. From your personal network or on social media (e.g. in the 'Managing Responsibly Network' group on LinkedIn), identify and interview an employee of a small- or medium- sized business about the nature of relationships in their upstream and downstream supply flows.

12. Think of an EOL design for a product of your choice. Write an e-mail to a producer of such a product, describing your idea and asking for advice regarding its feasibility.

Being

13. In 60 seconds, write down as many terms as possible that come to mind when you think about 'good' supply and demand. How does the result reflect your views?

14. What supply system issues do you personally care about most?

15. Use an online tool to analyse the impact of your consumption in the supply system – e.g. the CO_2 footprint, biodiversity impact, or slavery footprint resulting from your personal consumption. How does the process and result make you feel?

Becoming

16. During your life at work, how could you contribute to the construction of more ethical, responsible, or sustainable supply and demand?

17. Change your personal 'procurement' practices related to one product or service you typically use (e.g. food, household items, clothing, haircuts), to make it more ethical, responsible, and sustainable.

18. What kind of organization could you work in that contributes to 'better' supply systems?

Laasch, O., Moosmayer, D., & Antonacopoulou, E. P. (2023). The interdisciplinary responsible management competence framework: An integrative review of ethics, responsibility, and sustainability competences. *Journal of Business Ethics, 187,* 733–757.

PIONEER INTERVIEW
MICHAEL BRAUNGART

INTERVIEWED BY: OLIVER LAASCH

Michael Braungart and William McDonough are the creators of the cradle-to-cradle (C2C) concept, which has become the underlying principle and credo of sustainable supply system management. Central concepts related to 'C2C' are the triple top line and eco-effectiveness.

Biological versus technological nutrients and systems. From my perspective there is no limitation because there are two types of products – the products which can be consumed like food, shoes, or detergent – which can be designed as part of the biological system, and the second type, like a washing machine or like a TV set, that can be designed as a technical nutrient for the technosphere.

'Michael Braungart' by Mario A. P. is licensed under CC BY-SA 2.0

The first thing is to look if the products are either going into biological or technical systems. You need to define the type of product because if you mix technical and biological systems you will contaminate the biosphere dramatically. Just to give you an example, the copper is extremely dangerous in biological systems but in technical systems it can be used endlessly. So that's why the first thing is to define technical cycle, biological cycle, technical nutrient, biological nutrient.

Sprinting towards C2C. There are some difficulties when you have very complex supply chains that you need to organize differently. The only real difficulty is that the expertise and knowledge, which we have based on only 40 years of environmental discussion, basically starting 50 years ago with Rachel Carson's book *Silent spring* and 40 years ago and with *Limits of growth* by the Club of Rome.

We will be able to handle these issues. It is amazing how fast people learn about C2C thinking compared to other learning curves. If you see between the declaration of human rights and women's right to vote in Germany, it took 130 years. So people didn't understand that women are humans for 130 years. We can be really happy how fast C2C thinking actually becomes implemented, thanks to great scientific work.

The dangers of 'efficiency' thinking. People think it is environmental protection when they destroy less, please protect the environment, reduce your water consumption, please

(Continued)

protect the environment, reduce your waste production, reduce your energy bill but that's not protecting. It is only minimizing damage. This leads in a lot of cases to optimizing wrong things. You make the wrong things perfectly wrong. As an example, it is not really protection of your child when you beat your child only five times instead of ten times. So you need to reinvent things, not just optimize existing things.

So don't optimize wrong things. That is why the first important thing to understand is not about efficiency; it is not about resource efficiency. It is about what is the right thing to do instead of doing things right and that's really important to understand because otherwise efficiency gains always lead to rebound effects.

Make sure that people are not just managing what they see. All people who are in management positions need to first ask: 'What is the right thing?' *If you optimize wrong things you make them badly wrong.* If we are able to learn from natural systems and learn it's not about efficiency gains because it's really about effectiveness that is one of the key things.

Needs-based reinvention. From there it is important to find out what people actually want if they buy something to what is the intention of what people have, for example if you really want to have a carpet or you only want a different acoustic or different optics. So do you really want to have a washing machine or want to wash your clothes? It is about understanding intentions.

The next thing is to define the status quo. You need to find out how good the product is, which you have right now from that benchmarking perspective and then you need to look at a product from the whole supply chain in a way in which you include your customer as your partner. That means you can reinvent everything that you see around you.

A carbon-positive human habitat? First of all, what I use as a picture for innovation that has been picked up by a lot of architects. Let's talk about the built environment around us as a system; let's have buildings like trees; buildings which clean the air, buildings which clean water, buildings which become habitable for other species, buildings which are carbon positive not carbon neutral. Secondly, what is important is to look at the culture and social needs of people even before that. The key thing is to understand the human role on this planet. A lot of people in the field who see humans as a burden for this planet end up with minimizing damage but they threaten human dignity by that. So the first thing is to understand that, if we are able to manage material flows differently, we could even be 20 billion people, easily, on this planet. People have fear when you question their existence, for instance, if you say let's minimize your impact to zero; you tell somebody it's better not to exist. Out of fear, when you question the existence of people they become greedy and aggressive. On the other hand, people are willing to share if they feel safe and accepted.

But the real key question behind that is really not the system per se but it's a discussion about what is the human role and impact on this planet. For being that bad we are far too many people on this planet. So that's why before we go on to specific systems, it is more about asking:

(Continued)

What is our role? How can we celebrate the human footprint on this planet? The key question is: How can we become native to this planet? This question will then change our lifestyles. So it is key to ask, what do we really want for this planet? What is our role on it? How can we be supportive of other species and supportive of other humans as well?

QUESTIONS

1. Highlight all of the points Michael makes that relate to sustainable supply and demand. Briefly elaborate on the relationship you see for each.

2. Reflect on whether you have ever 'optimized' the wrong thing, or witnessed someone else doing it.

3. Michael talks about how we should keep biological and technical systems apart. Conversely, do you think there might actually be sustainable 'cyborg' systems combining elements from both? If so, give an example of what that might look like.

PROFESSIONAL PROFILE
DINAH MADIADIPURA

I am a sustainability and corporate responsibility professional with around 20 years of experience. Having conducted numerous worker empowerment trainings in Indonesia, social compliance audits in Asia, and managed sustainability programmes when working in global fashion companies such as S. Oliver and the Gap Inc., US-based social monitoring organizations STR and UL Sourcing, and the International Labour Organization. I am highly skilled in CSR, sustainability audit, project and operations management, and ethical business practices.

Courtesy of Dinah Madiadipura

(Continued)

I have founded the Indonesia Labour Database, a community organization working to increase knowledge and capability of individuals, scholars, industries, civil societies, labour practitioners and enthusiasts about sustainability and labour in Indonesia. I have law degrees from Universitas Pakuan and the University of Sydney.

My responsibilities. In my previous organizations I was responsible for managing the day-to-day business of sustainability and social compliance, including programme strategizing, delivering worker empowerment training, conducting social compliance audits in the supply chains and supporting external stakeholder engagement such as the relevant governmental agencies and trade unions. In my current role, I manage a website on sustainability in Indonesia, in particular labour and human rights topics, and providing consultancy and legal construction.

My day. A typical day at work consists of team touch base and alignment meetings, coordination meetings with other departments, stakeholders' meetings, programme analysis, regulation construction, training or assessment preparation and site visits for training or assessments, and report writing. Concrete activities strongly depend on what role I am working on that day:

Assessor/auditor:

- Audit preparation and site visit

- Report writing

- Participating in training on client standards or related regulations

- Team touch base

Programme manager/adviser:

- Team alignment meetings

- Stakeholders' meetings and collaboration

- Coordination meetings

- Programme development, implementation and analysis

- Regulations or standards construction

- Site visits for training and facilitation

Challenges. As an auditor working either at a third party monitoring agency or a multinational corporation, a sound understanding about local and national regulations of a host country is very important. As an auditor who conducts audits on site in Indonesia and other Asian countries perhaps the most challenging aspect is to work out the applicable

(Continued)

law and regulations in the country and accurately interpret them. To add to the challenge, there are language barriers and different legal systems to consider when construing and understanding regulations.

Other challenges include demanding work travel schedules. Four to five audits a week are very common in a monitoring agency. Overseas audits can often take about one week to one month. This was not always the case when I worked as an auditor in a corporation conducting internal audits. The work timetable was not as packed as in a third party monitoring agency.

Ever-changing standards and industry initiatives also possess their own challenges as it takes time to have a handle on new standards and initiatives.

Lastly, working with external stakeholders that have different fundamental interests is challenging as well. Adversarial relationships, uneven power relations and political agendas between opposing external stakeholders demand plenty of time, patience and resources to get a programme going.

Tips and tricks. First and foremost, find a speciality that you want to be an expert of. Sustainability is a very big and wide subject. Ranging from environment, chemical, health and safety, labour to ethics, some of the components in sustainability require diverse, specific, technical knowledge and experience. It is not easy for a practitioner to master everything at once. Second, knowledge about the industry, its supply chains and the primary external stakeholders will take you far and beyond. The development of sustainability in every industry is very distinct and highly influenced by its unique business dynamics. A sound understanding of the industry will support your success in this field of work. As the day-to-day work of a practitioner can be demanding, mental agility such as resilience and adaptability is needed to thrive.

QUESTIONS

1. What aspects of Dinah's job do you find exciting? Which ones wouldn't you enjoy so much?

2. Following Dinah's advice, what kind of sustainability speciality and industry could you imagine yourself focusing on?

3. Do you think Dinah's job is more that of a legal professional or that of a manager? What kind of competences do you think it requires?

TRUE STORY
IT'S ALL ABOUT 'THE GREEN'

EDITED BY ALEXANDRA LEONOR BARRUETA SACKSTEDER

Who I am. My name is Callie. I have been working at my company for 11 years now and generally am really happy with my job. At our company we deal with mannequins and have two brands: the high brand makes *haute couture* mannequins and the second brand functions as a well-developed e-commerce with the possibility of more economical products. I was the person who originally opened the international purchasing and production for our company. Our high-end brand mannequins are made in Italy while the second brand purchased products from European importers. Initially, foreign production and direct importation regarded the second brand followed by some production for the high brand.

Context matters. In an SME the expectation is often that if we are respecting the laws of the supplier country and our own national laws regarding importation, that is our only true obligation. In a company with limited staff and a variety of real and diverse operational problems every day, it is not so incredible that this would be standard operational procedure.

The context for the search of more sustainable and responsible/ethical practices in this type of environment either comes from a like-minded company owner or is operator dependent stemming from initiatives taken by the person handling the international supply system. For me personally, it was a matter of bringing my values into my job and having the good fortune to work with a company owner with a sympathetic ear, willing to make changes like the ones I proposed, as long as we are of course staying on track and hitting our targets.

(Continued)

It has not been possible to implement more sustainable and ethical ideas while I've been here, although maybe I will be able to adapt more of these in the future if I stay at the company. A new person has arrived to help handle foreign production, a new type of job for her. Her mindset does not go beyond respecting national laws and those of the country we are importing from. I am trying to help her understand certain issues and to do that it is also important to understand production materials and processes.

Our challenge. Recent factory inspections by Chinese authorities in regard to pollution have constituted the biggest challenge for organizations like mine, generating incredible delays and shortage of materials as it is incredibly difficult for an SME to have any say over third-party suppliers. Our direct production was alright with our supplier factories but one issue, for instance, was that the cardboard box factories were being shut down (so no packaging). The ones with government approval were overloaded and either couldn't take new orders or the orders were greatly delayed. This was widely publicized internationally. Another issue arose with the few chrome components we had. They were taking an incredibly long time to produce for the same reasons; only a few chroming facilities remained open. Other third party facilities, such as one working with plastic recyclable products, had a small issue and were temporarily shut down too.

Because of all these inconveniences caused by the authorities actually attempting to meet industry standards, people began proclaiming that the age of production in China was over and that it would be necessary to take manufacturing to other countries. That honestly made me ill. Finally, China is getting its act together and we all walk out? Discussing this with our company owner we agreed that the best thing to do was to support our suppliers during that time with great encouragement towards compliance on all fronts and as a consequence took a terrible hit in delays and scheduling. One supplier is also being eliminated because it is evident that they do not wish to comply as they should.

It's all about 'the green' after all. For those more sensitive to ethical and sustainable issues we created a completely biodegradable display bust and base made from recycled paper materials, made completely in the EU. It was offered at a competitive price. Just the same, customers didn't really take notice of it. Initially I'd thought it was because we weren't publicizing it enough but then we realized that the problem was something much more basic.

An important multinational had discussed a large purchase from us that we believed could help us move in the direction of 'going green' which we wanted. They said that they wished to have an environmentally conscious product 100 per cent in respect of EU laws on labour and the environment as the benchmark. We proposed a blown plastic mannequin (recyclable) made in an Italian factory respecting all EU labour and environmental laws without even minimal doubt. The cost was just a couple of dollars higher than a fibreglass mannequin made in China.

(Continued)

Ultimately, even the Chinese mannequins were too expensive so they purchased from Vietnam. When we followed up and asked for feedback hoping to see what had gone wrong and how to improve in this area, the person told us that it would be lovely to respect the standards they initially proposed but price was the ultimate factor. It all came down 'to the green, the money'.

QUESTIONS

1. What is your spontaneous reaction to the story told in this case and how would you feel if you were in Callie's shoes?

2. How would you interpret this situation through a circular economy lens?

3. If you were Callie, what would be your next move in order to become a more responsible supplier?

4. Prepare an elevator pitch for members of the board from the case story company. Come up with a new sales strategy for the 'green' mannequins and present it to at least one other person.

DIGGING DEEPER: CIRCULAR ECONOMY SYSTEM DIAGRAM

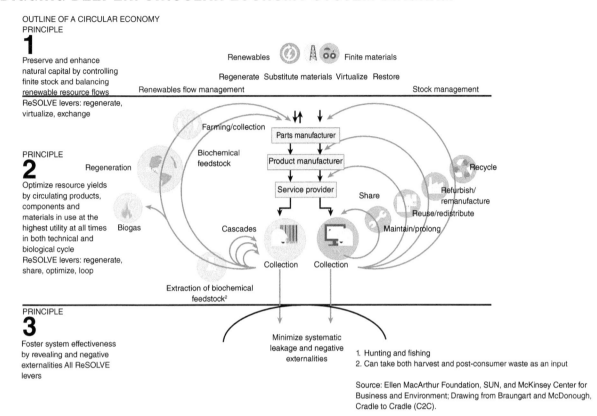

FIGURE 16.8

SOURCE: © Copyright Ellen MacArthur Foundation 2020 (www.ellenmacarthurfoundation.org). This is an unofficial translation by SAGE and we do not suggest or imply that the content has been endorsed or approved by the Ellen MacArthur Foundation.

POINTERS

You could use this diagram to dig deeper into the different layers, stages and actors of the circular economy; to follow the different pathways that resources flow through the circular economy; or map different practices. You could also use this map as an orientation for mapping an actual case or a circular economy project that you are working on – for instance, to map out the current state of your (non) circular economy supply network and to see what additional elements could be added to improve its circularity.

WORKSHEET

SUPPLY–DEMAND SYSTEM MAPPING

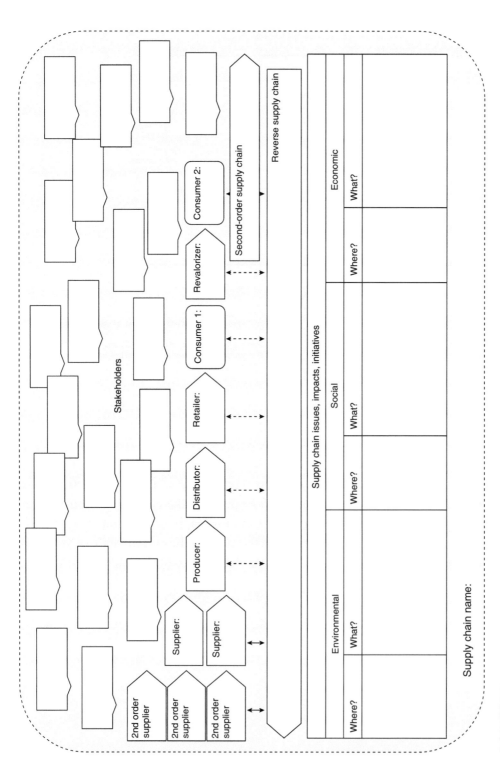

POINTERS

You could use this worksheet to map a complex dynamic supply–demand network. Exemplary applications are planning a more sustainable system for a product or an industry. Conduct a baseline assessment of the sustainability of a supply system, or find and address weak or problematic areas. The worksheet could also be used to improve your resource flows in order to increase the system's circularity. You may find relevant information to fill in the worksheet in annual reports and on company websites, or from speaking to people in companies, or from industry experts.

REFERENCES

1. Stiffler D, Watt S, Chumakov C. *Women in supply chain survey highlights consumer value chain progress*. Stamford: Gartner, 2020.
2. Tetra Pak. Planet positive. www.tetrapak.com/sustainability/planet-positive Published 2020. Accessed July 23 2020.
3. Tetra Pak. What is the low-carbon circular economy? www.tetrapak.com/sustainability/circular-economy Published 2020. Accessed July 23 2020.
4. Tetra Pak. Our sustainable offering. www.tetrapak.com/sustainability/sustainable-offering Published 2020. Accessed July 23 2020.
5. Tetra Pak. Post consumer recycling. www.tetrapak.com/sustainability/recycling Published 2020. Accessed July 23 2020.
6. Jia F, Wu Z. Creating competitive advantage by greening the supply chain: Tetra Pak in China. European Case Clearinghouse (ECCH), 2012.
7. Seuring S, Müller M. From a literature review to a conceptual framework for sustainable supply chain management. *Journal of Cleaner Production*. 2008, 16: 1699–1710.
8. Mollenkopf D, Stolze H, Tate WL, Ueltschy M. Green, lean, and global supply chains. *International Journal of Physical Distribution & Logistics Management*. 2010, 40(1–2): 14–41.
9. Hyatt DG, Johnson JL. Expanding boundaries: Nongovernmental organizations as supply chain members. *ELEMENTA Science of the Anthropocene*. 2016, 4: 1–14.
10. Wu Z, Jia F. Toward a theory of supply chain fields: Understanding the institutional process of supply chain localization. *Journal of Operations Management*. 2018, 58: 27–41.
11. https://digitalnewsroom.media/houdini/houdini-menu
12. Choi TY, Hong Y. Unveiling the structure of supply networks: Case studies in Honda, Acura, and Daimler Chrysler. *Journal of Operations Management*. 2002, 20(5): 469–493.
13. Choi TY, Dooley KJ, Rungtusanatham M. Supply networks and complex adaptive systems: Control versus emergence. *Journal of Operations Management*. 2001, 19(3): 351–366.
14. Laasch O, Conaway RN. *Responsible business: Managing for sustainability, ethics and global citizenship*. Monterrey: Editorial Digital, 2013.
15. Martinko K. Zara's 'sustainable' hoodie is anything but. www.treehugger.com/zaras-sustainable-hoodie-anything-4855387 Published 2018. Accessed July 24 2020.
16. Taylor K, Martin W. Who is Amancio Ortega – the richest man in the world? www.independent.co.uk/life-style/wealth-amancio-ortega-richest-man-world-zara-founder-retail-tycoon-bill-gates-a7924241.html Published 2017. Accessed July 24 2020.
17. Cervantes G. A methodology for teaching industrial ecology. *International Journal of Sustainability in Higher Education*. 2007, 8(2): 131–141.
18. Laasch O, Conaway RN. *Responsible business: The textbook for management learning, competence, innovation*. Sheffield: Greenleaf, 2016.
19. Cohen E. *CSR for HR*. Chichester: Wiley, 2010.
20. Crane A. Modern slavery as a management practice: Exploring the conditions and capabilities for human exploitation. *Academy of Management Review*. 2013, 38(1): 49–69.
21. Bales K. *Blood and earth: Modern slavery, ecocide, and the secret to saving the world*. New York: Spiegel & Grau, 2016.
22. Deloitte Development. *Selected sustainable value chain research findings*. Deloitte Development, 2012.
23. Iwundu A. Five rules for sustainable supply chain management. In: Pohl M, Tolhurst N, eds. *Responsible business: How to manage a CSR strategy successfully*. Chichester: Wiley, 2010: 239–250.
24. WWW Risk Filter Suite. Biodiversity risk filter. https://riskfilter.org/biodiversity/home Last accessed July 31 2023.
25. Rodrigue J-P, Slack B, Comtois C. Green logistics (The Paradoxes of). In *The handbook of logistics and supply-chain management*. London: Pergamon/Elsevier, 2001.
26. Edwards JB, McKinnon AC, Cullinane SL. Comparative analysis of the carbon footprints of conventional and online retailing. *International Journal of Physical Distribution and Logistics Management*. 2010, 40(1/2): 103–123.
27. DEFRA. *Comparative life-cycle assessment of food commodities procured for UK consumption through a diversity of supply chains – FO0103*. United Kingdom: Department for Environment Food and Rural Affairs (DEFRA), 2008.

28. Edgeman RL. Circular and sustainable enterprise excellence Businessmodellen Duurzaamheid. *Sigma*. 2018, 4: 16–19.
29. Fiksel J. *Design for environment*. New York, NY: McGraw-Hill, 2010.
30. Pagell M, Wu Z, Murthy NN. The supply chain implications of recycling. *Business Horizons*. 2007, 50: 133–143.

CHAPTER 17

OPERATIONS MANAGEMENT

RICK EDGEMAN, OLIVER LAASCH AND ZHAOHUI WU

LEARNING GOALS

1. Analyse professional management activities and create processes for managing triple bottom line, stakeholder value, and moral excellence

2. Organize production and transformation processes to match supply and demand ethically, responsibly, and sustainably

3. Use lean management to create triple bottom line efficiency and quality management to optimize stakeholder value

IMPRESSIVE FACT

'Ninety-six percent of CEOs believe that sustainability issues should be fully integrated into the operations of their Company' [1].

SPOTLIGHT

PPP OPERATIONS MANAGEMENT AT IKEA

"IKEA, furniture warehouse store. Location" is marked with CC0 1.0.

Resource consumption and carbon emissions growth proportional to the growth of the overall business is unacceptable to management at the Swedish furniture corporation IKEA. This value led IKEA to launch the People & Planet Positive (PPP) sustainability strategy in 2012, aimed at becoming energy independent and helping people live an affordable and sustainable home life. PPP emphasized global trends, such as growing solar and wind energy markets, recycling, smart home energy management, and circular economy principles and practices [2]. Core to PPP are replacement of energy-consuming goods with solutions that benefit customers, society, and the natural environment. IKEA is committed to the circular economy principles of efficient resource use and to transformation of waste into resources.

Motivated by accelerating global environmental and social challenges, IKEA built on PPP in 2020 with 10 Jobs in Three Years – strategies and actions essential to further reducing

'IKEA' by Gabriel White is licensed under CC BY-SA 2.0

IKEA's environmental impact and elevating its positive social impact. For instance, there is the job of promoting sustainable living, to 'bring products and services to more people when wanted, where wanted, in sustainable and affordable ways to enable more sustainable living'. Also, there is the change from unsustainable products to sustainable services, to 'co-create sustainable living solutions and circular services'. In addition, internally IKEA's management uses their operations management practices to role model change they hope to see in society, namely for stores to 'become a best destination for beautiful, smart and sustainable homes' and 'ensuring that IKEA is a good example of equality, diversity and inclusion' [3].

(Continued)

PPP and the 10 Jobs are foundational to IKEA's long-term growth strategy with numerous operations intersections. Effective execution of these will help IKEA address climate change and resource scarcity internally through its policies and operations, through its supply chain, in the communities it operates, and for customers through product and process design and optimization, choice, and efficient consumption of materials, materials acquisition, product distribution, and energy generation, and reduced consumption of both water and energy.

Still, actively embracing responsible and sustainable operations did not render IKEA immune to criticism, when it built its most sustainable store in early 2019. Why? To do so, IKEA demolished a Sainsbury's supermarket at the Greenwich, United Kingdom site that had been the UK's most sustainable supermarket facility [4].

OPERATIONS AND PROFESSIONAL MANAGEMENT

Mission Zero ... To understand how everything we do, take, make and waste affects nature's balance and, ultimately, our children and the children of all species. From this knowledge, we can build processes throughout our business that mimic nature and support the environment [5].

Can we build companies that use zero natural resources instead of consuming them? John Elkington calls managers of companies pursuing this mission zero 'Zeronauts' [6]. If such Zeronauts are to achieve their mission, they must begin at the process level. Processes are well-confined, manageable series of activities. Companies are systems of interconnected processes, and operations management is the management of these processes. This is why **professional operations management** must be at the core of any professional management effort.

Professional operations management
a process-based framework that aims at creating efficiency, zero resource consumption, and optimum stakeholder value through process effectiveness

Professional operations management is not only crucial for the triple bottom line (TBL) [7], but also to stakeholder value creation. Stakeholder value is created through the output of processes. Thus, processes must be designed to optimize stakeholder value.

Operations management (OM) explicitly addresses the design and management of products, processes, services, systems, and supply chains. It considers the acquisition, development, and use of resources that enterprises need to deliver services, information, and tangible goods desired by the various customer and market segments they serve. The purview of OM spans operational, tactical, and strategic levels. At the strategic level operations are concerned with larger issues such as facility location and size determinations, designing technology supply chains, and determination of service or telecommunications networks structures. At the operational level, issues addressed by OM include materials acquisition, handling, and transportation; production planning and control; quality control; and logistics, including inventory management. Tactical OM issues include facility layout and structure; equipment selection, maintenance and replacement; and project management.

This chapter will develop through the three main phases of professional operations management using the simplified process model illustrated in Figure 17.1. In Phase 1, we will provide basic insights into how to integrate ethics, responsibility, and sustainability management into existing processes and the design of specialized professional management processes. In Phase 2, we will explore key elements of organizing production processes, such as facilities layout, technologies, and process control. In Phase 3, we will more closely examine efficiency, and how to use lean enterprise methods to minimize waste, as well as continuous improvement methods to improve process effectiveness for key stakeholders.

As illustrated in Figure 17.1, an organization's performance is the sum of all outcomes of all its processes. If those outcomes are excellent, we may speak of enterprise excellence. Of most obvious import relative to operations is the emphasis on **operational performance**, but operational performance is – of course – substantially driven by, for example, innovation and human capital and in turn impacts customer-related, financial, marketplace, societal, and environmental performance.

Beyond exceptional operational performance, excellence in professional management must combine excellent TBL outcomes, optimum stakeholder value, and moral excellence in all processes. Thus, **professional enterprise excellence** is exceptional operational performance for the TBL, stakeholder value, and moral excellence. Enterprise excellence employs the systematic use of quality management strategies, principles, practices and tools in the management of the enterprise with the objective of improving performance.

Operations management (OM)
the area of management concerned with the effectiveness and efficiency of processes for the production of goods and services

Operational performance
describes the effectiveness and efficiency of processes for the production of goods and services

Professional enterprise excellence
refers to above-average operational performance for the triple bottom line, stakeholder value, and moral excellence

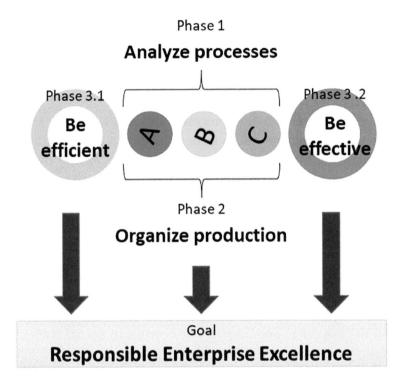

FIGURE 17.1 Elements of professional operations management

Foundational to enterprise excellence are customer focus, stakeholder value, strong emphasis on process management, and a strong measurement orientation.

PHASE 1: ANALYSE THE PROCESS

To create professional excellence and performance you need to map, understand and transform processes. Processes are the DNA of a business. They define the whole by every little decision, sustainable or unsustainable, ethical or not, responsible or irresponsible that is taken on the way. Thus, to create a truly professional business, managers have to have a close look at the DNA of the business, at the processes to build in, instead of just bolting on sustainability, responsibility, and ethics [8]. In this first section we will look closely at business processes to understand where professional management can attach.

MAPPING THE PROCESS

Process maps are powerful tools that enable basic understanding of how the company works and where to transform and integrate sustainability, responsibility, and ethics to create a truly professional business. Processes consist of one or several activities that with the help of resources transform inputs to outputs [9]. Businesses are made of processes. An example is the process

Process
a set of activities that uses resources to transform inputs to outputs

Effectiveness
the extent to which planned activities are realized and planned results achieved

Efficiency
the relationship between result achieved and resources used

of recruiting a new employee, of preparing an expense sheet or managing a certain production line.

To evaluate the process quality or performance, one must analyse process **effectiveness** and **efficiency**. High-performing processes need to be effective to make sure that planned activities are executed and planned results achieved. Efficient and excellent processes also require strong relationships between resources used and results achieved. One could say that an effective process achieves results, and an efficient one uses up exactly the minimum amount of resources necessary to create a given result; hence it produces no waste. Sustainability, responsibility, and ethics play an important role from both effectiveness and efficiency perspectives. Eco-efficiency, for instance, aims to minimize the environmental resources used to produce a product or service and, in this way, make the process more eco-efficient [10]. Similarly, one might imagine 'ethics efficiency', whereby companies aim to reduce the amount of non-compliance or ethical misconduct per product or service produced. Process effectiveness can be seen as the TBL output of a process, as explained in Chapter 5. The question is: how much social, environmental, and economic value is created by the process?

MAPPING INTERNAL PROCESSES

Processes can be described on many levels. Like viewing something under a microscope, with every further level the process becomes closer and more detailed. Figure 17.2 illustrates how an organization can be viewed at six levels of increasing detail [11]. Levels 1 (Organization) and 2 (Function) describe the basic structure typically reflected in organizational architectures, as illustrated in Chapter 6.

From Level 3 onward, the work of process mapping begins. Functions typically consist of many sub-functions. A people management department of a medium-sized company, for instance, will have one person or a group of people in charge of onboarding and offboarding employees or, more plainly, of 'hiring and firing'. Another sub-function might be in charge of the employee training and development process. Each sub-function is embedded in one or several processes, which are described at Level 4. For instance, the training and development sub-function will be involved in conducting in-company training as one process, and in keeping track of employee qualifications as another sub-function.

Processes often exceed the boundaries of functions or sub-functions, which is why in a Level 5 business process description, often more than one player [11] is mentioned in the left sidebar of the Level 5 description. On this level of 'business process detail' mapping, each process step is described for all players involved. In our example, the business process detail map describes how to conduct in-house training for employees who will work together as a 'green office team' that needs to be introduced to environmental management basics.

The closest and last look at a process is at Level 6, 'supporting details'. It describes the process through information gathered during its operation. For the employee training process, for example, the records required might be attendance lists to single training sessions and final exam grades on the subject. We will now look more closely at how to establish a Level 5 process detail map that integrates ethics, responsibility, and sustainability.

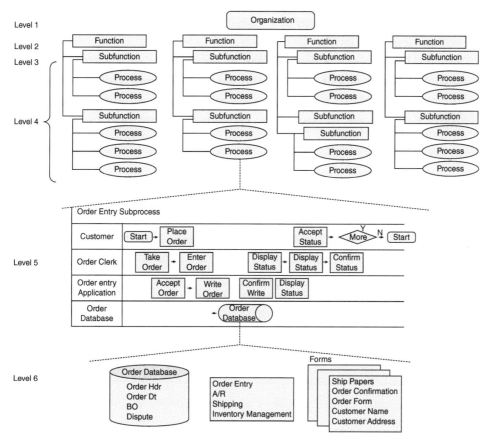

FIGURE 17.2   Zooming into organizations and their processes

SOURCE: [11]

DESCRIBING DETAILED PROCESSES

Mapping business processes requires and creates detailed and profound understanding of how companies work and, more importantly, shows where management intervention is required to make the overall process more professional. We will illustrate via an adjusted version of Level 5 process detail maps, introduced in the preceding section. This type of map is customarily used in mainstream business.

Process detail map
describes how activities in a process are related, sequenced, and how process flow is controlled

A Level 5 **process detail map** is the right tool to understand specific process steps where environmental impacts can be mitigated, stakeholder value can be created, and ethical misconduct can be avoided. Once this understanding is created, managers are able to specifically address those hotspots in their management activity. Process maps facilitate understanding of mainstream business processes such as implementing a marketing campaign or screening a new supplier, and drive deeper understanding and improvement of specialized professional management processes, such as a volunteering campaign or an eco-efficiency initiative.

Figure 17.3 provides a process map as an example of the embedding of professional management considerations into the process of developing a mainstream market. In the diagram we see the characteristics of **shared processes**, which are a constituting element of professional processes. The professional marketing process extensively involves customers and broader civil society as main stakeholders.

Shared process
integrates internal and external stakeholders in a value creating series of activities

There are many different methodologies for business process modelling, covering different application areas, focal points, and uses [12]. Due to the scope of this book, we focus on one general, intuitive, and broadly applicable approach, called a swimlane diagram that depicts activities undertaken by different involved groups and individuals. The legend in Figure 17.3 summarizes typical icons of a process description, including start and stop, activities, flows, information/data elements and conditions and connections. To those standard icons we added three professional management icons describing considerations such as stakeholder value creation, environmental impacts, and ethical dilemma situations.

BUNDLING PROCESSES TO MANAGEMENT SYSTEMS

Management systems
establish policies and objectives and provide the framework to control achievement of these objectives

Quality **management systems**, systems for organizational health and safety, or environmental management systems, such as the ones described by the EMAS and ISO 14000 standards are well known, but how can we build a management system for something as complex and seemingly intangible as professional management?

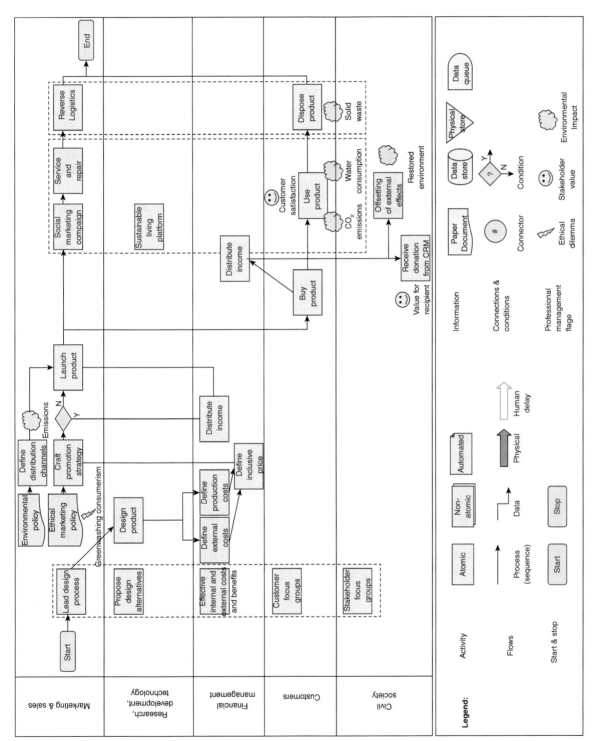

FIGURE 17.3 Mapping professional operations on the process level

SOURCE: Adapted from [11]

Imagine, for instance, the complexity of controlling your CO_2 footprint per customer if you run an operation as complex as an airport. Bristol airport's sustainability director explains that 'reduction in our demand for energy, switching to lower carbon energy and off-setting any residual emissions will get us to carbon neutrality… The CO2 footprint for a Bristol Airport passenger now stands at 0.69kg, a huge reduction from 1.2kg in 2008' [13]. While such operations management successes are laudable, the crucial open management challenge in the aviation industry is, however, to decarbonize the flights themselves [14].

Managing towards zero carbon emissions in airport operations at Bristol airport.

"Control Tower, Bristol Airport - geograph.org.uk – 3738102" by M J Richardson is licensed under CC BY-SA 2.0.

Different types of management systems share basic commonalities. First, they handle topics that permeate all functions and every company process. As an example, the quality of the final product or service depends on every step and activity throughout all the business processes from controlling a specific customer account, to the logistics of delivering the product or service. The same holds true for the topics subsumed under professional management, sustainability, responsibility, and ethics. Every process will have a TBL impact (sustainability), affect and be affected by stakeholders (responsibility), and potentially involve moral dilemmas (ethics). This is why management systems increasingly include systems for managing professionally, such as sustainable operating systems [15], a total responsibility management system [16], or mainstream management control systems [17].

Second, those systems consist of organizational documents of a normative and descriptive nature that describe what good performance in the intended system means and how it is achieved. Such documents include texts as broad as the company mission, and others as narrow as a concrete checklist for a specific process step, such as checking a customer request. Figure 17.4 illustrates the documents constituting a management system in hierarchical order.

Third, management systems involve a continuous improvement mechanism, often through internal and external audits, and use of well-defined performance indicators and tools for performance analysis and improvement. In a later section of this chapter we will illustrate continual improvement mechanisms, such as Six Sigma's Define, Measure, Analyze, Improve, and Control (DMAIC) framework.

Management systems for sustainability, responsibility, and ethics are usually integrated into already existing management systems, most commonly into a company's quality and environmental management. An

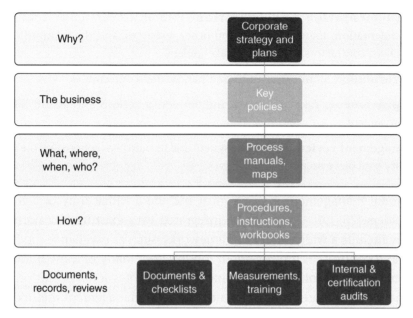

FIGURE 17.4   Document structure constituting a management system

SOURCE: Adapted from Conger [11]. Adapted with permission.

integrated management system houses several – in the most advanced case all – components of a business in one coherent system in order to enable the achievement of organizational purpose and mission [18]. The important task for professional operations managers is to either establish new management systems for sustainability, responsibility and ethics, or to integrate these into existing management systems to create an integrated 'professional' management system. Designing an integrated management system is a unique task for each organization as it requires substantial customization. Guidance in the process can be provided by standards for the development of integrated management systems, such as the ISO 72 guide on management systems development [19, 20] and the PAS 99 standard for establishing integrated management systems [21].[1] The valid steps that should generally be taken to develop a management system such as the ISO 9000 standard for quality management are listed below [23, 24].

1. **Policy.** Establish policies and principles.

2. **Planning.** Identify needs, resources, requirements, relevant organizational structures, potential contingencies, issues to be addressed through the management system, and relevant processes.

Integrated management system
houses all components of a business in one coherent system in order to enable the achievement of organizational purpose and mission

---

[1]For a practical guide to building management systems, written in plain language, have a look at the Bizmanualz website [22].

3. **Implementation and operation.** Establish operational control and documentation, manage human and other resources, and the relationship with suppliers, contractors, and related stakeholders.

4. **Performance**. Monitor, measure, and handle non-conformities.

5. **Improvement.** Take preventive and corrective actions and assure continual improvement.

6. **Management review.** Review the system and its outcomes concerning the system's ability to achieve established objectives.

Professional management systems must include a wider array of actors and stakeholders [25, 26]. They can be integrated into existing ISO norms [36] and may include a wide variety of frameworks, such as excellence models, Six Sigma, and continuous improvement models [28]. Many of these frameworks are described in the following two phases of the professional operations management process. Phase 2 focuses mainly on lean management methods.

PHASE 2: ORGANIZING PRODUCTION

After understanding the process there are a variety of practices we can engage to set up and organize processes. Here we will focus on the essential considerations of designing transformation (production) systems, organizing sites, as well as process planning and control.

TRANSFORMATION SYSTEMS DESIGN

Transformation systems transfer inputs (resources) into output offers for stakeholders, in particular goods and services

Transformation systems are also known as production systems. They are typical combinations of process elements, well suited to different purposes. For instance, Greyston Bakery (see Case Study Zone VI) built their baking production system for the purpose of employing as many low-skilled 'unemployable' people (e.g. previously incarcerated, homeless, or single mothers) as possible.

More commonly, the main purpose of designing a particular transformation system is to produce a particular type of product or service for a paying customer. However, the Greyston example reminds us of how such systems can equally importantly be designed to create value for a particular stakeholder group, unrelated to products, services, customers, or clients. Basic characteristics and the strengths and weaknesses of transformation systems differ substantially across their different types, based on variety-volume considerations. Figure 17.5 offers an overview of the most common transformation system types, which can be divided into continuously running processes, and by the two Vs of volume of goods and services produced, and their variety.

For instance, at Greyston Bakery they originally baked varieties of pastries and tarts in low volumes in a job shop system, each batch of pastry being a unique work of art. However, this type of system required very skilled and experienced workers, which the people stigmatized as 'unemployable' usually would not be. This kind of production system and corresponding product also only allowed them to hire comparatively small numbers. Accordingly, they moved on to a continuous flow system focused on only one type of product, producing large quantities of brownies [29]). Their company slogan is 'We don't hire people to bake brownies, we bake brownies to hire people' [30]) is closely aligned with this production system design.

This example also illustrates the close interrelatedness between product design and production system design. Mostly, a different offer (product or service) or changes in a portfolio of offers will require a different production system. However, sometimes the same or a very similar product can be produced in different systems. For instance, the German automotive and aerospace industries supplier Allsafe could produce the load-securing parts that are their main product in batch production or assembly line, but have instead chosen a manufacturing cells design, in which smaller teams flexibly self-organize mini production lines for their different customized products [31]). This decision suits Allsafe's unique management philosophy which is centred on giving employees freedom and expecting them to use it responsibly (see chapter 8).

While you would probably first associate a production system with the production of physical products, services also require such systems. When designing service transformation systems, however, we need to keep in mind that there are important differences between product and service transformation systems. For instance, customers are mostly present during the service transformation process (e.g. there is a greater need to manage customer input during process and wait times) and services are intangible (e.g. there are no stocks of finished goods and there is often hidden, intangible value). In services, we typically speak about degree of customization instead of variety and the degree of labour intensity instead of volume. For instance, professional services like those of sustainability consultants are typically very labour intensive and highly customized, which makes them likely to be suitable for a project or job shop transformation system (also frequently called 'service factories' [32]). However, as illustrated in Figure 17.6, they also share similarities.

It is easy to imagine how each of these different transformation systems needs to be very differently managed and organized to set up and maintain. For instance, in service factories or assembly lines, a typically salient organizing element is operational procedures or technologies as guiderails that ensure

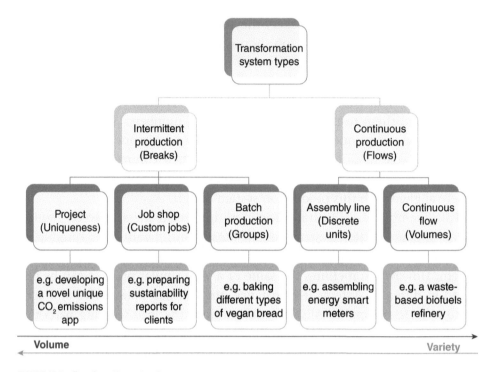

FIGURE 17.5   Transformation system types

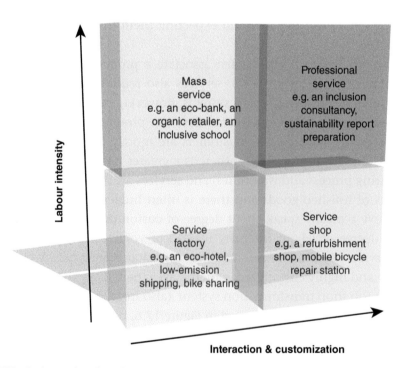

FIGURE 17.6   Service transformation systems

SOURCE: Adapted from [33])

efficiency and consistent quality. In professional services transformation systems and project production systems, it is essential to ensure that the highly skilled people working on these projects are able to use their professional competence and creativity while also sticking to basic parameters, such as timeliness and assessable product and service quality, in spite of the uniqueness of the systems. Different transformation systems are also characterized by different physical sites and their respective layouts, as we will explore next.

Production sites are the physical or virtual spaces in which a transformation process takes place

PRODUCTION FACILITIES AND SITES

The sites where transformation takes place are not only crucial for efficient and effective production processes, but can also be powerful levers for ethics, responsibility, and sustainability, or conversely, for thwarting one's efforts to achieve professional operations management. Think, for instance, of the dramatic and largely inevitable environmental impacts of a mining operation, or conversely, about how such an operation may bring socio-economic development by employing people from local communities, often in remote sites where work opportunities are scarce. Where to place your site may also be important in relation to environmental impact – for instance, if you decide to move closer to other companies that can use the waste from your operations, which we call site co-location in Chapter 16.

Once the place for a particular site has been chosen, it is important to design the physical or virtual (for online and blended operations) layout of a production site. Sites need to be aligned with the type and dynamics of the production system they are hosting. Key considerations are proximity and connectivity, optimizing physical material or information flows, and separation when confidential information is handled, or production involves the use of trade secrets and other types of proprietary knowledge. The four types illustrated in Table 17.1 are common site layouts.

However, sites also need to be designed to generate positive socio-environmental affordances of the facilities. For instance, community boards and space in retail stores often play an important role in community lives, or repair workshops in Patagonia's stores offer a space for mending products to reduce waste, and there are the positive health impacts of ergonomic workplace designs. The environmental performance of facilities can often make an important difference. Great examples are the sustainable cleaning products company Ecover's French and Belgian factories, which have a plethora of built-in environmentally friendly features. They run exclusively on renewables, their architecture maximizes daylight use to minimize artificial lighting, and machines are designed to waste only minuscule amounts of the cleaning liquids they produce [34]).

TABLE 17.1   Common facilities layouts

	Fixed position	Functional	Cellular	Line
Description	Process happens in one place, workers and equipment move there	Process distributed across multiple uni-functional units	Multiple independent micro-units within facility, each equipped with multiple functions	Workers and equipment organized in sequence of the stages of the transformation process
Best for...	Processes that are immobile and where workers and technologies are mobile	Similar areas grouped based on their function or shared equipment used	Creating semi-autonomous groups responsible for the entire transformation process of a particular offer or part-offer	Straightforward, linear transformation processes with little necessary wait time
ERS examples	A vegan restaurant with table service; a zero-emissions building construction project; a livestream production of an environmental education class; a sustainable facilities management service	A sustainable lifestyle store might have areas to refill detergents, a second-hand products sales area, a repair area, and checkouts	A sustainability consultancy's offices that are laid out to create different smaller groups each centred on a different offer (e.g. reporting, energy efficiency solutions, net zero strategies)	A plastic separation plant; an assembly line for an energy smart meter; ChopValue's chopstick recycling process; production of an integrative annual report (from data collection, to writing and imaging, to layout, and dissemination)

It is also crucial to consider the human aspects of site layout – for instance, to accommodate colleagues with diverse abilitites in inclusive manufacturing designs. Increasing the number of people with disabilities in our transformation system may have important productivity implications. For instance, in garment manufacturing it has been found that it is better for productivity to place people with different types of disabilities evenly across the range of production 'cells', rather than in the same one [35]). This kind of assessment, however, needs to be complemented by an understanding of the job satisfaction and wellbeing implications of different placement patterns for all involved.

Sites where transformation processes take place can be understood as **socio-technical systems,** due to the close interconnectedness between human and technological elements. Such systems can be of physical or virtual nature. For the physical kind, think of industrial weaving looms in the first industrial revolution, Henry Ford's mass-production use of conveyor belt technology, and the most recent 'industry 4.0' or 'smart manufacturing' fully automated robotic or blended 'cyber-physical sites' [36]).

The many dynamics between humans and non-humans in physical and virtual sites are a key concern for professional operations management. On the one

Socio-technical systems are characterized by the close interaction between human and technological transformation system elements

hand, technologies are often hyped for their productivity promises and can bring substantial human benefits. For instance, the use of exoskeletons in manufacturing has been found to have the potential to both increase productivity and to improve human worker wellbeing due to their ergonomic support benefits [37]. On the other hand, technologies may also underperform, or even keep humans from performing. For instance, hundreds of workers were re-hired at Tesla's fully robotic 'machines build machines' factories, because machines did not deliver on the production quota [38]). Similarly, in blended online–offline environments, paradoxically AI 'colleagues', which are meant to make humans' work easier or more effective, may create additional tasks that reduce overall productivity [39].

Exoskeletons are at the core of Volkswagen's operational strategy and are 'production processes … focusing on the future of work. This includes physical and behavioral ergonomic support systems …'. Volkswagen suggests that these technologies support both their increasingly older worker 'demographics and ergonomics. Ergonomically unfavorable workplaces are being continually reduced. Where the ergonomics of an operation cannot be improved, devices such as "exoskeletons" can provide support for production workers', which they trialled first in their Slovakian factory in Bratislava [40])

www.volkswagen-newsroom.com/en/press-releases/the-production-process-of-the-future-exoskeletons-provide-support-for-employees-at-the-bratislava-plant-3836

PROCESS PLANNING AND CONTROL

Process planning and control's core task is to match the amount of demand for our products or services with our capacity to produce them at any given point in time. To be able to answer these questions, we need to be able to forecast demand and to competently manage our capacity to match it as accurately as possible. As you can see in Figure 17.7, this is no easy feat as it requires monitoring and forecasting the varieties of flows (e.g. materials, products, information, and money), as well as adjusting deliveries, production, and warehousing activities to match supply and demand at a particular point in time. It becomes even more complex when doing so in order to optimize this production and consumption system's environmental and social impacts. There are many trade-offs to be made. For instance, you might decide to practice 'load shifting', to shift your production to full capacity at night when there is an excess of energy in the grid, or, if you are using local solar or wind power, you would shift it to particularly windy or sunny times. Such load shifting practices have been found to reduce energy costs by a third, and environmental

Process planning and control is concerned with the management of process capacity in relationship to demand for process outputs.

emissions by one quarter [41, 42]. However, a production controller would also have an eye on social impacts (e.g. employees' health or family lives) and on the scheduling (possibly less flexibility to respond to demand quickly in the short run). Load shifting, if done in the right way, could also open up production facilities for other non energy-intensive activities during the daytime, such as preparing production, packaging, warehousing, shipping orders, or receiving inputs.

Matching supply and demand requires forecasting the different streams of goods and services – for instance, of suppliers' or the production company's own capacity, or of delivery times. In particular, accurate **demand forecasting** is challenging as most businesses have little control over their customers'

Demand forecasting
is a predictive process estimating demand for a product or service at future points or periods in time

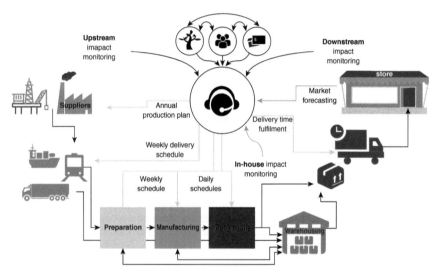

FIGURE 17.7   How process control management brings together supply and demand

buying behaviour. Demand forecasting methods can be qualitative (e.g. consumer surveys or expert panels) or quantitative (e.g. time series analysis or causal modelling).

The interplay of resulting forecasts and production capacity is not trivial. Producing too much leads to the negative effects of over-supply, such as immediate disposal of unsold and unused goods and services. All the environmental resources and negative impacts realized in their production will have been in vain. Producing too little in turn can lead to societally catastrophic shortages in, for instance, food, housing, or medicines.

Bullwhip effect
is dynamic in which a small inaccuracy in forecasting is amplified through tiers of production and supply systems, leading to over- or under-supply

One particularly problematic phenomenon is the **bullwhip effect**. Imagine a major retailer reporting back to their suppliers that customers had increased their consumption of charcoal for barbecuing by 20 per cent in comparison to the previous year. To be on the safe side, producers might decide to increase their production by 25 per cent and their suppliers in turn by 30 per cent. However, it might then turn out that the increase was due to a 'super summer' caused by global warming, and that the next summer, again due to global warming fluctuations, it is extremely cold and wet, and that for environmental concerns there is less barbecuing and lower consumption of meat products.

Figure 17.8 illustrates how sophisticated forecasting can be used to be mindful of such inaccuracies, and in service of more ethical, responsible, and sustainable supply and demand matching.

FIGURE 17.8   Steps of demand forecasting and examples of ERS considerations

SOURCE: Based on the structure of Reid RD and Sanders NR. *Operations management: An integrated approach*. Hoboken, NJ: Wiley, 2010.

On the supply side, capacity management is crucial for supply–demand matching. **Capacity** management revolves around questions of 'How much to do?' (loading), 'In what order to do things?' (sequencing), 'When to do things?' (scheduling), 'Are things going according to plan?' (monitoring), and 'What corrective actions to take?' (controlling) [43].

As an example, a core question in capacity management's scheduling task is identifying and managing process bottlenecks, where production activity slows down or is vulnerable and risks leading to a standstill or unnecessary wait times. Critical path analyses are often used to map bottlenecks and identify measures for managing them. Bottlenecks are important in managing a lack of output, and respectively throughput. Inventory management can be

Capacity
is the ability to supply a particular process output (product or service) over a certain period of time

used to bypass the temporary lack of output as a result of bottlenecks, or to absorb excess output at times of lower demand.

Inventories can be physical (e.g. production inputs) or virtual (e.g. data storage). In the manufacturing context, the three main types of inventories are raw materials, part-finished components, and finished goods. Holding inventories may be costly and bind capital that might be needed elsewhere. In addition, some types of finished goods might become outdated. As a result, inventories might use their value and de facto become waste. This kind of waste often has severe environmental consequences – for instance, when electronic goods become outdated before they are ever used, or fashion items are thrown out before they are ever sold and worn [44].

A key consideration in managing capacity and inventories is to be prepared for **variability** in produced supply, or realized demand in comparison to forecasts. One tactic a programme manager might use as protection against the variability of lower than forecasted demand is to operate at low base capacity and to buy in capacity from the gig economy, which is quickly available if necessary. While reducing fixed costs and tied capital this tactic also comes with ethics and responsibility issues, such as the negative impacts on many workers of uncertain gigs versus stable continuous employment. On the other hand, if demand exceeds supply there also is a social cost, in terms of unsatisfied demand and wait times. Quite literally, managing variability well can save lives, for instance, as a process manager in a hospital's emergency department in charge of bed management [45]. Managing variability is also at the core of some of our most pressing socio-environmental problems, such as food waste management responding to seasonal variety in food production.

PHASE 3: EFFICIENT THROUGH LEAN AND EFFECTIVE THROUGH QUALITY MANAGEMENT

EFFICIENCY AND LEAN MANAGEMENT

Increasing efficiency to make and do more with less has long been a management theory and practice mantra, and plays a major role in professional management. The best-known form of this is **eco-efficiency**, which aims to minimize environmental resource consumption and ecological damage by optimizing the efficiency of the firm's production processes. We could also consider stakeholder efficiency, which aims to create as little stakeholder cost and as much stakeholder benefit as possible through processes. Moral efficiency that minimizes ethical misconduct is another form.

Inventories
are accumulations of process resources and/or outputs

Variability
refers to differences between planned and actual production or demand

Eco-efficiency
aims to minimize environmental resource consumption and ecological damage by optimizing the efficiency of the firm's production processes

Efficiency primarily focuses on the process input side with the goal of minimizing the input necessary to create a fixed output. Lean management methods focus on efficiency, while quality management tools illustrated in Phase 3 focus on process output needed to yield the highest possible customer (stakeholder) satisfaction. In practice, both lean and quality management have efficiency and effectiveness components, but complexity is reduced by focusing on the use of lean management methods for efficiency and quality management methods for effectiveness.

Professional operations management requires commitment to lean management, manufacturing, and service methods that are often collectively referred to simply as 'lean'. **Lean management methods** consider efficient and effective use of resources through a lens that regards resources used for any objective other than value creation for the end customer as waste generated through formulation and execution of flawed strategies, processes, and practices. Lean management targets all identified waste for reduction or elimination to enhance quality, performance, and profit.

Imagine you are an upcycling retailer working out of ReTuna in Sweden, which is the world's first recycling shopping mall. Shops in such a mall only sell recycled or upcycled items from the public waste recycling centre that they are located right next to. Most of the upcycling production happens in the very same location [46].What kinds of complexities and challenges for operations management, but also advantages, do you think this operational design could bring?

www.retuna.se/english

Lean management methods aim to increase process efficiency by reducing non value-adding activities, so-called wastes

Resource consumption describes all resources used as inputs into a process

Lean management methods extend beyond this common definition of stewardship since both service and enterprise-level self-interest are in play. Responsible stewardship of **resources** resulting in reduced **consumption** of material, time, transport, energy, and human capital is central to lean management. In principle, these should yield social, environmental, and stakeholder benefits while increasing profitability.

In the lean context, 'value' is regarded as any action, process, or product that an end user or – more generally – customer or stakeholder would be willing to pay for: anything else is waste. This must be thoroughly considered in view of the primary sustainable enterprise excellence goal of effectively, efficiently, and profitably transforming TTL (triple top line) strategy into TBL (triple bottom line) results, with ten principles of the Shingo Model for operational excellence.[2]

---

[2]See www.shingo.org

These are based on three insights of enterprise excellence, are divided into cultural enablers, continuous improvement, enterprise alignment, and results categories, which are especially useful. The principles and insights are summarized in Table 17.2.

TABLE 17.2   Shingo model principles and insights of enterprise excellence

Cultural Enabler Principles
• Respect every individual
• Lead with humility
Continuous Improvement Principles
• Embrace critical and scientific thinking
• Focus on processes
• Assure quality at the source
• Flow and pull value
• Pursue excellence
Enterprise Alignment Principles
• Create shared vision and unity of purpose
• Think and act systemically
Results Principles
• Create value for stakeholders
Insights of Enterprise Excellence
• Principles inform behaviours
• Systems drive behaviours
• Ideal results require ideal behaviours

SOURCE: Adapted from [47]

While most of the foregoing principles and insights are self-explanatory, a few are worthy of brief elaboration. Flow and pull value resides at the heart of 'single-piece flow', a cornerstone of the Toyota Production System or TPS [48] that – in its ideal form – means that nothing is produced except to actual demand. This relies on the practice of assuring quality at the source – that is, never knowingly passing on a defect. Embracing critical and scientific thinking requires willingness to 'experiment', that is to make and study the results of logical changes in systems or processes (scientific thinking), and to establish whether and to what extent any change in process behaviour is a consequence of changes made (critical thinking).

Thinking and acting systemically requires thinking and seeing beyond individual actions or processes to the larger context within which multiple actions and processes interact. Note that the principles of respecting every individual and leading with humility are intended to extend beyond the enterprise, into its supply chain and, more broadly, into society. Humility implies being teachable and being teachable is at the core of being a learning organization. Respect for every individual opens the door to possibilities of being more inclusive and to reinterpretation of management responsibilities to communities, to marginalized individuals or groups, and towards care for the environment.

Improving processes and their outputs means serving customers and prioritized stakeholders better, faster, and less expensively so that the overall essence of lean management practice focuses on preservation or enhancement of value based on reduced consumption or more effective and efficient use of resources.

This philosophy derives from the TPS, a system intent on **waste** reduction to improve overall value. Seven *mudas*, types of waste, can be more easily remembered by the acronym NOW TIME [48] (see Table 17.3). An eighth waste – unused or underused human abilities – is commonly often regarded as an eighth source of waste. Simply put, non value-adding efforts are waste.

Of all waste, food waste is arguably one of the most interesting topics, located at the very intersection between operational efficiency and quality management. For instance, one-quarter of perfectly edible apples produced are thrown away

Waste
is any effort or resource that does not add-stakeholder value

TABLE 17.3   NOW TIME lean enterprise *muda*

	Muda (waste)	Muda description
N	Non-quality	These are 'defects'. Defects incur additional costs associated with rework, rescheduling production, replacement, poorly calculated investments, etc.
O	Overproduction	Overproduction occurs when more product or service is produced than customers require at that time. This is contrary to the Shingo principle of 'flow and pull value'. Production of large batches often leads to this waste, which can become truly significant when there are major changes to customer needs or expectations. Overproduction is considered the worst *muda* because it hides and/or generates all other *mudas*.
W	Waiting	Goods not in transport or being processed are in waiting. In traditional inefficient processes, a large part of an individual product's life is spent waiting to be worked on.
T	Transportation	Each time a product is moved it is vulnerable to possible damage, delay, or being lost. No value is added since transportation doesn't positively transform the product.
I	Inventory	Inventory represents capital expenditures not yet producing income for the producer or value for the consumer – capital that could otherwise be dedicated to value-added use(s).
M	Motion	Motion is damage inflicted by the production process to any entity creating the product.
E	Excess processing	Excess or over-processing occurs when more work is done on a piece than the customer requires. This includes use of more precise, complex or expensive tools than are required.

before they ever leave the farm, as they don't look 'perfect' according to society's and supermarkets' aesthetic quality standards [49]. The world's biggest fruits and vegetables producer Dole has committed to an ambitious continuous improvement campaign to eliminate all food waste, what they call 'zero fruit loss' in their operations within just five years [50]. Meanwhile, other companies like Flawsome! have tapped into the value that is in food waste by producing fruit juices with the purpose of 'saving wonky fruit' from being wasted [51].

EFFECTIVENESS AND QUALITY MANAGEMENT

The juice maker Flawsome! has built a thriving business built on the management practice of extracting value from the non-quality muda of 'wonky' fruit.

Courtesy of Flawsome! Drinks

Effectiveness refers to the output part of the process. Different from efficiency, here we do not ask how much input we need, but rather, how can we create the optimum output? We stress 'optimum' output, not maximum output, as the goal is to deliver the output required by priority stakeholders, to balance the TBL, or to create moral excellence. While the focus of Phase 2 was mostly on environmental sustainability, through the concept of eco-efficiency, this Phase 3 will primarily deal with the question of how to tune in processes to create optimum value for stakeholders. We call this **stakeholder effectiveness**. While we focus on stakeholder effectiveness, it is not the only type of effectiveness that matters in professional management. Processes that lead to good ethical results can be called morality effective. Processes that restore ecosystems could be called eco-effective. One crucial difference between effectiveness and efficiency has to be taken into consideration. Efficiency minimizes resource consumption, while effectiveness maximizes performance creation. The latter creates positive outcomes, while the former minimizes negative ones.

At the system engineering level, product and service requirements are often reviewed with marketing and customer representatives or with customer focus groups to carefully elaborate customer needs and to eliminate less desired, yet costly, requirements. In this way, compromise solutions that are pleasing to customers, of appropriate quality, yet profitable, are selected from a larger and more complex set of potential solutions.

Stakeholder effectiveness refers to creating operational outcomes that satisfy stakeholder requirements

Total responsibility management gears operations towards stakeholder effectiveness

Quality management a framework that aims to create products and services that are perfectly aligned with customer (stakeholder) needs by reducing non-conformities with customer requirements

Customer needs assessment and fulfilment are consistent with the **COPIS** ⇨ *SIPOC* concept-to-conduct flow [47] that begins with careful elaboration of customer needs (C) that precisely communicates outputs (O) desired by stakeholders. Outputs result from processes (P) that should be optimally configured to yield those outputs. Processes require inputs (I) that must be transformed by processes and those inputs are obtained from carefully selected suppliers (S) or vendors, with the end result always in view. Once business is conceived in this way, it is executed, beginning with suppliers that provide inputs transformed by processes into outputs produced for customers: SIPOC. This strategy may yield a departure from awarding contracts to lowest cost vendors towards a more professional approach that 'begins with the end in mind' (see Figure 17.9).

COPIS
an algorithm for quality management, formed by the words Customer, Outputs, Processes, Inputs, and Suppliers

Any approach used should begin with a detailed assessment of customer (stakeholder) needs that may be derived through **voice-of-the-customer (VOC)** tools such as surveys, focus groups, customer complaint systems or other approaches. Customers are commonly unable to articulate what they are unaware of, so that exploratory dialogue may be required. Similarly, enterprises shouldn't expect customers to be familiar with their full range of technological solutions or capabilities, thus necessitating exploration of 'if we could … what uses might you have …?' questions.

Voice-of-the-customer (VOC) describes efforts to identify customer needs. For professional management this should rather be voice-of-the-stakeholder (VOS)

The Kano customer needs model [52] classifies needs as dissatisfiers, satisfiers, and delighters. Dissatisfiers are 'must haves' that are absolutely expected, satisfiers are one-dimensional aspects such as fuel efficiency (more is better) or processing time (less is better), and delighters are 'attractive' or positively surprising aspects of the product, process or system. Generally, products or services should possess all must haves, excel relative to one-dimensional needs, and include some delighters (see Figure 17.10). For instance, the home appliances producer Gorenje engages in total responsibility management. The practice includes the voice of employees, particularly related to intergenerational management, which is key to creating value for and with an ageing workforce [53].

Satisfying one need may inhibit the ability to satisfy another, so that a 'best compromise solution' nearest to an *ideal final result* (IFR) must be derived. Once customer/stakeholder needs are identified and confirmed, they must be fulfilled via appropriate products, services, processes, and systems. Needs fulfilment methods range from basic to complex in nature and include PDSA (plan, do, study, act) when incremental improvement of an existing product or service is needed; Six Sigma's DMAIC approach when moderate improvement is needed; and benchmarking, quality function deployment or QFD [54], or the DMADV (define, measure, analyse, design,

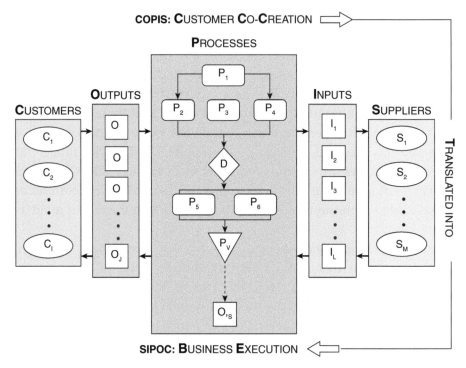

FIGURE 17.9   COPIS ⇨ SIPOC business conception to business conduct connection

Capturing the voice of employees at Slovenian home appliance producer Gorenje.

PDSA
the abbreviation of the improvement cycle following the stages plan, do, study, and act

verify) algorithm of Design for Six Sigma (DFSS) methodology when significant improvement or innovation in an existing product or development of a new product or service is required. Regardless of the approach employed, the goal is to elaborate and fulfil the VOC in a way consistent with enterprise purpose and values, which is profitable to the organization, and leads satisfied and loyal customers to be open to continued or future engagement with the enterprise.

These approaches are systematic and philosophically similar. To illustrate, briefly consider PDSA and Six Sigma's DMAIC and DMADV approaches to improvement and design.

PDSA is often referred to as the Deming Cycle or Deming Wheel [55] and is often attributed to W. Edwards Deming, though Dr Deming credited the method to his mentor, Dr Walter A. Shewhart [56]. Deming's management

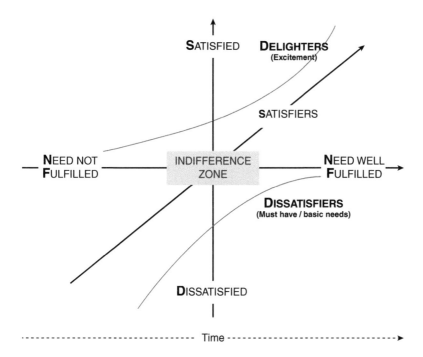

FIGURE 17.10 Kano customer/stakeholder needs model

theory and practices – like the Shingo model and principles – are in widespread use. The PDSA cycle plays a key role in implementing Deming's approach and its application to professional management [16] (see Table 17.4).

This should continue until **continuous PDSA improvement cycle** improvements become untenable due to competing opportunities, return on improvement is outstripped by investments required to achieve improvements, or further improvement is subject to hard constraints such as technological limitations. Figure 17.11 portrays a mildly modified version of the PDSA process that reflects the need to standardize a solution prior to broad implementation, a step that renders the solution more portable while also mitigating the likelihood of increased variation that infiltrates processes without standardization. A second modification emphasizes the importance of 'holding the gains' of any implemented changes while pursuing further improvement.

> Continuous improvement cycle is one in which after each pass through the cycle a new planning phase is initiated and the cycle is repeated to continue improving the product, process, or system

BENCHMARKING FOR BREAKTHROUGH IMPROVEMENT

Benchmarking is most commonly used when breakthrough improvement is needed or when the potential benefit of improvement warrants the sort of investment benchmarking often requires. Among well-known varieties of

TABLE 17.4   Plan–do–study–act (PDSA) cycle applied on responsibility management

Phase	Original cycle	Professional management PDSA
P	**PLAN.** Recognize the change opportunity and plan a specific beneficial change.	Define stakeholders, issues, assess relevant norms, create a guiding coalition of stakeholders, and define objectives.
D	**DO.** Implement the change, possibly on a smaller initial scale in the event that change does not accomplish the anticipated results either directionally or at the needed magnitude.	Identify gaps in stakeholder performance; implement measures to bridge them, train employees to empower them to perform responsibly.
S	**STUDY.** Study implementation results by observing and analysing changes in process performance. Identify that which has been learned in relation to the motivation for change.	Review progress with the guiding coalition, communicate to internal and external stakeholders, calculate stakeholder benefits from improvements.
A	**ACT.** Take action based on the results of the study phase. This may involve full implementation, scaled back implementation, or reversion to prior conditions.	Revise responsibility objectives and start the cycle all over again.

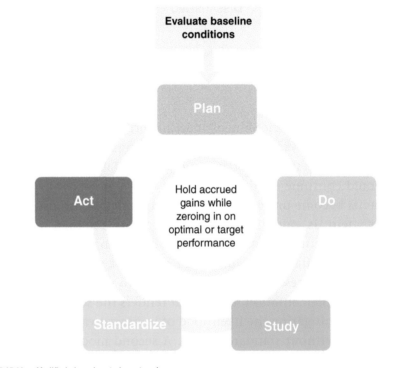

FIGURE 17.11   Modified plan–do–study–act cycle

Best practices benchmarking the process of continually searching for and studying, and adopting internal and external methods, practices, and processes that yield superior performance to become the 'best of the best'

benchmarking are competitive, functional, internal, product, process, best practices, strategic, and parameter benchmarking. **Best practice benchmarking** resides at the intersection of competitive, functional, and internal benchmarking, as portrayed in Figure 17.12

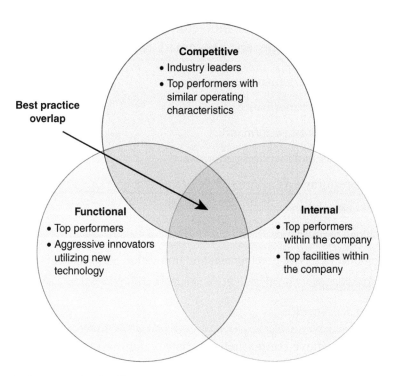

Best practice overlap

Competitive
- Industry leaders
- Top performers with similar operating characteristics

Functional
- Top performers
- Aggressive innovators utilizing new technology

Internal
- Top performers within the company
- Top facilities within the company

FIGURE 17.12   Best practices benchmarking

Benchmarking typically delivers at least 15 per cent performance improvement by comparing performance levels, determining what best practices are and how they deliver superior performance, adoption, or adaptation of best practices to improve one's own performance, and identifying means of sustaining improved performance.

Benchmarking has a distinct measurement focus and it is important to determine and measure where processes both create and detract from customer value. Benchmarking efforts typically use both lagging measures that describe past performance, and leading measures capable of forecasting future performance. In contrast to lagging measures that are inherently reactive in nature, leading measures enable upstream intervention. Benchmarks or measures designed for performance improvement should be constructed to empower individuals or teams to implement change and control subsequent performance.

Among enablers of improved performance are so-called soft, medium, and hard enablers. Soft enablers include training, communication, and human capital empowerment. Medium enablers include (SMART) goals and objectives, controls, measures, and policies and procedures. Hard enablers are tangible resources such as manufacturing plants, suppliers, money, technology, and equipment. Generic benchmark categories include:

1. Customer service performance

2. Product or service performance

3. Core business process performance

4. Support processes and services performance

5. Employee performance

6. Supplier performance

7. Technology performance

8. New product or service development and innovation performance

9. Cost performance

10. Financial performance

Many enterprises have contextualized their benchmarking processes and use benchmarking to advance both tactical and strategic aims. Perhaps the most well-known benchmarking process is that developed and applied by Xerox Corporation, an overview of which is provided in Table 17.5 [57].

PRINCIPLES OF PROFESSIONAL OPERATIONS MANAGEMENT

I.   The goal of professional operations management is **professional enterprise excellence,** which refers to above-average operational performance for the TBL, stakeholder value, and moral excellence.

II.   **Operational performance** describes the **effectiveness and efficiency** of processes for the production of goods and services.

III. For professional operational performance, **processes** must integrate stakeholder value, environmental impacts and ethical dilemmas in their description and management.

IV.   Different **transformation systems** (e.g. job shops, assembly lines, or service factories) are best suited to particular **facilities layouts** (e.g. cellular or functional).

V.   **Production control** aims to bring together produced supply and customer/stakeholder demand at a given point in time, while optimizing ethics, responsibility, and sustainability impacts.

TABLE 17.5 Xerox benchmarking process (left column) and the example of eco-efficiency benchmarking (right column)

Phase 1. Planning		
1	Identify what to benchmark	Tier 2 CO_2 emissions per unit produced
2	Identify comparative enterprises	Other enterprises globally of our size and in the same industry
3	Determine data collection method and obtain data	Extract relevant measure from the Carbon Disclosure Project database or from annual reports
Phase 2. Analysis		
4	Determine current performance gap	Compare our own carbon impact per unit produced with that of the most carbon-efficient companies benchmarked
5	Forecast future performance levels	Explore if the journey towards net zero is likely to lead to even further improvement of the benchmarked companies' carbon efficiency
Phase 3. Integration		
6	Communicate and archive findings in easily accessible form. Gain acceptance	Share informative overview of the emissions achieved by benchmarked companies, and discuss how similar could be achieved in your company
7	Establish functional goals	Work with functional experts on achievable stretch goals for reduced CO_2 emissions per product unit
Phase 4. Action		
8	Develop plans	Co-develop feasible, evidence-based plans for achieving the desired carbon reduction
9	Implement specific actions and monitor progress	Set, implement, and monitor reduction actions and measure if they lead to projected emissions reduction results
10	Recalibrate benchmarks	Revisit and update your carbon efficiency companies database.
Phase 5. Maturity		
11	Attain leadership position	Keep repeating 1–10 until your CO_2 emissions per unit are among the very best of the benchmarked companies
12	Fully integrate practices into processes	Deeply anchor the key practices leading to the CO_2 emissions reduction excellence in all your organizational processes and keep up the benchmarking effort

SOURCE: Adapted from [57]

VI. **Lean enterprise** methods aim to increase the efficiency of a process by reducing non-value adding activities, so-called **wastes**. Lean thinking is the basis for **eco-efficiency**, which reduces pollution and resource consumption from existing processes.

VII. **Quality management** aims to create products and services that are perfectly aligned with customer (stakeholder) needs by reducing nonconformities (errors) with customer requirements.

VIII. A **continuous improvement** cycle is one that, after each pass through the cycle, initiates a new planning phase and the cycle is repeated to continue improving the product, process, or system. A prominent cycle is **PDSA** (plan, do, study, and act).

MANAGEMENT GYM: TRAINING YOUR PROFESSIONAL SIX-PACK

Knowing

1. Define the following terms and explain how they are related: performance, efficiency, effectiveness, process, output, and input.

2. Explain the differences between quality management and lean management, and describe for each how they apply to professional management.

3. Search online or in operations management books for at least three numeric metrics used in demand forecasting (e.g. mean forecast error) and capacity management (e.g. lead time).

Thinking

4. WaterHope is a social enterprise that provides clean and affordable drinking water to poor communities in the Philippines. Water stations fostered by WaterHope distribute clean drinking water at low cost to the community, provide educational programmes on sanitation and health, and micro-finance services through which water dealers may obtain credit to purchase gallons and start their water distribution business. What do you think are the main processes of WaterHope? What are the core practices and activities, resources, and outputs?

5. Reflect on how mainstream operations management and professional operations management are different and where they overlap.

6. Tom Szaki, CEO of TerraCycle claims that 'Waste is an entirely human concept. There is really no such thing in nature as waste. Everything is used; everything decomposes to become the building blocks of something else … The idea is to focus on what is "waste", and find a way to use it.' How does this understanding of waste relate to how waste is presented in the operations management context?

Acting

7. Prepare a table in which you brainstorm about the satisfiers, dissatisfiers, and delighters of three stakeholder groups of your choice. Based on your analysis, write a half-page 'Voice of the stakeholder' statement for one of the stakeholders to define the requirements to be fulfilled for this stakeholder.

8. Choose one operational process in a type of business or industry of your choice. Prepare a one-page benchmarking report by identifying and comparing best practices and choosing the 'best of the best'.

9. Identify a process that you are very familiar with. Construct a COPIS map for the process.

Interacting

10. Search annual sustainability reports of three leading organizations in relation to the lean enterprise concepts of muda, muri, and mura. In a small group, discuss your findings and ideas for avoiding further waste.

11. Organize one of your group work projects using frameworks related to transformation systems, demand forecasting, or capacity management.

12. Identify someone who works in operations management (e.g. from your personal acquaintances, by recommendation from family or friends, or on a professional social media network like LinkedIn) and ask them about their experience (or lack thereof) in integrating ethics, responsibility, or sustainability.

Being

13. Reflect about your personal values as they relate to your purchasing habits. How might these relate to professional operations management?

14. Consider a service that is familiar to you. Identify at least one personal dissatisfier, one satisfier, and one delighter. Outline at least one operations management action that would improve the value you get out of the service.

15. Think about one of your personal habits and try to describe one or more wastes associated with each of the seven NOW TIME wastes.

Becoming

16. Try to improve one of your personal habits or practices by describing how you currently do it, including weaknesses and opportunities for improvement (baseline conditions). Then run through two rounds of the plan–do–study–act cycle documenting both process and outcomes.

17. How might routine practices of 'embracing critical and scientific thinking' and 'thinking systemically' impact on your personal behaviour and your professional experiences? Give at least one example of where you have used each of these and reflect on both process and outcomes.

18. If you were to use total responsibility management to improve your personal relations, what type of value would you want to create and who for?

SOURCE: Adapted from [58]

PIONEER INTERVIEW
SANDRA WADDOCK

INTERVIEWED BY: OLIVER LAASCH

Sandra Waddock is arguably the most prolific academic author on corporate social responsibility (CSR). She has been an influential player in developing the field of CSR for decades on many different topics. In her recent work in collaboration with Charles Bodwell, she provides practical advice on how (total) quality management, one of the main tools of operations management, can be applied to become 'total responsibility management'.

Courtesy of Sandra Waddock

What responsibility practitioners can learn from quality management. The main lesson as I see it is that you can manage responsibilities just as you can manage quality. You may remember (from reading if not experience) that there was a lot of scepticism about quality management when it was first introduced. Managers raised issues like – our customers don't care about quality. You can't measure quality. You can't manage quality. Well, along came the quality movement, and today it turned out that you could, in fact, do all those things. Indeed, today quality management is a fundamental imperative for companies – you can't do business in most markets without paying attention to quality. I would argue that the same dynamic is affecting responsibility management, particularly with respect to the integration process.

So, responsibility practitioners can begin to think systematically about managing responsibilities to stakeholders and the natural environment, just as they manage quality and, increasingly, environmental issues. The processes and steps are actually quite similar.

Similarities between quality and responsibility. There are great similarities between the ways in which managers in companies learned to manage quality and the way that they now need to learn to manage their responsibilities to stakeholders and the natural environment. If you think of responsibility management as something totally new, it can become totally overwhelming. But if you view it as managing the company's relationships with a variety of stakeholders much as you have already learned to manage, for example, your employee relationships (and indeed, responsibility management includes employee relationships), then you realize that you are *already* managing those responsibilities. It's just that without explicit

(Continued)

attention to the whole system of important stakeholder/natural environment relationships, you may not be doing that management process very well.

So you can think of responsibility management, which my collaborator Charlie Bodwell and I called TRM for total responsibility management (in our book by that name), just to make the connection to TQM or total quality management, as another set of managerial processes, though I'm going to make this sound more linear than it actually is.

Stages of TRM. You begin with envisioning what you see as the company's important responsibilities, and identifying who the key stakeholders are (including the natural environment as one of them, even though it's not a person). Then you construct a vision, based on the core values of the company, that articulates how you want to treat those stakeholders, and you can even begin a stakeholder engagement process at that point to determine what they see as the issues, if any, in their current relationship to the company. We call this stage the inspiration process. When you've got a clearer sense of what you think the company stands for with respect to stakeholders, you can articulate your vision for managing stakeholder and environmental responsibilities, and move to the next stage.

The next stage we called integration, because it is the process of more deeply embedding explicit responsibility management into the company's people management practices as well as the other systems that support the mission of the firm. So, you have to think about the processes and practices of the company that affect each stakeholder group and what the responsibility issues embedded in those practices are. How well are you treating your employees, customers, local communities, shareholders, and suppliers? Do they trust you? If not, why not? Where are the problems? What needs to be done to resolve those problems? Which are signals that some sort of responsibility is falling through the cracks? What are your environmental practices? Is there waste? Are there activists raising concerns that need attention? Yes, the integration process is more complex than with managing quality because there are more stakeholders involved. With quality, you are mostly concerned about employees and customers, but that list does expand considerably when you think about your responsibilities. It is through integration that quality and responsibility practices get embedded into the firm – and where the most changes need to take place.

And, of course, as with quality, you can't determine how well you're doing with responsibility management unless you develop appropriate metrics. As my colleague Charlie Bodwell would point out, you're already gathering a lot of the relevant metrics, though probably not all of them, but they are typically not consolidated into a systematic approach to managing responsibility until you begin to think about developing the whole approach to responsibility management. And, also as with managing quality, responsibility management does not lend itself to perfection – it is a process of continuous improvement based on ongoing assessments and feedback loops to see how well you are living up to your own standards and vision.

(Continued)

The responsibility imperative. Since that time, corporate responsibility has indeed become more of a business imperative, although it doesn't always seem so when we look at all the scandals associated with corporations. But surveys show today that most of the world's largest corporations are now issuing multiple bottom line reports of some sort and virtually all of them have actively engaged CSR – what I call the new CSR, corporate sustainability and responsibility – programmes. So, especially in the realm of large multinational firms, yes, I think that there has been continued growth in that direction. Are we fully there – where 'there' means fully responsible firms? Obviously not, but the external pressures on firms, the visibility that creates transparency, and the demands for accountability are like the genie that has been let out of the bottle – and is now too big to get back in.

QUESTIONS

1. What are the main similarities and differences between managing responsibility and managing quality that you can spot in Sandra's interview? Which ones does she leave unmentioned?

2. From what Sandra explains, is there a perfect way of implementing responsible management that ensures it stays stable once and for all, or does it need continuous tinkering and adjustment? Which is it and why?

3. Do you agree with Sandra that responsibility is a management imperative nowadays, or is it rather a 'nice to have' that you can easily do without?

PROFESSIONAL PROFILE
CECILIA DEL CASTILLO

Hi, my name is Cecilia Castillo, and I am an Environmental, Health and Safety (EHS) Coordinator in the Mexican state of San Luis Potosí. I work at Eaton, a global company focused on electrical, hydraulic, and mechanical power technologies.

(Continued)

Courtesy of Cecilia del Castillo

What I am responsible for. I coordinate safety, environmental and hygiene projects as well as maintenance work related to buildings, offices and services to ensure continuity of plant operations and safe working conditions with a significant impact reduction on the environment. On a daily basis I am responsible for implementing, promoting, and maintaining a safe work environment by implementing a culture of accident prevention, investigation, equipment maintenance, and application of rules.

A normal day at work. Typical activities include reviewing the daily safety status, coordinating with EHS staff activities planned during the year to maintain a zero accident exposure culture, and communication of plants and areas status for environmental impact. Every activity planned during the day corresponds to a greater plan that has been developed through the year, which involves having in mind the priority of the mission and vision of the company. Safety and environmental issues have always been important but the impacts of these issues on production matters have taken more importance in the last few years.

Strategic operations and EHS. In order to promote the company's mission and vision I actively support Eaton's ethics and values as well as quality policies. We motivate and coach employees to maintain high levels of satisfaction, productivity, and quality through effectively utilizing available rewards and recognition channels to encourage and promote desired behaviours and results.

As we strive to become the most admired company in its markets as measured by customers, shareholders, and employees, environment, health and safety (EHS) will be an integral part of this process by adding value and enhancing the company's competitive advantage in the marketplace. We direct our efforts in the following areas: sustainable business, employees, business integration, compliance, customers, suppliers and contractors, community.

I believe that one of the most important tools is related to Six Sigma – standardization tools. One of the most important in order to complete the implementation of a strategy is DMAIC – this tool will give you structure and will help you to have a greater view of your business plan so your metrics will be simple, traceable, reasonable, all with a view to continuous improvement.

QUESTIONS

1. What content covered in the chapter can you spot in Cecilia's text? What new content does she introduce?

2. How does Cecilia describe the role of people in operations management?

3. How would you imagine the role of an EHS manager like Cecilia in a factory? What relationship do you think she will have with other managers and production workers?

TRUE STORY

MANAGING PRIVACY INVASION ... RESPONSIBLY

My name is Xiling and I am a residential building manager. After my education, I did a couple of internships in real-estate-related services and got my first full-time job managing the day-to-day operations of a residential building in Ningbo, China, mostly inhabited by foreign expats. I was originally not very interested in responsible management, but recent events and continuous tensions in my job have made me think about questions of responsibility and ethics in managing our building operations.

The practice. One of my main tasks is to accompany maintenance staff into the apartments to maintain, for instance, air conditioners, to upgrade electronic appliances, or to check on fire alarms. All of these things are quite important, as the maintenance workers are not always very cautious. They might break something or, in extreme cases, even steal.

Our common practice is to send an email to apartment residents a couple of days before the maintenance visit, and ask them to send us an email back if they do not want us to conduct the maintenance. If we do not hear back from tenants, we simply enter their apartment and do what needs doing. Typically, we knock once to make clear we will come in, then quickly let ourselves in because there is no time. We sometimes have to visit up to a hundred apartments in a day.

The beef. However, tenants often get quite upset when we enter their apartments. Sometimes, they are in the shower or on the toilet. One tenant recently yelled at me and told me not only was I invading his privacy, but also violating the rent contract. It appears we have a clause in there saying we can only enter into tenants' apartments when they have let us in or explicitly given permission to enter. I have heard that in their cultures, they are more focused on privacy, but they are in China after all, right? Shouldn't they accept how things are done here?

(Continued)

So the contract doesn't matter? I asked my line manager, but she just said we have to get it done and this is the only way. The contract doesn't matter, because we have always done it this way. Personally, I don't know what to do. In Chinese culture, it is very bad to question our superiors, but also, I don't want to be yelled at by the tenants. I like many of them and for us Chinese our Chi, the good personal relationship between people we are close to, is very important.

QUESTIONS

1. How would you interpret the problem posed in this case through a quality management lens?

2. If you were Xiling, how could you use VOS and PDSA to improve the situation?

3. Who are the different stakeholders involved? How would you try to harmonize their needs through total responsibility management?

4. If you were Xiling, what would you do?

DIGGING DEEPER: THE TOYOTA PRODUCTION SYSTEM

Toyota production system
(TPS)
a management method that led
to the lean enterprise methods

Lean management implementation flows from the **Toyota production system**. Although the most obvious opportunities for lean implementation are found in manufacturing, other opportunities for improving overall enterprise performance and reducing cost may be just as fruitful, though less easily discovered. TPS practice has been translated into 14 principles that are thoroughly elaborated in the landmark book *The Toyota way* [48]. These principles – briefly stated on the right side of Figure 17.13 – closely correspond to the Shingo Principles positioned on the left side.

Though criticized as limiting creativity and innovation, the focus of TPS and other lean management methods on waste doesn't hinder creativity and innovation per se, but more carefully defines and constrains the range of viable solutions within which creativity and innovation occur.

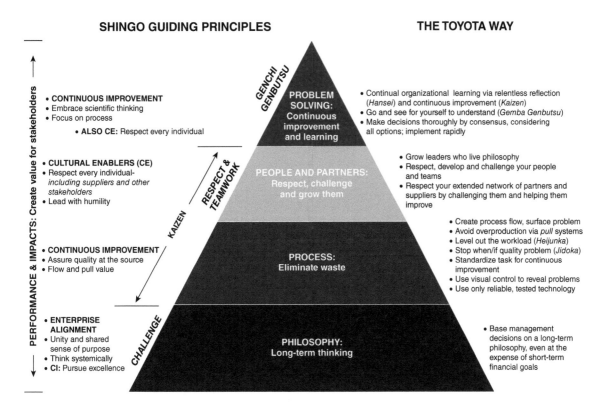

FIGURE 17.13 Toyota and Shingo principles

POINTERS

As an example, you could use this section to have a closer look at the elements and context of the Toyota Production System and how it might relate to professional operations management. You could read *The Toyota way* or have a closer look at elements of the TPS like Kaizen, pull systems, or Jidoka.

WORKSHEET

PROCESS SWIMLANE DIAGRAM

POINTERS

You could use this worksheet to map a process (actual process or planned) of your choice and see how and where it connects to ethical, social, and environmental issues or opportunities. You could also use it to redesign an existing process – for instance, by making improvements to some parts of it.

REFERENCES

1. Lacey P, Cooper T, Hayward R, Neuberger L. *A new era of sustainability: UN global compact-accenture CEO study 2010.* New York: Accenture Institute for High Performance, 2010.

2. McDonough W, Braungart M. *The upcycle: Beyond sustainability – designing for abundance.* New York: North Point Press, 2013.

3. Ingka. Retail direction: 10 jobs in three years. www.ingka.com/what-we-do/ikea-retail Published 2020. Accessed July 13 2020.

4. Ravenscroft T. There's something seriously wrong with IKEA's most sustainable store. www.dezeen.com/2019/02/28/ikea-most-sustainable-store-greenwich-sainsburys-chetwoods-opinion Published 2019. Accessed July 13 2020.

5. Interface Recruiting and Careers. *Mission zero.* www.interfaceglobal.com/careers/mission_zero.html Published 2012. Accessed December 24 2012.

6. Elkington J. *The Zeronauts: Breaking the sustainability barrier.* New York: Routledge, 2012.

7. Elkington J. *Cannibals with forks: The triple bottom line of 21st century business.* Gabriola Island, BC: New Society Publishers, 1998.

8. Laszlo C, Zhexembayeva N. *Embedded sustainability: The next big competitive advantage.* Stanford: Stanford University Press, 2011.

9. International Organization for Standardization. *Quality management systems – fundamentals and vocabulary.* Geneva: ISO, 2005.

10. *Eco-efficiency: Creating more value with less impact.* Geneva: World Business Council for Sustainable Development, 1999.

11. Conger S. *Process mapping and management.* New York: Business Expert Press, 2011.

12. List B, Korherr B. An evaluation of conceptual business process modelling languages. Paper presented at: Proceedings of the 2006 ACM Symposium on Applied Computing, New York, 2006.

13. Earles S. Sustainable operations: Bristol Airport's decade of transformation. www.internationalairportreview.com/article/101818/brist(ol-airport-sustainable-procedures Published 2019. Accessed July 14 2020.

14. International Airport Review. European aviation association's call for sustainable COVID-19 recovery. www.internationalairportreview.com/news/119594/european-aviation-sustainable-covid-19-recovery Published 2020. Accessed July 14 2020.

15. Blackburn WR. *The sustainability handbook: The complete management guide to achieving social, economic and environmental responsibility.* Washington: Earthscan, 2007.

16. Waddock S, Bodwell C. *Total responsibility management: The manual.* Sheffield: Greenleaf Publishing, 2007.

17. Morsing M, Oswald D. Sustainable leadership: Management control systems and organizational culture in Novo Nordisk A/S. *Corporate Governance.* 2009, 9(1): 83–99.

18. Dalling I. *Integrated management system: Definition and structuring guidance.* London: Chartered Quality Institute, 2007.

19. International Organization for Standardization. ISO guide 72: 2001. www.iso.org/iso/catalogue_detail?csnumber=34142 Published 2012. Accessed December 22 2012.

20. International Organization for Standardization. New ISO guide for writers of management system standards. www.iso.org/iso/home/news_index/news_archive/news.htm?refid=Ref812 Published 2002. Accessed December 22 2012.

21. The British Standards Institution. PAS 99 integrated management. www.bsiamerica.com/en-us/Assessment-and-Certification-services/Management-systems/Standards-and-schemes/PAS-99 Published 2012. Accessed December 22 2012.

22. bizmanualz. How to build effective management systems. www.bizmanualz.com/blog/how-to-build-effective-management-systems.html Published 2005. Accessed December 24 2012.

23. Integrated management system framework (ISO Guide 72). Hong Kong: i-VAC Certification, 2008.

24. *Guidelines for the justification and development of management system standards.* Geneva: ISO, 2001.

25. Jørgensen TH, Remmen A, Mellado MD. Integrated management systems – three different levels of integration. *Journal of Cleaner Production.* 2006, 14(8): 713–722.

26. Karapetrovic S. Musings on integrated management systems. *Measuring Business Excellence*. 2003, 7(1): 4–13.

27. Castka P, Bamber CJ, Bamber DJ, Sharp JM. Integrating corporate social responsibility (CSR) into ISO management systems – in search of a feasible CSR management system framework. *The TQM Magazine*. 2004, 16(3): 216–224.

28. Mertins K, Orth R. Intellectual capital and the triple bottom line: Overview, concepts and requirements for an integrated sustainability management system. Paper presented at: Proceedings of the European Conference on Intellectual Capital, Helsinki, 2012.

29. Glassman, B., & Fields, R. Instructions to the cook: A Zen master's lessons in living a life that matters. New York: Harmony, 2010.

30. Aziz A. the power of purpose: How Greyston is championing radical inclusivity through open hiring. www.forbes.com/sites/afdhelaziz/2019/05/16/the-power-of-purpose-how-greyston-is-championing-radical-inclusivity-through-open-hiring/?sh=6d249a092ced Published 2019. Last accessed July 31 2023.

31. Allsafe. Secure your cargo, undertake sustainably. www.allsafe-group.com/unternehmen Last accessed July 31 2023.

32. Chase RB., & Erikson WJ. The service factory. *Academy of Management Perspectives*. 1988, 2(3): 191–196.

33. Schmenner RW How can service businesses survive and prosper? *Sloan Management Review*. 1986, 27(3): 21.

34. Slack N, Brandon-Jones A., & Burgess N. *Operations management* (10th edition). Pearson: Harlow, 2022.

35. Narayanan S, Terris E. Inclusive manufacturing: The impact of disability diversity on productivity in a work integration social enterprise. *Manufacturing & Service Operations Management*. 2020, 22(6):1112–1130.

36. Marr B. What is Industry 4.0? Here's a super easy explanation for anyone. www.forbes.com/sites/bernardmarr/2018/09/02/what-is-industry-4-0-heres-a-super-easy-explanation-for-anyone/?sh=597590499788 Published 2018. Last accessed July 31 2023.

37. Fox S, Aranko O, Heilala, J, & Vahala, P. Exoskeletons: Comprehensive, comparative and critical analyses of their potential to improve manufacturing performance. *Journal of Manufacturing Technology Management*. 2019, 31(6), 1261–1280.

38. Pearson J. How Tesla used robotics to survive 'production hell' and became the world's most advanced car manufacturer. www.roboticstomorrow.com/article/2022/06/2022-top-article-how-tesla-used-robotics-to-survive-production-hell-and-became-the-worlds-most-advanced-car-manufacturer/18908 Published 2022. Last accessed July 31 2023.

39. Ribeiro B, Meckin R, Balmer A, & Shapira, P. The digitalisation paradox of everyday scientific labour: How mundane knowledge work is amplified and diversified in the biosciences. *Research Policy*. 2023, 52(1): 104607.

40. Volkswagen. The production process of the future: exoskeletons provide support for employees at the Bratislava plant. www.volkswagen-newsroom.com/en/press-releases/the-production-process-of-the-future-exoskeletons-provide-support-for-employees-at-the-bratislava-plant-3836 Published 2018. Last accessed August 21 2023.

41. Harding M, Kettler, K, Lamarche C. Environmental and social benefits of time of use electricity pricing. www.chapman.edu/research/institutes-and-centers/economic-science-institute/_files/ifree-papers-and-photos/harding-benefits-time-use-electricity-pricing-2019.pdf Published 2019. Last accessed August 21 2023.

42. Slipstream and MN Center for Energy and Environment. *Market potential for saving energy and carbon emissions with load shifting measures*. https://slipstreaminc.org/sites/default/files/documents/research/load-shifting-measures-can-save-energy-and-carbon-together.pdf Published 2020. Last accessed July 31 2023.

43. Slack N, Brandon-Jones A., & Burgess N. *Operations management* (10th edition). Harlow: Pearson, 2022.

44. HKTDC Research. European organisations call for ban on destruction of unsold goods including clothing and electronics. https://research.hktdc.com/en/article/OTE5NDM2OTA2 Published 2021. Last accessed July 31 2023.

45. Proudlove NC, Gordon K, & Boaden, R. Can good bed management solve the overcrowding in accident and emergency departments? *Emergency Medicine Journal*. 2003, 20(2): 149–155.

46. Retuna. Welcome to the world's first recycling mall. www.retuna.se/english Last accessed July 31 2023.

47. Edgeman R. *Complex management systems and the Shingo Model: Foundations of operational excellence and supporting tools*. Abingdon: Routledge, 2019.

48. Liker J. *The Toyota way: 14 management principles from the world's greatest manufacturer*. New York: McGraw-Hill, 2004.

49. Dobson MC, Edmondson JL. Ugly vegetables are a major cause of food waste. www.independent.co.uk/life-style/food-and-drink/ugly-vegetable-food-waste-fruit-vegetable-a8825311.html Published 2019. Accessed July 14 2020.

50. Peters A. Banana leaf packaging and pineapple powder: How Dole plans to eliminate food waste by 2025. www.fastcompany.com/90522466/banana-leaf-packaging-and-pineapple-powder-how-dole-plans-to-eliminate-food-waste-by-2025 Published 2020. Accessed July 14 2020.

51. Flawsome! Fruit saved by our juices so far. https://flawsomedrinks.com Published 2020. Accessed July 13 2020.

52. Kano N, Seraku N, Takahashi F, Tsuji S. Attractive quality and must-be quality. *Journal of the Japanese Society for Quality Control*. 1984, 14(2): 39–48.

53. Gorenak S, Bobek V. Total responsibility management indicators and sustainable development. *International Journal of Sustainable Society*. 2010, 2(3): 248–264.

54. Edgeman R, Hensler D. QFD and the BEST paradigm: Deploying sustainable solutions. *World Review of Science, Technology and Sustainable Development*. 2005, 2(1): 49–59.

55. Moen R, Norman C. Circling back: Clearing up myths about the Deming Cycle and seeing how it keeps evolving. *Quality Progress*. 2010, 43(11): 22–28.

56. Deming WE. *Out of the crisis*. Cambridge: MIT Center for Advanced Engineering Study, 1986.

57. Bogan C, English M. *Benchmarking for best practices*. New York: McGraw-Hill, 1994.

58. Laasch, O., Moosmayer, D., & Antonacopoulou, E. P. (2023). The interdisciplinary responsible management competence framework: An integrative review of ethics, responsibility, and sustainability competences. *Journal of Business Ethics, 187*, 733–757.

CHAPTER 18

MARKETING MANAGEMENT

OLIVER LAASCH, DIRK C. MOOSMAYER,
NATASHA CLENNELL AND ROGER N. CONAWAY

LEARNING GOALS

1. Promote ethical, responsible, and sustainable consumption
2. Engage in ethical, responsible, and sustainable marketing management
3. Master the seven Ps of marketing and ERS marketing tools

STAGGERING FACT

'Brands with the highest reputations for sustainability are around 60 per cent more valuable than brands with the lowest reputations for sustainability. And brands with the highest reputations for sustainability grow value over ten times faster than brands with the lowest reputations for sustainability' [1].

MANAGING MARKETING FOR THE HOMELESS AT BOMBAS

Clean socks are crucial for the homeless. Their socks are often quickly worn out from walking miles every day. Dirty, threadbare, socks can result in foot problems including blisters, cuts, frostbite, athlete's foot, and other debilitating infections. Although something as simple as a new pair of socks may seem insignificant, they make a huge difference to the homeless community. When Randy Goldberg and David Heath came across a Facebook post, which highlighted the need for socks at homeless shelters, the idea for their company Bombas was born [2]. The company would revolve around the one-for-one marketing practice where a brand-new pair of socks would be donated to a homeless person for every pair purchased [2].

Bombas has created a line of first class, fashionable socks, priced at between US$12 and $18 [3]. They spent two years researching, to appreciate what paying customers sought in a

Joni Hanebutt / shutterstock.com

pair of well-designed socks [3]. They prioritized quality materials including merino wool, which is temperature regulating. Their innovations included a honeycomb design across the mid-foot to help with arch support [2]. Emily Hofsetter, head of communications at Bombas, highlights that their interactions with the homeless made the firm realize that their initial belief, to provide exactly the same socks as sold to customers, was inappropriate. The homeless have different needs, she said: '...

(Continued)

our regular collection wasn't serving them well' [4]. The standard Bombas socks are stitched by hand at the top, which eliminates the bump at the toe [3]. For extra comfort, the donation socks have a reinforced seam, which makes them more durable. They are also treated with anti-microbial technology; this means they do not need to be washed as often. In addition, the donation socks are made in black, making wear and tear less visible [3].

While Bombas sends thousands of pairs of socks to homeless shelters directly, employees also donate socks to the homeless in person [2]. Hofsetter described an event whereby Bombas staff not only took socks, but also lunch to a shelter, serving and making the homeless sandwiches to their own design [4]. The visits enable employees to connect with the people they are trying to support, providing meaning when they returned to the office to carry out their routine tasks.

Bombas

Management at Bombas recently created an event called: '60K day' [4]. The context for this is that on any given night approximately 60,000 people seek refuge in a New York homeless shelter. Bombas encouraged 60 New York firms to visit a shelter and donate 60,000 pairs of socks. While they met their goal, the staff of the firms involved (from Gap and Kenneth Cole to ShakeShack) were able to start conversations with vulnerable people in their local communities, enabling each firm to contribute in a unique way [4].

PROFESSIONAL MARKETING

As marketers, we recognize that we not only serve our organizations but also act as stewards of society in creating, facilitating and executing the transactions that are part of the greater economy … to embrace the highest professional ethical norms and the ethical values implied by our responsibility toward multiple stakeholders.

American Marketing Association [5]

Marketing management revolves around the exchange of organizational offerings and value with varieties of societal stakeholders referred to as customers

Marketing the practice of connecting organizational value creation to customer needs and of influencing consumer behaviour

Marketing management is placed at the interface between business and society, between management and customers. This prominent position gives **marketing** a powerful role in a company's success, and in translating management practice into having a positive impact in society.

This societal role is also reflected in the evolution of the definition of marketing practice. It has moved away from a narrow focus on advertising, sales, and the promotion of consumption in the dawn of modern marketing in the 1920s [6–8], to satisfying 'individual and organizational objectives', to generating 'value to customers and for managing customer relationships in ways that benefit the organization and its stakeholders', to 'offerings that have value for customers, clients, partners, and society at large' [9]. In the working definition used for this chapter, we go one step further by highlighting marketing's unique capacity to influence consumer behaviour and, with it, lifestyles and societal trends, both positively and negatively.

Professional marketing means proficiently engaging in practices that enable healthy consumption, while engaging in 'good' conduct

Professional marketing therefore includes but goes beyond simply being a competent and effective marketing practitioner or marketer. It also means assuming a positive role in society by promoting healthy consumption, be it aiding in the transition to sustainable lifestyles or in helping people to curb unhealthy consumerism. It also means abstaining from unethical marketing practices, like targeting vulnerable groups or engaging in deceptive communication.

In this context, customers are not only end consumers in a supermarket or buyers in business-to-business marketing. In a wider sense this also covers customers of internal processes, such as customers of people management delivering payroll services to the employees of a firm or a production unit supplying parts to the firm's assembly unit. **Customers** also include stakeholders in the wider society to which management offers some kind of value – for instance the value of employment sought by governments and wider society.

In a narrow view, **customers** are external users and buyers of a product or service; in a broader view they are all stakeholders for whom value is generated internally and externally

In this chapter we will first explore fundamental ideas of and concepts of marketing. We will then have a close look at market segmentation practices and the market positioning 'Ps' also known as the marketing mix. Finally, we will circle back to questions of ethics, responsibility, and sustainability in marketing by exploring the role of marketing in society.

FIGURE 18.1   Areas of professional marketing practice

CREDIT: Slidemodel.com

FUNDAMENTALS OF MARKETING

In this section we will have a close look at some of the central underlying ideas and concepts of marketing, starting from how the marketing world-view has developed. We will then explore how marketing relates to consumer behaviour and close this section by discussing marketing's most common framework, segmentation, targeting and positioning (STP).

MARKETING'S CORE IDEAS

In the same way as marketing definitions have developed, its core ideas have evolved over time. We will now briefly explore which ideas have been dominant at different times before focusing on the most recent core idea of service marketing.

EVOLVING CORE IDEAS

The following three core ideas exist in parallel in marketing theory and practice:

1. **Duality.** Since the beginning of marketing thought and practice, there has been a strong emphasis on the duality of the customer process as an external process and the internal firm process which serves to support the customer process.

2. **Relationality.** Since the 1990s, marketing thinking has emphasized the relationality of business and the necessity of managing business not as a project to sell products but as a project to shape profitable long-term customer relationships [10]. Seen from

this perspective, marketing becomes customer relationship management. This perspective opens up marketing to sustainability thinking as the long-term view on the relationship is inherent in it.

3. **Service**. Since the early 2000s, marketing thinking has centred on a service-dominant logic, emphasizing services and on the service component of products (e.g. products as service) [11]. The move from products to services holds a strong promise of fulfilling people's needs with higher environmental resource efficiency. The same product and its environmental production impacts (e.g. water, carbon emissions and other natural resources) are ideally spread over a longer time of use and across a larger number of users. For instance, a bike in a well-managed bike sharing service will be in continuous use, while a privately owned bike is likely to spend much of its useful life being stored away.

As the service dominant logic of marketing is currently the dominant marketing worldview, we will now have a closer look at it.

SERVICE MARKETING

The most influential marketing paper published to date in this century suggests a fundamental shift in worldview away from product thinking towards a service-dominant logic [12]. The main characteristics of services have been summarized using the abbreviation IHIP: intangibility, heterogeneity, inseparability, and perishability [13, 14]:

1. Services are **intangible** as they are not physical and therefore cannot be possessed, transported, or stored. Think of a train ride as a transportation service. You cannot possess a train ride; you can own the physical ticket but not the ride itself.

2. Services are **heterogeneous** as it is much more difficult to standardize their quality than physical products, which can be mass produced and thus reach a specific quality level quite easily. Standardizing services is more difficult because they are produced in interaction between customer and service provider. Take getting a haircut, for example. The quality of the service depends on your ability to explain to the hairdresser what you want. It also depends on the ability, mood, and daily performance of the hairdresser. When you come to the same hairdresser on a different day, you may have a very different experience.

3. Services are **inseparable**. For physical products, production and consumption can be separated. A football is produced in one place. It can then be stored and sold later in a different place, and be used even later in yet another place. This is not possible for services. If you have a bus ticket from Boston to Montreal on Wednesday morning at 10:00 o'clock, you have to be there in order to use the service. The service of transporting you from Boston to Montreal cannot be delivered without you and without the transportation firm being present at the same time and in the same place.

4. Services are **perishable**. This means that services can only be used at the specific time they are made available. The service is consumed at the time of its production. For the transportation company, this means that seats that remain empty are lost revenue as they cannot be resold.

One central idea of this shift is that even products can be understood and managed as services. This accounts for the fact that in most cases value is not created by ownership of a product but by the service that a product delivers to its owner. For example, a car does not create value by being owned but it creates value when it's used in order to transport its owner from one place to another. This idea is also the fundamental logic of the sharing economy.

CONSUMER BEHAVIOUR

Consumer behaviour helps us to understand how groups and individuals consume [15]. Consumer behaviour consists of varieties of consumer behaviours and practices related to purchasing, use and disposal of products. Figure 18.2 provides a high-level overview of consumer behaviour processes and what influences them. The green parts of the map describe the entangled interaction between marketing, consumers, and their lifestyles. Consumers' lifestyles and their decision processes are influenced, first, by personal consumer characteristics (yellow). Secondly, there are also contextual influences (blue) such as governmental incentives or environmental trends. An interesting example of how external political stimuli come together was the UK government's 'Fix Your Bike' scheme. It gave anyone the right to claim a £50 voucher to repair their unused bikes, incentivizing a healthier and more sustainable lifestyle, which in turn influenced the consumption of bike repair services [16]. Marketing stimuli, therefore, are only one influence on the consumption process, albeit a powerful one.

A particularly controversial use of marketers' knowledge about consumer behaviour is **impulse buying** [18, 19]. Impulse marketing taps into this unhealthy behaviour by using means such as product placements or repeated sales attempts (even after a consumer has said no rationally). Impulse marketing often leads to overconsumption, or to buying offers that do not serve the customer as well as the ones they would have bought if they had thought twice, or that are simply overpriced. However, marketers can also use their knowledge of consumer behaviour to help consume well. An example is when marketing helps to bridge the intention behaviour gap that keeps many of us from buying green.

In principle, the vast majority of people agree with pro-environmental behaviour and ethical consumerism; however, changes in consumption

Consumer behaviour
describes the psychological and sociological processes of how consumers select, purchase, use, and dispose of goods, services, ideas, or experiences to satisfy their needs and desires

Impulse buying
happens when consumers give in to an urge to consume without deliberation, often driven by impulse marketing aimed at fostering such behaviour

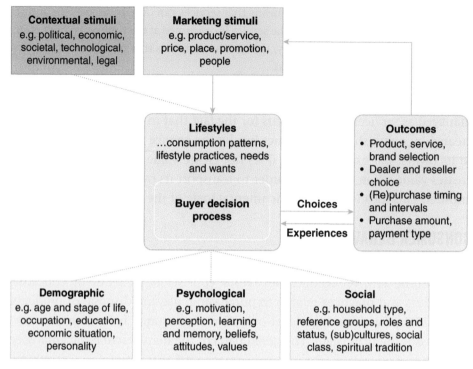

FIGURE 18.2 Mapping consumer behaviour processes and influences

SOURCE: Adapted from [17]

behaviour have been small. This **gap between consumption intention and behaviour** has been observed in contexts particularly relevant to 'good' marketing, such as pro-environmental behaviour [20], sustainable consumption [21], and ethical purchasing behaviour.

Figure 18.3 helps us to understand the dynamics and roots of the intention–behaviour gap. It builds on theories of planned behaviour and is interested in the complex relationship between values and action, intentions, and behaviours. If a consumer evaluates a suggested behaviour (e.g. an advertisement suggesting purchase of an environmentally friendly product) as positive (attitude), and if they think people important to them want them to perform the behaviour (subjective norm), this results in a higher intention (motivation) to engage in the behaviour. Both the intention and the actual behaviour are also influenced by the degree to which the person believes they can actually carry out the behaviour (perceived behavioural control) [23]. However, there are varieties of barriers in the space (gap) between intention and carrying out that behaviour [20]:

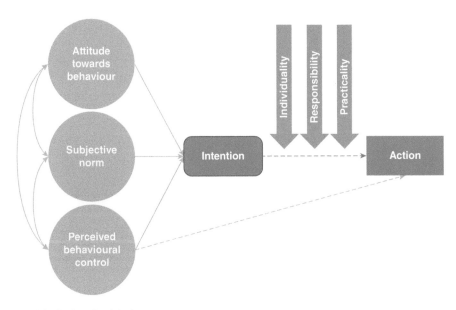

FIGURE 18.3   The intention–behaviour gap

SOURCE: Adapted from [20, 22]

1. **Individual barriers** relate to personal attitudes that conflict either with the behaviour or with carrying it out, such as a personal value that keeps you from engaging in the behaviour, or simply laziness.

2. **Responsibility barriers** relate to a person not believing they are responsible for carrying out a behaviour, or that someone else is more responsible for it.

3. **Practical constraints** consist of issues like not having the financial resources or time to engage in a certain behaviour, or a lack of infrastructure, such as recycling facilities, or bike paths.

Marketing can be geared towards bridging this gap [24]. It can also consist of directly tackling the barriers causing the gap. An example is when influencers on social media explain how they have used certain products, which in turn decreases the practicality barrier. Conversely, we might have a positive attitude (to the left of our model), but not yet a formed intention (middle). People might never have formed an intention as their positive attitude might have been neutralized – for instance, by opposing subjective norms in their environment or because they don't think they have control over carrying out the behaviour. In this case, marketing could foster an intention such as 'you can do it' type of messaging to increase the perceived behavioural control. In the last section of this chapter, we will discuss further how to use social marketing to support customers through different stages of behaviour change.

THE SEGMENTATION, TARGETING, AND POSITIONING (STP) PROCESS

The marketing process can be understood as running through stages of **segmentation, targeting, and positioning (STP)** (see Figure 18.4).

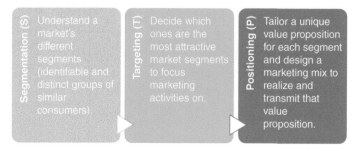

FIGURE 18.4   The marketing process of segmentation, targeting, and positioning (STP)

SEGMENTATION

Understanding customers' needs is a crucial activity in marketing. **Market segmentation** practice generates an understanding of groups of customers with similar needs (a segment), and of the different needs between groups. As an example, marketing management at Bombas, which featured in this chapter's introductory case, is built on an intimate understanding of two distinct segments. The company found out that the segments of homeless people ('clothing that meets the needs of people who don't have the luxury of putting on clean clothes every day' [25]) and paying customers had a different product need due to the specific conditions under which they each use socks. Common criteria for segmenting consumer markets are:

1. **Demographic** segmentation is centred on variables such as age and gender, geographies including different countries and cultures, but also climatic areas – for instance, to distinguish where snow compatible vehicles would be needed and where selling such vehicles might be irresponsible to the environment.

2. A further criterion is **behavioural** segmentation, whereby companies can segment their customers by purchase intensity or the different types of products they have used before.

3. Finally, and probably most important in our context, is **psychographic** segmentation, identifying segments by practices and lifestyles. There may be segments such as the successful businessperson, the parent, the grandparent couple, or the single consumer. People are grouped according to a similar life situation, therefore likely to consume in a similar way.

A useful way of thinking about segmentation is also an appreciation of the attitude members of the segment have towards the type of offer being made. We can distinguish between three broad types, which we introduce using examples of 'green' consumption:

1. **Committed consumers** *care deeply* about ethics, responsibility, and sustainability (ERS) and are willing to put an extra effort or money into acquiring related offers.

2. **Casual consumers** are willing to *acquire an offer as long as it is not of substantial effort*. They are willing to choose a sustainable product if it is of similar quality and does not cost more.

3. **Indifferent consumers** *do not care at all*, and might even include consumers who avoid sustainable products. They might feel that adding 'green' features might increase the price without increasing functional product quality, leading to poor value for money.

Finally, ethical, responsible, and sustainable consumption practices can also serve to identify consumer segments with particular needs, consumer behaviour patterns, and related marketing implications. Here are three of the most common specialized segments:

1. **Lifestyles of health and sustainability (LOHAS)** consumers' consumption choices are geared towards sustainability and well-being products and services. They are often willing to pay an additional price premium for such offers, mainly because they would aim to avoid unsustainable and unhealthy offers, or because increasingly green offers have become symbols of sophistication and status.

2. **Lifestyles of voluntary simplicity (LOVOS)** are related to simple living where people consume less, more slowly, or don't consume some products at all (e.g. no car, television, or meat). They do so, first, in order to reduce their environmental footprint – to avoid social, environmental, and ethical issues related to consumption. Secondly, they often have an underlying desire to make life simpler and more meaningful; they are less driven by consumerist wants. Often, there is also an underlying intention to reduce pressures to work in order to afford consumption and social status. There are many subgroups to this lifestyle, like freegans (people who only consume free products) or localvores (only consuming local produce), as well as slow food, vegetarian, and vegan practices.

3. The **bottom of the pyramid (BoP)** [26] refers to consumption based on a very low income (the 'bottom of the socio-economic income pyramid'). This enormous segment and the related market at the bottom of the pyramid, in the past, has not been served well, if at all. BoP marketing has to consider the different needs of people with low incomes (e.g. more basic, but functional offers), spending patterns (e.g. smaller amounts and package sizes), and availability of disposable income.

LOVOS consumption might be driven by the need to 'avoid the rat race' of work and consumption.

'Banksy no stopping' by thecardinaldelaville is licensed under CC BY 2.0

TARGETING: WHICH SEGMENT(S) TO FOCUS ON?

As part of **targeting practices**, marketing management connects to strategizing by identifying the segments that are both a good fit with the company strategy and are attractive. For instance, a social enterprise with a strategy for poverty reduction is likely to target a BoP customer segment (fit) that benefits substantially from their service (attractive). A company with a stronger commercial strategy is likely to target the segment that promises the greatest economic return (attractive), but which also matches the company culture (fit) [27]. Criteria that play a role when deciding which particular segment(s) to target are also practical considerations for the attractiveness of a segment [17, 28]:

Targeting practices seek to identify which customer segment to serve

1. **Measurable**. How well can segment size and purchasing power be assessed? It might be difficult to get the necessary information to assess the attractiveness of a segment.

2. **Accessible**. How well can segment members be reached? Members of a segment might not be easily distinguishable.

3. **Substantial**. Can the segment sustain activity required to serve it? A segment might be too small or have too little profit potential to sustain the activity required.

4. **Differentiable**. Is the segment distinct enough to develop a unique offer for it? The segment might already be served by an offer that had been shaped for a similar segment.

5. **Actionable**. Is targeting the segment feasible? It might not be feasible to target members of a segment that is widely dispersed.

Once a market has been found to be attractive and a fit, the question is how many and which of the suitable markets should be targeted? Different types of targeting can be distinguished based on the number and heterogeneity of customer groups to be targeted [29]:

1. **Concentrated** targeting is centred on just one narrowly defined customer segment.

2. **Differentiated** targeting instead is focused on a small group of often similar segments.

3. **Undifferentiated** targeting, also called mass-market targeting, aims to please all customer segments.

In the context of sustainable marketing, a related targeting question is: Do we want to sell sustainably to the mass market, or do we want to sell to a consumer segment particularly attracted by ethics, responsibility, and sustainability? Another important question is whom not to target for moral reasons. For instance, it is considered irresponsible to target the children segment, especially with harmful or unhealthy products, to target addicts, such as alcoholics with alcohol advertisements, or others 'vulnerable' to marketing messaging. Vulnerability will be addressed further in the marketing ethics section of this chapter.

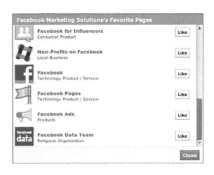

Negative targeting in the Facebook buycott by their business-to-business advertising customers.

'Facebook Data Team – Religious Organization' by gywst is licensed under CC BY-SA 2.0

The targeting question may quickly reverse, from Which segment does a company target? to Which customer segment targets which company? **Activist consumers** may target companies in order to affect the consumption of their offers [30–32] on the basis of strategic consumption: '… every time you spend money, you're casting a vote for the kind of world you want' [33].

Activist consumption
a practice that targets companies to influence demand for their offers positively or negatively

1. **Positive targeting** practices aim at increasing the consumption of products from 'good' companies – for instance, through consumer advocacy, or by strategically buying only from companies considered worthy.

2. **Negative targeting** practices are aimed at reducing demand for an offer. This could consist in simply not buying products (e.g. not buying products with palm oil, or from a company known for bad labour practices), or even organizing large-scale boycotts (or rather 'buycotts').

An intriguing example of negative targeting is when a sizeable share of Facebook's advertising customers (including giants like Verizon and Patagonia) decided to stop buying advertising space. They protested against Facebook's alleged practice of leaving up hate speech messages due to the advertising revenue they generate. The buycott related to the Stop Hate for Profit campaign led to a 7 per cent devaluation of Facebook's shares [34]. One of the buycotters, Unilever's marketing management, released a statement asserting that 'continuing to advertise on these platforms at this time would not add value to people and society'.

POSITIONING

Successfully **positioning** an offer in the targeted segment requires the development of a unique value proposition for that segment, sometimes also called

Positioning practices determine how targeted customer segments will be served by developing a unique value proposition

a 'unique selling point' (USP) [35–37]. Constructing this unique value proposition requires distinct positioning efforts for each market segment.

Imagine you are positioning your product in both the LOHAS segment consisting of both committed and casual green consumers and in the mass market of 'normal' consumers. Effective positions will differ due to the unique characteristics of the consumers in each segment, particularly their attitude towards ethics, responsibility, and sustainability. For the LOHAS consumer segment the USP would require foregrounding an offer's sustainability features, and the company's ethical, responsible, and sustainable practices. For the mass market, however, the USP will need to be distinct. Consumers here may only 'buy green' if they see features they care about, such as a lower price, functionality, luxury, comfort, but not the green features. In order to reach a large portion of the mass market through sustainable and responsible market offers, these would need to be offered through USPs that focus on value dimensions other than ethics, responsibility, or sustainability. This means they would need to be positioned as high quality, high functionality, high performance, high value for money, affordability, and so on.

A great example is the purchasing of remanufactured car engines in China. Considering the substantially reduced environmental impact in comparison between a new or a remanufactured engine, one would assume that these are predominantly bought for environmental reasons. Surprisingly, remanufacturing companies have mainly positioned their engines in a segment that has a very low environmental attitude. They achieved this by building their unique value proposition around remanufactured engines with equal, often higher functionality than new engines [38].

Branding
to generate a unique and consistent perception in the consumer's mind, to establish a differentiated market presence

Positioning your product in a particular market or in a particular customer segment not only requires positioning your offer, but also positioning the organization behind it through **branding**. Such brand positioning has two main components:

- **Brand awareness**. Brand awareness means that a specific company's brand(s) come to mind when consumers begin the purchasing process. For example, when you think about fast food, sports apparel, or organic food, which firms do you immediately think of? This will tell you which firms are important and what their position is in the marketplace.

- **Brand image.** Brand image refers to the thoughts and feelings consumers have about a company's brand(s). When **positioning** themselves in a socially or environmentally responsible consumer segment, marketing needs to develop a related brand image. For instance, consumers might think of a product as 'eco-friendly', 'fair', or 'organic', representing a sustainability brand image.

Positioning
practices determine how targeted customer segments will be served by developing a unique value proposition

Instead of just positioning themselves in an existing segment, **marketing management could also develop**, shape, and grow segments in order to create a new or a larger market to position their offers in. This way, positioning does not mean identifying existing segments that fit, but generating a desired segment that fits the offer. In the ethics, responsibility, and sustainability context particularly, you might want to develop the 'goodness' of a segment to make it receptive for your 'good' offer, rather than just 'positioning' it in a ready-made segment. Such market development would mean marketing sustainable consumption involving your offers to customers in a segment currently not consuming sustainably.

Once a position has been identified, the marketing management task becomes fine tuning the positioning Ps of the marketing mix so that together they deliver the unique value proposition. Positioning of an offer in the targeted marketing segment requires a set of interrelated practices. These practices are often described as the positioning 'Ps', together forming the marketing mix. There are several different frameworks of the **marketing mix** with different underlying uses and assumptions (see Figure 18.5), typically distinguished by the number and type of Ps each has.

Market development
aims to transform non-buying customers in a segment to buying customers

Marketing mix
the backbone of positioning and comes in different versions of 4, 7, or 8 Ps for different areas of application

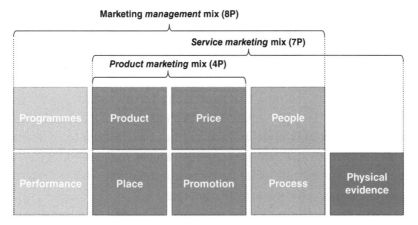

FIGURE 18.5 Versions of the marketing mix and their distinct Ps

1. The ***product* marketing mix (4Ps)** was devised in the 1960s when firms tended to sell products rather than services and when customer service was not widely embraced [39]. These 4Ps include product, price, promotion, and place.

2. The ***services* marketing mix (7Ps)** originated in 1981 when three Ps were added to do justice to the rising importance of services [40]. This 'service mix' originally included participants, physical evidence, and processes [40]. 'Participants' was later updated to 'people'. The 7Ps facilitate the definition and review of issues, which

Branded waste relates to the marketing P of 'Physical evidence', in this case generating negative brand awareness.

impact on product and service marketing. An alternative to the services marketing Ps are the 4 Cs of service marketing (customer solutions, cost, convenience, and communication).

3.   The **marketing *management* mix (8Ps)** [41] serves to create a closer connection between marketing inside and outside the company. Such a holistic marketing management perspective understands marketing as integrated into every part of business management as opposed to seeing marketing as a standalone business unit within a firm. All the departments in the firm work together to produce a unified and confident

brand image in the customer's mind. Marketing is the responsibility of everyone in the firm, not just people in the marketing department [42]. It adds the Ps of performance and programmes.

'GOOD' MARKETING IN SOCIETY AND FOR THE PLANET

Marketing system
facilitates the exchange of goods and services between production and consumption

Marketing systems, systems that are the foundation of growth, may be seen to facilitate a tremendous increase of well-being through increased individual income – more food, better health provision, more resources for individual fulfilment. At the same time, the availability of resources that exceed fundamental needs do have negative effects in terms of promoting the collective use of environmental resources that exceed the Earth's capacity by 75 per cent (see Chapter 5). It may well create societal tensions – for instance, through the promotion of gaming consoles that are fun for children to play with, but might cause difficult situations for parents. Parents may feel obliged to buy a console to allow their child social participation (gaming with friends) despite this being challenging for the family's finances.

The field of macro-marketing is concerned with the marketing system's role in society, and society's role on the planet [43]. As illustrated in Table 18.1, there are two fundamental approaches to understanding these relationships [44, 45]:

The content throughout this chapter has been related to both developmental and critical perspectives on marketing. The underlying motivation is to make sure both to use marketing's strength for good, and also to rethink the parts of marketing that are fundamentally bad and require transformation. The following sections have elements of both approaches. For instance, sustainability marketing is critical in the sense that it rules out marketing practices that

TABLE 18.1 Views on the role of marketing in society and on the planet

	Developmental school	Critical school
View of marketing system	Marketing systems can be important parts of the solution to the precarious human condition.	Marketing systems are part of the problems causing the precarious human condition.
View of consumption	Problems can be solved through more consumption.	Problems are caused by bad consumption.
Key dynamics	Marketing drives socio-economic development and the efficient satisfaction of consumer needs by matching supply and demand.	Marketing leads to destructive consumption patterns, including socially exploitative consumption and environmentally unsustainable overconsumption.
Conditions for a functioning system	Develop institutions that help to construct and control a marketing system that is good for society and the planet.	Markets and the 'normal' marketing systems cannot be sustainable, implying that a functioning system has to be one that is fundamentally different.
Implied actions	Work the paradigm: work within the current system of marketing, improve lives, solve problems, and foster sustainable lifestyles.	Transform the paradigm: engage in reflexive practice and think about what could be changed in the system, how and where.
Implications for marketers	Use marketing practices as a force for good – for instance, design a cause-related marketing campaign to raise funds for good social and environmental causes, or use marketing as a tool to promote the consumption of organic products.	Transform the system, one marketing practice at a time – for instance, by using alternative practices like 'demarketing', or reimagine marketing practices that can reinforce radical alternative lifestyles like LOVOS.

SOURCE: Adapted from [44]

promote unsustainable consumption. Marketing ethics work within the current system by institutionalizing moral rules for how they can produce a 'good' system. The behaviour change facilitated through social marketing could fit into both schools. It could be used to create 'good' consumption behaviours that can be addressed by good marketing in the current system. Alternatively, social marketing could be used 'subversively', to help people reduce consumption and 'exit' the marketing system in the critical school's tradition.

We will now briefly discuss four main marketing frameworks related to ethics, responsibility, and sustainability. Each of these tools is characterized by different intended outcomes of the marketing process. The intended outcome of social marketing, for instance, is a change in a stakeholder's behaviour, while cause-related marketing usually aims at increasing sales revenues.

MARKETING ETHICS

Moral issues in marketing are many, ranging from the promotion of unhealthy consumption and irresponsible marketing to vulnerable groups, deceptive marketing communications, excluding fringe groups, promoting stereotypes, and excluding segments of society from consumption opportunities. The American Marketing Association (AMA) suggests the following ethical norms for professional marketers [6]:

1. **Do no harm**. This means consciously avoiding harmful actions or omissions by embodying high ethical standards and adhering to all applicable laws and regulations in the choices we make.

2. **Foster trust in the marketing system**. This means striving for good faith and fair dealing so as to contribute towards the efficacy of the exchange process as well as avoiding deception in product design, pricing, communication, and delivery of distribution.

3. **Embrace ethical values**. This means building relationships and enhancing consumer confidence in the integrity of marketing by affirming these core values: honesty, responsibility, fairness, respect, transparency, and citizenship.

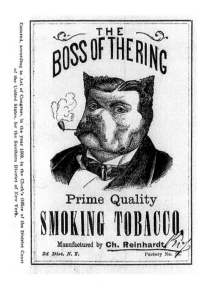

This antique advertisement is an excellent example of marketing's long history of ethical issues like promoting gender stereotypes and unhealthy consumption.

'The Boss of the Ring' by Double--M is licensed under CC BY 2.

According to the AMA, 'values also serve as the criteria for evaluating our own personal actions and the actions of others', implying that marketers should also hold each other responsible for complying with these ethical principles. The principles establish a moral code for 'good conduct' for marketing professionals, which is introduced at greater depth in Table 18.2 [6]. Salient moral issues and corresponding ethical judgements (see Chapter 3) may differ considerably across locations and industries, and this is documented in varieties of industry guides like one from the extractives industry, and local marketing ethics codes like one from the UK Chartered Institute of Marketing[69].

CAUSE-RELATED MARKETING (CRM)

The relationship between a cause and marketing activities can be established in different forms. We

Cause-related marketing (CRM) the promotion of a product by linking its sales with the contribution to a good cause

will discuss three types of **CRM**, the traditional product + cause programme, product as cause, and cause branding.

PRODUCT+CAUSE MARKETING

The traditional donation-based CRM is to channel a certain part of a product's sales revenue to a donation. For instance, in arguably the first ever documented

TABLE 18.2 Professional ethical norms of the American Marketing Association

Value	Honesty	Responsibility	Fairness	Respect	Transparency	Citizenship
Definition	Be forthright in dealings with customers and stakeholders.	Accept the consequences of our marketing decisions and strategies.	Balance justly the needs of the buyer with the interests of the seller.	Acknowledge the basic human dignity of all stakeholders.	Create a spirit of openness in marketing operations.	Fulfil the economic, legal, philanthropic and societal responsibilities that serve stakeholders.
Behaviours	– Strive to be truthful in all situations and at all times. – Offer products of value that do what we claim in our communications. – Stand behind our products if they fail to deliver their claimed benefit. – Honour our explicit and implicit commitments and promises.	– Strive to serve the needs of customers. – Avoid using coercion with all stakeholders. – Acknowledge the social obligations to stakeholders that come with increased marketing and economic power. – Recognize our special commitments to vulnerable market segments such as children, seniors, the economically impoverished, market illiterates and others who may be substantially disadvantaged. – Consider environmental stewardship in our decision-making.	– Represent products in a clear way in selling, advertising and other forms of communication; this includes the avoidance of false, misleading and deceptive promotion. – Reject manipulations and sales tactics that harm customer trust. – Refuse to engage in price fixing, predatory pricing, price gauging or 'bait-and-switch' tactics. – Avoid knowing participation in conflicts of interest. – Seek to protect the private information of customers, employees and partners.	– Value individual differences and avoid stereotyping customers or depicting demographic groups (e.g. gender, race, sexual orientation) in a negative or dehumanizing way. – Listen to the needs of customers and make all reasonable efforts to monitor and improve their satisfaction on an ongoing basis. – Make every effort to understand and respectfully treat buyers, suppliers, intermediaries and distributors from all cultures. – Acknowledge the contributions of others, such as consultants, employees, and coworkers, to marketing endeavours. – Treat everyone, including our competitors, as we would wish to be treated.	– Strive to communicate clearly with all constituencies. – Accept constructive criticism from customers and other stakeholders. – Explain and take appropriate action regarding significant product or service risks, component substitutions or other foreseeable eventualities that could affect customers or their perception of the purchase decision. – Disclose list prices and terms of financing as well as available price deals and adjustments.	– Strive to protect the ecological environment in the execution of marketing campaigns. – Give back to the community through volunteerism and charitable donations. – Contribute to the overall betterment of marketing and its reputation. – Urge supply chain members to ensure that trade is fair for all participants, including producers in developing countries.

SOURCE: Adapted from [6]

cause-related marketing campaign, American Express in 1983 donated 1 cent for the renovation of the Statue of Liberty every time customers used their cards and cheques [46]. This traditional type of CRM is probably the most direct link between creating social value and tangible business benefits in the form of revenues, 'to do well by doing good' [47]. Traditional CRM may be technically defined as 'the process of formulating and implementing marketing activities that are characterized by an offer from the firm to contribute a specified amount to a designated cause when customers engage in revenue-providing exchanges that satisfy organizational and individual objectives' [47]. Cause-related marketing is 'a strategic positioning and marketing tool which links a company or brand to a relevant social cause or issue, for mutual benefit' [48]. An important factor when planning cause-related marketing activities is the thematic link between the chosen cause and a company's core business or product. While a close connection brings operational advantages and allows for a more 'natural connection' (e.g. Bombas donating their own product socks), consumers interestingly respond more positively to product-unrelated causes (e.g. Danone making donations for cancer treatment) [49].

PRODUCTS-AS-CAUSE

The traditional type of CRM relates to causes mostly unconnected to the product's characteristics and socio-environmental life-cycle performance. Product-based CRM instead is focusing on causes directly connected to the product's life cycle. Products with improved socio-environmental life-cycle performance, also called sustainable innovation products have a built-in cause relation. The two consumer packaged-goods industry giants P&G and Unilever have both launched a wide variety of sustainable innovation products with mostly environmental life-cycle improvements. Fair-trade products use added social value in the supply chain as a sales argument. Organic products combine a wide variety of different causes such as local production, customer health, and support of sustainable agriculture among others.

CAUSE-BRANDING

Cause-branding is the type of CRM that relates whole brands to a good cause and supports the marketing of all products under the brand umbrella. The high-end products or luxury items market, including brands such as Gucci or IWC, traditionally required differentiated products and expensive items. A study published by the World Wildlife Federation – United Kingdom [50] ranked the world's top luxury companies on their green performance and assessed relevant attitudes in the industry. Their analysis revealed a compelling reason for the top luxury brands to incorporate social and environmental excellence, and to communicate this excellence to consumers in all markets: 'Brand and marketing professionals on both client and agency sides can unlock the latent commercial potential of sustainable luxury brands, provided that they do so in an authentic and systematic way.' Their report concluded with a ten-point plan with an emphasis on communication as one of the points. There is a larger question, however, as to whether luxury brands themselves should even exist, let alone be marketed in the current environment. By definition, such brands and their products are both socially exclusionary, although they might prefer the world 'exclusive' (by price), and generate an enormous negative environmental footprint from creating and satisfying unnecessary wants.

SOCIAL MARKETING

In contrast to cause-related marketing, social marketing is directed at change in a stakeholder's behaviour [51]. **Social marketing** has traditionally been a tool of governments and civil society organizations to promote aspired behaviour patterns, such as not smoking, using condoms, and healthier nutrition. Business marketers can use social marketing to change customers' and employees' behaviour towards responsible behaviour patterns. Figure 18.6 illustrates how the product marketing mix can be applied to achieve behaviour change.

Social marketing
an application of traditional marketing techniques to effect a behaviour change, which benefits the individual or society at large

Product	Price
The behaviour the target audience should adopt; preferably this behaviour is directly observable and offers a solution to a problem.	The behaviour the target audience has to give up to adopt the aspired behaviour; involves intangible costs, such as time, effort, and emotional costs, as well as the tangible costs of realizing the change in behaviour.
Place	**Promotion**
The place of behaviour change should be where the target audience is acting the behaviour to be given up, and where the audience experiences the highest possible aperture to a potential behaviour change.	The marketing promotion of behaviour change involves the communication of the aspired behaviour, throughout manifold audiences (Publics), involving Partnerships, and taking into consideration public Policies.

FIGURE 18.6   The social marketing mix

SOURCE: Adapted from [52]

The difference between commercial marketing and social marketing is that 'the benefits accrue to the individual or society rather than to the marketer's organization … social marketing applies to individuals rather than organizations' [52]. Nevertheless, marketing management can simultaneously change people's behaviour for the better and improve their company's reputation or even tangibly increase sales in a combined social and cause-related marketing campaign. The Volkswagen 'Fun Theory' contest is an iconic example of a social marketing campaign that combines positive behaviour change for health, sustainability, and responsibility, while tangibly changing people's behaviour [53].

Social marketing is often misunderstood as awareness raising. However, increased awareness of the necessity to change behaviour is merely the first step towards behaviour adoption, followed by the consideration, adoption, and maintenance of a new behaviour pattern [52]. Social marketing has to address all stages of behaviour change (see Figure 18.7). It has to be tuned in to the behaviour stage that most of the targeted group are in and then adjust marketing as they progress. Or it could provide marketing activities that have elements applicable to the next step on all of these stages.

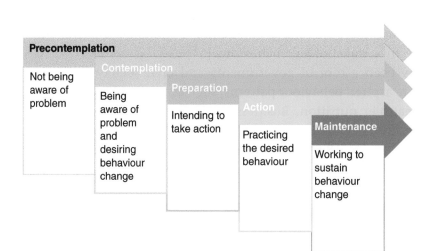

FIGURE 18.7   Stages of behaviour change

SOURCE: Adapted from [54]

SUSTAINABLE MARKETING

Sustainability marketing is marketing directed at the ultimate goal of creating a sustainable production– consumption system, operating within the environmental limits of the planet

Sustainability is a megatrend in marketing [44]. Sustainable or **sustainability marketing** [55, 56] is a combination of elements from the following three marketing traditions [57]:

1. **Green marketing**. Developing and marketing more sustainable products and services while introducing sustainability efforts at the core of the marketing and business process

2. **Social marketing**. Using the power of upstream and downstream marketing interventions to encourage sustainable behaviour.

3. **Critical marketing**. Analysing marketing using a critical theory-based approach to guide marketing practice.

Having grown out of the green marketing tradition, sustainability marketing emphasizes the environmental dimension of sustainability. Therefore, sustainability marketing does not ignore the social and economic dimensions of sustainability, but rather considers them as part of what is necessary for the achievement of environmental sustainability. Sustainability marketing's underlying goal is to connect environmentally sustainable production and consumption, supply, and demand through the market [58]. This way it aims to normalize sustainable behaviour both on the management and consumer sides of the market [59].

Sustainability marketing is guided by the ultimate goal of humanity as a whole consuming sustainably well within the resource limits of our planet. Therefore, sustainability marketing deviates from many of the usual tenets of mainstream marketing:

1. Sustainability marketing is deeply critical of consumption, particularly excessive consumerist tendencies, and of conspicuous consumption (buying products to display status), 'hyper consumerism' (buying goods for non-functional purposes), and recreational shopping practices, leading to 'unnecessary', avoidable environmental impacts: 'Trying to reduce environmental pollution without reducing consumerism is like combatting drug trafficking without reducing the drug addiction … the pandemic of consumerism' [60].

2. While marketing as usual largely reduces consumers to their purchase, sustainability marketing assumes a more 'holistic approach to consumer behaviour' interested in a human being's entire (un)sustainable lifestyle as well as humanity's lifestyles as a species [58]. Sustainability marketing emphasizes the importance of 'making sustainable consumption work' for everyone, even the poorest of the poor [61].

PRINCIPLES OF PROFESSIONAL MARKETING

I.   **Marketing management** revolves around the exchange of organizational offerings and value with varieties of societal stakeholders referred to as customers.

II. **Professional marketing** means proficiently engaging in marketing practices in order to promote healthy consumption while engaging in 'good' conduct.

III. **Foundations** of marketing include the core ideas of marketing such as **duality, relationality, and service**, and its deep roots in the understanding of **consumer behaviour**.

IV. An underlying core process of marketing management is **segmentation, targeting, and positioning (STP)**.

V.   The **marketing mix(es)** (for product marketing, service marketing, and marketing management), consists of the elements, also called **Ps, of marketing:** product, price, place, promotion, people, process, physical evidence, programmes, and performance.

VI.   Approaches to **marketing in society** include the **developmental approach** (marketing is part of the solution) and the **critical approach** (marketing as part of the problem).

VII. Specialized responsible **marketing management** tools and frameworks serving different purposes include **marketing ethics, cause-related marketing, social marketing, and sustainability marketing**.

MANAGEMENT GYM: TRAINING YOUR PROFESSIONAL SIX-PACK

Knowing

1. What connections can you spot between the consumer purchasing behaviour model, the theory of planned behaviour, and stages of behaviour change model?

2. Associate social marketing, sustainability marketing, and cause-related marketing with either critical marketing and/or developmental marketing in a mindmap.

3. Look up the marketing ethics code or code of conduct of a local marketing association or of a company and compare it with the AMA code of ethics.

Thinking

4. Brainstorm to identify ethical dilemmas throughout the marketing management process. Then briefly write down what are ethical dos and don'ts for each dilemma.

5. What core beliefs and practices would need to change and how for marketing to become deeply ethical, responsible, and sustainable?

6. Think about one product of your choice. How could the same need of the product be satisfied through a service, ideally one that is more sustainable?

Acting

7. Prepare a one-page outline of a social marketing campaign for a desired behaviour change of your choice.

8. Construct a list of marketing performance metrics for a marketing management activity of your choice.

9. Prepare an STP (segmentation, targeting, and positioning) infographic for a real or fictitious product or service of your choice.

Interacting

10. Think of three alternative marketing promotion slogans or taglines for a product/service promotion or an organizational branding of your choice. Then talk about the alternatives with five different people, document their comments, and decide which one is the best slogan.

11. Buycott or endorse a company for a reason you have informed yourself well about (you could use an app like 'buycott' for it). Let the company know via social media or in person by visiting one of their branches.

12. Follow and interact (e.g. comment, like) with an (integrated) marketing campaign of your choice through at least five different online media.

Being

13. What kind of consumption style are you most likely to engage in – LOVOS, LOHAS, strategic consumption, boycotting, or buycotting?

14. Do you think you would prefer to work in business-to-business or business-to-consumer marketing? Why?

15. Which one is the worst, and which one the best advertisement you can remember? Why do you think so, and what does that say about your values?

Becoming

16. What kind of world do you want to live in and how could you use the power of your purchasing to help construct that world?

17. Think about a situation where you had the strong intention to do something, but didn't do it after all. What barriers did you encounter and how could you avoid or overcome them next time?

18. Which one of the ethical norms of the American Marketing Association do you find most challenging to comply with, and what could you do to make it easier for yourself?

SOURCE: Adapted from [62]

PIONEER INTERVIEW
PHILIP KOTLER

INTERVIEWED BY OLIVER LAASCH

Philip Kotler has been called the father of modern marketing. Early on, he covered social and cause-related marketing in his standard textbook. He has published stand-alone textbooks on social marketing, and on corporate social responsibility. He focuses on creating a new area of marketing called 'Marketing 3.0', which has many characteristics of what might be considered responsible marketing for a sustainable future.

Marketing 3.0! Marketing has been moving through three stages. Marketing 1.0 involved marketers appealing to the *mind* of their target audience trying to establish the idea that their product was best for the customer. Marketing 2.0 involved marketers moving their appeal to the *heart* of the target customer by adding emotion. Marketing 3.0 involves marketers moving their appeal to the *spirit*, or 'caring quality' of the audience. More members of the middle class are caring about the environment and sustainability and are increasingly able to evaluate which companies have this set of values.

Demarketing consumerism. Our concept of demarketing originally dealt with responding to shortages. For example, when California faced a water shortage, the State ran several campaigns to persuade people and companies to use less water. We believe that demarketing campaigns will increase as we overuse scarce resources and face resource limits to growth. In a city such as Beijing, good quality air is becoming scarce and 9,000 persons needed to be hospitalized because of respiratory problems. The underlying issue is whether we are overselling consumerism, namely that the good life consists of accumulating more and more material goods. I can imagine the startup of campaigns to demarket our current consumerist lifestyle. These campaigns will be fought by business but I favour 'airing' the issue of how much consumption the Earth can support.

Reconsidering the purpose of a company through cause marketing. I am in favour of companies offering consumers a 'cause' incentive to buy their products. Cause marketing received its big boost when American Express offered to donate money to help rebuild the Statue of Liberty in proportion to how much people charged their American Express card instead of competitor's credit cards in paying for their purchases. I like the shoe company that will give

(Continued)

a pair of shoes to a poor person somewhere in the world when you buy a pair of their shoes. Even though some 'greenwashing' is occurring, where the effort is more about image-making than really caring about the cause, I think most of it is sincere and leads competitors to reconsider their purpose as a company and what they can contribute to the social good.

QUESTIONS

1. How would you connect Marketing **1.0, 2.0,** and **3.0** to the aspects we discussed about the transformation of the marketing definition and of the marketing worldview over time?

2. Do you think demarketing consumerism could work and possibly even save the planet from our overconsumption? Is it possible? Why? Why not?

3. Do you share Philip's enthusiasm for cause-related marketing?

PROFESSIONAL PROFILE
ADELA METLICKA LUSTYKOVA

Hi, my name is Adela and I am a Marketing and PR specialist at Chládek *a* Tintěra, Inc., a construction company with a universal production schedule operating in the Czech market.

Responsibilities and activities. I am responsible for treating brand, reputation and the visual face of the company (including paperback presentations, business cards, e-commerce, and CSR activities), active sales role in key sales opportunities, direct B2B communication, fair representative, managing CSR activities. Typical activities are to seek potential business partners and ventures with the target of private investors mainly, direct communication with investors,

(Continued)

partners, and customers, making reference sheets and other graphic presentation materials, development of online presentations.

Integrated marketing and stakeholder communication. External stakeholder communication is a topic that is very important for my company. For a proper marketing communication, we are very sensitive about building close relationships with investors, business partners and governmental organizations. In this case effective communication must be applied and creating positive awareness shows a part of our brand image. That is also connected to the marketing mix that we shape in a responsible manner. But firstly, we care about proper internal communication that must be effective. Otherwise the further processes are not.

Don't invite disaster! Even though I have heard a lot that CSR is only another trend and marketing fad, I do believe that when responsibility in all terms is not settled in the key governing documents as well as the strategy of the company, or at least at the consciousness of the top management and the owners, it sooner or later causes a disaster. For this reason I would recommend not trying to engage with any CSR topics when there is no belief in that. Also, it is important to clarify that CSR is not just a part of marketing but should be integrated within the whole company, across all departments, with the support of the top management, owners, and other employees.

The tricky case of 'construction'. The construction business is a completely different case. Behaving responsibly reflects mainly the good intentions of the owners. Even an irresponsible company may stay in the market for a long time. In some cases I see is it hard to find strong arguments for why the construction company should be responsible.

QUESTIONS

1. How is it that marketing, public relations, and social responsibility are integrated in Adela's job?

2. What can we learn from Adela about integrative marketing communication? How is what Adela does in her job 'integrative'?

3. Connecting to Adela's statement about the construction industry, how do you think industry characteristics may influence responsible marketing management?

❝ TRUE STORY
HAVOC IN MARKETING HEAVEN

EDITED BY ALEXANDRA LEONOR BARRUETA SACKSTEDER AND JUDY NAGY

Hi there. My name is Toby and I work in the marketing department at my organization's headquarters. I'm very proud of my accomplishments in this department as I was recruited from the US where I was a brand manager for a clothing company. For the past two years I've been growing the marketing department and we now have five category groups: paint and frames, scrapbooking, yarn and thread, baking, and party themes. I also incorporated a full graphic design team and two translators into the department. I hope to become vice-president one day and because of this I am aware that I have to make a strong mark in this family business. Everything was going according to plan … until I hired Amelie.

The big mistake. Eight months ago I was desperate for help. As director of marketing I needed a right-hand person, someone who could organize all the operations of the marketing department. Amelie's resume was brought to me by the people manager, who was excited about Amelie's experience and credentials. She had an MBA, several years of experience running her own marketing agency, had worked for a large Canadian multinational in the same industry and could speak both English and French fluently.

I met with Amelie and was impressed. She was a bit bossy and overconfident and her salary expectations were quite high, but I knew she could handle the job easily and I needed someone immediately. I hired her on the spot. She was up to date on trends and competitive forces and

(Continued)

she was helpful in organizing the marketing team. In fact, it was her idea to centralize the product categories so that the marketing operations could function more seamlessly.

Too good to be true? Soon after Amelie began working for me, the senior executives began to notice her progress. The brand managers called her online portal for marketing operations 'brilliant' and the graphic designers were relieved that everything was finally running more smoothly, and everything seemed to be going wonderfully.

That's when Bertil, one of the original founders of the company, who now sat as an honorary chairman at the company meetings, boomed, 'Amelie, you are doing a great job!' He pointed to me and said, 'We can send this guy to our Eastern Europe branch! Not much going on there so he can sit back and let everyone else work!' Everyone laughed but I felt it in the pit of my stomach.

I met with my friend Andy from the paint and frames product group. We got along well and often had lunch together. I began to think that it would have been a better idea to have Andy on board as marketing operations manager instead of Amelie. We had a lot in common and even though Andy was younger and less experienced, I liked the idea of being able to train him from the ground up. However, Amelie was getting the job done and I couldn't just replace her.

A crack in the paint. Over the next few weeks, I watched Amelie very closely. I noticed that she wasn't as perfect as everyone thought. She really dropped the ball on some promotional items by not double checking the spelling and they had been printed with spelling mistakes. She was working on a corporate video project at the time and had written a script and hired videographers to film employees saying a line of a corporate mission story, which was taking up a lot of her time.

On several occasions, my employees told me they couldn't find Amelie after lunch to discuss important matters with her. She had been enjoying the company yoga programme during lunchtime and taking advantage of the programme to come back late, affecting the entire department's productivity. I had no choice but to file a complaint with HR as it was more than one employee with the same issue. I tried to explain to Amelie that it was affecting her colleagues and tried to come up with suggestions to fix the problem: shorter showers or skipping them altogether as the type of yoga taught didn't cause people to sweat that much.

To relieve some of her pressure and allow her time to get her work done I discontinued my weekly meetings with her. She had spent so much time in the yoga programme and with work that she hadn't really established a connection with the other employees and became quiet and sullen around everyone. Shortly after she began to have 'migraines', which affected her work performance.

The end. Just before Christmas, I realized that the job wasn't working out and so I called a meeting with Amelie and HR and informed her that her performance just wasn't cutting it. She was making too many mistakes at the company's expense and we couldn't afford to keep correcting them. Amelie became defensive and claimed that her performance had been good

(Continued)

so I reminded her of the times I had been disappointed in her work despite the fact that in Quebec, we are not legally obligated to provide a reason for termination as she'd been working with us for less than a year.

The company was offering her a generous $5,000 package to ease her transition; all she had to do was sign. Amelie became agitated and refused to sign the paper, stating that she first had to talk to an attorney. She then walked out of the room, cleared her desk and left the building.

QUESTIONS

1. This story might sound like one you would expect to find in the people management or leadership context. How is this a story of marketing management? How do marketing management and people management connect here?

2. What can we learn from the story about the hierarchies, organizational structures, and internal practices of marketing management?

3. Is there anything you would have done differently if you had been in Toby's shoes?

DIGGING DEEPER: B2B VERSUS B2C MARKETING

The business-to-business (B2B) market consists of 'all the organisations that acquire goods and services used in the production of other products or services that are sold, rented or supplied to others. Any firm that supplies components for products is in the business-to-business marketplace' [65]

Business-to-business (B2B) marketing [63, 64] is different from business-to-consumer (B2C) marketing primarily due to the transaction process between the buyer and seller. B2B transactions are often more complicated than B2C transactions. Generally, they involve more people, more decision makers, and more expenditure. Buyers of B2B products and services often need to deliver a return on investment for their purchase, highlighting the more complex nature of B2B purchases.

Examples of industries that rely heavily on the B2B market include banking, energy, communication, technology, and finance [65]. Some firms in the top 20 of all B2B firms include Microsoft, Wells Fargo, Accenture, and ExxonMobil [66]. Due to increased cooperation and disruption, the difference between B2B and B2C firms is blurred. For example, the rise of the Internet of Things and autonomous cars has sped up collaboration. Additionally, cloud computing has disrupted traditional workplace

IT infrastructure with the utilization of consumer devices [66]. B2B marketing is crucial for sustainability marketing.

Table 18.3 shows the general differences between B2B and B2C **buying** behaviours. The widespread use of personal selling in B2B markets can be understood by observing the common market structure and buying behaviour characteristics, as opposed to the predominant use of advertising in B2C markets [63]. In B2B transactions, demand is concentrated in the hands of a few dominant buyers (market structure) who utilize their teams of professional buyers (buying behaviour), whereas in consumer markets, demand is generally more widely scattered throughout the buying public (market structure) and buyers are not skilled professionals (buying behaviour). Personal selling is therefore typical in B2B settings (strong demand, influential buyers, skilled professionals) primarily because organizational buyers seek an articulate response tailored to their needs. The cost of a sales executive is justified by the potential high order values, whereas in B2C markets (scattered demand, no influential buyers) advertising is more applicable due to the typically low value of each transaction [63]. Despite this, it is easier to tailor messages to individual customer needs with modern IT and customer relationship management software tools [67]. Such tools engender convergence between B2B and B2C markets.

Organizational buying (B2B) is centred on 'the decision making process by which formal organisations establish the need for purchased products and services, and identify, evaluate and choose among alternative brands and suppliers' [65]

TABLE 18.3 Salient differences in B2B and B2C marketing and buying

B2B	B2C
Fewer, larger buyers	Many individual buyers
Multiple sales calls	Few or no sales calls
Direct purchasing	Purchasing can be direct (website, high street shops) or indirect (e.g. via wholesalers, intermediaries, agents, or brokers).
Professional purchasing for the firm	Purchasing is carried out by individuals for personal use
Inelastic demand (when the quantity demanded of the product changes very little when its price fluctuates)	Elastic demand (when the quantity demanded of the product changes drastically when the price increases or decreases)
Derived demand – demand for a commodity, service, etc., which is a consequence of the demand for something else, e.g. demand for houses creates demand for cement, iron, and wood, etc.	Final demand – the individual makes a purchase for personal use
Geographically concentrated buyers	Buyers are scattered throughout the public
Close supplier–customer relationships. Customers are likely to know the supplier well	Distant supplier–customer relationships. Customers will not personally know the suppliers
The organizational buying/decision-making process is generally more complex	The buying/decision-making process is generally simpler and more straightforward. The buyer will usually make the decision themselves using their own finances

A core difference mentioned as the last point in Table 18.4 is that the B2B buying decision-making context is more complex. Salient points to be considered relate to the considerations presented in Table 18.3.

TABLE 18.4   Checklist for analysing a B2B buying situation

How many decisions are to be made?	What's the buying situation?	Who are the multiple people involved in the buying decision?
▶ Depends on the complexity of the problem to be solved	▶ Rebuy	▶ Which person identifies that the business needs the product/service?
▶ Newness of the buying requirement	▶ Modified rebuy	▶ Who makes the decision to pay?
▶ Number of people involved	▶ New task	▶ Who will collect it and integrate it into the firm?
▶ Time required		

Due to these unique aspects of B2B marketing in comparison to B2C marketing, particularly the close long-term relationship between marketers and buyers allows for the advancements of impactful and transformative sustainability marketing practices [68].

POINTERS

You could dig deeper into B2B marketing – for instance, by looking up the sources mentioned in this text, or by using the text as a basis for brainstorming all the further ways B2B and B2C marketing are distinct. You could also reflect on the different roles that ethics, responsibility, and sustainability play in B2B and B2C.

WORKSHEET

HOLISTIC HUMANISTIC MARKETING

Marketing management activities	Mind — Marketing through rational advantages	Heart — Marketing by evoking emotions	Spirit — Marketing by connecting to something bigger

POINTERS

The purpose of this matrix is to support the design of holistic marketing activities that connect to the whole human being, rationally, emotionally, and spiritually. Activities to be planned could be related to product or service offers, branding initiatives, or a promotional campaign.

REFERENCES

1. Schept K. Brandz top 100 most valuable brands 2020. London: Brandz & Kantar, 2020.
2. Bombas. About us. https://bombas.com/pages/about-us Published 2020. Accessed July 10 2020.
3. Leighton M. Bombas makes the best socks we've ever worn: The brand has also donated over 33 million pairs to homeless shelters to date. www.businessinsider.com/bombas-socks-review?r=US&IR=T Published 2020. Accessed July 10 2020.
4. Segran E. Getting startups fired up about social justice: One sock at a time. https://www.fastcompany.com/40445016/how-one-sock-brand-is-helping-startups-step-up-their-social-good-game Published 2017. Accessed July 10 2020.
5. AMA. Codes of conduct: AMA statement of ethics. www.ama.org/codes-of-conduct Published 2020. Accessed July 31 2020.
6. Campaign. Birth of marketing in the 1930s. www.campaignlive.co.uk/article/birth-marketing-1930s/637105?src_site=marketingmagazine Published 2007. Accessed August 2 2020.
7. Bartels R. *The history of marketing thought* (2nd edn). Columbus: Grid, 1988.
8. Hollander SC, Rassuli KM, Jones DB, Dix LF. Periodization in marketing history. *Journal of Macromarketing*. 2005, 25(1): 32–41.
9. American Association of Marketing. Definition of marketing. http://wwwmarketingpowercom/AboutAMA/Pages/DefinitionofMarketingaspx?sq=definition Published 2013.
10. Hennig-Thurau T, Hansen U. Relationship marketing: Some reflections on the state-of-the-art of the relational concept. In: *Relationship marketing*. Heidelberg: Springer, 2000: 3–27.
11. Zeithaml VA, Bitner MJ, Gremler DD. *Services marketing: Integrating customer focus across the firm*. New York: McGraw-Hill Education, 2018.
12. Vargo SL, Lusch RF. Evolving to a new dominant logic for marketing. *Journal of Marketing*. 2004, 68(1): 1–17.
13. Zeithaml VA, Parasuraman A, Berry LL. Problems and strategies in services marketing. *Journal of Marketing*. 1985, 49(2): 33–46.
14. Edgett S, Parkinson S. Marketing for service industries: A review. *Service Industries Journal*. 1993, 13(3): 19–39.
15. Solomon M, Russell-Bennett R, Previte J. *Consumer behaviour.* Frenchs Forest: Pearson Higher Education AU, 2012.
16. Reid C. U.K. government rolls out £50 'Fix Your Bike' voucher scheme. www.forbes.com/sites/carltonreid/2020/06/23/uk-government-rolls-out-50-fix-your-bike-voucher-scheme-one-month-after-first-announcing-it/#3882c8205448 Published 2020. Accessed August 2 2020.
17. Kotler P, Armstrong G. *Principles of marketing.* Upper Saddle River, NJ: Prentice Hall, 2006.
18. Rook DW. The buying impulse. *Journal of Consumer Research.* 1987, 14(2): 189–199.
19. Stern H. The significance of impulse buying today. *Journal of Marketing.* 1962, 26(2): 59–62.
20. Blake J. Overcoming the 'value-action gap' in environmental policy: Tensions between national policy and local experience. *Local Environment.* 1999, 4(3): 257–278.
21. Vermeir I, Verbeke W. Sustainable food consumption: Exploring the consumer 'attitude–behavioral intention' gap. *Journal of Agricultural and Environmental Ethics.* 2006, 19(2): 169–194.
22. Ajzen I. The theory of planned behavior. *Organizational Behavior and Human Decision Processes.* 1991, 50(2): 179–211.
23. Ajzen I. From intentions to actions: A theory of planned behavior. In: *Action control.* Heidelberg: Springer, 1985: 11–39.
24. Fennis BM, Adriaanse MA, Stroebe W, Pol B. Bridging the intention–behavior gap: Inducing implementation intentions through persuasive appeals. *Journal of Consumer Psychology.* 2011, 21(3): 302–311.
25. Bombas. Giving back. https://bombas.com/pages/giving-back Published 2020. Accessed August 2 2020.
26. Prahalad CK. *The fortune at the bottom of the pyramid.* Upper Saddle River, NJ: Pearson, 2004.

27. Kotler P. Marketing management: Analysis, planning, implementation and control. Upper Saddle River, NJ: Prentice Hall, 1997.
28. Dolnicar S, Matus K. Are green tourists a managerially useful target segment? *Journal of Hospitality & Leisure Marketing.* 2008, 17(3–4): 314–334.
29. Kotler P. *Marketing management* (1st edn). Englewood Cliffs: Prentice Hall, 1967.
30. Hustad TP, Pessemier EA. Will the real consumer activist please stand up: An examination of consumers' opinions about marketing practices. *Journal of Marketing Research.* 1973, 10(3): 319–324.
31. Portwood-Stacer L. Anti-consumption as tactical resistance: Anarchists, subculture, and activist strategy. *Journal of Consumer Culture.* 2012, 12(1): 87–105.
32. Littler J. Radical consumption: Shopping for change in contemporary culture. London: McGraw-Hill, 2008.
33. Lappé FM, Lappé A. *Hope's edge: The next diet for a small planet.* New York: Tarcher/ Penguin, 2002.
34. BBC. Facebook to tag 'harmful' posts as boycott widens. www.bbc.co.uk/news/ business-53196487 Published 2020. Accessed August 2 2020.
35. Payne A, Frow P, Eggert A. The customer value proposition: Evolution, development, and application in marketing. *Journal of the Academy of Marketing Science.* 2017, 45(4): 467–489.
36. Frow P, Payne A. A stakeholder perspective of the value proposition concept. *European Journal of Marketing.* 2011, 45(1–2): 223–240.
37. Osterwalder A, Pigneur Y, Bernarda G, Smith A. *Value proposition design: How to create products and services customers want.* Chichester: Wiley, 2014.
38. Moosmayer DC, Abdulrahman MD-A, Subramanian N, Bergkvist L. Strategic and operational remanufacturing mental models. *International Journal of Operations & Production Management.* 2020, 40(2): 173–195.
39. McCarthy EJ. *Basic marketing.* Homewood, IL: Richard D. Irwin, 1964.
49. Booms BH, Bitner MJ. Marketing strategies and organization structures for service firms. In: Donnelly JH, George WR, ed. *Marketing of services.* Chicago: American Marketing Association, 1981: 47–51.
41. Kotler P, Keller KL. *Marketing management* (15th edn). Harlow: Pearson, 2016.
42. Keller KL, Kotler P. Holistic marketing. In: Sheth JN, Sisodia RS, eds. *Does marketing need reform? Fresh perspectives on the future.* Armonk, NY: Sharpe, 2015: 300–305.
43. Hunt S. Macromarketing as a multidimensional concept. *Journal of Macromarketing.* 1981, 1(1): 7–8.
44. Mittelstaedt JD, Shultz CJ, Kilbourne WE, Peterson M. Sustainability as megatrend: Two schools of macromarketing thought. *Journal of Macromarketing.* 2014, 34(3): 253–264.
45. Tadajewski M, Brownlie DT. *Critical marketing: Contemporary issues in marketing.* Chichester: Wiley, 2008.
46. Gottlieb, M. Cashing in on a higher cause. *New York Times.* www.nytimes. com/1986/07/06/business/cashing-in-on-higher-cause.html Published 1986. Last accessed August 22 2023.
47. Varadarajan PR, Menon A. Cause-related marketing: A coalignment of marketing strategy and corporate philanthropy. *Journal of Marketing.* 1988, 52(3): 58–74.
48. Pringle H, Thompson M. *How cause-related marketing builds brands.* Chichester: John Wiley & Sons, 1999.
49. Moosmayer DC, Fuljahn A. Corporate motive and fit in cause related marketing. *Journal of Product & Brand Management.* 2013, 22(3): 200–207.
50. Bendell J, Kleanthous A. Deeper luxury. *World Wildlife Federation-UK.* https://de.scribd. com/doc/207085714/Deeper-Luxury-Report# Published 2007. Accessed September 14 2023.
51. Armstrong G, Kotler P. *Marketing: An introduction.* Upper Saddle River, NJ: Pearson Education, 2009.
52. Weinreich NK. *Hands-on social marketing: A step-by-step guide to designing change for good.* Thousand Oaks, CA: Sage, 2011.
53. The Fun Theory. www.thefuntheory.com Published 2010. Last accessed August 22 2023.
54. DiClemente CC, Prochaska JO. Toward a comprehensive, transtheoretical model of change: Stages of change and addictive behaviors. In: Miller WR, Heather N, eds. *Applied clinical psychology: Treating addictive behaviors.* New York: Plenum Press, 1998.

55. Belz F-M, Peattie K. *Sustainability marketing.* Hoboken, NJ: John Wiley & Sons, 2009.

56. McDonagh P, Prothero A. Sustainability marketing research: Past, present and future. *Journal of Marketing Management.* 2014, 30(11–12): 1186–1219.

57. Gordon R, Carrigan M, Hastings G. A framework for sustainable marketing. *Marketing Theory.* 2011, 11(2): 143–163.

58. Peattie K, Belz F-M. Sustainability marketing: An innovative conception of marketing. *Marketing Review St Gallen.* 2010, 27(5): 8–15.

59. Rettie R, Burchell K, Riley D. Normalising green behaviours: A new approach to sustainability marketing. *Journal of Marketing Management.* 2012, 28(3–4): 420–444.

60. Majfud J. The pandemic of consumerism. *UN Chronicle.* 2009, 46(3–4): 89–90.

61. Kirchgeorg M, Winn MI. Sustainability marketing for the poorest of the poor. *Business Strategy and the Environment.* 2006, 15(3): 171–184.

62. Laasch, O., Moosmayer, D., & Antonacopoulou, E. P. (2023). The interdisciplinary responsible management competence framework: An integrative review of ethics, responsibility, and sustainability competences. *Journal of Business Ethics, 187,* 733–757.

63. Brennan R, Canning L, McDowell R. *Business-to-business marketing.* London: Sage, 2020.

64. Ellis N. *Business to business marketing: Relationships, networks and strategies.* Oxford: Oxford University Press, 2010.

65. Kotler PT. *Marketing management.* Harlow: Pearson, 2019.

66. Kantar M-B. Brands continue to blur border dividing B2B, B2C. www.brandz.com/articlenew/brands-continue-to-blur-border-dividing-b2b-b2c-1753 Published 2020. Accessed July 24 2020.

67. Pass MW, Evans KR, Schlacter JL. Sales force involvement in CRM information systems: Participation, support, and focus. *Journal of Personal Selling & Sales Management.* 2004, 24(3): 229–234.

68. Sharma A, Iyer GR, Mehrotra A, Krishnan R. Sustainability and business-to-business marketing: A framework and implications. *Industrial Marketing Management.* 2010, 39(3): 330–341.

69. https://eiti.org/guide-implementing-eiti-standard and https://www.cim.co.uk/media/7393/cim-code-of-professional-conduct-february-2020.pdf

CHAPTER 19

PEOPLE MANAGEMENT

ROGER N. CONAWAY, ELAINE COHEN
AND OLIVER LAASCH

LEARNING GOALS

1. Get to know five main areas of the people management process
2. Explore the main tools of professional people management
3. Manage people from an ethical, responsible, and sustainable perspective
4. Understand the role of professional people management

STUNNING FACT

'In the US and UK, almost two thirds of employees say efforts by business to tackle environmental and societal challenges do not go far enough ... Nearly half of employees say they would consider resigning if the company's values don't align with their own, even in these difficult economic times. A third of employees say they have already resigned for this reason ... an era of conscious quitting' [1].

SPOTLIGHT

SPOTLIGHT

OPEN HIRING® AT GREYSTON BAKERY

OLIVER LAASCH, REUT LIVNE-TARANDACH, MICHAEL PIRSON

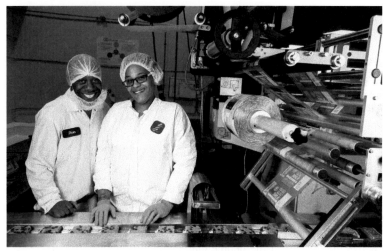

Courtesy of Greyston

Imagine companies were hiring anyone willing to work – no questions asked. This innovative personnel management practice is called open hiring. It was pioneered and perfected at Greyston Bakery. 'We don't hire people to bake brownies. We bake brownies to hire people' is their motto.

Open hiring has had an immense positive social impact on the challenged community of Yonkers close to New York City, Greyston's home turf. Open hiring provides a stepping-stone for a variety of people into work–life who find themselves excluded otherwise, in a neighbourhood where one third of residents live below the poverty line. Greyston's valued employees are people of all colours, of all faiths, sexual orientations, immigrants and refugees, those living in poverty or who have spent time in prison, and anyone else who has faced barriers to employment, including single parents or people with long gaps in their work history.

(Continued)

Courtesy of Greyston

Open hiring also has deep implications for how personnel management beyond hiring practices is performed. This includes social worker support for employees on site, and an unusual focus on 'offboarding' successful employees to find jobs elsewhere, so that more new hirees can be accepted to fill their place. As outlandish as this might sound in comparison to 'normal' personnel management, similar practices related to inclusion and diversity management have become a normal part of contemporary personnel management.

One might be tempted to assume that a company with such a strong focus on the social impact of their professional management practices might be less geared towards economic recognition. However, Greyston is at the top of its commercial bakery game. Its corporate customers include, among others, Whole Foods, Ben & Jerry's, and Delta Airlines. Anecdotal evidence points at the differentiation gained through open hiring as a significant success factor in Greyston's commercial relationships [2] (see also Case Study Zone VI).

PROFESSIONAL PEOPLE MANAGEMENT

> Human resource development (HRD) is increasingly expected to play a facilitative role in corporate social responsibility (CSR), sustainability, and ethics in organizations. However, it is criticized for moving away from its mission to advocate humanistic values in organizations to totally embracing a short-term business agenda [3].

This introductory quote expresses the interesting tension that people management professionals face on a daily basis. On the one hand, they can make a major contribution to ethics, responsibility, and sustainability through their work. On the other hand, their work is also meant to make humans 'resources' for the achievement of business goals, human resources or in short, HR. From a humanistic perspective, doing so means 'instrumentalizing' human beings as mere resources for production.

People management
practices dealing with the management of and management for people employed by an organization

It is for this very reason that throughout this chapter we refer to the less common term **people management** (PM). Language matters as it creates and recreates realities, and we have decided not to further contribute to the recreation of the term human *resources*. We believe 'using' people as resources too often justifies irresponsible practices like pressuring people into working overtime to achieve business goals, or to compromise on workplace safety for the sake of saving some costs.

PM–PM symbiosis
refers to the mutually reinforcing relationship in which professional management (PM) needs employees' engagement, and similarly, people management (PM) benefits from professional management activities with employees as a main group of stakeholders

Professional people management differs from traditional perspectives of PM, in particular that of strategic human 'resources' management, because of its focus on outcomes of decisions on people, society, and the environment, and not just on business outcomes related to efficiency and growth. Traditional perspectives of PM performance seek more efficient management, organizational development, and economic growth. Professional PM may seek these similar goals, but differs because it also integrates ethics, responsibility, and sustainability throughout the employee life cycle from start to end of their employment.

We will first discuss the relationship between people management and professional management. Then, by examining five traditional core areas of PM practices, we will show how enhanced value for business, employees and society in general is delivered through a professional PM approach (see Figure 19.1).

The goal of professional PM in any organization is to provide tools and processes, which enable and support the embedding of a responsibility culture and practices at all levels in the organization. This is done by both supporting professional management objectives and by performing the PM function in a responsible way. This is a dual role: on the one hand, PM must understand how the organization implements social responsibility and provides appropriate

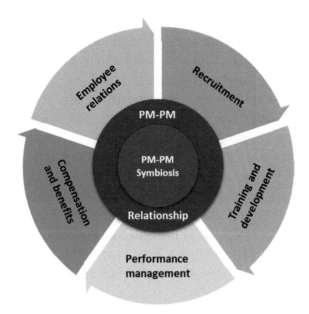

FIGURE 19.1 Professional people management practices

PM solutions; on the other hand, PM must understand the wider implications of PM actions on wider stakeholders and society.

1. First, people management must **support professional management objectives**. Most organizations realize that the achievement of ethics, responsibility, and sustainability relies on the collaboration of employees in a wide range of practices. Examples are reducing energy consumption in offices, recycling of waste, reducing business travel and adopting virtual tools for meetings, and using alternative transportation to get to and from work. In addition, companies that market 'green' products need employees who are capable and competent to engage with customers in the environmental responsibility arena.

2. Second, people management must implement responsibility in its own department and **perform PM responsibly**. Professional management begins at home and the PM function has a role in ensuring that employees are treated responsibly in order that they will be able to perform their roles and engage with each other and external stakeholders in a responsible way. PM policies can affect the quality of employees' lives – for example, in relation to managing stress, health and wellness, work–life balance, long-term skill development and employability, and much more. The Digging Deeper section at the end of this chapter gives an in-depth insight into the important topic of employability.

Performing PM responsibly requires **people managers** to think about the broader effects of their strategies on local communities – for example, hiring policies, approach to diversity and inclusion, compensation levels, managing

Professional people management includes the responsibility of managing and protecting the employee stakeholder, and helping them thrive as human beings at work, as well as optimizing PM's contribution to ethics, responsibility, and sustainability

layoffs, and more can have significant local consequences. In addition, PM has an opportunity to engage employees through measures that connect them to the organization's agenda and also benefit them in a direct way. For example, employees who learn about environmental management in the workplace are likely to take this learning home and generate benefits in their home lives.

Occupational bodies, like the Society for Human Resources Management have offered further orientation for people managers' ethical behaviour. Such professional codes of ethics cover many important aspirational behaviours of people managers, such as acting in the public interest and maintaining confidentiality. However, one could argue that codes like the one shown here don't go far enough, as they still clearly instrumentalize employees for the benefit of the employer. People managers as presented in these codes are not impartial, and much less so on the employees' side. Many of the items in this particular code of ethics are not strong enough, such as the very meek suggestion to 'encourage' one's employer's fair and equitable treatment. Shouldn't truly professional people managers note that their professional integrity is at risk if they stand by without interfering in the inequitable practices of an employer?

THE SOCIETY FOR HUMAN RESOURCE MANAGEMENT'S CODE OF ETHICS

As a member of the Society for Human Resource Management, I pledge to:

- Maintain the highest standards of professional and personal conduct.

- Strive for personal growth in the field of human resource management.

- Support the Society's goals and objectives for developing the human resource management profession.

- Encourage my employer to make the fair and equitable treatment of all employees a primary concern.

- Strive to make my employer profitable both in monetary terms and through the support and encouragement of effective employment practices.

- Instill in the employees and the public a sense of confidence about the conduct and intentions of the employer.

- Maintain loyalty to my employer and pursue its objectives in ways that are consistent with the public interest.

- Uphold all laws and regulations relating to my employer's activities.

- Refrain from using my official positions, either regular or volunteer, to secure special privilege, gain or benefit for myself.

- Maintain the confidentiality of privileged information.

- Improve public understanding of the role of human resource management.

  Source: ([4])

THE PM–PM RELATIONSHIP

The role of the traditional PM function is to add business value through developing and managing activities, processes, and tools to enhance organizational and individual capability, and drive a culture designed to deliver organizational objectives. This includes a spectrum of activities ranging from organizational development to attraction, recruitment, development and retention of talented employees, maintaining healthy employee relations, providing performance management tools and support, and ensuring compensation systems which serve business competitiveness.

Recruitment costs and effectiveness, hours of training provided, number of employees trained and training budget size, employer costs and competitiveness of compensation and benefits, and maintaining business continuity through positive employee relations are all examples of traditional ways of measuring the PM contribution. However, this approach is narrow and these objectives and measures serve the interests of only two primary internal groups:

1. Owners/shareholders (represented by management) whose interest lies generally in the short-term financial returns to be gained from a business

2. Employees, who must achieve a certain level of satisfaction in the working environment in order to continue to contribute and remain with the organization

Wider stakeholder considerations in PM should include the impacts of PM practices on society in general.

PROFESSIONAL PM LEADERSHIP

Professional PM goes beyond the traditional role of PM in supporting business value. Four key areas of professional PM can be distilled into the following headlines (adapted from [5]:

1. Developing the ability of PM to develop and maintain an organization's resource base to **support business sustainability**

2. Supporting the long-term survival of the organization through managing the **impacts of PM activities on employees and on external stakeholders**

3. Developing **mutual trustful 'resourcing partnerships'** by understanding and considering the specific conditions of people development, care, and regeneration

4. Supporting sustaining **social legitimacy (the 'licence to operate')**

The key implications are that PM must go beyond the immediate concern with the management of work and organizations to adopt a broader approach. This includes responsibility for the impact of PM processes on the way in which managers fulfil their role as responsible citizens and PM's contribution to social development by:

1. Taking both moral and ethical **responsibility for the way PM is delivered** in an organization while ensuring that the broader needs of society, communities, employees, and other stakeholders are included

2. Take responsibility for **assisting business leadership** to assume greater awareness of PM issues and the impact of PM policies on the organization

3. **Being role models for ethical conduct, stakeholder inclusion, and social impact**.

Important guidance for people managers when reshaping workplaces are professional PM norms and certification like those presented in Table 19.1.

TABLE 19.1   Comparing professional PM norms

ILO (International Labour Organization)	Social Accountability (SA) 8000	Great Place to Work	Quality of Life in the Business (part of Empresa Socialmente Responsable, ESR)
1. Freedom of association and the effective recognition of the right to collective bargaining	1. Child labour	1. Credibility of management	1. Employability and labour relations
2. Elimination of all forms of forced or compulsory labour	2. Forced and compulsory labour	2. Respect in employee relationships	2. Social dialogue
3. Effective abolition of child labour	3. Health and safety	3. Fairness in work-related matters	3. Work conditions and social security
4. Elimination of discrimination in respect of employment and occupation	4. Freedom of association and the right to collective bargaining	4. Pride in ones' work	4. Work–family balance
	5. Discrimination	5. Camaraderie among coworkers	5. Training and human development
	6. Disciplinary practices		6. Security and health
	7. Working hours		
	8. Remuneration		
	9. Management systems		

THE BUSINESS CASE FOR PROFESSIONAL PM

The following are some examples of how PM can adapt its approach to deliver business benefits:

- **Advancing diversity**. PM processes can be leveraged to create an inclusive culture where the entire workforce can contribute to greater innovation, improved customer relationships, reduced workplace conflict and enjoy higher motivation, productivity, and workplace loyalty. This means designing PM processes that actively seek out candidates from diverse backgrounds, proactively training managers to hire with an inclusive mindset, purposefully creating a workplace that respects the needs of different employees, especially minority groups, and sensitively promoting diversity in internal communications.

- **Going green**. Reducing environmental impacts is one of the most serious business challenges of the day. Business can gain advantage only when the entire workforce is engaged. PM support for the employee-driven 'green teams' to enhance employee practices related to electricity usage, use of paper for printing, recycling, waste reduction, and more delivers benefits such as reduced operating costs, improved environmental protection, and employees who derive satisfaction from becoming ambassadors for a more sustainable planet. An excellent example is the case of Coronation Street discussed in Chapter 2.

- **Employee well-being**. Investment in employee well-being delivers big returns. In Unilever's 'Lamplighter' programme, employees voluntarily participate in programmes for managing stress, nutrition, exercise, and other lifestyle habits. It not only delivered amazing results in terms of reducing health risk factors for thousands of employees but also delivered a return of more than four times the amount invested in the programme [6]. It contributed directly to profit whilst protecting business continuity and improved employee productivity. PM policies that help employees to manage their own well-being deliver an ROI in reduced absenteeism, reduced health care costs, higher productivity, and longer job tenure.

- **Human rights**. There are hundreds of millions of children illegally employed around the world, tens of millions of people in forced labour, and millions of employees who do not enjoy the basic right to freedom of association. People managers need to identify the human rights risks in their internal and extended supply chains and ensure robust PM policies to uphold these rights, including risk assessment and awareness and training programmes. Creating a culture in which these issues can be openly addressed protects and advances the business, employees, and communities.

RECRUITMENT

A primary function of PM is **recruiting**, screening, and hiring employees competent to perform the intended role, and to enable new employees to succeed and support the company culture. The hiring process must lead to a positive triple bottom line by protecting, creating, and sustaining social, environmental, and economic business value. The hiring process must also be ethical, where decisions are morally desirable in both its process and its outcome.

Recruitment refers to practices of attracting, screening, and selecting employees

Social media and employee referrals are today's recruitment hotspots [7]. Thus, recruitment efforts by people management through its own company website and public advertisements seem to account for only a small portion of successful new recruits. Clearly, ethics are central to the decisions of professionals when they follow non-discrimination policies. Responsible practices ensure zero discrimination on any basis and should be incorporated into recruiting and screening practices. A particularly helpful framework to map and critically probe for potential **unconscious bias** (e.g. against particular sexual preferences, ages, or ethnicities) in the recruitment process is the implicit association test [8]. Taking a test like this can help us to make our own and others' unconscious biases conscious and, by doing so, make them manageable. It is also important to be aware of how such personal qualities, against which recruiters might be biased, might intersect with some potential recruitees possibly being affected by multiple biases. Thinking **about intersectionality** [9], as illustrated in Figure 19.2, leads to a better understanding of how a person's characteristics may result in discrimination or privilege in the recruitment process and in management practices more widely.

Unconscious bias
refers to the influence of previous experiences, prejudices, or stereotypes on our decision-making without being aware of it

Intersectionality
is a concept that allows us to explore how a combination of multiple sensitive personal characteristics may lead to advantages and disadvantages

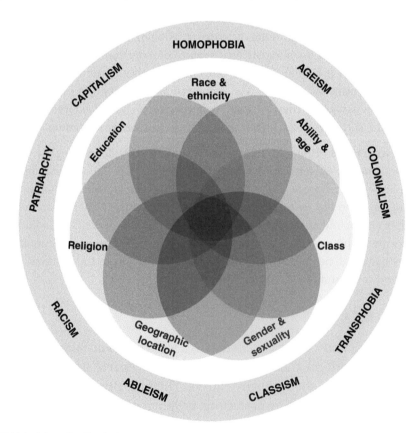

FIGURE 19.2   Intersectionality wheel
SOURCE: Adapted from [10]

DEVELOPING THE RESPONSIBLE JOB DESCRIPTION

Professional PM is not simply a receiver of **job descriptions** and candidate profiles, which are unilaterally determined by the business manager's needs, or sometimes, personal preferences. The professional PM recruitment process starts with awareness and training for business managers in the business value of diversity in recruitment; the need for managers to be ready and willing to embrace candidates representing the full range of diversity. 'Blind hiring' tools that ensure anonymity while assessing candidates' suitability are an important and relevant tool [11].

A job description defines the responsibilities associated with a job position

In fact, there may even be a case for demanding that no hiring may take place without a gender-diverse shortlist being presented and at least one or two candidates from minority groups. There is also 'positive' discrimination, a practice that aims to benefit marginalised groups by giving preference to individuals from such groups when hiring, as practiced by PM at Nadeshiko, the female-only Sushi restaurant in Tokyo [12].

Managers must know that to define candidate profiles in a way which excludes groups of the population is discriminatory. It represents not only a legal and reputational risk, but also poor management practice, limiting the potential talent pool and therefore harming the organization's ability to fulfil its purpose.

PM at Nadeshiko challenges gender discrimination by exclusively hiring female sushi chefs. Women have traditionally been excluded from this profession. That menstrual cycle affects women's sense of smell and that their higher body temperature affects ingredients are just two of the stigmatizing myths.

Copyright: Justin McCurry/The Guardian

ATTRACTING CANDIDATES

Once the definition of the role and candidate profile have been agreed, the people manager will typically advertise the vacancy through traditional channels such as the corporate website, newspapers, online sites and recruitment agencies. In most cases, jobs are advertised as being 'equal opportunity', meaning that anyone with relevant experience and qualifications may apply.

Often, seeking candidates through traditional routes is exclusionary, as the stated experience and qualification thresholds may put those who do not meet the exact criteria off from applying. A responsible approach to recruitment demands that PM seek out potential candidates through developing a broader range of recruitment channels and retain some flexibility around education and experience.

Collaboration with local government employment offices or specialist organizations which assist minority groups may help to discover a wider range of candidates with potential, even if some additional efforts will need to be made upfront.

Recruitment agencies must be fully briefed and trained in the organization's social responsibility requirements and instructed to actively seek diverse candidates. By ensuring a proactive approach to ensuring a diverse pool of applicants, PM can contribute to more equitable and effective recruitment processes.

SELECTING HIRES

Typically, candidates who are successful in the initial screening process will be asked to undertake a series of tasks until final hiring decisions are made. These may include personal interviews, group interviews, participation in assessment centres that test different forms of mental ability, leadership skills, personal traits and more. Tasks might also include practical exercises or participation in a work process. Some companies even use handwriting analysis in order to understand the candidate's personal traits.

In the responsible selection process, PM must ensure that the candidates' abilities and values are carefully explored, and gain a clear understanding of their preferences and aspirations. A company must hire employees who are aligned with its objectives, and this means finding not only the most capable employees but also the most suitable employees. This turns the screening process into one which offers a balance between obtaining information about the candidate and enabling the candidate to obtain information about the company. A recruitment decision is made not only by the company – the candidate must also make a decision about whether to join the company.

A positive process for the dialogue-based interview is the behavioural interview approach, in which candidates are asked to describe how they have demonstrated the desired behaviours as an indication of their potential to reapply them in your company. This kind of approach requires skill and training, so the responsible screening process must include managers who can apply this approach when they interview. Managers must learn how to navigate personal preferences or preconceptions that might lead to discriminatory decisions in the selection process. It is the role of PM to ensure that this is put into practice.

Additionally, PM must ensure that candidates have the opportunity to learn enough about the company. This means that the employer brand must accurately reflect the company's practice and that managers have enough information to be able to respond to candidates' queries.

In developing the employment contract, the company must proactively ensure that the candidate has all the information about the company's terms and conditions of employment in writing. Employment contracts offered must be fair and represent the interests of the employee and not only the company.

TRAINING AND DEVELOPMENT

People management defines **training and development** needs in line with those required to support business objectives. This is no different with professional PM, though, of course, the responsible organization's business objectives may include new areas of activity such as employees' contribution to zero-carbon goals or the adaptation of products to address social issues. In addition, professional PM seeks to ensure that employees are well versed in additional organizational aspects such as values, ethical conduct and social responsibility.

Training and development also reflect the responsibility an organization has to advance the personal development and employability of its people, enabling them to grow and develop so that they will be better able to contribute to the organization or any organization that they may work for in the future. Professional PM sees beyond the very immediate needs of the business and aims to add to the long-term value of employees as an added benefit of their current employment. This is part of the contribution of a responsible business to a sustainable society. Immediate business needs change and skills become obsolete. By preparing employees for the future, a company is taking out an insurance policy against the possible negative effects of business changes, layoffs, and damage to local communities.

The remainder of this section considers orientation, training, and development (see Figure 19.3) [13].

Training and development educational activities within an organization that aim to increase personal growth and the performance of employees

- **Orientation:** orients, directs, and guides employees toward socially responsible and ethical practices, and to understand the sustainable mission or areas of work, firm, and colleagues.

- **Training:** helps employees learn to do their current work better and participate in sustainable activities and to produce competitive, high-quality product(s) or service.

- **Development:** prepares ethical individuals for the future. It focuses on sustainable learning and responsible personal development.

FIGURE 19.3   Training and development practices

SOURCE: Adapted from [13].

EMPLOYEE ORIENTATION AND SOCIALIZATION

When new employees enter an organization, the process is complex and neither automatic nor instant. Newcomers often have to face expectations unknown to them and they discover unwritten rules about the organizational culture. They soon learn whether the business 'walks the talk' in terms of ethics, responsibility, and sustainability.

Employee orientation
the process of introducing new employees to an organization

Typical goals of a good **orientation** programme include reducing newcomer anxiety, minimizing turnover, saving time, and developing realistic expectations [13]. Organizations want to see new employees succeed because of the time and costs involved, and PM carries the responsibility for this transition process to prepare the newcomer.

Organizational assimilation is the entire transition of ongoing behavioural and cognitive processes that begin before employees join the organization and continues until they become insiders [14]. In professional PM contexts, there are opportunities to go beyond traditional orientation models that aim to familiarize employees with the company, the job, key processes, and colleagues. As the orientation phase shapes the way employees will succeed in their immediate role in the short term, and may help them develop within the organization in the long term, this is a unique opportunity to ensure that the responsibility of business is understood and that employees know how their work connects to broader social and environmental impacts.

Additionally, the orientation phase is one in which all other employees must be supportive and offer constructive help and guidance, especially if the new employee is from a minority or has special needs. In many companies, there are affinity groups, or employee resource groups, which may play an active role in employees feeling they have a 'support group' of colleagues with similar needs to help them integrate and grow with the company. Other companies may assign mentors or coaches to help new employees find their feet. The orientation and socialization transition happens in three phases: anticipatory socialization, encounter, and metamorphosis [15]. In Table 19.2 we suggest professional PM practices for each stage.

TABLE 19.2   Stages of the responsible socialization process

Stage	Descriptions
Anticipatory socialization	**Socialization occurs before entry into the organization. It encompasses both socialization to an occupation and socialization to an organization.** **Responsible principles:** • Communicate responsible, sustainable, and ethical business practices and performance widely to external stakeholders through a range of channels. This might include use of social media to engage in dialogue with potential employees.

- Develop a robust employer brand that reflects social responsibility principles.

- Integrate responsible objectives throughout the recruitment process, in the interview, and during induction. This might also include participation in careers fairs or community involvement of employees in educational projects.

- Manage the recruitment process in a fair, open, and respectful way to all candidates, including those the company decides not to hire.

Encounter	**Sensemaking is the stage that occurs when a new employee enters the organization. The newcomer must let go of old roles and values in adapting to the expectations of the new organization.** **Responsibility principles:** - Clearly communicate company sustainability objectives at the 'point of entry'. - Ensure the new employee has a clear understanding of expectations and an internal company support system (people manager, employee resource group, mentor, etc.). - Help the new employee feel involved in the company's social purpose by offering opportunities to participate in social or environmental activities. - 'Start or maintain their professional development … through training in initial company requirements, corporate culture, processes which empower the new hire, and establishment of a supportive network …' [6]
Metamorphosis	**The state reached at completion of the socialization process. The new employee is now accepted as an organizational insider.** **Responsibility principles:** - Ensure continued support through supportive management, opportunities for open dialogue and feedback, and continued training and development. - Ensure continued engagement of the employee in social responsibility activities and recognize good contribution and 'ownership' of the company's culture of responsibility.

SOURCE: Adapted from [15].

TRAINING

The **training** process may provide focus on knowledge of the job or help with specific job skills or abilities, and may apply to individuals or dedicated groups who specialize in a particular task. In the context of professional PM, training should be designed to impart the wider implications of business activities in sustainability contexts and an understanding of the social and environmental impacts of both the organization and the roles of individuals. For instance, the Chinese semi-conductor business Good-Ark's people management runs an eight-module 'happy company' training, based on life lessons from Chinese sages like Confucius, that impacts positively employees behaviours towards others and the environment [16].

In Figure 19.4, we present a roadmap of responsible training recommendations for integrating sustainability principles into people management departments [6]. While the roadmap displays training and communication in two separate areas, the two are intimately interlinked.

> Training
> a process of changing the performance of employees to better achieve organizational goals and objectives

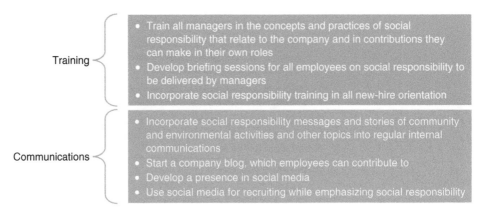

FIGURE 19.4   Responsibility training and communications practices

SOURCE: Adapted from [6]

Training in social responsibility should also include training relating to employee rights from a human rights perspective. Excellent source documents for employers include the Universal Declaration of Human Rights and the *Labour Principles of the UN Global Compact.* The labour principles apply specifically to freedom of association and the right to collective bargaining for employees, the elimination of forced or compulsory labour, the abolition of child labour, and the elimination of discrimination in respect of employment and occupation. Child labour or forced and compulsory labour issues may come to mind when reflecting on Nike during the 1990s, and Apple's supply chain issues in recent years. People managers need to set the following guidelines for training in human rights in supplier companies as well as their own. This employee training must be inclusive of all employees, adapt to laws of local countries, and be reinforced frequently (minimally on an annual basis):

1.   Ensure existence of policies and systems that maintain human and employee rights in the business and its supply chain.

2.   Ensure awareness and training for all employees in company policies on human rights.

3.   Proactively inform employees and assist them to understand and realize all of their rights. [6]

Employee development
the process of planning and implementing activities to develop employees' competencies in the medium and long run

DEVELOPING EMPLOYEES

PM may use a variety of tools to **develop employees**, both on and off the job. Westpac Banking Corp. serving Australia, New Zealand, and the Pacific islands ran an organizational mentoring programme that matched high performing employees with community organizations. The purpose was to bring about measurable change to community partners while exposing 'our employees to different types of organization and to a range of social issues' Ilana Atlas, Group Executive, People and Performance at Westpac explained [6].

The value of **employee volunteering** in the community is often over-looked as an employee development (and empowerment) opportunity. Volunteering can serve as a framework for personal development and acquisition of competences for employees who may not be able to gain these skills in the workplace, due to the limitations of company-based opportunities.

Employee volunteering voluntary engagement of personnel from an organization

Skill-based volunteering means that employees volunteer in a way that enables them to utilize the professional competence they bring with them from the workplace. Rather than accounting professionals handing out food to needy people, they can offer pro-bono financial advice to the finance department of not-for-profit organizations. Thereby they both utilize their core skills for community benefit and gain experience of a different working culture with its own challenges.

PERFORMANCE MANAGEMENT

Creating processes and tools for evaluating the performance of employees, and ensuring the embedding of such processes and tools in the organization is a third major function of people management. Such performance management practices are centred on 'the process by which executives, managers, and supervisors work to align employee performance with the firm's goals' [13].

Performance management the process of monitoring and improving employees' work performance

PERFORMANCE EVALUATION PRACTICES

Performance management tools often include some form of performance evaluation, which serves several purposes:

1. It provides a basis for **dialogue between an employee and line manager** to ensure there is alignment around shared mission, objectives, and goals. It enables a discussion about behaviours and not only results. In professional management, the way in which goals are achieved is no less important than the performance results. A performance evaluation dialogue is instrumental in reinforcing the messages related to the impact an employee has in the organization and work interactions, internally and externally, through the way in which the employee conducts themself.

2. It provides the employee with an **opportunity to hear how their performance is rated by superiors** and often also by peers and subordinates (in the form of a 360 degree appraisal). This evaluation opens up possibilities to review ways of offering support to the employee for the development of a performance improvement and professional/personal development plan.

3. It provides the employee with an **opportunity to give feedback to the manager**, including the way in which the company is assisting, or hindering, them in reaching their full potential and delivering best performance.

This open dialogue can be a strong tool for engaging employees, building trust, refocusing, and realigning the employee with what matters most, and in ensuring that the company develops talent in a sustainable way. Performance evaluation may contribute to business sustainability as it focuses on performance improvement and alignment of contribution, reinforcing sustainable behaviours.

NEW TYPES OF PERFORMANCE

Activities that had not traditionally been on the PM radar can provide valuable tools for people development in any organization while delivering benefits for society and the environment. Involvement in the community – in the form of volunteering, for example – provides opportunities for employees. Volunteering in the community motivates employees and may drive greater loyalty and commitment, which may be translated into work productivity. Many of these benefits can be quantified, such as:

- **Employee job satisfaction**. When employees are given time within their working day to volunteer, their overall motivation increases. This can be assessed in performance evaluation conversations and in employee surveys.

- **Recruitment effectiveness**. More employees want to apply to work at a responsible company. When this is used as part of the employer brand, and applicants or new hires are surveyed, we can measure the impact.

- **Employee competence building**. This can be tracked through the employee performance evaluation process.

We should also count the benefits for society resulting from employee contribution, and the benefit to the business of enhanced reputation. Developing an effective employee volunteering programme requires clear policy, planning, and careful implementation. It is a terrific tool for people managers to advance business objectives through new ways of engaging and motivating employees in a way which brings benefits back to the workplace. There are some that say a business has a responsibility to 'give back' to the communities in which they operate and many companies take this approach. Whatever the motivation, values or strategy based, creating positive community impacts through employee volunteering is a feature of a responsible workplace. A great example is Ericsson's volunteering programme through which employees set up needed communication infrastructure in regions affected by humanitarian crises [17].

Another example for alternative employee performance relates to 'going green'. PM support for driving a culture of environmental efficiency is crucial. Engaged employees can advance all forms of efficiencies, not only around energy, but in reducing water consumption (another cost that businesses will see increasing in coming years), reducing waste, earning new revenues from recycling and more.

Skill-based volunteering staff of the Swedish telecommunications company Ericsson, setting up communication infrastructure in south Sudan.
Copyright: Ericsson

COMPENSATION, BENEFITS, AND EMPLOYEE WELL-BEING

Compensation can be either financial or non-financial. Financial compensation includes wages and salaries, and it takes the form of any monetary return to the employee, such as bonuses, commissions, or non-salary benefits. These may include health or medical insurance, sick leave, vacation time, childcare, or higher education subsidies for children of employees. Companies who offer long-term benefits may provide retirement plans, stock options, ownership plans, or profit sharing, a form of compensation that distributes a percentage of organizational profit among employees in the form of cash or deferred bonuses. Non-financial compensation can be just as attractive to employees. Prominent examples are flexible work schedules, four-day-work weeks, personal development opportunities, and employee recognition practices (e.g., most environmental-friendly employee of the month).

Compensation
the financial and nonfinancial remuneration received for the work done

A company's approach to compensation relates to the way a firm provides for the health and prosperity of its employees, which has a significant impact on society. Typical compensation plans encompass major categories of a base pay system, a short-term incentive plan, a long-term incentive plan, and benefit plans.

DRIVING PRINCIPLES OF A COMPENSATION SYSTEM

The two key principles of fairness and equality should guide any compensation system. These principles result in eight policies that should be incorporated into any sustainable compensation plan [6]:

1. Compensation should be **legal**, obeying all laws and regulations in the host country. When laws differ among countries in a supply chain, companies should follow the laws of the country with the stricter or higher standards.

2. Compensation should be **fair and equitable** and not discriminate on the basis of gender or other elements of diversity. Employees with the same levels of experience, skill, or training should be paid equitably. Opportunities for non-financial compensation to earn awards or participate in activities should be fair and equitable.

3. Compensation should be **supportive** of employees by offering wages and benefits beyond the minimum wage, fixed standards, or basic working conditions.

4. **Engaging** compensation plans treat employees as partners in the achievement of company objectives. Any type of financial compensation package that allows employees to participate in stock options, ownership plans, or in distribution of company profits will provide incentives that engage employees. The purpose of treating employees as partners is for motivation and increased productivity. Firms with compensation plans tend to have more joint consultative committees, quality circles, and company-level information with employees [18].

5. Compensation should be **attractive** to employees and future employees who consider working for the company. A company should be at no disadvantage when recruiting new employees because of a non-competitive salary.

6. Compensation should be **flexible**, taking into account individual employee needs. Financial status, health condition, or educational needs will require a flexible choice of benefits. People management must offer professional advice and counselling. Centralized management works better for compensation *procedures* whereas decentralized decision-making works best for such issues as long-term incentives and employee benefits [19].

7. PM should be **proactive** with its compensation package by annually reviewing what it offers. Cost of living increases and pay rises must be adjusted. The company can ensure costs of insurance do not become prohibitive if employees contribute to their insurance plan.

8. Finally, and perhaps most importantly, compensation plans should be **transparent**. Does this issue matter to you and how transparent should a company be internally with employee pay? Opinions differ widely on this issue, and in many countries, laws determine the level of transparency of public institutions such as federal governmental offices and public universities.

LIVING WAGE

Living wage
describes the minimum hourly wage necessary for an individual in full-time employment to meet basic needs

The phenomenon of the 'working poor' is becoming more prevalent. The idea that one can spend most of one's waking hours working diligently and still not be able to afford a reasonable quality of life that includes basic life essentials should be offensive to all leaders and especially PM professionals. The level of the **living wage** necessary to meet basic needs, including housing, food, utilities, transport, health care and education, will differ from country to country. However, it is almost always higher than local minimum wage levels established by law.

It is not ethical, responsible, or sustainable to pay employees at a level that does not enable them to maintain a decent, safe, and healthy lifestyle. It erodes the basic fabric of our society and ultimately creates an environment in which it is harder to do business. Fairly rewarded employees are more committed, more productive, more stable, and less prone to sickness absence. These issues have an impact on costs but the return on paying a living wage is usually positive. People management has

Dan Price, CEO of the online payment company Gravity announces his radical decision to pay at least 70,000 USD to each employee in 2015. This move doubled the wage of a third of all employees, while cutting Dan's own salary by over 1 million USD. He took the decision inspired by research that suggested that a person in the US needed on average an income of 70k to stop worrying about money and to be happy. This minimum wage was adjusted because of inflation to 80,000 USD from 2022 onwards.

a responsibility to lead on responsible compensation practice for the long-term benefit of all. There is even a practice popular among progressive CEOs to cut their own wages in order to increase employee wages to a 'happiness wage', inspired by Dan Price at the Seattle-based online payment company Gravity [20].

EMPLOYEE WELL-BEING

A lack of attention to employee well-being can carry significant risk. There have been high-profile cases of employee suicides, notably at France Telecom where the toll reached 46, and at Foxconn, the Chinese manufacturer of electronic products, where nine suicides were counted in a year [21]. Employees resorted to this drastic action because they were under pressure to deliver more and more, under tighter deadlines, in an unsupportive working environment that was not responsive to their personal needs and pressures.

At the other end of the spectrum, investing in employee well-being delivers business benefits. In a programme to advance employee health and address stress issues at Unilever [22], Dean Patterson, global health and productivity manager for Unilever, said when taking stock that 'not only did we see impressive improvements to the health and energy levels of our people, the business also benefited from a financial return on investment of £3.73: 1. So for every £1 ($1.64) Unilever invested in its employees, it got back almost £4 ($6.59) through reduced health care costs and increased productivity'.

Such risks and opportunities make it imperative that people managers accept responsibility for promoting a sustainable approach. This typically means addressing work–life balance issues such as flexible working hours, tele-commuting options, child care leave and support, and other support services, each of which can be proven to deliver a positive return in terms of reduced absenteeism, improved productivity, and more.

NAVIGATING EMPLOYEE RELATIONS

Employee relations are centred on tensions between an organization and its employees, including its relationship with unions, downsizing, and employee offboarding.

LABOUR UNIONS

Unionization refers to any organized group of employees who work together collectively to promote their interests. As labour or trade unions, these groups engage in collective bargaining to accomplish member goals, and provide a vehicle for employees to ensure their rights are upheld in the workplace. The union grants employees an organized voice and strength for their causes. The communication that occurs between managers and labour unions is called labour relations.

Unions exist in most countries, industries and sectors today and are closely regulated by laws. PM professionals must be knowledgeable about relevant laws and regulations. The right to collective bargaining is one of the basic rights of employees, embodied in the 1998 ILO Declaration of Fundamental Principles and Rights at Work [23] and the fundamental Convention covering collective bargaining as the Right to Organise and Collective Bargaining Convention, 1949 (No. 98), which has been ratified as law by most countries. Professional PM embraces the value that employee associations can bring to the development of a shared commitment to business objectives and ensures that employee representatives are treated with respect, and that negotiations are conducted in a spirit of fair and equal opportunity.

Despite the right afforded in law for employees to organize and engage in collective bargaining, PM might prefer not to be chained to union agreements or the requirement to negotiate terms and conditions on a collective basis for employees. Management may regard this as restrictive, possibly obstructive to the decision-making process, and also risk escalation of employee costs. While these fears may be justified in some cases, the fact is that collective bargaining is a right and, if well managed, can actually support business development rather than hinder it. It is the role of people managers to ensure that labour relations are conducted within the law, first and foremost, which means ensuring that an organization does not obstruct employees' rights in this respect in any way. By taking a positive view of labour relations, PM can lead a respectful, constructive relationship with employee representatives, and ensure business continuity and a positive reputation, as well as alignment of employee demands with management objectives. This does not always work out smoothly, as in the case of the fashion retailer Everlane. Their people management was accused of **union busting** by US senator Bernie Sanders [24, 25].

Union busting
refers to the employer practice of disrupting or preventing the formation or expansion of trade unions

DOWNSIZING

Organizational restructuring and downsizing may be inevitable steps for some businesses. The way in which such downsizing is managed can destroy business continuity and create negative social burdens, especially in small communities if layoffs are concentrated in specific areas or affect a particular age group. Responsible downsizing makes a difference:

1. To **employees**, leaving the organization with a programme of assistance to manage re-entry into the job market

2. To **society**, by reducing the burden of unemployment or local recession through improved planning and consideration of local downsizing impacts

3. To **the business** and its financial stability and economic contribution to society, through maintenance of business continuity by ensuring that retained employees remain motivated and engaged

4. To all **other stakeholders**, who daily assess their relationships with a company and have a preference for doing business with those who behave in a responsible manner towards society

The way in which PM manages such processes, considering the broader implications, can build or destroy business value.

OFFBOARDING

PM's scope of responsibility is relevant to employees who leave the company, and an ethical, responsible, and sustainable approach ensures that layoffs due to restructuring changes and business downsizing are dealt with in a fair manner. After having done whatever possible to minimize the need for layoffs, PM has a responsibility to ensure this offboarding process is as positive as possible. **Offboarding** refers to managing the way employees leave the company. Professional PM policy and processes will ensure offboarding is as constructive as possible so that the best possible outcomes can be achieved for departing employees. This is important for several reasons:

Offboarding
refers to the management of employees leaving a company

1. Helping employees who are laid off to **navigate their way back into the job market**, or transition into retirement, makes a strong contribution to society by helping people continue to be productive members of the workforce or local communities.

2. Employees leave companies, but **more stay**. The employees that stay with companies need to see that colleagues are treated ethically, fairly, and in a positive way at the time of leaving. Not doing so can damage employee morale considerably and risk business continuity.

3. Ex-employees can **promote or damage your reputation** after they leave in many ways. By considering them as future ambassadors, and ensuring their departure is a positive process, the reputational risk to the business is reduced.

4. Ex-employees who **remain positive about the company** may be re-hired at a future date if business needs change. Rehiring ex-employees often offers advantages over completely new employees, as they are experienced and understand the organizational culture, so onboarding time is reduced.

Offboarding usually includes 'outplacement' programmes that support employees' re-entry into the job market by providing practical tools such as applying for jobs, writing résumés, interview skills and more, as well as personal tools such as managing personal finances during and after the transition, or coping with stress.

PRINCIPLES OF PEOPLE MANAGEMENT

I.   **Professional PM** includes responsibility for managing the employee stakeholder, and contributing to larger ethics, responsibility, and sustainability performance.

II. The goal of professional people management is a **PM–PM symbiosis**, a mutually reinforcing relationship in which professional management (PM) needs employees' engagement, and the other way around, people management (PM) benefits from professional management activities taking care of the employee stakeholder.

III. For understanding the **people management–professional management relationship** one should consider the main norms for professional PM, the business case for professional people management, and the role of the people manager.

IV. **Recruitment** involves including employee competences for professional management in job descriptions, attracting candidates with such competences, and selecting them on that basis.

V.   **Training and development** begins with new employee orientation, ongoing training for professional management performance, development of employees and close external stakeholders with the underlying goal of increasing trained people's employability.

V. **Performance management** includes the evaluation of employees' contribution to organizational goals, and their professional management performance.

VI. **Compensation and benefits** should be based on an ethical, responsible, and sustainable compensation system that pays at least a decent living wage, and contributes to employee well-being through other benefits.

VII. **Employee relations** include the relationship to labour unions and responsible 'offboarding' of employees when they leave.

MANAGEMENT GYM: TRAINING YOUR PROFESSIONAL SIX-PACK

Knowing

1. Explain the symbiosis and relationship between people management and ERS (ethics, responsibility, and sustainability).

2. Briefly explain the stages of the employee socialization process and how they interrelate.

3. Briefly describe the main areas of practices of people management and search online for two real-life examples for each, one responsible and one an irresponsible practice.

Thinking

4. Which do you think has more professional people management practices, the Brazilian company Semco or the USA's SAS? Why do you think so?

5. Compare the four professional PM norms presented in this chapter and think about how their coverage differs. Should an organization apply all norms simultaneously or is compliance with one norm sufficient to create professional people management?

6. How should professional people management practices differ between home company and suppliers, between developed countries and developing countries, between large companies and small and medium-sized enterprises?

Acting

7. Write an anti-discrimination policy for a company of your choice. Define the groups that are likely to face discrimination, the type of discrimination they might face and the potential practices and principles to help counter that discrimination.

8. Write an advertisement for a job of your choice at a company of your choice and make sure it integrates ethics, responsibility and sustainability.

9. You are the health and safety manager of a food delivery company at the beginning of the Coronavirus outbreak. Write an email to all staff about the actions that will be taken to keep everyone safe and healthy.

Interacting

10. Look up the responsibility report of a company of your choice and find examples for (un)professional people management practices. Propose one measure to improve the company's professional people management practices. Send your proposal to the company using the contact information on the report or on their website.

11. Have a look at the websites and social media accounts of Net Impacts, Oikos, or another student organization that focuses on ethics, responsibility, and sustainability. Get in touch with them and attend one of their activities online or at a location near to you.

12. Interview one person about their employer's people management practices and ask what they think would be worth improving.

Being

13. What are your main needs as an individual in the workplace? How do you want to be treated? How do you want to treat others, and what kind of practices would you not engage in?

14. Do you personally agree that we need to stop saying human resources to stress that we should not instrumentalize people, or is this going too far?

15. You have two job offers, one that requires you to engage in practices you consider irresponsible, and another one that doesn't. How much more would the first company have to pay you to accept their job?

Becoming

16. Think about what it would mean for you to have a 'responsible' career. What would be your ideal career path? What competences do you think would be worth developing so that you can walk that path and what first step could you take to start doing so?

17. It can be quite tempting to 'use' interns in ways other than those intended. Could you see yourself being tempted to ask an intern to pick up your dry cleaning, run to the pharmacy 'just this one time', or make the coffee every day?

18. What personal characteristics do you find hard to accept in others and what could you do to become more tolerant?

SOURCE: Adapted from [26]

PIONEER INTERVIEW
LIZ MAW

INTERVIEWER: OLIVER LAASCH

Liz Maw was founding CEO of Net Impact, a large network of students and practitioners of 'more than 30,000 changemakers using our [their] jobs to tackle the world's toughest problems'. Net Impact aims to foster the CSR profession and to create careers with a positive impact.

Courtesy of Liz Maw

Young professionals' and students' roles in changing the economic system. Recruiting and retaining talent is a top priority and concern for global CEOs. CEOs know that their growth and market leadership will be delivered by ensuring talented people are fully engaged in their company priorities.

Young professionals and grad students care deeply about making an impact on social and environmental causes. And even though these young hirees have less experience than their colleagues and bosses, they have the attention of the leadership. They are the talent pipeline that will drive growth and results. That's a powerful position to be in.

Responsibility skills. In the study, *Business skills for a changing world*, published by Net Impact and the World Environment Center, we outlined a number of critical competencies that leaders in Fortune 500 companies told us they needed from MBA graduates. One set of skills we termed 'inside-out' skills, which refer to the technical and behavioural skills for day-to-day business management that enable an employee to make responsible decisions with a sustainable lens. In addition, leaders spoke of the need for 'outside-in' skills that help an employee understand and process external realities and factors that can reshape its business strategy. Finally, 'traverse' skills are necessary to apply systems thinking, communicate with stakeholders, and manage social interactions and networks to influence change.

Towards a responsible management profession? Several leading practitioners in the field are currently in discussion about 'professionalizing' the corporate responsibility profession. These positions have evolved organically in many companies, and as the demands on these positions become more complex, some believe the field would benefit from greater formal training and standardization. That said, the corporate responsibility or responsible management function has also been integrated into many business positions. For example, supply chain

(Continued)

professionals are increasingly asked to understand ethical supply chain opportunities, and operations professionals must learn about energy efficiency.

As a result of these two trends, students who are passionate about responsible management will have the opportunity to both enter into a more defined 'profession' with CSR colleagues as well as choose to work on sustainability from many different day jobs. The most important step students can take is to ensure that they work for companies authentically committed to a holistic and integrated approach to sustainability – companies that engage employees at all levels with responsible management. In the right kind of open culture, all employees are able to meaningfully contribute to responsible management progress.

QUESTIONS

1. To what extent do you agree with Liz's observation that recent graduate students' favour for responsibility changes means that companies adjust their behaviour for the better, or do they simply mention 'the same old' CSR initiatives they are doing anyway to attract employees?

2. What do you think is the role of student organizations like Net Impact, Oikos, or PRME in fostering responsible people management?

3. Could you imagine working in a specialized corporate responsibility role like the ones Liz described? If so, what attracts you to a role like this? If not, why not?

PROFESSIONAL PROFILE
ERIKA GUZMÁN

Hi, my name is Erika Guzmán and I am the Human Resources Director of INNOVATION, a Mexican contract manufacturer providing co-packing solutions for the food and beverage industry.

(Continued)

Typical activities during a day at work. Human Resources is a 100 per cent service area, and our functions are focused on meeting this. Some of the main activities of a 'typical' day are:

- Recruiting, screening and hiring. Looking rather for attitude than knowledge; in other words, we choose people whose principles match those of INNOVATION. 'The company will be like its people.'

- Training and development of employees. We maximize efforts because development never ends. 'If we train half as much, people will work half as well.'

Courtesy of Erika Guzmán

- Managing high performance teams. Lots of communication and continuous effort with the teams, working with a focus on results, common good, and continuous improvement.

Professional people management initiatives. We feature a well-defined business philosophy with the highest values and principles, and we are responsible for communication across the organization:

- In terms of quality of life. Having decent facilities, a safe working environment and health campaigns for our people and their families. Practising inclusive recruitment, without discrimination, fostering teamwork, continuous training and integration activities.

- Promoting our Ethics Code as a commitment throughout our value chain, from fair competition with honest market practices and transparency, to respecting human rights, confidentiality agreements for our clients, staff, and security audits, etc.

- We bond with our community, creating safe and stable jobs, supporting social welfare causes, philanthropy, with a focus on health and the nutrition of our products.

- The link with the environment we achieved through compliance with national and international codes, controlling our emissions and recycling all our major waste.

Concentrating on diversity and inclusion. Currently, everything related to the concepts of diversity and inclusion is very important to us in our journey to professional people management. INNOVATION is a company created with the goal of generating welfare for its people and its community; in fact it is part of our Mission. One of our greatest strengths is that we have the opportunity to have men and women of different skills, age, social conditions, backgrounds, etc. ... and one of our biggest challenges this year will be the formal incorporation of people with disabilities.

(Continued)

Recommendations to people management practitioners. It is essential to have the commitment and support of the company's top leaders if you want social responsibility as part of the organizational culture. Extend the company values to all stakeholders. 'See what others do not see.' Have the ability to reconcile constantly, promoting openness and communication at all levels and in all directions. Remember that the basis and essence of our work is the service culture. Do not stop learning, growing. Be authentic and have integrity.

Job challenges? View employees as people with qualities, abilities, needs, interests and motivations, and adapt this to the policies and activities of the company. Involve people in the organization so that they are satisfied with what they do and keep it as a constant. The transformation of the company is through the leaders. It takes time, preparation, awareness, and vision, so that the changes are accepted and well kept.

People as ends, not means. It is very important to see people 'as an end and not a means' to achieve corporate growth and become fully human, in which only through the cooperation and commitment of all those who make up the organization can we achieve planned targets. Fundamental is the basic principle of respect for people. Do not deceive, do not take advantage of them. Not using people – either the community or customers, or suppliers, or employees. It seems a simple practice, but many companies forget this. Successful organizations maintain this in first place.

QUESTIONS

1. Which of the typical people management practices mentioned in this chapter does Erika engage in? Which ones are missing and what additional ones are there?

2. Discuss the tension between Erika's role called human 'resources' and her focus on never treating people as means.

3. How would you describe the role that Erika's work plays for her employer INNOVATION, for the local community, and for society at large?

TRUE STORY
INTERNSHIP ISSUES

EDITED BY ALEXANDRA LEONOR BARRUETA SACKSTEDER

Me exploring the field. My name is Baruk and I am a 23-year-old aspiring social entrepreneur. Throughout my academic journey, I have been involved with different social projects, which have allowed me to travel to a lot of places across the world to see the living and working conditions of many and the whole experience has definitely broadened my scope of understanding on social entrepreneurship in general. In 2016, my colleagues and I launched our first social enterprise in Zambia. But due to my inquisitive and hardworking nature, I have also worked in different sectors beforehand, such as the education sector, commodity retail, food industry, medical industry and various positions held in different domestic and international organizations. However, it is important to note that having an inquisitive and hardworking nature can be a double-edged sword in a working environment that may lead to overworking or even exploitation. This case will explain how that notion came to be as I was working for a medical company as an intern.

A dream come true … or is it? During my third year as an undergraduate student, I did my internship in a newly launched medical and diagnostic firm. The company had recently

(Continued)

been launched, and it was a well-established, well-marketed initiative where a lot of people from different corners of the city came to the firm to get their health checked. The firm was unparalleled when it came to customer service perfection, sophisticated machinery used and the medical personnel in charge of handling all the diagnoses in the firm.

Upon my arrival at the firm, the management in charge placed me in the accounting and finance department. Working in the said department was a great platform for me to get a glimpse of the accounting profession in handling middle- to large-sized enterprises, which later on contributed immensely in managing the financial aspect of my own startup. In the finance department, interns were grouped into teams, and each team was the responsibility of a full-time employee in the firm. So the interns underwent onsite job training under the supervision of their team leaders.

The plot thickens. Filled with enthusiasm and eager to learn, I was determined to work very hard, not only to equip myself with the necessary knowledge but also to let my presence be felt by the managers and to give back to the firm for giving me the opportunity that I wanted. My initial goal was to blend in, so as to make the learning process as smooth as possible. So the learning process started and we were taught several things like handling the daily expenditure and revenue of a large-sized firm or handling medical orders.

However, as the days progressed, the tasks were becoming more and more difficult, we were being asked to complete tasks too complex for our level. After a month of interning there, a few of us were assigned tasks by the team leaders to handle monthly bank reconciliation statements from several banks in collaboration with the firm. We were in charge of handling delicate matters like national and medical insurance payments. To a certain extent, I knew the more knowledge we gained during our time there the better. However, the management was orchestrated in a way that it forced a few of us to stay over time, working for up to ten hours a day instead of seven.

What was really going on. A couple of weeks into the internship, it came to my knowledge that team leaders and full-time employees were taking a step back from their responsibilities once they had identified an intern with two specific characteristics. Once an intern showed charisma and enthusiasm with what they were assigned to do and also once they had proven themselves to be hardworking individuals, team leaders began entrusting them with their tasks, knowing that the interns were able to get the job done effectively, thus utilizing their capabilities to their own benefit. And it is only natural that most interns will comply with the requests from their leaders out of fear and out of the need to appease and impress them. However, the question one should be asking is, was it right for the team leaders to push the interns past their limit or beyond their expectations?

Are you kidding me? A few years later, I got to know the following: the team leaders weren't allowed to share confidential information with anyone outside contract who wasn't hired full time

(Continued)

in the firm. Upon learning this a few years later, I still think I should have asked questions as to why things were happening the way they were. But I guess when you are an intern or an entry level employee, sometimes the fear of losing the job makes you do things or put up with things you shouldn't.

QUESTIONS

1. When managing interns, is it ethically correct to categorize who gets to handle complex tasks based on their enthusiasm and achievements? Why or why not?

2. What would you have done if faced with such a dilemma? Would you continue to work and learn as much as you can or would you quit to avoid further exploitation?

3. If you were a people manager in this firm, what new ways would you come up with to avoid any future exploitation of the interns and promote fairness in task allocation?

4. Have you ever had an internship or job where you felt you were being taken advantage of? How did you deal with it?

5. What kind of risks do you think there are with this practice of 'using' interns, and for whom?

DIGGING DEEPER: EMPLOYABILITY

Historically, at the heart of the perception of a good and responsible workplace was the concept of jobs for life, or job security. People were hired for a lifetime of work, and retired from companies they worked in after 30 years or more of loyal service. This was often the height of people's ambition – to achieve stability and develop within the company they joined after leaving school, college, or university.

Employability describes how well a person is qualified to work

Over the past three decades or so, things have changed. Markets have become much more dynamic, globalization has transformed business models, companies undergo change at an unprecedented pace, skills required some years ago are no longer needed and new skills are sought at a rapid pace.

Not only that, job-seekers have changed, Gen Ys (those born in the 1980s–2000s) are the currently dominant group of young professionals who seek meaning as well as money, and who demand much more from their employers than the previous generation ever did. There is in fact an expectation of not staying with a company for life, but instead gaining skills and moving on to the next company that can provide a different environment for personal and professional growth. Today, you advance your career by moving to another company, not waiting for your boss to retire or to promote you.

The implications of these changes for people managers are far-reaching and touch on the way people managers can create sustainable organizations through advancing employability in favour of employment:

1. Employability can often refer to the **ability of a person who is not employed** or never has been employed to enter the job market for the first time, such as graduates, or people from disadvantaged groups in the community [6]. There are examples in many countries of government and corporate programmes, which provide vocational training and upskilling for people who need help in penetrating the job market. Similarly, those who are laid off and find themselves in between jobs may undertake professional retraining so as to pursue another career as they find the skills they have developed at their former place of work becoming obsolete.

2. Employability, however, can also be **something you acquire while you are working**. A company that offers training and professional development, and internal career opportunities inherently makes their employees more employable and more attractive to another potential employer. This protects employees from the risks of layoffs, as if they are more employable, they will be able to compete in today's markets. Ironically, those very Gen Ys who have less long-term loyalty to a single company will tend to stay with a company that invests in them. Despite the fact that they are more employable, they will change companies less frequently because their need for professional development is being met. Employability then is an insurance policy, or personal asset, which employees often choose to retain to protect themselves against future uncertainty of their job stability and also enhance their personal value in the job market, should they need to cash in.

Employability has inherent advantages for society because more qualified and skilled people are able to make a positive contribution to local economies through maintaining their relevance in the marketplace. By investing in people, companies strengthen societies. The ripple effect is incalculable, but it is significant. Therefore, in this respect, PM policy directly affects communities. At the same time, by focusing on employability, PM protects its business against high attrition levels and contributes to professional management. Finally, by investing in potential employees and enhancing their employability, and subsequently hiring them, people managers are delivering a great benefit to their own company and their communities.

People managers should understand these trends and consider how they can develop policies and practices that meet the development needs of existing and potential employees. Investing in employees is a powerful tool, which meets the needs of professional management at many different levels and helps companies with the 'war for talent' while delivering a benefit for society as a whole.

POINTERS

Digging deeper into employability could, for instance, serve to reflect on the changed nature of work and employment with people often moving on from one company to another, often between industries and countries, the importance of transferable skills, work in the 'gig economy', precarious jobs, and a changed relationship between employers and employees.

WORKSHEET

DIVERSE EMPLOYEE VOICES

Credit: Slidemodel.com

Employee voice on: _____

POINTERS

Start by writing down what topic you want to explore relating to diverse employee voices and perspectives (e.g. a what would they say about a particular new policy of your choice?). Then, inspired by the different employees, give each a name and think about who they might be. Write down a short statement in the speech bubbles that represents this employee's take on the topic (e.g. relating to their unique needs, well-being, competence, interests, performance). This exercise would be particularly useful in the context of diversity management. While doing it, be mindful of any unconscious biases you might have.

REFERENCES

1. Polman, P. Net positive employee barometer. www.paulpolman.com/wp-content/uploads/2023/02/MC_Paul-Polman_Net-Positive-Employee-Barometer_Final_web.pdf Published 2023. Accessed March 20 2023.

2. Greyston. Our mission is to create thriving communities through the practice and promotion of Open Hiring®. www.greyston.org Published 2020. Accessed March 31 2020.

3. Garavan TN, McGuire D. Human resource development and society: Human resource development's role in embedding corporate social responsibility, sustainability, and ethics in organizations. *Advances in Developing Human Resources*. 2010, 12(5): 487–507.

4. www.ecsu.edu/documents/human-resources/hrcodeofethics.pdf

5. Ehnert I. Sustainability and HRM: A model and suggestions for future research. In: Wilkinson A, Townsend K, eds. *The future of employment relations*. Basingstoke: Palgrave, 2011: 215–237.

6. Cohen E. *CSR for HR*. Chichester: Wiley, 2010.

7. Zojceska A. Top 50 hiring and recruitment statistics for 2020. www.talentlyft.com/en/blog/article/364/top-50-hiring-and-recruitment-statistics-for-2020 Published 2020. Accessed July 30 2020.

8. Project Implicit. https://implicit.harvard.edu/implicit/takeatest.html Published 2011. Last accessed August 23 2023.

9. Collins PH., & Bilge S. (2020). *Intersectionality*. Chichester: Wiley, 2020.

10. United Nations. *Intersectionality resource guide and toolkit* www.unwomen.org/sites/default/files/2022-02/Intersectionality-resource-guide-and-toolkit-large-print-en.pdf Last accessed August 23 2023.

11. Applied. The hiring process of tomorrow is unbiased. www.beapplied.com Published 2020. Accessed July 30 2020.

12. McCurry J. A raw deal: The female chefs challenging sushi sexism in Japan. www.theguardian.com/world/2015/dec/25/a-raw-deal-the-female-chefs-challenging-sushi-sexism-in-japan Published 2015. Accessed April 6 2020.

13. Ivancevich JM. *Human resource and personnel management*. New Delhi: Tata Mcgraw- Hill, 2003.

14. Jablin FM. *Organizational entry, assimilation, and exit*. In: Jablin FM, Putnam LL, Roberts KH, Porter LW, eds, *Handbook of organizational communication: An interdisciplinary perspective*. Sage Publications, 1987: 679–740.

15. Miller K. *Organizational communication: Approaches and processes*. Wadsworth: Cengage, 2012.

16. Good-Ark. About Happy Company. www.goodark.com/en/happy_company/happy_introduce Published 2020. Accessed April 6 2020.

17. Ericsson. Humanitarian response. www.ericsson.com/en/about-us/sustainability-and-corporate-responsibility/technology-for-good/humanitarian-response Published 2020. Accessed April 6 2020.

18. Gollan PJ. High involvement management and human resource sustainability: The challenges and opportunities. *Asia Pacific Journal of Human Resources*. 2005, 43(1): 18–33.

19. Baeten X. Global compensation and benefits management: The need for communication and coordination. *Compensation & Benefits Review*. 2010, 42(5): 392–402.

20. Hegarty S. The boss who put everyone on 70K. www.bbc.co.uk/news/stories-51332811# Published 2020. Accessed April 5 2020.

21. Foremski T. Suicides at France Telecom are 5 times higher than at Foxconn – the human cost of cheap bandwidth and gadgets? *Silicon Valley Watcher*. www.siliconvalleywatcher.com/suicides-at-france-telecom-are-5-times-higher-than-at-foxconn--the-human-cost-of-cheap-bandwidth-and-gadgets Published 2010. Accessed December 22 2012.

22. HC Online. Unilever gets down to business with health. www.hrleader.net.au/articles/E6/0C0690E6.asp. Published 2010. Accessed December 22 2012.

23. International Labour Organization. About the declaration. www.ilo.org/declaration/thedeclaration/lang--en/index.htm Published 2012. Accessed December 22 2012.

24. Pearl D. Everlane workers were laid off at a busy time – and days after asking for union recognition. www.adweek.com/retail/everlane-workers-laid-off-after-asking-union-recognition Published 2020. Accessed April 6 2020.

25. Bjella B. Bernie Sanders accused Everlane of 'union busting' following staff cuts amid COVID-19 crisis. www.teenvogue.com/story/bernie-sanders-accused-everlane-of-union-busting-staff-cuts-covid-19 Published 2020. Accessed April 6 2020.

26. Laasch O, Moosmayer D. & Antonacopoulou EP. The interdisciplinary responsible management competence framework: An integrative review of ethics, responsibility, and sustainability competences. *Journal of Business Ethics*. 2022, https://doi.org/10.1007/s10551-022-05261-4

27. Report: Global Estimates of Modern Slavery: Forced Labour and Forced Marriage (ilo.org), Global Estimates of Modern Slavery: Forced Labour and Forced Marriage, ILO (2022).

CHAPTER 20

ACCOUNTING AND CONTROLLING

ULPIANA KOCOLLARI, ANDREA
GIRARDI AND OLIVER LAASCH

LEARNING GOALS

1. Create holistic accountability through sustainability accounting
2. Develop and produce responsible key performance indicators and balance sheets
3. Understand the basics of management controlling

FACTS AND FIGURES

Only 16 per cent of S&P500 companies' market value was represented by physical and financial assets, while 84 per cent were intangible assets, only a few of which are explained in traditional financial statements [1].

SPOTLIGHT

SOCIAL AND ENVIRONMENTAL REPORTING AT CLP

© 2014 CLP Holdings Limited

Reporting by CLP's management illustrates excellence in integrating social, environmental, and economic accounting in a way that creates holistic accountability. CLP is a Hong Kong-based business providing electricity in the Asia-Pacific region (including Hong Kong, Australia, Chinese Mainland, India, Southeast Asia, and Taiwan). CLP's mission is to produce and supply energy with minimal environmental impact to create value for shareholders, customers, employees and the wider community [2].

CLP's annual report opens with a '5-Minute Annual Report' that gives a snapshot of CLP's financial, social, and environmental performance. CLP reports more than 60 assets and investments, including wind power, hydropower, biomass power and solar power, as well as existing

© 2014 CLP Holdings Limited

assets, such as its nuclear power plant. Ever since 2011, CLP's operating and financial performance has combined the Annual Report with varieties of other tools to bring information to stakeholders, including the Sustainability Report and the CLP website. CLP stated '... these, taken together, are designed to give you a coherent and integrated picture of CLP and to demonstrate our ability to create value now and in the future' [3]. To make it accessible for stakeholders, areas of the annual report are highlighted by symbols that indicate where further information is available online and in the sustainability report. These links are displayed through-

(Continued)

out all sections of the report: Chairman's statement, CEO's strategic review, assets/partnership chart, performance and business outlook, resources, process, and financials, except the section on economic value where these two dimensions are integrated indirectly in the traditional financial approach.

In the performance section, environmental and social performance are integrated with financial and operational performance indicators. Performance is measured for each geographical area in which the group operates. Main sustainability measurements are reported in the final part of Chapter 19 ('Financial Management')

'File:HK Yau Ma Tei MTR Station shop CLPa Power Oct-2012.JPG' by Heleikoanoofutei is licensed under CC BY-SA 3.0

where the data is reported in a five-year summary for the CLP Group as a whole. Some of the environmental performance indicators included are resource use and emissions, carbon dioxide equivalent (CO_2e) emissions, water withdrawal, hazardous waste produced and recycled, etc. In particular, CLP's Climate Vision 2050 Target Performance provides an interesting long-term orientation. The social indicators are subdivided into three main categories: employees, safety, and governance. For each of these indicators, reference to the Global Reporting Initiative is highlighted, demonstrating the harmonization of the information with this standard.

PROFESSIONAL ACCOUNTING AND CONTROLLING

An organization should account for: The impacts of its decisions and activities on society, the environment and the economy, especially significant negative consequences; and the actions taken to prevent repetition of unintended and unforeseen negative impacts.

ISO 26000 Standard [4]

Professional management is impossible without **accounting** practice that delivers information regarding the triple bottom line, stakeholders, and ethical issues. The management proverb 'What cannot be measured cannot be managed', which is often attributed to the quality management pioneer William Edwards Deming, holds true for professional management. Many managers are not yet used to measuring ethical, responsible, and sustainable management activity and performance. The second line of the proverb might be even more important: 'What cannot be managed cannot be improved.' Only if we

Accounting
practices of systematically recording, measuring, analysing, and communicating information

learn to measure and manage ethics, responsibility, and sustainability management can we assume its positive role in society and for the planet. This chapter aims to provide a basis of concepts and practices for practitioners to build upon, to measure, manage, and improve management activity and performance, to 'make it count' positively for society and the planet.

Ethical standards in accounting have always been important. In 1494, Luca Pacioli, a Franciscan friar, and 'the father of accounting' wrote the first manifesto for formal accounting, *Summa de arithmetica, geometria, proportioni et proportionalita*. He wrote not only about double-entry accounting, and the interconnected system for capital, income, liability, and expenses, but he also elaborated on accounting ethics [5]. Nowadays, in the field of **professional accounting**, good and ethical practices and routines are statutorily specified through rules that are defined by a body of professional accountants [6, 7]. The ethical behaviour of accountants is also part of the auditing process, where auditors have a responsibility to evaluate the results of other accountants in terms of truthfulness and accuracy. Only in this way can accountants fulfil the purposes of their profession – 'to meet the needs of the clients or companies they work for, or to serve the best interests of those stockholders and stakeholders who are entitled to accurate financial pictures of organizations with which they are involved' [8]. The International Federation of Accountants (IFAC) ethical accounting framework in Figure 20.1 offers an even fuller picture of what practicing accounting ethically comprises.

> **Professional accounting** is centred on collecting and presenting the most truthful and accurate information possible, while engaging in ethical accounting practices

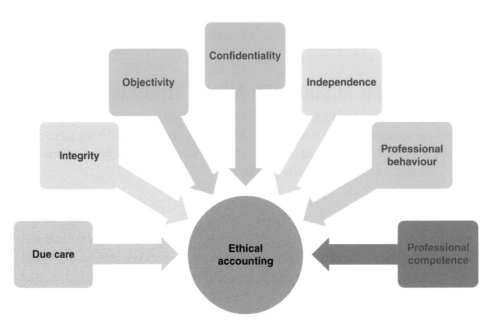

FIGURE 20.1   The IFAC Framework for Professional Accountants' Ethical Accounting

Source: Adapted from [10]

Figure 20.2 illustrates the accounting process holistically, its main phases of accounting and controlling and, at the same time, describes the way this chapter is structured. We illustrate basic elements, quality criteria, and concepts of accounting, and apply them to professional management. While *gathering data*, we identify the groups of data, environmental, social, ethics, and stakeholder information to be gathered, and prioritize them. During *evaluation*, we measure environmental, social and economic benefits, and costs and consider impacts. When *reporting*, we disseminate the information to stakeholders. In **management control**, we use data internally in order to manage what was measured, which closes the cycle illustrated in the proverb mentioned earlier. The underlying goal of the accounting process is to create *stakeholder accountability*, to be able to account for and to be held accountable for the triple bottom line, stakeholder impacts, and ethical outcomes of one's management activity by a broad set of stakeholders.

Management control both supports managerial work by providing relevant information and serves to evaluate and improve management performance

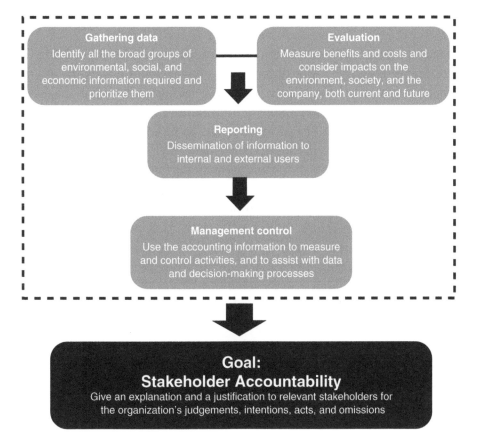

FIGURE 20.2   The professional accounting process

Accountability
is defined as readiness
or preparedness to give
an explanation and a
justification for judgements,
intentions, acts, and
omissions when appropriately
called upon to do so

Stakeholder accountability
recognizes that every stakeholder
has a basic right to be informed
and participate in decisions on
matters that might impact upon
them, irrespective of the power
which that stakeholder holds

Main accounting practitioners
are the recipient (accountee)
and the provider (accountor)
of information

This function of accounting information is developed through the concept of **accountability** [9] 'as the duty to provide an account (by no means necessarily a financial account) or reckoning of those actions for which one is held responsible. It is about identifying what one is responsible for and then providing information about that responsibility to those who have rights to that information' [11]. **Stakeholder accountability**, or rather accountability to stakeholders, consists of practices providing relevant information to stakeholders. It empowers stakeholders to hold management accountable for activities and outcomes [12]. In order to reflect a sustainability and stakeholder focus in daily activities and to constantly monitor the attainment of 'good' management goals, an appropriate accounting process that individuates measurement systems and management tools should be put in place. Together with its provision of relevant and decision-useful data to management, holistic accounting information must also embrace the qualitative attributes of accounting processes and practices in a relevant sustainability context to enable stakeholders to assess the environmental, social, and economic impact of the organization [13]. A core element of this process is the interaction between the main **accounting practitioners**.

We distinguish between stakeholders' contributions and their claims. The first category highlights what information management expects to get from its stakeholders; the latter refers to what stakeholders need from management. Considering this bidirectional flow of information, the crucial question from a stakeholder accountability perspective has to be the engagement and dialogue processes they are invited to participate in [14]. Stakeholder accountability must consider both giving and receiving information. The giving of an account is only one part of the accountability framework, as this also requires the accountee to have 'the power to hold to account the person who gives the account' [15]. Therefore, if accountability is to be achieved, stakeholders need to be empowered in such a way that they can hold the accountors to account [14]. This conception of accountability requires not only the provision of information, but also its value in terms of 'facilitating action' [16]. In addition to the concerns as to whether stakeholders are able to enter into communicative action with management, it must also consider the potential for new corporate environmental and social disclosure initiatives to enhance stakeholder accountability via empowerment, in terms of facilitating action through adequate tools.

THE 'NEW' ACCOUNTING AND CONTROLLING

A new normal of accounting and controlling is quickly emerging, as it moves from an exclusive focus on financial information to an imperative for the integration of social and environmental information.

FROM TRADITIONAL ACCOUNTING TO SUSTAINABILITY ACCOUNTING

Traditional accounting involved the identification, acquisition, measurement, and analysis of financial data in order to support companies' decision-making processes [17]. Accounting has therefore provided the shared language used for economic and financial information for stakeholders, both external (shareholders, creditors, etc.) and internal (owners and managers), or institutions and regulatory bodies (such as tax authorities and stock exchanges). It provides information on how a company pursues its economic and overall returns in the short and long run. This information is usually supplied by means of formal documents such as financial statements, business plans, and industrial plans. These provide quantitative and qualitative explanations of how economic resources are managed. The functions assigned to the accounting system are expressed as the concept of financial accountability [18]. Related obligations for disclosure are determined in regulations or legislation and verified by the institutions assigned to monitor them. As well as fulfilling a reporting function for a variety of commercial players, in traditional accounting the results of the measurement processes can be used for planning and controlling processes, to bring behaviours in line with the company's overall objectives and strategy [19].

Traditional accounting was centred on providing financial information to commercial stakeholders and for purposes of management control

Sustainability accounting [20] as a broader concept embraces the social, environmental, and ethical accounting (the so-called SEEA) supporting and monitoring an organization's contribution towards or away from sustainability [21, 22]. In particular, using the broader conception of sustainability accounting we describe a goal-driven, stakeholder engagement process that attempts to build up a company specific measuring tool for sustainability issues and links between its social, environmental, and economic dimensions [23].

Sustainability accounting controlling and reporting revolves around environmental, social, and economic information

Therefore, 'rather than being concerned with profits and financial accountability, accountability demonstrates corporate acceptance of its ethical, social and environmental responsibility. As such the "account" given should reflect corporate ethical, social and environmental performance' [22].

A stakeholder engagement session at the Italian multi-utilities (sewerage, aqueduct, purification, electricity, and gas) company Heralab.

Credit: HeraLAB

ORIGINS OF SUSTAINABILITY ACCOUNTING

Drivers behind the emergence of social and environmental accounting (and controlling) reflect the increased importance of stakeholders, the realization that companies have responsibilities, which cannot always only be expressed in traditional financial terms. Further, financial accounting has turned out to be of limited usefulness in the context of the economy's transition towards environmental and social sustainability. In other ways, though, the pace and development of social and environmental accounting has challenged the way companies measure success and, in turn, transformed the professional field of accounting itself. Figure 20.3 illustrates the main drivers and issues behind this rise.

Business	Government	Society
• Increased demand for more complex and accurate management information • Measurability and transparency of economic, social and environmental factors, and trade-offs per unit produced	• Pre-emptive and preparatory policies for regulatory regime and changes • Increased business and legal responsibility • Global/national economy externalities valuation	• Increased power of society and lobbying groups • Enhanced awareness of inter-connectedness, impact, 'trade-offs' and moral responsibilities of business/society

FIGURE 20.3   Main drivers of sustainability accounting

The start of this process can be traced back to the socially liberal activism of the 1970s. In the 'first wave' of socially liberal activism, a number of companies in the US and Western Europe adopted practices of social accounting concerned with 'the identification, measurement, monitoring, and reporting of the social and economic effects of an institution on society ... intended for both internal managerial and external accountability purposes' [24]. With the advent of the more economically laissez-faire 1980s, social reporting declined [25] until the process gained a new impetus in a 'second wave' in the early 1990s with a more particular focus on environmental issues and specific attention on external, accountability dimensions. A quoted example of a first mover in this second wave is Norsk Hydro, which first published an environmental report in 1989. Since then, of course, social and environmental reporting has grown exponentially to the point where most large (or even small- and medium- sized) companies are, in some way, audited and reported.

REGULATORY SHIFTS

Many countries in the world are progressively undertaking the introduction of regulations to ensure influential companies communicate financial and non-financial information, in an attempt to reach a level of harmonization regarding non-financial accounting metrics [23, 26–28].

A very recent example of upcoming legislation will require large and transnational companies and financial institutions to regularly monitor, and assess and disclose risks, dependencies, and impacts on biodiversity, and to provide that information to consumers. The 196 countries that signed the Kunming-Montreal Global Biodiversity Frmework have committed to implementing corresponding regulation [29]. Another important example is the European Commission's innovative directive [30] that requires mandatory disclosure of non-financial impacts for big companies (more than 500 people employed) [27, 30, 31]: 'Disclosure of non-financial information helps the measuring, monitoring and managing of undertakings' performance and their impact on society [with] a sufficient level of comparability to meet the needs of investors and other stakeholders as well as the need to provide consumers with easy access to information on the impact of businesses' [30]. Its aim is 'to provide investors and other stakeholders with a more complete picture of an organization's financial and non-financial, as well as social, environmental and economic performance' [32]. The directive encourages companies to rely on existing recognized frameworks. Adoption of the GRI's Sustainability Reporting Guidelines, the ISO 26000, the OECD Guidelines for Multinational Enterprises or the UN Global Compact is recommended. In contrast to the EU, in the US sustainability reports are not yet mandatory. However, legislators have shown a clear sign of political attention to non-financial reporting through the formation of a high-level committee [33]. Interestingly, large public companies have independently developed sustainability reports in the US: in 2018, 86 per cent of the S&P500 companies had a sustainability reporting system (compared to only 20 per cent in 2011) [33].

While governments seem to have undertaken non-financial reporting regulation, professionals and scholars are still not sure about its effectiveness in terms of reporting quality and tend to debate widely on the trade-off between government regulation and business self-regulation. Self-regulation should provide more tailored, sector-specific, and flexible sustainability reports depicting the actual performance of the company. On the other hand, this may allow companies too much freedom, and the lack of external pressure can lead to self-interested poor practices [27].

The European Commission has recently recognized the existence of these issues and discovered a gap between the sustainability information disclosed by companies and the actual information needs of stakeholders. A new related directive, the Corporate Sustainability Reporting Directive (CSRD), obliges large companies to report on the social and environmental impacts of their activities. It prescribes not only what information large companies are to publish (such as environmental and social protection, respect of human rights, diversity, corruption, etc.) but also how this information should be collected, organized and presented in non-financial reports. It introduces the following additional requirements:

- Double materiality concept

- Procedural notices to select material topics

- Inclusion of forward-looking information (like targets)

- Inclusion of information related to social, human, and intellectual capital intangibles

- Reporting in compliance with the Sustainable Finance Disclosure Regulation (SFDR) and the Taxonomy Regulation of the European Union

Furthermore, the new directive (2022/2464) prescribes, for the first time, the mandatory adoption of a specific non-financial reporting standard, the European Sustainability Reporting Standard (ESRS) [34].

IDENTIFYING THE ACCOUNT AND GATHERING DATA

In the first phase, it is necessary for organizations to identify a suitable framework to reflect the responsible management strategy as well as other factors like the sector or location. This framework will depend on the main sustainability accounting drivers facing the company. In traditional accounting most indicators (although not necessarily all) are based around economic performance indicators such as business performance (sales, profit, return on investment, etc.) or market presence (e.g. market penetration). In social and environmental accounting, a wider set of indicators must be used. These indicators will include environmental factors such as energy and water used in production, the percentage of recycled waste, or the amount of carbon dioxide emitted. Social factors may include labour indicators such as diversity, training, or health and safety. External social factors might cover items such as product safety or community involvement. A wide range of sustainability issues are organized under stakeholder categories (see Figure 20.4).

'It is difficult to determine exactly which of the many facts and figures that make up the full range of sustainability data […] should be disclosed' [35]. Therefore accounting must first identify all the broad groups of sustainability information required using the stakeholder accountability approach. The different stakeholder issues should then be prioritized. This process depends on how organizations decide their level of **sustainability disclosure**,[1] communicating performance on material matters relating to financial, **environmental, social and governance (ESG)** activities [36].

Sustainability disclosure is aimed at enabling stakeholders' informed assessment of management's sustained value creation. Disclosures are required and, if not furnished, the company should explain why not

ESG stands for environmental, social, and governance

---

[1]Sustainability disclosure is also referred to as Environment Social Governance or ESG disclosure, an old concept for the description of non-financial data.

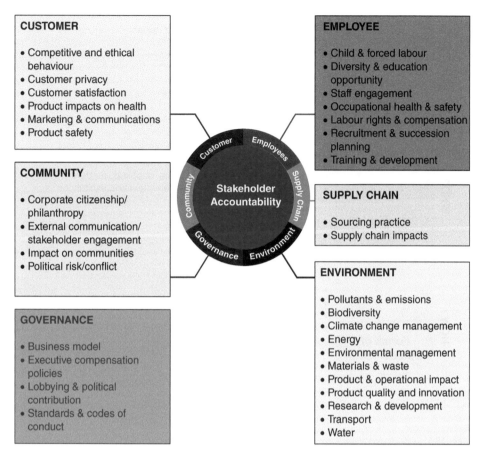

CUSTOMER

- Competitive and ethical behaviour
- Customer privacy
- Customer satisfaction
- Product impacts on health
- Marketing & communications
- Product safety

COMMUNITY

- Corporate citizenship/philanthropy
- External communication/stakeholder engagement
- Impact on communities
- Political risk/conflict

GOVERNANCE

- Business model
- Executive compensation policies
- Lobbying & political contribution
- Standards & codes of conduct

EMPLOYEE

- Child & forced labour
- Diversity & education opportunity
- Staff engagement
- Occupational health & safety
- Labour rights & compensation
- Recruitment & succession planning
- Training & development

SUPPLY CHAIN

- Sourcing practice
- Supply chain impacts

ENVIRONMENT

- Pollutants & emissions
- Biodiversity
- Climate change management
- Energy
- Environmental management
- Materials & waste
- Product & operational impact
- Product quality and innovation
- Research & development
- Transport
- Water

Stakeholder Accountability

FIGURE 20.4   Responsible stakeholder accountability issues
SOURCE: Adapted from [35]

An important part of sustainability accounting is to explain how stakeholder issue prioritization has been achieved [13]. This process is different from case to case because of the different drivers of sustainable accounting. Also there are manifold variables in terms of geographical influences, sector specificities, ethical and cultural values, activities, and services. This selection is influenced by and influences the degree and type of sustainability disclosure. Social and environmental disclosures have been increasing in both size and complexity over the last decades. International studies, although indicating variations between countries, [37–39] sectors [40, 41] and variation over time in the areas of disclosure [42, 43], confirm the rise in the volume and importance of these disclosures [44]. Considering the complexity of this process, a three-step test (Figure 20.5) can be useful to target every single sustainability issue to the account that management aims to represent in data.

The first step defines the accounting entity for which the account is to be developed. The accounting entity is an area of activities where information

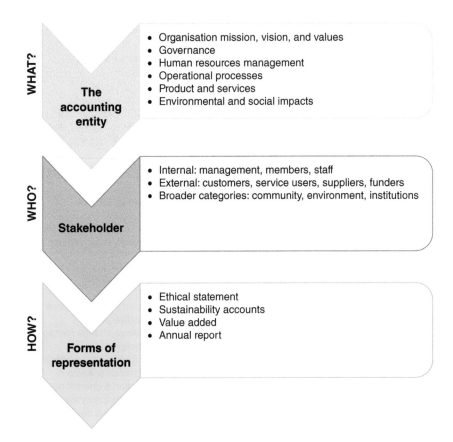

FIGURE 20.5   Individuation of disclosure content

has the potential to be useful for existing and potential stakeholders. These are stakeholders who cannot directly obtain the information they need to make decisions about providing resources to the entity. Or they cannot assess whether the management and the governing board of that entity have made efficient and effective use of the resources provided [17]. This test helps to select the basic issues that determine the impact that different organizations' entities may have on sustainability issues, orienting the process to the purpose of the accounting data.

The second step is identification of the stakeholders who are the potential recipients of the data. It responds to the second question: Who will receive the information? The distinction among internal, external, and broader stakeholders is important for the construction of the data. The information recorded should be made available in a manner that is understandable and accessible to stakeholders.

The third step, 'forms of representation', identifies the form the data must be presented in, examining how the information can be modelled and generated. This final stage considers quantification of the sustainability-related flows. These flows may include the number of people employed, emissions from product manufacture and use, resource use and amount of product or service generated, among others [45]. But not all the issues referring to the social and environmental dimensions can be expressed quantitatively. Qualitative tools, such as narratives to describe social and environmental impacts, should be used as a critical qualitative part of sustainability accounting [46].

MATERIALITY

Materiality describes the shared importance of a specific issue to both company and stakeholders and is an important principle for defining the content of sustainability accounting data. In Chapter 4 we illustrated a methodology to assess materiality. Many international regulators and standard setters, and public and private sector organizations have issued guidelines defining materiality for non-financial information. In general, they are in line with the definition of materiality for financial information by 'describing it in terms relevant to decision-making, putting it in the context of other information, and assessing its qualitative and quantitative importance with respect to this other information and decision-making' [45]. Here the attention is placed on defining the recipient of the information, usually a category of stakeholders beyond just shareholders. Importance is placed on the justification of not providing material information.

Materiality
describes the shared importance
of a specific issue to both
company and stakeholders

An important methodology for defining the materiality of the sustainability data is the sector-based framework of the Sustainability Accounting Standards Board (SASB). The SASB **engages** in the creation and dissemination of sustainability accounting standards for use by publicly listed corporations in disclosing material sustainability issues for the benefit of investors and the public. The SASB offers a materiality test, which includes five criteria for the inclusion of issues:

1. **Financial impacts/risks.** Issues that may have a financial impact or may pose a risk to the sector in the short, medium, or long term.

2. **Legal/regulatory/policy drivers.** Sectoral issues that are being shaped by emerging or evolving government policy and regulation.

3. **Peer-based norms.** Sustainability issues that companies in the sector tend to report on and accept as important drivers for their business activities.

4. **Stakeholder concerns and societal trends.** Issues that are of high importance to stakeholders, including communities, non-governmental organizations and the general public, and/or reflect social and consumer trends.

5. **Opportunity for innovation.** Areas where the potential exists to explore innovative solutions that benefit the environment, customers, and other stakeholders, establish sector leadership, and create competitive advantage.

To identify sector-specific material issues, the SASB methodology calculates a hypothetical score for each issue on a four-point Likert-type scale using each of the five materiality dimensions. These scores are then added together to give to each issue an overall score of 0–15, with the higher scoring issues considered to be more material. An example of the SASB materiality map constructed for the healthcare sector is represented in Figure 20.6.

The scores presented are not the result of a comprehensive and transparent assessment process but can be indicative. This exercise helps stakeholders identify key issues, and allows organizations to efficiently allocate resources to those issues most material to their sustainability performance [35].

A recent development of the concept of materiality is the European Union's directive 2022/2464 on mandatory non-financial reporting which introduces the requirement to perform a 'double materiality' process when selecting relevant non-financial information for disclosure. Double materiality refers to the idea of combining the analysis of the impacts of environmental and social risks on the company and the impacts of the company on society and the environment together [34].

EVALUATING AND ELABORATING DATA

The metrics of sustainability data should be part of a clear articulation of the causal relationships leading from the inputs to the process and then flowing to the identified outputs and outcomes [49], covering everything related to each of the sustainability issues selected:

> Specific and appropriate measures that reflect the sustainability strategy are essential to monitor the key performance drivers (inputs and processes) and assess whether the implemented sustainability strategy is achieving its stated objectives (outputs) and thus contributing to the long-term success of the corporation (outcomes) [49].

Measurability
expresses accounting's search and preference for tangible, quantifiable information

When evaluating and elaborating on data, we measure a broad set of social and environmental benefits and costs and consider impacts on the company, society, and planet. This phase includes costs and benefits related to both current and future operations but should not include current costs related to past operations. The adoption of these models and measures, and the systems to implement them, can help managers make more effective decisions to increase both sustainability and financial performance.

Measurability means expressing the indicator in terms that *can* be measured, rather than finding an indicator that is *easy* to measure [50]. This process of evaluation is often referred to as monetization because in traditional financial accounting, the measurement is intended as the process for determining the monetary

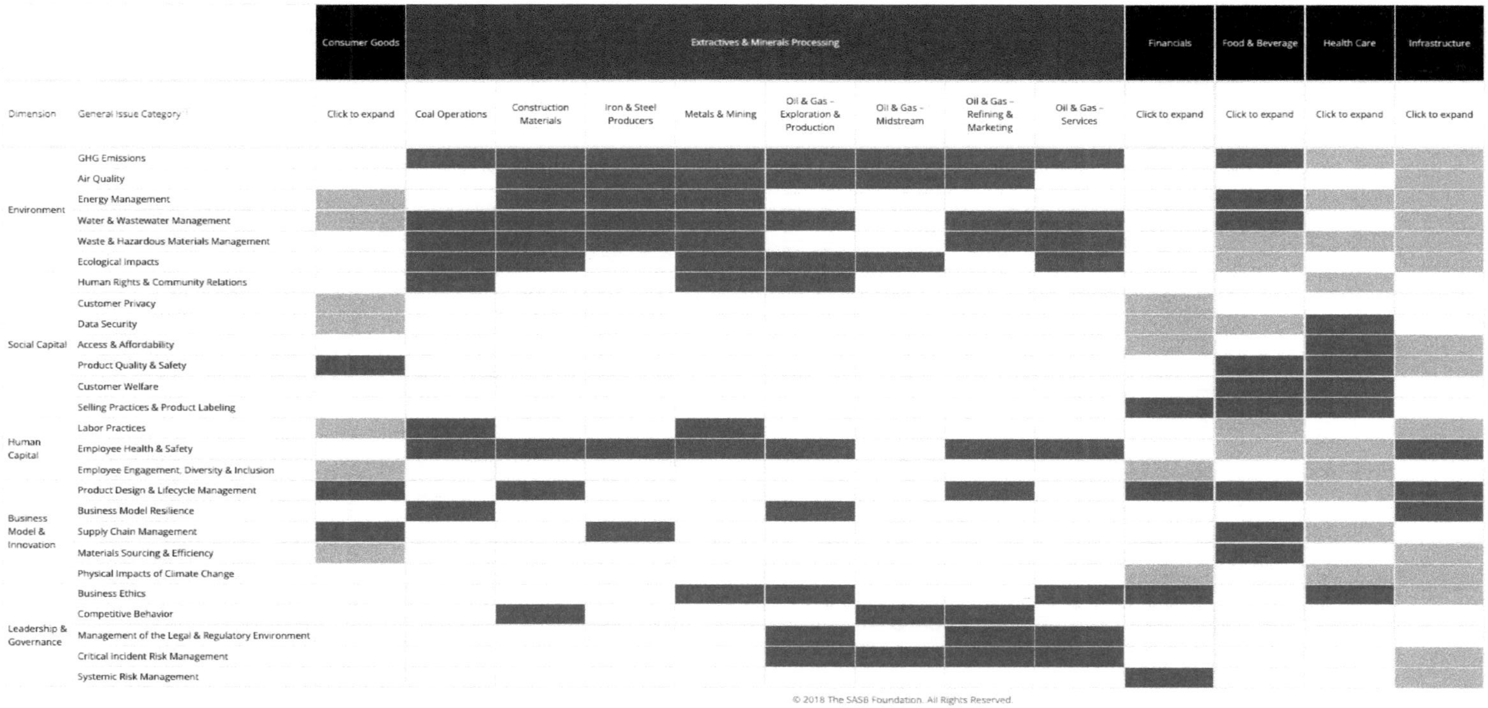
Consumer Goods
Extractives & Minerals Processing
Financials
Food & Beverage
Health Care
Infrastructure
Dimension
General Issue Category
Click to expand
Coal Operations
Construction Materials
Iron & Steel Producers
Metals & Mining
Oil & Gas - Exploration & Production
Oil & Gas - Midstream
Oil & Gas - Refining & Marketing
Oil & Gas - Services
Click to expand
Click to expand
Click to expand
Click to expand
Environment
GHG Emissions
Air Quality
Energy Management
Water & Wastewater Management
Waste & Hazardous Materials Management
Ecological Impacts
Social Capital
Human Rights & Community Relations
Customer Privacy
Data Security
Access & Affordability
Product Quality & Safety
Customer Welfare
Selling Practices & Product Labeling
Human Capital
Labor Practices
Employee Health & Safety
Employee Engagement, Diversity & Inclusion
Business Model & Innovation
Product Design & Lifecycle Management
Business Model Resilience
Supply Chain Management
Materials Sourcing & Efficiency
Physical Impacts of Climate Change
Leadership & Governance
Business Ethics
Competitive Behavior
Management of the Legal & Regulatory Environment
Critical Incident Risk Management
Systemic Risk Management
© 2018 The SASB Foundation. All Rights Reserved.

FIGURE 20.6 The SASB Materiality Map™ by industries

SOURCE: [48]. © 2020. Reprinted with permission from the SASB Foundation. All rights reserved.

amounts at which the elements of the financial statements are to be recognized and carried in the balance sheet and income statement [17]. In the sustainability accounting context, there are three main issues with this process:

1. Financial units of measurement are not necessarily suitable for **capturing social and ecological impacts**, which require an array of measurement tools to capture nature's multiplicity [51].

2. Many social and environmental impacts may appear to have **no immediate consequences** on the market and no financial effect. However, many of these externalities (impacts on others) are internalized in future periods and do affect operations and profitability of the firm in the long term.

3. We often see **economic benefits of sustainability as intangible** and therefore difficult to measure. As a consequence, although some forms of sustainability accounting rely on monetary units to measure environmental and social impacts, an increasing trend is the use of multiple units of measurement to assess performance in relation to the three dimensions of sustainability [13].

We will now illustrate several holistic accounting frameworks for sustainability data elaboration and evaluation, starting with costing models.

COSTING MODELS

Although it is difficult to precisely measure sustainability performance, there are economic and financial analysis techniques that provide reasonable estimates for social and environmental performance:

- **Full cost accounting** allocates all direct and indirect costs to a product or product line for inventory valuation, profitability analysis, and pricing decisions. Full cost accounting, such as Mathews' total impact accounting [52], attempts to capture the total costs resulting from an organization's economic activities, including social and environmental costs [53] and to value these impacts in financial terms.

- **Activity-based costing (ABC)** assumes that any activities related to products, services, and customers cause costs. ABC first assigns costs to the activities performed by the organization (direct labour, employee training, regulatory compliance) and then attributes these costs to products, customers, and services based on a cause-and-effect relationship [49].

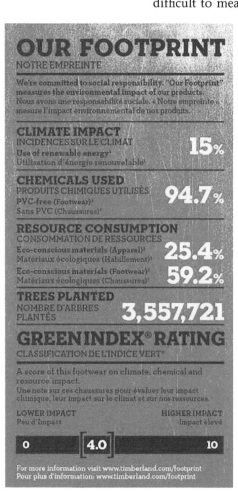

Accounting at the shoes company Timberland was able to account for varieties of environmental indicators (most of them per pair of shoes), which they, in turn communicate to their customers when buying a pair of shoes.

- **Life-cycle assessment** is aimed at minimizing the environmental impacts of products, technologies, materials, processes, industrial systems, activities, and services [54]. Life-cycle cost has been defined as the amortized annual cost of a product, including capital costs and disposal costs discounted over the lifetime of a product.

- **Natural capital inventory accounting** involves the recording of stocks of natural capital over time, with changes in stock levels used as an indicator for the (declining) quality of the natural environment. Various types of natural capital stocks are distinguished enabling the recording, monitoring, and reporting of depletions or enhancements within distinct categories [55].

SUSTAINABILITY PERFORMANCE METRICS

After evaluating the inputs and their effects on sustainability and financial performance, managers develop the appropriate processes to measure results. The sustainability accounting model in Figure 20.7 illustrates how managerial actions lead to sustainability performance and stakeholder reactions (outputs) that at a final stage affect long-term corporate (financial) performance (outcomes) [49]. Indicators are developed and used to collect evidence on the outputs and outcomes and assess their importance by valuing them.

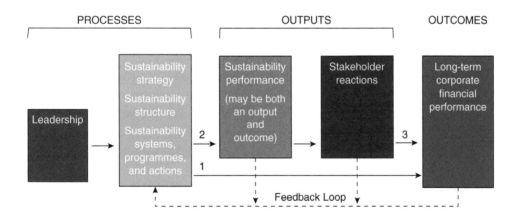

1. **Corporate financial costs/benefits of actions**
2. **Social impact**
3. **Financial impact through sustainable performance**

FIGURE 20.7   Individuation of consequences of sustainability actions on performance

SOURCE: Adapted from [49]

Arrow 1 in the figure represents processes that have immediate, identifiable costs and benefits that affect long-term financial performance. Some methods for its measurement were shown in the previous paragraph. Arrow 2 shows how the various inputs impact sustainability performance through processes. Finally, Arrow 3 illustrates how financial performance is impacted by stakeholder reactions to an organization's sustainability performance. We can distinguish between two categories of **sustainability assessments** [56]: the first tends to be all-encompassing ('stronger') and the second one tends to be limited ('weaker'). All-encompassing assessments will set broader physical boundaries to the sustainability model, will refer to longer time frames for measuring stability and success, and will minimize trade-offs among the sustainability interest of competing components in the system, while limited assessments do less so. The broader the range of the activities involved and the longer the duration, the more likely the outcome will be affected by other factors and the measurement becomes complex. Codifying of the information is an important issue in this phase. The information is elaborated on so that it is intelligible to the stakeholder to whom it is addressed [57]. Codifying enables the transmission of the information and the decision of the tools that will be selected for the data transfer.

Strong sustainability assessments
are all-encompassing assessments involving broad physical boundaries, longer time frames, and minimize trade-offs

SUSTAINABILITY INDICATORS

Sustainability indicator
a qualitative or quantitative metric used to assess social, environmental, and economic activity and performance

Accounting also derives indicators for the definition of performance targets [58] and their ongoing measurement. In sustainability accounting, **indicators** measure environmental, social, and economic dimensions. The use of indicators to estimate variables that cannot be measured precisely has a long history in environmental science [59]. It is considered appropriate where variables that are inherently complex cannot be observed directly.

In particular, the Global Reporting Initiative (GRI) indicators framework [60] on standard disclosures, which we will have a closer look at later on, is organized by economic, environmental, and social categories. Each of the categories includes a set of core and additional performance indicators. Core indicators have been developed through GRI's multi-stakeholder engagement.

1. **Environmental** indicators for behaviour and performance are, for instance, materials used by weight or volume, percentage of recycled materials, total water withdrawal, and initiatives to mitigate environmental impacts of products and services.

2. **Social** performance indicators are divided into four different categories: labour practices, human rights, society, and product responsibility. Within each category there is a requirement to elaborate on more specific topics. For instance, labour practices performance indicators provide data about employment, labour/management relations, occupational health and safety, training and education, and diversity and equal opportunity.

3. **Economic** dimension indicators address impacts on the economic status of commercial stakeholders and on economic systems at local, national, and international levels. The economic performance indicators category includes seven core plus two additional indicators. The core indicators report on, for example, financial implications for the organization's activities due to climate change, significant financial assistance received from government, and development of infrastructure investments.

Figure 20.8 provides a variety of further examples from the companies Iberdrola (environmental), Ferrero (social), and Deutsche Bank (economic) GRI Sustainability Indicators.

THE VALUE ADDED MODEL

The **value added** statement (VAS) is a supplemental report, which analyses 'value added in production and its source or distribution among the organization participants' [62]. It is a way for management to fulfil its accounting duties to the various interest groups by providing more information than is possible with the income statement and balance sheet.

The value added is the value created by the organization carrying out its activities and managing the contribution of its employees. Take the example of a manufacturing company calculating sales less production costs. The value-added statement reports on the calculation of value added and its

Value added
describes the economic value created by the organization, and how it is distributed among stakeholders

Goal of the 2030 Agenda (SDGs)	GRI Indicator	Description	P.
13.a Implement the commitment undertaken by developed-country parties to the United Nations Framework Conversation on Climate Change 13.1. - **Strengthen resilience** and adaptive capacity to climate-related hazards and natural disasters in all countries.	302–1	Proportion of energy consumption derived from renewable energy	190
	302–4	Reduction of energy consumption (efficiency)	192
	302–5	Energy savings of green products and services	195
	305–1	Direct GHG emissions. Scope 1 (per GHG Protocol)	199
	305–2	Indirect GHG emissions. Scope 2 (per GHG Protocol)	201
	305–3	Other indirect GHG emissions. Scope 3 (per GHG Protocol)	202
	EU30	Average plant availability	109
	Own indicator	Installed capacity from renewable sources (MW or %)	22
	Own indicator	Power produced from renewable sources (MWh or %)	23
	201–2	Financial implications and other risks and opportunities for the organisation's activities due to climate change	70
13.3. - Improve education, awareness-raising and human and institutional capacity on climate change mitigation, adaptation, impact reduction and early warning.	Own indicator	Awareness-raising activities regarding climate change and renewable energy	71

(Continued)

Topic	Where the impacts occur	Type of involvement
Human rights	Ferrero Group, Suppliers, Farmers, NGOs	Generated, contributed by the Group and directly linked through the Group's business relationships
Nutrition	Ferrero Group, Consumers, Consumer associations and NGOs, Institutions, Government and regulators	Generated by the Group
Employee rights	Ferrero Group, Suppliers	Generated by the Group and directly linked through the Group's business relationships
Products and ingredients safety and quality	Production plants, Suppliers, Distributors and Retailers, Consumers, Consumer associations and NGOs, Government and regulators	Generated and contributed by the Group
Talent and development	Ferrero Group	Generated by the Group
Consumer rights	Ferrero Group, Distributors and Retailers, Consumers, Consumer associations and NGOs	Generated by the Group and directly linked through the Group's business relationships
Responsible marketing	Ferrero Group, Institutions and regulators	Generated by the Group
Employee health, safety and well-being	Ferrero Group, Suppliers	Generated by the Group
Fair and inclusive workplace	Ferrero Group	Generated by the Group
Local community support	Production plants, HCo, Kinder + Sport, suppliers, Ferrero Foundation, Michele Ferrero Entrepreneurial Project, NGOs, Institutions, Governments	Generated and contributed by the Group
Inclusion and accessibility	Ferrero Group, Farmers, Local Communities	Generated by the Group and directly linked through the Group's business relationships

Topic specific standard disclosures			
GRI 200 Economy			
GRI 201: Economic performance			
103–1	Explanation of the material topic and its Boundary	7 – Identifying material topics 65 – Materiality and risk assessment	SDG 8
103–2	The management approach and its components	5ff.- Purpose and management approach	
103–3	Evaluation of the management approach	6 – Globally challenging and emerging trends 8 – Validating our performance	
201–1	Direct economic value generated and distributed	AR – The Group at a glance AR 212ff. – Consolidated Financial Statements	SDG 5, 7, 8, 9
201–2	Financial implications and other risks and opportunities due to climate change	6 – Globally challenging and emerging trends 29ff. – ESG due diligence 38ff. – Climate risks 62 – Implementing carbon neutrality DWS Report 10f. – Clients and products	Partially reported. We have not identified substantial changes required in operations, revenue or expenditure posed by climate change. Therefore, financial implications or costs of actions are not reported for 2018.	SDG 13 UNGC 7

Topic specific standard disclosures			
GRI 205: Anti-corruption			
103–1	Explanation of the material topic and its boundary	7 – Identifying material topics	SDG 16
		65 – Materiality and risk assessment	
		20 – Anti-financial crime	
103–2	The management approach and its components	20f. – Managing financial crime risks	
103–3	Evaluation of the management approach	20f. – Managing financial crime risks	

FIGURE 20.8   Exemplary indicators by sustainability dimension

SOURCES: [61]

application among the stakeholders in an organization. The information included in the VAS is the same as the one already contained in the income statement – salaries and wages used to be the only additional information, but it presents the information in a more comprehensible format (see Figure 20.9). In contrast to profit, which is the wealth created only for the owners or shareholders, value added represents the wealth created for several groups of stakeholders [63, 64]. It provides the wider stakeholder implications activities beyond just profits or losses [65].

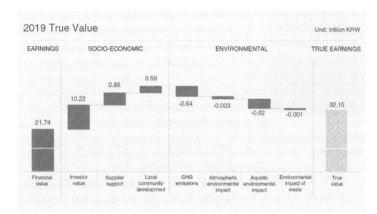

	2017	2018	2019	Unit
Economic Value Distribution				
[Supplier] Procurement costs	135.2	156.0	173.3	KRW trillion
[Local Community] Social contributors1	0.47	0.44	0.53	KRW trillion
[Shareholder & Investor] Dividends	5.8	96	9.6	KRW trillion
[Shareholder & Investor] Pay-out ratio	14	22	45	%
[Creditors] Interest expenses	0.7	0.7	0.7	KRW trillion
[Employee] Remuneration	27.2	27.8	28.1	KRW trillion
[Government] Taxes and dues by region	15.1	17.8	9.7	KRW trillion
Asia	10	6	15	%
South Korea	81	86	69	%
Americas & Europe	8	7	14	%
Others	1	1	2	%

FIGURE 20.9   Samsung's value added (Source [66])

Reporting
a formalized practice of disclosing information and giving account

REPORTING

To achieve accountability, stakeholders require access to information. Therefore, accounting cannot be separated from **reporting** or from the management of sustainability issues [67]. Once the information is elaborated on, the third component of the sustainability accounting process concerns the dissemination of information to internal and external users. It is based upon three key questions:

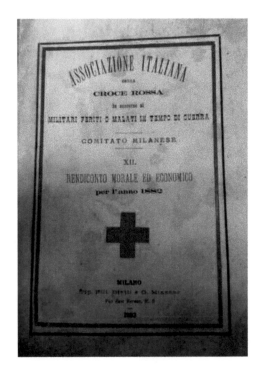

One of the first examples of social reporting, the 'Moral and Economic Report' of the Italian Red Cross in 1883

SOURCE: Ulpiana Kocollari

1. Based on what **criteria** should sustainability accounting information be represented?

2. What is the appropriate **format** of sustainability accounting reports?

3. What **dissemination mechanisms** should sustainability accounting use internally and externally?

Sustainability reporting can be subdivided into two broad categories based on the different relationships between financial and non-financial information:

1. **Supplemental reporting** to traditional financial reports use both quantitative and qualitative data, catering to the expectations of broader categories of stakeholders [68]. The main difficulty in supplemental reporting is evaluating the relative materiality of social and environmental actions with respect to economic performance.

2. **Integrated reporting** combines social, environmental, and economic information. Social and environmental dimensions are not supplemental to the financial accounts, but rather integrated with each other.

We will now look at the GRI as the main standard for supplemental reporting and the IIRC (International Integrated Reporting Council) guidance for integrated reporting. Finally, we will illustrate the auditing and assurance practices used to verify both types of reporting.

GLOBAL REPORTING INITIATIVE (GRI)

According to the **GRI** [60], 'sustainability reporting is the practice of measuring, disclosing, and being accountable to internal and external stakeholders for organizational performance towards the goal of sustainable development'

[60]. In the GRI Sustainability Reporting Guidelines, the term of sustainability reporting is considered synonymous with others used to define reporting on economic, environmental, and social impacts (e.g. triple bottom line, corporate responsibility reporting).

Currently, over 10,000 organizations from 110 countries regularly use the GRI standard as orientation for their sustainability reporting process and outcomes (see Figure 20.10). Moreover, 73 per cent of the biggest 250 companies in the world use the GRI as the main sustainability standard [69]. You can have a look at their open database, often including many years' worth of GRI reports from a variety of companies.

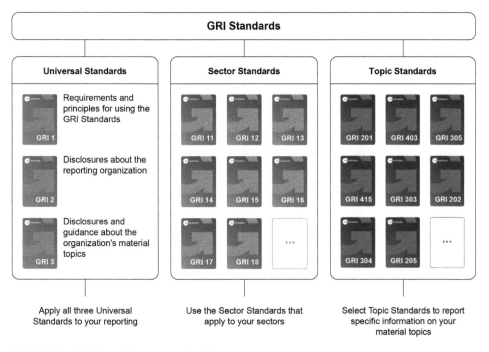

FIGURE 20.10 The GRI reporting process and guidelines

SOURCE: [70]

In the GRI's most recent version, standards are now structured into three main blocks [60]:

1. **Universal standards** (GRI 1, 2, and 3)

2. **Sector standards** (GRI 11, 12, 13, 14, 15, 16, 17, 18)

3. **Topic standards** (GRI 201–7, 301–8, and 401–18)

The central document is the GRI 1, which serves as a normative foundation of the GRI's approach and provides the conceptual framework for GRI's approach and structure. We will now introduce two core practices, defining the boundary and materiality assessment.

A crucial practice is defining the **report boundary**. We must determine which entities' performance will be represented in the report. For this reason, the process of boundary definition represents a crucial decision in the process of reporting on sustainability. The guidelines state that the report should include entities over which the reporting organization exercises control or significant influence.

The **materiality assessment** is a crucial component of the process of sustainability reporting. There is a wide range of topics that organizations could include in a sustainability report, and a materiality assessment assists in prioritizing the ones to be reported on. The GRI standard proposes a reporting process for which materiality assessment has been achieved by using a combination of internal and external factors (such as stakeholder concerns), which we discussed in Chapter 4.

EUROPEAN SUSTAINABILITY REPORTING STANDARD (ESRS)

The ESRS framework has received a boost from a new European Union directive (2022/2464), which prescribes its mandatory adoption as a non-financial reporting standard for large companies [34]. The framework introduces the idea of double materiality, mentioned earlier in this chapter – that is, evaluating the company's impact on the environment and society alongside their impact on the company. The ESRS framework comprises 13 standards including climate change, workforce, governance, risk management and internal control [71].

INTEGRATED REPORTING

According to the IIRC framework [72], integrated reporting brings together the material information on an organization's strategy, governance, performance, and prospects. It should reflect the commercial, social and environmental context of organizational activities. The IIRC is an international cross-section of leaders from the corporate, investment, accounting, securities, regulatory, academic, civil society, and standard-setting sectors [73].

Integrated reporting gives a broader picture of performance than traditional financial reporting. It makes visible the use of and dependence on different resources and relationships or 'capitals', its interaction with external factors, relationships, and resources, and access to and impact on them. The IIRC distinguishes six capitals that a business might rely on when considering the financial and non-financial types of capital:

- **Financial.** The wide-ranging funds available to the organization

- **Manufactured.** Manufactured physical objects, distinct from natural physical objects

- **Human.** People's skills and experience, and their motivations to innovate

---

Report boundary
defines information on which organization(s) is to be included

Materiality assessment
serves to identify the relevant (material) topics to be included

14 LIFE BELOW WATER

Combined Assurance

The Audit Comittee, on behalf of the Board, should ensure the credibility of all information included in the Integrated Report

Principles	Elements	Content
Strategic focus: An Integrated Report provides insight into the organization's strategic objectives, and how those objectives relate to its ability to create and sustain value over time, and the resources and relationships on which the organization depends.	Group profile	• First few pages of the report to introduce the business • In which sector does the business operate? What type of business is this? What are the products? • What is the structure of the Group and company? • Where does the business operate?
	Impact of scope and boundary	• Indicate the reporting period to which the report pertains • Focus on comparability between different reporting periods (i.e. the impact of acquisitions, disposals or restructuring on the comparability of financial and non-financial information) • Focus on comparability between financial and non-financial information (more often than not the boundary for financial and non-financial information differs)
Connectivity of information: An Integrated Report shows the connections between the different components of the organization's business model, external factors that affect the organization, and the various resources and relationships on which the organization and its performance depend.	Key features	• Illustrate the company's main achievements and key features • Ensure a balance between financial and non-financial information • Utilize graphs, illustrations and pictures to deliver a clear message to the reader (too many words drown out the message)
	Strategy Vision Values	• Use this part of the report to inform the reader of the character and values of the business • Clearly describe the strategic goals and objective of the business in plain language (this is a key feature of the report since risks, opportunities, key performance indicators and targets will all be linked to the strategic objectives of the business)
Future orientation: An Integrated Report includes management's expectations about the future, as well as other information to help report users understand and assess the organizations prospects and the uncertainties it faces.	Governance structure	• Set out the governance structure of the group and the company, including the committee structure • Provide details on directors (qualifications, experience, age, other Board appointments, etc.) • Describe the governance structures to manage risk and sustainability respectively • Governance report should provide clear feedback on the performance of the Board and each committee, as well as specific disclosures as required in terms of King III (composition of the Board, statement on adequacy of internal controls and internal financial controls, ethics performance, etc.)
	Stakeholders	• The Integrated Report is directed at the business's key stakeholders (remember, the Integrated Report cannot be everything to everybody, but should rather focus on providing key stakeholders with relevant and material information) • Identify the key stakeholders of the business (based on influence and dependency) • Identify the key interests and concerns of the key stakeholders and indicate where in the report these concerns are being addressed • Describe the strategy and methodology to ensure effective stakeholder communication
Responsiveness and stakeholder inclusiveness: An Integrated Report provides insight into the organizations relationships with its key stakeholders and how and to what extent the organization understands, takes into account and responds to their needs.	Material risks and opportunities	• Identify the risks and opportunities facing the business (linked to the strategic objectives) • Indicate the mitigation plans in place to mitigate the risks and capitalize on opportunities • Ensure a balance between financial and other risks and opportunities (think people, product, supply chain, governance, and environment)
	Key performance indicators and targets	• Identify the key performance indicators as they pertain to the strategy, risks and stakeholder concerns • Ensure a balance between financial and non-financial indicators • Identify measurable targets linked to the key performance indicators and report back on the progress to achieve these targets
Conciseness, reliability and materiality: An Integrated Report provides concise, reliable information that is material to assessing the organization's ability to create and sustain value in the short-, medium- and long-term.	Remuneration	• Explain the business's remuneration strategy • How is remuneration used to ensure delivery on the business' strategy? Include information of long-term and short-term incentives, as well as any other incentives

FIGURE 20.11 Integrated reporting framework

SOURCE: [74]

- **Intellectual.** Intangibles that provide competitive advantage

- **Natural.** Water, land, minerals, and forests; biodiversity and ecosystem health

- **Social and relationship**. The institutions and relationships established within and between each community, stakeholders, and other networks to enhance individual and collective well-being, including an organization's social licence to operate [72]

An overview on the guiding principles supporting the preparation of an integrated report is shown in Figure 20.11.

MANAGEMENT CONTROL

Controlling
is the process of assessing and steering management activities and outcomes towards a set of pre-defined goals

Sustainability measurement and management systems
are centred on controlling interactions between management, society, and the environment

Reporting and communicating accounts are also used widely in internal **management control** practices. Internal uses of accounting information arise from the need to measure and control activities and to provide data for decision-making processes. The management of sustainability performance requires a sound management framework, which links environmental and social management with the commercial strategy. It also integrates environmental and social information with economic business information and sustainability reporting [20]. Such alignment of strategy, structure, management systems, and performance measures is fundamental for organizations to coordinate activities and motivate employees to practice sustainability strategies [49].

Social and environmental concerns, as well as stakeholders' expectations, must be integrated with traditional financial and economic goals, developing a multi-dimensional and balanced **sustainability measurement and management** system [20]. This integration can help sustainability performance to be evaluated using a holistic approach, assisting managers to guide decision-making and behaviour. Once data is reported, management control practices evaluate sustainability performance. We compare the results achieved with the objectives set. This assessment practice can identify important improvements or shortcomings. It may also serve to revisit the targets and set out the new objectives (see Figure 20.12).

In this phase, the role of accounting and accountants is seen to:

1. Support the process of **engaging management** in the development and improvement of sustainability

2. **Review results, processes and inputs** as well as to relate these areas to each other

3. **Support and challenge management** in their choice of sustainability measures

4. **Facilitate communication** and review of reports [67]

Such control can also be practiced for a single process or product and services, giving an individual measure for the sustainability of the unit analysed. We will now look further into two prominent sustainability controlling practices:

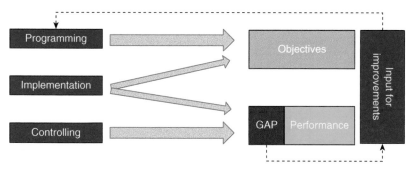

FIGURE 20.12   The process of management control

sustainability dashboards and strategic controls like the balanced score card and key performance indicators.

SUSTAINABILITY DASHBOARDS

Sustainability accounting utilized for management control purposes is designed to support and facilitate the achievement of objectives through the utilization of management information tools. An instrument that can provide overall, concise, and real-time information internally and externally is the **dashboard**. The sustainability metrics can then be sent to a dashboard (see example in Figure 20.13), which dynamically elaborates and summarizes social, environmental, and ethical performance through quantitative indicators providing real-time information.

A dashboard can automatically organize data according to the chosen category and level, or use different graphics to display achievement levels. This system allows qualitative estimation of sustainability based on manifold types of organizations and quantitative measurements that allow for customization, enabling sophisticated value judgements by end users.

The Ellen MacArthur foundation has verified and offers assurance that the medium-sized German cleaning products manufacturer Werner & Mertz has achieved record levels when it comes to plastic recycling levels and best practices. The next management control task relates to caps of these plastic bottles.

IMAGE SOURCE: https://wmprof.com/blog/ellen-macarthur-foundation

Sustainability dashboard summarizes social, environmental, and ethical performance through quantitative indicators

STRATEGIC CONTROLS

Evaluating strategies entails practices that measure and control the formulated and executed strategy against the strategic purpose and objectives. A chosen strategy's effectiveness has to be checked not only against the company's aspirational goal structure, but also against the overarching goal of

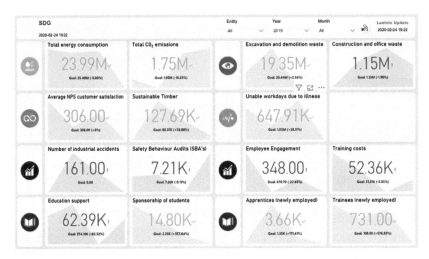

FIGURE 20.13   Sustainability dashboard solution

SOURCE: [75]

Strategic controls
guide ongoing strategizing to
indicate how to compare actual
results with expected results
and to suggest corrective
actions for strategy execution

the achievement of a responsible competitive advantage. **Strategic controls** aim to track the performance of the implemented strategy and provide the basis for corrective actions.

The point of departure for an effective control of strategic outcomes is the definition of quantitative and qualitative goals, metrics, and milestones leading to the achievement of the set of strategic objectives, so-called key performance indicators. If an adequate strategy has been chosen and executed, the pursuit of these indicators will lead to responsible competitiveness. An effective accounting of social and environmental business performance is the necessary condition to make the evaluation of an implemented strategy work. Management information systems such as enterprise resource planning systems are increasingly being adapted to deliver information on social and environmental performance as well.

The balanced scorecard
breaks down strategies for
implementation into key
performance indicators of
four types: customer, learning
and growth, internal process,
and financial perspective

The **balanced scorecard** is arguably the most popular strategy execution and control tool. Balanced scorecards are increasingly used to explicitly plan and track how ethics, responsibility, and sustainability are integrated into professional strategizing. Strategic objectives are translated into key performance indicators for the entire organization, individual units, and often even to evaluate managers' performance against the strategic objectives in personal performance reviews. The original balanced scorecard triggered a revolutionary development from a purely financial goal structure to the integration of goals and metrics related to learning and growth, internal business processes, and customer. Now those categories experience a renewed review, integrating professional management-related indicators [78].

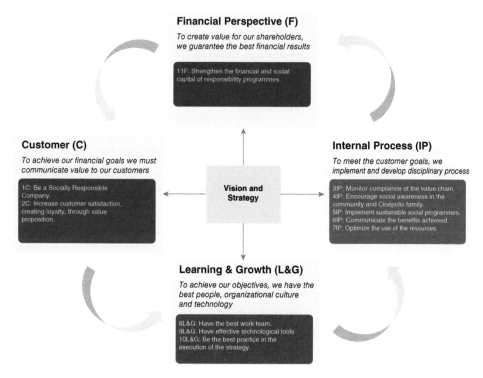

FIGURE 20.14 Responsibility balanced scorecard at Cinépolis

SOURCE: Adapted from [76, 77]

As an example (see Figure 20.14), Cinépolis, the world's third largest cinema theatre chain has extensively integrated social and environmental performance indicators into their company-wide-applied balanced scorecard [79].

PRINCIPLES OF PROFESSIONAL ACCOUNTING AND CONTROLLING

I. One of the main goals of professional accounting is the verification of a high level of the organization's **stakeholder accountability**, providing quantitative and qualitative information oriented to the long-term achievement of organizational ethical, social, and environmental performance.

II. The **accounting process** consists of four phases: (1) gathering data, (2) elaboration and evaluation of the data, (3) reporting both internally and externally, and (4) implementing and controlling.

III. **The disclosure of information** is one of the main criteria for accounting activity and should integrate social and environmental data with economic accounting data.

IV. **Materiality** is an important principle for defining the content of sustainability accounting data, describing all stakeholder-relevant information the firm may have.

V.   Sustainability accounting measures a broad set of **social and environmental benefits and costs**, and considers impacts on the company, society, and the environment. Although some of these forms of sustainability accounting rely on monetary units to measure environmental and social impacts, the use of **multiple units of measurement** to assess performance towards the three dimensions of sustainability is the most representative.

VI. The dissemination of accounting information to internal and external users is made through appropriate reports on ethical values, sustainability, and responsibility. The **Global Reporting Initiative** (GRI) – process-oriented standards with a particular focus on the document, is the world's most widely used sustainability reporting framework.

VII. The **integrated approach** to the accounting process can be an important framework for reporting the social, environmental, and economic indicators leading to accountability to stakeholders.

VIII. The responsible **management control process** evaluates the sustainability accounting data, comparing the results achieved with the values and objectives from the programming phase.

MANAGEMENT GYM: TRAINING YOUR PROFESSIONAL SIX-PACK

Knowing

1. Describe the four phases of accounting and give an example of the formulation of data passing through each phase.

2. Explain connections and differences between the following terms: Global Reporting Initiative, integrated reporting, and triple bottom line accounting.

3. Look up the most recent sustainability or responsibility report of a company from your country and answer the following questions:

(a) Who are the primary stakeholders of the company?

(b) Which are the most material lines of action?

Thinking

4. Research the practice of 'Hollywood accounting' and think about what the motivation behind it is, which stakeholders are affected and how.

5. Look up the list of performance indicators proposed by the Global Reporting Initiative. Which indicators do you think are the easiest ones to gather quantifiable data for? Which ones are the most difficult?

6. What do you think accounting should look like in 15 years time to make a maximum contribution to sustainable development, stakeholder value, and moral excellence?

Acting

7. Pick five UN Sustainable Development Goals of your choice. For each goal, design one key performance indicator that a manager could use to measure and control their sustainability performance.

8. What data could you gather to establish an accounting system for Tayo Akinyede, a Nigerian career mum. She sells Save80 stoves, a highly efficient cooking device, which reduces indoor pollution, deforestation, and carbon emissions. It also reduces time spent cooking. So that it remains accessible to low earners, the individual product cannot be sold for more than 17,000 NGN. Quantity discounts are available, though [80, 81].

9. Imagine you were asked to provide internal 'assurance' for the last draft of an annual report. After reviewing an actual annual report of your choice, write down five points that could have been improved – e.g. because they are ambiguous, misleading, or not credible.

Interacting

10. Identify and watch a movie that features an accountant. Write down the script of a conversation for an additional scene in this movie in which you discuss with the accountant what they could do better. Include their responses arguing against your points.

11. Conduct a role-play in which one group member plays a management controller, one a middle-level manager, and one a corporate strategist (you can invent more roles for bigger groups). Discuss what role key performance indicators play in your work. Do you like them?

12. Identify a company's most recent integrated annual report or GRI report and comment on it in a social media post, tagging the company.

(Continued)

Being

13. Think about what role accounting plays or will play in your (future) professional life.

14. What does it mean to you personally to do responsible accounting? Which one of your values plays the biggest role? What kind of role is that?

15. If you were to transform what matters most into performance indicators, what would be your top three KPIs?

Becoming

16. What challenges do you think there are in being a responsible accountant? How would you approach these challenges personally?

17. What good and bad behaviours do accounting codes of conduct stipulate, and which ones of these would you find easiest and most difficult to follow? How would you stay in line with all professional accounting practices?

18. How do you think you might be affected by 'bad' accounting, reporting, or controlling practices? What could you do to avoid this from happening?

Laasch, O., Moosmayer, D., & Antonacopoulou, E. P. (2023). The interdisciplinary responsible management competence framework: An integrative review of ethics, responsibility, and sustainability competences. *Journal of Business Ethics, 187,* 733–757.

PIONEER INTERVIEW
STEFAN SCHALTEGGER

INTERVIEWER: OLIVER LAASCH

Stefan Schaltegger is one of the earliest pioneers to study and shape the field of sustainability accounting, and has done ground-breaking work in sustainability strategy, ecopreneurship, and sustainability-oriented innovation as well. He founded the world's first Sustainability MBA at the Leuphana University Lüneburg.

Sustainability accounting change? For the last couple of years, research and corporate practice have been specialized more, and aim to analyse and develop different areas of sustainability accounting, such as carbon, water, biodiversity, accounting, material flow cost accounting or human rights accounting and reporting. Sustainability management control has developed, and more specialized

Courtesy of Stefan Schaltegger

accounting tools are being discussed. Overall, this is a development from philosophical and engineering approaches focusing on the organizational level, and reporting to stakeholders to management approaches how accounting could contribute to sustainable development.

What is the role of sustainability accounting? Cutting edge research is challenged to deal with how accounting could (i) better support companies not only to become less unsustainable but

(Continued)

to contribute effectively to sustainability transitions of markets and the economy acting in the 'safe operating space of planetary boundaries'. Better consider specific contexts of social and environmental topics, complexities of phenomena of unsustainability, as well as contexts of industry, culture, country, time period, etc. (ii) The role of accounting as enabler of sustainable development needs to be brought more into focus. Here a deeper understanding needs to be achieved of how accounting could be developed for different types of profit, non-profit, or hybrid organizations, as well as how links to planetary boundaries and UN SDGs could be established much more explicitly.

Conventional vs sustainability accounting? Conventional accounting and reporting develop too slowly and incrementally, and I dare say, often into the wrong direction, requiring ever more bureaucratic processes and structures. Conventional accounting still fosters many sustainability problems, is outdated and deals with too many irrelevant issues while largely ignoring highly relevant sustainability topics. Sustainability accounting is largely in parallel to conventional accounting and performed by non-accountants. So far, I cannot find sufficiently strong signals that this will change fast.

Sustainability accounting challenges? First, accounting methods still need to be developed for complex topics like biodiversity or human rights. This involves approaches, which take an inter- and transdisciplinary approach to sustainability management, accounting, and reporting. Second, more research progress on accounting considering the impacts of an organization beyond its boundaries is needed. Third, the benefit of applying sustainability accounting methods needs to be developed better and communicated more clearly. This includes a better understanding of how to develop business cases for sustainability to create effective contributions to sustainable development at the macro scale and benefits at the organizational level. However, this also involves research on purpose and motivational aspects of accounting.

QUESTIONS

1. How does Stefan imply that accounting can contribute to sustainable development?

2. Thinking forward from Stefan's point about different types of accounting for different organizations, how do you think accounting will be different between, for instance, a commercial business, B Corp, and an NGO?

3. Which one of the challenges of sustainability accounting are you most likely to encounter in your work, and in what form?

PROFESSIONAL PROFILE
DANIEL ETTE

Hi, my name is Daniel and I am working as a sustainability controller for the high-end sanitary fittings manufacturer Grohe.

Responsibilities of a sustainability controller.
My main responsibility as a sustainability controller is to be seen introducing sustainability into management accounting and controlling thinking. The methodological competence of controlling must be extended from simply a financial focus towards the recognition of economic, ecological, and social topics, so that our controlling can be a holistic business partner for the management board. In order to achieve that, my

responsibilities include setting up a valid database and agreeing on KPIs together with the management. Moreover, it is my responsibility to convince co-workers, management and employees that responsible thinking is important. As a sustainability controller I strive towards a mindset change within the corporation.

A day at work. For me, being a sustainability controller meant setting up an IT-based solution to generate reliable triple bottom line data. Now, sustainability data can be reported in the same cycles as key financial figures, by using SAP-based tools. That led to the implementation of automatically available KPIs within a customized sustainability dashboard, which we called 'Hansgrohe sustainability KPIs'.

In the day-to-day business, deviations from targets are evaluated in order to be able to take effective corrective actions. The result is that respect for the environment, social factors, and economic success are combined efficiently and integrated systematically into business processes.

Moreover, since we have implemented sustainability investment criteria, investments are being evaluated not only on a monetary basis, but also with a social and environmental understanding. Last but not least, the evaluation of environmental footprints of more and more products requires the support of sustainability controlling.

Accounting and stakeholders. The goal of sustainability controlling is to be seen in maintaining the long-term viability of the corporation and at the same time showing respect for the members of our society and the environment. It is not about doing some

(Continued)

philanthropic actions. Rather, sustainability controlling deals with the question of how the interests of shareholders, as well as the interests of other stakeholders like the employees or the neighbourhood can be satisfied. The triple bottom line comes into play by extending investment evaluation towards a holistic picture. Controlling itself has a lot to do with accountability and honesty. Controlling is required to support management with accurate and reliable data.

Phases and tools of sustainability controlling. The work of a sustainability controller is linked to all phases mentioned in the chapter. I am highly involved in gathering suitable data and in evaluating it. At the beginning, which of the indicators are material and help to steer the corporation must be clarified. Questions of *what*, *who* and *how* help a lot to not lose sight in the complex context of sustainability controlling. In this sense, the *materiality map* is also helpful. As always in controlling, a sustainability controller deals with gap analyses and supports management to take corrective measures – in my position, corrective measures with respect to social, environmental, and economic issues.

The key role of controlling. It is important to realize that controlling and management accounting is in a crucial position when it comes to the question of how sustainability can be introduced into a corporation. Controlling, with its cross-departmental tasks and connections, can be a driver towards sustainability. To do so, methodological competences are necessary, as shown in this book. A valid database is one of the most important aspects. Only in this way can targets be set, deviations evaluated and measures derived.

However, it is of substantial importance to understand that one cannot make a corporation responsible by only taking hard facts into account. Controlling is required to change its own mindset and to nudge management and employees towards holistic thinking in terms of responsibility and sustainability. Hence, sustainability controlling is not number crunching. It is about steering a corporation towards responsible behaviour by making responsibility a central issue.

Main challenges of my job. One of the most challenging points can be seen in convincing managers and employees that environmental and social factors are of importance – besides monetary ones. Moreover, as a sustainability controller, one must master the balancing act of being a trustworthy business partner for management and of being an enthusiastic driver towards more responsibility and sustainability.

QUESTIONS

1.   Would you have thought the work of a sustainability controller would be like Daniel has described? What aspects are different and which ones are similar to what you thought it was about?

(Continued)

2. What do you think might be the top social, environmental, and economic sustainability indicators for management in a business like Grohe?

3. What stakeholders do you think Daniel may consider when doing his work and what indicators do you think he might use to provide relevant information for them?

TRUE STORY

AM I THERE YET? ACCOUNTING AND CONTROLLING FOR A 1 TONNE CARBON LIFESTYLE

EDITED BY OLIVER LAASCH

Who I am and who I want to become. Hi everyone, my name is Geetika from Scotland, where I am currently studying to become a certified management accountant. Something that has defined me for the last couple of years now is this feeling of anxiety about the future. In particular, I feel super anxious about climate change. So naturally, I felt maybe I can use what I am good at, accounting, to understand and control my own carbon impact. Maybe, this can even give me back a feeling of being able to do something about the cause of my climate anxiety; the very least I hope

'Go vegan and cut your climate footprint by 50%. (23310836832).jpg' by Alisdare Hickson from Canterbury, United Kingdom is licensed under CC BY-SA 2.0

(Continued)

to be able to say one day is that I stopped being part of the problem, maybe, even becoming part of the solution.

One tonne carbon lifestyle. Even if I was able to properly account for and calculate my carbon emissions impact, what should be the goal? Quite quickly my internet search is saturated with terms like 'net zero' and the 'one tonne' per year lifestyle. I learnt that net zero refers to the goal of being able to emit just as much carbon directly and indirectly as one can offset (think planting trees for the sake of simplicity). I also learnt that 0.7 metric tonnes of carbon emissions per person per year would get us to net zero globally. Typically, this is then rounded up to 1 tonne. Bang, the one tonne carbon lifestyle was my goal.

Reality check! Once I started reading about actual carbon impacts, my anxiety came back. Is this actually possible, for me, and more importantly, for everyone else on this planet? For instance, I learnt that the average person in the United Kingdom lives on 13 tonnes, and even people in countries with some of the least carbon intensive lifestyles like in the Congo with 1.4 metric tonnes did not meet this essential goal. What frustrated me most was that even just the carbon emission from governmental activities per person was 800 kgs, implying that if I was to take this seriously I had just 200 kg left for everything else I was doing. This corresponds to the amount of carbon emitted from taking a long hot shower every day.

Accounting for the lowest-hanging carbon fruits. I decided to go for it anyway. I like challenges. Once I did that I found that there were a couple of low-hanging fruits. Luckily, I never qualified for a driving licence and therefore am not even tempted to buy a car. This alone means I am not emitting the 1.6 metric tonnes the average car in the UK emits per year. Then I noticed the enormous impact of plant-based eating, which in my family and home culture was the normal diet anyway. This meant that my eating habits were already over 70 per cent less carbon intensive than that of the average meat eater! But then I learnt that even a typical vegan diet meant over a tonne of carbon per year. So it would need to even be a low-carbon vegan diet. Uff, I am in trouble!

Now that's a biggie! And it got even worse, I hadn't even thought about my less frequent, but super big travel impacts. I always very much enjoyed connecting back to my family's Indian roots, and visiting relatives who are still there on an annual basis. I would have to account 2.1 tonnes for that. Also, I was hoping to become that kind of travelling controller for a multinational company who checks in on a different factory in a different location every two weeks or so. If I was to take this seriously, I might have to rethink my career plans to go online, but then I learnt that even working from home on average means 1 tonne of carbon emissions per year, mostly related to the energy used in the home and as 'every click we do' emits humongous amounts of carbon in the infrastructure on which the internet runs. And this doesn't even include the carbon emissions going into the production of my equipment. Not two screens, one. Maybe I should only work from my laptop?

(Continued)

Offsetting is the saviour ... or wait, is it? Then I got excited about offsetting, but yes right, the 'net' in net zero meant that even if I emit more than that dang tonne, I can reduce that number by taking carbon out of the air. Very conveniently, I learnt I can actually pay others for it. So maybe, visits to India are back on the table?! Then I had a closer look and got suspicious about the enormous difference in pricing, and some of the projects I would pay these companies to use to offset my emissions didn't feel quite right. Then I got into all the scandals and ways the accounting behind how much is actually being offset is 'not straightforward' to say the least. Can I really trust the numbers of offsetting? Maybe I could do my own carbon 'insetting' to do the offset myself, rather than paying someone else for it. I learnt that, for instance, composting is a 'carbon sink', meaning that it stores more carbon in the soil than it emits.

Does it have to be that difficult?! After all that research and my first account estimates, I am now living a 7 tonnes lifestyle, far below average, but still way too high. I will take on the challenge, but also feel what is happening around me is a crucial element, and maybe, I should actively work towards changing my life's 'infrastructure' as well. For instance, I could approach companies to suggest they disclose the carbon impacts of their products and services, maybe even start a petition for legislation? I even read somewhere that personal carbon accounting one day might become a mandatory thing, just as businesses do their tax return every year. If it was too high, you might be forced to pay for offsets. Something like that would surely create very well needed pressure, and probably a much better infrastructure for our personal carbon accounting and controlling.

QUESTIONS

1. If you were trying to find out your exact personal impact, where would you begin your accounting efforts? What would be the main lifestyle practices that you would need to assess in order to capture the CO_2 impacts?

2. Which main causes of CO_2 emissions in your personal life do you anticipate being the most difficult ones to reduce sufficiently? Do you think once you know your emissions, you would be able to get to a 1 tonne lifestyle? What personal sacrifices are you open to making for the sake of your CO_2 impact?

3. What big moves and lifestyle choices do you think one could make to be in the best place for a low carbon emission lifestyle? Moving house, maybe, DIY carbon offsetting in your own garden, changing jobs, only using a bicycle ...?

DIGGING DEEPER: GENDER ISSUES INSTRUMENTS IN ACCOUNTING

Gender budgeting is defined by the Council of Europe as an assessment of budgets that incorporates a gender perspective at all levels of the process of budget setting and that reallocates revenues and expenditures in order to promote gender equality [82]. The underlying idea is to address the need for social equality between men and women by focusing on how resources are collected, managed, and spent. Using a gender budgeting logic moves gender equality to the forefront of resource allocation practices. By doing this, the issue of reducing gender gaps is addressed using financial tools like different types of gender budgeting (see Table 20.1) [83].

TABLE 20.1   Gender budgeting typology

Gender budgeting categories	1. Gender-informed resource allocation
	2. Gender-assessed budgets
	3. Needs-based gender budgeting
Gender budgeting tools	• Ex ante and/or ex post gender impact assessment
	• Gender perspective in resource allocation, performance setting and/or spending review
	• Gender-related budget incident assessment
	• Gender budget baseline analysis
	• Gender audit of the budget
	• Gender needs assessment

SOURCE: Adapted from [83]

Another tool is a **gender equality action plan** (see Table 20.2), which represents a set of actions that articulate a strategic view in order to achieve gender equality. The scope and structure of gender equality plans may vary widely depending on the organizational context. This is due to the peculiarities of each context and differences in diagnosis.

However, a proper gender equality plan should include a set of actions including these four phases at least [84]:

1. **Analysis.** Conducting audits and impact assessments of practices with the aim of identifying gender bias

2. **Planning.** Identifying strategies that could correct bias in an innovative way

3. **Implementation.** Activities are implemented

4. **Monitoring.** Setting proper targets and monitoring progress using indicators

TABLE 20.2 Sample indicators for a gender equality action plan

Inequality identified in mapping	Action to be undertaken	Specific measures and targets to achieve change	Responsible
Numerical gender inequality in the staff at all levels	• Increase the number of women in mid- and senior- level management positions • Determine whether legal reform is required	• Agree a target for the proportion of mid- and senior-level management positions to be held by women (such as gender balance over the next five years) • Provide all mid-level women executives with leadership and management training within a certain time period • Entrust a group of individuals in the EMB with the responsibility to monitor progress on the target	• Executive management board (EMB) leadership • People management department • Training department and/or public service ministry or equivalent
No formal equal opportunity policy or anti-discrimination and harassment policy	• Develop policies on equal opportunity and anti-discrimination and harassment	• Review all existing policies and procedure manuals from a gender equality perspective • Survey staff about their recruitment and workplace experiences • Adopt a policy and review periodically	• EMB management • People management department • Gender focal point(s)
Lack of gender-disaggregated data	• Commit to ensuring that voter turnout data collected and reported by the EMB is disaggregated by gender	• Review existing laws and regulations and amend any clauses that may prevent collecting gender-disaggregated data • Review all data collection methods and forms • Where needed, add 'gender' as a variable on all electronic databases that deal with voter registration and turnout • Where needed, add 'gender' as a variable on all forms that collect turnout data, such as polling station results forms • Ensure that instructions on collecting gender-disaggregated data are included in training manuals or other directives for polling staff	• EMB management • Parliament • Electoral operations section • Training section • Voter information section

SOURCE: [85]

POINTERS

You could use these materials to look in depth into the principles and practices of gender accounting – for instance, starting with the OECD's gender budgeting website, or digging deeper into the different types of gender budgeting. You could also use gender accounting practices to brainstorm about how other accounting practices could be introduced to address a different social or environmental issue.

WORKSHEET

IDENTIFYING AND DOCUMENTING SUSTAINABILITY INDICATORS

Indicator name	Period 1:				Period 2:				Period 3:			
	Overall	Per product	Per person	Change compared to previous period in %	Overall	Per product	Per person	Change compared to previous period in %	Overall	Per product	Per person	Change compared to previous period in %
Social												
_____												
_____												
Environmental												
_____												
_____												
Economic												
_____												
_____												

POINTERS

You could use this table to identify sustainability indicators and document their development over three periods (e.g. a day, month, quarter, or year). You present the indicator value overall (e.g. for the entire company) and/or divide it by the number of products or people involved. You could fill this table in, for instance, based on data you measure yourself (e.g. related to your job, business, or private life) or you could use an organization's sustainability and/or integrated reports to procure data (e.g. on the value of indicators across different periods, and total number of employees, or units of products/services produced).

REFERENCES

1. AON. *Financial impact of intellectual property & cyber assets.* New York: AON-Ponemon, 2020.
2. CLP. www.clpgroup.com Published 2020. Accessed July 20 2020.
3. CPL. Annual report. *Annual report and accounts.* CPL, 2011.
4. ISO 26000 Social responsibility, 2012.
5. Pacioli L. Summa de arithmetica, geometria, proportioni et proportionalita. Venica, 1494.
6. Barton A. Professional accounting standards and the public sector: A mismatch. *Abacus.* 2005, 41(2): 138–158.
7. Parker LD. Professional accounting body ethics: In search of the private interest. *Accounting, Organizations and Society.* 1994, 19(6): 507–525.
8. Duska RF, Duska BS. *Accounting ethics.* Malden, MA: Blackwell, 2003.
9. Crane A, Matten D, Moon J. Stakeholders as citizens? Rethinking rights, participation, and democracy. *Journal of Business Ethics.* 2004, 53(1–2): 107–122.
10. Jules, D., & Erskine, R. *The international code of ethics for professional accountants: Key areas of focus for SMEs and SMPs.* International Federation of Accountants, 2018. www.ifac.org/knowledge-gateway/supporting-international-standards/discussion/international-code-ethics-professional-accountants-key-areas-focus-smes-and-smps Accessed March 20 2023.
11. Gray R, Owen D, Adams C. *Accounting and accountability: Changes and challenges in corporate social and environmental reporting.* London: Prentice Hall, 1996.
12. Unerman J, Bennett M. Increased stakeholder dialogue and the internet: Towards greater corporate accountability or reinforcing capitalist hegemony? *Accounting, Organizations and Society.* 2004, 29(7): 685–707.
13. Lamberton G. Sustainability accounting – a brief history and conceptual framework. Paper presented at Accounting Forum, 2005, 29(1): 7-26.
14. Cooper SM, Owen DL. Corporate social reporting and stakeholder accountability: The missing link. *Accounting, Organizations and Society.* 2007, 32(7–8): 649–667.
15. Stewart JD. The role of information in public accountability. in Hopwood, A. and Tomkins, C. (Eds), Issues in Public Sector Accounting, Philip Allan, Oxford, pp. 13-34..
16. Bailey D, Harte G, Sugden R. Corporate disclosure and the deregulation of international investment. *Accounting, Auditing & Accountability Journal.* 2000, 13(2): 197–218.
17. IASB Conceptual Framework. *The conceptual framework for financial reporting.* London: IASB (IASB International Accounting Standards Board), 2010.
18. Kocollari U, Ennio L. Social accounting at work: An analysis of social impact measurement models. *Journal of Modern Accounting and Auditing.* 2020, 16(1): 31–43.
19. Cerbioni F, Cinquini L, Sòstero U. *Contabilità e bilancio.* Milan: McGraw-Hill, 2011.
20. Schaltegger S, Wagner M. Integrative management of sustainability performance, measurement and reporting. *International Journal of Accounting, Auditing and Performance Evaluation.* 2006, 3(1): 1–19.
21. Gray R, Milne M. Sustainability reporting: Who's kidding whom? *Chartered Accountants Journal of New Zealand.* 2002, 81(6): 66–70.
22. Adams CA. The ethical, social and environmental reporting–performance portrayal gap. *Accounting, Auditing & Accountability Journal.* 2004, 17(5): 731–757.
23. Mion G, Adaui CRL. Mandatory nonfinancial disclosure and its consequences on the sustainability reporting quality of Italian and German companies. *Sustainability (Switzerland).* 2019, 11(17): 1–28.
24. Epstein M, Flamholtz E, McDonough JJ. Corporate social accounting in the United States of America: State of the art and future prospects. *Accounting, Organizations and Society.* 1976, 1(1): 23–42.
25. Dierkes M, Antal AB. The usefulness and use of social reporting information. *Accounting, Organizations and Society.* 1985, 10(1): 29–34.
26. Baboukardos D, Rimmel G. Value relevance of accounting information under an integrated reporting approach: A research note. *Journal of Accounting and Public Policy.* 2016, 35(4): 437–452.
27. Jackson G, Bartosch J, Avetisyan E, Kinderman D, Knudsen JS. Mandatory non-financial disclosure and its influence on CSR: An international comparison. *Journal of Business Ethics.* 2019, 162(2): 323–342.

28. La Torre M, Sabelfeld S, Blomkvist M, Tarquinio L, Dumay J. Harmonising non-financial reporting regulation in Europe: Practical forces and projections for future research. *Meditari Accountancy Research.* 2018, 26(4): 598–621.

29. European Commission *COP15: Historic global deal for nature and people.* European Commission of the European Union. https://ec.europa.eu/commission/presscorner/detail/en/ip_22_7834 Published 2022. Accessed March 20 2023.

30. Directive 2014/95/EU. Directive /95/Eu, Union The European Parliament. The Council of the European Union. *Official Journal of the European Union.* 2014, 330: 1–9.

31. Maas KEH, & Vermeulen MC. *A systemic view on the impacts of regulating non-financial reporting.* PBL Netherlands Environmental Agency, 2015.

32. Busco F, Izzo MF, Grana C. *Sustainable development goals and integrated reporting.* London: Routledge, 2019.

33. Robinson C, Vodovoz I, Sullivan K, Burns J. Sustainability disclosure goes mainstream. *Deloitte ESG.* 2019, 26(21): 1–8.

34. Directive (EU) 2022/2464 of the European Parliament and of the Council of 14 December 2022 amending Regulation (EU) No 537/2014, Directive 2004/109/EC, Directive 2006/43/EC and Directive 2013/34/EU, as regards corporate sustainability reporting.

35. Lydenberg S, Rogers J, Wood D. *From transparency to performance: Industry-based sustainability reporting on key issues.* The Hauser Center for Nonprofit Organizations, Initiative for Responsible Investment.

36. Deloitte. Deloitte debate. *Disclosure of long-term business value: What matters?* www2.deloitte.com/content/dam/insights/us/articles/disclosure-of-long-term-business-value/DUP150_Reporting_What_Matters.pdf Published 2012. Accessed April 2012.

37. Michelon G, Parbonetti A. The effect of corporate governance on sustainability disclosure. *Journal of Management & Governance.* 2012, 16(3): 477–509.

38. Gamerschlag R, Möller K, Verbeeten F. Determinants of voluntary CSR disclosure: Empirical evidence from Germany. *Review of Managerial Science.* 2011, 5(2–3): 233–262.

39. Burritt RL, Schaltegger S, Orij R. Corporate social disclosures in the context of national cultures and stakeholder theory. *Accounting, Auditing & Accountability Journal.* 2010, 23(7): 868–889.

40. Toppinen A, Li N, Tuppura A, Xiong Y. Corporate responsibility and strategic groups in the forest-based industry: Exploratory analysis based on the Global Reporting Initiative (GRI) framework. *Corporate Social Responsibility and Environmental Management.* 2012, 19(4): 191–205.

41. Pollach I, Scharl A, Weichselbraun A. Web content mining for comparing corporate and third-party online reporting: A case study on solid waste management. *Business Strategy and the Environment.* 2009, 18(3): 137–148.

42. Reverte C. Determinants of corporate social responsibility disclosure ratings by Spanish listed firms. *Journal of Business Ethics.* 2009, 88(2): 351–366.

43. Pava ML, Krausz J. The association between corporate social-responsibility and financial performance: The paradox of social cost. *Journal of Business Ethics.* 1996, 15(3): 321–357.

44. Gray R, Javad M, Power DM, Sinclair CD. Social and environmental disclosure and corporate characteristics: A research note and extension. *Journal of Business Finance & Accounting.* 2001, 28(3–4): 327–356.

45. Bebbington J, Brown J, Frame B, Thomson I. Theorizing engagement: The potential of a critical dialogic approach. *Accounting, Auditing & Accountability Journal.* 2007, 20(3): 356–381.

46. Lehman G. Disclosing new worlds: A role for social and environmental accounting and auditing. *Accounting, Organizations and Society.* 1999, 24(3): 217–241.

47. Eccles RG, Krzus MP, Watson LA. Integrated reporting requires integrated assurance. In J Oringel (ed.) *Effective auditing for corporates: Key developments in practice and procedures.* London: Bloomsbury, 2012, pp. 161–178.

48. SASB. SASB Materiality map. https://materiality.sasb.org Published 2020. Accessed July 14 2020.

49. Epstein M. Implementing corporate sustainability: Measuring and managing social and environmental impacts. *Strategic Finance.* 2008, 89(7): 24–31.

50. SROI Guide. *A guide to social return on investment*, 2012.
51. Cooper C. The non and nom of accounting for (m)other nature. *Accounting, Auditing & Accountability Journal.* 1992, 5(3).
52. Mathews MR. *Socially responsible accounting.* London: Chapman & Hall, 1993.
53. Deegan C, Newson M. *Environmental performance evaluation and reporting for private and public organisations.* New South Wales: Environmental Protection Authority and New South Wales Department of State and Regional Development, 1996.
54. Klöpffer W. Life-cycle based methods for sustainable product development. *The International Journal of Life Cycle Assessment.* 2003, 8(3): 157–159.
55. Gray R. Corporate reporting for sustainable development: Accounting for sustainability in 2000AD. *Environmental Values.* 1994, 3(1): 17–45.
56. Bell S, Morse S. *Sustainability indicators measuring the immeasurable?* London: Earthscan, 2008.
57. Zavani M. *Il valore della comunicazione aziendale: rilevanza e caratteri dell'informativa sociale a ambientale.* G. Giappichelli, 2000.
58. Rasche A, Esser DE. From stakeholder management to stakeholder accountability. *Journal of Business Ethics.* 2006, 65(3): 251–267.
59. Moldan B, Billharz S, Matravers R. *Sustainability indicators: A report on the project on indicators of sustainable development.* Vol. 58: Chichester: John Wiley & Sons, 1997.
60. GRI. Gri 101: Foundation 2016 101. *GRI standards.* 2016, GRI101(1): 29–29.
61. *Iberdrola sustainability report. Statement of non-financial information sustainability report*, 2022.
62. Suojanen WW. Accounting theory and the large corporation. *The Accounting Review.* 1954, 29(3): 391–398.
63. Riahi-Belkaoui A. *Value added reporting and research: State of the art.* Westport, CT: Quorum Books, 1999.
64. Burchell S, Clubb C, Hopwood AG. Accounting in its social context: Towards a history of value added in the United Kingdom. *Accounting, Organizations and Society.* 1985, 10(4): 381–413.
65. Meek GK, Gray SJ. The value added statement: An innovation for US companies. *Accounting Horizons.* 1988, 2(2): 73.
66. Samsung. *A journey towrads a sustainable future: Samsung Electronics sustainability report 2022 – Executive summary.* https://images.samsung.com/is/content/samsung/assets/uk/sustainability/overview/Samsung_Electronics_Sustainability-Report-2022_Executive_Summary.pdf Accessed March 20 2023.
67. Schaltegger S, Burritt RL. Sustainability accounting for companies: Catchphrase or decision support for business leaders? *Journal of World Business.* 2010, 45(4): 375–384.
68. Coupland C. Corporate social and environmental responsibility in web-based reports: Currency in the banking sector? *Critical Perspectives on Accounting.* 2006, 17(7): 865–881.
69. GRI. *GRI's disclosure database.* 2022.
70. GRI. Using the GRI standards for sustainability reporting. www.globalreporting.org/standards/media/1381/using-the-gri-standards-reporting-process.pdf Published 2020. Accessed July 22 2020.
71. EFRAG. www.efrag.org
72. IIRC. *The international integrated reporting framework*, 2013.
73. IIRC. www.theiirc.org Published 2020. Accessed July 14 2020.
74. Integrated Reporting (2023) Get to grips with the six capitals. www.integratedreporting.org/what-the-tool-for-better-reporting/get-to-grips-with-the-six-capitals Published 2023. Accessed March 20 2023.
75. Rockfeather. Beezzz – sustainability app. https://rockfeather.com/cases/beezzz-sustainability-app Published 2020. Accessed July 14 2020.
76. Kaplan RS, Norton DP. Using the balanced scorecard as strategic management system. *Harvard Business Review.* 1996, 74(1): 75–85.
77. Presentación de caso 'Del amor nace la vista' [Presentation of the case 'Love gives birth to eyesight'] [PowerPoint]. Mexico City: Cinépolis Foundation, 2010.
78. Figge F, Hahn T, Schaltegger S, Wagner M. The sustainability balanced scorecard – linking sustainability management to business strategy. *Business Strategy and the Environment.* 2002, 11(5): 269–284.

79. Kaplan RS, Norton DP. *Strategy maps*. Boston: Harvard Business School Press, 2004.

80. Adejo T. Save 80 stove: Curbing desertification, carbon emission. *Environews Nigeria*. www.environewsnigeria.com/2012/10/07/save-80-stove-curbing-desertification-carbon-emission Published 2012. Accessed February 2 2013.

81. Akinyede T. *Interview by Ogunyemi with a save 80 stove distributor in Nigeria*, Personal Communication. 2012.

82. Council of Europe. *Final report of the group of specialists on gender budgeting (EG-S-GB), EG-S-GB (2004) RAP FIN, equality division, directorate general of human rights*. Strasbourg: Council of Europe, 2015.

83. Downes R, Von Trapp L, Nicol S. Gender budgeting in OECD countries. *OECD Journal on Budgeting*. 2017, 16(3): 71–107.

84. EIGE Europe. What is a gender equality plan. https://eige.europa.eu/gender-mainstreaming/toolkits/gear/what-gender-equality-plan-gep Published 2020. Accessed July 14 2020.

85. Women U. *Inclusive electoral processes: A guide for electoral management bodies on promoting gender equality and women's participation*. New York: UN Women Policy Division, 2015.

CHAPTER 21

FINANCIAL MANAGEMENT

OLIVER LAASCH AND NICK TOLHURST

LEARNING GOALS

1. Understand how to access external financing for responsible management activities
2. Make capital budgeting decisions based on ethics, responsibility, and sustainability
3. Practice good corporate governance

IMPRESSIVE FACT

A majority, 57 per cent, of managers believe that environmental, social, and governance (ESG) initiatives create financial value. Only 3 per cent believe it reduces value. Among the believers, 71 per cent think it increases brand equity, 49 per cent see positive HR impacts, and 34 per cent believe it strengthens their organization's competitive position [1].

SPOTLIGHT

COOPERATIVE FINANCIAL MANAGEMENT AT MONDRAGON
RORY RIDLEY-DUFF, MICHAEL BULL, AND OLIVER LAASCH

Credit: Mondragon Corporation

Imagine a type of financial management in a business with the foundational management principle that capital is of an 'instrumental subordinate nature of capital … an instrument subordinate to labour'. Money is a mere means to the end of social welfare, to paying people wages, and to developing the community [2]. This is the setting of financial management at the Mondragon Corporation, Spain's tenth biggest business. Mondragon was originally founded as a motor of social development for Spain's Basque region after World War II and is active in finance, retail, and knowledge industries.

Ever since its foundation in 1953, financial management at Mondragon has been centred on cooperative management principles, an 'economic democracy', where workers are the principal owners of the company. Through a general assembly, all workers, as members and owners of the cooperative, receive their corresponding share of profit, on top of

(Continued)

their wage, actively elect representatives into their governing bodies, and make main decisions collectively [2].

Credit: Mondragon Corporation

The CEO wages are also decided by vote. To widen the starting differential of 3:1, the CEO earns three times as much as a common worker, all capital account holders have to approve the change on a one-member, one-vote basis. In the last 57 years, no workforce has approved a differential of more than 9:1. The average is 5:1. As a comparison, in the US, wage differentials between CEOs and workforce members have grown to 450:1.

Mondragon now has over 12 billion euros in revenues, from 264 sub businesses, and over 8,100 employees, most of whom are member owners [3]. At the height of the 2008/9 recession, membership still grew by 6.1 per cent. New growth is supported by expansion of Eroski, a chain of retail outlets that extends ownership and profit sharing to both staff and customers. Mondragon now has a presence in 43 countries, and sales in more than 150 [3].

PROFESSIONAL FINANCIAL MANAGEMENT

Money is important: I have got to make red blood cells to live, but the purpose of my life is not to make red blood cells. Business has to make profits to live, but making profits isn't the purpose of business.

R. Edward Freeman [4]

Financial management involves the planning, organizing, budgeting, directing, controlling, and governance of financial activities such as the procurement and utilization of funds of an organization. Financial management is so important because it is the very lifeblood of management: 'You have to make red blood cells to live.'

Financial management consists of practices related to financing of and investing in activities and of distributing financial results

Why is **professional financial management** so important? Financial management provides resources to implement and drive responsible management activities [5]. Financial management has increasingly become engaged in social and environmental performance on financial managers' to-do lists [6]. Financial reporting, controlling, and risk management now explicitly connect to ESG criteria.

Secondly, professional financial management needs to navigate **fiduciary responsibilities** related to the potential impact of financial managers' decisions when handling[1] large amounts of money. Even financial managers who are not in the highest-ranking positions often move considerable amounts of capital [7].

Third, financial management has been blamed for harming society. This includes company collapses such as Enron and Worldcom. It has been argued that the last global financial crisis was caused by a lack of fiduciary responsibility by bank staff, from sales people to fund managers, who ignored the potential negative consequences of selling subprime loans to people who

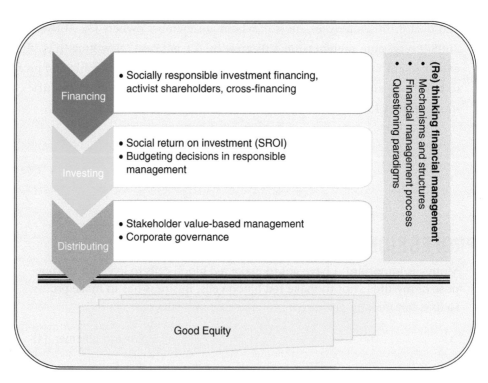

FIGURE 21.1 The professional financial management process

---

[1]Fiduciary is derived from the Latin word *fidere* (to trust).

could not pay them back. Further, the financial sector has been blamed by the global Occupy Wall Street movement of reinforcing an unfair elitist capitalist system that only serves the 1 per cent super rich, but not the 99 per cent of 'normal' people.

This chapter both introduces the main practices of financial management and integrates ethics, responsibility, and sustainability throughout (see Figure 21.1) in order to build **good equity**, firm value that is produced through ethical, responsible, and sustainable financial management practices.

Good equity
firm value built ethically, responsibly, and sustainably

(RE)THINKING FINANCIAL MANAGEMENT

In order to re-think and re-construct financial management, we first need to understand how traditional financial management works and where it malfunctions. Key to this understanding is to appreciate how financial management in an organization is intimately associated with mechanisms in the broader financial system, most notably the public sector and financial markets (see Figure 121.2).

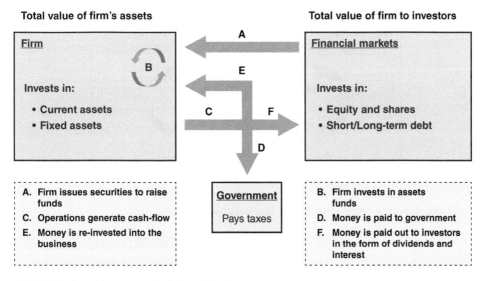

FIGURE 21.2   Financial management in the financial system

FINANCIAL MANAGEMENT PROCESS

One might be tempted to think that decisions in **financial management** are very rational, based on a broad set of highly standardized quantitative analysis tools. Interestingly, it has been found that financial decision-making is dominated by qualitative and non-financial criteria, and that financial managers are

Practices of financial management
are to externally procure funds, to internally invest into activities, and to distribute the financial results

often heavily influenced by the expectations of external and internal stake-holders. Ethical considerations and sustainability are also important factors influencing financial managers' decisions [8]. What are the typical practices and related decisions that financial managers engage in as part of their work (see Figure 21.3)?

1. A first area of practices is centred on **procuring funds**, '**financing**'. Financing is concerned with how to raise funds from various sources, to choose the right capital structure, to define the period of financing, and the costs of funding.

2. A second area is **internally investing** the capital, channelling financial resources to management activities and assets. It is concerned with how to distribute capital between fixed assets and current assets, to manage working capital, to control financial performance, and to define budgets for different areas of the business.

3. The last area is **distributing financial results**. This pay-out decision includes the distribution of net profits through shareholders' and owners' pay-out or retained profits to be further re-invested in the company. It relates to the payment of taxes and documentation of the results in reports and balance sheets, corporate governance, and how the distribution creates value for particular stakeholders.

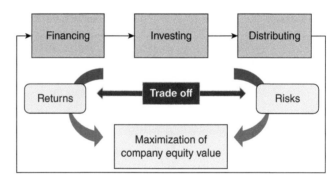

FIGURE 21.3   Financial management process

These practices aim to achieve the following objectives:

a. **Procurement of funding.** Investment in fixed assets and current assets as well as the management of working capital (current assets minus current liabilities)

b. **Investment optimization.** Ensuring that any funds procured are utilized in the best possible way

c. **Investment security.** Ensuring that investment of any funds is in safe ventures that guarantee the best long-term returns

d. **Sound capital structure.** Ensuring that there is a sustainable composition of debt and equity capital

e. **Shareholder returns**. Appropriate returns to shareholders depend on earning capacity, share price, and shareholder expectations

Shareholder returns are closely related to mainstream financial management's underlying purpose, which is the maximization of the equity, the value of the organization. This value translates into maximization for the company owners and shareholders.

QUESTIONING PARADIGMS OF FINANCIAL MANAGEMENT

There are many paradigms built into traditional financial management that inherently lead to ethical issues, which stand in the way of creating optimum stakeholder value and a sustainable company.

Members of the Occupy Wall Street movement criticizing greed as an underlying paradigm of 'normal' financial management.

'Occupy Wall Street at Zuccotti Park' by VideoPhotoholic is licensed under CC BY-SA 2.0

Sticking to traditional financial management tenets and not taking social and environmental concerns seriously is a dangerous thing to do in today's context. A case in point is when the bank HSBC's head of socially responsible investing saw himself forced to resign after his speech at a *Financial Times* event entitled 'Why investors need not worry about climate risk', in which he publicly ridiculed climate movements by sharing that 'there was always some nut job telling me about the end of the world … unsubstantiated, shrill, partisan, self-serving, apocalyptic warnings' [9]. The following financial management paradigms are most prominently criticized.

1. **Profit paradigm.** Seeing profit maximization as the ultimate end of business reflects a skewed picture of reality. Businesses do not need to be profit maximizers to take their functional role in society of providing needed goods and services. Financial management should move from profit maximization, to profit optimization, where the profit paradigm is balanced with stakeholder value and the triple bottom.

2. **Growth paradigm.** Financial management has built-in growth mechanisms: growing revenues, growing markets, growing consumption. Professional financial management has to find ways to replace the growth paradigm by an 'optimum size' paradigm, where the need to grow, maintain or even shrink is based on defining the point in time where the company has its optimum size for society and the environment. Financial management can help companies that can increase their positive impact, such as renewable energies or organic agriculture to grow, and the ones that have a negative impact like petroleum companies or tobacco to de-grow or transform.

3. **Short-term paradigm.** It is easier to consider short-term (or short-term) results from decision-making. They are safer to estimate than long-term (or long-term) factors, and more likely to influence financial decision makers' own fate. Inherently, sustainability

is a long-term concept. Only if the outcomes of decisions are considered in the long run can they be evaluated with regard to a decision's social, environmental, and economic sustainability.

4. **Money paradigm.** Primacy of financial factors leads to an underrepresentation of social, environmental, and ethical considerations. Professional finance has to move away from the skewed money paradigm by giving social, environmental, and ethical indicators equal importance, and/or by monetizing those non-financial indicators so that they become comparable in the money paradigm.

5. **Shareholder paradigm.** Responsible financial management has to manage the company for the benefit of all stakeholders. This does not mean that owners or more specifically shareholders become disowned. The goal is for owners to become one among many important stakeholders.

6. **Internality paradigm.** Financial management with its traditional tools has a tendency to over-consider so-called internalities. Internalities are the effects of one's own activity on oneself, in this case on the organization. A positive internal effect is, for instance, increased profit. A negative internal effect, an internal cost, is spending on production. Internalities neglect many external costs and benefits not carried by the company, such as pollution created by a production practice. An example of external benefits is the social welfare created for employees' families through wage payments. Decision-making in financial management has to include both external costs and benefits. It has to move from internality thinking to inclusivity thinking.

These paradigms are deeply anchored into the DNA of financial management and of financial managers. Solutions to dismantle those paradigms require creativity and management innovation.

FINANCING

The **financing** function of financial management in bigger companies is usually managed by the department for investor relations. Financing does not end with the answer to the question 'Where do we get the money from?' At least equally important is the question, 'Who do we want to own and control our organization?'

Financing
refers to the practice of procuring necessary capital

• Organizations owned by **institutional investors** are more likely to show good social performance. This might change with the location of the company [10].

• Shareholding by **top managers** is negatively associated with social performance [11].

• In developing countries, **foreign ownership** is positively related with higher responsible management performance.

• **State-owned** companies, depending on the location, could either be significantly less, or more socially responsible [11].

- **Publicly traded** companies experience higher scrutiny than privately held companies, which might drive them to higher social performance [12].

- **Privately owned** companies with higher ownership dispersion are more likely to achieve better social performance [13, 14].

As illustrated in Figure 21.4, there is a wide variety of financing mechanisms tied to ethics, responsibility, and sustainability.

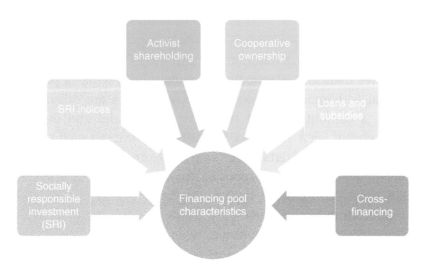

FIGURE 21.4   Financing practices

   In the following paragraphs, we will provide a more detailed picture of those different financing mechanisms, which are crucial for either procuring capital for responsible management or discouraging management from behaving irresponsibly. Financial managers are well advised to know how their responsible actions may affect access to capital.[2]

SOCIALLY RESPONSIBLE INVESTMENT (SRI)

SRI is an investment practice that involves screening, through which investors assess investment possibilities. Guidance for such analysis is provided in the UN Principles for Responsible Investment (PRI) [15]:

1.   We will incorporate environmental, social and corporate governance issues into investment analysis and decision-making processes.

Socially responsible investment (SRI) is a practice that involves the evaluation of social, environmental, and/or ethical issues when investing

---

[2]While the financing mechanisms in this chapter mostly relate to financial management in mature established businesses, Chapter 15 provides a set of complementary financing mechanisms tuned in to financing new ventures.

2. We will be active owners and incorporate ESG issues into our ownership policies and practices.

3. We will seek appropriate disclosure on ESG issues by the entities in which we invest.

4. We will promote acceptance and implementation of the Principles within the investment industry.

5. We will work together to enhance our effectiveness in implementing the Principles.

6. We will each report on our activities and progress towards implementing the Principles.

Negative screening
excludes investment in organizations deemed unworthy on ethical, social or environmental criteria

Divestment
is the opposite of investment, and describes the process by which investments are removed from a portfolio

Positive screening
identifies exemplary responsible businesses for investment purposes

SRI principles have a long tradition. For instance, Quakers avoided dealings with the slave trade and Islamic finance is built on a series of principles on how to deal with money responsibly. Such practices are called **negative screening**, a commitment not to invest in industries and organizations deemed unworthy. Such 'sin stocks' typically include items such as gambling, arms, tobacco or adult entertainment, but increasingly also key polluters like petroleum or aviation. When responsible investors identify sin stocks in their portfolios, a common practice is **divestment**. Divestment has been particularly significant in large publicly held funds and pensions such as those of university endowments and labour union pension funds.

Positive screening is the process of identifying exemplary companies engaging in responsible management. As increasingly aware and prosperous consumers have progressively embraced responsible consumption, it was inevitable that the focus would also be placed on financial products.

SRI and ethical funds have become increasingly professionalized, proving that ethical investment can be just as profitable as investment based purely on financial performance. There is little difference in returns compared with 'non-ethical' portfolios. Indeed, one of the oldest ethical funds – the Domino 400 – has, since its inception in 1990, consistently outperformed the S&P 500.

The trend to increase the capital available to 'good' companies, and to withdraw it from 'sin industries' is ongoing. Annual increases in total SRI funds under management continuously outperform those of traditional investments to a total of over $12 trillion in the US only [16]. This has led to a further cumulative effect that ethical funds and SRI now pack enough punch in financial markets to influence mainstream investment behaviour [17].

A particularly powerful SRI practice is that of decarbonizing investment portfolios. It may involve a variety of strategies, such as divesting from carbon sin companies and whole industries like fossil fuels or tourism, or conversely, to strategically invest in sin industries' leading companies that are most aggressively reducing their carbon emissions [18, 19].

SRI INDICES

As the amount of funds geared to sustainable investment has increased exponentially, so have sustainability indices such as the Dow Jones Sustainability Index or the FTSE4Good and others emerged in order to provide information on companies' responsible business performance. Inclusion into sustainability stock exchanges has been found to channel a significant amount of additional capital to the company at the time it enters the **SRI index** [20] as it makes an organization visible for positive screening.

SRI index
a ranking of companies, based on their responsible management performance

Responsible managers often know SRI indices by heart, as they are frequently involved in gathering the data necessary to be included and maintained in the index. For instance, the Dow Jones Sustainability Index (DJSI) applies criteria from the economic, environmental, and social dimensions to calculate a maximum score of 100. For inclusion in FTSE4Good, for example, companies need to satisfy standards in three types of criteria: environmental, social and stakeholder interests, and human rights. These criteria address three key questions:

- What is the company doing to protect and reduce its impact on the environment?

- How well is the company safeguarding the interests of the society in which it operates and the interests of its stakeholders e.g. employees, suppliers and customers?

- How far does the company comply with the requirements of human rights legislation?

The criteria for inclusion in the FTSE4Good index are detailed but important features consisting of:

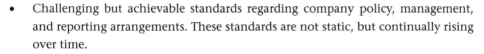

- Challenging but achievable standards regarding company policy, management, and reporting arrangements. These standards are not static, but continually rising over time.

- A detailed environmental policy covering all parts of the company. It should be noted that they are more demanding in those sectors that tend to have a higher impact – for example, chemicals and agriculture tend to have higher impact on the environment than do those in the media sector.

- Reporting procedures that provide data on social and environmental indicators as well as an effective system for managing the company's social and environmental footprint.

Ultimately, sustainability indices can be seen as an extension of 'investor relations', which has institutionalized interaction with investors, another example of which is activist shareholding.

ACTIVIST SHAREHOLDING

Activist shareholder
an investor who buys company shares in order to target and influence company behaviour by being granted access to shareholder participation mechanisms

Activist shareholders are not a significant source of funding as they typically buy a small number of stocks of companies that are 'bad' as an 'entrance fee' for speaking rights at annual shareholder meetings, shareholder resolutions, and direct access to top management. Shareholder activism is a more aggressive type of influence that involves negative screening, and turns boycott strategies on their heads by actively investing in 'bad' companies. In theory, such minority investors have little quantifiable power, but their ability to influence other shareholders, stakeholders, and the media is immense.

For instance, Amazon employee shareholders tried to force Amazon's leadership's hand to lead on tackling the climate crisis through a shareholder resolution [21]. Management at Amazon, however, threatened to fire employees if they should speak up again, and put in place stricter policies restricting employees' political engagement [22]. Social hedge funds are another example. They seek a decline in a company's stock price in order to drive a particular agenda.

User experience designer Emily, backed up by 28 employee-shareholders, and over 7700 Amazon employees pushing a shareholder resolution.

Jade Prevost Manuel / Shutterstock.com

Activist shareholders have been found to be successful in influencing concrete company practices, but have only limited influence in companies' share

prices, and performance [23, 24]. The dividing line between the previously 'nice' and 'modest' world of SRI and these more activist groups is disappearing as SRI funds seek to hold companies more accountable, and proactively challenge companies' operating strategies rather than relying on screening criteria.

COOPERATIVE OWNERSHIP

Cooperatives
are owned and run by and for their members

Our introductory case of Mondragon is an example of a **cooperative**. Members of cooperatives could be virtually any stakeholder. Typically, customers, employees or community members, or suppliers own a cooperative [25]. Members of cooperatives contribute capital to fund the operations [26]. Stakeholder ownership and control of cooperatives makes them an interesting funding model for responsible management. Figure 21.5 illustrates the basic structure, operating principles and financing mechanism of cooperatives.

Cooperatives share many commonalities with traditional ownership models. Examples include the elected board or the different member financing models that resemble those of shareholders in a publicly traded corporation. A number of variations of traditional cooperatives have been developed [28, 29]. What makes cooperatives different is their open membership model, the underlying values of mutuality and not-for-profit thinking, and the strong

Structure & Control	Operating Principles	Member Financing
• Ownership through **cooperative members** • **Democratic decision-making** through voting mechanisms • A member-nominated and **elected board** supervises operations • **Earnings** are either re-invested into the business or paid out to members	• **Voluntary and open** membership • **Democratic** member **control** • Member **economic participation** • **Autonomy** and independence • **Education**, training and information • **Cooperation** among cooperatives • Concern for **community**	• **Direct investment**: Members decide to invest a lump-sum. • **Retained margins**: Surplus is retained and re-invested instead of paid out to members. • **Per-unit capital retains:** A fixed amount of money is invested 'per unit' or through percentage calculations.*

FIGURE 21.5 Characteristics of cooperatives

*Units here refer, for instance, to a product sold per customer, or a work contract per employee, while percentage can refer to a fraction of a revenue created through a customer, or the wage received by an employee.

SOURCE: Adapted from [27]

concern for communities and members. Cooperative models have become a large-scale global phenomenon. According to the International Co-operative Alliance, the organization represents one billion members of cooperatives worldwide [30].

LOANS AND SUBSIDIES

Financing responsible management activities can rely on varieties of external funding mechanisms that do not involve giving up ownership for funds. Both bank loans and corporate bonds are mechanisms of borrowing money, to be paid back with interest over a predetermined period of time. While the planned nature of such arrangements is helpful for stability, they are typically not very flexible and pricy financing mechanisms, tied into payment schemes, often with high interest rates, particularly for short-term loans.

However, financial managers in companies engaging in responsible management might find themselves in an advantageous position. First, ethical, responsible, and sustainable management practices drive down environmental, social and governance risks, which in turn might be rewarded with a lower interest rate. Secondly, as with socially responsible investment, there are also socially responsible lenders, who offer preferential loans at better conditions to companies meeting their criteria. Third, you might find yourself in a position where governments or development agencies financially support responsible management initiatives. These loans are often offered at a lower interest rate, only have to be paid back partially, or sometimes are subsidies that do not have to be paid back at all.

However, these forms of special financing may be tied to strict criteria that have to be met. Accessing such financing might require lengthy, elaborate, competitive application procedures.

CROSS-FINANCING

Cross-financing
a method that uses the income of income-generating activities to subsidize activities that do not generate income

Cross-financing uses income from an organization's activity to subsidize activities that do not generate income. Responsible management can in various ways generate cash flows internally, which can then be used to cover the cost of other responsible management activities:

- **Savings from cost reductions.** Responsible management has great potential to reduce operational costs. A cost decrease, such as from an eco-efficiency project, that reduces both environmental impact and operational costs could be re-invested internally.

- **Revenues from products.** Additional income from sustainable innovation products could be used to cross-finance a new sustainability department.

- **Corporate foundations.** Many companies have their own foundation which donates money to philanthropic purposes. Why not design an internal philanthropic programme, based on the strengths and competences of the business, to be financed by the foundation?

Getting cross-financing in responsible management right implies both creating responsible management activities that generate income and optimizing the social value created through cross-financed activities. A portfolio approach to responsible management aligns activities in a way that balances these aspects.

INVESTING IN INTERNAL ACTIVITIES

Capital budgeting
the process of analysing alternative projects and activities to decide which ones to accept and budget for

Investing in activities and allocation of funds internally relies on capital budgeting practices [31]. **Capital budgeting** is an internal financing or investment process that involves making decisions by analysing the internal return on investment of alternative actions. Capital budgeting is of primary importance for responsible management:

1. Responsible managers have to convince decision-makers that responsible management activities are worthwhile. In mainstream business logic, it helps to claim that the *financial return on investment* of a certain responsible management activity is positive, or even higher than a competing activity.

2. If we solely make decisions on the basis of financial return on investment, strategically important responsible management activities that have a high *social return on investment* would not take place [32]. Responsible managers have to show that they are spending money in the best of social value creation.

Only if we work with both types of return on investment, can financial management be a driver of ethics, responsibility, and sustainability [5].

Financial management is deeply involved in the evaluation of company portfolios of activities according to their social, environmental, and economic returns for an optimized triple-bottom-line performance [33]. Financial management is not only crucial to the allocation of funds, it can also boost the positive impact of activities. Examples are microfinance, fintech, or 'insetting' practices like the ones at Burberry, and might even attract further external financing related to carbon credits [34].

ASSESSING BLENDED VALUE

An assessment of the **blended value** of an internal activity that takes both financial and social profitability into consideration requires the following practices [35]:

Blended value describes value creation as a blend of economic, social, and environmental value to optimize total returns

1. **Qualitative** assessment considers stakeholder value, triple bottom line, and ethics as additional intangible values that complement financial decision instruments: the decision to enter into a joint venture with either a defence company or an electric car producer might be informed by the intangible factor of those two businesses' ethical implications.

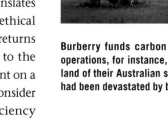

2. **Quantified** assessment measures ethical, social, and environmental value and translates them into a social, environmental, or ethical return on investment. Those alternative returns on investment can then be compared to the traditional financial return on investment on a quantitative basis. Management might consider either a traditional operational efficiency project that will result in a cost decrease, or

Burberry funds carbon capture activities in their operations, for instance, through reforestation on the land of their Australian suppliers' sheep farms, which had been devastated by bush fires.

in an eco-efficiency project that achieves the same decrease in cost, but which additionally reduces the company's CO_2 emissions. Both the financial cost decrease and the reduction in CO_2 can be measured.

3. **Monetized** assessment attributes financial value to traditionally non-monetary metrics to provide a financial basis for comparison. The evaluation of a community volunteering scheme that involves employees teaching classes in a local school might measure the hourly wage costs of the time spent by volunteers and the financial value of the education received by students.

Monetization refers to attributing a financial value to non-financial factors

In the following section we will illustrate the social return on investment, a fully monetized assessment method, which also includes qualitative and quantitative activities.

SOCIAL RETURN ON INVESTMENT (SROI)

The social return on investment (SROI) quantifies and monetizes stakeholder value costs and benefits of an activity in one single ratio

The **SROI** can provide a holistic assessment of either mainstream or responsible management activity. In the responsible management context, for instance, a volunteering programme with an SROI of 35 per cent could be compared with an eco-efficiency activity of 40 per cent or a cause-related marketing campaign of 20 per cent. While those numbers cannot describe all aspects necessary to decide upon which of the three activities should be implemented, it is still a powerful tool to describe the value of different alternatives. In addition, once the SROI has been established, we can deduct other metrics from it – for instance, the payback period of an activity to find out when an activity has paid for itself.

Figure 21.6 illustrates ten guidelines for rigorously calculating an SROI [36]. In the 'Digging deeper' section of this chapter you will find an exemplary calculation of a social return on investment of the fictional green office programme 'GreenO'.

Construction	Guideline 1. Include both positive and negative impacts in the assessment.
	Guideline 2. Consider impacts made by and on all stakeholders, including those inside the company itself, before deciding which are significant enough to be included in the assessment.
	Guideline 3. Include only impacts that are clearly and directly attributable to the company's activities. Be conservative with leaps of faith and don't take credit for more than your organization can realistically affect.
	Guideline 4. Avoid double counting the value (financial and social) created by the company and avoid using market valuations of social impacts where they do not reflect full costs and benefits.
Content	Guideline 5. In industries or geographic areas in which impacts would be created by the existence of any business, do not count these impacts. The SROI should describe what makes the company different from a standard venture in the industry (i.e., from its competition).
	Guideline 6. Only monetize impacts if it is logical given the context of the impact, business, or industry.
	Guideline 7. Put numeric metrics into context (e.g., this period versus last period, this company versus similar companies) to give the social return on investment meaning.
Certainty	Guideline 8. Address risk factors affecting the SROI in the assumptions and carefully consider and document the choice of discount rate for social cash flows.
	Guideline 9. Carry out a sensitivity analysis to identify key factors influencing projected outcomes.
Continuity	Guideline 10. Include ongoing tracking of social impact.

FIGURE 21.6   SROI guidelines

SOURCE: [36]

So far we have mostly discussed responsible management activities as objects of the SROI calculation. In practice the SROI evaluation can be used to assess virtually any business activity:

- **Diversification.** SROI can play a role with regard to a corporation's structure. For instance, Clorox founded the ecological cleaning products producer Greenworks for its positive SROI in comparison to other businesses in the corporation's portfolio.

- **Programmes.** SROI can be used to assess responsible management programmes. As an example, the retailer M&S estimates that their sustainability flagship programme Plan A generated a benefit of £70 million from one year to another [37].

- **Single campaigns.** Selecting the campaign that creates the highest social return for the money invested is crucial. For instance, M&S's one-day-wardrobe cleanout campaign raised over £2.2 million for Oxfam [37]. The sum is one important component of the SROI.

- **Projects.** Projects are defined for a fixed period of time, budget, and outcome, which provides a clearly delineated boundary for SROI assessment [38]. As an example, single eco-efficiency projects in Mexican companies were able to achieve payback periods of often less than half a year [39].

- **Processes.** As processes are mostly well described and their parameters are well established, here a measurement of the SROI is less complex than in less structured activities.

- **Products (goods and services).** Comparing the SROI of one product alternative with another might reveal dramatic differences. A product SROI may support inclusion of the full costs in prices and develop offsetting schemes for negative impacts.

- **Departments.** Crucial in successful company-wide implementation of responsible management practices is the establishment of a department in charge. The SROI can be used to make the case for it.

- **Employee performance.** An SROI summing up the value created for stakeholders of employees' work can provide insights that can be used to incentivize employees for both financial and social performance.

DISTRIBUTING RESULTS AND GOVERNANCE

The outcome of financial management must be aligned with the interests of the main stakeholders, among them the shareholders or owners of the organization. In the following two sections we will first emphasize the importance of developing stakeholder value drivers through value-based management. We will then discuss corporate governance aiming to assure consistency between managers' actions and stakeholders' needs.

STAKEHOLDER VALUE-BASED MANAGEMENT

The ultimate objective of mainstream financial management is the maximization of shareholder value through so-called value drivers [40]. These drivers have become a controversial topic in the general public perception, associated with a concentration on short-term share price, profits, and dividends at the expense of all other factors [41]. Even those most closely connected with the concept of shareholder value, such as former General Electric CEO Jack Welch, have emphasized the importance of focusing on long-term value, instead of self-defeating immediate share-price movements. Shareholder value has been found to be influenced by the drivers illustrated in Figure 21.7 [42]. Even a cursory glance at these value drivers may not specifically be what one associates with pure short-term profit maximization.

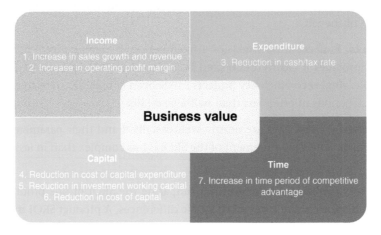

FIGURE 21.7   Value drivers

SOURCE: Adapted from [42]

Responsible management frequently leads to tangible advantages, a 'business case', including cost reduction, higher productivity, and the attraction of investors [43]. All those advantages can be drivers of shareholder value. Research has found that it is possible to build a positive relationship between corporate social performance (CSP), and corporate financial performance (CFP) [44, 45]. In financial management terms, responsible management can, and should, be consistent with sound financial practice. It should not just be 'good publicity', but influence financial value drivers such as lower costs of capital, higher sales income, and longer time periods of competitive advantage. As a next step, financial management needs to move away from emphasizing drivers for shareholder value, towards creating a list of drivers for each of the primary stakeholders.

CORPORATE GOVERNANCE

Corporate governance
aims to ensure that managers
lead an organization in the
best interests of its owners
and other main stakeholders

Corporate governance is centred on the relationship between the company and its owners, respectively shareholders. In the early stages of a company, the owners are simultaneously the managers of a company. The need for corporate governance arises when companies' management and ownership become separated and the ones managing the company are different people from those owning the company.

This is called a **principal–agent problem**, when managers and owners may have different interests regarding how the company should be managed. A conflict of interest might arise where managers who are closer to the daily operations use their knowledge advantage, or asymmetric information, to steer it differently from the owner's wishes. Such a situation in which the agent abuses his position to the disadvantage of the principal is called moral hazard. In a wider understanding of corporate governance, the agent keeps being the manager, but the principal might be any other stakeholder beyond owners. However, the 'shareholder primacy' myth [46] that shareholders are to be treated with preference among other stakeholders has often led to perverse outcomes. An example is EasyJet claiming they are legally obliged to pay out horrendously high dividends to shareholders while planning to stop giving employees food on shifts to save money, and asking for taxpayer support [47, 48].

Principal–agent problems arise under conditions of incomplete, uncertain, and asymmetric information when principals (such as shareholders) hire agents (such as managers). Incentives have to be calibrated to minimize problems of moral hazard and conflicts of interest

The declared goal of the US activist and impact investing firm Engine No. 1 is to 'bring common sense back into capitalism' [49]. Their biggest 'coup' so far was arguably to force Exxon Mobil's hand to add three environmental and social investment speclialists to the oil giant's board. With only a 0.2 per cent share in the company, Engine No. 1 was able to mobilize other large institutional investors to join their shareholder resolution for a turn towards sustainability on the Exxon board [50].

SOURCE: https://time.com/collection/time100-companies-2022/6159495/engine-no-1

While the standards and regulations in corporate governance traditionally differ from country to country, corporate governance principles in general have been sharply influenced by three documents released over the last two decades: The Cadbury report [51], the OECD *Principles of corporate governance* [52], and the Sarbanes-Oxley Act [53]. They are based on five common principles:

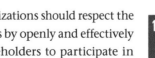

1. **Shareholder rights and equitable treatment.** Organizations should respect the rights of shareholders and help them to exercise those rights by openly and effectively communicating information and by encouraging shareholders to participate in general meetings.

2. **Interests of stakeholders**. Organizations should recognize that they have legal, contractual, social, and market-driven obligations to non-shareholder stakeholders, including investors, employees, creditors, suppliers, local communities, customers, and governments.

3. **Boards' role and responsibilities.** Boards should have the relevant skills and understanding to oversee management as well as having appropriate levels of independence and commitment.

4. **Ethical behaviour and professional integrity.** Organizations should emphasize corporate integrity as well as developing a code of conduct for their directors and executives that promotes ethical and responsible decision-making.

5. **Disclosure and transparency.** Organizations should clarify and make publicly known the roles and responsibilities of board and management to provide stakeholders with a proper level of accountability. The integrity of the company's financial reporting should be guaranteed and procedures to independently verify them should be put in place. Information concerning the organization should be disclosed in a timely and balanced fashion to ensure that all investors have access to clear, factual information.

As illustrated in Figure 21.8, the disciplines and pressure on company management no longer just come internally from the shareholders, the management and the board, but also externally through private as well as regulatory actors. The traditional mix of shareholders voting on a board that appoints and monitors management, which in return is obliged to report to the board, has now been extended through a complex mix of statutory and non-regulatory disciplines. Despite global regulatory models, corporate governance structures still retain significant national differences.

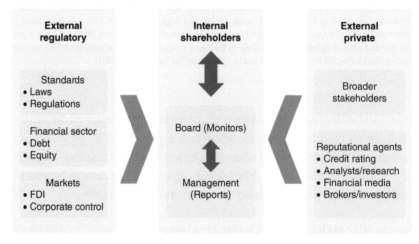

FIGURE 21.8   Corporate governance relationships

The **board of directors**
is an institution that controls
the managers of a company

The most prominent governance mechanism may be the **board of directors**. It is a hybrid organization with a body of individuals from within and external to the organization, who have the task of monitoring if the company is managed in the best interests of stakeholders, including shareholders. The composition of the board of directors is critical to the authority it has to control management's actions. There is a major difference between the Anglo-American style unitary board system and the Continental European model of dual tiers split between 'supervisory' and 'executive' boards.

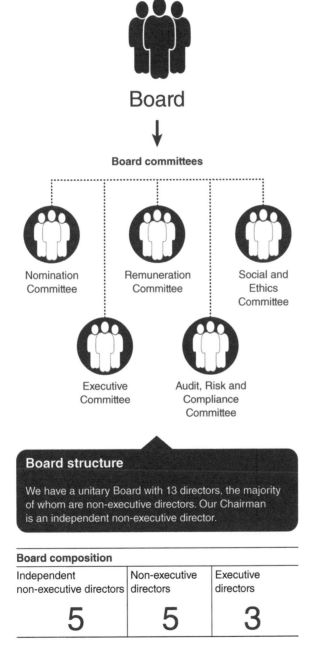

FIGURE 21.9   Exemplary board structure at Vodacom

SOURCE: [54]

The competing strands and views of corporate governance can best be illustrated by the combinations of, and trade-offs between, differing orientations to 'stewardship' and 'agency' in Figure 21.10 [55]. Governance structure and culture, as they developed, tended traditionally to emphasize either strong stewardship or agency orientation. With the emergence of a global understanding of sustainability, and the increasing demands and scope of accountability, corporate governance culture is settling into a combination of the two around high stewardship and agency orientation.

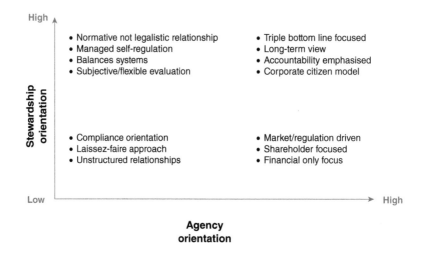

FIGURE 21.10   Corporate governance orientation mix

SOURCE: Adapted from [55]

The board of directors is probably the most powerful and most prominent corporate governance mechanism. Other mechanisms include:

- Compensation and bonuses

- Transparency and reporting

- Create accountability

- Auditing

- Due diligence

- Authority and power abuse

- (Legal) compliance and standards

PRINCIPLES OF PROFESSIONAL FINANCIAL MANAGEMENT

I.   **Professional financial management** integrates ethics, responsibility, and sustainability, fulfils fiduciary responsibilities, and offers a positive contribution to society.

II. The goal is **'good' equity**, produced ethically, responsibly, and sustainably.

III. Six main paradigms of financial management have to be questioned: **profit** maximization, continuous **growth**, **short-term thinking**, **money** as a main decision-making indicator, the dominance of **shareholders** and the **internality thinking** that leads to incomplete decisions.

IV. **Financing** describes the process of procuring funds for business activities. Financing in responsible management has a set of attractive additional **financing tools**, due to its special characteristics.

V. **Investing** is the process of internally allocating financial resources to company activities and projects. Capital budgeting is crucial to providing responsible management with the financial resources required.

VI. The **social return on investment (SROI)** is a method that quantifies and monetizes all stakeholder costs and benefits, the social, environmental, and economic ones, of an activity in one single ratio.

VII. **Corporate governance** describes a set of mechanisms and structures intended to ensure that managers lead an organization to comply with its responsibility to owners and other main stakeholders.

MANAGEMENT GYM: TRAINING YOUR PROFESSIONAL SIX-PACK

Knowing

1. Describe the differences between mainstream and professional financial management.

2. Define and interrelate the following terms: SROI, monetization, fiduciary responsibilities.

3. Find the integrated financial reports of three companies, and identify if/how they calculate some types of social return on investment.

Thinking

4. What would be the consequences for financial management if each of the three bottom lines, economic, social, environmental, were equally important?

5. Look up the structure of the board of directors for three different companies. Which company has the best board? Why?

6. Think outside of the box: What innovative financial management practice do you think would be more ethical, responsible or sustainable than current practice?

Acting

7. Assess the social return on investment of one aspect of your life, for instance, of your choice of breakfast cereal.

8. Think about the employee and the community as stakeholders. For each come up with four main value drivers, similar to the drivers for shareholder value.

9. Imagine a fictional responsible business activity and develop its SROI. Then think about ways to increase the SROI, based on the numbers that you used for the calculation.

Interacting

10. Ask one person currently employed the following question: 'Should companies be managed for shareholders or stakeholders?' Do you agree with the person's answer?

11. Search for a recent social return on investment calculation. Have a close look and ask the organization that issued the report a question about their methodology via social media.

12. Post your view on a recent financial management scandal on social media and ask for views and feedback from your network.

(Continued)

Being	Becoming
13. How do you feel about the enormous gap between CEO pay and worker pay?	16. If you were in a management position where you had to handle large budgets, how would you ensure that you fulfil your fiduciary responsibilities?
14. Which would you personally be more inclined to engage in, activist shareholding, or positive screening and investment?	17. Can you imagine some of your friends or family being critical about your work in (financial) management, maybe, even someone who is 'against business'? How would you respond to them criticizing your job?
15. Do you feel financial management is more part of the problem or part of the solution? Which problem? What solution?	18. Imagine you have noticed some misconduct of your financial management, like the payment of bribes, embezzlement, or short-sighted profit-seeking behaviour. How could you do something about it?

SOURCE: Adapted from [56]

PIONEER INTERVIEW
ROBERT COSTANZA

INTERVIEWER: OLIVER LAASCH

Robert Costanza is a pioneer of the monetary evaluation of environmental factors. He made the topic of ecosystems services and their financial evaluation famous. Monetizing non-monetary indicators is one of the main pre-conditions for responsible financial management.

Courtesy of Robert Costanza

Rethinking capital(s). We should all recognize that there are *four basic types of assets or capital that contribute to sustainable human well-being and to sustainable business practice*: (1) conventional 'built' capital like buildings and factories – the kind of capital that businesses usually worry about; **(2)** human capital – the individual people that make up the community or company and their skills, knowledge, health, and creativity; **(3)** social capital – the networks, relationships, cultures, and institutions that connect people – the business culture embedded in the larger regional, national, and global cultures; and **(4)** natural capital – ecosystems that produce a range of valuable and essential goods and services upon which our economy and society depend. All human benefits depend on a combination of these assets, and sustainable

(Continued)

business practice must recognize and understand these interactions, even though most social and natural capital assets are 'off the books'.

Managing non-financial capitals. I'm the chair of the advisory board of Trucost, a company that estimates the external environmental costs of businesses based on a sophisticated model of the complex interactions in the economy and environment. Trucost estimates both the environmental costs of the companies' operations and the indirect cost of the companies' entire supply chains. Puma has used Trucost to estimate their environmental costs and has made this information public. Companies can use this information to recognize and then decrease their environmental impacts. This will *prevent companies from confusing externalized costs with profits* and allow them to pursue truly sustainable social profits. It will also allow investors to recognize companies that are behaving in truly sustainable ways and not just 'greenwashing'.

How can companies restore natural capital? By recognizing the value of natural capital assets, companies can begin to invest in conserving and restoring those assets. If these assets can be brought 'on the books', companies will have a much easier time of doing this. Imagine a company shareholder report that includes all four types of capital assets mentioned above. Even though most social and natural capital assets are (and should not be) owned by companies, these common assets are extremely important to everyone's well-being. *We need to harmonize our social and private books in order to manage all or our assets sustainably.*

Ecosystems creating economic value? If anything, this value has only increased. Even though global GDP has increased over this time [since 1997 when Robert published a report about the economic value of ecosystems services], ecosystems have continued to be depleted, and the services they provide have become more scarce and valuable. We have estimated the benefit/cost ratio of preserving and restoring global natural capital as at least 100:1. There are not many better investments than that. If we adequately account for *all* our assets, we would put much less emphasis on GDP (which was never designed as a measure of economic well-being and is a very misleading proxy) and think more about maximizing the value of our total global portfolio of assets. An Earth Shareholder Report would do something like that and would be a better guide to investment policies.

QUESTIONS

1. What implications does Robert's work have for financial management?

2. How could financial management connect to natural capital?

3. What does Robert mean regarding companies understanding external costs as profits? What's the mechanism behind it?

PROFESSIONAL PROFILE
DARMINDER TIWANA

Hi, my name is Darminder Tiwana and I am a director and chief financial officer (CFO) at Legrand, a global specialist in electrical and digital building infrastructure.

My responsibilities. I am responsible for helping the company strategize the way forward, enabling it to grow in a sustained way. It remains key that I try to balance the needs of all the stakeholders in trying to achieve this. As well as being the CFO, I am also the compliance officer of the company, thus ensuring that we follow good business practices, such as fair competition and ensuring ethics remains a key consideration in each decision taken. It is paramount that when evaluating new business opportunities and/or new product launches, we keep the environmental impacts and sustainable solutions of our products at the heart of the decision-making process.

Courtesy of Darminder Tiwana

A typical day at work. As well as managing the core areas of finance and IT such as financial reporting and controlling, cash management, legal, audit, and tax, I focus on meeting external stakeholders such as banks, consultants, and lawyers to explore new business opportunities and to stay connected with new developments in the industry. Automation and digitalization remain a focal point but consequently retraining and upskilling of employees to work on more added value activities remain key to balancing both employee and business considerations. Mergers and acuisitions (M&A) are also a focus area, and when identifying the target, as well as financial performance, we give weight to the values of the target company and brand, thus ensuring smooth integration.

Challenges. I am lucky to interact with all departments of the company and many external stakeholders, but the biggest challenge is always to balance the various needs of all of them. Being compliant, competitive, productive, and efficient are just a prerequisite to the bigger picture whereby we need to ensure we remain socially responsible in our actions while achieving success. In this responsibility we work in three main areas. Regarding people, we give high regard to human rights, health, safety and well-being, skill development, and equality. For the environment, to limiting greenhouse gases and combat pollution. Regarding the business ecosystem, it is challenging to provide sustainable solutions, ensure sustainable procurement and, obviously, to act ethically.

(Continued)

Tips and tricks. It remains relatively easy to deliver good results quickly; however, it is much more difficult to sustain them. I would discourage short-termism, as often you would not have thought through the complete cycle in your decision-making process and the possible repercussions due to them on the various stakeholders of the company. Business equity is built over many years but can easily become tarnished, especially at times of economic difficulties, such as a recession.

QUESTIONS

1. Is Darminder's professional life as a financial manager the way you would have imagined it? What is surprising, what isn't?

2. Into which different areas beyond just financial management do Darminder's work activities and practices reach?

3. What relationships can you spot between the financial, social, and environmental dimensions in Darminder's work?

4. How would you describe Darminder's way of describing his stakeholders?

TRUE STORY

MONEY BEFORE PEOPLE?

EDITED BY ALEXANDRA LEONOR BARRUETA SACKSTEDER

(Continued)

A lawyer turned manager. My name is Xiao. I hold both bachelor's and master's degrees in law, and I am qualified as a Chinese lawyer. After graduation, I joined a bank and have been working there for nine years. Currently, I am working as a senior manager in the legal department in the headquarters. My work mainly includes compliance consulting in the banking business, the management of legal risks, and the disposal of non-performing loans.

From my actual working experience, I found that inclusive finance has become the most important aspect of social responsibility in the Chinese banking industry. It seems that the protection of the rights and interests of financial consumers is becoming another important part of corporate social responsibility (CSR), which also receives the special attention of regulatory authorities.

Stories from the frontline. The common disputes that clients have with the banks and their services serve to highlight issues and gaps in the consumer protection services that banks tote as their CSR initiatives. But when rules are bent and consumer protection skirted, it leads to banks promising CSR and not delivering and furthermore, undervaluing their stakeholders and their investments. Although I have experienced these issues with the bank's clients on several occasions, I can remember two of them particularly vividly.

Blank contracts. Mr Ren wanted to help his friend who needed a loan from the bank. In China, Guanxi (social relationships facilitating) is very important and people tend to do everything they can to help their friends, even if it could potentially put them at risk. In this case, Mr Ren provided collateral for his friend's bank loan.

When the loan had almost expired, the bank put a blank guarantee contract in the documents he was to sign without informing him of this. He signed all the documents without really reading them, trusting the bank to adhere to what had been discussed. Once this was discovered, legal actions were taken but ultimately the court ruled that he had the obligation of guaranteeing responsibility for the loan. The bank added the blank guarantee contract because the initial collateral wasn't enough to cover the loans exposure and Mr Ren had strong assets. So, by using a blank guarantee they had essentially forced him into repayment obligations in order to reduce their losses. This case could not be more black and white and serves to exemplify how the bank often stoops to dishonest actions and misinformation when conducting business.

It would be easy to single out the bank and say that it is a particular problem of this branch. However, these stories are passed around at meetings, conferences, and retreats and often as a badge of honour: 'Look how many clients I bamboozled this month!' It is an unfortunate trend in the banking industry in China, particularly amongst those banks that claim consumer protection as a CSR initiative.

Single house. Another memorable client, Mrs Ye, used the bank's mortgage loan business in order to purchase a house. This is a common issue in China as there is still an underlying belief that one must have a house before one can get married, although this is changing more every

(Continued)

day. Unfortunately, due to circumstances unforeseen and out of her control, Mrs Ye was unable to meet her scheduled payment a few times. Rather than contacting her to set up an alternative payment plan or even approach her with a warning, the bank took Mrs Ye to court in order to seize and auction off the house to the highest bidder. The issue here is simple: Mrs Ye only owned the one house and if it were sold she would be left homeless, despite already having paid some money to the bank, albeit not the whole sum. On the other hand, if the house can't be sold, how can the bank's interests be protected?

In this case, as it often is, we can see a direct contradiction between the right to personal residence and the bank's interests. Which party should be given priority protection? And when a bank is relying so heavily on 'consumer protection and rights' in order to avoid other CSR practices, how can it justify the said treatment?

On top of this, in a country where most banks are regulated by the State council, how can one expect to go to court and get a fair hearing? Wouldn't they judge in favour of the banks, which belong to the same entity?

QUESTIONS

1. What kinds of behaviours on the part of banks have the potential to infringe the rights of financial consumers?

2. Can you think of a win–win solution where neither bank nor customers lose?

3. What would you do if you were in this situation and knew about these incidents and practices? Is there anything you could do?

4. Can you think of a new financial practice or mechanism that deals with defaulted mortgages in a way other than auctioning off a person's home?

DIGGING DEEPER: RETHINKING RETURNS ON INVESTMENT

As illustrated early on in this chapter, rethinking the maximization of short-term return on investment (profit) is a core aspect of responsible financial management. In this section, we will both proceed to dig deeper into the components of a responsible return on investment (RROI) and provide a hands-on example of how to calculate a social return on investment.

ETHICS, RESPONSIBILITY, AND SUSTAINABILITY IN THE RROI

Responsible return on investment (RROI) measures success as the long-term optimization of returns in the form of an optimum triple bottom line and stakeholder value creation, as well as minimizing ethical misconduct

The declared goal of most common financial management activity is to maximize profit. What is wrong with profit thinking? Nothing per se, but profit can and should be one of the many indicators used to assess the performance of a company. Short-term profit maximization leads to results that may be counterproductive to the long-term goals of sustainability. Also, profit-first thinking skews financial management towards primarily satisfying the needs of the owner stakeholder, while neglecting the needs of equally legitimate other stakeholder groups.

Triple bottom line return on investment (ROI_{TBL}) measures the amount of economic, social, and environmental value created, per dollar spent

Therefore, in professional financial management, the goal is what we call a responsible return on investment (RROI). To optimize the RROI, companies must make sure they achieve a maximum triple bottom line (sustainability) in the long run to create maximum stakeholder value (responsibility) and to minimize ethical misconduct per dollar spent. Equation 1 below illustrates how the responsible return on investment (ROI_{Res}) is composed of the **triple bottom line return** (ROI_{TBL}), the stakeholder value return (ROI_{SHV}), and the ethical return (ROI_{ETH}):

$$ROI_{Res} = ROI_{TBL} + ROI_{SHV} + ROI_{ETH}$$

Stakeholder return on investment measures the amount of stakeholder value created per dollar spent

Equation 2 shows how the ROI_{TBL} is composed of the sum of all three types of triple bottom line value, economic (V_{Econ}), social (V_{Soc}) and environmental (V_{Env}) value per dollar spent, how the **stakeholder value return** is a sum of all stakeholder value created ($\sum_{i=0}^{n} SHV_n$), and how the **ethical return** is the sum of all ethical dilemmas per dollar spent ($\sum_{i=0}^{n} EM_n$).

Ethical return on investment measures the amount of ethical (mis)behaviours per dollar spent

$$= \frac{V_{Econ} + V_{Soc} + V_{Env}}{1\$} + \frac{\sum_{i=0}^{n} SHV_n}{1\$} + \frac{\sum_{i=0}^{n} EM_n}{1\$}$$

In order to maximize the responsible return on investment, what companies have to do is to optimize the triple bottom line (*opt TBL*), optimize the sum of stakeholder value (*opt ΣSHV*), and minimize the sum of ethical misconduct:

$$\rightarrow ROI_{RES}^{MAX} = optTBL + opt \sum SHV - min \sum EM$$

In contrast to the mainstream financial *maximization* paradigm, RROI in responsible management has to be optimized, as there is often a built-in trade-off between the three dimensions of the triple bottom line and competing stakeholder claims. For example, the company might have two competing courses of action, one of which is highly profitable financially, while the other one creates much stakeholder value. Thus, in this case, there is a trade-off between the social and economic dimensions. In another situation, a company might encounter two activities competing for capital, one being exceptionally good for the company's employees, the other one for the company communities. Again the trade-off exists, but this time between the value created for the two different stakeholder groups. Sometimes, you can't have your cake and eat it, as they say [57].

The preceding algebraic description numerically illustrates a responsible return on investment. In practice, measuring and calculating the three elements of an RROI is very complex. One well-developed method is the social return on investment.

CALCULATING THE SROI

How can you calculate a social return on investment (SROI) in practice? As illustrated in Figure 21.11, the first stage is assessing the basic parameters of the SROI. The second is quantifying the costs and benefits, and the third using the established SROI. We will illustrate the three stages by applying them to the example of a fictional green office programme called 'GreenO', which has the goal of reducing the amount of CO_2 emissions from paper use. The programme is built around two lines of action: (1) substituting an old printer for a new one that uses less energy and avoids paper jams; (2) providing a two-hour weekend training session on the topic of green printing by an external trainer who specializes in green office programmes.

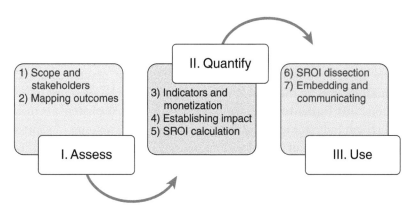

FIGURE 21.11   Stages in establishing an SROI

SOURCE: Based on [58]

STAGE I ASSESS SCOPE AND STAKEHOLDERS, AND MAP OUTCOMES

The first stage in establishing an SROI consists of defining the boundaries of what should be included.

1. **Scope and stakeholders.** An initial step is to define the *scope*, asking questions such as: What activities do you want to calculate the SROI for? Are you looking at a single action or a whole programme? Will you consider only one location or an array of activities at different locations? A concise description of the scope of what you evaluate will greatly facilitate all subsequent steps. Once you have described the scope you can proceed to identify the *stakeholders* who affect and are affected by the activity you are calculating the SROI for. In the SROI calculation, stakeholders are not only important as the ones providing inputs to the activity, and the ones for whom value is created, but also as an important source of information. It is for this reason that even at this early stage a successful SROI calculation needs you to establish stakeholder communication channels and to decide

how to involve stakeholders in the process. Chapter 4 provides deeper insight into how to manage stakeholder relations.

2. **Mapping outcomes.** During this second step, the main goal is to define and have a clear understanding of the mechanics of the activity. First make a list of the **inputs** provided by the different stakeholders involved in the activity and value the inputs monetarily:

- The price for a new printer (310 euro) and the cost of hiring an external trainer (300 euro) are inputs provided by the company.

- The employee stakeholders provide their free time at a weekend as an input (2h x 40 employees x 11 euro/h = 880 euro).

Inputs
resources that are used up in the process of an activity

Outputs
quantitative, immediately measurable effects of an activity

Outcomes
long-term changes, achieved through an activity

Second, the direct **outputs** and final **outcomes** of the activity are evaluated. Outputs are direct, often quantifiable consequences of an activity, while outcomes are the long-term impacts and achievements of an activity. An outcome of our green office programme, for instance, would be the number of employees who participated in the weekend training session. The outcome of this same activity would be a long-term reduction in environmental inputs like paper, or energy and a reduction in office waste.

STAGE II QUANTIFY

3. **Indicators and monetization.** In Stage I, we developed a good sense of what and how to measure. Here, it is time to work with the numbers. First, develop measurable input, output, and outcome indicators for the activities that could not easily be measured in Stage I, the so-called soft indicators. **Soft indicators** require more effort than **hard indicators** to make them measurable. One such soft indicator to be defined as an output is the amount of paper saved and, as a related outcome, the amount of CO_2 emissions saved because of reduced paper usage. It is important to assign a monetary value (so-called **monetization**) to the outcome created and to find out how long the outcome will probably last. Let us imagine that GreenO achieved a reduction of 2.3 tons of CO_2 in the first month. One ton can be attributed to the new printer, 1.3 tons stem from the change in employees' printing behaviour [59]. At the time you do this assessment one ton of CO_2 is valued at 7.43 euro [60], which translates into a monetary value of 17.09^3 for the 2.3 tons. As employees progressively forget the lessons learnt in the green printing training, the effect of the training wears off by 25 per cent every year after the first year. After five years the effect of the training is zero.

Soft indicators
qualitative in nature and difficult to be quantified

Hard indicators
indicators that can be easily measured quantitatively

Monetization
describes the process of defining a financial value for non-financial indicators

Social value is often perceived as harder to monetize. How can we measure how much a certain activity is worth for a stakeholder? The answer is simple: ask them. For instance, to know how much employees value the responsible business activities of their company, a typical question is: 'If you could have the choice to work for two almost identical companies, but one is known to be a responsible business, how much wage would you forfeit to work for the responsible organization?' The answer represents a **financial proxy**, an estimation of the monetary value created for the

Financial proxy
an estimate of the financial value represented by a social or environmental factor

---

[3]Less pollution (here less CO_2) is not a value created in the strict sense, but an environmental cost avoided, which is why we describe it here as a positive impact.

employee stakeholder to the company's responsible business conduct. Proxies for many types of social value are also available externally. For instance, a financial proxy for improved health might be the cost of treatment of health issues. To evaluate the social value of the input given by employees to the weekend training, we used the proxy of an average hourly remuneration. While monetization and the use of financial proxies still require refinement, which will come with increased usage in practice, the importance of implementing responsible business practices must be highlighted. Monetization is the one crucial condition needed to be able to integrate social, environmental, and ethical factors into financial decision-making tools, such as the return on investment in this section.

4. **Establishing impact.** The fourth step isolates the **impact** of the organization's activity from the parts of the outcome created by other factors. The impact is the total outcome achieved minus 'what would have happened anyway' [61]. In most cases, only parts of the overall outcome can be attributed to the activity of the organization. From the overall impact, we have to deduct the following four external factors:

    Impact
    the total outcome achieved minus 'what would have happened anyway'

    *   The **deadweight** is the fraction of the outcome that would have been achieved anyway, whether the activity would have taken place or not. Can some parts of the outcome be attributed to former activities or general trends?

    *   **Displacement** describes a situation where a positive outcome is achieved but creates a negative cost, a trade-off somewhere else. For instance, the new printer bought in our example on the one hand saves CO_2 emission from jammed paper but creates additional CO_2 emissions in its production and transportation. Here, for the sake of simplicity, we will omit this consideration.

    *   **Attribution** is the attempt to define how much of the outcome has been created by other actors.

    *   The **drop-off** explains how the outcomes wear off over time. Earlier we described the self-reducing effect of the GreenO training session, which is a typical example of a drop-off.

5. **Calculating the SROI.** Here we reach the core piece of the SROI calculation. The goal at this stage is to come up with a concrete number for the SROI. To do so, we use the net present value calculation and the internal rate on investment (IRR), both common tools in mainstream financial management. The following chain of events summarizes inputs, outputs, and outcomes realized in the GreenO programme:

    *   **Inputs.** The company buys a new printer (310 euro) and hires the trainer (300 euro). Forty employees invest two hours of free time in the training (11 euro per hour, per employee) (total input 880 euro). They are not paid for their time, which we add as inputs to the employee stakeholder, not to the company's inputs.

    *   **Employee motivation.** Employees were motivated by the new GreenO programme. Via a questionnaire it was found that they would forfeit an average yearly 1000 euro to work for a company with such a programme. The effect wears off in the first year to 500 euro and disappears from the third year on.

- **CO_2 and cost savings.** The activities of the GreenO programme lead to constant yearly reductions in CO_2 of 1000 tons from the new printer until the fourth year in which the printer has to be substituted with a new one. The change in employees' printing behaviour results in a reduction of 1.3 tons of CO_2 emissions in the first year. The effect drops off by 25 per cent in each following year. The mentioned CO_2 reduction resulted from of 1.36 tons of paper, and of 569 kWh annually for the company. In the first year, the paper reduction saves the company 2067 euro (1520 euro/t) and the reduction in energy consumption results in savings of 61.96 euro (0.1089 euro/kWh).

In a traditional net present value (NPV) calculation, businesses summarize the cash flows related to an activity. Cash flows only represent the flow of financial value. In order to include the social and environmental value categories as well, we broaden the term cash flow to value flow. Thus, counterintuitively to its title 'social' return on investment, the SROI includes not only social but also environmental and financial value. The upper half of Table 21.1 illustrates the flows of social, environmental, and economic value and sums them up per year period, including the inputs, outputs, and outcomes of all stakeholders.

TABLE 21.1   Value flows in the GreenO example

Period		0			1	2	3	4
Value flows per stakeholder	Company	−310 € −300 €		Energy saving	569 kWh x 0.1089 €/kWh= 61.96 €	569 kWh x 0.1089 €/kWh= 61.96 €	569 kWh x 0.1089 €/kWh= 61.96 €	569 kWh x 0.1089 €/kWh= 61.96 €
				Paper saving	1.36 t x 1520 €/t =2067 €	1.15 t x 1520 €/t =1748 €	1.00 t x 1520 €/t =1520 €	0.86 t x 1520 €/t =1307 €
	Employees	−880 €		Wage equivalent	1000 €	500 €	0 €	0 €
	Environment	0€		CO_2 savings	1.3 t x 7.43 €/t= 9.66 €	0.98 t x 7.43 €/t= 7.28 €	0.73 t x 7.43 €/t= 5.42 €	0.55 t x 7.43 €/t= 4.09 €
Value flow sums per period		−1490 €			3146.05 €	2324.67 €	1594.81 €	1380.48 €

We have to take into account that money has a cost. Typically, this cost is represented by the average market interest rate for borrowing money. It is for this reason that in the NPV calculation, we now have to discount later value flows after period 0 by the market interest rate (r), which we assume to be 5 per cent.

$$NPV = V_0 + \frac{V_1}{1+r} + \frac{V_n}{(1+r)^n}$$

In our example, the basic formula translates into the following equation:

$$NPV_S^{GreenO} = -1490 + \frac{3146.05\square}{1,05} + \frac{2324.67\square}{1,05^2} + \frac{1594.81\square}{1,05^3} + \frac{1380.48\square}{1,05^4} = 6210\lbrack$$

To calculate the SROI we use the internal rate of return (IRR) method, which is used in capital budgeting to evaluate projects. The IRR is the SROI. The IRR of a project or activity is the interest rate (r) with which the NPV of all cash flows becomes 0. The algebraic calculation of the IRR is beyond the scope of this book. In our case all social value created accounts for 2.96 euro per every euro spent. The IRR respectively the SROI is 1.96, in a percentage of 196 per cent.

$SROI = IRR = 1.96 \triangleq SROI\ Ratio = 2.96\ € \ per\ 1\ € \ spent$

Another standard calculation is to find out when an activity breaks even, which means at which point in time the costs of an activity equal its benefits. The **break even point** (BEP) is calculated by establishing the ratio between the initial costs caused by an activity and the benefits created by them. An activity breaks even at the point in time in which the benefits realized from the activity equal the initial costs. After the BEP an activity is profitable.

Break even point is calculated by establishing the ratio between the initial costs caused by an activity and the benefits created by them

STAGE III USE

6. **Dissecting the SROI.** While the traditional financial return on investment does not include enough information regarding the true costs and benefits of an activity, the social return on investment runs the risk of including too much information in one number, which might cause problems in interpretation. It is for this reason that the last stage of the process of establishing an SROI is to dissect it into its components in order to enrich the practice value and analysis possibilities of the SROI. Table 21.2 shows how the SROI can be split for different evaluation purposes.

    In order to evaluate we need to split the costs and benefits and resulting cash flows into private and social cash flows. *Private cash flows* are incurred by the respective actor (company or employee) for whom the calculation is carried out. *Social cash-flows* are all costs and benefits that have been incurred by any stakeholder in the calculation, not only the actor.

    As an example, a for-profit-company will probably be inclined not merely to base its decision on the social return on investment, which might lead it to establish two criteria, one based on the purely private return and another one on the overall social return on investment. The company might say, we do not do any responsible management activity that does not have at least neutral private net present value ($\mathbf{NPV_P}^{Comp}$). There are many responsible management activities that are at least able to recover their costs. The second criterion might then be to pick the ones that have the highest overall social return on investment ($\mathbf{NPV_s}$). Of course, the two criteria mentioned are an oversimplification. In practice, many more decision factors play a role. The company in our example might also have to decide, because of budget restrictions, to either buy the new printer or to conduct employee training. Comparing the social net present value of the printer purchase ($\mathbf{NPV_s^{Print}}$), its social return on investment ($\mathbf{IRR_s^{\ Print}}$), and its social value break-even point ($\mathbf{BEP_s^{Print}}$) with the respective indicators for the training programme can inform such a decision. Among the many other techniques of dissecting and interpreting the SROI we would like to highlight one last example. Calculating the return on investment of just one specific stakeholder group provides a measure of how much the different stakeholder groups benefit from the activity and how well incentivized they are to cooperate.

In our example, we calculated the social return on investment for the employees as the main stakeholder group involved. Those values can then be compared with the private value created for the company to get a quantified idea of the fairness of distribution of value between the company and the main stakeholders involved in the activity.

7. **Embedding and communicating.** Based on the dissected indicators for the return on investment, responsible managers may pick the indicator most aligned with the respective stakeholder. Communication could be used both for informing external stakeholders on the company's social performance, and for the internal controlling process. Chapter 10 provides further insight and Chapter 20 illustrates internal controlling systems and the use of indicators.

POINTERS

Look again at the different returns of investment illustrated and exemplified here. Which ones are more abstract, which ones more hands-on? For the more abstract ones, are there any more practical ways you can think of to calculate them?

TABLE 21.2 Dissecting the SROI

Question 1: Is the GreenO programme good for society?

Total social value	$NPVS^{GreenO}$	6210 €	$IRR\ S^{GreenO}$	196%	BEPS	5.4 months

Answer 1: Yes GreenO (printer and training activities) is excellent from a social standpoint. NPV and IRR are very high. The overall cost for company and employees is recovered in only 5.4 months.

Question 2: Will the two actors involved carry out the activities?

Private value for the company (printer and training)	NPV_S^{Comp}	5553 €	IRR_S^{Comp}	334%	BEP_S^{Comp}	3.4 months
Private value for the employee (training)	NPV_S^{Emp}	3868 €	IRR_S^{Emp}	252%	BEP_S^{Emp}	4.1 months

Answer 2: Yes, both actors will, if they are rational and perfectly informed, carry out the activity. Both encounter high NPV and IRR and very short periods until their activities break even. All values look slightly better from a company perspective, which is why the company incentives to carry out the activities is higher than the one of the employees.

Question 3: If we had to decide which of the two activities (training or printer) to carry out, which one should we choose?

Private value of printer for the company	$NPV_P^{Comp/Print}$	2598 €	$IRR_P^{Comp/Print}$	263%	$BEP_P^{Comp/Print}$	4.5 months
Private value of training for the company	$NPV_P^{Comp/Train}$	2938 €	$IRR_P^{Comp/Train}$	411%	$BEP_P^{Comp/Train}$	2.8 months
Social value of printer	NPV_S^{Print}	2624 €	IRR_S^{Print}	265%	BEP_S^{Print}	4.5 months
Social value of training	NPV_S^{Train}	3568 €	IRR_S^{Train}	172%	BEP_S^{Train}	5.7 months

Answer 3: From the company's private perspective, the training beats the printer in all three metrics. From a social perspective, the training has a higher NPV, but the printer is better in IRR and BEP. The answer here is not completely clear.

(Continued)

WORKSHEET

VALUE FLOWS ASSESSMENT

TABLE 21.2

Actors and stake-holders	Initial expenditure	Types of stakeholder value obtained	Monetized value flows per period				
			1	2	3	4	5
Stakeholder 1: ___		Value 1.1: ___					
		Value 1.2: ___					
Stakeholder 2: ___		Value 2.1: ___					
		Value 2.2: ___					

TABLE 21.2 (Continued)

Stakeholder 3:	Value 3.1: _____
	Value 3.2: _____
Sums of value per period:	

POINTERS

You might want to conduct a value flow analysis, for instance, to assess how much value stakeholders get out of an action over time, or as a basis for calculating its social return on investment. For further details and an example of how to calculate an activity's stakeholder value flows, have a look at this chapter's 'Digging Deeper' section. As the number of stakeholders, types of different value flows, and periods that value is affected by vary considerably across activities, you might want to create your own customized version of this worksheet.

REFERENCES

1. Delevingne L, Gründler A, Kane S, Koller T. *The ESG premium: New perspectives on value and performance.* New Jersey: McKinsey, 2020.
2. Mondragon. Our principles. www.mondragon-corporation.com/en/co-operative-experience/our-principles Published 2020. Accessed April 8 2020.
3. Mondragon. www.mondragon-corporation.com/en Published 2020. Accessed April 8 2020.
4. Freeman RE, Laasch O. From 'management sucks' to 'management rocks' through responsible management. In: Laasch O, Suddaby R, Freeman RE, Jamali D, eds. *The research handbook of responsible management.* Cheltenham: Edward Elgar, 2020: 113–120.
5. Scholtens B. Finance as a driver of corporate social responsibility. *Journal of Business Ethics.* 2006, 68(1): 19–33.
6. LeBlanc B. Sustainability rises: On the CFO's 'to-do' list. *Financial Executive.* 2012, 28(2): 54–57.
7. Kaufman A. Managers' double fiduciary duty: To stakeholders and to freedom. *Business Ethics Quarterly.* 2002, 12(2): 189–214.
8. Coleman L, Maheswaran K, Pinder S. Narratives in managers' corporate finance decisions. *Accounting and Finance.* 2010, 50(3): 605–633.
9. Owen, W., (2022, Jul. 7), HSBC banker quits over climate change furore. www.ft.com/content/5ff24114-5777-4d00-a014-ad36ce948d64
10. Fauzi H, Mahoney L, Rahman AA. Institutional ownership and corporate social performance: Empirical evidence from Indonesian companies. *Issues in Social and Environmental Accounting.* 2007, 1(2): 334–347.
11. Oh WY, Chang YK, Martynov A. The effect of ownership structure on corporate social responsibility: Empirical evidence from Korea. *Journal of Business Ethics.* 2011, 104(2): 283–297.
12. Min-Dong PL. Does ownership form matter for corporate social responsibility? A longitudinal comparison of environmental performance between public, private, and joint-venture firms. *Business and Society Review.* 2009, 114(4): 435–456.
13. Prado-Lorenzo JM, Gallego-Alvarez I, Garcia-Sanchez IM. Stakeholder engagement and corporate social responsibility reporting: The ownership structure effect. *Corporate Social Responsibility and Environmental Management.* 2009, 16(2): 94–107.
14. Li W, Zhang R. Corporate social responsibility, ownership structure, and political interference: Evidence from China. *Journal of Business Ethics.* 2010, 96(4): 631–645.
15. UNPRI. What are the principles for responsible investment? www.unpri.org/pri/an-introduction-to-responsible-investment/what-are-the-principles-for-responsible-investment Published 2020. Accessed April 9 2020.
16. Field A. SRI investing in the US now $12 trillion in AUM. www.forbes.com/sites/annefield/2018/11/26/sri-investing-in-the-us-now-12-trillion-in-aum/#22119952a3bc Published 2019. Accessed April 9 2020.
17. USISFI. *Report on socially responsible investing trends in the United States.* Washington, DC: Social Investment Forum Foundation, 2010.
18. Sprague M. Decarbonising investment portfolios on the journey to Net Zero. www.southpole.com/blog/decarbonising-investment-portfolios-net-zero Published 2021. Last accessed August 1 2023.
19. Insights Institute. Investing to enable an economy-wide evolition to a low-carbon future. www.cppinvestments.com/insight-institute/investing-to-enable-an-economy-wide-evolution-to-low-carbon-future Published 2021. Last accessed August 1 2023.
20. Capelle-Blancard G, Couderc N. The impact of socially responsible investing: Evidence from stock index redefinitions. *The Journal of Investing.* 2009, 18(2): 76–86.
21. Amazon employees challenge Bezos over inaction on the climate crisis at shareholder meeting [press release], 2019.
22. BBC News. Amazon 'threatens to fire' climate change activists. www.bbc.co.uk/news/business-50953719 Published 2020. Accessed April 9 2020.
23. Karpoff JM. The impact of shareholder activism on target companies: A survey of empirical findings. Working paper, University of Washington, 1998.

24. Smith MP. Shareholder activism by institutional investors: Evidence from CalPERS. *The Journal of Finance*. 1996, 51(1): 227–252.
25. The International Co-operative Alliance. *What Is a Co-op?* 2012. https://www.ica. coop/en#:~:text=Cooperatives%20are%20people%2Dcentred%20enterprises,and%20 cultural%20needs%20and%20aspirations.
26. The International Co-operative Alliance. Factsheet: Differences between co-operatives, corporations and non-profit organisations. http://2012.coop/sites/default/files/ Factsheet%20-%20Differences%20between%20Coops%20Corps%20and%20NFPs%20 -%20US%20OCDC%20-%202007.pdf Published 2007. Accessed December 10 2012.
27. The International Co-operative Alliance. Differences between co-operatives, corporations and non-profit organisations. http://2012.coop/sites/default/files/Factsheet%20-%20 Differences%20between%20Coops%20Corps%20and%20NFPs%20-%20US%20 OCDC%20-%202007.pdf. Published 2007. Accessed 11 December 2012.
28. Chaddad FR, Cook ML. Understanding new cooperative models: An ownership-control rights typology. *Review of Agricultural Economics*. 2004, 26(3): 348–360.
29. Chaddad FR, Cook ML. An ownership rights typology of cooperative models. Department of Agricultural Economics working paper AEWP 2002–06, 2002.
30. The International Co-operative Alliance. *Co-operative facts & figures*. http://2012.coop/en/ ica/co-operative-facts-figures Published 2012. Accessed December 11 2012.
31. Berk J, DeMarzo P. *Corporate finance*. Boston, MA: Pearson Addison Wesley, 2007.
32. Mansdorf Z. Sustainability and return on investment. *EHS Today*. 2010: 49–52.
33. Dorfleitner G, Utz S. Safety first portfolio choice based on financial and sustainability returns. *European Journal of Operational Research*. 2012, 221(1): 155–164.
34. Burberry. Burberry introduces carbon insetting and Autumn/Winter 2020 runway show certified carbon neutral. www.burberryplc.com/en/news/news/corporate/2020/burberry-introduces-carbon-insetting-and-autumn-winter-2020-runw.html Published 2020. Accessed April 9 2020.
35. Emerson J. The blended value proposition: Integrating social and financial returns. *California Management Review*. 2003, 45(4): 35–51.
36. Lingane A, Olsen S. Guidelines for social return on investment. *California Management Review*. 2004, 46(3): 116–135.
37. Informa Bringing Knowledge to Life. Annual report and financial statements 2011. London: Marks & Spencer Group, 2012.
38. Keeble JJ, Topiol S, Berkeley S. Using indicators to measure sustainability performance at a corporate and project level. *Journal of Business Ethics*. 2003, 44(2–3): 149–158.
39. Secretaría de Medio Ambiente y Recursos Naturales. *Liderazgo Ambiental para la Competitividad*. http://liderazgoambiental.gob.mx/portel/libreria/pdf/ PresentacinLACJulio2012.pdf Published 2012. Accessed December 27 2012.
40. Rappaport A. *Creating shareholder value: A guide for managers and investors*. New York: The Free Press, 1998.
41. Brigham EF, Houston JF. *Fundamentals of financial management*. Mason, OH: South-Western, Cengage Learning, 2011.
42. Bender R, Ward K. *Corporate financial strategy*. Oxford: Butterworth-Heinemann, 2008.
43. Laasch O. Strategic CSR. In: *The A-Z of corporate social responsibility* (2nd edition). Chichester: Wiley, 2010: 378–380.
44. Orlitzky M, Schmidt FL, Rynes SL. Corporate social and financial performance: A meta-analysis. *Organization Studies*. 2003, 24(3): 403–441.
45. Waddock SA, Graves SB. The corporate social performance-financial performance link. *Strategic Management Journal*. 1997, 18(4): 303–319.
46. Chandler D. *Corporate social responsibility: A strategic perspective*. New York: Business Expert Press, 2014.
47. Peat J. Easyjet shareholders get £174 million dividends as airline appeals for taxpayer support. www.thelondoneconomic.com/travel/easyjet-shareholders-get-174-million-dividends-as-airline-appeals-for-taxpayer-support-181739 Published 2020. Accessed April 9 2020.
48. Leggett T. Coronavirus: EasyJet staff may no longer be given food on shifts. www.bbc. co.uk/news/business-51962981 Published 2020. Accessed April 9 2020.
49. Engine No.1. https://engine1.com

50. Walt V. Can capitalism save the planet? Engine No.1's Jennifer Grancio thinks so. https://time.com/collection/time100-companies-2022/6159495/engine-no-1 Published 2022. Last accessed August 1 2023.

51. Report of the Committee on *The financial aspects of corporate governance*. London, UK: Gee, Professional Publishing, 1992. [The Cadbury report]

52. *OECD principles of corporate governance*. Paris: OECD Publications Service, 1998. https://www.oecd.org/corporate/principles-corporate-governance

53. Sarbanes-Oxley. Corporate responsibility (Public Law 107–204, 2002).

54. Vodacom Group Limited Integrated Report, 2012.

55. Balasubramanian B, Satwalekar D. *Corporate governance: An emerging scenario.* Mumbai: National Stock Exchange of India, 2010.

56. Laasch, O., Moosmayer, D., & Antonacopoulou, E. P. 2022. The interdisciplinary responsible management competence framework: An integrative review of ethics, responsibility, and sustainability competences. Journal of Business Ethics. https://doi.org/10.1007/s10551-022-05261-4.

57. Hahn T, Figge F, Pinkse J, Preuss L. Trade-offs in corporate sustainability: You can't have your cake and eat it. *Business Strategy and the Environment.* 2010, 19(4): 217–229.

58. A guide to social return on investment. Liverpool, UK: SROI, 2012.

59. Hewlett-Packard Development Company. HP carbon footprint calculator for printing. www.hp.com/large/ipg/ecological-printing-solutions/carbon-footprint-calc.html Published 2012. Accessed December 10 2012.

60. The exchange of SENDECO2. *CO2 prices.* www.sendeco2.com/index-uk.asp Published 2012. Accessed December 17 2012.

61. Measuring social impact: The foundation of social return on investment (SROI). London: SROI Primer, 2004.

CASE STUDY ZONE

I   **New-World Management at Patagonia**   853

    Oliver Laasch

II   **Yash Pakka: Naturally Inspired to Change the World**   863

    Daniel A. Diaz

III   **Fairphoning Management**   875

    Oliver Laasch

IV   **Managing According to the Sages at Good-Ark**   889

    Pingping Fu and Qing Qu

V   **Managing by the Gram at Algramo**   901

    Daniel A. Diaz

VI   **Greyston's Bakers on a Mission to Scale Open Hiring®**   913

    Oliver Laasch, Reut Livne-Tarandach, and Michael Pirson

I NEW-WORLD MANAGEMENT AT PATAGONIA

OLIVER LAASCH

The attitude. 'Screw Mars. We gotta do this,' says Yvon Chouinard founder of the billion dollar outdoor clothing company Patagonia in an interview for Fast Company Magazine. This was his answer when asked what he thought of Jeff Bezos' and Elon Musk's pursuits of interplanetary travel and colonies on Mars 'because they don't believe we can save our home planet' [1]. Yvon Chouinard has been called an 'iconoclast' who breaks with old, taken-for-granted management paradigms [2], an 'intelligent fanatic' [3] who dances 'at the edge' of management [4], at least the edge of old-world management that has created and keeps recreating many of the problems we are in nowadays. He is not alone in this attitude, not at Patagonia for sure.

The purpose. Rose Marcario, back then the CEO of Patagonia, prominently tweeted 'the plain truth is that capitalism needs to evolve if humanity is going to survive' [5]. Many management practices at Patagonia appear to be evolved 'new-world management practices', which are breaking away from 'normal' old-world management and related practices. They might well be a blueprint for new-world management practices. Patagonia's care for the natural world is not new and can be traced back in their history. Patagonia started as a rock climbing company, but stopped selling their original gear in 1976, just three years after the company was founded. The reasons were that their equipment was damaging natural rock surfaces [6]. The company has recently changed its mission statement to a 'mission to save the planet', and has declared that 'Earth is now our only stakeholder' after all of its stock was donated to nonprofits fighting climate change, which now effectively own the company [7]. How do you manage a business that is there to save the Earth, not Wall Street? It is a type of management where 'important decisions [are] based on wanting to be here 100 years from now' [8]. Here are a couple of the new world-management practices pioneered by the managers at Patagonia.

Demarketing. First, there is a set of practices that break with many of the usual marketing paradigms such as maximizing sales and promoting consumerism, with many of them related to 'green demarketing' [9, 10]. For example, there are ads stating 'reduce what you buy' or more specifically 'Don't buy this jacket!' [11, 12]. Such marketing practices may be counterintuitive and appear 'much like something out of an anti-capitalism rally' [11] as one journalist noticed. However, Rose Marcario would probably claim that they are instead management practices necessary for an evolution of capitalism. Such capitalism would be built on practices aimed at slowed-down 'controlled growth' [3]. Yvon Chouinard calls the underlying paradigm 'economies of abundance … there is enough. Not too much. Not too little. Enough. Most importantly, there is enough time for the things that matter: relationships, delicious food, art, games and the rest. … At Patagonia, we are dedicated to abundance … Our idea is to make the best product so you can consume less and consume better … We want to make the best clothes and make them so they will last a long, long time' [13]. Another practice is to purposefully increase price, so that people both buy less and pay the full cost of the product, including the environmental cost that may be borne by ecosystems [3].

Extending product life and use. Patagonia also made headlines by integrating used eBay products along with new Patagonia products, actively providing used alternatives that do not generate any income for them [3]. Similar to these initiatives, store management at Patagonia engages in repair, re-use, and recycling practices, helping customers to repair their clothing or to return used items , receiving store credit that can be used for future purchases, including used clothing [14]. These practices are a challenge to the dominant old-world management practices of fast fashion. Patagonia's efforts to extend the product life cycle stand in steep contrast to the common practice of planned obsolescence whereby products are designed to break or become useless so that customers have to buy new ones in ever shorter cycles. Rick Ridgeway, Patagonia's environment VP explains: 'We want to ask them [managers in fast fashion companies] to start thinking about their business practices and create a dialogue … to ask where they are going to be in five, 10, 20 years time, when the natural resources of this planet are in increasingly critical condition' [11].

Restorative sourcing. Patagonia has pioneered organic cotton sourcing practices and production practices since 1994, including an overhaul of their entire sourcing system, organic cotton clothing lines, and their 'footprint chronicles', which provide personalized insight into their suppliers' practices through an interactive map of the world [15–17]. However, they have begun to go one big step further. As Yvon Chouinard explains, 'We're doubling down on regenerative organic agriculture' that not only does less harm but regenerates the environment – 'With cotton now, we're sequestering [collecting] carbon' and have 'invested in companies that are working on growing synthetic fibers, stuff made from plants rather than petroleum' [1]. Such practices contradict the logic of normal business sourcing practices of a petroleum-based economy and the fundamental tenet of our 'normal' agriculture, which is large-scale monoculture and crucially relies on herbicides and pesticides. Yvon Chouinard puts it like this: 'These people [the farmers] are getting rid of their bugs by squashing them with their fingers' [1].

Activist venturing. Such agricultural management practices are a feasible alternative, as Patagonia's recent move into the sustainable food business shows [18]. Yvon Chouinard explains:

We also believe there is great opportunity – and an urgent need – for positive change in the food industry … today, modern technology, chemistry and transportation combine to put more distance between people and their food than ever before. We harvest salmon indiscriminately or farm them in open-water feedlots, putting wild salmon in peril. We overgraze our prairies, fill our livestock with antibiotics, and drain fossil aquifers to water unsustainable crops. Chemicals reign supreme to maximize production, and the unknown impact of genetically modified organisms hovers over the entire industry. In short, our food chain is broken … Patagonia Provisions is about finding solutions to repair the chain. We'll start, as we always do, by rolling up our sleeves and learning everything we can about the sourcing of each product. In some cases, we'll adopt the best practices already in existence;

in others, we'll have to find new ways of doing things, which, as we might have guessed, frequently end up being the old ways … as the Zen master might say, 'turn around and take a step forward' [19].

Birgit Cameron, senior director for Patagonia Provisions, elaborates:

The food industry is one of the biggest industries on earth and a massive contributor to global warming. Most of our food is produced using methods that reduce biodiversity, decimate soil and contribute to climate change … Yet food done differently holds a special potential not only to reduce our negative impacts on the planet – but to reverse them entirely. That's why Patagonia started a food business [19].

Humanistic management. It is well known that people management practices at Patagonia are humanistic, letting people be their authentic selves and supporting them to be fulfilled as human beings with all types of needs, professional and private, spiritual and economic, both introspective and very much 'out-there' activists. These practices respond to what humans need [20]. Yvon Chouinard's book explaining his management practices is, after all, entitled *Let my people go surfing* [21]. Related practices include hiring highly educated MBAs as well as itinerant rock climbers who can learn to do the job [21, 22]. Patagonia actively supports managers, customers, and even people with no direct relationship to become activists for environmental causes … climate lobbying for everyone [23].

How can I get involved?

We built Patagonia Action Works to connect committed individuals to organizations working on environmental issues in the same community. It's now possible for anyone to discover and connect with environmental action groups and get involved with the work they do.

Find out about **events** happening in your area

Sign **petitions** supporting issues you care about

Have a skill that an organization is looking for? Find out how to **volunteer** your time

Donate money to local causes

Care-giving people management. Another set of humanistic management practices is centred on employees flourishing as human beings with families, particularly young children. 'It lets you be the kind of parent you want to be', reflects Phil Graves, head of Patagonia's venture fund [24]. Patagonia's work travel practices include paying the costs for breast-feeding mothers who take their child with them on business trips, as well as the travel costs of an additional family member. Alternatively, employees can leave their children in the care of professional carers employed by Patagonia [25]. Holly Morrissette, who works in recruitment, shares her thoughts after having received very positive feedback from her manager on her breast-feeding in a meeting: 'With a bit of creativity, and a whole lot of guts, companies can create a workplace where mothers aren't hiding in broom closets pumping milk, but rather visiting their babies for large doses of love and serotonin before returning to their work and kicking ass'. Holly's boss had commented when seeing her breast-feeding in a meeting as follows: 'I don't know how high the ROI on this, but it is huge' [26]. A hard-to-believe perfect score in terms of the retention rate of women during and after pregnancy implies that the company is reaping the rewards for engaging in such practices. 'I wish it was 97.5 per cent because 100 per cent just doesn't sound accurate', comments Dean Carter, Vice President leading HR, Finance, and Legal. He further suggests that 'business leaders (and their CFOs) should take note' [24]. Rose Marcario adds to this by claiming that 'the answer is really not that difficult, or expensive … you have to value care-giving … Can businesses have the imagination to figure this out?' She actively challenges others to engage in similar practices: 'We support paid leave, you should too!'

Reparative financial management. There is also a set of new-world financial management practices at Patagonia. For instance, closing the financial year at Patagonia means donating 1 per cent of sales (not profit!) to protect and restore the natural environment. While most companies try to pay

as little tax as possible, Patagonia has actively assumed responsibility to pay this 'self-imposed tax' as stated on their website [2]. While most companies use Black Friday sales to boost their income, the practice of Black Friday sales at Patagonia has been used to donate 100 per cent of the proceeds to environmental charities [27]. They have even closed their stores at times in alignment with the Fridays for the Future protests, so that potential protesters (employees and customers) can be on the streets campaigning against climate inaction [5]. In addition, financial management and ownership practices played a vital role in Patagonia becoming one of the very first certified B Corps [2]. Rick Ridgeway explains such practices by observing that Patagonia is 'owned by people who aren't looking to get wealthy' [11]. Yvon Chouinard once stated that 'we don't want to grow larger, but want to remain lean and quick' [13].

Spreading good practices. Yvon Chouinard reiterates how Patagonia's mission reverberates in financial practices: 'We're in business to save our home planet. We aim to use … our investments … to do something about it' [28]. 'Since 1985, Patagonia has given over $100 million to their grantees, business ventures that address the transformation of business and management' [29]. Patagonia has started its own venture fund to multiply new-world business management practices complementary to their own. The website of this fund called Tin Shed Ventures explains how its investment practices are aimed at fixing bad practices:

> We started the fund because we felt existing models for start-up capital were broken. Traditional investors tend to focus on short-term growth and profit, then quickly flip the companies in which they invest. We take a completely different approach to investing. We place environmental and social returns on equal footing with financial returns and provide long-term, patient capital that helps to support forward-thinking entrepreneurs for the long haul … Tin Shed Ventures is funding the next generation of responsible business leaders who share these core values [29].

It might well be that Patagonia does not have to invest in business to inspire new practices. A recently founded organization called 'Screw Mars', inspired by Yvon Chouinard's words, sells t-shirts and bumper stickers spreading this very message: 'Screw Mars' and 'There's no rainbow trout on Mars' [30].

STUDY QUESTIONS

1. **Management as unusual?** What do management at Patagonia mean by 'radical' and 'revolution'? Do you agree that their management practices are radically different? Or is what they do just more of the same in a different packaging? Which

of the above-mentioned practices do you consider old-world management and which ones new-world management?

2. **Professional management competence.** What does it mean to be a professional manager at Patagonia? What competences do you need to engage in these practices? What kind of professional service and professional conduct would you engage in? Why?

3. **Zooming in.** Gather additional information to scrutinize one of Patagonia's management practices. Find out what elements (meaning, materials, and competences) the practice is made of. What is necessary to make it work? How does the practice connect with other practices inside and outside Patagonia?

4. **A critical eye.** Do you think 'they really mean it', or are these practices 'just a marketing stunt' carried out for very normal commercial reasons? How could you possibly reconcile the company's rapid growth in past years with talk of planned growth and demarketing? What light could 'smaller' observations like free global shipping of products shine on their intentions and the depth to which these practices are a lived business reality?

REFERENCES

1. Beer J. Patagonia founder Yvon Chouinard talks about the sustainability myth, the problem with Amazon – and why it's not too late to save the planet. www.fastcompany.com/90411397/exclusive-patagonia-founder-yvon-chouinard-talks-about-the-sustainability-myth-the-problem-with-amazon-and-why-its-not-too-late-to-save-the-planet Published 2019. Accessed January 1 2020.
2. 1% for the Planet. Yvon Chouinard. www.onepercentfortheplanet.org/yvon-chouinard Published 2019. Accessed January 6 2020.
3. Iddings S. Yvon Chouinard of Patagonia on controlled growth. https://community.intelligentfanatics.com/t/yvon-chouinard-of-patagonia-on-controlled-growth/266 Published 2017. Accessed January 7 2020.
4. Chouinard Y. *Some stories: Lessons from the edge of business and sport*. Ventura, CA: Patagonia, 2019.
5. Patagonia. The plain truth is that capitalism needs to evolve if humanity is going to survive. In: Chouinard Y, ed. *Some stories: Lessons from the edge of business and sport*. Ventura, CA: Patagonia, 2019.
6. Patagonia. Company history. www.patagonia.com/company-history.html Published 2019. Accessed January 6 2020.
7. Chouinard Y. Earth is now our only shareholder. https://eu.patagonia.com/gb/en/ownership Last accessed August 1 2023.
8. Stifler-Wolfe E. Patagonia founder Yvon Chouinard is in business to save the Earth – not Wall Street. www.esquire.com/style/mens-fashion/a27153682/patagonia-yvon-chouinard-sustainability-wall-street Published 2019. Accessed January 1 2020.
9. Armstrong Soule CA, Reich BJ. Less is more: Is a green demarketing strategy sustainable? *Journal of Marketing Management*. 2015, 31(13–14): 1403–1427.
10. Kotler P, Levy SJ. Demarketing, yes, demarketing. *Harvard Business Review*. 1971, 49: 74–80.
11. Schiller B. Patagonia asks its customers to buy less. www.fastcompany.com/1678676/patagonia-asks-its-customers-to-buy-less Published 2011. Accessed January 7 2020.
12. Allchin J. Case study: Patagonia's 'Don't buy this jacket' campaign. www.marketingweek.com/case-study-patagonias-dont-buy-this-jacket-campaign Published 2013. Accessed January 1 2020.
13. Chouinard Y, Gallagher N. Don't buy this shirt unless you need it. www.patagonia.com/us/patagonia.go?assetid=2388 Published 2004. Accessed March 16 2016.
14. Patagonia. Worn wear. https://wornwear.patagonia.com/?_ga=2.203954768.1332802338.1577484719–1722527096.1577484719 Published 2020. Accessed January 1 2020.

15. Patagonia. 20 years of organic cotton. www.patagonia.com/20-years-of-organic-cotton. html Published 2015. Accessed January 8 2020.
16. Patagonia. Organic cotton clothing. www.patagonia.com/shop/organic-cotton-clothing Published 2020. Accessed January 8 2020.
17. Patagonia. The footprint chronicles. www.patagonia.com/footprint.html Published 2019. Accessed January 8 2020.
18. Simpson C. Patagonia Provisions releases a documentary detailing the critical role food will play in solving the environmental crisis. www.patagoniaworks.com/press/2016/8/1/ patagonia-provisions-releases-a-documentary-detailing-the-critical-role-food-will-play-in-solving-the-environmental-crisis Published 2016. Accessed January 8 2020.
19. Patagonia. Patagonia enters food market. www.thebusinessofsurf.com/patagonia-enter-food-market Published 2017. Accessed January 8 2020.
20. Anderson J. This is what work-life balance looks like at a company with 100% retention of moms. https://qz.com/work/806516/the-secret-to-patagonias-success-keeping-moms-and-onsite-child-care-and-paid-parental-leave Published 2016. Accessed January 9 2020.
21. Chouinard Y. *Let my people go surfing: The education of a reluctant businessman – including 10 more years of business unusual.* New York: Penguin, 2016.
22. Patagonia. Culture/life. www.patagonia.com/culture.html Published 2020. Accessed January 9 2020.
23. Patagonia. Patagonia action works. www.patagonia.com/actionworks/about Published 2020. Accessed January 9 2020.
24. Carter D. Strong families build strong businesses. www.patagonia.com/blog/2016/03/ strong-families-build-strong-businesses Published 2016. Accessed January 7 2020.
25. Barney A. 16 companies with innovative parent-friendly policies. www.parents.com/ parenting/work/parent-friendly-companies Published 2015. Accessed January 9 2020.
26. Scagell J. Patagonia accommodates employee's breastfeeding schedule: 'Huge ROI'. www. scarymommy.com/breastfeeding-mom-patagonia Published 2019. Accessed January 9 2020.
27. Leighton M. 5 companies that buck the Black Friday trend: From donating 100% of their proceeds to shutting their websites down for the day. www.businessinsider.in/5-companies-that-buck-the-black-friday-trend-from-donating-100-of-their-proceeds-to-shutting-their-websites-down-for-the-day/articleshow/66700534.cms Published 2018. Accessed January 10 2020.
28. For the Planet. Building a better future together. www.onepercentfortheplanet.org Published 2020. Accessed January 10 2020.
29. Tin Shed Ventures. About history. www.tinshedventures.com Published 2020. Accessed January 10 2020.
30. Screw Mars. Screw Mars: Let's save the planet we have. https://screwmars.com Published 2020. Accessed January 10 2020.

II YASH PAKKA

NATURALLY INSPIRED, MANAGING TO CHANGE THE WORLD

DANIEL A. DIAZ

There were only problems. In 2012, after almost 40 years, the paper company Yash Pakka was on a survival track, essentially relying on the trust of its suppliers. The teams missed the previous boss, and the manager was going through an existential crisis trying to find his way in life. Not a big deal. It was the perfect storm from which you either come out with a great idea or empty hands. Ved Krishna, CEO at that time, says that in 2012:

> we had gone through a corporate debt restructuring, financially we were not doing well at all. We were trying to do a lot of things, but we went through this vicious cycle, a downward spiral where you know we were not getting the support we needed. We were losing a lot of people in our business who were unable to stay with us as we were not sustaining ourselves. I also had on the personal front, I had recently gone through a divorce. I had two children who I was trying to build a bond with. [1]

The solution came in the form of a slogan that became a mantra: 'You can produce a superior product that is both good for people and good for the Earth.' [2]. In his words, 'We didn't know whether the company will run the next day or not. I realised that all the work I wanted to do was towards the ecology and environment.' [3]

Who is Ved? Ved Krishna was born in Faizabad, northern India, to two adventurous, nature-loving parents who instilled in him a love of the outdoors. A significant change came when, at the age of 16, he spent time at a survival camp in the north of Scotland. He realised the importance of leaving people and the planet better than he found them and focused on making a positive contribution. Ved attended his high school at Welham Boys' School, Dehradun. He completed his bachelor's degree from London Metropolitan University in 1999. In 2012 Ved Krishna studied Business Administration and Management at the Indian School of Business. He returned to India to help his father, KK Jhunjhunwala, run Yash Pakka, a pulp and paper business.

Established in 1981 by entrepreneur KK Jhunjhunwala, Yash Pakka started by producing low grammage grades of paper [4]. KK's call to action was, 'When my father decided that he wanted to travel the world on his motorcycle and neither of his sons was interested, and he was not even able to sell the business and go on this journey, I decided to come back and get into it, and I felt maybe that had happened just by chance' [1].

https://restaurant.indianretailer.com

The year was 1999. Ved took control of the company. After years of building his role, , it was a matter of survival every year. 'I didn't know when the company would shut down,' [2] recounts Krishna. What helped was that 'The buyers, suppliers and team stood by me' [2]. During with this period of struggling, he started to reflect on his purpose in life, 'I always wanted to do something with nature' [2]. By then, he began to see his company as a vehicle for that purpose. Thus, 2010 was the year when these threads began to braid together. That year the company started the R&D that led to the development of CHUCK in 2014, a compostable tableware series of products and brands launched in 2017 [5]. That was just the beginning.

The starting point. Inspired by the motto of 'never think small', Ved's purpose became 'Leave the earth cleaner through nature-based packaging' [1]. In that stated purpose, the presence of packaging was not accidental because 'what I inherited was a pulp and paper company which was making packaging material; most of you actually do use our packaging material on a daily basis' [1]. The problem with that inheritance was that it clashed with the new purpose because

> most of the packaging that we were doing got plastic added to it, so if you look at soap wrappers, there's plastic on top and plastic in the bottom and a paper is mainly merely a carrier of that plastic which also means that when it's thrown away, it has the same consequences as any other plastic would. [1]

But the solution was very much at hand. Quite literally. According to the Encyclopedia Britannica, the word bagasse derives from the French bagage via the Spanish bagazo, which

> originally meant 'rubbish,' 'refuse,' or 'trash'. Applied first to the debris from the pressing of olives, palm nuts, and grapes, the word was subsequently used to mean residues from other processed plant materials such as sisal, sugarcane, and sugar beets. In modern use, the word is limited to the by-product of the sugarcane mill. [6]

And there was plenty of that in Ved's factories right there in Uttar Pradesh.

SOURCE: www.followingthefootprints.com/p/newsletter-3

India is the world's second-largest sugar producer [7], making more than 25 million metric tonnes only in 2020, which accounts for nearly 15 per cent of the world's total sugar production. For over 40 years, Ved Krishna's family turned sugarcane waste into paper in Yash Pakka [4]. Apart from producing paper, they burnt it to produce electricity. But then the elements aligned. Ved says that Bagasse 'has other uses, too. We were told this is a very good fibre for moulding' [3].

Used with kind permission of Yash Pakka

Inspiration. The primary source of inspiration was nature itself. 'Nothing packages as well as nature does. You just must open your eyes and look around you. As soon as you start looking, you find that there are so many things that nature offers in packaging.' [1] That inspiration involved observing how in nature it is easy to tell from the outside what is on the inside:

> You can never mistake an orange for a banana. That's the way it is shaped, that's the texture, that's the whole idea. It's in your mind as soon as you see a watermelon, you know what it is; as soon as you see a pea, you know what is inside. It so you know it is designed in a way where you know it shows what it is. [1]

Likewise, the unpacking process must be exceptional:

> Look at when you peel an orange you put that thumb in, and it's just sort of fun peels; you look at the eggs, you know you press it from the top and to the bottom nothing is going to happen to it; and you take a little … a little knife or fork can crack it on the side and there it opens out. [1]

Another central aspect is that in nature it is possible to see packaging for all types of contents: solids, liquids, and gases: 'You probably drink coconuts; it carries that liquid for so many months and years within it and nothing happens' [1].

And one essential aspect he notes is the source of energy. 'Nature uses only a single source of energy. It's only using sun. There is no high-powered coal going into producing packaging from nature; water usage is minimal, and it gives back what it is taking in' [1]. All these ideas are drawn from the general concept of biomimicry-based innovations. The Biomimicry Institute defines this as 'a practice that learns from and mimics the strategies found in nature to solve human design challenges' [8]. It explains that 'Biomimicry is about valuing nature for what we can learn, not what we can extract, harvest, or domesticate. In the process, we learn about ourselves, our purpose, and our connection to each other and our home on earth' [8].

Making the purpose moving forward. Ved and the company needed to challenge several well-established assumptions in the industry to make his purpose work. The change was not something new for the company since, in the past, Ved's father had already implemented innovative practices in the industry. During that process, 'decision-making became a democratic process, and the assigning of roles was based on skills. Teams strove to remain cross-functional and self-organised with other teams to create more efficient structures. For example, while all teams operated independently, teams like mechanical/maintenance decided to form a small operations team to oversee their practices [4]. In their time, all these innovations were revolutionary for the practices of industry within Indian society [4].

As well as this new wave of purpose-inspired changes led by Ved, there was a simple but very complex one:

> We were told that the market only accepts white. Especially in India we are used to wanting nice and clean things, and brown doesn't look clean. But we were again challenging and being close to our purpose of making more earth-friendly things. As soon as you want to make it white, you will add bleaching chemicals, which has two problems. One is you're adding more chemicals, and the second is that you're losing more fibre, so in the end, you are damaging yourself, you're not optimising the usage of fibre, so we said we are going to challenge that. Why not make it more natural-looking as well? [1]

They also started to realise that packaging doesn't need to be round in shape:

> We're going to give the power of usage to the customer; the customer can decide whether they want to use two-compartment or the three-compartment by fitting these two bowls into everything, but that also meant that geometry had to shift, it had to be a square or a rectangle instead of a circle [1].

Probably one of the most monumental challenges was to rethink what the company should look like to make this purpose a real thing in the long run: 'We're going to do that by making the pulp ourselves, designing and making the product ourselves, and then also trying to make a brand and marketing it ourselves, which again was going against the trade norms' [1].

Used with kind permission of Yash Pakka/CHUK

Ved argues that:

[the] whole motive is to find solutions which are compostable in nature and that get into food service sector. We want to serve a product with a certain ethos because it creates a different experience altogether. All our products are made up of sugarcane base. We mould them into shape keeping in mind that if any person throws it away then it should not harm nature but go back to the earth itself. People today are getting much more conscious about not only what they eat but how they eat and that is where we come in. We create joy by being friendly with the environment. [9]

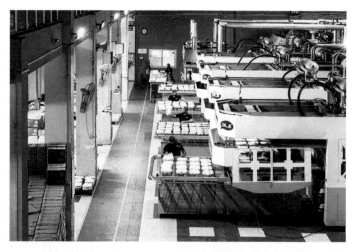

Used with kind permission of Yash Pakka

Ved's role. After taking control of the company, he says, 'I tried very hard to be like my father for 14 years' [2]. But the differences between the two became apparent. Ved's father 'had very little resources' [2], resulting in a mindset of maximisation at the minimum cost. On the other hand, Ved invested in the best machines and offered high salaries to attract and retain talent. He tried to end this tension by moving himself from CEO to Managing Director. But evidence proved that this was only the first step. He struggled to give up control to colleagues. 'I would leave, come back, leave and come back', [2] he says, alluding to his practice of interfering in the role of senior managers. 'At some point, you realise the world doesn't revolve around you' [2]. Ved left operations, focusing on innovations, collaboration, designs, strategy, new products, and new businesses. 'These are the things that I loved doing. My life was finally changing' [2]. He ended up in the position of Strategy Head, where he is described as an 'eternal optimist. Nothing seems to bring him down. He has been with the organisation for over 14 years, and he has grown the company over four times' [10].

https://businessagility.institute/learn/challenging-times/306

WHAT LIES AHEAD?

Ved says:

> the world is clearly progressing, and a lot of interesting developments are happening. We need renewable resources and regenerative solutions, and both are needed at scale … We need to realise that there is no such thing as 'recycling', there is only 'downcycling', and that reaches a stage when it cannot be in the system. Nature has a fundamental law that each material decomposes to contribute to life, and so must our materials. [11]

Ved sees that 'the greatest challenge is that of scale, along with performance and cost, and we need to find solutions with sustainable processes to overcome all three' [11].

He explains that Yash Pakka alone has little impact:

> We know we cannot make a big enough impact on our own; hence we are working for ways to bring the ecosystem together. We have been encouraging the creation of a solutions platform called the Global Compostables Alliance by investing in Pakka PTE. This will enable others interested in the sector to face much fewer challenges as it will provide transparency in supply chains, innovation, funding, and marketplaces. [11]

That is why in 2020 they started a collaboration with a Swedish company to develop a strong paper for food packaging that is 'water resistant, grease resistant, oil resistant, and it can take a lot of weight' [12] ,eliminating the need for plastic films to be added. They are also working with the American company Biomimicry 3.8, exploring ways to further their technological solutions [10].

It is in that same line that Ved sees the role of regulators:

> We must keep evolving materials, and the rest will evolve in response. We all function as parts of a singular whole. Our purpose is to do our best to build and disseminate more regenerative materials and then to encourage and collaborate with policymakers, composters, and the public to bring change. [11]

The future looks bright. On July 1 2022, a new opportunity opened up in the field:

The Government of India has taken resolute steps for mitigation of pollution caused by littered Single Use Plastics. The list of banned items includes earbuds with plastic sticks, plastic sticks for balloons, plastic flags, candy sticks, ice-cream sticks, polystyrene (Thermocol) for decoration, plastic plates, cups, glasses, cutlery such as forks, spoons, knives, straw, trays, wrapping or packing films around sweet boxes, invitation cards, cigarette packets, plastic, or PVC banners less than 100 microns, stirrers. [13]

Ravi Agarwal, director of environmental NGO Toxics Link, stressed that alternatives to SUPs were needed: 'Availability of cheap alternatives to cater the demand of these banned products are critical challenges which need to be looked into' [14].

"bottle recycling," by ella novak is licensed under CC BY 2.0.

At an international level, 'the world has come together to act against plastic pollution – a serious threat to our planet. International partnerships will be crucial in tackling a problem that affects all of us, and the progress made at UNEA reflects this spirit of collaboration', Jeanne d'Arc Mujawamariya, Rwanda's Minister of Environment [15] commented on the agreement reached by 175 countries participating in the United Nations Environment Assembly (UNEA-5.2) in Nairobi, Kenya in March 2022 to end plastic pollution and formulate an internationally binding treaty by 2024. This occurred in a context where 'across 34 countries, a global average of 70% of citizens support the creation of global rules for governments to end plastic pollution' [16].

At a personal level, Ved has not stopped developing skills. That is why in 2021, he completed part of a Master's degree in Biomimicry from Arizona State University in the United States of America. This programme seemed to fit perfectly with his pursuits, as it expects 'graduates from the program to transform the ways in which we conduct business, design buildings and products, run governments, provide healthcare, manufacture goods, grow food and educate future generations' [17].

STUDY QUESTIONS

1. **How environmentally friendly?** Yash Pakka recommends leaving its products for 90 to 180 days in a backyard composting bin that maintains moisture and good oxygen flow. But these products can still harm the environment if they end up in landfill, where they won't decompose as quickly. What could be done?

2. **What else can management learn from nature?** Yash Pakka's product innovation built on nature-based principles can be an inspiration for exploring what management can learn from nature more widely. What natural principles could you use to rethink what management practices and how?

3. **The role of purpose.** This story is very much about a manager finding their purpose and shaping their management practice accordingly. What purpose do you think you could find in your (current or future) management role?

4. **In getting ready for the role.** As described, Ved went through several formative experiences on both academic and personal levels. How do you see that these different experiences helped him to engage in his responsibilities running his father's company? How possible is it to train someone to become a manager who leads ethically, responsibly, and sustainably?

5. **On finding the right place.** In this case study , Ved tried leading the company from different roles, starting as CEO and finishing in his current position as Strategy Head. How do you think a leader can become aware of the need for their role to change as part of a broader company transformation?

6. **How bright is the future actually**? Use a PESTEL analysis or the five forces model to analyse Yash Pakka's competitive environment.

REFERENCES

1. Krishna V. Nature based packaging/Ved Krishna/TEDxPSITKanpur. www.youtube.com/watch?v=cxQc6Mz_c3U 2018. Last accessed August 1 2023.
2. Singh R. How letting go brought 40-year-old family Biz Yash Pakka back from the brink. *Forbes India*. Published online August 2022.
3. Insider Business. How plates made from sugarcane could help India's plastic problem. *Insider Business*. www.youtube.com/watch?v=HcqCWiGyDvw 2022. Last accessed August 1 2023.

4. Ruz C. Challenging times: Self-management through religious strife and hierarchy of caste. https://businessagility.institute/learn/challenging-times/306 2020. Accessed December 13 2022.
5. Chuck. CHUCK: About Us. https://chuk.in/about-us Published 2022. Accessed January 1 2023.
6. Encyclopaedia Britannica. Bagasse. In: *Encyclopaedia Britannica*. www.britannica.com/technology/bagasse Last accessed August 1 2023.
7. Walton J. The 5 countries that produce the most sugar. Investopedia. www.investopedia.com/articles/investing/101615/5-countries-produce-most-sugar.asp Published 2022. Accessed April 12 2022.
8. Biomimicry Institute. Biomimicry. https://biomimicry.org/what-is-biomimicry Published 2022. Accessed December 2 2022.
9. Sharma C. This supplier is promoting recyclable products for eating. Restaurant India. https://restaurant.indianretailer.com/article/This-Supplier-is-Promoting-Recyclable-Products-for-Eating.10097 Published 2017. Accessed December 25 2022.
10. Yash Pakka. Our Team. www.yashpakka.com/our-team Accessed December 11 2022.
11. In conversation with Ved Krishna, founder of Pakka Inc. https://rethinkingmaterials.com/qa-ved-krishna-founder-of-pakka-inc Published 2022. Last accessed August 1 2023.
12. Krishna V. Yash Pakka steps up with three kind of paper domains to serve food segment. www.youtube.com/watch?v=aQtx1v4ETJU&t=158s 2020. Accessed December 7 2022.
13. Government of India. Ban on identified single use plastic items from 1st July 2022. Press Information Bureau – Government of India. https://pib.gov.in/PressReleasePage.aspx?PRID=1837518 Published 2022. Accessed November 8 2022.
14. Krishnan M. Why is India's single-use plastic ban failing? *Deutsche Welle*. www.dw.com/en/why-is-indias-single-use-plastic-ban-failing/a-63625217 Published 2022. Accessed November 12 2022.
15. Pandey K. 175 countries commit to forge internationally binding treaty on plastic pollution by 2024. DownToEarth. www.downtoearth.org.in/news/pollution/175-countries-commit-to-forge-internationally-binding-treaty-on-plastic-pollution-by-2024-81776 Published 2022. Last accessed August 1 2023.
16. IPSOS. Global attitudes towards a plastic pollution treaty. www.ipsos.com/sites/default/files/ct/news/documents/2022-11/Ipsos%20global%20report%20-%20Attitudes%20towards%20SUP%20%2820221110%29%20GLOBAL%20VERSION.pdf2022. Published 2022. Last accessed August 1 2023.
17. Arizona State University. MS in Biomimicry. https://biomimicry.asu.edu/education/asu-online-masters-degree Accessed December 7 2022.

III FAIRPHONING MANAGEMENT

OLIVER LAASCH

Backstory. 'Change is in your hand' is printed on the back of the phone my colleague Stefan is using. 'What does this mean?' I ask him when he hangs up. After an excited ten-minute monologue on all the 'awesome practices' of the Amsterdam-based company Fairphone, I was hooked. Looking at Fairphone's website, I learnt that they claim 'from the Earth to your pocket, a smartphone's journey is filled with unfair practices. We believe a fairer electronics industry is possible' [1]. CEO Eva Gouwens describes the Fairphone as 'a proof of concept for a future that's kinder to humans and to the Earth. A statement that a better world is possible. That change is in your hands' [2]. Lofty claims, I thought, but anyone can criticize. It's much harder to actually do things differently. How do they practice 'Fairphoning management'? Are they actually achieving change? Let's take a closer look.

Anti-business activists. One of Fairphone's founders Bas van Abel explains that 'we didn't want to start a company. Actually, we wanted to do a campaign to start discourses and debates. It became much bigger than we had originally thought. Well the debate is: What does fairness mean?' [3]. Bas further shares his change strategy by saying that in order to achieve change you have to 'start with human beings. A big company is a system, not a human being. Companies are socio-paths that pretend to act human' [3]. Co-founder Tessa Wernink, however, illustrates the problem with this strategy: 'We started out as a campaign raising awareness about the use of conflict minerals in electronics. But it quickly became apparent that … there was no "fair" alternative on the market for people to buy' [4].

Fairphone for your business

The perfect match for your company's values

- Fair and recycled materials
- Fast, safe and reliable
- Modular, repairable design
- Removable long-life battery
- Committed to fairness

Joining the dark side? Fairphone's founding team decided to build an organization around their goal, first an NGO, then a social business. As Bas explains:

> Our goal was to understand the system and see if things could be done differently … That made Fairphone both a storytelling artefact (our campaign), but also a real product that could function as a catalyst to change the way products are made and eventually positively influence an economic system based mainly on profit maximization … Our goal has never been and never will be to maximize profits. [5]

After seed funding from a social impact investor, the cash flow necessary for kick-starting the first Fairphone version was obtained through crowdfunding. Five thousand future customers were needed to pre-pay a phone which had never been produced. Bas explains that the founders thought that 'crowdfunding the investment necessary to go into production fits … buyers not only buy the phone, but actually make Fairphone possible' [5]. Over 10,000 customers pre-paid 325 euro to pre-order what industry specialists called 'a mid-range Android device, with no specs that would catch the eye of a technophile' [6]. The Fairphone was born … well, at least financed. Within just two years the social activist group had become the social enterprise Fairphone [7], a transformation enterprise taking on giants like Apple and Samsung.

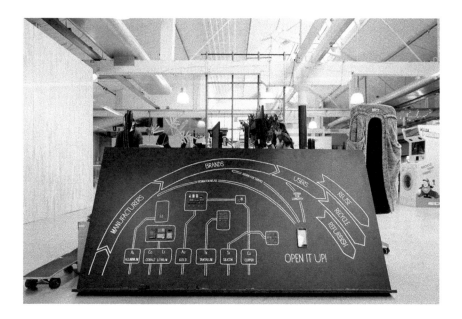

Changing the basis of competition? 'You're paying more for less. Performance is subpar across the board' was the defeating verdict of a leading mobile tech expert [8], a competitive death sentence for any 'normal' technology company competing on specs. However, Fairphone's strategists take 'a break from the standard smartphones available on the market with flashy features like glass designs and extensive camera capabilities … the focus is on creating phones that have reduced environmental impact, using conflict-free, recyclable and Fairtrade materials' [9]. They compete on making a 'phone that cares … caring is a radical act in a world that doesn't care' [10]. This includes a move into the corporate phones market by suggesting that 'with the Fairphone 3, employees can proudly showcase your company's values to the outside world' [11]. Usual strategizing practices would require preventing others from copying the luxurious competitive advantage from Fairphone's unique practices. However, Fairphone's CEO Eva Gowens, who was hired to scale Fairphone [12], wants competitors to emulate these practices:

We envision an economy where consideration for people and the planet is a natural part of doing business. This is why we are creating scalable and replicable models in our impact areas for the industry ... we need to transform the industry. The strongest signal that we can send is that there is a market. [9]

Another transformational move was to offer a 'phone as service', Fairphone 4 using a monthly subscription model. It came with maximum physical protection of the phone (screen protector and case), a repair and 48-hour replaced-if-broken guarantee, and a reduced monthly fee for every year without damage [13].

Creating products that last

We design for longevity, easy repair, and modular upgrades. Our goal is to make your phone's hardware last as long as possible, and to provide the support to keep its software up to date. The longer you can keep your phone, the smaller its environmental footprint.

Our approach to long-lasting design ›

Our impact with the Fairphone 2 ›

Extending your phone's lifespan ›

Reducing e-waste

We want to make the most of the materials used in consumer electronics. We're moving one step closer to a circular economy by encouraging the reuse and repair of our phones, researching electronics recycling options and reducing electronic waste worldwide.

Our programs and progress ›

Our takeback initiative ›

Rethinking plastic waste ›

Choosing fairer materials

We go straight to the source to make sure we're creating positive change. One material at a time, we're working to incorporate fairer, recycled, and responsibly mined materials in our phones – to increase industry and consumer awareness.

Our focus on fair materials explained ›

Responsible sourcing from conflict areas ›

Partnership for responsible gold sourcing ›

Putting people first

We're innovating ways to improve job satisfaction for workers in the industry. Together with our suppliers, we're listening to workers and creating better working conditions with employee representation, income and growth opportunities for all.

Learn about our initiatives ›

Our partnership with Arima ›

Paying living wages in the electronics supply chain ›

What's under the hood? From the outside this all sounds great, but what does 'Fairphoning management' actually look like in practice? Management at Fairphone orients its decisions and actions according to four main principles: creating products that last, reducing e-waste, choosing fairer materials, and putting people first [14]. These management principles apply differently across different stages of the Fairphone's life cycle. As brand manager Jan reminds us, 'Your phone isn't born in a store' [15]. What are the Fairphoning management practices 'from cradle to grave' [16]? Managerial practices that 'make' a truly fair phone, connect design practices with raw material procurement, suppliers' operations management, and customers' use and re-use of a phone, including what happens 'when your phone dies' and after.

Fairphone 2 Battery
€20.00

Fairphone 2 Bottom Module
€25.00

Fairphone 2 Camera Module
€45.00

Fairphone

Conceiving the Fairphone. James, industrial design lead manager, elaborates on the philosophy behind the Fairphone design:

> Our goal has always been to design a tough, well-made, repairable phone that lasts as long as possible. The prevailing industry trend is beautiful, sleek tech that is glued together and impossible to repair … so what happens if something breaks? Most of this tech is disposable. We design our Fairphone with modules, so if anything breaks, the module can be easily swapped, instead of replacing the whole phone. To make this easier our phone has guidance and instructions on the inside, directing the user to the part that needs to be replaced. [17]

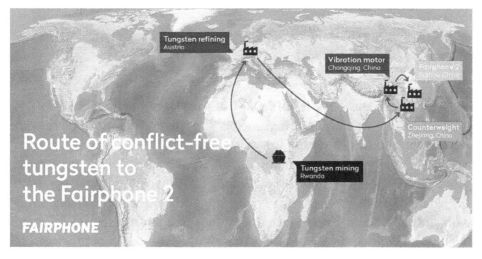

Fairphone

Replicating the modular DNA. Modular design is in Fairphone's DNA – even accessories follow the same principle – as stressed by Leon who works in commercial management: 'New earphones deserve an extra-special shout-out: just like our phones, they have a modular design. That means the cable and the earbuds can be replaced separately if anything happens' [18]. These features of the Fairphone and of the practices it's made of simultaneously address customers' 'right to repair' and the environmental impact from 'throw-away phones' [1, 8]. And customers are demanding it and challenging management to always go one step further, as illustrated by Leon's questioning of the headphones: 'Earbuds … it would make most sense if they were **offered individually** (left earbud vs. right earbud). I am probably succumbing to wishful thinking here though' [18]. Another user asks: 'What is the story behind the earphones exactly? … Where are they made? Is their production on par with the motivations and standards set?' 18].

In the cradle. The very starting point of Fairphone's journey was the criticism related to the mining of the metals and minerals that the phones are made from. The core criticism was that money spent on sourcing from conflict zones often ended up funding armed conflict. A timeline on the Fairphone website presents its main achievements in working towards 'responsible sourcing from conflict areas', particularly in central Africa, from which many crucial materials are procured [19]. Responsible sourcing management practices include, for instance, the certification of the origin of major metals and minerals' as being 'conflict free' or fair trade; on-site work with suppliers to uphold and raise responsible management standards; and strategic planning for continuous 'responsibilization' of supply [19]. However, achieving responsible sourcing practices is a complex and sticky managerial challenge. For instance, impact innovation manager Monique stresses that

> We are well aware that human rights abuses routinely occur in the ASM [artisanal and small-scale mining] sector, especially in the DRC [Democratic Republic of Congo] and neighboring countries. Up to 20 per cent of the cobalt mining in the DRC falls under the category of ASM, which is extremely informal, non-industrialized and often lacking even the most basic health and safety measures. Because of the current mining, trading and smelting processes in materials supply chains, at the moment, it's impossible for companies to ensure that irresponsibly sourced materials don't end up in their products. The first step to remedying these issues is for everyone in our industry to acknowledge that this is actually happening … We need to admit that this cobalt may be integrated into our supply chains, whether we like it or not. [20]

In addition, Fairphone founder Bas is open about the moving-target-like nature of fair management practices: 'If you think that a Fairphone is 100 per cent fair, then you have to ask yourself, what is actually fair? Is this actually possible? … Yes, there is child labour in the mines and we cannot change that from one day to another' [3].

Challenges downstream. Bas explains that 'if you have customers and materials, then you go to China where smartphones are manufactured. That's straightforward. What is not so easy is to improve or change supply chains' [3]. A particular focus of improvement efforts are the conditions in phone assembly factories, which have been making headlines, for instance, in the form of repeated worker suicides at Apple's main manufacturer Foxconn [21]. Fairphone is working with the assembly partner Arima in the Chinese city of Suzhou where, as Bas tells us, Fairphone were now able to introduce 'practices to facilitate employee voice'. This might be perceived as a baby step from a Western perspective. However, this is a significant, almost revolutionary move in the Chinese context, especially if you consider the small size and bargaining power of the industry newcomer Fairphone. 'At Foxconn, they would probably have laughed at us and kicked us out', speculates Bas [3].

Spotting the win–wins. The smaller supplier Arima, however, did have an incentive to accept Fairphone's order of '25.000 phones ... not a particularly high number. Until then the company [Arima] had not delivered into the European market. Therefore, our manufacturer [Arima] gained a strategic benefit by bringing their products to Europe. It's about win–win situations' [3]. Remco, working in value chain management, introduces some of 'the makers' at Arima in the context of another move towards more responsible sourcing practices:

> We're proud to announce that as of November this year, Xu Shang, Li Su, and other workers at Arima's factory **receive a living wage bonus.** This quarterly bonus will help improve their quality of life and employee satisfaction, and in the long term, it will help reduce the need to work overtime. As advised by the workers themselves, this bonus will be shared with all of this factory's employees, not just those on the Fairphone 3 production line.

It's a small but significant step towards bridging the living wage gap, and is paid directly by Fairphone 3 owners as part of the cost of the phone – €1.50 to be exact. [22].

www.weforum.org/agenda/2019/08/india-due-to-ban-multiple-single-use-plastics

When phones die and are reborn. E-waste is a major global issue: hard to recycle, potentially harmful if disposed of incorrectly, and full of non-renewable materials. So ideally, any phone, once it has been disposed of, would be recycled in its entirety. And, ideally, any new Fairphone would be made of such recycled materials. Miquel, one of the co-founders and circular innovation lead manager provides some insight into Fairphone's related managerial practices and challenges:

While the demand for recycled materials grows, the amount of such materials available will not be enough to meet the increasing demands … We must therefore acknowledge that the mining of raw materials will still play a very important role … We have to keep improving conditions in mining in order to bring focus to the topic in our industry's agenda, in tandem with examining how to increase the share of recycled material supplies … seeking more transparency around bottlenecks in the recycling industry … At Fairphone we work with the industry (and with you, as our community) to increase both 'fair' demand and 'fair' supply; both need to come hand in hand … more recycled materials in your products could, in the long run, lead to an increase in the use of recycled materials. But this alone isn't enough; we also need to ensure that an increase in supply comes from fair and sustainable sources. [23].

Fairphone-created plastic waste is one of the areas in search of creative managerial solutions. Jan from brand management discusses a pilot run by Fairphone aimed at making practical use of the Fairphone shell:

Plastic waste as raw material for their 3D printing techniques to create furniture for our office, giving our old cases a new life … and function. We're excited … closing the loop and using the upcycled furniture in our office … 3700 plastic slim cases gathered for recycling, to 73kg worth of raw materials, to some great upcycled conversation starters for our office and events. [24]

Blurring boundaries between managers and users. Bas gives us insight into his theory of change by suggesting that 'you have to start with human beings … as consumers you can influence what companies do. Therefore, we address consumers directly' [3]. However, management at Fairphone treats users not as mere customers, but rather as 'the key superpower in our amazing community of supporters and advocates. We want to shine a light on the local Fairphone pioneers, change-makers and innovators that are shaping the future of the industry with us' [25]. Fairphone users have become an actual part of Fairphone's operations, for instance, through the Fairphone Angels programme. Fairphone Angels are local volunteers who provide hands-on advice, and often even engage in repair practices for other Fairphone users [26]. Another common community activity is 'urban mining', where Fairphone users use guidance provided by Fairphone to take apart and 'mine' precious materials from old phones [27]. These materials may again become part of new Fairphones – for instance, the 50 per cent of recycled Tungsten that the vibration motor is made from. Such engaged user practices blur the boundaries between business management and user practices, and allow us to recycle the message that led us into this case study: 'Change is in *your* hands!'.

STUDY QUESTIONS

1. **Fairphoning practices.** List the unique practices that make Fairphoning. List the practitioners involved in them. Reflect on how different practices connect, and how practitioners co-enact the practices.

2. **Professional management instruments.** How do you see management at Fairphone apply typical ethics, responsibility, and sustainability management tools?

3. **Stakeholder assessment.** Prepare a stakeholder assessment and an initial list of Fairphoning stakeholder management practices. If you were a manager at Fairphone, what else would you do?

4. **Changing and innovating.** What types of innovations does Fairphone engage in and how do these innovations relate to their larger strategy of change?

5. **Entrepreneurial practices.** What stage of an entrepreneurial business venture is Fairphone currently at? What typical entrepreneuring practices and processes can you identify? How did Fairphoning management practices change at different stages? Do you think they are able to scale-up their venture, and if so, how?

6. **Are they actually 'better'?** Do you think Fairphone is a competitive company? How (not) and why (not)? What are main strategizing practices and how do these relate to the (non-) achievement of their strategic goals?

7. **Integrated marketing-communication.** For whom do you think Fairphoning creates value and how? How would you describe the relationship between Fairphoning management and Fairphoning customers? How would you describe their marketing management and managerial communicating practices?

8. **ERS management upstream and downstream.** How does management at Fairphone manage ethics, responsibility, and sustainability in different sections of their supply and demand chain?

9. **Glocalized Fairphoning.** What glocalizing practices does Fairphone engage in, how, and where? What glocal strengths, weaknesses, threats and opportunities can you identify and how would you manage in order to address them?

10. **Is it *really* that good?** Do you buy it? Is this a perfect company? What issues, controversies or criticism of Fairphoning management might you raise?

REFERENCES

1. Fairphone. Our mission. www.fairphone.com/en/story Published 2020. Accessed February 4 2020.
2. Gouwens E. Launching Fairphone 3: Dare to care. www.fairphone.com/en/2019/08/27/launching-fairphone-3 Published 2019. Accessed February 27 2020.
3. Kim J-H. 'Das Problem ist das Wachstum.' Fairphone-Macher Bas van Abel im Interview. http://dasfilter.com/gesellschaft/das-problem-ist-das-wachstum-fairphone-macher-bas-van-abel-im-interview Published 2014. Accessed February 27 2020.
4. Georgi W. Fairphone: Calling for change. www.homerun.co/interviews/fairphone Published 2020. Accessed February 27 2020.
5. Joe. Fairphone's crowdfunded model and social impact. www.fairphone.com/en/2013/05/24/crowdfunded-model Published 2013. Accessed March 1 2020.
6. Best J. The gadget with a conscience: How Fairphone crowdfunded its way to an industry-changing smartphone. www.techrepublic.com/article/the-gadget-with-a-conscience-how-fairphone-crowdfunded-its-way-to-an-industry-changing-smartphone Published 2014. Accessed February 4 2020.
7. Akemu O, Whiteman G, Kennedy S. Social enterprise emergence from social movement activism: The Fairphone case. *Journal of Management Studies.* 2016, 53(5): 846–877.
8. Martin A. Fairphone 3 review: The only way is ethics? www.expertreviews.co.uk/mobile-phones/1411365/fairphone-3-review Published 2020. Accessed February 4 2020.
9. Heathman A. Is the Fairphone 3 the most sustainable smartphone on the market? www.standard.co.uk/tech/fairphone-3-phone-specs-features-uk-price-and-release-date-a4221756.html Published 2019. Accessed February 4 2020.
10. Fairphone. The phone that cares for people and planet. www.fairphone.com/en Published 2020. Accessed February 4 2020.
11. Fairphone. Fairphone for your business: The perfect match for your company's values. www.fairphone.com/en/business/?ref=footer Published 2020. Accessed February 27 2020.
12. van Abel B. From founder leadership to growth leadership. www.fairphone.com/en/2018/10/17/from-founder-leadership-to-growth-leadership Published 2018. Accessed February 27 2020.
13. Fairphone. Fairphone Easy: The sustainable smartphone subscription. https://shop.fairphone.com/en/fairphone-easy Last accessed August 1 2023.
14. Fairphone. Our impact: Changing the electronics industry from the inside. www.fairphone.com/en/impact/?ref=header Published 2020. Accessed February 27 2020.
15. Jan. Your phone isn't born in a store: Meet the makers. www.fairphone.com/en/2019/12/09/your-phone-isnt-born-in-a-store-meet-the-makers Published 2019. Accessed February 27 2020.
16. McDonough W, Braungart M. *Cradle to cradle: Remaking the way we make things.* New York: North Point Press, 2002.
17. James. Going against the grain to design a sustainable phone. www.fairphone.com/en/2020/01/17/going-against-the-grain-to-design-a-sustainable-phone Published 2020. Accessed February 27 2020.
18. Leon. Show your Fairphone some love with brand new accessories. www.fairphone.com/en/2020/01/30/brand-new-accessories Published 2020. Accessed February 27 2020.

19. Fairphone. Responsible sourcing from conflict areas. www.fairphone.com/en/project/responsible-sourcing Published 2020. Accessed March 3 2020.

20. Monique. Cobalt mining: It's time to face the facts and invest in making improvements. www.fairphone.com/en/2019/12/20/cobalt-mining-its-time-to-face-the-facts-and-invest-in-making-improvements Published 2019. Accessed February 27 2020.

21. Merchant B. Life and death in Apple's forbidden city. www.theguardian.com/technology/2017/jun/18/foxconn-life-death-forbidden-city-longhua-suicide-apple-iphone-brian-merchant-one-device-extract Published 2017. Accessed January 26 2020.

22. Remco. Meet the makers: The people behind your Fairphone. www.fairphone.com/en/2019/12/30/meet-the-makers-the-people-behind-your-fairphone Published 2019. Accessed February 27 2020.

23. Miquel. Digging into the recycled material chains. www.fairphone.com/en/2018/04/26/digging-into-the-recycled-material-chains Published 2018. Accessed February 27 2020.

24. Jan. Rethinking plastic waste. www.fairphone.com/en/2019/07/19/rethinking-plastic-waste Published 2019. Accessed February 27 2020.

25. Fairphone. Welcome to the Fairphone community. www.fairphone.com/en/community/?ref=header Published 2020. Accessed February 27 2020.

26. Stefan. The Fairphone Angels Program (Local support by community members). https://forum.fairphone.com/t/the-fairphone-angels-program-local-support-by-community-members/33058 Published 2017. Accessed February 27 2020.

27. Fairphone. *Urban mining manual: Leader's guide*. Amsterdam, 2014.

IV MANAGING ACCORDING TO THE SAGES AT GOOD-ARK

PINGPING FU AND QING QU

This case study has been written based on original interviews conducted by the authors.

How does this make any sense? 'How can people run a business without talking about business?' was one of the critical questions that MBA students at the Chinese University of Hong Kong asked when listening to an introduction about Mr Wu, Chairman and founder of Good-Ark Electronics Ltd before visiting his company in Suzhou, China. They did not think that the management of a for-profit commercial company could follow a mission 'to bring the culture of the sages to the world to benefit mankind'.

The inscription on this boulder at the Good-Ark headquarters says, 'Yong Bu Cai Yuan' – never to lay off employees.

The practice. Good-Ark started as a small diodes factory in 1992 with 68 people in Suzhou. With over 1600 employees, the company is now China's largest and the world's third largest diodes manufacturer.

The new mission was set in 2009. Mr Wu believed the first step was to show the effect of learning from Chinese sages – most prominently Confucius – by transforming themselves into a happy enterprise, led by inspiration from the sages' wisdom. He introduced eight training modules based on Chinese sages' principles, which also form core areas of action across the company. Since 2009, the modules have been systematically implemented, first through activities organized by a special department. Later, in 2015, shop floor workers took charge of the activities under different modules. The change made the 1600+ workers more passionately engaged in the different activities, even throughout the Covid pandemic. To be consistent with these modules and their intended learning, the company publicly pledged in June 2021 never to lay off employees and eliminated over 93 per cent of its night shifts to increase workers' morale. The company's stock performance has remained strong and stable.

Module 1. Humanistic care. Mr Wu, who is now the permanent educational officer, thinks genuine care is the most fundamental act an employer should engage in, because only through this can a company win trust from employees. For many employees who come from remote areas in China to work in the cities, the income they earned was very limited. This meant that leaving children with grandparents was often a financial necessity. To enable these employees to see their children more often, Good-Ark has since allowed two additional six- to eight-day paid vacations annually and employees can choose their own time to take national holidays. Pregnant employees have a table with cushioned seats in the dining room and are offered specially cooked meals. Employees also have flexible work times. The company offers a

monthly stipend of 200RMB Yuan to each child left behind, and parents who are 80 or older. Mr. Wang, a middle manager in the factory, said he used to yell at and be rude to team members, but now explains and persuades, and gets to know employees' families, including understanding the physical conditions of their parents. 'You put yourself into others' shoes. When others care about you, you work harder,' he said.

Module 2. Humanistic education. Mr Wu believes that 'employees have to be educated if they are to understand why they need to behave in certain ways and for what purposes they should work and live'. Therefore, 'Societal organizations, companies, schools, hospitals, shopping malls, even government agencies, should all be offering moral education to enhance employees' outlook on life; only when they do that can they enable employees to make sense of things,' he said. Liu, who joined Good-Ark in 2010 as a technician, said he was particularly thankful because of the many different classics he has learned, including Confucius' Analects, *Di Zi Gui* (Guiding Principles for Behaviours), *Qun Shu Zhi Yao* (Collections of Guiding Principles) and *Liao Fan Si Xun* (Four Pieces of Advice from Liao Fan to His Son). He said employees in Good-Ark learn every day:

> After lunch from 12:30 to 1, we learn and share our own thoughts within our own section every day; we are paid to learn together with other people for a whole day every other week. Every year, we take turns to join the week-long (5.5 days and evenings) learning programme (also paid) to learn different classics and to identify what can be improved.

Module 3. Green environment. Mr. Wu believes everything on Earth is inter-connected. Human beings can only live well if they take care of the environment well. As an effort to promote a green environment, Good-Ark tries every possible way to minimize waste. People use their own cups and hand-kerchiefs instead of paper cups or napkins provided by the company. Visitors are offered handkerchiefs upon arrival. In the dining room, all food is eaten to reduce foodwaste. In the bathroom, water from hand washing is collected into bowls placed in the sinks and poured into big buckets underneath, which is then used to flush the toilets or water the plants and crops in the farm. The company occupies 8.3 hectares in a science park, of which a little less than half is used for the factory, including a farm of 4,200 sqm that the workers can use to grow vegetables and fruits in their spare time. The other 4.4 hectares is still a wetland, home to many animals. Song, a worker who joined in 2013, said she felt strange at first to find so many things that other companies did not offer. 'For example,' she said, 'the company uses videos, lectures, and post-ers to educate us about the benefits of eating vegetables, reducing pollution and increase health, and we are all happy to switch to eating vegetables only at work and eat less meat at home.'

Module 4. Health promotion. Driven by the desire to care, Good-Ark maintains a health record for each employee and puts up posters in the hall-ways and dining room about the benefits of a healthy diet and the dangers

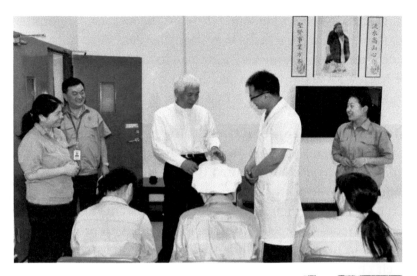

of smoking to raise awareness of these issues. The company has got rid of the smoking room because most smokers have quit. The few who still do only smoke when at home. Many have chosen to reduce or quit eating meat. However, the company chefs do such a good job that visitors who get the free meals on the Company Open Day frequently say they would be very happy not to eat meat if they could make vegetarian meals as delicious as these. The company also offers dozens of different programmes teaching employees how to maintain good health, including First Aid, CPR (cardiopulmonary resuscitation)and use of an AED (automated external defibrillator). There is an on-site Chinese medicine practitioner, offering free medical help to employees, including massage and acupuncture. He refers them to regular hospitals when needed, for which employees are very happy because most hospital trips can be avoided as a result. 'We are very fortunate to have such convenient services and we learn a lot about how to stay healthy,' Ms Wu, an HR staff member who joined the company in 2009, told us.

Module 5. Philanthropic actions. Offering philanthropic services is a big part of what Good-Ark does for society. In addition to donations to areas hit by natural disasters, it sponsored the establishment of three public primary schools in Yunnan, a remote province in Southern China, for children left to the care of their grandparents while parents relocated to work in urban areas. Good-Ark works with local volunteers to provide educational programmes to help mothers understand the importance of spending time with their children and, at the same time, tries to create opportunities for them, such as garment factory work and treating soil to grow special crops, to ensure that mothers or parents who have returned to their home villages can continue earning an income. They have also set up an art school for kids. Ms Chen, a mother of two, said she was among the first to return because her daughter refused to call her after she had been away for a few years. 'Life is now so different. I am very thankful to *Wu Da Jia Zhang* for all he has done for us.'

Module 6. Voluntary services. Good-Ark believes that receiving care softens the heart and offering care enables people to appreciate what they have and encourages them to become more caring and loving themselves. The company is very particular about having the right attitude. It tries very hard to encourage its employees to be thankful for having the opportunity to serve, rather than giving to employees as a means of offering help. Every employee has to go through a training programme and get certified before they join any voluntary services. Now over 90 per cent of them have been certified and frequently participate in various activities, including helping elderly people in retirement homes, children in rehabilitation centres, children with conditions such as Down's syndrome and autism, and cleaning public parks and neighborhoods. Liu, one of the volunteers, told us, 'Before "having a loving heart" was only mentioned verbally, you would not feel anything; but now through those services, you can see what you have done and you can also feel the effects after you do them.'

Module 7. Publicizing humanistic activities. Mr Wu believes that education should be delivered in three ways: *verbal* (including reading texts, watching recorded lectures, and listening to and discussing talks), *role* models (leaders setting examples for followers), and *physical* (through posters featuring quotes from sages or famous people, and photos of various activities). Different sections take turns to replace the posters regularly, the content being different each time. Sometimes, individual workers offer their personal post-learning thoughts, or stories from the classics they've read. Other times, the content delivered relates to changes in the workplace, improvements or innovations by different groups. Walking by these posters, one could learn something new inadvertently. Liang, who chose to accept the job offer from Good-Ark over another from a Japanese firm offering higher pay, better benefits package and better working conditions, said, 'I chose to work for Good-Ark because I like the company culture. I enjoy being reminded about the correct way to live by those posters. You feel inspired and encouraged. When you pass them to other people, you can also influence others.'

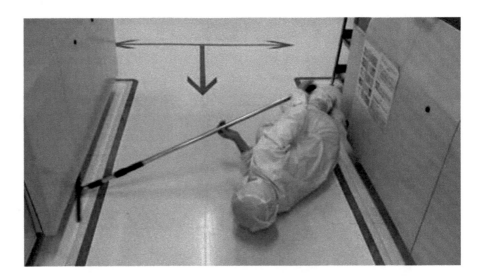

Module 8. Dun Lun Jin Fen (敦伦尽分). The four Chinese characters mean to do one's best to play well every role one plays, including being a good child, sibling, or parent at home, a dedicated employee or a responsible manager at work, and a good citizen in the community. The word *lun* refers to morals in the five cardinal relationships (leader–follower, father–son, husband–wife, siblings, and friends). Of the five, three occur within the family, which is why Mr. Wu urges all employees to be filial and pious, and play the family roles well. He also regards the company as a big family and plays the role of 'big family head', encouraging all employees to treat each other as brothers and

sisters. He believes love is the most important key for solving all problems in the world, and family is the source that generates and nourishes love. Employees in Good-Ark not only enjoy working together, they also love the equipment they use, the chairs they sit on, and everything around them. Visitors who saw the photo showing workers lying on the floor to clean the bottom of the machines asked Mr Wu how Good-Ark managed to get such dedication from the workers. Mr Wu said 'genuine love'. 'If you show them genuine love, they pass on the love to everything they do'.

Mr Wu talking in UNESCO in 2017.

Global influence. Since 2011, Good-Ark has been attracting visitors from all over China and the world. Harvard Business School has written a case on the company. Mr Wu has also been invited by many Chinese and international organizations to share his experiences. UNESCO, for example, has invited him back almost every year. He has also met with the Pope three times and been invited to the World Religious Conference a few times. Many foreign guests have also visited and all expressed admiration for the company. When sharing their thoughts after the visit, Mr George Kell, founder of UN Global Compact, said he was deeply touched by what he saw. 'I've never seen something like this before. This is very precious, very important, especially in today's world, where in many parts of the world, capitalism is in crisis,' he said. Dr Nasaruddin Umar, Deputy Minister of Indonesian Religious Affairs, said what he saw in Good-Ark brought tears to his eyes and changed his biases towards China. Former prime minister of Japan, Mr Yukio Hatoyama, said the experience made him realize 'only with humanity, could science help us achieve what we want'.

Connecting the Eight Modules with the UNSDG. In 2019, Good-Ark received the award for best practice of the United Nations Sustainable Development Goals (UNSDGs). While attending the UNSDG meeting, Mr Wu proposed that moral education, rather than knowledge or science and technology, be the key to sustainable development. He pointed out that the 17 SDGs lack a core, and although the goals include other content, the focus is on economy, which only worsens the world's problems. To him, moral education is that of genuine love, which involves role models, verbal as well as physical (visual) education, and is different from general education on knowledge. Mr. Wu discovered that Good-Ark's eight modules echo the 17 SDGs. If we place humanistic education at the centre, the connections between the other seven modules and the 17 SDGs become apparent. For instance, Good Ark's philanthropic actions connect with SDG 1 No Poverty and SDG 2 Zero Hunger. Humanistic care and *Dun Lun Jin Fen* corresponds to SDG 8 Decent Work and Economic Growth.

STUDY QUESTIONS

1. **The modules.** Do you think the eight modules connect with each other? If yes, how? How do you think management in other organizations could benefit from implementing these or similar modules?

2. **Management as (un)usual?** How are Good-Ark practices different from management in other companies? To what degree do you think Mr. Wu's practices can be transferred to other organizations, maybe, in other sectors, industries, or countries?

3. **A critical eye.** What challenges can you foresee Good-Ark encountering going forward? Do you think Good-Ark's practices are feasible and sustainable in the long run? If you were asked to revise and improve these practices, what would you propose?

4. **Connecting with other practices.** How do you think other practices in the organization and outside Good-Ark are connected to the eight modules? For instance, how do the 'sage practices' influence people management, or operations management? How do they translate to their suppliers, customers, communities, or employee families' practices?

5. **Take home messages.** What are your take-home messages from the case? Is there anything that you could do differently in your personal or professional life based on these? How would you describe this case in a sentence? How in three words?

V MANAGING BY THE GRAM AT ALGRAMO

DANIEL A. DIAZ

Discovering the poverty premium. In 2012, José Manuel Moller was studying Business Administration at the Catholic University of Chile. He was looking for a place to live with three of his friends in Santiago, the capital city of Chile. Santiago is the largest city in Chile and has over six million residents [1]. Many residents live on less than $4 a day, the continent's average wage [2]. Being socially motivated, the four students engaged in their university's volunteer programme. They chose to live in the commune of La Granja, home to more than 132,000 people in the southern part of the capital. José Manuel tells us what happened next: 'While we worked and studied, we started to have problems. Problems that we wouldn't have seen if we weren't living there … I called these problems "the punishment of poverty" … when we buy in small package size we pay a lot more than if we had bought the larger format' [3]. Even though there were four people living in the same household, their joint

income was so low that they were forced to buy what they needed in smaller quantities. These purchases were made in an 'almacén', as local grocery stores are known in Chile: 'Affordable food is hard to come by in the outskirts of Santiago de Chile. There are few supermarkets and the produce at small stores can often be up to 40 per cent more expensive than in larger outlets' [4].

Deconstructing unhealthy business school teachings. In a TEDx talk José explained:

> This is what is being taught in business schools in Chile: maximization of profit. Look for an optimum that through a mathematical formula says what the manager should do. This formula has been the cause of many of the problems that we face today. Chile is among the more unequal countries; Latin America is the most unequal continent in the world. And all because of formulas like this one. What we say is that we cannot look only at this formula but have to see the people behind it, and manage to incorporate other variables that are not usually taken into consideration. It is because of this that we got a country that actually grows, but just for the few … We were told that when companies are doing well, that trickles down. There hasn't been such a thing in 20 years. In those 20 years inequality just grew [3].

This inequality is the reason why many people do not have a stable monthly salary. Salvador Achondo, Algramo's Development Manager explains:

> We have a monthly salary with which we can access the supermarket once a month and plan our purchases to be able to buy in large formats. What happens to thousands of families in Chile is that they cannot have a budget and do not plan. They are forced to buy in packages of small size, to buy in neighbourhood stores and to pay up to 40 per cent more for these products. [5]

The idea. José Manuel explains: 'We at Algramo buy essential products such as rice, beans, lentils and sugar in bulk from suppliers and distribute them directly to local grocery stores, through our unique mechanical dispensers. This results in a considerably cheaper product for consumers' [4]. They install machines that fill reusable containers with basic products such as rice, lentils, chickpeas, and beans. Located in about 1200 local grocery stores in popular neighborhoods in Santiago de Chile, each vending machine is installed free of charge and the profits are shared equally between the company and the storekeeper. Through this practice they aim to reduce what the founder calls the 'poverty tax': 'whoever cannot buy in bulk, today buys in small packages and pays about 40 per cent or 50 per cent more'. The practice also helps the local grocery stores: 'Why in the almacén? It is there, where neighbours meet to buy their bread. Their owners are entrepreneurs who can't compete with supermarkets, and they are neighbours themselves, who have the same problems' [3]. A particular advantage of Algramo's approach is that it also reduces single-use plastics. Brian Bauer, who is in charge of circular economy at Algramo explains:

> When you buy in small packages, you also produce a lot of packaging waste. That's typically the type of packaging waste that's most likely to end up in the environment because it's smaller, and it's also in low-income areas where waste management systems in place are not very good. So, there's a lot of that packaging that ends up in the environment, ultimately, in oceans or other places it shouldn't be. [6]

The organization around the practice. With funding from his university's student union, José Manuel was able to develop prototypes of a device that both took payment and dispensed goods. He then won two entrepreneurship competitions and used the prize money to develop the first detergent dispensing machine in a joint venture with an industrial designer who went on to become the second partner of the company. They went on to name their company 'Algramo', a name which means quite literally 'by the gram' [7]. By the end of 2013 they had detergent dispensing machines in 20 *almacenes* and were developing prototypes for another four products with funding from several other entrepreneurship competitions [8, 9].

Striking an environmental chord. Hernán Albornoz, owner of 'Almacén Nelson' explains how he bought into the project's goals: 'Some time ago the owner of Algramo came here, he was doing a survey of whether we had confidence in a project that they presented to us. It was about eliminating polyethylene and I found it fantastic because I had just seen reports of pollution in the seas' [1]. This environmental awareness is shared by his customers. Constanza Dorr, customer of Algramo says: 'We had a big problem a few years ago with the Santa Marta landfill, and to think that I contributed week by week by throwing plastics into that landfill, and that it is going to take a century until it degrades, is something that worries me a lot' [1].

Making more out of less. The logic of Algramo's general approach is to reduce processes and intermediaries between the product and the consumer. The benefits of this supply chain model are explained by Hernán Albornoz: 'Costs are reduced because thanks to Algramo I buy directly from the producer. They don't pack it for me. We skip that step that makes the product more expensive. Then people, apart from not polluting, get a much cheaper product' [1]. The installation of the machines is free, and the profits generated are divided equally between the storekeeper and Algramo. The products Algramo dispenses are non-perishable items of common consumption in Chile like lentils and rice. This reduces the risk of stock expiration when there is a reduction in demand or when large purchases are made from suppliers [10]. They made efforts to align their technology with the purpose [11]. The engineering of the machines means that they can be adapted to different products, responding to the needs of each particular almacén. Also, the packaging that customers buy is designed to be durable, without the need for frequent replacement.

Looking after the organizational purpose. One of the concerns José Manuel had was to be able to establish an organizational structure that would safeguard the social purpose that had motivated Algramo's creation and was fostering its development. This is why they were incorporated as a B Corporation: 'Algramo is a company that does not seek to maximize shareholder profits, but rather aims to solve social and environmental problems in a sustainable manner' [12]. As José Manuel explains:

> Algramo is a triple-impact project. Economic, because it generates an attractive margin for both us and the storekeeper. Social, because it reduces prices

by around 40 per cent and also helps the stores to compete with the large supermarket chains. And sustainable, because it reduces the carbon footprint by reusing packaging. This is why Algramo has a sustainable model in economic terms, because by obtaining a margin by sales, we can put those sales to work for the growth of the project and be able to reach many more places. [13]

Widening the portfolio. Management at Algramo saw that their achievements went hand in hand with what was happening in the local grocery store and not only in their machine. They needed to detect opportunities that would strengthen the relationship between storekeepers, their customers, and the company [14]. In 2015 they created a sister company called ALCOM, which used the wired internet service that connects the dispensing devices with Algramo's head office to offer high-speed wireless internet through a prepaid subscription [15]. In 2016 they launched a third company, ALTECH, the purpose of which was to identify, incubate and introduce new technologies that could enhance the relationship between Algramo and its primary stakeholders – the shop owners and their customers [12]. As a consequence, Algramo is now a group of companies – the Algramo Group. Juan José explains that: 'we want to be an attractive company, a company that is profitable, but not at the expense of people. That's the case with many companies that are just maximizing profits. Today people are demanding from companies to be different' [1]. By 2020 1200 local grocery stores belonged to Algramo's network, reaching 220,000 people [12].

The packaging challenge. The next challenge is to increase the reuse rate of the containers customers use to receive their dispensed goods. This had been a challenge since the firm's inception. José Manuel explains:

> Many people said that people who have little money are given a smaller package size, but no one realized that we are giving them a much more expensive package. The first four years were not easy. In the beginning few people came back with the packaging, only 5–6 per cent. I was super transparent when I said that if they don't bring the package none of this makes sense. Today we are around 80 per cent return of packaging … plastic that would otherwise end up in the landfill. [1]

Management at Algramo frames their approach as follows: 'The root problem with single-use bottle pollution (and other plastic packaging) is that single-use plastic is inexpensive and convenient. A promising solution that can eliminate the need for 1/5 of the world's single-use plastic are innovative reusable packaging distribution systems (RPDS)' [16].

"...we strongly believe that is a fair solution to a problem of millions"
José Manuel Moller, **TEDGlobal 2014**

"The word's 50 most innovative companies 2015 for filling an ignored food gap"

"...he is creating the channels to revive not only local grocery stores but also the very social fabric of these failing communities"
José Manuel Moller, **elected as Ashoka Fellow 2014.**

Algramo 2.0 in Web 3.0. What management branded as Algramo 2.0 began with a pilot programme that takes advantage of the 'Internet of Things technology' in partnership with Unilever [17]. Brian Bauer explains the model:

> We are supporting our refill model by creating something that we call 'packaging as a wallet'. In our bottles which are co-branded with Unilever and that get delivered to people's houses by a tricycle. So, this packaging unit has radio-frequency identification technology (RFID) … which basically turns the bottle, the packaging, into a digital wallet. It enables people to buy their products, and the packaging encourages people to use the packaging over and over again. The brands are creating what we call a sustainable consumption credit, that means that when they buy a litre of the product, they get X amount of money put on the packaging that gets discounted in a future purchase. [18]

Pedro Alamos, CEO of Algramo explains: 'We started the pilot in three communes of Santiago and then we will expand it throughout the city' [1]. The technology is expected to generate an additional incentive for the use of the same package, reducing plastic waste and at the same time the cost for the final consumer [18]. Unilever's work with Algramo is part of their corporate strategy, as Richard Slater, Unilever's Chief R&D Officer, explains:

> This is a really exciting area and one where we're aiming to take a leading role. While we've been designing potential solutions and experimenting for some time, it's a new and very different concept for consumers. We're trialing various approaches to tackle the issue, as there is unlikely to be a one-size-fits-all solution. We're determined to make a real difference on the plastics challenge, and so we'll continue to experiment and to test, learn and refine. [19]

Decoupling consumption from plastic waste. The purpose that guides all this effort is explained by Brian Bauer: 'We offer a solution where we decouple consumption from packaging waste' [6]. To this end, the partnership with Unilever will now incorporate Nestlé to assist in the development of this type of product in what has been called a 'New Plastics Economy' [20]. 'With our Unilever model, Omo laundry detergent is about 30 per cent less expensive than what you'd pay for them in a corporate supermarket at the regular price. Brands are excited to be able to lower their product costs, as this gives them a significant competitive advantage' [21]. To which Heather Clancy, Editorial director of the journal *GreenBiz* comments: 'Why is Algramo's approach striking a chord? Not only can Unilever reach new customers by teaming up, but the company also will save substantially on the cost of that single-use packaging' [22]. Its expansion plans include developing all the technology and offering it as a franchise, so that major brands or retailers around the world can use it [18]. This is a move that is already showing results, as Lidl in the UK introduced a trial programme of on-shelf refills for the laundry detergent Formil. A press note says, 'They will take up space equivalent to 66 standard Formil single-use bottles but have the potential of filling over 245 individual pouches, increasing capacity by nearly 300%' [23]. About the trial Mark Newbold, CSR Manager at Lidl GB said: 'We believe you shouldn't have to pay more for doing the right thing. It's why we're especially proud to be trialling this pioneering refill technology that not only helps customers reduce their plastic usage, but also their weekly shopping bill' [24]. The same kind of agreements have been reached in 2021 with Walmart and Target in the U.S., where other trials are being conducted.

STUDY QUESTIONS

1. **Focus**. Do their alliances with Walmart, Target or Lidl move away from the original local grocery store focus, where they served to promote more local and smaller scale economies?

2. **Just another channel?** Do Algramo's alliances with Unilever and Nestlé mean that they are at risk of becoming a new distribution channel that can be acquired by large transnationals?

3. **The technology or the people?** Initially it was all about reducing the final cost to customers and revamping local grocery stores. The creation of an app which can be used to call an electric vehicle housing a vending machine seems a reorientation towards the technological side in terms of making life easier for people, but it might contribute to further reductions in the market share of local grocery stores. Is this the case?

4. **What 'makes' the practice?** What are the main elements (meanings, materials, competences) of Algramo's managing by the grain practice required in order for it to work?

5. **Breaking paradigms?** Would you consider any of Algramo's management practice(s) paradigm-breaking? If so, what paradigm(s) do you think they break?

6. **Good strategizing?** What kind of strategic advantage does Unilever get from their collaboration with Algramo and vice versa?

REFERENCES

1. CNN Chile. Algramo, empresa que ofrece ventas al detalle con menor precio y cuida al medioambiente. www.youtube.com/watch?v=DC1X4KzBvTI Published 2020. Accessed March 17 2020.

2.   Leonard A. This vending machine could feed people living on $4 a day. BRIT+CO. www.
     brit.co/affordable-food-vending-machine Published 2015. Accessed March 24 2020.
3.   Moller JM. Algramo, economía familiar/Jose Manuel Moller/TEDxUFRO. www.youtube.
     com/watch?v=exvu5OLrGSw 2014. Accessed March 18 2020.
4.   Moller JM. The Venture – Algramo, Chile. www.indiegogo.com/projects/the-venture-
     algramo-chile# Published 2020. Accessed March 13 2020.
5.   CNN Chile. 'Algramo' busca potenciar la venta a granel en almacenes. www.youtube.com/
     watch?v=bAaGqkhscEQ 2015. Accessed March 24 2020.
6.   Fastcompany. This startup is ditching plastic waste by bringing the refills to you.
     Fastcompany. www.fastcompany.com/90416401/this-startup-is-ditching-plastic-waste-by-
     bringing-the-refills-to-yo Published 2019. Accessed March 13 2020.
7.   Bustos Báez S, Wastavino Muñoz F. ¿De qué manera las Empresas B generan impactos
     positivos en el ámbito social y medioambiental? *Gestión las Pers y Tecnol*. 2016, 9(27):
     21–33.
8.   El Mercurio. Algramo afina su expansión por América Latina y busca inversionistas
     en EE.UU. El Mercurio. www.economiaynegocios.cl/noticias/noticias.asp?id=169085
     Published 2015. Accessed March 17 2020.
9.   Portales L. *Social innovation and social entrepreneurship. Fundamentals, concepts, and tools*.
     Cham: Palgrave Macmillan, 2019.
10. Algramo: The value-add vending machine. *Algramo: The value-add vending machine*.
     Boston. https://digital.hbs.edu/platform-rctom/submission/algramo-the-value-add-
     vending-machine Published 2020. Last accessed August 1 2023.
11. Bauer B. Building a sustainable supply chain for a food startup. www.extension.harvard.
     edu/inside-extension/building-sustainable-supply-chain-food-startup Published 2020.
     Accessed April 3 2021.
12. Algramo. Algramo: Nuestra historia. www.algramoalmacenes.com/nuestra-historia.html
     Published 2020. Accessed March 13 2020.
13. AshokaSwitzerland. Algramo, Jose Manuel Moller. www.youtube.com/
     watch?v=wVjBlyfdrT4 2016. Accessed March 24 2020.
14. Luzardo A. Algramo: La revolución de la compra inteligente. IQLatino. https://iqlatino.
     org/2015/algramo-la-revolucion-de-la-compra-inteligente Published 2015. Accessed March
     22 2020.
15. Capital. Algramo y Alcom, primero porotos, ahora Internet. www.capital.cl/algramo-y-
     alcom-primero-porotos-ahora-internet Published 2015. Accessed March 18 2020.
16. Bauer B. Rethink plastic challenge. https://solve.mit.edu/challenges/RethinkPlastics-en/
     solutions/15297 Published 2020. Accessed March 16 2020.
17. New Plastic Economy. Algramo: Access the right amount of product without the need
     for non-recyclable single-use sachets. www.newplasticseconomy.org/innovation-prize/
     winners/algramo Published 2020. Accessed March 13 2020.
18. Ellen MacArthur Foundation. Reuse for plastic packaging in action: Algramo. www.
     youtube.com/watch?v=jIizIVK8fUs 2019. Accessed March 20 2020.
19. Unilever. We're innovating for a reuse-refill revolution. www.unilever.com/news/
     news-and-features/Feature-article/2019/we-are-innovating-for-a-reuse-revolution.html
     Published 2019. Accessed March 23 2020.
20. Defruyt S. Towards a new plastics economy. *Field Actions Science Reports*. 2019 (Special
     Issue 19): 78–81.
21. Sustainable brands. Chilean startup eliminating packaging waste, 'Poverty tax' in
     Latin American product market. https://sustainablebrands.com/read/defining-the-next-
     economy/chilean-startup-eliminating-packaging-waste-poverty-tax-in-latin-american-
     product-market Published 2020. Accessed March 23 2020.
22. Clancy H. The startup disrupting Unilever. www.greenbiz.com/article/startup-disrupting-
     unilever Published 2019. Accessed March 17 2020.
23. Moore, D. Lidl becomes first UK supermarket to trial on-shelf smart refills. www.
     circularonline.co.uk/news/lidl-becomes-first-uk-supermarket-to-trial-on-shelf-smart-refills
     Published 2022 Accessed March 27 2023.
24. Lidl. Save a load: Lidl trials UK's first supermarket 'smart' refill station to help customers
     cut plastic and costs. https://corporate.lidl.co.uk/media-centre/pressreleases/2022/refill-
     trial Published April 2022. Accessed March 27 2023.

VI GREYSTON'S BAKERS ON A MISSION TO SCALE OPEN HIRING®

OLIVER LAASCH, REUT LIVNE-TARANDACH AND MICHAEL PIRSON

This case study has been written based on original interviews conducted by the authors.

The practice. You might have heard about open innovation, or open source software, but Open Hiring? Sascha, a production manager at Greyston Bakery explains Open Hiring in a nutshell: 'People whoever, wherever they came from, walk in and will be employed without any questions'. Roger, an executive in the bakery elaborates further:

> Somebody just happens to walk by the bakery and they put their name on a list. At some point [once there is an opening], we call them up and say hey, do you want to come in for a job? I'm sure the new bakers coming in are thinking that they're going to have to be asked questions on all this. No, we won't ask them anything. We just say here is the basic training that you get before you can go on the floor. If you like everything you hear you're going to come to work in the next couple of days.

Our bakers are on a mission.

Our bakers operate a world-class food processing facility that produces 35,000 pounds of brownies every day. They all joined our team through Open Hiring.

Greyston

An easy start. Carla, who is now a production controller, reports her personal experience as a hiree:

> When I came in for orientation they asked for two picture IDs, social security, and are you legal to work in the United States? Then the orientation is about four to five hours. They take us all around Greyston. They show us how the equipment runs, where we'll be working, the process of the brownies. They actually pay us for the orientation. Then the next day, we're hired. They don't do criminal background checks. They don't ask for résumés. I think it's really awesome.

Greyston's mission is to create thriving communities through the practice and promotion of Open Hiring.

Greyston

The purpose. Anna, a personnel management employee fills us in on the deeper meaning behind Open Hiring, and why it is so different from other hiring practices: 'Here, we are not looking for a perfect employee. We're looking for a long-term relationship both with us and for their communities, making sure that we have a responsible citizen that goes back home and is a working citizen. If we don't give them the opportunity, who will?'

Sally, one of the production coordinators at Greyston explains that Open Hiring represents a life-changing opportunity for many, including herself:

> I went through a series of looking for a job, filling out applications. I'm 38 years old and in a lot of places – that age is pretty old for them. Also the gap in my employment history. I didn't graduate from high school. It was really hard. I have been turned down by McDonald's and that was devastating. They didn't even want me. They didn't want to give me a chance. Everything, I exhausted, everything, every bit of me trying to get a job.

It's a yes!

> I got the phone call and they asked me if I was still interested in the job at Greyston Bakery. Of course I said yes and I have been with them ever since. I haven't missed a day. I want them to know that I really appreciate the fact that they gave me the opportunity to take care of my family. Everyone else told me no, but they told me yes.

A job can change everything.

A pioneering social enterprise, Greyston practices Open Hiring in our world-class commercial bakery. Through The Center for Open Hiring at Greyston, you can learn more about our model and how it can change your workplace, community, and the world.

Greyston

35

years building inclusive business practices.

176

individuals employed through Open Hiring.

6.5M

pounds of brownies baked annually.

Greyston

The management. Anna, one of the personnel management employees, gives us an insight into the unusual practices related to Open Hiring: 'I have been in human resources over 23 years in the corporate environment, in non-profit and academic. The structure is different here, well it's Open Hiring and I am not your typical HR person'. Roger, an executive of Greyston Bakery exemplifies Open Hiring's disruptive logic: 'Typical hiring practices, of interview[ing] 100 people for one or two openings: You take the ones that are the best of the best and sift out people who have issues'. In Open Hiring, instead, 'You come in, you put your name on a list and we call you for a job. No questions asked, no experience, no background check, we don't care about your past. You just come in and you get a job,' explains Leslie who supports Greyston's social programmes. Kimberley, who is another personnel management employee at Greyston: 'It's a self-selection process. You decide you're going to come put your name on the list. You decide whether or not you're going to follow the rules. You have to also decide if you're going to stay'. Ina, who works in the promotion of Open Hiring among other organizations reiterates that 'instead of us deciding that somebody is [a] fit or not [a] fit, the employee decides. Instead of ruling out people, people rule themselves [out]. You take people seriously. You trust them. You don't judge. You respect their choices ... giving people back their own responsibility and dignity'.

Greyston

The power of pathmaking. Open Hiring requires a different set of unusual practices and roles. An excellent example is Emma: 'There are always folks who have personal issues, personal trauma. It helps to have someone who they can talk to … I provide support for employees, to improve employee retentions and to help the bakers connect them to services in the community. I counsel them'. Such caring practices 'make sure we give everyone every opportunity to be able to be on that journey to become a productive worker, and that things outside of their life don't impact their ability to do that … housing, childcare, travel, mental health', says Manfred, one of Greyston's executives. Daniela, who works in one of Greyston's social programmes, elaborates on how such practices relate to Greyston's Buddhist guiding principle of 'pathmaking, to make sure that each person had their needs met. We are human beings and we do bring issues to work. It is not to be frowned upon. It should be embraced. Just like you and I, they have families, they have feelings, they have personal aspirations as well as professional ones.'

PathMaking Programs

We all need support to stay on our path and succeed.

PathMaking is a critical part of our Open Hiring Model. People need more than a job to be successful. More than 5,400 members of our community benefit annually from Greyston programming designed to build skills and opportunities.

Greyston

Rethinking retention. Practices related to employee retention and 'offboarding' are unusual, particularly once employees have matured sufficiently to be employable elsewhere and may not have adequate growth opportunities at Greyston. Manfred explains:

> The retention I'm focused on is the period when someone is not a productive worker. Once someone is a productive worker, then we want people to move on, frankly. Then they open up another spot for someone else. Is it bad that I would want my team members to leave my company? The idea of them leaving to take a better job elsewhere is what? That's an amazing social contribution to the community. A couple of things to chew on. It is completely upside down.

A history of inclusion.

Greyston was founded in 1982 as a place of opportunity for everyone. Our founders created a social enterprise based on the Buddhist tenets of non-judgement and loving action.

Greyston

The backstory. The practice of Open Hiring was first grounded in Greyston founder Bernie Glassman's Buddhist philosophy of Social Action Zen. Greyston as an organization formed around it. Samantha, who is responsible for the relationship with a core customer, elaborates further:

> At Greyston Open Hiring is foundational for the business model. Bernie initially did not create [the bakery] with Open Hiring in mind. It was founded to support his then Buddhist community to just have a business to provide them with a source of income. But I think the minute he changed focus and saw the need in Southwest Yonkers he just started hiring people that he met, creating this training model on the go to bring people in. It fundamentally shifted who we were and it has been so ingrained in how the business has operated ever since. I think for us, it's just a critical and foundational piece of how we run the business. The radically inclusive hiring model will always be a part of what we do.

Open Hiring has made Greyston unique, as Anna explains: 'Different next to another bakery is that we give an opportunity to the person.'

What can we do for the community? As Bernie Glassman, Greyston's late founder stressed in his book *Instructions to the cook*, 'It seemed obvious that

1982   Greyston Bakery is founded

1987   Partners with Ben & Jerry's to create its Chocolate Fudge Brownie ice cream

Greyston

there was no single solution to the problem of homelessness and unemployment. Our approach had to include housing, childcare, job training, counselling and the creation of jobs all at once.' The Greyston Foundation supports the community through programmes complementing the social impacts of Open Hiring. Their workforce development programme is open to community members, providing 'hard skills trainings in culinary arts, building and construction trade safety certifications, security guard licensing'. Another key community programme is Issan House where chronically homeless people living with HIV/AIDS find a home, and may find their way back into work life. Ellie, who works in Greyston's social programmes, explains by telling the story of:

... a tenant at Issan House, who we nurtured along the way. First, a peer educator then a volunteer, then he worked for our day programme. He's now been case managing ... since 2004. Also, one of ... [the] security guards who had started off in workforce development and we put her as a security guard trainee. She became the security guard supervisor.

1992   Launch of Greyston Foundation to strengthen the governance of its unique hybrid organization   **GREYSTON**

2004   Greyston Bakery opens a new LEED® Certified 21,000 square foot bakery on the Yonkers waterfront

Greyston

Fostering learning. The third main programme is Greyston's Community Gardens, which not only makes a contribution to community health and food security, but also provides volunteering work opportunities. Lilly explains the integrative impact of the gardens with this story: 'I have a lady that came out of jail. She spent 12 years in jail. That lady worked for me for five years. You see, she learned.'

2008   Workforce Development Program
        launches to serve hard-to-employ
        workers

2015   Greyston Bakery ranked in the top
        10% of all B Corporations in the
        world

Certified

Corporation

Greyston

Hybrid enterprise management. Greyston's wider set of 'good' business practices is shown by their leading role among the B Corps. These are social purpose businesses that commit to a wider set of responsible management practices. They are run by people using 'business as a force for good', which implies that they are 'hybrid', 'a new kind of business that balances purpose and profit' (https://bcorporation.net). Gemma says:

> I think the board members, are committed to running a B Corp, an organization that for many people is new. That's exciting. And then there is a whole community of B Corp companies and Greyston for them has been a leader. They [Greyston] have been the initial B Corp member.

Manfred emphasizes the uniqueness of a B Corp's organically grown:

> … hybrid structure meaning that our bakery is a for-profit that's serving people and community but at the same time if we do things right and run efficiently, we can then generate money that goes towards funding the non-for-profit activities whether that's directly for our bakers or for the other community area and people that we do support. I think that's unique'.

As Amanda from the Greyston Foundation stresses, what unifies this hybrid organization is the underlying purpose of empowering people at Greyston's 'Mandala' [see the Greyston Logo]. 'People can be in the gardens or in the Issan House and workforce development programmes. It's just complete acceptance to use your potential to go to the next steps.'

2016   Bakery invited to the White House for launch of Fair Chance Business Pledge

2018   The Center for Open Hiring at Greyston launches

Greyston

The challenge. Today, Greyston is Open Hiring and Open Hiring is Greyston. This is a great achievement, but how can Greyston transplant this practice elsewhere to scale positive impacts? Amanda describes this challenge as follows:

> A lot of people are asking us about this practice in the bakery. Why don't we see if we can try to help other organizations how to practice? We open[ed] a Centre for Open Hiring, then study our process, then design teaching materials, and then teach those materials as best as possible to other organizations; to businesses with the goal to impact the employment space and help individuals with barriers to employment. Open Hiring as applied in Yonkers is for formerly incarcerated, homeless, individuals without work history. But it could be applied in different contexts. That's the hope of Open Hiring that you can apply to the different populations in need.

5.4M   Million cannot find a job in the United States

$30K   Annual cost of imprisonment in the United States

$4K   Saved per individual hire through Open Hiring

Greyston

Staying on our toes. Manfred further outlines the need for adaptation of Open Hiring, stressing that:

> Even though we have been doing some form of Open Hiring for 35 years, we still learn stuff. The world changes and I think it's important that whatever the model is, it has to be dynamic. It has to adjust. What is important here in Yonkers might be different in another location. It's important to say: This is how you approach it and then you have to do your situation analysis of the market and say what do we need? What do the people need, who this particular business is going to be in the locale of? Every location has different barriers, different challenges, different needs.

PERSPECTIVE

With New Hiring Models, Corporations (Including Amazon) Can Spur Positive Change

Everybody, including the formerly incarcerated and refugees, deserves a spot in corporate America. CEOs should develop hiring models that reflect that.

Passing it on. One of the initiatives to spread Open Hiring around the world consists of a move to the Netherlands. This move not only relates to Greyston's new bakery there, but also consists of a larger initiative to spread Open Hiring throughout Europe in the early 2020s. Ina tells us more:

> Open Hiring is a great way to get people back to work, especially the people that are sitting at home, but are able to work. This is a big problem in the Netherlands. We have 1.6 million that can work, but people don't hire them because they are too old. If you're 50 plus, then it's difficult to get a job in the Netherlands. And also people from Syria, the people that do have a working permit, but they have the wrong last name. They are highly motivated and still find it hard to find a job. Start Foundation … [has] this programme for the next three to five years … time to prove it … to prove the theory [that Open Hiring can work in the Netherlands]. We decided that we will start right from the beginning; a couple of companies are willing to give it a try. And then we are spreading the word. Hopefully, we get more and more companies who will form a network and will strengthen each other. We make a movement out of it. I think we have a good chance because a lot of companies, also big companies, really want to go for it. They want to step up and join this movement. Hopefully, they'll make it happen.

Protecting the practice. While promoting the adaptation of Open Hiring to others by highlighting its business case, there is also a concern that Open Hiring could be hijacked. As a protective measure, Greyston's leadership has registered Open Hiring as a trademark. Amanda describes both the rationale behind this move and its criticism: 'Individuals are asking: Are you guys going to trademark that? Shouldn't it be free? The idea was to create intellectual property around [Open Hiring]. We are going [to] build materials and concepts that we can actually own in a way that empowers what we do. You know, someone starts doing what they call Open Hiring but they're not treating people well. They're not compassionate. Then that wouldn't be right. So we want to know that people, if they're gonna do Open Hiring, they're going to do it right. Similar, probably to our way. But obviously we know that there's going to be adjustments. There's obviously gonna be adaptations'.

Open Hiring can solve today's business challenges.

Recruitment, Screening, and Retention Costs

Consider the cost of trying to find the right employee for the job.

Tight Labor Market

Companies are overlooking a group of individuals who are eager to fill entry-level positions.

Demand for Corporate Responsibility

Today's businesses need to pay attention to more than the financial bottom line. Customers are demanding it.

Greyston

STUDY QUESTIONS

1. **Management as unusual.** How are Open Hiring management practices different from 'normal' personnel management?

2. **Ripple effects.** How might it affect practices like performance evaluation, training, or compensation?

3. **Managerial implications.** What challenges and opportunities do you think Open Hiring can bring for managers across an organization?

4. **Making it work.** What do you think Open Hiring needs in order for it to work? What might be challenges or synergies? Where does it work, where does it not?

5. **The management challenge.** How would you scale the Open Hiring practice? What strategies and activities would you employ to convince others to adopt Open Hiring?

APPENDIX: THE SDGS AND THEIR TARGETS

Goal 1 NO POVERTY
End poverty in all its forms everywhere

TARGETS
1.1 By 2030, eradicate extreme poverty for all people everywhere, currently measured as people living on less than $1.25 a day
1.2 By 2030, reduce at least by half the proportion of men, women and children of all ages living in poverty in all its dimensions according to national definitions
1.3 Implement nationally appropriate social protection systems and measures for all, including floors, and by 2030 achieve substantial coverage of the poor and the vulnerable
1.4 By 2030, ensure that all men and women, in particular the poor and the vulnerable, have equal rights to economic resources, as well as access to basic services, ownership and control over land and other forms of property, inheritance, natural resources, appropriate new technology and financial services, including microfinance
1.5 By 2030, build the resilience of the poor and those in vulnerable situations and reduce their exposure and vulnerability to climate-related extreme events and other economic, social and environmental shocks and disasters
1.a Ensure significant mobilization of resources from a variety of sources, including through enhanced development cooperation, in order to provide adequate and predictable means for developing countries, in particular least developed countries, to implement programmes and policies to end poverty in all its dimensions
1.b Create sound policy frameworks at the national, regional and international levels, based on pro-poor and gender-sensitive development strategies, to support accelerated investment in poverty eradication actions

Goal 2 ZERO HUNGER
End hunger, achieve food security and improved nutrition and promote sustainable agriculture

TARGETS
2.1 By 2030, end hunger and ensure access by all people, in particular the poor and people in vulnerable situations, including infants, to safe, nutritious and sufficient food all year round
2.2 By 2030, end all forms of malnutrition, including achieving, by 2025, the internationally agreed targets on stunting and wasting in children under 5 years of age, and address the nutritional needs of adolescent girls, pregnant and lactating women and older persons
2.3 By 2030, double the agricultural productivity and incomes of small-scale food producers, in particular women, indigenous peoples, family farmers, pastoralists and fishers, including through secure and equal access to land, other productive resources and inputs, knowledge, financial services, markets and opportunities for value addition and non-farm employment
2.4 By 2030, ensure sustainable food production systems and implement resilient agricultural practices that increase productivity and production, that help maintain ecosystems, that strengthen capacity for adaptation to climate change, extreme weather, drought, flooding and other disasters and that progressively improve land and soil quality
2.5 By 2020, maintain the genetic diversity of seeds, cultivated plants and farmed and domesticated animals and their related wild species, including through soundly managed and diversified seed and plant banks at the national, regional and international levels, and promote access to and fair and equitable sharing of benefits arising from the utilization of genetic resources and associated traditional knowledge, as internationally agreed
2.a Increase investment, including through enhanced international cooperation, in rural infrastructure, agricultural research and extension services, technology development and plant and livestock gene banks in order to enhance agricultural productive capacity in developing countries, in particular least developed countries
2.b Correct and prevent trade restrictions and distortions in world agricultural markets, including through the parallel elimination of all forms of agricultural export subsidies and all export measures with equivalent effect, in accordance with the mandate of the Doha Development Round
2.c Adopt measures to ensure the proper functioning of food commodity markets and their derivatives and facilitate timely access to market information, including on food reserves, in order to help limit extreme food price volatility

Goal 3 GOOD HEALTH AND WELL-BEING
Ensure healthy lives and promote well-being for all at all ages

TARGETS
3.1 By 2030, reduce the global maternal mortality ratio to less than 70 per 100,000 live births
3.2 By 2030, end preventable deaths of newborns and children under 5 years of age, with all countries aiming to reduce neonatal mortality to at least as low as 12 per 1,000 live births and under-5 mortality to at least as low as 25 per 1,000 live births
3.3 By 2030, end the epidemics of AIDS, tuberculosis, malaria and neglected tropical diseases and combat hepatitis, water-borne diseases and other communicable diseases
3.4 By 2030, reduce by one third premature mortality from non-communicable diseases through prevention and treatment and promote mental health and well-being
3.5 Strengthen the prevention and treatment of substance abuse, including narcotic drug abuse and harmful use of alcohol
3.6 By 2020, halve the number of global deaths and injuries from road traffic accidents
3.7 By 2030, ensure universal access to sexual and reproductive health-care services, including for family planning, information and education, and the integration of reproductive health into national strategies and programmes
3.8 Achieve universal health coverage, including financial risk protection, access to quality essential health-care services and access to safe, effective, quality and affordable essential medicines and vaccines for all
3.9 By 2030, substantially reduce the number of deaths and illnesses from hazardous chemicals and air, water and soil pollution and contamination
3.a Strengthen the implementation of the World Health Organization Framework Convention on Tobacco Control in all countries, as appropriate
3.b Support the research and development of vaccines and medicines for the communicable and non-communicable diseases that primarily affect developing countries, provide access to affordable essential medicines and vaccines, in accordance with the Doha Declaration on the TRIPS Agreement and Public Health, which affirms the right of developing countries to use to the full the provisions in the Agreement on Trade-Related Aspects of Intellectual Property Rights regarding flexibilities to protect public health, and, in particular, provide access to medicines for all
3.c Substantially increase health financing and the recruitment, development, training and retention of the health workforce in developing countries, especially in least developed countries and small island developing States
3.d Strengthen the capacity of all countries, in particular developing countries, for early warning, risk reduction and management of national and global health risks

Goal 4 QUALITY EDUCATION
Ensure inclusive and equitable quality education and promote lifelong learning opportunities for all

TARGETS
4.1 By 2030, ensure that all girls and boys complete free, equitable and quality primary and secondary education leading to relevant and effective learning outcomes
4.2 By 2030, ensure that all girls and boys have access to quality early childhood development, care and pre-primary education so that they are ready for primary education
4.3 By 2030, ensure equal access for all women and men to affordable and quality technical, vocational and tertiary education, including university
4.4 By 2030, substantially increase the number of youth and adults who have relevant skills, including technical and vocational skills, for employment, decent jobs and entrepreneurship
4.5 By 2030, eliminate gender disparities in education and ensure equal access to all levels of education and vocational training for the vulnerable, including persons with disabilities, indigenous peoples and children in vulnerable situations
4.6 By 2030, ensure that all youth and a substantial proportion of adults, both men and women, achieve literacy and numeracy
4.7 By 2030, ensure that all learners acquire the knowledge and skills needed to promote sustainable development, including, among others, through education for sustainable development and sustainable lifestyles, human rights, gender equality, promotion of a culture of peace and non-violence, global citizenship and appreciation of cultural diversity and of culture's contribution to sustainable development
4.a Build and upgrade education facilities that are child, disability and gender sensitive and provide safe, non-violent, inclusive and effective learning environments for all
4.b By 2020, substantially expand globally the number of scholarships available to developing countries, in particular least developed countries, small island developing States and African countries, for enrolment in higher education, including vocational training and information and communications technology, technical, engineering and scientific programmes, in developed countries and other developing countries
4.c By 2030, substantially increase the supply of qualified teachers, including through international cooperation for teacher training in developing countries, especially least developed countries and small island developing States

Goal 5 GENDER EQUALITY
Achieve gender equality and empower all women and girls

TARGETS
5.1 End all forms of discrimination against all women and girls everywhere
5.2 Eliminate all forms of violence against all women and girls in the public and private spheres, including trafficking and sexual and other types of exploitation
5.3 Eliminate all harmful practices, such as child, early and forced marriage and female genital mutilation
5.4 Recognize and value unpaid care and domestic work through the provision of public services, infrastructure and social protection policies and the promotion of shared responsibility within the household and the family as nationally appropriate
5.5 Ensure women's full and effective participation and equal opportunities for leadership at all levels of decision-making in political, economic and public life
5.6 Ensure universal access to sexual and reproductive health and reproductive rights as agreed in accordance with the Programme of Action of the International Conference on Population and Development and the Beijing Platform for Action and the outcome documents of their review conferences
5.a Undertake reforms to give women equal rights to economic resources, as well as access to ownership and control over land and other forms of property, financial services, inheritance and natural resources, in accordance with national laws
5.b Enhance the use of enabling technology, in particular information and communications technology, to promote the empowerment of women
5.c Adopt and strengthen sound policies and enforceable legislation for the promotion of gender equality and the empowerment of all women and girls at all levels

Goal 6 CLEAN WATER AND SANITATION
Ensure availability and sustainable management of water and sanitation for all

TARGETS
6.1 By 2030, achieve universal and equitable access to safe and affordable drinking water for all
6.2 By 2030, achieve access to adequate and equitable sanitation and hygiene for all and end open defecation, paying special attention to the needs of women and girls and those in vulnerable situations
6.3 By 2030, improve water quality by reducing pollution, eliminating dumping and minimizing release of hazardous chemicals and materials, halving the proportion of untreated wastewater and substantially increasing recycling and safe reuse globally
6.4 By 2030, substantially increase water-use efficiency across all sectors and ensure sustainable withdrawals and supply of freshwater to address water scarcity and substantially reduce the number of people suffering from water scarcity
6.5 By 2030, implement integrated water resources management at all levels, including through transboundary cooperation as appropriate
6.6 By 2020, protect and restore water-related ecosystems, including mountains, forests, wetlands, rivers, aquifers and lakes
6.a By 2030, expand international cooperation and capacity-building support to developing countries in water- and sanitation-related activities and programmes, including water harvesting, desalination, water efficiency, wastewater treatment, recycling and reuse technologies
6.b Support and strengthen the participation of local communities in improving water and sanitation management

Goal 7 AFFORDABLE AND CLEAN ENERGY
Ensure access to affordable, reliable, sustainable and modern energy for all

TARGETS
7.1 By 2030, ensure universal access to affordable, reliable and modern energy services
7.2 By 2030, increase substantially the share of renewable energy in the global energy mix
7.3 By 2030, double the global rate of improvement in energy efficiency
7.a By 2030, enhance international cooperation to facilitate access to clean energy research and technology, including renewable energy, energy efficiency and advanced and cleaner fossil-fuel technology, and promote investment in energy infrastructure and clean energy technology
7.b By 2030, expand infrastructure and upgrade technology for supplying modern and sustainable energy services for all in developing countries, in particular least developed countries, small island developing States and landlocked developing countries, in accordance with their respective programmes of support

Goal 8 DECENT WORK AND ECONOMIC GROWTH
Promote sustained, inclusive and sustainable economic growth, full and productive employment and decent work for all

TARGETS
8.1 Sustain per capita economic growth in accordance with national circumstances and, in particular, at least 7 per cent gross domestic product growth per annum in the least developed countries
8.2 Achieve higher levels of economic productivity through diversification, technological upgrading and innovation, including through a focus on high-value added and labour-intensive sectors
8.3 Promote development-oriented policies that support productive activities, decent job creation, entrepreneurship, creativity and innovation, and encourage the formalization and growth of micro-, small- and medium-sized enterprises, including through access to financial services
8.4 Improve progressively, through 2030, global resource efficiency in consumption and production and endeavour to decouple economic growth from environmental degradation, in accordance with the 10-Year Framework of Programmes on Sustainable Consumption and Production, with developed countries taking the lead
8.5 By 2030, achieve full and productive employment and decent work for all women and men, including for young people and persons with disabilities, and equal pay for work of equal value
8.6 By 2020, substantially reduce the proportion of youth not in employment, education or training
8.7 Take immediate and effective measures to eradicate forced labour, end modern slavery and human trafficking and secure the prohibition and elimination of the worst forms of child labour, including recruitment and use of child soldiers, and by 2025 end child labour in all its forms
8.8 Protect labour rights and promote safe and secure working environments for all workers, including migrant workers, in particular women migrants, and those in precarious employment
8.9 By 2030, devise and implement policies to promote sustainable tourism that creates jobs and promotes local culture and products
8.10 Strengthen the capacity of domestic financial institutions to encourage and expand access to banking, insurance and financial services for all
8.a Increase Aid for Trade support for developing countries, in particular least developed countries, including through the Enhanced Integrated Framework for Trade-related Technical Assistance to Least Developed Countries
8.b By 2020, develop and operationalize a global strategy for youth employment and implement the Global Jobs Pact of the International Labour Organization

Goal 9 INDUSTRY, INNOVATION AND INFRASTRUCTURE
Build resilient infrastructure, promote inclusive and sustainable industrialization and foster innovation

TARGETS
9.1 Develop quality, reliable, sustainable and resilient infrastructure, including regional and transborder infrastructure, to support economic development and human well-being, with a focus on affordable and equitable access for all
9.2 Promote inclusive and sustainable industrialization and, by 2030, significantly raise industry's share of employment and gross domestic product, in line with national circumstances, and double its share in least developed countries
9.3 Increase the access of small-scale industrial and other enterprises, in particular in developing countries, to financial services, including affordable credit, and their integration into value chains and markets
9.4 By 2030, upgrade infrastructure and retrofit industries to make them sustainable, with increased resource-use efficiency and greater adoption of clean and environmentally sound technologies and industrial processes, with all countries taking action in accordance with their respective capabilities
9.5 Enhance scientific research, upgrade the technological capabilities of industrial sectors in all countries, in particular developing countries, including, by 2030, encouraging innovation and substantially increasing the number of research and development workers per 1 million people and public and private research and development spending
9.a Facilitate sustainable and resilient infrastructure development in developing countries through enhanced financial, technological and technical support to African countries, least developed countries, landlocked developing countries and small island developing States
9.b Support domestic technology development, research and innovation in developing countries, including by ensuring a conducive policy environment for, inter alia, industrial diversification and value addition to commodities
9.c Significantly increase access to information and communications technology and strive to provide universal and affordable access to the Internet in least developed countries by 2020

Goal 10 REDUCED INEQUALITIES
Reduce inequality within and among countries

TARGETS
10.1 By 2030, progressively achieve and sustain income growth of the bottom 40 per cent of the population at a rate higher than the national average
10.2 By 2030, empower and promote the social, economic and political inclusion of all, irrespective of age, sex, disability, race, ethnicity, origin, religion or economic or other status
10.3 Ensure equal opportunity and reduce inequalities of outcome, including by eliminating discriminatory laws, policies and practices and promoting appropriate legislation, policies and action in this regard
10.4 Adopt policies, especially fiscal, wage and social protection policies, and progressively achieve greater equality
10.5 Improve the regulation and monitoring of global financial markets and institutions and strengthen the implementation of such regulations
10.6 Ensure enhanced representation and voice for developing countries in decision-making in global international economic and financial institutions in order to deliver more effective, credible, accountable and legitimate institutions
10.7 Facilitate orderly, safe, regular and responsible migration and mobility of people, including through the implementation of planned and well-managed migration policies
10.a Implement the principle of special and differential treatment for developing countries, in particular least developed countries, in accordance with World Trade Organization agreements
10.b Encourage official development assistance and financial flows, including foreign direct investment, to States where the need is greatest, in particular least developed countries, African countries, small island developing States and landlocked developing countries, in accordance with their national plans and programmes
10.c By 2030, reduce to less than 3 per cent the transaction costs of migrant remittances and eliminate remittance corridors with costs higher than 5 per cent

Goal 11 SUSTAINABLE CITIES AND COMMUNITIES
Make cities and human settlements inclusive, safe, resilient and sustainable

TARGETS
11.1 By 2030, ensure access for all to adequate, safe and affordable housing and basic services and upgrade slums
11.2 By 2030, provide access to safe, affordable, accessible and sustainable transport systems for all, improving road safety, notably by expanding public transport, with special attention to the needs of those in vulnerable situations, women, children, persons with disabilities and older persons
11.3 By 2030, enhance inclusive and sustainable urbanization and capacity for participatory, integrated and sustainable human settlement planning and management in all countries
11.4 Strengthen efforts to protect and safeguard the world's cultural and natural heritage
11.5 By 2030, significantly reduce the number of deaths and the number of people affected and substantially decrease the direct economic losses relative to global gross domestic product caused by disasters, including water-related disasters, with a focus on protecting the poor and people in vulnerable situations
11.6 By 2030, reduce the adverse per capita environmental impact of cities, including by paying special attention to air quality and municipal and other waste management
11.7 By 2030, provide universal access to safe, inclusive and accessible, green and public spaces, in particular for women and children, older persons and persons with disabilities
11.a Support positive economic, social and environmental links between urban, peri-urban and rural areas by strengthening national and regional development planning
11.b By 2020, substantially increase the number of cities and human settlements adopting and implementing integrated policies and plans towards inclusion, resource efficiency, mitigation and adaptation to climate change, resilience to disasters, and develop and implement, in line with the Sendai Framework for Disaster Risk Reduction 2015–2030, holistic disaster risk management at all levels
11.c Support least developed countries, including through financial and technical assistance, in building sustainable and resilient buildings utilizing local materials

Goal 12 RESPONSIBLE CONSUMPTION AND PRODUCTION
Ensure sustainable consumption and production patterns

TARGETS
12.1 Implement the 10-Year Framework of Programmes on Sustainable Consumption and Production Patterns, all countries taking action, with developed countries taking the lead, taking into account the development and capabilities of developing countries
12.2 By 2030, achieve the sustainable management and efficient use of natural resources
12.3 By 2030, halve per capita global food waste at the retail and consumer levels and reduce food losses along production and supply chains, including post-harvest losses
12.4 By 2020, achieve the environmentally sound management of chemicals and all wastes throughout their life cycle, in accordance with agreed international frameworks, and significantly reduce their release to air, water and soil in order to minimize their adverse impacts on human health and the environment
12.5 By 2030, substantially reduce waste generation through prevention, reduction, recycling and reuse
12.6 Encourage companies, especially large and transnational companies, to adopt sustainable practices and to integrate sustainability information into their reporting cycle
12.7 Promote public procurement practices that are sustainable, in accordance with national policies and priorities
12.8 By 2030, ensure that people everywhere have the relevant information and awareness for sustainable development and lifestyles in harmony with nature
12.a Support developing countries to strengthen their scientific and technological capacity to move towards more sustainable patterns of consumption and production
12.b Develop and implement tools to monitor sustainable development impacts for sustainable tourism that creates jobs and promotes local culture and products
12.c Rationalize inefficient fossil-fuel subsidies that encourage wasteful consumption by removing market distortions, in accordance with national circumstances, including by restructuring taxation and phasing out those harmful subsidies, where they exist, to reflect their environmental impacts, taking fully into account the specific needs and conditions of developing countries and minimizing the possible adverse impacts on their development in a manner that protects the poor and the affected communities

Goal 13 CLIMATE ACTION
Take urgent action to combat climate change and its impacts

TARGETS
13.1 Strengthen resilience and adaptive capacity to climate-related hazards and natural disasters in all countries
13.2 Integrate climate change measures into national policies, strategies and planning
13.3 Improve education, awareness-raising and human and institutional capacity on climate change mitigation, adaptation, impact reduction and early warning
13.a Implement the commitment undertaken by developed-country parties to the United Nations Framework Convention on Climate Change to a goal of mobilizing jointly $100 billion annually by 2020 from all sources to address the needs of developing countries in the context of meaningful mitigation actions and transparency on implementation and fully operationalize the Green Climate Fund through its capitalization as soon as possible
13.b Promote mechanisms for raising capacity for effective climate change-related planning and management in least developed countries and small island developing States, including focusing on women, youth and local and marginalized communities

Goal 14 LIFE BELOW WATER
Conserve and sustainably use the oceans, seas and marine resources for sustainable development

TARGETS
14.1 By 2025, prevent and significantly reduce marine pollution of all kinds, in particular from land-based activities, including marine debris and nutrient pollution
14.2 By 2020, sustainably manage and protect marine and coastal ecosystems to avoid significant adverse impacts, including by strengthening their resilience, and take action for their restoration in order to achieve healthy and productive oceans
14.3 Minimize and address the impacts of ocean acidification, including through enhanced scientific cooperation at all levels
14.4 By 2020, effectively regulate harvesting and end overfishing, illegal, unreported and unregulated fishing and destructive fishing practices and implement science-based management plans, in order to restore fish stocks in the shortest time feasible, at least to levels that can produce maximum sustainable yield as determined by their biological characteristics
14.5 By 2020, conserve at least 10 per cent of coastal and marine areas, consistent with national and international law and based on the best available scientific information
14.6 By 2020, prohibit certain forms of fisheries subsidies which contribute to overcapacity and overfishing, eliminate subsidies that contribute to illegal, unreported and unregulated fishing and refrain from introducing new such subsidies, recognizing that appropriate and effective special and differential treatment for developing and least developed countries should be an integral part of the World Trade Organization fisheries subsidies negotiation
14.7 By 2030, increase the economic benefits to small island developing States and least developed countries from the sustainable use of marine resources, including through sustainable management of fisheries, aquaculture and tourism
14.a Increase scientific knowledge, develop research capacity and transfer marine technology, taking into account the Intergovernmental Oceanographic Commission Criteria and Guidelines on the Transfer of Marine Technology, in order to improve ocean health and to enhance the contribution of marine biodiversity to the development of developing countries, in particular small island developing States and least developed countries
14.b Provide access for small-scale artisanal fishers to marine resources and markets
14.c Enhance the conservation and sustainable use of oceans and their resources by implementing international law as reflected in the United Nations Convention on the Law of the Sea, which provides the legal framework for the conservation and sustainable use of oceans and their resources, as recalled in paragraph 158 of "The future we want"

Goal 15 LIFE ON LAND
Protect, restore and promote sustainable use of terrestrial ecosystems, sustainably manage forests, combat desertification, and halt and reverse land degradation and halt biodiversity loss

TARGETS
15.1 By 2020, ensure the conservation, restoration and sustainable use of terrestrial and inland freshwater ecosystems and their services, in particular forests, wetlands, mountains and drylands, in line with obligations under international agreements
15.2 By 2020, promote the implementation of sustainable management of all types of forests, halt deforestation, restore degraded forests and substantially increase afforestation and reforestation globally
15.3 By 2030, combat desertification, restore degraded land and soil, including land affected by desertification, drought and floods, and strive to achieve a land degradation-neutral world
15.4 By 2030, ensure the conservation of mountain ecosystems, including their biodiversity, in order to enhance their capacity to provide benefits that are essential for sustainable development
15.5 Take urgent and significant action to reduce the degradation of natural habitats, halt the loss of biodiversity and, by 2020, protect and prevent the extinction of threatened species
15.6 Promote fair and equitable sharing of the benefits arising from the utilization of genetic resources and promote appropriate access to such resources, as internationally agreed
15.7 Take urgent action to end poaching and trafficking of protected species of flora and fauna and address both demand and supply of illegal wildlife products
15.8 By 2020, introduce measures to prevent the introduction and significantly reduce the impact of invasive alien species on land and water ecosystems and control or eradicate the priority species
15.9 By 2020, integrate ecosystem and biodiversity values into national and local planning, development processes, poverty reduction strategies and accounts
15.a Mobilize and significantly increase financial resources from all sources to conserve and sustainably use biodiversity and ecosystems
15.b Mobilize significant resources from all sources and at all levels to finance sustainable forest management and provide adequate incentives to developing countries to advance such management, including for conservation and reforestation
15.c Enhance global support for efforts to combat poaching and trafficking of protected species, including by increasing the capacity of local communities to pursue sustainable livelihood opportunities

Goal 16 PEACE, JUSTICE AND STRONG INSTITUTIONS
Promote peaceful and inclusive societies for sustainable development, provide access to justice for all and build effective, accountable and inclusive institutions at all levels

TARGETS
16.1.1 Number of victims of intentional homicide per 100,000 population, by sex and age
16.1.2 Conflict-related deaths per 100,000 population, by sex, age and cause
16.1.3 Proportion of population subjected to (a) physical violence, (b) psychological violence and (c) sexual violence in the previous 12 months
16.1.4 Proportion of population that feel safe walking alone around the area they live after dark
16.2.1 Proportion of children aged 1–17 years who experienced any physical punishment and/or psychological aggression by caregivers in the past month
16.2.2 Number of victims of human trafficking per 100,000 population, by sex, age and form of exploitation
16.2.3 Proportion of young women and men aged 18–29 years who experienced sexual violence by age 18
16.3.1 Proportion of victims of violence in the previous 12 months who reported their victimization to competent authorities or other officially recognized conflict resolution mechanisms
16.3.2 Unsentenced detainees as a proportion of overall prison population
16.3.3 Proportion of the population who have experienced a dispute in the past two years and who accessed a formal or informal dispute resolution mechanism, by type of mechanism
16.4.1 Total value of inward and outward illicit financial flows (in current United States dollars)
16.4.2 Proportion of seized, found or surrendered arms whose illicit origin or context has been traced or established by a competent authority in line with international instruments
16.5.1 Proportion of persons who had at least one contact with a public official and who paid a bribe to a public official, or were asked for a bribe by those public officials, during the previous 12 months
16.5.2 Proportion of businesses that had at least one contact with a public official and that paid a bribe to a public official, or were asked for a bribe by those public officials during the previous 12 months
16.6.1 Primary government expenditures as a proportion of original approved budget, by sector (or by budget codes or similar)
16.6.2 Proportion of population satisfied with their last experience of public services
16.7.1 Proportions of positions in national and local institutions, including (a) the legislatures; (b) the public service; and (c) the judiciary, compared to national distributions, by sex, age, persons with disabilities and population groups
16.7.2 Proportion of population who believe decision-making is inclusive and responsive, by sex, age, disability and population group
16.8.1 Proportion of members and voting rights of developing countries in international organizations
16.9.1 Proportion of children under 5 years of age whose births have been registered with a civil authority, by age
16.10.1 Number of verified cases of killing, kidnapping, enforced disappearance, arbitrary detention and torture of journalists, associated media personnel, trade unionists and human rights advocates in the previous 12 months
16.10.2 Number of countries that adopt and implement constitutional, statutory and/or policy guarantees for public access to information
16.a.1 Existence of independent national human rights institutions in compliance with the Paris Principles
16.b.1 Proportion of population reporting having personally felt discriminated against or harassed in the previous 12 months on the basis of a ground of discrimination prohibited under international human rights law

Goal 17 PARTNERSHIPS FOR THE GOALS
Strengthen the means of implementation and revitalize the Global Partnership for Sustainable Development

TARGETS
17.1.1 Total government revenue as a proportion of GDP, by source
17.1.2 Proportion of domestic budget funded by domestic taxes
17.2.1 Net official development assistance, total and to least developed countries, as a proportion of the Organization for Economic Cooperation and Development (OECD) Development Assistance Committee donors' gross national income (GNI)
17.3.1 Additional financial resources mobilized for developing countries from multiple sources
17.3.2 Volume of remittances (in United States dollars) as a proportion of total GDP
17.4.1 Debt service as a proportion of exports of goods and services
17.5.1 Number of countries that adopt and implement investment promotion regimes for developing countries, including the least developed countries
17.6.1 Fixed Internet broadband subscriptions per 100 inhabitants, by speed
17.7.1 Total amount of funding for developing countries to promote the development, transfer, dissemination and diffusion of environmentally sound technologies
17.8.1 Proportion of individuals using the Internet
17.9.1 Dollar value of financial and technical assistance (including through North-South, South-South and triangular cooperation) committed to developing countries
17.10.1 Worldwide weighted tariff-average
17.11.1 Developing countries' and least developed countries' share of global exports
17.12.1 Weighted average tariffs faced by developing countries, least developed countries and small island developing States
17.13.1 Macroeconomic Dashboard
17.14.1 Number of countries with mechanisms in place to enhance policy coherence of sustainable development
17.15.1 Extent of use of country-owned results frameworks and planning tools by providers of development cooperation
17.16.1 Number of countries reporting progress in multi-stakeholder development effectiveness monitoring frameworks that support the achievement of the sustainable development goals
17.17.1 Amount in United States dollars committed to public-private partnerships for infrastructure
17.18.1 Statistical capacity indicator for Sustainable Development Goal monitoring
17.18.2 Number of countries that have national statistical legislation that complies with the Fundamental Principles of Official Statistics
17.18.3 Number of countries with a national statistical plan that is fully funded and under implementation, by source of funding
17.19.1 Dollar value of all resources made available to strengthen statistical capacity in developing countries
17.19.2 Proportion of countries that (a) have conducted at least one population and housing census in the last 10 years; and (b) have achieved 100 per cent birth registration and 80 per cent death registration

Source: https://sdgs.un.org/goals

POINTERS

The targets listed can be used to get a much more nuanced and concrete idea as to what can and should be done to achieve each SDG (sustainable development goal). You can, for instance, use the indicators to assess if something presented as contributing to SDG achievement really is in line with the targets, or might rather be a case of 'SDG washing' (using an SDG for communication, but not or inconsistently implementing action that addresses the SDG). Also, you can use these targets to explore how particular actions or practices could be changed to contribute to a particular SDG more explicitly. On the United Nations' official SDG website, you can dig even deeper by looking for the quantifiable indicators that correspond to each of the targets.

INDEX

Page numbers in *italics* refer to figures; page numbers in **bold** refer to tables.

4Ocean, 440

Abel B van, 875–877, 881–882, 884
absorptive capacity, 514–515
abusive supervisors, **246**
accountability, 770
accounting and controlling
  overview of, 767–770, *768–769*
  digitalizing and, 408
  evaluating and elaborating data for,
      778–785, *781*, **783–785**, *785*, 804
  facts and figures, 765
  gender budgeting and, 802–803, **802–803**
  identifying the account and gathering data for,
      774–778, *775–776*, *779*
  management control and, 790–793, *791–793*
  management gym, 794–797
  new normal of, 770–774, *772*
  old-world management and, 11
  pioneer: Schaltegger, 797–798
  principles of, 793–794
  profile: Ette, 797–801
  reporting and, 785–790, *787*, *789*
  spotlight: CLP, 766–767
  true story, 801–801
accounting practitioners, 770
Achondo S, 902
act utilitarianism, 82
activism, 255–257
activist consumption, 705
activist shareholding, 820
activist venturing, 856–857
activity-based costing (ABC), 780
additive manufacturing, **391**
Adler NJ, 288–290
Agarwal R, 871
Agle BR, 130–131
Alamos P, 908
Albornoz H, 904–905
ALCOM, 906
Algramo, 901–910
alienated followers, 276
Allsafe, 268–269, 471–472, 661
ALTECH, 906
Amazon, 405–406, 820
ambidextrous management, 511–518, **512**, *513–514*,
    516–517
American Marketing Association (AMA), 696,
    710, **711**

anal retentiveness, 197
Ansoff I, 470
anti-global trade movements, 436
Apple, 490, 744
appreciative inquiry, 329
ARIA framework for responsible innovation, 530, *530*
Aristotle, 85
Arkwright R, 8–9
artificial intelligence (AI), 334, **392**, 393–394, 405,
    406–407, 530–531
Arustamyan N, 30–31
aspirational talk, 364
assessing, 478
assimilation, 515
Atlas I, 745
Attenborough D, 518
attributes, 450–451
attribution, 841
authentic leadership, **284**
authoritarian behaviour, **246**
autocratic leadership, **283**
Azuara M, 291–292

backcasting, **521**
balanced scorecard, 792–793, *793*
bankruptcy, 588
barriers, 355–356
Bartlett CA, 53–54, 438
Bauer B, 903, 908–909
behaving
  overview of, 236, *236*
  extreme workplace behaviours and,
      243–245, *243*, **245**, 259–260
  group and team behaviours and, 245–250,
      248–249, *251*
  management gym, 251–252
  motivation and, 236–240, *237*, **238**
  pioneer: Rousseau, 252–254
  power and, 240–242, **242**
  principles of, 250–251
  problematic behaviours and, 261–262
  profile: Hogan, 255–257
  spotlight: Google, 234–235
  true story, 257–259
  worrying behavioural fact, 233
behavioural interviews, 740
behavioural psychology. *See* descriptive ethics
behavioural segmentation, 702
Ben and Jerry's, 473

benchmarking, 675–678, *677*, **679**
Bentham J, 80
best practice benchmarking, 676–677, *677*
Beugelsdijk S, 457
Beyoncé, 523
big data, 394–395
bioeconomy, **22**
bioinspiration, **521**
biomimicry, **521**, 537, 866–872
Bitcoin, 408
Black-owned enterprises, 523
Blanchard KH, 282
blended value, 823
blending, 401–402
blockchain technology, **391**, 405,
    407–408
Bluegogo, 588
Blueland, 527
board of directors, 203–204,
    828–829, *829*
Bodwell C, 681–682
The Body Shop, 589
Bombas, 694–695
Boston Consulting Group (BCG) matrix,
    483–484
bottom of the pyramid (BoP) market,
    441–442, 444, 703
bounded rationality, 318
BRAC, 573
Bragues G, 85
brand awareness, 706
brand image, 706
branding, 706
Braungart M, 289, 637–639
break even point (BEP), 843–844
BrewDog, 315
Brick S, 248–250
bricolage, **521**, 563
BRICS (Brazil, Russia, India, China, and South
    Africa), 435
Buddhism, 917
bullwhip effect, 667–667
bureaucratic leadership, **283**
Burt's Bees, 483
business analytics, 394–395
business ethics, 76. *See also* ethical
    management
business incubators and accelerators, 576
business model innovation, **522**, 540–543,
    541, **542–543**
business models
    digitalizing and, 403–408, **404**
    entrepreneuring and, 578–580, *580*,
        600–601
    strategizing and, 489–491
business-to-business (B2B) marketing,
    722–724, **723–724**
business unit level strategies, 482,
    484–485, *484*

business venture life cycle, 578–590,
    579–580, **581–582**, *583–585*, *587*, **588**,
    600–601
by-products, 631

Cadbury report, 827–828
Caguan Expedition, 577–578
Cameron B, 857
capacity management, 667–668
capital budgeting, 824–823
Carbon Disclosure Project, 161
carbon labelling, 517–518
Carroll AB, 121, *122*, 135–137
Carson R, 637
Carter D, 858
Castillo C, 683–684
Castillo H, 573
causation, 562
cause-branding, 712–713
cause-centred programmes, 207
cause-related marketing (CRM), 710–713,
    717–718
Caux Round Table Principles for Responsible
    Globalization, **462**
certification, 623, 625–626, **625**
cha bu duo (just good enough), 197
change management, 217–220, *218*, *220*, 228
channels, 354–356, *355*
charismatic leadership, **283**
Charles III, 12, 50
chatbots, **392**, 406
China Eastern, 368
choice situations, 312–316, *313*
Chouinard Y, 5, 853–861
Christensen C, 174
Christensen LT, 371
Cinépolis, 377
circular economy (CE), 630–632, *632*, *645*
Clancy H, 909
climate change, 13–14, 255–257, 259–260,
    801–801, 815
Clise L, 458–459
Clorox, 482–483, *483*
closed-loop supply networks, 632–633, *633*
closing the loop, 629–635, **629**, *630*, *632*,
    633, *645*
cloud computing, 393
CLP, 766–767
co-opetition, 472
co-responsibility, 529
Coca Cola, 590
codes of conduct, 96, **96**
codes of ethics, 206, 734. *See also* ethics
    management
coercive power, 242
collaborative practices, 55–57, *56*
collaborative strategic advantage, 472
collective bargaining, 750
collectivism, 451–452, **452–453**

commercial innovation, **522**
communicating
  overview of, 351–353, *353*
  entrepreneuring and, 571–572
  good communication and, 353–360,
    354–355, 380
  management gym, 369–370
  paradoxical fact, 349
  pioneer: Cooren, 370–373
  principles of, 369
  profile: Hügli, 373–374
  spotlight: Haier, 350–351
  stakeholder communication and, 365–369,
    366, *368*, 377–379, **377**
  true story, 375–376
  twalking and, 360–366, *362*
communication process, *353*, 354–356
communication tools, *203*, 210
communicative constitution, 363–364
community-based engagement, 209
compensation, 747–749
competence building, 746
competences, 51–53, **53**, 66, 479–481, *480*
competitive strategic advantage, 471–472
complex adaptive systems, 619
Confucianism, 84
conscious capitalism, **22**
consequentialism, 79–82, *81*, 84, 86, 110
constraint, 451–452, **452–453**
consumer behaviour, 699–701, *700–701*
consumerist marketing practices, 10
content theories of motivation, 237–239,
  237, **238**
continuous company growth, 10
continuous PDSA improvement cycle, 675
cooperative ownership, 820–823, *823*
Cooren F, 370–373
COPIS (Customer, Outputs, Processes, Inputs,
  and Suppliers), 673–674, *674*
Coronation Street (soap opera), 42–43, 49, 51,
  52, 53, 55
corporate entrepreneuring, 589–590
corporate foundations, 824
corporate governance, 826–830, *828–830*
corporate level strategies, 482–484
corporate social performance (CSP), 826
corporate social responsibility (CSR), 681–683
corporate strategic renewal, 590
Corporate Sustainability Reporting Directive
  (CSRD), 773–774
Costanza R, 832–833
costing models, 780–781
Council of Europe, 802
courage, 85
Covey S, 192
cradle-to-cradle (C2C), 632, 637–639
creative decision-making, 316–317, **317**,
  323–325, *324*
creativity, 518, 572

critical marketing, 714
cross-cultural ethics, 454–455
cross-financing, 824
cross-sectorial alliances, 447
crowd workers, **400**
cryptocurrency, 408
cultural dimensions, 451–452, **452–453**,
  456–458
culturally inclusive management, 453
culturally responsive management, 450–451
culture, 98, 214–216, 450–455, **452–453**,
  456–458
customers, 696
Cycle.Land, 586

deadweight, 841
decarbonizing investment portfolios, 818
deciding
  overview of, 310–311, *311*
  challenging nature of, 311–316, *313*
  fishbone diagram and, 341–342
  management gym, 331
  modes of, 316–330, **317**, *319*, *321–322*, *324*,
    326, *329*
  pioneer: Suddaby, 331–333
  principles of, 330
  profile: Weir, 333–335
  responsible decision-making and, 337–340,
    338–339
  spotlight: Yash Pakka, 308–309
  true story, 335–337
  what a fact! 307
Deciem, 567
decision trees, 319–320, *319*
Declaration of Fundamental Principles and
  Rights at Work (ILO, 1998), 750
decluttering, *194*, 195, *196*
decoding, 356
decoupling, 360
deliberate strategies, 498–499, *499*
delineating, *194*, 195–197, *197*
delivering, *194*, 197–198, *198*
Dell, 485–486
Delphi technique, 328–329
demand forecasting, 667–667, *667*
demarketing, 4–5, 717, 854–855
dematerialization, 527
Deming WE, 674, 767–768
Democratic Republic of the Congo, 623
demographic segmentation, 702
deontology, 79–80, *81*, 82–84, 86, 110
departments, *203*, 207–208
dependency, 128
descriptive ethics, 78, *78*, 86–89, *88*, 108–109
Design for Environment, 527, *528*
Design for Six Sigma (DFSS) methodology,
  673–674
design innovation, **521**
detoxification, 527

development and training management, 407
deviant behaviour, 243–244, *243*
devil's advocate technique, 329–330
Diamond Model, 448–450, *448*
digital competences, 396, *397*
digital nomads, **399**
digital technologies, 390–396, **391–392**, *395*
digital transformation, 389, *390*
digital well-being, 402–403, *402*
digital workers, 396–401, **398–400**
digitalization, 389, *390*
digitalizing
    overview of, 388–389, *389*
    business models and, **404**
    business models and functions and,
        403–408
    fact for thought, 385
    key concepts in, 389–396, *390*,
        391–392, *395*
    management gym, 409–410
    pioneer: Kaplan, 410–413
    principles of, 409
    profile: Hu, 413–414
    spotlight: Lenzing, 386–387
    stakeholders and, 420
    true story, 415–418
    web communication and, 418–419, **419**
    work life and, 396–403, *397*,
        398–400, *402*
digitization, 389, *390*
dimensions of professional management,
    22–27, *23*, **25**. *See also* ethical
    management; responsible management;
    sustainable management
displacement, 841
distributed innovation, **520**
distributed leadership, **283**
distributing results and governance,
    814, 827–830, *826, 828–830*
distribution fairness, 82
diversification, 482–483, 826
diversity
    behaving and, 248–250
    folleading and, 289
    glocalizing and, 453
    people management (PM) and, 730–731,
        737, 739, 756, 762
    strategizing and, 485–486
diversity management, 453
divestment, 482, 818
DMADV (define, measure, analyse, design,
    verify) algorithm, 673–674
DMAIC approach, 673–674
Dole, 672
Domino 400 (ethical fund), 818
Donham WB, 9–10, *10*, 52
Dorr C, 904
double materiality, 778

Doughnut model for sustainable
    development, 156–157, *158*
Dow Jones Sustainability Index (DJSI), 19, 819
downcycling, 634
downsizing, 751
drop-off, 841
Drucker P, 43, 523–524, 556
duality, 697
Dubai, 526
due diligence, 446

e-commerce, 627–628
e-waste, 883–884
eco-efficiency
    overview of, 47–48
    innovating and, **521**
    logistics and, 628
    operations management and, 654, 668
ecological economics, **22**
economic capital, 160
economic dimension indicators, 783
economically developed countries, 180–181
economically developing countries, 180–181
economically underdeveloped countries,
    180–181
economy of the common good (Gemeinwohl
    Ökonomie), **22**
Ecover, 527, 663
effective communication, 352–353, 356–357
effective followers, 276–277
effectiveness
    overview of, 45, 46–47
    deciding and, 325
    folleading and, 271, 276–277
    operations management and, 654, 669,
        672–678, *674–677*, **676**
effectuation, 562
efficiency
    overview of, 45, 47–48
    glocalizing and, 442
    operations management and, 654, 668–672,
        670–671
Eisenhower matrix, 195–197, *197*
elancers, **399**
Elkington J, 154, 173–174, 651
EMAS (Eco-Management and Audit
    Scheme), **625**
emergent strategies, 498–499, *499*
emotionally disconnected behaviour, **245**
employability, 760–761
employee competence building, 746
employee development, 744–745
employee-driven innovation, **521**
employee job satisfaction, 746
employee motivation, 841–842. *See also*
    motivation
employee orientation and socialization,
    742, **742–743**

employee performance, 827
employee relations, 750–752
employee volunteering, 745, 895
employee well-being, 402–403, *402*, 737, 749–750
Empresa Socialmente Responsible (ESR), **736**
encoding, 356
end-of-life (EOL) design, 634–635
engagement platforms, *203*, 209–210
engagement practices, 623, 624–625, *624*
Engine No. 1, 827
entrepreneurial acts, 564
entrepreneurial ecosystem, 575–578, *576–577*
entrepreneurial exit, 589
entrepreneurial managers, 560–562, *561*
entrepreneurial teams, 575
entrepreneuring
    overview of, 556–557, *557*
    business venture life cycle and, 578–590, *579–580*, **581–582**, *583–585*, *587*, **588**, 600–601
    encouraging fact, 553
    logics of action and, 557–563, **558–559**, *561*, *563*
    management gym, 591
    pioneer: Yunus, 592–593
    principles of, 590–591
    process of, 571–578, *572*, *576–577*
    profile: Mitrana, 594–595
    small and medium sized enterprises (SMEs) and, 598–600, **598–599**
    spotlight: Fusion Festival, 554–555
    true story, 595–597
    varieties of, 564–571, **564**, *566*, *569*, **570**
environmental capital (natural capital), 160, 781, 832–833
environmental impacts, 737
environmental indicators, 782
environmental integrity, 442
environmental life-cycle assessment (ELCA), 167
environmental margin, 478
environmental overshoot, 157
environmental scanning, 477
environmental, social and governance (ESG) activities, 774
episodic change, 218
equity, 442
equity theory of motivation, 240
ethical behaviour of managers, 94
ethical culture, 98
ethical folleading, 272
ethical leadership, **284**
ethical management
    overview of, 22–27, *23*, **25**, 75–78, *76–78*
    cross-cultural ethics and, 454–455
    descriptive ethics and, 78, *78*, 86–89, *88*, 108–109

ethics management and, 78, *78*, 89–100, *90*, *92–93*, **96**, *99*
impactful fact, 73
innovation and, 531–533
management gym, 101–102
marketing management and, 709–710, **711**
normative ethics and, 77, 78–82, *78*, *81*, 110
pioneer: Treviño, 102–103
principles of, 100–101
profile: Poppenreiter, 104–105
spotlight: Fairphone, 74–75
supply management and, 616, 620–622
true story, 106–107
ethical misconduct, 95
ethical problems, 77, *77*
ethical return, 838
ethical trade, 443
ethical value creation, 90–100, *90*, *92–93*
ethics and compliance (E&C) departments, 98
ethics management, 78, *78*, 89–100, *90*, *92–93*, **96**, *99*
ethics performance, 211–213, *212*
ethics programmes, 98
Ethics Resource Center, 88–89, 94
ethnocentrism, 437–438, 463
Ette D, 797–801
European Commission (EC), 773–774
European Sustainability Reporting Standard (ESRS), 774, 788
European Union (EU), 778, 788
Everlane, 751
evidence-based management, 253–254
expectancy theory, 239
expert power, 242
explicit responsibility, 448
exploitation, 511–512, **512**, 514–518, *516*
exploration, 511–514, **512**, *513–514*
export businesses (EBs), 438, **439**
external corporate venturing, 590
external environment analysis, 476–478
external operational communication, 378
externalities, 440
extreme workplace behaviours, 243–245, *243*, **245**, 259–260
Exxon, 827
eye-level leadership, 268–269

Facebook, 705
failure, 588–589, **588**
Fair Labor Association, 435
fair trade, 443
fairness in distribution maxim, 127
fairness of distribution, 440
Fairphone, 74–75, 875–888
Fairtrade International, 443
Fayol H, 53
feedback, 356
feedback mechanisms, 97

femininity, 451–452, **452–453**
feminist economics, **22**
fiduciary responsibilities, 812
Fiedler F, 280–282
financial management
  overview of, 811–815, *812*
  distributing results and governance and,
    814, 827–830, *826, 828–830*
  financing and, 814, 816–824, *817, 823*
  impressive fact, 809
  investing in internal activities and, 814,
    824–827, **826**, 837–844, *839*, **842**,
    845–846
  management gym, 831–832
  pioneer: Costanza, 832–833
  principles of, 830–831
  profile: Tiwana, 834–835
  as reparative, 858–859
  responsible return on investment (RROI)
    and, 837–839
  spotlight: Mondragon Corporation, 810–811
  traditional vs. new, 813–816, *813–814*
  true story, 835–837
  value flows assessment and, 847
financial management process, 813–815, *814*
financial proxy, 840–841
financing, 814, 816–824, *817, 823*
fishbone diagram, 341–342
Fix Your Bike scheme, 699
Flawsome! 672
fluid dynamics, 211–213, *212*
focal companies, 617
folleading
  overview of, 270–273, *271–272, 274*
  disconcerting fact, 267
  following and, 274–279, *275–276*
  innovating and, 572
  leading and, 279–285, *281*, **283–284**, *286*,
    298–299
  management gym, 287
  management theory and, 295–297,
    295–297
  people management and, 735–736
  pioneer: Adler, 288–290
  principles of, 285–287
  profile: Azuara, 291–292
  spotlight: Allsafe, 268–269
  toxic followership and leadership and,
    244–245, **245–246**
  true story, 292–294
Follett MP, 9, *10*
follower activism, 277–279, *277*
follower opposition, 278–279
following, 274–279, *275–276. See also*
  folleading
food waste, 672
footprinting, 13, 160–161, *162–163*
forecasting, 477

foreign direct investment (FDI), 445
foreign markets, **441**, 443–444
foreign ownership, 816
Foxconn, 749–750
free speech, 358
Freeman E, 473
Freeman RE, 469, 534–536, 811
Freud S, 197
Friedman argument, 19
Friedman M, 19, 118
frugal innovation, **521**
FTSE4Good Index, 19, 819
full cost accounting, 780
functional level strategies, 482, 485–486
funding, 580–583, **581–582**, *583*
Fusion Festival, 554–555

Gaiha, A., 405
Gantt charts, 197–198, *198*
Gaur, V., 405
Gedik C, 494–495
gender budgeting, 802–803, **802–803**
gender equality action plans, 802–803, **803**
gender inequality, 11, 802–803, **802–803**, **803**
General Electric (GE), 483
generosity, 85
geocentrism, 437–438, 463
Ghoshal S, 48, 53–54
gig workers, **400**
Glassman B, 917–918
global companies, 438–439, **439**
Global Entrepreneurship Monitor (GEM),
  575, *576*
global organizations, 435
Global Reporting Initiative (GRI), 19, 773,
  782–783, **783–785**, 786–788, *787*
global sourcing, 441–442, **441**
global-sourcing companies (GSC), 438, **439**
global trade, **441**, 442–443
globalization, 434–435
globalized supply chain management, 11
glocal leadership, 285
glocalizing
  overview of, 432–437, *433*
  core practices of, 448–455, *449*,
    452–453, *452*
  encouraging fact, 429
  guidelines for, 461–463, **462**
  international businesses and, 437–439,
    439, 463
  management gym, 456
  management practices and, 440–448, **441**
  pioneer: Hofstede, 456–458
  principles of, 455
  profile: Clise, 458–459
  spotlight: Natura, 430–431
  true story, 459–461
goal and scope (G&S), 168, *169*

goal-setting theory, 239
goals, 45–46
Goldberg R, 694
golden rule, 83
Good-Ark, 743, 889–899
good communication, 353–360, *354–355*, 380
good equity, 813
'good' innovation, 522–533, *524–526, 528, 530*
Google, 234–235, 241–242
Gorenje, 673
Gouwens E, 875, 877–878
Grameen Bank, 476, 556, 570–571, 592–593
Graves P, 858
Gravity, 749
Great Place to Work, **736**
green collar workers, 209
green marketing, 714
Greenstar, 586
greenwash trapdoor, 361–362, *362*
greenwashing, 19–20, 361–362
Greyston Bakery, 660–661, 730–731, 913–922
GRI (Global Reporting Initiative), 19, 773, 782–783, **783–785**, 786–788, *787*
group and team behaviours, 245–250, *248–249, 251*
groupthink, 327–330
growth paradigm, 815
growth phase. *See* take-off phase
growth strategies, 584–585, *585*
Guidelines for Multinational Enterprises (OECD), **462**, 773
Guzmán E, 755–757

H&M, 438–439
Haier, 350–351, 368–369
Hamel G, 20, 510
Hang Seng Sustainability Index, 19
hard indicators, 840
hardwiring, 486–488
Hatoyama Y, 897
Heath D, 694
hereditary succession, 589
Hersey P, 282
Herzberg F, 238
heterodox economics, **22**
hierarchy of needs, 237, *237*
high-level pay, 11
Hofsetter E, 694–695
Hofstede G, 456–458
Hogan C, 255–257
holistic humanistic marketing, 724
hollow organizations, 201–202, *201*
honesty, 454
Honeywell, 633
horizontal alliances, 447
horizontal integration, 482
Houdini, 618

Houten F von, 432
HSBC, 815
Hu Y, 413–414
Huawei, 532–533
hub and spoke logistical networks, 627
Hügli T, 223–224, 373–374
Hulme Community Garden Centre (Manchester), 527
human rights, 737
humanistic management, 857–858
humanistic view on motivation, 240
hybrid competence, 393
hybrid entrepreneuring, 568–570, *569*, **570**
hype cycle, 517–518, *517*

Iberdrola, 367
IBM, 590
ICT-based mobile workers, **399**
ideal final result (IFR), 673–674
ideal speech situations, 358
IFLYTEK, 368
IKEA, 212, 650–651
ILO (International Labour Organization), **736**, 750
impact, 841. *See also* environmental impacts
impact assessment and management, 164–171, *166*, **167**
implementation stages, 121, **121**, 123–124
implemented ethics, *90*, 91–92
implicit responsibility, 448
impulse buying, 699
inclusive workplace, 453
inclusiveness, 326
incremental changes, 217–218
incremental innovations, 519
independent foundations, 208
indigenous leadership, 285
Inditex, 619–620
individual factors, 87–88, *88*, 108–109
individualism, 451–452, **452–453**
indulgence, 451–452, **452–453**
industrial ecology, 629–630, **629**, *630*
industry clusters, 576
influence, 129
informal communication, 379
infrastructure, 444, 631
ingroup favouritism, 245
Innocent, 590
Innocent Drinks, 163
innovating
   overview of, 8, 508–509, *509*
   ambidextrous management and, 511–518, **512**, *513–514, 516–517*
   entrepreneuring and, 572
   fact for thought, 505
   as 'good,' 522–533, *524–526, 528, 530,* 540–545, *541*, **542–543**
   management gym, 533–534

as mode of management, 509–511, *511*
pioneer: Freeman, 534–536
principles of, 533
profile: Krishna, 536–538
spotlight: Tesla, 506–507
true story, 538–540
varieties of, 518–520, **520–522**
innovation ethics, 531–533
innovation for sustainability, **522**
innovation funnel, 512–514, *513–514*
innovative management, 509
innovative work behaviour, **520**
innovator's dilemma, 516
inputs, 45–46, 840, 841
inside-out linkages, 475
institutional entrepreneurship, 564–568, **564**
institutional innovation, **522**
institutional investors, 816
institutional leadership, **283**
institutional work, 17
integrated foundations, 208
integrated management systems, 658–659
integrated processes, 210
integrated reporting, 786, 788–790, *789*
integrative stakeholder communication,
    377–379, **377**
intellectual property, 532
intention–behaviour gap, 699–701, *701*
Intercontinental Hotel Group (IHG), 142
intercultural management competence,
    450–451
Interface, 152–153, 635
internal corporate venturing, 590
internal environment analysis, 478–481, *479*,
    480–481, 500
internal operational communication, 378
internality paradigm, 816
international businesses, 437–439, **439**, 463
international cooperation, 443
international development, 440
International Federation of Accountants
    (IFAC), 768, *768*
International Integrated Reporting Council
    (IIRC), 788
International Labour Organization (ILO),
    736, 750
international mentality, 438, **439**
international strategic alliances, **441**, 447–448
international subsidiaries, **441**, 445–446
Internet of Things (IoT), **391**, 404–405,
    406–407, 908
internships, 758–760
intersectionality, 738, *738*
interviews, 740
intrapreneuring, 564–568, **564**
intuitive decision-making, 316–317, **317**,
    320–322, *321–322*
inventions, 518

inventory management, 667–668
investing in internal activities, 814, 824–827,
    826, 837–844, *839*, **842**, **845–846**
irresponsible competitiveness, 472
ISO 72 standard, 659
ISO 9000 standard, **625**, 626, 659–660
ISO 14000 standard, 19, **625**, 626
ISO 26000 standard, 19, **625**, 767, 773
issues maturity, 121, **121**, 123

Jhunjhunwala, KK, 308
job crafting, **520**
job descriptions, 739
job interviews, 740
job positions, *203*, 208–209
job satisfaction, 746
Jong E de, 457
just-in-time logistics, 627
justice, 85, 454
justification problem of intuition,
    321–322, *322*

Kano customer needs model, 673, *675*
Kant I, 82–83
Kaplan A, 410–413
Kell G, 897
Kelley RE, 270, 275–277, *275*
Kelliher, C, 398
Khurana R, 28–29
King ML, 473
kingdom of ends, 83
knowledge, 450–451
knowledge acquisition, 515
Kobo360, 568
Kohlberg L, 91, *92*
Kondo M, 195
Kotler P, 717–718
Kotter JP, 228
Kramer M, 470, 493–494
Krishna V, 308–309, 313, 536–538, 863–872
Kunming-Montreal Global Biodiversity
    Framework, 77
Kuznets S, 179–180, *179*

labour unions, 750–751
laissez-faire leadership, 282–283
leadership
    process and styles of, 279–285, *281*,
        283–284, *286*, 298–299
    See also folleading
lean management, 668–672, **670–671**
Least Preferred Coworker (LPC) scale, 280–282
legislation and regulations, 577, 772–773
legitimate power, 242
LEGO, 116–117, 118–119
Lenzing, 386–387
LG Corporation, 407–408
licensing, 140–142

life-cycle assessment and impact inventory, 165–171, *166*, **167**, *168–170*, 182, 781
life-cycle costing (LCC), 167
life-cycle impact assessment (LCIA), 169–170
life-cycle interpretation (LCI), 170
life-cycle inventory (LCI), 169
Lifestyles of Health and Sustainability (LOHAS), 18, 477, 519, 703, 706
Lifestyles of Voluntary Simplicity (LOVOS), 519, 703
line management, 203–204, 209
link alliances, 447
listening, 371
living wage, 748–749
loans, 823–824
localization, 436–437. *See also* glocalizing
Locke J, 83
logic of appropriateness, 315–316
logic of consequences, 315–316
logistics, 626–629
Lohmann D, 268–269
long-term orientation, 451–452, **452–453**
low-cost production, 10

Machiavellian leadership, **283**
machine learning, 393
Mackey J, 559
macro-marketing, 708–709, **709**
Madiadipura D, 639–641
magnanimity, 85
magnificence, 85
mainstream ethics management tools, 94–96
management buy-in, 589
management buy-out, 589
management control, 769, 790–793, *791–793*
management in context
    overview of, 6–8, *7*
    new-world management and, 20–27, **22**, *23*, **25**, *26*, 33–35
    old-world management and, 8–12, *10*, 33–35
    pioneer: Khurana, 28–29
    principles of, 27
    professional management oath and, 36
    professional profile: Arustamyan, 30–31
    scary fact, 3
    spotlight: Patagonia, 4–5
    transition world management and, 12–20, *14*
    true story, 31–33
management in practice
    overview of, 43–44, *44*
    fun fact, 41
    management gym, 57–58, 67
    management practices and, 48–57, *50*, **53**, *56*, 66
    modes of management and, 54–55, *54*. *See also specific modes*

pioneer: Mintzberg, 58–60
principles of, 57
process of, 44–48, *45*
profile: Umeasiegbu, 61–62
spotlight: *Coronation Street* (soap opera), 42–43
true story, 63–65
management innovation, 510–511, *511*, **521**
management innovators, 8. *See also* innovating
management practices, 8, 10–12, 48–57, *50*, **53**, *56*, 66
management systems, 656–660, *659*
management's social performance (MSP), 120–124, **121**, *122*
managing innovation, 509–510
manic depressive behaviour, **245**
Marcario R, 853–854
Marine Stewardship Council, 435
market development, 707
market pull, 519
market segmentation, 702–703, *702*. *See also* segmentation, targeting, and positioning (STP) process
marketing ethics, 709–710, **711**
market(ing) innovation, 520
marketing management
    overview of, 696
    business-to-business (B2B) market and, 722–724, **723–724**
    digitalizing and, 406
    fundamentals of, 697–701, *700–701*
    as 'good' for society and planet, 708–715, **709**, **711**, *713*
    holistic humanistic marketing and, 724
    management gym, 715–716
    pioneer: Kotler, 717–718
    principles of, 715–716
    profile: Metlicka Lustykova, 718–719
    segmentation, targeting, and positioning (STP) process and, 702–708, *702*, *707*
    spotlight: Bombas, 694–695
    staggering fact, 693
    true story, 720–722
marketing mix, 707–708, *707*
marketing systems, 708–709, **709**
Marks and Spencer, 213–214
masculinity, 451–452, **452–453**
Maseland R, 457
Maslow A, 237, *237*
materiality, 777–778, *779*
materiality assessment, 132, *132*, 788
materials, 51
Maw L, 754–755
MAX Burgers, 318
maximization of stakeholder value maxim, 127
McCrary-Ruiz-Esparz E, 94–95

McDonald's, 247
McDonough W, 289, 637
McGregor D, 238–239
McKinsey, 311, 314–315
McMullen A, 116
meanings, 50
measurability, 778–780
mechanistic organizing, 199–200
mergers and acquisitions (M&A),
    445–446, 589
messages, 354–356
Meta, 406
Metlicka Lustykova A, 718–719
middle management, 209
Mill JS, 80
Mintzberg H, 20, 43, 44, 53, 58–60, 351
mission statements, 206, 474
Mitchel R, 130–131
Mitrana D, 594–595
mobile access acceleration, 392–393
mobile knowledge workers, **399**
modern slavery, 622–623
modes of management, 54–55, *54. See also*
    specific modes
modular design, 880
modular organizations, *201*, 202
Moller JM, 901–910
Mondragon Corporation, 810–811, 820
monetization, 840
monetized assessment, 823–826
money paradigm, 816
Mongolian Hard Rock Band, 390
monitoring, 477
moral development, 90–91, *90, 92*
moral dilemmas, 76–77
moral excellence, 90
moral leadership, 96, **96**
moral philosophy. *See* normative ethics
morality, 76
Morrissette H, 858
motivation, 236–240, *237*, **238**, 841–842
motivation–hygiene theory, 238
Mujawamariya Jd'A, 871
Müller M, 615
multi-cause programmes, 206–207
multinational firms, 435, 438, **439**
Musk E, 480–481, 506–507, 562
mutual respect, 454

Nadeshiko, 739
narcissist behaviour, **245–246**
National Health Service (NHS), 124
nationalism, 436
Natura, 430–431, 589
natural capital (environmental capital), 160,
    781, 832–833
natural capital inventory accounting, 781
Natural Step, 526–527

negative screening, 818
Net Impact, 754–755
net present value (NPV), 842–844
new business venturing, 564–568, **564**
new-world management, 20–27, *22, 23,* **25,**
    26, 33–35
Newbold M, 909
Nike, 744
nine to fivers, **398**
nominal group technique, 328
non-instrumentalization, 83
non-urgent decisions, 314–315
non-violent communication (NVC),
    359–360, 380
normative documents, *203,* 204–206
normative ethics, 77, 78–82, *78, 81,* 110
Norsk Hydro, 772
novelties, 508, 518–519
NOW TIME, 671–672, **671**

observed behaviour, *90,* 92–93
Ochs P, 289
OECD (Organisation for Economic
    Co-operation and Development), 435,
    462, 773, 827–828
offboarding, 751–752
offshoring, 442
old-world management, 8–12, *10,* 33–35
Omalla JA, 284–285
on-demand workers, **400**
open access, 358
open hiring, 730–731, 913–922
open innovation, 513–514, *513–514,* **520**
open patenting, 506–507
openness, 443
operational performance, 652
operations management (OM)
    overview of, 651–653
    digitalizing and, 405–406
    impressive fact, 649
    lean management and, 668–672,
        670–671
    management gym, 679
    organization of production and, 662–668,
        662, **664,** *667–667*
    pioneer: Waddock, 681–683
    principles of, 678–679
    process analysis and, 653–660, *655, 657,*
        659, 688–689
    profile: Castillo, 683–684
    quality management and, 669, 672–678,
        674–677, **676**
    spotlight: IKEA, 650–651
    Toyota Production System (TPS) and,
        670–671, 686–687, *687*
    true story, 685–686
opportunities, 573–574
organic organizing, 199–200

Organisation for Economic Co-operation and Development (OECD), 435, **462**, 773, 827–828
organizational architecture, 202–211, *203, 205, 207*
organizational behaviour. *See* behaving
organizational citizenship behaviours, 244
organizational culture, 98, 214–216
organizational development, 211
organizational innovation, 520, **522**
organizational institutionalism, 331–333
organizational learning, 216–217, *217*
organizational structure, 97, 198–202, *201*
organizations, 192
organizing
   overview of, 192–193, *193*
   encouraging fact, 189
   fluid dynamics and, 211–213, *212*
   'hard' structures and, 198–211, *201, 203, 205, 207*, 226–227
   management gym, 221
   ourselves and, 193–198, *194, 196–198*
   patterns of, 213–220, *215–218*, **220**, 228
   pioneer: Zadek, 221–222
   principles of, 220
   profile: Hügli, 223–224
   spotlight: SEMCO, 190–191
   true story, 224–226
orientation, 742, **742–743**
Ortega A, 619–620
Oslo typology, 519–520
Otto's Coffee House and Kitchen, 363–364
outcomes, 840
outputs, 48, 840
outside-in linkages, 475–476
outsourcing, 442
Oxfam, 473

Pacioli L, 768
Parker M, 8
participative decision-making, 326–327, *326*
partnership-based engagement, 209
PAS 99 standard, 659
passive aggressive behaviour, **245**
Patagonia, 4, 17, 21, 590, 853–861
Patterson D, 749–750
PDSA (plan, do, study, act) cycle, 673–675, **676**, *676*
people, 46
people management (PM)
   overview of, 732–735, *733*
   compensation and, 747–749
   digitalizing and, 406–408
   diversity and, 730–731, 737, 739, 756, 762
   employability and, 760–761
   employee relations and, 750–752
   employee well-being and, 402–403, *402*, 737, 749–750

   humanistic management practices and, 858
   management gym, 753
   old-world management and, 11
   performance management and, 745–747
   pioneer: Maw, 754–755
   PM–PM relationship and, 735–737, **736**
   principles of, 752–753
   profile: Guzmán, 755–757
   recruitment and, 737–741, *738*
   spotlight: Greyston Bakery, 730–731
   stunning fact, 729
   training and development and, 741–745, *741, 744*
   true story, 758–760
performance, 48. *See also* employee performance; ethics performance; responsibility performance; sustainability performance
performance evaluation practices, 745–746
performance management, 407, 745–747
performative communication, 363–364
PESTLE (Political, Economic, Social, Technological, Legal and Environmental factors) analysis, 476
Pink D, 510, 535
planetary boundaries, 14–15, *14*
planned obsolescence, 531
Plastic Free Planet, 162
PM–PM relationship, 735–737, **736**
policies, 206
polycentrism, 437–438, 463
polyphony, 365
Poppenreiter P, 104–105
Porter M, 470, 476, 493
positioning, 705–708. *See also* segmentation, targeting, and positioning (STP) process
positive deviance, *243*, 244
positive screening, 818
power, 240–242, **242**
power distance, 451–452, **452–453**
power over, 241–242, **242**
power to, 241–242
power with, 241–242, **242**
practices innovation, **522**
precaution, 443
Premium, 468–469
Price D, 749
principal–agent problem, 827
Principles for Responsible Investment (PRI), 817–818
Principles of Corporate Governance (OECD), 827–828
privately owned companies, 817
problematic behaviours, 261–262
procedures, *203*, 210–211
process detail maps, 656
process innovation, 520, **522**
process maps, 653–656, *657*, 688–689

process planning and control, 665–668, *667*, *667*

process theories of motivation, 239–240

processes, 46–48, *203*, 210

Procter and Gamble (P&G), 487

product innovation, 520, **522**

product marketing mix (4Ps), 707

product+cause marketing, 710–712

production facilities and sites, 663–665, **664**

production systems (transformation systems), 660–663, *662*

products-as-cause, 712

professional enterprise excellence, 652–653

professional management competence, 52–53

professional management conduct, 24–27

professional management oath, 36

professional management performance, 48

professional management service, 24–27

professional managers, 46

professional practices, 6

professions, 6

profit paradigm, 815

programmed decisions, 312–313

programmes, *203*, 206–207, *207*

prosumer workers, **400**

psychographic segmentation, 702

psychological contract (PC), 252–254

psychological safety, 250, *251*

Public Eye, 619

publicly traded companies, 817

purpose economy, **22**

qualitative assessment, 120–124, **121**, *122*, 823

quality management, 623, 669, 672–678, *674–677*, **676**

Quality of Life in the Business, **736**

quantified assessment, 823

quantitative corporate social performance assessment, 142–144, *143*

quarterly reporting, 11

R&D management, **521**

radical innovations, 519

rational decision-making, 316–320, **317**, *319*

receivers, 354–356

recruitment, 406–407, 737–741, *738*

recycling, 631

referent power, 242

regiocentrism, 437–438, 463

related diversification, 482–483

relational decision-making, 316–317, **317**, 325–330, *326*, *329*

relationality, 697–698

renewable energy, 631

renovation, **521**

report boundary, 788

resource-based view of strategizing, 475, 479–482

resource cascading, 631

resource consumption, 669

resources, 11, 46, 574–575

responsibility, 129. *See also* responsible management

responsibility category, 121–122, **121**, *122*

responsibility performance, 211–213, *212*

responsible communication, 358–360

responsible competitiveness, 449–450, 471–472

responsible decision-making, 337–340, **338–339**

responsible folleading, 272–273, *274*

responsible innovation, **522**, 527–531, *530*, 544–545

responsible leadership, **284**, 288–290

responsible management
    overview of, 22–27, *23*, **25**, 118–120, *119*
    concept and definitions of, 120–124, **121**, *122*
    folleading and, 288–290
    intriguing fact, 115
    management gym, 134–135
    pioneer: Carroll, 135–137
    principles of, 133–134
    profile: Sinha, 138–139
    quantitative corporate social performance assessment and, 142–144, *143*
    spotlight: LEGO, 116–117
    stakeholder management and, 125–133, *126*, *130–132*, **133**, 142
    supply management and, 620–622
    true story, 140–142

responsible return on investment (RROI), 837–839

responsible sourcing management, 880–883

responsible trade, 442–443

restorative sourcing, 855–856

retrovation, **521**

revalorization, 527, 633

reverse logistics, 628

reverse supply flow, 633

reward power, 242

Robertson R, 327–328

Rousseau D, 252–254

rule utilitarianism, 82

Ruppert J, 175–176

SA 8000, **625**

Sage, 530

Sanders B, 751

Sarbanes-Oxley Act, 827–828

Sasol, 360–361

scale alliances, 447

Schaltegger S, 795–798

science, 443

second-order supply loops, 619
Sedlácek T, 457
segmentation, targeting, and positioning (STP) process, 702–708, *702, 707*
self-control, 85
self-determination theory, 239
self-management, 276–277
self-promoters, **246**
self-regulation, 773
SEMCO, 190–191, 200–201
senders, 354–356
Senge P, 20
servant leadership, **284**
service-dominant logic, 698–699
services innovation, **522**
services marketing mix (7Ps), 707–708
servitization logistics, 628
settling down phase, 586–590, **588**
Seuring S, 615
shared leadership, **283**
shared processes, 656
shared value, 493–494
shareholder paradigm, 816
shareholder returns, 814–815
shareholder-value-based management practices, 11
shareholders, 820, 827–830, *828–830*
Shaw GB, 173
sheeple (sheep people), 276
Shewhart DA, 674
Shingo Model for operational excellence, 669–671, **670**
short-term orientation, 451–452, **452–453**
short-term paradigm, 815–816
Simon H, 310, 320
Sinha SK, 138–139
SIPOC (Suppliers, Inputs, Processes, Outputs, and Customer), 673–674, *674*
site co-location, 663
situational factors, 88–89, *88*, 108–109
situational leadership, 280–282, *281*
Skilich C, 386
skills, 450–451
Slater R, 908
small and medium sized enterprises (SMEs), 598–600, **598–599**
Smart Air, 563
sociability, 85
Social Accountability (SA) 8000, **736**
social capital, 160
social, environmental, and ethical accounting (SEEA), 771
social franchising, 586
social innovation, **522**, 523–525, *524–525*
social life-cycle assessment (SLCA), 167–168
social margin, 478
social marketing, 713–714, *713*
social movements, 277–278

social performance indicators, 782
social return on investment (SROI), 824–827, **824**, 839–844, *839*, **842**, **845–846**
social sustainability, 622–623
socialization, 742, **742–743**
socially liberal activism, 772
socially responsible investment (SRI), 817–819
Society for Human Resources Management, 734–735
socio-technical systems, 664–665
soft indicators, 840
softwiring, 486–488
Solzhenitsyn A, 410
Soul Food Supermarket, 122
SpaceX, 507
specialized ERS managers, 55–56, *56*
specialized ethics management tools, 96–97, **96**
specialized processes, 210
spiritual leadership, **284**
staff function, 203–204
stakeholder accountability, 770
stakeholder assessment, 128–132, *130–131*
stakeholder audience analysis, 366–367, **366**
stakeholder co-creation strategy, 368–369
stakeholder communication, 365–369, **366**, *368*, 377–379, **377**
stakeholder effectiveness, 672–673
stakeholder efficiency, 668–669
stakeholder engagement, 132, *132*, **133**
stakeholder information strategy, 367
stakeholder involvement strategy, 368
stakeholder management, 125–133, *126, 130–132*, **133**, 142
stakeholder response strategy, 367–368
stakeholder responsiveness, 121, **121**, 122–123
stakeholder thinking, 534–536
stakeholder value, 125–128, *126*
stakeholder value-based management, 825–826
stakeholder value return, 838
stakeholders
    accounting and, 769–770, *769*, 774–778, 783–785
    communicating and, 357–358, 361–362, *362. See also* stakeholder communication
    deciding and, 326–330, *326, 329*
    digitalizing and, 420
    entrepreneuring and, 575, *576*
    financial management and, 825–828, 839–844
    glocalizing and, 440, 445–446, 450
    innovating and, 513–514
    leadership and, 280
    strategizing and, 471–474, 487–488

supply management and, 616, 617,
    631–632, *632*
transition world management and, 17–18
See also responsible management
stand-alone ERS departments, 207–208
standardization, 623, 625–626, **625**
Starbucks, 142, 488–489, *489*
start-up phase, 578–583, *579–580*
state-owned companies, 816
stewardship, 454
Stone L, 523
strategic alliances, 447
strategic controls, 791–792
strategic human resources management, 11
strategic objectives and goals, 474
strategizing
    overview of, 469–470, *471*
    context of, 474–481, *475, 477, 479,
        480–481,* 500
    executing, 486–491, *489–490*
    formulating strategies for, 481–486, *483–484*
    impressive fact, 467
    management gym, 492
    pioneer: Kramer, 493–494
    principles of, 491
    profile: Gedik, 494–495
    responsible competitiveness and, 471–472
    spotlight: Premium, 468–469
    strategic purpose and objectives and,
        473–474
    true story, 496–498
    types of strategies and, 498–499, *499*
Strategyzer business model, 489–490
strengths weaknesses opportunities threats
    (SWOT) analysis, 481, *481,* 500
subsidiarity, 442
subsidies, 821–822
Suddaby R, 331–333
supplemental reporting, 786
supply architectures, 619–622, *620–621,* **622**
supply loops, 619
supply management
    overview of, 615–616, *617*
    closing the loop in, 629–635, **629,** *630, 632,*
        633, 645
    digitalizing and, 404–405
    management gym, 636
    old-world management and, 11
    pioneer: Braungart, 637–639
    positive signs? 613
    practices in, 623–629, *624,* **625**
    principles of, 635
    profile: Madiadipura, 639–641
    spotlight: Tetra Pak, 614–615
    supply system and, 617–623, *620–621,*
        622, *646*
    true story, 642–644
supply networks, 618–623, *620–621*

supply system engagement tools,
    624–625, *624*
supply systems, 617–623, *620–621,* **622,** *646*
survivors, 276
sustainability. *See* sustainable management
sustainability accounting, 771–772, *772,*
    795–796
Sustainability Accounting Standards Board
    (SASB), 777, *779*
sustainability assessments, 782
sustainability dashboards, 791, *792*
sustainability disclosure, 774
sustainability footprints, 160–161, *162–163*
sustainability indicators, 782–783,
    783–785, 804
sustainability leadership, **284**
sustainability measurement and management
    systems, 790–791
sustainability-oriented innovation, 525–527,
    526, 528, 540–543, *541,* **542–543**
sustainability performance, 211–213, *212*
sustainability performance metrics,
    781–782, *781*
sustainability reporting, 785–790, *787, 789*
Sustainability Reporting Guidelines (GRI),
    773, 782–783, **783–785,** 786–788, *787*
Sustainable Development Goals (SDGs),
    14–15, *15,* 388, 528, 897–898
sustainable development indicators,
    179–181, *179*
sustainable folleading, 272
sustainable infrastructure, 444
sustainable leadership, **284**
sustainable management
    overview of, 22–27, *23,* **25,** 154–157,
        155–158
    concepts of, 157–162, *159, 162–163*
    management gym, 172
    pioneer: Elkington, 173–174
    principles of, 171
    profile: Ruppert, 175–176
    spotlight: Interface, 152–153
    staggering fact, 151
    supply management and, 620–622, **622**
    sustainable development indicators and,
        179–181, *179*
    true story, 176–178
    See also triple bottom line (TBL)
        management
sustainable market innovation, 444
sustainable marketing, 714–715
sustainable trade, 442–443
sustainably developed countries, 180–181
sustainably developing countries, 180–181
SWOT (strengths weaknesses opportunities
    threats) analysis, 481, *481,* 500
systems innovation, **522**
systems thinking, 631

take-make-waste production management, 11
take-off phase, 583–586, *584–585*, *587*
Taobao, 563
targeting practices, 704–705. *See also*
    segmentation, targeting, and positioning
    (STP) process
Taylorism, 238
teams, 247–250, *248*, *251*
technical skills, 519
techniques, 519
technology, 519
technology push, 519
tension, 129
Tesco, 55, 518, 562
Tesla, 480–481, 506–507, 562
testing, 531–532
Tetra Pak (TP), 614–615
textual agency, 364–365
Theory X, 238–239, **238**
Theory Y, 238–239, **238**
Theory Z, 238–239, **238**
thinking hats method, 330
Thomas Aquinas, 84
Thunberg G, 6, 13, 277–278, 567
Tin Shed Ventures, 860
Tiwana D, 834–835
TOMS business model, 491
TOMS Shoes, 565, 585
Top Glove, 124
top management, 11, 203–204, 208
top managers, 816
total responsibility management (TRM), 682
toxic workplace behaviours, 244–245,
    245–246
Toyota, 477
Toyota Production System (TPS), 434, 510,
    670–671, 686–687, *687*
traceability, 619–620, 625, 628
trade, 442–443
traditional accounting, 771
training and development, 741–745, *741*, *744*
transactional leadership, 282–283
transfer pricing, 445, 446
transformation, 515
transformation systems (production systems),
    660–663, *662*
transformational leadership, 282–283
transition world management, 12–20,
    14–16
transnational firms, 439, **439**
transparency, 357, 625, 628, 828
Treviño LK, 75, 102–103
triple bottom line return on investment, 838
triple bottom line (TBL) management
    overview of, 154, 163–165, *165*
    life-cycle assessment and impact inventory
        and, 165–171, *166*, **167**, *168–170*, 182
    operations management and, 652, 669

strategizing and, 478
supply management and, 616
triple-layered business model canvas, 600–601
triple top line (TTL), 616, 669
Tru Earth, 527
Trump D, 50
twalking, 360–366, *362*
Twitter (now X), 507

Umar N, 897
Umeasiegbu K, 55, 61–62
UMICORE, 51
un-programmed decisions, 312–313
uncertainty, 313–314
uncertainty avoidance, 451–452, **452–453**
unconscious bias, 738
UNESCO, 897
Unilever, 749–750, 908–909
union busting, 751
unionization, 750–751
Uniqlo, 432
unique selling point (USP), 705–706
United Nations (UN). *See* Sustainable
    Development Goals (SDGs)
United Nations Environment Assembly
    (UNEA), 871
United Nations Global Compact, 19, **462**, 773
universal law, 83
unpredictable ones, **246**
unprofessional management practices,
    10–12
unrealized strategies, 498–499, *499*
unrelated diversification, 482–483
urgent decisions, 314–315
user/customer innovation, **521**
utilitarianism, 80–82

value added statement (VAS), 783–785, *785*
value capture, 490, *490*
value chain, 478–479, *479*
value creation, 490, *490*
value exchange, 490, *490*
value flows assessment, 847
value proposition, 490, *490*
values statements, 206
variability, 668
ventriloquism, 365, 372
Verschlimmbessern, 258
vertical alliances, 447
vertical integration, 482
Vestas, 483
virtual organizations, *201*, 202
virtue ethics, 79, *81*, 84–86, 110
vision statements, 206, 473–474
voice-of-the-customer (VOC) tools,
    673–675
Volkswagen, 665
volunteering, 745, 895

Waddock S, 681–683
Wahaha, 510–511
Wakefield L, 573–574
Walmart, 485
warehousing, 627
waste, 631, 671–672, **671**
web communication, 418–419, **419**
Weber M, 332
Weir T, 333–335
Welch J, 825–826
well-being, 402–403, *402*, 737, 749–750
Wernink T, 876
Westpac Banking Corp., 744–745
WhatsApp, 273
whole-person decision-making, 310
wikinomics, **400**
Wintour A, 274–275, 278–279
Wood DJ, 130–131
work life. *See* behaving
working poor, 748–749
workplace innovation, **520**
World Business Council for Sustainable
    Development (WBCSD), 156
World Commission on Environment and
    Development, 157–158
World Economic Forum (WEF), 12, 50, 388,
    441–442
World Trade Organization (WTO), 435, 442

X (formerly Twitter), 507
Xerox, 633

Yanai T, 432
Yash Pakka, 308–310, 312–313, 536–538,
    863–873
yes people, 276
Youon, 586
Yunus M, 476, 556, 570–571, 592–593

Zadek S, 221–222
Zara, 619–620
Zeitz J, 174
Zeronauts, 651
Zhang R, 350–351
Zong Q, 510–511
Zuckerberg M, 273, 351–352